Brockway
The American
Reformatory (1910)

Mabbott
Punishment (1939)

Andenaes
General Preventive Effects
of Punishment (1966)

Martinson
What Works (1974)

Packer
The Limits of Criminal Sanction (1968)

Newman
Defensible Space
(1973)

Kretschmer
Physique and Character
(1921)

Hooton
American Criminal (1939)

Montagu
Man and
Aggression
(1968)

Jeffery
Crime Prevention
(1971)

E. O. Wilson
Sociobiology (1975)

Goring
The English Convict (1913)

Sheldon
Varieties of Delinquent Youth (1949)

Dalton
The Premenstrual Syndrome (1971)

Tarde
Penal
Philosophy
(1912)

Freud
General Introduction
to Psychoanalysis (1920)

Friedlander
Psychoanalytic
Approach to
Delinquency (1947)

Eysenck
Crime and Personality (1964)

Bandura
Aggression (1973)

Healy
The Individual Deliquent (1915)

Bonger
Criminality and
Economic Conditions (1916)

Rusche & Kircheimer
Punishment and Social
Structure (1939)

Vold
Theoretical Criminology (1958)

Chambliss & Seidman
Law, Order & Power (1971)

Dahrendorf
Class and Class Conflict
in Industrial Society (1959)

Taylor, Walton, & Young
The New Criminology
(1973)

Park, Burgess, & McKenzie
The City (1925)
Shaw et al.
Delinquency Areas (1925)
Thrasher
The Gang (1926)

Merton
Social Structure
and Anomi (1938)

Sellin
Culture, Conflict and Crime (1938)

Cloward & Ohlin
Delinquency and Opportunity (1960)

Lewis
The Culture of Poverty (1966)

Mead
The Psychology of
Punitive Justice (1917)

Sutherland
Principles of
Criminology (1939)

Lemert
Social
Pathology (1951)

Hirschi
Causes of
Delinquency (1969)

Schur
Labeling Deviant
Behavior (1972)

Sutherland
Criminology (1924)

Sutherland
The Professional Thief (1937)

Becker
Outsiders (1963)

Glueck & Glueck
500 Criminal Careers
(1930)

Glueck & Glueck
Unraveling Juvenile Delinquency
(1950)

Hathaway & Monachesi
Analyzing and Predicting
Juvenile Delinquency
with the MMPI (1953)

Eysenck
Crime and Personality
(1964)

Wolfgang, Figlio, & Sellin
Delinquency in
Birth Cohorts
(1972)

1925	1940	1950	1969	1975
World War I Depression	World War II	Cold War	Vietnam War	Watergate

Time Line of Criminological Theories (continued)

Cohen & Felson
Routine Activities (1979)

Clarke
Situational Crime Prevention (1992)

Lott
*More Guns,
Less Crime* (2000)

Felson
*Crime and Everyday
Life*, 3rd (2002)

J.Q. Wilson
Thinking About Crime (1975)

Katz
Seductions of Crime (1988)

Mednick & Volavka
Biology and Crime (1980)

Rowe
*The Limits of
Family Influence*
(1995)

Harris
The Nurture Assumption (1998)

Ellis
*Evolutionary
Sociobiology* (1989)

Schoenthaler
*Intellegence, Academic Performance
and Brain Function* (2000)

Hirschi & Hindelang
*Intelligence and
Delinquency* (1977)

Henggeler
*Delinquency in
Adolescence*
(1989)

Moffitt
*Neuropsychology
of Crime* (1992)

Wilson & Daly
Evolutionary Psychology (1997)

Murray & Herrnstein
The Bell Curve (1994)

Bushman & Anderson
Media Violence (2001)

Lea & Young
Left Realism
(1984)

Hagan
Structural Criminology (1989)

Zehr & Mika
*Fundamental Concepts
of Restorative Justice* (1998)

Sullivan & Tifft
Restorative Justice (2001)

Daly & Chesney-Lind
Feminist Theory
(1988)

Quinney & Pepinsky
*Criminology as
Peacemaking* (1991)

Barak & Henry
An Integrative-Constitutive Theory of Crime (1999)

Kornhauser
*Social Sources
of Delinquency* (1978)

Wilson
*The Truly
Disadvantaged*
(1987)

Agnew
General Strain Theory
(1992)

Courtwright
Violent Land (1996)

Anderson
Code of the Street (1999)

Blau & Blau
The Cost of Inequality (1982)

Messner & Rosenfeld
*Crime and the American
Dream* (1994)

LaFree
Losing Legitimacy
(1998)

Akers
Deviant Behavior (1977)

Kaplan
*General Theory
of Deviance* (1992)

Akers
*Social Learning
and Social Structure* (1998)

Heimer & Matsueda
Differential Social Control (1994)

West & Farrington
Delinquent Way of Life
(1977)

Thornberry
Interactional Theory
(1987)

Sampson & Laub
Crime in the Making (1993)

Loeber
Pathways to Delinquency (1998)

Weis
*Social Development
Theory* (1981)

Moffitt
*Adolescence-Limited and Life-Course
Persistent Antisocial Behavior* (1995)

Wilson & Herrnstein
*Crime and Human
Nature* (1985)

Tittle
*Control Balance: Toward a General
Theory of Deviance* (1995)

Colvin
Crime and Coercion (2000)

Gottfredson & Hirschi
General Theory of Crime (1990)

Herrnstein & Murray
The Bell Curve (1996)

1980	1991	1995	1997	2000	2002
Reagan Era	Fall of European Communism	Clinton Administration			

www.wadsworth.com

wadsworth.com is the World Wide Web site for Wadsworth and is your direct source to dozens of online resources.

At *wadsworth.com* you can find out about supplements, demonstration software, and student resources. You can also send e-mail to many of our authors and preview new publications and exciting new technologies.

wadsworth.com
Changing the way the world learns®

LARRY J. SIEGEL

University of Massachusetts—Lowell

CRIMINOLOGY

EIGHTH EDITION

THOMSON

WADSWORTH

Australia · Canada · Mexico · Singapore · Spain · United Kingdom · United States

THOMSON
WADSWORTH

Senior Executive Editor, Criminal Justice: SABRA HORNE
Development Editor: JULIE SAKAUE
Assistant Editor: DAWN MESA
Editorial Assistant: PAUL MASSICOTTE
Technology Project Manager: SUSAN DEVANNA
Marketing Manager: DORY SCHAEFFER
Marketing Assistant: NEENA CHANDRA
Advertising Project Manager: BRYAN VANN
Project Manager, Editorial Production: JENNIE REDWITZ
Print/Media Buyer: KAREN HUNT
Permissions Editor: CHARLES HODGKINS

Production Service: CECILE JOYNER, THE COOPER COMPANY
Text Designer: JOHN WALKER
Photo Researcher: LINDA RILL
Copy Editor: KAY MIKEL
Illustrators: JOHN AND JUDY WALLER
Indexer: KAY BANNING
Cover Designer: JEANNE CALABRESE
Cover Image: © TEOFILO OLIVIERI/SIS
Compositor: R&S BOOK COMPOSITION
Text and Cover Printer: TRANSCONTINENTAL/BEAUCEVILLE
Photo credits appear on page 652.

For more information about our products, contact us at:
Thomson Learning Academic Resource Center
1-800-423-0563
For permission to use material from this text, contact us by:
Phone: 1-800-730-2214   **Fax:** 1-800-730-2215
Web: http://www.thomsonrights.com

Library of Congress Control Number: 2002103355

Student Edition ISBN 0-534-52654-3
Instructor's Edition ISBN 0-534-52655-1

Wadsworth/Thomson Learning
10 Davis Drive
Belmont, CA 94002-3098
USA

Asia
Thomson Learning
5 Shenton Way #01-01
UIC Building
Singapore 068808

Australia
Nelson Thomson Learning
102 Dodds Street
South Melbourne, Victoria 3205
Australia

Canada
Nelson Thomson Learning
1120 Birchmount Road
Toronto, Ontario M1K 5G4
Canada

Europe/Middle East/Africa
Thomson Learning
High Holborn House
50/51 Bedford Row
London WC1R 4LR
United Kingdom

Latin America
Thomson Learning
Seneca, 53
Colonia Polanco
11560 Mexico D.F.
Mexico

Spain
Paraninfo Thomson Learning
Calle/Magallanes, 25
28015 Madrid, Spain

This book is dedicated to my children, Julie, Andrew, Eric, and Rachel, and to my wife, Therese J. Libby.

CONTENTS

PART IV The Criminal Justice System

CHAPTER 15 **Overview of the Criminal Justice System**   458

My kids have a long tradition of serving me breakfast in bed on my birthday, and this year was no exception. As I was having my toast and coffee, with the family gathered round me, I put the TV on and the screen showed a jet plane crashing into a familiar building, causing it to burst into flames. For a moment I thought I was catching the tail end of some science fiction film, maybe *Independence Day* or *Battlefield Earth*. I soon realized I was, in fact, tuned to the news station. You see, my birthday is September 11.

Like most Americans, the attack left me reeling. I was born and raised in New York and went to City College. As a criminologist, I am used to trying to explain why people commit horrendous acts, but this was so enormous and outrageous that it left me stumped. What could cause someone to engage in a conspiracy to kill so many innocent people? Some experts speculate that the attack was a result of politically motivated anger directed at American foreign policy. Others view it simply as a crazed plot carried out by deranged, twisted minds. Whatever its cause, the World Trade Center attack will be for most of us the most devastating crime of our lifetime. The terrorists may have had political or religious motivations, but their act was a violent crime, albeit of immense proportions.

Criminologists spend their career trying to understand what drives people to commit crime. Why do people behave the way they do? What causes one person to become violent and antisocial while another channels his or her energy into work, school, and family? Why would a terrorist kill innocent people and himself to express his anger at the United States? Why do some adolescents who live in high crime areas grow up to become law-abiding citizens while others join gangs and enter into a criminal career? And what accounts for the behavior of the multimillionaire who cheats on his or her taxes or engages in fraudulent schemes? Why are some people who live in extreme circumstances able to resist crime while others who have every form of material wealth fall prey to its lure?

My goal in writing this text is to help students gain insight into the answers behind these questions and to generate the same interest in criminology that has sustained me during my 30 years in college teaching. The text itself is meant as a broad overview of the field of criminology, designed in such a way as to whet the reader's appetite and encourage further in-depth exploration while covering this compelling area of study in an organized and comprehensive manner.

■ Recurrent Themes and Noteworthy Changes

Criminology is a dynamic field, changing constantly with the release of major research studies, Supreme Court rulings, and governmental policy, not to mention the current events of everyday life. Because of its evolutionary nature, I have updated *Criminology* to reflect important and noteworthy changes that have occurred since the Seventh Edition was written. In addition to these changes, several major themes recur throughout the text. It is my hope that these changes together with these recurring themes present criminology in such a way that students not only gain a comprehensive understanding of criminology but learn to think critically about criminological issues and to create informed opinions of their own.

Current Theory and Research

Throughout the book, every attempt is made to use the most current research to show students the major trends in criminological research and policy. In fact, most people who have used previous editions of the book have told me that this is one of its strongest features. In keeping with this tradition, you will find up-to-date research throughout the text, with additional in-depth coverage of recent important criminology research in the Criminological Enterprise features. For example, in Chapter 3 "Explaining Crime Trends" discusses research that helps explain why crime rates rise and fall.

Competing Viewpoints

In every chapter an effort is made to introduce students to the diversity of thought that characterizes the discipline. Current research is presented in a balanced fashion, although this sometimes can be frustrating to students. For example, some experts find that a defendant's race negatively affects sentencing in the criminal courts, but other criminologists conclude that race has little influence on sentencing. Which position is correct? Although it is comforting to reach an unequivocal conclusion about an important topic, sometimes that is simply not possible. In an effort to be objective and fair, each side of important criminological debates is presented in full.

Critical Thinking

It is important for students to think critically about law and justice and to develop a critical perspective toward the social and legal institutions entrusted with crime control. Throughout the book, students are asked to critique issues highlighted in the boxed material and prompted to think outside the box, so to speak. To aid in this task, each chapter ends with a section titled "Thinking Like a Criminologist," which presents a scenario that can be analyzed with the help of material found in the chapter. Connections boxes, which link issues and questions addressed in one chapter to topics covered in another, are found throughout each chapter. Such cross-references allow students to jump quickly to other areas of the text to learn more about a particular topic; this helps highlight how issues related to one area apply to other areas.

To encourage students to think critically even more, I also include critical thinking questions at the end of each boxed feature, where we take a look at specific topics or events in greater detail, and also at the end of each chapter.

Diversity

Diversity is a key issue in criminology, and the text attempts to integrate issues of racial, ethnic, gender, and cultural diversity throughout. I include material on international issues, such as the use of the death penalty abroad, as well as gender issues, such as the rising rate of female criminality. Moreover, Race, Culture, Gender, and Criminology boxes address a multitude of diversity issues in greater depth. Chapter 17, for example, includes an in-depth discussion on how race influences sentencing in criminal courts.

Public Policy

There is a focus on public policy throughout the book to show students how criminological theory translates into crime prevention programs. Policy and Practice in Criminology boxes, for instance, show how criminological ideas and research can be put into action. For example, in Chapter 7 a feature titled "Reentry Blues: Problems with Locking People Up and Then Letting Them Go" discusses the long-term effects of an increasing prison population. Rather than deterring or preventing crime, this feature dis-

cusses the rather provocative view that imprisoning large numbers of offenders has an opposite effect—it causes the crime rate to increase. What is the cause of this unexpected phenomenon?

Use of Techonology

The book attempts to interweave even more current research and events by incorporating the Internet into each chapter's coverage. Within each chapter, I have provided a number of links that will take students to relevant and timely Web sites, which will further inform discussions on the material presented in each chapter. In addition, the text makes extensive use of InfoTrac College Edition, a powerful online library provided exclusively by Wadsworth Publishing Company, which contains hundreds of thousands of full-length text articles. You will find InfoTrac College Edition exercises interspersed throughout each chapter and at the end of all the boxed features to encourage critical thinking and expand students' points of reference beyond the text and the classroom.

■ Organization of the Text

Criminology is a thorough introduction to this fascinating field. It is divided into four main sections or topic areas.

Part I provides a framework for studying criminology. The first chapter defines the field and discusses its most basic concepts: the component areas of criminology, the history of criminology, criminological research methods, the definition of crime, and the ethical issues that confront the field. Chapter 2 covers some of the basic concepts of criminal law, including its origins, key concepts, and recent developments. Chapter 3 covers the nature, extent, and patterns of crime. It has sections on crime measurement, recent trends in crime rates, and key structural variables that correlate with criminal behavior. Chapter 4 is devoted to the concept of victimization, including the nature of victims, theories of victimization, and programs designed to help crime victims.

Part II contains six chapters that cover criminological theory: why do people behave the way they do? These views include choice (Chapter 5), biology and psychology (Chapter 6), structure and culture (Chapter 7), social process and socialization (Chapter 8), social conflict (Chapter 9), and human development (Chapter 10).

Part III is devoted to the major forms of criminal behavior. The chapters in this section cover violent crime (Chapter 11), common theft offenses (Chapter 12), white-collar and organized crimes (Chapter13), and public order crimes, including sex offenses and substance abuse (Chapter 14).

Part IV contains four chapters that describe the criminal justice system. Chapter 15 provides an overview of the entire justice system, including the process of justice, the major organizations that make up the justice system, and concepts and perspectives of justice. Chapter 16 focuses on the police in society, tracing the history of law enforcement and the current state of policing. Chapter 17 covers the court process, and Chapter 18 provides an overview of the correctional process.

■ What's New in This Edition

Each new edition of this book integrates the most recent cases, research, and data. Following are a few of the important, exciting changes new to this edition.

In Chapter 1, Crime and Criminology, I've included a discussion of the concept of social harm and how it relates to criminal behavior and updated the Race, Culture, Gender, and Criminology box "Is Crime an International Phenomenon?" which presents recent changes in cross-national crime.

Chapter 2, The Criminal Law and Its Processes, begins with discussion of a 2001 case in which a man murdered his former girlfriend on her wedding; this case highlights the concept of a criminal responsibility of the accused. There is also an enhanced discussion of self-defense, with material on the Junta "Hockey Dad" case in which a coach was beaten to death after a kids' hockey game. The chapter also contains recent material on the insanity defense, using the example of the Andrea Yates case (the mother who drowned her five children and was charged with murder despite a plea of postpartum depression).

Chapter 3, The Nature and Extent of Crime, begins with a new introduction: a 2001 school violence case involving an alleged victim of bullying who killed two students. The introduction relates school violence to public policy and perceptions. It includes updated UCR, NCVS, and self-report trends. A new Policy and Practice in Criminology box, "Gun Control Issues," reflects in part the findings of Anthony Braga and David Kennedy on the illicit acquisition of firearms by youth and juveniles and those of Anthony Hoskin on the impact of firearm availability on national homicide rates. There is also new material on the characteristics that predict chronic offending and a new table that looks at delinquency types and the probability of becoming an adult offender.

Chapter 4, Victims and Victimization, opens with a new introduction that helps students understand the victim's role in the crime process, spotlighting the case of Waterbury, Connecticut, mayor Philip Giordano, accused of child sexual abuse. It has a new in-depth analysis of the long-term costs of victimization and a discussion on moral guardianship, the idea that moral beliefs and socialization may influence the routine activities that produce crime. The chapter has two new boxes, a Policy and Practice in Criminology box, "Combating Elderly Abuse," and a Criminological Enterprise box, "Siblicide," which discusses the relatively rare but shocking phenomenon of kids killing their brothers and sisters.

I begin Chapter 5, Choice Theory, with a new introduction that demonstrates rational choice theory, showing how drug dealers use carefully calculated market risk assessment techniques to determine where to sell their illegal drugs. There is a discussion of crime as a method of solving problems. A new Criminological Enterprise box looks at the benefits of crime, and I also address new evidence on the pros and cons of capital punishment as a crime deterrent.

In Trait Theories, Chapter 6, there is a discussion on recent findings examining "the contagion effect" on twin behavior. I have also addressed new findings from the Minnesota Study of Twins Reared Apart, which shows the similarity of twin behavior. I have also added material on the theory that human traits that produce violence and aggression are part of the long process of human evolution. The chapter now also presents evidence on how this evolutionary model can explain female criminality.

Chapter 7, Social Structure Theories, now begins by examining a gang killing in Boston. This vignette exemplifies how gang membership is a function of cultural and social pressures. A new Policy and Practice in Criminology box, "The Reentry Blues: Problems with Locking People Up and Then Letting Them Out," discusses the problem of returning inmates and how their presence may destabilize neighborhoods. I also added a new discussion on the relationship between self-image and relative deprivation as well as a new Gender, Culture, Race, and Criminology box, "Bridging the Racial Divide," which presents an analysis of the most recent work by famed sociologist William Julius Wilson.

In Chapter 8, Social Process Theories, I present recent material on parenting, self-control, and delinquency, including the relationship between parental efficacy and delinquent behavior. I also added new sections on the effect of religion on crime, the impact of maternal employment on delinquency, and the relationship between law violation and depression.

Chapter 9, Conflict Theory, now includes more on the concept of restorative justice as a noncoercive, nonconflict method of crime control. There is also a discussion on the role of "reintegrative shaming" and its relationship to crime control as well as a discussion of the challenges and perils of restorative justice.

I begin Chapter 10, Developmental Theories, with the case of a 41-year-old chronic offender and look at the factors that may have contributed to his offending career. I also added new discussions on differential coercion theory and control balance theory.

Chapter 11, Violent Crime, begins with a profile of the psychological implications of Osama bin Laden's murderous actions. I included new sections on school shootings, acquaintance robbery, and stalking, and updated the material on terrorism. The Race, Culture, Gender, and Criminology box, "Transnational Terrorism in the New Millennium," includes a discussion of al-Qaeda and Osama bin Laden.

In Chapter 12, Property Crimes, I added a new Criminological Enterprise box, "Operation American Dream: The Anatomy of a Professional Criminal Enterprise," and in Chapter 13, White-Collar and Organized Crime, I begin with an analysis of the Gold Club case in Atlanta in which a strip club controlled by criminal syndicates provided prostitutes to professional athletes. There are also new sections on Internet crime, Internet securities fraud, and Eastern European crime groups in the United States. I also added a Race, Culture, Gender, and Criminology box that discusses Russian organized crime and a Policy and Practice in Criminology box on controlling techno-crime.

Chapter 14, Public Order Crimes, has an added discussion on child pornography, the international sex trade, newly emerging drugs including Ecstasy and OxyContin, and sexual abuse/prostitution. Pornography and sexual violence is discussed further in a new Criminological Enterprise box on this issue.

I begin Chapter 15, Overview of the Criminal Justice System, with a discussion of the Brian Dalton case, the young man whose diary entries about sexual fantasies led to a seven-year prison term. I also updated numbers on the cost and size of criminal justice and reexamine material on the abolition of the juvenile court.

Chapter 16, Police and Law Enforcement, has been updated extensively. I include material on the case of racial profiling of a Secret Service agent of Middle Eastern descent and new material from the most recent national survey of police contacts with civilians. I also added new sections covering the changing role of the FBI, findings on the effectiveness of Operation CeaseFire, a gun control project in Boston, and up-to-date material on the control of deadly force by police officers. The chapter covers the newest forms of policing, problem-oriented and community-oriented policing, and addresses the questions of whether community-oriented policing is changing the basic functions of policing. Findings from a study of 200 police agencies reveal the answer.

Chapter 17, The Judiciary Process, begins with the case of two boys in Florida charged with murder for giving their friend OxyContin. There is added material on specialty courts, such as drug courts and gun courts, as well as new data on prosecutors in large courts (population 500,000+) and state-funded indigent defense. I also cover recent events related to the death penalty abroad, including China's "Strike Hard" campaign against crime during which more than 1,700 people were executed in three months! I have also added new data on race and sentencing to the chapter.

Chapter 18, Corrections, includes recent data on size and trends in the correctional system. There is also an update on the use of ultra-maximum-security prisons, including concerns about the long-term effects of prolonged solitary confinement on inmates. The chapter covers the 2001 case *Shaw v. Murphy* in which the Supreme Court ruled that inmates do not have a right to correspond with other inmates even concerning legal advice. I also take a look at changes in the parole system, including recent developments in parole release mechanisms.

■ Supplements

Criminology, Eighth Edition, is accompanied by a wide array of supplements, prepared for both instructor and student, which creates the best learning environment inside as well as outside the classroom. All the continuing supplements for *Criminology*, Eighth Edition, have been thoroughly revised and updated, and several are new to this edition. Especially noteworthy are the new media- and Internet-based supplements. I invite you to examine and take full advantage of the teaching and learning tools available to you.

For the Instructor

Instructor's Resource Manual   This revised and updated *Instructor's Resource Manual* includes the following for every text chapter: learning objectives, key terms, detailed chapter outlines, discussion topics, InfoTrac College Edition activities, and a test bank. The completely new test bank features the following for each text chapter: 40 multiple-choice, 15 true/false, 15 fill-in-the-blank, and 5 essay questions.

ExamView® Computerized Testing   *ExamView* helps you create and customize tests in minutes! You can easily edit and import your own questions and graphics, edit and maneuver existing questions, and change test layouts. Tests appear on screen just as they will when printed. *ExamView* offers flexible delivery and the ability to test and grade online.

InfoTrac® College Edition   With InfoTrac College Edition, the premier online library of current publications, instructors can ignite discussions and augment lectures with the latest developments in corrections and criminal justice. Available free with this newly purchased text, InfoTrac College Edition gives instructors and students four months of free access to an extensive online database of reliable, full-length articles (not just abstracts) from hundreds of top academic journals and popular sources that go back as far as 22 years. By entering a single key word, users instantly search the entire InfoTrac College Edition database for related articles that can be read online or printed. Available only to colleges and universities.

Classroom Presentation Tools for the Instructor

Criminology 2003: A Microsoft® PowerPoint® Presentation Tool   This set of more than 500 slides will help you enhance your classroom presentations quickly and easily.

Transparency Acetates for Criminology, Eighth Edition This set of 50 full-color transparencies will help you effortlessly enhance your discussion of key concepts and research findings.

CNN® Today: Criminal Justice Video Series Now you can integrate the up-to-the-minute programming power of CNN and its affiliate networks right in your course. These videos feature short, high-interest clips perfect for launching your lectures. A current new volume is available to adopters each year. Ask your Thomson/Wadsworth representative about our video policy by adoption size. Vol. I: 0-534-53520-8. Vol. II: 0-534-53529-1. Vol. III: 0-534-53530-5. Vol. IV: 0-534-53539-9. Vol. V: 0-534-53540-2.

Customized Criminal Justice Videos Produced by Wadsworth and *Films for the Humanities,* these videos include short 5- to 10-minute segments that encourage classroom discussion. Topics include white-collar crime, domestic violence, forensics, suicide and the police officer, the court process, the history of corrections, prison society, and juvenile justice. Vol. I: 0-534-52528-5. Vol. II: 0-534-57335-5.

The Wadsworth Criminal Justice Video Library So many exciting, new videos . . . so many great ways to enrich your lectures and spark discussion of the material in this text! Your Thomson/Wadsworth representative will be happy to provide details on our video policy by adoption size. The library includes these selections and many others: *Court TV Videos,* one-hour videos presenting seminal and high-profile court cases; plus videos from the A & E American Justice Series, Films for the Humanities, and the National Institute of Justice Crime File Videos.

For the Student

Study Guide For each chapter of the book, this helpful guide contains learning objectives, detailed chapter outlines, chapter summaries, key terms with definitions, and a practice test. The practice test questions include 25 multiple choice, 15 true/false, 10 fill-in-the-blank, 10 matching, and 3 essay questions.

Internet Activities for Criminal Justice, Second Edition This completely updated booklet shows how to best utilize the Internet for research through fun and informative exercises, searches, and activities.

Internet Guide for Criminal Justice, Second Edition Intended for the less-experienced Internet user, the first part of this completely revised booklet explains the background and vocabulary necessary for navigating the Internet, and the second part focuses on Internet applications in criminal justice, doing criminal justice research online, and criminal justice career information on the Web.

InfoTrac College Edition Student Guide for Criminal Justice This booklet provides detailed user guidelines for students, illustrating how to use the InfoTrac College Edition database. Special features include log-in help, a complete search tips worksheet, and a topic list of suggested key word search terms for criminal justice.

The Criminal Justice Internet Investigator, Third Edition This colorful tri-fold brochure lists some of the most popular Internet addresses for criminal justice–related Web sites.

Internet-based Supplements

WebTutor® Advantage This Web-based software for students and instructors takes a course beyond the classroom to an anywhere, anytime environment. Students gain access to a full array of study tools, including chapter outlines, chapter-specific quiz material, interactive games, and videos. With WebTutor Advantage, instructors have access to an array of communication and class management tools. They can provide virtual office hours, post syllabi, track student progress with the quiz material, and even customize the content to suit their needs. They can also do such things as set up threaded discussions and conduct "real-time" chats. "Out of the box" or customized, WebTutor Advantage provides powerful tools for instructors and students alike.

Criminal Justice Resource Center at http://cj. wadsworth.com This Web site provides instructors and students alike with a wealth of FREE information and resources:

- The Criminal Justice Timeline
- What Americans Think
- BookFinder
- Terrorism: An Interdisciplinary Perspective
- National Criminal Justice Reference Service Calendar of Events

The Criminal Justice Resource Center also includes text-specific Web sites with chapter-specific resources for instructors and students. For instructors, the Web sites offer password-protected instructor's manuals, Microsoft PowerPoint presentation slides, and more. For students, there is a multitude of text-specific study aids.

These chapter-specific features are available for students using many of Wadsworth's criminal justice and criminology texts:

- Tutorial practice quizzes that can be scored and emailed to the instructor
- Internet links and exercises
- InfoTrac College Edition exercises
- Flashcards

- Crossword puzzles
- And much more!

To access all of these exciting text-specific Web resources, go to *The Wadsworth Criminal Justice Resource Center* at http://cj.wadsworth.com and follow these steps:

- Click either **Student Resources** or **Instructor Resources** on the left navigation bar. If you are an instructor, you will be prompted to enter a user name and password.
- Click the text cover that you use.

■ Acknowledgments

The preparation of this text would not have been possible without the aid of my colleagues who helped by reviewing the previous editions and gave me important suggestions for improvement.

Reviewers of the Eighth Edition:

Dorothy Goldsborough
Chaminade University

Gary Perlstein
Portland State University

Mark Stetler
Montgomery College

Kathleen Sweet
St. Cloud State University

Angela West
University of Louisville

Cecil Willis
University of North Carolina—Wilmington

Reviewers of previous editions include M.H. Alsikafi, Alexander Alvarez, Thomas Arvanites, Patricia Atchison, Timothy Austin, Agnes Baro, Bonnie Berry, James Black, Joseph Blake, David Bordua, Stephen Brodt, Thomas Calhoun, Mike Carlie, Mae Conley, Thomas Courtless, Mary Dietz, Edna Erez, Stephen Gibbons, Edward Green, Julia Hall, Marie Henry, Denny Hill, Alfred Himelson, Dennis Hoffman, Gerrold Hotaling, Joseph Jacoby, Casey Jordan, John Martin, Pamela Mayhall, James McKenna, Steven Messner, Linda O'Daniel, Hugh O'Rourke, Nikos Passos, William Pridemore, Jim Ruiz, Louis San Marco, Kip Schelgel, Theodore Skotnick, Gregory Talley, Kevin Thompson, Charles Tittle, Paul Tracy, Charles Vedder, Joesph Vielbig, Ed Wells, Michael Wiatkowski, Janet Wilson, and Janne Ziembo-Vogl.

My colleagues at Wadsworth did their typical outstanding job of aiding me in the preparation of the text and putting up with my seasonal angst. Sabra Horne, my wonderful editor is always there with encouragement, enthusiasm, and advice; Julie Sakaue is a terrific developmental editor who has become a good friend. Linda Rill did her usual thorough, professional job in photo research; and Cecile Joyner, the book's production editor, is a joy to work with. Karen Austin Keith helped in keeping things in order and everything moving; the sensational Jennie Redwitz somehow pulled everything together as production manager; and Dory Schaeffer, the marketing manager, tirelessly explains to people what the book is all about.

Larry Siegel
Bedford, New Hampshire

How is crime defined? How much crime is there, and what are the trends and patterns in the crime rate? How many people fall victim to crime, and who is likely to become a crime victim? How did our system of criminal law develop, and what are the basic elements of crimes? What is the science of criminology all about? These are some of the core issues that will be addressed in the first four chapters of this text. Chapter 1 introduces students to the field of criminology: its nature, area of study, methodologies, and historical development. Concern about crime and justice has been an important part of the human condition for more than 5,000 years, since the first criminal codes were set down in the Middle East. Although criminology—the scientific study of crime—is considered a modern science, it has existed for more than 200 years.

PART I Concepts of Crime, Law, and Criminology

Chapter 2 introduces students to one of the key components of criminology—the development of criminal law. It discusses the social history of law, the purpose of law, and how law defines crime, and it briefly examines criminal defenses and the reform of the law. The final two chapters of this section review the various sources of crime data to derive a picture of crime in the United States. Chapter 3 focuses on the nature and extent of crime, and Chapter 4 is devoted to victims and victimization. Important, stable patterns in the rates of crime and victimization indicate that these are not random events. The way crime and victimization are organized and patterned profoundly influences how criminologists view the causes of crime.

AP/Wide World Photos

CHAPTER 1 Crime and Criminology

Introduction

On May 10, 2001, two men broke into a midtown Manhattan apartment located above the famed Carnegie Deli, with the intention of robbing its owner Jennifer Stahl, a former actress who had become a dealer in high-priced marijuana. Words were exchanged, and one of the robbers shot Ms. Stahl in the forehead, killing her instantly. The two gunmen then decided they would have to kill the four other people in the apartment, friends who were having dinner with Ms. Stahl, to cover their tracks. Though all four were shot, two recovered and later helped police put together the crime.

After committing the robbery and killing three people, the two men fled with $1,000 and 12 quarter-ounce bags of marijuana, leaving behind an additional six pounds of marijuana and $1,800 in cash. As the robbers left, their images were captured by security cameras. When the images were shown on the media, an acquaintance recognized Andre Smith of Irvington, New Jersey, and notified the New York detectives investigating the case. After his arrest, Smith confessed to the crime and identified his partner as Sean Salley. Able to avoid capture at first, Salley was

AP/Wide World Photos

■ Paramedics on the scene of the Carnegie Deli murders prepare to remove the five victims left in the wake of a botched robbery. Incidents such as this one convince the general public that crime is an ever-present aspect of American life.

later arrested outside a Miami homeless shelter after being profiled on Fox television's *America's Most Wanted*.

Both suspects had extensive prior records. Sean Salley had been arrested in Brooklyn and Buffalo, New York, and in Massachusetts and Georgia, on charges including assault, robbery, weapons possession, and fare evasion. Andre Smith was on parole for a 1993 robbery. Ironically, Smith should have been incarcerated at the time of the crime. He had been arrested three months earlier in New Jersey on charges of possessing 311 grams of marijuana near a public school. Despite the fact that he had an extensive criminal record that included nine arrests on charges ranging from weapons possession to drug offenses, corrections officials never moved to revoke his parole. Gov. George E. Pataki said the case showed the wisdom of eliminating parole for all violent felons. "We had revolving-door justice for too long," he told the press.[1]

The Carnegie Deli murders underscore a number of issues that help define the crime problem in America. The robbers used handguns to kill their victims. Should such weapons be strictly controlled or even banned outright? This case, like so many others, involved substance abuse and drug dealing. Would the violent crime rate be reduced if drugs were legalized? The case also illustrates the powerful attraction crime has on the media. Without the publicity given this tragedy, the suspects might never have been caught, yet the media help fan the fear of crime. Cases such as the Carnegie Deli murders get widespread media attention and help convince the public that crime is rampant despite evidence that in reality rates have been trending downward. Such stories have even greater impact when people have personally experienced crime or live in neighborhoods where crime is a problem.[2]

Finally, the perpetrators in the Carnegie Deli murders were career criminals with many prior offenses who should have been incarcerated. Yet they were free to commit crime again. New York's governor used the case as a forum to express his views on toughening criminal penalties. Should measures be adopted to prevent repeat offenders from earning early release via parole? Would such measures help reduce repeat criminality? Or would such a "get tough" approach reduce the likelihood that an offender can "go straight"?

Highly publicized criminal events such as the Carnegie Deli murders have become a routine occurrence, creating concern among the public, political figures, and those responsible for administering justice in the United States. Concern about crime and the need for effective measures to control criminal behavior have spurred the development of criminology as an academic discipline. This discipline is devoted to the development of valid and reliable information that addresses the causes of crime as well as crime patterns and trends. **Criminologists** use scientific methods to study the nature, extent, cause, and control of criminal behavior. Unlike media commentators, whose opinions about crime may be colored by personal experiences, biases, and values, criminologists remain objective as they study crime and its consequences. The field of criminology has gained prominence as an academic area of study due to the constant threat of crime and the social problems it represents.

This text analyzes criminology and its major subareas of inquiry. It focuses on the nature and extent of crime, the causes of crime, crime patterns, and crime control. This chapter introduces and defines criminology: What are its goals? What is its history? How do criminologists define crime? How do they conduct research? What ethical issues face those wishing to conduct criminological research?

■ What Is Criminology?

Criminology is the scientific approach to studying criminal behavior. In their classic definition, criminologists Edwin Sutherland and Donald Cressey state:

> Criminology is the body of knowledge regarding crime as a social phenomenon. It includes within its scope the processes of making laws, of breaking laws, and of reacting toward the breaking of laws.... The objective of criminology is the development of a body of general and verified principles and of other types of knowledge regarding this process of law, crime, and treatment.[3]

Sutherland and Cressey's definition includes the most important areas of interest to criminologists: (1) the development of criminal law and its use to define crime, (2) the cause of law violation, and (3) the methods used to control criminal behavior. This definition also makes reference to the term *verified principles*, which implies that the scientific method should be used in studying criminology. Criminologists use objective research methods to pose research questions (hypotheses), gather data, create theories, and test their validity. They also use every method of established social science inquiry, including analysis of existing records, experimental designs, surveys, historical analysis, and content analysis. Criminology is essentially an **interdisciplinary science**; criminologists have been trained in diverse fields, most commonly sociology, but also criminal justice, political science, psychology, economics, and the natural sciences. Criminology has evolved into an independent field of study, although it is still sometimes mistakenly confused with the related disciplines of criminal justice and deviance (see Exhibit 1.1).

■ A Brief History of Criminology

The scientific study of crime and criminality is a relatively recent development. Although written criminal codes have existed for thousands of years, these were restricted to defining crime and setting punishments. What motivated people to violate the law remained a matter for conjecture.

Exhibit 1.1 Criminology, Criminal Justice, and Deviance

Criminology explains the etiology (origin), extent, and nature of crime in society. Criminologists are concerned with identifying the nature, extent, and cause of crime.

Criminal justice refers to the study of agencies of social control that handle criminal offenders. Criminal justice scholars engage in describing, analyzing, and explaining the operations of the agencies of justice, specifically the police departments, courts, and correctional facilities. They seek more effective methods of crime control and offender rehabilitation.

Overlapping areas of concern: Criminal justice experts cannot begin to design effective programs of crime prevention or rehabilitation without understanding the nature and cause of crime. They require accurate criminal statistics and data to test the effectiveness of crime control and prevention programs.

Deviance refers to the study of behavior that departs from social norms. Included within the broad spectrum of deviant acts are behaviors ranging from violent crimes to joining a nudist colony. Not all crimes are deviant or unusual acts and not all deviant acts are illegal.

Overlapping areas of concern: Under what circumstances do deviant behaviors become crimes? For example, when does sexually oriented material cross the line from merely suggestive to obscene and therefore illegal? If an illegal act becomes a norm, should society reevaluate its criminal status? For example, there is still debate over the legalization and/or decriminalization of abortion, recreational drug use, possession of handguns, and assisted suicide.

CONNECTIONS

English Common Law is the immediate antecedent of our own legal system, but the influence of some of the earliest written codes, such as those of the Hebrews and Babylonians, can still be detected. Chapter 2 traces the history of the law in some detail. ■

During the Middle Ages (1200–1600), superstition and fear of satanic possession dominated thinking. People who violated social norms or religious practices were believed to be witches or possessed by demons. The prescribed method for dealing with the possessed was burning at the stake, a practice that survived into the seventeenth century. For example, between 1575 and 1590, Nicholas Remy, head of the Inquisition in the French province of Lorraine, ordered 900 sorcerers and witches burned to death; likewise, a contemporary, Peter Binsfield, the bishop of the German city of Trier, ordered the death of 6,500 people. An estimated 100,000 people were prosecuted throughout Europe

■ During the Middle Ages, superstition and fear of satanic possession dominated thinking. People who violated social norms or religious practices were believed to be witches or possessed by demons. The prescribed method for dealing with the possessed was burning at the stake, a practice that survived into the seventeenth century. This painting, *The Trial of George Jacobs, August 5, 1692* by T. H. Matteson (1855), depicts the ordeal of Jacobs, a patriarch of Salem, Massachusetts. During the witch craze, he had ridiculed the trials, only to find himself being accused, tried, and executed.

for witchcraft during the sixteenth and seventeenth centuries. It was also commonly believed that some families produced offspring who were unsound or unstable and that social misfits were inherently damaged by reason of their "inferior blood."[4] It was common practice to use cruel tortures to extract confessions, and those convicted of violent or theft crimes suffered extremely harsh penalties including whipping, branding, maiming, and execution.

Classical Criminology

By the mid-eighteenth century, social philosophers began to rethink the prevailing concepts of law and justice. They argued for a more rational approach to punishment, stressing that the relationship between crimes and their punishment should be balanced and fair. This view was based on the prevailing philosophy of the time called **utilitarianism**, which emphasized that behavior occurs when the actor considers it useful, purposeful, and reasonable. It stands to reason that criminal behaviors can be eliminated or controlled if people begin to view them as troublesome and disappointing and not easily rewarding. Reformers called for a more moderate and just approach to penal sanctions, which could substitute for the cruel public executions designed to frighten people into obedience. The most famous of these was Cesare Beccaria (1738–1794), whose writings described both a motive for committing crime and methods for its control.

Beccaria believed people want to achieve pleasure and avoid pain. Therefore, he concluded, crimes must provide some pleasure to the criminal. To deter crime, he believed one must administer pain in an appropriate amount to counterbalance the pleasure obtained from crime. Beccaria stated his famous theorem like this:

> In order for punishment not to be in every instance, an act of violence of one or many against a private citizen, it must be essentially public, prompt, necessary, the least possible in the given circumstances, proportionate to the crimes, and dictated by the laws.[5]

The writings of Beccaria and his followers form the core of what today is referred to as **classical criminology**. As originally conceived in the eighteenth century, classical criminology theory had several basic elements:

- In every society people have free will to choose criminal or lawful solutions to meet their needs or settle their problems.
- Criminal solutions may be more attractive than lawful ones because they usually require less work for a greater payoff; if left unsanctioned, crime has greater utility than conformity.
- A person's choice of criminal solutions may be controlled by his or her fear of punishment.
- The more severe, certain, and swift the punishment, the better able it is to control criminal behavior.

This classical perspective influenced judicial philosophy during much of the late eighteenth and nineteenth centuries. Prisons began to be used as a form of punishment, and sentences were geared proportionately to the seriousness of the crime. Executions were still widely used but slowly began to be employed for only the most serious crimes. The catch phrase was "let the punishment fit the crime."

During the nineteenth century, a new vision of the world challenged the validity of classical theory and presented an innovative way of looking at the causes of crime.

Nineteenth-Century Positivism

The classical position served as a guide to crime, law, and justice for almost 100 years, but during the late nineteenth century a change in the way knowledge was being gathered created a challenge to its dominance. The scientific method was beginning to take hold in Europe. Rather than rely on pure thought and reason, careful observation and analysis of natural phenomena was being undertaken to understand the way the world worked. This movement inspired new discoveries in biology, astronomy, and chemistry. If the scientific method could be applied to the study of nature, then why not use it to study human behavior?

Positivism can be used as an orientation in shaping the content of the law. To learn about this perspective, use InfoTrac College Edition to find and read: Claire Finkelstein. Positivism and the notion of an offense. *California Law Review* March 2000 v88 i2 p335 ■

Auguste Comte (1798–1857), considered the founder of sociology, applied scientific methods to the study of society. According to Comte, societies pass through stages that can be grouped on the basis of how people try to understand the world in which they live. People in primitive societies consider inanimate objects as having life (for example, the sun is a god); in later social stages, people embrace a rational, scientific view of the world. Comte called this final stage the positive stage, and those who followed his writings became known as positivists.

As we understand it today, **positivism** has two main elements. The first is the belief that human behavior is a function of internal and external forces. Some of these forces are social, such as the effect of wealth and class, and others are political and historical, such as war and famine. Other forces are more personal and psychological, such as an individual's brain structure and his or her biological makeup or mental ability. Each of these forces influences human behavior.

The second aspect of positivism is embracing the scientific method to solve problems. Positivists rely on the strict use of empirical methods to test hypotheses. That is, they believe in the factual, firsthand observation and meas-

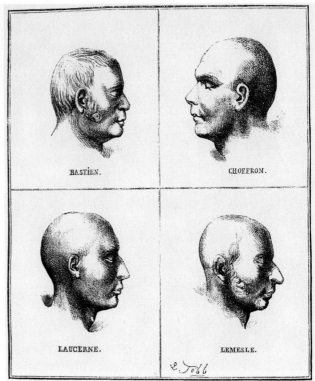

La *Phrénologie* criminelle.

■ Early positivists believed the shape of the skull was a key determinant of behavior. These drawings from the nineteenth century illustrate "typical" criminally shaped heads.

urement of conditions and events. Positivists would agree that an abstract concept such as "intelligence" exists because it can be measured by an IQ test. They would challenge a concept such as the "soul" because it is a condition that cannot be verified by the scientific method. The positivist tradition was popularized by Charles Darwin (1809–1882), whose work on the evolution of man encouraged a nineteenth-century "cult of science" that mandated that all human activity could be verified by scientific principles.

Positivist criminology The earliest "scientific" studies examining human behavior were biologically oriented. **Physiognomists,** such as J. K. Lavater (1741–1801), studied the facial features of criminals to determine whether the shape of ears, nose, and eyes and the distance between them were associated with antisocial behavior. **Phrenologists,** such as Franz Joseph Gall (1758–1828) and Johann K. Spurzheim (1776–1832), studied the shape of the skull and bumps on the head to determine whether these physical attributes were linked to criminal behavior. Phrenologists believed that external cranial characteristics dictate which areas of the brain control physical activity. Though their primitive techniques and quasi-scientific methods have been thoroughly discredited, these efforts were an early attempt to use a "scientific" method to study crime.

By the early nineteenth century, abnormality in the human mind was being linked to criminal behavior patterns. Philippe Pinel, one of the founders of French psychiatry, claimed that some people behave abnormally even without being mentally ill. He coined the phrase *"manie sans delire"* to denote what eventually was referred to as a **psychopathic personality.** In 1812, an American, Benjamin Rush, described patients with an "innate preternatural moral depravity."[6] Another early criminological pioneer, English physician Henry Maudsley (1835–1918), believed that insanity and criminal behavior were strongly linked. He stated: "Crime is a sort of outlet in which their unsound tendencies are discharged; they would go mad if they were not criminals, and they do not go mad because they are criminals."[7] These early research efforts shifted attention to brain functioning and personality as the keys to criminal behavior.

Biological determinism   In Italy, Cesare Lombroso (1835–1909) was studying the cadavers of executed criminals in an effort to scientifically determine whether law violators were physically different from people of conventional values and behavior. Lombroso, known as the "father of criminology," was a physician who served much of his career in the Italian army. That experience gave him ample opportunity to study the physical characteristics of soldiers convicted and executed for criminal offenses. Later, he studied inmates at institutes for the criminally insane at Pavia, Pesaro, and Reggio Emilia.[8]

James Cook at the University of Australia has an interesting Web page devoted to health issues that covers the work of Lombroso and cross references it with views of his contemporaries. Visit this page at:
    http://www.cimm.jcu.edu.au/hist/stats/lomb/
For an up-to-date list of Web links, go to
    http://info.wadsworth.com/siegel ▪

Lombrosian theory can be outlined in a few simple statements.[9] First, Lombroso believed that serious offenders—those who engaged in repeated assault- or theft-related activities—inherited criminal traits. These "born criminals" inherited physical problems that impelled them into a life of crime. This view helped stimulate interest in a **criminal anthropology.**[10] Second, Lombroso held that born criminals suffer from **atavistic anomalies**—physically, they are throwbacks to more primitive times when people were savages. For example, criminals were believed to have the enormous jaws and strong canine teeth common to carnivores and savages who devour raw flesh.

Lombroso compared the behavior of criminals to that of the mentally ill and those suffering some forms of epilepsy. According to Lombrosian theory, criminogenic traits can be acquired through indirect heredity, from a degenerate family whose members suffered from such ills as insanity, syphilis, and alcoholism. He believed that direct heredity—being related to a family of criminals—is the second primary cause of crime.

Lombroso's version of criminal anthropology was brought to the United States via articles and textbooks that adopted his ideas. He attracted a circle of followers who expanded on his vision of **biological determinism.** His work was actually more popular in the United States than it was in Europe. By the turn of the century, American authors were discussing "the science of penology" and "the science of criminology."[11]

Lombroso's version of strict biological determinism is no longer taken seriously. Later in his career even he recognized that not all criminals were biological throwbacks. Today, those criminologists who suggest that crime has some biological basis also believe that environmental conditions influence human behavior. Hence, the term **biosocial theory** has been coined to reflect the assumed link between physical and mental traits, the social environment, and behavior.

Social positivism   At the same time that biological views were dominating criminology, another group of positivists were developing the field of sociology to scientifically study the major social changes that were taking place in nineteenth-century society.

Sociology seemed an ideal perspective from which to study society. After thousands of years of stability, the world was undergoing a population explosion: the population estimated at 600 million in 1700 had risen to 900 million by 1800. People were flocking to cities in ever-increasing numbers. Manchester, England, had 12,000 inhabitants in 1760 and 400,000 in 1850; during the same period, the population of Glasgow, Scotland, rose from 30,000 to 300,000.

The development of machinery such as power looms had doomed cottage industries and given rise to a factory system in which large numbers of people toiled for extremely low wages. The spread of agricultural machines increased the food supply while reducing the need for a large rural workforce; these excess laborers further swelled city populations. At the same time, political, religious, and social traditions continued to be challenged by the scientific method.

Foundations of Sociological Criminology

The foundations of sociological criminology can be traced to the works of pioneering sociologists L. A. J. (Adolphe) Quetelet (1796–1874) and (David) Émile Durkheim (1858–1917). Quetelet instigated the use of data and statistics in performing criminological research. Durkheim, considered one of the founders of sociology,[12] defined crime as a normal and necessary social event. These two perspectives have been extremely influential on modern criminology.

L. A. J. (Adolphe) Quetelet   Quetelet was a Belgian mathematician who began (along with a Frenchman, Andre-Michel Guerry) what is known as the **cartographic school of criminology.**[13] This approach made use of social statistics that were being developed in Europe in the early nineteenth century. Statistical data provided important demographic information on the population, including density, gender, religious affiliations, and wealth.

Quetelet studied data gathered in France (called the *Comptes generaux de l'administration de la justice*) to investigate the influence of social factors on the propensity to commit crime. In addition to finding a strong influence of age and sex on crime, Quetelet also uncovered evidence that season, climate, population composition, and poverty were related to criminality. More specifically, he found that crime rates were greatest in the summer, in southern areas, among heterogeneous populations, and among the poor and uneducated. He also found crime rates to be influenced by drinking habits.[14] Quetelet identified many of the relationships between crime and social phenomena that still serve as a basis for criminology today.

Émile Durkheim   According to Durkheim's vision of social positivism, crime is part of human nature because it has existed during periods of both poverty and prosperity.[15] Crime is normal because it is virtually impossible to imagine a society in which criminal behavior is totally absent. Such a society would almost demand that all people be and act exactly alike. Durkheim believed that the inevitability of crime is linked to the differences (heterogeneity) within society. Since people are so different from one another and employ such a variety of methods and forms of behavior to meet their needs, it is not surprising that some will resort to criminality. Even if "real" crimes were eliminated, human weaknesses and petty vices would be elevated to the status of crimes. As long as human differences exist, then, crime is inevitable and one of the fundamental conditions of social life.

Durkheim argued that crime can be useful and, on occasion, even healthy for society. He held that the existence of crime paves the way for social change and that the social structure is not rigid or inflexible. Put another way, if crime did not exist, it would mean that everyone behaved the same way and agreed on what is right and wrong. Such universal conformity would stifle creativity and independent thinking. To illustrate this concept, Durkheim offered the example of the Greek philosopher Socrates, who was considered a criminal and put to death for corrupting the morals of youth simply because he expressed ideas that were different from what people believed at that time.

Durkheim reasoned that another benefit of crime is that it calls attention to social ills. A rising crime rate can signal the need for social change and promote a variety of programs designed to relieve the human suffering that may have caused crime in the first place. For example, national surveys conducted since the 1970s show that a surprising number of teens are substance abusers. This has prompted

school systems to develop school-based anti-drug programs, which may have helped lower use rates in the teenage population.[16]

In his famous book, *The Division of Labor in Society*, Durkheim described the consequences of the shift from a small, rural society, which he labeled "mechanical," to the more modern "organic" society with a large urban population, division of labor, and personal isolation.[17] From this shift flowed **anomie,** or norm and role confusion, a powerful sociological concept that helps describe the chaos and disarray accompanying the loss of traditional values in modern society. Durkheim's research on suicide indicated that anomic societies maintain high suicide rates; by implication, anomie might cause other forms of deviance as well.

CONNECTIONS

Durkheim's writing and research has had a profound effect on criminology. His vision of anomie and its influence on contemporary criminological theory will be discussed further in Chapter 7. ■

The Chicago School and Beyond

The primacy of sociological positivism was secured by research begun in the early twentieth century by Robert Ezra Park (1864–1944), Ernest W. Burgess (1886–1966), Louis Wirth (1897–1952), and their colleagues in the Sociology Department at the University of Chicago. The scholars who taught at this program created what is still referred to as the **Chicago School,** in honor of their unique style of doing research. These urban sociologists pioneered research on the **social ecology** of the city. Their work inspired a generation of scholars to conclude that social forces operating in urban areas create criminal interactions; some neighborhoods become "natural areas" for crime.[18] These urban neighborhoods maintain such a high level of poverty that critical social institutions, such as the school and the family, break down. The resulting social disorganization reduces the ability of social institutions to control behavior, and the outcome is a high crime rate.

The Chicago School sociologists and their contemporaries focused on the functions of social institutions, such as the school and family, and how their breakdown influenced deviant and antisocial behavior. Criminal behavior, they argued, was not a function of personal traits or characteristics but rather a reaction to an environment that was inadequate for proper human relations and development. They initiated the ecological study of crime by examining how neighborhood conditions, such as poverty levels, influenced crime rates. Their findings substantiated their belief that crime was a function of where one lived.

During the 1930s and 1940s, another group of sociologists—strong believers in a social-psychological link to criminological behavior—conducted research to support their beliefs. They concluded that the individual's relationship to important social processes, such as education, family life, and peer relations, was the key to understanding human behavior. For example, they found that children who grow up in homes wracked by conflict, attend inadequate schools, and/or associate with deviant peers become exposed to procrime forces. One position, championed by the preeminent American criminologist Edwin Sutherland, was that people learn criminal attitudes from older, more experienced law violators. Another view, developed by Chicago School sociologist Walter Reckless, was that crime occurs when children develop an inadequate self-image, which renders them incapable of controlling their own misbehavior. Both of these views linked criminality to the failure of **socialization,** the interactions people have with the various individuals, organizations, institutions, and processes of society that help them mature and develop.

By mid-century, most criminologists had embraced either the **ecological view** or the **socialization view** of crime. However, these were not the only views of how so-

cial institutions influence human behavior. In Europe, the writings of another social thinker, Karl Marx (1818–1883), had pushed the understanding of social interaction in another direction and sowed the seeds for a new approach in criminology.[19]

Use InfoTrac College Edition to learn more about how socialization affects human development. Use "socialization" as a key word. You might also want to look at this article to learn how TV affects socialization:
Susan D. Witt. The influence of television on children's gender role socialization. *Childhood Education* Mid-Summer 2000 v76 i5 p322 ■

Conflict Criminology

In his *Communist Manifesto* and other writings, Marx described the oppressive labor conditions prevalent during the rise of industrial capitalism. His observations of the economic structure convinced Marx that the character of every civilization is determined by its mode of production—the way its people develop and produce material goods (materialism). The most important relationship in industrial culture is between the owners of the means of production, the capitalist **bourgeoisie,** and the people who do the actual labor, the **proletariat.** The economic system controls all facets of human life; consequently, people's lives revolve around the means of production. The exploitation of the working class, he believed, would eventually lead to class conflict and the end of the capitalist system.

CONNECTIONS

Marx did not attempt to develop a theory of crime and justice, but his writings were applied to legal studies by a few social thinkers, including Ralf Dahrendorf, George Vold, and Willem Bonger. Their attempts to mold a Marxist conflict criminology will be discussed in some detail in Chapter 9. ■

Though these writings laid the foundation for a Marxist criminology, decades passed before the impact of Marxist theory was realized. In the United States during the 1960s, social and political upheaval was fueled by the Vietnam War, the development of an anti-establishment counterculture movement, the civil rights movement, and the women's movement. Young sociologists who became interested in applying Marxist principles to the study of crime began to analyze the social conditions in the United States that promoted class conflict and crime. What emerged from this intellectual ferment was a Marxist-based radical criminology that indicted the economic system as producing the conditions that support a high crime rate. The radical tradition has played a significant role in criminology ever since.

■ Firefighters and rescue workers struggle to put out fires in the aftermath of the 9/11 attack. According to conflict theory, violence is a function of the political, economic, and social conflict that divides people. The 9/11 attack is an extreme instance of the violent effects of political rage.

AP/Wide World Photos

Figure 1.1 Criminological Perspectives

The major perspectives of criminology focus on individual (biological, psychological, and choice theories), social (structural and process theories), political and economic (conflict theory), and multiple (developmental theory) factors.

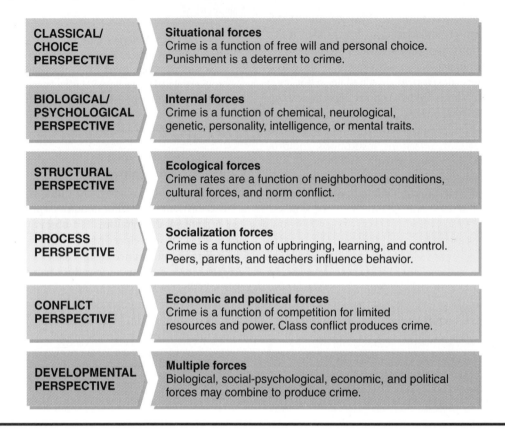

CLASSICAL/ CHOICE PERSPECTIVE
Situational forces
Crime is a function of free will and personal choice. Punishment is a deterrent to crime.

BIOLOGICAL/ PSYCHOLOGICAL PERSPECTIVE
Internal forces
Crime is a function of chemical, neurological, genetic, personality, intelligence, or mental traits.

STRUCTURAL PERSPECTIVE
Ecological forces
Crime rates are a function of neighborhood conditions, cultural forces, and norm conflict.

PROCESS PERSPECTIVE
Socialization forces
Crime is a function of upbringing, learning, and control. Peers, parents, and teachers influence behavior.

CONFLICT PERSPECTIVE
Economic and political forces
Crime is a function of competition for limited resources and power. Class conflict produces crime.

DEVELOPMENTAL PERSPECTIVE
Multiple forces
Biological, social-psychological, economic, and political forces may combine to produce crime.

Contemporary Criminology

The various schools of criminology developed over 200 years. Though they have evolved, each continues to have an impact on the field. For example, classical theory has evolved into rational choice and deterrence theories. Choice theorists today argue that criminals are rational and use available information to decide if crime is a worthwhile undertaking; deterrence theory holds that this choice is structured by the fear of punishment. Biological positivism has undergone similar transformation. Although criminologists no longer believe that a single trait or inherited characteristic can explain crime, some are convinced that biological and psychological traits interact with environmental factors to influence all human behavior, including criminality. Biological and psychological theorists study the association between criminal behavior and such traits as diet, hormonal makeup, personality, and intelligence.

Sociological theories, tracing back to Quetelet and Durkheim, maintain that individuals' lifestyles and living conditions directly control their criminal behavior. Those at the bottom of the social structure cannot achieve success and thus experience anomie, strain, failure, and frustration.

Some sociologists have added a social-psychological dimension to their views of crime causation and believe that individuals' learning experiences and socialization directly control their behavior. In some cases, children learn to commit crime by interacting with and modeling their behavior after others they admire, whereas other criminal offenders are people whose life experiences have shattered their social bonds to society.

The writings of Marx and his followers continue to be influential. Many criminologists still view social and political conflict as the root cause of crime. The inherently unfair economic structure of the United States and other advanced capitalist countries is the engine that drives the high crime rate.

Some criminologists are now integrating each of these concepts into more complex developmental theories of crime. Each of the major perspectives is summarized in Figure 1.1.

Figure 1.2   The Criminological Enterprise

These subareas constitute the field/discipline of criminology.

SUBAREA	PRIMARY FOCUS
CRIMINAL STATISTICS	**Gathering valid crime data** Devising new research methods Measuring crime patterns and trends
SOCIOLOGY OF LAW	**Determining the origin of law** Measuring the forces that can change laws and society
THEORY CONSTRUCTION	**Predicting individual behavior** Understanding the cause of crime rates and trends
CRIMINAL BEHAVIOR SYSTEMS	**Determining the nature and cause of specific crime patterns** Studying violence, theft, organized, white-collar, and public order crimes
PENOLOGY	**Studying the correction and control of criminal behavior**
VICTIMOLOGY	**Studying the nature and cause of victimization** Aiding crime victims

---

CONNECTIONS

The modern versions of the various schools of criminological thought will be discussed in greater detail throughout the book. Choice theories, the modern offshoot of Beccaria, are reviewed in Chapter 5. Current biological and psychological theories are the topic of Chapter 6. Contemporary theories based on Durkheim's views as well as theories based on the writings of the Chicago School are contained in Chapter 7. The social process view will be discussed in Chapter 8, and Marxist views are contained in Chapter 9. Developmental views are discussed in Chapter 10. ■

■ **What Criminologists Do: The Criminological Enterprise**

Regardless of their background or training, criminologists are primarily interested in studying crime and criminal behavior. As two noted criminologists, Marvin Wolfgang and Franco Ferracuti, put it: "A criminologist is one whose pro-fessional training, occupational role, and pecuniary reward are primarily concentrated on a scientific approach to, and study and analysis of, the phenomenon of crime and criminal behavior."[20]

Several subareas of criminology exist within the broader arena of criminology. Taken together, these subareas make up the **criminological enterprise.** Criminologists may specialize in a subarea in the same way that psychologists might specialize in a subfield of psychology, such as child development, perception, personality, psychopathology, or sexuality. Some of the more important criminological specialties are described next and summarized in Figure 1.2.

Criminal Statistics

The subarea of criminal statistics involves measuring the amount and trends of criminal activity. How much crime occurs annually? Who commits it? When and where does it occur? Which crimes are the most serious?

Criminologists interested in criminal statistics try to create valid and reliable measurements of criminal behavior.

Is Crime an International Phenomenon?

In a recent book, *Crime and Social Change in Middle England*, Evi Girling, Ian Loader, and Richard Sparks studied the effects of crime in one of Britain's typical small towns, Macclesfield. Crime rates there are still relatively low, but people are becoming increasingly concerned about incivility and disorder. Not unlike small-town residents in the United States, Macclesfield's citizenry equate civil disorder with wayward youth. Their main concern is the rowdy groups of kids who congregate in public places to drink, take drugs, and vandalize property. Local citizens blame parents for falling down on the job, yet they are unsure of what to do to control the problem: they are hesitant about giving more power to the police and/or installing security devices to monitor local activities.

Although the United States may still have a relatively high violence rate compared to many other nations, our crime rates have been on a decline while there is evidence of a disturbing upswing in crime abroad. For example, there has been a sharp increase in the murder rates in England, Germany, and Sweden. Racial assaults and hate crime have increased dramatically in Germany and England. Meanwhile, in the United States, in some instances, crime rates have declined to a point where they are actually lower than in some European nations. The most recent data available indicate that robbery, assault, burglary, and motor vehicle theft rates are lower in the United States today than they are in England and Wales.

Russia and the former Soviet republics have experienced an increase in large-scale organized crime gangs, who commonly use violence and intimidation. In other European nations, violence has been fueled by a dramatic growth in the number of illegal guns smuggled into these countries from the former Soviet republics. In addition, unrestricted immigration has brought newcomers who face cultural differences, lack of job prospects, and racism. Social and economic pressures, including unemployment and cutbacks in the social welfare system, have also been contributing factors to an increase of violence. Especially in the former communist countries in Eastern Europe, weak law enforcement institutions, rapid changes in economic laws, deteriorating economic conditions, incomplete reforms, and destabilization of social norms have contributed to rising criminality.

Youth crime has become a serious issue all over the world. Russia has experienced a significant increase in delinquency; the number of reported acts doubled during the past 10 years and delinquents account for nearly 20 percent of all serious criminal activity. Germany has been wracked by well-publicized outbursts of violence against immigrants and minorities by youth gangs of "skinheads." The "skins" are reacting to unemployment and competition for jobs between Germans and immigrants. Juveniles have been involved in about 20 percent of all violent crime in Germany and 33 percent of all property offenses. These trends show that juvenile delinquency and youth crime is a worldwide phenomenon.

Reports of increased criminal activity in Asia are also erupting. For example, Japan, a nation that prides itself on low crime rates, has experienced an upsurge in juvenile crime. It is estimated that 45 percent of all crimes are committed by people under 20, about double what it is in the United States. With so much Japanese crime committed by youths, and with the juvenile crime rate escalat-

---

For example, they create techniques to access the records of police and court agencies. They develop paper-and-pencil survey instruments and then use them on large samples of citizens to determine the percentage of people who actually commit crime and the number of law violators who escape detection by the justice system. They also develop techniques to identify the victims of crime to establish more accurate indicators of the "true" number of criminal acts: How many people are victims of crime, and what percentage reports crime to police? The study of criminal statistics is a crucial aspect of the criminological enterprise, because without valid and reliable data sources, efforts to conduct research on crime and create criminological theories would be futile.

Criminal statistics are used to evaluate crime rates all over the world. The Race, Culture, Gender, and Criminology feature looks at international crime rates.

To better understand the nature of crime in Eastern European nations that have transitioned from Communism to democracy and the efforts now being made for its control, use InfoTrac College Edition to find these articles: Christian Caryl. The very long arm of American law. *U.S. News & World Report* July 7, 1997 v123 p49
Richard Lotspeich. Crime in the transition economies. *Europe-Asia Studies* June 1995 v47 p555 ∎

How can gang activity be prevented? To find out, go to the Office of Juvenile Justice Web site at:
  http://www.ncjrs.org/html/ojjdp/2000_9_2/page3.html
For an up-to-date list of Web links, go to
  http://info.wadsworth.com/siegel ∎

ing, experts predict an overall increase in future crime rates.

Juvenile delinquency is also increasing in the island nation of Singapore. It is ironic that Singapore's "crime wave" occurred after the government became notorious for its draconian justice policies when, in 1993, an American teen, Michael Fay, was flogged after being convicted of vandalism. One would think that a nation that applies severe criminal punishments would never experience a "crime wave."

Singapore and Japan are not the only Asian nations experiencing an upsurge in crime. Authorities in Vietnam report a troubling increase in street crimes such as burglary and theft. Many crimes are drug related; there are an estimated 200,000 opium addicts in the country. Almost 50,000 acres of land are now being cultivated for growing the poppy from which heroin is produced.

Though it is difficult to obtain accurate crime data from China, the world's largest nation seems to be cracking down on crime. In recent years, Chinese courts annually sentenced more than 100,000 street criminals. Death sentences are doled out to thousands of criminals, and many thousands more are sentenced to life in prison. The current wave of punishments is in response to a significant increase in street crimes, including robberies and drug trafficking.

Violence rates are also increasing in other parts of the Americas. The homicide rate in Jamaica is 32 per 100,000; in Colombia, homicide rates are about 70 per 100,000, about 10 times the U.S. average! As in Asia and Europe, high murder rates in the region are tied to the flourishing drug trade.

Critical Thinking Questions

1. Will countries such as Japan experience growth in their crime rates as they become more economically dominant?

2. What factors do you think contribute to the high U.S. crime rate?

InfoTrac College Edition Research

To find out about the factors causing an increase in crime rates in Eastern European countries, check out these articles:

Richard Lotspeich. Crime in the transition economies. *Europe-Asia Studies* June 1995 v47 n4 p555 (35)

Tom Fenton. "Mafia" targets journalists abroad. *Editor & Publisher* July 2, 1994 v127 n27 p15 (2)

SOURCES: Evi Girling, Ian Loader, and Richard Sparks, *Crime and Social Change in Middle England: Questions of Order in an English Town* (New York: Routledge, 2000); Patrick A. Langan and David P. Farrington, *Crime and Justice in the United States and in England and Wales, 1981–96* (Washington, D.C.: Bureau of Justice Statistics, 1998); James Finckenauer, *Russian Youth, Law, Deviance and the Pursuit of Freedom* (New Brunswick, N.J.: Transaction Books, 1995); Michael Zielenziger, "Juvenile Crime Jumps to Record High in Japan," *Boston Globe*, 19 April 1998, p. A16; John King, "Paradise Lost? Crime in the Caribbean: A Comparison of Barbados and Jamaica," *Caribbean Journal of Criminology and Social Psychology* 2 (1997): 30–44; "With Women's Liberation Comes a Growing Involvement in Crime," *CJ International* 12 (1996): 19; "Crime Crackdown Continues as Statistics Increase," *CJ International* 12 (1996): 8; Sean Malinowski, "Battling an Emerging Crime Problem," *CJ International* 12 (1996): 3–4; "Singapore Says Delinquency Up," *Boston Globe*, 17 February 1996, p. 4; James Lynch, "A Serious Crime Cross-National Comparison of the Length of Custodial Sentences for Juveniles," *Justice Quarterly* 10 (1993); Gunther Kaiser, "Juvenile Delinquency in the Federal Republic of Germany," *International Journal of Comparative and Applied Criminal Justice* 16 (1992): 185–97; Marc Mauer, *Americans Behind Bars: The International Use of Incarceration* (Washington, D.C.: Sentencing Project, 1994); Elizabeth Neuffer, "Violent Crime Rise Fueling Fears in a Changing Europe," *Boston Globe*, 10 April 1994, p. 1.

Sociology of Law

The sociology of law is a subarea of criminology concerned with the role social forces play in shaping criminal law and, concomitantly, the role of criminal law in shaping society. Criminologists study the history of legal thought in an effort to understand how criminal acts, such as theft, rape, and murder, evolved into their present form.

Often, criminologists are asked to join in the debate when a new law is proposed to banish or control behavior. For example, across the United States, a debate has been raging over the legality of art works, films, photographs, and even rock albums that some people find offensive and lewd and others consider harmless. Criminologists help determine the role that the law will take in curbing the public's access to media and culture. They help answer questions such as these: Should society curb actions that some people consider immoral but by which no one is ac-

tually harmed? How is harm defined? Is a child who reads a pornographic magazine "harmed"?

Using InfoTrac College Edition to learn more about the sociology of law, use "sociological jurisprudence" as a subject guide. You might also want to check out this article: George P. Fletcher. The nature and function of criminal theory. *California Law Review* May 2000 v88 i3 p687 ■

Criminologists are also active participants in updating the content of the criminal law. In making key decisions, all involved in making laws must take into account that the law must be flexible; it must respond to changing times and conditions. For example, computer fraud, airplane hijacking, theft from automatic teller machines, Internet scams, and illegally tapping into TV cable lines are all behaviors that did not exist when the criminal law was originally conceived. Consequently, the law must be constantly revised to reflect cultural, societal, and technological adaptations to common acts. For example, Dr. Jack Kevorkian made headlines for helping people to kill themselves by using his "suicide machine." Some believe Dr. Kevorkian's actions are criminal, immoral, and socially harmful, and national media coverage made his actions widely known. However, even though many tried to take him to court, there was no law banning second-party help in suicides. In response to the national media coverage, however, Michigan passed legislation making it a felony to help anyone commit suicide, and in the November 1998 election Michigan voters defeated an attempt to legalize physician-assisted suicide.[21] Kevorkian was convicted for his acts and sent to prison. Is he a criminal?

Theory Construction

One question has tormented criminologists from the beginning: Why do people engage in criminal acts? When they know their actions can bring harsh punishment and social disapproval, why do people steal, rape, and murder? In short, why do people behave the way they do? Does crime have a social or an individual basis? Is it a psychological, biological, social, political, or economic phenomenon?

Criminologists bring their personal beliefs and backgrounds to bear when they study criminal behavior, so there are diverse theories of crime causation. Some criminologists have a psychological orientation and view crime as a function of personality, development, social learning, or cognition. Others investigate the biological correlates of antisocial behavior and study the biochemical, genetic, and neurological linkages to crime. Sociologists look at the social forces producing criminal behavior, including neighborhood conditions, poverty, socialization, and group interaction.

Understanding the true cause of crime remains a difficult problem. Criminologists are still unsure why, given similar conditions, one person elects criminal solutions to his or her problems while another conforms to accepted social rules of behavior. Further, understanding crime rates and trends has proven difficult: Why do rates rise and fall? Why are crime rates higher in some areas or regions than in others? Why are some groups more crime-prone than others? These questions motivate theories that address all of these issues.

Criminal Behavior Systems

The criminal behavior systems subarea of criminology involves research on specific criminal types and patterns: violent crime, theft crime, public order crime, and organized crime. Numerous attempts have been made to describe and understand particular crime types. For example, Marvin Wolfgang's famous 1958 study, *Patterns in Criminal Homicide,* is considered a landmark analysis of the nature of homicide and the relationship between victim and offender.[22] Edwin Sutherland's analysis of business-related offenses helped coin a new phrase—**white-collar crime**—to describe economic crime activities. The study of criminal behavior also involves research on the links between different types of crime and criminals. This is known as **crime typology.** Unfortunately, because people often disagree about types of crimes and criminal motivation, no standard exists within the field. Some typologies focus on the criminal, suggesting the existence of offender groups, such as professional criminals, psychotic criminals, occasional criminals, and so on. Others focus on the crimes, clustering them into categories such as property crimes, sex crimes, and so on.

Penology

The study of penology involves the correction and control of known criminal offenders. Penologists formulate strategies for crime control and then help implement these policies in the "real world." Today penology is most commonly referred to as the study of criminal justice. Although the field of criminal justice overlaps this area, criminologists have continued their efforts to develop new crime-control programs and policies. Some criminologists view penology as involving rehabilitation and treatment. Their efforts are directed at providing behavior alternatives for would-be criminals and treatment for individuals convicted of law violations. This view portrays the criminal as someone society has failed; someone under social, psychological, or economic stress; someone who can be helped if society is willing to pay the price. Others argue that crime can only be prevented through a strict policy of social control. They advocate such strict penological measures as the death penalty (capital punishment) and mandatory prison sentences. Criminologists also help evaluate correctional initiatives to determine if they are effective and how they impact people's lives.

Victimology

In two classic criminological studies, one by Hans von Hentig and another by Stephen Schafer, the critical role of the victim in the criminal process was first identified. These authors were among the first to suggest that victim behavior is often a key determinant of crime and that victims' actions may actually precipitate crime. Both men believe that the study of crime is not complete unless the victim's role is considered.[23]

CONNECTIONS

In recent years, criminologists have devoted ever-increasing attention to the victim's role in the criminal process. It has been suggested that a person's lifestyle and behavior may actually increase the risk that they will become crime victims. Some have suggested that living in a high-crime neighborhood increases risk; others point their finger at the problems caused by associating with dangerous peers and companions. For a discussion of victimization risk, see Chapter 4. ■

For those studying the role of the victim in crime, these areas are of particular interest:

- Using victim surveys to measure the nature and extent of criminal behavior, calculating the actual costs of crime to victims
- Creating probabilities of victimization risk
- Studying victim culpability or precipitation of crime
- Designing services for the victims of crime, such as counseling and compensation programs

Victimology has taken on greater importance as more criminologists focus their attention on the victim's role in the criminal event.

■ How Criminologists View Crime

Professional criminologists usually align themselves with one of several schools of thought or perspectives in their field. Each perspective maintains its own view of what constitutes criminal behavior and what causes people to engage in criminality. This diversity of thought is not unique to criminology; biologists, psychologists, sociologists, historians, economists, and natural scientists disagree among themselves about critical issues in their fields. Considering the multidisciplinary nature of the field of criminology, fundamental issues such as the nature and definition of crime itself is cause for disagreement among criminologists.

A criminologist's choice of orientation or perspective depends, in part, on his or her definition of crime: the beliefs and research orientations of most criminologists are related to this definition. This section discusses the three most common concepts of crime used by criminologists.

The Consensus View of Crime

According to the **consensus view,** crimes are behaviors believed to be repugnant to all elements of society. The **substantive criminal law,** which is the written code that defines crimes and their punishments, reflects the values, beliefs, and opinions of society's mainstream. The term *consensus* is used because it implies that there is general agreement among a majority of citizens on what behaviors should be outlawed by the criminal law and henceforth viewed as crimes. Several attempts have been made to create a concise, yet thorough and encompassing, consensus definition of crime. The eminent criminologists Edwin Sutherland and Donald Cressey have taken the popular stance of linking crime with the criminal law:

> Criminal behavior is behavior in violation of the criminal law. . . . [I]t is not a crime unless it is prohibited by the criminal law [which] is defined conventionally as a body of specific rules regarding human conduct which have been promulgated by political authority, which apply uniformly to all members of the classes to which the rules refer, and which are enforced by punishment administered by the state.[24]

This approach to crime implies that it is a function of the beliefs, morality, and rules established by the existing legal power structure. According to Sutherland and Cressey's statement, criminal law is applied "uniformly to all members of the classes to which the rules refer." This statement reveals the authors' faith in the concept of an "ideal legal system" that deals adequately with all classes and types of people. For example, laws banning burglary and robbery

■ According to the consensus view of crime, criminal acts reflect public opinion. Do you agree with the artist's implied sentiment that spraying graffiti on a wall is not really a crime? Why do you think this remains an outlawed behavior?

are directed at controlling the neediest members of society, whereas laws banning insider trading, embezzlement, and corporate price-fixing are aimed at controlling the wealthiest. The reach of the criminal law is not restricted to any single element of society.

Social harm The consensus view of crime links illegal behavior to the concept of **social harm.** Though people generally enjoy a great deal of latitude in their behavior, it is agreed that behaviors that are harmful to other people and society in general must be controlled. Social harm is what sets strange, unusual, or **deviant behavior**—or any other action that departs from social norms—apart from criminal behaviors.[25] According to the consensus view, many deviant acts are not criminal even though they may be shocking or immoral: for example, watching sexually explicit films. Though religious leaders would probably condemn this behavior as immoral and decadent, it is not considered a crime and no legal action can be taken because the general consensus is that watching adult films does not cause sufficient harm to the person doing the watching and/or the performers who made the film. However, if the film involved children, its production and sale would be outlawed because making such films is considered extremely harmful to minors.

The principal purpose of the Office on National Drug Control Policy (ONDCP) is to establish policies, priorities, and objectives for the nation's drug control program, the goals of which are to reduce illicit drug use, manufacturing, and trafficking; reduce drug-related crime and violence; and reduce drug-related health consequences. To read more about their efforts, go to their Web site at:

    http://www.whitehousedrugpolicy.gov
For an up-to-date list of Web links, go to
    http://info.wadsworth.com/siegel ■

Creating crimes Many acts that are legally forbidden today were once considered merely unusual or deviant behavior. For example, the sale and possession of marijuana was legal in this country until 1937, when it was prohibited under federal law. In the 1930s, Harry Anslinger, head of the Federal Bureau of Narcotics, spearheaded an extensive lobbying effort that resulted in marijuana use being banned. He used magazine articles, public appearances, and public testimony to sway public opinion against using marijuana.[26] In one famous article, which appeared in 1937, Anslinger told how "an entire family was murdered by a youthful [marijuana] addict in Florida...[who] with an axe had killed his father, mother, two brothers, and a sister."[27] Due to Anslinger's efforts to show the social harm caused by smoking marijuana, a harmless deviant act was transformed into a criminal act; previously law-abiding citizens were now defined as criminal offenders.

CONNECTIONS

Some of the drugs considered highly dangerous today were once sold openly and considered medically beneficial. For example, the narcotic drug heroin, now considered extremely addicting and dangerous, was originally named in the mistaken belief that its pain-killing properties would prove "heroic" to medical patients. The history of drug and alcohol abuse will be discussed further in Chapter 14. ■

This position is not without controversy. Although it is clear that rape, robbery, and murder are inherently harmful and their control justified, behaviors such as drug use and prostitution are more problematic because the harm they inflict is only on those who are willing participants. According to the consensus view, however, society is justified in controlling these so-called victimless crimes because public opinion holds that they undermine the social fabric and threaten the general well-being of society. Moreover, they may potentially bring harm to participants, and society has a duty to protect all its members—even those who choose to engage in high-risk behaviors.

The Conflict View of Crime

Central to the radical approach to crime is the proposition that criminal law reflects and protects established economic, racial, gendered, and political power and privilege.[28] The **conflict view** depicts society as a collection of diverse groups—owners, workers, professionals, students—who are in constant and continuing conflict. Groups able to assert their political power use the law and the criminal justice system to advance their economic and social position. Criminal laws, therefore, are viewed as acts created to protect the haves from the have-nots. Conflict criminologists often compare and contrast the harsh penalties exacted on the poor for their "street crimes" (burglary, robbery, and larceny) with the minor penalties the wealthy receive for their white-collar crimes (securities violations and other illegal business practices), which cause considerably more social harm. While the poor go to prison for minor law violations, the wealthy are given lenient sentences for even the most serious breaches of law.

According to the conflict view, the definition of crime is controlled by those who possess wealth, power, and position. Crime is shaped by the values of the ruling class and not by an objective moral consensus that reflects the needs of all people. Crime, according to this definition, is a political concept designed to protect the power and position of the upper classes at the expense of the poor. Even crimes prohibiting violent acts, such as armed robbery, rape, and murder, may have political undertones. Banning violent acts ensures domestic tranquility and guarantees that the anger of the poor and disenfranchised classes will not be directed at their wealthy capitalist exploiters.

According to this conflict view of crime, "real" crimes would include the following acts:

- Violations of human rights due to racism, sexism, and imperialism.
- Unsafe working conditions.
- Inadequate child care.
- Inadequate opportunities for employment and education and substandard housing and medical care.
- Crimes of economic and political domination.
- Pollution of the environment.
- Price-fixing.
- Police brutality.
- Assassinations and war-making.
- Violations of human dignity.
- Denial of physical needs and necessities, and impediments to self-determination.
- Deprivation of adequate food and blocked opportunities to participate in political decision making.[29]

Although this list might be criticized as containing vague and subjectively chosen acts, conflict theorists counter that consensus law also contains crimes that have vague and subjective definitions. Consider the case of substance abuse. Narcotics and similar drugs are illegal, but alcohol, which causes far more social harm, is readily available. Similarly, gambling among friends is prohibited, but the state sells lottery tickets and licenses horse tracks. The sale of obscene material is illegal, but people can buy magazines featuring sex and nudity such as *Penthouse* and *Hustler* at every newsstand.

The Interactionist View of Crime

The **interactionist view** of crime traces its antecedents to the symbolic interaction school of sociology, first popularized by pioneering sociologists George Herbert Mead, Charles Horton Cooley, and W. I. Thomas.[30] This position holds that (1) people act according to their own interpretations of reality, through which they assign meaning to things; (2) they observe the way others react to it, either positively or negatively; and (3) they reevaluate and interpret their own behavior according to the meaning and symbols they have learned from others.

According to this perspective, there is no objective reality. People, institutions, and events are viewed subjectively and labeled either good or evil according to the interpretation of the evaluator. For example, some people might consider the film *Pulp Fiction* obscene, foul-mouthed, and degrading, but another observer may consider the same film an imposing work of art.

In the interactionist view, the definition of crime reflects the preferences and opinions of people who hold social power in a particular legal jurisdiction. These people use their influence to impose their definition of right and wrong on the rest of the population. Conversely, criminals are individuals who society chooses to label as outcasts or deviants because they have violated social rules. In a classic statement, sociologist Howard Becker argued, "The deviant is one to whom that label has successfully been applied; deviant behavior is behavior people so label."[31] Crimes are outlawed behaviors because society defines them that way and not because they are inherently evil or immoral acts.

The interactionist view of crime is similar to the conflict perspective; both suggest that behavior should be outlawed when it offends people who maintain the social, economic, and political power necessary to have the law conform to their interests or needs. However, unlike the conflict view, the interactionist perspective does not attribute capitalist economic and political motives to the process of defining crime. Instead, interactionists see the criminal law as conforming to the beliefs of "moral crusaders" or **moral entrepreneurs,** who use their influence to shape the legal process in the way they see fit.[32] Laws against pornography, prostitution, and drugs are believed to be motivated more by moral crusades than by capitalist sensibilities. Consequently, interactionists are concerned with shifting moral and legal standards.

To the interactionist, crime has no meaning unless people react to it negatively. The one-time criminal, if not caught or labeled, can simply return to a "normal" way of life with little permanent damage. For example, consider the college student who tries marijuana. He does not view himself, nor do others view him, as a criminal or a drug addict. Only when prohibited acts are recognized and sanctioned do they become important, life-transforming events.

CONNECTIONS

Because of the damage caused by the stigma of official criminal justice processing, interactionists believe society should intervene as little as possible in the lives of law violators lest they be labeled and stigmatized. Labeling theory, discussed in Chapter 8, is based on interactionist views and holds that applying negative labels leads first to a damaged identity and then to a criminal career. ■

■ Defining Crime

The consensus view of crime dominated criminological thought until the late 1960s. Criminologists devoted themselves to learning why lawbreakers violated the rules of society. The criminal was viewed as an outlaw who, for one reason or another, flouted the rules defining acceptable conduct and behavior. In the 1960s, the interactionist perspective gained prominence. The rapid change U.S. society was experiencing made traditional law and values questionable.

Figure 1.3   The Definition of Crime

The definition of crime affects how criminologists view the cause and control of illegal behavior and shapes their research orientation.

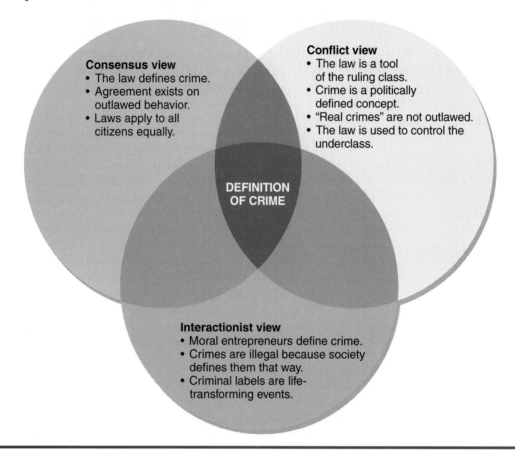

Consensus view
- The law defines crime.
- Agreement exists on outlawed behavior.
- Laws apply to all citizens equally.

Conflict view
- The law is a tool of the ruling class.
- Crime is a politically defined concept.
- "Real crimes" are not outlawed.
- The law is used to control the underclass.

DEFINITION OF CRIME

Interactionist view
- Moral entrepreneurs define crime.
- Crimes are illegal because society defines them that way.
- Criminal labels are life-transforming events.

Many criminologists were swept along in the social revolution of the 1960s and likewise embraced an ideology that suggested that crimes reflected rules imposed by a conservative majority on nonconforming members of society. At the same time, more radical scholars gravitated toward conflict explanations, which they believed were a more accurate assessment of the social harms caused by crime (see Figure 1.3).

Today, each position still has many followers. This is important because criminologists' personal definitions of crime dominate their thinking, research, and attitudes toward their profession. Because of their diverse perspectives, criminologists have taken a variety of approaches in explaining the causes of crime and suggesting methods for its control. Considering these differences, it is possible to take elements from each school of thought to formulate an integrated definition of crime, such as this one:

> Crime is a violation of societal rules of behavior as interpreted and expressed by a criminal legal code created by people holding social and political power. Individuals who violate these rules are subject to sanctions by state authority, social stigma, and loss of status.

This definition combines the consensus position that the criminal law defines crimes with the conflict perspective's emphasis on political power and control and the interactionist concept of stigma. Thus crime, as defined here, is a political, social, and economic function of modern life.

■ How Criminologists Study Crime

Criminologists use a wide variety of research techniques to measure the nature and extent of criminal behavior. To understand and evaluate theories and patterns of criminal behavior, it is important to understand how these data are collected. It is also important to understand the methods used to gain insight into how professional criminologists approach various problems and questions in their field.

Survey Research

Survey research can be designed to measure the attitudes, beliefs, values, personality traits, and behavior of participants. A great deal of crime measurement is based on analysis of survey data, which is gathered using techniques such as self-report surveys and interviews. Both types of surveys involve **sampling,** which refers to the process of selecting for study a limited number of subjects who are representative of entire groups sharing similar characteristics, called **populations.** For example, a criminologist might interview a sample of 3,000 prison inmates drawn from the population of more than 1 million inmates in the United States; in this case, the sample represents the entire population of U.S. inmates. Or a sample of burglary incidents could be taken from Miami; here, the sample would represent the population of Miami burglaries. It is assumed that the characteristics of people or events in a carefully selected sample will be quite similar to those of the population at large.

One common type of survey includes simultaneously interviewing or questioning a diverse sample of subjects who represent a cross section of a community. This method is referred to as **cross-sectional research.** For example, all youths in the tenth grade in a public high school can be surveyed about their substance abuse. Since most youths in the community are currently in school, the survey will contain a sample that represents a cross section of the community—the rich and the poor, males and females, users and nonusers, and so on.

Self-report surveys ask participants to describe, in detail, their recent and lifetime criminal activity. For example, victimization surveys seek information from people who have been victims of crime. Likewise, **attitude surveys** measure the attitudes, beliefs, and values of different groups, such as prostitutes, students, drug addicts, police officers, judges, or juvenile delinquents.

Surveys are among the most widely used methods of criminological study. They are an excellent and cost-effective technique for measuring the characteristics of large numbers of people. Because questions and methods are standardized for all subjects, uniformity is unaffected by the perceptions or biases of the person gathering the data. Statistical analysis of data gathered from carefully drawn samples enables researchers to generalize their findings from small groups to large populations. Though surveys measure subjects at a single point in their life span, questions can elicit information on subjects' prior behavior as well as their future goals and aspirations.[33]

Cohort Research: Longitudinal and Retrospective

Cohort research involves observing a group of people who share a like characteristic over time. For example, researchers might select all girls born in Albany, New York, in 1970 and then follow their behavior patterns for 20 years. The research data might include their school experiences, arrests, hospitalizations, and information about their family life (divorces, parental relations). The subjects might be given repeated intelligence and physical exams; their diets might be monitored. Data could be collected directly from the subjects, or without their knowledge, from schools, police, and other sources. If the research is carefully conducted, it may be possible to determine which life experiences, such as growing up in an intact home or failing at school, typically preceded the onset of crime and delinquency.

It is extremely difficult, expensive, and time-consuming to follow a cohort over time. Another approach for obtaining this kind of information is to take an intact cohort of known offenders and look back into their early life experiences by checking their educational, family, police, and hospital records. This format is known as a **retrospective cohort study.**[34]

To carry out cohort studies, criminologists frequently investigate records of social organizations, such as hospitals, schools, welfare departments, courts, police departments, and prisons. School records contain data on students' academic performance, attendance, intelligence, disciplinary problems, and teacher ratings. Hospitals record incidents of drug use and suspicious wounds, which may be indicative of child abuse. Police files contain reports of criminal activity, arrest data, personal information on suspects, victim reports, and actions taken by police officers. Court records enable researchers to compare the personal characteristics of offenders with the outcomes of their court appearances, for example, conviction rates and types of sentence. Prison records contain information on inmates' personal characteristics, adjustment problems, disciplinary records, rehabilitation efforts, and length of sentence served.

CONNECTIONS

Some critical criminological research has been based on cohort studies, such as the important research conducted by University of Pennsylvania criminologist Marvin Wolfgang and his colleagues. Their findings have been instrumental in developing an understanding about the onset and development of a criminal career. Wolfgang's cohort research is discussed in Chapter 3. Wolfgang's pioneering efforts helped identify the "chronic criminal offender." ■

Aggregate Data Research

Aggregate data can tell us about the effect of social trends and patterns on the crime rate. Criminologists use large government agency and research foundation databases, such as those from the U.S. Census Bureau, Labor Department (on employment), state correctional departments, and so on. The most important of these sources is the **Uniform Crime Report (UCR),** compiled by the **Federal Bureau of Investigation (FBI).**[35] The UCR is an annual report that reflects the number of crimes reported by citizens to local police departments and the number of arrests made by police agencies in a given year. The UCR is probably the most important single source of official crime statistics, and it will be discussed more completely in Chapter 3.

Aggregate data can be used to focus on the social forces that affect crime. For example, to study the relationship between crime and poverty, criminologists use the Census Bureau's data, which provides information about income, the number of people on welfare, and the number of single-parent families in an urban area. They then cross reference this information with official crime statistics from the same locality.

Experimental Research

Sometimes criminologists want to see the direct effect of one factor on another. For example, they may wish to directly test whether (a) watching a violent TV show will (b) cause viewers to act aggressively. This requires them to carry out experimental research. To conduct experimental research, criminologists manipulate or intervene in the lives of their subjects to see the outcome or the effect of the intervention. True experiments usually have three elements: (1) random selection of subjects, (2) a control or comparison group, and (3) an experimental condition. To find out the effects of violent TV, a criminologist might have one group of randomly chosen subjects watch an extremely violent and gory film (*Scream; Psycho*) while another randomly selected group viewed something more mellow (*Babe; Princess Diaries*). The behavior of both groups would be monitored; if the subjects who had watched the violent film were significantly more aggressive than those who had watched the nonviolent film, an association between media content and behavior would be supported. The fact that both groups were randomly selected would prevent some preexisting condition from invalidating the results of the experiment.

When it is impossible to randomly select subjects or manipulate conditions, a different type of experiment is done. For example, a criminologist may want to measure the change in driving fatalities and drunk driving arrests brought about by a new state law that mandates jail sentences for persons convicted of driving while intoxicated (DWI). Since police cannot randomly arrest drunk drivers, criminologists need to find an alternative strategy, such as comparing the state's DWI arrest and fatality trends with those of nearby states that have more lenient DWI statutes. This is not a "true experiment," but this approach would give an indication of the effectiveness of mandatory sentences because the states are comparable except for their drunk driving legislation.

Another type of experimental research is referred to as **time-series design.** Applying this approach to the above example, consider this strategy: Criminologists would record statewide DWI arrest and fatality data for the months and years preceding and following passage of the mandatory jail statute. The effectiveness of mandatory jail terms as a deterrent to DWI would be supported if a drop in the arrest and fatality rates coincided with the bill's adoption.

Criminological experiments are relatively rare because they are difficult and expensive to conduct; they involve manipulating subjects' lives, which can cause ethical and legal roadblocks; and they require long follow-up periods to verify results. Nonetheless, they have been an important source of criminological data.

Observational and Interview Research

Sometimes criminologists focus their research on relatively few subjects, interviewing them in depth or observing them as they go about their activities. This research often results in the kind of in-depth data absent in large-scale surveys. For example, a recent study by Claire Sterk-Elifson focused on the lives of middle-class female drug abusers.[36] The 34 interviews she conducted provide insight into a group whose behavior might not be captured in a large-scale survey. Sterk-Elifson found that these women were introduced to cocaine at first "just for fun": "I do drugs," one 34-year-old lawyer told her, "because I like the feeling. I would never let drugs take over my life."[37] Unfortunately, many of these subjects succumbed to the power of drugs and suffered both emotional and financial stress.

Another common criminological method is to observe criminals firsthand to gain insight into their motives and activities. This may involve going into the field and participating in group activities; this was done in sociologist William Whyte's famous study of a Boston gang, *Street Corner Society*.[38] Other observers conduct field studies but remain in the background, observing but not being part of the ongoing activity.[39]

Still another type of observation involves bringing subjects into a structured laboratory setting and observing how they react to a predetermined condition or stimulus. This approach is common in experimental studies testing the effect of observational learning on aggressive behavior. For example, experiments such as the one described previously, in which subjects view violent films and their subsequent behavior is monitored, would typically be conducted in a laboratory setting.[40]

Criminology, then, relies on many of the basic research methods common to other fields, including sociology, psychology, and political science. Multiple methods are needed to ensure that the goals of criminological inquiry can be achieved.

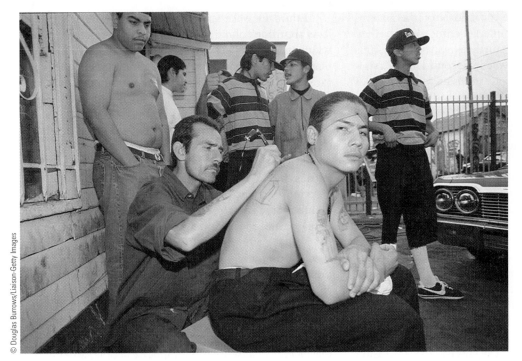

■ Making firsthand observations of criminals to gain insight into their motives and activities is an important aspect of criminological investigation. These Los Angeles gang members may become research subjects for criminologists who go into the field and participate in group activities. Some observers conduct field studies but remain in the background, observing but not taking part in the ongoing activity.

© Douglas Burrows/Liaison-Getty Images

■ Ethical Issues in Criminology

A critical issue facing students of criminology involves recognizing the field's political and social consequences. All too often, criminologists forget the social responsibility they bear as experts in the area of crime and justice. When government agencies request their views of issues, their pronouncements and opinions become the basis for sweeping social policy. The lives of millions of people can be influenced by criminological research data.

Debates over gun control, capital punishment, and mandatory sentences are ongoing and contentious. Some criminologists have successfully argued for social service, treatment, and rehabilitation programs to reduce the crime rate, but others consider them a waste of time, suggesting instead that a massive prison construction program coupled with tough criminal sentences can bring the crime rate down. By accepting their roles as experts on law-violating behavior, criminologists place themselves in a position of power; the potential consequences of their actions are enormous. Therefore, they must be aware of the ethics of their profession and be prepared to defend their work in the light of public scrutiny. Major ethical issues include these:

- What is to be studied?
- Who is to be studied?
- How are studies to be conducted?

Under ideal circumstances, when criminologists choose a subject for study, they are guided by their own scholarly interests, pressing social needs, the availability of accurate data, and other similar concerns. Nonetheless, in recent years, a great influx of government and institutional funding has influenced the direction of criminological inquiry. Major sources of monetary support include the Justice Department's National Institute of Justice and the Office of Juvenile Justice and Delinquency Prevention. Both the National Science Foundation and the National Institute of Mental Health have been prominent sources of government funding. Private foundations, such as the Edna McConnell Clark Foundation, have also played an important role in supporting criminological research.

Though the availability of research money has spurred criminological inquiry, it has also influenced the direction research has taken. State and federal governments provide a significant percentage of available research funds, and they may also dictate the areas that can be studied. In recent years, for example, the federal government has spent millions of dollars funding long-term cohort studies of criminal careers. Consequently, academic research has recently focused on criminal careers. Other areas of inquiry may be ignored because there is simply not enough funding to pay for or sponsor the research.

A potential conflict of interest may arise when the institution funding research is itself one of the principal subjects of the research project. For example, governments may be reluctant to fund research on fraud and abuse of power by government officials. They may also exert a not-so-subtle influence on the criminologists seeking research funding: if criminologists are too critical of the government's efforts to reduce or counteract crime, perhaps they will be barred from receiving further financial help. This situation is even more acute when we consider that criminologists typically work for universities or public agencies and are under pressure to bring in a steady flow of research funds or to maintain the continued viability of their agency. Even when criminologists maintain discretion of choice, the direction of their efforts may not be truly objective.

A second major ethical issue in criminology concerns who will be the subject of inquiries and study? Too often, criminologists focus their attention on the poor and minorities while ignoring the middle-class criminal who may be committing white-collar crime, organized crime, or government crime. Critics have charged that by "unmasking" the poor and desperate criminologists have justified any harsh measures taken against them. For example, a few social scientists have suggested that criminals have lower intelligence quotients than the average citizen, and that because minority group members have lower than average IQ scores, their crime rates are high.[41] This was the conclusion reached in the *The Bell Curve,* a popular though highly controversial book written by Richard Herrnstein and Charles Murray.[42] Although such research is often methodologically unsound, it brings to light the tendency of criminologists to focus on one element of the community while ignoring others. The question that remains is whether or not it is ethical for criminologists to publish biased or subjective research findings, paving the way for injustice.

Ethics are once again questioned in cases where subjects are misled about the purpose of the research. When white and African American youngsters are asked to participate in a survey of their behavior or an IQ test, they are rarely told in advance that the data they provide may later be used to prove the existence of significant racial differences in their self-reported crime rates. Should subjects be told about the true purpose of a survey? Would such disclosures make meaningful research impossible? How far should criminologists go when collecting data? Is it ever permissible to deceive subjects to collect data? Criminologists must take extreme care when they select subjects for their research studies to ensure that they are selected in an unbiased and random manner.[43]

When criminological research efforts involve experimentation and treatment, care must be taken to protect those subjects who have been chosen for experimental and control groups. For example, it may be unethical to provide a special treatment program for one group while depriving others of the same opportunity. Conversely, criminologists must be careful to protect subjects from experiments that may actually cause them harm. For example, an examination of the highly publicized "Scared Straight" program, which brought youngsters into contact with hardcore prison inmates who gave them graphic insights into prison life (to scare them out of a life of crime), discovered that the young subjects may have been harmed by their experience. Rather than being frightened into conformity, subjects actually increased their criminal behavior.[44]

■ Summary

Criminology is the scientific approach to the study of criminal behavior and society's reaction to law violations and violators. It is essentially an interdisciplinary field; many of its practitioners were originally trained as sociologists, psychologists, economists, political scientists, historians, and natural scientists.

Criminology has a rich history with roots in the utilitarian philosophy of Beccaria, the biological positivism of Lombroso, the social theory of Durkheim, and the political philosophy of Marx. A number of fields are related to criminology. In the late 1960s, criminal justice programs were created to examine and improve the U.S. system of justice. Today, many criminologists work in criminal justice educational programs. Criminology and criminal justice are mutually dedicated to understanding the nature and control of criminal behavior. The study of deviant behavior also overlaps with criminology because many "deviant" acts are violations of the criminal law.

The criminological enterprise is comprised of subareas, including criminal statistics, the sociology of law, theory construction, criminal behavior systems, penology, and victimology.

Criminologists believe in one of three perspectives: the consensus view, the conflict view, or the interactionist view. The consensus view dictates that crime is illegal behavior defined by the existing criminal law, which reflects the values and morals of a majority of citizens. The conflict view states that crime is behavior created so that economically powerful individuals can retain their control over society. The interactionist view portrays criminal behavior as a relativistic, constantly changing concept that reflects society's current moral values. According to the interactionist view, criminal behavior is behavior so labeled by those in power; criminals are people society chooses to label as outsiders or deviants.

Criminologists use a variety of research methods to gather information that will shed light on criminal behavior. Each method focuses on a different aspect of the research. These include surveys, longitudinal studies, record studies, experiments, and observations. Questions about ethical standards arise when information-gathering methods appear biased or exclusionary. These types of issues may cause serious consequences because their findings can have a significant impact on individuals and groups.

■ Thinking Like a Criminologist

You have been experimenting with various techniques to identify a sure-fire method to predict violence-prone behavior in delinquents. Your procedure involves brain scans, DNA testing, and blood analysis. Used with samples of incarcerated adolescents, your procedure has been able to distinguish with 80 percent accuracy between youths with a history of violence and those who are exclusively property offenders.

Your research indicates that if any youth were tested with your techniques, potentially violence-prone career criminals easily could be identified for special treatment. For example, children in the local school system could be tested, and those who are identified as violence prone carefully monitored by teachers. Those at risk to future violence could be put into special programs as a precaution.

Some of your colleagues argue that this type of testing is unconstitutional because it violates the subjects' Fifth Amendment right against self-incrimination. There is also the problem of error: some kids may be falsely labeled as violence prone. How would you answer your critics? Is it fair and/or ethical to label people as "potentially" criminal and violent even though they have not yet exhibited any antisocial behaviors? Do the risks of such a procedure outweigh its benefits?

■ Key Terms

- criminologists (3)
- criminology (4)
- interdisciplinary science (4)
- utilitarianism (5)
- classical criminology (5)
- positivism (6)
- physiognomist (6)
- phrenologist (6)
- psychopathic personality (7)
- criminal anthropology (7)
- atavistic anomalies (7)
- biological determinism (7)
- biosocial theory (7)
- cartographic school of criminology (8)

- anomie (8)
- Chicago School (8)
- social ecology (8)
- socialization (9)
- ecological view (9)
- socialization view (9)
- bourgeoisie (9)
- proletariat (9)
- criminological enterprise (11)
- white-collar crime (14)
- crime typology (14)
- consensus view (15)
- substantive criminal law (15)
- social harm (16)
- deviant behavior (16)

- conflict view (16)
- interactionist view (17)
- moral entrepreneurs (17)
- sampling (19)
- population (19)
- cross-sectional research (19)
- self-report survey (19)
- attitude survey (19)
- cohort (19)
- retrospective cohort study (19)
- Uniform Crime Report (UCR) (20)
- Federal Bureau of Investigation (FBI) (20)
- time-series design (20)

■ Critical Thinking Questions

1. Beccaria argued that the threat of punishment controls crime. Are there other forms of social control? Aside from the threat of legal punishments, what else controls your own behavior?

2. What research method would you employ if you wanted to study drug and alcohol abuse at your own school?

3. Would it be ethical for a criminologist to observe a teenage gang by "hanging" with them, drinking, and watching as they steal cars? Should he report that behavior to the police?

4. Can you identify behaviors that are deviant but not criminal? What about crimes that are not deviant?

5. Do you agree with conflict theorists that some of the most damaging acts in society are not punished as crimes? If so, what are they?

Notes

1. Kevin Flynn, "New Jersey Parolee Is Arrested in Killings of 3 Above Carnegie Deli," *New York Times*, 23 May 2001.

2. Ted Chiricos, Kathy Padgett, and Marc Gertz, "Fear, TV News, and the Reality of Crime," *Criminology* 3 (2000): 755–85.

3. Edwin Sutherland and Donald Cressey, *Principles of Criminology*, 6th ed. (Philadelphia: J. B. Lippincott, 1960), p. 3.

4. Eugene Weber, *A Modern History of Europe* (New York: W. W. Norton, 1971), p. 398.

5. Marvin Wolfgang, *Patterns in Criminal Homicide* (Philadelphia: University of Pennsylvania Press, 1958).

6. Described in David Lykken, "Psychopathy, Sociopathy, and Crime," *Society* 34 (1996): 29–38.

7. See Peter Scott, "Henry Maudsley," in *Pioneers in Criminology*, ed. Hermann Mannheim (Montclair, N.J.: Prentice-Hall, 1981).

8. Howard Becker, *Outsiders: Studies in the Sociology of Deviance* (New York: Free Press, 1963), p. 21.

9. Ibid., p. 9.

10. Nicole Hahn Rafter, "Criminal Anthropology in the United States," *Criminology* 30 (1992): 525–47.

11. Ibid., p. 535.

12. See, generally, Robert Nisbet, *The Sociology of Émile Durkheim* (New York: Oxford University Press, 1974).

13. L. A. J. Quetelet, *A Treatise on Man and the Development of His Faculties* (Gainesville, Fla.: Scholars' Facsimilies and Reprints, 1969), pp. 82–96.

14. Ibid., p. 85.

15. Émile Durkheim, *Rules of the Sociological Method*, reprint ed., trans. W. D. Halls (New York: Free Press, 1982).

16. See Jerald Bachman, Lloyd Johnston, and Patrick O'Malley, *Monitoring the Future: Questionaire Responses from the Nation's High School Seniors, 2000* (Ann Arbor, Mich.: Institute for Social Research, 2001).

17. Émile Durkheim, *The Division of Labor in Society*, reprint ed. (New York: Free Press, 1997).

18. Robert Park and Ernest Burgess, *The City* (Chicago: University of Chicago Press, 1925).

19. Karl Marx and Friedrich Engels, *Capital: A Critique of Political Economy*, trans. E. Aveling (Chicago: Charles Kern, 1906); Karl Marx, *Selected Writings in Sociology and Social Philosophy*, trans. P. B. Bottomore (New York: McGraw Hill, 1956). For a general discussion of Marxist thought, see Michael Lynch and W. Byron Groves, *A Primer in Radical Criminology* (New York: Harrow and Heston, 1986), pp. 6–26.

20. Marvin Wolfgang and Franco Ferracuti, *The Subculture of Violence* (London: Social Science Paperbacks, 1967), p. 20.

21. Associated Press, "Michigan Senate Acts to Outlaw Aiding Suicides," *Boston Globe*, 20 March 1994, p. 22.

22. Marvin Wolfgang, *Patterns in Criminal Homicide* (Philadelphia: University of Pennsylvania Press, 1958).

23. Hans von Hentig, *The Criminal and His Victim* (New Haven: Yale University Press, 1948); Stephen Schafer, *The Victim and His Criminal* (New York: Random House, 1968).

24. Edwin Sutherland and Donald Cressey, *Criminology*, 8th ed. (Philadelphia: J. B. Lippincott, 1960), p. 8.

25. Charles McCaghy, *Deviant Behavior* (New York: MacMillan, 1976), pp. 2–3.

26. Edward Brecher, *Licit and Illicit Drugs* (Boston: Little, Brown, 1972), pp. 413–16.

27. Ibid., p. 414.

28. Michael Lynch, Raymond Michalowski, and W. Byron Groves, *The New Primer in Radical Criminology: Critical Perspectives on Crime, Power and Identity*, 3rd ed. (Monsey, N.Y.: Criminal Justice Press, 2000), p. 59.

29. Michael Lynch and W. Byron Groves, *A Primer in Radical Criminology* (Albany, N.Y.: Harrow and Heston, 1989).

30. See Herbert Blumer, *Symbolic Interactionism* (Englewood Cliffs, N.J.: Prentice-Hall, 1969).

31. Becker, *Outsiders*, p. 9.

32. Ibid.

33. Michael Gottfredson and Travis Hirschi, "The Methodological Adequacy of Longitudinal Research on Crime," *Criminology* 25 (1987): 581–614.

34. See, generally, David Farrington, Lloyd Ohlin, and James Q. Wilson, *Understanding and Controlling Crime* (New York: Springer-Verlag, 1986), pp. 11–18.

35. The most recent version available at the time of this writing is *Federal Bureau of Investigation, Crime in the United States, 1997* (Washington, D.C.: U.S. Government Printing Office, 1998).

36. Claire Sterk-Elifson, "Just for Fun?: Cocaine Use among Middle-Class Women," *Journal of Drug Issues* 26 (1996): 63–76.

37. Ibid., p. 63.

38. William F. Whyte, *Street Corner Society* (Chicago: University of Chicago Press, 1955).

39. Herman Schwendinger and Julia Schwendinger, *Adolescent Subcultures and Delinquency* (New York: Praeger, 1985).

40. For a review of these studies, see L. Rowell Huesmann and Neil Malamuth, eds., "Media Violence and Antisocial Behavior," *Journal of Social Issues* 42 (1986): 31–53.

41. See, for example, Michael Hindelang and Travis Hirschi, "Intelligence and Delinquency: A Revisionist Review," *American Sociological Review* 42 (1977): 471–86.

42. Richard Herrnstein and Charles Murray, *The Bell Curve* (New York: Free Press, 1994).

43. Victor Boruch, Timothy Victor, and Joe Cecil, "Resolving Ethical and Legal Problems in Randomized Experiments," *Crime and Delinquency* 46 (2000): 330–53.

44. Anthony Petrosino, Carolyn Turpin-Petrosino, and James Finckenauer, "Well-Meaning Programs Can Have Harmful Effects! Lessons from Experiments of Programs Such as Scared Straight," *Crime and Delinquency* 46 (2000): 354–79.

A. C. Cooper Ltd.; by permission of The Inner Temple, London

CHAPTER 2 The Criminal Law and Its Processes

Introduction

On October 22, 2001, a New Jersey jury found Agustin Garcia, 49, a successful businessman and neighborhood leader, guilty of murder.[1] There was no question that Mr. Garcia had committed the crime. During his trial, the jury was shown a homemade videotape in which he could be seen shooting former girlfriend Gladys Ricart, 39, in her living room in Ridgefield, New Jersey, as she presented bouquets to her bridesmaids at her wedding. The question the jury was forced to decide was Mr. Garcia's degree of criminal responsibility.

During the trial, Mr. Garcia argued that the shock of suddenly learning that his longtime girlfriend was marrying someone else induced a temporary mental illness known as acute adjustment disorder. His altered mental state made it impossible for him to control his emotions and behavior. He claimed that he believed Ms. Ricart still had feelings for him, and he was shocked to walk in on her wedding. The defense produced videotape evidence from a security camera showing Mr. Garcia and Ms. Ricart embracing at a supermarket on the morning of the killing. They claimed that the two remained romantically linked right up to her wedding day. Mr. Garcia testified that he drove by Ms. Ricart's house on the way to the opening of an art show and was puzzled to see signs of a celebration. At first he left the scene but returned an hour later. When he entered the home, he was assaulted by her relatives. Overcome by shock, confusion, and fear, he drew his gun, which fired during the struggle.

To be found guilty of manslaughter, which he had hoped, rather than murder, the jurors would have to conclude that, among other things, Mr. Garcia had reasonable provocation to kill Ms. Ricart. The jury rejected this reasoning: "Even if she did have a relationship with him, it made no difference in him killing her," said the jury forewoman. "He saw the love of his life slipping away, and he couldn't deal with it. You know, 'If I can't have her, nobody will.'" Some members felt that Garcia must have known a wedding was under way because there were limousines parked in front of the house and people in formal wear. Others were swayed by the fact that Garcia had an hour to think about the crime before he shot Ms. Ricart.

The Garcia case illustrates the complexity of the criminal law. Under the rule of law, it is not enough to commit an illegal act, the offender's mental state and his or her relationship to the victim may also come into play. Criminal law dictates what constitutes a crime and how criminal acts are defined. Having evolved over many generations, today's definition of criminal law incorporates historical traditions, moral beliefs, and social values as well as political and economic developments and conditions. The criminal law is a living concept, constantly changing to keep pace with society. It governs the form and direction of almost all human interaction. Business practices, family life, education, property transfers, inheritance, and other common forms of social relations must conform to the rules set out by the **legal code,** which are the specific laws that fall within the scope of "criminal law." As we examine this topic throughout this chapter, you will begin to see how the law defines behaviors that society labels as "criminal." Consequently, it is important for students of criminology to have a basic understanding of the law and

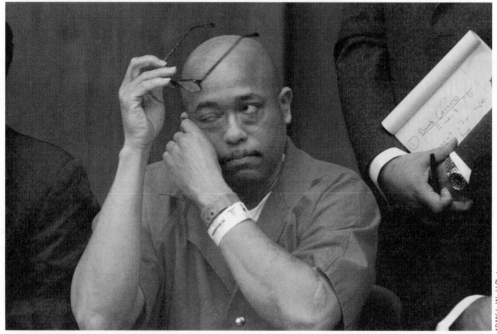

■ Agustin Garcia weeps in court as he watches a videotape showing him shooting his former girlfriend, Gladys Ricart, while she posed for wedding pictures just hours before the ceremony. The Garcia case illustrates the complexity of the criminal law and shows how an offender's mental state and his relationship to the victim may influence the outcome of a case.

AP/Wide World Photos

its relationship to crime and deviance. This chapter reviews the nature and purpose of the law, charts its history, and discusses its components.

The Origin of Law

We know that crimes and criminal behavior were recognized in many early societies.[2] In preliterate societies, common custom and tradition (**mores** and **folkways**) were the equivalents of law. Each group had its own set of customs, which were created to deal with situations that arose daily. These customs would often be followed long after the reason for their origin was forgotten. In some cases, customs had become such an integral part of the way a culture functioned that eventually they became formal, or written, law.

The concept of crime was first recognized in the earliest surviving legal codes, which were developed by the Babylonians and the Hebrews, and later in legal codes developed by the Romans. King Dungi of Sumer (an area that is part of present-day Iraq) is credited with developing one of the first legal codes in about 2000 B.C. Its content is known today because it was later adopted by Hammurabi (1792–1750 B.C.), the sixth king of Babylon, in his famous set of written laws that is today known as the **Code of Hammurabi.** Preserved on basalt rock columns, the code establishes crimes and their correction. Punishment was based on physical retaliation or *lex talionis* ("an eye for an eye"). The severity of punishment depended on class standing: for assault, slaves would be put to death; freemen might lose a limb.

CONNECTIONS

Although not exactly an "eye for an eye," efforts are now being made to make punishments "fit the crime." In Chapter 5, the sections on "just desert" present the perspective that crime and punishment should be closely aligned. Chapter 17 picks up on this again in the discussion on determinate sentencing, which shows how the just desert model has been put into practice. ■

Judges, who were controlled by advisers to the king, strictly enforced Babylonian laws. Crimes such as burglary and theft were common in ancient Babylon, and officials responsible for enforcing these laws had to take their duties seriously. Local officials were expected to apprehend criminals. If they failed in their duties, they had to personally replace lost property; if murderers were not caught, the responsible official paid a fine to the deceased's relatives.

The second of the ancient legal codes still surviving is the **Mosaic Code** of the Israelites (1200 B.C.). According to tradition, God entered into a covenant or contract with the tribes of Israel in which they agreed to obey his law (The

---

 Exhibit 2.1   Table VIII of the Twelve Tables: Torts or Delicts

- If any person has sung or composed against another person a song such as was causing slander or insult to another, he shall be clubbed to death.
- If a person has maimed another's limb, let there be retaliation in kind unless he makes agreement for settlement with him.
- Any person who destroys by burning any building or heap of corn deposited alongside a house shall be bound, scourged, and put to death by burning at the stake, provided that he has committed the said misdeed with malice aforethought; but if he shall have committed it by accident, that is, by negligence, it is ordained that he repair the damage, or, if he be too poor to be competent for such punishment, he shall receive a lighter chastisement.

---

613 laws of the Old Testament, including the Ten Commandments), as presented to them by Moses, in return for God's special care and protection. The Mosaic Code is not only the foundation of Judeo-Christian moral teachings, but it also is a basis for the U.S. legal system: prohibitions against murder, theft, perjury, and adultery precede, by several thousand years, the same laws found in the U.S. legal system.

Also surviving is the Roman law contained in the **Twelve Tables** (451 B.C.). The *Decemviri Consulari Imperio Legibus Scribundis,* a special commission of ten noble Roman men, formulated the Twelve Tables in response to pressure from the lower classes, who were referred to as **plebeians.** The plebeians believed that an unwritten code gave arbitrary and unlimited power to the wealthy classes, known as **patricians,** who served as magistrates. The original code was written on bronze plaques, which have been lost, but records of sections, which were memorized by every Roman male, survive. The remaining laws deal with debt, family relations, property, and other daily matters. A sample section of this code is set out in Exhibit 2.1.

 To read some of the original elements of the Twelve Tables, go to:

    http://members.aol.com/pilgrimjon/ private/LEX/12tables.html

For an up-to-date list of Web links, go to

    http://info.wadsworth.com/siegel ■

Early Crime, Punishment, and Law

The early formal legal codes were lost during the Dark Ages, which lasted for hundreds of years after the fall of Rome (around A.D. 500–1000). During this period, superstition and fear of magic and satanic black arts dominated thinking.

Some attempts were made to regulate the definition and punishments of crime during the early feudal period. Those that still exist feature monetary payments as punishments for crimes. Some early German and Anglo-Saxon societies developed legal systems featuring compensation, **wergild** (in Old English = man's price; *wer* means worth and refers to what the person, and therefore the crime, was worth), for criminal violations. For example, under the sixth-century legal code of the Salic Franks (a tribe that lived in what is today France), if someone were to kill a freewoman of childbearing age, the murderer was punished by wergild in the amount of 24,000 denars (a form of Frankish currency) to the woman's family. If the woman was past childbearing age, the wergild was reduced to 8,000 denars.

Guilt was determined by two methods, **compurgation** and **ordeal.** Compurgation involved having the accused person swear to an oath of innocence while being backed up by a group of 12–25 "oathhelpers," who would attest to his character and claims of innocence. In contrast, the ordeal was based on the principle of divine intervention and the then-prevalent belief that divine forces would not allow an innocent person to be harmed. Determining guilt by ordeal involved such measures as having the accused place his or her hand in boiling water or hold a hot iron to see if God would intervene and heal the wounds. If the wound healed, the person wasn't found guilty; conversely, if the wound didn't heal, the accused was deemed guilty of the crime for which he or she was being punished.

Trial by combat was another method for establishing guilt or innocence. Using this method, one could challenge an accuser to a duel, with the outcome determining the legitimacy of the accusation. These measures continued to be used in Europe until the thirteenth century. For example, when William of Normandy (better known as "the Conqueror") assumed the English crown in 1066, the rules of conduct code stated, in part:

> It was decreed there that if a Frenchman shall charge an Englishman with perjury or murder or theft or homicide or "ran," as the English call open rapine which cannot be denied, the Englishman may defend himself, as he shall prefer, either by the ordeal of hot iron or by wager of battle. But if the Englishman be infirm, let him find another who will take his place. If one of them shall be vanquished, he shall pay a fine of 40 shillings to the king. If an Englishman shall charge a Frenchman and be unwilling to prove his accusation either by ordeal or by wager of battle, I will, nevertheless, that the Frenchman shall acquit himself by a valid oath.[3]

CONNECTIONS

It was possible in trial by combat to have a "champion" fight for you if the combat was obviously one-sided. This evened the odds a bit! The development of the jury trial and the end of the use of the ordeal are discussed in Chapter 17. ■

■ Trial by fire was a common practice during the Middle Ages. Guilt was determined by ordeals, such as having the accused place his or her hand in boiling water or hold a hot iron to see if God would intervene and heal the wounds. This painting illustrates an account given by the twelfth-century historian Godfrey of Viterbo. A count in the court of Holy Roman Emperor Otto the III (890–1002) was accused and executed for adultery with the Empress. Otto forced her to undergo trial by fire. She is shown here holding a piece of red-hot metal that has been heated in the fire at her feet. When her hand is burned, the test "proves" her guilt. Her burning at the stake is shown at the top of the panel.

Despite such "reforms," the systems of crime, punishment, law, and justice were chaotic. The lords of the great manors, who tried cases according to local custom and rule, controlled the law. Although there was general agreement that such acts as theft, assault, treason, and blasphemy constituted crimes, the penalties were often arbi-

Musees Royaux Des Beaux-Arts. Art Resource, NY.

trary, discretionary, and cruel. Punishments included public flogging, branding, beheading, and burning. Peasants who violated the rule of their masters were violently punished and rebellions were put down with extreme cruelty and loss of lives.

According to a fourteenth-century Norman chronicle, disobedient peasants or those who stole from their masters were treated harshly. "Some had their teeth pulled out; others [were] impaled, with their eyes torn out, hands cut off, ankles charred; others were burnt alive or plunged in boiling lead."[4] Even simple wanderers and vagabonds were viewed as dangerous and were subject to these extreme penalties.

Origins of Common Law

Because the ancient legal codes had been lost during the Dark Ages (Middle Ages), the concept of law and crime during this long 500-year period was in disarray and often guided by superstition and local custom. After the Norman conquest of England in 1066, a **common law** developed, which helped standardize law and justice. Before the Norman Conquest, the legal system among the early English (Anglo-Saxons), like elsewhere in Europe, was decentralized. Each county, also known as a **shire,** was divided into units called **hundreds,** which were groups of one hundred families. The hundred was further divided into groups of ten called **tithings.** The **reeve** was the head law enforcement official in the shire. However, within these smaller groups, the tithings were responsible for maintaining order among themselves and dealing with minor disturbances such as fires, wild animals, and so on. Early law enforcement organized along the lines of the tithing, hundred, and shire.

CONNECTIONS

The shire reeve is embodied today in the county sheriff. For more on the history of law enforcement see Chapter 16. ■

Petty cases were tried by courts of the hundred group, the **hundred-gemot.** More serious and important cases could be heard by an assemblage of local landholders, or the **shire-gemot,** or by the local nobleman in a manorial court, sometimes called the the **hali-gemot.** If the act concerned any type of spiritual matter, it could be judged by clergymen and church officials in courts known as **holy-motes** or **ecclesiastics.** Although the law was becoming more standardized than it had been in past generations, it still varied from county to county, hundred to hundred, and tithing to tithing.

Compensation for Crime

To a great degree, criminal law was designed to provide an equitable solution to what was considered a private dispute. Crimes during this period, before the Conquest in 1066, were viewed as a violation of the victim's personal rights, and compensation therefore was paid directly to the victim and/or the victim's family. In this way, medieval criminal law was similar to modern civil law, where victims are compensated for their loss and suffering by the party that brought them to harm. If payment was not made, the victim's family would attempt to forcibly collect damages or seek revenge. The result could be a blood feud between two families. Crimes warranting these types of feuds included treason, homicide, rape, property theft, **assault** (putting another in fear), and **battery** (wounding another). For **treasonous acts,** such as siding with an enemy in a dispute over territory or succession, the punishment was death. Theft during the period before the Conquest could result in slavery for the thieves and their families. If caught in the act of fleeing with the stolen goods, the thief could be killed.

For many other acts, including both theft and violence, compensation could be paid to the victim. For example, even a homicide could be settled by paying wergild to the deceased's family, unless the crime was carried out by poison or ambush—in which case, it was punished by death.

Eventually, wergild was divided so that of the sum (**bot**) paid, part (**wer**) went to the king, and the remainder (**wite**) went to the victim or, in the case of death, the deceased's kin (Figure 2.1). The nobility began to see the value in the wer, and it became the predominant portion of the bot. This arrangement is, in fact, the precursor of the modern-day criminal fine. A scale of compensation existed for lesser injuries, such as the loss of an arm or an eye. Important persons, such as churchmen and nuns, received greater restitution than the general population, yet they paid more if they were the criminal defendant.

CONNECTIONS

Monetary compensation is used today as a criminal sanction. Criminal forfeiture is used to punish white-collar criminals and organized crime figures and is discussed in Chapter 13. Today, experiments are under way to see whether adjusting fines according to what people earn would work as a deterrent. See the section on fines in Chapter 18. ■

The Norman Conquest

In 1066, Edward Confessor, King of England, died without an heir, and the kingship was assumed by Harold Godwinson, a son of one of England's great noble families. His rule was soon disputed by William, Duke of Normandy (a province of France), and William and his followers invaded and defeated Harold's forces at the famed Battle of Hastings.

After the Conquest, William did not immediately change the substance of Anglo-Saxon law. At the outset of

Figure 2.1   **The Distribution of Wergild**

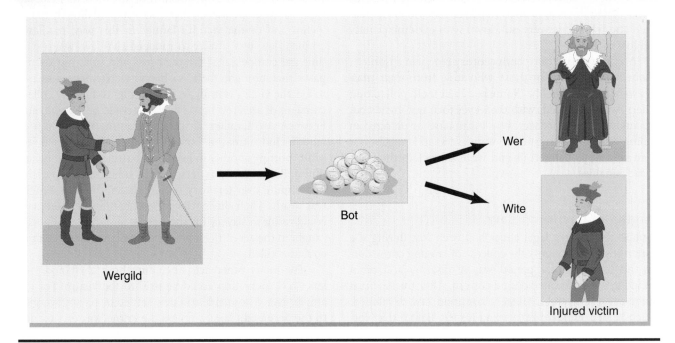

William's reign, justice was administered as it had been in previous centuries. The church courts handled acts that might be considered sinful, and the local hundred or **manorial courts** dealt with most secular violations. However, to secure control of the countryside and to ensure military supremacy over his newly won lands, William established royal courts, which dealt with the most serious breaches of the peace.

Royal courts could not be present in each community, so a system was developed in which the king's judicial representatives traveled throughout the land, holding court in each county several times a year. When court was in session, the royal administrator, or judge, would summon a number of citizens who would, on their oath, tell of the crimes and serious breaches of the peace that had occurred since the judge's last visit. The royal judge then would decide what to do in each case, using local custom and rules of conduct as his guide. If, for example, a local landholder was convicted of theft, he might be executed if those before him had suffered that fate for a similar offense. However, if in previous cases the thief had been forced to make restitution to the victim, then that judgment would be rendered in the present case. This system, known as *stare decisis* (Latin for "to stand by decided cases"), was used by the early courts to determine the outcome of future cases. Courts were bound to follow the law established in previously decided cases unless a higher authority, such as the king or the pope, overruled the law.

Some scholars view this period as chaotic and assume that the content of the law varied from place to place and from year to year, without any sort of centralized control, but contemporary legal scholars suggest that even during this early period there was some degree of continuity in the way the law was administered and that attention was given to the creation of a detailed and formal body of rules.[5] However, it was not until the twelfth century that the present form of the English legal system developed.

The Common Law

The present English system of law came into existence during the reign of Henry II (1154–1189). Henry, one of England's greatest monarchs, instituted many reforms to weaken traditional feudal ties and strengthen the position of the king. Among them was the creation of a new class of government clerks that were given independence to operate effectively in the king's absence. Henry's reforms also allowed for the emergence of a body of common law to replace the disparate customs of feudal and county courts. Jury trials were initiated to end the old Germanic trials by ordeal or battle. Henry also used traveling judges, better known as **circuit judges.** These judges followed a specific route known as a **circuit** and heard cases that previously had been under the jurisdiction of local courts. Professional jurists could be found in three central royal courts— The Exchequer, King's Bench, and Common Pleas—and their judges developed a reputation for fairness and the ability to systematize the law across the land. **Juries,** which began to develop about this time, were groups of local

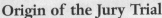

Origin of the Jury Trial

In early medieval Europe and England, disputed criminal charges were often decided by an ordeal. In a trial by fire, the accused individuals would have a hot iron placed in their hand, and if the wound did not heal properly, it was considered proof of their guilt. In a trial by combat, the defendant could challenge his accuser to a duel; the accuser had the option of finding an alternate to fight in his place.

Settling trials by ordeal fell out of favor when the Catholic Church, at the Fourth Lateran Council (1215), decreed that priests could no longer participate in trials by ordeal. Without the use of the ordeal in disputed criminal cases, courts both in England and in the rest of Europe were not sure how to proceed.

In England, the Church ban on ordeal meant that a new method of deciding criminal trials needed to be developed. To fill the gap, British justices adapted a method that had long been used to determine real estate taxes. Since the time of William the Conqueror, 12 knights in each district had been called before an "in-quest" of the king's justices to give local tax information. Instead of the slow determination of feudal taxes by judges, these "twelve free and lawful men of the neighbourhood" would view the land and testify as to who last had peaceful possession so that accurate accounting could be made. Since they were available when the king's justices were present on circuit, the Writ of Novel Disseisin, first established in 1166 under Henry II, also required them to settle "claim jumping" disputes over land.

By 1219 the jury (from the Latin term *jurati*, to be sworn) called to decide land cases also began to hear criminal cases. At first jurors were like witnesses, telling the judge what they knew about the case; these courts were known as assise or assize (from the Latin *assideo*, to sit together). By the fourteenth century, jurors had become the deciders of fact. Over the centuries, the English jury came to be seen as a check on the government. The great case that established the principle of jury independence, *Bushell's* case (1670), arose when a London jury acquitted William Penn, a leading Quaker and later the founder of Pennsylvania, of unlawful assembly in connection with his preaching in the street after a Quaker church was padlocked. The jurors were imprisoned by an angry royalist judge. They were freed when British Chief Judge Vaughn held that unless a jury was corrupt it was free to reach a verdict based on the evidence, or else the jury would be nothing but a useless rubber stamp.

Critical Thinking Questions

1. Do you think that the common-law development of a jury trial is relevant in today's world?
2. Should a jury of one's peers be replaced by professionals who are schooled in the law?

InfoTrac College Edition Research

The jury trial continues to be the centerpiece of the legal system. In some ways it is almost like a theater experience. To learn more about this, read this article:

Mark I. Bernstein, Laurence R. Milstein. Trial as theater. *Trial*, Oct 1997 33 n10 p64(5)

SOURCE: Marvin Zalman and Larry Siegel, *Criminal Procedure, Constitution and Society* (St. Paul: West Publishing, 1991).

---

landholders whom the judges called not only to decide the facts of cases but also to investigate the crimes, accuse suspected offenders, and even give testimony at trials (see the Policy and Practice in Criminology feature titled "Origin of the Jury Trial" for more on this).

Gradually, **royal prosecutors** were established as key players in the court proceedings. These representatives of the Crown submitted evidence and brought witnesses to testify before the jury. Few formal procedures existed at this time, however, and both the judge and the prosecutor felt free to intimidate witnesses and jurors when they considered it necessary. The development of these routine judicial processes heralded the beginnings of the common law.

As it is used today, the term *common law* refers to a law applied to all subjects of the land, without regard for geographic or social differences. As best they could, Henry's judges began to apply a national law instead of the law that only held sway in local jurisdictions. This attempt was somewhat confused at first because the judges and prosecutors had to take into account both local custom and the Norman conquerors' feudal law, which were not always in sync. As new situations arose, however, judges took advantage of legal uncertainty by either inventing new solutions or borrowing from the laws of European countries.

As time went on, judicial decisions began to be written and published. This allowed judicial precedents to be established, and more concrete examples of common-law decisions began to emerge. Together these cases and decisions filtered through the national court system and eventually produced a fixed body of legal rule and principles.

This approach to common law, or judge-made law, is defined as **case law.** Judicial decisions were made on a case-by-case basis. Working with customary rules, the judges applied them to new situations as they arose. Legal rules could be merged or expanded and new varieties tried out. If the new rules could be successfully applied in a number of different cases, they would become precedents, which would then be commonly applied in all similar cases. The legal definitions of crimes such as murder, burglary, arson, and rape are common-law crimes—they were initially defined and created by judges.

Common Law and Statutory Law

The common law was and still is the law of the land in England. In most instances, the common law retained traditional Anglo-Saxon concepts. For example, the common law originally defined murder as the unlawful killing of another human being with malice aforethought.[6] According to this definition, for offenders to be found guilty of murder, they must (1) have planned the crime and (2) have intentionally killed the victim out of spite or hatred. This general definition proved inadequate to deal with many situations in which one person took another's life, however. To bring the law closer to the realities of human behavior, over time judges began to differentiate between deaths caused by passion (manslaughter), negligence (involuntary manslaughter), rage (second degree murder), or cunning (capital or first degree murder). Using this revised definition, someone who caused the death of another during the course of committing another crime, such as a robbery, could be convicted of capital murder even though the death was unintentional. Each form of murder warranted a different degree of punishment. Thus, the common law was a constantly evolving legal code.

CONNECTIONS

Common-law practices still guide modern legal codes. For example, murder statutes still retain different degrees of seriousness based on intent. Each degree is correlated with a level of punishment commensurate with its seriousness. The degrees of murder and other defining issues are discussed in Chapter 11. ■

In some instances, creation of a new common-law crime can be traced back to a particular case. For example, an unsuccessful attempt to commit an illegal act was not considered a crime under early common law. The modern doctrine, that criminal attempt can be punished under law, can be traced directly back to 1784 and the case of *Rex v. Scofield*. In that case, Scofield was charged with having put a lit candle and combustible material in a house he was renting with the intention of burning it down; however, the house did not burn. He defended himself by arguing that a failed attempt to break the law could not be considered a criminal offense. In rejecting this argument, the court stated: "The intent may make an act, innocent in itself, criminal; nor is the completion of an act, criminal in itself, necessary to constitute criminality."[7] After *Scofield*, attempt became a common-law crime, and today, most U.S. jurisdictions have enacted some form of **criminal attempt law** also known as **inchoate crimes.**

When the situation required it, the English Parliament enacted legislation to supplement the judge-made common law. Violations of these laws are referred to as **statutory crimes**. Statutory laws usually reflect existing social conditions. For example, in 1723, a statutory law, known as the Waltham Black Act, was created to provide the British ruling class with a mechanism for protecting its property and position of social power. This act was intended to punish, with death, offenses against rural property, such as poaching small game or arson, if the criminal was armed or disguised.[8] Moreover, the act eroded the rights of the accused; it allowed the death sentence to be carried out without a trial if the accused failed to surrender when ordered to do so. The underlying purpose of the act was Parliament's desire to control the behavior of peasants whose poverty forced them to poach on royal lands.

Other statutory laws dealt with issues of morality, such as gambling, sexual activity, and drug-related offenses. For example, a whole series of statutory laws were created to protect the well-being of British and, later, U.S. business enterprise.[9] These laws took into account crimes such as **embezzlement,** which is when someone takes the possessions of others that have been entrusted to him or her, such as a bank teller taking the bank deposits; and **fraud,** which is when someone takes the possessions of another through deception.

Common Law and Statutory Law in America

Before the American Revolution, the colonies, then under British rule, were subject to the law handed down by English judges. Once the colonies acquired independence, they adapted and changed English law to fit their needs. State legislatures standardized common-law crimes such as murder, burglary, arson, and rape by putting them into statutory form in criminal codes.

Conversion to statutory law allowed common-law principles to be modified and modernized. An example of this process of modifying the common law can be found in the Massachusetts statute defining arson. The common-law definition of **arson** is "the malicious burning of the dwelling of another." Massachusetts has expanded this definition by passing legislation defining arson as "the willful and malicious setting fire to, or burning of, *any building or contents thereof even if they were burned by the owner*" (emphasis added).[10] As in England, whenever the common law proved inadequate to deal with changing social and moral issues, the states and Congress supplemented it with legislative statutes, creating new elements in the various state and federal legal codes.

Early in the nation's history, it was both legal and relatively easy to obtain narcotics, such as heroin, opium, and cocaine.[11] As information about drugs became known, however, drug use began to herald trouble. Drug use became a habit of the middle class, and public and governmental concern arose over the use of narcotics by immigrants, such as the Chinese, who had come to the United States to build railroads and work in mines. Eventually, changes in public sentiment resulted in the 1914 passage of the Harrison Act, which outlawed trade in opium and its derivatives. Later, in 1937, pressure from federal law enforcement officials led to passage of the Marijuana Tax Act, which outlawed the sale or possession of that drug. This case illustrates how the statutory law is subject to change. When use of "pot" became widespread among the middle class in the 1960s, several states revised their laws and effectively decriminalized the possession of marijuana. The statutory law began to reflect the views of individual state legislatures on the use of soft drugs by their citizens. In some states, marijuana possession is still punished by many years in prison; in others, the punishment is only a small fine.

■ Classification of Law

Laws can be classified in a number of different ways, and these categories help us understand their nature and purpose. Three of the most important classifications are discussed next.

Crimes and Torts

Law can be divided into two broad categories—criminal law and **civil law.** Civil law is all law other than criminal law, and it includes such legal areas as **property law,** which is the law governing transfer and ownership of property; and **contract law,** which is the law of personal agreements. Of all areas of the civil law, **tort law,** the law of personal wrongs and damage, is most similar in intent and form to the criminal law.

A **tort** is a civil action in which an individual asks to be compensated for personal harm. The harm may be either physical or mental and includes such acts as trespassing, assault and battery, invasion of privacy, **libel** (false and injurious writings), and **slander** (false and injurious statements). A tort can occur when someone is injured by the actions of another. As the O. J. Simpson civil trial illustrates, a person can be sued for damages even if not found guilty of a criminal act. Damages may also be awarded when a behavior is an indirect cause of injury; that is, when it sets off a chain of events that leads to injury or death. In 1990, for example, the families of two youths who had attempted suicide sued the heavy metal rock group Judas Priest and CBS Records because they claimed the group had put the subliminal message "do it" in its albums to effect "mind control" over the band's fans. Though the group was vindicated, the judge ruled that the First Amendment right to free speech, if indeed they had employed privacy-invading mind-control messages, did not protect its recordings.[12]

Because some torts are similar to some criminal acts, a person can possibly be held both criminally and civilly liable for one action. For example, if one man punches another, it is possible for the assailant to be charged by the state with assault and battery—and imprisoned if found guilty—and be sued by the victim in a tort action of as-

sault in which he could be required to pay monetary damages. In a Massachusetts case, Jennifer Hoult received an award of $500,000 from her father, David, after a federal court accepted her claim that he had raped her at least 3,000 times from the time she was a child of 4 until she reached age 16. The case is a milestone because the **statute of limitations** (which specifies the amount of time by which action must be taken by the state in a criminal matter) for bringing a tort action in a rape case was three years. However, in the Hoult case, the jury found that because the plaintiff had repressed her memory of the rapes the statute of limitations did not start running until she had regained her memory through psychological therapy.[13]

Perhaps the most important similarity between criminal law and civil law is that they have a common purpose. Both attempt to control people's behavior by setting limits on what acts are permissible; and both accomplish this through state-imposed sanctions.

There are also several differences between criminal law and civil law. First, the main purpose of criminal law is to give the state the power to protect the public from harm by punishing individuals whose actions threaten the social order. In tort law, the harm or injury is considered a private wrong, and the main concern is to compensate victims for harm that others have inflicted on them.

In a criminal action, the state initiates the legal proceedings by bringing charges and prosecuting the violator. If it is determined that the criminal law has been broken, the state can impose punishment, such as imprisonment; **probation,** which is community supervision by the court; or a fine payable to the state. In a civil action, however, the injured person must file an action to initiate proceedings. In a successful action, the injured individual usually receives financial compensation for the harm done.

Another major difference between these types of law is the burden of proof required to establish the defendant's liability. In criminal matters, the defendant's guilt must be proven **beyond a reasonable doubt.** This standard means that the jury must consider all of the evidence presented to them and be entirely satisfied that the party is guilty as charged. If there is any doubt, the jury must find for the defendant by returning a verdict of "not guilty." In a civil case, the defendant is required to pay damages if by a **preponderance of the evidence** the trier of fact (either judge or jury) finds that he or she committed the wrong. According to this doctrine, while both parties may share some blame, the defendant (the target of the civil action) is at fault if he or she contributed more than 50 percent to the cause of the dispute. Establishing guilt by a preponderance of the evidence is easier than establishing it beyond a reasonable doubt.[14]

Felony and Misdemeanor

In addition to being a separate branch of law from civil law, criminal laws can be further classified either as felonies or misdemeanors. The distinction is based on seriousness. A **felony** (from the term *felonia,* an act by which a vassal forfeited his fee) is a serious offense; a misdemeanor is a minor or petty crime. Crimes such as murder, rape, and burglary are felonies; crimes such as unarmed assault and battery, petty larceny, and disturbing the peace are misdemeanors.

Most states distinguish between a felony and a misdemeanor on the basis of the punishment that is dispensed to the guilty party. Time sentenced and the place of imprisonment will differ significantly. Under this model of classification, a felony is usually defined as a crime punishable by death or imprisonment for more than one year in a **state prison**; this is an institution where felony offenders are held. A misdemeanor is defined as a crime punished by less than a year in a local county facility, which houses convicted misdemeanants, usually called a jail or **house of correction.** Some common felonies and misdemeanors are described in Exhibit 2.2.

Exhibit 2.2   Common-Law Crimes

Crimes Against the Person

First-degree murder. Unlawful killing of another human being with malice aforethought and with premeditation and deliberation.

Voluntary manslaughter. Intentional killing committed under extenuating circumstances that mitigate the killing, such as killing in the heat of passion after being provoked.

Battery. Unlawful touching of another with intent to cause injury.

Assault. Intentional placing of another in fear of receiving an immediate battery.

Rape. Unlawful sexual intercourse with a female without her consent.

Robbery. Wrongful taking and carrying away of personal property from a person by violence or intimidation.

Examples

A woman buys some poison and pours it into a cup of coffee her husband is drinking, intending to kill him. The motive—to get the insurance benefits of the victim.

A husband coming home early from work finds his wife in bed with another man. The husband goes into a rage and shoots and kills both lovers with a gun he keeps by his bedside.

A man seeing a stranger sitting in his favorite seat in a cafeteria goes up to that person and pushes him out of the seat.

A student aims an unloaded gun at her professor, who believes the gun is loaded. She says she is going to shoot.

After a party, a man offers to drive a young female acquaintance home. He takes her to a wooded area and, despite her protests, forces her to have sexual relations with him.

A man armed with a loaded gun approaches another man on a deserted street and demands his wallet.

Inchoate (Incomplete) Offenses

Attempt. An intentional act for the purpose of committing a crime that is more than mere preparation or planning of the crime. The crime is not completed, however.

Conspiracy. Voluntary agreement between two or more persons to achieve an unlawful object or to achieve a lawful object using means forbidden by law.

Examples

A person intending to kill another person places a bomb in the intended victim's car so that it will detonate when the ignition key is used. The bomb is discovered before the car is started. Attempted murder has been committed.

A drug company sells larger-than-normal quantities of drugs to a doctor, knowing that the doctor is distributing the drugs illegally. The drug company is guilty of conspiracy.

Crimes Against Property

Burglary. Breaking and entering of a dwelling house of another in the nighttime with the intent to commit a felony.

Arson. Intentional burning of a dwelling house of another.

Larceny. Taking and carrying away the personal property of another with the intent to keep and possess the property.

Examples

Intending to steal some jewelry and silver, a young man breaks a window and enters another's house at 10 P.M.

A secretary, angry that her boss did not give her a raise, goes to her boss's house and sets fire to it.

While a woman is shopping, she sees a diamond ring displayed at the jewelry counter. When no one is looking, the woman takes the ring and walks out of the store.

SOURCE: Developed by Therese J. Libby, J.D.

Mala in Se and Mala Prohibitum

A third way to classify crimes is as **mala in se** or **mala prohibitum.** Some illegal acts, referred to as *mala in se* crimes, are rooted in the core values inherent in Western civilization, which are referred to as **natural law.** These are designed to control such behaviors as inflicting physical harm on others (assault, rape, murder), taking possessions that rightfully belong to another (larceny, burglary, robbery), or harming another person's property (malicious damage, trespass). These have traditionally been considered violations of Western civilization's morals.

Mala prohibitum crimes refer to statutory crimes, which involve violations of laws that reflect current public opinion and social values. In essence, these crimes are acts that conflict with contemporary standards of morality. Crimes are periodically created to control behaviors that conflict with the way society functions. *Mala prohibitum* offenses include drug use and possession of unlicensed handguns. It is relatively easy to link *mala in se* crimes to an objective concept of morality, but it is much more difficult to do so if the acts are *mala prohibitum* because so many average people willingly engage in these behaviors.

■ Functions of the Criminal Law

Substantive criminal law refers to a written code defining crimes and their punishments. In the United States, state and federal governments have developed their own unique criminal codes. Though all the codes have their differences, most use comparable terms, and the behaviors they are designed to control are often quite similar. Regardless of which culture or jurisdiction created them or when, criminal codes have several distinct functions. The most important of these are described in the following sections.

Enforcing Social Control

The primary purpose of the criminal law is to control the behavior of people within its jurisdiction. The criminal law is a written statement of rules to which people must conform. Every society also maintains unwritten rules of conduct—ordinary customs and conventions referred to as *folkways* and universally followed behavior referred to as **norms** and **morals,** or *mores.*

Those in political power rely on criminal law to formally prohibit behaviors believed to threaten societal well-being and that challenge their own authority. For example, in U.S. society, the criminal law incorporates centuries-old prohibitions against the following behaviors harmful to others: taking another person's possessions, physically harming another person, damaging another person's property, and cheating another person out of his or her possessions. Similarly, the law prevents actions that challenge the legitimacy of the government, such as planning its

overthrow, collaborating with its enemies, and so on. Any person can informally punish violations of mores and folkways, but control of the criminal law is given to those in political power.

Discouraging Revenge

By delegating enforcement to others, the criminal law controls an individual's need to seek revenge or vengeance against those who violated his or her rights. By punishing people who infringe on the rights, property, and freedom of others, the law shifts the burden of revenge from the individual to the state. As Oliver Wendell Holmes stated, this prevents "the greater evil of private retribution."[15] Though state retaliation may offend the sensibilities of many citizens, it is greatly preferable to a system in which individuals would have to seek justice themselves.

Expressing Public Opinion and Morality

The criminal law also reflects constantly changing public opinions and moral values. *Mala in se* crimes, such as murder and forcible rape, are almost universally prohibited; however, the prohibition of legislatively created *mala prohibitum* crimes, such as traffic law and gambling violations, changes according to the overriding social conditions and attitudes. The criminal law is used to codify these changes. For example, if a state government decides to legalize certain outlawed behaviors, such as gambling or marijuana possession, it will amend the state's criminal code. The criminal law then has the power to define the boundaries of moral and immoral behavior. Nonetheless, it has proven difficult to legally control public morality because of the problems associated with (1) gauging the will of the majority, (2) respecting the rights of the minority, and (3) enforcing laws that many people consider trivial or self-serving. For example, controlling the sale of pornographic and obscene material has proven to be difficult because (1) it violates people's first amendment rights to "free speech" and (2) control efforts devote important resources to eliminating a behavior that many people view as benign and harmless.

CONNECTIONS

Though it is generally considered a "victimless" crime, is there actually a victim in the production and sale of pornography? This question is addressed in Chapter 14 in a discussion of public order crimes. ■

The power of the law to express norms and values can be viewed in the context of the crime of **vagrancy.** A *vagrant* (whose crime is vagrancy) is a person who goes from place to place without visible means of support and who, though able to work for his or her maintenance, refuses to do so. In a famous 1964 treatise, criminologist William

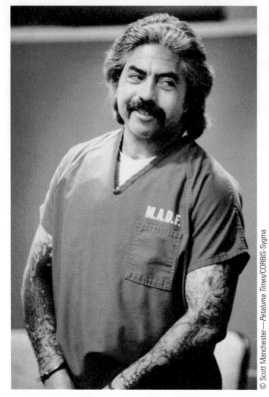

■ Some illegal acts, referred to as *mala in se* crimes, are rooted in the core values inherent in Western civilization. These "natural laws" are designed to control behaviors that have traditionally been considered a violation of the morals of Western civilization. There is little debate about the seriousness of these acts or their need for control. When Richard Allen Davis was convicted of the abduction and killing of 12-year-old Polly Klaas, the revulsion felt toward his behavior was universal and absolute. During a sentencing hearing, Polly's father, Marc Klaas, said, "Mr. Davis, when you get to where you're going, say hello to Hitler, to Dahmer, and to Bundy. Good riddance, and the sooner you get there the better we'll all be." Davis was sentenced to death on September 26, 1996.

Chambliss linked the historical development of the law of vagrancy to the prevailing economic interests of the ruling class. He argued that the original vagrancy laws were formulated in the fourteenth century after the bubonic plague had killed significant numbers of English peasants, threatening the labor-intensive feudal economy. The first vagrancy laws were aimed at preventing workers from leaving their estates to secure higher wages elsewhere. They punished migration and permissionless travel, thereby mooring peasants to their manors and aiding wealthy landowners by limiting the wages of workers, who could not leave their employers to seek higher earnings elsewhere.[16]

In an opposing view of the social conditions that influenced the creation of vagrancy laws, social historian Jeffrey Adler argues that early English vagrancy laws were less concerned with maintaining capitalism than with controlling beggars and relieving the overburdened public relief and welfare systems.[17] Adler suggests that early American vagrancy laws provided town officials with a mechanism to repel the moral threat to the community posed by vagrants, "sabbath breakers," paupers, and the

wandering poor. Adler contends that economic demands had little to do with the content of the law.

Deterring Criminal Behavior

The criminal law has a **social control function.** This refers to the ability to control, restrain, and direct human behavior through its ability to punish and correct law violators. The threat of punishment associated with violating the law is designed to prevent crimes before they occur. During the Middle Ages, public executions were held to drive this point home. Today, the criminal law's impact is felt through news accounts of long prison sentences and an occasional execution.

Punishing Wrongdoing

The deterrent power of the criminal law is tied to the authority it gives the state to sanction or punish offenders. Violations of folkways and mores are controlled informally, but breaches of the criminal law are left to the jurisdiction of political agencies. Those violating mores and folkways can be subject to social disapproval, whereas criminal law violators alone are subject to physical coercion and punishment.

Although the criminal law is society's instrument of punishment, it need not fulfill a utilitarian purpose to justify its existence. It serves as a barometer of the public's vision of right and wrong. There are firmly entrenched beliefs that some acts are evil and should be punished, regardless of whether their punishment serves any practical purpose. The need for punishment may transcend any practical purpose such as deterrence.[18]

CONNECTIONS

The social control function of the criminal law assumes that the threat of punishment will deter crime. This assumption is actually the subject of significant debate: If the criminal law can deter crime, then why is there so much crime today? For the answer, see the discussion on deterrence in Chapter 5. ■

Maintaining the Social Order

All legal systems are designed to support and maintain the boundaries of the social system they serve. In medieval England, the law protected the feudal system by defining an orderly system of property transfer and ownership. Laws in some socialist nations protect the primacy of the state by strictly curtailing profiteering and individual enterprise. Our own capitalist system is also supported and sustained by the criminal law. In a sense, the content of the criminal law is more a reflection of the needs of those who control the existing economic and political system than a representation of some idealized moral code.

In U.S. society, by meting out punishment to those who damage or steal property, the law promotes the activities needed to sustain an economy based on the accumulation of wealth. It would be impossible to conduct business through the use of contracts, promissory notes, credit, banking, and so on unless the law protected private capital. Maintaining a legal climate in which capitalism can thrive is an underlying goal of the criminal law.

The criminal law has not always protected commercial enterprise; if one merchant cheated another, it was considered a private matter. This changed in 1473 due to the *Carrier's Case,* when an English court ruled that a merchant who held and transported merchandise for another was guilty of theft if he kept the goods for his own purposes.[19] Before the *Carrier's Case,* the law did not consider it a crime for people to keep something that was voluntarily given to them by their rightful owners. Breaking with legal precedent, the British court recognized that the new English mercantile trade system could not be sustained if property rights had to be individually enforced. To this day, the substantive criminal law prohibits such business-related acts as **larceny,** fraud, embezzlement, and **commercial theft.** Without the law to protect it, the free enterprise system could not exist.

■ The Legal Definition of a Crime

In the media, we occasionally hear about people who admit at trial that they committed the act of which they are accused, yet they are not found guilty of the crime. For example, there was little question that John Hinckley attempted to assassinate President Ronald Reagan in 1981; the act was shown on national television. Yet Hinckley was not found guilty of a crime because he lacked one of the legal requirements needed to prove his guilt—mental competency. The jury concluded that he was not mentally competent at the time of the crime. In most instances, this occurs because state or federal prosecutors have not proven that the defendant's behavior falls within the legal definition of a crime. To fulfill the legal definition, all elements of the crime must be proven. For example, in Massachusetts, the common-law crime of burglary in the first degree is defined this way:

> Whoever breaks and enters a dwelling house in the nighttime, with intent to commit a felony, or whoever, after having entered with such intent, breaks into such dwelling house in the nighttime, any person being lawfully therein, and the offender being armed with a dangerous weapon at the time of such breaking or entry, or so arriving himself in such house or making an actual assault on a person lawfully therein, commits the crime of burglary.[20]

Note that burglary in the first degree has the following elements:

* It happens at night.
* It involves breaking, entering, or both.
* It happens at a dwelling house.
* The accused is armed or arms him- or herself after entering the house or commits an actual assault on a person who is lawfully in the house.
* The accused intends to commit a felony.

For the state to prove a crime occurred, and that the defendant committed it, the prosecutor must show that the accused engaged in the guilty act (*actus reus*) and had the intent to commit the act (*mens rea*). Under common law, both the *actus reus* and the *mens rea* must be present for the act to be considered a crime. Thoughts of committing an act do not alone constitute a crime; there must also be an illegal act. Let us now look more closely at these issues.

Actus Reus

The *actus reus* is an aggressive act, such as taking someone's money, burning a building, or shooting someone. The action must be voluntary for an act to be considered illegal;

an accident or involuntary act would not be considered criminal. For example, if a person has a convulsion while walking down the street and as a result strikes another person in the face, he cannot be held criminally liable for assault. But if he knew beforehand that he could have a seizure and unreasonably put himself in a position where he was likely to harm others—for instance, by driving a car—he would be criminally liable for his behavior.

In addition, here are some occasions when the failure to act can be considered a crime:

1. *Failure to perform a legally required duty, which is based on relationship or status.* These relationships include parent and child and husband and wife. If a husband finds his wife unconscious because she took an overdose of sleeping pills, he is obligated to save her life by seeking medical aid. If he fails to do so and she dies, he can be held responsible for her death. Parents are required to look after the welfare of their children; failure to provide adequate care can be a criminal offense.

2. *Imposition by statute.* Some states have passed laws that require a person who observes an automobile accident to stop and help the other parties involved.

3. *A contractual relationship.* These relationships include lifeguard and swimmer, doctor and patient, and babysitter or au pair and child. Because lifeguards have been hired to ensure the safety of swimmers, they have a legal duty to come to the aid of drowning persons. If a lifeguard knows a swimmer is in danger and does nothing about it and the swimmer drowns, the lifeguard is legally responsible for the swimmer's death.

The duty to act is a legal and not a moral duty. The obligation arises from the relationship between the parties or from explicit legal requirements. For example, a private citizen who sees a person drowning is under no legal obligation to save that person. Although we may find it morally reprehensible, the private citizen could walk away and let the swimmer drown without facing legal sanctions.

Mens Rea

In most situations, for an act to constitute a crime, it must be done with criminal intent. A person entering a store with a gun with the intention of stealing money indicates by his actions his intent to commit a robbery. However, the definition also encompasses situations in which recklessness or negligence establishes the required criminal intent. For example, a drunk driver may not have intended to kill his or her victim, yet the driver's negligent and reckless behavior (driving while drunk) creates a condition a reasonable person can assume will lead to injury.

Criminal intent also exists if the results of an action, though originally unintended, are certain to occur. For example, when Timothy McVeigh planted a bomb in front of the Murrah Federal Building in Oklahoma City, he did not intend to kill any particular person in the building. Yet

■ The law requires that a mother obtain medical attention for a sick child. Failure to do so can result in criminal charges. Here, Rebecca Corneau is escorted out of Bristol County District Court in Attleboro, Massachusetts, by two police officers. Corneau, who is pregnant and is suspected of covering up the death of her last child, was ordered into custody after she refused to submit to a court-ordered medical exam. Corneau is a member of a fundamentalist religious sect that rejects conventional medical treatment, and prosecutors are looking into whether Corneau's last baby and another infant in the sect died because they did not receive needed care.

the law would hold that McVeigh, or any other person, would be substantially certain that people in the building would be killed in the blast, and therefore McVeigh had the criminal intent to commit the crime of murder.

Strict Liability

Both the *actus reus* and the *mens rea* must be present before a person can be convicted of a crime. However, several crimes defined by statute do not require *mens rea*. In these cases, the person accused is guilty simply by doing what the statute prohibits; mental intent does not enter the picture. These offenses are known as **strict-liability crimes,** or public welfare offenses. Health and safety regulations, traffic laws, and narcotic control laws are strict-liability statutes. For example, a person stopped for speeding is guilty of breaking the traffic laws regardless of whether he or she had intended to go over the speed limit or had done it by accident. The underlying purpose of these laws is to protect the public; therefore, intent is not required.[21]

CONNECTIONS

Many white-collar crimes, such as polluting the environment, are considered strict-liability crimes. A person found dumping toxic wastes is guilty of a crime. For an analysis of white-collar law enforcement, see Chapter 13. ■

Criminal Defenses

When people defend themselves against criminal charges, they must refute one or more of the elements of the crime of which they have been accused. A number of different approaches can be taken to create this defense.

First, defendants may deny the *actus reus* by arguing that they were falsely accused and the real culprit has yet to be identified. Defendants may also claim that they did engage in the criminal act they are accused of but lacked the *mens rea,* or mental intent needed, to be found guilty of the crime. If a person whose mental state is impaired commits a criminal act, it is possible for the person to excuse his or her criminal actions by claiming he or she lacked the capacity to form sufficient intent to be held criminally responsible. Insanity, intoxication, and ignorance are among other types of excuse defenses.

Another type of defense is **justification.** Here, the individual usually admits committing the criminal act but maintains that the act was justified and that he or she, therefore, should not be held criminally liable. Among the justification defenses are *necessity, duress, self-defense,* and *entrapment.* Persons standing trial for criminal offenses may defend themselves by claiming either that their actions were justified under the circumstances or that their behavior can be excused by their lack of *mens rea.* If either the physical or mental elements of a crime cannot be proven, then the defendant cannot be convicted. We will now examine some of these defenses and justifications in greater detail.

AP/Wide World Photos

■ Thomas Junta at his arraignment in Middlesex Superior Court in Cambridge, Massachusetts. Junta failed to convince a jury that his attack on his son's hockey coach was a matter of self-defense, and he was sentenced to prison.

Self-Defense

On July 5, 2000, Thomas Junta, a 42-year-old truck driver with no previous criminal record, assaulted Michael Costin at a hockey rink in Reading, Massachusetts, a town north of Boston. The beating followed a pickup hockey game refereed by Mr. Costin in which Mr. Junta's 10-year-old son was playing alongside Costin's own child. As the game came to a close, an argument ensued over Costin's ability to control the game. Junta, who is six feet two inches tall and weighs 275 pounds, assaulted Costin, who was five foot eleven inches tall and weighed 170 pounds, as he left the ice. After being ordered out of the rink by a rink manager, Junta returned and slammed Costin to the ground beside a soda machine, a blow that caused immediate brain death but which did not stop Junta from pushing his knee into Costin's chest and continuing to beat and punch his head until he was virtually unrecognizable.[22] At his trial, Junta claimed that because Costin had thrown the first punch his actions amounted to self-defense. However, on January 11, 2002, a jury convicted him of involuntary manslaughter on the grounds that even though Junta did not mean to kill Costin he should have known that the amount of force he used could be fatal.[23]

As a general legal rule, a person defending him- or herself may use only such force as is reasonably necessary to prevent personal harm. For example, a person who is assaulted by another with no weapon is ordinarily not justified in hitting the assailant with a baseball bat. A person verbally threatened by another is not justified in striking the other party. If a woman hits a larger man, generally speaking the man would not be justified in striking the woman and causing her physical harm. In other words, to

Exhibit 2.3 **Various Insanity Defense Standards**

Test	Legal Standard Because of Mental Illness	Final Burden of Proof	Who Bears Burden of Proof
M'Naghten rule	"didn't know what he was doing or didn't know it was wrong"	Varies, from proof by a balance of probabilities on the defense to proof beyond a reasonable doubt on the prosecutor, depending on state jurisdiction	
Irresistible impulse test	"could not control his conduct"		
Substantial capacity test	"lacks substantial capacity to appreciate the wrongfulness of his conduct or to control it"	Beyond reasonable doubt	Prosecutor
Present federal law	"lacks capacity to appreciate the wrongfulness of his conduct"	Clear and convincing evidence	Defense

SOURCE: National Institute of Justice, *Crime Study Guide: Insanity Defense* by Norval Morris (Washington, D.C.: U.S. Department of Justice, 1986), 3.

exercise the self-defense privilege, the danger to the defendant must be immediate. In addition, the defendant is obligated to look for alternative means of avoiding the danger, such as escape, retreat, or assistance from others. In the Junta case, the jury reasoned that Junta could have restrained the smaller man and called for assistance without the need to repeatedly punch and pummel him until he died.

Ignorance or Mistake

Ignorance or mistake can be an excuse if it negates an element of a crime. As a general rule, however, ignorance of the law is no excuse. Some courts have had to accept this excuse in cases where the government failed to make enactment of a new law public. It is also a viable justification when the offender relies on an official statement of the law that is later deemed incorrect. Barring that, even immigrants and other new arrivals to the United States are required to be aware of the content of the law. For example, on October 7, 1998, Chris Ahamefule Iheduru, a Nigerian immigrant, was convicted of sexual assault on the ground that he had intimate relations with his 14-year-old stepdaughter after signing a contract with the girl to bear him a son (she gave birth to a daughter in September 1998).[24] At trial, Iheduru testified that it is not illegal in his native country to have sex with a juvenile and that he did not know it was against the law in the United States. His ignorance of U.S. law did not shield him from conviction.

The Insanity Plea

Insanity is a defense to criminal prosecution in which the defendant's state of mind negates his or her criminal responsibility. A successful insanity defense results in a verdict of "not guilty by reason of insanity." Insanity, in this case, is a legal category. As used in U.S. courts, it does not

necessarily mean that anyone who suffers from a form of mental illness can be excused from legal responsibility. Many people who are depressed, suffer mood disorders, or have a psychopathic personality can be found legally sane.

CONNECTIONS

For more on the relationship between mental illness, personality disorders, and crime, read the section on crime and mental illness in Chapter 6. ■

Insanity means that the defendant's state of mind at the time the crime was committed made it impossible for the person to have the necessary intent, or *mens rea*, to satisfy the legal definition of a crime. Thus, a person can be undergoing treatment for a psychological disorder but still be judged legally sane if it can be proven that at the time the person committed the crime he or she had the capacity to understand the wrongfulness of his or her actions.

If a defendant uses the insanity plea, it is usually left to psychiatric testimony to prove that a person understood the wrongfulness of his or her actions and was therefore legally sane or, conversely, was mentally incapable of forming intent. The jury will then be asked to weigh the evidence in light of the test for sanity currently used in the jurisdiction. These vary throughout the United States; the commonly used tests are listed in Exhibit 2.3. Because the issue of insanity is so controversial, it is discussed further in the Policy and Practice in Criminology feature.

■ Changing the Criminal Law

In recent years, many states and the federal government have been examining their substantive criminal law. Since the law, in part, reflects public opinion and morality

The Insanity Controversy

In June of 2001, Mrs. Andrea Yates, 37, confessed to the police that she had methodically drowned her five children, ranging in age from 7 years to 6 months. Charged with murder, she plead not guilty by reason of insanity on the ground that her act was a function of her severe psychotic depression.

Yates attempted suicide after her fourth child was born in 1999. Warned by doctors not to have any more children, she had become pregnant once again. The birth of her fifth child and the death of her father triggered an emotional episode during which she killed her children. Her lawyers claimed, "but for the psychosis, she would never have considered, much less acted upon, any thought to take the lives of the children she bore into this world and dearly loved as their mother." The prosecutor charged her with murder in the first degree and recommended the death penalty. Could Andrea Yates' horrendous act have been the product of a sound mind? Despite her apparent mental instability, Yates was convicted of murder in 2002 and sentenced to life in prison.

The insanity defense has been the source of debate and controversy. Many critics of the defense maintain that inquiry into a defendant's psychological makeup is inappropriate at the trial stage; they would prefer that the issue be raised at the sentencing stage, after guilt has been determined. Opponents also charge that criminal responsibility is separate from mental illness and that the two should not be equated. It is a serious mistake, they argue, to consider criminal responsibility as a trait or quality that can be detected by a psychiatric evaluation. Moreover, some criminals avoid punishment because they are erroneously judged by psychiatrists to be mentally ill. Conversely, some people who are found not guilty by reason of insanity because they suffer from a mild personality disturbance are then incarcerated in mental health facilities far longer than they would have been imprisoned if they had been convicted of a criminal offense.

Advocates of the insanity defense say that it serves a unique purpose. Most successful insanity verdicts result in the defendant being committed to a mental institution until he or she has recovered. The general assumption is that the insanity defense makes it possible to single out for special treatment certain persons who would otherwise be subjected to further penal sanctions following conviction.

The insanity plea was thrust into the spotlight when John Hinckley's unsuccessful attempt to kill President Ronald Reagan was captured by news cameras. Hinckley was found not guilty by reason of insanity. Public outcry against this seeming miscarriage of justice prompted some states to revise their insanity statutes. New Mexico, Georgia, Alaska, Delaware, Michigan, Illinois, and Indiana, among other states, have created the plea of guilty but insane, in which the defendant is required to serve the first part of his or her sentence in a hospital and, once "cured," is then sent to prison.

In 1984 the federal government revised its criminal code to restrict insanity as a defense solely to individuals who are unable to understand the nature and wrongfulness of their acts. The burden of proof has made an important shift from the prosecutor's need to prove sanity to the defendant's need to prove insanity. About 11 states have followed the federal government's lead and made significant changes in their insanity defenses, such as shifting the burden of proof from prosecution to defense; three states (Idaho, Montana, and Utah) no longer use evidence of mental illness as a defense in court, although psychological factors can influence sentencing. On March 28, 1994, the U.S. Supreme Court failed to overturn the Montana law (*Cowan v. Montana,* 93-1264) thereby giving the states the right to abolish the insanity defense if they so choose.

Although this backlash against the insanity plea is intended to close supposed legal loopholes that allow dangerous criminals to go free, the public's fear may be misplaced. It is estimated that the insanity plea is used in less than 1 percent of all cases. Moreover, evidence shows that relatively few insanity defense pleas are successful.

If the insanity defense is successful, the offender must be placed in a secure psychiatric hospital or the psychiatric ward of a state prison. Because many defendants who successfully plead insanity are nonviolent offenders, it is certainly possible that their hospital stay will be longer than the prison term they would have received if they had been convicted of the crimes of which they were originally accused.

Despite efforts to ban its use, the insanity plea is probably here to stay. Most crimes require *mens rea,* and unless we are willing to forgo that standard of law, we will be forced to find not guilty those people whose mental state makes it impossible for them to rationally control their behavior.

Critical Thinking Questions

1. Is it fair to excuse the criminal responsibility of someone who acted under an "irresistible impulse"?

2. Couldn't we argue that all criminals are impulsive people who lack the capacity to control their behavior? If not, why would they commit crimes in the first place?

3. Is it possible that child molesters, for example, are rational creatures who do not have "irresistible impulses"?

InfoTrac College Edition Research

To research the impact of the insanity plea on criminal defenses, check out the following article:

Richard J. Bonnie, Norman G. Poythress, Steven K. Hoge, John Monahan, and Marlene Eisenberg. Decision-making in criminal defense: an empirical study of insanity pleas and the impact of doubted client competence. *Journal of Criminal Law and Criminology* Fall 1996 v87 n1 p48–62

SOURCE: Daniel N. Robinson, *Wild Beasts & Idle Humours: The Insanity Defense from Antiquity to the Present* (Cambridge, Mass.: Harvard University Press, 1996); Ralph Slovenko, *Psychiatry and Criminal Culpability* (New York: John Wiley & Sons, 1995).

■ Dr. Jack Kevorkian was sentenced to prison for assisting one of his patients to commit suicide. The criminal law is constantly changing to reflect changes in public morality and opinion.

regarding various forms of behavior, what was considered criminal 40 years ago may not be considered so today. In some states, crimes such as possession of marijuana have been **decriminalized**—given reduced penalties. Such crimes may be punishable by a fine instead of a prison sentence. Other former criminal offenses, such as vagrancy, have been legalized—all criminal penalties have been removed. And, in some jurisdictions, penalties have been toughened, especially for violent crimes, such as rape and spousal assault.

In some instances, new criminal laws have been created to conform to emerging social issues. For example, physician-assisted suicide became the subject of a national debate when Dr. Jack Kevorkian began practicing what he calls **obitiatry,** helping people take their lives.[25] In an attempt to stop Kevorkian, Michigan passed a statutory ban on assisted suicide, reflecting what lawmakers believed to be prevailing public opinion.[26] Kevorkian was convicted on this law and is currently serving a long prison sentence.

Assisted suicide is but one of many emerging social issues that has prompted change in the criminal law. More than 25 states have enacted **stalking** statutes, which prohibit and punish acts described typically as "the willful, malicious and repeated following and harassing of another person."[27] Stalking laws were originally formulated to protect women terrorized by former husbands and boyfriends, although celebrities are often plagued by stalkers as well. In celebrity cases, however, the stalkers are usually strangers or casual acquaintances of their victims.

CONNECTIONS

Stalking is a relatively new concept in both law and criminology. The nature and extent of stalking is discussed in Chapter 11. ■

Community notification laws are a response to concern about sexual predators moving into neighborhoods. These are usually referred to as Megan's Law, named after 7-year-old Megan Kanka of Hamilton Township, New Jersey, who was killed in 1994. Charged with the crime was a convicted sex offender who the Kanka family was unaware lived across the street from them. The New Jersey law requires that neighbors in the community be notified if an offender is living near them. In 1996, the federal government passed legislation requiring that the general public be informed of local **pedophiles** (sexual offenders who target children). It was left up to the officials to determine how much public warning was necessary, based on the danger posed by the offender.[28]

Similarly, new laws have been passed to keep the sexually dangerous under control. California's new **sexual predator law** allows authorities to keep some criminals in custody even after their sentences are served. The law, which took effect January 1, 1996, states that people convicted of sexually violent crimes against two or more victims can be committed to another institution once their prison term is served. Civil juries may recommend commitment to a mental institution, which would be reviewed every two years. The law already has been upheld by **appellate court** judges in the state.[29] Appellate courts are those that review trial procedures to determine whether the outcome was influenced by the fact that the judge made a legal mistake: for example, if the judge allowed evidence to be considered that violated the defendant's rights.

The federal government has also revised the U.S. legal code to reflect changing social conditions. The Brady Handgun Control Law of 1993, requiring a five-business-day waiting period before an individual can buy a handgun, reflects the nation's concern with gun violence and the easy access to handguns. The future direction of the criminal law in the United States remains unclear. Certain actions will be adopted as criminal and given more attention, such as crimes by corporations and political corruption. Other offenses, such as recreational drug use, may be reduced in importance or removed entirely from the criminal law system. In addition, changing technology and its ever-increasing role in our lives, globally and locally, will require modification in the criminal law. For example, such technologies as automatic teller machines and cellular phones have already spawned a new generation of criminal acts involving "theft" of access numbers and cards and software piracy. As the "information highway" sprawls toward new expanses, the nation's computer network advances, and biotechnology produces new substances, the criminal law will be forced to address threats to the public safety that are today unknown.

CONNECTIONS

Chapter 13 contains sections on technological crimes, including the newly emerging area of computer crime. The criminal law must be constantly modified to include areas that only a few years earlier were unknown. ■

■ Changing Defenses

Criminal defenses are also undergoing rapid change. As society becomes more aware of existing social problems that may contribute to crime, it has become commonplace for defense counsels to raise a variety of new defenses based on preexisting conditions or syndromes with which their clients are afflicted. Examples might include Battered Woman Syndrome, Vietnam Syndrome, Child Sexual Abuse Syndrome, Holocaust Survivor Syndrome, and Adopted Child Syndrome. In using these defenses, attorneys are asking judges either to recognize a new excuse for crime or to fit these conditions within preexisting defenses. For example, a person who used lethal violence in self-defense may argue that the trauma of serving in the war in Vietnam caused him to overreact to provocation. A victim of child abuse may use these experiences to mitigate his or her culpability in a crime, asking a jury, for example, to consider this background when making a death penalty decision. In some cases, these defenses have been successful; this defense was almost successfully used in the prominent Menendez brothers' case. The two bothers were tried for killing their parents. They claimed that their actions were the product of earlier sexual and physical abuse. This defense tactic led to a hung jury, but they were later convicted after a second trial.

In some instances, exotic criminal defenses have been gender specific. Attorneys have argued that their female clients' behavior was a result of Premenstrual Syndrome (PMS) and that male clients were aggressive because of an imbalance in their testosterone levels. These defenses have achieved relatively little success in the United States.[30] Others contend that attorneys can turn the tables and use these defenses against the defendant. For example, some commentators have suggested that courts will ultimately view PMS as an aggravating condition in a crime, prompting harsher penalties.

■ Summary

The substantive criminal law is a set of rules that specifies the behavior society has outlawed. The criminal law can be distinguished from the civil law on the basis that the former involves powers given to the state to enforce social rules, whereas the latter controls interactions between private citizens. The criminal law serves several important purposes: it represents public opinion and moral values, it enforces social controls, it deters criminal behavior and wrongdoing, it punishes transgressors, and it banishes private retribution.

The criminal law used in U.S. jurisdictions traces its origin to the English common law. Common law was formulated during the twelfth and thirteenth centuries in the Middle Ages, when English royal judges began to use precedents set in one case to guide actions in another; this system is called *stare decisis*.

In the U.S. legal system, lawmakers have codified common-law crimes into state and federal penal codes. Today, most crimes fall into the category of felony or misdemeanor. Felonies are serious crimes usually punished by a prison term, whereas misdemeanors are minor crimes that carry a fine or a light jail sentence. Common felonies include murder, rape, assault with a deadly weapon, arson, and robbery; misdemeanors include larceny, simple assault, and possession of small amounts of drugs.

Every crime has specific elements. In most instances, these elements include the *actus reus* (guilty act), which is the actual physical part of the crime: for example, taking money or burning a building. In addition, most crimes also contain a second element, the *mens rea* (guilty mind), which refers to the state of mind of the individual who commits a crime—more specifically, the person's intent to do the act.

At trial accused persons can defend themselves by claiming to have lacked *mens rea* and, therefore, not to be responsible for the criminal actions. One type of defense is justification by reason of self-defense or entrapment. Ignorance or mistake can be an excuse if it negates an element of a crime. Another defense is excuse for mental reasons, such as insanity, intoxication, necessity, or duress. Of all defenses, insanity is perhaps the most controversial. In most states, persons using an insanity defense claim that they did not know what they were doing when they committed a crime or that their mental state did not allow them to tell the difference between right and wrong. Regardless of the insanity defense used, critics charge that mental illness is separate from legal responsibility and that the two should not be equated. Supporters counter that the insanity defense allows mentally ill people to avoid penal sanctions.

The criminal law is undergoing constant reform. Some acts are being decriminalized—their penalties are being reduced—while laws are being revised to make penalties for some acts more severe. The law must continue to evolve to confront social and technological change.

■ Thinking Like a Criminologist

Congress is considering passing some new laws designed to meet the changing social and economic landscape. They have asked you to make an appearance before the joint legislative committee on criminal code reform to identify some of the emerging areas in which legal controls are needed. One area of concern is whether laws should be passed to control the use of the Internet—for example, regulating the sale of digital information, including text, images, sounds, computer programs, software, and databases. The danger may be that unscrupulous entrepreneurs will use the Internet to sell such undesirable material as pornography.

Would you advise Congress to control the Internet closely? What dangers might be presented by such an attempt at regulation?

■ Key Terms

- legal code *(26)*
- mores *(27)*
- folkways *(27)*
- Code of Hammurabi *(27)*
- *lex talionis* *(27)*
- Mosaic Code *(27)*
- Twelve Tables *(27)*
- plebeians *(27)*
- patricians *(27)*
- wergild *(28)*
- compurgation *(28)*
- ordeal *(28)*
- common law *(29)*
- shire *(29)*
- hundreds *(29)*
- tithings *(29)*
- reeve *(29)*
- hundred-gemot *(29)*
- shire-gemot *(29)*
- hali-gemot *(29)*
- holy-motes *(29)*
- ecclesiastics *(29)*
- assault *(29)*
- battery *(29)*
- treasonous acts *(29)*
- bot *(29)*
- wer *(29)*
- wite *(29)*
- manorial courts *(30)*
- *stare decisis* *(30)*
- circuit judges *(30)*
- circuit *(30)*
- juries *(30)*
- royal prosecutors *(31)*
- case law *(31)*
- criminal attempt law *(32)*
- inchoate crimes *(32)*
- statutory crimes *(32)*
- embezzlement *(32)*
- fraud *(32)*
- arson *(32)*
- civil law *(33)*
- property law *(33)*
- contract law *(33)*
- tort law *(33)*
- tort *(33)*
- libel *(33)*
- slander *(33)*
- statute of limitations *(33)*
- probation *(33)*
- beyond a reasonable doubt *(33)*
- preponderance of the evidence *(33)*
- felony *(34)*
- state prison *(34)*
- house of correction *(34)*
- *mala in se* *(35)*
- *mala prohibitum* *(35*
- natural law *(35)*
- substantive criminal law *(35)*
- norms *(35)*
- morals *(35)*
- vagrancy *(35)*
- social control function *(36)*
- larceny *(37)*
- commercial theft *(37)*
- *actus reus* *(37)*

- *mens rea* (37)
- strict-liability crimes (39)
- justification (39)
- decriminalize (42)

- obitiatry (42)
- stalking (42)
- community notification laws (42)
- pedophiles (42)

- sexual predator law (42)
- appellate court (43)

■ Critical Thinking Questions

1. What are the specific aims and purposes of the criminal law? To what extent is the criminal law aimed at controlling social harm?

2. What kinds of activities should be labeled criminal in contemporary society? Do you believe some acts that are now legal should be criminalized and some that are now criminal should be legalized?

3. Under common law a person must have *mens rea* to be guilty of a crime. Would society be better off if criminal intent was not considered? After all, aren't we merely guessing about a person's actual motivation for committing crime?

4. When is it permissible to use force in self-defense? Considering that the law seeks to prevent crime, not promote it, should the permissible use of self-defense be tightened?

5. Should a person's past history of abuse be considered in judging criminal responsibility? Should the fact that a person was sexually abused as a child be used to defend his or her actions as an adult?

■ Notes

1. "Jury Returns Murder Verdict in Wedding-Day Killing of Ex-Girlfriend," *New York Times*, 23 October 2001, B2.

2. The historical material in the following sections was derived from a number of sources. The most important include Rene Wormser, *The Story of Law*, rev. ed. (New York: Simon and Schuster, 1962); Jackson Spielvogel, *Western Civilization* (St. Paul, Minn.: West Publishing, 1991); Eugene Weber, *A Modern History of Europe* (New York: W. W. Norton, 1971); James Heath, *Eighteenth-Century Penal Theory* (New York: Oxford University Press, 1963); David Jones, *History of Criminology* (Westport, Conn.: Greenwood Press, 1986); Fred Inbau, James Thompson, and James Zagel, *Criminal Law and Its Administration* (Mineola, N.Y.: Foundation Press, 1974); Wayne LaFave and Austin Scott, *Criminal Law*, 2d ed. (St. Paul: West Publishing, 1986); and Sanford Kadish and Monrad Paulsen, *Criminal Law and Its Processes* (Boston: Little, Brown, 1975).

3. Internet Medieval Sourcebook, *The Laws of William the Conqueror, Set down what William, king of the English, established in consultation with his magnates after the conquest of England.* [Online] Available at http://www.fordham.edu/halsall/sbook.html

4. Weber, *A Modern History of Europe*, p. 9.

5. John Hudson, *The Formation of the English Common Law. Law and Society in England from the Norman Conquest to Magna Carta* (London: Longman, 1996).

6. Wayne LaFave and Austin Scott, *Handbook on Criminal Law* (St. Paul, Minn.: West Publishing, 1982), pp. 528–29.

7. Caldwell 397 (1784), cited in LaFave and Scott, *Handbook on Criminal Law*, p. 422.

8. 9 George I, C. 22, 1723, cited in Douglas Hay, "Crime and Justice in Eighteenth and Nineteenth Century England," in *Crime and Justice*, vol. 2, eds. Norval Norris and Michael Tonry (Chicago: University of Chicago Press, 1980), p. 51.

9. Jerome Hall, *Theft, Law, and Society* (Indianapolis: Bobbs-Merrill, 1952); chap. 1 is generally considered the best source for the history of common-law theft crimes.

10. Mass. Gen. Laws Ann. (West 1982) ch. 266, pp. 1–2.

11. See, generally, Alfred Lindesmith, *The Addict and the Law* (New York: Vintage Books, 1965), chap. 1.

12. William Henry, "Did the Music Say 'Do It'?" *Time*, 30 July 1990, p. 65.

13. Mathew Brelis, "Man Must Pay $500,000 for Raping Daughter," *Boston Globe*, 2 July 1993, p. 1.

14. For example, see *Brinegar v. United States*, 388 U.S. 160 (1949); *Speiser v. Randall*, 357 U.S. 513 (1958); *In re Winship*, 397 U.S. 358 (1970).

15. Oliver Wendell Holmes, *The Common Law*, ed. Mark De Wolf (Boston: Little, Brown, 1881), p. 36.

16. William Chambliss, "A Sociological Analysis of the Law of Vagrancy," *Social Problems* 12 (1964): 67–77; idem, "On Trashing Marxist Criminology," *Criminology* 27 (1989): 231–39.

17. Jeffrey Adler, "A Historical Analysis of the Law of Vagrancy," *Criminology* 27 (1989): 209–30; idem, "Vagging the Demons and Scoundrels: Vagrancy and the Growth of St. Louis, 1830–1861," *Journal of Urban History* 13 (1986): 3–30.

18. Todd Clear, *Harm in American Penology: Offenders, Victims and Their Communities* (Albany: State University of New York Press, 1994), pp. 73–74.

19. *Carrier's Case*, Y.B. 13 Edw. 4, f. 9, pl. 5 (Star Chamber and Exchequer Chamber, 1473), discussed at length in Jerome Hall, *Theft, Law and Society* (Indianapolis: Bobbs-Merrill, 1952), chap. 1.

20. Mass. Gen. Laws Ann. (West 1983) ch. 266, p. 14.

21. 320 U.S. 277 (1943).

22. Fox Butterfield, "A Fatality, Parental Violence and Youth Sports," *New York Times*, 11 July 2000, p. 1.

23. Brian MacQuarrie and Kathleen Burge, "Jury Convicts Him of Involuntary Manslaughter; Sentencing Jan. 25," *Boston Globe*, 12 January 2002, p. 1.

24. Associated Press, "Nigerian Used Stepdaughter, 14, for a Son, Jury Finds," *Boston Globe*, 8 October 1998, p. 9.

25. Marvin Zalman, John Strate, Denis Hunter, and James Sellars, "Michigan Assisted Suicide Three Ring Circus: The Intersection of Law and Politics," *Ohio Northern Law Review* 23 (1997): 211–48.

26. 1992 P.A. 270 as amended by 1993 P.A.3, M.C. L. ss. 752.1021 to 752. 1027.

27. National Institute of Justice, *Project to Develop a Model Anti-Stalking Statute* (Washington, D.C.: National Institute of Justice, 1994).

28. "Clinton Signs Tougher 'Megan's Law,'" CNN News Service, 17 May 1996.

29. Associated Press, "Judge Upholds State's Sexual Predator Law," *Bakersfield Californian*, 2 October 1996.

30. Deborah W. Denno, "Gender, Crime, and the Criminal Law Defenses," *Journal of Criminal Law and Criminology*, Summer 85 (1994): 80–180.

CHAPTER 3 The Nature and Extent of Crime

Introduction

School violence has become an all too common phenomenon in the United States. In a recent incident, on March 5, 2001, a student in Santee, California—an alleged victim of schoolyard bullies—brought a gun to school and killed two students. Soon after the school shootings took place, the county school board adopted a zero-tolerance policy mandating that any student who makes a threat, even in jest, must be disciplined. When a 10-year-old girl whimpered, "I could kill her!" after she wet her pants because a teacher had refused to let her go to the bathroom, she was suspended for three days. A 10-year-old who muttered, "I oughtta murder his face!" when someone left his desk in disarray got the same punishment.

At least 50 children were suspended for similar acts, most in kindergarten to third grade. All those suspended, including kindergartners, now have their names in police files. The Santee experience is not unique. School boards around the nation have adopted similar zero-tolerance policies. In Louisiana, a boy was suspended for two days after warning his peers in the lunch line not to eat all the potatoes or "I'm gonna get you!" In West Windsor, New Jersey, a 9-year-old boy was suspended for threatening to shoot a wad of paper with a rubber band.

The response has become so extreme that in February 2001 the American Bar Association felt compelled to pass a resolution opposing zero-tolerance policies, saying they have "redefined students as criminals." In Santee, parents of some of the suspended children were so outraged that they hired lawyers and threatened to sue. Confronted by an angry public, the school board agreed to stop the automatic suspensions and leave decisions about discipline to teachers and principals. A policy that had looked good on paper had not worked well in practice.[1]

In some shooting incidents, the perpetrators claim to have been picked on and bullied by the school's star athletes. Did you know that in sports a team reflects the personality of the coach? If the coach is very aggressive, players may follow this example. To research the effects of coaching on team violence, use InfoTrac College Edition and type in "sports violence" as key words. You may want to read this article as well:
Edgar Shields. Intimidation and violence by males in high school athletics. *Adolescence,* Fall 1999 v34 i135 p503 ■

School shootings such as the Santee case and the Columbine High School massacre, which resulted in the deaths of 15 students and one teacher, get widespread media coverage and give the general public the impression that violence is out of control. Is this impression accurate? Is violent behavior an everyday event? Should people barricade themselves behind armed guards? Are crime rates rising or falling? Where do most crimes occur? To answer these and similar questions, criminologists have devised elaborate methods of crime data collection and analysis. Without accurate data on the nature and extent of crime, it would not be possible to formulate theories that explain

■ On March 5, 2001, a student in Santee, California—an alleged victim of schoolyard bullies—brought a gun to school and killed two students. Here visitors place flowers at a memorial to the victims. School shootings such as the Santee case get widespread media attention and give the general public the mistaken impression that violence is out of control. Criminologists must collect accurate crime data to provide a more informed and valid appraisal of crime trends.

AP/Wide World Photos

the onset of crime or to devise social policies that facilitate its control or elimination.

To read about some of the more publicized school shooting instances, go to:
> **http://www.washingtonpost.com/wp-srv/national/ longterm/juvmurders/timeline.htm**

For an up-to-date list of Web links, go to
> **http://info.wadsworth.com/siegel** ∎

This chapter reviews data collected on criminal offenders in some detail. The data provide a summary of crime patterns and trends. We also examine the concept of criminal careers and discover what available crime data can tell us about the onset, continuation, and termination of criminality. We begin with a discussion of the most important sources of crime data.

■ Measuring Crime

Today three significant methods are used to measure the nature and extent of crime: official data, victim data, and self-report data. In the next sections, these three methods are reviewed in some detail.

Official Data: The Uniform Crime Report

Official data on crime refers to those crimes known to and recorded by the nation's police departments. The Federal Bureau of Investigation's **Uniform Crime Report (UCR)** is the best known and most widely cited source of official criminal statistics.[2] The FBI receives and compiles records from more than 17,000 police departments serving a majority of the U.S. population. Its major unit of analysis involves **index crimes,** or **Part I crimes**: murder and nonnegligent manslaughter, forcible rape, robbery, aggravated assault, burglary, larceny, arson, and motor vehicle theft. Table 3.1 defines these crimes.

Table 3.1 Part I Index Crime Offenses

Crime	Description
Criminal homicide	a. Murder and nonnegligent manslaughter: the willful (nonnegligent) killing of one human being by another. Deaths caused by negligence, attempts to kill, assaults to kill, suicides, accidental deaths, and justifiable homicides are excluded. Justifiable homicides are limited to (1) the killing of a felon by a law enforcement officer in the line of duty and (2) the killing of a felon, during the commission of a felony, by a private citizen. b. Manslaughter by negligence: the killing of another person through gross negligence. Traffic fatalities are excluded. Although manslaughter by negligence is a Part I crime, it is not included in the Crime Index.
Forcible rape	The carnal knowledge of a female forcibly and against her will. Included are rapes by force and attempts or assaults to rape. Statutory offenses (no force used—victim under age of consent) are excluded.
Robbery	The taking or attempting to take anything of value from the care, custody, or control of a person or persons by force or threat of force or violence and/or by putting the victim in fear.
Aggravated assault	An unlawful attack by one person upon another for the purpose of inflicting severe or aggravated bodily injury. This type of assault usually is accompanied by the use of a weapon or by means likely to produce death or great bodily harm. Simple assaults are excluded.
Burglary/breaking or entering	The unlawful entry of a structure to commit a felony or a theft. Attempted forcible entry is included.
Larceny/theft (except motor vehicle theft)	The unlawful taking, carrying, leading, or riding away of property from the possession or constructive possession of another. Examples are thefts of bicycles or automobile accessories, shoplifting, pocket picking, or the stealing of any property or article that is not taken by force and violence or by fraud. Attempted larcenies are included. Embezzlement, con games, forgery, worthless checks, and so on are excluded.
Motor vehicle theft	The theft or attempted theft of a motor vehicle. A motor vehicle is self-propelled and runs on the surface and not on rails. Specifically excluded from this category are motorboats, construction equipment, airplanes, and farming equipment.
Arson	Any willful or malicious burning or attempt to burn, with or without intent to defraud, a dwelling house, public building, motor vehicle or aircraft, personal property of another, or the like.

SOURCE: FBI, Uniform Crime Report, 2000.

The FBI tallies and annually publishes the number of reported offenses by city, county, standard metropolitan statistical area, and geographical divisions of the United States. In addition to these statistics, the UCR shows the number and characteristics (age, race, and gender) of individuals who have been arrested for these and all other crimes, except traffic violations (**Part II crimes**).

You can access the Uniform Crime Report at the FBI Web site, at:

http://www.fbi.gov/

For an up-to-date list of Web links, go to

http://info.wadsworth.com/siegel ■

Collecting the Uniform Crime Report The methods used to compile the UCR are quite complex. Each month law enforcement agencies report the number of index crimes known to them. These data are collected from records of all crime complaints that victims, officers who discovered the infractions, or other sources reported to these agencies.

Whenever criminal complaints are found through investigation to be unfounded or false, they are eliminated from the actual count. However, the number of actual offenses known is reported to the FBI whether or not anyone is arrested for the crime, the stolen property is recovered, or prosecution ensues.

In addition, each month law enforcement agencies also report how many crimes were **cleared.** Crimes are cleared in two ways: (1) when at least one person is arrested, charged, and turned over to the court for prosecution; or (2) by exceptional means, when some element beyond police control precludes the physical arrest of an offender (for example, the offender leaves the country). Data on the number of clearances involving the arrest of only juvenile offenders, data on the value of property stolen and recovered in connection with Part I offenses, and detailed information pertaining to criminal homicide are also reported. Traditionally, slightly more than 20 percent of all reported index crimes are cleared by arrest each year (see Figure 3.1).

CONNECTIONS

The 20 percent clearance rate is a sore point with police. Despite years of effort, the clearance rate has not changed measurably. This has prompted many police departments to adopt new techniques. See Chapter 16 for more on this topic. ■

Violent crimes are more likely to be solved than property crimes because police devote more resources to these more serious acts. For these types of crime, witnesses (including the victim) are frequently available to identify offenders, and in many instances the victim and offender were previously acquainted.

Figure 3.1 Crimes Cleared by Arrest, 2000

More serious crimes such as murder and rape are cleared at much higher rates than less serious crimes such as larceny. Factors may include that police spend more resources solving serious crimes and there is more likely to be an association between victim and offender in serious crimes.

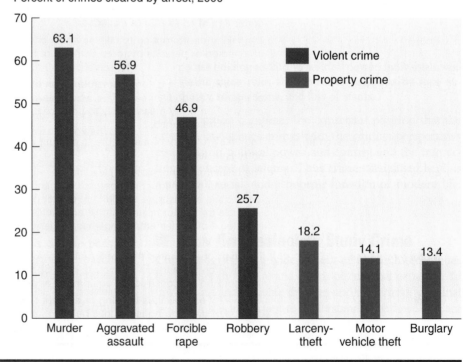

SOURCE: FBI, Uniform Crime Report, 2000.

The UCR uses three methods to express crime data. First, the number of crimes reported to the police and arrests made are expressed as raw figures (for example, 15,517 murders occurred in 2000). Second, crime rates per 100,000 people are computed. That is, when the UCR indicates that the murder rate was 5.5 in 2000, it means that about 6 people in every 100,000 were murdered between January 1 and December 31 of 2000. This is the equation used:

$$\frac{\text{Number of Reported Crimes}}{\text{Total U.S. Population}} \times 100,000 = \text{Rate per } 100,000$$

Third, the FBI computes changes in the number and rate of crime over time. For example, murder rates hardly changed at all between 1999 and 2000, declining less than 0.1 percent.

How accurate are the Uniform Crime Reports?

Despite criminologists' continued reliance on the UCR, its accuracy has been suspect. The three main areas of concern are reporting practices, law enforcement practices, and methodological problems.

Reporting practices Some criminologists claim that victims of many serious crimes do not report these incidents to police; therefore, these crimes do not become part of the UCR. The reasons for not reporting vary. Some victims do not trust the police or have confidence in their ability to solve crimes. Others do not have property insurance and therefore believe it is useless to report theft. In other cases, victims fear reprisals from an offender's friends or family. According to surveys of crime victims, less than 40 percent of all criminal incidents are reported to the police. Some of these victims justify nonreporting by stating that the incident was "a private matter," that "nothing could be done," or that the victimization was "not important enough."[3] These findings indicate that the UCR data may significantly underrepresent the total number of annual criminal events.

Law enforcement practices The way police departments record and report criminal and delinquent activity also affects the validity of UCR statistics. This effect was recognized more than 40 years ago, when between 1948 and 1952 the number of burglaries in New York City rose from 2,726 to 42,491, and larcenies increased from 7,713 to 70,949.[4] These increases related to the change from a precinct-based to a centralized statewide reporting system for crime statistics.[5]

How law enforcement agencies interpret the definitions of index crimes may also affect reporting practices. Some departments define crimes loosely—for example, reporting a trespass as a burglary or an assault on a woman as an attempted rape—whereas others pay strict attention to FBI guidelines. These reporting practices may help explain interjurisdictional differences in crime.[6] For example, arson may be seriously underreported because many fire departments do not report to the FBI, and those that do define as "accidental" or "spontaneous" many fires that may well have been set by arsonists.[7]

Some local police departments make systematic errors in UCR reporting. Some count an arrest only after a formal booking procedure, although the UCR requires arrests to be counted if the suspect is released without a formal charge. One survey of arrests found an error rate of about 10 percent in every Part I offense category.[8] More serious allegations claim that in some cases police officials may deliberately alter reported crimes to improve their department's public image. Police administrators interested in lowering the crime rate may falsify crime reports by, for example, classifying a burglary as a nonreportable trespass.[9]

Ironically, boosting police efficiency and professionalism may actually help increase crime rates; as people develop confidence in the police, they may be more motivated to report crime. For example, a recent New York City police program provided special services (such as follow-up visits and education) to a select sample of domestic violence victims.[10] Evaluation of the program showed that households that received the extra attention were more likely to report new incidences of violence than those that received no special services. Although it is possible that the follow-ups encouraged violence, a more realistic assessment is that the interventions increased citizens' confidence in the ability of the police to handle domestic assaults and encouraged greater crime reporting.

Higher crime rates may occur as departments adopt more sophisticated computer technology and hire better-educated, better-trained employees. Crime rates also may be altered based on the way law enforcement agencies process UCR data. As the number of employees assigned to dispatching, record keeping, and criminal incident reporting increases, so too will national crime rates. What appears to be a rising crime rate may be simply an artifact of improved police record-keeping ability.[11]

Methodological problems Methodological issues also contribute to questions pertaining to the UCR's validity. The most frequent issues include the following:
1. No federal crimes are reported.
2. Reports are voluntary and vary in accuracy and completeness.
3. Not all police departments submit reports.
4. The FBI uses estimates in its total crime projections.
5. If an offender commits multiple crimes, only the most serious is recorded. Thus, if a narcotics addict rapes, robs, and murders a victim, only the murder is recorded. Consequently, many lesser crimes go unreported.
6. Each act is listed as a single offense for some crimes but not for others. If a man robbed six people in a bar, the offense is listed as one robbery; but if he assaulted or murdered them, it would be listed as six assaults or six murders.

7. Incomplete acts are lumped together with completed ones.

8. Important differences exist between the FBI's definition of certain crimes and those used in a number of states.[12]

The complex scoring procedure means that many serious crimes are not counted. For example, during an armed bank robbery, the offender strikes a teller with the butt of a handgun. The robber runs from the bank and steals an automobile at the curb. Although the offender has technically committed robbery, aggravated assault, and motor vehicle theft, which are three Part I offenses, because robbery is the most serious, it would be the only one recorded in the UCR.[13]

The future of the Uniform Crime Report Clearly there must be a more reliable source for crime statistics than the UCR as it stands today. For the past 15 years, the FBI has been implementing some important changes in the Uniform Crime Report. An attempt is being made to provide more detailed information on individual criminal incidents by using a uniform, comprehensive program called the **National Incident-Based Reporting System (NIBRS).** Instead of submitting statements of the kinds of crime that individual citizens reported to the police and summary statements of resulting arrests, the new program will require local police agencies to provide at least a brief account of each incident and arrest within 22 crime patterns, including the incident, victim, and offender information. These expanded crime categories would include numerous additional crimes, such as blackmail, embezzlement, drug offenses, and bribery; this would allow a national database on the nature of crime, victims, and criminals to be developed.[14] Other information to be collected includes statistics gathered by federal law enforcement agencies, as well as data on hate or bias crimes. In 1999, 3,396 police agencies in 17 states submitted NIBRS reports, representing 13 percent of the total population. When this new UCR program is fully implemented and adopted across the nation, it should bring about greater uniformity in cross-jurisdictional reporting and improve the accuracy of official crime data.

To read more about NIBRS, go to:
   http://www.ojp.usdoj.gov/bjs/nibrs.htm
For an up-to-date list of Web links, go to
   http://info.wadsworth.com/siegel ∎

Victim Surveys: The National Crime Victimization Survey

The second source of crime data is surveys that ask crime victims about their encounters with criminals. Because many victims do not report their experiences to the police, victim surveys are considered a method of getting at the unknown figures of crime. The most important and widely used victim survey—the **National Crime Victimization Survey**

(NCVS)—is sponsored by the Bureau of Justice Statistics of the U.S. Department of Justice. In these national surveys, housing units are selected using a complex, multistage sampling technique. Each year data are obtained from a large nationally representative sample; in 2000, 86,800 households and 159,420 people age 12 or older were interviewed.[15] They are asked to report on the frequency, characteristics, and consequences of criminal victimization for such crimes as rape, sexual assault, robbery, assault, theft, household burglary, and motor vehicle theft. The total sample is interviewed twice a year about victimizations suffered in the preceding six months. Households remain in the sample for about three years, and new homes rotate into the sample continually. The NCVS reports that the interview completion rate in the national sample is usually more than 90 percent in any given period. NCVS data are considered to be a relatively unbiased, valid estimate of all victimizations for the target crimes included in the survey because of the care with which the samples are drawn and the high completion rate.

To access the most recent NCVS data, go to:
   http://www.ojp.usdoj.gov/bjs/pub/pdf/cv00.pdf
For an up-to-date list of Web links, go to
   http://info.wadsworth.com/siegel ∎

The NCVS finds that many crimes go unreported to police. For example, the UCR shows that about 408,000 robberies or attempted robberies occurred in 2000, but the NCVS estimates that about 810,000 actually occurred. The reason for such discrepancies is that less than half of all violent crimes, one-third of personal theft crimes (such as pocket picking), and only half of household thefts are reported to police. The reasons most often given by victims for not reporting crime include believing that "the police can do nothing about it," that it was a "private matter," or that they did not want to "get involved." Victims seem to report to the police only crimes that involve considerable loss or injury.

CONNECTIONS

Victim surveys provide information about criminal incidents that have occurred, but they can also describe the individuals who are most at risk of falling victim to crime, where the crime might occur, and when they are most likely to become victimized. Data from recent NCVS surveys are used in Chapter 4 to draw a portrait of the nature and extent of victimization in the United States. ∎

Like the UCR, the NCVS may also suffer from some methodological problems. As a result, its findings must be interpreted with caution. Among the potential problems are these:

• Overreporting due to victims' misinterpretation of events. For example, a lost wallet may be reported as stolen, or an open door may be viewed as a burglary attempt.

Figure 3.2 Self-Report Survey Questions

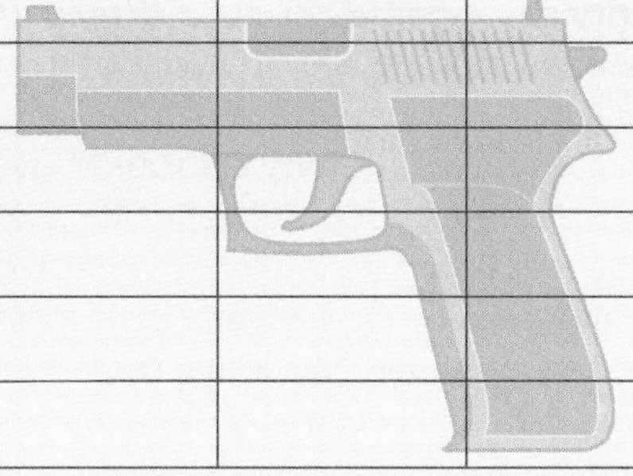

PLEASE INDICATE HOW OFTEN IN THE PAST 12 MONTHS YOU DID EACH ACT. (CHECK THE BEST ANSWER.)

	Never did act	One time	2–5 times	6–9 times	10+ times
Stole something worth less than $50					
Stole something worth more than $50					
Used cocaine					
Been in a fistfight					
Carried a weapon such as a gun or knife					
Fought someone using a weapon					

- Underreporting due to the embarrassment of reporting crime to interviewers, fear of getting in trouble, or simply forgetting an incident.
- Inability to record the personal criminal activity of those interviewed, such as drug use or gambling; murder is also not included for obvious reasons.
- Sampling errors, which produce a group of respondents who do not represent the nation as a whole.
- Inadequate question format that invalidates responses. Some groups, such as adolescents, may be particularly susceptible to error because of the question format.[16]

Self-Report Surveys

The problems associated with official statistics have led many criminologists to seek alternative sources of information in assessing the true extent of crime patterns. The data provided by the NCVS are important, but they cannot tell us much about the personality, attitudes, and behavior of individual offenders. Neither the NCVS nor UCR is of much value in charting the extent of one of the nation's most important social problems—substance abuse in the teenage population. To address these issues, criminologists have developed the **self-report survey.**

Most often, self-report surveys are administered to groups of subjects through a mass distribution of questionnaires. Although some surveys are able to identify the subjects, most are given anonymously so that respondents are free to tell the truth about their behaviors. The basic assumption of self-report studies is that because anonymity and confidentiality is assured, people will be encouraged to accurately describe their illegal activities. Figure 3.2 illustrates some typical self-report items.

Because most self-report instruments contain items measuring subjects' attitudes, values, personal characteristics, and behaviors, the data obtained from them can be used for various purposes. These include testing theories, measuring attitudes toward crime, and computing the association between crime and important social variables, such as family relations, educational attainment, and income. They also enable criminologists to evaluate the distribution of criminal behavior across racial, class, and gender lines. It is then possible to determine whether official arrest data truly represent the offender population or if they reflect bias, discrimination, and selective enforcement. For example, if black and white respondents report equal amounts of crime, but official data indicate that minorities are arrested more often than whites, the results would indicate the presence of racial bias in the arrest rate. In sum, self-reports provide an appreciable amount of information about offenders that official statistics and victimization surveys fail to provide.

Are self-reports accurate? Although self-report data have profoundly affected criminological inquiry, some important methodological issues have been raised about their accuracy. Critics of self-report studies frequently suggest that it is unreasonable to expect people to candidly admit illegal acts. They have nothing to gain, and the ones taking the greatest risk are the ones with official records who may be engaging in the most criminality. In addition, some people may exaggerate their criminal acts, forget some of them, or be confused about what is being asked. Some surveys contain an overabundance of trivial offenses, such as shoplifting small amounts of items or using false identification, which are often lumped together with serious crimes to form a total crime index. Consequently, comparisons between groups can be highly misleading.

Various techniques have been used to verify self-report data.[17] The "known group" method compares incarcerated youths with "normal" groups to see whether the former report more delinquency. Another approach is to use peer informants who can verify the honesty of a subject's answers. Subjects can be tested twice to see if their answers remain stable. Sometimes questions are designed to reveal respondents who are lying on the survey; for example, an item might say, "I have never done anything wrong in my life." Polygraphs, commonly known as lie detectors, have also been used to verify the responses given on self-report surveys. The results often validate the accuracy of self-report survey data.[18]

It is also possible to compare the answers youths give with their official police records. A typical approach is to ask youths if they have ever been arrested for or convicted of a delinquent act and then check their official records against their self-reported responses.[19] Research studies indicate a substantial association between official processing and self-reported crime.[20] For example, kids who report being involved with the justice system are much more likely to have a juvenile court record than those who deny contact with the system.[21]

Questioning self-report accuracy Although these findings are encouraging, nagging questions still remain about the validity of self-reports. Even if 90 percent of a school population voluntarily participates in a self-report study, researchers can never be sure whether the few who refuse to participate or are absent that day comprise a significant portion of the school's population of persistent high-rate offenders. Research indicates that offenders with the most extensive prior criminality are also the most likely to be "poor historians of their own crime commission rates."[22] It is also unlikely that the most serious chronic offenders in the teenage population are the ones most willing to cooperate with university-based criminologists administering self-report tests.[23] Institutionalized youths, who are not generally represented in the self-report surveys, are not only more delinquent than the general youth population but also are considerably more misbehaving than the most delinquent youths identified in the typical self-report survey.[24] Consequently, self-reports may measure only nonserious, occasional delinquents while ignoring hard-core chronic offenders who may be institutionalized and unavailable for self-reports.

CONNECTIONS

Criminologists suspect that a few high-rate offenders are responsible for a disproportionate share of all serious crime. Results would be badly skewed if even a few of these chronic offenders were absent or refused to participate in schoolwide self-report surveys. For more on chronic offenders, see the sections at the end of this chapter. ■

Self-reports are the accepted method of measuring substance abuse by the nation's high school population. Nonetheless, criminologists suspect that substance abusers tend to underreport the frequency of their drug use.[25] For example, in studies of juvenile detainees, many children who tested positive for drug use in physical exams failed to mention using any drugs in self-report surveys.[26] Although this research involves a sample of incarcerated youth who might be expected to underreport drug use, the findings call into question the validity of self-report surveys. Similar research with adult pretrial detainees also found that self-reports significantly undercounted substance abuse.[27]

Although self-reports continue to be used to measure criminal behavior, their accuracy is not assured. The least reliable self-reports are those of two offending populations—chronic offenders and persistent drug abusers. These groups may be among the most frequent and serious criminal offenders. Although these criticisms are troubling, self-reports continue to be widely used in the criminological community. In what is probably the most thorough analysis of self-report methodologies, respected criminologists Michael Hindelang, Travis Hirschi, and Joseph Weis evaluated the reliability and validity of self-reports and concluded that they are accurate and quite compatible with official statistics.[28]

CONNECTIONS

Self-report data are used as the standard measure of U.S. youthful drug use. When reading the results of national drug use surveys in Chapter 14, keep in mind the limited validity of these self-report surveys. ■

Compatibility of Crime Statistics Sources

Are the various sources of crime statistics compatible? Each has strengths and weaknesses. The FBI survey is carefully tallied and contains data on the number of murders and people arrested, information that the other data sources lack. However, this survey omits the many crimes victims choose not to report to police, and it is subject to the reporting caprices of individual police departments.

The NCVS contains unreported crime and important information on the personal characteristics of victims, but the data consist of estimates made from relatively limited samples of the total U.S. population. Because of this, even narrow fluctuations in the rates of some crimes can have a major impact on findings. It also relies on personal recollections that may be inaccurate. The NCVS does not include data on important crime patterns, including murder and drug abuse.

Self-report surveys can provide information on the personal characteristics of offenders, such as their attitudes, values, beliefs, and psychological profiles, which is unavailable from any other source. Yet at their core, self-reports rely on the honesty of criminal offenders and drug abusers, a population not generally known for accuracy and integrity.

Despite these differences, a number of prominent criminologists have concluded that the data sources are more compatible than was first believed. Although their tallies of crimes are certainly not in sync, the crime patterns and trends they record are often quite similar.[29] For example, all three sources generally agree about the personal characteristics of serious criminals (such as age and gender) and where and when crime occurs (such as urban areas, nighttime, and summer months).

This may be persuasive, but some criminologists still question the compatibility between the data sources and point out that they measure separate concepts (for example, reported crimes, actual crimes, and victimization rates).[30] This ongoing academic debate accentuates the fact that interpreting crime data is often problematic. Because each source of crime data uses a different method to obtain results, differences inevitably will occur among them. These differences must be carefully considered when criminologists interpret data on the nature and trends in crime.[31]

■ Crime Trends

Crime is not new to this century.[32] Studies have indicated that a gradual increase in the crime rate, especially in violent crime, occurred from 1830 to 1860. Following the Civil War, this rate increased significantly for about 15 years. Then, from 1880 up to the time of the First World War, with the possible exception of the years immediately preceding and following the war, the number of reported crimes decreased. After a period of readjustment, the crime rate steadily declined until the Depression (about 1930), when another crime wave was recorded. Crime rates increased gradually following the 1930s until the 1960s, when the growth rate became much greater. The homicide rate, which had actually declined from the 1930s to the 1960s, also began a sharp increase that continued through the 1970s.

In 1981 the number of index crimes peaked at about 13.4 million and then began a consistent decline until 1984, when police recorded 11.1 million crimes. By the following year, however, the crime rate once again began an upward trend, so that by 1991 police recorded about 14.6 million crimes. Both the number and rate of crimes have been declining ever since (Figure 3.3).

In 2000 about 11.6 million crimes were reported to the police, a decrease of about 0.2 percent from the preceding year. Though the crime rate stabilized between 1999 and 2000, there has been a decade-long decline in the number and rate of crimes in the United States. The overall crime rate has declined more than 22 percent since 1991; the number of reported crimes has declined more than 3 million from the 1991 peak. Even the teen murder rate, which had remained stubbornly high, has undergone decline during the past few years.[33] The factors that help explain the upward and downward movements in crime rates are discussed in the Criminological Enterprise feature.

Figure 3.3   Crime Rate Trends

After years of steady increase, crime rates declined from 1993 through 1999 and leveled off through 2001.

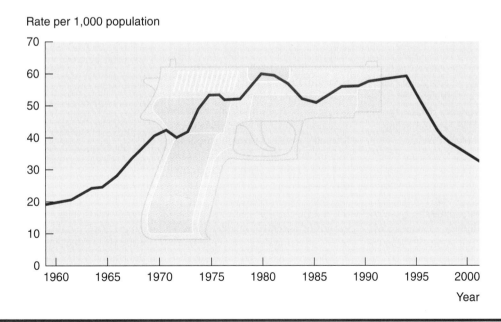

SOURCE: FBI, Uniform Crime Report, 2000.

Explaining Crime Trends

Criminologists have identified a variety of social, economic, personal, and demographic factors that influence crime rate trends. Although criminologists are still uncertain about how these factors impact crime rate trends, change in their direction seems to be associated with changes in crime rates.

Age

Because teenagers have extremely high crime rates, criminologists view change in the population age distribution as having the greatest influence on crime trends: as a general rule, the crime rate follows the proportion of young males in the population. With the "graying" of society in the 1980s and a decline in the birth rate, it is not surprising that the overall crime rate declined between 1991 and 2000. The number of juveniles should be increasing over the next decade, and some criminologists fear that this will signal a return to escalating crime rates. However, the number of senior citizens is also expanding, and their presence in the population may have a moderating effect on crime rates (seniors do not commit much crime), offsetting the effect of teens.

Economy

There is debate over the effect the economy has on crime rates. Some criminologists believe a poor economy actually helps lower crime rates because unemployed parents are at home to supervise children and guard their possessions. Because there is less to spend, a poor economy reduces the number of valuables worth stealing. Also, it seems unlikely that law-abiding, middle-aged workers will suddenly turn to a life of crime if they are laid off during an economic downturn.

A poor economy may lower crime rates in the short run, but long periods of sustained economic weakness and unemployment can eventually lead to increased rates. Crime rates fell when the economy surged during the 1990s. A long-term economic recession may produce increases in the crime rate.

Social Malaise

As the level of social problems increases—such as single-parent families, dropout rates, racial conflict, and teen pregnancies—so too do crime rates. For example, crime rates are correlated with the number of unwed mothers in the population. It is possible that children of unwed mothers need more social services than children in two-parent families. As the number of kids born to single mothers increases, the child welfare system will be taxed and services depleted. The teenage birth rate began to increase in the late 1980s and 1990s, and so too have crime rates.

Racial conflict may also increase crime rates. Areas undergoing racial change, especially those experiencing an in-migration of minorities into predominantly white neighborhoods, seem prone to significant increases in their crime rate. Whites in these areas may be using violence to protect what they view as their home turf. Racially motivated crimes actually diminish as neighborhoods become more integrated and power struggles are resolved.

Abortion

In a controversial work, John J. Donohue III and Steven D. Levitt found empirical evidence that the recent drop in the crime rate can be attributed to the availability of legalized abortion. In 1973, *Roe v. Wade* legalized abortion nationwide. Within a few years of *Roe v. Wade*, more than 1 million abortions were being performed annually, or roughly one abortion for every three live births. Donohue and Levitt suggest that the crime rate drop, which began approximately 18 years later, in 1991, can be tied to the fact that at that point the first groups of potential offenders affected by the abortion decision began reaching the peak age of criminal activity.

They find that states that legalized abortion before the rest of the nation were the first to experience decreasing crime rates and that states with high abortion rates have seen a greater fall in crime since 1985.

The abortion-related reduction in crime rates is predominantly attributable to a decrease in crime among the young. It is possible that the link between crime rates and abortion is the result of two mechanisms: (1) selective abortion on the part of women most at risk to have children who would engage in criminal activity, and (2) improved child-rearing or environmental circumstances caused by better maternal, familial, or fetal circumstances because women are having fewer children. If abortion were illegal, they find, crime rates might be 10 to 20 percent higher than they currently are with abortion. If these estimates are correct, legalized abortion can explain about half of the recent fall in crime. All else equal, they predict that crime rates will continue to fall slowly for an additional 15 to 20 years as the full effects of legalized abortion are gradually felt.

Guns and Teens

The availability of firearms may influence the crime rate, especially the proliferation of weapons in the hands of teens. There is evidence that more guns than ever before are finding their way into the hands of young people. Surveys of high school students indicate that between 6 and 10 percent carry guns at least some of the time. Guns also cause escalation in the seriousness of crime. As the number of gun-toting students increases, so too will the seriousness of violent crime as, for example, a schoolyard fight turns into murder.

Gangs

Another factor that affects crime rates is the explosive growth in teenage gangs. Surveys indicate that there are more than 850,000 gang members in the United States. Boys who are members of gangs are far more likely to possess guns than non–gang members; criminal activity increases when kids join gangs. According to Alfred Blumstein, gangs involved in the urban drug trade recruit juveniles because they work cheaply, are immune from heavy criminal penalties, and are "daring and willing to take risks." Arming themselves for protection, these drug-dealing children present a menace to their community, which persuades non–gang-affiliated neighborhood adolescents to arm themselves for protection. The result is an arms race that produces an increasing spiral of violence.

The recent decline in the crime rate may be tied to changing gang values. Some streetwise kids have told researchers that they now avoid gangs because of the "younger brother syndrome"—they have watched their older siblings or parents caught in gangs or drugs and want to avoid the same fate.

Drug Use

Some experts tie increases in the violent crime rate between 1980 and 1990 to the crack cocaine epidemic, which swept the nation's largest cities, and drug-trafficking gangs that fought over drug turf. These well-armed gangs did not hesitate to use violence to control territory, intimidate rivals, and increase market share. As the crack epidemic has subsided, so too has the violence in New York City and other metropolitan areas where the crack epidemic was rampant.

Justice Policy

Some law enforcement experts have suggested that a reduction in crime rates may be attributed to aggressive police practices that target "quality of life" crimes such as panhandling, graffiti, petty drug dealing, and loitering. By showing that even the smallest infractions will be dealt with seriously, aggressive police departments may be able to discourage potential criminals from committing more serious crimes.

It is also possible that tough laws targeting drug dealing and repeat offenders with lengthy prison terms can affect crime rates. The fear of punishment may inhibit some would-be criminals. Lengthy sentences also help boost the nation's prison population. Placing a significant number of potentially high-rate offenders behind bars may help stabilize crime rates. Some ex-criminals have told researchers that they stopped committing crime because they perceive higher levels of street enforcement and incarceration rates.

Crime Opportunities

Crime rates may drop (a) when market conditions change or (b) when an alternative criminal opportunity develops. For example, the decline in the burglary rate over the past decade may be explained in part by the abundance and subsequent decline in price of commonly stolen merchandise such as VCRs, TVs, and cameras. Improving home and commercial security devices may also turn off would-be burglars, convincing them to turn to other forms of theft such as theft from motor vehicles. These are non-index crimes and do not contribute to the national crime rate.

Critical Thinking Questions

While crime rates have been declining in the United States, they have been increasing in Europe. Is it possible that factors that correlate with crime rate changes in the United States have little utility in predicting changes in other cultures? What other factors may increase or reduce crime rates?

InfoTrac College Edition Research

Gang activity may have a big impact on crime rates. To read about the effect, see:

John M. Hagedorn, Jose Torres, Greg Giglio. Cocaine, kicks, and strain: patterns of substance use in Milwaukee gangs. *Contemporary*

Drug Problems, Spring 1998 v25 n1 p113–145

Mary E. Pattillo. Sweet mothers and gangbangers: managing crime in a black middle-class neighborhood. *Social Forces,* March 1998 v76 n3 p747(28)

SOURCES: Steven Messner, Lawrence Raffalovich, and Richard McMillan, "Economic Deprivation and Changes in Homicide Arrest Rates for White and Black Youths, 1967–1998: A National Time-Series Analysis," *Criminology* 39 (2001): 591–614; John Laub, "Review of the Crime Drop in America," *American Journal of Sociology* 106 (2001): 1820–22; John J. Donohue III and Steven D. Levitt, "Legalized Abortion and Crime" (University of Chicago, June 24, 1999, unpublished paper); Donald Green, Dara Strolovitch, and Janelle Wong, "Defended Neighborhoods, Integration, and Racially Motivated Crime," *American Journal of Sociology* 104 (1998): 372–403; Robert O'Brien, Jean Stockard, and Lynne Isaacson, "The Enduring Effects of Cohort Characteristics on Age-Specific Homicide Rates, 1960–1995," *American Journal of Sociology* 104 (1999): 1061–95; Darrell Steffensmeier and Miles Harer, "Making Sense of Recent U.S. Crime Trends, 1980 to 1996/1998: Age Composition Effects and Other Explanations," *Journal of Research in Crime and Delinquency* 36 (1999): 235–74; Desmond Ellis and Lori Wright, "Estrangement, Interventions, and Male Violence toward Female Partners," *Violence and Victims* 12 (1997): 51–68; Richard Rosenfeld, "Changing Relationships between Men and Women: A Note on the Decline in Intimate Partner Homicide," *Homicide Studies* 1 (1997): 72–83; Bruce Johnson, Andrew Golub, and Jeffrey Fagan, "Careers in Crack, Drug Use, Drug Distribution, and Nondrug Criminality," *Crime and Delinquency* 41 (1995): 275–95; Alfred Blumstein, "Violence by Young People: Why the Deadly Nexus," *National Institute of Justice Journal* 229: 2–9 (1995); Joseph Sheley and James Wright, *In the Line of Fire: Youth, Guns, and Violence in Urban America* (New York: Aldine de Gruyter, 1995); Alan Lizotte, Gregory Howard, Marvin Krohn, and Terence Thornberry, "Patterns of Illegal Gun Carrying among Young Urban Males," *Valparaiso University Law Review* 31 (1997): 376–94; and Rosemary Gartner, "Family Structure, Welfare Spending, and Child Homicide in Developed Democracies," *Journal of Marriage and the Family* 53 (1991): 231–40.

Figure 3.4   Homicide Rate Trends, 1900–2000

Rate per 100,000 population

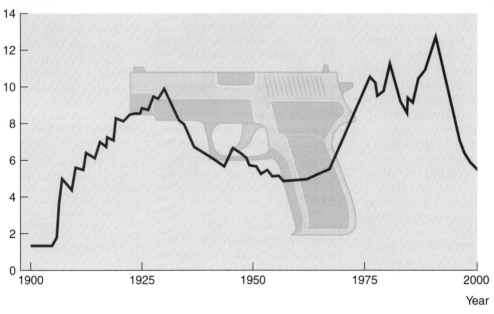

SOURCE: FBI, Uniform Crime Report, 2000.

Trends in Violent Crime

The violent crime rate has been trending downward. In the year 2000, violent crimes (murder, forcible rape, robbery, and aggravated assault) hit their lowest level since 1985. The 1.4 million violent crimes reported to the police in 2000 were down about 15.6 percent from the number reported in 1996 and 25.5 percent from the 1991 amounts. In 2000, there were 506 violent offenses for every 100,000 citizens in the population, a 20.5 percent decline from the 1996 rate, and a 33.2 percent decline from the 1991 rate. However, the decline in violent crimes seems to be stabilizing; the number of crimes recorded in 2000 decreased only 0.1 percent from the 1999 volume.

Particularly encouraging has been the decrease in the number and rate of murders. The murder statistics are generally regarded as the most accurate aspect of the UCR. Figure 3.4 illustrates homicide rate trends since 1900. Note how the rate peaked around 1930, then fell, rose dramatically around 1960, and peaked once again in 1991, when the number of murders topped 24,000 for the first time in the nation's history. There were an estimated 15,517 murders in 2000, 21 percent less than in 1996 and 37.2 percent less than in 1991. Some major cities, such as New York, report significant declines of more than 50 percent in their murder rates through the 1990s. Like other violent crimes, the number of murders occurring in 1999 and 2000 was relatively unchanged.

Trends in Property Crime

The property crimes reported in the UCR include burglary, larceny, and motor vehicle theft. An estimated 10.2 million property offenses were recorded in 2000, 13.8 percent less than in 1996 and 21.4 percent lower than in 1991. There were about 3,618 offenses for every 100,000 residents, 18.7 percent below the 1996 rate and 29.6 percent fewer than the 1991 rate. As was the case for violence, property crime declines may be stabilizing. Between 1999 and 2000 there was a decrease of 0.3 percent in reported crimes, and the property crime rate was 3.4 percent less than the 1999 rate.

Trends in Victimization Data

In 2000 (the latest data available), an estimated 26 million victimizations were recorded in the United States, a significant decline from the 28.8 million property and violent crimes experienced in 1999. The decline in victimizations parallels changes in the official crime rate: a downward trend that began in 1994 has brought the number of victimizations to the lowest ever recorded since 1973 when the NCVS began and measured 44 million victimizations (Figure 3.5).

Self-Report Findings

In general, self-reports indicate that the number of people who break the law is far greater than the number projected

Figure 3.5 Victimization Rate Trends, 1973–2000

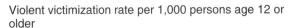

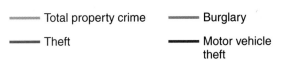

Violent victimization rate per 1,000 persons age 12 or older

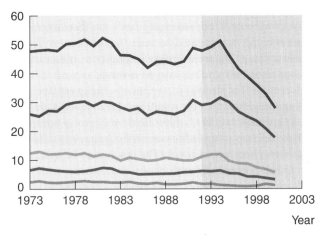

Property crime rate per 1,000 households

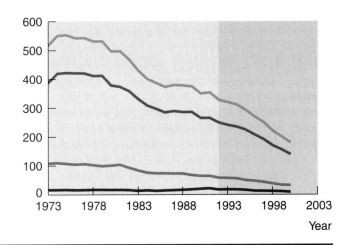

NOTE: The darker background shade after 1992 indicates the data were collected by redesigned methods.

SOURCE: National Crime Victimization Survey, 2000, p. 2.

by official statistics. Almost everyone questioned is found to have violated some law.[34] Furthermore, self-reports dispute the notion that criminals and delinquents specialize in one type of crime or another; offenders seem to engage in a "mixed bag" of crime and deviance.[35]

Self-report studies indicate that the most common offenses are truancy, alcohol abuse, use of a false ID, shoplifting or larceny under $50, fighting, marijuana use, and damage to the property of others. It is not unusual for self-reports to find combined substance abuse, theft, violence, and damage rates of more than 50 percent among suburban, rural, and urban high school youths. What is surprising is the consistency of these findings in samples taken around the United States.

Table 3.2 contains data from a self-report study called *Monitoring the Future,* which researchers at the University of Michigan Institute for Social Research (ISR) conduct annually. This national survey of more than 2,500 high school seniors, one of the most important sources of self-report data, shows a widespread yet stable pattern of youth crime since 1978.[36] Young people self-report a great deal of crime: about 30 percent of high school seniors now report stealing in the last 12 months; 20 percent said they were involved in a gang fight, and more than 10 percent injured someone so badly that the victim had to see a doctor; almost 25 percent engaged in breaking and entering. The

Table 3.2 Self-Reported Delinquent Activity During the Past 12 Months Among High School Seniors, 2000

Crime Category	Percentage Engaging in Offenses	
	At Least One Offense	Multiple Offenses
Serious fight	7	5
Gang fight	11	9
Hurt someone badly	7	5
Used a weapon to steal	1	2
Stole less than $50	12	18
Stole more than $50	6	7
Did breaking and entering	10	13
Committed arson	1	2
Damaged school property	7	6

SOURCE: *Monitoring the Future, 2000* (Ann Arbor, Mich.: Institute for Social Research, 2001).

fact that so many—at least 33 percent—of all U.S. high school students engaged in theft and about 20 percent committed a serious violent act during the past year shows that criminal activity is widespread and is not restricted to a few "bad apples."

■ What the Future Holds

It is risky to speculate about the future of crime trends because current conditions can change rapidly, but some criminologists have tried to predict future patterns. Criminologist James A. Fox predicts a significant increase in teen violence if current trends persist. There are approximately 50 million school-age children in the United States and many are under age 10; this is more than we have had for decades. Many come from stable homes, but some lack stable families and adequate supervision. These children will soon enter their prime crime years. As a result, Fox predicts a wave of youth violence that will be even worse than that of the past 10 years. If current trends persist, the number of juvenile homicides should grow from fewer than 4,000 today to about 9,000 in 2004.[37] Such predictions are based on population trends and other factors discussed previously.

Fox's predictions are persuasive, but not all criminologists believe we are in for an age-driven crime wave. Some, such as Steven Levitt, dispute the fact that the population's age makeup contributes as much to the crime rate as suggested by Fox and others.[38] Even if teens commit more

crime in the future, he finds that their contribution may be offset by the aging of the population, which will produce a large number of senior citizens and elderly, a group with a relatively low crime rate.

Criminologists Darrell Steffensmeier and Miles Harer predict a much more moderate increase in crime than previously believed possible.[39] Steffensmeier and Harer agree that the age structure of society is one of the most important determinants of crime rates, but they believe the economy, technological change, and social factors help moderate the crime rate.[40] For example, they note that American culture is being transformed because "baby boomers," now in their 40s and 50s, are exerting a significant influence on the nation's values and morals. As a result, the narcissistic youth culture that stresses materialism is being replaced by "kinder and gentler" cultural values.[41] Positive social values have a "contagion effect"; those held by the baby boomers will have an important influence on the behavior of all citizens, even crime-prone teens. The result may be a moderation in the potential growth of the crime rate.

Such prognostication is reassuring, but there is, of course, no telling what changes are in store that may influence crime rates either up or down. Technological developments such as the rapid expansion of E-commerce on the Internet have created new classes of crime. Concern about the environment in rural areas may produce a rapid upswing in environmental crimes ranging from vandalism to violence.[42] Although crime rates have trended downward, it is too early to predict that this trend will continue into the foreseeable future.

■ Even though official crime data tell us that the violence rate is in steep decline, highly publicized cases such as the shootings at Columbine High School in Colorado help convince the general public that U.S. society is extremely violent. Politicians seize on these tragedies to advocate a quick fix for teen violence: ban violent TV; encourage school prayers; prohibit rap music with offensive lyrics. Can such measures possibly deter violent outbursts such as Columbine?

© Rodolfo Gonzalez/Rocky Mountain News/CORBIS-Sygma

Crime Patterns

Criminologists look for stable crime rate patterns to gain insight into the nature of crime. If crime rates are consistently higher at certain times, in certain areas, and among certain groups, this knowledge might help explain the onset or cause of crime. For example, if criminal statistics show that crime rates are consistently higher in poor neighborhoods in large urban areas, then crime may be a function of poverty and neighborhood decline. If, in contrast, crime rates are spread evenly across society, this would provide little evidence that crime has an economic basis. Instead, crime might be linked to socialization, personality, intelligence, or some other trait unrelated to class position or income. In this section we examine traits and patterns that may influence the crime rate.

The Ecology of Crime

Patterns in the crime rate seem to be linked to temporal and ecological factors. Some of the most important of these are discussed here.

Day, season, and climate   Most reported crimes occur during the warm summer months of July and August. During the summer, teenagers, who usually have the highest crime levels, are out of school and have greater opportunity to commit crime. People spend more time outdoors during warm weather, making themselves easier targets. Similarly, homes are left vacant more often during the summer, making them more vulnerable to property crimes. Two exceptions to this trend are murders and robberies, which occur frequently in December and January (although rates are also high during the summer).

Crime rates also may be higher on the first day of the month than at any other time. Government welfare and Social Security checks arrive at this time, and with them come increases in such activities as breaking into mailboxes and accosting recipients on the streets. Also, people may have more disposable income at this time, and the availability of extra money may relate to behaviors associated with crime such as drinking, partying, gambling, and so on.[43]

Temperature   Although weather effects (such as temperature swings) may have an impact on violent crime rates, laboratory studies suggest that the association between temperature and crime resembles an inverted U-shaped curve. Crime rates increase with rising temperatures and then begin to decline at some point (85 degrees) when it may be too hot for any physical exertion[44] (see Figure 3.6). However, field studies indicate that the rates of some crimes (such as domestic assault), but not all of them (for example, rape), continue to increase as temperatures rise.[45] Research has also shown that a long stretch of highly uncomfortable weather is related to homicide rates, indicating that the stress of long-term exposure to extreme temperatures may prove sufficiently unpleasant and increase violence rates.[46]

Figure 3.6   The Relationship between Temperature and Crime

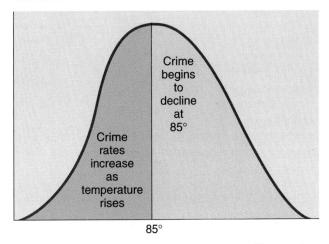

In their study of the relationship of temperature to assault, criminologists Ellen Cohn and James Rotton found evidence of a highly significant effect, especially during morning and evening hours. They found that a person is four times more likely to be assaulted at midnight when the temperature exceeds 90 degrees than when the temperature is 10 degrees below zero.[47]

Population density   Large urban areas have by far the highest violence rates. Areas with low per capita crime rates tend to be rural. These findings are also supported by victim data. Exceptions to this trend are low population resort areas with large transient or seasonal populations—such as Atlantic City, New Jersey, and Nantucket, Massachusetts.

Region   Crime rates vary by region. For many years, southern states have had consistently higher crime rates in almost all crime categories than those found in other regions of the country; these data convinced some criminologists that there was a "southern subculture of violence." Though the "lead" has flipped-flopped in recent years between the South and the West, the latest UCR data, illustrated in Figure 3.7, indicate that southern crime rates once again lead the nation.

CONNECTIONS

The "southern subculture of violence" theory will be discussed in greater detail in Chapter 11. Some criminologists dispute that cultural values produce high crime rates and explain regional differences as due to other factors, such as the economy. ■

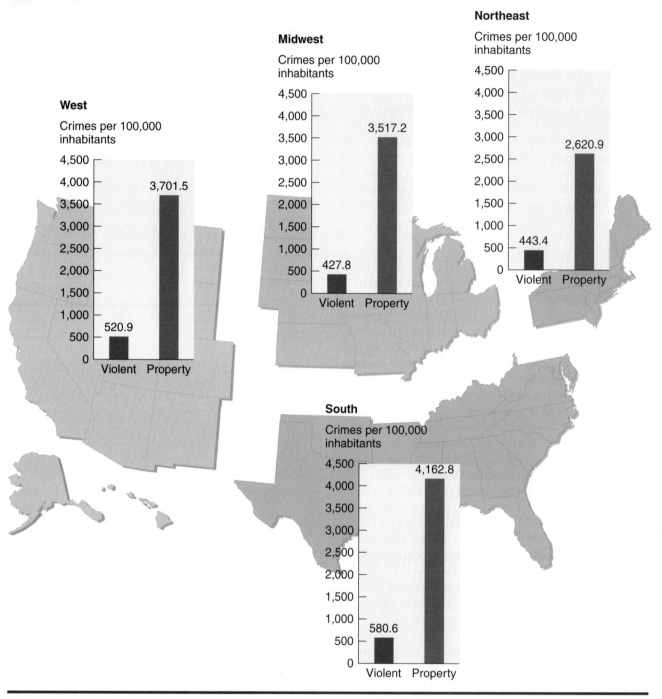

SOURCE: FBI, Uniform Crime Report, 2000, p. 10.

Use of Firearms

Firearms play a dominant role in criminal activity. According to the NCVS, firearms are typically involved in about 20 percent of robberies, 10 percent of assaults, and 6 percent of rapes. In 2000 the UCR reported that almost 70 percent of all murders involved firearms; most of these weapons were handguns.

According to international criminologists Franklin Zimring and Gordon Hawkins, the proliferation of handguns and the high rate of lethal violence they cause is the single most significant factor separating the crime problem in the United States from the rest of the developed world.[48] Differences between the United States and Europe in non-lethal crimes are only modest at best.[49] Because this issue is so important, the Policy and Practice in Criminology feature discusses gun control issues in some detail.

Some experts, such as Gary Kleck and Marc Gertz, maintain that handguns may be more of an effective deterrent to crime than gun control advocates are ready to admit. Their research indicates that as many as 400,000 people per year use guns in situations in which they later claim that the guns almost "certainly" saved lives. Even if these estimates are off by a factor of 10, it means that armed citizens may save 40,000 lives annually. Although Kleck and Gertz recognize that guns are involved in homicides, suicides, and accidents, which claim more than 30,000 lives per year, they believe their benefit as a crime prevention device should not be overlooked.[50]

AP/Wide World Photos

■ At a press conference in Los Angeles, Margaret Ensley, president of Mothers against Violence in Schools, stands with a picture of her son Michael, a victim of gun violence. Handguns are used in a significant number of all violent crimes, and some cities, led by Los Angeles and San Francisco, have gone as far as suing gun manufacturers to get them to compensate victims for gun-related injuries and deaths.

Social Class and Crime

A still-unresolved issue in criminological literature is the relationship between social class and crime. Traditionally crime has been thought of as a lower-class phenomenon. After all, people at the lowest rungs of the social structure have the greatest incentive to commit crimes. Those unable to obtain desired goods and services through conventional means may consequently resort to theft and other illegal activities—such as selling narcotics—to obtain them. These activities are referred to as **instrumental crimes**. Those living in poverty are also believed to engage in disproportionate amounts of **expressive crimes**, such as rape and assault, as a means of expressing their rage, frustration, and anger against society. Alcohol and drug abuse, common in impoverished areas, help fuel violent episodes.[51]

When measured with UCR data, official statistics indicate that crime rates in inner-city, high-poverty areas are generally higher than those in suburban or wealthier areas.[52] Surveys of prison inmates consistently show that prisoners were members of the lower class and unemployed or underemployed in the years before their incarceration.

An alternative explanation for these findings is that the relationship between official crime and social class is a function of law enforcement practices, not actual criminal behavior patterns. Police may devote more resources to poor areas, and consequently apprehension rates may be higher there. Similarly, police may be more likely to formally arrest and prosecute lower-class citizens than those in the middle and upper classes, which may account for the lower class's overrepresentation in official statistics and the prison population.

Class and self-reports   Self-report data have been used extensively to test the class–crime relationship. If people in all social classes self-report similar crime patterns, but only those in the lower class are formally arrested, that would explain higher crime rates in lower-class neighborhoods. However, if lower-class people report greater criminal activity than their middle- and upper-class peers, it would indicate that official statistics accurately represent the crime problem. Surprisingly, early self-report studies conducted in the 1950s, specifically those conducted by James Short and F. Ivan Nye, did not find a direct relationship between social class and youth crime.[53] They found that socioeconomic class was related to official processing by police, courts, and correctional agencies but not to the actual commission of crimes. In other words, although lower- and middle-class youth self-reported equal amounts of crime, the lower-class youths had a greater chance of being arrested, convicted, and incarcerated and becoming official delinquents. In addition, factors generally associated with lower-class membership, such as broken homes, were found to be related to institutionalization but not to admissions of delinquency. Other studies of this period reached similar conclusions.[54]

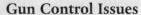

Gun Control Issues

More than 200 million guns are in private hands; half of U.S. households possess a gun. An estimated 50 million of these guns are illegal. Handguns are linked to many violent crimes, including 20 percent of all injury deaths (second to autos) and 60 percent of all homicides and suicides. They are also responsible for the deaths of about two-thirds of all police officers killed in the line of duty. Cross-national research conducted by Anthony Hoskin found that nations, including the United States, that have high levels of privately owned firearms also have the highest levels of homicide.

The association between guns and crime has spurred many Americans to advocate controlling the sale of handguns and banning the cheap mass-produced handguns known as "Saturday night specials." In contrast, gun advocates view control as a threat to personal liberty and call for severe punishment of criminals rather than control of handguns. They argue that the Second Amendment of the U.S. Constitution protects the right to bear arms. A 2001 survey by Robert Jiobu and Timothy Curry found that the typical gun owner has a deep mistrust of the federal government; to them, a gun is an "icon for democracy and personal empowerment" (p. 87).

Efforts to control handguns have come from many different sources. The states and many local jurisdictions have laws banning or restricting sales or possession of guns; some regulate dealers who sell guns. The Federal Gun Control Act of 1968, which is still in effect, requires that all dealers be licensed, fill out forms detailing each trade, and avoid selling to people prohibited from owning guns such as minors, ex-felons, and drug users. Dealers must record the source and properties of all guns they sell and

carefully account for their purchase. Gun buyers must provide identification and sign waivers attesting to their ability to possess guns. Unfortunately, the resources available to enforce this law are meager.

On November 30, 1993, the Brady Handgun Violence Prevention Act was enacted, amending the Gun Control Act of 1968. The bill was named after former Press Secretary James Brady, who was severely wounded in the attempted assassination of President Ronald Reagan by John Hinckley in 1981. The Brady Law imposes a waiting period of five days before a licensed importer, manufacturer, or dealer may sell, deliver, or transfer a handgun to an unlicensed individual. The waiting period applies only in states without an acceptable alternate system of conducting background checks on handgun purchasers. Beginning November 30, 1998, the Brady law changed, providing an instant check on whether a prospective buyer is prohibited from purchasing a weapon. Federal law bans gun purchases by people convicted of or under indictment for felony charges, fugitives, the mentally ill, those with dishonorable military discharges, those who have renounced U.S. citizenship, illegal aliens, illegal drug users, and those convicted of domestic violence misdemeanors or who are under domestic violence restraining orders (individual state laws may create other restrictions). The Brady Law now requires background approval not just for handgun buyers but also for those who buy long guns and shotguns.

Although gun control advocates see this legislation as a good first step, some question whether such measures will ultimately curb gun violence. For example, when Jens Ludwig and Philip Cook compared two sets of states, 32 that installed the Brady Law in 1994 and 18 states plus the District of Columbia, which already had simi-

lar types of laws prior to 1994, they found that there was no evidence that implementing the Brady Law contributed to a reduction in homicide.

Another approach is to severely punish people caught with unregistered handguns. The most famous attempt to regulate handguns using this method is the Massachusetts Bartley-Fox Law, which provides a mandatory one-year prison term for possessing a handgun (outside the home) without a permit. A detailed analysis of violent crime in Boston after the law's passage found that the use of handguns in robberies and murders did decline substantially (in robberies by 35 percent and in murders by 55 percent in a two-year period). However, these optimistic results must be tempered by two facts: rates for similar crimes dropped significantly in comparable cities that did not have gun control laws, and the use of other weapons, such as knives, increased in Boston.

Some jurisdictions have tried to reduce gun violence by adding extra punishment, such as a mandatory prison sentence for any crime involving a handgun. California's "10-20-life" law requires an additional 10 years in prison for carrying a gun while committing a violent felony, 20 years if the gun is fired, and if someone is injured the penalty increases to from 25 years to life in prison. Aiding this effort is a recent decision by the U.S. Supreme Court, *U.S. v. Rodriguez-Moreno* (97.1139, 1998), which held that a person can be prosecuted for using an illegal handgun to commit a crime even if the person did not use the gun in the prosecuting jurisdiction. *Rodriguez-Moreno* means, for example, that a person who uses a gun in Kansas to steal drugs and then sells the drugs in California can be prosecuted for gun possession in California because both the theft and sale of the drugs are considered part of the same crime.

Even if outlawed or severely restricted, the government's ability to control guns is problematic. Even if legitimate gun stores were strictly regulated, private citizens could still sell, barter, or trade handguns. Unregulated gun fairs and auctions are common throughout the United States; many gun deals are made at gun shows with few questions asked. When Anthony Braga and David Kennedy reviewed illegal firearms trafficking involving youth and juveniles, they found that most kids obtained firearms illegally through a multitude of unauthorized sources including unlicensed dealers, corrupt licensed dealers, and "straw" purchasers.

If handguns were banned or outlawed, they would become more valuable; illegal importation of guns might increase as it has for another controlled substance, narcotics. Increasing penalties for gun-related crimes has also met with limited success because judges may be reluctant to alter their sentencing policies to accommodate legislators. Regulating dealers is difficult, and tighter controls on them would only encourage private sales and bartering. Relatively few guns are stolen in burglaries, but many are sold to licensed gun dealers who circumvent the law by ignoring state registration requirements or making unrecorded or misrecorded sales to individuals and unlicensed dealers. Even a few corrupt dealers can supply tens of thousands of illegal handguns.

Not all experts are convinced that strict gun control is a good thing. Gary Kleck, a leading advocate of gun ownership, argues that guns may actually inhibit violence. In many assaults, he reasons, the aggressor does not wish to kill but only scare the victim. Possessing a gun gives aggressors so much killing power that they may actually be inhibited from attacking. For example, during a robbery they can control the situation without the need for illegal force. Guns may also

enable victims to escape serious injury. They may be inhibited from fighting back without losing face; it is socially acceptable to back down from a challenge if the opponent is armed with a gun. Guns then can deescalate a potentially violent situation. Kleck, along with Michael Hogan, finds that people who own guns are only slightly more likely to commit homicide than nonowners. The benefits of gun ownership, he concludes, outweigh the costs.

Kleck's findings have been supported by research conducted by John Lott and David Mustard. Using cross-sectional data for the United States, they found that jurisdictions that allow citizens to carry concealed weapons also have lower violent crime rates. If all states allowed citizens to carry concealed weapons, their analysis indicates that 1,500 murders, 4,000 rapes, 11,000 robberies, and 60,000 aggravated assaults would be avoided yearly. The annual social benefit from each additional concealed handgun permit is as high as $5,000, saving society more than $6 billion per year.

Kleck's arguments are persuasive, but many have been critical of the methodology used and question the reliability of the findings. The recent spate of gun violence in schools and in the workplace makes a powerful statement against gun ownership. Research shows that people who want to buy guns legally and/or purchase licenses to carry concealed weapons often have prior criminal records and engage in patterns of heavy drinking. Facilitating their access to weapons may increase rather than reduce violent crime levels.

Critical Thinking Questions

1. Should the sale and possession of handguns be banned?
2. Which of the gun control methods discussed do you feel would be most effective in deterring crime?

 InfoTrac College Edition Research

One method of reducing gun violence may be to make guns safer. Read more about this plan in:

Krista D. Robinson, Stephen P. Teret, Susan DeFrancesco, Stephen W. Hargarten. Making guns safer. *Issues in Science and Technology* Summer 1998 v14 n4 p37(4)

SOURCES: John Lott Jr., "More Guns, Less Crime: Understanding Crime and Gun-Control Laws," *Studies in Law and Economics,* 2d ed. (Chicago, Ill.: University of Chicago Press, 2001); John Lott Jr. and David Mustard, "Crime, Deterrence, and Right-to-Carry Concealed Handguns," *Journal of Legal Studies* 26 (1997): 1–68; Anthony A. Braga and David M. Kennedy, "The Illicit Acquisition of Firearms by Youth and Juveniles," *Journal of Criminal Justice* 29 (2001): 379–88; Anthony Hoskin, "Armed Americans: The Impact of Firearm Availability on National Homicide Rates," *Justice Quarterly* 18 (2001): 569–92; J. Robert Jiobu and Timothy Curry, "Lack of Confidence in the Federal Government and the Ownership of Firearms," *Social Science Quarterly* 82 (2001): 77–87; Jens Ludwig and Philip Cook, "Homicide and Suicide Rates Associated with the Implementation of the Brady Violence Prevention Act," *Journal of the American Medical Association* 284 (2000): 585–91; Julius Wachtel, "Sources of Crime Guns in Los Angeles, California," *Policing* 21 (1998): 220–39; Gary Kleck and Michael Hogan, "National Case-Control Study of Homicide Offending and Gun Ownership," *Social Problems* 46 (1999): 275–93; Garen Wintemute, Mora Wright, Carrie Parham, Christina Drake, and James Beaumont, "Denial of Handgun Purchase: A Description of the Affected Population and a Controlled Study of Their Handgun Preferences," *Journal of Criminal Justice* 27 (1999): 21–31; Shawn Schwaner, L. Allen Furr, Cynthia Negrey, and Rachelle Seger, "Who Wants a Gun License?" *Journal of Criminal Justice* 27 (1999): 1–10; "Gun Crime Mandatory Sentences Take Effect in California," *Criminal Justice Newsletter* 28 (December 15, 1997); Gary Kleck and Marc Gertz, "Armed Resistance to Crime: The Prevalence and Nature of Self-Defense with a Gun," *Journal of Criminal Law and Criminology* 86 (1995): 150–87; Colin Loftin, David McDowall, Brian Wiersma, and Talbert Cottey, "Effects of Restrictive Licensing of Handguns on Homicide and Suicide in the District of Columbia," *New England Journal of Medicine* 325 (1991): 1615–20; Gary Kleck, "The Incidence of Gun Violence among Young People," *Public Perspective* 4 (1993): 3–6.

For more than 20 years after the use of self-reports became widespread, a majority of self-report studies concluded that a class–crime relationship did not exist: if the poor possessed more extensive criminal records than the wealthy, this difference was attributed to differential law enforcement and not to class-based behavior differences. That is, police may be more likely to arrest lower-class offenders and treat the affluent more leniently.

More than 20 years ago, Charles Tittle, Wayne Villemez, and Douglas Smith published what is still considered the definitive review of the relationship between class and crime.[55] They concluded that little if any support exists for the contention that crime is primarily a lower-class phenomenon. Consequently, Tittle and his associates argued that official statistics probably reflect class bias in processing lower-class offenders. In a subsequent article written with Robert Meier, Tittle once again reviewed existing data on the class–crime relationship and found little evidence of a consistent association between class and crime.[56] More recent self-report studies generally support Tittle's conclusions: there is no direct relationship between social class and crime.[57]

Tittle's findings have sparked significant debate in the criminological community. Many self-report instruments include trivial offenses such as using a false ID or drinking alcohol, which may invalidate findings. It is possible that affluent youths frequently engage in trivial offenses such as petty larceny, using drugs, and simple assault but rarely escalate their criminal involvement. Those who support a class–crime relationship suggest that if only serious felony offenses are considered a significant association can be observed.[58] Some studies find that when only serious crimes, such as burglary and assault, are considered lower-class youths are significantly more delinquent.[59]

i Why does social class have such a great impact on individual behavior? To find out go to InfoTrac College Edition and use "social class" as a subject guide. ■

The class–crime controversy The relationship between class and crime is an important one for criminological theory. If crime is related to social class, then it follows that economic and social factors, such as poverty and neighborhood disorganization, cause criminal behavior.

CONNECTIONS

If class and crime are unrelated, then the causes of crime must be found in factors experienced by members of all social classes—psychological impairment, family conflict, peer pressure, school failure, and so on. Theories that view crime as a function of problems experienced by members of all social classes are reviewed in Chapter 8. ■

One reason that a true measure of the class–crime relationship has so far eluded criminologists is that the methods now employed to measure social class vary widely. Some widely used measures of social class, such as father's occupation and education, are only weakly related to self-reported crime, but others, such as unemployment or receiving welfare, are more significant predictors of criminality.[60]

It is also possible that the association between class and crime is more complex than a simple linear relationship (i.e., the poorer you are, the more crime you commit).[61] Class may affect some subgroups in the population (e.g., women, African Americans) more than it does others (e.g., males, whites).[62] Sally Simpson and Lori Elis found that

■ Youngsters watch the scene of a shooting in West Philadelphia where four people in ski masks burst into a dilapidated row house where drugs were being sold and gunned down six people and wounded three. The debate over the true relationship between class and crime continues. Nonetheless, most criminologists recognize that the most serious violent crimes take place in disorganized, deteriorated neighborhoods.

white females are more likely to be influenced by social class than are minority females. They speculate that white females have had their financial expectations significantly raised because of the women's movement but that the women's movement has had less effect on minority women. Therefore, white females are more likely to turn to crime when their expectations of wealth are not achieved.[63]

In light of these findings, it is not surprising that the true relationship between class and crime is difficult to determine. The effect may be obscured because its impact varies within and between groups.

Does class matter?   Like so many other criminological controversies, the debate over the true relationship between class and crime will most likely persist. The weight of recent evidence seems to suggest that serious, official crime is more prevalent among the lower classes, whereas less serious and self-reported crime is spread more evenly throughout the social structure.[64] Income inequality, poverty, and resource deprivation are all associated with the most serious violent crimes, including homicide and assault.[65] Members of the lower class are more likely to suffer psychological abnormality including high rates of anxiety and conduct disorders, conditions that may promote criminality.[66]

Communities that lack economic and social opportunities also produce high levels of frustration; their residents believe they are relatively more deprived than residents in more affluent areas and may then turn to criminal behavior to relieve their frustration.[67] Family life is disrupted and law-violating youth groups thrive in a climate that undermines adult supervision.[68] Conversely, when the poor are provided with economic opportunities via welfare and public assistance, crime rates drop.[69] Although crime rates may be higher in lower-class areas, poverty alone cannot explain why a particular individual becomes a chronic violent criminal; if it could, the crime problem would be much worse than it is now.[70]

Age and Crime

There is general agreement that age is inversely related to criminality. Criminologists Travis Hirschi and Michael Gottfredson state, "Age is everywhere correlated with crime. Its effects on crime do not depend on other demographic correlates of crime."[71] Regardless of economic status, marital status, race, sex, and so on, younger people commit crime more often than their older peers; research indicates this relationship has been stable across time periods ranging from 1935 to the present.[72] Official statistics tell us that young people are arrested at a disproportionate rate to their numbers in the population; victim surveys generate similar findings for crimes in which assailant age can be determined. Whereas youths ages 13 to 17 collectively make up about 6 percent of the total U.S. popula-

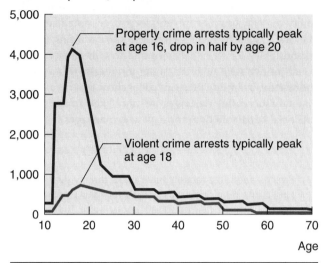

Figure 3.8   The Relationship between Age and Serious Crime Arrests

Arrest rate per 100,000 persons

Property crime arrests typically peak at age 16, drop in half by age 20

Violent crime arrests typically peak at age 18

SOURCE: FBI, Uniform Crime Report, 2000, p. 226.

tion, they account for about 25 percent of index crime arrests and 17 percent of arrests for all crimes. As a general rule, the peak age for property crime is believed to be 16, and for violence 18 (see Figure 3.8). In contrast, adults 45 and over, who make up 32 percent of the population, account for only 7 percent of index crime arrests. The elderly are particularly resistant to the temptations of crime; they make up more than 12 percent of the population and less than 1 percent of arrests. Elderly males 65 and over are predominantly arrested for alcohol-related matters (public drunkenness and drunk driving) and elderly females for larceny (shoplifting). The elderly crime rate has remained stable for the past 20 years.[73]

The age and crime controversy   There are two positions on the relationship between age and crime. The first is that the relationship is constant: all people, regardless of their demographic characteristics (race, gender, class, family structure, domicile, work status, and so on), commit less crime as they age.[74] How can this phenomenon be explained? Psychologists note that young people, especially the indigent and antisocial, tend to discount the future.[75] They are impatient, and because their future is uncertain they are unwilling or unable to delay gratification. As they mature, troubled youths are able to develop a long-term life view and resist the need for immediate gratification.[76] James Q. Wilson and Richard Herrnstein argue that **aging out** is a function of the natural history of the human life cycle.[77] Deviance in adolescence is fueled by the need for money and sex and reinforced by close relationships with peers who defy conventional morality. At the same time, teenagers are becoming independent from parents and other adults who enforce conventional standards of morality and behavior. They have a new sense of energy and strength and are involved with peers who are similarly vigorous and frustrated. Adults, on the other hand, develop the ability to delay gratification and forgo the immediate gains that law violations bring. They also start wanting to take responsibility for their behavior and to adhere to conventional mores, such as establishing long-term relationships and starting a family.[78] Research does show that people who maintain successful marriages are more likely to desist from antisocial behaviors than those whose marriages fail.[79]

CONNECTIONS

Hirschi and Gottfredson have used their views on the age–crime relationship as a basis for their General Theory of Crime. This important theory holds that the factors that produce crime change little after birth and that the association between crime and age is constant. For more on this view, see the section on the General Theory of Crime in Chapter 10. ■

Early onset   Those who oppose the Hirschi and Gottfredson view argue that most people age out of crime but that a small group continues on into old age as chronic or persistent offenders. People who commit crimes at a very early age (**early onset**) and who establish official criminal records are most likely to become chronic offenders.[80] These "early starters" may accumulate delinquent friends who support their deviant behavior and encourage the continuity of criminal behaviors.[81] Their decision to remain criminals into their maturity may be influenced by the type of crimes they commit. For example, people who commit crimes that provide significant economic gain, such as gambling, embezzlement, and fraud, are less likely to desist with maturity; people who commit high-risk, low-profit offenses such as assaults and robberies quit sooner.[82] People who frequently use cocaine and heroin continue to commit criminal acts 10 years or more past the age when nonaddicts have terminated their criminal activity.[83]

It is possible that both positions are correct. The population may contain different sets of criminal offenders: one or more groups whose criminality declines with age; another whose criminal behavior remains constant through maturity.[84]

CONNECTIONS

A discussion of how life events influence behavioral choices is presented in more depth in Chapter 10. ■

Gender and Crime

The three data-gathering criminal statistics tools support the fact that male crime rates are much higher than those

of females. Victims report that their assailant was male in more than 80 percent of all violent personal crimes. The Uniform Crime Report arrest statistics indicate that the overall male–female arrest ratio is about 3.5 male offenders to 1 female offender; for serious violent crimes, the ratio is closer to 5 males to 1 female; murder arrests are 8:1 male. Recent self-report data collected by the Institute for Social Research at the University of Michigan also show that males commit more serious crimes, such as robbery, assault, and burglary, than females. However, although the patterns in self-reports parallel official data, the ratios are smaller. In other words, males self-report more criminal behavior than females—but not to the degree suggested by official data.

There are many explanations for the gender differences in the crime rate. To research this topic on InfoTrac College Edition, use "gender" and "crime" as key words. ■

Explaining gender differences: biological views
Early criminologists pointed to emotional, physical, and psychological differences between males and females to explain the differences in crime rates. Cesare Lombroso's 1895 book, *The Female Offender,* argued that a small group of female criminals lacked "typical" female traits of "piety, maternity, undeveloped intelligence, and weakness."[85] In physical appearance as well as in their emotional makeup, delinquent females appeared closer to men than to other women. Lombroso's theory became known as the **masculinity hypothesis**; in essence, a few "masculine" females were responsible for the handful of crimes women commit.

Another early view of female crime focused on the supposed dynamics of sexual relationships. Female criminals were viewed as either sexually controlling or sexually naive, either manipulating men for profit or being manipulated by them. The female's criminality was often masked because criminal justice authorities were reluctant to take action against a woman.[86] This perspective is known as the **chivalry hypothesis,** which holds that much female criminality is hidden because of our culture's generally protective and benevolent attitude toward women.[87] In other words, police are less likely to arrest, juries are less likely to convict, and judges are less likely to incarcerate female offenders.

Although these early writings are no longer taken seriously, some criminologists still consider trait differences a key determinant of crime rate differences. For example, some criminologists link antisocial behavior to hormonal influences by arguing that male sex hormones (androgens) account for more aggressive male behavior and that gender-related hormonal differences can also explain the gender gap in the crime rate.[88]

Gender differences in the crime rate may be a function of androgen levels because these hormones cause areas of the brain to become less sensitive to environmental stimuli, making males more likely to seek high levels of stimulation and to tolerate more pain in the process. Chapter 6 discusses the biosocial causes of crime and reviews this issue in greater detail. ■

Explaining gender differences: socialization By the mid-1900s criminologists commonly portrayed gender differences in the crime rate as a function of socialization. Textbooks explained the relatively low female crime rate by citing the fact that, in contrast to boys, girls were supervised more closely and protected from competition.[89] The few female criminals were described as troubled individuals, alienated at home, who pursued crime as a means of compensating for their disrupted personal lives.[90] The streets became a "second home" to girls whose physical and emotional adjustment was hampered by a strained home life marked by such conditions as absent fathers, overly competitive mothers, and so on.

Some experts continue to explain gender-based crime differences as a function of socialization. Most girls, they argue, are socialized to be less aggressive than boys and are supervised more closely by parents.[91] Females usually learn to respond to provocation by feeling anxious and depressed, whereas boys are encouraged to retaliate with aggression.[92] Overall, women are much more likely to feel distressed than men, experiencing sadness, anxiety, uneasiness, and low self-esteem.[93] Although females get angry as often as males, many have been taught to blame themselves for harboring such negative feelings. Females are therefore much more likely than males to respond to anger with feelings of depression, anxiety, fear, and shame. Whereas females are socialized to fear that their anger will harm valued relationships, males react with "moral outrage" and look to blame others for their discomfort.[94] It is not surprising then that girls develop moral values that strongly discourage antisocial behavior. These values help shield them from the influence of delinquent peers, an influence to which boys are decidedly more vulnerable.[95]

The relatively few females who commit violent crimes report having home and family relationships that are more troubled than those experienced by male delinquents.[96]

Explaining gender differences: feminist views In the 1970s **liberal feminist theory** focused attention on the social and economic role of women in society and its relationship to female crime rates.[97] This view suggested that the traditionally lower crime rate for women could be explained by their "second-class" economic and social position. As women's social roles changed and their lifestyles became more like those of males, it was believed that their crime rates would converge.

To read about the history and nature of the women's movement in the United States, go to InfoTrac College Edition and use "liberal feminism" as a subject guide. ■

Criminologists, responding to this research, began to refer to the "new female criminal." The rapid increase in the female crime rate during the 1960s and 1970s, especially in what had traditionally been male-oriented crimes (such as burglary and larceny), supported the liberal feminist view. In addition, self-report studies seem to indicate that (1) the pattern of female criminality, if not its frequency, is quite similar to that of male criminality; and (2) the factors that predispose male criminals to crime have an equal impact on female criminals.[98] Criminologists began to assess the association between economic issues, gender roles, and criminality.

Critical criminologists view gender inequality as stemming from the unequal power of men and women in a capitalist society and the exploitation of females by fathers and husbands. This perspective, along with radical feminism, is considered more fully in Chapter 9. ■

Is convergence likely? Will the gender differences in the crime rate eventually dissolve? Some criminologists find that gender-based crime rate differences remain significant and argue that the emancipation of women has had relatively little influence on female crime rates.[99] They dispute that increases in the female arrest rate reflect economic or social change brought about by the women's movement. For one thing, many female criminals come from the socioeconomic class least affected by the women's movement; their crimes seem more a function of economic inequality than women's rights. For another, the offense patterns of women are still quite different from those of men, who still commit a disproportionate share of serious crimes such as robbery, burglary, murder, and assault.[100] This view is supported by recent research showing that women who are living in poverty (e.g., on welfare and unemployed) are much more likely than their more affluent sisters to get involved in assaults and engage in petty property crime such as fraudulently claiming welfare benefits, credit card fraud, and public order crimes such as prostitution.[101]

Perhaps it is too soon for criminologists to write off "the new female criminal." Although male arrest rates are still considerably higher than female rates, female arrest rates seem to be increasing at a faster pace. For example, between 1991 and 2000 the male arrest rate actually declined by 3.8 percent while the female rate increased by 17.6 percent. Male arrests for violent crimes actually dropped by 17.1 percent while the female rate rose 32.7 percent. One reason for this convergence is the increasing female participation in crimes that traditionally have been a male enterprise. For example, although at one time a rare occurrence, females are now joining teen gangs in record numbers. Recent national surveys indicate that about 8 percent of females report gang membership (as compared to 14 percent of males); the male–female gang membership ratio is now less than 2:1.[102]

Race and Crime

Official crime data indicate that minority group members are involved in a disproportionate share of criminal activity. According to UCR reports, African Americans make up about 12 percent of the general population, yet they account for about 40 percent of Part I violent crime arrests and 34 percent of property crime arrests. They also are responsible for a disproportionate number of Part II arrests (except for alcohol-related arrests, which detain primarily white offenders).

It is possible that these data reflect racial differences in the crime rate, but it is also possible that they reflect police bias in the arrest process. We can evaluate this issue by comparing racial differences in self-report data with those found in official delinquency records. Charges of racial discrimination in the arrest process would be substantiated if whites and blacks self-reported equal numbers of crimes but minorities were arrested far more often.

Early efforts by noted criminologists Leroy Gould in Seattle, Harwin Voss in Honolulu, and Ronald Akers in seven midwestern states found virtually no relationship between race and self-reported delinquency.[103] These research efforts supported a case for police bias in the arrest decision. Other, more recent self-report studies that use large national samples of youths have also found little evidence of racial disparity in crimes committed. For example, one effort conducted by the Institute for Social Research at the University of Michigan found that, if anything, black youths self-report less delinquent behavior and substance abuse than whites.[104] Another nationwide study of youth, conducted by social scientists at the Behavioral Science Institute at Boulder, Colorado, found few interracial differences in crime rates, although black youths were much more likely to be arrested and taken into custody.[105] These and other self-report studies seem to indicate that the delinquent behavior rates of black and white teenagers are generally similar and that differences in arrest statistics may indicate a differential selection policy by police.[106]

Racial differences in the crime rate remain an extremely sensitive issue. Although official arrest records indicate that African Americans are arrested at a higher rate than members of other racial groups, some question whether this is a function of crime rate differences, racism by police, or faulty data collection.[107] Research shows that suspects who are poor, minority, and male are more likely to be formally arrested than suspects who are white, af-fluent, and female.[108] Some critics charge that police officers routinely use "racial profiling" to stop African Americans and search their cars without probable cause or reasonable suspicion. Some cynics have gone so far as suggesting that police officers have created a new form of traffic offense called DWB, "Driving While Black."[109]

Although the UCR may reflect discriminatory police practices, African Americans are arrested for a disproportionate amount of violent crime, such as robbery and murder, and it is improbable that police discretion alone could account for these proportions. It is doubtful that police routinely ignore white killers, robbers, and rapists while arresting violent black offenders.[110] How can these racial differences be explained?

Racism and discrimination   Most criminologists focus on the impact of economic deprivation and the legacy of racism and discrimination on personality and behavior.[111] The fact that U.S. culture influences African American crime rates is underscored by the fact that black violence rates are much lower in other nations—both those that are predominantly white, such as Canada, and those that are predominantly black, such as Nigeria.[112]

Some criminologists view black crime as a function of socialization in a society where the black family was torn apart and black culture destroyed in such a way that recovery has proven impossible. Early experiences, beginning with slavery, have left a wound that has been deepened by racism and lack of opportunity.[113] Children of the slave society were thrust into a system of forced dependency and ambivalence and antagonism toward one's self and group.

In an important work, *All God's Children: The Bosket Family and the American Tradition of Violence*, crime reporter Fox Butterfield chronicles the history of the Boskets, a black family, through five generations.[114] He focuses on Willie Bosket, who is charming, captivating, and brilliant. He is also one of the worst criminals in the New York State penal system. By the time he was in his teens, he had committed more than 200 armed robberies and 25 stabbings. Butterfield shows how early struggles in the South, with its violent slave culture, led directly to Willie Bosket's rage and violence on the streets of New York City. Beginning in South Carolina in the 1700s, the southern slave society was a place where white notions of honor demanded immediate retaliation for the smallest slight. According to Butterfield, contemporary black violence is a tradition inherited from white southern violence. The need for respect has turned into a cultural mandate that can provoke retaliation if even a slight insult is sensed.

CONNECTIONS

According to some criminologists, racism has created isolated subcultures that espouse violence as a way of

AP/Wide World Photos

■ Empirical evidence shows that, in at least some jurisdictions, young African American males are treated more harshly by the criminal and juvenile justice system than are members of any other group. Elements of institutional racism have become so endemic that terms such as "DWB" (Driving While Black) are now part of the vernacular, used to signify the fact that young African American motorists are routinely stopped by police.

coping with conflict situations. Exasperation and frustration among minority group members who feel powerless to fit within middle-class society are manifested in aggression. This view is discussed further in Chapter 11, which reviews the subculture of violence theory. ■

Institutional racism   Racism is still an element of daily life in the African American community, a factor that undermines faith in social and political institutions and weakens confidence in the justice system. Such fears are supported by empirical evidence that, at least in some jurisdictions, young African American males are treated more harshly by the criminal and juvenile justice systems than are members of any other group.[115] There is evidence that African Americans, especially those who are indigent or unemployed, receive longer prison sentences than

whites with the same employment status. It is possible that judges impose harsher punishments on unemployed African Americans because they view them as "social dynamite," considering them more dangerous and more likely to recidivate than white offenders.[116] Yet when African Americans are victims of crime, their predicament receives less public concern and media attention than that afforded white victims.[117]

In his book *Search and Destroy*, correctional reformer Jerome Miller spells out how millions of young African Americans acquire a criminal record each year because big-city police officers abuse their authority. Conservative politicians complain about providing welfare because they believe government should stay out of people's lives, but they do not mind the traumatic intrusion to the black community being made by agents of the criminal justice system who seem bent on "identifying and managing unruly groups."[118] Differential enforcement practices take their toll on the black community. For example, a national survey found that more that 13 percent of all African American males have lost the right to vote, that in seven states 25 percent have been disenfranchised, and in two states, Florida and Alabama, 33 percent of black males have lost their voting privileges.[119] It is not surprising then that African Americans of all social classes hold negative attitudes toward the justice system and view it as an arbitrary and unfair institution.[120]

Economic and social disparity   Racial differentials in crime rates may also be tied to economic disparity. Blacks and whites face different economic and social realities. African Americans typically have higher unemployment rates and lower incomes than whites. They face a greater degree of social isolation and economic deprivation, a condition that has been linked by empirical research to high murder rates.[121] Not helping the situation is the fact that during tough economic times blacks and whites may find themselves competing for shrinking job opportunities. As economic competition between the races grows, interracial homicides do likewise; economic and political rivalries lead to greater levels of interracial violence.[122]

Even during times of economic growth, lower-class African Americans are left out of the economic mainstream, a fact that meets with a growing sense of frustration and failure.[123] As a result of being shut out of educational and economic opportunities enjoyed by the rest of society, this population may be prone, some believe, to the lure of illegitimate gain and criminality. Young African American males in the inner city often are resigned to a lifetime of little if any social and economic opportunity. Even when economic data say they are doing better, news accounts of "protests, riots, and acts of civil disobedience" tell them otherwise.[124] African Americans living in lower-class slums may be disproportionately violent because they are exposed to more violence in their daily lives than other racial and economic groups. This exposure is a significant risk factor for violent behavior.[125]

Family dissolution   Family dissolution in the minority community is tied to low employment rates among African American males, which places a strain on marriages. The relatively large number of single, female-headed households in these communities may be tied to the high mortality rate among African American males due in part to their increased risk of early death by disease and violence.[126] When families are weakened or disrupted, their social control is compromised. It is not surprising, then, that divorce and separation rates are significantly associated with homicide rates in the African American community.[127]

Is convergence possible?   Considering these overwhelming social problems, is it possible that racial crime rates will soon converge? One argument is that if economic conditions improve in the minority community, then differences in crime rates will eventually disappear.[128] A trend toward residential integration, under way since 1980, may also help reduce crime rate differentials.[129] Despite economic disparity, there are actually few racial differences in attitudes toward crime and justice today. Convergence in crime rates will occur if economic and social obstacles can be removed.

CONNECTIONS

The concept of relative deprivation refers to the fact that people compare their success to those with whom they are in immediate contact. Even if conditions improve, they still may feel as if they are falling behind. A sense of relative deprivation, discussed in Chapter 7, may lead to criminal activity. ■

In sum, the weight of the evidence shows that although there is little difference in the self-reported crime rates of racial groups, African Americans are more likely to be arrested for serious violent crimes. The causes of minority crime have been linked to poverty, racism, hopelessness, lack of opportunity, and urban problems experienced by all too many African American citizens.

Criminal Careers

Crime data show that most offenders commit a single criminal act, and upon arrest discontinue their antisocial activity. Others commit a few less-serious crimes. A small group of criminal offenders, however, account for a majority of all criminal offenses. These persistent offenders are referred to as **career criminals** or **chronic offenders.**

The concept of the chronic or career offender is most closely associated with the research efforts of Marvin Wolfgang, Robert Figlio, and Thorsten Sellin.[130] In their landmark 1972 study, *Delinquency in a Birth Cohort*, they used official records to follow the criminal careers of a cohort of 9,945 boys born in Philadelphia in 1945 from the time of their birth until they reached 18 years of age in 1963. Official police records were used to identify delinquents. About one-third of the boys (3,475) had some police contact. The remaining two-thirds (6,470) had none. Each delinquent was given a seriousness weight score for every delinquent act.[131] The weighting of delinquent acts allowed the researchers to differentiate, for example, between a simple assault requiring no medical attention for the victim and serious battery in which the victim needed hospitalization. The best known discovery of Wolfgang and his associates was that of the so-called chronic offender. The cohort data indicated that 54 percent (1,862) of the sample's delinquent youths were repeat offenders, whereas the remaining 46 percent (1,613) were one-time offenders. The repeaters could be further categorized as nonchronic recidivists and chronic recidivists. The former consisted of 1,235 youths who had been arrested more than once but fewer than five times and who made up 35.6 percent of all delinquents. The latter were a group of 627 boys arrested five times or more, who accounted for 18 percent of the delinquents and 6 percent of the total sample of 9,945.

The chronic offenders (known today as "the chronic 6 percent") were involved in the most dramatic amounts of delinquent behavior: they were responsible for 5,305 offenses, or 51.9 percent of all the offenses committed by the cohort. Even more striking was the involvement of chronic offenders in serious criminal acts. Of the entire sample, they committed 71 percent of the homicides, 73 percent of the rapes, 82 percent of the robberies, and 69 percent of the aggravated assaults.

Wolfgang and his associates found that arrests and court experience did little to deter the chronic offender. In fact, punishment was inversely related to chronic offending: the more stringent the sanction chronic offenders received, the more likely they would be to engage in repeated criminal behavior.

In a second cohort study, Wolfgang and his associates selected a new, larger birth cohort, born in Philadelphia in 1958, which contained both male and female subjects.[132] Although the proportion of delinquent youths was about the same as that in the 1945 cohort, they again found a similar pattern of chronic offending. Chronic female delinquency was relatively rare—only 1 percent of the females in the survey were chronic offenders. Wolfgang's pioneering effort to identify the chronic career offender has been replicated by a number of other researchers in a variety of locations in the United States.[133] The chronic offender has also been found abroad.[134]

Who are chronic offenders?   Who is at risk of becoming a chronic offender? As might be expected, kids who have been exposed to a variety of personal and social problems at an early age are the most at risk to repeat of-

Exhibit 3.1   Characteristics that Predict Chronic Offending

School Behavior/ Performance Factor	Attendance Problems (truancy or a pattern of "skipping" school)
	Behavior Problems (recent suspensions or expulsion)
	Poor Grades (failing two or more classes)
Family Problem Factor	Poor Parental Supervision and Control
	Significant Family Problems (illness, substance abuse, discord)
	Criminal Family Members
	Documented Child Abuse, Neglect or Family Violence
Substance Abuse Factor	Alcohol or Drug Use (by minors in any way but experimentation)
Delinquency Factor	Stealing Pattern of Behavior
	Runaway Pattern of Behavior
	Gang Member or Associate

SOURCE: Michael Schumacher and Gwen Kurz, *The 8% Solution: Preventing Serious Repeat Juvenile Crime* (Thousand Oaks, Calif.: Sage, 1999).

fending. One important study of delinquent offenders in Orange County, California, conducted by Michael Schumacher and Gwen Kurz, found seven factors (see Exhibit 3.1) that characterized the chronic offender, including problems in the home and at school.[135] Other research studies have found that involvement in criminal activity (e.g., getting arrested before age 15), relatively low intellectual development, and parental drug involvement were key predictive factors for chronicity.[136]

CONNECTIONS

It is evident that chronic offenders suffer from a profusion of social problems. Some criminologists believe that accumulating a significant variety of these social deficits is the key to understanding criminal development. For more on this topic, see the discussion on problem behavior syndrome in Chapter 10. ■

Persistence: the continuity of crime   One of the most important findings from the cohort studies is that persistent juvenile offenders are the ones most likely to continue their criminal careers into adulthood.[137] In one important study, Paul Tracy and Kimberly Kempf-Leonard followed up all subjects in the second 1958 cohort and found that most (two-thirds) delinquent offenders desisted

from crime, but those who started their delinquent careers early and who committed serious violent crimes throughout adolescence were the most likely to persist as adults.[138] This phenomenon is referred to as **persistence** or the **continuity of crime**. In another effort, Kempf-Leonard and her associates found that chronic delinquents can be further subdivided into independent subgroups and that those falling into the most serious category (chronic delinquents who commit violent acts) have a much greater chance of becoming adult offenders than other delinquent youth; this phenomenon was observed for both males and females (see Table 3.3).[139]

Children who are found to be disruptive and antisocial as early as age 5 or 6 are the most likely to exhibit stable, long-term patterns of disruptive behavior throughout adolescence.[140] They have measurable behavior problems in areas such as learning and motor skills, cognitive abilities, family relations, and other areas of social, psychological, and physical functioning.[141] Youthful offenders who persist are more likely to abuse alcohol, get into trouble while in military service, become economically dependent, have lower aspirations, get divorced or separated, and have a weak employment record.[142] They do not specialize in one type of crime; rather, they engage in a variety of criminal acts, including theft, drugs, and violent offenses.

Apprehension and punishment seem to have little effect on the offending behavior of these youths. A recent study that followed the offending careers of nearly 2,000 serious, chronic youthful offenders for 10 years after their release from the California Youth Authority found they were arrested on 24,615 occasions over the following decade, an average of 22 arrests each. More than 90 percent

Table 3.3   Delinquency Types and Probability of Becoming an Adult Offender

Delinquent Type	Probability of Becoming an Adult Criminal (percent)	
	Male	Female
Nondelinquent	14	2.5
Total All Delinquents	42	12
Serious Delinquent	52	25
Violent Delinquent	56	26
Chronic Delinquent	63	29
Serious and Chronic	64	44
Violent and Chronic	64	44

SOURCE: Kimberly Kempf-Leonard, Paul Tracy, and James Howell, "Serious, Violent, and Chronic Juvenile Offenders: The Relationship of Delinquency Career Types to Adult Criminality," *Justice Quarterly* 18 (2001): 449–78.

■ Not all chronic offenders commit serious crimes. Here Cindy, a repeat offender, pleads for a break with Nashville Police officer Nicki Harakas while being taken in for processing at police headquarters. Kids who have been exposed to a variety of personal and social problems at an early age are the most at risk for repeat offending.

AP/Wide World Photos

had been rearrested during the following decade, and their arrests were for an average of 9 property crimes, 4 violent offenses, 3 drug crimes, and 6 other types crimes.[143] This recent research suggests the axiom, "The best predictor of future behavior is past behavior."

Implications of the chronic offender concept The findings of the cohort studies and the discovery of the chronic offender have revitalized criminological theory. If relatively few offenders become chronic, persistent criminals, then perhaps they possess some individual trait that is responsible for their behavior. Most people exposed to troublesome social conditions, such as poverty, do not become chronic offenders, so it is unlikely that social conditions alone can cause chronic offending. Traditional theories of criminal behavior have failed to distinguish between chronic and occasional offenders. They concentrate more on explaining why people begin to commit crime and pay scant attention to why people stop offending. The discovery of the chronic offender 25 years ago forced criminologists to

consider such issues as persistence and desistance in their explanations of crime; more recent theories account for not only the onset of criminality but also its termination.

The chronic offender has become a central focus of crime control policy. Concern about repeat offenders has been translated into programs at various stages of the justice process. For example, police departments and district attorneys' offices around the nation have set up programs to focus resources on capturing and prosecuting dangerous or repeat offenders.[144] Legal jurisdictions are developing sentencing policies designed to incapacitate chronic offenders for long periods of time without hope of probation or parole. Among the policies spurred by the chronic offender concept are mandatory sentences for violent or drug-related crimes and **"three strikes and you're out"** policies, which require people convicted of a third felony offense to serve a mandatory life sentence. Whether such policies can reduce crime rates or are merely "get tough" measures designed to placate conservative voters remains to be seen.

■ Summary

There are three primary sources of crime statistics: the Uniform Crime Report based on police data accumulated by the FBI, self-reports from criminal behavior surveys, and victim surveys. They tell us that there is quite a bit of crime in the United States, although the amount of violent crime is decreasing. Each data source has its strengths and weaknesses, and although quite different from one another, they actually agree on the nature of criminal behavior.

The data sources show stable patterns in the crime rate. Ecological patterns show that some areas of the country are more crime prone than others, that there are seasons and times for crime, and that these patterns are quite stable. There is also evidence of gender and age gaps in the crime rate: men commit more crime than women, and young people commit more crime than the elderly. Crime data show that people commit less crime as they age, but the significance and cause of this pattern is still not completely understood.

Similarly, racial and class patterns appear in the crime rate. However, it is still unclear whether these are true differences or a function of discriminatory law enforcement.

One of the most important findings in the crime statistics is the existence of the chronic offender, a repeat criminal responsible for a significant amount of all law violations. Chronic offenders begin their careers early in life and, rather than aging out of crime, persist into adulthood. The discovery of the chronic offender has led to the study of developmental criminology—why people persist, desist, terminate, or escalate their deviant behavior.

■ Thinking Like a Criminologist

The planning director for the State Department of Juvenile Justice has asked for your advice on how to reduce the threat of chronic offenders. Some of the more conservative members of her staff seem to believe that these kids need a strict dose of rough justice if they are to be turned away from a life of crime. They believe juvenile delinquents who are punished harshly are less likely to recidivate than youth who receive lesser punishments, such as community corrections or probation. In addition, they believe that hard-core, violent offenders deserve to be punished; excessive concern for offenders and not their acts ignores the rights of victims and society in general.

The planning director is unsure whether such an approach can reduce the threat of chronic offending. Can tough punishment produce deviant identities that lock kids into a criminal way of life? She is concerned that a strategy stressing punishment will have relatively little impact on chronic offenders and, if anything, may cause escalation in serious criminal behaviors.

She has asked you for your professional advice. On one hand, the system must be sensitive to the adverse effects of stigma and labeling. On the other hand, the need for control and deterrence must not be ignored. Is it possible to reconcile these two opposing views?

■ Key Terms

- **Uniform Crime Report (UCR)** (49)
- **index crimes** (49)
- **Part I crimes** (49)
- **Part II crimes** (50)
- **cleared** (50)
- **National Incident-Based Reporting System (NIBRS)** (52)
- **National Crime Victimization Survey (NCVS)** (52)
- **self-report survey** (53)
- **instrumental crimes** (63)
- **expressive crimes** (63)
- **aging out** (67)
- **early onset** (68)
- **masculinity hypothesis** (68)
- **chivalry hypothesis** (68)
- **liberal feminist theory** (69)
- **career criminal** (72)
- **chronic offender** (72)
- **persistence** (73)
- **continuity of crime** (73)
- **"three strikes and you're out"** (74)

■ Critical Thinking Questions

1. Would you answer honestly if a national crime survey asked you about your criminal behavior, including drinking and drug use? If not, why not? If you said "no," do you question the accuracy of self-report surveys?

2. How would you explain gender differences in the crime rate? Why do you think males are more violent than females?

3. Assuming that males are more violent than females, does that mean crime has a biological rather than a social basis (because males and females share a similar environment)?

4. The UCR reports that crime rates are higher in large cities than in small towns. What does that tell us about the effects of TV, films, and music on teenage behavior?

5. What social and environmental factors do you believe influence the crime rate? For example, do you think a national emergency would increase or decrease crime rates?

Notes

1. Kate Zernike, "Crackdown on Threats in Schools Fails a Test," *New York Times,* 17 May 2001, B3.

2. Federal Bureau of Investigation, *Crime in the United States, 2000* (Washington, D.C.: U.S. Government Printing Office, 2001). Herein cited in notes as FBI, Uniform Crime Report, and referred to in text as Uniform Crime Report or UCR.

3. Callie Marie Rennison, *Criminal Victimization 2000: Changes 1999–2000 with Trends 1993–2000* (Washington, D.C.: Bureau of Justice Statistics, 2001). Hereinafter cited as NCVS, 2000.

4. Paul Tappan, *Crime, Justice and Corrections* (New York: McGraw-Hill, 1960).

5. Daniel Bell, *The End of Ideology* (New York: Free Press, 1967), p. 152.

6. Duncan Chappell, Gilbert Geis, Stephen Schafer, and Larry Siegel, "Forcible Rape: A Comparative Study of Offenses Known to the Police in Boston and Los Angeles," in *Studies in the Sociology of Sex,* ed. James Henslin (New York: Appleton Century Crofts, 1971), pp. 169–93.

7. Patrick Jackson, "Assessing the Validity of Official Data on Arson," *Criminology* 26 (1988): 181–95.

8. Lawrence Sherman and Barry Glick, "The Quality of Arrest Statistics," *Police Foundation Reports* 2 (1984): 1–8.

9. David Seidman and Michael Couzens, "Getting the Crime Rate Down: Political Pressure and Crime Reporting," *Law and Society Review* 8 (1974): 457.

10. Robert Davis and Bruce Taylor, "A Proactive Response to Family Violence: The Results of a Randomized Experiment," *Criminology* 35 (1997): 307–33.

11. Robert O'Brien, "Police Productivity and Crime Rates: 1973–1992," *Criminology* 34 (1996): 183–207.

12. Leonard Savitz, "Official Statistics," in *Contemporary Criminology,* ed. Leonard Savitz and Norman Johnston (New York: John Wiley, 1982), pp. 3–15.

13. FBI, *UCR Handbook* (Washington, D.C.: U.S. Government Printing Office, 1998), p. 33.

14. Roger Hood and Richard Sparks, *Key Issues in Criminology* (New York: McGraw-Hill, 1970), p. 72.

15. Rennison, NCVS, 2000. Data in this section come from this report.

16. L. Edward Wells and Joseph Rankin, "Juvenile Victimization: Convergent Validation of Alternative Measurements," *Journal of Research in Crime and Delinquency* 32 (1995): 287–307.

17. See, for example, Spencer Rathus and Larry Siegel, "Crime and Personality Revisited: Effects of MMPI Sets on Self-Report Studies," *Criminology* 18 (1980): 245–51; John Clark and Larry Tifft, "Polygraph and Interview Validation of Self-Reported Deviant Behavior," *American Sociological Review* 31 (1966): 516–23.

18. Clark and Tifft, "Polygraph and Interview Validation of Self-Reported Deviant Behavior."

19. See, for example, Harwin Voss, "Ethnic Differences in Delinquency in Honolulu," *Journal of Criminal Law, Criminology and Police Science* 54 (1963): 322–27; Maynard Erickson and LaMar Empey, "Court Records, Undetected Delinquency and Decision Making," *Journal of Criminal Law, Criminology and Police Science* 54 (1963): 456–59; H. B. Gibson, Sylvia Morrison, and D. J. West, "The Confession of Known Offenses in Response to a Self-Reported Delinquency Schedule," *British Journal of Criminology* 10 (1970): 277–80; and John Blackmore, "The Relationship between Self-Reported Delinquency and Official Convictions amongst Adolescent Boys," *British Journal of Criminology* 14 (1974): 172–76.

20. David Farrington, Rolf Loeber, Magda Stouthamer-Loeber, Welmoet Van Kammen, and Laura Schmidt, "Self-Reported Delinquency and a Combined Delinquency Seriousness Scale Based on Boys, Mothers, and Teachers: Concurrent and Predictive Validity for African-Americans and Caucasians," *Criminology* 34 (1996): 501–25.

21. Mallie Paschall, Miriam Ornstein, and Robert Flewelling, "African-American Male Adolescents' Involvement in the Criminal Justice System: The Criterion Validity of Self-Report Measures in Prospective Study," *Journal of Research in Crime and Delinquency* 38 (2001): 174–87.

22. Leonore Simon, "Validity and Reliability of Violent Juveniles: A Comparison of Juvenile Self-Reports with Adult Self-Reports Incarcerated in Adult Prisons." Paper presented at the American Society of Criminology meeting, Boston, Mass., November 1995, p. 26.

23. Stephen Cernkovich, Peggy Giordano, and Meredith Pugh, "Chronic Offenders: The Missing Cases in Self-Report Delinquency Research," *Journal of Criminal Law and Criminology* 76 (1985): 705–32.

24. Terence Thornberry, Beth Bjerregaard, and William Miles, "The Conse-

quences of Respondent Attrition in Panel Studies: A Simulation Based on the Rochester Youth Development Study," *Journal of Quantitative Criminology* 9 (1993): 127–58.

25. Minu Mathur, Richard Dodder, and Harjit Sandhu, "Inmate Self-Report Data: A Study of Reliability," *Criminal Justice Review* 17 (1992): 258–67.

26. Eric Wish, Thomas Gray, and Eliot Levine, *Recent Drug Use in Female Juvenile Detainees: Estimates from Interviews, Urinalysis and Hair Analysis* (College Park, Md.: Center for Substance Abuse Research, 1996); Thomas Gray and Eric Wish, *Maryland Youth at Risk: A Study of Drug Use in Juvenile Detainees* (College Park, Md.: Center for Substance Abuse Research, 1993).

27. Eric Wish and Christina Polsenberg, "Arrestee Urine Tests and Self-Reports of Drug Use: Which Is More Related to Rearrest?" Paper presented at the annual meeting of the American Society of Criminology, Phoenix, Arizona, November 1993.

28. Michael Hindelang, Travis Hirschi, and Joseph Weis, *Measuring Delinquency* (Beverly Hills: Sage, 1981).

29. Alfred Blumstein, Jacqueline Cohen, and Richard Rosenfeld, "Trend and Deviation in Crime Rates: A Comparison of UCR and NCVS Data for Burglary and Robbery," *Criminology* 29 (1991): 237–48. See also Hindelang, Hirschi, and Weis, *Measuring Delinquency.*

30. For a critique, see Scott Menard, "Residual Gains, Reliability, and the UCR–NCVS Relationship: A Comment on Blumstein, Cohen and Rosenfield (1991)," *Criminology* 30 (1992): 105–15.

31. David McDowall and Colin Loftin, "Comparing the UCR and NCVS over Time," *Criminology* 30 (1992): 125–33.

32. Clarence Schrag, *Crime and Justice: American Style* (Washington, D.C.: U.S. Government Printing Office, 1971), p. 17.

33. Thomas Bernard, "Juvenile Crime and the Transformation of Juvenile Justice: Is There a Juvenile Crime Wave?" *Justice Quarterly* 16 (1999): 336–56.

34. For example, the following studies have noted the great discrepancy between official statistics and self-report studies: Martin Gold, "Undetected Delinquent Behavior," *Journal of Research in Crime and Delinquency* 3 (1966): 27–46; James Short and F. Ivan Nye, "Extent of Undetected Delinquency, Tentative Conclusions," *Jour-*

nal of Criminal Law, Criminology and Police Science 49 (1958): 296–302; Michael Hindelang, "Causes of Delinquency: A Partial Replication and Extension," Social Problems 20 (1973): 471–87.

35. D. Wayne Osgood, Lloyd Johnston, Patrick O'Malley, and Jerald Bachman, "The Generality of Deviance in Late Adolescence and Early Adulthood," American Sociological Review 53 (1988): 81–93.

36. Lloyd Johnston, Patrick O'Malley, and Jerald Bachman, Monitoring the Future, 1990 (Ann Arbor, Mich.: Institute for Social Research, 1991); Timothy Flanagan and Kathleen Maguire, Sourcebook of Criminal Justice Statistics, 1989 (Washington, D.C.: U.S. Government Printing Office, 1990), pp. 290–91.

37. James A. Fox, Trends in Juvenile Violence: A Report to the United States Attorney General on Current and Future Rates of Juvenile Offending (Boston, Mass.: Northeastern University, 1996).

38. Steven Levitt, "The Limited Role of Changing Age Structure in Explaining Aggregate Crime Rates," Criminology 37 (1999): 581–99.

39. Darrell Steffensmeier and Miles Harer, "Did Crime Rise or Fall During the Reagan Presidency? The Effects of an 'Aging' U.S. Population on the Nation's Crime Rate," Journal of Research in Crime and Delinquency 28 (1991): 330–39.

40. Darrell Steffensmeier and Miles Harer, "Making Sense of Recent U.S. Crime Trends, 1980 to 1996/1998: Age Composition Effects and Other Explanations," Journal of Research in Crime and Delinquency 36 (1999): 235–74.

41. Ibid., p. 265.

42. Ralph Weisheit and L. Edward Wells, "The Future of Crime in Rural America," Journal of Crime and Justice 22 (1999): 1-22.

43. Ellen Cohn, "The Effect of Weather and Temporal Variations on Calls for Police Service," American Journal of Police 15 (1996): 23–43.

44. R. A. Baron, "Aggression as a Function of Ambient Temperature and Prior Anger Arousal," Journal of Personality and Social Psychology 21 (1972): 183–89.

45. Ellen Cohn, "The Prediction of Police Calls for Service: The Influence of Weather and Temporal Variables on Rape and Domestic Violence," Journal of Environmental Psychology 13 (1993): 71–83.

46. Derral Cheatwood, "The Effects of Weather on Homicide," Journal of Quantitative Criminology 11 (1995): 51–70.

47. Ellen Cohn and James Rotton, "Assault as a Function of Time and Temperature: A Moderator-Variable Time-Series Analysis." Paper presented at the annual meeting of the American Society of Criminology, Chicago, Ill., November 1996, p. 23.

48. See generally Franklin Zimring and Gordon Hawkins, Crime Is Not the Problem: Lethal Violence in America (New York Oxford University Press, 1997).

49. Ibid., p. 36.

50. Gary Kleck and Marc Gertz, "Armed Resistance to Crime: The Prevalence and Nature of Self-Defense with a Gun," Journal of Criminal Law and Criminology 86 (1995).

51. Robert Nash Parker, "Bringing 'Booze' Back In: The Relationship between Alcohol and Homicide," Journal of Research in Crime and Delinquency 32 (1995): 3–38.

52. Victoria Brewer and M. Dwayne Smith, "Gender Inequality and Rates of Female Homicide Victimization across U.S. Cities," Journal of Research in Crime and Delinquency 32 (1995): 175–90.

53. Short and Nye, "Extent of Undetected Delinquency."

54. Ivan Nye, James Short, and Virgil Olsen, "Socio-economic Status and Delinquent Behavior," American Journal of Sociology 63 (1958): 381–89; Robert Dentler and Lawrence Monroe, "Social Correlates of Early Adolescent Theft," American Sociological Review 63 (1961): 733–43. See also Terence Thornberry and Margaret Farnworth, "Social Correlates of Criminal Involvement: Further Evidence of the Relationship between Social Status and Criminal Behavior," American Sociological Review 47 (1982): 505–18.

55. Charles Tittle, Wayne Villemez, and Douglas Smith, "The Myth of Social Class and Criminality: An Empirical Assessment of the Empirical Evidence," American Sociological Review 43 (1978): 643–56.

56. Charles Tittle and Robert Meier, "Specifying the SES/Delinquency Relationship," Criminology 28 (1990): 271–301.

57. R. Gregory Dunaway, Francis Cullen, Velmer Burton, and T. David Evans, "The Myth of Social Class and Crime Revisited: An Examination of Class and Adult Criminality," Criminology 38 (2000): 589–632.

58. Delbert Elliott and Suzanne Ageton, "Reconciling Race and Class Differences in Self-Reported and Official Estimates of Delinquency," American Sociological Review 45 (1980): 95–110.

59. See also Delbert Elliott and David Huizinga, "Social Class and Delinquent Behavior in a National Youth Panel: 1976–1980," Criminology 21 (1983): 149–77. For a similar view, see John Braithwaite, "The Myth of Social Class and Criminality Reconsidered," American Sociological Review 46 (1981): 35–58; Hindelang, Hirschi, and Weis, Measuring Delinquency, p. 196.

60. David Brownfield, "Social Class and Violent Behavior," Criminology 24 (1986): 421–39.

61. Douglas Smith and Laura Davidson, "Interfacing Indicators and Constructs in Criminological Research: A Note on the Comparability of Self-Report Violence Data for Race and Sex Groups," Criminology 24 (1986): 473–88.

62. Dunaway, Cullen, Burton, and Evans, "The Myth of Social Class and Crime Revisited."

63. Sally Simpson and Lori Elis, "Doing Gender: Sorting Out the Case and Crime Conundrum," Criminology 33 (1995): 47–81.

64. Judith Blau and Peter Blau, "The Cost of Inequality: Metropolitan Structure and Violent Crime," American Sociological Review 147 (1982): 114–29; Richard Block, "Community Environment and Violent Crime," Criminology 17 (1979): 46–57; Robert Sampson, "Structural Sources of Variation in Race-Age-Specific Rates of Offending across Major U.S. Cities," Criminology 23 (1985): 647–73.

65. Chin-Chi Hsieh and M. D. Pugh, "Poverty, Income Inequality, and Violent Crime: A Meta-Analysis of Recent Aggregate Data Studies," Criminal Justice Review 18 (1993): 182–99.

66. Richard Miech, Avshalom Caspi, Terrie Moffitt, Bradley Entner Wright, and Phil Silva, "Low Socioeconomic Status and Mental Disorders: A Longitudinal Study of Selection and Causation during Young Adulthood," American Journal of Sociology 104 (1999): 1096–1131; Marvin Krohn, Alan Lizotte, and Cynthia Perez, "The Interrelationship between Substance Use and Precocious Transitions to Adult Sexuality," Journal of Health and Social Behavior 38 (1997): 87–103, at 88; Richard Jessor, "Risk Behavior in Adolescence: A Psychosocial Framework for Understanding and Action," in Adolescents at Risk: Medical and Social Perspectives, eds. D. E. Rogers and E. Ginzburg (Boulder, Colo.: Westview, 1992).

67. Robert Agnew, "A General Strain Theory of Community Differences in Crime Rates," *Journal of Research in Crime and Delinquency* 36 (1999): 123–55.

68. Bonita Veysey and Steven Messner, "Further Testing of Social Disorganization Theory: An Elaboration of Sampson and Groves's Community Structure and Crime," *Journal of Research in Crime and Delinquency* 36 (1999): 156–74.

69. Lance Hannon and James Defronzo, "Welfare and Property Crime," *Justice Quarterly* 15 (1998): 273–88.

70. Alan Lizotte, Terence Thornberry, Marvin Krohn, Deborah Chard-Wierschem, and David McDowall, "Neighborhood Context and Delinquency: A Longitudinal Analysis," in *Cross National Longitudinal Research on Human Development and Criminal Behavior*, eds. E. M. Weitekamp and H. J. Kerner (Stavernstr, Netherlands: Kluwer, 1994), pp. 217–27.

71. Travis Hirschi and Michael Gottfredson, "Age and the Explanation of Crime," *American Journal of Sociology* 89 (1983): 552–84, at 581.

72. Darrell Steffensmeier and Cathy Streifel, "Age, Gender, and Crime across Three Historical Periods: 1935, 1960 and 1985," *Social Forces* 69 (1991): 869–94.

73. For a comprehensive review of crime and the elderly, see Kyle Kercher, "Causes and Correlates of Crime Committed by the Elderly," in *Critical Issues in Aging Policy*, eds. E. Borgatta and R. Montgomery (Beverly Hills: Sage, 1987), pp. 254–306; Darrell Steffensmeier, "The Invention of the 'New' Senior Citizen Criminal," *Research on Aging* 9 (1987): 281–311.

74. Hirschi and Gottfredson, "Age and the Explanation of Crime."

75. Margo Wilson and Martin Daly, "Life Expectancy, Economic Inequality, Homicide, and Reproductive Timing in Chicago Neighbourhoods," *British Journal of Medicine* 314 (1997): 1271–74.

76. Edward Mulvey and John LaRosa, "Delinquency Cessation and Adolescent Development: Preliminary Data," *American Journal of Orthopsychiatry* 56 (1986): 212–24.

77. James Q. Wilson and Richard Herrnstein, *Crime and Human Nature* (New York: Simon and Schuster, 1985), pp. 126–47.

78. Ibid., p. 219.

79. Erich Labouvie, "Maturing Out of Substance Use: Selection and Self-Correction," *Journal of Drug Issues* 26 (1996): 457–74.

80. Marvin Wolfgang, Robert Figlio, and Thorsten Sellin, *Delinquency in a Birth Cohort* (Chicago: University of Chicago Press, 1972); Lyle Shannon, *Assessing the Relationship of Adult Criminal Careers to Juvenile Careers: A Summary* (Washington, D.C.: U.S. Department of Justice, 1982); D. J. West and David P. Farrington, *The Delinquent Way of Life* (London: Hienemann, 1977); Donna Hamparian, Richard Schuster, Simon Dinitz, and John Conrad, *The Violent Few* (Lexington, Mass.: Lexington Books, 1978).

81. Lening Zhang, William Wieczorek, and John Welte, "The Impact of Age of Onset on Substance Use on Delinquency," *Journal of Research in Crime and Delinquency* 34 (1997): 253–68.

82. Darrell Steffensmeier, Emilie Andersen Allan, Miles Harer, and Cathy Streifel, "Age and the Distribution of Crime: Variant or Invariant?" Paper presented at the American Society of Criminology meeting, Montreal, Canada, November 1987.

83. Hilary Saner, Robert MacCoun, and Peter Reuter, "On the Ubiquity of Drug Selling among Youthful Offenders in Washington, D.C., 1985–1991: Age, Period, or Cohort Effect?" *Journal of Quantitative Criminology* 11 (1995): 362–73.

84. Arnold Barnett, Alfred Blumstein, and David Farrington, "Probabilistic Models of Youthful Criminal Careers," *Criminology* 25 (1987): 83–107.

85. Cesare Lombroso, *The Female Offender* (New York: Appleton, 1920), p. 122.

86. Otto Pollack, *The Criminality of Women* (Philadelphia: University of Pennsylvania, 1950).

87. For a review of this issue, see Darrell Steffensmeier, "Assessing the Impact of the Women's Movement on Sex-Based Differences in the Handling of Adult Criminal Defendants," *Crime and Delinquency* 26 (1980): 344–57.

88. Alan Booth and D. Wayne Osgood, "The Influence of Testosterone on Deviance in Adulthood: Assessing and Explaining the Relationship," *Criminology* 31 (1993): 93–118.

89. Darrell Steffensmeier and Robert Clark, "Sociocultural versus Biological/Sexist Explanations of Sex Differences in Crime: A Survey of American Criminology Textbooks, 1918–1965," *American Sociologist* 15 (1980): 246–55.

90. Gisela Konopka, *The Adolescent Girl in Conflict* (Englewood Cliffs, N.J.: Prentice-Hall, 1966); Clyde Vedder and Dora Somerville, *The Delinquent Girl* (Springfield, Ill.: Charles C. Thomas, 1970).

91. Dennis Giever, "An Empirical Assessment of the Core Elements of Gottfredson and Hirschi's General Theory of Crime." Paper presented at the American Society of Criminology meeting, Boston, Mass., November 1995.

92. John Mirowsky and Catherine Ross, "Sex Differences in Distress: Real or Artifact?" *American Sociological Review* 60 (1995): 449–68.

93. Kristen Kling, Janet Shibley Hyde, Carolin Showers, and Brenda Buswell, "Gender Differences in Self-Esteem: a Meta Analysis," *Psychological Bulletin* 125 (1999): 470–500.

94. For a review of this issue, see Anne Campbell, *Men, Women and Aggression* (New York: Basic Books, 1993).

95. Daniel Mears, Matthew Ploeger, and Mark Warr, "Explaining the Gender Gap in Delinquency: Peer Influence and Moral Evaluations of Behavior," *Journal of Research in Crime and Delinquency* 35 (1998): 251–66.

96. Robert Hoge, D. A. Andrews, and Alan Leschied, "Tests of Three Hypotheses Regarding the Predictors of Delinquency," *Journal of Abnormal Child Psychology* 22 (1994): 547–59.

97. Freda Adler, *Sisters in Crime* (New York: McGraw-Hill, 1975); Rita James Simon, *The Contemporary Woman and Crime* (Washington, D.C.: U.S. Government Printing Office, 1975).

98. David Rowe, Alexander Vazsonyi, and Daniel Flannery, "Sex Differences in Crime: Do Mean and Within-Sex Variation Have Similar Causes?" *Journal of Research in Crime and Delinquency* 32 (1995): 84–100; Michael Hindelang, "Age, Sex, and the Versatility of Delinquency Involvements," *Social Forces* 14 (1971): 525–34; Martin Gold, *Delinquent Behavior in an American City* (Belmont, Calif.: Brooks/Cole, 1970); Gary Jensen and Raymond Eve, "Sex Differences in Delinquency: An Examination of Popular Sociological Explanations," *Criminology* 13 (1976): 427–48.

99. Darrell Steffensmeier and Renee Hoffman Steffensmeier, "Trends in Female Delinquency," *Criminology* 18 (1980): 62–85; see also Darrell Steffensmeier and Renee Hoffman Steffensmeier, "Crime and the Contemporary Woman: An Analysis of Changing Levels of Female Property Crime, 1960–1975," *Social Forces* 57 (1978): 566–84; Joseph Weis, "Liberation and Crime: The Invention of the New Female Criminal," *Crime and Social Justice*

1 (1976): 17–27; Carol Smart, "The New Female Offender: Reality or Myth," *British Journal of Criminology* 19 (1979): 50–59; Steven Box and Chris Hale, "Liberation/Emancipation, Economic Marginalization or Less Chivalry," *Criminology* 22 (1984): 473–78.

100. Meda Chesney-Lind, "Female Offenders: Paternalism Reexamined," in *Women, the Courts and Equality,* eds. Laura Crites and Winifred Hepperle (Newbury Park, Calif.: Sage, 1987), pp. 114–39, at 115.

101. Anne Campbell, Steven Muncer, Daniel Bibel, "Female–Female Criminal Assault: An Evolutionary Perspective," *Journal of Research in Crime and Delinquency* 35 (1998): 413–28.

102. Finn-Aage Esbensen and Elizabeth Piper Deschenes, "A Multisite Examination of Youth Gang Membership: Does Gender Matter?" *Criminology* 36 (1998): 799–828.

103. Leroy Gould, "Who Defines Delinquency: A Comparison of Self-Report and Officially Reported Indices of Delinquency for Three Racial Groups," *Social Problems* 16 (1969): 325–36; Voss, "Ethnic Differentials in Delinquency in Honolulu"; Ronald Akers, Marvin Krohn, Marcia Radosevich, and Lonn Lanza-Kaduce, "Social Characteristics and Self-Reported Delinquency," in *Sociology of Delinquency,* ed. Gary Jensen (Beverly Hills: Sage, 1981), pp. 48–62.

104. Institute for Social Research, *Monitoring the Future* (Ann Arbor, Mich.: Author, 2000).

105. David Huizinga and Delbert Elliott, "Juvenile Offenders: Prevalence, Offender Incidence, and Arrest Rates by Race," *Crime and Delinquency* 33 (1987): 206–23. See also Dale Dannefer and Russell Schutt, "Race and Juvenile Justice Processing in Court and Police Agencies," *American Journal of Sociology* 87 (1982): 1113–32.

106. Paul Tracy, "Race and Class Differences in Official and Self-Reported Delinquency," in *From Boy to Man, from Delinquency to Crime,* eds. Marvin Wolfgang, Terence Thornberry, and Robert Figlio (Chicago: University of Chicago Press, 1987), p. 120.

107. Phillipe Rushton, "Race and Crime: An International Dilemma," *Society* 32 (1995): 37–42; for a rebuttal, see Jerome Neapolitan, "Cross-National Variation in Homicides: Is Race a Factor?" *Criminology* 36 (1998): 139–56.

108. Miriam Sealock and Sally Simpson, "Unraveling Bias in Arrest Decisions: The Role of Juvenile Offender Type-

scripts," *Justice Quarterly* 15 (1998): 427–57.

109. "Law Enforcement Seeks Answers to 'Racial Profiling' Complaints," *Criminal Justice Newsletter* 29 (1998): 5.

110. Daniel Georges-Abeyie, "Definitional Issues: Race, Ethnicity and Official Crime/Victimization Rates," in *The Criminal Justice System and Blacks,* ed. D. Georges-Abeyie (New York: Clark Boardman, 1984), p. 12; Robert Sampson, "Race and Criminal Violence: A Demographically Disaggregated Analysis of Urban Homicide," *Crime and Delinquency* 31 (1985): 47–82.

111. Barry Sample and Michael Philip, "Perspectives on Race and Crime in Research and Planning," in *The Criminal Justice System and Blacks,* ed. Georges-Abeyie, (pp. 21–36.

112. Candace Kruttschnitt, "Violence by and against Women: A Comparative and Cross-National Analysis," *Violence and Victims* 8 (1994): 4.

113. James Comer, "Black Violence and Public Policy," in *American Violence and Public Policy,* ed. Lynn Curtis (New Haven: Yale University Press, 1985), pp. 63–86.

114. Fox Butterfield, *All God's Children: The Bosket Family and the American Tradition of Violence* (New York: Avon, 1996).

115. Michael Leiber and Jayne Stairs, "Race, Contexts and the Use of Intake Diversion," *Journal of Research in Crime and Delinquency* 36 (1999): 56–86; Darrell Steffensmeier, Jeffery Ulmer, and John Kramer, "The Interaction of Race, Gender, and Age in Criminal Sentencing: The Punishment Cost of Being Young, Black, and Male," *Criminology* 36 (1998): 763–98.

116. Tracy Nobiling, Cassia Spohn, and Miriam DeLone, "A Tale of Two Counties: Unemployment and Sentence Severity," *Justice Quarterly* 15 (1998): 459–86.

117. Alexander Weiss and Steven Chermak, "The News Value of African-American Victims: An Examination of the Media's Presentation of Homicide," *Journal of Crime and Justice* 21 (1998): 71-84.

118. Jerome Miller, *Search and Destroy: African American Males in the Criminal Justice System* (New York: Cambridge University Press, 1996), p. 226.

119. *The Sentencing Project, Losing the Vote: The Impact of Felony Disenfranchisement Laws in the United States* (Washington, D.C.: Sentencing Project, 1998).

120. Ronald Weitzer and Steven Tuch, "Race, Class, and Perceptions of Dis-

crimination by the Police," *Crime and Delinquency* 45 (1999): 494–507.

121. Karen Parker and Patricia McCall, "Structural Conditions and Racial Homicide Patterns: A Look at the Multiple Disadvantages in Urban Areas," *Criminology* 37 (1999): 447–69.

122. David Jacobs and Katherine Woods, "Interracial Conflict and Interracial Homicide: Do Political and Economic Rivalries Explain White Killings of Blacks or Black Killings of Whites?" *American Journal of Sociology* 105 (1999): 157–90.

123. Melvin Thomas, "Race, Class and Personal Income: An Empirical Test of the Declining Significance of Race Thesis, 1968–1988," *Social Problems* 40 (1993): 328–39.

124. Gary LaFree, Kriss Drass, and Patrick O'Day, "Race and Crime in Postwar America: Determinants of African-American and White Rates, 1957–1988," *Criminology* 30 (1992): 157–88.

125. Mallie Paschall, Robert Flewelling, and Susan Ennett, "Racial Differences in Violent Behavior among Young Adults: Moderating and Confounding Effects," *Journal of Research in Crime and Delinquency* 35 (1998): 148–65.

126. R. Kelly Raley, "A Shortage of Marriageable Men? A Note on the Role of Cohabitation in Black-White Differences in Marriage Rates," *American Sociological Review* 61 (1996): 973–83.

127. Julie Phillips, "Variation in African-American Homicide Rates: An Assessment of Potential Explanations," *Criminology* 35 (1997): 527–59.

128. Roy Austin, "Progress toward Racial Equality and Reduction of Black Criminal Violence," *Journal of Criminal Justice* 15 (1987): 437–59.

129. Reynolds Farley and William Frey, "Changes in the Segregation of Whites from Blacks During the 1980s: Small Steps toward a More Integrated Society," *American Sociological Review* 59 (1994): 23–45.

130. Marvin Wolfgang, Robert Figlio, and Thorsten Sellin, *Delinquency in a Birth Cohort* (Chicago: University of Chicago Press, 1972).

131. See Thorsten Sellin and Marvin Wolfgang, *The Measurement of Delinquency* (New York: Wiley, 1964), p. 120.

132. Paul Tracy and Robert Figlio, "Chronic Recidivism in the 1958 Birth Cohort." Paper presented at the American Society of Criminology meeting, Toronto, October 1982; Marvin Wolfgang, "Delinquency in Two Birth Cohorts," in *Perspective Studies of Crime and Delinquency,* eds. Katherine Teil-

mann Van Dusen and Sarnoff Mednick (Boston: Kluwer-Nijhoff, 1983),
pp. 7–17. The following sections rely
heavily on these sources.

133. Lyle Shannon, *Criminal Career Opportunity* (New York: Human Sciences
Press, 1988).

134. D. J. West and David P. Farrington,
The Delinquent Way of Life (London:
Hienemann, 1977).

135. Michael Schumacher and Gwen Kurz,
The 8% Solution: Preventing Serious Repeat Juvenile Crime (Thousand Oaks,
Calif., Sage, 1999).

136. Peter Jones, Philip Harris, James Fader,
and Lori Grubstein, "Identifying
Chronic Juvenile Offenders," *Justice
Quarterly* 18 (2001): 478–507.

137. See, generally, Wolfgang, Thornberry,
and Figlio, eds., *From Boy to Man, from
Delinquency to Crime*.

138. Paul Tracy and Kimberly Kempf-
Leonard, *Continuity and Discontinuity in
Criminal Careers* (New York: Plenum
Press, 1996).

139. Kimberly Kempf-Leonard, Paul Tracy,
and James Howell, "Serious, Violent,
and Chronic Juvenile Offenders: The
Relationship of Delinquency Career
Types to Adult Criminality," *Justice
Quarterly* 18 (2001): 449–78.

140. R. Tremblay, R. Loeber, C. Gagnon,
P. Charlebois, S. Larivee, and M.
LeBlanc, "Disruptive Boys with Stable
and Unstable High Fighting Behavior
Patterns During Junior Elementary
School," *Journal of Abnormal Child Psychology* 19 (1991): 285–300.

141. Jennifer White, Terrie Moffitt, Felton
Earls, Lee Robins, and Phil Silva,
"How Early Can We Tell? Predictors
of Childhood Conduct Disorder and
Adolescent Delinquency," *Criminology*
28 (1990): 507–35.

142. John Laub and Robert Sampson, "Unemployment, Marital Discord, and Deviant Behavior: The Long-Term Correlates of Childhood Misbehavior."
Paper presented at the annual meeting
of the American Society of Criminology, Baltimore, November 1990; rev.
version.

143. Michael Ezell and Amy D'Unger,
"Offense Specialization among Serious
Youthful Offenders: A Longitudinal
Analysis of a California Youth Authority Sample" (Durham, N.C.: Duke
University, 1998, unpublished report).

144. Susan Martin, "Policing Career Criminals: An Examination of an Innovative
Crime Control Program," *Journal of
Criminal Law and Criminology* 77 (1986):
1159–82.

© David Young-Wolff/Photo Edit

CHAPTER 4 Victims and Victimization

■ In 2001, the state of Connecticut was rocked when Waterbury Mayor Philip Giordano, shown here, a married father of three, was arrested for engaging in sexual relations with minors as young as 9 years old.

■ Introduction

In 2001, the state of Connecticut was rocked when Waterbury Mayor Philip Giordano, a married father of three, was arrested for engaging in sexual relations with minors as young as 9 years old. Giordano was a highly respected officeholder who had been the Republican candidate for U.S. Senator in the 2000 campaign (he lost to incumbent Joseph Lieberman). During an FBI investigation into city corruption, a 17-year-old girl came forward and charged that Giordano had paid her to have sex with him in his private law office and to watch him have sex with her aunt, known in the case as "Jane Doe." The teenager told state officials that from the time she was 12 Jane Doe often arranged for sexual encounters between her and men for pay, a practice that Doe called "going to wash windows." Jane Doe is the mother of two girls, ages 9 and 10. She was arrested when the FBI found out that she was providing them to Giordano for sexual encounters. A 14-count federal indictment says the mayor repeatedly arranged for Jane Doe to deliver the two young girls to him for sex at his home, his private law office, and his office at city hall. The children are under the care of state authorities, and at the time of this writing, Jane Doe is jailed on federal child sex charges while Giordano remains in jail awaiting trial.[1]

The Giordano case is shocking because it involves a high public official. And though it is unusual for its sordidness, it is not unique or uncommon. A recent multinational survey concluded that each year in the United States 325,000 children are subjected to some form of sexual exploitation, which includes sexual abuse, prostitution, use in pornography, or molestation by adults.[2]

These incidents illustrate the importance of understanding the victim's role in the crime process. Criminologists who focus their attention on crime victims refer to themselves as **victimologists.** This chapter examines victims and their relationship to the criminal process. First, using available victim data, we analyze the nature and extent of victimization. We then discuss the relationship between victims and criminal offenders. During this discussion, we look at the various theories of victimization that attempt to explain the victim's role in the crime problem. Finally, we examine how society has responded to the needs of victims and discuss the special problems they still face.

■ Problems of Crime Victims

The National Crime Victimization Survey (NCVS) indicates that in 2000 (the latest data available), U.S. residents age 12 or older experienced approximately 25.9 million crimes. Of these, 75 percent (19.3 million) were property crimes, 24 percent (6.3 million) were crimes of violence, and 1 percent were personal thefts.[3] Being the target or victim of a rape, robbery, or assault is a terrible burden and one that can have considerable long-term consequences.[4] In this section we explore some of the effects of these incidents.

Loss

Based on estimates of property taken during larcenies, burglaries, and other reported crimes, the FBI estimates that victims lose about $12 billion per year. Of that amount, after the crime has been cleared, they recover about $4 billion of their losses.[5] When added to productivity losses caused by injury, pain, and emotional trauma, the cost of victimization is estimated to be more than $100 billion each year. If the cost of long-term suffering, trauma, and risk of death is included, the total loss due to crime amounts to $450 billion annually, or about $1,800 per U.S. citizen[6] (see Table 4.1).

Crime produces social costs that must be paid by nonvictims as well. For example, each heroin addict is estimated to cost society more than $135,000 per year (see Figure 4.1); an estimated half-million addicts cost society about $68 billion per year.[7]

In addition to these societal costs, victims may suffer long-term losses in earnings and occupational attainment. Research by Ross Macmillan shows that Americans who suffer a violent victimization during adolescence earn about $82,000 less annually than nonvictims; Canadian victims earn $237,000 less! Macmillan reasons that victims bear psychological and physical ills that first inhibit their academic achievement and later their economic and professional success.[8]

Suffering

Millions of crime victims suffer injury each year, ranging from a scratch to a gunshot. According to a recent analysis on crime-related injuries conducted by the Bureau of Justice Statistics, there are on average about 10 million victims of violent crime in the United States each year, and of these, 2.6 million suffer some form of injury. About 20 percent received minor wounds including bruises, black eyes, cuts, scratches, swelling, chipped teeth, and other similar injuries that required less than two days of hospitalization. About 3 percent have severe injuries, including gunshot or knife wounds, broken bones, loss of teeth, internal injuries, loss of consciousness, and undetermined injuries that required two or more days of hospitalization. About 1 percent are rape and sexual assault victims. It is easy to see why violent crime is so costly to society: Nearly 1 in 5 injured violent crime victims, or an average of just under 480,000 persons per year, were treated in an

Table 4.1 Costs per Victimization

Crime	Tangible Costs	Intangible Costs	Total Costs
Murder	$1,030,000	$1,910,000	$2,940,000
Rape/sexual assault	5,100	81,400	86,500
Robbery/attempt with injury	5,200	13,800	19,000
Assault or attempt	1,550	7,800	9,350
Burglary or attempt	1,100	300	1,400

SOURCE: Ted Miller, Mark Cohen, and Brian Wiersema, *The Extent and Costs of Crime Victimization: A New Look* (Washington, D.C.: National Institute of Justice, 1996), p. 2.

Figure 4.1 The Costs of Heroin Addiction

Each heroin addict incurs the following losses annually:

Lost employment earnings	$11,918.12
Value of premature death	$6,909.59
Crime costs	$56,974.91
Costs to the criminal justice system	$30,000.00
Cost of spreading addiction to other users	$29,624.73
Total	**$135,427.35**

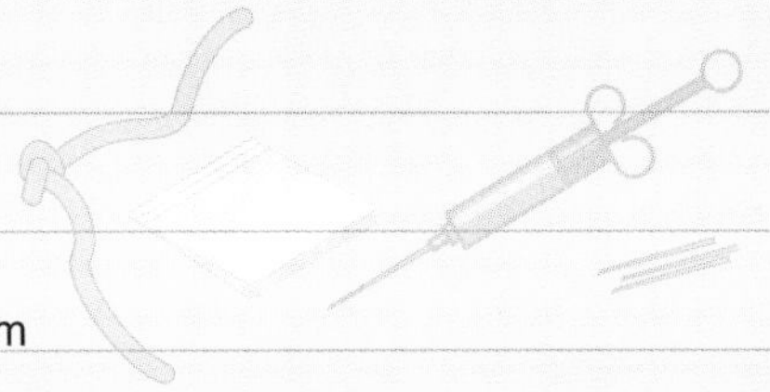

SOURCE: George Rengert, *The Geography of Illegal Drugs* (Boulder, Colo.: Westview Press, 1996), p. 5.

emergency department or hospital for violence-related injuries.

The suffering endured by crime victims does not end when their attacker leaves the scene of the crime. They may suffer more **victimization** by the justice system. While the crime is still fresh in their minds, victims may find that the police interrogation following the crime is handled callously, with innuendos or insinuations that they were somehow at fault. They have difficulty learning what is going on in the case; property is often kept for a long time as evidence and may never be returned. Some rape victims report that the treatment they receive from legal, medical, and mental health services is so destructive that they can't help but feel "re-raped."[9] Victims may also suffer economic hardship due to wages lost while they testify in court, and they may find that authorities are indifferent to their fear of retaliation if they cooperate in their offenders' prosecution.[10]

Victims may suffer stress and anxiety long after the incident is over and the justice process has been forgotten. For example, girls who were psychologically, sexually, or physically abused as children are more likely to have lower self-esteem and be more suicidal as adults than those who were not abused.[11] Kids who are victimized in the home are more likely to run away to escape their environment, which puts them at risk for juvenile arrest and involvement with the justice system.[12]

The long-term suffering of victims does not end in childhood. Spousal abuse victims suffer an extremely high prevalence of depression, **posttraumatic stress disorder** (an emotional disturbance following exposure to stresses outside the range of normal human experience), anxiety disorder, and **obsessive-compulsive disorder** (an extreme preoccupation with certain thoughts and compulsive performance of certain behaviors).[13] One reason may be that abusive spouses are as likely to abuse their victims psychologically, with threats and intimidation, as they are to use physical force; psychological abuse can lead to depression and other long-term disabilities.[14]

Some victims are physically disabled due to the serious wounds sustained during episodes of random violence, including a growing number who suffer paralyzing spinal cord injuries. And, if victims have no insurance, the long-term effects of the crime may have devastating financial ramifications as well as the emotional and physical desolation.[15]

The mission of the National Center for Victims of Crime is to forge a national commitment to help victims of crime rebuild their lives: "We are dedicated to serving individuals, families, and communities harmed by crime." Visit their Web site at:
   http://www.ncvc.org/
For an up-to-date list of Web links, go to
   http://info.wadsworth.com/siegel ■

Fear

Victims of violent crime are the most deeply affected, fearing a repeat of their attack. The effects of fear are critical considering that forms of victimization are so widespread. For example, one study of sexual harassment among Cana-

■ Communities may live in fear when news of a violent incident grips the neighborhood. Sometimes local incidents become national news. The 1999 shooting of Amadou Diallo by New York City police officers was a graphic example of urban violence that can put an entire city in fear. Here, Vickie Smith of the Capital Region Justice for Diallo Committee stands in front of the Albany County (New York) Courthouse near a door painted with a body and bullet holes to symbolize the fatal wounds of Amadou Diallo.

© Albany Times Union/The Image Works

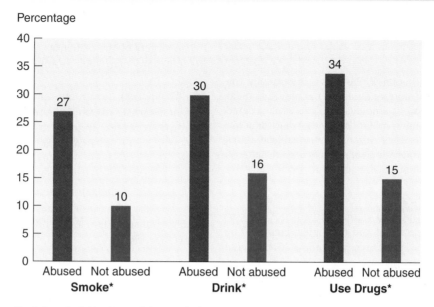

Smoke*: smoked at least several cigarettes in the past week; Drink: drank at least once a month; Use drugs: used illegal drugs at least once in the past month.

NOTE: The survey was an in-class questionnaire completed by 3,162 boys in grades 5–12 at a nationally representative sample of 265 public, private, and parochial schools from December 1996 to June 1997. The survey included roughly equal samples of adolescent boys in grades 5–8 and 9–12. All responses were weighted to reflect grade, region, race and ethnicity, and gender.

SOURCE: Cathy Schoen et al., *The Health of Adolescent Boys: Commonwealth Fund Survey Findings* (New York: Commonwealth Fund, 1998). Figure prepared by The Center for Substance Abuse Research, University of Maryland, College Park.

dian women found that more than 80 percent have experienced some form of sexual harassment by strangers and many remain fearful of being sexually victimized long after the attack.[16]

There may also be a spillover effect in which victims become fearful of other forms of crime they have not yet experienced; people who have been assaulted, for example, may develop fears that their house will be burglarized.[17] Many go through a fundamental life change, viewing the world more suspiciously and less as a safe, controllable, and meaningful place. These people are more likely to suffer psychological stress for extended periods of time.[18]

Fear of crime may also be more complex than simply resolving issues of personal safety. Many people fear for the safety of others in their lives—children, spouses, and friends whose safety they value—this is referred to as **altruistic fear** (fear for others).[19] Altruistic fear may be more common and often more intense than personal fear and may cause people to take everyday precautions sometimes erroneously assumed to be motivated by *self*-protection.

Antisocial Behavior

There is growing evidence that people who are crime victims also seem more likely to commit crime themselves. There is strong evidence that being abused or neglected as

a child increases the odds of being arrested both as a juvenile and as an adult.[20] People, especially young males, who were physically or sexually abused are much more likely to smoke, drink, and take drugs than are nonabused youth (see Figure 4.2). Incarcerated offenders report significant amounts of posttraumatic stress disorder as a result of prior victimization, which may in part explain their violent and criminal behaviors.[21]

The abuse–crime phenomenon is referred to as the **cycle of violence**.[22] Research shows that both boys and girls were more likely to engage in violent behavior if they were (1) the targets of physical abuse and were (2) exposed to violent behavior among adults they know or live with or were exposed to weapons.[23]

■ The Nature of Victimization

How many crime victims are there in the United States, and what are the trends and patterns in victimization? In 2000, an estimated 25.9 million victimizations occurred, a decline from 28.8 million property and violent crimes experienced in 1999. Violent crime rates fell 15 percent between 1999 and 2000, the greatest annual percentage decline since the NCVS was begun. The 2000 level of violent crime continued a downward trend that began in 1994, and the 2000 level of property crime is the lowest since 1974. The number of criminal victimizations estimated for 2000 is the lowest recorded since 1973 when the NCVS began and measured 44 million victimizations.

| CONNECTIONS

As discussed in Chapter 3, the NCVS is currently the leading source of information about the nature and extent of victimization. It employs a highly sophisticated and complex sampling methodology to collect data annually from thousands of citizens. Statistical techniques then estimate victimization rates, trends, and patterns that occur in the entire U.S. population. ■

Patterns in victimization survey findings are stable and repetitive, demonstrating that victimization is not random but is a function of personal and ecological factors. The stability of these patterns allows judgments to be made about the nature of victimization; policies can then be created in an effort to reduce the victimization rate.

Who are victims? Where does victimization take place? What is the relationship between victims and criminals? The following sections discuss some of the most important victimization patterns and trends.

The Social Ecology of Victimization

The NCVS shows that violent crimes are slightly more likely to take place in an open, public area, such as a street, a park, or a field, in a school building, or at a commercial establishment, such as a tavern during the daytime or early evening hours. The more serious forms of these crimes, such as rape and aggravated assaults, typically take place after 6 P.M. Less serious forms of violence, such as unarmed robberies and personal larcenies like purse snatching, are more likely to occur during the daytime. Approximately two-thirds of rapes and sexual assaults occur at night—6 P.M. to 6 A.M.

Did you know that a great deal of victimization occurs in school buildings? Although school violence may be declining, about one-third of all students are injured in a physical altercation each year. To learn more about this phenomenon, using InfoTrac College Edition, read: Violence decreasing in U.S. high schools. *The Brown University Child and Adolescent Behavior Letter,* Dec 1999 v15 i12 p3 ■

Neighborhood characteristics influence the chances of victimization. Those living in the central city had significantly higher rates of theft and violence than suburbanites; people living in nonmetropolitan rural areas had a victimization rate almost half that of city dwellers. The risk of murder for both men and women is significantly higher in disorganized inner-city areas where gangs flourish and drug trafficking is commonplace.[24]

The Victim's Household

The NCVS tells us that larger, low-income, African American, western, and urban areas are the most vulnerable to crime. In contrast, affluent, rural, white homes in the Northeast are the least likely to contain crime victims or to be targets of theft offenses, such as burglary or larceny. People who own their homes are less vulnerable than renters.

Population movement and changes may account for recent decreases in crime victimization. U.S. residents have become extremely mobile, moving from urban areas to suburban and rural areas. In addition, family size has been reduced; more people than ever before are living in single-person homes (about 25 percent of households). It is possible that the decline in household victimization rates during the past 15 years can be explained by the fact that smaller households in less populated areas have a lower victimization risk.

Victim Characteristics

Social and demographic characteristics also distinguish victims and nonvictims. The most important of these involve gender, age, social status, and race.

Gender Gender affects victimization risk: except for the crimes of rape and sexual assault, males are much more likely than females to suffer violent crime. Men were twice as likely as women to experience aggravated assault and robbery. Women, however, were six times more likely than men to be victims of rape or sexual assault. According to NCVS estimates, about 230,000 women and 40,000 men suffer sexual assault each year.

When men are the victims of violent crime, the perpetrator is described as a stranger; women are much more likely to be attacked by a relative than are men. About two-thirds of all attacks against women are committed by a husband, boyfriend, family member, or acquaintance.[25] In two-thirds of sexual assaults, the victim knew or was acquainted with her attacker.

Age Victim data reveal that young people face a much greater victimization risk than do older persons. As Table 4.2 shows, victim risk diminishes rapidly after age 25. The elderly, who are thought of as the helpless targets of predatory criminals, are actually much safer than their grandchildren. People over age 65, who make up about 15 percent of the population, account for only 1 percent of violent victimizations; teens 12–19, who also make up 15 percent of the population, typically account for more than 30 percent of victimizations.

Data gathered in the emergency rooms of the nation's hospitals further confirm that young people have a much greater chance of victimization than the elderly and that more often than not their attackers are people they know or with whom they are acquainted.[26] Children under age 12 are significantly more likely to be assaulted by people

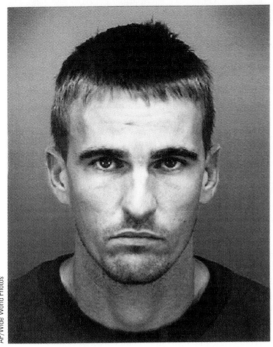

AP/Wide World Photos

PINELLAS COUNTY
SHERIFF'S OFFICE

SUSPECT DATABASE

Name: CARR
JASON
DOB: 12 / 30 / 74
Race: MALE
Sex: WHITE
Hgt/Wgt: 6' 02" 160 lbs.
Eyes: BLUE Hair: BROWN
Image#: 1070245
Type: BOOKING RECORD
Picture Date/Time:
10 / 10 / 00 20 : 05

■ Men are typically attacked by strangers, but about two-thirds of all attacks against women are committed by a husband, boyfriend, family member, or an acquaintance. Jason Carr, shown here in his booking photograph in Pinellas County, Florida, was placed under house arrest after his tenth felony conviction. He was then arrested and charged with domestic violence and child abuse—committed while serving his sentence at home!

	Table 4.2	Number of Violent Crimes per 1,000 Persons Age 12 or Older		
Age of victim	1999	2000		Percent change
12–15 years	74.4	60.1		–19.2
16–19 years	77.4	64.3		–16.9
20–24 years	68.5	49.4		–27.9
25–34 years	36.3	34.8		–4.1
35–49 years	25.2	21.8		–13.5
50–64 years	14.4	13.7		–4.9
65+ years	3.8	3.7		–2.6

SOURCE: NCVS, 2000.

they know or are related to than teens or adults; teens between 12 and 19 are more likely to be victimized by acquaintances; people over 20 have the highest level of stranger attacks.

Did you know that Australia, the United States, and other developed countries offer elementary school programs that heighten children's awareness about the possibility of abduction? To read about these and other programs on InfoTrac College Edition, use "crime victims" as a subject guide and look for the subcategory "youth–crimes against." ■

CONNECTIONS

The association between age and victimization is undoubtedly tied to lifestyle: adolescents often stay out late at night, go to public places, and hang out with other kids who have a high risk of criminal involvement. Teens also face a high victimization risk because they spend a great deal of time in the most dangerous building in the community—the local school! As Chapter 3 indicated, adolescents have the highest crime rates. It is not surprising that people who associate with these high-crime-rate individuals (other adolescents) have the greatest victimization risk. ■

Although the elderly are less likely to be victimized by strangers than the young, they have increasingly become the target of a disturbing form domestic violence, **elder abuse**, by children and other relatives with whom they live. A New York City program designed to combat this growing social problem is discussed in the Policy and Practice in Criminology feature.

Social status As Table 4.3 shows, people in the lowest income categories are much more likely to become crime victims than those who are more affluent. The poorest Americans appear to be the most likely victims of crime because they live in crime-prone areas: inner-city, urban neighborhoods.

Although the poor are more likely to suffer violent crimes, the wealthy are more likely to be targets of personal theft crimes such as pocket picking and purse snatching.

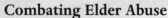

Combating Elder Abuse

Because of shifts in the U.S. population, the issue of elderly victimization and abuse is taking on greater importance. The Bureau of the Census predicts that by 2030 the population over age 65 will nearly triple to more than 70 million people, and older people will make up more than 20 percent of the population (up from 12.3 percent in 1990). The saliency of elder abuse is underscored by reports from the National Center on Elder Abuse, which show an increase of 150 percent in reported cases of elder abuse nationwide since 1986.

In an attempt to counteract this rising tide of elderly victimization, an innovative program was instituted in New York City. Using techniques first implemented to battle spousal abuse, researchers chose as their target population persons who reported elder abuse incidents to the police in selected public housing units of New York City. Thirty of 60 public housing projects were randomly assigned to receive public education. Posters were placed in public areas, leaflets were distributed to all elderly residents, and project staff made presentations that discussed definitions of abuse, the legal rights of victims, and assistance available from the police and social service agencies. In addition, in all 60 housing projects, half of the households reporting elder abuse to the police were randomly assigned to receive home visits by a team of a police officer and a domestic violence counselor. The team discussed legal options and police procedures and attempted to

link the households to social services. Victims were also encouraged to call the police if repeated violence occurred. In the few cases in which the abusers were present, the police officer made it clear to them that police would monitor the household.

Results of the Study

To determine whether abuse continued to occur, police records were checked and victims were interviewed 6 and 12 months after the trigger incident. According to both interview results and official measures, new incidents of abuse were more frequent among households that both received home visits and were in housing projects that received public education. Households that received home visits called the police significantly more often than controls, both in the housing projects that received public education and in those that did not. Contrary to expectation, however, victims who received both interventions were more likely to report more physical abuse to the police.

What could account for this surprising and somewhat disappointing finding? The researchers believed there were three possible explanations for these findings:

• Persons who received both interventions did not suffer more abuse but had become more sensitized to abuse.

• Persons who received both interventions were more willing to report abuse both to police and to research interviewers.

• Receiving both interventions caused more abuse to occur.

The thought that intervention may actually increase abuse is troubling, but the effect cannot be ruled out. It is possible that abusers may be angered by intervention and lash out at their victims. Unlike spousal abuse victims, the victims of elder abuse may be "stuck" in their home situation. They are more likely to be dependent, both physically and financially, on the abuser and to find it extremely difficult to sever ties if the abuse continues. If abusers of elderly relatives become angered by attempts to intervene, victims may have no options for escape.

Critical Thinking Questions

1. If the intervention has the potential to bring about more abuse, should such programs be discontinued? Or should a different approach be tried? What would you suggest?

2. Is it possible that while creating more abuse in the short term home visits and public education bring issues associated with abuse to a head that in the long run will reduce violence against the elderly?

InfoTrac College Edition Research

To find out more about the nature and extent of elder abuse, use it as a subject guide on InfoTrac College Edition.

SOURCE: Robert C. Davis and Juanjo Medina-Ariza, *Results from an Elder Abuse Prevention Experiment in New York* (Washington, D.C.: National Institute of Justice, September 2001).

Perhaps the affluent, who sport more expensive attire and drive better cars, attract the attention of thieves.

Marital status Marital status also influences victimization risk. Divorced and never-married males and females are victimized more often than married people. Widows and widowers have the lowest victimization risk. This as-

sociation between marital status and victimization is probably influenced by age, gender, and lifestyle:

• Many young people, who have the highest victim risk, are too young to have been married.

• Young single people also go out in public more often and sometimes interact with high-risk peers, increasing their exposure to victimization.

Table 4.3   Number of Violent Crimes per 1,000 Persons Age 12 or Older

Income of victim	1999	2000	Percent change
Less than $7,500	57.5	60.3	4.9
$7,500–$14,999	44.5	37.8	–15.1
$15,000–$24,999	35.3	31.8	–9.9
$25,000–$34,999	37.9	29.8	–21.4
$35,000–$49,999	30.3	28.5	–5.9
$50,000–$74,999	33.3	23.7	–28.8
$75,000 or more	22.9	22.3	–2.6

SOURCE: NCVS, 2000.

- Widows and widowers suffer much lower victimization rates because they are older, interact with older people, and are more likely to stay home at night and avoid public places.

Married women seem to be at much greater risk of domestic violence than single people who are living together. A possible cause may be that domestic relationships among single people tend to be less stable and more short-lived, insulating these couples from the pressures and conflicts that come with building longer-term marriages.[27] Nonetheless, the rate of domestic violence appears to be declining among both married couples and single cohabitants. One reason is that females now find it easier to get high-paying jobs, to obtain legal divorces, and to receive domestic violence counseling. Financial independence and emotional support enable women to leave a bad marriage before interspousal conflict leads to violence and death. And even if partners stay together in troubled relationships, newly emerging social interventions empower women to end male partner violence.[28]

Race and ethnicity   African Americans are more likely than whites to be victims of violent crime: African Americans are three times more likely to be the victims of robbery and twice as likely as whites to experience aggravated assault. Young African American males face a murder risk 4 or 5 times greater than that of young African American females, 5 to 8 times higher than that of young white males, and 16 to 22 times higher than that of young white females.

Other ethnic minorities also share a high risk of victimization. For example, Hispanics are twice as likely as non-Hispanics to fall victim to robbery and personal theft. Hispanics are also more likely to suffer completed violent crimes than are non-Hispanics.

Why do these discrepancies exist? Because of income inequality, racial and ethnic minority group members are

often forced to live in deteriorated urban areas beset by alcohol and drug abuse, poverty, racial discrimination, and violence. Consequently, their lifestyle places them in the most "at risk" population group.

Repeat victimization   Does prior victimization enhance or reduce the chance of future victimization? Individuals who have been crime victims maintain a significantly higher chance of future victimization than people who have remained nonvictims.[29] Households that have experienced victimization in the past are most likely to experience it again in the future.[30]

What factors predict **chronic victimization**? Most repeat victimizations occur soon after a previous crime has occurred, suggesting that repeat victims share some personal characteristic that makes them a magnet for predators.[31] For example, kids who are shy, physically weak, or socially isolated may be prone to being bullied in the schoolyard.[32] David Finkelhor and Nancy Asigian find that three specific types of characteristics increase the potential for victimization:

1. *Target vulnerability:* Victims' physical weakness or psychological distress renders them incapable of resisting or deterring crime and makes them easy targets.
2. *Target gratifiability:* Some victims have some quality, possession, skill, or attribute that an offender wants to obtain, use, have access to, or manipulate. Having attractive possessions such as a leather coat may make one vulnerable to predatory crime.
3. *Target antagonism:* Some characteristics increase risk because they arouse anger, jealousy, or destructive impulses in potential offenders. Being gay or effeminate, for example, may bring on undeserved attacks in the street; being argumentative and alcoholic may provoke barroom assault.[33]

Repeat victimization may occur when the victim does not take defensive action. For example, if an abusive husband finds out that his battered wife will not call police, he repeatedly victimizes her; if a hate crime is committed and the police do not respond to reported offenses, the perpetrators learn they have little to fear from the law.[34]

Victims and Their Criminals

The victim data also tell us something about the relationship between victims and criminals. For example, victims reported that most crimes were committed by a single offender over age 20. About one-quarter of the victims indicated that their assailant was a young person under 30 years of age.

Crime tends to be intraracial: African American offenders victimize African Americans, and whites victimize whites. However, because the country's population is predominantly white, it stands to reason that criminals of all races will be more likely to target white victims.

Siblicide

On April 15, 2002, the body of Jackson Carr, a 6-year-old boy, was found buried in mud in Lewisville, Texas; he had been stabbed to death. Later that day, Jackson's 15-year-old sister and 10-year-old brother confessed to the crime and were charged with murder. The Carr family had lived in the rural subdivision in a suburb north of Dallas for about four months. The motive for the crime baffled police.

A recent study by criminologist Erika Gebo focuses attention on an important yet relatively unfamiliar aspect of family violence: sibling homicide, or siblicide. Although 82 percent of the U.S. population has siblings, murder among siblings is quite rare, constituting about 2 percent of annual homicides in the United States. Nonetheless, the shocking, almost biblical nature of siblicide makes it an important area of study.

Analysis of the FBI's homicide data show that most known siblicides (78 percent) occur between adults who are fewer than five years apart. The median age of sibling homicide offenders is 23 years old, and the median age of their victims is 25 years old. The vast majority of sibling homicide offenders are males (87 percent), and they are most likely to kill their brothers. When lethal violence by brothers against their sisters occurs, it is more likely in juvenile sibling relationships rather than adult sibling relationships (31 percent versus 14 percent). Sisters killing their brothers or sisters are relatively rare events.

How Can Siblicide Be Explained?

It is still uncertain why brothers and sisters are driven to lethal violence. One possibility is that sociobiological factors may help explain the nature and extent of siblicide. Individuals share an average of one-half of their genes with their siblings. Consequently, siblings are given genetic preferential treatment over others, including other kin. Nonetheless, sociobiologists believe people possess a self-interested drive to dominate or even kill those who threaten their future existence and their ability to procreate. Siblings would seem likely targets because they compete for shelter, food, and/or parental nurturance. The Bible and early mythological tales are replete with examples of sibling rivalries leading to death: for example, Cain and Abel, Remus and Romulus, Loki and Baldur. Recognizing this danger, most societies have strict prohibitions within their moral codes against sibling harm, mediating the incidence of siblicide. Thus, even when there is a biological stake in killing another, avoidance of sanctions is a strong deterrent, thereby explaining the relatively low siblicide rate.

The nature of siblicide may also be influenced by the opportunity to commit crime and the capability of parents to protect their children. The opportunity to commit siblicides will most likely occur in the late teen and early adulthood years, when the guardianship capacities of parents and other adults have decreased. In other words, in their younger years, siblings who are close in age are more likely

to be cared for and watched by adults. As they grow older, adult supervision decreases, allowing siblings more freedom. This freedom, in turn, creates the opportunity for deadly conflict, explaining in part why most siblicide occurs among adults rather than children, though the latter typically are more likely to be in close proximity to one another for longer periods of time and to have more fights and squabbles.

Critical Thinking Questions

1. Will the incidence of siblicide increase as American families undergo change and blended and nontraditional families become the norm?

2. Would it be relevant for future research to look at the issue of family size and violence? If the need for nurturance can produce conflict, might not larger families have more violent episodes than smaller ones?

InfoTrac College Edition Research

Use "family violence" and "sibling rivalry" as subject guides on InfoTrac College Edition to learn more about the factors that produce violence and conflict within the family structure.

Sources: Associated Press, Texas Siblings Accused of Killing 6-Year-Old Brother, *New York Times,* April 16, 2002; Erika Gebo, "A Contextual Exploration of Siblicide," *Violence & Victims,* 17 (2002): in press.

Victims reported that substance abuse was involved in about one-third of violent crime incidents.[35]

Although many violent crimes are committed by strangers, a surprising number of violent crimes were committed by relatives or acquaintances of the victims. In fact, about 40 percent of all violent crimes were committed by people who were described, at least, as being "well known" to the victim. Victimization commonly occurs within families and involves parents, children, and extended family. One disturbing form of victimization that

occurs within families, **siblicide,** is the topic of the Criminological Enterprise feature.

■ Theories of Victimization

For many years criminological theory focused on the actions of the criminal offender; the role of the victim was virtually ignored. But more than 50 years ago scholars began to realize that the victim was not a passive target in crime, but someone whose behavior can influence his or her own fate, who "shapes and molds the criminal."[36] These early works helped focus attention on the role of the victim in the crime problem and led to further research efforts that have sharpened the image of the crime victim. Today a number of different theories attempt to explain the cause of victimization; the most important are discussed here.

Victim Precipitation Theory

According to the **victim precipitation view,** some people may actually initiate the confrontation that eventually leads to their injury or death. Victim precipitation can be either active or passive.

Active precipitation occurs when victims act provocatively, use threats or fighting words, or even attack first.[37] In 1971, Menachem Amir suggested female victims often contribute to their attacks by dressing provocatively or pursuing a relationship with the rapist.[38] Although Amir's findings are controversial, courts have continued to return not-guilty verdicts in rape cases if a victim's actions can in any way be construed as consenting to sexual intimacy.[39]

In contrast, **passive precipitation** occurs when the victim exhibits some personal characteristic that unknowingly either threatens or encourages the attacker. The crime can occur because of personal conflict—for example, when two people compete over a job, promotion, love interest, or some other scarce and coveted commodity. For example, a woman may become the target of intimate violence when she increases her job status and her success results in a backlash from a jealous spouse or partner.[40] Although the victim may never have met the attacker or even know of his or her existence, the attacker feels menaced and acts accordingly.[41]

Passive precipitation may also occur when the victim belongs to a group whose mere presence threatens the attacker's reputation, status, or economic well-being. For example, hate crime violence may be precipitated by immigrant group members arriving in the community to compete for jobs and housing. Research indicates that passive precipitation is related to power: if the target group can establish themselves economically or gain political power in the community, their vulnerability will diminish. They are still a potential threat, but they become too formidable a target to attack; they are no longer passive precipitators.[42] By implication, economic power reduces victimization risk.

Lifestyle Theory

Some criminologists believe people may become crime victims because their lifestyle increases their exposure to criminal offenders. Victimization risk is increased by such behaviors as associating with young men, going out in public places late at night, and living in an urban area. Conversely, one's chances of victimization can be reduced by

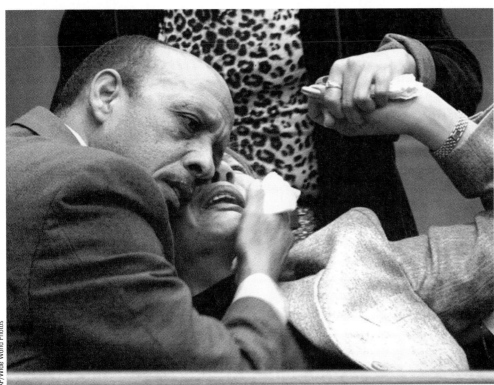

■ The family of crime victim Gladys Ricart is overcome with grief after watching a video in court of her shooting by her ex-boyfriend. Although Gladys had done little to provoke her victimization, could it be argued that her involvement with a violence-prone person ultimately led to her death?

staying home at night, moving to a rural area, staying out of public places, earning more money, and getting married. The basis of this theory is that crime is not a random occurrence but rather a function of the victim's lifestyle.

High-risk lifestyles People who have high-risk lifestyles—drinking, taking drugs, getting involved in crime—maintain a much greater chance of victimization.[43] For example, young runaways are at high risk for victimization; the more time they are exposed to street life, the greater their risk of becoming crime victims.[44] Teenage males have an extremely high victimization risk because their lifestyle places them at risk both at school and once they leave the school grounds.[45] They spend a great deal of time hanging out with friends and pursuing recreational fun.[46] Their friends may give them a false ID so they can go drinking in the neighborhood bar; or they may hang out in taverns at night, which places them at risk because many fights and assaults occur in places that serve liquor. Those who have histories of engaging in serious delinquency, getting involved in gangs, carrying guns, and selling drugs have an increased chance of being shot and killed themselves.[47]

Lifestyle risks continue into young adulthood. College students who spend several nights each week partying and who take recreational drugs are much more likely to suffer violent crime than those who avoid such risky academic lifestyles.[48] As adults, those who commit crimes increase their chances of becoming the victims of homicide.[49]

Victims and criminals One element of lifestyle that may place people at risk for victimization is ongoing involvement in a criminal career. Analysis of data from the Rochester and Pittsburgh Youth Studies, two ongoing longitudinal surveys tracking thousands of at-risk youth, indicates that kids who became victims of serious crime were more likely than nonvictims to have participated in such criminal activities as gang/group fights, serious assaults, and drug dealing. They are also more likely to carry a weapon and associate with delinquent peers. An adolescent characterized by any one of these risk factors was generally 2 to 4 times more likely to become a crime victim than a noncriminal youth. For example, between 24 and 40 percent of males involved in gang/group fights had themselves been seriously injured; among females, 27 percent of those involved in gang/group fights had been seriously injured. Carrying a weapon was another surefire way to become a crime victim. Males who carried weapons were approximately 3 times more likely to be victimized than those who did not carry weapons—between 27 and 33 percent of the weapon carriers became victims, as opposed to only 10 percent who did not carry weapons.[50] These data indicate that criminals and victims may not be two separate and distinct groups. Rather, the risk of victimization is directly linked to the high-risk lifestyle of young, weapon-toting gang boys.

Deviant Place Theory

According to deviant place theory, victims do not encourage crime but are victim prone because they reside in socially disorganized high-crime areas where they have the greatest risk of coming into contact with criminal offenders, irrespective of their own behavior or lifestyle.[51] Consequently, there may be little reason for residents in lower-class areas to alter their lifestyle or take safety precautions because personal behavior choices do not influence the likelihood of victimization.[52] Neighborhood crime levels, then, may be more important for determining the chances of victimization than individual characteristics.

Deviant places are poor, densely populated, highly transient neighborhoods in which commercial and residential property exist side by side.[53] The commercial property provides criminals with easy targets for theft crimes, such as shoplifting and larceny. Successful people stay out of these stigmatized areas; they are homes for "demoralized kinds of people" who are easy targets for crime: the homeless, the addicted, the retarded, and the elderly poor.[54] People who live in more affluent areas and take safety precautions significantly lower their chances of becoming crime victims; the effect of safety precautions is less pronounced in poor areas. Residents of poor areas have a much greater risk of becoming victims because they live in areas with many motivated offenders; to protect themselves, they have to try harder to be safe than the more affluent.[55]

Sociologist William Julius Wilson has described how people who can afford to leave dangerous areas do so. He suggests that affluent people realize that criminal victimization can be avoided by moving to an area with greater law enforcement and lower crime rates. Because there are significant interracial income differences, white residents are able to flee inner-city high-crime areas, leaving members of racial minorities behind to suffer high victimization rates.[56]

Routine Activities Theory

Routine activities theory was first articulated in a series of papers by Lawrence Cohen and Marcus Felson.[57] They concluded that the volume and distribution of predatory crime (violent crimes against a person and crimes in which an offender attempts to steal an object directly) are closely related to the interaction of three variables that reflect the routine activities of the typical American lifestyle (see Figure 4.3):

- The availability of **suitable targets,** such as homes containing easily salable goods
- The absence of **capable guardians,** such as police, homeowners, neighbors, friends, and relatives
- The presence of **motivated offenders,** such as a large number of unemployed teenagers

The presence of each of these components increases the likelihood that a predatory crime will take place. Targets are more likely to be victimized if they engage in risky behaviors, are poorly guarded, and are exposed to a large

Figure 4.3   Routine Activities Theory: The Interaction of Three Factors

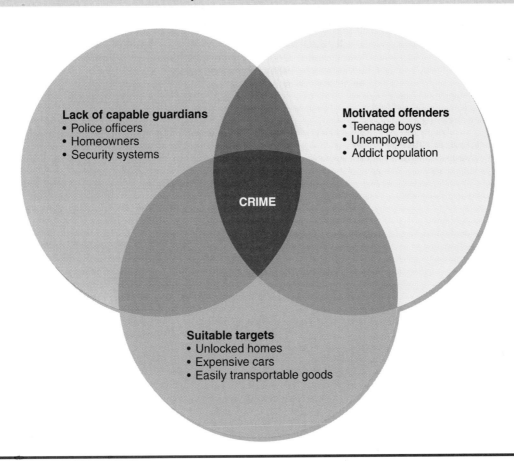

Lack of capable guardians
• Police officers
• Homeowners
• Security systems

Motivated offenders
• Teenage boys
• Unemployed
• Addict population

CRIME

Suitable targets
• Unlocked homes
• Expensive cars
• Easily transportable goods

group of motivated offenders such as substance abusing young men.[58] For example, young women who drink to excess in bars and frat houses may elevate their risk of **date rape** because (1) they are perceived as easy targets and (2) their attackers can rationalize the attack because they view intoxication as a sign of immorality ("She's loose, so I didn't think she'd care.").[59] Conversely, people can reduce their chances of victimization if they adopt a lifestyle that limits their exposure to danger: for example, by getting married, having children, and moving to a small town.[60]

Hot spots   Motivated people—such as teenage males, drug users, and unemployed adults—are the ones most likely to commit crime. If they congregate in a particular neighborhood, it becomes a "hot spot" for crime and violence. People who live in these hot spots elevate their chances of victimization. For example, people who live in public housing projects may have high victimization rates because their fellow residents, mostly indigent, are extremely motivated to commit crime.[61] Yet motivated criminals must have the opportunity to find suitable undefended targets before they commit crime. Even the most desperate criminal might hesitate to attack a well-defended

target, whereas a group of teens might rip off an unoccupied home on the spur of the moment.[62] In hot spots for crime, therefore, an undefended yet attractive target becomes an irresistible objective for motivated criminals. Given these principles, it is not surprising that (1) people who live in high-crime areas and (2) go out late at night (3) carrying valuables such as an expensive watch and (4) engage in risky behavior such as drinking alcohol, (5) without friends or family to watch or help them, have a significant chance of becoming crime victims.[63]

Moral guardianship   Some criminologists believe moral beliefs and socialization may influence the routine activities that produce crime. Even in the presence of criminal opportunities, people may refrain from crime if they are bonded and or attached to conventional peers and have been socialized to hold conventional attitudes. The strength of social bonds may serve as a buffer, a form of moral guardianship, sufficient to counteract the lure of criminal opportunities.[64]

When Martin Schwartz and his associates studied date rape on college campuses, they found that men whose peer group supported emotional and physical violence against

Figure 4.4   The Opportunity Structure of Crime

SOCIOECONOMIC STRUCTURE
Demography, geography, industrialization, urbanization, welfare/health/education/ legal institutions

Lifestyle/routine activity
Leisure/work, shopping/residence

Physical environment
Urban form, housing type, technology, communications, vehicles

Subcultural influences
Social control, lack of love, etc.
(i.e. traditional criminological theory)

Crime opportunity structure

Victims
Women alone, drunks, strangers

Targets
Cars, banks, convenience stores, etc.

Facilitators
Guns, cars, drugs, alcohol

Information/modeling

Search/perception

Lack of supervision
Freedom of movement ("unhandled" offender)

Potential offenders

Numbers motivation

SOURCE: Ronald Clarke, "Situational Crime Prevention," in *Building a Safer Society: Strategic Approaches to Crime Prevention*, vol. 19 of *Crime and Justice: A Review of Research*, eds. Michael Tonry and David Farrington (Chicago: University of Chicago Press, 1995), p. 103. Reprinted with permission.

women were the ones most likely to engage in date rape (especially if they drank on a weekly basis). Those who believed their peers would reject and disapprove of their behavior were deterred from victimizing women. Peer rejection and disapproval may be a form of moral guardianship that can deter even motivated offenders from engaging in law-violating behavior.[65]

Lifestyle, opportunity, and routine activities   Routine activities theory is bound up in opportunity and

lifestyle. A person's living arrangements can affect victim risk; people who live in unguarded areas are at the mercy of motivated offenders. Lifestyle affects the opportunity for crime because it controls a person's (1) proximity to criminals, (2) time of exposure to criminals, (3) attractiveness as a target, and (4) ability to be protected.[66]

Ronald Clarke shows the relationship among opportunity, routine activities, and environmental factors in Figure 4.4. Criminal opportunities (like suitable victims and targets) abound in urban environments where facilitators (such as guns and drugs) are also readily found. Environmental factors, such as physical layout and cultural style, may either facilitate or restrict criminal opportunity. Motivated offenders living in these urban hot spots continually learn about criminal opportunities from peers, the media, and their own perceptions; such information may either escalate their criminal motivation or warn them of its danger.[67]

Empirical support Cohen and Felson argue that crime rates increased between 1960 and 1980 because the number of adult caretakers at home during the day (guardians) had decreased as a result of increased female participation in the workforce. While mothers are at work and children in day care, homes are left unguarded. A recent study by Steven Messner and his associates found that between the years of 1967 and 1998, as unemployment rates increased, juvenile homicide arrest rates decreased, a finding that supports the effects of adult supervision on juvenile crime predicted by routine activities theory.[68]

Similarly, with the growth of suburbia during the 1960s, traditional urban neighborhoods were in transition and/or decline, and the number of such familiar guardians as family, neighbors, and friends had diminished. At the same time, the volume of easily transportable wealth increased, creating a greater number of available targets.[69] These structural changes in society led to 30 years of increasing crime rates. To counteract these forces, some communities are becoming better organized, restricting traffic, changing street patterns, and limiting neighborhood entrances to control the opportunity to commit crime and reduce the chances of residents' victimization.[70]

Skyrocketing drug use in the 1980s created an excess of motivated offenders, and the rates of some crimes, such as robbery, increased dramatically. Crime rates may have fallen in the 1990s because a robust economy decreased the pool of motivated offenders and the growing number of police officers increased guardianship.[71] If crime is rational, criminal motivation should be reduced if potential offenders perceive alternatives to crime; in contrast, the perception of opportunities for crime should increase criminal motivation. The Criminological Enterprise feature on crime in everyday life shows how these relationships can be influenced by cultural and structural change.

■ Caring for the Victim

National victim surveys indicate that almost every American age 12 and over will one day become the victim of a common-law crime, such as larceny or burglary, and in the aftermath suffer financial problems, mental stress, and physical hardship.[72] Surveys show that upward of 75 percent of the general public has been victimized by crime at least once in their lives; as many as 25 percent of the victims develop posttraumatic stress syndrome, and their

symptoms last for more than a decade after the crime occurred.[73] The long-term effects of sexual victimization can include years of problem avoidance, social withdrawal, and self-criticism.[74]

Helping the victim to cope is the responsibility of all of society. Law enforcement agencies, courts, and correctional and human service systems have come to realize that due process and human rights exist for both the defendant and the victim of criminal behavior.

The Government's Response

Because of public concern over violent personal crime, President Ronald Reagan created a Task Force on Victims of Crime in 1982.[75] This group suggested that a balance be achieved between recognizing the victim's rights and providing the defendant with due process. Recommendations included providing witnesses and victims with protection from intimidation, requiring restitution in criminal cases, developing guidelines for fair treatment of crime victims and witnesses, and expanding programs of victim compensation.[76] Consequently, the Omnibus Victim and Witness Protection Act was passed, which required the use of victim impact statements at sentencing in federal criminal cases, greater protection for witnesses, more stringent bail laws, and the use of restitution in criminal cases.

The Office for Victims of Crime (OVC) was established by the 1984 Victims of Crime Act (VOCA) to oversee diverse programs that benefit victims of crime. OVC provides substantial funding to state victim assistance and compensation programs and supports training designed to educate criminal justice and allied professionals regarding the rights and needs of crime victims. For more information on this topic, go to:
  http://www.ojp.usdoj.gov/ovc/welcovc/
  welcome.html
For an up-to-date list of Web links, go to
  http://info.wadsworth.com/siegel ■

In 1984 the Comprehensive Crime Control Act and the Victims of Crime Act authorized federal funding for state victim compensation and assistance projects.[77] With these acts, the federal government began to aid the plight of the victim and make victim assistance an even greater concern of the public and the justice system.

The National Center for Victims of Crime (NCVC) in Arlington, Virginia, conducts research on the the effectiveness of state constitutional amendments and other laws designed to protect victims. To learn more about its work on InfoTrac College Edition, read:
Julie Brienza. Crime victim laws sometimes ignored. *Trial* May 1999 v35 i5 p103 ■

Crime and Everyday Life

A core premise of routine activities theory is that all things being equal, the greater the *opportunity* to commit crime, the *higher* the crime and victimization rate. This thesis is cogently presented by Marcus Felson in *Crime and Everyday Life*. Using a routine activities perspective, Felson shows why he believes U.S. crime rates are so high and why U.S. citizens suffer such high rates of victimization.

According to Felson, there are always impulsive, motivated offenders who are willing to take the chance, if conditions are right, of committing crime for profit. Therefore, crime rates are a function of changing social conditions. Crime in the United States grew as the country changed from a nation of small villages and towns to one of large urban environments. In a village, not only could a thief be easily recognized but the commodities stolen could be identified long after the crime occurred. Cities provided the critical population mass, which allowed predatory criminals to hide and evade apprehension. After the crime, criminals could blend into the crowd, disperse their loot, and make a quick escape using the public transportation system.

The modern-day equivalent of the urban center is the shopping mall. Here, strangers converge in large numbers and youths "hang out." The interior is filled with people, so drug deals can be concealed in the pedestrian flow. Stores have attractively displayed goods, which encourage shoplifting and employee pilferage. Substantial numbers of cars are parked in areas that make larceny and car theft virtually undetectable. Cars that carry away stolen merchandise have an undistinguished appearance. Who notices people placing items in a car in a shopping mall lot? Also, shoppers can be attacked in parking lots as people go in isolation to and from their cars.

As the suburbs grew in importance, the divergent metropolis was created. Labor and family life began

to be scattered away from the household, decreasing guardianship (see Exhibit A). The convenience of microwave ovens, automatic dishwashers, and increased emphasis on fast food offerings now free adolescents from common household chores. Rather than help prepare the family dinner and wash dishes afterward, adolescents have the freedom to meet with their peers and avoid parental controls. As car ownership increases, teens have greater access to transportation outside of parental control. Greater mobility and access to transportation make it impossible for neighbors to know if a teen belongs in an area or is an intruder planning to commit a crime. As schools become larger and more complex, they provide ideal sites for crime. The many hallways and corridors prevent teachers from knowing who belongs where; spacious school grounds reduce teacher supervision.

Felson believes these changes in the structure and function of society have been responsible for changes in the crime rates. He concludes that rather than change people crime prevention strategies must be established to reduce the opportunity to commit crime.

Exhibit A How Development of the Divergent Metropolis Has Increased Crime Levels

1. It has become more difficult to protect people from criminal entry because homes have been dispersed over larger areas, huge parking lots have been created, and building heights lowered.
2. There are fewer people in each household and consequently less intrapersonal and intrafamily supervision.
3. By spreading people and vehicles over larger areas as they travel and park, people are more exposed to attack.
4. As shopping, work, and socializing are spread farther from home, people are forced to leave their immediate neighborhood, and, as strangers, they become more vulnerable to attack.
5. By spreading vast quantities of retail goods throughout huge stores and malls, with fewer employees to watch over them, the divergent metropolis creates a retail environment that invites people of all ages to shoplift.
6. Commuting to the inner city for work requires that millions of dollars worth of vehicles be left in parking lots without supervision.

Critical Thinking Questions

1. What recent technological changes influence crime rates? The Internet? Video and computer games? Paging systems? Fax machines? Automatic teller systems?
2. Would increased family contact decrease adolescent crime rates, or would it increase the opportunity for child abuse?

 InfoTrac College Edition Research

To see how the routine activities approach is used to explain violent victimizations, see:

Thoroddur Bjarnason, Thordis J. Sigurdardottir, and Thorolfur Thorlindsson. Human agency, capable guardians, and structural constraints: a lifestyle approach to the study of violent victimization. *Journal of Youth and Adolescence* Feb 1999 v28 i1 p105(1)

SOURCE: Marcus Felson, *Crime and Everyday Life, Insights and Implications for Society* (Thousand Oaks, Calif.: Pine Forge Press, 1994; 3d ed., 2002), Exhibit A at pp. 57–59.

Victim Service Programs

An estimated 2,000 **victim-witness assistance programs** have developed around the United States.[78] Victim-witness assistance programs are organized on a variety of governmental levels and serve a variety of clients. We will look at the most prominent forms of victim services operating in the United States.[79]

The National Organization for Victim Assistance is a private, nonprofit organization of victim and witness assistance programs and practitioners, criminal justice agencies and professionals, mental health professionals, researchers, former victims and survivors, and others committed to the recognition and implementation of victim rights and services. To learn more about these services, go to:

> **http://www.try-nova.org/**

For an up-to-date list of Web links, go to
> **http://info.wadsworth.com/siegel** ■

Victim compensation One of the primary goals of victim advocates has been to lobby for legislation creating crime **victim compensation** programs.[80] As a result of such legislation, the victim ordinarily receives compensation from the state to pay for damages associated with the crime. Rarely are two compensation schemes alike, however, and many state programs suffer from lack of both adequate funding and proper organization within the criminal justice system. Compensation may be made for medical bills, loss of wages, loss of future earnings, and counseling. In the case of death, the victim's survivors can receive burial expenses and aid for loss of support.[81] Awards are typically in the $100 to $15,000 range. Occasionally programs will provide emergency assistance to indigent victims until compensation is available. Emergency assistance may come in the form of food vouchers or replacement of prescription medicines.

It is the Mission of the Crime Victims Board of New York to provide compensation to innocent victims of crime in a timely, efficient, and compassionate manner, to fund direct services to crime victims via a network of community-based programs, and to advocate for the rights and benefits of all innocent victims of crime. You can learn more about this program at:

> **http://www.cvb.state.ny.us/**

For an up-to-date list of Web links, go to
> **http://info.wadsworth.com/siegel** ■

Court services A common victim program service helps victims deal with the criminal justice system. One approach is to prepare victims and witnesses by explaining court procedures: how to be a witness, how bail works, and what to do if the defendant makes a threat. Lack of

■ Antonio Jorge, center, sits next to his wife, Laura Jorge, while being comforted by Elaine Rendine, director of the Victim's Assistance Program, as the jury announces on February 13, 1998, that it has found Charles Smith guilty of first-degree murder in the death of Jorge's 16-year-old stepdaughter, Kristen M. Jorge.

such knowledge can cause confusion and fear, making some victims reluctant to testify in court proceedings. Many victim programs also provide transportation to and from court and counselors, who remain in the courtroom during hearings to explain procedures and provide support. Court escorts are particularly important for elderly and disabled victims, victims of child abuse and assault, and victims who have been intimidated by friends or relatives of the defendant.

Public education More than half of all victim programs include public education programs that help familiarize the general public with their services and with other agencies that help crime victims. In some instances, these are primary education programs, which teach methods of dealing with conflict without resorting to violence. For example, school-based programs present information on spousal and dating abuse followed by discussions of how to reduce violent incidents.[82]

Crisis intervention Most victim programs refer victims to specific services to help them recover from their ordeal. Clients are commonly referred to the local network of public and private social service agencies that can provide emergency and long-term assistance with transportation, medical care, shelter, food, and clothing. In addition, more than half of victim programs provide **crisis intervention** to victims, many of whom feel isolated, vulnerable, and in need of immediate services. Some programs counsel at their offices, and others visit victims' homes, the crime scene, or a hospital.

Victim–offender reconciliation programs Victim–offender reconciliation programs (VORPs) use mediators to facilitate face-to-face encounters between victims and their attackers. The aim is to engage in direct negotiations that lead to **restitution agreements** and, possibly, reconciliation between the two parties involved.[83] More than 120 reconciliation programs are currently in operation, and they handle an estimated 16,000 cases per year. Designed at first to handle routine misdemeanors such as petty theft and vandalism, programs now commonly hammer out restitution agreements in more serious incidents such as residential burglary and even attempted murder.

CONNECTIONS

Reconciliation programs are based on the concept of restorative justice, which rejects punitive correctional measures and instead suggests that crimes of violence and theft should be viewed as interpersonal conflicts that need to be settled in the community through noncoercive means. See Chapter 8 for more on this approach. ■

Victims' Rights

Legal scholar Frank Carrington suggests that crime victims have legal rights that should assure them of basic services from the government.[84] According to Carrington, just as the defendant has the right to counsel and a fair trial, society is also obliged to ensure basic rights for law-abiding citizens. These rights range from adequate protection from violent crimes to victim compensation and assistance from the criminal justice system. Some suggested changes that might enhance the relationship between the victim and the criminal justice system are included in Exhibit 4.1.

About 14 states have actually incorporated language similar to that shown in Exhibit 4.1 in their legal codes in a "Victims' Bill of Rights." Victims are now entitled to find out about the progress of their cases in 22 states and to be

---

Exhibit 4.1   Proposed Victims' Rights

- Liberally using preventive detention (pretrial jailing without the right to bail) for dangerous criminals awaiting trial
- Eliminating delays between the arrest and the initial hearing and between the hearing and the trial, which would limit the opportunity an offender has to intimidate victims or witnesses
- Eliminating plea bargaining, or if that proves impossible, allowing victims to participate in the plea negotiations
- Controlling defense attorneys' cross-examination of victims
- Allowing hearsay testimony of police at the preliminary hearing instead of requiring the victim to appear

- Abolishing the exclusionary rule, which allows the guilty to go free on technicalities
- Allowing victims to participate in sentencing
- Creating minimum mandatory sentences for crimes
- Prohibiting murderers given life sentences from being freed on parole
- Making criminals serve time for each crime they are convicted of and reducing the use of concurrent sentences, which allows them to simultaneously serve time for multiple crimes
- Tightening the granting of parole and allowing victims to participate in parole hearings
- Providing full restitution or compensation to victims in all crimes

SOURCE: Frank Carrington, "Victim's Rights Litigation: A Wave of the Future," in *Perspectives on Crime Victims*, eds. Burt Galaway and Joe Hudson (St. Louis: C.V. Mosby Co., 1981).

present at sentencing hearings in 37 states and at parole hearings in 36 states.[85]

Victim Advocacy

Assuring victims' rights can involve an eclectic group of advocacy groups, some independent, others government-sponsored, and some self-help. Advocates can be especially helpful when victims need to interact with the agencies of justice. For example, advocates can lobby police departments to keep investigations open as well as request the return of recovered stolen property. They can demand from prosecutors and judges protection from harassment and reprisals by, for example, making "no contact" a condition of bail. They can help victims make statements during sentencing hearings as well as probation and parole revocation procedures. Victim advocates can also interact with news media, making sure that reporting is accurate and that victim privacy is not violated. Victim advocates can be part of an independent agency similar to a legal aid society. If successful, top-notch advocates may eventually open private offices, similar to attorneys, private investigators, or jury consultants.[86]

To read about how health care providers can help the victims of domestic violence, read this article by Nancy E. Isaac and V. Pualani Enos, "Documenting Domestic Violence: How Health Care Providers Can Help Victims," at:

http://www.ncjrs.org/pdffiles1/nij/188564.pdf

For an up-to-date list of Web links, go to

http://info.wadsworth.com/siegel ■

Self-Protection

Although the general public mostly approves of the police, fear of crime and concern about community safety have prompted many people to become their own "police force," taking an active role in community protection and citizen crime control groups.[87] The more crime in an area, the greater the amount of fear, and the more likely residents will be to engage in self-protective measures.[88]

Research indicates that a significant number of crimes may not be reported to police simply because victims prefer to take matters into their own hands.[89] One manifestation of this trend is the concept of **target hardening,** or making one's home and business crime proof through locks, bars, alarms, and other devices.[90] Other commonly used crime prevention techniques include a fence or barricade at the entrance; a doorkeeper, guard, or receptionist in an apartment building; an intercom or phone to gain access to the building; surveillance cameras; window bars; warning signs; and dogs chosen for their ability to guard the house. The use of these measures was inversely proportional to perception of neighborhood safety: people who feared crime were more likely to use crime-prevention techniques.

Although the true relationship is still unclear, there is mounting evidence that people who protect their homes are less likely to be victimized by property crimes.[91] One study conducted in the Philadelphia area found that people who install burglar alarms are less likely to suffer burglary than those who forgo similar preventive measures.[92]

Some people take self-protection to its ultimate end by preparing to fight back when criminals attack them. How successful are victims when they fight back? Research indicates that victims who fight back often frustrate their attackers but also face increased odds of being physically harmed during the attack.[93] In some cases, fighting back decreases the odds of a crime being completed but increases the victim's chances of injury.[94] Resistance may draw the attention of bystanders and make a violent crime physically difficult to complete. It can also cause offenders to escalate their violence.[95]

What about the use of firearms? Each year victims use guns for defensive purposes 2.5 million times, a number that is not surprising considering that about one-third of U.S. households contain guns.[96] Gary Kleck has estimated that armed victims kill between 1,500 and 2,800 potential felons each year and wound between 8,700 and 16,000. Kleck's research shows, ironically, that by fighting back victims kill far more criminals than the estimated 250 to 1,000 killed annually by police.[97] Kleck has found that the risk of collateral injury is relatively rare and that potential victims should be encouraged to fight back.[98] According to Kleck, empirical research studies unanimously show that defensive gun use is associated with both lower rates of crime completion and lower rates of injury to the victim.[99]

Community Organization

Not everyone is capable of buying a handgun or semiautomatic weapon and doing battle with predatory criminals. An alternative approach has been for communities to organize on the neighborhood level against crime. Citizens have been working independently and in cooperation with local police agencies in neighborhood patrol and block watch programs. These programs organize local citizens in urban areas to patrol neighborhoods, watch for suspicious people, help secure the neighborhood, lobby for improvements (such as increased lighting), report crime to police, put out community newsletters, conduct home security surveys, and serve as a source for crime information or tips.[100] Although such programs are welcome additions to police services, there is little evidence that they appreciably affect the crime rate. There is also concern that their effectiveness is spottier in low-income, high-crime areas, which need the most crime prevention assistance.[101] Block watches and neighborhood patrols seem more successful when they are part of general-purpose or multi-issue community groups rather than when they focus directly on crime problems.[102]

Table 4.4   Victimization Theories

Theory	Major Premise	Strengths
Victim precipitation	Victims trigger criminal acts by their provocative behavior. Active precipitation involves fighting words or gestures. Passive precipitation occurs when victims unknowingly threaten their attacker.	Explains multiple victimizations. If people precipitate crime, it follows that they will become repeat victims if their behavior persists over time.
Lifestyle	Victimization risk is increased when people have a high-risk lifestyle. Placing oneself at risk by going out to dangerous places results in increased victimization.	Explains victimization patterns in the social structure. Males, young people, and the poor have high victimization rates because they have a higher-risk lifestyle than females, the elderly, and the affluent.
Deviant place theory	People who live in deviant places are at high risk for crime. Victim behavior has little influence over the criminal act.	Places the focus of crime on deviant places. Shows why people with conventional lifestyles become crime victims.
Routine activities	Crime rates can be explained by the availability of suitable targets, the absence of capable guardians, and the presence of motivated offenders.	Can explain crime rates and trends. Shows how victim behavior can influence criminal opportunity. Suggests that victimization risk can be reduced by increasing guardianship and/or reducing target vulnerability.

Summary

Criminologists now consider victims and victimization a major focus of study. More than 25 million U.S. citizens suffer from crime each year, and the social and economic costs of crime are in the billions of dollars. Like crime, victimization has stable patterns and trends. Violent crime victims tend to be young, poor, single males living in large cities, although victims come in all ages, sizes, races, and genders. Many victimizations occur in the home, and many victims are the target of relatives and loved ones.

There are a number of theories of victimization. One view, called victim precipitation, is that victims provoke criminals. More common are lifestyle theories, which suggest that victims put themselves in danger by engaging in high-risk activities, such as going out late at night, living in a high-crime area, and associating with high-risk peers. Deviant place theory argues that victimization risk is related to neighborhood crime rates. The routine activities theory maintains that a pool of motivated offenders exists and that these offenders will take advantage of unguarded, suitable targets. The major theories of victimization are summarized in Table 4.4.

Numerous programs help victims by providing court services, eco-nomic compensation, public education, and crisis intervention. Some people suggest that the U.S. Constitution should be amended to include protection of victims' rights. Rather than depend on the justice system, some victims have attempted to help themselves. In some instances, this self-help means community organization for self-protection. In other instances, victims have armed themselves and fought back against their attackers. There is evidence that fighting back reduces the number of completed crimes but is also related to victim injury.

Thinking Like a Criminologist

The director of the state's department of human services has asked you to evaluate a self-report survey of adolescents ages 10 to 18. She has provided you with the following information on physical abuse:

Adolescents experiencing abuse or violence are at high risk of immediate and lasting negative effects on health and well-being. Of the high school students surveyed, an alarming one in five (21 percent) said they had been physically abused. Of the older students, ages 15 to 18, 29 percent said they had been physically abused. Younger students also reported significant rates of abuse: 17 percent responded "yes" when asked whether they had been physically abused. Although girls were far less likely to report abuse than boys,

12 percent said they had been physically abused. Most abuse occurs at home, occurs more than once, and the abuser is usually a family member. More than half of those physically abused had tried alcohol and drugs, and 60 percent had admitted to a violent act. Nonabused children were significantly less likely to abuse sub-

stances, and only 30 percent indicated they had committed a violent act.

How would you interpret these data? What factors might influence their validity? What is your interpretation of the association between abuse and delinquency?

■ Key Terms

- **victimologists** *(82)*
- **victimization** *(84)*
- **posttraumatic stress disorder** *(84)*
- **obsessive-compulsive disorder** *(84)*
- **altruistic fear** *(85)*
- **cycle of violence** *(85)*
- **elder abuse** *(87)*
- **chronic victimization** *(89)*

- **siblicide** *(90)*
- **victim precipitation view** *(91)*
- **active precipitation** *(91)*
- **passive precipitation** *(91)*
- **suitable targets** *(92)*
- **capable guardians** *(92)*
- **motivated offenders** *(92)*
- **date rape** *(93)*

- **victim-witness assistance program** *(97)*
- **victim compensation** *(97)*
- **crisis intervention** *(98)*
- **restitution agreements** *(98)*
- **target hardening** *(99)*

■ Critical Thinking Questions

1. Considering what we learned in this chapter about crime victimization, what measures can you take to better protect yourself from crime?

2. Do you agree with the assessment that a school is one of the most dangerous locations in the com-

munity? Did you find your high school to be a dangerous environment?

3. Does a person bear some of the responsibility for his or her victimization if the person maintains a lifestyle that contributes to the chances of becoming a crime vic-

itm? That is, should we "blame the victim"?

4. Have you ever experienced someone "precipitating" crime? If so, did you do anything to help the situation?

■ Notes

1. Mark Pazniokas, "Mayor again Denied Bail, Giordano Remains Flight Risk, Judge Says," *Hartford Courant,* 9 November 2001, A1; Associated Press, "Waterbury Mayor Paid Teenager for Sex, Reports Say," *New York Times,* 16 August 2001, p.1.

2. Richard Estes and Neil Alan Weiner, *The Commercial Sexual Exploitation of Children in the U.S., Canada and Mexico* (Philadelphia, Pa.: University of Pennsylvania, 2001).

3. Data in this secton are based on Callie Marie Rennison, *Criminal Victimization 2000 Changes 1999–2000 with Trends 1993-2000* (Washington, D.C.: Bureau of Justice Statistics, 2001).

4. Arthur Lurigio, "Are All Victims Alike? The Adverse, Generalized, and Differential Impact of Crime," *Crime and Delinquency* 33 (1987): 452–67.

5. FBI, *Crime in the United States, 2000* (Washington, D.C.: U.S. Government Printing Office, 2001), p. 201. Hereinafter cited as FBI, Uniform Crime Report, 2000.

6. Ted Miller, Mark Cohen, and Brian Wiersema, *The Extent and Costs of Crime Victimization: A New Look* (Washington, D.C.: National Institute of Justice, 1996).

7. George Rengert, *The Geography of Illegal Drugs* (Boulder, Colo.: Westview Press, 1996), p. 5.

8. Ross Macmillan, "Adolescent Victimization and Income Deficits in Adulthood: Rethinking the Costs of Criminal Violence from a Life-Course Perspective," *Criminology* 38 (2000): 553–88.

9. Rebecca Campbell and Sheela Raja, "Secondary Victimization of Rape Victims: Insights from Mental Health Pro-

fessionals Who Treat Survivors of Violence," *Violence and Victims* 14 (1999): 261–74.

10. Peter Finn, *Victims* (Washington, D.C.: Bureau of Justice Statistics, 1988), p. 1.

11. Michael Wiederman, Randy Sansone, and Lori Sansone, "History of Trauma and Attempted Suicide among Women in a Primary Care Setting," *Violence and Victims* 13 (1998): 3–11; Susan Leslie Bryant and Lillian Range, "Suicidality in College Women Who Were Sexually and Physically Abused and Physically Punished by Parents," *Violence and Victims* 10 (1995): 195–215; William Downs and Brenda Miller, "Relationships between Experiences of Parental Violence During Childhood and Women's Self-Esteem," *Violence and Victims* 13 (1998): 63–78; Sally Davies-Netley, Michael Hurlburt, and Richard Hough, "Childhood Abuse as a Precursor to Home-

lessness for Homeless Women with Severe Mental Illness," *Violence and Victims* 11 (1996): 129–42.

12. Jeanne Kaufman and Cathy Spatz Widom, "Childhood Victimization, Running Away, and Delinquency," *Journal of Research in Crime and Delinquency* 36 (1999): 347–70.

13. Dina Vivian and Jean Malone, "Relationship Factors and Depressive Symptomology Associated with Mild and Severe Husband-to-Wife Physical Aggression," *Violence and Victims* 12 (1997): 19–37; Walter Gleason, "Mental Disorders in Battered Women," *Violence and Victims* 8 (1993): 53–66. Daniel Saunders, "Posttraumatic Stress Symptom Profiles of Battered Women: A Comparison of Survivors in Two Settings," *Violence and Victims* 9 (1994): 31–43.

14. K. Daniel O'Leary, "Psychological Abuse: A Variable Deserving Critical Attention in Domestic Violence," *Violence and Victims* 14 (1999): 1–21.

15. James Anderson, Terry Grandison, and Laronistine Dyson, "Victims of Random Violence and the Public Health Implication: A Health Care of Criminal Justice Issue," *Journal of Criminal Justice* 24 (1996): 379–93.

16. Ross Macmillan, Annette Nierobisz, and Sandy Welsh, "Experiencing the Streets: Harassment and Perceptions of Safety among Women," *Journal of Research in Crime and Delinquency* 37 (2000): 306–22.

17. Pamela Wilcox Rountree, "A Reexamination of the Crime–Fear Linkage," *Journal of Research in Crime and Delinquency* 35 (1998): 341–72.

18. Robert Davis, Bruce Taylor, and Arthur Lurigio, "Adjusting to Criminal Victimization: The Correlates of Postcrime Distress," *Violence and Victimization* 11 (1996): 21–34.

19. Mark Warr and Christopher G. Ellison, "Rethinking Social Reactions to Crime: Personal and Altruistic Fear in Family Households," *American Journal of Sociology* 106 (2000): 551–79.

20. Timothy Ireland and Cathy Spatz Widom, *Childhood Victimization and Risk for Alcohol and Drug Arrests* (Washington, D.C.: National Institute of Justice, 1995).

21. Brigette Erwin, Elana Newman, Robert McMackin, Carlo Morrissey, Danny Kaloupek, "PTSD, Malevolent Environment, and Criminality among Criminally Involved Male Adolescents," *Criminal Justice and Behavior* 27 (2000): 196–215.

22. Cathy Spatz Widom, *The Cycle of Violence* (Washington, D.C.: National Institute of Justice, 1992), p. 1.

23. Steve Spaccarelli, J. Douglas Coatsworth, and Blake Sperry Bowden, "Exposure to Serious Family Violence among Incarcerated Boys: Its Association with Violent Offending and Potential Mediating Variables," *Violence and Victims* 10 (1995): 163–80; Jerome Kolbo, "Risk and Resilience among Children Exposed to Family Violence," *Violence and Victims* 11 (1996): 113–27.

24. M. Dwayne Smith and Victoria Brewer, "A Sex-Specific Analysis of Correlates of Homicide Victimization in United States Cities," *Violence and Victims* 7 (1992): 279–87.

25. Ronet Bachman, *Violence against Women* (Washington, D.C.: Bureau of Justice Statistics, 1994).

26. Michael Rand, *Violence-Related Injuries Treated in Hospital Emergency Departments* (Washington, D.C.: Bureau of Justice Statistics, 1997).

27. Richard Rosenfeld, "Changing Relationships between Men and Women: A Note on the Decline in Intimate Partner Homicide," *Homicide Studies* 1 (1997): 72–83.

28. Desmond Ellis and Lori Wright, "Estrangement, Interventions, and Male Violence toward Female Partners," *Violence and Victims* 12 (1997): 51–68.

29. Karin Wittebrood and Paul Nieuwbeerta, "Criminal Victimization During One's Life Course: The Effects of Previous Victimization and Patterns of Routine Activities," *Journal of Research in Crime and Delinquency* 37 (2000): 91–122; Janet Lauritsen and Kenna Davis Quinet, "Repeat Victimizations among Adolescents and Young Adults," *Journal of Quantitative Criminology* 11 (1995): 143–63.

30. Denise Osborn, Dan Ellingworth, Tim Hope, and Alan Trickett, "Are Repeatedly Victimized Households Different?" *Journal of Quantitative Criminology* 12 (1996): 223–45.

31. Graham Farrell, "Predicting and Preventing Revictimization," in *Crime and Justice: An Annual Review of Research*, Vol. 20, eds. Michael Tonry and David Farrington (Chicago: University of Chicago Press, 1995), pp. 61–126.

32. Ibid., p. 161.

33. David Finkelhor and Nancy Asigian, "Risk Factors for Youth Victimization: Beyond a Lifestyles/Routine Activities Theory Approach," *Violence and Victimization* 11 (1996): 3–19.

34. Graham Farrell, Coretta Phillips, and Ken Pease, "Like Taking Candy: Why Does Repeat Victimization Occur?" *British Journal of Criminology* 35 (1995): 384–99.

35. Christopher Innes and Lawrence Greenfeld, *Violent State Prisoners and Their Victims* (Washington, D.C.: Bureau of Justice Statistics, 1999).

36. Hans Von Hentig, *The Criminal and His Victim: Studies in the Sociobiology of Crime* (New Haven, Conn.: Yale University Press, 1948), p. 384.

37. Marvin Wolfgang, *Patterns of Criminal Homicide* (Philadelphia: University of Pennsylvania Press, 1958).

38. Menachem Amir, *Patterns in Forcible Rape* (Chicago: University of Chicago Press, 1971).

39. Susan Estrich, *Real Rape* (Cambridge: Harvard University Press, 1987).

40. Edem Avakame, "Female's Labor Force Participation and Intimate Femicide: An Empirical Assessment of the Backlash Hypothesis," *Violence and Victims* 14 (1999): 277–83.

41. Martin Daly and Margo Wilson, *Homicide* (New York: Aldine de Gruyter, 1988).

42. Rosemary Gartner and Bill McCarthy, "The Social Distribution of Femicide in Urban Canada, 1921–1988," *Law and Society Review* 25 (1991): 287–311.

43. Lening Zhang, John W. Welte, and William F. Wieczorek, "Deviant Lifestyle and Crime Victimization," *Journal of Criminal Justice* 29 (2001): 133–43.

44. Dan Hoyt, Kimberly Ryan, and Mari Cauce, "Personal Victimizaton in a High-Risk Environment: Homeless and Runaway Adolescents," *Journal of Research in Crime and Delinquency* 36 (1999): 371–92.

45. See, generally, Gary Gottfredson and Denise Gottfredson, *Victimization in Schools* (New York: Plenum Press, 1985).

46. Gary Jensen and David Brownfield, "Gender, Lifestyles, and Victimization: Beyond Routine Activity Theory," *Violence and Victims* 1 (1986): 85–99.

47. Rolf Loeber, Mary DeLamatre, George Tita, Jacqueline Cohen, Magda Stouthamer-Loeber, and David Farrington, "Gun Injury and Mortality: The Delinquent Backgrounds of Juvenile Offenders," *Violence and Victims* 14 (1999): 339–51.

48. Bonnie Fisher, John Sloan, Francis Cullen, and Chunmeng Lu, "Crime in the Ivory Tower: The Level and Sources of Student Victimization," *Criminology* 36 (1998): 671–710.

49. Adam Dobrin, "The Risk of Offending on Homicide Victimization: A Case Control Study," *Journal of Research in Crime and Delinquency* 38 (2001): 154–73.

50. Rolf Loeber, Larry Kalb, and David Huizinga, *Juvenile Delinquency and Serious Injury Victimization* (Washington, D.C.: Office of Juvenile Justice and Delinquency Prevention, 2001).

51. James Garofalo, "Reassessing the Lifestyle Model of Criminal Victimization," in *Positive Criminology*, eds. Michael Gottfredson and Travis Hirschi (Newbury Park, Calif.: Sage, 1987), pp. 23–42.

52. Terance Miethe and David McDowall, "Contextual Effects in Models of Criminal Victimization," *Social Forces* 71 (1993): 741–59.

53. Rodney Stark, "Deviant Places: A Theory of the Ecology of Crime," *Criminology* 25 (1987): 893–911.

54. Ibid., p. 902.

55. Pamela Wilcox Rountree, Kenneth Land, and Terance Miethe, "Macro–Micro Integration in the Study of Victimization: A Hierarchical Logistic Model Analysis across Seattle Neighborhoods." Paper presented at the annual meeting of the American Society of Criminology, Phoenix, Arizona, November 1993.

56. William Julius Wilson, *The Truly Disadvantaged* (Chicago: University of Chicago Press, 1990); see also, Allen Liska and Paul Bellair, "Violent-Crime Rates and Racial Composition: Convergence over Time," *American Journal of Sociology* 101 (1995): 578–610.

57. Lawrence Cohen and Marcus Felson, "Social Change and Crime Rate Trends: A Routine Activities Approach," *American Sociological Review* 44 (1979): 588–608.

58. Teresa LaGrange, "The Impact of Neighborhoods, Schools, and Malls on the Spatial Distribution of Property Damage," *Journal of Research in Crime and Delinquency* 36 (1999): 393–422.

59. Georgina Hammock and Deborah Richardson, "Perceptions of Rape: The Influence of Closeness of Relationship, Intoxication, and Sex of Participant," *Violence and Victimization* 12 (1997): 237–47.

60. Wittebrood and Nieuwbeerta, "Criminal Victimization During One's Life Course," pp. 112–13.

61. Don Weatherburn, Bronwyn Lind, Simha Ku, "'Hotbeds of Crime?' Crime and Public Housing in Urban Sydney," *Crime and Delinquency* 45 (1999): 256–71.

62. Andy Hochstetler, "Opportunities and Decisions: Interactional Dynamics in Robbery and Burglary Groups," *Criminology* 39 (2001): 737–63.

63. Richard Felson, "Routine Activities and Involvement in Violence as Actor, Witness, or Target," *Violence and Victimization* 12 (1997): 209–23.

64. Jon Gunnar Bernburg and Thorolfur Thorlindsson, "Routine Activities in Social Context: A Closer Look at the Role of Opportunity in Deviant Behavior," *Justice Quarterly* 18 (2001): 543–68.

65. Martin Schwartz, Walter DeKeseredy, David Tait, and Shahid Alvi, "Male Peer Support and a Feminist Routine Activities Theory: Understanding Sexual Assault on the College Campus," *Justice Quarterly* 18 (2001): 623–50.

66. Terence Miethe and Robert Meier, *Crime and Its Social Context: Toward an Integrated Theory of Offenders, Victims, and Situations* (Albany, N.Y.: State University of New York Press, 1994).

67. Ronald Clarke, "Situational Crime Prevention," in *Building a Safer Society, Strategic Approaches to Crime Prevention, Vol. 19 of Crime and Justice, A Review of Research,* eds. Michael Tonry and David Farrington (Chicago: University of Chicago Press, 1995), 91–151.

68. Steven Messner, Lawrence Raffalovich and Richard McMillan, "Economic Deprivation and Changes in Homicide Arrest Rates for White and Black Youths, 1967–1998: A National Time-Series Analysis," *Criminology* 39 (2001): 591–614.

69. Lawrence Cohen, Marcus Felson, and Kenneth Land, "Property Crime Rates in the United States: A Macrodynamic Analysis, 1947–1977, with Ex-ante Forecasts for the Mid-1980s," *American Journal of Sociology* 86 (1980): 90–118.

70. Patrick Donnelly and Charles Kimble, "Community Organizing, Environmental Change, and Neighborhood Crime," *Crime and Delinquency* 43 (1997): 493–511.

71. Simha Landau and Daniel Fridman, "The Seasonality of Violent Crime: The Case of Robbery and Homicide in Israel," *Journal of Research in Crime and Delinquency* 30 (1993): 163–91.

72. Patricia Resnick, "Psychological Effects of Victimization: Implications for the Criminal Justice System," *Crime and Delinquency* 33 (1987): 468–78.

73. Dean Kilpatrick, Benjamin Saunders, Lois Veronen, Connie Best, and Judith Von, "Criminal Victimization: Lifetime Prevalence, Reporting to Police, and Psychological Impact," *Crime and Delinquency* 33 (1987): 479–89.

74. Mark Santello and Harold Leitenberg, "Sexual Aggression by an Acquaintance: Methods of Coping and Later Psychological Adjustment," *Violence and Victims* 8 (1993): 91–103.

75. U.S. Department of Justice, *Report of the President's Task Force on Victims of Crime* (Washington, D.C.: U.S. Government Printing Office, 1983).

76. Ibid., pp. 2–10; and "Review on Victims—Witnesses of Crime," *Massachusetts Lawyers Weekly,* 25 April 1983, p. 26.

77. Robert Davis, *Crime Victims: Learning How to Help Them* (Washington, D.C.: National Institute of Justice, 1987).

78. Peter Finn and Beverly Lee, *Establishing a Victim-Witness Assistance Program* (Washington, D.C.: U.S. Government Printing Office, 1988).

79. This section leans heavily on Albert Roberts, "Delivery of Services to Crime Victims: A National Survey," *American Journal of Orthopsychiatry* 6 (1991): 128–37; see also Albert Roberts, *Helping Crime Victims: Research, Policy, and Practice* (Newbury Park, Calif.: Sage, 1990).

80. Randall Schmidt, "Crime Victim Compensation Legislation: A Comparative Study," *Victimology* 5 (1980): 428–37.

81. Ibid.

82. Pater Jaffe, Marlies Sudermann, Deborah Reitzel, and Steve Killip, "An Evaluation of a Secondary School Primary Prevention Program on Violence in Intimate Relationships," *Violence and Victims* 7 (1992): 129–45.

83. Andrew Karmen, "Victim–Offender Reconciliation Programs: Pro and Con," *Perspectives of the American Probation and Parole Association* 20 (1996): 11–14.

84. See Frank Carrington, "Victim's Rights Litigation: A Wave of the Future," in *Perspectives on Crime Victims,* eds. Burt Galaway and Joe Hudson (St. Louis: C.V. Mosby Co., 1981).

85. Andrew Karmen, "Toward the Institutionalization of a New Kind of Justice Professional: The Victim Advocate," *The Justice Professional* 9 (1995): 2–15.

86. Ibid., pp. 9–10.

87. Sara Flaherty and Austin Flaherty, *Victims and Victims' Risk* (New York: Chelsea House, 1998).

88. Pamela Wilcox Rountree and Kenneth Land, "Burglary Victimization, Perceptions of Crime Risk, and Routine Activities: A Multilevel Analysis across Seattle Neighborhoods and Census Tracts," *Journal of Research in Crime and Delinquency* 33 (1996): 1147–80.

89. Leslie Kennedy, "Going It Alone: Unreported Crime and Individual Self-Help," *Journal of Criminal Justice* 16 (1988): 403–13.

90. Ronald Clarke, "Situational Crime Prevention: Its Theoretical Basis and Practical Scope," in *Annual Review of Criminal Justice Research*, eds. Michael Tonry and Norval Morris (Chicago: University of Chicago Press, 1983).

91. See generally, Dennis P. Rosenbaum, Arthur J. Lurigio, and Robert C. Davis, *The Prevention of Crime: Social and Situational Strategies* (Belmont, Calif.: Wadsworth, 1998).

92. Andrew Buck, Simon Hakim, and George Rengert, "Burglar Alarms and the Choice Behavior of Burglars," *Journal of Criminal Justice* 21 (1993): 497–507; for an opposing view, see James Lynch and David Cantor, "Ecological and Behavioral Influences on Property Victimization at Home: Implications for Opportunity Theory," *Journal of Research in Crime and Delinquency* 29 (1992): 335–62.

93. Alan Lizotte, "Determinants of Completing Rape and Assault," *Journal of Quantitative Criminology* 2 (1986): 213–17.

94. Polly Marchbanks, Kung-Jong Lui, and James Mercy, "Risk of Injury from Resisting Rape," *American Journal of Epidemiology* 132 (1990): 540–49.

95. Caroline Wolf Harlow, *Robbery Victims* (Washington, D.C.: Bureau of Justice Statistics, 1987).

96. Gary Kleck, "Guns and Violence: An Interpretive Review of the Field," *Social Pathology* 1 (1995): 12–45, at p. 17.

97. Ibid.

98. Gary Kleck, "Rape and Resistance," *Social Problems* 37 (1990): 149–62.

99. Personal communication with Gary Kleck, 10 January 1997; see also Kleck, "Guns and Violence: An Interpretive Review of the Field."

100. James Garofalo and Maureen McLeod, *Improving the Use and Effectiveness of Neighborhood Watch Programs* (Washington, D.C.: National Institute of Justice, 1988).

101. Peter Finn, *Block Watches Help Crime Victims in Philadelphia* (Washington, D.C.: National Institute of Justice, 1986).

102. Ibid.

An important goal of the criminological enterprise is to create valid and accurate theories of crime causation. A *theory* can be defined as an abstract statement that explains why certain things do (or do not) happen. To be called a theory, this statement must have empirical (observable) implications—that is, it must make predictions that something observable will (or will not) happen under certain specified circumstances.*

Criminologists have sought to collect vital facts about crime and interpret them in a scientifically meaningful fashion. By developing empirically verifiable statements, or hypotheses, and organizing them into theories of crime causation, they hope to identify the causes of crime.

PART II Theories of Crime Causation

Since the late nineteenth century, criminological theory has pointed to various underlying causes of crime. The earliest theories generally attributed crime to a single underlying cause: atypical body build, genetic abnormality, insanity, physical anomalies, or poverty. Later theories attributed crime causation to multiple factors: poverty, peer influence, school problems, and family dysfunction.

In this section, theories of crime causation are grouped into five chapters. Chapters 5 and 6 focus on theories based on individual traits. They hold that crime is either a free-will choice made by an individual, a function of personal psychological or biological abnormality, or both. Chapters 7 through 9 investigate theories based in sociology and political economy. These theories portray crime as a function of the structure, process, and conflicts of social living. Chapter 10 is devoted to theories that combine or integrate these various concepts into a cohesive, complex view of crime.

*Rodney Stark, *Sociology,* 8th ed. (Belmont, Calif.: Wadsworth, 2001), p. 2.

© L. Clarke/CORBIS

CHAPTER 5 Choice Theory

■ Introduction

In May 2001, officials of the United States Drug Enforcement Agency (DEA) announced that despite pouring in more than $1 billion in military aid to Colombia there was little sign that the amount of cocaine entering the United States was in decline. In fact, the price per kilo, about $36,000, had been stable since the U.S.-backed Plan Colombia offensive on drugs began in December of 2000. The plan involved supplying 14 Black Hawk helicopters and training an elite Colombian army battalion to provide cover for crop dusters and to destroy drug labs. Despite these efforts, Colombia produced almost 600 tons of cocaine in 2000, more than double the 1995 crop. Drug dealers are able to avoid the government's antidrug forces by paying a percentage of their profits in "taxes" to left-wing or right-wing warlords who supply them with protection. More than 40,000 lives have been lost in the civil war that rages in Colombia. The destruction of drug cartels in Cali and Medellin have done little to slow the drug trade, and supply now outstrips demand in the United States. As a result, cocaine traffickers no longer seek to increase their presence in the U.S. market and instead are looking toward Europe and the former Soviet Union to create new markets.[1]

Some criminologists consider the complex intrigues of international drug dealers as an indicator that criminal acts are not a matter of random chance but are cool, calculated actions designed to maximize profit and minimize loss. The Colombian drug dealers seem to be carefully analyzing market conditions before deciding on the proper course of action. Is it cheaper to pay off warlords than to try to fight them?—the excess costs can be passed on to consumers. When their marketing people tell them that the U.S. market is saturated, they seek new territories in Europe and Russia. Calculating market risks and rewards seems more like a job for the management team at Microsoft, McDonald's, or Intel rather than for violent drug dealing gangs. The fact that drug traffickers consider the same kinds of information as computer makers or restaurant operators suggests that their decisions to commit crimes are complex and well planned.

If international drug dealers use rational decision making in their daily activities, is it possible that such common crimes as theft, fraud, and even murder are a function of detailed planning and decision making? Are these random, senseless acts or a matter of personal choice, designed to maximize gain and minimize loss? The view that crime is a matter of **rational choice** is held by a number of criminologists who believe the decision to violate any law—commit a robbery, sell drugs, attack a rival, fill out a false tax return—is made for a variety of personal reasons, including greed, revenge, need, anger, lust, jealousy, thrill-seeking, or vanity. Regardless of the motive, criminal actions occur only after individuals careful weigh the potential benefits and consequences of crime. The jealous suitor, for example, concludes that the risk of punishment is worth the satisfaction of punching a rival. The greedy shopper considers the chance of apprehension by store detectives so small that she takes a "five-finger discount" on a new sweater. The drug dealer concludes that the huge profit from a single shipment of cocaine far outweighs the possible costs of apprehension. In the final analysis, people choose crime because it is rewarding, satisfying, easy, or fun.

This chapter reviews the philosophical underpinnings of choice theory, tracing it back to the classical school of criminology. We then turn to more recent theoretical models that flow from the concept of choice. These models hold that because criminals are rational their behavior can be controlled or deterred by the fear of punishment; desistance can then be explained by a growing and intense fear of criminal sanctions. These views include situational crime control, general deterrence theory, specific deterrence theory, and incapacitation. Finally, the chapter briefly reviews how choice theory has influenced criminal justice policy.

■ The Development of Rational Choice Theory

Rational choice theory has its roots in the classical school of criminology developed by the Italian social thinker Cesare Beccaria.[2] In keeping with his utilitarian views, Beccaria called for fair and certain punishment to deter crime. He believed people are egotistical and self-centered, and therefore they must be motivated by the fear of punishment, which provides a tangible motive for them to obey the law and suppress the "despotic spirit" that resides in every person.[3]

CONNECTIONS

As you may recall from Chapter 1, classical criminology is based on the work of Cesare Beccaria and other utilitarian philosophers. Its core concepts are that (1) people choose all behavior, including criminal behavior; (2) their choices can be controlled by fear of punishment; and (3) the more severe, certain, and swift the punishment, the greater its ability to control criminal behavior. ■

To deter people from committing more serious offenses, Beccaria believed crime and punishment must be proportional; if not, people would be encouraged to commit more serious offenses. For example, if robbery, rape, and murder were all punished by death, robbers or rapists would have little reason to refrain from killing their victims to eliminate them as witnesses to the crime.

To read about Beccaria's life history and the formulation of his ideas, go to:

http://www.criminology.fsu.edu/crimtheory/ beccaria.htm

For an up-to-date list of Web links, go to **http://info.wadsworth.com/siegel** ■

The Classical Theory of Crime

Beccaria's ideas and writings inspired social thinkers to believe that criminals choose to commit crime and that crime can be controlled by judicious punishment. His vision was widely accepted throughout Europe and the United States.[4]

To learn more about the influence of Beccaria's views, go to InfoTrac College Edition and read: Richard Bellamy. Crime and punishment. *History Review,* Sept 1997 n28 p24(2) ■

In Britain, philosopher Jeremy Bentham (1748–1833) helped popularize Beccaria's views in his writings on **utilitarianism.** Bentham believed that people choose actions on the basis of whether they produce pleasure and happiness and help them avoid pain or unhappiness.[5] The purpose of law is to produce and support the total happiness of the community it serves. Because punishment is in itself harmful, its existence is justified only if it promises to prevent greater evil than it creates. Punishment, therefore, has four main objectives:

1. To prevent all criminal offenses
2. When it cannot prevent a crime, to convince the offender to commit a less serious crime
3. To ensure that a criminal uses no more force than is necessary
4. To prevent crime as cheaply as possible[6]

To read more about the life of Jeremy Bentham, go to:
http://www.blupete.com/Literature/Biographies/ Philosophy/Bentham.htm
For an up-to-date list of Web links, go to
http://info.wadsworth.com/siegel ■

This vision was embraced by France's postrevolutionary Constituent Assembly (1789) in its Declaration of the Rights of Man:

> [T]he law has the right to prohibit only actions harmful to society. . . . The law shall inflict only such punishments as are strictly and clearly necessary . . . no person shall be punished except by virtue of a law enacted and promulgated previous to the crime and applicable to its terms.

Similarly, a prohibition against cruel and unusual punishment was incorporated in the Eighth Amendment to the U.S. Constitution.

Beccaria's writings have been credited as the basis of the elimination of torture and severe punishment in the nineteenth century. The practice of incarcerating criminals and structuring prison sentences to fit the severity of crime was a reflection of his classical criminology.

By the end of the nineteenth century, the popularity of the classical approach began to decline, and by the middle of the twentieth century, this perspective was neglected by mainstream criminologists. During this period, positivist criminologists focused on internal and external factors—poverty, IQ, education, home life—which were believed to be the true causes of criminality.

CONNECTIONS

The rise of positivist criminology is discussed in Chapter 1. Positivist theories of criminology, which stress that people are influenced by internal and external forces beyond their control, are analyzed in Chapters 6, 7, 8, and again in Chapter 10. ■

Because these conditions could not be easily manipulated, the concept of punishing people for behaviors beyond their control seemed both foolish and cruel. Although classical principles still controlled the way police, courts, and correctional agencies operate, most criminologists rejected classical criminology as an explanation of criminal behavior.

Choice Theory Emerges

Beginning in the mid-1970s, the classical approach began to enjoy resurging popularity. First, the rehabilitation of known criminals—considered a cornerstone of positivist policy—came under attack. According to positivist criminology, if crime was caused by some social or psychological problem, such as poverty, then crime rates could be reduced by providing good jobs and economic opportunities. Despite some notable efforts to provide such opportunities, a number of national surveys (the most well-known being Robert Martinson's "What Works?") failed to find examples of rehabilitation programs that prevented future criminal activity.[7] A well-publicized book, *Beyond Probation,* by Charles Murray and Louis Cox, went as far as suggesting that punishment-oriented programs could suppress future criminality much more effectively than those that relied on rehabilitation and treatment efforts.[8]

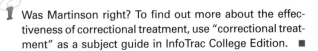

Was Martinson right? To find out more about the effectiveness of correctional treatment, use "correctional treatment" as a subject guide in InfoTrac College Edition. ■

A significant increase in the reported crime rate, as well as serious disturbances in the nation's prisons, frightened the general public. The media depicted criminals as callous and dangerous rather than as needy people deserving of public sympathy. Some criminologists began to suggest that it made more sense to frighten these cold calculators with severe punishments than to waste public funds by futilely trying to improve entrenched social conditions linked to crime such as poverty.[9]

Thinking about crime Beginning in the late 1970s, a number of criminologists began producing books and monographs expounding the theme that criminals are rational actors who plan their crimes, fear punishment, and deserve to be penalized for their misdeeds. In a 1975 book that came to symbolize renewed interest in classical views, *Thinking about Crime,* political scientist James Q. Wilson debunked the positivist view that crime was a function of external forces, such as poverty, that could be altered by government programs. Instead, he argued, efforts should be made to reduce criminal opportunity by deterring would-be offenders and incarcerating known criminals. Persons who are likely to commit crime, he maintained, lack inhibition against misconduct, value the excitement and thrills of breaking the law, have a low stake in conformity, and are willing to take greater chances than the average person. If they could be convinced that their actions will bring severe punishment, only the totally irrational would be willing to engage in crime.[10] Wilson made this famous observation:

> Wicked people exist. Nothing avails except to set them apart from innocent people. And many people, neither wicked nor innocent, but watchful, dissembling, and calculating of their chances, ponder our reaction to wickedness as a clue to what they might profitably do.[11]

Here Wilson is saying that unless we react forcefully to crime, those "sitting on the fence" will get a clear message—crime pays.

To read a famous talk given by Wilson, "Two Nations," the 1997 Francis Boyer lecture delivered at the annual dinner of the American Enterprise Institute, go to:
http://www.aei.org/boyer/jwilson.htm
For an up-to-date list of Web links, go to
http://info.wadsworth.com/siegel ▪

Impact on crime control   Coinciding with the publication of Wilson's book was a conservative shift in U.S. public policy, which resulted in Ronald Reagan's election to the presidency in 1980. Political decision makers embraced Wilson's ideas as a means to bring the crime rate down. Tough new laws were passed, creating mandatory prison sentences for drug offenders; the nation's prison population skyrocketed. Critics decried the disproportionate number of young minority men being locked up for drug law violations.[12] Despite liberal anguish, conservative views of crime control have helped shape criminal justice policy for the past two decades.[13] Many Americans, some of whom are passionate opponents of abortion on the ground that it takes human life, became, ironically, ardent supporters of the death penalty![14] This "get tough" attitude was supported by the fact that while the prison population has grown to new heights the crime rate has been in a steep decline.

From these roots, a more contemporary version of classical theory evolved that is based on intelligent thought processes and criminal decision making; today this is referred to as the *rational choice* approach to crime causation.[15]

The Concepts of Rational Choice

According to the rational choice approach, law-violating behavior occurs when an offender decides to risk breaking the law after considering both personal factors (such as the need for money, revenge, thrills, and entertainment) and situational factors (how well a target is protected and the efficiency of the local police force). Before choosing to commit a crime, the **reasoning criminal** evaluates the risk of apprehension, the seriousness of expected punishment, the potential value of the criminal enterprise, and his or her immediate need for criminal gain. Conversely, the decision to forgo crime may be based on the criminal's perception that the economic benefits are no longer there or that the risk of apprehension is too great.[16]

Rational choice theorists view crime as both offense- and offender-specific.[17] When they say that crime is **offense-specific,** they mean that offenders will react selectively to the characteristics of particular offenses. The decision of whether to commit burglary, for example, might involve evaluating the target's likely cash yield, the availability of resources such as a getaway car, and the probability of capture by police.[18]

When they say that crime is **offender-specific,** they mean that criminals are not simply automatons who, for one reason or another, engage in random acts of antisocial behavior. Before deciding to commit crime, individuals must decide whether they have the prerequisites to commit a successful criminal act, including the proper skills, motives, needs, and fears. Criminal acts might be ruled out if potential offenders perceive that they can reach a desired personal goal through legitimate means or if they are too afraid of getting caught.[19]

Note the distinction made here between crime and criminality.[20] **Crime** is an event; **criminality** is a personal trait. Professional criminals do not commit crime all the time, and even ordinary citizens may, on occasion, violate the law. Some people considered "high risk" because they are indigent or disturbed may never violate the law, whereas others who are seemingly affluent and well adjusted may risk criminal behavior given enough provocation and/or opportunity. What conditions promote crime and enhance criminality?

Structuring Criminality

A number of personal factors condition people to choose criminality. Among the more important factors are economic opportunity, learning and experience, and knowledge of criminal techniques.

Economic opportunity   Perceptions of economic opportunity may influence the decision to commit crime. Crime occurs when an individual believes he or she will successfully profit from an act even if it results in a law violation. Research shows that criminals may be motivated to commit crime when they know people who have made "big scores" and are quite successful at crime. Though the prevailing wisdom is that "crime does not pay," a small but significant subset of criminals actually enjoy earnings of close to $50,000 per year from crime, and their success may help motivate other would-be offenders.[21] However, offenders are likely to desist from crime if they believe that (1) their future criminal earnings will be relatively low and that (2) attractive and legal opportunities to generate income are available.[22] In this sense, rational choice is a function of a person's perception of conventional alternatives and opportunities.

CONNECTIONS

Lack of conventional opportunity is a persistent theme in sociological theories of crime. The frustration caused by a perceived lack of opportunity explains the high crime rates in lower class areas. Chapter 7 discusses strain and cultural deviance theories, which provide alternative explanations of how lack of opportunity is associated with crime. ■

Learning and experience Learning and experience may be important elements in structuring the choice of crime.[23] Career criminals may learn the limitations of their powers; they know when to take a chance and when to be cautious. Experienced criminals may turn from a life of crime when they develop a belief that the risk of crime is greater than its potential profit.[24] Patricia Morgan and Karen Ann Joe's three-city (San Francisco, San Diego, and Honolulu) study of female drug abusers found that experience helped dealers avoid detection. One dealer who earns $50,000 per year explained her strategy this way:

> I stayed within my goals, basically . . . I don't go around doing stupid things. I don't walk around telling people I have drugs for sale. I don't have people sitting out in front of my house. I don't have traffic in and out of my house . . . I control the people I sell to.[25]

Morgan and Joe found that these female dealers consider drug distribution a positive experience that gives them economic independence, self-esteem, increased ability to function, professional pride, and the ability to maintain control over their lives. These women often seemed more like yuppies opening a boutique than out-of-control addicts:

> I'm a good dealer. I don't cut my drugs, I have high-quality drugs insofar as it's possible to get high-quality drugs. I want to be known as somebody who sells good drugs, but doesn't always have them, as opposed to someone who always has them and sometimes the drugs are good.[26]

Here we see how experience in the profession shapes criminal decision making.

CONNECTIONS

The role economic needs plays in the motivation of white-collar criminals is discussed in Chapter 13. Research

AP/Wide World Photos

■ According to choice theory, crime occurs when an individual believes he or she will successfully profit from an act even if it results in a law violation. Shown here is Susan Almgren, a first-grade teacher, after she pled guilty in a Lexington, Kentucky, court to charges of prostitution and running an illegal escort service. Almgren, a first-time offender, was fined $300. Could greed alone cause an educated woman such as Almgren to engage in such a risky scheme as running a shady escort service?

shows that even consistently law-abiding people may turn to criminal solutions when faced with overwhelming economic needs. They make the rational decision to commit crimes to solve some economic crisis. ■

Knowledge of criminal techniques Criminals report learning techniques that help them avoid detection, a sure sign of rational thinking and planning. In his studies of drug dealers, criminologist Bruce Jacobs found that crack dealers learn how to stash crack cocaine in some undisclosed location so that they are not forced to carry large amounts of product on their persons. Dealers carefully evaluate the security of their sales area before setting up shop.[27] Most consider the middle of a long block the best place for drug deals because they can see everything in

Exhibit 5.1   Female Crack Dealers' Arrest-Avoidance Techniques

Projected Self-Image Female crack dealers learn the art of conveying a sense of normalcy and ordinariness in their demeanor and physical appearance to avoid attention. Female crack dealers avoid typical male behavior. They refuse to dress provocatively or to wear flashy jewelry, instead they dress down, wearing blue jeans and sweat pants, to look like a "resident." Some affected the attire of crack users, figuring that the police would not think them worth the trouble of an arrest.

Stashing Dealers learn how to hide drugs on their person, in the street, or at home. One dealer told how she hid drugs in the empty shaft of a curtain rod; another wore hollow earmuffs to hide crack. Knowing that a female officer had to do body cavity searches gave the dealers time to get rid of their drugs before they got to the station house. Dealers are aware of legal definitions of possession. One said she stashed her drugs 250 feet from her home because that was beyond the distance (150 feet) police considered a person legally to be in "constructive possession" of drugs.

Selling Hours The women were aware of the danger of dealing at the wrong time of day. For example, it would be impossible to tell police you were out shopping at 3 A.M. If liquor stores were open, a plausible story could be concocted: I was out buying beer for a party. Dealers who sold from their homes cultivated positive relations with neighbors who might otherwise be tempted to tip off police. Some had barbecues and even sent over plates of ribs and pork to those who did not show up for dinner.

Routine Activities/Staged Performances Dealers camouflaged their activities within the bustle of their daily lives. They would sell crack while hanging out in a park or shooting hoops at a playground. They would meet their customers in a lounge and try to act normal, having a good time, anything not to draw attention to themselves and their business. They used props to disguise drug deals.

SOURCE: Bruce Jacobs and Jody Miller, "Crack Dealing, Gender, and Arrest Avoidance," *Social Problems* 45 (1998): 550–66.

---

both directions; police raids can be spotted before they develop.[28] If a buyer seems dangerous or unreliable, the dealer would require that they do business in spaces between apartment buildings or in back lots. Although dealers lose the tactical edge of being on a public street, they gain a measure of protection because their associates can watch over the deal and come to the rescue if the buyer tries to "pull something."[29] Similar detection avoidance schemes were found by Gordon Knowles in his study of crack dealers in Honolulu, Hawaii. Knowles found that drug dealers often use pornographic film houses as their base of operations because they offer both privacy and convenience.[30]

When Jacobs, along with Jody Miller, studied female crack dealers, they discovered a variety of defensive moves used by the dealers to avoid detection; these are set out in Exhibit 5.1.[31] Criminals who learn the proper techniques may be able to prolong their criminal careers.

Jacobs found that these offenders use specific techniques to avoid being apprehended by police. They play what they call the "peep game" before dealing drugs, scoping out the territory to make sure the turf is free from anything out of place that could be a potential threat (such as police officers or rival gang members).[32] One crack dealer told Jacobs:

> There was this red Pontiac sittin' on the corner one day with two white guys inside. They was just sittin' there for an hour, not doin' nothin'. Another day, diff'rent people be walkin' up and down the street you don't really recognize. You think they might be kin of someone but then you be askin' around and they [neighbors] ain't never seen them before neither. When ya' see strange things like that, you think somethin' be goin' on [and you don't deal].[33]

Drug dealers told Jacobs that they also carefully consider whether they should deal alone or in groups; large groups draw more attention from police but can offer more protection. Drug-dealing gangs and groups can help divert the attention of police: if their drug dealing is noticed by detectives, a dealer can slyly walk away or dispose of evidence while confederates distract the cops.[34]

Experienced burglars also report having to learn detection avoidance techniques. Some check to make sure that no one is home, either by calling ahead or ringing the doorbell, preparing to claim they had the wrong address if someone answers. Others seek unlocked doors and avoid the ones with deadbolts; houses with dogs are usually considered off limits.[35] Most burglars prefer to commit crimes in **permeable neighborhoods**—those with a greater than usual number of access streets from traffic arteries into the neighborhood.[36] These areas are chosen for theft and break-ins because they are familiar and well traveled, they appear more open and vulnerable, and they offer more potential escape routes.[37]

Structuring Crime

Not only do criminals structure their careers, but they rationally choose where and when to commit crime and whom to target. According to the rational choice approach, the decision to commit crime is structured by analysis of (1) the type of crime, (2) the time and place of crime, and (3) the target.

Choosing the type of crime Some criminals are specialists, for example, professional car thieves. Others are generalists who sell drugs one day and commit burglaries the next. Their choice of crime may be dictated by a rational analysis of market conditions. For example, they may rob the elderly on the first of the month when they know that Social Security checks have been cashed.

Sometimes the choice of crime is structured by the immediacy of the need for funds. Eric Baumer and his associates found that cities with greater levels of crack cocaine often experience an increase in robbery and a corresponding decrease in burglary rates. Baumer reasons that crack users need a quick influx of cash to purchase drugs and are in no position to plan a burglary and take the time to sell their loot; street robberies are designed to provide a quick influx of cash that meets their lifestyle needs.[38]

Do drug dealers make rational decisions? Use "drug dealing" as a subject guide on InfoTrac College Edition to find out. ■

Choosing the time and place of crime   There is evidence of rationality in the way criminals choose the time and place of their crimes. Burglars seem to prefer "working" between 9 A.M. and 11 A.M. and in mid-afternoon, when parents are either working or dropping off or picking up kids at school.[39] Burglars avoid Saturdays because most families are at home; Sunday morning during church hours is considered a prime time for weekend burglaries.[40] Some find out which families have star high school athletes because those that do are sure to be at the weekend game, leaving their houses unguarded.[41]

Evidence of rational choice may also be found in the way criminals choose target locations. Thieves seem to avoid freestanding buildings because they can more easily be surrounded by police; they like to select targets that are known to do a primarily cash business, such as bars, supermarkets, and restaurants.[42] Burglars appear to monitor car and pedestrian traffic and avoid selecting targets on heavily traveled streets.[43] Corner homes, usually near traffic lights or stop signs, are the ones most likely to be burglarized: stop signs give criminals a legitimate reason to stop their cars and look for an attractive target.[44] Secluded homes, such as those at the end of a cul-de-sac or surrounded by wooded areas, make suitable targets.[45] Thieves also report being concerned about target convenience. They are more apt to choose familiar burglary sites that are located in easily accessible and open areas.[46]

Because criminals often go on foot or use public transportation, they are unlikely to travel long distances to commit crimes and are more likely to drift toward the center of a city than move toward outlying areas.[47] Some may occasionally commute to distant locations to commit crimes, but most prefer to stay in their own neighborhood where they are familiar with the terrain. They will only travel to unfamiliar areas if they believe the new location contains a worthy target and lax law enforcement. They may be encouraged to travel when the police are cracking down in their own neighborhood and the "heat is on."[48] Evidence is accumulating that predatory criminals are in fact aware of law enforcement capabilities and consider them closely before deciding to commit crimes. Communities with the reputation of employing aggressive "crime-fighting" cops are less likely to attract potential offenders than areas perceived to have passive law enforcers.[49]

Choosing the target of crime   Criminals may also be well aware of target vulnerability. For example, there is evidence that people engaging in deviant or antisocial behaviors are also the most likely to become crime victims.[50] Perhaps predatory criminals sense that people with "dirty hands" make **suitable targets** because they are unlikely to want to call police or get entangled with the law.

Criminals tend to shy away from victims who are perceived to be armed and potentially dangerous.[51] In a series of interviews with career property offenders, Kenneth Tunnell found that burglars avoid targets if they feel there are police in the area or if "nosy neighbors" might be suspicious and cause trouble.[52]

Can private security measures reduce the likelihood of burglary? Use "private security" as a key word in Info-Trac College Edition to research this issue. ■

CONNECTIONS

Rational choice theory dovetails with routine activities theory, which you learned about in Chapter 4. Although not identical, these approaches both claim that crime rates are a normal product of criminal opportunity. Both suggest that criminals consider such elements as guardianship and target attractiveness before they decide to commit crimes.

The routine activities and rational choice views also agree that criminal opportunity is a key element in the criminal process. The overlap between these two viewpoints may help criminologists suggest means for effective crime control. ■

■ Is Crime Rational?

It is relatively easy to show that some crimes are the product of rational, objective thought, especially when they involve an ongoing criminal conspiracy centered on economic gain. When prominent bankers in the savings and loan industry were indicted for criminal fraud, their elaborate financial schemes not only showed signs of rationality but exhibited brilliant, though flawed, financial expertise.[53] The stock market manipulations of Wall Street insiders such as Ivan Boesky and Michael Milken, and the drug dealings of organized crime bosses, demonstrate a reasoned analysis of market conditions, interests, and risks. Even small-time wheeler-dealers, such as the female drug dealers discussed earlier in the chapter, are guided by their rational assessment of the likelihood of apprehension and take pains to avoid detection.

Are Street Crimes Rational?

Street crimes—larcenies, robberies, muggings, purse snatchings—seem more likely to be random acts of criminal opportunity than well-thought-out conspiracies. However, there is evidence that even these seemingly "unplanned" events may be the product of careful risk assessment, including environmental, social, and structural factors. For example, research shows that robbers are likely to choose victims who are vulnerable, have low coercive power, and do not pose any threat.[54] In their survey of violent felons, James Wright and Peter Rossi found that robbers avoid victims who may be armed and dangerous. About three-fifths of all felons interviewed were more afraid of armed victims than police; about two-fifths had

© John T. Barr/Liaison-Getty Images

■ Is drug use rational? If so, how can persistent abuse by such well-known celebrities as Robert Downey Jr., shown here in court during a hearing on charges of drug possession, be explained? After all, they have everything to lose and nothing to gain from their behavior.

avoided a victim because they believed the victim was armed; and almost one-third reported that they had been scared off, wounded, or captured by armed victims.[55] It comes as no surprise that cities with higher than average gun-carrying rates generally have lower rates of unarmed robbery.[56]

Robbers also tend to pick the time and day of crimes carefully. When they rob a commercial establishment, they choose the time when there is the most cash on hand to increase their take from the crime. For example, robbery rates increase in the winter partly because the Christmas shopping season means more money in the cash registers of potential targets.[57] Targets are generally found close to robbers' homes or in areas in which they routinely travel. Familiarity with the area gives them ready knowledge of escape routes; this is referred to as their "awareness space."[58] Robbers may be wary of people who are watching the community for signs of trouble: research by Paul Bellair shows that robbery levels are relatively low in neighborhoods where residents keep a watchful eye on their neighbors' property.[59] Robbers avoid freestanding buildings because they can more easily be surrounded by police; others select targets that are known to do a primarily cash business, such as bars, supermarkets, and restaurants.[60] Their activities show clear signs of rational choice.

Is Drug Use Rational?

Did actor Robert Downey Jr. make an objective, rational choice to abuse drugs and potentially sabotage his career? Did comedian Chris Farley make a rational choice when he abused alcohol and other drugs to the point that it killed him? Is it possible that drug users and dealers, a group not usually associated with clear thinking, make rational choices? Research does in fact show that from its onset drug use is controlled by rational decision making. Users report that they begin taking drugs when they believe that the benefits of substance abuse outweigh its costs (for example, they believe that drugs will provide a fun, exciting, thrilling experience). Their entry into substance abuse is facilitated by their perception that valued friends and family members endorse and encourage drug use and abuse substances themselves.[61]

In adulthood, heavy drug users and dealers show signs of rationality and cunning in their daily activity, approaching drug dealing as a business proposition. Research conducted by Leanne Fiftal Alarid and her partners provides a good illustration of this phenomenon because it focused on how women drawn into dealing drugs learn the trade in a businesslike manner. One young dealer told them how she learned the techniques of the trade from an older male partner: "He taught me how to 'recon' [reconstitute] cocaine, cutting and repacking a brick from 91 proof to 50 proof, just like a business. He treats me like an equal partner, and many of the friends are business associates. I am a catalyst. . . . I even get guys turned on to

In the Drug Business

According to criminologist George Rengert's study of drug markets, drug dealers face many of the same problems as legitimate retailers. If they are too successful in one location, rivals will be attracted to the area, and stiff competition may drive down prices and cut profits. The dealer can fight back by discounting drugs or increasing quality, but this too will reduce profit margins.

Of course, drug dealing differs from other kinds of retail sales. Police can arrest you and your customers, and it is difficult to collect unpaid bills. Drug markets become stabilized in areas that offer the minimum risk and the maximum sales potential. Whereas dealers like to sell in familiar areas that they can control, many customers are willing to pay higher prices to buy close to home.

Rengert notes that there are a variety of levels or stages of drug marketing:

- *Mutual societies* involve drugs shared among friends at parties or teenage hangouts. Drug distribution here is for casual or recreational use.

- *Periodic markets* are drug sites that provide relatively low incomes because sales can be made only at limited times during the day. For example, a dealer may travel to the site to sell to students on their way home from school. Dealers may establish a number of retail outlets and spend a short amount of time each day at different locations. If an area has enough customers, competitors may set up shop to take advantage of the trade.

- *Fixed-site neighborhoods* are neighborhoods in which demand is so great that dealers will remain in a single location all day. Consumers know where the drug dealerships are in the neighborhood and simply travel there on foot to buy merchandise.

- *Drug marts* are neighborhoods that are so drug-infested that law-abiding citizens have moved out and competing drug dealers have taken over. The drug mart's notoriety, heightened by media coverage, helps dealers obtain a steady flow of customers who know where to shop.

Here we can see the parallels between drug dealing and commercial sales. Fixed sites seem like a convenience store that stays open 24 hours a day because there are sufficient customers to make a profit. The drug mart seems similar to the shopping mall, which occupies a large area, has numerous retailers under one roof, and attracts customers without the need for advertising. Service stations and fast food restaurants may sprout up around shopping malls to provide for customers' needs. Similarly, drug marts may attract gun dealers, prostitutes, and fences, who buy stolen merchandise for cash in order to provide for the "customers" (that is, burglars who "shop" at drug marts). If retail purchases and sales are rational and market driven, so too are drug sales and purchases.

Critical Thinking Questions

If drug dealing is similar to any type of commercial sales, can it be controlled or eliminated in the same way a competitor is put out of business—for example, by driving down the price of goods and offering a much cheaper alternative? If so, what sort of legal alternative could you suggest?

InfoTrac College Edition Research

Are we getting too tough on criminals in a futile effort to control the drug trade? To find out, read:

John J. DiIulio Jr. Against mandatory minimums. *National Review* May 17, 1999 v51 p46

SOURCE: George Rengert, *The Geography of Illegal Drugs* (Boulder, Colo.: Westview Press, 1996).

---

drugs."[62] Note the business terminology used. This coke dealer could be talking about taking a computer training course at a major corporation! If criminal acts are treated as business decisions, in which profit and loss potential must be carefully calculated, then crime must indeed be a rational event. This phenomenon is discussed in the Criminological Enterprise feature titled "In the Drug Business."

Can Violence Be Rational?

In 1998, Brandon Wilson, 21, slashed the throat of Matthew Cecchi, a 9-year-old California boy, then stabbed him in the back and left him to bleed to death. After his conviction on murder charges, Wilson told the jury that he would "do it again in a second if I had the chance." When the jury later met to consider the death penalty, Wilson told them, "My whole purpose in life is to help destroy your society. You people are here as representatives of that society. As such, you should do everything in your power to rid the world of me, execute me." Granting him his wish, the jury foreman told reporters, "If there was ever a case that deserved the death penalty, this one fits."[63]

Though seemingly a demented child killer, Brandon Wilson's statements indicate that he is a rational and calculating killer who may have carefully chosen his victim. Is it possible that violent acts, through which the offender gains little material benefit, are the product of reasoned decision making?

AP/Wide World Photos

■ Brandon Wilson, shown here, killed 9-year-old Matthew Cecchi. Is it possible that such a seemingly irrational act could be the product of rational thought and deliberation? Did Wilson choose Cecchi to be his victim because he was young and vulnerable and unlikely to fight back?

Rational killers? Hollywood likes to portray deranged people killing innocent victims at random, but people who carry guns and are ready to use them typically do so for more rational reasons. They may perceive that they live in a dangerous environment and carry a weapon for self-protection.[64] Some are involved in dangerous illegal activities such as drug dealing and carry weapons as part of the job.[65] Even in apparently senseless killings among strangers, the conscious motive is typically revenge for a prior dispute or disagreement among the parties involved or their families.[66] Many homicides are motivated by offenders' desire to avoid retaliation from a victim they assaulted or to avoid future prosecutions by getting rid of witnesses.[67] Although some killings are the result of anger and aggression, others are the result of rational planning.

Even serial murderers, outwardly the most irrational of all offenders, tend to pick their targets with care. Most choose victims who are either defenseless or cannot count on police protection: prostitutes, gay men, hitchhikers, children, hospital patients, the elderly, the homeless. Rarely do serial killers target weightlifters, martial arts experts, or any other potentially powerful group.[68]

Rational rapists? Serial rapists also show rationality in their choice of targets. They travel, on average, three miles from their homes to commit their crimes. This indicates that they are careful, for the most part, to avoid victims who might recognize them later.

The desire to avoid detection supersedes the wish to obtain a victim with little effort. Older, more experienced rapists who have extensive criminal histories are willing to travel farther; younger rapists who have less experience committing crimes travel less and are therefore more at risk of detection.[69]

For many people, then, crime is attractive; it brings rewards, excitement, prestige, or other desirable outcomes without lengthy work or effort.[70] Whether it is violent or profit-oriented, crime has an allure that some people cannot resist. Crime may produce a natural "high" and other positive sensations that are instrumental in maintaining and reinforcing criminal behavior.[71] Some law violators describe the "adrenaline rush" that comes from successfully executing illegal activities in dangerous situations. This has been described as **edgework,** the "exhilarating, momentary integration of danger, risk, and skill" that motivates people to try a variety of dangerous criminal and noncriminal behaviors.[72] Crime is not some random act but a means that can at the same time both provide pleasure and offer a solution to vexing personal problems. The view that crime can solve problems is discussed in the Criminological Enterprise feature titled "The Benefits of Crime."

CONNECTIONS

In Chapter 6 we discuss the thrill-seeking aspect of crime as a biological process. This view of crime, called arousal theory, holds that thrill-seeking is a function of such biological processes as abnormal brain chemistry and brain structure. It is possible that people commit crime because they have a biologically based need to engage in risky behaviors. ■

■ Eliminating Crime

If crime is rational and people choose to commit crime, then it follows that crime can be controlled or eradicated by convincing potential offenders that crime is a poor choice that will not bring them rewards but pain, hardship, and deprivation instead. Evidence shows that jurisdictions with relatively low incarceration rates also experience the highest crime rates.[73] As we have seen, according to rational choice theory, street-smart offenders know which

The Benefits of Crime

The criminal lifestyle fits well with people who organize their life around risk taking and partying. Criminal events provide money for drugs and are ideal for displaying courage and fearlessness to one's running mates. Rather than create overwhelming social problems, a criminal way of life may be extremely beneficial to some people, helping them overcome the problems and stress they face in their daily lives.

According to sociologist Timothy Brezina, crime helps some people achieve a sense of control or mastery over their environment. Adolescents, in particular, may find themselves feeling "out of control" because society limits their opportunities and resources. Antisocial behaviors give them the opportunity to exert control over their own lives and destiny by helping them avoid situations they find uncomfortable or repellant (for example, cutting school or running away from an abusive home) or obtain resources for desired activities and commodities (for example, stealing or selling drugs to buy stylish outfits).

Crime may help them boost their self-esteem by attacking, symbolically or otherwise, perceived enemies (for example, vandalizing the property of an adult who has given them grief). Drinking and drug taking may help some people to ward off depression and compensate for a lack of positive experiences; they learn how to self-medicate themselves. Some, angry at their mistreatment, may turn to violence to satisfy a desire for revenge or retaliation.

Brezina finds that there is a great deal of evidence that people engage in antisocial acts to solve problems. The literature on drug and alcohol abuse is replete with examples of research showing how people turn to substance abuse to increase their sense of personal power, to become more assertive, and to reduce tension and anxiety. Some people embrace deviant lifestyles, such as joining a gang, to offend conventional society while at the same time compensating for their feelings of powerlessness or ordinariness. Engaging in risky behavior helps people to feel alive and competent.

There is also evidence that antisocial acts can provide positive solutions to problems. Violent kids, for example, may have learned that being aggressive with others is a good means to control the situation and get what they want; counterattacks may be one means of controlling people who treat them poorly.

Why do people age out of crime? As a short-run problem-solving solution, crime may be appealing to adolescents; it becomes less attractive as people mature and begin to appreciate the dangers of using crime to solve problems. Going to a drunken frat party may sound appealing to sophomores who want to improve their social life, but the risks involved to safety and reputation make them off limits to older grads. As people mature, their thinking extends farther into the future and risky behavior is a threat to long-range plans.

The Seductions of Crime

Sociologist Jack Katz also argues that there are immediate benefits to criminality, which he labels the *seductions of crime*. These are situational inducements that directly precede the commission of a crime and draw offenders into law violations. For example, someone challenges their authority and they vanquish their opponent with a beating; or they want to do something exciting, so they break into and vandalize a school building.

According to Katz, choosing crime can help satisfy personal needs. For some people, shoplifting and vandalism are attractive because getting away with crime is a thrilling demonstration of personal competence; Katz calls this "sneaky thrills." Even murder can have an emotional payoff. Killers behave like the avenging gods of mythology, choosing to have life-or-death control over their victims.

Katz finds that crimes can help soothe the strain produced by emotional upheaval. For example, when a person is rebuked for his or her behavior, violence may be a method for restoring self-esteem. When a person gets drunk and rowdy at a party and is told to tone it down by a rival, the aggrieved person may respond, "So, I'm acting like a fool, am I?" and attack.

Public embarrassment leads to action; the person must "sacrifice" or injure the body of the victim to maintain his or her "honor." A number of research studies have supported Katz's view that situational inducements play an important role in causing adolescent misbehavior. People are most likely to be "seduced" if they fear neither the risk of apprehension nor its social consequences. People who either (1) fear losing the respect of their peers or (2) suffer legal punishment are most likely to forgo the "seductions of crime."

Critical Thinking Questions

1. If crime is "seductive," how can the fear of punishment control criminal tendencies? Are people thinking rationally when they commit crimes?
2. According to Brezina, as people mature their thinking extends farther into the future and risky behavior is a threat to long-range plans. Does this vision adequately explain the aging-out process? If so, why do some people continue to commit crime in their adulthood?

InfoTrac College Edition Research

How do people learn to solve problems? To find out, go to InfoTrac College Edition and use "problem solving" as a subject guide.

SOURCES: Timothy Brezina, "Delinquent Problem-Solving: An Interpretive Framework for Criminological Theory and Research," *Journal of Research in Crime and Delinquency* 37 (2000): 3–30; Andy Hochstetler, "Opportunities and Decisions: Interactional Dynamics in Robbery and Burglary Groups," *Criminology* 39 (2001): 737–63; Jack Katz, *Seductions of Crime* (New York: Basic Books, 1988); Bill McCarthy and John Hagan, "Mean Streets: The Theoretical Significance of Situational Delinquency among Homeless Youths," *American Journal of Sociology* 3 (1992): 597–627; Christopher Birkbeck and Gary LaFree, "The Situational Analysis of Crime and Deviance," *American Review of Sociology* 19 (1993): 113–37; Karen Heimer and Ross Matsueda, "Role-Taking, Role Commitment, and Delinquency: A Theory of Differential Social Control," *American Sociological Review* 59 (1994): 400–437; Peter Wood, Walter Gove, James Wilson, and John Cochran, "Nonsocial Reinforcement and Habitual Criminal Conduct: An Extension of Learning," *Criminology* 35 (1997): 335–66; Jeff Ferrell, "Criminological Versthen: Inside the Immediacy of Crime," *Justice Quarterly* 14 (1997): 3–23, at 12; Bill McCarthy, "Not Just 'For the Thrill of It': An Instrumentalist Elaboration of Katz's Explanation of Sneaky Thrill Property Crime," *Criminology* 33 (1995): 519–39.

Exhibit 5.2 Crime Control Strategies Based on Rational Choice

1. *Situational crime prevention* is aimed at convincing would-be criminals to avoid specific targets. It relies on the doctrine that crime can be avoided if motivated offenders are denied access to suitable targets. When people install security systems in their homes or hire security guards, they are broadcasting the message that guardianship is great here, stay away; the potential reward is not worth the risk of apprehension.

2. *General deterrence strategies* are aimed at making potential criminals fear the consequences of crime. The threat of punishment is aimed at convincing rational criminals that crime does not pay.

3. *Specific deterrence* refers to punishing known criminals so severely that they will never be tempted to repeat their offenses. If crime is rational, then painful punishment should reduce its future allure.

4. *Incapacitation strategies* attempt to reduce crime rates by denying motivated offenders the opportunity to commit crime. If, despite the threat of law and punishment, some people still find crime attractive, then the only way to control their behavior is to incarcerate them for extended periods.

---

areas offer the least threat and plan their crimes accordingly. Strategies for crime control based on this premise are illustrated in Exhibit 5.2. The following sections discuss each of these crime reduction or control strategies.

Situational Crime Prevention

Because criminal activity is offense-specific, rational choice theory suggests that crime prevention, or at least crime reduction, should be achieved through policies that convince potential criminals to desist from criminal activities, delay their actions, or avoid a particular target. Criminal acts will be avoided if (1) potential targets are carefully guarded, (2) the means to commit crime are controlled, and (3) potential offenders are carefully monitored. Desperate people may contemplate crime, but only the truly irrational would attack a well-defended, inaccessible target and risk strict punishment. Crime prevention can be achieved by reducing the opportunities people have to commit particular crimes, a practice known as **situational crime prevention.**

Situational crime prevention was first popularized in the United States in the early 1970s by Oscar Newman, who coined the term **defensible space.** This term signifies that crime can be prevented or displaced through the use of residential architectural designs that reduce criminal opportunity, such as well-lit housing projects that maximize surveillance.[74] C. Ray Jeffery wrote *Crime Prevention through Environmental Design*, which extended Newman's concepts and applied them to nonresidential areas, such as schools and factories.[75] According to this view, mechanisms such

as security systems, deadbolt locks, high-intensity street lighting, and neighborhood watch patrols should reduce criminal opportunity.[76]

Crime Prevention through Environmental Design is a branch of situational crime prevention that has as its basic premise that the physical environment can be changed or managed to produce behavioral effects that will reduce the incidence and fear of crime. To read more about the concept, go to:

> **http://www.cpted.com.au/**

For an up-to-date list of Web links, go to

> **http://info.wadsworth.com/siegel** ■

In 1992 Ronald Clarke published *Situational Crime Prevention*, which compiled the best-known strategies and tactics to reduce criminal incidents.[77] Criminologists have suggested using a number of situational crime prevention efforts that might reduce crime rates. One approach is not to target a specific crime but to create an environment that can reduce the overall crime rate by limiting the access to tempting targets for a highly motivated offender group (such as high school students). Notice that this approach is designed not to eliminate a specific crime but to reduce the overall crime rate. Such a strategy might include some or all of the elements contained in Exhibit 5.3.[78]

Targeting specific crimes Situational crime prevention can also involve developing tactics to reduce or eliminate a specific crime problem (such as shoplifting in an

Exhibit 5.3 A Total Community Situational Crime Prevention Model

- Schedule school release uniformly so that there is no doubt when kids belong in school and when they are truant.
- Control truancy.
- Organize after-school activities to keep kids under adult supervision.
- Organize weekend activities with adult supervision.
- Offer school lunches to keep kids in school and away from shopping areas.
- Prohibit cash in schools to reduce kids' opportunity either to be a target or to consume drugs or alcohol.
- Keep shopping areas and schools separate.
- Construct housing to maximize guardianship and minimize illegal behavior.
- Encourage neighborhood stability so that residents will be acquainted with one another.
- Encourage privatization of parks and recreation facilities so that people will be responsible for their area's security.

SOURCE: Marcus Felson, "Routine Activities and Crime Prevention," in National Council for Crime Prevention, *Studies on Crime and Crime Prevention, Annual Review*, vol. 1 (Stockholm: Scandinavian University Press, 1992), pp. 30–34.

Exhibit 5.4 Sixteen Techniques of Situational Prevention

Increasing Perceived Effort	Increasing Perceived Risks	Reducing Anticipated Rewards	Inducing Guilt or Shame
1. *Target hardening* Slug rejector devices Steering locks Bandit screens	5. *Entry/exit screening* Automatic ticket gates Baggage screening Merchandise tags	9. *Target removal* Removable car radio Women's refuges Phone card	13. *Rule setting* Harassment codes Customs declaration Hotel registrations
2. *Access control* Parking lot barriers Fenced yards Entry phones	6. *Formal surveillance* Burglar alarms Speed cameras Security guards	10. *Identifying property* Property marking Vehicle licensing Cattle branding	14. *Strengthening moral condemnation* "Shoplifting is stealing" Roadside speedometers "Bloody idiots drink and drive"
3. *Deflecting offenders* Bus stop placement Tavern location Street closures	7. *Surveillance by employees* Pay phone location Park attendants CCTV systems	11. *Reducing temptation* Gender-neutral phone lists Off-street parking	15. *Controlling disinhibitors* Drinking age laws Ignition interlock Server intervention
4. *Controlling facilitators* Credit card photo Caller ID Gun controls	8. *Natural surveillance* Defensible space Street lighting Cab driver ID	12. *Denying benefits* Ink merchandise tags PIN for car radios Graffiti cleaning	16. *Facilitating compliance* Improved library checkout Public lavatories Trash bins

SOURCE: Ronald Clarke and Ross Homel, "A Revised Classification of Situation Crime Prevention Techniques," in *Crime Prevention at a Crossroads*, ed. Steven Lab (Cincinnati: Anderson, 1997), p. 4.

urban mall or street-level drug dealing). According to criminologists Ronald Clarke and Ross Homel, crime prevention tactics used today generally fall in one of four categories:

- Increase the effort needed to commit crime.
- Increase the risks of committing crime.
- Reduce the rewards for committing crime.
- Induce guilt or shame for committing crime.

Exhibit 5.4 lists sixteen strategies to limit opportunities for crime based on these categories of prevention.

Some of the tactics to increase effort include target-hardening techniques such as putting unbreakable glass on storefronts, locking gates, and fencing yards. Technological advances can make it more difficult to commit crimes; for example, having an owner's photo on credit cards should reduce the use of stolen cards. The development of new products, such as steering locks on cars, can make it more difficult to commit crimes. Empirical evidence indicates that using steering locks has helped reduce car theft in the United States, Britain, and Germany.[79] Installing a locking device on cars that prevents inebriated drivers from starting the vehicle significantly reduces drunk-driving rates.[80] Removing signs from store windows, installing brighter lights, and instituting a pay-first policy can help reduce thefts from gas stations and convenience stores.[81]

Target reduction strategies are designed to reduce the value of crime to the potential criminal. These include making car radios removable so they can be kept in the home at night, marking property so that it is more difficult to sell when stolen, and having gender-neutral phone listings to discourage obscene phone calls. Tracking systems, such as those made by the Lojack Corporation, help police locate and return stolen vehicles.

Inducing guilt or shame might include such techniques as setting strict rules to embarrass offenders. For example, publishing "John lists" in the newspaper punishes those arrested for soliciting prostitutes. Facilitating compliance by providing trash bins might shame chronic litterers into using them. Ronald Clarke shows how caller ID in New Jersey resulted in significant reductions in the number of obscene phone calls. Caller ID displays the telephone number of the party placing the call; the threat of exposure had a deterrent effect on the number of obscene calls reported to police.[82] The Policy and Practice in Criminology feature titled "Reducing Subway Crime" describes how these ideas have been implemented to protect passengers on the Washington, D.C. subway system.

Crime discouragers The success of situational crime prevention may also rest on the behavior of people whose actions directly influence crime prevention. These people are known as **crime discouragers**.[83]

Discouragers can be grouped into three categories: guardians, who monitor targets (such as store security guards); handlers, who monitor potential offenders (such

Reducing Subway Crime

Washington, D.C.'s subway system has experienced less crime than expected since it began operations in 1976. One reason is that the system, called the "Metro," employs design characteristics, management practices, and maintenance policies that incorporate principles of situational crime prevention. Here are some of the crime-reducing strategies included:

- High, arched ceilings not only are architecturally sound and aesthetically pleasing but also create a feeling of openness that reduces passenger fears and provides an open view of the station. Long, winding corridors and corners were avoided to reduce shadows and nooks that criminals and panhandlers could occupy.

- Passengers buy multiple-use fare cards in any dollar amount, reducing the time money is exposed to pickpockets and robbers. Fare cards also must be used on entry and exit from the system, reducing the likelihood of fare evasion.

- Metro trains are equipped with graffiti- and vandal-resistant materials to discourage potential offenders. When graffiti artists or vandals do cause damage, maintenance workers clean and repair damaged property promptly.

- No public restrooms, lockers, or excess seats allow potential offenders to loiter. Fast food establishments are prohibited because customers generate litter and provide victims for robbers and pickpockets.

- Rules prohibiting "quality of life" violations, such as smoking or eating on trains are enforced, and all vandalism and graffiti are promptly reported to maintenance personnel to ensure a safe and clean environment.

- Entrance kiosks are continuously staffed while Metro is open. Station attendants are aided by closed-circuit televisions at all unattended entrances, tunnels, and platforms, and they carry two-way radios to report crime and maintenance problems.

Metro's crime rates have been stable and far lower than those experienced in the subway systems in Atlanta, Boston, and Chicago. Applying Metro's design, maintenance, and crime prevention strategies may help new or existing systems reduce subway crime.

Critical Thinking Questions

1. Is it possible that the Metro policies do not actually reduce crime but shift it above ground (crime displacement)? Explain your response.

2. Which methods employed by the Metro system might other government institutions adopt to reduce their own crime problems? For example, which techniques might school systems employ?

InfoTrac College Edition Research

To read about the most famous incident of subway crime in recent memory, check out this article:

Michael Brooks. Stories and verdicts: Bernhard Goetz and New York in crisis. *College Literature* 1998 v25 p77

SOURCE: Nancy LaVigne, *Visibility and Vigilance: Metro's Situational Approach to Preventing Subway Crime* (Washington, D.C.: National Institute of Justice, 1997).

as parole officers and parents); and managers, who monitor places (such as homeowners and doorway attendants). According to this view, crime requires a desirable target without an effective guardian, a motivated offender without an effective handler, and a facilitating place that lacks an attentive manager.[84]

Crime discouragers also have different levels of responsibility, ranging from highly personal involvement, such as the home owner protecting her house and the parent controlling his children, to the most impersonal general involvement, such as a stranger who stops someone from shoplifting in the mall (see Exhibit 5.5).

Felson suggests that the concept of crime discouragement can be useful in planning situational crime prevention tactics. More effective crime reduction may occur if (1) managers are given better tools to monitor places, (2) guardians are better equipped to protect targets, and (3) handlers are allowed to exert greater control over offenders. For example, a store clerk is in a better position to discourage offenders if armed with a mirror to watch merchandise and a button to summon supervisory help. Handlers become more effective when supplied with hidden cameras and eavesdropping devices.

Research indicates that crime discouragers can have an impact on crime rates. An evaluation of a police initiative in Oakland, California, found that an active working partnership with residents and businesspeople who have a stake in maintaining order in their places of work or residences can reduce levels of drug dealing while at the same time increasing civil behavior. Collective action and cooperation in solving problems were effective in controlling crime, whereas individual action (such as calling 911) seemed to have little effect.[85]

Diffusion and discouragement There may also be hidden benefits to situational crime prevention: diffusion and discouragements.[86] **Diffusion** occurs (1) when efforts to prevent one crime unintentionally prevent another and (2) when crime control efforts in one locale reduce crime in other nontarget areas. Diffusion may be produced by

Exhibit 5.5 Crime Discouragers

Types of Supervisors and Objects of Supervision

Level of Responsibility	A. Guardians (monitoring suitable targets)	B. Handlers (monitoring likely offenders)	C. Managers (monitoring amenable places)
1. *Personal* (owners, family, friends)	Student keeps eye on own bookbag	Parent makes sure child gets home	Homeowner monitors area near home
2. *Assigned* (employees with specific assignment)	Store clerk monitors jewelry	Principal sends kids back to school	Doorman protects building
3. *Diffuse* (employees with general assignment)	Accountant notes shoplifting	School clerk discourages truancy	Hotel maid impairs trespasser
4. *General* (strangers, other citizens)	Bystander inhibits shoplifting	Stranger questions boys at mall	Customer observes parking structure

SOURCE: Marcus Felson, "Those Who Discourage Crime," in John Eck and David Weisburd, *Crime and Place* (Monsey, N.Y.: Criminal Justice Press, 1995), p. 59. Reprinted by permission.

two independent effects. Crime control efforts may deter criminals by causing them to fear apprehension. For example, video cameras set up in a mall to reduce shoplifting can also reduce property damage because would-be vandals fear they are being caught on camera. One recent police program targeting drugs in areas of Jersey City, New Jersey, also reduced public morals crimes.[87]

Discouragement occurs when efforts to eliminate one type of crime convinces would-be lawbreakers to forgo other criminal activity because crime no longer pays. In her study of the effects of the SMART program (a drug enforcement program in Oakland, California, that enforces municipal codes and nuisance abatement laws), criminologist Lorraine Green found that not only did drug dealing decrease in targeted areas but improvement was found in surrounding areas as well. She suggests that the program most likely discouraged buyers and sellers who saw familiar hangouts closed. This sign that drug dealing would not be tolerated probably decreased the total number of people involved in drug activity even though they did not operate in the targeted areas.[88]

Another example of this effect can be found in evaluations of the Lojack auto protection system, which uses a hidden radio transmitter to track stolen cars. Lojack also seems to disrupt the operation of chop shops, where stolen vehicles are taken apart for the resale of parts. Police can trace the Lojack signals directly to the chop shop; in Los Angeles alone Lojack has resulted in the breakup of more than 50 chop shops. Car theft rings are afraid to buy stolen cars because they cannot be sure if they contain Lojack.[89] A device designed to protect cars from theft also has the benefit of disrupting the sale of stolen car parts.

Displacement, extinction, and fear Although situational crime prevention appears to work in some situa-

tions, there are also problems that limit the success of these methods. Preventing crime in one location does not address or deter criminal motivation. People who desire the benefits of crime may choose alternative targets, so that crime is not prevented but deflected or displaced.[90] For example, beefed-up police patrols in one area may shift crimes to a more vulnerable neighborhood.[91] Although **crime displacement** does not solve the general problem of crime, under some circumstances deflection efforts can partially reduce the frequency of crime or produce less serious offense patterns.[92]

There is also the problem of **extinction**: crime reduction programs may produce a short-term positive effect, but benefits dissipate as criminals adjust to new conditions. They learn to dismantle alarms or avoid patrols; they may try new offenses they had previously avoided. For example, if every residence in a neighborhood has a foolproof burglar alarm system, motivated offenders may turn to armed robbery, a riskier and more violent crime.

Situational crime prevention efforts may also be compromised in a climate where fear and social disorganization are overwhelming. For example, a recent effort employing situational crime prevention techniques to reduce gang crime and drug dealing in some of Chicago's most troubled housing projects failed to meet its objectives. Evaluation of the program found that residents feared retaliation from gang boys and possible loss of relationships; joining an effort to organize against crime placed them at extreme risk.[93]

General Deterrence

According to the rational choice view, motivated, rational people will violate the law if left free and unrestricted. The concept of **general deterrence** holds that crime rates are

■ Crime discouragers are people whose actions directly influence crime prevention. Here, School Resource Officer (SRO) Joe Hoffar adjusts the controls of a television monitor that displays images from several security cameras placed at Atwater High School in Atwater, California, June 14, 2001. Following the 1999 shootings at Colorado's Columbine High School, the legislature passed a law aimed at limiting school violence by providing additional funds for safety-related items, such as security cameras, and for police officers on campus, known as school resource officers. Hoffar is supervisor of the SROs for the Merced Union High School District.

influenced and controlled by the threat of criminal punishment. If people fear being apprehended and punished, they will not risk breaking the law. An inverse relationship should then exist between crime rates and the *severity, certainty,* and *speed* of legal sanctions. If, for example, the punishment for a crime is increased and the effectiveness and efficiency of the criminal justice system are improved, then the number of people engaging in that crime should decline. The factors of severity, certainty, and speed of punishment may also influence one another. For example, if a crime—say, robbery—is punished severely, but few robbers are ever caught or punished, the severity of punishment for robbery will probably not deter people from robbing. However, if the certainty of apprehension and conviction is increased by modern technology, more efficient police work, or some other factor, then even minor punishment might deter the potential robber. Do these factors actually affect the decision to commit crime and, consequently, general crime rates?

Certainty of punishment According to **deterrence theory,** if the probability of arrest, conviction, and sanctioning increases, crime rates should decline. Rational offenders will soon realize that the increased likelihood of punishment outweighs any benefit they perceive from committing crimes. Crime persists because most criminals believe (a) that there is only a small chance they will be arrested for committing a particular crime, (b) that police officers are sometimes reluctant to make arrests even when they are aware of crime, and (c) that even if apprehended there is a good chance of receiving a lenient punishment.[94] Considering these problems, it is not surprising that research efforts have found little relationship between the

likelihood of being arrested or imprisoned and corresponding crime rates.[95]

While these results contradict deterrence theory, there is evidence that people who believe that they will be punished for future crimes also say that they will not commit those crimes.[96] Some criminologists link certainty to a concept they refer to as the "tipping point": being certain of punishment will only work if the likelihood of getting caught reaches a specific level. For example, research shows that the crime rate would significantly decline if police could increase their effectiveness and make an arrest in at least 30 percent of all reported crimes.[97]

Does increasing police activity deter crime? If certainty of apprehension and punishment deters criminal behavior, then increasing the number of police officers on the street should cut the crime rate. Moreover, if these police officers are active, aggressive crime fighters, would-be criminals should be convinced that the risk of apprehension outweighs the benefits they can gain from crime.[98]

In the past, criminologists questioned whether simply increasing the number of police officers in a community could lower crime rates. There was little evidence that adding additional officers could produce a deterrent effect.[99] One problem is that as crime rates increase communities add police officers. Consequently, the number of officers increases along with the crime rate, making it appear that adding police actually increases crime rates rather than lowering them. However, recent research using sophisticated methodological tools has found evidence that increasing levels of crime only cause small increases in the number of police officers, whereas increased police levels cause substantial reductions in crime over time.[100] It is therefore possible that the presence of police officers does in fact have a substantial deterrent effect.

Some police departments have conducted experiments to determine whether increasing police activities or allocation of services can influence crime rates. Perhaps the most famous experiment was conducted by the Kansas City, Missouri, police department.[101] To evaluate the effectiveness of police patrols, 15 independent police beats or districts were divided into three groups: the first retained a normal police patrol; the second (proactive) was supplied with two to three times the normal amount of patrol forces; the third (reactive) eliminated its preventive patrol entirely, and police officers responded only when summoned by citizens to the scene of a crime.

Surprisingly, these variations in patrol techniques had little effect on the crime patterns. The presence or absence of patrol forces did not seem to affect residential or business burglaries, auto thefts, larcenies involving auto accessories, robberies, vandalism, or other criminal behavior. Variations in police patrol techniques appeared to have little effect on citizens' attitudes toward the police, their satisfaction with police, or their fear of future criminal behavior. It is possible that as people traveled around the city they noticed large number of police officers in one area and relatively few in another; the two effects may have cancelled each other out!

Other police departments have instituted **crackdowns**—sudden changes in police activity designed to increase the communicated threat or actual certainty of punishment—to lower crime rates. For example, a police task force might target street-level narcotics dealers by using undercover agents and surveillance cameras in known drug-dealing locales. Or they may actively enforce public nuisance laws in an effort to demonstrate the department's crime fighting resolve. These efforts have yielded mixed results: some have not proven to be successful mechanisms for lowering crime rates;[102] others initially deterred crime rates but evaluations found that crime returned to normal levels once the crackdown ended.[103] However, a recent analysis of a crackdown and cleanup initiative in seven city neighborhoods in Richmond, Virginia, found that crime rates declined by 92 percent during the month-long crackdown period, the effects persisted up to six months after the crackdown ended, and no displacement was observed.[104] Clearly more research is needed on this important area of deterrence.

Police seem to have more luck deterring crime when they use more focused approaches such as aggressive problem-solving and community improvement techniques (increased lighting and cleaning up vacant lots, for example) to fight particular crimes in selected places.[105] A recent initiative by the Dallas Police Department to aggressively pursue truancy and curfew enforcement resulted in lower rates of gang violence.[106] The evidence shows that merely saturating an area with police may not deter crime, but focusing efforts at a particular problem area may have a deterrent effect.

Severity of Punishment and Deterrence

According to deterrence theory, the severity of punishment is inversely proportional to the level of crime rates. Increasing punishments should lower crime rates. Some studies have in fact found that increasing sanction levels can control common criminal behaviors. For example, a 1997 study by the National Center for Policy Analysis uncovered evidence of a direct correlation between the probability of imprisonment for a particular crime and a subsequent decline in the rate of that crime.[107] The probability of going to prison for murder increased 17 percent between 1993 and 1997, and the murder rate dropped 23 percent during that time period; robbery declined 21 percent as the probability of prison increased 14 percent.

These data seem persuasive, but there is little consensus that the severity of criminal sanctions alone can reduce criminal activities.[108] Because the likelihood of getting caught for some crimes is relatively low, the impact of deterrent measures is negligible over the long term.[109] Although some findings show that toughening laws can lower crime rates, others question their deterrent effect.[110] In summary, it has not been proven that just increasing the punishment for specific crimes can reduce their occurrence.

Capital punishment It stands to reason that if severity of punishment can deter crime, then fear of the death penalty, the ultimate legal deterrent, should significantly reduce murder rates. Because no one denies its emotional impact, failure of the death penalty to deter violent crime jeopardizes the validity of the entire deterrence concept.

Various studies have tested the assumption that capital punishment deters violent crime. The research can be divided into three types: immediate impact studies, comparative research, and time-series analysis.

1. **Immediate impact:** If capital punishment is a deterrent, the reasoning goes, then its impact should be greatest after a well-publicized execution. Robert Dann began testing this assumption in 1935 when he chose five highly publicized executions of convicted murderers in different years and determined the number of homicides in the 60 days before and after each execution.[111] Each 120-day period had approximately the same number of homicides, as well as the same number of days on which homicides occurred. Dann's study revealed that an average of 4.4 more homicides occurred during the 60 days following an execution than during those preceding it, suggesting that the overall impact of executions might actually be an increase in the incidence of homicide.

2. **Comparative research:** Another type of research compares the murder rates in jurisdictions that have abolished the death penalty with the rates of those that employ the death penalty. Studies using this approach have found little difference in the murder rates of adjacent states, regardless of their use of the death

penalty; capital punishment did not appear to influence the reported rate of homicide.[112] Research conducted in 14 nations around the world found little evidence that countries with a death penalty have lower violence rates than those without; homicide rates actually decline after capital punishment is abolished, a direct contradiction to its supposed deterrent effect.[113]

3. **Time-series studies:** Time-series studies look at the long-term association between capital sentencing and murder. If capital punishment is a deterrent, then periods that have an upswing in executions should also experience a downturn in violent crime and murder.[114] Most research efforts have failed to show such a relationship. For example, a recent test of the deterrent effect of the death penalty in Texas found no association between the frequency of execution during the years 1984 to 1997 and murder rates.[115]

Rethinking the deterrent effect of capital punishment Those who oppose the death penalty view these studies as providing conclusive evidence that executing convicted criminals has relatively little influence on behavior.[116] Although it is still uncertain why the threat of capital punishment has failed as a deterrent, the cause may lie in the nature of homicide itself. Murder is often an expressive "crime of passion" involving people who know each other and who may be under the influence of drugs and alcohol; murder is also a by-product of the criminal activity of people who suffer from the burdens of poverty and income inequality.[117]

Although many criminologists question the utility of capital punishment, claiming that it either has little effect on murder rates or may even cause more harm than it prevents, there are a few who still maintain that, in the short run, executing criminals can bring the murder rate down.[118] Criminologist Steven Stack has conducted a number of research studies that show that the immediate impact of a well-publicized execution can lower the murder rate during the following month.[119] Criminologist James Yunker, using a national data set, has found evidence that there is a deterrent effect of capital punishment that may be hidden when state-by-state comparisons are made. The most significant effect has been achieved in recent years when the pace of executions has accelerated.[120] Although the majority of criminologists disagree, some still believe that use of the death penalty has helped reduce murder rates.

CONNECTIONS

Those who favor the death penalty today question the claims that capital punishment has no deterrent effect. Nor do they believe it is cruel and unusual punishment or state-sponsored vengeance. They consider it a reasonable application of sufficient force to convince would-be killers not to take the life of another. Chapter 17 discusses the legal and philosophical issues involved in the use of the death penalty. ■

Even if the death penalty were an effective deterrent, does it present ethical problems that make its use morally dubious? Read what the American Civil Liberties Union has to say at:
   http://www.aclu.org/death-penalty/
For an up-to-date list of Web links, go to
   http://info.wadsworth.com/siegel ■

Informal sanctions Evidence is accumulating that the fear of **informal sanctions** may have a greater crime-reducing impact than the fear of formal legal punishment.[121] Informal sanctions occur when significant others, such as parents, peers, neighbors, and teachers, direct their disapproval, stigma, anger, and indignation toward an offender. If this happens, law violators run the risk of feeling shame, being embarrassed, and suffering a loss of respect.[122] Can the fear of public humiliation deter crime?

Research efforts have in fact established that the threat of informal sanctions can be a more effective deterrent than the threat of formal sanctions.[123] The reason for this is that social control is influenced by the way people perceive negative reactions from interpersonal acquaintances. Legal sanctions may act as a supplement to informal control processes. In other words, a combination of informal and formal social control may have a greater impact on the decision to commit crime than either deterrent measure alone.[124] Other studies have found that people who are committed to conventional moral values or believe crime to be sinful are unlikely to violate the law.[125] For example, British efforts to control drunk driving by shaming offenders produced a moral climate that helped reduce its incidence.[126]

Shame and humiliation Fear of shame and embarrassment can be a powerful deterrent to crime. Those who fear being rejected by family and peers are reluctant to engage in deviant behavior.[127] These factors manifest themselves in two ways: (1) personal shame over violating the law and (2) the fear of public humiliation if the deviant behavior becomes public knowledge. People who say that their involvement in crime will cause them to feel ashamed are less likely to commit theft, fraud, motor vehicular, and other offenses than people who report they will not feel ashamed.[128]

Anticrime campaigns have been designed to play on this fear of shame; they are most effective when they convince the general public that being accused of crime will make them feel ashamed or embarrassed.[129] For example, spouse abusers report they are more afraid of the social costs of crime (like loss of friends and family disapproval) than they are of legal punishment (such as going to jail). Women are more likely to fear shame and embarrassment than men, a finding that may help explain gender differences in the crime rate.[130]

The effect of informal sanctions may vary according to the cohesiveness of community structure and the type of crime. Informal sanctions may be most effective in highly unified areas where everyone knows one another and the crime cannot be hidden from public view. The threat of informal sanctions seems to have the greatest influence on instrumental crimes, which involve planning, and not on impulsive or expressive criminal behaviors or those associated with substance abuse.[131]

Critique of general deterrence   Some experts believe that the purpose of the law and justice system is to create a "threat system."[132] That is, the threat of legal punishment should, on the face of it, deter lawbreakers through fear. Nonetheless, as we have already discussed, the relationship between crime rates and deterrent measures is far less than choice theorists might expect. Despite efforts to punish criminals and make them fear crime, there is little evidence that the fear of apprehension and punishment can reduce crime rates. How can this discrepancy be explained?

1. **Rationality:** Deterrence theory assumes a rational offender who weighs the costs and benefits of a criminal act before deciding on a course of action. In many instances, criminals are desperate people who suffer from personality disorders that impair their judgment and render them incapable of making truly rational decisions. As you learned in Chapter 3, a relatively small group of chronic offenders commits a significant percentage of all serious crimes. Some psychologists believe this select group suffers from an innate or inherited emotional state that renders them both incapable of fearing punishment and less likely to appreciate the consequences of crime.[133] For example, people who are easily aroused sexually also say that they will be more likely to act in a sexually aggressive fashion and not consider the legal consequences of their actions.[134] Their heightened emotional state negates the deterrent effect of the law.

2. **Need:** Many offenders are members of what is referred to as the underclass—people cut off from society, lacking the education and skills they need to be in demand in the modern economy.[135] Such desperate people may not be deterred from crime by fear of punishment because, in reality, they perceive few other options for success. Among poor, high-risk groups, such as teens living in economically depressed neighborhoods, the threat of formal sanctions is irrelevant.[136] Young people in these areas have less to lose because their opportunities are few and they have little attachment to social institutions such as school or family. In their environment, they see many people who appear relatively well off (the neighborhood drug dealer) committing crimes without getting caught or punished.[137]

3. **Greed:** Some may be immune to deterrent effects because they believe the profits from crime are worth the risk of punishment; it may be their only significant chance for gain and profit. When criminologists Alex Piquero and George Rengert studied active burglars, they found that the lure of criminal profits outweighed their fears of capture and subsequent punishment. Perceived risk of punishment may deter some potential and active criminal offenders, but only if they doubt that they can make a "big score" from committing a crime.[138]

4. **Severity and speed:** As Beccaria's famous equation tells us, the threat of punishment involves not only its severity but its certainty and speed. Our legal system is not very effective. Only 10 percent of all serious offenses result in apprehension (half go unreported and police make arrests in about 20 percent of reported crimes). Police routinely do not arrest suspects in personal disputes even when they lead to violence.[139] As apprehended offenders are processed through all the stages of the criminal justice system, the odds of their receiving serious punishment diminish. As a result, some offenders believe they will not be severely punished for their acts and consequently have little regard for the law's deterrent power.

Criminologist Raymond Paternoster found that adolescents, a group responsible for a disproportionate amount of crime, may be well aware that the juvenile court is generally lenient about imposing meaningful sanctions on even the most serious juvenile offenders.[140] Even those accused of murder are often convicted of lesser offenses and spend relatively short amounts of time behind bars.[141] In making their "rational choice," offenders may be aware that the deterrent effect of the law is minimal.

The Concept of Specific Deterrence

The general deterrence model focuses on future or potential criminals. In contrast, the theory of **specific deterrence** (also called *special* or *particular deterrence*) holds that criminal sanctions should be so powerful that known criminals will never repeat their criminal acts. For example, the drunk driver whose sentence is a substantial fine and a week in the county jail should, according to this theory, be convinced that the price to be paid for drinking and driving is too great to consider future violations. Similarly, burglars who spend five years in a tough, maximum security prison should find their enthusiasm for theft dampened.[142] In principle, punishment works if a connection can be established between the planned action and memories of its consequence; if these recollections are adequately intense, the action will be unlikely to occur again.[143]

At first glance, specific deterrence does not seem to work because a majority of known criminals are not deterred by their punishment. As you have already seen, arrest and punishment seem to have little effect on experienced criminals and may even increase the likelihood that first-time offenders will commit new crimes.[144] Chronic offender research indicates that a stay in a juvenile justice facility does little to deter a persistent delinquent from becoming an adult criminal.[145] It follows that most prison inmates had prior records of arrest and conviction before their current offenses.[146] About two-thirds of all convicted felons are rearrested within three years of their release from prison, and those who have been punished in the past are the most likely to recidivate.[147] Incarceration may sometimes slow down or delay recidivism in the short term, but the overall probability of rearrest does not change following incarceration.[148]

■ Simply put, if dangerous criminals were incapacitated, they would never have the opportunity to prey upon others. One of the most dramatic examples of the utility of incapacitation is the case of Lawrence Singleton, who in 1978 raped a young California girl, Mary Vincent, and then chopped off her arms with an axe. He served eight years in prison for this vile crime. Upon his release, he moved to Florida, where in 1997 he killed a woman, Roxanne Hayes. Vincent is shown here as she testifies at the penalty phase of Singleton's trial; he was sentenced to death. Should a dangerous predator such as Singleton ever be released from incapacitation? Is rehabilitation even a remote possibility?

Research also shows that offenders sentenced to prison do not have lower rates of recidivism than those receiving community sentences for similar crimes. For example, white-collar offenders who receive prison sentences are as likely to recidivate as a matched group of offenders who receive community-based sanctions.[149] Rather than reducing the frequency of crime, some research efforts have actually shown that punishment increases re-offending rates.[150] Punishment may bring defiance rather than deterrence, or perhaps the stigma of apprehension may help lock offenders into a criminal career instead of convincing them to avoid one.

A few empirical research studies indicate that some offenders who receive harsh punishments will be less likely to recidivate, or if they do commit crimes again, they may do so less frequently. But the consensus is that the association between crime and specific deterrent measures remains uncertain at best.[151] Only the most severe, draconian punishments seem to influence experienced criminals.[152]

CONNECTIONS

Theoretically, experiencing punishment should deter future crime. However, punishment stigmatizes people and spoils their identity, a turn of events that may encourage antisocial behavior. The two factors may cancel one another out, helping to explain why punishment does not substantially reduce future criminality. The effects of stigma and negative labels are discussed further in Chapter 8. ■

The effects of specific deterrence on preventing domestic violence are discussed in the Race, Culture, Gender, and Criminology feature titled "Deterring Domestic Violence."

Incapacitation

It stands to reason that if more criminals are sent to prison the crime rate should go down. Because most people age out of crime, the duration of a criminal career is limited. Placing offenders behind bars during their prime crime years should lessen their lifetime opportunity to commit crime. The shorter the span of opportunity, the fewer offenses they can commit during their lives; hence crime is reduced. This theory, known as the **incapacitation effect,** seems logical, but does it work? The past 20 years have witnessed significant growth in the number and percentage of the population held in prison and jails; today more than 2 million Americans are incarcerated. Advocates of incapacitation suggest that this effort has been responsible for the long decline in the crime rate that began in 1993.

This argument is persuasive, but not all criminologists buy into the incapacitation effect. Michael Lynch, for one, shows that as the prison population expanded during another period of time, 1972 to 1993, there was little if any

Deterring Domestic Violence

Is it possible to use a specific deterrence strategy to control domestic violence? Would the memory of a formal police arrest reduce the incidence of spousal abuse? Despite the fact that domestic violence is a prevalent, serious crime, police departments have been accused of rarely arresting suspected perpetrators. Lack of forceful action may contribute to chronic episodes of violence, which obviously is of great concern to women's advocacy groups. Is it possible that prompt, formal action by police agencies might prevent the reoccurrence of this serious crime that threatens and even kills so many women?

In the famous Minneapolis domestic violence study, Lawrence Sherman and Richard Berk had police officers randomly assign treatments to the domestic assault cases they encountered on their beats. One approach was to give some sort of advice and mediation; another was to send the assailant from the home for a period of eight hours; and the third was to arrest the assailant. When police took formal action (arrest), they found that the chance of recidivism was substantially less than with less punitive measures,

such as warning offenders or ordering offenders out of the house for a cooling-off period. A six-month follow-up found that only 10 percent of those who were arrested repeated their violent behavior, whereas 19 percent of those advised and 24 percent of those sent away repeated their offenses. Sherman and Berk's interviews of 205 victims demonstrated that arrests were somewhat effective in controlling domestic assaults: 19 percent of the women whose attackers had been arrested reported their mates had assaulted them again; in contrast, 37 percent of those whose mates were advised and 33 percent of those whose mates were sent away reported further assaults. Sherman and Berk concluded that a formal arrest was the most effective means of controlling domestic violence, regardless of what happened to the offender in court.

The Minneapolis experiment deeply affected police operations around the nation. Atlanta, Chicago, Dallas, Denver, Detroit, New York, Miami, San Francisco, and Seattle, among other large cities, adopted policies encouraging arrests in domestic violence cases. A number of states adopted legislation mandating that police either take formal action in domestic abuse cases or explain in writing their failure to act.

Although the findings of the Minneapolis experiment received quick acceptance, government-funded research replicating the experimental design in five other locales, including Omaha, Nebraska, and Charlotte, North Carolina, failed to duplicate the original results. In these locales, formal arrest was not a greater deterrent to domestic abuse than warning or advising the assailant. A recent analysis conducted by Christopher Maxwell and his associates pooled the findings from all the replication sites to provide an overall picture of the arrest/deterrence relationship. Maxwell found that, although arrested batterers did reduce subsequent aggression against female partners, the overall size of the relationship between arrest and repeat offending was at best modest. What seemed more important predictors of repeat offending were the batterers' prior criminal record and/or his age.

Why Is the Deterrent Effect Minimal?

There are a number of reasons arrests do not deter domestic violence. Sherman and his associates found that in some instances the effect of arrest quickly decays and, in the long run, may escalate the frequency of repeat domestic violence.

---

drop in crime rates.[153] Other criminologists believe the association is illusory and that a stable crime rate is actually controlled by factors such as these:

- The size of the teenage population
- The threat of tough new mandatory sentences
- A healthy economy
- Tougher gun laws
- The end of the crack epidemic
- The implementation of tough, aggressive policing strategies in large cities such as New York[154]

CONNECTIONS

Chapter 3 discussed the factors that control crime rates. What appears to be an incapacitation effect may actually reflect the effect of some other legal phenomena

and not the incarceration of so many criminals. If, for example, the crime rate drops as more people are sent to prison, it would appear that incapacitation works. However, crime rates may really be dropping because potential criminals now fear punishment and are being deterred from crime. What appears to be an incapacitation effect may actually be an effect of general deterrence. Similarly, people may be willing to build new prisons because the economy is robust. If the crime rate drops, it may be because of economic effects and not because of prison construction. ■

Can incapacitation reduce crime? Research on the direct benefits of incapacitation has been inconclusive. A number of studies have set out to measure the precise effect of incarceration rates on crime rates, and the results have not supported a strict incarceration policy.[155] If the

Explaining why the initial deterrent effect of arrest decays over time is difficult. It is possible that offenders who are arrested initially fear punishment, but eventually they replace fear with anger and violent intent toward their mates when their cases do not result in severe punishment. Many repeat abusers do not fear arrest, believing formal police action will not cause them harm. They may be aware that police are reluctant to make arrests in domestic violence cases unless there is a significant chance of injury to the victim, for example, when a weapon is used.

It is also possible that the threat of future punishment may have little impact on repeat offenders who have already become involved in the justice system. For example, when they surveyed men in an abuse prevention program, D. Alex Heckert and Edward Gondolf found that the subjects were aware of potential punishment but it was unlikely to deter their spousal abuse. Similarly, Robert Davis and his associates also found little association between severity of punishment for past spousal abuse and re-arrest on subsequent charges. Men were just as likely to recidivate if their case was dismissed, if they were given probation, or even if they were sent to jail. It is possible that some

men who have already experienced arrest and punishment on spouse abuse charges perceive the law as less severe than they had imagined, encouraging rather than deterring future violations.

Critical Thinking Questions

1. Why do arrests seem to have little effect on future domestic violence? Could it be that getting arrested increases feelings of strain and hostility and does little to reduce the problems that led to domestic conflict in the first place? Explain how you think this works.

2. What policies would you suggest to reduce the recurrence of domestic violence?

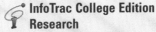
InfoTrac College Edition Research

Would police be more efficient in combating domestic violence if they feared lawsuits from victims? To find out, read:

Lisa Gelhaus. Civil suits against police change domestic violence response. *Trial* Sept 1999 v35 p103

SOURCES: Christopher D. Maxwell, Joel H. Garner, and Jeffrey A. Fagan, *The Effects of Arrest in Intimate Partner Violence: New Evidence from the Spouse Assault Replication Program* (Washington, D.C.: National Institute of Justice, 2001); D. Alex Heckert and Edward Gondolf, "The Effect of Perceptions of Sanctions on Batterer Program Outcomes," *Journal of Research in Crime and Delinquency* 37 (2000) 369–91; Robert Kane, "Patterns of Arrest in Domestic Violence Encounters: Identifying a Police Decision-Making Model," *Journal of Criminal Justice* 27 (1999): 65–79; Dana Jones and Joanne Belknap, "Police Responses to Battering in a Progressive Pro-Arrest Jurisdiction," *Justice Quarterly* 16 (1999): 249–73; Robert Davis, Barbara Smith, and Laura Nickles, "The Deterrent Effect of Prosecuting Domestic Violence Misdemeanors," *Crime and Delinquency* 44 (1998): 434–42; Amy Thistlethwaite, John Wooldredge, and David Gibbs, "Severity of Dispositions and Domestic Violence Recidivism," *Crime and Delinquency* 44 (1998): 388–98; J. David Hirschel, Ira Hutchison, and Charles Dean, "The Failure of Arrest to Deter Spouse Abuse," *Journal of Research in Crime and Delinquency* 29 (1992): 7–33; Franklyn Dunford, David Huizinga, and Delbert Elliott, "The Role of Arrest in Domestic Assault: The Omaha Experiment," *Criminology* 28 (1990): 183–206; Lawrence Sherman, Janell Schmidt, Dennis Rogan, Patrick Gartin, Ellen Cohn, Dean Collins, and Anthony Bacich, "From Initial Deterrence to Long-Term Escalation: Short-Custody Arrest for Domestic Violence," *Criminology* 29 (1991): 821–50; Lawrence Sherman and Richard Berk, "The Specific Deterrent Effects of Arrest for Domestic Assault," *American Sociological Review* 49 (1984): 261–72; Michael Steinman, "Lowering Recidivism among Men Who Batter Women," *Journal of Police Science and Administration* 17 (1990):124–31; and Susan Miller and Leeann Iovanni, "Determinants of Perceived Risk of Formal Sanction for Courtship Violence," *Justice Quarterly* 11 (1994): 282–312.

prison population were cut in half, it has been estimated that the crime rate would most likely go up only 4 percent; if prisons were entirely eliminated, crime might increase 8 percent.[156] Looking at this relationship from another perspective, if the average prison sentence were increased 50 percent, the crime rate might be reduced only 4 percent.[157]

A few criminologists, however, have found an inverse relationship between incarceration rates and crime rates. In a frequently cited study, Reuel Shinnar and Shlomo Shinnar's research on incapacitation in New York led them to conclude that mandatory prison sentences of five years for violent crime and three for property offenses could reduce the reported crime rate by a factor of four or five.[158] In a more recent analysis of incarceration effects, Steven Levitt found that a one-prisoner reduction in the correctional population is associated with an increase of 15 index crimes per year. Although calculations of the costs of

crime are inherently uncertain, Levitt concludes that it appears that the social benefits associated with crime reduction equal or exceed the social costs of incarceration for the marginal prisoner.[159]

The logic behind incarceration   Incarceration as a crime control strategy should work, considering that the criminals who commit crimes are unable to continue from prison or jail. For example, a recent study of 201 heroin abusers in New York City found that if these abusers were incarcerated for one year they would not have been able to commit their yearly haul of crimes: 1,000 robberies, 4,000 burglaries, 10,000 shopliftings, and more than 3,000 other property crimes.[160]

Nonetheless, evaluations of incarceration strategies reveal that their impact may be less than expected. For one thing, there is little evidence that incapacitating criminals will deter them from future criminality and even more reason to believe they may be more inclined to commit crimes upon release. In fact, the more prior incarceration experiences inmates have, the more likely they are to recidivate (and return to prison) within 12 months of their release.[161]

CONNECTIONS

The problems of inmate reentry are discussed in detail in Chapter 7. As millions of former inmates reenter their old neighborhoods, they may become a destabilizing force, driving up crime rates. ∎

By its nature, the prison experience exposes young, first-time offenders to higher risk, more experienced inmates who can influence their lifestyle and help shape their attitudes. Novice inmates also run an increased risk of becoming infected with AIDS and other health hazards and that exposure reduces their life chances after release.[162] The short-term crime reduction effect of incapacitating criminals is negated if the prison experience has the long-term effect of escalating frequency of criminal behavior upon release. Furthermore, the economics of crime suggest that if money can be made from criminal activity, there will always be someone to take the place of the incarcerated offender. New criminals will be recruited and trained, offsetting any benefit accrued by incarceration. Imprisoning established offenders may likewise open new opportunities for competitors who were suppressed by more experienced criminals. For example, incarcerating organized crime members may open drug markets to new gangs; the flow of narcotics into the country may increase after organized crime leaders are imprisoned.

Another reason incarceration may not work is that most criminal offenses are committed by teens and very young adult offenders who are unlikely to be sent to prison for a single felony conviction. In addition, incarcerated criminals, aging behind bars, are already past the age where they are likely to commit crime. As a result, a strict incarceration policy may keep people in prison beyond the time they are a threat to society while a new cohort of high-risk adolescents is on the street. It is possible that the most serious criminals are already behind bars and that adding more to the population will have little appreciable effect while adding tremendous costs to the correctional system.[163]

An incapacitation strategy is also terribly expensive. The prison system costs billions of dollars each year. Even if incarceration could reduce the crime rate, the costs would be enormous. Are U.S. taxpayers willing to spend billions more on new prison construction and annual maintenance fees? A strict incarceration policy would result in a growing number of elderly inmates whose maintenance costs, estimated at $69,000 per year, are three times higher than those of younger inmates. By the year 2001 there will be more than 125,000 of these elderly inmates, and by 2005 about 16 percent of the prison population will be over age 50.[164]

Selective incapacitation: three strikes and you're out A more efficient incapacitation model has been suggested that is based on discovering who the chronic career criminals are. The premise for this model is that if a small number of people account for a relatively large percentage of the nation's crime, then an effort to incapacitate these few troublemakers might have a significant payoff. In an often-cited work, Peter Greenwood of the Rand Corporation suggests that **selective incapacitation** could be an effective crime reduction strategy.[165] In his study of more than 2,000 inmates serving time for theft in California, Michigan, and Texas, he found that selective incapacitation of chronic offenders could reduce the rate of robbery offenses by 15 percent and the inmate population by 5 percent. According to Greenwood's model, chronic offenders can be distinguished on the basis of their offending patterns and lifestyle (for example, their employment record and history of substance abuse). Once identified, high-risk offenders would be eligible for sentencing enhancements that would substantially increase the time they serve in prison.

Another concept receiving widespread attention is the **three strikes and you're out** policy of giving people convicted of three violent offenses a mandatory life term without parole. Many states already employ habitual offender laws that provide long (or life) sentences for repeat offenders. Criminologists retort that although such strategies are politically compelling they will not work for these reasons:

- Most three-time losers are at the verge of aging out of crime anyway.
- Current sentences for violent crimes are already severe.
- An expanding prison population will drive up already high prison costs.
- There would be racial disparity in sentencing.
- Police would be in danger because two-time offenders would violently resist a third arrest knowing they face a life sentence.[166]
- The prison population probably already contains the highest-frequency criminals.

Those who support a selective incapacitation strategy argue that criminals who are already in prison (high-rate offenders) commit significantly more crimes each year than the average criminal who is on the outside (low-rate offenders). If a broad policy of incarceration were employed, requiring mandatory prison sentences for all those convicted of crimes, more low-rate criminals would be placed behind bars.[167] It would be both costly and nonproductive to incarcerate large groups of people who commit relatively few crimes. It makes more economic sense to focus incarceration efforts on known high-rate offenders by lengthening their sentences.

Public Policy Implications of Choice Theory

From the origins of classical theory to the development of modern rational choice views, the belief that criminals choose to commit crime has influenced the relationship between law, punishment, and crime. Although research on the core principles of choice theory and deterrence theories produces mixed results, these models have had an important impact on crime prevention strategies.

When police patrol in well-marked cars, it is assumed that their presence will deter would-be criminals. When the harsh realities of prison life are portrayed in movies and TV shows, the lesson is not lost on potential criminals. Nowhere is the idea that the threat of punishment can control crime more evident than in the implementation of tough mandatory criminal sentences to control violent crime and drug trafficking.

Despite its questionable deterrent effect, some advocates argue that the death penalty can effectively restrict criminality; at least it ensures that convicted criminals never again get the opportunity to kill. Many observers are dismayed because people who are convicted of murder sometimes kill again when released on parole. One study of 52,000 incarcerated murderers found that 810 had been previously convicted of murder and had killed 821 people following their previous release from prison.[168] About 9 percent of all inmates on death row have had prior convictions for homicide. Death penalty advocates argue that if these criminals had been executed for their first offenses hundreds of people would be alive today.[169]

Just Desert

The concept of criminal choice has also prompted the creation of justice policies referred to as **just desert.** The just desert position has been most clearly spelled out by crim-

inologist Andrew Von Hirsch in his book *Doing Justice.*[170] Von Hirsch suggests the concept of desert as a theoretical model to guide justice policy. This utilitarian view purports that punishment is needed to preserve the social equity disturbed by crime. Nonetheless, he claims that the severity of punishment should be commensurate with the seriousness of the crime.[171] Von Hirsch's views can be summarized in these three statements:

1. Those who violate others' rights deserve to be punished.
2. We should not deliberately add to human suffering; punishment makes those punished suffer.
3. However, punishment may prevent more misery than it inflicts; this conclusion reestablishes the need for desert-based punishment.[172]

Desert theory is also concerned with the rights of the accused. It alleges that the rights of the person being punished should not be unduly sacrificed for the good of others (as with deterrence). The offender should not be treated as more (or less) blameworthy than is warranted by the character of his or her offense. For example, Von Hirsch asks the following question: If two crimes, A and B, are equally serious, but if severe penalties are shown to have a deterrent effect only with respect to A, would it be fair to punish the person who has committed crime A more harshly simply to deter others from committing the crime? Conversely, imposing a light sentence for a serious crime would be unfair because it would treat the offender as less blameworthy than he or she is.

In sum, the just desert model suggests that retribution justifies punishment because people deserve what they get for past deeds. Punishment based on deterrence or incapacitation is wrong because it involves an offender's future actions, which cannot accurately be predicted. Punishment should be the same for all people who commit the same crime. Criminal sentences based on individual needs or characteristics are inherently unfair because all people are equally blameworthy for their misdeeds. The influence of Von Hirsch's views can be seen in sentencing models that give the same punishment to all people who commit the same type of crime.

Summary

Choice theories assume that criminals carefully choose whether to commit criminal acts. These theories are summarized in Table 5.1. People are influenced by their fear of the criminal penalties associated with being caught and convicted for law violations. The more severe, certain, and swift the punishment, the more likely it is to control crime. The choice approach is rooted in the classical criminology of Cesare Beccaria and Jeremy Bentham. These eighteenth-century social philosophers argued that punishment should be certain, swift, and severe enough to deter crime.

The growth of positivist criminology, which stressed external causes

Table 5.1   Choice Theories

Theory	Major Premise	Strengths
Rational choice	Law-violating behavior occurs after offenders weigh information on their personal needs and the situational factors involved in the difficulty and risk of committing a crime.	Explains why high-risk youths do not constantly engage in delinquency. Relates theory to delinquency control policy. It is not limited by class or other social variables.
Routine activities	Crime and delinquency are functions of the presence of motivated offenders, the availability of suitable targets, and the absence of capable guardians.	Can explain fluctuations in crime and delinquency rates. Shows how victim behavior influences criminal choice.
General deterrence	People will commit crime and delinquency if they perceive that the benefits outweigh the risks. Crime is a function of the severity, certainty, and speed of punishment.	Shows the relationship between crime and the threat of punishment. Suggests that crime can be controlled by the efficient applications of criminal justice.
Specific deterrence	If punishment is severe enough, criminals will not repeat their illegal acts.	Provides a strategy to reduce crime. Suggests the utility of punishments.
Incapacitation	Keeping known criminals out of circulation will reduce crime rates.	Recognizes the role opportunity plays in criminal behavior. Provides solution to chronic offending.

of crime and rehabilitation of known offenders, reduced the popularity of the classical approach in the twentieth century. However, in the late 1970s the concept of criminal choice once again became an important criminological perspective. Today choice theorists view crime as offense- and offender-specific. Research shows that offenders consider their targets carefully before deciding on a course of action. By implication, crime can be prevented or displaced by convincing potential criminals that the risks of violating the law exceed the benefits.

Deterrence theory holds that, if criminals are indeed rational, an inverse relationship should exist between punishment and crime. However, a number of factors confound the relationship. For example, if people do not believe they will be caught, even harsh punishment may

not deter crime. Deterrence theory has been criticized on the grounds that it wrongfully assumes that criminals make a rational choice before committing crimes, ignores the intricacies of the criminal justice system, and does not take into account the social and psychological factors that may influence criminality. Research designed to test the validity of the deterrence concept has not indicated that deterrent measures actually reduce the crime rate.

Specific deterrence theory holds that the crime rate can be reduced if known offenders are punished so severely that they never commit crimes again. However, there is little evidence that harsh punishment actually reduces the crime rate. Incapacitation theory maintains that if deterrence does not work the best course of action is to incarcerate known offenders

for long periods so that they lack criminal opportunity. Research efforts, however, have not proved that increasing the number of people in prison—and increasing prison sentences—will reduce crime rates.

Choice theory has been influential in shaping public policy. Criminal law is designed to deter potential criminals and fairly punish those who have been caught in illegal acts. Some courts have changed sentencing policies to adapt to classical principles, and the U.S. correctional system seems geared toward incapacitation and specific deterrence. The just desert view is that criminal sanctions should be geared precisely to the seriousness of the crime. People should be punished on the basis of whether they deserve to be punished for what they did and not because it may affect or deter their future behavior.

■ Thinking Like a Criminologist

The attorney general has recently funded a national survey of state sentencing practices. The table provided here shows the

most important findings from the survey.

The attorney general wants you to make some recommendations

about criminal punishment. Is it possible, she asks, that both the length of criminal sentences and the way they are served can have an impact on crime rates? What could be gained by either increasing punishment or requiring inmates to spend more time behind bars before their release? Are we being too lenient or too punitive? As someone who has studied choice theory, how would you interpret these data, and what do they tell you about sentencing patterns? How might crime rates be affected if the way we punished offenders was radically changed?

Type of Offense	Average Sentence	Average Sentence Served Before Release	Average Percentage of Sentence Served
All violent	89 months	43 months	48%
Homicide	149 months	71 months	48%
Rape	117 months	65 months	56%
Kidnapping	104 months	52 months	50%
Robbery	95 months	44 months	6%
Sexual assault	72 months	35 months	49%
Assault	61 months	29 months	48%
Other	60 months	28 months	47%

■ Key Terms

- **rational choice** *(107)*
- **utilitarianism** *(108)*
- **reasoning criminal** *(109)*
- **offense-specific** *(109)*
- **offender-specific** *(109)*
- **crime** *(109)*
- **criminality** *(109)*
- **permeable neighborhood** *(111)*
- **suitable targets** *(112)*
- **edgework** *(115)*
- **situational crime prevention** *(117)*
- **defensible space** *(117)*
- **crime discouragers** *(118)*
- **diffusion** *(119)*
- **discouragement** *(120)*
- **crime displacement** *(120)*
- **extinction** *(120)*
- **general deterrence** *(120)*
- **deterrence theory** *(121)*
- **crackdowns** *(122)*
- **informal sanctions** *(123)*
- **specific deterrence** *(124)*
- **incapacitation effect** *(125)*
- **selective incapacitation** *(128)*
- **three strikes and you're out** *(128)*
- **just desert** *(129)*

■ Critical Thinking Questions

1. Are criminals rational decision makers, or are they motivated by uncontrollable psychological and emotional drives?

2. Would you want to live in a society where crime rates are quite low because criminals are subjected to extremely harsh punishments, such as flogging for vandalism?

3. If you were caught by the police while shoplifting, which would you be more afraid of: receiving criminal punishment or having to face your friends or relatives?

4. Is it possible to create a method of capital punishment that would actually deter murder, for example, by televising executions? What might be some of the negative consequences of such a policy?

■ Notes

1. Phil Stewart, Cocaine Price in US Stable, Official Says," *Boston Globe,* 24 May 2001, p. 15.

2. Francis Edward Devine, "Cesare Beccaria and the Theoretical Foundations of Modern Penal Jurisprudence," *New England Journal on Prison Law* 7 (1982): 8–21.

3. Ibid.

4. Bob Roshier, *Controlling Crime* (Chicago: Lyceum Books, 1989), p. 10.

5. Jeremy Bentham, *A Fragment on Government and an Introduction to the Principle of Morals and Legislation,* ed. Wilfred Harrison (Oxford: Basil Blackwell, 1967).

6. Ibid., p. xi.

7. Robert Martinson, "What Works?— Questions and Answers about Prison Reform," *Public Interest* 35 (1974): 22–54.

8. Charles Murray and Louis Cox, *Beyond Probation* (Beverly Hills: Sage, 1979).

9. Ronald Bayer, "Crime, Punishment, and the Decline of Liberal Optimism," *Crime and Delinquency* 27 (1981): 190.

10. James Q. Wilson, *Thinking about Crime,* rev. ed. (New York: Vintage Books, 1983), p. 260.

11. Ibid., p. 128.

12. Michael Tonry, *Malign Neglect: Race, Crime and Punishment in America* (New York: Oxford University Press, 1995).

13. John Irwin and James Austin, *It's about Time: America's Imprisonment Binge* (Belmont, Calif.: Wadsworth, 1997).

14. Kimberly Cook, "A Passion to Punish: Abortion Opponents Who Favor the Death Penalty," *Justice Quarterly* 15 (1998): 329–46.

15. See, generally, Derek Cornish and Ronald Clarke, eds. *The Reasoning Criminal: Rational Choice Perspectives on Offending* (New York: Springer Verlag, 1986); Philip Cook, "The Demand and Supply of Criminal Opportunities," in *Crime and Justice*, vol. 7, eds. Michael Tonry and Norval Morris (Chicago: University of Chicago Press, 1986), pp. 1–28; Ronald Clarke and Derek Cornish, "Modeling Offender's Decisions: A Framework for Research and Policy," in *Crime and Justice*, vol. 6, eds. Michael Tonry and Norval Morris (Chicago: University of Chicago Press, 1985), pp. 147–87; and Morgan Reynolds, *Crime by Choice: An Economic Analysis* (Dallas: Fisher Institute, 1985).

16. George Rengert and John Wasilchick, *Suburban Burglary: A Time and Place for Everything* (Springfield, Ill.: Charles Thomas, 1985).

17. Derek Cornish and Ronald Clarke, "Understanding Crime Displacement: An Application of Rational Choice Theory," *Criminology* 25 (1987): 933–47.

18. Lloyd Phillips and Harold Votey, "The Influence of Police Interventions and Alternative Income Sources on the Dynamic Process of Choosing Crime as a Career," *Journal of Quantitative Criminology* 3 (1987): 251–74.

19. Ibid.

20. Michael Gottfredson and Travis Hirschi, *A General Theory of Crime* (Stanford, Calif.: Stanford University Press, 1990).

21. Pierre Tremblay and Carlo Morselli, "Patterns in Criminal Achievement: Wilson and Abrhamse Revisited," *Criminology* 38 (2000): 633–60.

22. Liliana Pezzin, "Earnings Prospects, Matching Effects, and the Decision to Terminate a Criminal Career," *Journal of Quantitative Criminology* 11 (1995): 29–50.

23. Ronald Akers, "Rational Choice, Deterrence and Social Learning Theory in Criminology: The Path Not Taken," *Journal of Criminal Law and Criminology* 81 (1990): 653–76.

24. Neal Shover, *Aging Criminals* (Beverly Hills, Calif.: Sage, 1985).

25. Patricia Morgan and Karen Ann Joe, "Citizens and Outlaws: The Private Lives and Public Lifestyles of Women in the Illicit Drug Economy," *Journal of Drug Issues* 26 (1996): 125–42, at 132.

26. Ibid., p. 136.

27. Bruce Jacobs, "Crack Dealers' Apprehension Avoidance Techniques: A Case of Restrictive Deterrence," *Justice Quarterly* 13 (1996): 359–81.

28. Ibid., p. 367.

29. Ibid., p. 372.

30. Gordon Knowles, "Deception, Detection, and Evasion: A Trade Craft Analysis of Honolulu, Hawaii's Street Crack Cocaine Traffickers," *Journal of Criminal Justice* 27 (1999): 443–55.

31. Bruce Jacobs and Jody Miller, "Crack Dealing, Gender, and Arrest Avoidance," *Social Problems* 45 (1998): 550–66.

32. Jacobs, "Crack Dealers' Apprehension Avoidance Techniques."

33. Ibid., p. 367.

34. Ibid., p. 368.

35. Paul Cromwell, James Olson, and D'Aunn Wester Avary, *Breaking and Entering, An Ethnographic Analysis of Burglary* (Newbury Park, Calif.: Sage, 1989), pp. 30–32.

36. Garland White, "Neighborhood Permeability and Burglary Rates," *Justice Quarterly* 7 (1990): 57–67.

37. Ibid., p. 65.

38. Eric Baumer, Janet Lauritsen, Richard Rosenfeld, and Richard Wright, "The Influence of Crack Cocaine on Robbery, Burglary, and Homicide Rates: A Cross-City, Longitudinal Analysis," *Journal of Research in Crime and Delinquency* 35 (1998): 316–40.

39. George Rengert and John Wasilchick, *Space, Time, and Crime: Ethnographic Insights into Residential Burglary* (Washington, D.C.: National Institute of Justice, 1989); see also Rengert and Wasilchick, *Suburban Burglary*.

40. Cromwell, Olson, and Avary, *Breaking and Entering*.

41. Ibid., p. 24.

42. John Gibbs and Peggy Shelly, "Life in the Fast Lane: A Retrospective View by Commercial Thieves," *Journal of Research in Crime and Delinquency* 19 (1982): 229–30.

43. Matthew Robinson, "Lifestyles, Routine Activities, and Residential Burglary Victimization," *Journal of Criminal Justice* 22 (1999): 27–52.

44. Cromwell, Olson, and Avary, *Breaking and Entering*.

45. Andrew Buck, Simon Hakim, and George Rengert, "Burglar Alarms and the Choice Behavior of Burglars: A Suburban Phenomenon," *Journal of Criminal Justice* 21 (1993): 497–507.

46. Ralph Taylor and Stephen Gottfredson, "Environmental Design, Crime, and Prevention: An Examination of Community Dynamics," in *Communities and Crime*, eds. Albert Reiss and Michael Tonry (Chicago: University of Chicago Press, 1986), pp. 387–416.

47. Michael Costanzo, William Halperin, and Nathan Gale, "Criminal Mobility and the Directional Component in Journeys to Crime," in *Metropolitan Crime Patterns*, eds. Robert Figlio, Simon Hakim, and George Rengert (Monsey, N.Y.: Criminal Justice Press, 1986), pp. 73–95.

48. Joseph Deutsch and Gil Epstein, "Changing a Decision Taken Under Uncertainty: The Case of the Criminal's Location Choice," *Urban Studies* 35 (1998): 1335–44.

49. Robert Sampson and Jacqueline Cohen, "Deterrent Effects of the Police on Crime: A Replication and Theoretical Extension," *Law and Society Review* 22 (1988): 163–88.

50. Elizabeth Ehrhardt Mustaine and Richard Tewksbury, "Predicting Risks of Larceny Theft Victimization: A Routine Activity Analysis Using Refined Lifestyle Measures," *Criminology* 36 (1998): 829–58.

51. Gary Kleck and Don Kates, *Armed: New Perspectives on Guns* (Amherst, N.Y.: Prometheus Books, 2001).

52. Kenneth Tunnell, *Choosing Crime* (Chicago: Nelson-Hall, 1992), p. 105.

53. Associated Press, "Thrift Hearings Resume Today in Senate," *Boston Globe*, 2 January 1991, p. 10.

54. Richard Felson and Steven Messner, "To Kill or Not to Kill? Lethal Outcomes in Injurious Attacks," *Criminology* 34 (1996): 519–45, at 541.

55. James Wright and Peter Rossi, *Armed and Considered Dangerous: A Survey of Felons and Their Firearms* (Hawthorne, N.Y.: Aldine De Guyer, 1983), pp. 141–59.

56. Gary Kleck and Marc Gertz, "Carry Guns for Protection: Results from the National Self-Defense Survey," *Journal of Research in Crime and Delinquency* 35 (1998): 193–224.

57. Peter Van Koppen and Robert Jansen, "The Time to Rob: Variations in Time and Number of Commercial Robberies," *Journal of Research in Crime and Delinquency* 36 (1999): 7–29.

58. William Smith, Sharon Glave Frazee, and Elizabeth Davison, " Furthering the Integration of Routine Activity and Social Disorganization Theories: Small Units of Analysis and the Study of Street Robbery as a Diffusion Process," *Criminology* 38 (2000): 489–521.

59. Paul Bellair, "Informal Surveillance and Street Crime: A Complex Relationship," *Criminology* 38 (2000): 137–67.

60. John Gibbs and Peggy Shelly, "Life in the Fast Lane: A Retrospective View by Commercial Thieves," *Journal of Research in Crime and Delinquency* 19 (1982): 229–30.

61. John Petraitis, Brian Flay, and Todd Miller, "Reviewing Theories of Adolescent Substance Use: Organizing Pieces in the Puzzle," *Psychological Bulletin* 117 (1995): 67–86.

62. Leanne Fiftal Alarid, James Marquart, Velmer Burton, Francis Cullen, and Steven Cuvelier, "Women's Roles in Serious Offenses: A Study of Adult Felons," *Justice Quarterly* 13 (1996): 431–54, at 448.

63. Ben Fox, "Jury Recommends Death for Convicted Child Killer," *Boston Globe*, 6 October 1999, p. 3.

64. Alan Lizotte, James Tesoriero, Terence Thornberry, and Marvin Krohn, "Patterns of Adolescent Firearms Ownership and Use," *Justice Quarterly* 11 (1994): 51–74.

65. Alan Lizotte, Marvin Krohn, James Howell, Kimberly Tobin, and Gregory Howard, "Factors Influencing Gun Carrying among Young Urban Males over the Adolescent–Young Adult Life Course," *Criminology* 38 (2000): 811–34.

66. Scott Decker, "Deviant Homicide: A New Look at the Role of Motives and Victim–Offender Relationships," *Journal of Research in Crime and Delinquency* 33 (1996): 427–49.

67. Felson and Messner, "To Kill or Not to Kill?"

68. Eric Hickey, *Serial Murderers and Their Victims* (Pacific Grove, Calif.: Brooks/Cole, 1991), p. 84.

69. Janet Warren, Roland Reboussin, Robert Hazlewood, Andrea Cummings, Natalie Gibbs, and Susan Trumbetta, "Crime Scene and Distance Correlates of Serial Rape," *Journal of Quantitative Criminology* 14 (1998): 35–58.

70. Christopher Birkbeck and Gary LaFree, "The Situational Analysis of Crime and Deviance," *American Review of Sociology* 19 (1993): 113–37;

Karen Heimer and Ross Matsueda, "Role-Taking, Role Commitment, and Delinquency: A Theory of Differential Social Control," *American Sociological Review* 59 (1994): 400–37.

71. Peter Wood, Walter Gove, James Wilson, and John Cochran, "Nonsocial Reinforcement and Habitual Criminal Conduct: An Extension of Learning," *Criminology* 35 (1997): 335–66.

72. Jeff Ferrell, "Criminological Versthen: Inside the Immediacy of Crime," *Justice Quarterly* 14 (1997): 3–23, at 12.

73. George Rengert, "Spatial Justice and Criminal Victimization," *Justice Quarterly* 6 (1989): 543–64.

74. Oscar Newman, *Defensible Space: Crime Prevention through Urban Design* (New York: Macmillan, 1973).

75. C. Ray Jeffery, *Crime Prevention through Environmental Design* (Beverly Hills: Sage, 1971).

76. See also Pochara Theerathorn, "Architectural Style, Aesthetic Landscaping, Home Value, and Crime Prevention," *International Journal of Comparative and Applied Criminal Justice* 12 (1988): 269–77.

77. Ronald Clarke, *Situational Crime Prevention: Successful Case Studies* (Albany, N.Y.: Harrow and Heston, 1992).

78. Marcus Felson, "Routine Activities and Crime Prevention," in National Council for Crime Prevention, *Studies on Crime and Crime Prevention, Annual Review*, vol. 1 (Stockholm: Scandinavian University Press, 1992), pp. 30–34.

79. Barry Webb, "Steering Column Locks and Motor Vehicle Theft: Evaluations for Three Countries," in *Crime Prevention Studies*, ed. Ronald Clarke (Monsey, N.Y.: Criminal Justice Press, 1994), pp. 71–89.

80. Barbara Morse and Delbert Elliott, "Effects of Ignition Interlock Devices on DUI Recidivism: Findings from a Longitudinal Study in Hamilton County, Ohio," *Crime and Delinquency* 38 (1992): 131–57.

81. Nancy LaVigne, "Gasoline Drive-Offs: Designing a Less Convenient Environment," in *Crime Prevention Studies*, vol. 2, ed. Ronald Clarke (New York: Criminal Justice Press, 1994), pp. 91–114.

82. Ronald Clarke, "Deterring Obscene Phone Callers: The New Jersey Experience," *Situational Crime Prevention*, ed. Ronald Clarke (Albany, N.Y.: Harrow and Heston, 1992), pp. 124–32.

83. Marcus Felson, "Those Who Discourage Crime," in *Crime and Place, Crime Prevention Studies*, vol. 4 eds., John Eck and David Weisburd (New York: Criminal Justice Press, 1995), pp. 53–

66; John Eck, Drug Markets and Drug Places: A Case-Control Study of the Spatial Structure of Illicit Drug Dealing, Ph.D. diss. University of Maryland, College Park, 1994.

84. Eck, Drug Markets and Drug Places, p. 29.

85. Lorraine Green Mazerolle, Colleen Kadleck, and Jan Roehl, "Controlling Drug and Disorder Problems: The Role of Place Managers," *Criminology* 36 (1998): 371–404.

86. Ronald Clarke and David Weisburd, "Diffusion of Crime Control Benefits: Observations of the Reverse of Displacement," in *Crime Prevention Studies*, vol. 2, ed. Ronald Clarke (New York: Criminal Justice Press, 1994).

87. David Weisburd and Lorraine Green, "Policing Drug Hot Spots: The Jersey City Drug Market Analysis Experiment," *Justice Quarterly* 12 (1995): 711–34.

88. Lorraine Green, "Cleaning Up Drug Hot Spots in Oakland, California: The Displacement and Diffusion Effects," *Justice Quarterly* 12 (1995): 737–54.

89. Ian Ayres and Steven D. Levitt, "Measuring Positive Externalities from Unobservable Victim Precaution: An Empirical Analysis of Lojack," *Quarterly Journal of Economics* 113 (1998): 43–78.

90. Robert Barr and Ken Pease, "Crime Placement, Displacement, and Deflection," in *Crime and Justice, A Review of Research*, vol. 12, eds. Michael Tonry and Norval Morris (Chicago: University of Chicago Press, 1990), pp. 277–319.

91. Clarke, *Situational Crime Prevention*, p. 27.

92. Ibid., p. 35.

93. Susan Popkin, Victoria Gwlasda, Dennis Rosenbaum, Jean Amendolla, Wendell Johnson, and Lynn Olson, "Combating Crime in Public Housing: A Qualitative and Quantitative Longitudinal Analysis of the Chicago Housing Authority's Anti-Drug Initiative," *Justice Quarterly* 16 (1999): 519–57.

94. R. Steven Daniels, Lorin Baumhover, William Formby, and Carolyn Clark-Daniels, "Police Discretion and Elder Mistreatment: A Nested Model of Observation, Reporting and Satisfaction," *Journal of Criminal Justice* 27 (1999): 209–25.

95. Robert Bursik, Harold Grasmick, and Mitchell Chamlin, "The Effect of Longitudinal Arrest Patterns on the Development of Robbery Trends at the Neighborhood Level," *Criminology* 28 (1990): 431–50; Theodore Chiricos and Gordon Waldo, "Punishment and

Crime: An Examination of Some Empirical Evidence," *Social Problems* 18 (1970): 200–17.

96. Daniel Nagin and Greg Pogarsky, "Integrating Celerity, Impulsivity, and Extralegal Sanction Threats into a Model of General Deterrence: Theory and Evidence," *Criminology* 39 (2001): 865–92.

97. Charles Tittle and Alan Rowe, "Certainty of Arrest and Crime Rates: A Further Test of the Deterrence Hypothesis," *Social Forces* 52 (1974): 455–62.

98. David Bayley, *Policing for the Future* (New York: Oxford, 1994).

99. For a review, see Thomas Marvell and Carlisle Moody, "Specification Problems, Police Levels, and Crime Rates," *Criminology* 34 (1996): 609–46.

100. Tomislav V. Kovandzic and John J. Sloan, "Police Levels and Crime Rates Revisited, A County-Level Analysis from Florida (1980–1998)," *Journal of Criminal Justice* 30 (2002): 65–76; Steven Levitt, "Using Electoral Cycles in Police Hiring to Estimate the Effect of Police on Crime," *American Economic Review* 87 (1997): 70–91; Marvell and Moody, "Specification Problems, Police Levels, and Crime Rates."

101. George Kelling, Tony Pate, Duane Dieckman, and Charles Brown, *The Kansas City Preventive Patrol Experiment: A Summary Report* (Washington, D.C.: Police Foundation, 1974).

102. Kenneth Novak, Jennifer Hartman, Alexander Holsinger, and Michael Turner, "The Effects of Aggressive Policing of Disorder on Serious Crime," *Policing* 22 (1999): 171–90.

103. Lawrence Sherman, "Police Crackdowns," *NIJ Reports* March/April 1990: 2–6, at 2.

104. Michael Smith, "Police-Led Crackdowns and Cleanups: An Evaluation of a Crime Control Initiative in Richmond, Virginia," *Crime and Delinquency* 47 (2001): 60–68.

105. Anthony Braga, David Weisburd, Elin Waring, Lorraine Green Mazerolle, William Spelman, and Francis Gajewski, "Problem-Oriented Policing in Violent Crime Places: A Randomized Controlled Experiment," *Criminology* 37 (1999): 541–80.

106. Eric Fritsch, Tory Caeti, and Robert Taylor, "Gang Suppression through Saturation Patrol, Aggressive Curfew, and Truancy Enforcement: A Quasi-Experimental Test of the Dallas Anti-Gang Initiative," *Crime and Delinquency* 45 (1999): 122–39.

107. Crime and Punishment in America: 1997 Update. National Center for Policy Analysis, Dallas, Texas, 1997.

108. Nagin and Pogarsky, "Integrating Celerity, Impulsivity, and Extralegal Sanction Threats into a Model of General Deterrence," pp. 884–85.

109. H. Laurence Ross, "Implications of Drinking-and-Driving Law Studies for Deterrence Research," in *Critique and Explanation, Essays in Honor of Gwynne Nettler*, eds. Timothy Hartnagel and Robert Silverman (New Brunswick, N.J.: Transaction Books, 1986), pp. 159–71; H. Laurence Ross, Richard McCleary, and Gary LaFree, "Can Mandatory Jail Laws Deter Drunk Driving? The Arizona Case," *Journal of Criminal Law and Criminology* 81 (1990): 156–67.

110. Ed Stevens and Brian Payne, "Applying Deterrence Theory in the Context of Corporate Wrongdoing: Limitations on Punitive Damages," *Journal of Criminal Justice* 27 (1999) 195–209; Jeffrey Roth, *Firearms and Violence* (Washington, D.C.: National Institute of Justice, 1994); and Thomas Marvell and Carlisle Moody, "The Impact of Enhanced Prison Terms for Felonies Committed with Guns," *Criminology* 33 (1995): 247–81.

111. Robert Dann, "The Deterrent Effect of Capital Punishment," *Friends Social Service Series* 29 (1935).

112. Thorsten Sellin, *The Death Penalty* (Philadelphia: American Law Institute, 1959); Walter Reckless, "Use of the Death Penalty," *Crime and Delinquency* 15 (1969): 43–51.

113. Dane Archer, Rosemary Gartner, and Marc Beittel, "Homicide and the Death Penalty: A Cross-National Test of a Deterrence Hypothesis," *Journal of Criminal Law and Criminology* 74 (1983): 991–1014.

114. Ibid.

115. Jon Sorenson, Robert Wrinkle, Victoria Brewer, and James Marquart, "Capital Punishment and Deterrence: Examining the Effect of Executions on Murder in Texas," *Crime and Delinquency* 45 (1999): 481–93.

116. William Bailey, "Disaggregation in Deterrence and Death Penalty Research: The Case of Murder in Chicago," *Journal of Criminal Law and Criminology* 74 (1986): 827–59.

117. Steven Messner and Kenneth Tardiff, "Economic Inequality and Level of Homicide: An Analysis of Urban Neighborhoods," *Criminology* 24 (1986): 297–317.

118. David Phillips, "The Deterrent Effect of Capital Punishment," *American Journal of Sociology* 86 (1980): 139–48; Hans Zeisel, "A Comment on the 'Deterrent Effect of Capital Punishment' by Phillips," *American Journal of Sociology* 88 (1982): 167–69; see also Sam McFarland, "Is Capital Punishment a Short-Term Deterrent to Homicide? A Study of the Effects of Four Recent American Executions," *Journal of Criminal Law and Criminology* 74 (1984): 1014–32.

119. Steven Stack, "Publicized Executions and Homicide, 1950–1980," *American Sociological Review* 52 (1987): 532–40; for a study challenging Stack's methods, see William Bailey and Ruth Peterson, "Murder and Capital Punishment: A Monthly Time-Series Analysis of Execution Publicity," *American Sociological Review* 54 (1989): 722–43; Steven Stack, "The Effect of Well-Publicized Executions on Homicide in California," *Journal of Crime and Justice* 21 (1998): 1–12.

120. James Yunker, "A New Statistical Analysis of Capital Punishment Incorporating U.S. Postmoratorium Data," *Social Science Quarterly* 82 (2001): 297–312.

121. Wanda Foglia, "Perceptual Deterrence and the Mediating Effect of Internalized Norms among Inner-City Teenagers," *Journal of Research in Crime and Delinquency* 34 (1997): 414–42.

122. Harold Grasmick, Robert Bursik, and Karyl Kinsey, "Shame and Embarrassment as Deterrents to Noncompliance with the Law: The Case of an Anti-Littering Campaign." Paper presented at the annual meeting of the American Society of Criminology, Baltimore, November 1990, p. 3.

123. Charles Tittle, *Sanctions and Social Deviance* (New York: Praeger, 1980).

124. For an opposite view, see Steven Burkett and David Ward, "A Note on Perceptual Deterrence, Religiously Based Moral Condemnation, and Social Control," *Criminology* 31 (1993): 119–34.

125. Ibid.

126. John Snortum, "Drinking–Driving Compliance in Great Britain: The Role of Law as a 'Threat' and as a 'Moral Eye-Opener,'" *Journal of Criminal Justice* 18 (1990): 479–99.

127. Donald Green, "Past Behavior as a Measure of Actual Future Behavior: An Unresolved Issue in Perceptual Deterrence Research," *Journal of Criminal Law and Criminology* 80 (1989): 781–804, at 803; Matthew Silberman, "Toward a Theory of Criminal Deterrence," *American Sociological Review* 41 (1976): 442–61; Linda Anderson, Theodore Chiricos, and Gordon

Waldo, "Formal and Informal Sanctions: A Comparison of Deterrent Effects," *Social Problems* 25 (1977): 103–114. See also Maynard Erickson and Jack Gibbs, "Objective and Perceptual Properties of Legal Punishment and Deterrence Doctrine," *Social Problems* 25 (1978): 253–64; and Daniel Nagin and Raymond Paternoster, "Enduring Individual Differences and Rational Choice Theories of Crime," *Law and Society Review* 27 (1993): 467–85.

128. Harold Grasmick and Robert Bursik, "Conscience, Significant Others, and Rational Choices: Extending the Deterrence Model," *Law and Society Review* 24 (1990): 837–61, at 854.

129. Grasmick, Bursik, and Kinsey, "Shame and Embarrassment as Deterrents to Noncompliance with the Law"; Harold Grasmick, Robert Bursik, and Bruce Arneklev, "Reduction in Drunk Driving as a Response to Increased Threats of Shame, Embarrassment, and Legal Sanctions," *Criminology* 31 (1993): 41–69.

130. Harold Grasmick, Brenda Sims Blackwell, and Robert Bursik, "Changes in the Sex Patterning of Perceived Threats of Sanctions," *Law and Society Review* 27 (1993): 679–99.

131. Thomas Peete, Trudie Milner, and Michael Welch, "Levels of Social Integration in Group Contexts and the Effects of Informal Sanction Threat on Deviance," *Criminology* 32 (1994): 85–105.

132. Ernest Van Den Haag, "The Criminal Law as a Threat System," *Journal of Criminal Law and Criminology* 73 (1982): 709–85.

133. David Lykken, "Psychopathy, Sociopathy, and Crime," *Society* 34 (1996): 30–38.

134. George Lowenstein, Daniel Nagin, and Raymond Paternoster, "The Effect of Sexual Arousal on Expectations of Sexual Forcefulness," *Journal of Research in Crime and Delinquency* 34 (1997): 443–73.

135. Ken Auletta, *The Under Class* (New York: Random House, 1982).

136. Foglia, "Perceptual Deterrence and the Mediating Effect of Internalized Norms among Inner-City Teenagers"; Raymond Paternoster, "Decisions to Participate in and Desist from Four Types of Common Delinquency: Deterrence and the Rational Choice Perspective," *Law and Society Review* 23 (1989): 7–29; Raymond Paternoster, "Examining Three-Wave Deterrence Models: A Question of Temporal Order and Specification," *Journal of Criminal Law and Criminology* 79 (1988): 135–63; Raymond Paternoster, Linda Saltzman, Gordon Waldo, and Theodore Chiricos, "Estimating Perceptual Stability and Deterrent Effects: The Role of Perceived Legal Punishment in the Inhibition of Criminal Involvement," *Journal of Criminal Law and Criminology* 74 (1983): 270–97; M. William Minor and Joseph Harry, "Deterrent and Experiential Effects in Perceptual Deterrence Research: A Replication and Extension," *Journal of Research in Crime and Delinquency* 19 (1982): 190–203; Lonn Lanza-Kaduce, "Perceptual Deterrence and Drinking and Driving among College Students," *Criminology* 26 (1988): 321–41.

137. Foglia, "Perceptual Deterrence and the Mediating Effect of Internalized Norms among Inner-City Teenagers," pp. 419–43.

138. Alex Piquero and George Rengert, "Studying Deterrence with Active Residential Burglars," *Justice Quarterly* 16 (1999): 451–62.

139. David Klinger, "Policing Spousal Assault," *Journal of Research in Crime and Delinquency* 32 (1995): 308–24.

140. Paternoster, "Decisions to Participate in and Desist from Four Types of Common Delinquency."

141. James Williams and Daniel Rodeheaver, "Processing of Criminal Homicide Cases in a Large Southern City," *Sociology and Social Research* 75 (1991): 80–88.

142. James Q. Wilson, *Thinking about Crime* (New York: Basic Books, 1975).

143. James Q. Wilson and Richard Herrnstein, *Crime and Human Nature* (New York: Simon and Schuster, 1985), p. 494.

144. Christina Dejong, "Survival Analysis and Specific Deterrence: Integrating Theoretical and Empirical Models of Recidivism," *Criminology* 35 (1997): 561–76.

145. Paul Tracy and Kimberly Kempf-Leonard, *Continuity and Discontinuity in Criminal Careers* (New York: Plenum Press, 1996).

146. Lawrence Greenfeld, *Examining Recidivism* (Washington, D.C.: U.S. Government Printing Office, 1985).

147. Allen Beck and Bernard Shipley, *Recidivism of Prisoners Released in 1983* (Washington, D.C.: Bureau of Justice Statistics, 1989).

148. Dejong, "Survival Analysis and Specific Deterrence," p. 573.

149. David Weisburd, Elin Waring, and Ellen Chayet, "Specific Deterrence in a Sample of Offenders Convicted of White-Collar Crimes," *Criminology* 33 (1995): 587–607.

150. Dejong, "Survival Analysis and Specific Deterrence"; Raymond Paternoster and Alex Piquero, "Reconceptualizing Deterrence: An Empirical Test of Personal and Vicarious Experiences," *Journal of Research in Crime and Delinquency* 32 (1995): 251–58.

151. Charles Murray and Louis Cox, *Beyond Probation* (Beverly Hills: Sage, 1979); Perry Shapiro and Harold Votey, "Deterrence and Subjective Probabilities of Arrest: Modeling Individual Decisions to Drink and Drive in Sweden," *Law and Society Review* 18 (1984): 111–49; Douglas Smith and Patrick Gartin, "Specifying Specific Deterrence: The Influence of Arrest on Future Criminal Activity," *American Sociological Review* 54 (1989): 94–105.

152. Eleni Apospori and Geoffrey Alpert, "Research Note: The Role of Differential Experience with the Criminal Justice System in Changes in Perceptions of Severity of Legal Sanctions over Time," *Crime and Delinquency* 39 (1993): 184–94.

153. Michael Lynch, "Beating a Dead Horse: Is There Any Basic Empirical Evidence for the Deterrent Effect of Imprisonment?" *Crime, Law and Social Change* 31 (1999): 347–62.

154. Andrew Karmen, Why Is New York City's Murder Rate Dropping So Sharply? Unpublished paper, John Jay College, New York City, 1996.

155. Isaac Ehrlich, "Participation in Illegitimate Activities: An Economic Analysis," *Journal of Political Economy* 81 (1973): 521–67; Lee Bowker, "Crime and the Use of Prisons in the United States: A Time Series Analysis," *Crime and Delinquency* 27 (1981): 206–12.

156. David Greenberg, "The Incapacitative Effects of Imprisonment: Some Estimates," *Law and Society Review* 9 (1975): 541–80.

157. Ibid., p. 558.

158. Reuel Shinnar and Shlomo Shinnar, "The Effects of the Criminal Justice System on the Control of Crime: A Quantitative Approach," *Law and Society Review* 9 (1975): 581–611.

159. Thomas Marvell and Carlisle Moody, "The Impact of Prison Growth on Homicide," *Homicide Studies* 1 (1997): 205–33.

160. David Greenberg and Nancy Larkin, "The Incapacitation of Criminal Opiate Users," *Crime and Delinquency* 44 (1998): 205–28.

161. John Wallerstedt, *Returning to Prison, Bureau of Justice Statistics Special Report*

(Washington, D.C.: U.S. Department of Justice, 1984).

162. James Marquart, Victoria Brewer, Janet Mullings, and Ben Crouch, "The Implications of Crime Control Policy on HIV/AIDS-Related Risk among Women Prisoners," *Crime and Delinquency* 45 (1999): 82–98.

163. Jose Canela-Cacho, Alfred Blumstein, and Jacqueline Cohen, "Relationship between the Offending Frequency of Imprisoned and Free Offenders," *Criminology* 35 (1997): 133–71.

164. Kate King and Patricia Bass, "Southern Prisons and Elderly Inmates: Taking a Look Inside." Paper presented at the American Society of Criminology meeting, San Diego, Calif., 1997.

165. Peter Greenwood, *Selective Incapacitation* (Santa Monica, Calif.: Rand Corp., 1982).

166. Marc Mauer, Testimony before the U.S. Congress, House Judiciary Committee, on "Three Strikes and You're Out," 1 March 1994.

167. Canela-Cacho, Blumstein, and Cohen, "Relationship between the Offending Frequency of Imprisoned and Free Offenders."

168. Stephen Markman and Paul Cassell, "Protecting the Innocent: A Response to the Bedeau-Radelet Study," *Stanford Law Review* 41 (1988): 121–70, at 153.

169. James Stephan and Tracy Snell, *Capital Punishment, 1994* (Washington, D.C.: Bureau of Justice Statistics, 1996), p. 8.

170. Andrew Von Hirsch, *Doing Justice* (New York: Hill and Wang, 1976).

171. Ibid., pp. 15–16.

172. Ibid.

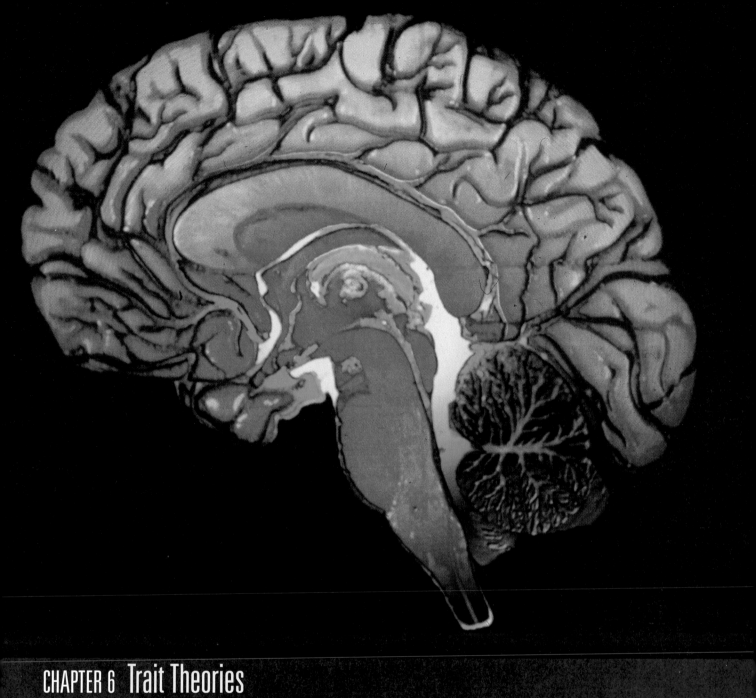

© Sovereign/PhotoTake

CHAPTER 6 Trait Theories

Introduction

Russell Eugene Weston Jr., 41, was a quiet loner who drifted back and forth between a cabin in the Montana mountains and a modest house in rural Illinois.[1] He became an increasingly troubled figure and was hospitalized in 1996 after he wrote threatening letters to government officials. On July 25, 1998, Weston entered the U.S. capitol building and went on a shooting rampage. Two capitol police officers were slain, and a female tourist was wounded. After his arrest, his parents told officials that their son had been diagnosed by a medical professional as a paranoid schizophrenic. His neighbors portrayed Weston as a withdrawn, introverted loner who had grown increasingly angry and alienated over the years. When invitations went out for a 20-year reunion to the 63 members of his 1974 graduating class at Valmeyer High School, Weston sent his invitation back scrawled with obscenities and a warning never to contact him again. "When he was on his medication, he was fine, he would wave and talk," said a neighbor who knew Weston during his youth, "When he was off the medication, he was paranoid; you just didn't know."

One of his former classmates remembered Weston from the seventh grade on, mostly as "one of the forgotten middle kids, kind of on the fat side, not a sports guy, never went out with any girls. Only had a couple of friends." Then, around the eleventh grade, "he started getting into the drug scene, smoking marijuana. He and a group of other kids, they all went out to this place in Montana. They wanted to get away, to be free. It was to be some kind of self-sufficient commune. I heard he had a gold claim out there."

Weston's case provides the public with an image of the criminal offender as a deeply disturbed individual who suffers from a garden variety of mental and physical abnormalities. In fact, he was later found to be mentally ill and incompetent to stand trial. The image of a disturbed, mentally ill offender seems plausible because a generation of Americans has grown up on films and TV shows that portray violent criminals as mentally deranged and physically abnormal.

Beginning with Alfred Hitchcock's film *Psycho*, producers have made millions depicting the ghoulish acts of people who at first seem normal and even friendly but turn out to be demented and dangerous. Lurking out there are crazed baby-sitters (*Hand That Rocks the Cradle*), frenzied airline passengers (*Turbulence*), deranged roommates (*Single, White Female*), psychotic tenants (*Pacific Heights*), demented secretaries (*The Temp*), unhinged police (*Maniac Cop*), irrational fans (*The Fan; Misery*), abnormal girlfriends (*Fatal Attraction*) and boyfriends (*Fear*), unstable husbands (*Sleeping with the Enemy*) and wives (*Black Widow*), loony fathers (*The Stepfather*) mothers (*Friday the 13th, Part 1*) and grandmothers (*Hush*), unbalanced crime victims (*I Know What You Did Last Summer*), maniacal children (*The Good Son*), lunatic high school friends (*Scream*) and college classmates (*Scream II*), and nutsy teenaged admirers (*The Crush*).

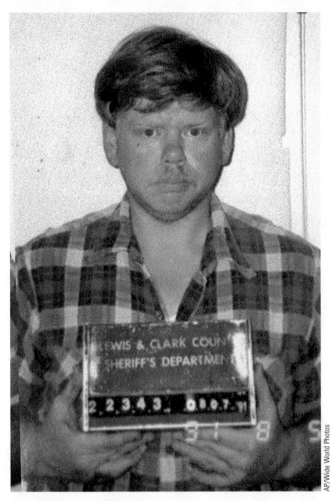

■ Russell Eugene Weston's violent shooting spree in the U.S. Capitol seemed to be the product of a deranged mind. Can people such as Weston who go on murderous rampages ever be considered "normal" or "sane"?

No one can ever be safe when the psychologists and psychiatrists who should be treating these disturbed people turn out to be demonic murderers themselves (*Silence of the Lambs, Dressed to Kill,* and *Never Talk to Strangers*). Is it any wonder that we respond to a particularly horrible crime by saying of the perpetrator, "That guy must be crazy" or "She is a monster!"?

CONNECTIONS

Some critics have called for the strict regulation of movies, videos, and TV shows, believing that viewing them is harmful to their mostly adolescent audience. Does watching all these aggressive, crazed people cause viewers to act violently themselves? For more on this issue, see the Criminological Enterprise feature on media violence later in this chapter. ■

The view that criminals bear physical and/or mental traits that make them "different" and "abnormal" is not restricted to the movie-going public. Since the nineteenth century, some criminologists have suggested that biological and psychological traits may influence behavior. Some people may develop physical or mental traits at birth or soon after that affect their social functioning over the life course and influence their behavior choices. For example, low birth weight babies have been found to suffer poor educational achievement later in life. Academic deficiency has been linked to delinquency and drug abuse, so it is possible that a condition present at birth will influence antisocial behavior during later adolescence.[2] Possessing these personal differences explains why, when faced with the same life situations, one person commits crime and becomes a chronic offender, whereas another attends school, church, and neighborhood functions and obeys the laws of society. To understand this view of crime causation, we begin with a brief review of the development of trait theories.

■ Foundations of Trait Theory

As you may recall, Cesare Lombroso's work on the "born criminal" was a direct offshoot of applying the scientific method to the study of crime. His identification of primitive, atavistic anomalies was based on what he believed was sound empirical research using established scientific methods.

CONNECTIONS

Biological explanations of criminal behavior first became popular during the middle part of the nineteenth century with the introduction of positivism—the use of the scientific method and empirical analysis to study behavior. Positivism was discussed in Chapter 1 when the history of criminology was described. ■

 To read more about Lombroso and his works, go to:
http://www.tld.jcu.edu.au/hist/stats/lomb/
For an up-to-date list of Web links, go to
http://info.wadsworth.com/siegel ■

Lombroso was not alone in the early development of biological theory. A contemporary, Raffaele Garofalo (1852–1934), shared the belief that certain physical characteristics indicate a criminal nature. For example, Garofalo stated that among criminals "a lower degree of sensibility to physical pain seems to be demonstrated by the readiness with which prisoners submit to the operation of tattooing."[3] Enrico Ferri (1856–1929), another student of Lombroso's, believed that a number of biological, social, and organic factors caused delinquency and crime.[4] Ferri added a social dimension to Lombroso's work and was a pioneer with his view that criminals should not be held personally or morally responsible for their actions because forces outside their control caused criminality.

 To read some chapters from Ferri's major books, go to this Web site provided by the University of Virginia:
**http://www.books-on-line.com/
BookDisplay.cfm?BookNum=997**
For an up-to-date list of Web links, go to
http://info.wadsworth.com/siegel ■

Advocates of the **inheritance school** traced the activities of several generations of families believed to have an especially large number of criminal members.[5] The body-build or **somatotype** school, developed more that 50 years ago by William Sheldon, held that criminals manifest distinct physiques that make them susceptible to particular types of delinquent behavior. *Mesomorphs,* for example, have well-developed muscles and an athletic appearance. They are active, aggressive, sometimes violent, and the most likely to become criminals. *Endomorphs* have heavy builds and are slow moving. They are known for lethargic behavior rendering them unlikely to commit violent crime and more willing to engage in less strenuous criminal activities such as fencing stolen property. *Ectomorphs* are tall and thin and less social and more intellectual than the other types.[6]

 Use "morphology" as a key word on InfoTrac College Edition to learn more about this topic. ■

The work of Lombroso and his contemporaries is regarded today as a historical curiosity, not scientific fact. In fact, their research methodology has been discredited because they did not use control groups from the general population to compare results. Many of the traits they assumed to be inherited are not really genetically determined but could be caused by deprivation in surroundings and diet. Even if most criminals shared some biological traits, they might be products not of heredity but of some environmental condition, such as poor nutrition or health care. It is equally likely that only criminals who suffer from biological abnormality are caught and punished by the justice system. In his later writings, even Lombroso admitted that the born criminal was just one of many criminal types. Because of these deficiencies in his theory, the validity of individual-oriented explanations of criminality became questionable and, for a time, was disregarded by the criminological mainstream.

Impact of Sociobiology

What seems no longer tenable at this juncture is any theory of human behavior which ignores biology and relies exclusively on socio-cultural learning.... Most social scientists have been wrong in their dogmatic rejection and blissful ignorance of the biological parameters of our behavior.[7]

Biological explanations of crime fell out of favor in the early twentieth century. During this period, criminologists became concerned about the sociological influences on crime, such as the neighborhood, peer group, family life, and social status. The work of biocriminologists was viewed as methodologically unsound and generally invalid by the sociologists who dominated the field and held the view, referred to as **biophobia,** that no serious consideration should be given to biological factors when attempting to understand human nature.[8]

In the early 1970s, spurred by the publication of *Sociobiology,* by biologist Edmund O. Wilson, the biological basis for crime once again emerged into the limelight.[9] Sociobiology differs from earlier theories of behavior in that it stresses that biological and genetic conditions affect how social behaviors are learned and perceived. These perceptions, in turn, are linked to existing environmental structures. Sociobiologists view the gene as the ultimate unit of life that controls all human destiny. Although they believe environment and experience also have an impact on behavior, their main premise is that most actions are controlled by a person's "biological machine." Most important, people are controlled by the innate need to have their genetic material survive and dominate others. Consequently, they do everything in their power to ensure their own survival and that of others who share their gene pool (relatives, fellow citizens, and so forth). Even when they come to the aid of others, which is called **reciprocal altruism,** people are motivated by the belief that their actions will be reciprocated and that their gene survival capability will be enhanced.

The study of sociobiology revived interest in finding a biological basis for crime and delinquency. If, as it suggests, biological (genetic) makeup controls human behavior, it follows that it should also be responsible for determining whether a person chooses law-violating or conventional behavior. This view of crime causation is referred to as **trait theory.**

___

Can sociobiology explain behavior patterns across all animal species and show how it is linked to mating behavior? To find out, read about the mechanism of natural selection in this InfoTrac College Edition article: Gerald Holton. The new synthesis? *Society* Jan–Feb 1998 v35 n2 p203(10) ■

Modern Trait Theories

Trait theorists today do not suggest that a single biological or psychological attribute is thought to adequately explain all criminality. Rather, each offender is considered unique, physically and mentally; consequently, there must be different explanations for each person's behavior. Some may have inherited criminal tendencies, others may be suffering from nervous system (neurological) problems, and still others may have a blood chemistry disorder that heightens their antisocial activity. Criminologists who focus on the individual see many explanations for crime, because, in fact, there are many differences among criminal offenders.

Trait theorists are not overly concerned with legal definitions of crime; they do not try to explain why people violate particular statutory laws such as car theft or burglary. To them, these are artificial legal concepts based on arbitrary boundaries (for example, speeding may be arbitrarily defined as exceeding 65 miles per hour). Instead, trait theorists focus on basic human behavior and drives—aggression, violence, and a tendency to act on impulse—that are linked to antisocial behavior patterns. They also recognize that human traits alone do not produce criminality and that crime-producing interactions involve both personal traits—such as intelligence, personality, and chemical and genetic makeup—and environmental factors, such as family life, educational attainment, economic factors, and neighborhood conditions. Physical or mental traits are, therefore, but one part of a large pool of environmental, social, and personal factors that account for criminality. Some people may have a predisposition toward aggression, but environmental stimuli can either suppress or trigger antisocial acts.

Even the most committed trait theorists recognize that environmental conditions in disadvantaged inner-city areas may have a powerful influence on antisocial behavior. Many people who reside in these areas experience poverty, racism, frustration, and anger, yet relatively few become delinquents and even fewer mature into adult criminals. Trait theorists argue that those who do become chronic offenders suffer some biological/psychological condition or trait that renders them incapable of resisting social pressures and problems.[10] As biocriminologists Anthony Walsh and Lee Ellis conclude, "If there is one takeaway lesson from studying biological bases of behavior, it is that the more we study them the more we realize how important the environment is."[11]

Trait theories have gained recent prominence because of what is now known about chronic recidivism and the development of criminal careers. If only a small percentage of all offenders go on to become persistent repeaters, then it is possible that what sets them apart from the criminal population is an abnormal biochemical makeup, brain structure, or genetic constitution.[12] Even if criminals do "choose crime," the fact that some repeatedly make that choice could well be linked to their physical and mental makeup.

All people may be aware of and even fear the sanctioning power of the law, but some are unable to control their urges and passions. Trait theories can be divided into two major subdivisions: one that stresses psychological functioning and another that stresses biological makeup. Although there is often overlap between these views (for example, brain functioning may have a biological basis), each branch has its unique characteristics and will be discussed separately.

Biosocial Trait Theories

Rather than view the criminal as a person whose behavior is controlled by biological conditions determined at birth, biosocial theorists believe physical, environmental, and social conditions work in concert to produce human behavior. Biosocial theory has several core principles.[13] First, it assumes that genetic makeup contributes significantly to human behavior. Further, it contends that not all humans are born with equal potential to learn and achieve (**equipotentiality**). **Biosocial theorists** argue that no two people are alike (with rare exceptions, such as identical twins) and that the combination of human genetic traits and the environment produces individual behavior patterns (see Figure 6.1). In contrast, social theorists suggest, either explicitly or implicitly, that all people are born equal and that thereafter behavior is controlled by social forces (parents, schools, neighborhoods, and friends).

Learning potential and its effect on individual behavior patterns Another critical focus of modern biological theory is the importance of brain functioning, mental processes, and learning. Social behavior, including criminal behavior, is learned, and each individual organism is believed to have a unique potential for learning. The physical and social environment interact to either limit or enhance an organism's capacity for learning. People learn through a process involving the brain and central nervous system. Learning is not controlled by social interactions but by biochemistry and cellular interaction. Learning can take place only when physical changes occur in the brain. There is a significant link, therefore, between behavior patterns and physical or chemical changes that occur in the brain, autonomic nervous system, and central nervous system.[14]

Instinct Some biosocial theorists also believe learning is influenced by instinctual drives. Developed over the course of human history, instincts are inherited, natural, unlearned dispositions that activate specific behavior patterns designed to reach certain goals. For example, people are believed to have a drive to "possess and control" other people and things. Some theft offenses may be motivated by the instinctual need to possess goods and commodities. Rape and other sex crimes may be linked to the primitive instinctual drive males have to "possess and control" females.[15]

The following subsections will examine some of the more important schools of thought within biosocial theory.[16] First, the biochemical factors that are believed to affect how proper behavior patterns are learned will be reviewed. Then the relationship of brain function and crime will be considered. Current ideas about the association between genetic and evolutionary factors and crime will be analyzed. Finally, evolutionary views of crime causation are evaluated.

Biochemical Conditions and Crime

Some trait theorists believe biochemical conditions, including both those that are genetically predetermined and those acquired through diet and environment, control and influence antisocial behavior. Some of the more important biochemical factors that have been linked to criminality are set out in detail here.

Chemical and mineral influences Biosocial criminologists maintain that minimum levels of minerals and chemicals are needed for normal brain functioning and growth, especially in the early years of life. If people with normal needs do not receive the appropriate nutrition, they will suffer from vitamin deficiency. If people have genetic conditions that cause greater than normal needs for certain chemicals and minerals, they are said to suffer from vitamin dependency. People with vitamin deficiency or dependency can manifest many physical, mental, and behavioral problems including lower intelligence test scores.[17] Alcoholics often suffer from thiamine deficiency because of their poor diets and consequently are susceptible to the serious, often fatal **Wernicke-Korsakoff disease,** a deadly neurological disorder.[18]

Diet and crime Research conducted over the past decade shows that the dietary inadequacy of certain chemicals and minerals, including sodium, potassium, calcium, amino acids, monoamines, and peptides, can lead to depression, mania, cognitive problems, memory loss, and

Figure 6.1 Biosocial Perspectives on Criminality

Perspective	Cause
BIOCHEMICAL	• Diet • Hormones • Environmental contaminants
NEUROPHYSIO-LOGICAL	• Brain structure • Brain damage • Brain chemicals
GENETIC	• Inherited aggressive predisposition • Inherited condition associated with crime such as impulsive personality
EVOLUTIONARY	• Aggression evolves over time • Aggressive males produce more offspsring

abnormal sexual activity.[19] Research studies examining the relationship between crime and vitamin deficiency and dependency have identified a close link between antisocial behavior and insufficient quantities of some B vitamins (B3 and B6) and vitamin C. In addition, studies have purported to show that a major proportion of all schizophrenics and children with learning and behavior disorders are dependent on vitamins B3 and B6.[20]

Stephen Schoenthaler has conducted some of the most important research on diet and crime. In one study of 803 New York City public schools, Schoenthaler found academic performance of 1.1 million school children rose 16 percent after the diets were modified.[21] The number of "learning disabled" children fell from 125,000 to 74,000 in one year. No other changes in school programs for the learning disabled were initiated that year. In a similar experiment conducted in a correctional institution, violent and nonviolent antisocial behavior fell, on average, 48 percent among 8,047 offenders after dietary changes were implemented. In both these studies, the improvements in behavior and academic performance were attributed to diets containing more vitamins and minerals than old diets. The greater amounts of these essential nutrients in the new diets were believed to have corrected impaired brain function caused by poor nutrition. Schoenthaler and his associates have also evaluated the relationship between nutrition and intelligence. These studies involved 1,753 children and young adults in California, Arizona, Oklahoma, Missouri, England, Wales, Scotland, and Belgium. In each study, the IQ of subjects taking dietary supplements rose more, on average 16 points, than the placebo control group. Furthermore, the differences in IQ could be attributed to about 20 percent of the children who were presumably inadequately nourished prior to supplementation.

> CONNECTIONS
>
> If there is a link between IQ and crime, as some experts believe, then the Schoenthaler research shows that proper diet is the key to lowering levels of antisocial behavior. See more on IQ and criminality later in this chapter. ■

Sugar and crime   Another suspected nutritional influence on behavior is a diet especially high in carbohydrates and sugar.[22] For example, some recent research found that the way the brain processed glucose was related to scores on tests measuring reasoning power.[23] In addition, sugar intake levels have been associated with attention span deficiencies.[24]

Diets high in sugar and carbohydrates also have been linked to violence and aggression. Experiments have been conducted in which children's diets were altered so that sweet drinks were replaced with fruit juices, table sugar with honey, molasses substituted for sugar in cooking, and so on. Results indicate that these changes can reduce aggression levels.[25] Those biocriminologists who believe in a diet–aggression association claim that in every segment of society there are violent, aggressive, and amoral people whose improper food, vitamin, and mineral intake may be responsible for their antisocial behavior. If diet could be improved, they believe the frequency of violent behavior would be reduced.[26]

Although these results are impressive, a number of biologists have questioned this association, and some recent research efforts have failed to find a link between sugar consumption and violence.[27] In one important study, a group of researchers had 25 preschool children and 23 school-age children described as sensitive to sugar follow a different diet for three consecutive three-week periods. One diet was high in sucrose, the second substituted Aspartame (Nutrasweet) for a sweetener, and the third relied on saccharin. Careful measurement of the subjects found little evidence of cognitive or behavioral differences that could be linked to diet. If anything, sugar seemed to have a calming effect on the children.[28]

In sum, while some research efforts allege a sugar–violence association, others suggest that many people who maintain diets high in sugar and carbohydrates are not violent or crime prone. In some cases, in fact, sugar intake has been found to possibly reduce or curtail violent tendencies.[29]

Glucose metabolism/hypoglycemia   Research shows that persistent abnormality in the way the brain metabolizes glucose (sugar) can be linked to antisocial behaviors such as substance abuse.[30] **Hypoglycemia** occurs when glucose in the blood falls below levels necessary for normal and efficient brain functioning. The brain is sensitive to the lack of blood sugar because it is the only organ that obtains its energy solely from the combustion of carbohydrates. Thus, when the brain is deprived of blood sugar, it has no alternate food supply to call upon, and brain metabolism slows down, impairing function. Symptoms of hypoglycemia include irritability, anxiety, depression, crying spells, headaches, and confusion.

Research studies have linked hypoglycemia to outbursts of antisocial behavior and violence.[31] Several studies have related assaults and fatal sexual offenses to hypoglycemic reactions.[32] Hypoglycemia has also been connected with a syndrome characterized by aggressive and assaultive behavior, glucose disturbance, and brain dysfunction. Some attempts have been made to measure hypoglycemia using subjects with a known history of criminal activity. Studies of jail and prison inmate populations have found a higher than normal level of hypoglycemia.[33] High levels of reactive hypoglycemia have been found in groups of habitually violent and impulsive offenders.[34]

Hormonal influences   Criminologist James Q. Wilson, in his book *The Moral Sense,* concludes that hormones, enzymes, and neurotransmitters may be the key to understanding human behavior. According to Wilson, they help explain gender differences in the crime rate. Males, he writes, are biologically and naturally more aggressive than females, whereas women are more nurturing toward the young and are important for survival of the species.[35] Hormone levels also help explain the aging-out process. Levels of testosterone, the principal male steroid hormone, decline during the life cycle and may explain why violence rates diminish over time.[36]

A number of biosocial theorists are now evaluating the association between violent behavior episodes and hormone levels, and the findings suggest that abnormal levels of male sex hormones (**androgens**) do in fact produce aggressive behavior.[37] Other androgen-related male traits include sensation seeking, impulsivity, dominance, and lesser verbal skills; all of these androgen-related male traits are also related to antisocial behaviors.[38] There is a growing body of evidence suggesting that hormonal changes are also related to mood and behavior and, concomitantly, that adolescents experience more intense mood swings, anxiety, and restlessness than their elders.[39] An association between hormonal activity and antisocial behavior is suggested because rates of both factors peak in adolescence.[40]

One area of concern has been **testosterone,** the most abundant androgen, which controls secondary sex characteristics, such as facial hair and voice timbre.[41] Research conducted on both human and animal subjects has found that prenatal exposure to unnaturally high levels of androgens permanently alters behavior. Girls who were unintentionally exposed to elevated amounts of androgens during their fetal development display an unusually high, long-term tendency toward aggression. Conversely, boys who were prenatally exposed to steroids that decrease androgen levels displayed decreased aggressiveness.[42] In contrast, samples of inmates indicate that testosterone levels were higher in men who committed violent crimes than in the other prisoners.[43] Gender differences in the crime rate then may be explained by the relative difference in androgens between the two sexes. Females may be biologically "protected" from deviant behavior in the same way they are immune from some diseases that strike males.[44]

How hormones may influence behavior

Hormones cause areas of the brain to become less sensitive to environmental stimuli. High androgen levels require people to seek excess stimulation and to be willing to tolerate pain in their quest for thrills. Androgens are linked to brain seizures that, under stressful conditions, can result in emotional volatility. Androgens affect the brain structure itself. They influence the left hemisphere of the **neocortex,** the part of the brain that controls sympathetic feelings toward others.[45] Here are some of the physical reactions produced by hormones that have been linked to violence:

- A lowering of average resting arousal under normal environmental conditions to a point that individuals

are motivated to seek unusually high levels of environmental stimulation and are less sensitive to harmful aftereffects resulting from this stimulation.

- A lowering of seizure thresholds in and around the limbic system, increasing the likelihood that stressful environmental factors will trigger strong and impulsive emotional responses.
- A rightward shift in neocortical functioning, resulting in an increased reliance on the brain hemisphere that is most closely integrated with the limbic system and is least prone to reason in logical-linguistic forms or to respond to linguistic commands.[46]

These effects promote violence and other serious crimes by causing people to seek greater levels of environmental stimulation and to tolerate more punishment, increasing impulsivity, emotional volatility, and antisocial emotions.[47]

Even though some research studies have been unable to demonstrate hormonal differences in samples of violent and nonviolent offenders, drugs that decrease testosterone levels are now being used to treat male sex offenders.[48] The female hormones, estrogen and progesterone, have been administered to sex offenders to decrease their sexual potency.[49] The long-term side effects of this treatment and the potential danger are still unknown.[50]

Premenstrual syndrome

Hormonal research has not been limited to male offenders. The suspicion has long existed that the onset of the menstrual cycle triggers excessive amounts of the female sex hormones, which affect antisocial, aggressive behavior. This condition is commonly referred to as **premenstrual syndrome,** or **PMS.**[51] The link between PMS and delinquency was first popularized more than 25 years ago by Katharina Dalton, whose studies of English women indicated that females are more likely to commit suicide and be aggressive and otherwise antisocial just before or during menstruation.[52]

Dalton's research is often cited as evidence of the link between PMS and crime, but methodological problems make it impossible to accept her findings at face value. There is still significant debate over any link between PMS and aggression. Some doubters argue that the relationship is spurious; it is equally likely that the psychological and physical stress of aggression brings on menstruation and not vice versa.[53]

Diana Fishbein, a noted expert on biosocial theory, concludes that there is in fact an association between elevated levels of female aggression and menstruation. Research efforts, she argues, show (a) that a significant number of incarcerated females committed their crimes during the premenstrual phase and (b) that at least a small percentage of women appear vulnerable to cyclical hormonal changes, which makes them more prone to anxiety and hostility.[54] While the debate is ongoing, it is important to remember that the overwhelming majority of females who do suffer anxiety reactions prior to and during menstruation do not actually engage in violent criminal behavior; so any link between PMS and crime is tenuous at best.[55]

Allergies   Allergies are defined as unusual or excessive reactions of the body to foreign substances.[56] For example, hay fever is an allergic reaction caused when pollen cells enter the body and are fought or neutralized by the body's natural defenses. The result of the battle is itching, red eyes, and active sinuses.

Cerebral allergies cause an excessive reaction in the brain, whereas **neuroallergies** affect the nervous system. Neuroallergies and cerebral allergies are believed to cause the allergic person to produce enzymes that attack wholesome foods as if they were dangerous to the body.[57] They may also cause swelling of the brain and produce sensitivity in the central nervous system, conditions linked to mental, emotional, and behavioral problems. Research indicates a connection between allergies and hyperemotionality, depression, aggressiveness, and violent behavior.[58]

Neuroallergy and cerebral allergy problems have also been linked to hyperactivity in children, which may portend antisocial behavior. The foods most commonly involved in producing such allergies are cow's milk, wheat, corn, chocolate, citrus, and eggs; however, about 300 other foods have been identified as allergens. The potential seriousness of the problem has been raised by studies linking the average consumption of one suspected cerebral allergen, corn, to cross-national homicide rates.[59]

Environmental contaminants   Dangerous amounts of copper, cadmium, mercury, and inorganic gases, such as chlorine and nitrogen dioxide, are found in the ecosystem. Research indicates that these environmental contaminants can influence behavior. At high levels, these substances can cause severe illness or death; at more moderate levels, they have been linked to emotional and behavioral disorders.[60] Some studies have linked the ingestion of food dyes and artificial colors and flavors to hostile, impulsive, and otherwise antisocial behavior in youths.[61] Lighting may be another important environmental influence on antisocial behavior. Research projects have suggested that radiation from artificial light sources, such as fluorescent tubes and television sets, may produce antisocial, aggressive behavior.[62]

Lead levels   A number of recent research studies have suggested that lead ingestion is linked to aggressive behaviors on both a macro and micro level. For example, on a macro level, when criminologists Paul Stretesky and Michael Lynch examined air lead concentrations across counties in the United States, they found that areas with the highest concentrations of lead also reported the highest levels of homicide.[63]

On a micro level, criminologist Deborah Denno investigated the behavior of more than 900 African American youth and found that lead poisoning was one of the most significant predictors of male delinquency and persistent adult criminality.[64] Herbert Needleman and his associates tracked 300 boys from ages 7 to 11 and found that those who had high lead concentrations in their bones were much more likely to report attention problems, delinquency, and aggressiveness.[65] High lead ingestion is also related to lower IQ scores, a factor also linked to aggressive behavior.[66]

Neurophysiological Conditions and Crime

Some researchers focus their attention on **neurophysiology,** the study of brain activity.[67] They believe neurological and physical abnormalities are acquired as early as the fetal or perinatal stage or through birth delivery trauma and that they control behavior throughout the life span.[68]

The relationship between neurological dysfunction and crime first received a great deal of attention in 1968 during a tragic incident in Texas. Charles Whitman killed his wife and mother, then barricaded himself in a tower at the University of Texas with a high-powered rifle where he proceeded to kill 14 people and wound 24 others before he was killed by police. An autopsy revealed that Whitman suffered from a malignant infiltrating brain tumor. Whitman had previously experienced uncontrollable urges to kill and had gone to a psychiatrist seeking help for his problems. He kept careful notes documenting his feelings and his inability to control his homicidal urges, and he left instructions for his estate to be given to a mental health foundation so it could study mental problems such as his own.[69]

Since the Whitman case, a great deal of attention has been focused on the association between neurological impairment and crime. Studies conducted in the United States and in other nations have indicated that the relationship is significant between impairment in executive brain functions (for example, abstract reasoning, problem-solving skills, and motor behavior skills) and aggressive behavior.[70] Research indicates that this relationship can be detected quite early and that children who suffer from measurable neurological deficits at birth are more likely to become criminals later in life.[71]

Neurological impairments and crime   There are numerous ways to measure neurological functioning, including memorization and visual awareness tests, short-term auditory memory tests, and verbal IQ tests. These tests have been found to distinguish criminal offenders from noncriminal control groups.[72]

Traditionally, the most important measure of neurophysiological functioning is the **electroencephalograph (EEG).** An EEG records the electrical impulses given off by the brain.[73] It represents a signal composed of various rhythms and transient electrical discharges, commonly called brain waves, which can be recorded by electrodes placed on the scalp. The frequency is given in cycles per second, measured in hertz (Hz), and usually ranges from 0.5 to 30 Hz. Measurements of the EEG reflect the activity of neurons located in the cerebral cortex. The rhythmic nature of this brain activity is determined by mechanisms that involve subcortical structures, primarily the thalamus portion of the brain. Studies using the EEG find that violent criminals have far higher levels of abnormal EEG recordings than nonviolent or one-time offenders.[74] Although about 5 percent of the general population has abnormal EEG readings, about 50 to 60 percent of adolescents with known behavior disorders display abnormal recordings.[75] Behaviors highly correlated with abnormal EEG included poor impulse control, inadequate social adaptation, hostility, temper tantrums, and destructiveness.[76] Studies of adults have associated slow and bilateral brain waves with hostile, hypercritical, irritable, nonconforming, and impulsive behavior.[77]

Newer brain scanning techniques, using electronic imaging such as Positron Emission Tomography (PET), Brain Electrical Activity Mapping (BEAM), and Superconducting Interference Device (SQUID), have made it possible to assess which areas of the brain are directly linked to antisocial behavior.[78] Violent criminals have been found to have impairment in the prefrontal lobes, thalamus, medial temporal lobe, superior parietal, and left angular gyrus areas of the brain.[79] A review of existing research by Nathaniel Pallone and James Hennessy finds that chronic violent criminals have far higher levels of brain dysfunction than the general population. Their most striking finding is that the incidence of brain pathology in homicide offenders is 32 times greater than in the general population.[80]

Minimal brain dysfunction (MBD)   MBD is related to an abnormality in cerebral structure. It has been defined as an abruptly appearing, maladaptive behavior that interrupts an individual's lifestyle and life flow. In its most serious form, MBD has been linked to serious antisocial acts, an imbalance in the urge-control mechanisms of the brain, and chemical abnormality. Included in the category of minimal brain dysfunction are several abnormal behavior patterns: dyslexia, visual perception problems, hyperactivity, poor attention span, temper tantrums, and aggressiveness. One type of minimal brain dysfunction is manifested through episodic periods of explosive rage. This form of the disorder is considered an important cause of such behavior as spouse beating, child abuse, suicide, aggressiveness, and motiveless homicide. One perplexing feature of this syndrome is that people who are afflicted with it often maintain warm and pleasant personalities between episodes of violence. Some studies measuring the presence of MBD in offender populations have found that up to 60 percent exhibit brain dysfunction on psychological tests.[81]

Criminals have been characterized as having dysfunction of the dominant hemisphere of the brain.[82] Researchers using brain wave data have predicted with 95 percent accuracy the recidivism of violent criminals.[83] More sophisticated brain scanning techniques, such as PET, have also shown that brain abnormality is linked to violent crime.[84]

Attention deficit hyperactivity disorder (ADHD)
Many parents have noticed that their children do not pay attention to them—they run around and do things in their own way. Sometimes this inattention is a function of age; in other instances, it is a symptom of **attention deficit hyperactivity disorder (ADHD),** in which a child shows a developmentally inappropriate lack of attention, impulsivity, and hyperactivity. The various symptoms of ADHD are described in Table 6.1.

About 3 percent of U.S. children, most often boys, are believed to suffer from this disorder, and it is the most common reason children are referred to mental health clinics. The condition has been associated with poor school performance, grade retention, placement in special needs classes, bullying, stubbornness, and lack of response to

Table 6.1   Symptoms of Attention Deficit Hyperactivity Disorder

Lack of Attention

Frequently fails to finish projects

Does not seem to pay attention

Does not sustain interest in play activities

Cannot sustain concentration on schoolwork or related tasks

Is easily distracted

Impulsivity

Frequently acts without thinking

Often "calls out" in class

Does not want to wait his or her turn in lines or games

Shifts from activity to activity

Cannot organize tasks or work

Requires constant supervision

Hyperactivity

Constantly runs around and climbs on things

Shows excessive motor activity while asleep

Cannot sit still; is constantly fidgeting

Does not remain in his or her seat in class

Is constantly on the go like a "motor"

SOURCE: Adapted from American Psychiatric Association, *Diagnostic and Statistical Manual of Mental Disorders,* 4th ed. (Washington, D.C.: American Psychiatric Press, 1994).

discipline.[85] Although the origin of ADHD is still unknown, suspected causes include neurological damage, prenatal stress, and even reactions to food additives and chemical allergies.

Recent research has also suggests a genetic link.[86] There are also links to family turmoil: Mothers of ADHD children are more likely to be divorced or separated and ADHD children are much more likely to move to new locales than non-ADHD children.[87] It may be possible then that emotional turmoil either produces symptoms of ADHD or, if they already exist, causes them to intensify.

A series of research studies now link ADHD to the onset and sustenance of a delinquent career.[88] Many ADHD children also suffer from **conduct disorder (CD)** and continually engage in aggressive and antisocial behavior in early childhood. The disorders are sustained over the life course: children diagnosed as ADHD are more likely to be suspended from school and engage in criminal behavior as adults. This ADHD–crime association is important because symptoms of ADHD seem stable through adolescence into adulthood.[89] Early diagnosis and treatment of children suffering ADHD may enhance their life chances. Today, the most typical treatment is doses of stimulants, such as Ritalin, which ironically help control emotional and behavioral outbursts. The relationship between chronic delinquency and attention disorders may also be mediated by school performance. Kids who are poor readers are the most prone to antisocial behavior; many poor readers also have attention problems.[90] Early school-based intervention programs may be of special benefit to those who suffer ADHD.

Other brain dysfunctions   Other brain dysfunctions have been related to violent crime. Persistent criminality has been linked to dysfunction in the frontal and temporal regions of the brain. These regions are believed to play an important role in regulating and inhibiting human behavior, including formulating plans and controlling intentions. It is also the brain center for regulating complex behaviors.[91] Brain lesions that occur at specific points of the neurological system, such as the auditory system, can have permanent effects on behavior.[92] Clinical evaluation of depressed and aggressive psychopathic subjects showed a significant number (more than 75 percent) had dysfunction of the temporal and frontal regions of the brain.[93]

Tumors, injury, and disease   The presence of brain tumors has also been linked to a wide variety of psychological problems, including personality changes, hallucinations, and psychotic episodes.[94] There is evidence that people with tumors are prone to depression, irritability, temper outbursts, and even homicidal attacks (for example, the Whitman case). Clinical case studies of patients suffering from brain tumors indicate that previously docile people may undergo behavior changes so great that they attempt to seriously harm their families and friends. When

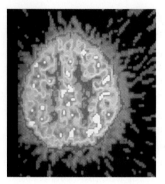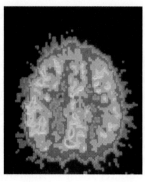

■ This scan compares a normal brain (left) and an ADHD brain (right). The areas of orange and white demonstrate a higher rate of metabolism; the areas of blue and green represent an abnormally low metabolic rate. Why is ADHD so prevalent in the United States today? Some experts believe our immigrant forebearers were risk-takers who impulsively left their homelands for a life in the new world. They also may have brought with them a genetic predisposition for ADHD.

the tumor is removed, their behavior returns to normal.[95] In addition to brain tumors, head injuries caused by accidents, such as falls or auto crashes, have been linked to personality reversals marked by outbursts of antisocial and violent behavior.[96]

A variety of central nervous system diseases have also been linked to personality changes. Some of these conditions include cerebral arteriosclerosis, epilepsy, senile dementia, Korsakoff's syndrome, and Huntington's chorea. Associated symptoms of these diseases are memory deficiency, orientation loss, and affective (emotional) disturbances dominated by rage, anger, and increased irritability.[97]

Brain chemistry   Neurotransmitters are chemical compounds that influence or activate brain functions. Those studied in relation to aggression include dopamine, norepinephrine, serotonin, monoamine oxidase, and GABA.[98] Evidence exists that abnormal levels of these chemicals are associated with aggression. For example, several researchers have reported inverse correlations between serotonin concentrates in the blood and impulsive and/or suicidal behavior.[99] Recent studies of habitually violent Finnish criminals show that low serotonin (5-hydroxytryptamine; 5-HT) levels are associated with poor impulse control and hyperactivity. In addition, a relatively low concentration of 5-hydroxyindoleactic acid (5-HIAA) is predictive of increased irritability, sensation seeking, and impaired impulse control.[100]

What is the link between brain chemistry and crime? Prenatal exposure of the brain to high levels of androgens can result in a brain structure that is less sensitive to environmental inputs. Affected individuals seek more intense and varied stimulation and are willing to tolerate more adverse consequences than individuals not so affected.[101] Such exposure also results in a rightward shift in (brain) hemispheric functioning and a concomitant diminution of cognitive and emotional tendencies. One result of this tendency is that left-handers are disproportionately represented in the criminal population since the movement of each hand tends to be controlled by the hemisphere of the brain on the opposite side of the body.

It has also been suggested that individuals with a low supply of the enzyme monoamine oxidase (MAO) engage in behaviors linked with violence and property crime, including defiance of punishment, impulsivity, hyperactivity, poor academic performance, sensation-seeking and risk-taking, and recreational drug use. Abnormal levels of MAO may explain both individual and group differences in the crime rate. For example, females have higher levels of MAO than males, a condition that may explain gender differences in the crime rate.[102]

The brain and neurological system can produce natural or endogenous opiates that are chemically similar to the narcotics opium and morphine. It has been suggested that the risk and thrills involved in crime cause the neurological system to produce increased amounts of these natural narcotics. The result is an elevated mood state, perceived as an exciting and rewarding experience that acts as a positive reinforcement for crime.[103] The brain then produces its own natural "high" as a reward for risk-taking behavior. Some people achieve this high by rock climbing and sky-diving; others engage in crimes of violence.

Because this linkage has been found, it is not uncommon for violence-prone people to be treated with antipsychotic drugs such as Haldol, Stelazine, Prolixin, and Risperdal, which help control levels of neurotransmitters (such as serotonin/dopamine); these are sometimes referred to as **chemical restraints** or **chemical straitjackets.**

Arousal Theory

It has long been suspected that obtaining "thrills" is a crime motivator. Adolescents may engage in crimes such as shoplifting and vandalism simply because they offer the attraction of "getting away with it"; from this perspective, delinquency is a thrilling demonstration of personal competence.[104]

CONNECTIONS

Jack Katz has written on the "seductions of crime." Perhaps some people may be "seduced" into crime because the experience produces the "natural high" they crave. Katz's work is discussed in Chapter 5. ■

According to **arousal theory,** for a variety of genetic and environmental reasons, some people's brains function differently in response to environmental stimuli. All of us seek to maintain a preferred or optimal level of arousal: too much stimulation leaves us anxious and stressed out; too little makes us feel bored and weary. There is, however, variation in the way people's brains process sensory input. Some nearly always feel comfortable with little stimulation, whereas others require a high degree of environmental input to feel comfortable. The latter group are "sensation seekers," who seek out stimulating activities, which may include aggressive, violent behavior patterns.[105]

The factors that determine a person's level of arousal are not fully determined, but suspected sources include brain chemistry (for example, serotonin levels) and brain structure. Some people have brains with many more nerve cells with receptor sites for neurotransmitters than others. Another view is that people with low heart beat rates are more likely to commit crime because they seek stimulation to increase their feelings of arousal to normal levels.[106]

Genetics and Crime

Early biological theorists believed that criminality ran in families. Although research on deviant families is not taken seriously today, modern biosocial theorists are still interested in the role of genetics. If some human behaviors are influenced by heredity, wouldn't that be the case for anti-social tendencies as well? There is evidence that animals can be bred to have aggressive traits: pit bulldogs, fighting bulls, and fighting cocks have been selectively mated to produce superior predators. Although no similar data exist with regard to people, a growing body of research is focusing on the genetic factors associated with human behavior.[107] There is evidence, for example, that personality traits including extraversion, openness, agreeableness, and conscientiousness are genetically determined.[108] There are also data suggesting that human traits associated with criminality have a genetic basis.[109] Personality conditions linked to aggression, such as psychopathy, impulsivity, and neuroticism, and psychopathology, such as schizophrenia, may be heritable.[110]

This line of reasoning was cast in the spotlight in the 1970s when genetic testing showed that Richard Speck, the convicted killer of eight nurses in Chicago, allegedly had an abnormal XYY chromosomal structure (XY is normal in males). There was much public concern that all people with XYYs were potential killers and should be closely controlled. Civil libertarians expressed fear that all XYYs could be labeled dangerous and violent regardless of whether they had engaged in violent activities.[111] When it was disclosed that neither Speck nor most violent offenders actually had an extra Y chromosome, interest in the XYY theory dissipated.[112] However, the Speck case drew researchers' attention to looking for a genetic basis of crime.

Researchers have carefully explored the heretability of criminal tendencies by looking at a variety of factors. Some of the most important are described here.

Parental deviance If criminal tendencies are inherited, then it stands to reason that the children of criminal parents should be more likely to become law violators than the offspring of conventional parents. A number of studies have found that parental criminality and deviance do, in fact, have a powerful influence on delinquent behavior.[113] Some of the most important data on parental deviance were gathered by Donald J. West and David P. Farrington as part of the long-term Cambridge Youth Survey. Now directed by Dr. Farrington, this research has followed a group of about 1,000 males from the time they were 8 years old until now as they are in their thirties. The boys in the study have been repeatedly interviewed and their school and police records evaluated. These cohort data indicate that a significant number of delinquent youths have criminal fathers.[114] While 8.4 percent of the sons of noncriminal fathers eventually became chronic offenders, about 37 percent of youths with criminal fathers were multiple offenders.[115] In another important analysis, Farrington found that one type of parental deviance, schoolyard aggression or bullying, may be both inter- and intragenerational. Bullies have children who bully others, and these "second-generation bullies" grow up to become the fathers of children who are also bullies, in a never-ending cycle.[116]

The cause of intergenerational deviance is still uncertain. It is possible that environmental, genetic, psychological, or child-rearing factors are responsible for the linkage between generations. The link might also have some biological basis. Research on the sons of alcoholic parents shows that these boys suffer many neurological impairments related to chronic delinquency.[117] These results may indicate (a) that prolonged parental alcoholism causes genetic problems related to developmental impairment or (b) that the children of substance-abusing parents are more prone to suffer neurological impairment before, during, or after birth.

The quality of family life may be key in determining children's behavior. Criminal parents should be the ones *least* likely to have close, intimate relationships with their offspring. Research shows that substance-abusing and/or criminal parents are the ones most likely to use harsh and inconsistent discipline, a factor closely linked to delinquent behavior.[118]

There is no certainty about the nature and causal relationship between parental and child deviance.[119] Nonetheless, recent evidence indicates that at least part of the association is genetic in nature.[120] It is also possible that the association is related to the labeling process and family stigma: social control agents may be quick to fix a delinquent label on the children of known law violators; "the acorn," the reasoning goes, "does not fall far from the tree."[121]

CONNECTIONS

For further discussion of the role "nature" may play in behavior, see the nature versus nurture discussion later in the chapter. ■

■ The genetic basis of criminal behavior became a topic of national debate in 1966 when Richard Speck, the convicted killer of eight nurses in Chicago, was alleged to have an abnormal XYY chromosomal structure (XY is normal in males). There was much public concern that all people with XYYs were potential killers and should be closely controlled. When it was disclosed that Speck did not actually have an extra Y chromosome, interest in the XYY theory dissipated.

Twin behavior If, in fact, inherited traits cause criminal behaviors, we might expect that twins would be quite similar in their antisocial activities. However, since twins are usually brought up in the same household and exposed to the same set of social conditions, determining whether their behavior is a result of biological, sociological, or psychological conditions would be difficult. Trait theorists have tried to overcome this dilemma by comparing identical, monozygotic (MZ), twins with fraternal, dizygotic (DZ), twins.[122] MZ twins are genetically identical, whereas DZ twins have only half their genes in common. If heredity does determine criminal behavior, we should expect MZ twins to be much more similar in their antisocial activities than DZ twins.

The earliest studies conducted on the behavior of twins detected a significant relationship between the criminal activities of MZ twins and a much lower association between those of DZ twins. A review of relevant studies conducted between 1929 and 1961 found that 60 percent of MZ twins shared criminal behavior patterns (if one twin was criminal, so was the other), whereas only 30 percent of DZ twin behavior was similarly related.[123] These findings may be viewed as powerful evidence that a genetic basis for criminality exists.

Other studies have supported these findings. In one well-known work, Danish criminologist Karl Christiansen studied 3,586 male twin pairs and found a 52 percent concordance for MZ pairs and a 22 percent concordance for DZ pairs. This result suggests that the identical MZ twins may share a genetic characteristic that increases the risk of their engaging in criminality.[124] Similarly, criminologists

David Rowe and D. Wayne Osgood analyzed the factors that influence self-reported delinquency in a sample of twin pairs and concluded that genetic influences actually have significant explanatory power.[125] Genetic effects have been found to be a significant predictor of problem behaviors in children as young as 3 years old.[126] While the behavior of some twin pairs seemed to be influenced by their environment, others displayed behavior disturbances that could only be explained by their genetic similarity.[127]

One famous study of twin behavior still under way is the Minnesota Study of Twins Reared Apart. This research compares the behavior of MZ and DZ twin pairs who were raised together with others who were separated at birth and in some cases did not even know of each other's existence. The study shows some striking similarities in behavior and ability for twin pairs raised apart. An MZ twin reared away from a co-twin has about as good a chance of being similar to the co-twin in terms of personality, interests, and attitudes as one who has been reared with his or her co-twin. The conclusion: similarities between twins are due to genes, not the environment. Because twins reared apart are so similar, the environment, if anything, makes them different (see Exhibit 6.1).[128]

Some experts, including David Rowe, conclude that individuals who share genes are alike in personality regardless of how they are reared; in contrast, environment induces little or no personality resemblance on twin pairs.[129]

Evaluating genetic research Twin studies also have their detractors. Some opponents suggest that available evidence provides little conclusive proof that crime is genetically predetermined. Not all research efforts have found that MZ twin pairs are more closely related in their crim-

inal behavior than DZ or ordinary sibling pairs, and some that have found an association note that it is at best "modest."[130] Those who oppose the genes–crime relationship point to the inadequate research designs and weak methodologies of supporting research. The newer, better-designed research studies, critics charge, provide less support than earlier, less methodically sound studies.[131]

It is also possible that what appears to be a genetic effect picked up by the twin research is actually the effect of sibling influence on criminality referred to as the **contagion effect**: genetic predispositions and early experiences make some people, including twins, susceptible to deviant behavior, which is transmitted by the presence of antisocial siblings in the household.[132] Sibling pairs who report warm, mutual relationships and share friends are the most likely to behave in a similar fashion; those who maintain a close relationship also have similar rates of drug abuse and delinquency.[133]

There are a number of ways to interpret these findings:

- Siblings who live in the same environment are influenced by similar social and economic factors.
- Deviant siblings may grow closer because of shared interests.
- Younger siblings who admire their older siblings may imitate the elder's behavior.

What seems to be a genetic effect may actually be the result of warm and close sibling interaction.

The contagion effect may explain in part the higher concordance of deviant behaviors found in identical twins as compared to fraternal twins or mere siblings. The relationship between identical twins may be stronger and more enduring than other sibling pairs so that contagion and not genetics explains their behavioral similarities. According to Marshall Jones and Donald Jones, the contagion effect may also help explain why the behavior of twins is more similar in adulthood than adolescence.[134] Youthful misbehavior is influenced by friends and peer group relationships. As adults, the influence of peers may wane as people marry and find employment. In contrast, twin influence is everlasting; if one twin is antisocial, it legitimizes and supports the criminal behavior in his or her co-twin. This effect may grow even stronger in adulthood because twin relations are more enduring than any other. What seems to be a genetic effect may actually be the result of sibling interaction with a brother or sister who engages in antisocial activity.

Adoption studies One way of avoiding the pitfalls of twin studies is to focus attention on the behavior of adoptees. It seems logical that if the behavior of adopted children is more closely aligned to that of their biological parents than to that of their adoptive parents, then the idea of a genetic basis for criminality would be supported. If, on the other hand, adoptees are more closely aligned to

---

Exhibit 6.1 Findings from the Minnesota Study of Twins Reared Apart

- *Minnesota Population Rate:* About 19 percent of Minnesota couples have been divorced.
- *Twin Family Rate:* About 20 percent of the twins had divorce in their families.
- *If Parent Divorced:* The risk of divorce climbs to about 29 percent if parents are divorced.
- *If Spouse's Parent Divorced:* The risk of divorce is about 31 percent if spouse's parent is divorced.
- *If Fraternal (DZ) Twin Divorced:* If you are a DZ twin and your co-twin is divorced, your risk of divorce is 30 percent.
- *If Identical (MZ) Twin Divorced:* If you are an MZ twin and your co-twin is divorced, your risk of divorce is 45 percent, which is 25 percent above the rate for the Minnesota population. Since this was not true for DZ twins, we can conclude that genes do influence the likelihood of divorce.

SOURCE: *Minnesota Study of Twins Reared Apart, 2001.*

the behavior of their adoptive parents than their biological parents, an environmental basis for crime would seem more valid.

Several studies indicate that some relationship exists between biological parents' behavior and the behavior of their children, even when their contact has been nonexistent.[135] In what is considered the most significant study in this area, Barry Hutchings and Sarnoff Mednick analyzed 1,145 male adoptees born in Copenhagen, Denmark, between 1927 and 1941. Of these, 185 had criminal records.[136] After following up on 143 of the criminal adoptees and matching them with a control group of 143 noncriminal adoptees, Hutchings and Mednick found that the criminality of the biological father was a strong predictor of the child's criminal behavior. When both the biological and the adoptive fathers were criminals, the probability that the youth would engage in criminal behavior greatly increased: 24.5 percent of the boys whose adoptive and biological fathers were criminals had been convicted of a criminal law violation. Only 13.5 percent of those whose biological and adoptive fathers were not criminals had similar conviction records.[137]

A more recent analysis of Swedish adoptees also found that genetic factors are highly significant, accounting for 59 percent of the variation in their petty crime rates. Boys who had criminal parents were significantly more likely to violate the law. Environmental influences and economic status were significantly less important, explaining about 19 percent of the variance in crime. Nonetheless, having a positive environment, such as being adopted into a more affluent home, helped inhibit genetic predisposition.[138]

The genes–crime relationship is quite controversial because it implies that the propensity to commit crime is present at birth and cannot be altered. It raises moral dilemmas. If in utero genetic testing could detect a gene for violence, and a violence gene was found to be present, what could be done as a precautionary measure?

Evolutionary Theory

Some criminologists believe the human traits that produce violence and aggression are produced through the long process of human evolution.[139] According to this evolutionary view, the competition for scarce resources has influenced and shaped the human species.[140] Over the course of human existence, people whose personal characteristics enable them to accumulate more than others are the most likely to breed and dominate the species. People have been shaped to engage in actions that promote their well-being and ensure the survival and reproduction of their genetic line. Males who are impulsive risk-takers may be able to father more children because they are reckless in their social relationships and have sexual encounters with numerous partners. If, according to evolutionary theories, such behavior patterns are inherited, impulsive behavior becomes intergenerational, passed down from father to son. It is not surprising then that human history has been marked by war, violence, and aggression.

For a broad overview of evolutionary psychology, read this article on InfoTrac College Edition: Linnda R. Caporael. Evolutionary psychology: toward a unifying theory and a hybrid science. *Annual Review of Psychology* 2001 p607 ∎

The evolution of gender and crime Evolutionary concepts that have been linked to the differences in violence rates according to gender are based loosely on the evolution of mammalian mating patterns. To ensure survival of the gene pool (and the species), it is beneficial for a male of any species to mate with as many suitable females as possible since each can bear his offspring. In contrast, because of the long period of gestation, females require a secure home and a single, stable nurturing partner to ensure their survival. Because of these differences in mating patterns, the most aggressive males mate most often and have the greatest number of offspring. Therefore, over the history of the human species, aggressive males have had the greatest impact on the gene pool. The descendants of these aggressive males now account for the disproportionate amount of male aggression and violence.[141] Crime rate differences between the genders, then, may be less a matter of socialization than inherent differences in mating patterns that have developed over time.[142] Among young men, reckless, life-threatening "risk proneness" is especially likely to evolve in cultures that force males to find suitable mates to ensure their ability to reproduce. Unless they are aggressive with potential mates and potential rivals for those suitable mates, they are doomed to remain childless.[143]

Violence and evolution In their classic book, *Homicide*, Martin Daly and Margo Wilson suggest that violent offenses are often driven by evolutionary and reproductive factors. High rates of spouse abuse in modern society may be a function of aggressive men seeking to control and possess "mates." When females are murdered by their spouses, the motivating factor is typically fear of infidelity and the threat of attachment to a new partner. Infidelity challenges male dominance and future reproductive rights. It comes as no surprise that in some cultures, including our own, sexual infidelity discovered in progress by the aggrieved husband is viewed legally as a provocation that justifies retaliatory killing.[144] Men who feel most threatened over the potential of losing mates to rivals are the ones most likely to engage in sexual violence. Research shows that women in common-law marriages, especially those who are much younger than their husbands, are at greater risk than older married women. Abusive males may fear the potential loss of their younger mates, especially if they are not bound by a marriage contract, and use force for purposes of control and possession.[145]

Armed robbery is another crime that may have evolutionary underpinnings. Though most robbers are caught and severely punished, it remains an alluring pursuit for men who both want to show their physical prowess and display resources with which to conquer rivals and attract mates. Violent episodes are far more common among men who are unemployed and unmarried, in other words those who may want to demonstrate their allure to the opposite sex but who are without the benefit of position or wealth.[146]

Evolution and female criminality Evolutionary factors may also influence female criminality. With the advent of agriculture and trade in prehistory, feminists have suggested that women were forced into a position of high dependence and limited power. They began to compete among themselves to secure partners who could provide necessary resources. As a result of these early evolutionary developments, intergender competition became greatest during periods of resource deprivation—times when women become most dependent on a male for support. These trends can still be observed. For example, during times of high female unemployment, female–female aggression rates increase as women compete with each other for men who can provide them with support. In contrast, as rates of social welfare increase, female–female aggression rates diminish because the state serves as a readily available substitute for a male breadwinner.[147] The Criminological Enterprise feature focuses on three popular (albeit controversial) evolutionary theories of crime.[148]

CONNECTIONS

The relationship between evolutionary factors and crime has just begun to be studied. Criminologists are now exploring how social organizations and institutions interact with biological traits to influence personal decision making, including criminal strategies. See the sections on latent trait theories in Chapter 10 for more on the integration of biological and environmental factors. ∎

Evaluation of the Biosocial Branch of Trait Theory

Biosocial perspectives on crime have raised some challenging questions. Critics find some of these theories to be racist and dysfunctional. If there are biological explanations for street crimes, such as assault, murder, or rape, the argument goes, and if, as the official crime statistics suggest, the poor and minority-group members commit a disproportionate number of such acts, then by implication biological theory says that members of these groups are biologically different, flawed, or inferior.

CONNECTIONS

Biosocial theory focuses on the violent crimes of the lower classes while ignoring the white-collar crimes of the upper and middle classes. It may seem logical to believe there is a biological basis to aggression and violence, but it is more difficult to explain how insider trading and fraud are biologically related. For the causes of white-collar crime, see Chapter 13. ∎

Biological explanations for the geographic, social, and temporal patterns in the crime rate are also problematic. Is it possible that there are more people genetically predisposed to crime in the South and West than in New England and the midwest? Furthermore, biological theory seems to divide people into criminals and noncriminals on the basis of their genetic and physical makeup, ignoring self-reports indicating that almost everyone has engaged in some type of illegal activity during his or her lifetime.

Biosocial theorists counter that their views should not be confused with Lombrosian, deterministic biology. Rather than suggest that there are born criminals and noncriminals, they maintain that some people carry the potential to be violent or antisocial and that environmental conditions can sometimes trigger antisocial responses.[149] This would explain why some otherwise law-abiding citizens engage in a single, seemingly unexplainable antisocial act, and conversely, why some people with long criminal careers often engage in conventional behavior. It also explains why there are geographic and temporal patterns in the crime rate: people who are predisposed to crime may simply have more opportunities to commit illegal acts in the summer in Los Angeles and Atlanta than in the winter in Bedford, New Hampshire, and Minot, North Dakota.

The biosocial view is that behavior is a product of interacting biological and environmental events.[150] Physical impairments may make some people "at risk" to crime, but it is when they are linked to social and environmental problems, such as family dysfunction, that they trigger criminal acts.[151] For example, Avshalom Caspi and his associates found that girls who reach physical maturity at an early age are the ones most likely to engage in delinquent acts. This finding might suggest a relationship between biological traits (hormonal activity) and crime. However, the Caspi research found that the association may also have an environmental basis. Physically mature girls are the ones most likely to have prolonged contact with a crime-prone group: older adolescent boys.[152] Here, the combination of biological change, social relationships, and routine opportunities may predict crime rates.

Theories of Evolutionary Criminology

There are a number of individual theories of evolutionary criminology, three of which are discussed in detail here.

Rushton's Theory of Race and Evolution

One of the most controversial versions of evolutionary theory was formulated by J. Phillippe Rushton and first appeared in his 1995 book, *Race, Evolution and Behavior*. According to Rushton, there is evidence that modern humans evolved in Africa about 200,000 years ago and then began to migrate outward to present-day Europe and Asia. He posits that the farther north elements of the populations migrated, the more they encountered harsher climates, which produce the need to gather and store food, gain shelter, make clothes, and raise children successfully during prolonged winters. As these populations evolved into present-day Europeans and Asians, their brain mass increased and they developed slower rates of maturation and lower levels of sex hormones. This physical change produced reductions in sexual potency and aggression and increases in family stability and longevity. These evolutionary changes are responsible for present-day crime rate differences between the races.

Rushton's work was received harshly by critics, who condemned his definitions of race and crime. Among the many criticisms hurled as Rushton has been his singular focus on street crimes, such as theft, while giving short shrift to white-collar and organized crimes, which are predominantly committed by whites. For example, criminologist Michael Lynch argues that Rushton ignores the fact that men are much more criminal than women even though there is little evidence of significant differences in intelligence or brain size between the genders.

R/K Selection Theory

R/K theory holds that all organisms can be located along a continuum based upon their reproductive drives. Those along the "R" end reproduce rapidly whenever they can and invest little in their offspring; those along the "K" end reproduce slowly and cautiously and take care in raising their offspring. Evolutionary theorists believe males today "lean" toward R-selection, because they can reproduce faster without the need for investing in their offspring; females are K-selected, because they have fewer offspring but give more care and devotion to them. K-oriented people are more cooperative and sensitive to others, whereas R-oriented people are more cunning and deceptive. Males, therefore, tend to partake in more criminal behavior. In general, people who commit violent crimes seem to exhibit R-selection traits, such as a premature birth and early and frequent sexual activity. They are more likely to have been neglected as children and to have a short life expectancy.

Cheater Theory

Cheater theory suggests that a subpopulation of men has evolved with genes that incline them toward extremely low parental involvement. They are sexually aggressive and use their cunning to gain sexual conquests with as many females as possible. Because females would not willingly choose them as mates, they use stealth to gain sexual access, including such tactics as mimicking the behavior of more stable males. They use devious and illegal means to acquire resources they need for sexual domination. Their deceptive reproductive tactics spill over into other endeavors, where their talent for irresponsible, opportunistic behavior supports their antisocial activities. Deception in reproductive strategies, then, is linked to a deceitful lifestyle.

Psychologist Byron Roth notes that cheater-type males may be especially attractive to those younger, less intelligent women who begin having children at a very early age. State sponsored welfare, claims Roth, removes the need for potential mates to have the resources needed to be stable providers and family caretakers. With the state meeting their financial needs, these women are attracted to men who are physically attractive and flamboyant. Their fleeting courtship process produces children with low IQs, aggressive personalities, and little chance of proper socialization in father-absent families. Because the criminal justice system treats them leniently, argues Roth, sexually irresponsible men are free to prey on young girls. Over time, their offspring will supply an ever-expanding supply of cheaters who are both antisocial and sexually aggressive.

Critical Thinking Questions

1. Can evolutionary processes, set in motion millions of years ago, influence contemporary human behavior? Although aggressive mating habits may have held sway a million years ago, can their effects still be felt today?

2. Wouldn't the effects of contemporary institutions such as government and media more than offset the influence of primitive mating regimes?

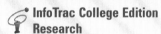 InfoTrac College Edition Research

For a review of similar takes on evolution and deviant behavior, go to InfoTrac College Edition and read this article:

Shotgun solutions for the family crisis: a survey of recent articles. *The Wilson Quarterly* Winter 1997 v21 n1 p113(2)

SOURCES: Byron Roth, "Crime and Child Rearing," *Society* 34 (1996): 39–45; Lee Ellis and Anthony Walsh, "Gene-Based Evolutionary Theories of Criminology, *Criminology* 35 (1997): 229–76; J. Phillipe Rushton, *Race, Evolution and Behavior*, abridged ed. (New Brunswick, N.J.: Transaction Books, 1999); Michael Lynch, "J. Phillipe on Crime: An Examination and Critique of the Explanation of Crime and Race," *Social Pathology* 6 (2000): 228–44; Lee Ellis, "Sex Differences in Criminality: An Explanation Based on the Concept of R/K Selection," *Mankind Quarterly* 30 (1990): 17–37.

CONNECTIONS

The routine activities approach was discussed in Chapters 4 and 5. Is it possible that a person's daily activities and opportunities to commit crime are structured by their biological makeup? This may be an important avenue of research for criminologists to pursue. ■

The most significant criticism of biosocial theory has been the lack of adequate empirical testing. In most research efforts, sample sizes are relatively small and nonrepresentative. A great deal of biosocial research is conducted with samples of adjudicated offenders who have been placed in clinical treatment settings. Methodological problems make it impossible to determine whether findings apply only to offenders who have been convicted of crimes and placed in treatment or to the population of criminals as a whole.[153] More research is needed to clarify the relationships proposed by biosocial researchers and to silence critics.

Psychological Trait Theories

The second branch of trait theory focuses on the psychological aspects of crime, including the association between intelligence, personality, learning, and criminal behavior.

CONNECTIONS

Chapter 1 discussed how some of the early founders of psychiatry, including Pinel and Rush, tried to develop an understanding of the "criminal mind." Later theories suggested that mental illness and insanity were inherited and that deviants were inherently mentally damaged by reason of their inferior genetic makeup. ■

Psychological theories of crime have a long history. In *The English Convict,* Charles Goring (1870–1919) studied the mental characteristics of 3,000 English convicts.[154] He found little difference in the physical characteristics of criminals and noncriminals, but he uncovered a significant relationship between crime and a condition he referred to as **defective intelligence,** which involves such traits as feeblemindedness, epilepsy, insanity, and defective social instinct.[155] Goring believed criminal behavior was inherited and could, therefore, be controlled by regulating the reproduction of families who produced mentally defective children.

Gabriel Tarde (1843–1904) is the forerunner of modern-day learning theorists.[156] Tarde believed people learn from one another through a process of imitation. Tarde's ideas are quite similar to modern social learning theorists who believe that both interpersonal and observed behavior, such as a movie or television, can influence criminality.

Since the pioneering work of people like Tarde and Goring, psychologists, psychiatrists, and other mental health professionals have long played an active role in for-

mulating criminological theory. In their quest to understand and treat all varieties of abnormal mental conditions, psychologists have encountered clients whose behavior falls within categories society has labeled as criminal, deviant, violent, and antisocial.

CONNECTIONS

Chapter 1 discussed the early history of the psychological branch of trait theory, including the work of Maudsley. He believed, as you may recall, that insanity and criminal behavior were strongly linked. ■

This section is organized along the lines of the predominant psychological views most closely associated with the causes of criminal behavior. These perspectives are outlined in Figure 6.2. Some psychologists view antisocial

Figure 6.2 Psychological Perspectives on Criminality

Theory	Cause
PSYCHODYNAMIC (psychoanalytic)	**Intrapsychic processes** • Unconscious conflicts • Defenses • Tendencies • Anger • Sexuality
BEHAVIORAL	**Learning processes** • Past experiences • Stimulus • Rewards and punishments
COGNITIVE	**Information processing** • Thinking • Planning • Memory • Perspective • Ethical values

Trait	Cause
PERSONALITY	**Personality processes** • Antisocial personality • Sociopath/psychopath temperament • Abnormal affect, lack of emotional depth
INTELLIGENCE	**Intellectual processes** • Low IQ • Poor school performance • Bad decision making

behavior from a **psychoanalytic** or **psychodynamic perspective:** their focus is on early childhood experience and its effect on personality. In contrast, **behaviorists** stress social learning and behavior modeling as the keys to criminality. **Cognitive theorists** analyze human perception and how it affects behavior.

CONNECTIONS

There is also a biological branch of psychology that holds that behavior is controlled by the effects of biochemical, neurological, and genetic influences on the brain. This latter viewpoint is quite similar to the biosocial views discussed earlier in this chapter. A great deal of biosocial research is conducted by people trained as psychologists and psychiatrists. ■

Psychodynamic Perspective

Psychodynamic or psychoanalytic psychology was originated by Viennese psychiatrist Sigmund Freud (1856–1939) and has since remained a prominent segment of psychological theory.[157] Freud believed that we all carry with us residue of the most significant emotional attachments of our childhood, which then guide future interpersonal relationships.

For a collection of links to libraries, museums, and biographical materials related to Sigmund Freud and his works, go to:
    http://users.rcn.com/brill/freudarc.html
For an up-to-date list of Web links, go to
    http://info.wadsworth.com/siegel ■

Psychodynamic theory holds that the human personality contains a three-part structure. The **id** is the primitive part of an individual's mental makeup present at birth. It represents unconscious biological drives for sex, food, and other life-sustaining necessities. The id follows the **pleasure principle:** it requires instant gratification without concern for the rights of others.

The **ego** develops early in life, when a child begins to learn that his or her wishes cannot be instantly gratified. The ego is that part of the personality that compensates for the demands of the id by helping the individual guide his or her actions to remain within the boundaries of social convention. The ego is guided by the **reality principle:** it takes into account what is practical and conventional by societal standards.

The **superego** develops as a result of incorporating within the personality the moral standards and values of parents, community, and significant others. It is the moral aspect of an individual's personality; it passes judgments on behavior. The superego is divided into two parts: **conscience** and **ego ideal.** Conscience tells what is right and wrong. It forces the ego to control the id and directs the

Table 6.2   Freud's Model of the Personality Structure

Personality Structure	Guiding Principle	Description
Id	Pleasure Principle	Unconscious biological drives. Requires instant gratification.
Ego	Reality Principle	Helps the personality refine the demands of the id. Helps person adapt to conventions.
Superego	The conscience	The moral aspect of personality.

individual into morally acceptable and responsible behaviors, which may not be pleasurable. Table 6.2 summarizes Freud's personality structure.

Psychosexual stages of human development The most basic human drive present at birth is **eros,** the instinct to preserve and create life. Eros is expressed sexually. Consequently, very early in their development, humans experience sexuality, which is expressed by seeking pleasure through various parts of the body. During the first year of life, a child attains pleasure by sucking and biting; Freud called this the **oral stage.** During the second and third years of life, the focus of sexual attention is on the elimination of bodily wastes—the **anal stage.** The **phallic stage** occurs during the third year when children focus their attention on their genitals. Males begin to have sexual feelings for their mothers (the **Oedipus complex**) and girls for their fathers (the **Electra complex**). **Latency** begins at age 6. During this period, feelings of sexuality are repressed until the genital stage begins at puberty; this marks the beginning of adult sexuality.

If conflicts are encountered during any of the psychosexual stages of development, a person can become **fixated** at that point. This means, as an adult, the fixated person will exhibit behavior traits characteristic of those encountered during infantile sexual development. For example, an infant who does not receive enough oral gratification during the first year of life is likely as an adult to engage in such oral behavior as smoking, drinking, or drug abuse or to be clinging and dependent in personal relationships. Thus, according to Freud, the roots of adult behavioral problems can be traced to problems developed in the earliest years of life.

Psychodynamics of abnormal behavior Psychodynamic theory originally referred to people who experience feelings of mental anguish and are afraid that they are losing control of their personalities as **neurotics.** Those people who had lost total control and were dominated by their primitive id were referred to as **psychotics.** Today, these terms have, for the most part, been replaced with the term **disorder.** There are a variety of disorders including anxiety disorder, mood disorders, and conduct disorders. The most serious disorder is **schizophrenia,** marked by hearing nonexistent voices, hallucinations, and inappropriate responses.

People with schizophrenia exhibit illogical and incoherent thought processes and a lack of insight into their behavior. They may experience delusions and hallucinate. For example, they may see themselves as agents of the devil, avenging angels, or the recipients of messages from animals and plants. David Berkowitz (the "Son of Sam" or the "44-calibre killer"), a noted serial killer who went on a rampage from 1976 to 1977, exhibited these traits when he claimed that his killing spree began when he received messages from a neighbor's dog. **Paranoid schizophrenics,** such as U.S. capitol slayer Eugene Weston, suffer complex behavior delusions involving wrongdoing or persecution—they think everyone is out to get them.

Psychologists have long linked criminality to abnormal mental states produced by early childhood trauma. For example, Alfred Adler (1870–1937), the founder of individual psychology, coined the term **inferiority complex** to describe people who have feelings of inferiority and compensate for them with a drive for superiority. Controlling others may help reduce personal inadequacies. Erik Erikson (1902–1984) described the **identity crisis**—a period of serious personal questioning people undertake in an effort to determine their own values and sense of direction. Adolescents undergoing an identity crisis might exhibit out-of-control behavior and experiment with drugs and other forms of deviance.

The psychoanalyst whose work is most closely associated with criminality is August Aichorn.[158] After examining many delinquent youths, Aichorn concluded that societal stress, though damaging, could not alone result in a life of crime unless a predisposition existed that psychologically prepared youths for antisocial acts. This mental state, which he labeled **latent delinquency,** is found in youngsters whose personality requires them to act in these ways:

- Seek immediate gratification (to act impulsively).
- Consider satisfying their personal needs more important than relating to others.
- Satisfy instinctive urges without considering right and wrong (that is, they lack guilt).

For a review of Aichorn's famous book, read this article on InfoTrac College Edition: Lynn E. Ponton. Wayward youth. *Journal of the American Academy of Child and Adolescent Psychiatry* July 1998 v37 n7 p793(3) ∎

Psychodynamics of criminal behavior Since Freud's original research, psychoanalysts have continued to view criminals as id-dominated persons who suffer from one or more disorders that render them incapable of controlling impulsive, pleasure-seeking drives.[159] The psychodynamic model of the criminal offender depicts an aggressive, frustrated person dominated by events that occurred early in childhood. Perhaps because they may have suffered unhappy experiences in childhood or had families that could not provide proper love and care, criminals suffer from weak or damaged egos that make them unable to cope with conventional society. Weak egos are associated with immaturity, poor social skills, and excessive dependence on others. People with weak egos may be easily led into crime by antisocial peers and drug abuse. Some offenders have underdeveloped superegos and consequently lack internalized representations of those behaviors that are punished in conventional society. They commit crimes because they have difficulty understanding the consequences of their actions.[160]

Offenders may suffer from a garden variety of mood and/or behavior disorders. They may be histrionic, depressed, antisocial, or narcissistic.[161] They may suffer from conduct disorders, which include long histories of antisocial behavior, or mood disorders characterized by disturbance in expressed emotions. Among the latter is **bipolar disorder,** in which moods alternate between periods of wild elation and deep depression.[162] Some offenders are driven by an unconscious desire to be punished for prior sins, either real or imaginary. As a result, they may violate the law to gain attention or to punish their parents.

Crime is a manifestation of feelings of oppression and people's inability to develop the proper psychological defenses and rationales to keep these feelings under control. Criminality enables troubled people to survive by producing positive psychic results: it helps them to feel free and independent, and it gives them the possibility of excitement and the chance to use their skills and imagination. Crime also provides them with the promise of positive gain; it allows them to blame others for their predicament (for example, the police), and it gives them a chance to rationalize their sense of failure ("If I hadn't gotten into trouble, I could have been a success").[163]

Behavioral Theories

Behavior theory maintains that human actions are developed through learning experiences. Rather than focusing on unconscious personality traits or cognitive development patterns produced early in childhood, behavior theorists are concerned with the actual behaviors people engage in during the course of their daily lives. The major premise of behavior theory is that people alter their behavior according to the reactions it receives from others. Behavior is supported by rewards and extinguished by negative reactions or punishments. Behaviorist theory is quite complex with many different subareas. With respect to criminal activity, the behaviorist views crimes, especially violent acts, as learned responses to life situations that do

■ According to behavioral theory, people learn to become violent when they learn to be aggressive through their life experiences. These experiences include personally observing others acting aggressively to achieve some goal or watching people being rewarded for violent acts on television or in movies. Here, on October 23, 2001, O.J. Simpson explains in a Miami court how he got into a confrontation with a motorist, Jeffrey Pattinson, which began when Pattinson flashed his lights and blared his horn. How would a behaviorist explain the onset of incidents of "road rage"?

not necessarily represent abnormal or morally immature responses.

Social Learning Theory

Social learning is the branch of behavior theory most relevant to criminology.[164] Social learning theorists, most notably Albert Bandura, argue that people are not actually born with the ability to act violently but that they learn to be aggressive through their life experiences. These experiences include personally observing others acting aggressively to achieve some goal or watching people being rewarded for violent acts on television or in movies. People learn to act aggressively when, as children, they model their behavior after the violent acts of adults. Later in life, these violent behavior patterns persist in social relationships. For example, the boy who sees his father repeatedly strike his mother with impunity is the one most likely to grow up to become a battering parent and husband.

Though social learning theorists agree that mental or physical traits may predispose a person toward violence, they believe that activating a person's violent tendencies is achieved by factors in the environment. The specific forms that aggressive behavior takes, the frequency with which it is expressed, the situations in which it is displayed, and the specific targets selected for attack are largely determined by social learning. However, people are self-aware and engage in purposeful learning. Their interpretations of behavior outcomes and situations influence the way they learn from

experiences. One adolescent who spends a weekend in jail for drunk driving may find it the most awful experience of her life—one that teaches her to never drink and drive again. Another person, however, may find it an exciting experience about which he can brag to his friends.

Social learning and violence   Social learning theorists view violence as something learned through a process called **behavior modeling.** In modern society, aggressive acts are usually modeled after three principal sources:

1. **Family members.** Bandura reports that studies of family life show that children who use aggressive tactics have parents who use similar behaviors when dealing with others.

2. **Environmental experiences.** People who reside in areas in which violence is a daily occurrence are more likely to act violently than those who dwell in low-crime areas whose norms stress conventional behavior.

3. **Mass media.** Films and television shows commonly depict violence graphically. Moreover, violence is often portrayed as an acceptable behavior, especially for heroes who never have to face legal consequences for their actions. For example, David Phillips found the homicide rate increases significantly immediately after a heavyweight championship prize fight.[165]

The Criminological Enterprise feature entitled "The Media and Violence" on pages 158–159 has more on the effects of the media and violent behavior.

Social learning theorists have tried to determine what triggers violent acts. One position is that a direct, pain-producing physical assault will usually trigger a violent response. Yet the relationship between painful attacks and aggressive responses has been found to be inconsistent. Whether people counterattack in the face of physical attack depends, in part, on their skill in fighting and their perception of the strength of their attackers. Verbal taunts and insults have also been linked to aggressive responses. People who are predisposed to aggression by their learning experiences are likely to view insults from others as a challenge to their social status and to react with violence. Still another violence-triggering mechanism is a perceived reduction in one's life conditions. Prime examples of this phenomenon are riots and demonstrations in poverty-stricken ghetto areas. Studies have shown that discontent also produces aggression in the more successful members of lower-class groups who have been led to believe they can succeed, but then have been thwarted in their aspirations. While it is still uncertain how this relationship is constructed, it is apparently complex. No matter how deprived some individuals are, they will not resort to violence. It seems evident that people's perceptions of their relative deprivation have different effects on their aggressive responses.

In summary, social learning theorists have said that the following four factors may contribute to violent and/or aggressive behavior:

1. **An event that heightens arousal:** such as a person frustrating or provoking another through physical assault or verbal abuse.

2. **Aggressive skills:** learned aggressive responses picked up from observing others, either personally or through the media.

3. **Expected outcomes:** the belief that aggression will somehow be rewarded. Rewards can come in the form of reducing tension or anger, gaining some financial reward, building self-esteem, or gaining the praise of others.

4. **Consistency of behavior with values:** the belief, gained from observing others, that aggression is justified and appropriate, given the circumstances of the current situation.

Cognitive Theory

One area of psychology that has received increasing recognition in recent years has been the cognitive school. Psychologists with a cognitive perspective focus on mental processes and how people perceive and mentally represent the world around them and solve problems. The pioneers of this school were Wilhelm Wundt (1832–1920), Edward Titchener (1867–1927), and William James (1842–1920). Today, there are several subdisciplines within the cognitive area. The **moral development** branch is concerned with the way people morally represent and reason about the world. **Humanistic psychology** stresses self-awareness and "getting in touch with feelings." The **information processing** branch focuses on the way people process, store, encode, retrieve, and manipulate information to make decisions and solve problems.

Moral and intellectual development theory The moral and intellectual development branch of cognitive psychology is perhaps the most important for criminological theory. Jean Piaget (1896–1980), the founder of this approach, hypothesized that people's reasoning processes develop in an orderly fashion, beginning at birth and continuing until they are 12 years old and older.[166] At first, children respond to the environment in a simple manner, seeking interesting objects and developing their reflexes. By the fourth and final stage, the formal operations stage, they have developed into mature adults who can use logic and abstract thought.

Lawrence Kohlberg first applied the concept of moral development to issues in criminology.[167] He found that people travel through stages of moral development during which their decisions and judgments on issues of right and wrong are made for different reasons. It is possible that serious offenders have a moral orientation that differs from that of law-abiding citizens. Kohlberg's stages of development are listed in Table 6.3.

Kohlberg classified people according to the stage on this continuum at which their moral development ceased to grow. Kohlberg and his associates conducted studies in which criminals were found to be significantly lower in their moral judgment development than noncriminals of the same social background.[168] Since his pioneering

Table 6.3 Kohlberg's Stages of Development

Stage 1 Right is obedience to power and avoidance of punishment.

Stage 2 Right is taking responsibility for oneself, meeting one's own needs, and leaving to others the responsibility for themselves.

Stage 3 Right is being good in the sense of having good motives, having concern for others, and "putting yourself in the other person's shoes."

Stage 4 Right is maintaining the rules of a society and serving the welfare of the group or society.

Stage 5 Right is based on recognized individual rights within a society with agreed-upon rules—a social contract.

Stage 6 Right is an assumed obligation to principles applying to all humankind—principles of justice, equality, and respect for human life.

SOURCE: Lawrence Kohlberg, *Stages in the Development of Moral Thought and Action* (New York: Holt, Rinehart and Winston, 1969).

The Media and Violence

On November 27, 1995, thieves ignited flammable liquid in a New York City subway token booth, seriously injuring the clerk. Their behavior was virtually identical to a robbery scene in the film *Money Train* (with Wesley Snipes and Woody Harrelson), which had been released a few days earlier. Then-Senator Robert Dole, a critic of media violence, said: "Those who work in Hollywood's corporate suites must also be willing to accept their share of blame. Is this how they want to make their livelihoods? Is this their contribution to society?" Dole made media violence a key issue in his unsuccessful 1996 presidential campaign.

Does the media influence behavior? Does broadcast violence cause aggressive behavior in viewers? This has become a hot topic because of the persistent theme of violence on television and in films. Critics have called for drastic measures, ranging from banning TV violence to putting warning labels on heavy metal albums because of a fear that listening to hard-rock lyrics produces delinquency.

If there is in fact a TV–violence link, the problem is indeed alarming. Systematic viewing of TV begins at 2-and-a-half years of age and continues at a high level during the preschool and early school years. It has been estimated that children ages 2 to 5 watch TV for 27.8 hours each week; children ages 6 to 11 watch 24.3 hours per week; and teens watch 23 hours per week. Marketing research indicates that adolescents ages 11 to 14 rent violent horror movies at a higher rate than any other age group. Children this age use older peers and siblings and apathetic parents to gain access to R-rated films. More than 40 percent of U.S. households now have cable TV, which features violent films and shows. Even children's programming is saturated with violence.

The fact that children watch so much violent TV is not surprising considering the findings of a well-publicized study conducted by UCLA researchers in 1995. They found that at least 10 network shows made heavy use of violence. Of the 161 television movies monitored (every one that aired that season), 23 raised concerns about their use of violence, violent theme, violent title, or inappropriate portrayals of a scene. Of the 118 theatrical films monitored (every one that aired that season), 50 raised concerns about their use of violence.

On-air promotions also reflect a continuing, if not worsening, problem. Some series may contain several scenes of violence, each of which is appropriate within its context. An advertisement for that show, however, will feature those violent scenes only without any of the context. Even some children's television programming had worrisome signs, featuring "sinister combat" as the theme of the show. The characters are usually happy to fight and frequently do so with little provocation. A University of Pennsylvania study also found that children's programming contained an average of 32 violent acts per hour, that 56 percent had violent characters, and that 74 percent had characters who became the victims of violence (though "only 3.3 percent had characters who were actually killed"). In all, the average child views 8,000 TV murders before finishing elementary school.

There have been numerous anecdotal cases of violence linked to TV and films. For example, in a famous incident, John Hinckley shot President Ronald Reagan due to his obsession with actress Jodie Foster, which developed after he watched her play a prostitute in the film *Taxi Driver*. Hinckley viewed the film at least 15 times.

A national survey conducted in the wake of the controversy found that almost 80 percent of the general public believes violence on TV can cause violence "in real life." Psychologists, however, believe media violence does not in itself *cause* violent behavior, because, if it did, there would be millions of daily incidents in which viewers imitated the aggression they watched on TV or in movies. But most psychologists agree that media violence *contributes* to aggression. There are several explanations for the effects of television and film violence on behavior:

- Media violence can provide aggressive "scripts" that children store in memory. Repeated exposure to these scripts can increase their retention and lead to changes in attitudes.

- Children learn from what they observe. In the same way they learn cognitive and social skills from their parents and friends, children learn to be violent from television.

- Television violence increases the arousal levels of viewers and makes them more prone to act aggressively. Studies measuring the galvanic skin response of subjects—a physical indication of arousal based on the amount of electricity conducted across the palm of the hand—show that viewing violent television shows led to increased arousal levels in young children.

- Watching television violence promotes such negative attitudes as suspiciousness and the expectation that the viewer will become involved in violence. Those who watch television frequently come to view aggression and violence as common and socially acceptable behavior.

- Television violence allows aggressive youths to justify their behavior. It is possible that, instead of causing violence, television helps violent youths rationalize their behavior as a socially acceptable and common activity.

- Television violence may disinhibit aggressive behavior, which is normally controlled by other learning processes. *Disinhibition* takes place when adults are viewed as being rewarded for violence and when violence is seen as socially acceptable. This contradicts previous learning experiences in which violent behavior was viewed as wrong.

Such distinguished bodies as the American Psychological Association, the National Institute of Mental Health, and the National Research Council support the TV–violence link. They base their conclusion on research efforts that indicate that watching violence on TV leads to increased levels of violence in laboratory settings as well as in natural settings.

A number of experimental approaches have been used. Some of these include:

- Having groups of subjects exposed to violent TV shows in a laboratory setting, then monitoring their behavior afterward compared to control groups who viewed non-violent programming.

- Observing subjects on playgrounds, athletic fields, and residences after they have been exposed to violent television programs.

- Requiring subjects to answer attitude surveys after watching violent TV shows.

- Using aggregate measures of TV viewing; for example, tracking the number of violent TV shows on the air during a given time period and comparing it to crime rates during the same period.

According to a recent analysis of all scientific data since 1975, Brad Bushman and Craig Anderson found that the weight of the evidence is that watching violence on TV is correlated to aggressive behaviors and that the newest most methodologically sophisticated works show the greatest amount of association. The weight of the experimental results indicates that violent media has an immediate impact on people with a preexisting tendency toward crime and violence.

There is also evidence that kids who watch TV are more likely to persist in aggressive behavior as adults. A recent study conducted by researchers at Columbia University found that kids who watch more than an hour of TV each day show an increase in assaults, fights, robberies, and other acts of aggression later in life. The team, led by Jeffery G. Johnson, studied more than 700 people for 17 years. Their data indicate that 5.7 percent of 14-year-olds who watched less than an hour of television a day became involved in aggressive acts between the ages of 16 and 22. The rate of aggressive acts skyrocketed to 22.5 percent when kids watched between one and three hours of TV. For kids who viewed more than three hours of TV per day, 28.8 percent were later involved in aggressive acts as adults. This association remained significant after previous aggressive behavior, childhood neglect, family income, neighborhood violence, parental education, and psychiatric disorders were controlled statistically. The Johnson research provides a direct link between TV viewing in adolescence and aggressive behavior in adulthood.

While this research is quite persuasive, not all criminologists accept that watching TV or movies and listening to heavy metal music eventually leads to violent and antisocial behavior. For example, criminologist Simon Singer found that teenage heavy metal fans were no more delinquent than nonlisteners. Candace Kruttschnitt and her associates found that an individual's exposure to violent TV shows is only weakly related to subsequent violent behavior.

There is also little evidence that areas that experience the highest levels of violent TV viewing also have rates of violent crime that are above the norm. Millions of children watch violence every night but do not become violent criminals. In fact, despite the prevalence of violent TV shows, films, and video games, which have become a universal norm, the violence rate among teens has been in a significant decline. If violent TV shows did, indeed, cause interpersonal violence, then there should be few ecological and regional patterns in the crime rate, but there are many. Put another way, how can regional differences in the violence rate be explained considering the fact that people all across the nation watch the same TV shows and films?

Critical Thinking Questions

1. Should the government control the content of TV shows and limit the amount of weekly violence? How could the national news be shown if violence were omitted? What about boxing matches or hockey games?

2. How can we explain the fact that millions of kids watch violent TV shows and remain nonviolent? If there is a TV–violence link, how can we explain the fact that violence rates may have been higher in the "Old West" than they are today? Do you think violent gang kids stay home and watch TV shows?

InfoTrac College Edition Research

For a different take on the effects of TV viewing on violence, check out these articles:

David Link. Facts about fiction: in defense of TV violence. *Reason* March 1994 v25 n10 p22

Mike Males. Who us? Stop blaming kids and TV. *The Progressive* Oct 1997 v61 n10 p25(3)

SOURCES: Jeffery Johnson, Patricia Cohen, Elizabeth Smailes, Stephanie Kasen, and Judith Brook, "Television Viewing and Aggressive Behavior During Adolescent and Adulthood," *Science* 295 (2002): 2468–71; Craig Anderson and Brad J. Bushman, "The Effects of Media Violence on Society," *Science* 295 (2002): 2377–79; Brad Bushman and Craig Anderson, "Media Violence and the American Public," *American Psychologist* 56 (2001): 477–89; UCLA Center for Communication Policy, *Television Violence Monitoring Project* (Los Angeles, Calif., 1995); Associated Press, "Hollywood Is Blamed in Token Booth Attack," *Boston Globe*, 28 November 1995, p. 30; Garland White, Janet Katz, and Kathryn Scarborough, "The Impact of Professional Football Games upon Violent Assaults on Women," *Violence and Victims* 7 (1992): 157–71; Simon Singer, "Rethinking Subcultural Theories of Delinquency and the Cultural Resources of Youth." Paper presented at the annual meeting of the American Society of Criminology, Phoenix, Arizona, November 1993; Albert Reiss and Jeffrey Roth, eds., *Understanding and Preventing Violence* (Washington, D.C.: National Academy Press, 1993); Reuters, "Seventy-nine Percent in Survey Link Violence on TV and Crime," *Boston Globe*, 19 December 1993, p. 17; Scott Snyder, "Movies and Juvenile Delinquency: An Overview," *Adolescence* 26 (1991): 121–31; Steven Messner, "Television Violence and Violent Crime: An Aggregate Analysis," *Social Problems* 33 (1986): 218–35; Candace Kruttschnitt, Linda Heath, and David Ward, "Family Violence, Television Viewing Habits, and Other Adolescent Experiences Related to Violent Criminal Behavior," *Criminology* 243 (1986): 235–67; Jonathan Freedman, "Television Violence and Aggression: A Rejoinder," *Psychological Bulletin* 100 (1986): 372–78; Wendy Wood, Frank Wong, and J. Gregory Chachere, "Effects of Media Violence on Viewers' Aggression in Unconstrained Social Interaction," *Psychological Bulletin* 109 (1991): 371–83.

efforts, researchers have continued to show that criminal offenders are more likely to be classified in the lowest levels of moral reasoning (Stages 1 and 2), whereas non-criminals have reached a higher stage of moral development (Stages 3 and 4).[169]

Recent research indicates that the decision not to commit crimes may be influenced by one's stage of moral development. People at the lowest levels report that they are deterred from crime because of their fear of sanctions. Those in the middle consider the reactions of family and friends. Those at the highest stages refrain from crime because they believe in duty to others and universal rights.[170]

CONNECTIONS

The deterrent effect of informal sanctions and feelings of shame discussed in Chapter 5 may hinge on the level of a person's moral development. The lower one's state of moral development, the less impact informal sanctions may have; increased moral development and informal sanctions may be better able to control crime. ■

Moral development theory suggests that people who obey the law simply to avoid punishment or have outlooks mainly characterized by self-interest are more likely to commit crimes than those who view the law as something that benefits all of society. Those at higher stages of moral reasoning tend to sympathize with the rights of others and are associated with conventional behaviors, such as honesty, generosity, and nonviolence.

Information processing When cognitive theorists who study information processing try to explain antisocial behavior, they do so in terms of mental perception and how people use information to understand their environment. When people make decisions, they engage in a sequence of cognitive thought processes. First, they encode information so that it can be interpreted. Next, they search for a proper response and decide on the most appropriate action. Finally, they act on their decision.[171]

According to this cognitive approach, people who use information properly, who are better conditioned to make reasoned judgments, and who can make quick and reasoned decisions when facing emotion-laden events are the ones best able to avoid antisocial behavior choices.[172] In contrast, violence-prone people may be using information incorrectly when they make decisions. One reason is that they may be relying on mental "scripts" learned in childhood that tell them how to interpret events, what to expect, how they should react, and what the outcome of the interaction should be.[173] Hostile children may have learned improper scripts by observing how others react to events; their own parents' aggressive and inappropriate behavior would have considerable impact. Some may have had early and prolonged exposure to violence (for example, child abuse), which increases their sensitivity to

slights and maltreatment. Oversensitivity to rejection by their peers is a continuation of sensitivity to rejection by their parents.[174] Violence becomes a stable behavior because the scripts that emphasize aggressive responses are repeatedly rehearsed as the child matures.

To violence-prone kids, people seem more aggressive than they actually are and intend them ill when there is no reason for alarm. According to information processing theory, as these children mature, they use fewer cues than most people to process information. Some use violence in a calculating fashion as a means of getting what they want; others react in an overly volatile fashion to the slightest provocation. Aggressors are more likely to be vigilant, on edge, or suspicious. When they attack victims, they may believe they are defending themselves, even though they are misreading the situation.[175]

Information processing theory has been used to explain the occurrence of date rape. Sexually violent males believe that when their dates say "No" to sexual advances the women are really "playing games" and actually want to be taken forcefully.[176]

Treatment based on how people process information takes into account that people are more likely to respond aggressively to a provocation because thoughts tend to intensify the insult or otherwise stir feelings of anger. Cognitive therapists, during the course of treatment, attempt to teach explosive people to control aggressive impulses by viewing social provocations as problems demanding a solution rather than retaliation. Programs are aimed at teaching problem-solving skills that may include self-disclosure, role-playing, listening, following instructions, joining in, and using self-control.[177]

Therapeutic interventions designed to make people better problem solvers may involve such measures as (1) enhancing coping and problem-solving skills; (2) enhancing relationships with peers, parents, and other adults; (3) teaching conflict resolution and communication skills and methods for resisting peer pressure related to drug use and violence; (4) teaching consequential thinking and decision-making abilities; (5) modeling prosocial behaviors, including cooperation with others, self-responsibility, respecting others, and public speaking efficacy; and (6) teaching empathy.[178]

Treatment interventions based on learning social skills are relatively new, but there are some indications that this approach can have long-term benefits for reducing criminal behavior.[179]

To learn more about information processing theory, go to these Web sites:

http://www.valdosta.edu/~whuitt/psy702/cogsys/infoproc.ht

http://www.a-levelpsychology.co.uk/pdf/as/17.pdf

For an up-to-date list of Web links, go to

http://info.wadsworth.com/siegel ■

Crime and Mental Illness

The nation was shocked on March 24, 1998, when a 13-year-old boy, who had vowed to kill all the girls who had broken up with him, and his 11-year-old cousin opened fire on students outside a middle school in Jonesboro, Arkansas, killing four girls and a teacher and wounding 11 other people.[180] The two boys, dressed in camouflage clothing, apparently lay in wait in a wooded area near the school after setting off a fire alarm, forcing students and faculty members outside. There have been similar multiple school shootings in the past few years including well-publicized ones in West Paducah, Kentucky, and Pearl, Mississippi.

When an obviously disturbed person commits an unfathomable violent act, it suggests a linkage between mental illness and crime. And while the association appears clear-cut, empirical evidence has been contradictory. A great deal of early research efforts found that many offenders who engage in serious, violent crimes suffer from some sort of mental disturbance. Juvenile murderers have been described in clinical diagnosis as "overtly hostile," "explosive or volatile," "anxious," and "depressed."[181] Studies of men accused of murder found that 75 percent could be classified as having some mental illness, including schizophrenia.[182] Abusive mothers have been found to have mood and personality disorders and a history of psychiatric diagnoses.[183] Also, the reported substance abuse among the mentally ill is significantly higher than that of the general population.[184] The diagnosed mentally ill appear in arrest and court statistics at a rate disproportionate to their presence in the population.[185]

Is the link valid? Despite this evidence, there are still questions about whether mental illness is a direct cause of crime and violence. The mentally ill may be more likely to withdraw or harm themselves than to act aggressively toward others.[186] Similarly, research shows that upon release prisoners who had prior histories of hospitalization for mental disorders were less likely to be rearrested than those who had never been hospitalized.[187] Mentally disordered inmates who do recidivate upon release appear to do so for the same reasons as the mentally sound—extensive criminal histories, substance abuse, and family dysfunction—rather than as a result of their illness.[188]

The National Mental Health Association (NMHA) is the country's oldest and largest nonprofit organization addressing all aspects of mental health and mental illness. It is dedicated to improving the mental health of all individuals and achieving victory over mental illnesses. Visit their Web site at:
   http://www.nmha.org/
For an up-to-date list of Web links, go to
   http://info.wadsworth.com/siegel ■

Although the existing data questions whether mental illness is a cause of crime per se, *particular symptoms* of mental illness may be connected to violence. People who suffer paranoid or delusional feelings, for example, and who believe others wish them harm or that their mind is dominated by forces beyond their control, seem to be violence prone.[189]

■ Susan Smith, Darlie Routier, and Andrea Yates all have been convicted of killing their children. Can such behavior be the product of a normal mind, or must their terrible acts be the result of some mental defect or illness?

CHAPTER 6 ■ *Trait Theories*   **161**

It is also possible that the link between mental illness and crime is spurious and an artifact of structural factors: mentally ill people lack the financial resources to live in affluent areas and are therefore more likely to reside in deteriorated high-crime neighborhoods, which are linked to violence (see Chapter 7).[190] Living in a stress-filled, urban environment may produce both symptoms of mental illness and crime.[191] It is also possible that a lack of resources may inhibit the mentally ill from obtaining the proper treatment, which, if made available, would result in reduced criminality. For example, a recent study conducted in North Carolina compared the outcomes for mentally ill patients who received outpatient treatment with an untreated comparison group; treatment significantly reduced arrest probability (12 percent versus 45 percent).[192]

Personality and Crime

Personality can be defined as the reasonably stable patterns of behavior, including thoughts and emotions, that distinguish one person from another.[193] One's personality reflects a characteristic way of adapting to life's demands and problems. The way we behave is a function of how our personality enables us to interpret life events and make appropriate behavioral choices. Can the cause of crime be linked to personality? This issue has long caused significant debate.[194] Sheldon Glueck and Eleanor Glueck identified a number of personality traits that they believe characterize antisocial youth:

self-assertiveness	sadism
defiance	lack of concern for others
extroversion	feeling unappreciated
ambivalence	distrust of authority
impulsiveness	poor personal skills
narcissism	mental instability
suspicion	hostility
destructiveness	resentment[195]

CONNECTIONS

The Glueck research is representative of the view that antisocial people maintain a distinct set of personal traits, which makes them particularly sensitive to environmental stimuli. Once dismissed by mainstream criminologists, the section on life course theories in Chapter 10 shows how the Gluecks' views still influence contemporary criminological theory. ■

Several other research efforts have attempted to identify criminal personality traits.[196] Suspected traits include impulsivity, hostility, and aggressiveness.[197] For example, Hans Eysenck identified two personality traits that he associated with antisocial behavior: *extroversion-introversion* and *stability-instability*. Extreme introverts are overaroused and avoid sources of stimulation; in contrast, extreme extroverts are unaroused and seek sensation. Introverts are slow to learn and be conditioned; extroverts are impulsive individuals who lack the ability to examine their own motives and behaviors. Those who are unstable, a condition Eysenck calls "neuroticism," are anxious, tense, and emotionally unstable.[198] People who are both neurotic and extroverted lack self-insight and are impulsive and emotionally unstable; they are unlikely to have reasoned judgments of life events. While extrovert neurotics may act self-destructively (for example, by abusing drugs), more stable people will be able to reason that such behavior is ultimately harmful and life threatening. Eysenck believes that personality is controlled by genetic factors and is heritable.

 To learn more about human personality and its effect on behavior, use "personality" as a key word on InfoTrac College Edition. ■

In a recent study evaluating the most widely used measures of personality, Joshua Miller and Donald Lynam found that variance within two dimensions—agreeableness and conscientious—seem most closely related to antisocial behaviors. *Agreeableness* involves the ability to use appropriate interpersonal strategies when dealing with others; *conscientiousness* involves a person's ability to control impulses, carry out plans and tasks, maintain organizational skills, and follow his or her internal moral code.[199] Miller and Lynam found that personality researchers now link antisocial behaviors to traits such as these: hostile, self-centered, spiteful, jealous, and indifferent to others. Law violators tend to lack ambition and motivation and perseverance, have difficulty controlling their impulses, and hold nonconventional values and beliefs. Miller and Lynam show that these personality traits are linked to crime, but there is still some question about the direction of the linkage. On one hand, it is possible that people who share these personality traits are programmed to commit crimes. On the other hand, it is possible that personality traits interact with environmental factors to alter behavior. For example, kids who are low in conscientiousness will most likely have poor educational and occupational histories, which limit their opportunity for advancement; this blocked opportunity renders them crime prone.[200]

CONNECTIONS

Miller and Lynam's view is similar to the one proposed by Michael Gottfredson and Travis Hirschi. They find that an impulsive personality is the key to understanding criminal behavior. To find out more about their viewpoint, read the section on the general theory of crime in Chapter 10. ■

Antisocial personality/psychopathy/sociopathy As a group, people who share these traits are believed to have a character defect referred to as antisocial, sociopathic, or psychopathic personality. Though these terms are often used interchangeably, some psychologists distinguish between sociopaths and psychopaths, suggesting that the former are a product of a destructive home environment whereas the latter are a product of a defect or aberration within themselves.[201] This condition is discussed in the Criminological Enterprise feature entitled "The Antisocial Personality."

Research on personality   Since maintaining a deviant personality has been related to crime and delinquency, numerous attempts have been made to devise accurate measures of personality and determine whether they can predict antisocial behavior. One of the most widely used psychological tests is the **Minnesota Multiphasic Personality Inventory,** commonly called the **MMPI.** This test has subscales designed to measure many different personality traits, including psychopathic deviation (Pd scale), schizophrenia (Sc), and hypomania (Ma).[202] Research studies have detected an association between scores on the Pd scale and criminal involvement.[203] Another frequently administered personality test, the **California Personality Inventory (CPI),** has also been used to distinguish deviants from nondeviant groups.[204] The **Multidimensional Personality Questionnaire (MPQ)** allows researchers to assess such personality traits as control, aggression, alienation, and well-being.[205] Evaluations using this scale indicate that adolescent offenders who are "crime prone" maintain "negative emotionality," a tendency to experience aversive affective states, such as anger, anxiety, and irritability. They also are predisposed to weak personal constraints, and they have difficulty controlling impulsive behavior urges. Because they are both impulsive and aggressive, crime-prone people are quick to take action against perceived threats.

Evidence that personality traits predict crime and violence is important because it suggests that the root cause of crime can be found in the forces that influence human development at an early stage of life. If these results are valid, rather than focus on job creation and neighborhood improvement, crime control efforts might be better focused on helping families raise children who are reasoned and reflective and enjoy a safe environment.

Intelligence and Crime

Many early criminologists maintained that many delinquents and criminals have a below-average intelligence quotient and that low IQ is a cause of their criminality. Criminals were believed to have inherently substandard intelligence, and thus, they seemed naturally inclined to commit more crimes than more intelligent persons. Furthermore, it was thought that if authorities could determine which individuals had low IQs, they might identify potential criminals before they committed socially harmful acts.

Social scientists had a captive group of subjects in juvenile training schools and penal institutions, and they began to measure the correlation between IQ and crime by testing adjudicated offenders. Thus, inmates of penal institutions were used as a test group around which numerous theories about intelligence were built, leading ultimately to the nature-versus-nurture controversy that is still going on today. These concepts are discussed in some detail in the following sections.

Nature theory   Nature theory argues that intelligence is largely determined genetically, that ancestry determines IQ, and that low intelligence, as demonstrated by low IQ, is linked to criminal behavior. When the newly developed IQ tests were administered to inmates of prisons and juvenile training schools in the first decades of the century, the nature position gained support because a very large proportion of the inmates scored low on the tests. During his studies in 1920, Henry Goddard found that many institutionalized persons were what he considered "feebleminded"; he concluded that at least half of all juvenile delinquents were mental defectives.[206] In 1926, William Healy and Augusta Bronner tested groups of delinquent boys in Chicago and Boston and found that 37 percent were subnormal in intelligence. They concluded that delinquents were 5 to 10 times more likely to be mentally deficient than normal boys.[207] These and other early studies were embraced as proof that low IQ scores indicated potentially delinquent children and that a correlation existed between innate low intelligence and deviant behavior. IQ tests were believed to measure the inborn genetic makeup of individuals, and many criminologists accepted the idea that individuals with substandard IQs were predisposed toward delinquency and adult criminality.

Nurture theory   The rise of culturally sensitive explanations of human behavior in the 1930s led to the nurture school of intelligence. The **nurture theory** states that intelligence must be viewed as partly biological but primarily sociological. Because intelligence is not inherited, low-IQ parents do not necessarily produce low-IQ children.[208] Nurture theorists discredited the notion that persons commit crimes because they have low IQs. Instead, they postulated that environmental stimulation from parents, relatives, social contacts, schools, peer groups, and innumerable others create a child's IQ level and that low IQs result from an environment that also encourages delinquent and criminal behavior. Thus, if low IQ scores are recorded among criminals, these scores may reflect criminals' cultural background, not their mental ability.

Studies challenging the assumption that people automatically committed criminal acts because they had below-average IQs began to appear as early as the 1920s. John Slawson studied 1,543 delinquent boys in New York institutions and compared them with a control group of New York City boys in 1926.[209] Slawson found that although 80 percent of the delinquents achieved lower scores in abstract verbal intelligence, delinquents were about normal

THE CRIMINOLOGICAL ENTERPRISE

The Antisocial Personality

Some violent offenders may have a disturbed character structure commonly and interchangeably referred to as psychopathy, sociopathy, or antisocial personality. Psychopaths exhibit a low level of guilt and anxiety and persistently violate the rights of others. Although they may exhibit superficial charm and above-average intelligence, this often masks a disturbed personality that makes them incapable of forming enduring relationships with others and continually involves them in such deviant behaviors as violence, risk-taking, substance abuse, and impulsivity.

From an early age, many psychopaths have had home lives that were filled with frustrations, bitterness, and quarreling. As a result of this instability and frustration, these individuals developed personalities that became unreliable, unstable, demanding, and egocentric. Most psychopaths are risk-taking, sensation seekers who are constantly involved in a garden variety of antisocial behaviors. They are often described as grandiose, egocentric, manipulative, forceful, and cold hearted, with shallow emotions and the inability to feel remorse, empathy with others, or anxiety over their misdeeds.

Hervey Cleckley, a leading authority on psychopathy, described them as follows:

[Psychopaths are] chronically antisocial individuals who are always in trouble, profiting neither from experience nor punishment, and maintaining no real loyalties to any person, group, or code. They are frequently callous and hedonistic, showing marked emotional immaturity, with lack of responsibility, lack of judgment and an ability to rationalize their behavior so that it appears warranted, reasonable and justified.

Considering these personality traits, it is not surprising that research studies show that people evaluated as psychopaths are significantly more prone to criminal and violent behavior when compared to nonpsychopathic control groups. Psychopaths tend to continue their criminal careers long after other offenders burn out or age out of crime. They are continually in trouble with the law and, therefore, are likely to wind up in penal institutions. Criminologists estimate that 10 percent or more of all prison inmates display psychopathic tendencies.

Though psychologists are still not certain of the cause of psychopathy, a number of factors are believed to contribute to its development. Some focus on family experiences, suggesting that the influence of an unstable parent, parental rejection, lack of love during childhood, and inconsistent discipline may be related to psychopathy. Children who lack the opportunity to form an attachment to a mother figure in the first three years of life, who suffer sudden separation

from the mother figure, or who see changes in the mother figure are most likely to develop psychopathic personalities. According to this view, the path runs from antisocial parenting to psychopathy to criminality.

Psychopathy may also be related to personal experiences. Donald Lynam finds that ADHD children are more likely to suffer from conduct problems in childhood, and as they mature, they fall prey to a serious form of conduct disorder he labels "fledgling psychopathy." This condition is, in turn, highly associated with chronic offending.

Psychopaths may also suffer from lower than normal levels of arousal. Research studies have revealed that psychopaths have lower skin conductance levels and fewer spontaneous responses than "normal" subjects. This finding may indicate that there is a link between psychopathy and autonomic nervous system (ANS) dysfunction. The ANS mediates physiological activities associated with emotions and is manifested in such measurements as heartbeat rate, blood pressure, respiration, muscle tension, capillary size, and electrical activity of the skin (called galvanic skin resistance).

Another view is that psychopathy is caused by a dysfunction of the limbic inhibitory system manifested through damage to the frontal and temporal lobes of the brain. Consequently, psychopaths may need

---

in mechanical aptitude and nonverbal intelligence. These results indicated the possibility of cultural bias in portions of the IQ tests. He also found that there was no relationship between the number of arrests, the types of offenses, and IQ.

In 1931, Edwin Sutherland evaluated IQ studies of criminals and delinquents and noted significant variation in the findings, which disproved Goddard's notion that criminals were "feebleminded."[210] Goddard attributed discrepancies to testing and scoring methods rather than to differences in the mental ability of criminals. However, Sutherland's research all but put an end to the belief that crime was caused by "feeblemindedness"; the IQ–crime link was all but forgotten in the criminological literature.

Rediscovering IQ and criminality The alleged IQ–crime link was dismissed by mainstream criminologists, but it once again became an important area of study when respected criminologists Travis Hirschi and Michael Hindelang published a widely read 1977 paper linking the two variables. After reexamining existing research data, Hirschi and Hindelang concluded that the weight of evidence is that IQ is a more important factor than race and socioeconomic class for predicting criminal and delinquent involvement.[211] Rejecting the notion that IQ tests are race and class biased, they concluded that major differences exist between criminals and noncriminals within similar racial and socioeconomic class categories. They proposed

greater than average stimulation to bring them up to comfortable levels (similar to arousal theory discussed earlier). The desire for this stimulation may originate in their physical differences. Psychologists have attempted to treat patients diagnosed as psychopaths by giving them adrenaline, which increases their arousal levels.

Psychologist David Lykken suggests that psychopaths have an inherited "low fear quotient," which inhibits their fear of punishment. All people have a natural or innate fear of certain stimuli, such as spiders, snakes, fires, or strangers. Psychopaths, as a rule, have few fears. Normal socialization processes depend on punishing antisocial behavior to inhibit future transgressions. Someone who does not fear punishment is simply harder to socialize.

Psychopaths may be less capable of regulating their activities than other people. While some people may become anxious and afraid when facing the prospect of committing a criminal act, psychopaths in the same circumstances feel no such fear. Ogloff and Wong conclude that their reduced anxiety levels result in behaviors that are more impulsive and inappropriate and in deviant behavior, apprehension, and incarceration.

The antisocial personality concept seems to jibe with what is known about chronic offending. In a recent paper, Lawrence Cohen and Bryan Vila argue that chronic offending should be conceived as a continuum of behavior at whose apex resides the most extremely dangerous and predatory criminals. As many as 80 percent of these high-end chronic offenders exhibit sociopathic behavior patterns. Though comprising about 4 percent of the total male population and less than 1 percent of the total female population, they are responsible for half of all serious felony offenses committed annually. Not all high-rate chronic offenders are sociopaths, but enough are to support a strong link between personality dysfunction and long-term criminal careers.

Critical Thinking Questions

1. Should people diagnosed as psychopaths be separated and treated even if they have not yet committed a crime?
2. Should psychopathic murderers be spared the death penalty because they lack the capacity to control their behavior?

 InfoTrac College Edition Research

To read more about the development of psychopathology check out these articles:

John V. Lavigne, Richard Arend, Diane Rosenbaum, Helen J. Binns, Katherine Kaufer Christoffel, Andrew Burns, and Andrew Smith. Mental health service use among young children receiving pediatric primary care. *Research Journal of the American Academy of Child and Adolescent Psychiatry* Nov 1998 v37 n11 p1175

Shirley Feldman, Jaime Waterman, Hans Steiner, and Elizabeth Cauffman. Posttraumatic stress disorder among female juvenile offenders. *Journal of the American Academy of Child and Adolescent Psychiatry* Nov 1998 v37 n11 p1209(8)

SOURCES: Grant Harris, Marnie Rice, and Martin Lalumiere, "Criminal Violence: The Roles of Psychopathy, Neurodevelopmental Insults, and Antisocial Parenting," *Criminal Justice and Behavior* 28 (2001): 402–15; David Lykken, "Psychopathy, Sociopathy, and Crime," *Society* 34 (1996): 30–38; Lawrence Cohen and Bryan Vila, "Self-Control and Social Control: An Exposition of the Gottfredson-Hirschi/Sampson-Laub Debate," *Studies on Crime and Crime Prevention* 5 (1996); Donald Lynam, "Early Identification of Chronic Offenders: Who Is the Fledgling Psychopath?" *Psychological Bulletin* 120 (1996): 209–34; James Ogloff and Stephen Wong, "Electrodermal and Cardiovascular Evidence of a Coping Response in Psychopaths," *Criminal Justice and Behavior* 17 (1990): 231–45; Laurie Frost, Terrie Moffitt, and Rob McGee, "Neuro-psychological Correlates of Psycho-pathology in an Unselected Cohort of Young Adolescents," *Journal of Abnormal Psychology* 98 (1989): 307–13; Hervey Cleckley, "Psychopathic States," in *American Handbook of Psychiatry*, ed. S. Aneti (New York: Basic Books, 1959), pp. 567–69; Spencer Rathus and Jeffrey Nevid, *Abnormal Psychology* (Englewood Cliffs, N.J.: Prentice-Hall, 1991), pp. 310–16; Helene Raskin White, Erich Labouvie, and Marsha Bates, "The Relationship between Sensation Seeking and Delinquency: A Longitudinal Analysis," *Journal of Research in Crime and Delinquency* 22 (1985): 197–211.

the idea that low IQ increases the likelihood of criminal behavior through its effect on school performance. That is, youths with low IQs do poorly in school, and school failure and academic incompetence are highly related to delinquency and later to adult criminality.

Hirschi and Hindelang's inferences have been supported by research conducted by both U.S. and international scholars.[212] Some studies have found a direct IQ–delinquency link among samples of adolescent boys.[213] When Alex Piquero examined violent behavior among groups of children in Philadelphia, he found that scores on intelligence tests were the best predictors of violent behavior and could be used to distinguish between groups of violent and nonviolent offenders.[214] In their influential book, *Crime and Human Nature*, James Q. Wilson and Richard Herrnstein also agreed that the IQ–crime link is an indirect one: low intelligence leads to poor school performance, which enhances the chances of criminality.[215] They conclude, "A child who chronically loses standing in the competition of the classroom may feel justified in settling the score outside, by violence, theft, and other forms of defiant illegality."[216]

Cross-national studies The IQ–crime relationship has also been found in cross-national studies. A significant relationship between low IQ and delinquency has been found among samples of youth in Denmark. Researchers found that Danish children with a low IQ tended to engage in delinquent behaviors because their poor verbal ability was a handicap in the school environment.[217] Research by Canadian neural-psychologist Lorne Yeudall and his associates found samples of delinquents possessed IQs about 20 points less than nondelinquent control groups on one of the standard IQ tests, the **Wechsler Adult Intelligence Scale.**[218] An IQ–crime link was also found in a longitudinal study of Swedish youth; low IQ measures taken at age 3 were significant predictors of later criminality over the life course.[219]

IQ and crime reconsidered The Hirschi-Hindelang research increased interest and research on the association between IQ and crime, but the issue is far from settled and is still a matter of significant debate. A number of recent studies find that IQ level has negligible influence on criminal behavior.[220] Also, a recent evaluation of existing knowledge on intelligence conducted by the American Psychological Association concluded that the strength of an IQ–crime link was "very low."[221]

In contrast, *The Bell Curve*, Richard Herrnstein and Charles Murray's influential albeit controversial book on intelligence, comes down firmly for an IQ–crime link. Their extensive review of the available literature shows that people with lower IQs are more likely to commit crime, get caught, and be sent to prison. Conversely, at-risk kids with higher IQs seem to be protected from becoming criminals by their superior ability to succeed in school and in social relationships. Taking the scientific literature as a whole, Herrnstein and Murray conclude that criminal offenders have an average IQ of 92, about 8 points below the mean; chronic offenders score even lower than the "average" criminal. To those who suggest that the IQ–crime relationship can be explained by the fact that only low IQ criminals get caught, they counter with data showing little difference in IQ scores between self-reported and official criminals.[222] This means that even criminals whose activities go undetected by the authorities have lower IQs than the general public; the IQ–crime relationship cannot be explained away by the fact that slow-witted criminals are the ones most likely to be apprehended by the police.

It is unlikely that the IQ–crime debate will be settled in the near future. Measurement is beset by many methodological problems. The well-documented criticisms suggesting that IQ tests are race and class biased would certainly influence the testing of the criminal population who are besieged with a multitude of social and economic problems. Even if it can be shown that known offenders have lower IQs than the general population, it is difficult to explain many patterns in the crime rate: Why are there more male than female criminals? (Are females three times smarter than males?) Why do crime rates vary by region, time of year, and even weather patterns? Why does aging

out occur? IQs do not increase with age, so why should crime rates fall?

■ Public Policy Implications of Trait Theory

For most of the twentieth century, biological and psychological views of criminality had an important influence on crime control and prevention policy. The result has been front-end or primary prevention programs that seek to treat personal problems before they manifest themselves as crime. To this end, thousands of family therapy organizations, substance abuse clinics, mental health associations, and so on are operating around the United States. Teachers, employers, courts, welfare agencies, and others make referrals to these facilities. These services are based on the premise that if a person's problems can be treated before they become overwhelming, some future crimes will be prevented. Secondary prevention programs provide treatment such as psychological counseling to youths and adults after they have violated the law. Attendance in such programs may be a mandatory requirement of a probation order, part of a diversionary sentence, or aftercare at the end of a prison sentence.

Biologically oriented therapy is also being used in the criminal justice system. Programs have altered diet, changed lighting, compensated for learning disabilities, treated allergies, and so on.[223] What is more controversial has been the use of mood-altering chemicals, such as lithium, pemoline, imipramine, phenytoin, and benzodiazepines, to control the behavior. Another practice that has elicited outcries of concern is the use of psychosurgery (brain surgery) to control antisocial behavior. These types of surgical procedures have been used to alter the brain structure of convicted sex offenders in an effort to eliminate or control their sex drive. Results are still in the preliminary stage, but some critics have argued these procedures are without scientific merit.[224]

Some criminologists view biologically oriented treatments as a key to solving the problem of the chronic offender. The biological analysis of criminal traits could pave the way for developing preventive measures, regardless of whether the trait is inherited or acquired. A number of inherited physical traits that cause disease have been successfully treated with medication after their genetic code had been broken; a similar method may lead to a genetic solution to crime.[225]

Although such biological treatment is a relatively new phenomenon, it has been commonplace since the 1920s to offer psychological treatment to offenders before, during, and after a criminal conviction. For example, beginning in the 1970s, pretrial programs have sought to divert offenders into nonpunitive rehabilitative programs designed to treat rather than punish them. Based on some type of counseling regime, diversion programs are commonly used with first offenders, nonviolent offenders, and so on. At the trial stage, judges often order psychological profiles of convicted offenders for planning a treatment program. Should these offenders be kept in the community? Do they need a more secure confinement to deal with their problems? If correctional confinement is called for, inmates are commonly evaluated at a correctional center to measure their personality traits or disorders. Correctional facilities almost universally require inmates to partake in some form of psychological therapy: group therapy, individual analysis, transactional analysis, and so on. Parole decisions may be influenced by the prison psychologist's evaluation of the offender's adjustment.

CONNECTIONS

The law recognizes the psychological aspects of crime when it permits the insanity plea as an excuse for criminal liability or when it allows trial delay because of mental incompetency. See Chapter 2 for more on the insanity defense. ■

■ Summary

The earliest positivist criminologists were biologists. Led by Cesare Lombroso, these early researchers believed some people manifested primitive traits that made them born criminals. Today, their research has been debunked because of poor methodology, testing, and logic. Biological views fell out of favor in the early twentieth century. In the 1970s, spurred by the publication of Edmund O. Wilson's *Sociobiology*, several criminologists again turned to the study of the biological basis of criminality. For the most part, the effort has focused on the cause of violent crime. Interest has centered on several areas: (1) biochemical factors, such as diet, allergies, hormonal imbalances, and environmental contaminants (such as lead); (2) neurophysiological factors, such as brain disorders, EEG abnormalities, tumors, and head injuries; and (3) genetic factors, such as the XYY syndrome and inherited traits. There is also an evolutionary branch, which holds that changes in the human condition, which have taken millions of years to evolve, may help explain crime rate differences. Biocriminology is in its infancy, and no definite studies have been undertaken.

Today there are three main psychological perspectives: the psychodynamic view, the cognitive view, and the social learning perspective. The psychodynamic view, the creation of Sigmund Freud, links aggressive behavior to personality conflicts developed in childhood. According to some psychoanalysts, psychotics are aggressive, unstable people who can easily become involved in crime. Cognitive psychology is concerned with human development and how people perceive the world. Criminality is viewed as a function of improper information processing and/or moral development. In contrast, behavioral and social learning theorists see criminality as a learned behavior. Children who are exposed to violence and see it rewarded may become violent as adults.

Psychological traits, such as personality and intelligence, have been linked to criminality. One important area of study has been the psychopath, a person who lacks emotion and concern for others. The controversial issue of the relationship of IQ to criminality has been resurrected once again with the publication of research studies purporting to show that criminals have lower IQs than noncriminals. Psychologists have developed standardized tests with which to measure personality traits. One avenue of research has been to determine whether criminals and noncriminals manifest any differences in their responses to test items.

Table 6.4 summarizes the biological and psychological trait theories that have been discussed in this chapter.

■ Thinking Like a Criminologist

The American Psychiatric Association believes a person should not be held legally responsible for a crime if his or her behavior meets the following standard developed by legal expert Richard Bonnie:

A person charged with a criminal offense should be found not guilty by reason of insanity if it is shown that as a result of mental disease or mental retardation he was unable to appreciate the wrongfulness of his conduct at the time of the offense.

As used in this standard, the terms "mental disease" and "mental retardation" include only those severely abnormal mental conditions that grossly and demonstrably impair a person's perception or understanding of reality and that are not attributable primarily to the voluntary ingestion of alcohol or other psychoactive substances.

As a criminologist with expertise on trait theories of crime, do you agree with this standard? What modifications, if any, might you make to include other categories of offenders who are not excused by this definition?

Table 6.4 Biological and Psychological Theories

Theory	Major Premise	Strengths
Biosocial		
Biochemical	Crime, especially violence, is a function of diet, vitamin intake, hormonal imbalance, or food allergies.	Explains irrational violence. Shows how the environment interacts with personal traits to influence behavior.
Neurological	Criminals and delinquents often suffer brain impairment, as measured by the EEG. Attention deficit/hyperactivity disorder and minimal brain dysfunction are related to antisocial behavior.	Explains irrational violence. Shows how the environment interacts with personal traits to influence behavior.
Genetic	Criminal traits and predispositions are inherited. The criminality of parents can predict the delinquency of children.	Explains why only a small percentage of youth in a high-crime area become chronic offenders.
Evolutionary	As the human race evolved, traits and characteristics have become ingrained. Some of these traits make people aggressive and predisposed to commit crime.	Explains high violence rates and aggregate gender differences in the crime rate.
Psychological		
Psychodynamic	The development of the unconscious personality early in childhood influences behavior for the rest of a person's life. Criminals have weak egos and damaged personalities.	Explains the onset of crime and why crime and drug abuse cut across class lines.
Behavioral	People commit crime when they model their behavior after others they see being rewarded for the same acts. Behavior is reinforced by rewards and extinguished by punishment.	Explains the role of significant others in the crime process. Shows how family life and media can influence crime and violence.
Cognitive	Individual reasoning processes influence behavior. Reasoning is influenced by the way people perceive their environment and by their moral and intellectual development.	Shows why criminal behavior patterns change over time as people mature and develop their moral reasoning. May explain the aging-out process.

■ Key Terms

- inheritance school *(139)*
- somatotype *(139)*
- biophobia *(140)*
- reciprocal altruism *(140)*
- trait theory *(140)*
- equipotentiality *(141)*
- biosocial theory *(141)*
- Wernicke-Korsakoff disease *(141)*
- hypoglycemia *(142)*
- androgens *(143)*
- testosterone *(143)*
- neocortex *(143)*
- premenstrual syndrome (PMS) *(143)*
- cerebral allergies *(144)*
- neuroallergies *(144)*
- neurophysiology *(144)*
- electroencephalograph (EEG) *(144)*

- attention deficit hyperactivity disorder (ADHD) *(145)*
- conduct disorder (CD) *(146)*
- chemical restraints *(147)*
- chemical straitjackets *(147)*
- arousal theory *(147)*
- contagion effect *(149)*
- defective intelligence *(153)*
- psychoanalytic or psychodynamic perspective *(154)*
- behaviorists *(154)*
- cognitive theorists *(154)*
- id *(154)*
- pleasure principle *(154)*
- ego *(154)*
- reality principle *(154)*
- superego *(154)*

- conscience *(154)*
- ego ideal *(154)*
- eros *(154)*
- oral stage *(154)*
- anal stage *(154)*
- phallic stage *(154)*
- Oedipus complex *(154)*
- Electra complex *(154)*
- latency *(154)*
- fixated *(154)*
- neurotic *(155)*
- psychotic *(155)*
- disorder *(155)*
- schizophrenia *(155)*
- paranoid schizophrenic *(155)*
- inferiority complex *(155)*
- identity crisis *(155)*

- latent delinquency *(155)*
- bipolar disorder *(155)*
- social learning *(156)*
- behavior modeling *(156)*
- moral development *(157)*
- humanistic psychology *(157)*

- information processing *(157)*
- personality *(162)*
- Minnesota Multiphasic Personality Inventory (MMPI) *(163)*
- California Personality Inventory (CPI) *(163)*

- Multidimensional Personality Questionnaire (MPQ) *(163)*
- nature theory *(163)*
- nurture theory *(163)*
- Wechsler Adult Intelligence Scale *(166)*

Critical Thinking Questions

1. What should be done with the young children of violent prone criminals if in fact research could show that the tendency to commit crime is inherited?

2. After considering the existing research on the subject, would you recommend that young children be forbidden from eating foods with a heavy sugar content?

3. Knowing what you do about trends and patterns in crime, how would you counteract the assertion that people who commit crime are physically or mentally abnormal? For example, how would you explain the fact that crime is more likely to occur in western and urban areas than in eastern or rural areas?

4. Aside from becoming a criminal, what other career paths are open to psychopaths?

5. Research shows that kids who watch a lot of TV in adolescence are more likely to behave aggressively in adulthood. This has led some to conclude that TV watching is responsible for adult violence. Can this relationship be explained in another way?

Notes

1. Based on James Brooke, Pam Belluck, and John Kifner, and written by James Brooke, "Man Hospitalized in 1996 for Writing Ominous Letters," *New York Times,* 26 July 1998, p. 1.

2. Dalton Conley and Neil Bennett, "Is Biology Destiny? Birth Weight and Life Chances," *American Sociological Review* 654 (2000): 458–67.

3. Raffaele Garofalo, *Criminology,* trans. Robert Miller (Boston: Little, Brown, 1914), p. 92.

4. Enrico Ferri, *Criminal Sociology* (New York: D. Appleton, 1909).

5. See Richard Dugdale, *The Jukes* (New York: Putnam, 1910); Arthur Estabrook, *The Jukes in 1915* (Washington, D.C.: Carnegie Institute of Washington, 1916).

6. William Sheldon, *Varieties of Delinquent Youth* (New York: Harper Bros., 1949).

7. Pierre van den Bergle, "Bringing the Beast Back In: Toward a Biosocial Theory of Aggression," *American Sociological Review* 39 (1974): 779.

8. Lee Ellis, "A Discipline in Peril: Sociology's Future Hinges on Curing Biophobia," *American Sociologist* 27(1996): 21–41.

9. Edmund O. Wilson, *Sociobiology* (Cambridge: Harvard University Press, 1975).

10. Anthony Walsh, "Behavior Genetics and Anomie/Strain Theory," *Criminology* 38 (2000): 1075–1108.

11. Anthony Walsh and Lee Ellis, "Shoring Up the Big Three: Improving Criminological Theories with Biosocial Concepts." Paper presented at the annual Society of Criminology meeting, San Diego, Calif., November 1997, p. 16.

12. Israel Nachshon, "Neurological Bases of Crime, Psychopathy and Aggression," in *Crime in Biological, Social and Moral Contexts,* eds. Lee Ellis and Harry Hoffman (New York: Praeger, 1990), p. 199. Herein cited as *Crime in Biological Contexts.*

13. See, generally, Lee Ellis, "Introduction: The Nature of the Biosocial Perspective," in *Crime in Biological Contexts,* pp. 3–18.

14. See, for example, Tracy Bennett Herbert and Sheldon Cohen, "Depression and Immunity: A Meta-Analytic Review," *Psychological Bulletin* 113 (1993): 472–86.

15. See, generally, Lee Ellis, *Theories of Rape* (New York: Hemisphere Publications, 1989).

16. Leonard Hippchen, "Some Possible Biochemical Aspects of Criminal Behavior," *Journal of Behavioral Ecology* 2 (1981): 1–6; Sarnoff Mednick and Jan Volavka, "Biology and Crime," in *Crime and Justice,* eds. Norval Morris and Michael Tonry (Chicago: University of Chicago Press, 1980), pp. 85–159; Saleem Shah and Loren Roth, "Biological and Psychophysiological Factors in Criminality," in *Handbook of Criminology,* ed. Daniel Glazer (Chicago: Rand McNally, 1974), pp. 125–40.

17. Ulric Neisser et al., "Intelligence: Knowns and Unknowns," *American Psychologist* 51 (1996): 77–101, at 88.

18. Leonard Hippchen, ed., *Ecologic-Biochemical Approaches to Treatment of Delinquents and Criminals* (New York: Von Nostram Reinhold, 1978), p. 14.

19. Michael Krassner, "Diet and Brain Function," *Nutrition Reviews* 44 (1986): 12–15.

20. Hippchen, *Ecologic-Biochemical Approaches to Treatment of Delinquents and Criminals.*

21. Stephen Schoenthaler, *Intelligence, Academic Performance, and Brain Function* (California State University, Stanislaus, 2000); see also, S. Schoenthaler and I. Bier, "The Effect of Vitamin-Mineral Supplementation on Juvenile Delinquency among American Schoolchildren: A Randomized Double-Blind Placebo-Controlled Trial," *Journal of Alternative and Complementary Medicine: Research on Paradigm, Practice, and Policy* 6 (2000): 7–18.

22. J. Kershner and W. Hawke, "Megavitamins and Learning Disorders: A Controlled Double-Blind Experiment," *Journal of Nutrition* 109 (1979): 819–26.

23. Richard Knox, "Test Shows Smart People's Brains Use Nutrients Better," *Boston Globe,* 16 February 1988, p. 9.

24. Ronald Prinz and David Riddle, "Associations between Nutrition and Behavior in 5-Year-Old Children," *Nutrition Reviews Supplement* 44 (1986): 151–58.

25. Stephen Schoenthaler and Walter Doraz, "Types of Offenses Which Can Be Reduced in an Institutional Setting Using Nutritional Intervention," *International Journal of Biosocial Research* 4 (1983): 74–84; and idem, "Diet and Crime," *International Journal of Biosocial Research* 4 (1983): 74–84. See also, A. G. Schauss, "Differential Outcomes among Probationers Comparing Orthomolecular Approaches to Conventional Casework Counseling." Paper presented at the annual meeting of the American Society of Criminology, Dallas, November 9, 1978); A. Schauss and C. Simonsen, "A Critical Analysis of the Diets of Chronic Juvenile Offenders, Part I," *Journal of Orthomolecular Psychiatry* 8 (1979): 222–26; A. Hoffer, "Children with Learning and Behavioral Disorders," *Journal of Orthomolecular Psychiatry* 5 (1976): 229.

26. Prinz and Riddle, "Associations between Nutrition and Behavior in 5-Year-Old Children."

27. H. Bruce Ferguson, Clare Stoddart, and Jovan Simeon, "Double-Blind Challenge Studies of Behavioral and Cognitive Effects of Sucrose-Aspartame Ingestion in Normal Children," *Nutrition Reviews Supplement* 44 (1986): 144–58; Gregory Gray, "Diet, Crime and Delinquency: A Critique," *Nutrition Reviews Supplement* 44 (1986): 89–94.

28. Mark Wolraich, Scott Lindgren, Phyllis Stumbo, Lewis Stegink, Mark Appelbaum, and Mary Kiritsy, "Effects of Diets High in Sucrose or Aspartame on the Behavior and Cognitive Performance of Children," *The New England Journal of Medicine* 330 (1994): 303–6.

29. Dian Gans, "Sucrose and Unusual Childhood Behavior," *Nutrition Today* 26 (1991): 8–14.

30. Diana Fishbein, "Neuropsychological Function, Drug Abuse, and Violence, a Conceptual Framework," *Criminal Justice and Behavior* 27 (2000): 139–59.

31. D. Hill and W. Sargent, "A Case of Matricide," *Lancet* 244 (1943): 526–27.

32. E. Podolsky, "The Chemistry of Murder," *Pakistan Medical Journal* 15 (1964): 9–14.

33. J. A. Yaryura-Tobias and F. Neziroglu, "Violent Behavior, Brain Dysrhythmia and Glucose Dysfunction: A New Syndrome," *Journal of Orthopsychiatry* 4 (1975): 182–88.

34. Matti Virkkunen, "Reactive Hypoglycemic Tendency among Habitually Violent Offenders," *Nutrition Reviews Supplement* 44 (1986): 94–103.

35. James Q. Wilson, *The Moral Sense* (New York: Free Press, 1993).

36. Walter Gove, "The Effect of Age and Gender on Deviant Behavior: A Biopsychosocial Perspective," in *Gender and the Life Course*, ed. A. S. Rossi (New York: Aldine, 1985), pp. 115–44.

37. Alan Booth and D. Wayne Osgood, "The Influence of Testosterone on Deviance in Adulthood: Assessing and Explaining the Relationship," *Criminology* 31 (1993): 93–118.

38. Anthony Walsh, "Genetic and Cytogenetic Intersex Anomalies: Can They Help Us to Understand Gender Differences in Deviant Behavior?" *International Journal of Offender Therapy and Comparative Criminology* 39 (1995): 151–66.

39. Christy Miller Buchanan, Jacquelynne Eccles, and Jill Becker, "Are Adolescents the Victims of Raging Hormones? Evidence for Activational Effects of Hormones on Moods and Behavior at Adolescence," *Psychological Bulletin* 111 (1992): 62–107.

40. Alex Piquero and Timothy Brezina, "Testing Moffitt's Account of Adolescent-Limited Delinquency," *Criminology* 39 (2001): 353–70.

41. Booth and Osgood, "The Influence of Testosterone on Deviance in Adulthood."

42. Albert Reiss and Jeffrey Roth, eds. *Understanding and Preventing Violence* (Washington, D.C.: National Academy Press, 1993), p. 118. Hereafter cited as *Understanding Violence*.

43. L. E. Kreuz and R. M. Rose, "Assessment of Aggressive Behavior and Plasma Testosterone in a Young Criminal Population," *Psychosomatic Medicine* 34 (1972): 321–32.

44. Walsh, "Genetic and Cytogenetic Intersex Anomalies."

45. Lee Ellis, "Evolutionary and Neurochemical Causes of Sex Differences in Victimizing Behavior: Toward a Unified Theory of Criminal Behavior and Social Stratification," *Social Science Information* 28 (1989): 605–36.

46. For a general review, see Lee Ellis and Phyllis Coontz, "Androgens, Brain Functioning, and Criminality: The Neurohormonal Foundations of Antisociality," in *Crime in Biological Contexts*, pp. 162–93.

47. Ibid., p. 181.

48. Robert Rubin, "The Neuroendocrinology and Neuro-chemistry of Antisocial Behavior," in *The Causes of Crime, New Biological Appoaches*, eds. Sarnoff Mednick, Terrie Moffitt, and Susan Stack (Cambridge: Cambridge University Press, 1987), pp. 239–62.

49. J. Money, "Influence of Hormones on Psychosexual Differentiation," *Medical Aspects of Nutrition* 30 (1976): 165.

50. Mednick and Volavka, "Biology and Crime."

51. For a review of this concept, see Anne E. Figert, "The Three Faces of PMS: The Professional, Gendered, and Scientific Structuring of a Psychiatric Disorder," *Social Problems* 42 (1995): 56–72.

52. Katharina Dalton, *The Premenstrual Syndrome* (Springfield, Ill.: Charles C. Thomas, 1971).

53. Julie Horney, "Menstrual Cycles and Criminal Responsibility," *Law and Human Nature* 2 (1978): 25–36.

54. Diana Fishbein, "Selected Studies on the Biology of Antisocial Behavior," in *New Perspectives in Criminology*, ed. John Conklin (Needham Heights, Mass.: Allyn and Bacon, 1996), pp. 26–38.

55. Ibid.; Karen Paige, "Effects of Oral Contraceptives on Affective Fluctuations Associated with the Menstrual Cycle," *Psychosomatic Medicine* 33 (1971): 515–37.

56. H. E. Amos and J. J. P. Drake, "Problems Posed by Food Additives," *Journal of Human Nutrition* 30 (1976): 165.

57. Ray Wunderlich, "Neuroallergy as a Contributing Factor to Social Misfits: Diagnosis and Treatment," in *Ecologic-Biochemical Approaches to Treatment of Delinquents and Criminals*, ed. Leonard Hippchen (New York: Von Nostram Reinhold, 1978), pp. 229–53.

58. See, for example, Paul Marshall, "Allergy and Depression: A Neurochemical Threshold Model of the Relation between the Illnesses," *Psychological Bulletin* 113 (1993): 23–39.

59. A. R. Mawson and K. J. Jacobs, "Corn Consumption, Tryptophan, and Cross-National Homicide Rates," *Journal of Orthomolecular Psychiatry* 7 (1978): 227–30.

60. Alexander Schauss, *Diet, Crime and Delinquency* (Berkeley, Calif.: Parker House, 1980).

61. C. Hawley and R. E. Buckley, "Food Dyes and Hyperkinetic Children," *Academy Therapy* 10 (1974): 27–32.

62. John Ott, "The Effects of Light and Radiation on Human Health and Behavior," in *Ecologic-Biochemical Approaches to Treatment of Delinquents and Criminals*, ed. Leonard Hippchen (New York: Von Nostram Reinhold, 1978), pp. 105–83. See also A. Kreuger and S.

Sigel, "Ions in the Air," *Human Nature* (July 1978): 46–47; Harry Wohlfarth, "The Effect of Color Psychodynamic Environmental Modification on Discipline Incidents in Elementary Schools over One School Year: A Controlled Study," *International Journal of Biosocial Research* 6 (1984): 44–53.

63. Paul Stretesky and Michael Lynch, "The Relationship between Lead Exposure and Homicide," *Archives of Pediatric Adolescent Medicine* 155 (2001): 579–82.

64. Deborah Denno, "Considering Lead Poisoning as a Criminal Defense," *Fordham Urban Law Journal* 20 (1993): 377–400.

65. Herbert Needleman, Julie Riess, Michael Tobin, Gretchen Biesecker, and Joel Greenohouse, "Bone Lead Levels and Delinquent Behavior," *Journal of the American Medical Assocation* 275 (1996): 363–69.

66. Ulric Neisser et al., "Intelligence: Knowns and Unknowns," *American Psychologist* 51 (1996): 77–101.

67. Terrie Moffitt, "The Neuropsychology of Juvenile Delinquency: A Critical Review," in *Crime and Justice, An Annual Review,* vol. 12, eds. Norval Morris and Michael Tonry (Chicago: University of Chicago Press, 1990), pp. 99–169.

68. Terrie Moffitt, Donald Lyman, and Phil Silva, "Neuropsychological Tests Predicting Persistent Male Delinquency," *Criminology* 32 (1994): 277–300; Elizabeth Kandel and Sarnoff Mednick, "Perinatal Complications Predict Violent Offending," *Criminology* 29 (1991): 519–29; Sarnoff Mednick, Ricardo Machon, Matti Virkkunen, and Douglas Bonett, "Adult Schizophrenia Following Prenatal Exposure to an Influenza Epidemic," *Archives of General Psychiatry* 44 (1987): 35–46; C. A. Fogel, S. A. Mednick, and N. Michelson, "Hyperactive Behavior and Minor Physical Anomalies," *Acta Psychiatrica Scandinavia* 72 (1985): 551–56.

69. R. Johnson, *Aggression in Man and Animals* (Philadelphia: Saunders, 1972), p. 79.

70. Jean Seguin, Robert Pihl, Philip Harden, Richard Tremblay, and Bernard Boulerice, "Cognitive and Neuropsychological Characteristics of Physically Aggressive Boys," *Journal of Abnormal Psychology* 104 (1995): 614–24; Deborah Denno, "Gender, Crime and the Criminal Law Defenses," *Journal of Criminal Law and Criminology* 85 (1994): 80–180.

71. Adrian Raine, Patricia Brennan, Brigitte Mednick, and Sarnoff Mednick, "High Rates of Violence, Crime, Academic Problems, and Behavioral Problems in Males with Both Early Neuromotor Deficits and Unstable Family Environments," *Archives of General Psychiatry* 53 (1966): 544–49.

72. Deborah Denno, *Biology, Crime and Violence: New Evidence* (Cambridge: Cambridge University Press, 1989).

73. Diana Fishbein and Robert Thatcher, "New Diagnostic Methods in Criminology: Assessing Organic Sources of Behavioral Disorders," *Journal of Research in Crime and Delinquency* 23 (1986): 240–67.

74. See, generally, David Rowe, *Biology and Crime* (Los Angeles: Roxbury Press, 2001).

75. Lorne Yeudall, "A Neuropsychosocial Perspective of Persistent Juvenile Delinquency and Criminal Behavior." Paper presented at the New York Academy of Sciences, September 26, 1979.

76. R. W. Aind and T. Yamamoto, "Behavior Disorders of Childhood," *Electroencephalography and Clinical Neurophysiology* 21 (1966): 148–56.

77. See, generally, Jan Volavka, "Electroencephalogram among Criminals," in *The Causes of Crime, New Biological Approaches,* eds. Sarnoff Mednick, Terrie Moffitt, and Susan Stack (Cambridge: Cambridge University Press, 1987), pp. 137–45; Z. A. Zayed, S. A. Lewis, and R. P. Britain, "An Encephalographic and Psychiatric Study of 32 Insane Murderers," *British Journal of Psychiatry* 115 (1969): 1115–24.

78. Nathaniel Pallone and James Hennessy, "Brain Dysfunction and Criminal Violence," *Society* 35 (1998): 21–27; P. F. Goyer, P. J. Andreason, and W. E. Semple, "Positronic Emission Tomography and Personality Disorders," *Neuropsychopharmacology* 10 (1994) 21–28.

79. Adrian Raine, Monte Buchsbaum, and Lori LaCasse, "Brain Abnormalities in Murderers Indicated by Positron Emission Tomography," *Biological Psychiatry* 42 (1997): 495–508.

80. Pallone and Hennessy, "Brain Dysfunction and Criminal Violence," p. 25.

81. D. R. Robin, R. M. Starles, T. J. Kenney, B. J. Reynolds, and F. P. Heald, "Adolescents Who Attempt Suicide," *Journal of Pediatrics* 90 (1977): 636–38.

82. R. R. Monroe, *Brain Dysfunction in Aggressive Criminals* (Lexington, Mass.: D.C. Heath, 1978).

83. L. T. Yeudall, *Childhood Experiences as Causes of Criminal Behavior* (Senate of Canada, Issue no. 1, Thirteenth Parliament, Ottawa, 1977).

84. Raine, Buchsbaum, and LaCasse, "Brain Abnormalities in Murderers Indicated by Positron Emission Tomography."

85. Leonore Simon, "Does Criminal Offender Treatment Work?" *Applied and Preventive Psychology* (Summer 1998); Stephen Faraone et al., "Intellectual Performance and School Failure in Children with Attention Deficit Hyperactivity Disorder and in Their Siblings," *Journal of Abnormal Psychology* 102 (1993): 616–23.

86. Ibid.

87. Simon, "Does Criminal Offender Treatment Work?"

88. Terrie Moffitt and Phil Silva, "Self-Reported Delinquency, Neuropsychological Deficit, and History of Attention Deficit Disorder," *Journal of Abnormal Child Psychology* 16 (1988): 553–69.

89. Elizabeth Hart et al., "Criterion Validity of Informants in the Diagnosis of Disruptive Behavior Disorders in Children: A Preliminary Study," *Journal of Consulting and Clinical Psychology* 62 (1994): 410–14.

90. Eugene Maguin, Rolf Loeber, and Paul LeMahieu, "Does the Relationship between Poor Reading and Delinquency Hold for Males of Different Ages and Ethnic Groups?" *Journal of Emotional and Behavioral Disorders* 1 (1993): 88–100.

91. Yeudall, "A Neuropsychosocial Perspective of Persistent Juvenile Delinquency and Criminal Behavior," p. 4; F. A. Elliott, "Neurological Aspects of Antisocial Behavior," in *The Psychopath: A Comprehensive Study of Antisocial Disorders and Behaviors,* ed. W. H. Reid (New York: Brunner/Mazel, 1978), pp. 146–89.

92. Lorne Yeudall, Orestes Fedora, and Delee Fromm, "A Neuropsychosocial Theory of Persistent Criminality: Implications for Assessment and Treatment," in *Advances in Forensic Psychology and Psychiatry,* ed. Robert Rieber (Norwood, N.J.: Ablex Publishing, 1987), pp. 119–91.

93. Ibid., p. 177.

94. Rita Shaushnessy, "Psychopharmacotherapy of Neuropsychiatric Disorders," *Psychiatric Annals* 25 (1995): 634–40.

95. H. K. Kletschka, "Violent Behavior Associated with Brain Tumor," *Minnesota Medicine* 49 (1966): 1853–55.

96. V. E. Krynicki, "Cerebral Dysfunction in Repetitively Assaultive Adolescents," *Journal of Nervous and Mental Disease* 166 (1978): 59–67.

97. C. E. Lyght, ed., *The Merck Manual of Diagnosis and Therapy* (West Point, Fla.: Merck, 1966).

98. Reiss and Roth, *Understanding Violence*, p. 119.

99. M. Virkkunen, M. J. DeJong, J. Bartko, and M. Linnoila, "Psychobiological Concomitants of History of Suicide Attempts among Violent Offenders and Impulsive Fire Starters," *Archives of General Psychiatry* 46 (1989): 604–06.

100. Matti Virkkunen, David Goldman, and Markku Linnoila, "Serotonin in Alcoholic Violent Offenders," *The Ciba Foundation Symposium, Genetics of Criminal and Antisocial Behavior* (Chichester, England: Wiley, 1995).

101. Lee Ellis, "Left- and Mixed-Handedness and Criminality: Explanations for a Probable Relationship," in *Left-Handedness, Behavioral Implications and Anomalies*, ed. S. Coren (Amsterdam: Elsevier, 1990): 485–507.

102. Lee Ellis, "Monoamine Oxidase and Criminality: Identifying an Apparent Biological Marker for Antisocial Behavior," *Journal of Research in Crime and Delinquency* 28 (1991): 227–51.

103. Walter Gove and Charles Wilmoth, "Risk, Crime and Neurophysiologic Highs: A Consideration of Brain Processes That May Reinforce Delinquent and Criminal Behavior," in *Crime in Biological Contexts*, pp. 261–93.

104. Jack Katz, *Seduction of Crime: Moral and Sensual Attractions of Doing Evil* (New York: Basic Books, 1988), pp. 12–15.

105. Lee Ellis, "Arousal Theory and the Religiosity-Criminality Relationship," in *Contemporary Criminological Theory*, eds., Peter Cordella and Larry Siegel (Boston, Mass.: Northeastern University, 1996), pp. 65–84.

106. Adrian Raine, Peter Venables, and Sarnoff Mednick, "Low Resting Heart Rate at Age 3 Years Predisposes to Aggression at Age 11 Years: Evidence from the Mauritius Child Health Project," *Journal of the American Academy of Adolescent Psychiatry* 36 (1997): 1457–64.

107. For a general view, see Richard Lerner and Terryl Foch, *Biological-Psychosocial Interactions in Early Adolescence* (Hilldale, N.J.: Lawrence Erlbaum Associates, 1987).

108. Kerry Jang, W. John Livesley, and Philip Vernon, "Heritability of the Big Five Personality Dimensions and Their Facets: A Twin Study," *Journal of Personality* 64 (1996): 577–89.

109. David Rowe, "As the Twig Is Bent: The Myth of Child-Rearing Influences on Personality Development," *Journal of Counseling and Development* 68 (1990): 606–11; David Rowe, Joseph Rogers, and Sylvia Meseck-Bushey, "Sibling Delinquency and the Family Environment: Shared and Unshared Influences," *Child Development* 63 (1992): 59–67.

110. Gregory Carey and David DiLalla, "Personality and Psychopathology: Genetic Perspectives," *Journal of Abnormal Psychology* 103 (1994): 32–43.

111. T. R. Sarbin and L. E. Miller, "Demonism Revisited: The XYY Chromosome Anomaly," *Issues in Criminology* 5 (1970): 195–207.

112. Mednick and Volavka, "Biology and Crime," p. 93.

113. For an early review, see Barbara Wooton, *Social Science and Social Pathology* (London: Allen and Unwin, 1959); John Laub and Robert Sampson, "Unraveling Families and Delinquency: A Reanalysis of the Gluecks' Data," *Criminology* 26 (1988): 355–80.

114. D. J. West and D. P. Farrington, eds., "Who Becomes Delinquent?" in *The Delinquent Way of Life* (London: Heinemann, 1977); D. J. West, *Delinquency, Its Roots, Careers, and Prospects* (Cambridge: Harvard University Press, 1982).

115. West, *Delinquency*, p. 114.

116. David Farrington, "Understanding and Preventing Bullying," in *Crime and Justice*, vol. 17, ed. Michael Tonry (Chicago: University of Chicago Press, 1993), pp. 381–457.

117. Philip Harden and Robert Pihl, "Cognitive Function, Cardiovascular Reactivity, and Behavior in Boys at High Risk for Alcoholism," *Journal of Abnormal Psychology* 104 (1995): 94–103.

118. Laub and Sampson, "Unraveling Families and Delinquency," p. 370.

119. See, generally, Wooton, *Social Science and Social Pathology*; H. Wilson, "Juvenile Delinquency, Parental Criminality, and Social Handicaps," *British Journal of Criminology* 15 (1975): 241–50.

120. David Rowe and David Farrington, "The Familial Transmission of Criminal Convictions," *Criminology* 35 (1997): 177–201.

121. D. P. Farrington, Gwen Gundry, and D. J. West, "The Familial Transmission of Criminality," in *Crime and the Family*, eds. Alan Lincoln and Murray Straus (Springfield, Ill.: Charles C. Thomas, 1985), pp. 193–206.

122. Ibid., p. 194.

123. Ibid., p. 195.

124. See Sarnoff A. Mednick and Karl O. Christiansen, eds., *Biosocial Bases in Criminal Behavior* (New York: Gardner Press, 1977).

125. David Rowe, "Genetic and Environmental Components of Antisocial Behavior: A Study of 265 Twin Pairs," *Criminology* 24 (1986): 513–32; David Rowe and D. Wayne Osgood, "Heredity and Sociological Theories of Delinquency: A Reconsideration," *American Sociological Review* 49 (1984): 526–40.

126. Edwin J. C. G. van den Oord, Frank Verhulst, and Dorret Boomsma, "A Genetic Study of Maternal and Paternal Ratings of Problem Behaviors in 3-Year-Old Twins," *Journal of Abnormal Psychology* 105 (1996): 349–57.

127. Michael Lyons, "A Twin Study of Self-Reported Criminal Behavior," and Judy Silberg, Joanne Meyer, Andrew Pickles, Emily Simonoff, Lindon Eaves, John Hewitt, Hermine Maes, and Michael Rutter, "Heterogeneity among Juvenile Antisocial Behaviors: Findings from the Virginia Twin Study of Adolescent Behavioral Development," in *The Ciba Foundation Symposium, Genetics of Criminal and Antisocial Behavior* (Chichester, England: Wiley, 1995).

128. Thomas Bouchard, "Genetic and Environmental Influences on Intelligence and Special Mental Abilities," *American Journal of Human Biology* 70(1998): 253–75; some findings from the Minnesota study can be accessed from their Web site. [Available online] http://www.cla.umn.edu/psych/psylabs/mtfs/mtfsspec.htm

129. David Rowe, *The Limits of Family Influence: Genes, Experiences and Behavior* (New York: Guilford Press, 1995), p. 64.

130. Gregory Carey, "Twin Imitation for Antisocial Behavior: Implications for Genetic and Family Environment Research," *Journal of Abnormal Psychology* 101 (1992): 18–25; David Rowe and Joseph Rodgers, "The Ohio Twin Project and ADSEX Studies: Behavior Genetic Approaches to Understanding Antisocial Behavior." Paper presented at the American Society of Criminology meeting, Montreal, Canada, November 1987.

131. Glenn Walters, "A Meta-Analysis of the Gene–Crime Relationship," *Criminology* 30 (1992): 595–613.

132. Marshall Jones and Donald Jones, "The Contagious Nature of Antisocial Behavior," *Criminology* 38 (2000): 25–46.

133. David Rowe and Bill Gulley, "Sibling Effects on Substance Use and Delinquency," *Criminology* 30 (1992): 217–32; see also, David Rowe, Joseph Rogers, and Sylvia Meseck-Bushey, "Sibling Delinquency and the Family Environment: Shared and Unshared Influences," *Child Development* 63 (1992): 59–67.

134. Jones and Jones, "The Contagious Nature of Antisocial Behavior" p. 31.

135. R. J. Cadoret, C. Cain, and R. R. Crowe, "Evidence for a Gene–Environment Interaction in the Development of Adolescent Antisocial Behavior," *Behavior Genetics* 13 (1983): 301–10.

136. Barry Hutchings and Sarnoff A. Mednick, "Criminality in Adoptees and Their Adoptive and Biological Parents: A Pilot Study," in *Biological Bases in Criminal Behavior*, eds. S. A. Mednick and K. O. Christiansen (New York: Gardner Press, 1977).

137. For similar results, see Sarnoff Mednick, Terrie Moffitt, William Gabrielli, and Barry Hutchings, "Genetic Factors in Criminal Behavior: A Review," in *Development of Antisocial and Prosocial Behavior*, ed. Dan Olweus (New York: Academic Press, 1986), pp. 3–50; Sarnoff Mednick, William Gabrielli, and Barry Hutchings, "Genetic Influences in Criminal Behavior: Evidence from an Adoption Cohort," in *Perspective Studies of Crime and Delinquency*, eds. Katherine Teilmann Van Dusen and Sarnoff Mednick (Boston: Kluver-Nijhoff, 1983), pp. 39–57.

138. Michael Bohman, "Predisposition to Criminality: Swedish Adoption Studies in Retrospect," in *Genetics of Criminal and Antisocial Behavior*, pp. 99–114.

139. Lawrence Cohen and Richard Machalek, "A General Theory of Expropriative Crime: An Evolutionary Ecological Approach," *American Journal of Sociology* 94 (1988): 465–501.

140. For a general review, see Martin Daly and Margo Wilson, "Crime and Conflict: Homicide in Evolutionary Psychological Theory," in *Crime and Justice, An Annual Edition*, ed. Michael Tonry (Chicago: University of Chicago Press, 1997), pp. 51–100.

141. Lee Ellis, "The Evolution of Violent Criminal Behavior and Its Nonlegal Equivalent," *Crime in Biological Contexts*, pp. 63–65.

142. David Rowe, Alexeander Vazsonyi, and Aurelio Jose Figuerdo, "Mating-Effort in Adolescence: A Conditional of Alternative Strategy," *Personal Individual Differences* 23 (1997): 105–15.

143. Ibid., p. 112.

144. Martin Daly and Margo Wilson, *Homicide* (New York: Aldine de Gruyter, 1988), p. 194.

145. Margo Wilson, Holly Johnson, and Martin Daly, "Lethal and Nonlethal Violence against Wives," *Canadian Journal of Criminology* 37 (1995): 331–61.

146. Daly and Wilson, *Homicide*, pp. 172–73.

147. Anne Campbell, Steven Muncer, and Daniel Bibel, "Female–Female Criminal Assault: An Evolutionary Perspective," *Journal of Research in Crime and Delinquency* 35 (1998): 413–29.

148. Lee Ellis and Anthony Walsh, "Gene-Based Evolutionary Theories of Criminology," *Criminology* 35 (1997): 229–76.

149. Deborah Denno, "Sociological and Human Developmental Explanations of Crime: Conflict or Consensus," *Criminology* 23 (1985): 711–41.

150. Israel Nachshon and Deborah Denno, "Violence and Cerebral Function," in *The Causes of Crime, New Biological Approaches*, eds. Sarnoff Mednick, Terrie Moffitt, and Susan Stack (Cambridge: Cambridge University Press, 1987), pp. 185–217.

151. Raine, Brennan, Mednick, and Mednick, "High Rates of Violence, Crime, Academic Problems, and Behavioral Problems in Males with Both Early Neuromotor Deficits and Unstable Family Environments."

152. Avshalom Caspi, Donald Lynam, Terrie Moffitt, and Phil Silva, "Unraveling Girl's Delinquency: Biological, Dispositional, and Contextual Contributions to Adolescent Misbehavior," *Developmental Psychology* 29 (1993): 283–89.

153. Glenn Walters and Thomas White, "Heredity and Crime: Bad Genes or Bad Research," *Criminology* 27 (1989): 455–86, at 478.

154. Charles Goring, *The English Convict: A Statistical Study, 1913* (Montclair, N.J.: Patterson Smith, 1972).

155. Edwin Driver, "Charles Buckman Goring," in *Pioneers in Criminology*, ed. Hermann Mannheim (Montclair, N.J.: Patterson Smith, 1970), p. 440.

156. Gabriel Tarde, *Penal Philosophy*, trans. R. Howell (Boston: Little, Brown, 1912).

157. See, generally, Donn Byrne and Kathryn Kelly, *An Introduction to Personality* (Englewood Cliffs, N.J.: Prentice-Hall, 1981).

158. August Aichorn, *Wayward Youth* (New York: Viking Press, 1935).

159. David Abrahamsen, *Crime and the Human Mind* (New York: Columbia University Press, 1944), p. 137; see, generally, Fritz Redl and Hans Toch, "The Psychoanalytic Perspective," in *Psychology of Crime and Criminal Justice*, ed. Hans Toch (New York: Holt, Rinehart and Winston, 1979), pp. 193–95.

160. See, generally, D. A. Andrews and James Bonta, *The Psychology of Criminal Conduct* (Cincinnati, Ohio: Anderson, 1994), pp. 72–75.

161. Paige Crosby Ouimette, "Psychopathology and Sexual Aggression in Nonincarcerated Men," *Violence and Victimization* 12 (1997): 389–97.

162. Robert Krueger, Avshalom Caspi, Phil Silva, and Rob McGee, "Personality Traits Are Differentially Linked to Mental Disorders: A Multitrait-Multidiagnosis Study of an Adolescent Birth Cohort," *Journal of Abnormal Psychology* 105 (1996): 299–312.

163. Seymour Halleck, *Psychiatry and the Dilemmas of Crime* (Berkeley: University of California Press, 1971).

164. This discussion is based on three works by Albert Bandura: *Aggression: A Social Learning Analysis* (Englewood Cliffs, N.J.: Prentice-Hall, 1973); *Social Learning Theory* (Englewood Cliffs, N.J.: Prentice-Hall, 1977); and "The Social Learning Perspective: Mechanisms of Aggression," in *Psychology of Crime and Criminal Justice*, ed. Hans Toch (New York: Holt, Rinehart and Winston, 1979), pp. 198–236.

165. David Phillips, "The Impact of Mass Media Violence on U.S. Homicides," *American Sociological Review* 48 (1983): 560–68.

166. See, generally, Jean Piaget, *The Moral Judgment of the Child* (London: Kegan Paul, 1932).

167. Lawrence Kohlberg, *Stages in the Development of Moral Thought and Action* (New York: Holt, Rinehart and Winston, 1969).

168. L. Kohlberg, K. Kauffman, P. Scharf, and J. Hickey, *The Just Community Approach in Corrections: A Manual* (Niantic: Connecticut Department of Corrections, 1973).

169. Scott Henggeler, *Delinquency in Adolescence* (Newbury Park, Calif.: Sage, 1989), p. 26.

170. Carol Veneziano and Louis Veneziano, "The Relationship between Deterrence and Moral Reasoning," *Criminal Justice Review* 17 (1992): 209–16.

171. K. A. Dodge, "A Social Information Processing Model of Social Competence in Children," in *Minnesota Symposium in Child Psychology*, vol. 18, ed. M. Perlmutter (Hillsdale, N.J.: Erlbaum, 1986), pp. 77–125.

172. Adrian Raine, Peter Venables, and Mark Williams, "Better Autonomic Conditioning and Faster Electrodermal Half-Recovery Time at Age 15 Years as Possible Protective Factors against Crime at Age 29 Years," *Developmental Psychology* 32 (1996): 624–30.

173. L. Huesman and L. Eron, "Individual Differences and the Trait of Aggression," *European Journal of Personality* 3 (1989): 95–106.

174. Rolf Loeber and Dale Hay, "Key Issues in the Development of Aggression and Violence from Childhood to Early Adulthood," *Annual Review of Psychology* 48 (1997): 371–410.

175. J. E. Lochman, "Self and Peer Perceptions and Attributional Biases of Aggressive and Nonaggressive Boys in Dyadic Interactions," *Journal of Consulting and Clinical Psychology* 55 (1987): 404–10.

176. D. Lipton, E. C. McDonel, and R. McFall, "Heterosocial Perception in Rapists," *Journal of Consulting and Clinical Psychology* 55 (1987): 17–21.

177. *Understanding Violence*, p. 389.

178. Kathleen. Cirillo, B. E. Pruitt, Brian Colwell, Paul M. Kingery, Robert S. Hurley, and Danny Ballard, "School Violence: Prevalence and Intervention Strategies for At-Risk Adolescents," *Adolescence* 33 (1998): 319–31.

179. *Understanding Violence*, p. 389.

180. Rick Bragg, "4 Girls and a Teacher Are Shot to Death in an Ambush at a Middle School in Arkansas," *New York Times*, 25 March 1998, p.1.

181. James Sorrells, "Kids Who Kill," *Crime and Delinquency* 23 (1977): 312–20.

182. Richard Rosner, "Adolescents Accused of Murder and Manslaughter: A Five-Year Descriptive Study," *Bulletin of the American Academy of Psychiatry and the Law* 7 (1979): 342–51.

183. Richard Famularo, Robert Kinscherff, and Terence Fenton, "Psychiatric Diagnoses of Abusive Mothers, A Preliminary Report," *Journal of Nervous and Mental Disease* 180 (1992): 658–60.

184. Richard Wagner, Dawn Taylor, Joy Wright, Alison Sloat, Gwynneth Springett, Sandy Arnold, and Heather Weinberg, "Substance Abuse among the Mentally Ill," *American Journal of Orthopsychiatry* 64 (1994): 30–38.

185. Bruce Link, Howard Andrews, and Francis Cullen, "The Violent and Illegal Behavior of Mental Patients Reconsidered," *American Sociological Review* 57 (1992): 275–92; Ellen Hochstedler Steury, "Criminal Defendants with Psychiatric Impairment: Prevalence, Probabilities and Rates," *Journal of Criminal Law and Criminology* 84 (1993): 354–74.

186. Robin Shepard Engel and Eric Silver, "Policing Mentally Disordered Suspects: A Reexamination of the Criminalization Hypothesis," *Criminology* 39 (2001): 225–52; Marc Hillbrand, John Krystal, Kimberly Sharpe, and Hilliard Foster, "Clinical Predictors of Self-Mutilation in Hospitalized Patients," *Journal of Nervous and Mental Disease* 182 (1994): 9–13.

187. Carmen Cirincione, Henry Steadman, Pamela Clark Robbins, and John Monahan, *Mental Illness as a Factor in Criminality: A Study of Prisoners and Mental Patients* (Delmar, N.Y.: Policy Research Associates, 1991). See also, idem, *Schizophrenia as a Contingent Risk Factor for Criminal Violence* (Delmar, N.Y.: Policy Research Associates, 1991).

188. James Bonta, Moira Law, and Karl Hanson, "The Prediction of Criminal and Violent Recidivism among Mentally Disordered Offenders: A Meta-Analysis," *Psychological Bulletin* 123 (1998): 123–42.

189. John Monahan, *Mental Illness and Violent Crime* (Washington, D.C.: National Institute of Justice, 1996).

190. Eric Silver, "Extending Social Disorganization Theory: A Multilevel Approach to the Study of Violence among Persons with Mental Illness," *Criminology* 38 (2000): 1043–74.

191. Stacy DeCoster and Karen Heimer, "The Relationship between Law Violation and Depression: An Interactionist Analysis," *Criminology* 39 (2001): 799–837.

192. Jeffrey Wanson, Randy Borum, Marvin Swartz, Virginia Hidaym, H. Ryan Wagner, and Barbara Burns, "Can Involuntary Outpatient Commitment Reduce Arrests among Persons with Severe Mental Illness?" *Criminal Justice and Behavior* 28(2001): 156–89.

193. See, generally, Walter Mischel, *Introduction to Personality*, 4th ed. (New York: Holt, Rinehart and Winston, 1986).

194. D. A. Andrews and J. Stephen Wormith, "Personality and Crime: Knowledge and Construction in Criminology," *Justice Quarterly* 6 (1989): 289–310; Donald Gibbons, "Comment—Personality and Crime: Non-Issues, Real Issues, and a Theory and Research Agenda," *Justice Quarterly* (1989): 311–24.

195. Sheldon Glueck and Eleanor Glueck, *Unraveling Juvenile Delinquency* (Cambridge: Harvard University Press, 1950).

196. See, generally, Hans Eysenck, *Personality and Crime* (London: Routledge and Kegan Paul, 1977).

197. Edelyn Verona and Joyce Carbonell, "Female Violence and Personality," *Criminal Justice and Behavior* 27 (2000): 176–95.

198. Hans Eysenck and M. W. Eysenck, *Personality and Individual Differences* (New York: Plenum, 1985).

199. Joshua Miller and Donald Lynam, "Personality and Antisocial Behavior," *Criminology* 39 (2001): 765–99.

200. Ibid., pp. 781–82.

201. David Lykken, "Psychopathy, Sociopathy, and Crime," *Society* 34 (1996): 30–38.

202. See, generally, R. Starke Hathaway and Elio Monachesi, *Analyzing and Predicting Juvenile Delinquency with the MMPI* (Minneapolis: University of Minnesota Press, 1953).

203. R. Starke Hathaway, Elio Monachesi, and Lawrence Young, "Delinquency Rates and Personality," *Journal of Criminal Law, Criminology, and Police Science* 51 (1960): 443–60; Michael Hindelang and Joseph Weis, "Personality and Self-Reported Delinquency: An Application of Cluster Analysis," *Criminology* 10 (1972): 268; Spencer Rathus and Larry Siegel, "Crime and Personality Revisited," *Criminology* 18 (1980): 245–51.

204. See, generally, Edward Megargee, *The California Psychological Inventory Handbook* (San Francisco: Josey-Bass, 1972).

205. Avshalom Caspi, Terrie Moffitt, Phil Silva, Magda Stouthamer-Loeber, Robert Krueger, and Pamela Schmutte, "Are Some People Crime-Prone? Replications of the Personality–Crime Relationship across Countries, Genders, Races and Methods," *Criminology* 32 (1994): 163–95.

206. Henry Goddard, *Efficiency and Levels of Intelligence* (Princeton, N.J.: Princeton University Press, 1920); Edwin Sutherland, "Mental Deficiency and Crime," in *Social Attitudes*, ed. Kimball Young (New York: Henry Holt, 1931), chap. 15.

207. William Healy and Augusta Bronner, *Delinquency and Criminals: Their Making and Unmaking* (New York: McMillan, 1926).

208. Joseph Lee Rogers, H. Harrington Cleveland, Edwin van den Oord, and David Rowe, "Resolving the Debate Over Birth Order, Family Size and Intelligence," *American Psychologist* 55 (2000): 599–612.

209. John Slawson, *The Delinquent Boys* (Boston: Budget Press, 1926).

210. Edwin Sutherland, "Mental Deficiency and Crime," in *Social Attitudes,* ed. Kimball Young (New York: Henry Holt, 1931), chap. 15.

211. Travis Hirschi and Michael Hindelang, "Intelligence and Delinquency: A Revisionist Review," *American Sociological Review* 42 (1977): 471–586.

212. Deborah Denno, "Sociological and Human Developmental Explanations of Crime: Conflict or Consensus," *Criminology* 23 (1985): 711–41; Christine Ward and Richard McFall, "Further Validation of the Problem Inventory for Adolescent Girls: Comparing Caucasian and Black Delinquents and Nondelinquents," *Journal of Consulting and Clinical Psychology* 54 (1986): 732–33; L. Hubble and M. Groff, "Magnitude and Direction of WISC-R Verbal Performance IQ Discrepancies among Adjudicated Male Delinquents," *Journal of Youth and Adolescence* 10 (1981): 179–83; Robert Gordon, "IQ Commensurability of Black–White Differences in Crime and Delinquency." Paper presented at the annual meeting of the American Psychological Association, Washington, D.C., August 1986; idem, "Two Illustrations of the IQ-Surrogate Hypothesis: IQ versus Parental Education and Occupational Status in the Race-IQ-Delinquency Model." Paper presented at the annual meeting of the American Society of Criminology, Montreal, Canada, November 1987.

213. Donald Lynam, Terrie Moffitt, and Magda Stouthamer-Loeber, "Explaining the Relation between IQ and Delinquency: Class, Race, Test Motivation, School Failure or Self-Control," *Journal of Abnormal Psychology* 102 (1993): 187–96.

214. Alex Piquero, "Frequency, Specialization, and Violence in Offending Careers," *Journal of Research in Crime and Delinquency* 37 (2000): 392–418.

215. James Q. Wilson and Richard Herrnstein, *Crime and Human Nature* (New York: Simon and Schuster, 1985), p. 148.

216. Ibid., p. 171.

217. Terrie Moffitt, William Gabrielli, Sarnoff Mednick, and Fini Schulsinger, "Socioeconomic Status, IQ, and Delinquency," *Journal of Abnormal Psychology* 90 (1981): 152–56, at 155. For a similar finding, see Hubble and Groff, "Magnitude and Direction of WISC-R Verbal Performance IQ Discrepancies among Adjudicated Male Delinquents."

218. Lorne Yeudall, Delee Fromm-Auch, and Priscilla Davies, "Neuropsychological Impairment of Persistent Delinquency," *Journal of Nervous and Mental Diseases* 170 (1982): 257–65.

219. Hakan Stattin and Ingrid Klackenberg-Larsson, "Early Language and Intelligence Development and Their Relationship to Future Criminal Behavior," *Journal of Abnormal Psychology* 102 (1993): 369–78.

220. H. D. Day, J. M. Franklin, and D. D. Marshall, "Predictors of Aggression in Hospitalized Adolescents," *Journal of Psychology* 132 (1998): 427–35; Scott Menard and Barbara Morse, "A Structuralist Critique of the IQ–Delinquency Hypothesis: Theory and Evidence," *American Journal of Sociology* 89 (1984): 1347–78; Denno, "Sociological and Human Developmental Explanations of Crime."

221. Neisser et al., "Intelligence: Knowns and Unknowns," p. 83.

222. Richard Herrnstein and Charles Murray, *The Bell Curve, Intelligence and Class Structure in American Life* (New York: Free Press, 1994).

223. Susan Pease and Craig T. Love, "Optimal Methods and Issues in Nutrition Research in the Correctional Setting," *Nutrition Reviews Supplement* 44 (1986): 122–31.

224. Mark O'Callaghan and Douglas Carroll, "The Role of Psychosurgical Studies in the Control of Antisocial Behavior," in *The Causes of Crime, New Biological Approaches,* eds. Sarnoff Mednick, Terrie Moffitt, and Susan Stack (Cambridge: Cambridge University Press, 1987), pp. 312–28.

225. Mednick, Moffitt, Gabrielli, and Hutchings, "Genetic Factors in Criminal Behavior: A Review," pp. 47–48.

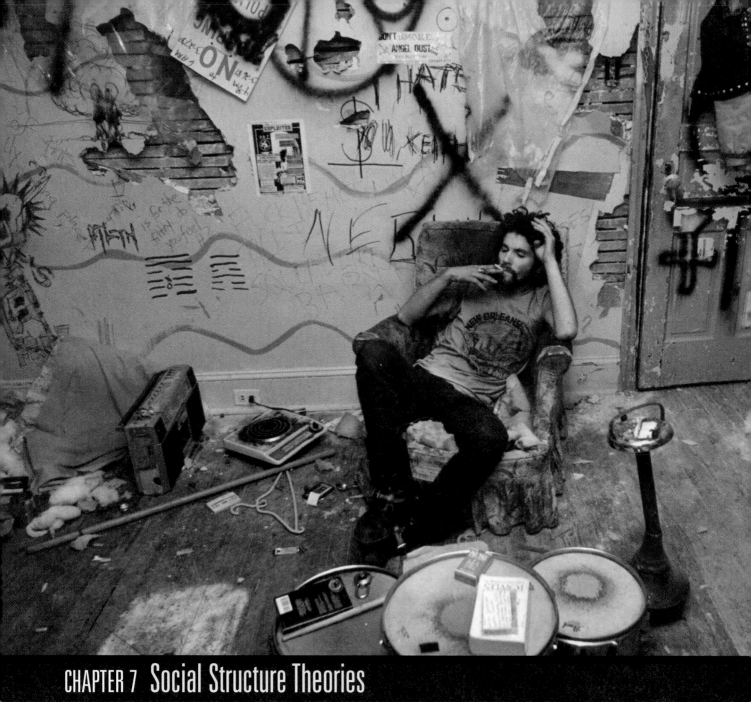

© David H. Wells/CORBIS

CHAPTER 7 Social Structure Theories

Introduction

On July 24, 2001, three young Boston men were charged with attempted murder for an attack in which a 13-year-old boy was clubbed and stabbed and left paralyzed.[1] The boys were believed to be members of La Mara Salvatrucha 13 or MS-13, a nationally known gang linked to murders, drug dealing, immigrant smuggling, and kidnapping. Their victim, Edwin Molina, thought to be a member of the rival Panocho-18 gang, suffered a severed spinal cord, a fractured jaw, several broken ribs, and bruises on his torso after being beaten with a baseball bat.

The incident stemmed from a simmering rivalry between the two gangs who were actively recruiting members and seeking power in the Boston area. It started at a party attended by MS-13 and Panocho-18 members, including Molina. Three carloads of MS-13 members parked outside the party. They started flashing gang signs and instigated a confrontation with their rivals. At about 1 A.M. Molina and three friends decided to try to get away before things got out of control. As they ran down the street, they were attacked by MS-13 members, who beat Molina as his friends ran away.

Both the MS-13 gang and its rival Panocho-18 began on the west coast and have migrated eastward, recruiting thousands of members in cities around the nation, including Newark, Boston, and Washington, D.C. The origins of MS-13 can be traced to the civil war in El Salvador. When members moved to Southern California, they soon became involved in drug smuggling and gun running. Membership is very appealing to poor boys like Edwin Molina because, despite the danger involved, gangs provide a sense of power and belonging for youths who may feel lost and alienated in our postmodern culture.

Many criminologists believe it would be a mistake to ignore social and environmental factors when trying to understand the causes of criminal behavior.[2] Most criminals are indigent and desperate, not calculating or evil. Many grew up in the most deteriorated part of town and lack the social support and economic resources familiar to more affluent members of society. To understand criminal behavior, we must analyze the influence of these destructive social forces on human behavior. According to this view, it is places—and not people—that cause crime.

Sociology has been the primary focus of criminology since the early twentieth century, when sociologists Robert Ezra Park (1864–1944), Ernest W. Burgess (1886–1966), Louis Wirth (1897–1952), and their colleagues were teaching and conducting criminological research in the sociology department at the University of Chicago. Their work on the social ecology of the city inspired a generation of scholars to conclude that social forces operating in urban areas create criminal interactions. This perspective came to be known as the **Chicago School.**

In 1915, Robert Ezra Park called for anthropological methods of description and observation to be applied to urban life.[3] He was concerned about how neighborhood structure developed, how isolated pockets of poverty formed, and what social policies could be used to alleviate urban problems. Later, Park, with Ernest Burgess, studied the social ecology of the city and found that some neighborhoods form so-called natural areas of wealth and affluence, while others suffered poverty and disintegration.[4] Regardless of their race, religion, or ethnicity, the everyday behavior of people living in these areas was controlled by the social and ecological climate.

To read more about Park's life, go to:
http://www2.pfeiffer.edu/~lridener/DSS/Park/ PARKPER.HTML
For an up-to-date list of Web links, go to
http://info.wadsworth.com/siegel ■

Over the next 20 years, Chicago School sociologists carried out an ambitious program of research and scholarship on urban topics, including criminal behavior patterns. Harvey Zorbaugh's *The Gold Coast and the Slum*,[5] Frederick Thrasher's *The Gang*,[6] and Louis Wirth's *The Ghetto*[7] are classic examples of objective, highly descriptive accounts of urban life. Their influence was such that most criminologists have been trained in sociology, and criminology courses are routinely taught in departments of sociology. As a result of this influence, many criminologists consider the social and economic structure as key determinants of the crime rate.

Socioeconomic Structure and Crime

People in the United States live in a **stratified society.** Social strata are created by the unequal distribution of wealth, power, and prestige. Social classes are segments of the population whose members have a relatively similar portion of desirable things and who share attitudes, values, norms, and an identifiable lifestyle. In U.S. society, it is common to identify people as upper-, middle-, and lower-class citizens, with a broad range of economic variations existing within each group. The upper-upper class is reserved for a small number of exceptionally well-to-do families who maintain enormous financial and social resources. In contrast, the indigent have scant, if any, resources and suffer socially and economically as a result. As Figure 7.1 shows, the lowest 20 percent of the population earns about 3.6 percent of all income, whereas the top 20 percent earns about 50 percent!

Fortunately, the proportion of indigent Americans has been in decline. In the year 2000, the poverty rate fell to 11.3 percent, the lowest rate since 1979 and statistically the same as the lowest poverty rate ever recorded—11.1 percent in 1973. The number of poor dropped significantly also, by 1.1 million people—from 32.3 million poor in 1999 to 31.1 million poor in 2000.[8] Though the decline in the poverty rate is welcome news, the fact that after more than eight years of a robust economy more than 30 million Americans still live in poverty is quite disturbing.

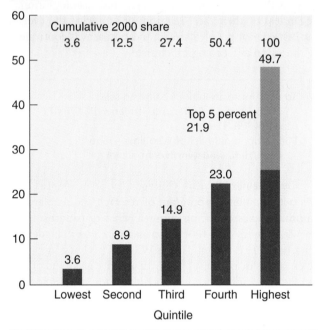

Figure 7.1 Measures of Household Income Inequality, 2000

Percent

Cumulative 2000 share

| | 3.6 | 12.5 | 27.4 | 50.4 | 100 |

Top 5 percent 21.9

49.7

23.0

14.9

8.9

3.6

Lowest Second Third Fourth Highest

Quintile

NOTES: No statistical change in shares of aggregate income from 1999 to 2000.
No statistical change in Gini Index from 1999 to 2000.

SOURCE: U.S. Census Bureau, Current Population Survey, March 2000 and 2001.

CONNECTIONS

The association between crime and economic class has been muddied by the ambiguous relationship between unemployment and crime. Crime rates sometimes go up during periods of full employment and drop during periods of relatively high unemployment. See the section titled Employment Opportunities later in this chapter to learn more about poverty and crime. ■

Lower-class areas are scenes of inadequate housing and health care, disrupted family lives, underemployment, and despair. Members of the lower class also suffer in other ways. They are more prone to depression, less likely to have achievement motivation, and less likely to put off immediate gratification for future gain. For example, they may be less willing to stay in school because the rewards for educational achievement are in the distant future.

Members of the lower class are constantly bombarded by the media with a flood of advertisements linking material possessions to self-worth, but they are often unable to attain desired goods and services through conventional means. Though they are members of a society that extols material success above any other, they are unable to satisfactorily compete for such success with members of the upper classes. As a result, they may turn to illegal solutions

to their economic plight: they may deal drugs for profit, steal cars and sell them to "chop shops," or commit armed robberies for desperately needed funds. They may become so depressed that they take alcohol and drugs as a form of self-tranquilization, and because of their poverty, they may acquire the drugs and alcohol through illegal channels.

Child Poverty

About 25 percent of children under age 6 now live in poverty, a frightening number considering America's self-image as the "richest country on earth." There is a distinct racial division in child poverty: only 6 percent of white children can be described as extremely poor, but about 50 percent of young black children live in extreme poverty.[9] Children are especially hard hit by poverty. Hundreds of studies have documented the association between family poverty and children's health, achievement, and behavior impairments.[10]

Kids Count, a project of the Annie E. Casey Foundation, is a national and state-by-state effort to track the relative status of children in the United States. Go to their Web site at:
  http://www.aecf.org/kidscount
For an up-to-date list of Web links, go to
  http://info.wadsworth.com/siegel ■

Children who grow up in low-income homes are less likely to achieve in school and are less likely to complete their schooling than children with more affluent parents.[11] Poor children are also more likely to suffer from health problems and receive inadequate health care. Unfortunately, more than 9 million children are not covered by health insurance, and nearly 90 percent of them are in working families.[12] With a lack of health benefits and without the means to afford doctors' care, chances are good that health problems that afflict these children may impede their long-term development. Children who live in extreme poverty or who remain poor for multiple years appear to suffer the worst outcomes. The timing of poverty also seems to be relevant. Findings suggest that poverty during early childhood may have a more significant impact on children than poverty during adolescence or teen years.[13]

Use "child poverty" as a key word in InfoTrac College Edition to find out more about this national problem. ■

In addition to having an increased chance of physical illness, poor children are also much more likely than wealthy children to suffer a garden variety of social and physical ills, ranging from low birth weight to a limited chance of earning a college degree. The social problems found in lower-class slum areas have been described as an

© Kevin Fleming/CORBIS

■ About 25 percent of children in the United States live in poverty. These children are less likely to achieve in school or to complete their education. They are more likely to have health problems and to receive inadequate health care. Children living in poverty suffer a variety of social and physical ills, ranging from low birth weight to dropping out of school or becoming teenage parents.

"epidemic" that spreads like a contagious disease, destroying the inner workings that enable neighborhoods to survive; they become "hollowed out."[14] As neighborhood quality decreases, the probability that residents will develop problems sharply increases. Adolescents in the worst neighborhoods share the greatest risk of dropping out of school and becoming teenage parents.

The Underclass

In 1966, sociologist Oscar Lewis argued that the crushing lifestyle of slum areas produces a **culture of poverty,** which is passed from one generation to the next.[15] Apathy, cynicism, helplessness, and mistrust of social institutions such as schools, government agencies, and the police mark the culture of poverty. This mistrust prevents slum dwellers from taking advantage of the meager opportunities available to them. Lewis's work was the first of a group that described the plight of **at-risk** children and adults. In 1970, Swedish economist Gunnar Myrdal described a worldwide **underclass** that was cut off from society, its members lacking the education and skills needed to be effectively in demand in modern society.[16]

 To read conservative social scientists' take on the "underclass," go to:
http://www.aei.org/ps/psmurray.htm
For an up-to-date list of Web links, go to
http://info.wadsworth.com/siegel ■

Economic disparity will continually haunt members of the underclass and their children over the course of their life span. Even if they value education and other middle-class norms, their desperate life circumstances (for example, high unemployment and nontraditional family structures) may prevent them from developing the skills, habits, and styles that lead first to educational success and later to success in the workplace. Both of these factors have been linked to incidents of crime and drug abuse.[17]

Unfortunately, minority group members are all too often members of the underclass who suffer a multitude of social problems. In some jurisdictions, up to half of all minority males are under criminal justice system control. Recent research by David Greenberg and Valerie West shows that states with a substantial minority population have a much higher imprisonment rate than those with predominantly white populations. They conclude that black males are considered a threat by the white majority disproportionate to the amount of crime they actually commit.[18] The costs of crime—paying for lawyers and court costs—perpetuate poverty by absorbing what money there is and depriving families and children of these funds.[19]

Sociologist William Julius Wilson has detailed the hardship faced by the African American underclass in the United States, whom he identified as the **truly disadvantaged.** His work is discussed in the Race, Culture, Gender, and Criminology feature.

The Northwestern University/University of Chicago Joint Center for Poverty Research examines what it means to be poor and live in America:
http://www.jcpr.org/
For an up-to-date list of Web links, go to
http://info.wadsworth.com/siegel ■

Bridging the Racial Divide

William Julius Wilson, one of the nation's most prominent sociologists, has produced an impressive body of work detailing racial problems and racial politics in American society. In 1987, he provided a description of the plight of the lowest levels of the underclass, which he labeled the "truly disadvantaged." Wilson portrayed members of this group as socially isolated people who dwell in urban inner cities, occupy the bottom rung of the social ladder, and are the victims of discrimination. They live in areas where the basic institutions of society—family, schools, housing—have long since declined. This decline triggers similar breakdowns in the strengths of inner-city areas, including loss of community cohesion and an inability of people living in the area to control the flow of drugs and criminal activity. For example, in a more affluent area, neighbors might complain to parents that their children are acting out. In distressed areas, this element of informal social control may be absent because parents are under stress or all too often absent. These effects magnify the isolation of the underclass from mainstream society and promote a ghetto culture and behavior.

Since the truly disadvantaged rarely come into contact with the ac-

tual source of their oppression, they direct their anger and aggression at those with whom they are in close and intimate contact, such as neighbors, businesspeople, and landlords. Members of this group, plagued by under- or unemployment, begin to lose self-confidence, a feeling supported by the plight of kin and friendship groups who also experience extreme economic marginality. Self-doubt is a neighborhood norm, overwhelming those forced to live in areas of concentrated poverty.

In his important book, *When Work Disappears,* Wilson assesses the effect of joblessness and underemployment on residents in poor neighborhoods on Chicago's south side. He argues that for the first time in the twentieth century most adults in inner-city ghetto neighborhoods are not working during a typical week. He finds that inner-city life is only marginally affected by the surge in the nation's economy, which has been brought about by new industrial growth connected with technological development. Poverty in these inner-city areas is eternal and unchanging and, if anything, worsening as residents are further shut out of the economic mainstream.

Wilson focuses on the plight of the African American community, which had enjoyed periods of relative prosperity in the 1950s and 1960s. As difficult as life was in the 1940s and

1950s for African Americans, he suggests that they at least had a reasonable hope of steady work. Now, because of the globalization of the economy, those opportunities have evaporated. In the past, racial segregation had limited opportunity, but growth in the manufacturing sector fueled upward mobility and provided the foundation of today's African American middle class. Those opportunities no longer exist as manufacturing plants have moved to inaccessible rural areas and overseas locations where the cost of doing business is lower. With manufacturing opportunities all but obsolete in the United States, service and retail establishments, which depended on blue-collar spending, have similarly disappeared, leaving behind an economy based on welfare and government supports. In less than 20 years, formerly active African American communities have become crime-infested slums.

The hardships faced by residents in Chicago's south side are not unique to that community. Beyond sustaining inner-city poverty, the absence of employment opportunities has torn at the social fabric of the nation's inner-city neighborhoods. Work helps socialize young people into the wider society, instilling in them such desirable values as hard work, caring, and respect for others. When work becomes scarce, however, the discipline and structure it provides are absent.

■ Social Structure Theories

Many criminologists view the disadvantaged economic class position as a primary cause of crime. This view is referred to as **social structure theory.** As a group, social structure theories suggest that social and economic forces operating in deteriorated lower-class areas push many of their residents into criminal behavior patterns. These theories consider the existence of unsupervised teenage gangs, high crime rates, and social disorder in slum areas as major social problems.

Lower-class crime is often the violent, destructive product of youth gangs and marginally and underemployed young adults. Underemployment means that many

working adults earn relatively low wages and have few benefits such as health insurance and retirement plans. Their ability to accumulate capital for home ownership is restricted and so, consequently, is their stake in society.

Although members of the middle and upper classes also engage in crime, social structure theorists view middle-class, or white-collar, crime as being of relatively lower frequency, seriousness, and danger to the general public. The real crime problem is essentially a lower-class phenomenon, which breeds criminal behavior that begins in youth and continues into young adulthood.

Most social structure theories focus on children's law-violating behavior. They suggest that the social forces that

Community-wide underemployment destroys social cohesion, increasing the presence of neighborhood social problems ranging from drug use to educational failure. Schools in these areas are unable to teach basic skills, and because desirable employment is lacking, there are few adults to serve as role models. In contrast to more affluent suburban households where daily life is organized around job and career demands, children in inner-city areas are not socialized in the workings of the mainstream economy.

In his newest book, *The Bridge Over the Racial Divide: Rising Inequality and Coalition Politics,* Wilson expands further on his views of race in contemporary society. He argues that despite economic gains there is a growing inequality in American society, and ordinary families of all races and ethnic origins are suffering. Whites, Latinos, African Americans, Asians, and Native Americans must therefore begin to put aside their differences and concentrate more on what they have in common—their aspirations, problems, and hopes. There needs to be mutual cooperation across racial lines.

One reason for this set of mutual problems is that the government tends to aggravate rather than ease the financial stress being placed on ordinary families. Monetary policy, trade policy, and tax policy are harmful to working-class families. A mul-

tiracial citizen's coalition could pressure national public officials to focus on the interests of ordinary people. As long as middle- and working-class groups are fragmented along racial lines, such pressure is impossible.

Wilson finds that racism is becoming more subtle and harder to detect. Whites believe African Americans are responsible for their inferior economic status because of their cultural traits. Because even affluent whites fear corporate downsizing, they are unwilling to vote for governmental assistance to the poor. Whites continue to be suburban dwellers, further isolating poor minorities in central cities and making their problems distant and unimportant. He continues to believe that the changing marketplace, with its reliance on sophisticated computer technologies, is continually decreasing demand for low-skilled workers, which has a more negative impact on African Americans than on other better educated and affluent groups.

Wilson argues for a cross-race, class-based alliance of working- and middle-class Americans to pursue policies that will benefit them rather than the affluent. These include full employment, programs to help families and workers in their private lives, and a reconstructed "affirmative opportunity" program that benefits African Americans without antagonizing whites.

Critical Thinking Questions

1. Is it unrealistic to assume that a government-sponsored public works program can provide needed jobs in this era of budget cutbacks?
2. What are some of the hidden costs of unemployment in a community setting?
3. How would a biocriminologist explain Wilson's findings?

InfoTrac College Edition Research

For more on Wilson's view of poverty, unemployment, and crime, check out:

Gunnar Almgren, Avery Guest, George Immerwahr, and Michael Spittel. Joblessness, family disruption, and violent death in Chicago, 1970–90. *Social Forces* June 1998 v76 n4 p1465

William Julius Wilson. Inner-city dislocations. *Society* Jan–Feb 1998 v35 n2 p270

SOURCES: William Julius Wilson, *The Truly Disadvantaged* (Chicago: University of Chicago Press, 1987); *When Work Disappears, The World of the Urban Poor* (New York: Alfred Knopf, 1996); *The Bridge Over the Racial Divide: Rising Inequality and Coalition Politics*, Wildavsky Forum Series, 2 (Berkeley: University of California Press, 1999).

cause crime begin to affect people while they are relatively young and continue to influence them throughout their lives. Though not all youthful offenders become adult criminals, many begin their training and learn criminal values as members of youth gangs and groups.

Social structure theorists challenge those who suggest that crime is an expression of psychological imbalance, biological traits, insensitivity to social controls, personal choice, or any other personal trait. They argue that people living in equivalent social environments tend to behave in a similar, predictable fashion. If the environment did not influence human behavior, then crime rates would be distributed equally across the social structure, which they are

not.[20] Since crime rates are higher in lower-class urban centers than in middle-class suburbs, social forces must be operating in urban slums that influence or control behavior.[21]

There are three independent yet overlapping branches within the social structure perspective—social disorganization, strain theory, and cultural deviance theory (outlined in Figure 7.2).

Social disorganization theory focuses on the conditions within the urban environment that affect crime rates. A disorganized area is one in which institutions of social control, such as the family, commercial establishments, and schools, have broken down and can no longer carry out their expected or stated functions. Indicators of social

Figure 7.2 **The Three Branches of Social Structure Theory**

Social disorganization theory focuses on conditions in the environment:
- Deteriorated neighborhoods
- Inadequate social control
- Law-violating gangs and groups
- Conflicting social values

Cultural deviance theory combines the other two:
- Development of subcultures as a result of disorganization and stress
- Subcultural values in opposition to conventional values

CRIME

Strain theory focuses on conflict between goals and means:
- Unequal distribution of wealth and power
- Frustration
- Alternative methods of achievement

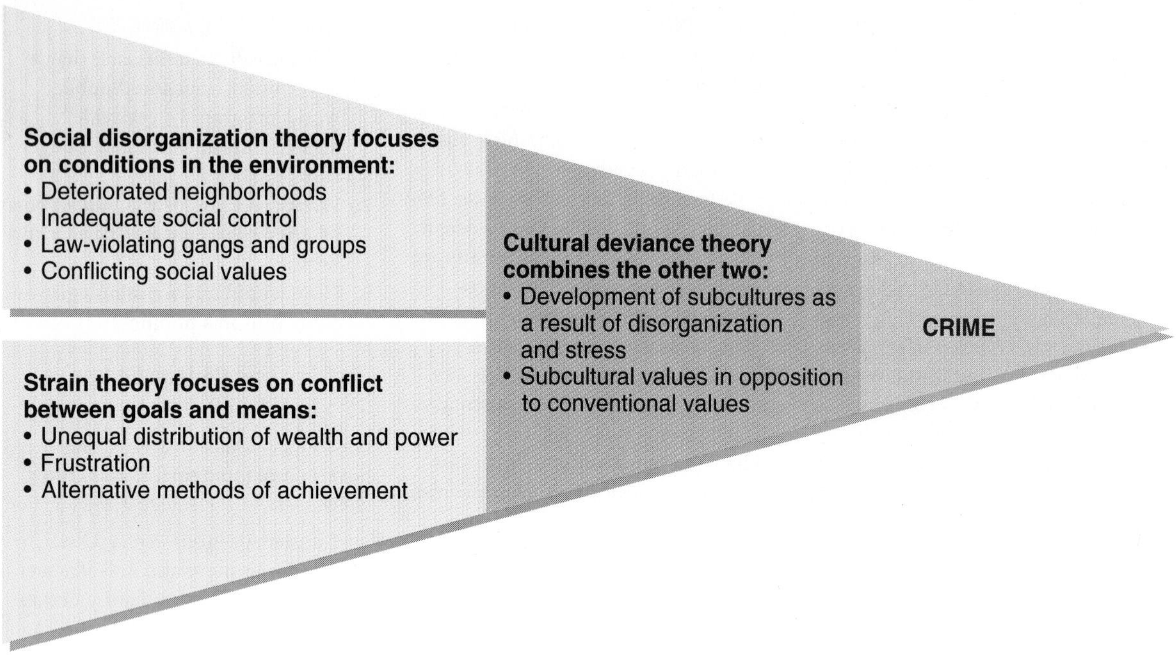

disorganization include high unemployment, school drop-out rates, deteriorated housing, low income levels, and large numbers of single-parent households. Residents in these areas experience conflict and despair, and as a result, antisocial behavior flourishes.

Strain theory, the second branch of social structure theory, holds that crime is a function of the conflict between the goals people have and the means they can use to legally obtain them. Although social and economic goals are common to people in all economic strata, strain theorists argue that the ability to obtain these goals is class-dependent. Most people in the United States desire wealth, material possessions, power, prestige, and other life comforts. Members of the lower class are unable to achieve these symbols of success through conventional means. Consequently, they feel anger, frustration, and resentment, which is referred to as **strain.** Lower-class citizens can either accept their condition and live out their days as socially responsible, if unrewarded, citizens, or they can choose an alternative means of achieving success, such as theft, violence, or drug trafficking.

Cultural deviance theory, the third variation of structural theory, combines elements of both strain and social disorganization. According to this view, because of strain and social isolation, a unique lower-class culture develops in disorganized neighborhoods. These independent **subcultures** maintain a unique set of values and beliefs that are in conflict with conventional social norms. Criminal behavior is an expression of conformity to lower-class sub-

cultural values and traditions and not a rebellion from conventional society. Subcultural values are handed down from one generation to the next in a process called **cultural transmission.**

Although each of these theories is distinct in critical aspects, each approach has at its core the view that socially isolated people, living in disorganized neighborhoods, are the ones most likely to experience crime-producing social forces. Each branch of social structure theory will now be discussed in some detail.

▇ Social Disorganization Theory

Social disorganization theory links crime rates to neighborhood ecological characteristics. Crime rates are elevated in highly transient, "mixed-use" (where residential and commercial property exist side by side) and/or "changing neighborhoods" in which the fabric of social life has become frayed. These localities are unable to provide essential services, such as education, health care, and proper housing and, as a result, experience significant levels of unemployment, single-parent families, and families on welfare and Aid to Dependent Children (ADC).

Social disorganization theory views crime-ridden neighborhoods as those in which residents are trying to leave at the earliest opportunity. Residents are uninterested in community matters, therefore, the common sources of control—the family, school, business community, social service agencies—are weak and disorganized. Personal relationships are strained because neighbors are constantly moving. Constant resident turnover weakens communications and blocks attempts at solving neighborhood problems or establishing common goals.[22] The elements of social disorganization theory are shown in Figure 7.3.

The Work of Shaw and McKay

Social disorganization theory was popularized by the work of two Chicago sociologists, Henry McKay and Clifford R. Shaw, who linked life in transitional slum areas to the inclination to commit crime. Shaw and McKay began their pioneering work on crime in Chicago during the early 1920s while working as researchers for a state-supported social service agency.[23] They were heavily influenced by Chicago School sociologists Ernest Burgess and Robert Park, who had pioneered the ecological analysis of urban life.

Shaw and McKay began their analysis during a period in the city's history that was fairly typical of the transition that was taking place in many other urban areas. Chicago had experienced a mid-nineteenth-century population expansion, fueled by a dramatic influx of foreign-born immigrants and, later, migrating southern families. Congregating in the central city, the newcomers occupied the oldest housing areas and therefore faced numerous health and environmental hazards.

Sections of the city started to physically deteriorate. This condition prompted the city's wealthy, established citizens to become concerned about the moral fabric of Chicago society. The belief was widespread that immigrants from Europe and the rural South were crime prone and morally dissolute. In fact, local groups were created with the very purpose of "saving" the children of poor families from moral decadence.[24] It was popular to view crime as the property of inferior racial and ethnic groups.

Transitional neighborhoods Shaw and McKay explained crime and delinquency within the context of the changing urban environment and ecological development of the city. They saw that Chicago had developed into distinct neighborhoods (natural areas), some affluent and others wracked by extreme poverty. These poverty-ridden, **transitional neighborhoods** suffered high rates of population turnover and were incapable of inducing residents to remain and defend the neighborhoods against criminal groups.

Low rents in these areas attracted groups with different racial and ethnic backgrounds. Newly arrived immigrants from Europe and the South congregated in these transitional neighborhoods. Their children were torn between assimilating into a new culture and abiding by the traditional values of their parents. They soon found that informal social control mechanisms that had restrained behavior in the "old country" or rural areas were disrupted. These urban areas were believed to be the spawning grounds of young criminals.

In transitional areas, successive changes in the population composition, disintegration of traditional cultures, diffusion of divergent cultural standards, and gradual industrialization of the area result in dissolution of neighborhood culture and organization. The continuity of conventional neighborhood traditions and institutions is broken, leaving children feeling displaced and without a strong or definitive set of values.

Concentric zones Shaw and McKay identified the areas in Chicago that had excessive crime rates. Using a model of analysis pioneered by Ernest Burgess, they noted that distinct ecological areas had developed in the city, comprising a series of five concentric circles, or zones, and that there were stable and significant differences in interzone

---

Figure 7.3 Social Disorganization Theory

Poverty
- Development of isolated lower-class areas
- Lack of conventional social opportunities
- Racial and ethnic discrimination

Social disorganization
- Breakdown of social institutions and organizations such as school and family
- Lack of informal social control

Breakdown of social control
- Development of gangs, groups
- Peer group replaces family and social institutions

Criminal areas
- Neighborhood becomes crime-prone
- Stable pockets of crime develop
- Lack of external support and investment

Cultural transmission
Adults pass norms (focal concerns) to younger generation, creating stable lower-class culture

Criminal careers
Most youths "age out" of delinquency, marry, and raise families, but some remain in life of crime

crime rates (see Figure 7.4). The areas of heaviest concentration of crime appeared to be the transitional inner-city zones, where large numbers of foreign-born citizens had recently settled.[25] The zones farthest from the city's center had correspondingly lower crime rates.

Analysis of these data indicated a surprisingly stable pattern of criminal activity in the five ecological zones over a 65-year period. Shaw and McKay concluded that, in the transitional neighborhoods, multiple cultures and diverse values, both conventional and deviant, coexist. Children growing up in the street culture often find that adults who have adopted a deviant lifestyle are the most financially successful people in the neighborhood: for example, the gambler, the pimp, or the drug dealer. Required to choose between conventional and deviant lifestyles, many slum kids see the value in opting for the latter. They join other like-minded youths and form law-violating gangs and cliques. The development of teenage law-violating groups is an essential element of youthful misbehavior in slum areas. The values that slum youths adopt are often in conflict with existing middle-class norms, which demand strict obedience to the legal code. Consequently, a value conflict occurs that sets the delinquent youth and his or her peer group even further apart from conventional society. The result is a more solid embrace of deviant goals and behavior. To justify their choice of goals, these youths seek support by recruiting new members and passing on the delinquent tradition.

Shaw and McKay's statistical analysis confirmed their theoretical suspicions. Even though crime rates changed, they found that the highest rates were always in Zones I and II (central city and a transitional area). The areas with the highest crime rates retained high rates even when their ethnic composition changed (in the areas Shaw and McKay examined, from German and Irish to Italian and Polish).[26]

The legacy of Shaw and McKay   Social disorganization concepts articulated by Shaw and McKay have remained prominent within criminology for more than 75 years. Most important among Shaw and McKay's findings was that crime rates corresponded to neighborhood structure and that crime is a creature of the destructive ecological conditions in urban slums. Their contention was that criminals are not, as some criminologists of the time believed, biologically inferior, intellectually impaired, or psychologically damaged. Their research supported their belief that crime is a constant fixture in areas of poverty regardless of the racial or ethnic identity of its residents. Because the basis of their theory was that neighborhood disintegration and slum conditions are the primary causes of criminal behavior, Shaw and McKay paved the way for the many community action and treatment programs developed in the last half-century.

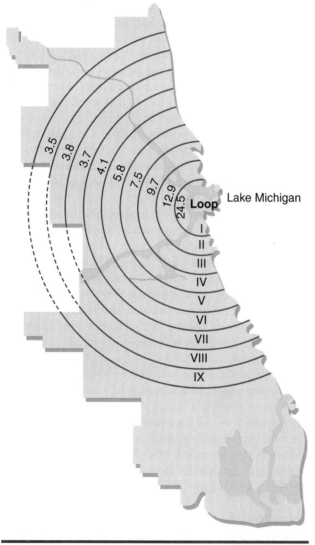

Figure 7.4   Shaw and McKay's Concentric Zones Map of Chicago

3.5 3.8 3.7 4.1 5.8 7.5 9.7 12.9 24.5

Loop   Lake Michigan

I
II
III
IV
V
VI
VII
VIII
IX

NOTE: Arabic numerals represent the rate of male delinquency.

SOURCE: Clifford R. Shaw et al., *Delinquency Areas* (Chicago: University of Chicago Press, 1929), p. 99. Reprinted with permission. Copyright 1929 by the University of Chicago. All rights reserved.

> ## CONNECTIONS
>
> Shaw was the founder of one very influential community-based treatment program, the Chicago Area Project, which will be discussed later in this chapter. The Chicago Area Project was the forerunner of many neighborhood revitalization programs that have been attempted since the 1960s. ■

Another important feature of Shaw and McKay's work is that it depicted both adult criminality and delinquent gang memberships as a normal response to the adverse social conditions in urban slum areas. Their findings mirror Émile Durkheim's concept that crime can be normal and useful.

Despite these noteworthy achievements, the validity of Shaw and McKay's findings have been challenged. Some have faulted their assumption that neighborhoods are essentially stable, and others have found their definition of social disorganization confusing.[27] The most important criticism, however, concerns their use of police records to calculate neighborhood crime rates. A zone's high crime rate may be a function of the level of local police surveillance and not interzone crime rate differences. Numerous studies indicate that police use extensive discretion when arresting people and that social status is one factor that influences their decisions.[28] It is possible that people in middle-class neighborhoods commit many criminal acts that never show up in official statistics, whereas people in lower-class areas face a far greater chance of arrest and court adjudication.[29] The relationship between ecology and crime rates, therefore, may reflect police behavior more than criminal behavior.

These criticisms aside, Shaw and McKay's theory provides a valuable contribution to our understanding of the causes of criminal behavior. By introducing a new variable—the ecology of the city—to the study of crime, they paved the way for a whole generation of criminologists to focus on the social influences of criminal and delinquent behavior.

The Social Ecology School

During the 1970s, criminologists were influenced by several critical analyses of the social disorganization theory, which presented well-thought-out challenges to its validity.[30] During this period, theories with a social-psychological orientation stressed offender socialization within the family, school, and peer group. These ideas dominated the criminological literature of that time.

Despite its "fall from grace," the social disorganization tradition was kept alive by "area studies" conducted by Bernard Lander in Baltimore, David Bordua in Detroit, and Roland Chilton in Indianapolis. These studies showed that such ecological conditions as substandard housing, low income, and unrelated people living together predicted a high incidence of delinquency.[31]

Beginning in the 1980s, a group of criminologists began to study ecological conditions, reviving concern about the effects of social disorganization.[32] These modern-day social ecologists developed a "purer" form of structural theory that emphasizes the association of community deterioration and economic decline to criminality but places less emphasis on value conflict. In the following sections, some of the more recent social ecological research is discussed in detail.

Community deterioration Crime rates have been associated with community deterioration: disorder, poverty, alienation, disassociation, and fear of crime.[33] For example, neighborhoods with a high percentage of deserted houses and apartments experience high crime rates; abandoned buildings serve as a "magnet for crime."[34] Areas in which houses are in poor repair, boarded-up and burned out, and whose owners are best described as "slumlords" are also the location of the highest violence rates and gun crime.[35] These are neighborhoods in which retail establishments often go bankrupt, are abandoned, and deteriorate physically.[36]

The concept of community deterioration and crime was the subject of a famous *Atlantic Magazine* article titled "Broken Windows," read it at:
> **http://www.theatlantic.com/politics/crime/windows.htm**
For an up-to-date list of Web links, go to
> **http://info.wadsworth.com/siegel** ■

Poverty concentration One aspect of community change may be the concentration of poverty in deteriorated neighborhoods. Although poverty rates or unemployment may not be a direct cause of crime, areas that are the most deteriorated, even within the context of inner-city poverty, seem to have much higher crime rates than more stable lower-class environments. William Julius Wilson describes how working- and middle-class families flee inner-city poverty areas, resulting in a **concentration effect,** in which elements of the most disadvantaged population are consolidated in urban ghettos. As the working and middle classes move out, they take with them their financial and institutional resources and support. Businesses are disinclined to locate in poverty areas; banks become reluctant to lend money for new housing or businesses.[37] Minority group members living in these areas also suffer race-based inequality such as income inequality and institutional racism.[38] Areas marked by concentrated poverty become isolated and insulated from the social mainstream and more prone to criminal activity and violence.[39]

The concentration effect contradicts, in some measure, Shaw and McKay's assumption that crime rates increase in transitional neighborhoods. Today, the areas that may be the most crime prone may be stable, homogenous areas whose residents are "trapped" in public housing and urban ghettos. Ethnically and racially isolated areas maintain the highest crime rates.[40]

CONNECTIONS

Later in this chapter the gang problem will be discussed in some detail. Today there are more than 500,000 gang members in the United States, a constant reminder of the nagging social problems found in disorganized inner-city neighborhoods. ■

Employment opportunities The relationship between unemployment and crime is still unsettled: aggregate crime rates and aggregate unemployment rates seem weakly related. In other words, crime rates sometimes rise during periods of economic prosperity and fall during periods of economic decline.[41] Yet, as Shaw and McKay claimed, neighborhoods that are continually wracked by unemployment also experience social disorganization and crime. Even though short-term economic trends may have little effect on crime,[42] it is possible that long-term unemployment rates will eventually produce higher levels of antisocial behaviors.[43]

Unemployment destabilizes households, and unstable families are the ones most likely to produce children who put a premium on violence and aggression as a means of dealing with limited opportunity. This lack of opportunity perpetuates higher crime rates, especially when large groups or cohorts of people of the same age compete for relatively scant resources.[44]

Limited employment opportunities also reduce the stabilizing influence of parents and other adults, who may have once been able to counteract the allure of youth gangs. Sociologist Elijah Anderson's analysis of Philadelphia neighborhood life found that "old heads" (respected neighborhood residents) who at one time played an important role in socializing youth have been displaced by younger street hustlers and drug dealers. While the old heads complain that these newcomers may not have "earned" or "worked for" their fortune in the "old-fashioned way," the old heads admire and envy these kids whose gold chains and luxury cars advertise their wealth amid poverty.[45] The old heads may admire the fruits of crime, but they disdain the violent manner in which it was acquired.

Community fear Disorganized neighborhoods suffer social and physical incivilities—rowdy youth, trash and litter, graffiti, abandoned storefronts, burned-out buildings, littered lots, strangers, drunks, vagabonds, loiterers, prostitutes, noise, congestion, angry words, dirt, and stench. The presence of such incivilities, especially when accom-

■ Residents in disorganized neighborhoods suffer social and physical isolation and experience a great deal of fear. People dread leaving their homes at night and withdraw from community life. Those who have already been victimized are more fearful of the future than those who have escaped crime.

panied by relatively high crime rates, convinces residents that their neighborhood is dangerous and that they face a considerable chance of becoming crime victims.[46]

Fear can become contagious. People tell others when they have been victimized, spreading the word that the neighborhood is getting dangerous and that the chances of future victimization is high.[47] As a result, people dread leaving their homes at night and withdraw from community life. Not surprisingly, people who have already been victimized are more fearful of the future than those who have escaped crime.[48]

CONNECTIONS

Fear of repeat victimization may be both instinctual and accurate. Remember that in Chapter 4 we discussed the fact that some people may be "victim prone" and fated to suffer repeated victimization over the life course. ■

When people live in areas where the death rates are high and life expectancies are short, they may alter their behavior out of fear. They may feel, "Why plan for the future when there is a significant likelihood that I may never see it?" In such areas, young boys and girls may psychologically assimilate by taking risks and discounting the future. Teenage birth rates soar and so do violence rates.[49] For these children, the inevitability of death skews their perspective of how they live their lives.

Fear is a powerful influence. When it grips a neighborhood, business conditions begin to deteriorate, population mobility increases, and a "criminal element" begins to drift into the area.[50] In essence, the existence of fear incites more crime, increasing the chances of victimization, producing even more fear, in a never-ending loop.[51] Fear is often associated with other community-level factors:

Race and fear: Fear of crime is also bound up in anxiety over racial and ethnic conflicts. Fear becomes most pronounced in areas undergoing rapid and unexpected racial and age-composition changes, especially when they are out of proportion to the rest of the city.[52] Whites become particularly fearful when they sense that they are becoming a racial minority in their neighborhood; African Americans seem less affected by racial change.[53] The fear experienced by whites may be based on racial stereotypes, but it may also be caused by the premonition that they will become less well protected because police do not provide adequate services in predominantly African American neighborhoods.[54]

Whites are not the only group to experience race-based fear. Fear can be found among other racial and ethnic groups, especially when they believe they are in the minority and vulnerable to attack. For example, recent research conducted in Florida by Ted Chiricos and his associates found that whites are threatened by Hispanics and blacks, but only in South Florida where whites are outnumbered by those two groups; in contrast, Hispanics are threatened by African Americans, but only outside of South Florida where Hispanics are the minority.[55]

Gangs and fear: Gangs flourish in deteriorated neighborhoods with high levels of poverty, lack of investment, high unemployment rates, and population turnover.[56] Unlike any other crime, however, gang activity is frequently undertaken out in the open, on the public ways, and in full view of the rest of the community.[57] Brazen criminal activity undermines community solidarity because it signals that the police must be either corrupt or inept. The fact that gangs are willing to openly engage in drug sales and other types of criminal activity shows their confidence that they have silenced or intimidated law-abiding persons in their midst. The police and the community alike become hopeless about their ability to restore community stability, producing greater levels of community fear.

To read more about the illegal activities of male and female gang members, use InfoTrac College Edition to access this article: John Hagedorn, Jose Torres, and Greg Giglio. Cocaine, kicks, and strain: patterns of substance use in Milwaukee gangs. *Contemporary Drug Problems* Spring 1998 v25 n1 p113–45 ■

Mistrust and fear: People who report living in neighborhoods with high levels of crime and civil disorder become suspicious and mistrusting.[58] They develop a sense of powerlessness, which amplifies the effect of neighborhood disorder and increases levels of mistrust. Some residents become so suspicious of authority that they develop a **siege mentality** in which the outside world is considered the enemy out to destroy the neighborhood. Elijah Anderson found that residents in the African American neighborhoods he studied believed in the existence of a secret plan to eradicate the population by such strategies as permanent unemployment, police brutality, imprisonment, drug distribution, and AIDS.[59] White officials and political leaders were believed to have hatched this conspiracy, and it was demonstrated by the lax law enforcement efforts in poor areas. Residents felt that police cared little about black-on-black crime because it helped reduce the population. Rumors abounded that federal government agencies, such as the CIA, controlled the drug trade and used profits to fund illegal overseas operations.

This siege mentality results in mistrust of critical social institutions, including business, government, and schools. Government officials seem arrogant and haughty. Residents become self-conscious, worried about garnering any respect, and are particularly attuned to anyone who disrespects or "disses" them. Considering this feeling of mistrust, when police ignore crime in poor areas or, conversely, when they are violent and corrupt, anger flares, and people take to the streets and react in violent ways.

Community change In our postmodern society, urban areas undergoing rapid structural changes in racial and economic composition also seem to experience the greatest change in crime rates. Recent studies recognize that change, not stability, is the hallmark of inner-city areas. A neighborhood's residents, wealth, density, and purpose are constantly evolving. Even disorganized neighborhoods acquire new identifying features. Some may become multiracial, while others become racially homogeneous. Some areas become stable and family-oriented, while in others, mobile, never-married people predominate.[60]

As areas decline, residents flee to safer, more stable localities. Those who can't leave because they cannot afford to live in more affluent communities face an increased risk of victimization. Because of racial differences in economic well-being, those "left behind" are all too often minority citizens.[61] Those who can't move find themselves surrounded by a constant influx of new residents. High population turnover can have a devastating effect on community culture because it thwarts communication and information flow.[62] In response to this turnover, a culture may develop that dictates standards of dress, language, and behavior to neighborhood youth that are in opposition to those of conventional society. All these factors are likely to produce increased crime rates.

The cycles of community change   During periods of population turnover, communities may undergo changes that undermine their infrastructure. Urban areas seem to have life cycles, which begin with building residential dwellings and are followed by a period of decline, with marked decreases in socioeconomic status and increases in population density.[63] Later stages in this life cycle include changing racial or ethnic makeup, population thinning, and finally, a renewal stage in which obsolete housing is replaced and upgraded (**gentrification**). Areas undergoing such change seem to experience an increase in their crime rates.[64]

To learn more about the effects of gentrification, use "housing rehabilitation" as a key word on InfoTrac College Edition. ■

As communities go through cycles, neighborhood deterioration precedes increasing rates of crime and delinquency.[65] Neighborhoods most at risk for crime rate increases contain large numbers of single-parent families and unrelated people living together, have gone from having owner-occupied to renter-occupied units, and have an economic base that has lost semiskilled and unskilled jobs (indicating a growing residue of discouraged workers who are no longer seeking employment).[66] These ecological disruptions strain existing social control mechanisms and inhibit their ability to control crime and delinquency.

A large body of research shows that changing lifestyles—including declining economic status, increasing population, and racial shifts—are associated with increased neighborhood crime rates.[67] Areas adjoining neighborhoods undergoing racial change will experience corresponding increases in their own crime rates.[68] This phenomenon may reflect community reaction to perceived racial conflict. In changing neighborhoods, adults may actually encourage the law-violating behavior of youths. They may express attitudes that justify violence as a means of protecting their property and way of life by violently resisting newcomers.

Collective efficacy   Most neighborhood residents share the common goal of living in a crime-free area. Some communities have the power to regulate the behavior of their residents through the influence of community institutions, such as the family and school. Communities that are cohesive and maintain high levels of social control develop **collective efficacy**—mutual trust and a willingness to intervene in the supervision of children and the maintenance

of public order.[69] It is the cohesion among neighborhood residents combined with shared expectations for informal social control of public space that promotes collective efficacy.[70] Communities with high collective efficacy generally experience low violence rates and low levels of physical and social disorder (for example, drinking in the street, spray-painting graffiti, and breaking windows). In contrast, neighborhoods with low collective efficacy suffer high rates of violence and significant physical and social disorder. Local organizations designed to control crime, such as neighborhood associations, may only be effective if they promote a sense of collective efficacy.[71] Moreover, it is rare to find neighborhoods with high collective efficacy surrounded by communities with low collective efficacy. This suggests that spillover effects extend beyond the geographic boundaries of a single neighborhood. There are actually three forms of collective efficacy:

Informal social control: Some elements of collective efficacy operate on the primary or private level and involve peers, families, and relatives. These sources exert informal control by either awarding or withholding approval, respect, and admiration. Informal control mechanisms include direct criticism, ridicule, ostracism, desertion, or physical punishment.[72] For example, families may exert control by corporal punishment, withholding privileges, or ridiculing lazy or disrespectful children.

In some neighborhoods, neighbors are willing to practice informal social control through surveillance practices: for example, by keeping an "eye out" for intruders when their neighbors go out of town. Informal surveillance has been found to reduce the levels of some crimes such as street robberies; however, if robbery rates remain high, surveillance may be terminated because people become fearful for their safety.[73]

Institutional social control: Social institutions such as schools and churches cannot work effectively in a climate of alienation and mistrust. Unsupervised peer groups and gangs, which flourish in disorganized areas, disrupt the influence of those neighborhood control agents that do exist.[74] Children who reside in these neighborhoods find that involvement with conventional social institutions, such as schools and afternoon programs, is blocked; they are instead at risk for recruitment into gangs and law-violating groups.[75] As crime flourishes, neighborhood fear increases, which in turn decreases a community's cohesion and thwarts the ability of its institutions to exert social control over its residents.[76]

To combat these influences, communities that have collective efficacy attempt to use their local institutions to control crime. Sources of institutional social control include businesses, stores, schools, churches, and social service and volunteer organizations.[77] Some institutions, such as recreation centers for teens, have been found to lower crime rates because they exert a positive effect; others, such as taverns and bars, can help destabilize neighborhoods and increase the rate of violent crimes such as rape and robbery.[78]

Public social control: Stable neighborhoods are also able to arrange for external sources of social control. If they can draw on outside help and secure external resources—a process referred to as public social control—they are better able to reduce the effects of disorganization and maintain lower levels of crime and victimization.[79] The level of policing, one of the primary sources of public social control, may vary between neighborhoods. The police presence is typically greatest when community organizations and local leaders have sufficient political clout to get funding for additional law enforcement personnel. The presence of police sends a message that the area will not tolerate deviant behavior. Because they can respond vigorously to crime, police prevent criminal groups from gaining a toehold in the neighborhood.[80] Criminals and drug dealers avoid such areas and relocate to easier and more appealing "targets."[81]

In more disorganized areas, the absence of political power brokers limits access to external funding and protection. Without money from the outside, the neighborhood lacks the ability to "get back on its feet."[82] In these areas, there are fewer police and those that do patrol the area are less motivated and their resources are stretched more tightly. These communities cannot mount an effective social control effort because, as neighborhood disadvantage increases, the level of informal social control decreases.[83]

The effects of collective efficacy The effects of collective efficacy are critical. In areas where collective efficacy is sufficient, children are less likely to become involved with deviant peers and engage in problem behaviors.[84] In disorganized areas, however, the population is transient so interpersonal relationships remain superficial.

When social control is weak, there may be an overreliance on formal punishment, such as arrest and prosecution, to control offenders, a situation that helps destabilize neighborhoods by putting many of its residents behind bars. This phenomenon is the subject of the Policy and Practice in Criminology feature titled "The Reentry Blues."

Social support/altruism Neighborhoods that can provide strong social supports for their members can help young people cope with life's stressors. Sometimes this is organized on the block level where neighbors meet face to face to deal with problems. Crime rates may be lower on

■ Neighborhoods that can provide strong social supports for their members can help young people cope with life's stressors. Here a police officer in Minot, North Dakota, works with kids by teaching them about forensic science.

AP/Wide World Photos

The Reentry Blues: Problems with Locking People Up and Then Letting Them Go

America is undergoing an incarceration boom, and the prison population is now well over one million. Criminologists Dina Rose and Todd Clear suggest that this imprisonment boom may have unforeseen effects on neighborhood stability. They maintain that imprisonment damages local and neighborhood levels of informal social control. By putting many parents in prison, the justice system is undermining the family, which is the primary source of informal social control. High levels of incarceration also undermine social, political, and economic systems, which are already weak in disorganized areas. Even though convicted criminals may not have been ideal parents, they do contribute to the financial support of their children, although they may provide fewer dollars than noncriminals. Families undergo increased stress if a parent is incarcerated; they are often forced to go on public assistance to survive. There is an increasing amount of literature indicating that family disruption and parental absence can have negative consequences for children. Losing a parent to state custody enhances the odds that children will engage in antisocial adolescent behaviors. Children who enter a life of crime as a result of a parent's incarceration may more than counterbalance the crime-reducing effect of incarcerating the parent.

Incarcerated adults are typically underemployed, but most do engage in some legitimate work, which they then supplement with their criminal activity. When they are incarcerated, this takes a worker from the neighborhood economy. Although another family may reap the benefit of the new employment opportunity, overall the community suffers a net loss of depleted economic strength. The incarcerated offender is neither bringing in outside resources (for example, state welfare money) nor consuming in the local economy. Instead, the offender is providing new jobs for correctional workers in upstate rural economies. The prison construction boom has artificially amplified the economy of rural communities while the urban economy has suffered deflation. The result is an increasing sense of income inequality, a condition often related to high crime rates.

Many incarcerated adults come from a relatively few urban neighborhoods. Removing large numbers of people from these already depleted areas adds to the neighborhood disorder. There are fewer adults to protect and support families. Then, when ex-offenders are released and returned to these neighborhoods, unemployed and angry, their contribution is adding yet another unemployed person to the economic instability. Because imprisonment hinders future employment possibilities, an important economic asset to the community is lost forever. Consequently, the more the prison system grows, the more it contributes to decay in the neighborhoods.

The Reentry Blues

Ironically, not only does a high incarceration rate undermine a community, so too does a high reentry rate! Because of America's two-decade-long imprisonment boom, more than 500,000 inmates are now being released into the community each year. Criminologist Joan Petersilia warns that there are a number of unfortunate collateral consequences of releasing people back into the community, many of whom have not received adequate treatment and are unprepared for life in conventional society. The risks they present to the community include increases in child abuse, family violence, spread of infectious diseases, homelessness, and community disorganization.

Reentry risks have increased and can be tied to legal changes in the way people are released from prison. In the past, offenders were granted early release only if a parole board believed they were rehabilitated and had ties to the community, such as a family or a job. Inmates were encouraged to enter treatment programs to earn parole. Changes in sentencing laws have resulted in the growth of mandatory release and limits on discretionary parole. People now serve a fixed sentence, and the discretion of parole boards has been blunted. Inmates may be discouraged from seeking involvement in rehabilitation programs (they do not influence the chance of parole), and the lack of incentive means that fewer inmates leaving prison having participated in programs to address work, education, and substance use deficiencies. For example, only 13 percent of inmates

blocks where people are committed to preserving their immediate environment by confronting destabilizing forces such as teen gangs and encouraging others to do so also.[85] By helping neighbors become more resilient and self-confident, adults in these areas can provide the external support systems that enable youth to desist from crime. For example, residents can teach one another that they have moral and social obligations to their fellow citizens; children can learn to be sensitive to the rights of others and

to respect differences. Residents may form neighborhood associations and self-help groups. In contrast, less altruistic areas stress individualism and self-interest.

Areas that place a greater stress on caring for fellow citizens are less crime prone than those that emphasize self-reliance. Even in the cities poorest areas, if people are generous and caring, their neighborhoods are also relatively crime free. **Social altruism** (for example, indications of generosity such as the ratio of contributions given to

who suffer addiction receive any kind of drug abuse treatment in prison. Nor does the situation improve upon release. Many inmates are not assigned to supervision caseloads once released into the community; about 100,000 released inmates go unsupervised each year.

Petersilia argues that offenders may increase their criminal activity once they are back in the community because they want to "make up for lost time" and resume their criminal careers. The majority leave prison with no savings, no immediate entitlement to unemployment benefits, and few employment prospects. One year after release, as many as 60 percent of former inmates are not employed in the regular labor market, and there is increasing reluctance among employers to hire ex-offenders. Unemployment is closely related to drug and alcohol abuse. Losing a job can lead to substance abuse, which in turn is related to child and family violence. Mothers released from prison have difficulty finding services such as housing, employment, and child care, and this causes stress for them and their children. Children of incarcerated and released parents often suffer confusion, sadness, and social stigma, and these feelings may result in school-related difficulties, low self-esteem, aggressive behavior, and general emotional dysfunction. If the parents are negative role models, children fail to develop positive attitudes about work and responsibility. Children of incarcerated parents are five times more likely to serve time in prison than are children whose parents are not incarcerated.

Prisoners have significantly more medical and mental health problems than the general population due to lifestyles that often include crowded or itinerant living conditions, intravenous drug use, poverty, and high rates of substance abuse. Inmates with mental illness (about 16 percent of all inmates) also are increasingly being imprisoned—and being released. Even when public mental health services are available, many mentally ill individuals fail to use them because they fear institutionalization, deny they are mentally ill, or distrust the mental health system. The situation will become more serious as more and more parolees are released back into the disorganized communities whose deteriorated conditions may have motivated their original crimes.

Fear of a prison stay has less of an impact on behavior than ever before. As the prison population grows, the negative impact of incarceration may be lessening. In neighborhoods where "doing time" is more a rule than the exception, it becomes less of a stigma and more of a badge of acceptance. It also becomes a way of life from which some ex-convicts do rebound. Teens may encounter older men who have gone to prison and have returned to begin their lives again. With the proper skills and survival techniques, prison is considered "manageable." A prison stay is still unpleasant, but it has lost the aura of shame and fear. By becoming commonplace and mundane, the "myth" and fear of the prison experience has been exposed and its deterrent power reduced.

Critical Thinking Questions

1. All too often, government leaders jump on the incarceration bandwagon as a panacea for the nation's crime problem. Is it a "quick fix" whose long-term consequences may be devastating for the nation's cities, or are Professor Clear's concerns counterbalanced by the positive effect of putting large numbers of high-rate offenders behind bars?

2. If you agree that incarceration undermines neighborhoods, can you think of some other indirect ways high incarceration rates help increase crime rates?

InfoTrac College Edition Research

Alternatives to prison are now being sought because high incarceration may undermine a community's viability. What do you think? For some interesting developments, check out these articles:

Joe Loconte. Making criminals pay: a New York county's bold experiment in biblical justice. *Policy Review* Jan–Feb 1998 n87 p26

Katarina Ivanko. Shifting gears to rehabilitation. *Corrections Today* April 1997 v59 n2 p20

SOURCES: Joan Petersilia, "When Prisoners Return to Communities: Political, Economic, and Social Consequences" *Federal Probation* 65 (2001): 3–9; Dina Rose and Todd Clear, "Incarceration, Social Capital, and Crime: Implications for Social Disorganization Theory," *Criminology* 36 (1998): 441–79; Todd Clear, "Backfire: When Incarceration Increases Crime," *Journal of the Oklahoma Criminal Justice Research Consortium* 3 (1996): 7–17.

the United Way charity by area income levels) has been found to be inversely related to crime rates.[86] This relationship can be interpreted in one of two ways: either crime rates are lower in altruistic areas because of the overall positive social climate, or well-funded charities in these areas help lower crime rates by providing a secure safety net for "at-risk" families.

The government can also be a force for social altruism by providing economic and social supports through publicly funded social support and welfare programs. Welfare programs are often criticized by conservative politicians as being "government handouts," but there is evidence of a significant negative association between the amount of welfare money people receive and crime rates.[87] Government assistance may help people improve their social status by providing them with the financial resources to clothe, feed, and educate their children while at the same time reducing stress, frustration, and anger.

People living in disorganized areas may also be able to draw on resources from their neighbors in more affluent surrounding communities, helping to keep crime rates down.[88] This phenomenon may explain, in part, why violence rates are high in poor African American neighborhoods cut off from outside areas for support.[89]

According to the social ecology school, then, the quality of community life, including levels of change, fear, incivility, poverty, and deterioration, has a direct influence on an area's crime rate. It is not some individual property or trait that causes people to commit crime but the quality and ambience of the community in which they reside. Conversely, in areas that have high levels of social control and collective efficacy, crime rates have been shown to decrease—no matter what the economic situation.

Strain Theories

Inhabitants of a disorganized inner-city area feel isolated, frustrated, ostracized from the economic mainstream, hopeless, and eventually angry and enraged. What effect do these feelings have on criminal activities?

Criminologists who view crime as a direct result of lower-class frustration and anger are referred to as **strain theorists.** They believe that most people share similar values and goals but that the ability to achieve personal goals is stratified by socioeconomic class. Strain is limited in affluent areas because educational and vocational opportunities are available. In disorganized areas, strain occurs because legitimate avenues for success are all but closed. To relieve strain, indigent people may be forced either to use deviant methods to achieve their goals, such as theft or drug trafficking, or to reject socially accepted goals outright and substitute other, more deviant goals, such as being tough and aggressive (Figure 7.5).

The Definition of Anomie

The roots of strain theories can be traced to Émile Durkheim's notion of **anomie** (from the Greek *a nomos,* without norms). According to Durkheim, an anomic society is one in which rules of behavior (norms) have broken down or become inoperative during periods of rapid social change or social crisis such as war or famine. An anomic society is not able to control human aspirations and demands. Anomie is most likely to occur in societies that are moving from mechanical to organic solidarity. **Mechanical solidarity** is a characteristic of a pre-industrial society, which is held together by traditions, shared values, and unquestioned beliefs. In postindustrial social systems, which are highly developed and dependent upon the division of labor, people are connected by their interdependent needs for each other's services and production (**organic solidarity**). The shift in traditions and values creates social turmoil. Established norms begin to erode and lose

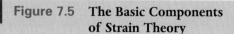

Figure 7.5 The Basic Components of Strain Theory

Poverty
- Development of isolated lower-class culture
- Lack of conventional social opportunities
- Racial and ethnic discrimination

Maintenance of conventional rules and norms
Residents of lower-class areas remain loyal to conventional values and rules of dominant middle-class culture.

Strain
Lack of opportunity coupled with desire for conventional success produces strain and frustration.

Formation of gangs and groups
Youths form law-violating groups to seek alternative means of achieving success.

Crime and delinquency
Methods of groups—theft, violence, substance abuse—are defined as illegal by dominant culture.

Criminal careers
Most youths "age out" of delinquency, marry, and raise families, but some remain in life of crime

meaning. If a division occurs between what the population expects and what the economic and productive forces of society can realistically deliver, a crisis situation develops which can manifest itself in normlessness or anomie.

To read more about the work of Émile Durkheim, go to:
http://www.hewett.norfolk.sch.uk/curric/soc/ durkheim/durk.htm
For an up-to-date list of Web links, go to
http://info.wadsworth.com/siegel

Anomie undermines society's social control function. Every society works to limit people's goals and desires. If a society becomes anomic, it can no longer establish and maintain control over its population's wants and desires. Since people find it difficult to control their appetites, their demands become unlimited. Under these circumstances, obeying legal codes may be strained, and alternative behavior choices, such as crimes, may be inevitable.

Theory of Anomie

Durkheim's ideas were applied to criminology in by sociologist Robert Merton in his **theory of anomie.**[90] Merton used a modified version of the concept of anomie to fit social, economic, and cultural conditions found in modern U.S. society.[91] He found that two elements of culture interact to produce potentially anomic conditions: culturally defined goals and socially approved means for obtaining them. For example, U.S. society stresses the goals of acquiring wealth, success, and power. Socially permissible means include hard work, education, and thrift.

In the United States, Merton argued, legitimate means to acquire wealth are stratified across class and status lines. Those with little formal education and few economic resources soon find that they are denied the ability to legally acquire wealth—the preeminent success symbol. When socially mandated goals are uniform throughout society and access to legitimate means is bound by class and status, the resulting strain produces anomie among those who are locked out of the legitimate opportunity structure. Consequently, they may develop criminal or delinquent solutions to the problem of attaining goals.

Social adaptations Merton argued that each person has his or her own concept of the goals of society and the means at his or her disposal to attain them. Whereas some people have inadequate means of attaining success, others who do have the means reject societal goals as being unsuited to them. Table 7.1 shows Merton's diagram of the hypothetical relationship between social goals, the means for getting them, and the individual actor. Here is a brief description of each of these modes of adaptation.

> **Conformity:** Conformity occurs when individuals both embrace conventional social goals and also have the means at their disposal to attain them. In a bal-

anced, stable society, this is the most common social adaptation. If a majority of its people did not practice conformity, the society would cease to exist.

Innovation: Innovation occurs when an individual accepts the goals of society but rejects or is incapable of attaining them through legitimate means. Many people desire material goods and luxuries but lack the financial ability to attain them. The resulting conflict forces them to adopt innovative solutions to their dilemma: they steal, sell drugs, or extort money. Of the five adaptations, innovation is most closely associated with criminal behavior.

If successful, innovation can have serious, long-term social consequences. Criminal success helps convince otherwise law-abiding people that innovative means work better and faster than conventional ones. The prosperous drug dealer's expensive car and flashy clothes give out the message that "crime pays." Merton claims, "The process thus enlarges the extent of anomie within the system, so that others, who did not respond in the form of deviant behavior to the relatively slight anomie which they first obtained, come to do so as anomie is spread and is intensified."[92] This explains why crime is initiated and sustained in certain low-income ecological areas.

Ritualism: Ritualists gain pleasure from practicing traditional ceremonies regardless of whether they have a real purpose or goal. The strict set of manners and customs in religious orders, feudal societies, clubs, and college fraternities encourage and appeal to ritualists. Ritualists should have the lowest level of criminal behavior because they have abandoned the success goal, which is at the root of criminal activity.

Retreatism: Retreatists reject both the goals and the means of society. Merton suggests that people who adjust in this fashion are "in the society but not of it." Included in this category are "psychotics, psychoneurotics, chronic autists, pariahs, outcasts, vagrants, vagabonds, tramps, chronic drunkards, and drug addicts." Because such people are morally or otherwise incapable of using both legitimate and illegitimate means, they attempt to escape their lack of success by withdrawing—either mentally or physically.

Rebellion: Rebellion involves substituting an alternative set of goals and means for conventional ones. Revolutionaries who wish to promote radical change in the existing social structure and who call for alternative lifestyles, goals, and beliefs are engaging in rebellion. Rebellion may be a reaction against a corrupt and hated government or an effort to create alternate opportunities and lifestyles within the existing system.

Table 7.1 Typology of Individual Modes of Adaptation

Modes of Adaptation	Cultural Goals	Institutionalized Means
I. Conformity	+	+
I. Innovation	+	−
II. Ritualism	−	+
V. Retreatism	−	−
V. Rebellion	±	±

SOURCE: Robert Merton, "Social Structure and Anomie," in *Social Theory and Social Structure* (Glencoe, Ill.: Free Press, 1957).

Evaluation of anomie theory According to anomie theory, social inequality leads to perceptions of anomie. To resolve the goals–means conflict and relieve their sense of strain, some people innovate by stealing or extorting money, others retreat into drugs and alcohol, others rebel by joining revolutionary groups, and still others get involved in ritualistic behavior by joining a religious cult. Merton's view of anomie has been one of the most enduring and influential sociological theories of criminality. By linking deviant behavior to the success goals that control social behavior, anomie theory attempts to pinpoint the cause of the conflict that produces personal frustration and consequent criminality. By acknowledging that society unfairly distributes the legitimate means to achieving success, anomie theory helps explain the existence of high-crime areas and the apparent predominance of delinquent and criminal behavior among the lower class. By suggesting that social conditions, not individual personalities, produce crime, Merton greatly influenced the direction taken to reduce and control criminality during the latter half of the twentieth century.

A number of questions are left unanswered by anomie theory.[93] Merton does not explain why people choose to commit certain types of crime. For example, why does one anomic person become a mugger and another deals drugs? Anomie may be used to explain differences in crime rates, but it cannot explain why most young criminals desist from crime as adults. Does this mean that perceptions of anomie dwindle with age? Is anomie short-lived?

Critics have also suggested that people pursue a number of different goals, including educational, athletic, and social success. Juveniles may be more interested in immediate goals, such as having an active social life or being a good athlete, than in long-term "ideal" achievements, such as monetary success. Achieving these goals is not a matter of social class alone; other factors, including athletic ability, intelligence, personality, and family life, can either hinder or assist goal attainment.[94] Anomie theory also assumes that all people share the same goals and values, which is false.[95] Because of these and other criticisms, the theory of anomie, along with other structural theories, fell into a period of decline for almost 20 years.

Anomie reconsidered Like other views of criminality that stressed the influence of the social structure, strain theories fell out of favor when criminologists turned their attention to social psychological views of criminality. Recently there has been a resurgence of interest in strain and anomie. Many Americans may be feeling anomic because of the economic displacement brought on by a shifting economy. The "truly disadvantaged" in society seem at grave risk to both normlessness and high crime rates. In addition, some researchers have begun to reexamine original concepts such as perceptions of anomie and have found that with more precise and valid measurements Merton's theory can in fact predict levels of criminal activity.[96] Cross-cultural research efforts have also linked anomic conditions to criminality, indicating that anomie is not unique to U.S. culture.[97]

Criminologists are now producing newer versions of Merton's visionary concepts. Some of these work on the general or macro level. They hold that the success goal integrated within American society influences the nature and extent of the aggregate crime rate. There are also individual or micro-level versions of the theory; these suggest that individuals who experience anomie are more likely to commit crime than those who are immune to feelings of strain or goal conflict. Each of these views is discussed in the sections that follow.

Institutional Anomie Theory

One addition to the strain literature is *Crime and the American Dream* by Steven Messner and Richard Rosenfeld.[98] Their macro-level version of anomie theory views antisocial behavior as a function of cultural and institutional influences in U.S. society. This is known as the **institutional anomie theory.**

Messner and Rosenfeld agree with Merton's view that the success goal is pervasive in American culture. They refer to this as the **American Dream,** a term they employ as both a goal and a process. As a goal, the American Dream involves accumulating material goods and wealth via open individual competition. As a process, it involves both being socialized to pursue material success and believing that prosperity is an achievable goal in American culture. In the United States, our capitalist system encourages innovation in pursuit of monetary rewards. Businesspeople such as Bill Gates, Warren Buffet, and Donald Trump are considered national heroes and leaders. Anomic conditions occur because the desire to succeed at any cost drives people apart, weakens the collective sense of community, fosters ambition, and restricts desires to achieve anything that isn't material wealth. Achieving a "good name" and respect is not sufficient.

What is distinct about American society, according to Messner and Rosenfeld, and what most likely determines the exceedingly high national crime rate, is that anomic conditions have been allowed to "develop to such an extraordinary degree."[99] There do not seem to be any alternatives that would serve the same purpose or strive for the same goal.

Impact of anomie Why does anomie pervade American culture? According to Messner and Rosenfeld, it is because institutions that might otherwise control the exaggerated emphasis on financial success, such as religious or charitable institutions, have been rendered powerless or obsolete.

There are three reasons social institutions have been undermined. First, noneconomic functions and roles have been devalued. Performance in other institutional settings—the family, school, or community—is assigned a lower priority than the goal of financial success. Second, when conflicts emerge, noneconomic roles become subordinate to and must accommodate economic roles. The schedules, routines, and demands of the workplace take priority over those of the home, the school, the community, and other aspects of social life. And third, economic language, standards, and norms penetrate into noneconomic realms. Economic terms become part of the common vernacular. People want to get to the "bottom line"; spouses view themselves as "partners" who "manage" the household. Retired people say they want to "downsize" their household; we "out source" home repairs instead of doing them ourselves. Corporate leaders run for public office promising to "run the country like a business."

According to Messner and Rosenfeld, the relatively high U.S. crime rates can be explained by the interrelationship between culture and institutions. At the cultural level, the dominance of the American Dream mythology ensures that many people will develop wishes and desires for material goods that cannot be satisfied by legitimate means. Anomie becomes a norm, and extra-legal means (crime) become a strategy for attaining material wealth. At the institutional level, the dominance of economic concerns weakens the informal social control exerted by the family, church, and school. These institutions have lost their ability to regulate behavior and have instead become a conduit for promoting material success. For example, schools are not evaluated for departing knowledge but for their ability to train students to get high-paying jobs. Social conditions reinforce each other in a never-ending loop: culture determines institutions, and institutional change influences culture. Crime rates may rise then in a healthy economy because national prosperity heightens the attractiveness of monetary rewards, encouraging people to gain financial success by any means possible, including illegal ones. Meanwhile, the importance of social institutions as a means of exerting social control is reduced. In this "culture of competition," self-interest prevails and generates amorality, acceptance of inequality, and disdain for the less fortunate.[100]

Supporting research A number of research efforts have found support for institutional anomie theory. Criminologists Mitchell Chamlin and John Cochran found that areas with high levels of church membership, lower levels of divorce, and high voter turnouts also enjoy lower crime rates. Strong institutional controls (family, church, and polity) may counteract the influence of economic deprivation, a finding in synch with institutional anomie theory.[101] In their analysis of survey data, Stephen Cernkovich and his associates found that people who valued the American Dream but failed to achieve economic success were crime prone. The effect was more substantial for whites than for African Americans. Cernkovich reasons that whites may have greater expectations of material success than African Americans, whose aspirations have been tempered by a long history of racial and economic deprivation. When whites experience strain, they are more apt to react with anger and antisocial behavior.[102]

The Messner-Rosenfeld version of anomie strain may be a blueprint for crime reduction strategies: if citizens are provided with an economic "safety net," they may be able to resist the influence of economic deprivation and commit less crime. Nations that provide such resources—welfare, pension benefits, health care—have significantly lower crime rates even though some of their citizens are beset by income inequality.[103]

To read research conducted by Messner and Rosenfeld on the utility of institutional anomie theory, use InfoTrac College Edition to access this article: Steven F. Messner and Richard Rosenfeld. Political restraint of the market and levels of criminal homicide: a cross-national application of institutional-anomie theory. *Social Forces* June 1997 v75 n4 p1393(24) ■

Relative Deprivation Theory

There is ample evidence that neighborhood-level income inequality is a significant predictor or neighborhood crime rates.[104] Sharp divisions between the rich and poor create an atmosphere of envy and mistrust. Criminal motivation is fueled both by perceived humiliation and the perceived right to humiliate a victim in return.[105] Psychologists warn that under these circumstances young males will begin to fear and envy "winners" who are doing very well at their expense. If they fail to take risky aggressive tactics, they are surely going to lose out in social competition and have little chance of future success.[106] These generalized feelings of **relative deprivation** are precursors to high crime rates.[107]

According to this view, lower-class people might feel both deprived and embittered when they compare their life circumstances to those of the more affluent. People who feel deprived because of their race or economic class standing eventually develop a sense of injustice and discontent. The less fortunate begin to distrust the society that has nurtured social inequality and obstructed their chances of progressing by legitimate means. The constant frustration that results from these feelings of inadequacy produces pent-up aggression and hostility and, eventually, leads to violence and crime. The effect of inequality may be greatest when the impoverished population believes they are becoming less able to compete in a society where the balance of economic and social power is shifting further toward the already affluent. Under these conditions, the likelihood that the relatively poor will choose illegitimate life enhancing activities will increase.[108] Ironically, if income inequality widens, crime rates may spiral upward even as the size of the indigent population is in decline.[109]

According to the relative deprivation view, a collective sense of social injustice directly related to income inequality tends to develop in communities or nations in which the poor and wealthy live in close proximity to one another. Adolescents raised in inner-city poverty areas, such as those in Boston, New York, Chicago, and Los Angeles, for example, experience frustration as they watch their neighborhood in comparison to the most affluent neighborhoods that are located in the same metropolitan area. Nor is relative deprivation unique to American cities.

Crime rates are high in underdeveloped nations that are also tourist havens. In the Caribbean, for example, their modest living standard becomes extremely frustrating to residents when significant numbers of affluent tourists arrive each year; this kind of frustration is often accompanied by high levels of property and violent crime.[110]

CONNECTIONS

It is possible that a sense of relative deprivation lowers self-esteem and leads people to seek methods to reduce their negative self-feelings. If conventional methods are unavailable to promote self-worth, they may seek out deviant modes of adaptation. For more on this view, see the sections on Howard Kaplan's self-enhancement theory in Chapter 8. ■

Relative deprivation is truly "relative." Even the most affluent Americans may feel deprived if they fail to achieve their lofty and unlimited goals.[111] Some affluent people may feel relatively deprived when they compare their accomplishments to those of their more successful peers. Their method for dealing with their feelings of deprivation may be to use illegal means to satisfy their "unrealistic" success goals.[112]

CONNECTIONS

Can relative deprivation concepts apply to white-collar crime? Perhaps some of the individuals involved in the savings and loan scandals or Wall Street stock fraud cases felt "relatively deprived" and socially frustrated when they compared the paltry few millions they had already accumulated with the hundreds of millions held by the "truly wealthy," whom they envied. For more on this issue, see the discussions in Chapter 13 on the causes of white-collar crime. ■

The relative deprivation model is important because it helps explain the ambiguous association between crime and the economy. It is possible that crime rates may increase even during an economic boom because some groups get left out of the job market. In contrast, during a recession, crime rates may fall because everyone is suffering and consequently there are relatively few of the "relatively deprived."

General Strain Theory

Sociologist Robert Agnew's **general strain theory (GST)** helps identify the micro-level or individual influences of strain. Whereas Merton tried to explain social class differences in the crime rate, Agnew tries to explain why individuals who feel stress and strain are more likely to commit crimes. Agnew also offers a more general explanation of criminal activity among all elements of society rather than restricting his views to lower-class crime.[113]

Multiple sources of stress   Agnew suggests that criminality is the direct result of **negative affective states**—the anger, frustration, and adverse emotions that emerge in the wake of negative and destructive social relationships. He finds that negative affective states are produced by a variety of sources of strain (Figure 7.6):

Failure to achieve positively valued goals: This category of strain, similar to what Merton speaks of in his theory of anomie, is a result of the disjunction between aspirations and expectations. This type of strain occurs when a youth aspires for wealth and fame but, lacking financial and educational resources, assumes that such goals are impossible to achieve.

Disjunction of expectations and achievements: Strain can also be produced when there is a disjunction between expectations and achievements. When people compare themselves to peers who seem to be doing a lot better financially or socially (such as making more money or getting better grades), even those doing relatively well feel strain. For example, when a high school senior is accepted at a good college, but not a "prestige school" like some of her friends, she will feel strain. Perhaps she is not being treated fairly because the "playing field" is tilted against her; "other kids have connections," she may say. Yet perceptions of inequity may result in many adverse reactions, ranging from running away from its source to lowering the benefits of others through physical attacks or vandalizing their property.

Removal of positively valued stimuli: Strain may occur because of the actual or anticipated removal or loss of a positively valued stimulus from the individual.[114] For example, the loss of a girl- or boyfriend can produce strain, as can the death of a loved one, moving to a new neighborhood or school, or the divorce or separation of parents. The loss of positive stimuli may lead to delinquency as the adolescent tries to prevent the loss, retrieve what has been lost, obtain substitutes, or seek revenge against those responsible for the loss.

Presentation of negative stimuli: Strain may also be caused by the presence of negative or noxious stimuli. Included within this category are such pain-inducing social interactions as child abuse and neglect, crime victimization, physical punishment, family and peer conflict, school failure, and interaction with stressful life events ranging from verbal threats to air pollution. For example, adolescent maltreatment has been linked to delinquency through the rage and anger it generates. Children who are abused at home may take their rage out on younger children at school or become involved in violent delinquency.[115]

According to Agnew, the greater the intensity and frequency of strain experiences, the greater their impact and the more likely they are to cause delinquency.

Figure 7.6 Elements of General Strain Theory (GST)

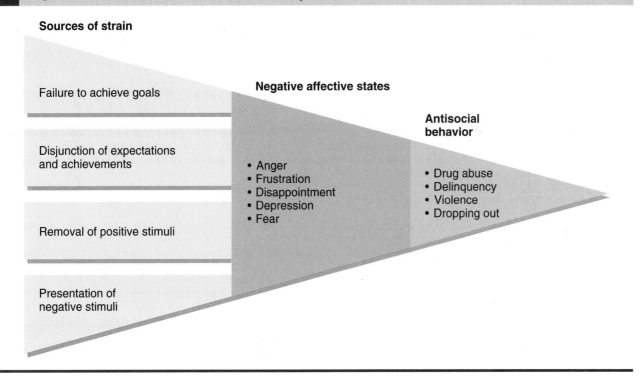

Each type of strain will increase the likelihood of experiencing such negative emotions as disappointment, depression, fear, and most important, anger. Anger increases perceptions of being wronged and produces a desire for revenge, energizes individuals to take action, and lowers inhibitions. Violence and aggression seem justified if you have been wronged and are righteously angry.

Because it produces these emotions, strain can be considered a predisposing factor for criminality when it is chronic and repetitive and creates a hostile, suspicious, and aggressive attitude. Individual strain episodes may serve as a situational event or trigger that produces crime, such as when a particularly stressful event ignites a violent reaction.

Sources of Strain

There are a variety of sources of strain. Sometimes, it can be a particular individual who is causing problems, such as an abusive parent or a peer group rival. When individuals identify a target to blame for their problems, they are more likely to respond with retaliatory action (for example, "Joe stole my girl away by lying about me, so I beat him up!"). When individuals internalize blame, delinquent behavior is less likely to occur (for example, "I lost my girlfriend because I was unfaithful; it's all my fault."). Sometimes the source of strain is difficult to pinpoint (for example, "I feel depressed because my parents got divorced."); this type of ambiguous strain is unlikely to produce an aggressive response.[116]

Social sources of strain People may begin to feel strain because of their membership in a peer or social group. The relationship may be reciprocal. Kids who report feelings of stress and anger are more likely to interact with delinquent peers and engage in criminal behaviors.[117] However, once in a deviant peer group, it is possible that membership conveys pressure to conform to peer expectations, which can produce more strain. Peer groups, deviant or otherwise, convey benefits such as friendship, companionship, and support, but they also force members into behavior patterns (for example, using drugs) that can be the source of unwelcome stress. Feelings of strain and being overwhelmed may become magnified as individuals attempt to comply with peer group demands. Kids may, for example, get involved in an unwanted shoplifting spree to pay for drugs, creating even more stress in their lives.[118]

Community sources of strain The GST generally focuses on individual level sources of strain, yet there are distinct ecological variations in the crime rate. Some regions, cities, and neighborhoods are more crime prone than others. Can ecological differences produce "negative affective states" in large segments of the population, which account for these differences? Agnew suggests that there are, in fact, community-level factors that produce feelings of strain. These strain-producing factors are set out in Exhibit 7.1.

According to Agnew, communities contribute to strain in several ways:

Exhibit 7.1 Community-Level Sources of Strain

Sources of Strain

1. Certain communities prevent residents from achieving desired levels of positively valued goals such as wealth, respect/status, and justice/fairness.
2. These communities also produce feelings of relative deprivation.
3. Deprived communities maintain levels of economic deprivation, family disruption, child abuse, overcrowding, and incivility that are much higher than those in surrounding areas. Residents not only experience these traits but witness close friends and family members enduring them; this is "vicarious strain."
4. These adverse community traits increase the likelihood of negative emotions, including anger and frustration.
5. Residence in these deprived communities increases the likelihood that angry, frustrated individuals will interact with one another, increasing stress levels.
6. Some communities will increase the likelihood that angry, frustrated people will commit crime.

Reasons Strain Produces Crime

1. Blocked opportunity for advancement or creation of new identities in some areas makes legitimate goals impossible to attain.

2. Densely populated communities make it impossible to keep activities and problems private. People may feel pressure to "save face" by acting tough or committing crimes.
3. Some communities develop subcultures whose members blame others for their misfortunes. This allows people to blame their aggressive illegal acts on others.
4. Residents in deprived areas are less able to develop noncriminal coping strategies for personal problems. They are less able to unite with others to solve their own or community-wide problems.
5. Residents in disorganized areas are less able to gain social support from others. They maintain weakened educational, religious, recreational, and other social institutions.
6. Deprived areas have weakened agencies of both formal and informal social control.
7. Residents of deprived areas are likely to hold values and beliefs conducive to crime.
8. The increased presence of criminal groups heightens the chance strain will lead to crime. Such groups serve as models and also reinforce criminal responses.

SOURCE: Robert Agnew, "A Macro-Strain Theory of Community Differences in Crime Rates." Paper presented at the American Society of Criminology meeting, San Diego, Calif., 1997.

- They influence the goals people pursue and the ability people have to meet these goals.
- They influence feelings of relative deprivation and exposure to aversive stimuli including family conflict, incivility, and economic deprivation.
- They influence the likelihood that angry, strain-filled individuals will interact with one another.

Consequently, not only does GST predict deviance on an individual level, but it can also account for community-level differences in the crime rate.

Coping with Strain

Not all people who experience strain fall into a life of crime and eventually resort to criminality. Some are able to marshal their emotional, mental, and behavioral resources to cope with the anger and frustration produced by strain. Coping ability may be a function of both individual traits and personal experiences over the life course. Personal temperament, prior learning of delinquent attitudes and behaviors, and association with criminal peers who reinforce anger are among other factors affecting the ability to cope.

Although it may be socially disapproved, criminality can provide relief and satisfaction for someone living an otherwise stress-filled life. Using violence for self-protection may increase feelings of self-worth among those who feel inadequate or intellectually insecure. Violent responses may also be used in response to negative stimuli, such as violence. For example, children who report that they hit or strike their parents also report that they had been the target of parental violence (hitting, slapping). In this case, assaulting parents may be viewed as a type of remedy for the strain caused by child abuse.[119]

Some defenses are cognitive; individuals may be able to rationalize frustrating circumstances. Not getting the career they desire is "just not that important"; they may be poor, but the "next guy is worse off"; and if things didn't work out, then they "got what they deserved." Others seek behavioral solutions: they run away from adverse conditions or seek revenge against those who caused the strain. Others will try to regain emotional equilibrium with techniques ranging from physical exercise to drug abuse.

Strain and criminal careers While some people can effectively cope with strain, how does GST explain both chronic offending and the stability of crime over the life course? GST recognizes that certain people have traits that may make them particularly sensitive to strain. These include an explosive temperament, being overly sensitive or emotional, low tolerance for adversity, and poor problem-solving skills. Kids who suffer from this form of "negative emotionality" are much more likely to engage in antisocial behaviors, especially if they also are lacking in self-control.[120]

Aggressive people who have these traits are likely to have poor interpersonal skills and are more likely to be treated negatively by others; their combative personalities make them feared and disliked. These people are likely to live in families whose caretakers share similar personality traits. They are also more likely to reject conventional peers and join deviant groups. Such individuals are subject to a high degree of strain over the course of their lives.

Crime peaks during late adolescence because this is a period of social stress caused by the weakening of parental supervision and the development of relationships with a diverse peer group. Many kids going through the trauma of family breakup and frequent changes in family structure find themselves feeling a high degree of strain. They may react by becoming involved in precocious sexuality or by turning to substance abuse to mask the strain. For example, research shows that young girls of any social class are more likely to bear out-of-wedlock children if they themselves experienced an unstable family life.[121] Adolescence is also a period during which hormone levels peak and the behavior moderating aspects of the brain have not fully developed, two factors that make adolescent males susceptible to environmental sources of strain.[122]

As they mature, children's expectations increase; some find that they are unable to meet academic and social demands. Adolescents are very concerned about their standing with peers. Those deficient in these areas may find they are social outcasts, another source of strain. In adulthood, crime rates drop because these sources of strain are reduced, new sources of self-esteem emerge, and adults seem more likely to bring their goals in line with reality.

CONNECTIONS

As you may recall in the discussion of cohort studies in Chapter 3, criminal behavior begins early in life, then remains stable over the life course. Considering that strain-producing interactions are not constant, explaining the stability of chronic offending is an important task for strain theory. That biological traits may predispose people to strain dovetails with the discussion of genetic influences on crime, which was covered in Chapter 6. ∎

Evaluating GST

Agnew's work is quite important because it both clarifies the concept of strain and directs future research agendas. It also adds to the body of literature describing how social and life history events influence offending patterns. Sources of strain vary over the life course; so too do delinquency rates.

CONNECTIONS

Explaining continuity and change in offending rates over the life course has become an important goal of criminologists. Analysis of latent trait and life course theories in Chapter 10 provides some recent thinking on this topic. ∎

There is also empirical support for GST. Adolescents who score high on self-report test items that measure per-

ceptions of strain (for example, "my classmates don't like me," "adults and friends don't respect my opinions") and negative life events (being a victim of crime, the death of a close friend, serious illness) are also the ones most likely to engage in crime.[123] Some research efforts show that indicators of strain—family breakup, unemployment, moving, feelings of dissatisfaction with friends and school—are positively related to criminality.[124] For example, middle-class youth who drop out of school are more likely to engage in criminal behavior than lower-class dropouts. It is possible that removing this positive stimulus (education) has a greater strain effect on those who are expected to succeed because of their class position than on those who already perceive more limited economic opportunities.[125]

Research shows that persistent drug abusers report feeling a great deal of "life stress." They also tend to associate with peers who are substance users.[126] In some cases, this interaction may actually help them reduce strain and anxiety. Criminality may serve as an effective coping mechanism, which helps relieve feelings of anger and resentment. Lashing out at others, for example, may reduce feelings of strain, as might stealing or vandalizing property.[127]

Gender issues One of the biggest question marks about GST is its ability to adequately explain gender differences in the crime rate. Females experience as much or more strain, frustration, and anger as males, but their crime rate is much lower. Is it possible that there are gender differences either (a) in the relationship between strain and criminality or (b) in the ability to cope with the effects of strain? Not all sources of strain produce the anger envisioned by Agnew.[128] For example, although females may experience more strain, males may be more deeply affected by interpersonal stress.[129]

There is evidence that stress influences both males and females equally: however, the degree to which it leads to criminal behavior is much higher among males than females.[130] When presented with similar types of strain, males and females respond with a different constellation of negative emotions.[131] Females may be socialized to internalize stress, blaming themselves for their problems; males may take the same type of strain and relieve it by striking out at others and deflecting criticism with aggression.[132] Consequently, males may resort to criminality in the face of stressors of any magnitude, but only extreme levels of strain produce violent reactions from women.[133]

∎ Cultural Deviance Theory

The third branch of social structure theory combines the effects of social disorganization and strain to explain how people living in deteriorated neighborhoods react to social isolation and economic deprivation. Because their lifestyle is draining, frustrating, and dispiriting, members of the lower class create an independent subculture with its own set of rules and values. Middle-class culture stresses hard work, delayed gratification, formal education, and being cautious; the lower-class subculture stresses excitement, toughness, risk-taking, fearlessness, immediate gratification, and "street smarts."

The lower-class subculture is an attractive alternative because the urban poor find that it is impossible to meet the behavioral demands of middle-class society. Unfortunately, subcultural norms often clash with conventional values. Slum dwellers are forced to violate the law because they obey the rules of the deviant culture with which they are in close and immediate contact. Figure 7.7 outlines the elements of cultural deviance theory.

Conduct Norms

The concept that the lower class develops a unique culture in response to strain can be traced to Thorsten Sellin's clas-

Figure 7.7   Elements of Cultural Deviance Theory

Poverty
• Lack of opportunity
• Feeling of oppression

Socialization
Lower-class youths are socialized to value middle-class goals and ideas. However, their environment inhibits proper socialization.

Subculture
Blocked opportunities prompt formation of groups with alternative lifestyles and values.

Success goal
Gangs provide alternative methods of gaining success for some, venting anger for others.

Crime and delinquency
New methods of gaining success involve law-violating behavior.

Criminal careers
Some gang boys can parlay their status into criminal careers; others become drug users or violent assaulters.

sic 1938 work, *Culture Conflict and Crime,* a theoretical attempt to link cultural adaptation to criminality.[134] Sellin's main premise is that criminal law is an expression of the rules of the dominant culture. The content of the law, therefore, may create a clash between conventional, middle-class rules and splinter groups, such as ethnic and racial minorities who are excluded from the social mainstream. These groups maintain their own set of **conduct norms**—rules governing the day-to-day living conditions within these subcultures.[135] Conduct norms can be found in almost any culture and are not the property of any particular group, culture, or political structure.

Complicating matters is the fact that most of us belong to several social groups. In a complex society, the number of groups people belong to—family, peer, occupational, and religious—is quite large. "A conflict of norms is said to exist when more or less divergent rules of conduct govern the specific life situation in which a person may find himself."[136] According to Sellin, **culture conflict** occurs when the rules expressed in the criminal law clash with the demands of group conduct norms. To make his point, Sellin cited the case of a Sicilian father in New Jersey who killed the 16-year-old boy who seduced his daughter and then expressed surprise at being arrested. He claimed that he had "merely defended his family honor in a traditional way."[137]

Focal Concerns

In his classic 1958 paper, "Lower Class Culture as a Generating Milieu of Gang Delinquency," Walter Miller identified the unique value system that defines lower-class culture.[138] Conformance to these **focal concerns** dominates life among the lower class. According to Miller, clinging to lower-class focal concerns promotes illegal or violent behavior. Toughness may mean displaying fighting prowess; street smarts may lead to drug deals; excitement may result in drinking, gambling, or drug abuse. Focal concerns do not necessarily represent a rebellion against middle-class values; rather, these values have evolved specifically to fit conditions in lower-class areas. The major lower-class focal concerns are set out in Exhibit 7.2.[139]

It is this adherence to the prevailing cultural demands of lower-class society that causes urban crime. Research, in fact, shows that members of the lower class value toughness and want to show they are courageous in the face of provocation.[140] A reputation for toughness helped them acquire social power while at the same time insulating them from becoming victims. Violence was also seen as a means to acquire the accouterments of wealth (nice clothes, flashy cars, or access to clubs), control or humiliate another person, defy authority, settle drug-related "business" disputes, attain retribution, satisfy the need for thrills or risk-taking, and respond to challenges to one's manhood.[141] Sociologist Elijah Anderson has written extensively on how lower-class areas maintain competing value systems.[142] One he labels "decent" and is commit-

Exhibit 7.2 Miller's Lower-Class Focal Concerns

Trouble	In lower-class communities, people are evaluated by their actual or potential involvement in trouble-making activity. Getting into trouble includes such behavior as fighting, drinking, and sexual misconduct. Dealing with trouble can confer prestige—for example, when a man establishes a reputation for being able to handle himself well in a fight. Not being able to handle trouble, and having to pay the consequences, can make a person look foolish and incompetent.
Toughness	Lower-class males want local recognition of their physical and spiritual toughness. They refuse to be sentimental or soft and instead value physical strength, fighting ability, and athletic skill. Those who cannot meet these standards risk getting a reputation for being weak, inept, and effeminate.
Smartness	Members of the lower-class culture want to maintain an image of being "street-wise" and savvy, using their "street smarts," and having the ability to outfox and "out-con" the opponent. Though formal education is not admired, knowing essential survival techniques, such as gambling, conning, and outsmarting the law, is a requirement.
Excitement	Members of the lower class search for fun and excitement to enliven an otherwise drab existence. The search for excitement may lead to gambling, fighting, getting drunk, and sexual adventures. In between, the lower-class citizen may simply "hang out" and "be cool."
Fate	Lower-class citizens believe their lives are in the hands of strong spiritual forces that guide their destinies. Getting lucky, finding good fortune, and hitting the jackpot are all slum dwellers' daily dreams.
Autonomy	Being independent of authority figures, such as the police, teachers, and parents, is required; losing control is an unacceptable weakness, incompatible with toughness.

SOURCE: Walter Miller, "Lower-Class Culture as a Generating Milieu of Gang Delinquency," *Journal of Social Issues* 14 (1958): 5–19.

ted to family and middle-class values; there is also an oppositional culture, that of "the streets," whose norms are often diametrically opposed to those of mainstream society. At the heart of the code is respect, which Anderson views as the need to be treated with the deference one deserves. Respect is hard-won but easily lost and so must constantly be guarded. Lower-class focal concerns seem as relevant today as when first identified by Miller more than 40 years ago.

Theory of Delinquent Subcultures

Albert Cohen first articulated the theory of delinquent subcultures in his classic 1955 book, *Delinquent Boys*.[143] Cohen's central position was that delinquent behavior of lower-class youths is actually a protest against the norms and values of middle-class U.S. culture. Because social conditions make them incapable of achieving success legitimately, lower-class youths experience a form of culture conflict that Cohen labels **status frustration**.[144] As a result, many of them join together in gangs and engage in behavior that is "non-utilitarian, malicious, and negativistic."[145]

Cohen viewed the delinquent gang as a separate subculture, possessing a value system directly opposed to that of the larger society. He describes the subculture as one that "takes its norms from the larger culture, but turns them upside down. The delinquent's conduct is right by the standards of his subculture precisely because it is wrong by the norms of the larger cultures."[146]

According to Cohen, the development of the delinquent subculture is a consequence of socialization practices found in the ghetto or slum environment. These children lack the basic skills necessary to achieve social and economic success in the demanding U.S. society. They also lack the proper education and therefore do not have the skills upon which to build a knowledge or socialization foundation. He suggests that lower-class parents are incapable of teaching children the necessary techniques for entering the dominant middle-class culture. The consequences of this deprivation include developmental handicaps, poor speech and communication skills, and inability to delay gratification.

Middle-class measuring rods   One significant handicap that lower-class children face is the inability to positively impress authority figures, such as teachers, employers, or supervisors. Cohen calls the standards set by these authority figures **middle-class measuring rods.** The conflict and frustration lower-class youths experience when they fail to meet these standards is a primary cause of delinquency. For example, the fact that a lower-class student is deemed by those in power to be substandard or below the average of what is expected can have an important impact on his or her future life chances. A school record may be reviewed by juvenile court authorities and by the military. Since a military record can influence whether or not someone is qualified for certain jobs, it is quite influential.[147] Negative evaluations become part of a permanent file that follows an individual for the rest of his or her life. When he or she wants to improve, evidence of prior failures is used to discourage advancement.

The formation of deviant subcultures   Cohen believes lower-class boys who suffer rejection by middle-class decision makers usually elect to join one of three existing subcultures: the corner boy, the college boy, or the delinquent boy. The **corner boy** role is the most common response to middle-class rejection. The corner boy is not a chronic delinquent but may be a truant who engages in petty or status offenses, such as precocious sex and recreational drug abuse. His main loyalty is to his peer group, on which he depends for support, motivation, and interest. His values, therefore, are those of the group with which he is in close personal contact. The corner boy, well aware of his failure to achieve the standards of the American Dream, retreats into the comforting world of his lower-class peers and eventually becomes a stable member of his neighborhood, holding a menial job, marrying, and remaining in the community.

The **college boy** embraces the cultural and social values of the middle class. Rather than scorning middle-class measuring rods, he actively strives to be successful by those standards. Cohen views this type of youth as one who is embarking on an almost hopeless path, since he is ill-equipped academically, socially, and linguistically to achieve the rewards of middle-class life.

The **delinquent boy** adopts a set of norms and principles in direct opposition to middle-class values. He engages in short-run hedonism, living for today and letting "tomorrow take care of itself."[148] Delinquent boys strive for group autonomy. They resist efforts by family, school, or other sources of authority to control their behavior. They may join a gang because it is perceived as autonomous, independent, and the focus of "attraction, loyalty, and solidarity."[149] Frustrated by their inability to succeed, these boys resort to a process Cohen calls **reaction formation.** Symptoms of reaction formation include overly intense responses that seem disproportionate to the stimuli that trigger them. For the delinquent boy, this takes the form of irrational, malicious, and unaccountable hostility to the enemy, which in this case are "the norms of respectable middle-class society."[150] Reaction formation causes delinquent boys to overreact to any perceived threat or slight. They sneer at the college boy's attempts at assimilation and scorn the corner boy's passivity. The delinquent boy is willing to take risks, violate the law, and flout middle-class conventions.

Cohen's work helps explain the factors that promote and sustain a delinquent subculture. By introducing the concepts of status frustration and middle-class measuring rods, Cohen makes it clear that social forces and not individual traits promote and sustain a delinquent career. By introducing the corner boy, college boy, delinquent boy triad, he helps explain why many lower-class youth fail to become chronic offenders: there is more than one social path open to indigent youth.[151] His work is a skillful integration of strain and social disorganization theories and has become an enduring element of the criminological literature.

Theory of Differential Opportunity

In their classic work *Delinquency and Opportunity,* written almost 40 years ago, Richard Cloward and Lloyd Ohlin combined strain and social disorganization principles into

■ Given the opportunity, kids who reside in some of the nation's toughest neighborhoods can achieve financial success through legitimate means. Here, John Paul DeJoria—the man who transformed John Paul Mitchell Systems from a company that couldn't afford to put color on its black-and-white label into the leading brand of professional salon hair care products in the United States—poses next to a sculpture at his office in Beverly Hills, California. DeJoria, 55, was born in Los Angeles and spent much of his youth as a member of an East Los Angeles street gang.

a portrayal of a gang-sustaining criminal subculture.[152] Cloward and Ohlin agreed with Cohen and found that independent delinquent subcultures exist within society. They consider a delinquent subculture to be one in which certain forms of delinquent activity are essential requirements for performing the dominant roles supported by the subculture.[153]

Youth gangs are an important part of the delinquent subculture. Although not all illegal acts are committed by gang youth, they are the source of the most serious, sustained, and costly criminal behaviors. Delinquent gangs spring up in disorganized areas where youths lack the opportunity to gain success through conventional means. True to strain theory principles, Cloward and Ohlin portray slum kids as individuals who want to conform to middle-class values but lack the means to do so.[154]

Differential opportunities The centerpiece of the Cloward and Ohlin theory is the concept of **differential opportunity,** which states that people in all strata of society share the same success goals but that those in the lower class have limited means of achieving them. People who perceive themselves as failures within conventional society will seek alternative or innovative ways to gain success. People who conclude that there is little hope for advancement by legitimate means may join with like-minded peers to form a gang. Gang members provide the emotional support to handle the shame, fear, or guilt they may develop while engaging in illegal acts. Delinquent subcultures then reward these acts that conventional society would punish. The youth who is considered a failure at school and is only qualified for a menial job at a minimum wage can earn thousands of dollars plus the respect of his or her peers by joining a gang and engaging in drug deals or armed robberies.

Cloward and Ohlin recognize that the opportunity for both successful conventional and criminal careers is limited. In stable areas, adolescents may be recruited by professional criminals, drug traffickers, or organized crime groups. Unstable areas, however, cannot support flourishing criminal opportunities. In these socially disorganized neighborhoods, adult role models are absent and young criminals have few opportunities to join established gangs or to learn the fine points of professional crime. Their most important finding, then, is that all opportunities for success, both illegal and conventional, are closed for the most "truly disadvantaged" youth.

Because of differential opportunity, kids are likely to join one of three types of gangs:

Criminal gangs: Criminal gangs exist in stable lower-class areas in which close connections among adolescent, young adult, and adult offenders create an environment for successful criminal enterprise.[155] Youths are recruited into established criminal gangs that provide a training ground for a successful criminal career. Gang membership provides a learning experience in which the knowledge and skills needed for success in crime are acquired. During this "apprenticeship stage," older, more experienced members of the criminal subculture hold youthful "trainees" on tight reins, limiting activities that might jeopardize the gang's profits (for example, engaging in nonfunctional, irrational violence). Over time, new recruits learn the techniques and attitudes of the criminal world and how to "cooperate successfully with others in criminal enterprises."[156] To become a fully accepted member of the criminal gang, novices must prove themselves reliable and dependable in their contacts with their criminal associates.

Conflict gangs: Conflict gangs develop in communities unable to provide either legitimate or illegitimate opportunities. These highly disorganized areas are marked by transient residents and physical deterioration. Crime in this area is "individualistic, unorganized, petty, poorly paid, and unprotected."[157] There are no successful adult criminal role models from whom youths can learn criminal skills. When such severe limitations on both criminal and conventional opportunity intensify frustrations of the young, violence is used as a means of gaining status. The image of the conflict gang member is the swaggering, tough adolescent who fights with weapons to win respect from rivals and engages in unpredictable and destructive assaults on people and property. Conflict gang members must be ready to fight to protect their own and their gang's integrity and honor. By doing so, they acquire a

"rep," which provides them with a means for gaining admiration from their peers and consequently helps them develop their own self-image. Conflict gangs, according to Cloward and Ohlin, "represent a way of securing access to the scarce resources for adolescent pleasure and opportunity in underprivileged areas."[158]

Retreatist gangs: Retreatists are double failures, unable to gain success through legitimate means and unwilling to do so through illegal ones. Some retreatists have tried crime or violence but are either too clumsy, weak, or scared to be accepted in criminal or violent gangs. They then "retreat" into a role on the fringe of society. Members of the retreatist subculture constantly search for ways of getting high—alcohol, pot, heroin, unusual sexual experiences, music. They are always "cool," detached from relationships with the conventional world. To feed their habit, retreatists develop a "hustle"—pimping, conning, selling drugs, and committing petty crimes. Personal status in the retreatist subculture is derived from peer approval.

Analysis of differential opportunity Cloward and Ohlin's theory is important because it integrates cultural deviance and social disorganization concepts and recognizes different modes of criminal adaptation. The fact that criminal cultures can be supportive, rational, and profitable seems to be a more realistic reflection of the actual world of the delinquent than Cohen's original view of purely negativistic, destructive delinquent youths who oppose all social values. Cloward and Ohlin's tripartite model of urban delinquency also relates directly to the treatment and rehabilitation of delinquents. While other social structure theorists portray delinquent youths as having values and attitudes in opposition to middle-class culture, Cloward and Ohlin suggest that many delinquents share the goals and values of the general society but lack the means to obtain success. This suggests that delinquency prevention can be achieved by providing youths with the means for obtaining the success they truly desire through employment opportunities without the need to change their basic attitudes and beliefs.[159]

Evaluating Social Structure Theories

The social structure approach has significantly influenced both criminological theory and crime prevention strategies. Its core concepts seem to be valid in view of the relatively high crime and delinquency rates and gang activity occurring in the deteriorated inner-city slum areas of the nation's largest cities.[160] The public's image of the disorganized inner city includes roaming bands of violent teenage gangs, drug users, prostitutes, muggers, and similar frightening examples of criminality. All of these are present today in inner-city areas.

Each branch of the general structural model seems to support and amplify others. Some theorists suggest that these concepts are actually interdependent.[161] Factors that cause strain, such as lack of access to legitimate economic opportunities and economic inequality, also produce social disorganization. Stress leads to alcohol abuse and unprotected sex outside of marriage, resulting in an increase of impaired households, dysfunctional families, urban hostility, and the deterioration of informal social controls.

Critics of the approach charge that we cannot be sure that it is lower-class culture itself that promotes crime and not some other force operating in society. Critics of this approach deny that residence in urban areas alone is sufficient to cause people to violate the law.[162] They counter with the charge that lower-class crime rates may be an artifact of bias in the criminal justice system. Lower-class areas seem to have higher crime rates because residents are arrested and prosecuted by agents of the justice system who, as members of the middle class, exhibit class bias.[163] Class bias is often coupled with discrimination against minority group members, who have long suffered at the hands of the justice system.

Even if the higher crime rates recorded in lower-class areas are valid, it is still true that most members of the lower class are not criminals. The discovery of the chronic offender indicates that a significant majority of people living in lower-class environments are not criminals and that a relatively small proportion of the population commits most crimes. If social forces alone could be used to explain crime, how can we account for the vast number of urban poor who remain honest and law abiding? Given these circumstances, law violators must be motivated by some individual mental, physical, or social process or trait.[164]

It is also questionable whether a distinct lower-class culture actually exists. Several researchers have found that gang members and other delinquent youths seem to value middle-class concepts, such as sharing, earning money, and respecting the law, as highly as middle-class youths. Criminologists contend that lower-class youths also value education as highly as middle-class students do.[165] Public opinion polls can also be used as evidence that a majority of lower-class citizens maintain middle-class values. National surveys find that people in the lowest income brackets want tougher drug laws, more police protection, and greater control over criminal offenders.[166] These opinions seem similar to conventional middle-class values rather than representative of an independent, deviant subculture. While this evidence contradicts some of the central ideas of social structure theory, the discovery of stable patterns of lower-class crime, the high crime rates found in disorganized inner-city areas, and the rise of teenage gangs and groups support a close association between crime rates and social class position.

■ Social Structure Theory and Public Policy

Social structure theory has had a significant influence on public policy. If the cause of criminality is viewed as a schism between lower-class individuals and conventional goals, norms, and rules, it seems logical that alternatives to criminal behavior can be provided by giving slum dwellers opportunities to share in the rewards of conventional society.

One approach is to give indigent people direct financial aid through welfare and Aid to Dependent Children (ADC). Although welfare has been curtailed through the Federal Welfare Reform Act of 1996, research shows that crime rates decrease when families receive supplemental income through public assistance payments.[167]

There are also efforts to reduce crime by improving the community structure in high-crime inner-city areas. Crime prevention efforts based on social structure precepts can be traced back to the Chicago Area Project, supervised by Clifford R. Shaw. This program attempted to organize existing community structures to develop social stability in otherwise disorganized slums. The project sponsored recreation programs for children in the neighborhoods, including summer camping. It campaigned for community improvements in such areas as education, sanitation, traffic safety, physical conservation, and law enforcement. Project members also worked with police and court agencies to supervise and treat gang youth and adult offenders. In a 25-year assessment of the project, Solomon Kobrin found that it was successful in demonstrating the feasibility of creating youth welfare organizations in high-delinquency areas.[168] Kobrin also discovered that the project made a distinct contribution to ending the isolation of urban males from the mainstream of society.

Social structure concepts, especially Cloward and Ohlin's views, were a critical ingredient in the Kennedy and Johnson administrations' "War on Poverty," begun in the early 1960s. Rather than organizing existing community structures, as Shaw's Chicago Area Project had done, this later effort called for an all-out attack on the crime-producing structures of slum areas. War on Poverty programs included the Job Corps; VISTA (the urban Peace Corps); Head Start and Upward Bound (educational enrichment programs); Neighborhood Legal Services; and the largest community organizing effort, the Community Action Program. War on Poverty programs were sweeping efforts to change the social structure of the slum area. They sought to reduce crime by developing a sense of community pride and solidarity in poverty areas and by providing educational and job opportunities for crime-prone youths. Some War on Poverty programs—Head Start, Neighborhood Legal Services, and the Community Action Program—have continued to help people.

Although it may be difficult to revive entire neighborhoods, the federal government continues to sponsor programs that have a total community focus. The Policy and Practice in Criminology feature on pages 206–207 entitled "Operation Weed and Seed" explores this issue in depth.

Summary

Sociology has been the main orientation of criminologists because they know that crime rates vary among elements of the social structure, that society goes through changes that affect crime, and that social interaction relates to criminality. Social structure theories suggest that people's places in the socioeconomic structure of society influence their chances of becoming criminals. Poor people are more likely to commit crimes because they are unable to achieve monetary or social success in any other way. Social structure theory has three schools of thought: social disorganization, strain, and cultural deviance theory (summarized in Table 7.2).

Social disorganization theory suggests that slum dwellers violate the law because they live in areas in which social control has broken down. The origin of social disorganization theory can be traced to the work of Clifford R. Shaw and Henry D. McKay. Shaw and McKay concluded that disorganized areas marked by divergent values and transitional populations produced criminality. Modern social ecology theory looks at such issues as community fear, unemployment, siege mentality, and deterioration.

Table 7.2 Social Structure Theories

Theory	Major Premise	Strengths
Social Disorganization Theory		
Shaw and McKay's concentric zone theory	Crime is a product of transitional neighborhoods that manifest social disorganization and value conflict.	Identifies why crime rates are highest in slum areas. Points out the factors that produce crime. Suggests programs to help reduce crime.
Social ecology theory	The conflicts and problems of urban social life and communities, including fear, unemployment, deterioration, and siege mentality, influence crime rates.	Accounts for urban crime rates and trends.
Strain Theory		
Anomie theory	People who adopt the goals of society but lack the means to attain them seek alternatives, such as crime.	Points out how competition for success creates conflict and crime. Suggests that social conditions and not personality can account for crime. Can explain middle- and upper-class crime.
General strain theory	Strain has a variety of sources. Strain causes crime in the absence of adequate coping mechanisms.	Identifies the complexities of strain in modern society. Expands on anomie theory. Shows the influence of social events on behavior over the life course.
Institutional anomie theory	Material goals pervade all aspects of American life.	Explains why crime rates are so high in American culture.
Relative deprivation theory	Crime occurs when the wealthy and poor live close to one another.	Explains high crime rates in deteriorated inner-city areas located near more affluent neighborhoods.
Cultural Deviance Theory		
Sellin's culture conflict theory	Obedience to the norms of their lower-class culture puts people in conflict with the norms of the dominant culture.	Identifies the aspects of lower-class life that produce street crime. Adds to Shaw and McKay's analysis. Creates the concept of culture conflict.
Miller's focal concern theory	Citizens who obey the street rules of lower-class life (focal concerns) find themselves in conflict with the dominant culture.	Identifies the core values of lower-class culture and shows their association to crime.
Cohen's theory of delinquent gangs	Status frustration of lower-class boys, created by their failure to achieve middle-class success, causes them to join gangs.	Shows how the conditions of lower-class life produce crime. Explains violence and destructive acts. Identifies conflict of lower class with middle class.
Cloward and Ohlin's theory of opportunity	Blockage of conventional opportunities causes lower-class youths to join criminal, conflict, or retreatist gangs.	Shows that even illegal opportunities are structured in society. Indicates why people become involved in a particular type of criminal activity. Presents a way of preventing crime.

Operation Weed and Seed

Operation Weed and Seed is a federal multilevel action plan for revitalizing communities. The thinking behind the conception of this program was that no single approach can reduce crime rates and that social service and law enforcement agencies must cooperate to be effective. There are four basic elements in this plan: law enforcement; community policing; prevention, intervention, and treatment; and neighborhood restoration.

Law Enforcement

No social program or community activity can survive in an atmosphere tainted by violent crime and drug abuse. Law enforcement must "weed out" the most violent offenders by coordinating and integrating the efforts of federal, state, and local law enforcement agencies in targeted high-crime neighborhoods. The law enforcement element consists primarily of suppression activities. These activities include enforcement, adjudication, prosecution, and supervision efforts designed to target, apprehend, and incapacitate violent street criminals who terrorize neighborhoods and account for a disproportionate percentage of criminal activity. One ex-

ample of an effective law enforcement strategy is Operation Triggerlock, a Department of Justice initiative that targets violent offenders for prosecution in federal court to take advantage of tough federal firearms laws.

Some of the suppression activities will focus on special enforcement operations such as repeat or violent offender removal programs, intensified narcotics investigations, targeted prosecutions, victim-witness protection, and elimination of narcotics trafficking organizations operating in these areas.

Community Policing

Community policing serves as the bridge between the "weeding" and "seeding" components. The community policing element operates in support of intensive law enforcement suppression and containment activities and provides a bridge to the prevention, intervention, and treatment component, as well as to the neighborhood reclamation and restoration components. Local police departments should implement community policing strategies in each of the targeted sites. Under community policing, law enforcement will work closely with community residents to develop solutions to violent and drug-related crime. In addition, community

policing will help foster a sense of responsibility within the community and serve as the stimulus for community mobilization. Community policing activities will focus on increasing police visibility and developing cooperative relationships between the police and citizenry in the target areas. Techniques such as foot patrols, problem solving, victim referrals to support services, and community relations activities will increase positive interaction between the police and the community. Special emphasis should be placed on addressing the needs of crime victims and minority communities that are disproportionately victimized by crime.

Community mobilization is also important to community policing in crime prevention. Programs that encourage community participation and help prevent crime include neighborhood watch, citizen marches and rallies, prayer services, drug-free zones, and graffiti removal.

Prevention, Intervention, and Treatment

The coordinated efforts of law enforcement and social service agencies, the private sector, and the community will help prevent crime from recurring. This can be accomplished by concentrating a broad array of

Strain theories comprise the second branch of the social structure approach. They view crime as a result of the anger people experience over their inability to achieve legitimate social and economic success. Strain theories hold that most people share common values and beliefs but the ability to achieve them is differentiated throughout the social structure. The best-known strain theory is Robert Merton's theory of anomie, which describes what happens when the means people have at their dis-

posal are not adequate to satisfy their goals. Steven Messner, Richard Rosenfeld, and Robert Agnew have extended this theory by showing that strain has multiple sources.

Cultural deviance theories hold that a unique value system develops in lower-class areas. Lower-class values approve of behaviors such as being tough, never showing fear, and defying authority. People perceiving strain will bond together in their own groups or subcultures for support and recognition. Albert Cohen links the

formation of subcultures to the failure of lower-class citizens to achieve recognition from middle-class decision makers, such as teachers, employers, and police officers. Richard Cloward and Lloyd Ohlin have argued that crime results from lower-class people's perception that their opportunity for success is limited. Consequently, youths in low-income areas may join criminal, conflict, or retreatist gangs.

human services on the target areas to create an environment where crime cannot thrive. Prevention, intervention, and treatment should include youth services, school programs, community and social programs, and support groups designed to develop positive community attitudes toward combating narcotics use and trafficking. The Safe Haven, for example, is a mechanism to organize and deliver an array of youth- and adult-oriented human services in a multi-service center setting such as a school. Another program in Durham, North Carolina, will attempt to reduce truancy using the following techniques:

- Both parent(s) and student will sign a contract with the school to guarantee attendance.
- Police officers will patrol school areas.
- Truant officers will be given daily information on truants.
- Truant officers will actively pursue truant students.
- Parents will be informed immediately if their children are truant and the consequences of their truancy will be explained.
- Human services agencies will be immediately involved.

- Truant officers will follow cases through the court system.
- Student populations will be educated about the costs of truancy to their lives.

Neighborhood Restoration

Neighborhood restoration can be achieved only through the coordinated use of federal, state, local, and private sector resources. This element of Weed and Seed is designed to revitalize distressed neighborhoods and improve the quality of life in the target communities. The neighborhood restoration element will focus on economic development activities designed to strengthen legitimate community institutions. Resources should be dedicated to economic development, provision of economic opportunities for residents, improved housing conditions, enhanced social services, and improved public services in the target area. Programs will be developed to improve living conditions: enhance home security; allow for low-cost physical improvements; develop long-term efforts to renovate and maintain housing; and provide educational, economic, social, recreational, and other vital opportunities. A key feature of this element will be fostering self-worth and individual responsibility among community members.

Critical Thinking Questions

1. What steps would you take if you were appointed to head a Weed and Seed program in your home town or in a neighboring city?
2. Would aggressive law enforcement tactics turn off residents and defeat the purpose of community restoration? Describe the reaction you would anticipate.

InfoTrac College Edition Research

To learn more about the techniques needed to redevelop communities, read these articles:

Elmer Johnson. The view from the metropolis. *Brookings Review* Fall 1998 v16 n4 p12

Mark R. Warren. Community building and political power. *American Behavioral Scientist* Sept 1998 v42 n1 p78

SOURCES: Information in this section was supplied by Operation Weed and Seed Executive Offices, U.S. Department of Justice, Washington, D.C., 1998; Executive Office for Weed and Seed, Weed and Seed In-sites, Series: Volume VI, Number 5, August/September 1998.

■ Thinking Like a Criminologist

You are criminologist from a local university who is serving as an adviser to the mayor of Central City, an industrial town with a population of 300,000. The mayor, up for reelection, is disappointed that efforts by the local police force to reduce public disorder and crime rates through a community police program do not seem to be working. He has recently read a report issued by the federal government suggesting that the key to reducing neighborhood crime is to create a sense of "collective efficacy" in city neighborhoods. The report defined collective efficacy as "cohesion among neighborhood residents combined with shared expectations for informal social control of public space." The report,* written by criminologists Robert Sampson and Stephen Raudenbush, found that when the rules of comportment are unclear and people mistrust one another they are unlikely to take action against disorder and crime. When there is cohesion and mutual trust among neighbors, the likelihood is greater that they will share a willingness to intervene for the common good. They found that in neighborhoods where this sense of collective efficacy was strong, rates of violence were low, regardless of neighborhood composition or socioeconomic conditions. Collective efficacy also appeared to deter disorder: where it was strong, observed levels of physical and social disorder were low.

The mayor wants to apply these concepts to Central City. He asks you to come up with a plan for increasing the collective efficacy of local neighborhoods and determine whether such measures can actually reduce crime. Your problem is twofold: (1) How can collective efficacy be improved? and (2) What test will show whether improvements in collective efficacy levels are responsible for lower violent crime rates?

*You can read the report (Robert J. Sampson and Stephen W. Raudenbush, "Disorder in Urban Neighborhoods: Does It Lead to Crime?") at the National Institute of Justice Web site: http://www.ncjrs.org/txtfiles1/nij/186049.txt

Key Terms

- Chicago School (177)
- stratified society (177)
- culture of poverty (179)
- at-risk (179)
- underclass (179)
- truly disadvantaged (179)
- social structure theory (180)
- social disorganization theory (181)
- strain theory (182)
- strain (182)
- cultural deviance theory (182)
- subcultures (182)
- cultural transmission (182

- transitional neighborhoods (183)
- concentration effect (185)
- siege mentality (187)
- gentrification (188)
- collective efficacy (188)
- social altruism (190)
- strain theorists (192)
- anomie (192)
- mechanical solidarity (192)
- organic solidarity (192)
- theory of anomie (193)
- institutional anomie theory (194)
- American Dream (194)

- relative deprivation (195)
- general strain theory (GST) (196)
- negative affective states (196)
- conduct norms (200)
- culture conflict (200)
- focal concerns (200)
- status frustration (201)
- middle-class measuring rods (201)
- corner boy (202)
- college boy (202)
- delinquent boy (202)
- reaction formation (202)
- differential opportunity (202)

Critical Thinking Questions

1. Is there a "transition" area in your town or city? Does the crime rate remain constant in this neighborhood regardless of the racial, ethnic, or cultural composition of its residents?

2. Do you believe a distinct lower-class culture exists? Do you know anyone who has the focal concerns Miller talks about? Did you experience elements of these focal concerns while you were in high school? Will emerging forms of communication such as the Internet reduce cultural differences and create a more homogenous society, or are subcultures resistant to such influences?

3. Do you agree with Agnew that there is more than one cause of strain? If so, are there other sources of strain that he did not consider?

4. How would a structural theorist explain the presence of middle-class crime?

5. How would biosocial theories explain the high levels of violent crime in lower-class areas?

Notes

1. Douglas Belkin and Cindy Rodriguez, "Gang Implicated in Beating of 13-Year-Old," Boston Globe, 25 July 2001, p. B1.

2. Steven Messner and Richard Rosenfeld, Crime and the American Dream (Belmont, Calif.: Wadsworth, 1994), p. 11.

3. Robert E. Park, "The City: Suggestions for the Investigation of Behavior in the City Environment," American Journal of Sociology 20 (1915): 579–83.

4. Robert Park, Ernest Burgess, and Roderic McKenzie, The City (Chicago: University of Chicago Press, 1925).

5. Harvey Zorbaugh, The Gold Coast and the Slum (Chicago: University of Chicago Press, 1929).

6. Frederick Thrasher, The Gang (Chicago: University of Chicago Press, 1927).

7. Louis Wirth, The Ghetto (Chicago: University of Chicago Press, 1928).

8. Dr. Daniel H. Weinberg, "Press Briefing on 2000 Income and Poverty Estimates," Chief, Housing and Household Economic Statistics Division, U.S. Census Bureau, 25 September 2001.

9. National Center for Children in Poverty, News Release, 11 December 1996.

10. Jeanne Brooks-Gunn and Greg J. Duncan, "The Effects of Poverty on Children," The Future of Children 7(1997): 34–39.

11. Greg Duncan, W. Jean Yeung, Jeanne Brooks-Gunn, and Judith Smith, "How Much Does Childhood Poverty Affect the Life Chances of Children?" American Sociological Review 63 (1998): 406–23.

12. Children's Defense Fund, *The State of America's Children, 2001 Yearbook* (Washington, D.C.: author, 2001), pp. 81–87.

13. Brooks-Gunn and Duncan, "The Effects of Poverty on Children."

14. Jonathan Crane, "The Epidemic Theory of Ghettos and Neighborhood Effects on Dropping Out and Teenage Childbearing," *American Journal of Sociology* 96 (1991): 1226–59; see also Rodrick Wallace, "Expanding Coupled Shock Fronts of Urban Decay and Criminal Behavior: How U.S. Cities Are Becoming 'Hollowed Out,'" *Journal of Quantitative Criminology* 7 (1991): 333–55.

15. Oscar Lewis, "The Culture of Poverty," *Scientific American* 215 (1966): 19–25.

16. Gunnar Myrdal, *The Challenge of World Poverty* (New York: Vintage Books, 1970).

17. James Ainsworth-Darnell and Douglas Downey, "Assessing the Oppositional Culture Explanation for Racial/Ethnic Differences in School Performances," *American Sociological Review* 63 (1998): 536–53.

18. David Greenberg and Valerie West, "State Prison Populations and Their Growth, 1971–1991," *Criminology* 39 (2001): 615–54.

19. Eric Lotke, "Hobbling a Generation: Young African-American Men in Washington, D.C.'s Criminal Justice System—Five Years Later," *Crime and Delinquency* 44 (1998): 355–66.

20. David Brownfield, "Social Class and Violent Behavior," *Criminology* 24 (1986): 421–38.

21. See Charles Tittle and Robert Meier, "Specifying the SES/Delinquency Relationship," *Criminology* 28 (1990): 271–95, at 293.

22. See Ruth Kornhauser, *Social Sources of Delinquency* (Chicago: University of Chicago Press, 1978), p. 75.

23. Clifford R. Shaw and Henry D. McKay, *Juvenile Delinquency and Urban Areas*, rev. ed. (Chicago: University of Chicago Press, 1972).

24. Anthony Platt, *The Child Savers: The Invention of Delinquency* (Chicago: University of Chicago Press, 1968).

25. Shaw and McKay, *Juvenile Delinquency and Urban Areas*, p. 52.

26. Ibid., p. 171.

27. For a discussion of these issues, see Robert Bursik, "Social Disorganization and Theories of Crime and Delinquency: Problems and Prospects," *Criminology* 26 (1988): 521–39.

28. Robert Sampson, "Effects of Socioeconomic Context of Official Reaction to Juvenile Delinquency," *American Sociological Review* 51 (1986): 876–85.

29. Jeffrey Fagan, Ellen Slaughter, and Eliot Hartstone, "Blind Justice? The Impact of Race on the Juvenile Justice Process," *Crime and Delinquency* 33 (1987): 224–58; Merry Morash, "Establishment of a Juvenile Police Record," *Criminology* 22 (1984): 97–113.

30. The best known of these critiques is Kornhauser, *Social Sources of Delinquency*.

31. Bernard Lander, *Towards an Understanding of Juvenile Delinquency* (New York: Columbia University Press, 1954); David Bordua, "Juvenile Delinquency and 'Anomie': An Attempt at Replication," *Social Problems* 6 (1958): 230–38; Roland Chilton, "Continuities in Delinquency Area Research: A Comparison of Studies in Baltimore, Detroit, and Indianapolis," *American Sociological Review* 29 (1964): 71–73.

32. For a general review, see James Byrne and Robert Sampson, eds., *The Social Ecology of Crime* (New York: Springer Verlag, 1985).

33. See, generally, Bursik, "Social Disorganization and Theories of Crime and Delinquency," pp. 519–51.

34. William Spelman, "Abandoned Buildings: Magnets for Crime?" *Journal of Criminal Justice* 21 (1993): 481–93.

35. Keith Harries and Andrea Powell, "Juvenile Gun Crime and Social Stress: Baltimore, 1980–1990," *Urban Geography* 15 (1994): 45–63.

36. Ellen Kurtz, Barbara Koons, and Ralph Taylor, "Land Use, Physical Deterioration, Resident-Based Control, and Calls for Service on Urban Streetblocks," *Justice Quarterly* 15 (1998): 121–49.

37. Jeffrey Morenoff, Robert Sampson, and Stephen Raudenbush, "Neighborhood Inequality, Collective Efficacy, and the Spatial Dynamics of Urban Violence," *Criminology* 39 (2001): 517–60.

38. Karen Parker and Matthew Pruitt, "Poverty, Poverty Concentration, and Homicide," *Social Science Quarterly* 81 (2000): 555–82.

39. Ibid.

40. Barbara Warner and Glenn Pierce, "Reexamining Social Disorganization Theory Using Calls to the Police as a Measure of Crime," *Criminology* 31 (1993): 493–519.

41. Steven Messner, Lawrence Raffalovich, and Richard McMillan, "Economic Deprivation and Changes in Homicide Arrest Rates for White and Black Youths, 1967–1998: A National Time Series Analysis," *Criminology* 39 (2001): 591–614.

42. Bursik, "Social Disorganization and Theories of Crime and Delinquency," p. 520.

43. Darrell Steffensmeier and Dana Haynie, "Gender, Structural Disadvantage, and Urban Crime: Do Macrosocial Variables Also Explain Female Offending Rates?" *Criminology* 38 (2000): 403–38; Richard McGahey, "Economic Conditions, Organization, and Urban Crime," in *Communities and Crime*, eds. Albert Reiss and Michael Tonry (Chicago: University of Chicago Press, 1986), pp. 231–70.

44. Scott Menard and Delbert Elliott, "Self-Reported Offending, Maturational Reform, and the Easterlin Hypothesis," *Journal of Quantitative Criminology* 6 (1990): 237–68.

45. Elijah Anderson, *Streetwise: Race, Class and Change in an Urban Community* (Chicago: University of Chicago Press, 1990), pp. 243–44.

46. Pamela Wilcox Rountree and Kenneth Land, "Burglary Victimization, Perceptions of Crime Risk, and Routine Activities: A Multilevel Analysis Across Seattle Neighborhoods and Census Tracts," *Journal of Research in Crime and Delinquency* 33 (1996): 147–80.

47. Wesley Skogan, "Fear of Crime and Neighborhood Change," in *Communities and Crime*, eds. Albert Reiss and Michael Tonry (Chicago: University of Chicago Press, 1986), pp. 191–232.

48. Stephanie Greenberg, "Fear and Its Relationship to Crime, Neighborhood Deterioration and Informal Social Control," in *The Social Ecology of Crime*, eds. James Byrne and Robert Sampson (New York: Springer Verlag, 1985), pp. 47–62.

49. Margo Wilson and Martin Daly, "Life Expectancy, Economic Inequality, Homicide, and Reproductive Timing in Chicago Neighborhoods," *BMJ* 314 (1997): 1271–74.

50. Skogan, "Fear of Crime and Neighborhood Change."

51. Ibid.

52. Ralph Taylor and Jeanette Covington, "Community Structural Change and Fear of Crime," *Social Problems* 40 (1993): 374–92.

53. Ted Chiricos, Michael Hogan, and Marc Gertz, "Racial Composition of Neighborhood and Fear of Crime," *Criminology* 35 (1997): 107–31.

54. Ibid., p. 125.

55. Ted Chiricos, Ranee Mcentire, and Marc Gertz, "Social Problems, Perceived Racial and Ethnic Composition of Neighborhood and Perceived Risk of Crime" *Social Problems* 48 (2001): 322–41.

56. G. David Curry and Irving Spergel, "Gang Homicide, Delinquency, and Community," *Criminology* 26 (1988): 381–407.

57. Lawrence Rosenthal, "Gang Loitering and Race," *Journal of Criminal Law and Criminology* 91 (2000): 99–160.

58. Catherine E. Ross, John Mirowsky, and Shana Pribesh, "Powerlessness and the Amplification of Threat: Neighborhood Disadvantage, Disorder, and Mistrust," *American Sociological Review* 66 (2001): 568–80.

59. Anderson, *Streetwise: Race, Class and Change in an Urban Community,* p. 245.

60. Esbensen Finn-Aage and David Huizinga, "Community Structure and Drug Use: From a Social Disorganization Perspective," *Justice Quarterly* 7 (1990): 691–709.

61. Allen Liska and Paul Bellair, "Violent-Crime Rates and Racial Composition: Convergence Over Time," *American Journal of Sociology* 101 (1995): 578–610.

62. Wesley Skogan, *Disorder and Decline: Crime and the Spiral of Decay in American Neighborhoods* (New York: Free Press, 1990), pp. 15–35.

63. Robert Bursik and Harold Grasmick, "Decomposing Trends in Community Careers in Crime." Paper presented at the annual meeting of the American Society of Criminology, Baltimore, November 1990.

64. Ralph Taylor and Jeanette Covington, "Neighborhood Changes in Ecology and Violence," *Criminology* 26 (1988): 553–89.

65. Leo Scheurman and Solomon Kobrin, "Community Careers in Crime," in *Communities and Crime,* eds. Albert Reiss and Michael Tonry (Chicago: University of Chicago Press, 1986), pp. 67–100.

66. Ibid.

67. See, generally, Robert Bursik, "Delinquency Rates as Sources of Ecological Change," in *The Social Ecology of Crime,* eds. James Byrne and Robert Sampson (New York: Springer Verlag, 1985), pp. 63–77.

68. Janet Heitgerd and Robert Bursik, "Extracommunity Dynamics and the Ecology of Delinquency," *American Journal of Sociology* 92 (1987): 775–87.

69. Felton Earls, *Linking Community Factors and Individual Development* (Washington, D.C: National Institute of Justice, 1998).

70. Robert J. Sampson and Stephen W. Raudenbush, *Disorder in Urban Neighborhoods: Does It Lead to Crime?* (Washington, D.C.: National Institute of Justice, 2001).

71. Robert J. Sampson, Jeffrey Morenoff, and Felton Earls, "Beyond Social Capital: Spatial Dynamics of Collective Efficacy for Children," *American Sociological Review* 64 (1999): 633–60.

72. Donald Black, "Social Control as a Dependent Variable," in *Toward a General Theory of Social Control,* ed. D. Black (Orlando: Academic Press, 1990).

73. Paul Bellair, "Informal Surveillance and Street Crime: A Complex Relationship," *Criminology* 38 (2000): 137–70.

74. Skogan, *Disorder and Decline.*

75. Robert Sampson and W. Byron Groves, "Community Structure and Crime: Testing Social Disorganization Theory," *American Journal of Sociology* 94 (1989): 774–802; Denise Gottfredson, Richard McNeill, and Gary Gottfredson, "Social Area Influences on Delinquency: A Multilevel Analysis," *Journal of Research in Crime and Delinquency* 28 (1991): 197–206.

76. Fred Markowitz, Paul Bellair, Allen Liska, and Jianhong Liu, "Extending Social Disorganization Theory: Modeling the Relationships between Cohesion, Disorder, and Fear," *Criminology* 39 (2001): 293–320.

77. Robert Bursik and Harold Grasmick, "The Multiple Layers of Social Disorganization." Paper presented at the annual meeting of the American Society of Criminology, New Orleans, November 1992.

78. Ruth Peterson, Lauren Krivo, and Mark Harris, "Disadvantage and Neighborhood Violent Crime: Do Local Institutions Matter?" *Journal of Research in Crime and Delinquency* 37 (2000): 31–63.

79. Maria Velez, "The Role of Public Social Control in Urban Neighborhoods: A Multi-Level Analysis of Victimization Risk," *Criminology* 39 (2001): 837–64.

80. David Klinger, "Negotiating Order in Patrol Work: An Ecological Theory of Police Response to Deviance," *Criminology* 35 (1997): 277–306.

81. Rodney Stark, "Deviant Places: A Theory of the Ecology of Crime," *Criminology* 25 (1987): 893–911.

82. Robert Bursik and Harold Grasmick, "Economic Deprivation and Neighborhood Crime Rates, 1960–1980," *Law and Society Review* 27 (1993): 263–78.

83. Delbert Elliott, William Julius Wilson, David Huizinga, Robert Sampson, Amanda Elliott, and Bruce Rankin, "The Effects of Neighborhood Disadvantage on Adolescent Development," *Journal of Research in Crime and Delinquency* 33 (1996): 389–426.

84. Ibid., p. 414.

85. Ralph Taylor, "Social Order and Disorder of Street Blocks and Neighborhoods: Ecology, Microecology, and the Systemic Model of Social Disorganization," *Journal of Research in Crime and Delinquency* 34 (1997): 113–55.

86. Mitchell Chamlin and John Cochran, "Social Altruism and Crime," *Criminology* 35 (1997): 203–27.

87. James DeFronzo, "Welfare and Homicide," *Journal of Research in Crime and Delinquency* 34 (1997): 395–406.

88. Robert Sampson, Jeffrey Morenoff, and Felton Earls, "Beyond Social Capital: Spatial Dynamics of Collective Efficacy for Children," *American Sociological Review* 64 (1999): 633–60.

89. Thomas McNulty, "Assessing the Race–Violence Relationship at the Macro Level: The Assumption of Racial Invariance and the Problem of Restricted Distribution," *Criminology* 39 (2001): 467–90.

90. Robert Merton, *Social Theory and Social Structure,* enlarged ed. (New York: Free Press, 1968).

91. For an analysis, see Richard Hilbert, "Durkheim and Merton on Anomie: An Unexplored Contrast in Its Derivatives," *Social Problems* 36 (1989): 242–56.

92. Ibid., p. 243.

93. Albert Cohen, "The Sociology of the Deviant Act: Anomie Theory and Beyond," *American Sociological Review* 30 (1965): 5–14.

94. Robert Agnew, "The Contribution of Social Psychological Strain Theory to the Explanation of Crime and Delinquency," in *Advances in Criminological Theory, Vol. 6, The Legacy of Anomie,* eds. Freda Adler and William Laufer (New Brunswick, N.J.: Transaction Press, 1995), pp. 111–22.

95. These criticisms are articulated in Messner and Rosenfeld, *Crime and the American Dream,* p. 60.

96. Scott Menard, "A Developmental Test of Mertonian Anomie Theory," *Journal of Research in Crime and Delinquency* 32 (1995): 136–74.

97. John Hagan, Hans Merkens, and Klaus Boehnke, "Delinquency and Disdain: Social Capital and Control of Right-

Wing Extremism among East and West Berlin Youth," *American Journal of Sociology* 100 (1995): 1028–52.

98. Messner and Rosenfeld, *Crime and the American Dream*.

99. Steven Messner and Richard Rosenfeld, "An Institutional-Anomie Theory of the Social Distribution of Crime." Paper presented at the annual meeting of the American Society of Criminology, Phoenix, Arizona, November 1993.

100. John Hagan, Gerd Hefler, Gabriele Classen, Klaus Boehnke, and Hans Merkens, "Subterranean Sources of Subcultural Delinquency Beyond the American Dream," *Criminology* 36 (1998): 309–40.

101. Mitchell Chamlin and John Cochran, "Assessing Messner and Rosenfelds' Institutional Anomie Theory: A Partial Test," *Criminology* 33 (1995): 411–29.

102. Stephen Cernkovich, Peggy Giordano, and Jennifer Rudolph, "Race, Crime, and the American Dream," *Journal of Research in Crime and Delinquency* 37 (2000): 131–70.

103. Jukka Savolainen, "Inequality, Welfare State and Homicide: Further Support for the Institutional Anomie Theory," *Criminology* 38 (2000): 1021–42.

104. Jeffrey Morenoff, Robert Sampson, and Stephen Raudenbush, "Neighborhood Inequality, Collective Efficacy, and the Spatial Dynamics of Urban Violence," *Criminology* 39 (2001): 517–60.

105. John Braithwaite, "Poverty Power, White-Collar Crime and the Paradoxes of Criminological Theory," *Australian and New Zealand Journal of Criminology* 24 (1991): 40–58.

106. Margo Wilson and Martin Daly, "Life Expectancy, Economic Inequality, Homicide, and Reproductive Timing in Chicago Neighbourhoods," *British Journal of Medicine* 314 (1997): 1271–74.

107. Judith Blau and Peter Blau, "The Cost of Inequality: Metropolitan Structure and Violent Crime," *American Sociological Review* 147 (1982): 114–29.

108. Gary LaFree and Kriss Drass, "The Effect of Changes in Intraracial Income Inequality and Educational Attainment on Changes in Arrest Rates for African Americans and Whites, 1957 to 1990," *American Sociological Review* 61 (1996): 614–34; Taylor and Covington, "Neighborhood Changes in Ecology and Violence," p. 582; Richard Block, "Community Environment and Violent Crime," *Criminology* 17 (1979): 46–57; Robert Sampson, "Structural Sources of Variation in Race-Age-Specific Rates of Offending across Major U.S. Cities," *Criminology* 23 (1985): 647–73; Richard Rosenfeld,

"Urban Crime Rates: Effects of Inequality, Welfare Dependency, Region and Race," in *The Social Ecology of Crime*, eds. James Byrne and Robert Sampson (New York: Springer Verlag, 1985), pp. 116–30.

109. Tomislav Kovandzic, Lynne Vieraitis, and Mark Yeisley, "The Structural Covariates of Urban Homicide: Reassessing the Impact of Income Inequality and Poverty in the Post-Reagan Era," *Criminology* 36 (1998): 569–600.

110. John King, "Paradise Lost? Crime in the Caribbean: A Comparison of Barbados and Jamaica," *Caribbean Journal of Criminology and Social Psychology* 2 (1997): 30–44.

111. Robert Agnew, "A Durkheimian Strain Theory of Delinquency." Paper presented at the annual meeting of the American Society of Criminology, Baltimore, November 1990.

112. Nikos Passas, "Anomie and Relative Deprivation." Paper presented at the annual meeting of the Eastern Sociological Society, Boston, 1987.

113. Robert Agnew, "Foundation for a General Strain Theory of Crime and Delinquency," *Criminology* 30 (1992): 47–87.

114. Ibid., p. 57.

115. Timothy Brezina, "Adolescent Maltreatment and Delinquency: The Question of Intervening Processes," *Journal of Research in Crime and Delinquency* 35 (1998): 71–99.

116. Paul Mazerolle and Alex Piquero, "Linking General Strain with Anger: Investigating the Instrumental, Escapist, and Violent Adaptations to Strain." Paper presented at the American Society of Criminology meeting, Boston, Mass., November 1995.

117. Paul Mazerolle, Velmer Burton, Francis Cullen, T. David Evans, and Gary Payne, "Strain, Anger, and Delinquent Adaptations Specifying General Strain Theory," *Journal of Criminal Justice* 28 (2000): 89–101; Paul Mazerolle and Alex Piquero, "Violent Responses to Strain: An Examination of Conditioning Influences," *Violence and Victimization* 12 (1997): 323–45.

118. George E. Capowich, Paul Mazerolle, and Alex Piquero, "General Strain Theory, Situational Anger, and Social Networks: An Assessment of Conditioning Influences," *Journal of Criminal Justice* 29 (2001): 445–61.

119. Timothy Brezina, "The Functions of Aggression: Violent Adaptations to Interpersonal Violence." Paper presented at the American Society of Criminology Meeting, San Diego, Calif., 1997.

120. Robert Agnew, Timothy Brezina, John Paul Wright, and Frances Cullen, "Strain, Personality Traits, and Delinquency: Extending General Strain Theory," *Criminology* 40 (2002): 43–72; Robert Agnew, "Stability and Change in Crime over the Life Course: A Strain Theory Explanation," in *Advances in Criminological Theory*, vol. 7, Developmental Theories of Crime and Delinquency, ed. Terence Thornberry (New Brunswick, N.J.: Transaction Books, 1995), pp. 113–37.

121. Lawrence Wu, "Effects of Family Instability, Income and Income Instability on the Risk of Premarital Birth," *American Sociological Review* 61 (1996): 386–406.

122. Anthony Walsh, "Behavior Genetics and Anomie/Strain Theory," *Criminology* 38 (2000): 1075–1108.

123. Robert Agnew and Helene Raskin White, "An Empirical Test of General Strain Theory," *Criminology* 30 (1992): 475–99.

124. John Hoffman and Alan Miller, "A Latent Variable Analysis of General Strain Theory," *Journal of Quantitative Criminology* 13 (1997) 111–13; Raymond Paternoster and Paul Mazerolle, "General Strain Theory and Delinquency: A Replication and Extension," *Journal of Research in Crime and Delinquency* 31(1994): 235–63.

125. G. Roger Jarjoura, "The Conditional Effect of Social Class on the Dropout–Delinquency Relationship," *Journal of Research in Crime and Delinquency* 33 (1996): 232–55.

126. Thomas Ashby Wills, Donato Vaccaro, Grace McNamara, and A. Elizabeth Hirky, "Escalated Substance Use: A Longitudinal Grouping Analysis from Early to Middle Adolescence," *Journal of Abnormal Psychology* 105 (1996): 166–80.

127. Timothy Brezina, "Adapting to Strain: An Examination of Delinquent Coping Responses," *Criminology* 34 (1996): 39–61.

128. Lisa Broidy, "A Test of General Strain Theory," *Criminology* 39 (2001): 9–36.

129. Robert Agnew and Timothy Brezina, "Relational Problems with Peers, Gender and Delinquency," *Youth and Society* 29 (1997): 84–111.

130. John Hoffmann and S. Susan Su, "The Conditional Effects of Stress on Delinquency and Drug Use: A Strain Theory in Assessment of Sex Differences," *Journal of Research in Crime and Delinquency* 34 (1997): 46–78.

131. Lisa Broidy, "The Role of Gender in General Strain Theory." Paper presented at the American Society of

Criminology meeting, Boston, Mass., November 1995.

132. Lisa Broidy and Robert Agnew, "Gender and Crime: A General Strain Theory Perspective," *Journal of Research in Crime and Delinquency* 34 (1997): 275–306.

133. Robbin Ogle, Daniel Maier-Katkin, and Thomas Bernard, "A Theory of Homicidal Behavior among Women," *Criminology* 33 (1995): 173–93.

134. Thorsten Sellin, *Culture Conflict and Crime,* Bulletin no. 41 (New York: Social Science Research Council, 1938).

135. Ibid., p. 22.

136. Ibid., p. 29.

137. Ibid., p. 68.

138. Walter Miller, "Lower-Class Culture as a Generating Milieu of Gang Delinquency," *Journal of Social Issues* 14 (1958): 5–19.

139. Ibid., pp. 14–17.

140. Fred Markowitz and Richard Felson, "Social-Demographic Attitudes and Violence," *Criminology* 36 (1998): 117–38.

141. Jeffrey Fagan, *Adolescent Violence: A View from the Street,* NIJ Research Preview (Washington, D.C.: National Institute of Justice, 1998)

142. Elijah Anderson, *Code of the Street: Decency, Violence, and the Moral Life of the Inner City* (New York: Norton, 2000).

143. Albert Cohen, *Delinquent Boys* (New York: Free Press, 1955).

144. Ibid., p. 25.

145. Ibid., p. 28.

146. Ibid.

147. Clarence Schrag, *Crime and Justice American Style* (Washington, D.C.: U.S. Government Printing Office, 1971), p. 74.

148. Cohen, *Delinquent Boys,* p. 30.

149. Ibid., p. 31.

150. Ibid., p. 133.

151. J. Johnstone, "Social Class, Social Areas, and Delinquency," *Sociology and Social Research* 63 (1978): 49–72; Joseph Harry, "Social Class and Delinquency: One More Time," *Sociological Quarterly* 15 (1974): 294–301.

152. Richard Cloward and Lloyd Ohlin, *Delinquency and Opportunity* (New York: Free Press, 1960).

153. Ibid., p. 7.

154. Ibid., p. 85.

155. Ibid., p. 171.

156. Ibid., p. 23.

157. Ibid., p. 73.

158. Ibid., p. 24.

159. Christopher Uggen, "Work as a Turning Point in the Life Course of Criminals: A Duration Model of Age, Employment and Recidivism," *American Sociological Review* 65 (2000): 529–46.

160. Finn-Aage Esbensen and David Huizinga, "Gangs, Drugs and Delinquency in a Survey of Urban Youth," *Criminology* 31 (1993): 565–87.

161. Robert Sampson and William Julius Wilson, "Toward a Theory of Race, Crime and Urban Inequality," in *Crime and Inequality,* eds. John Hagan and Ruth Peterson (Stanford, Calif.: Stanford University Press, 1995), pp. 37–54.

162. For a general criticism, see Kornhauser, *Social Sources of Delinquency.*

163. Charles Tittle, "Social Class and Criminal Behavior: A Critique of the Theoretical Foundations," *Social Forces* 62 (1983): 334–58.

164. James Q. Wilson and Richard Herrnstein, *Crime and Human Nature* (New York: Simon and Schuster, 1985).

165. Kenneth Polk and F. Lynn Richmond, "Those Who Fail," in *Schools and Delinquency,* eds. Kenneth Polk and Walter Schafer (Englewood Cliffs, N.J.: Prentice-Hall, 1974), p. 67.

166. Kathleen Maguire and Ann Pastore, *Sourcebook of Criminal Justice Statistics, 1996* (Washington, D.C.: U.S. Government Printing Office, 1996), pp. 150–66.

167. James DeFronzo, "Welfare and Burglary," *Crime and Delinquency* 42 (1996): 223–30.

168. Solomon Kobrin, "The Chicago Area Project—25-Year Assessment," *Annals of the American Academy of Political and Social Science* 322 (1959): 20–29.

CHAPTER 8 Social Process Theories

Introduction

Many criminologists question whether a person's place in the social structure alone can control or predict the onset of criminality. After all, the majority of people residing in the nation's most deteriorated urban areas are law-abiding citizens who hold conventional values and compensate for their lack of social standing and financial problems with hard work, frugal living, and keeping an eye to the future. Conversely, self-report studies tell us that many members of the privileged classes engage in theft, drug use, and other crimes.

The NCVS estimates that about 26 million serious crimes occur annually. If the average active criminal commits one serious crime every two weeks, about 2 million people could account for almost the entire serious crime problem (half being in prison or jail at any given time, and the other half committing crimes).[1] Today, more than 30 million Americans live below the poverty line. Even were it assumed that all criminals come from the lower class—which they don't—it is evident that the great majority of the most indigent Americans do not commit criminal acts even though they may have a great economic incentive to do so. As discussed in Chapter 7, neighborhood deterioration and disorganization alone cannot explain why one individual embarks on a criminal career while another, living in the same environment, obeys the law, gets an education, and seeks legitimate employment.[2]

Relatively few delinquent offenders living in the most deteriorated areas remain persistent, chronic offenders; most desist despite the continuing pressure of social decay. Some other social forces, then, must be at work to explain why the majority of at-risk individuals do not become persistent criminal offenders.

Socialization and Crime

To explain these contradictory findings, attention has been focused on social-psychological processes and interactions common to people at all segments of the social structure. **Social process theories** hold that criminality is a function of individual socialization. These theories draw attention to the interactions people have with various organizations, institutions, and processes of society such as education, employment, family life, and peer relations. As individuals pass through the life cycle, most are influenced by the direction of their familial relationships, peer group associations, educational experiences, and interactions with authority figures, including teachers, employers, and agents of the justice system. If these relationships are positive and supportive, individuals will be able to succeed within the rules of society; if these relationships are dysfunctional and destructive, conventional success may be impossible and criminal solutions may become a feasible alternative.

Social process theories share one basic concept: all people, regardless of their race, class, or gender, have the potential to become delinquents or criminals. Although members of the lower class may have the added burdens of poverty, racism, poor schools, and disrupted family lives, these social forces may be counteracted by positive peer relations, a supportive family, and educational success. In contrast, even the most affluent members of society may turn to antisocial behavior if their life experiences are intolerable or destructive.

The influence of social process theories has endured because the relationship between social class and crime is still uncertain. Most residents of inner-city areas refrain from criminal activity, and few of those who do commit crimes remain persistent chronic offenders into their adulthood. If poverty were the sole cause of crime, then indigent adults would be as criminal as indigent teenagers. The association between economic status and crime has been called "problematic" because class position alone cannot explain crime rates.[3]

CONNECTIONS

The analysis in Chapter 3 of the class–crime relationship shows why this is still a hotly debated topic. Although serious criminals may be disproportionately found in lower-class areas, self-report studies show that criminality cuts across class lines. The discussion of drug use in Chapter 14 shows that members of the middle class engage in recreational substance use and abuse; this indicates that many law violators are not necessarily economically motivated. ■

Criminologists have long studied the critical elements of socialization to determine how they contribute to a burgeoning criminal career. Prominent among these elements are the family, the peer group, and the school.

Family Relations

For some time, family relationships have been considered a major determinant of behavior.[4] In fact, there is abundant evidence that parenting factors, such as the ability to communicate and to provide proper discipline, may play a critical role in determining whether people misbehave as children, and even later as adults. This is one of the most replicated findings in the criminological literature.[5]

Use the term "parental deprivation" as a subject guide in InfoTrac College Edition to find out the effects of parental absence on children. ■

Youth who grow up in households characterized by conflict and tension, where parents are absent or separated, or where there is a lack of familial love and support, are susceptible to the crime-promoting forces in the environment.[6] Even those children living in so-called high-crime areas will be better able to resist the temptations of

© Tom McCarthy/Photo Edit

■ According to social process theory, youths who grow up in a household characterized by conflict and tension, where parents are absent or separated, or where there is a lack of familial love and support, are susceptible to the crime-promoting forces in the environment. In contrast, children will be able to resist crime if they receive fair discipline, care, and support from parents and other family members who provide them with strong, positive role models.

the streets if they receive fair discipline, care, and support from parents who provide them with strong, positive role models.[7] Nonetheless, living in a disadvantaged neighborhood places terrific strain on family functioning, especially in single-parent families that experience social isolation from relatives, friends, and neighbors. Children who are raised within such distressed families are at risk for delinquency.[8]

The relationship between family structure and crime is critical when the high rates of divorce and single parents are considered. The U.S. Census Bureau estimates that the percentage of children living in homes headed by married couples is on the decline and should be further reduced from about 35 percent today to about 29 percent in 2010.[9] This trend is important when we consider the fact that since 1960 the number of single-parent households in the population has been significantly related to arrest rates.[10]

For a site devoted to family issues of all types, go to:
http://www.unitedfamilyservices.com/
For an up-to-date list of Web links, go to
http://info.wadsworth.com/siegel ■

At one time, growing up in a so-called *broken home* was considered a primary cause of criminal behavior. However, many criminologists today discount the association between family structure and the onset of criminality, claiming that family conflict and discord are more important determinants of behavior than family structure.[11] Not all experts discount the effects of family structure on crime, however. Even if single mothers (or fathers) can

make up for the loss of a second parent, the argument goes, it is simply more difficult to do so and the chances of failure increase. Single parents may find it difficult to provide adequate supervision. Kids whose parents are divorced are more likely to engage in delinquency, especially if they hang out with peers who engage in criminal behaviors. The lack of supervision in the aftermath of divorce may expose some kids to the negative effects of antisocial peers.[12] There is evidence that children who live with single parents receive less encouragement and less help with schoolwork. Poor school achievement and limited educational aspirations have been associated with delinquent behavior. Also, because they are receiving less attention as a result of having just one parent, these children may be more prone to rebellious acts, such as running away and truancy.[13] Children in two-parent households, on the other hand, are more likely to want to go on to college than kids in single-parent homes.[14]

Does remarriage help the educational achievement of kids who live in single-parent households? To find out, read this article in InfoTrac College Edition: William Jeynes. Effects of remarriage following divorce on the academic achievement of children. *Journal of Youth and Adolescence* June 1999 v28 i3 p385(9) ■

Because their incomes may decrease substantially in the aftermath of marital breakup, some divorced mothers are forced to move to residences in deteriorated neighborhoods. Some of these disorganized neighborhoods may place children at risk of crime and drug abuse.[15] When a mother remarries, it does not seem to mitigate the effects of divorce on youth. Children living with a stepparent exhibit as many problems as youth in single-parent families and considerably more problems than those who are living with both biological parents.[16]

Other family factors with predictive value include inconsistent discipline, poor supervision, and the lack of a warm, loving, supportive parent–child relationship.[17] Parents who are supportive and effectively control their children in a noncoercive fashion (parental efficacy) are more likely to raise children who refrain from delinquency.[18] Delinquency will be reduced if parents provide the type of structure that integrates children into families while giving them the ability to assert their individuality and regulate their own behavior.[19] In contrast, children who have warm and affectionate ties to their parents report greater levels of self-esteem beginning in adolescence and extending into their adulthood; high self-esteem is inversely related to criminal behavior.[20] Conversely, when a parent exhibits deviant behavior, the children are more likely to follow suit. In fact, parental deviance has been linked to a child's criminal behavior.

Children growing up in homes where a parent suffers from mental impairment are also at risk for delinquency.[21] Even children as young as 2 years old who are the children of drug abusers exhibit personality defects such as excessive anger and negativity.[22] These children, and those who are older, are more likely to become persistent substance abusers than the children of nonabusers.[23] John Laub and Robert Sampson find that parents who engage in criminality and substance abuse are more likely to raise children who engage in law-violating behavior than the offspring of conventional law-abiding parents.[24]

CONNECTIONS

Sampson and Laub's research will be discussed more fully in Chapter 10. Although deviant parents may encourage offending, Sampson and Laub believe that life experiences can either encourage crime-prone people to offend or conversely aid them in their return to a conventional lifestyle. ■

Child Abuse and Crime

There is also a suspected link between child abuse, neglect, sexual abuse, and crime.[25] A number of studies show that there is a significant association between child maltreatment and serious self-reported and official delinquency, even when taking into account gender, race, and class.[26] Children who are subject to even minimum amounts of physical punishment may be more likely to use violence themselves in personal interactions.[27] In nonviolent societies, parents rarely punish their children physically; in more violent societies, there is a link between corporal punishment, delinquency, anger, spousal abuse, depression, and adult crime.[28]

CONNECTIONS

Chapter 4 noted that victims of abuse may suffer significant social problems and emotional stress related to criminal activity. Process theories recognize the role of family relations in escalating criminal activity. ■

The effect of the family on delinquency has also been observed in other cultures. Research conducted in 10 European countries shows that the degree to which parents and teachers approve of corporal punishment is related to the overall homicide rate and as well as the infant homicide rate.[29] Studies of Chinese families show that those who provide firm support inhibit delinquency, whereas families that have one or both parents who are deviant are more likely to have children who are involved in deviant activities.[30]

The goal of the Institute for Child and Family is to stimulate and coordinate the cross-disciplinary work required to make progress on the most difficult child and family policy issues facing the United States. Visit their Web site at:
  http://www.childpolicy.org/
For an up-to-date list of Web links, go to
  http://info.wadsworth.com/siegel ■

Educational Experience

The educational process and adolescent achievement in school have been linked to criminality. Studies show that children who do poorly in school, lack educational motivation, and feel alienated are the most likely to engage in criminal acts.[31] Children who fail in school have been found to offend more frequently than those who are successful in school. These children commit more serious and violent offenses and persist in their offending into adulthood.[32]

Schools contribute to criminality in that when they label problem youths they set them apart from conventional society. One way in which schools perpetuate this stigmatization is the "track system," which identifies some students as college bound and others as academic underachievers or potential dropouts.[33] Those children placed in tracks labeled "advanced placement," "college prep," or "honors" will develop positive self-images and achievement motivation, whereas those assigned to lower level or general courses of study may believe academic achievement is closed to someone of their limited skills. Research indicates that many school dropouts, especially those who have been expelled, face a significant chance of entering a criminal career.[34] In contrast, doing well in school and developing attachments to teachers has been linked to crime resistance.[35]

Does delinquency cause educational failure? Or does educational failure cause delinquency? To find out, read this article in InfoTrac College Edition: Julian Tanner, Scott Davies, and Bill O'Grady. Whatever happened to yesterday's rebels? Longitudinal effects of youth delinquency on education and employment. *Social Problems* May 1999 v46 i2 p250(1) ■

Efforts to keep children in school are discussed in the Policy and Practice in Criminology feature highlighting a program called Communities In Schools.

The association between the educational experience and crime is highlighted by the growing evidence that many criminal acts occur on school grounds. One national survey found that about 15 percent of students ages 12 through 19 report violent or property victimization at school each year.[36] Another study found that 190,000 fights occur on school grounds each year. In addition, there are about 116,000 incidents of theft, 98,000 incidents of vandalism, 4,000 rapes, 7,000 robberies, and 11,000 fights or attacks with a weapon.[37] One reason for a recent upsurge in school violence may be the number of students who are bringing weapons to school: by age 15, about 15 percent of students know a student who brought a gun to school.

Peer Relations

Psychologists have long recognized that the peer group has a powerful effect on human conduct and can have a dramatic influence on decision making and behavior choices.[38] Peer influence on behavior has been recorded in different cultures and may be a universal norm.[39]

Early in children's lives, parents are the primary source of influence and attention. Between the ages of 8 and 14, children begin to seek out a stable peer group. If all goes as it should, both the number and variety of friendships increase as children go through adolescence. Soon, friends begin having a greater influence over decision making than parents.[40]

By their early teens, children report that their friends give them emotional support when they are feeling badly and that they can confide intimate feelings to peers without worrying about their confidences being betrayed. In later adolescence, peer approval has a major impact on socialization. As they go through adolescence, children form cliques, small groups of friends who share activities and confidences. They also belong to crowds, loosely organized groups of children who share interests and activities. While clique members share intimate knowledge, crowds are brought together by mutually shared activities, such as sports, religion, or hobbies. Though bonds in this "wider circle of friends" may not be intimate, adolescents learn a lot about themselves and their world while navigating through these relationships.[41] Some adolescents who are considered "popular" may be members of a variety of cliques and crowds. The most popular youths, in general, tend to do well in school and are socially astute.

In contrast, children who are rejected by their peers are more likely to display aggressive behavior and disrupt group activities through bickering, bullying, or other antisocial behavior.[42] Peer relations, then, are a vital aspect of maturation.

Use "peers and delinquency" as key words in InfoTrac College Edition to find out more about the interrelationship between these two critical factors. ■

Because of the powerful influence adolescents feel from their peers, they feel a persistent pressure to conform to group values. When the peer pressure is exerted from positive relationships, peers guide each other and help their friends learn to share and cooperate, cope with aggressive impulses, and discuss feelings they would not dare bring up at home. In these relationships, youths can compare their own experiences and learn that others have similar concerns and problems. Through these friendships, they realize they are not alone. When the peer group is not among friends who are positive influences on each other, however, adolescent criminal activity can begin to be initiated as a group process.[43] Though experts have long debated the exact relationship between peer group interaction and delinquency, research shows that adolescents who report inadequate or strained peer relations, and who say they are not popular with the "opposite sex," are the ones most likely to become delinquent.[44]

Delinquent peers often exert tremendous influence on behavior, attitudes, and beliefs.[45] In every level of the social structure, youths who fall in with a "bad crowd" become more susceptible to criminal behavior patterns.[46] These deviant peers provide friendship networks that support delinquency and drug use.[47] Activities such as riding around, staying out late, and partying with deviant peers provide these groups with the opportunity to commit deviant acts.[48] Because delinquent friends tend to be, as criminologist Mark Warr puts it, "sticky" (once acquired, they are not easily lost), peer influence may continue throughout the life span.[49]

Some children join more than one deviant group, playing a leadership role in one and being a follower in another. Even when some of these groups are short lived, being exposed to so many deviant influences in multiple groups may help explain why deviant group membership is highly correlated with personal offending rates.[50] The more antisocial the peer group, the more likely its members will engage in delinquency; nondelinquent friends will help moderate delinquency.[51]

As children grow and move forward, friends will influence their behavior, and their behavior will influence their friends.[52] Antisocial friends guide delinquent careers so they withstand the aging-out process.[53] People who maintain close relations with antisocial peers will sustain their own criminal behavior into their adulthood.

Keeping Kids in School: The Communities In Schools Program

Millions of Americans have not completed high school; they are dropouts. Research indicates that they will earn less over their lifetimes and be at risk for criminality. Four in 10 dropouts said they left high school because they were failing or they did not like school; an equal number of males and females reported they were leaving school because of personality conflicts with teachers. More males than females dropped out because of school suspension or expulsion.

A popular government-supported program designed to reduce the number of students who drop out of school is the Communities In Schools (CIS) network (formerly known as Cities In Schools). This program includes a web of local, state, and national partnerships working together to bring at-risk youth four basic necessities to help motivate them to stay in school:

- A personal one-on-one relationship with a caring adult.
- A safe place to learn and grow.
- A marketable skill to use upon graduation.

- A chance to give back to peers and community.

A student's "decision" to drop out of school may result from a variety of social and emotional problems, such as family dissention, drug and alcohol abuse, illiteracy, or teenage pregnancy. Therefore, the entire community, not just the schools, must take responsibility for preventing youth from dropping out of school. CIS brings together businesses and public and private agencies in communities—welfare and health professionals, employment counselors, social workers and recreation leaders, the clergy, and members of community groups—in the schools. CIS caters to the student and his or her family, bringing together in one place a support system of caring adults. They ensure that the student has access to the resources that can help him or her build self-worth and the skills needed to embark on a productive and constructive life.

Most CIS programs take place inside traditional schools, but another method of service delivery is the CIS academy, an easily identifiable free-standing facility or wing of an existing school, sponsored largely by an individual corporation or organization.

In general, CIS projects are grouped into three broad categories:

- Traditional school site projects that pattern themselves as closely as possible after the normal classroom routine.
- Projects in which repositioned health and human services staff assume the primary role.
- Projects that function as alternative schools.

The first two categories apply to the classroom model; the third applies to the academy model.

The CIS *classroom model* enables students to sign up for the program as an elective class. Instruction focuses on life-skills education, such as employment, remedial education, and tutoring. CIS classrooms often involve community volunteers who mentor and tutor students. The classroom model also can provide in-school activities such as conflict resolution, violence abatement, and community service. The classroom structure is patterned closely after a normal routine. Teachers assigned by the school district to the CIS program lead these activities. In certain situations, repositioned health and human services staff assume the primary leadership role

The *academy model* has all the basic elements of the CIS classroom model but is organized as an alternative

Institutional Involvement and Belief

It follows that people who hold high moral values and beliefs, who have learned to distinguish "right from wrong," and who regularly attend religious services should also eschew crime and other antisocial behaviors. Religion binds people together and forces them to confront the consequences of their behavior. Committing crimes would violate the principles of all organized religions.

Sociologists Travis Hirschi and Rodney Stark found (in an often-cited study) that, contrary to expectations, the association between religious attendance and belief and delinquent behavior patterns is negligible and insignificant.[54] However, some recent research efforts have reached an opposite conclusion, find that attending religious services has a significant negative impact on crime.[55] Kids living in disorganized high-crime areas who attend religious services are better able to resist illegal drug use.[56]

Interestingly, participation seems to be a more significant inhibitor of crime than merely having religious beliefs and values.[57] Cross-national research shows that countries with high rates of church membership and attendance have lower crime rates than less "devout" nations.[58]

CONNECTIONS

Arousal theory would predict that church attendance is inversely correlated with crime rates because criminals are people who need large amounts of stimulation and would not be able to sit through religious services. See Chapter 6 for more on arousal theory. ■

The Effects of Socialization on Crime

To many criminologists, the elements of socialization described up to this point are the chief determinants of crim-

school. These academies can be "schools within schools," located in a separate wing or section of the school where the CIS students attend classes together, or can occupy a completely separate building. A student who meets CIS program eligibility criteria and has parental permission is assigned a case manager who assesses the student's needs. The case manager then contacts the proper agencies to provide the specific services needed. Through the CIS program, the young person can receive counseling either individually or as part of a group. If the CIS program cannot provide a needed service directly, the student, and sometimes parents and family members, are referred to an appropriate service agency.

CIS programs serve a target population of at-risk youth and youth who have already crossed the line into risky behaviors and consequences. If not for the CIS program, most of these students would be expected to leave school before graduation. Evaluations of the program show the following results:

- High proportions of CIS students remain in school or graduate.
- Of the students who participated in CIS services, 80 percent were still in school or had graduated.

- The cumulative dropout rate for CIS students is about 7 percent annually.
- CIS students who had had serious to moderately severe problems in attendance and academic performance improved their performance in these areas.

About 70 percent of students with high absenteeism prior to participation in CIS improved their attendance, and 60 percent with low initial grades improved. Of those students with the lowest grades (GPA below 1.0), 79 percent raised their GPA, with an average increase of a full grade point. The majority of the students believed they had benefited from CIS and expressed high levels of satisfaction with the program.

Today, almost 2 million students participate in the CIS program at 2500 different educational sites. The CIS program is a good example of how strengthening an adolescent's bond to a critical element of the social process can improve his or her chances of a successful life.

Critical Thinking Questions

1. Why does the CIS program seem to be making a difference for at-risk youth?
2. What is it about the way the program is structured that allows

students the opportunity to succeed?
3. What is it about the program that makes it possible for underachieving students to be successful in the CIS program?
4. What other alternative may be available to help motivate kids to stay in school? What other special programs may be helpful?

InfoTrac College Edition Research

To learn more, read these articles:

Adel Wassef, Gayle Mason, Melissa Lassiter Collins, Michael O'Boyle, and Denise Ingham. Student assessment of school-based support groups. *Adolescence* Spring 1996 v31 n121 p1

Clyde A. Winters. Learning disabilities, crime, delinquency, and special education placement. *Adolescence* Summer 1997 v32 p451–58

SOURCES: Susan Siegel, *Communities In Schools Network Report 2000–2001, a Year of Connections, Relations, and Results* (Alexandria, VA: 2002). Sharon Cantelon and Donni LeBoeuf, *Keeping Young People in School: Community Programs That Work* (Washington, D.C: National Institute of Justice, 1997).

inal behavior. According to this view, people living in even the most deteriorated urban areas can successfully resist inducements to crime if they have a positive self-image, learn moral values, and have the support of their parents, peers, teachers, and neighbors. The girl with a positive self-image who is chosen for a college scholarship has the warm, loving support of her parents and is viewed as someone "going places" by friends and neighbors. She is less likely to adopt a "criminal way of life" than another adolescent who is abused at home, lives with criminal parents, and whose bond to her school and peer group is shattered because she is labeled a "troublemaker."[59] The boy who has learned criminal behavior from his parents and siblings and then joins a neighborhood gang is much more likely to become an adult criminal than his next door neighbor who idolizes his hard working, deeply religious parents. It is socialization, not the social structure that de-

termines life chances. As Figure 8.1 shows, the more social problems encountered during the socialization process, the greater the likelihood that youths will encounter difficulties and obstacles as they mature, such as being unemployed or becoming a teenage mother.

Theorists who believe that an individual's socialization determines the likelihood of criminality adopt the **social process approach** to human behavior. The social process approach has several independent branches (see Figure 8.1). The first branch, **social learning theory,** suggests that people learn the techniques and attitudes of crime from close and intimate relationships with criminal peers; crime is a learned behavior. The second, **social control theory,** maintains that everyone has the potential to become a criminal but that most people are controlled by their bonds to society. Crime occurs when the forces that bind people to society are weakened or broken. The third branch, **social**

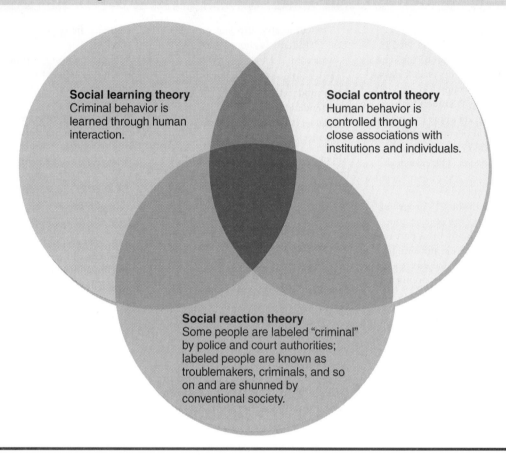

Social learning theory
Criminal behavior is learned through human interaction.

Social control theory
Human behavior is controlled through close associations with institutions and individuals.

Social reaction theory
Some people are labeled "criminal" by police and court authorities; labeled people are known as troublemakers, criminals, and so on and are shunned by conventional society.

reaction **(labeling) theory,** says people become criminals when significant members of society label them as such and they accept those labels as a personal identity.

Put another way, social learning theory assumes people are born "good" and learn to be "bad"; social control theory assumes people are born "bad" and must be controlled in order to be "good"; social reaction theory assumes that, whether "good" or "bad," people are controlled by the reactions of others. Each of these independent branches will be discussed separately.

■ Social Learning Theory

Social learning theorists believe crime is a product of learning the norms, values, and behaviors associated with criminal activity. Social learning can involve the actual techniques of crime—how to hot-wire a car or roll a joint—as well as the psychological aspects of criminality—how to deal with the guilt or shame associated with illegal activities. This section briefly reviews the three most prominent forms of social learning theory: differential association theory, differential reinforcement theory, and neutralization theory.

Differential Association Theory

One of the most prominent social learning theories is Edwin H. Sutherland's **differential association theory (DA).** Often considered the preeminent U.S. criminologist, Sutherland first put forth his theory in 1939 in his text, *Principles of Criminology.*[60] The final version of the theory appeared in 1947. When Sutherland died in 1950, Donald Cressey, his long-time associate, continued his work. Cressey was so successful in explaining and popularizing his mentor's efforts that DA remains one of the most enduring explanations of criminal behavior.

Sutherland's research on white-collar crime, professional theft, and intelligence led him to dispute the notion that crime was a function of the inadequacy of people in the lower classes.[61] To Sutherland, criminality stemmed neither from individual traits nor from socioeconomic position; instead, he believed it to be a function of a learning process that could affect any individual in any culture. Acquiring a behavior is a social learning process, not a political or legal process. Skills and motives conducive to crime are learned as a result of contacts with procrime values, attitudes, and definitions and other patterns of criminal behavior.

According to differential association theory, becoming a criminal is a learning process. Conversely, it may be possible to help troubled youth forgo criminality if they are taught prosocial behavior and attitudes. Here, brothers Hans (with daughter Jamile) and Irvin Hageman are shown outside the East Harlem School at Exodus House. The brothers gave up lucrative careers to run the school at the site of a former drug rehabilitation center. It has been described as a "nugget of hope within a neighborhood of despair."

Principles of differential association

The basic principles of differential association are explained as follows:[62]

- **Criminal behavior is learned.** This statement differentiates Sutherland's theory from prior attempts to classify criminal behavior as an inherent characteristic of criminals. By suggesting that delinquent and criminal behavior is learned, Sutherland implied that it can be classified in the same manner as any other learned behavior, such as writing, painting, or reading.

- **Learning is a by-product of interaction.** Criminal behavior is learned as a by-product of interacting with others. Sutherland believed individuals do not start violating the law simply by living in a crimogenic environment or by manifesting personal characteristics, such as low IQ or family problems, associated with criminality. People actively participate in the learning process as they interact with other individuals who serve as teachers and guides to crime. Thus, criminality cannot occur without the aid of others.

- **Learning occurs within intimate groups.** Learning criminal behavior occurs within intimate personal groups. People's contacts with their most intimate social companions—family, friends, peers—have the greatest influence on their deviant behavior and attitude development. Relationships with these influential individuals color and control the way individuals interpret everyday events. For example, research shows that children who grow up in homes where parents abuse alcohol are more likely to view drinking as being socially and physically beneficial.[63] The inti-

macy of these associations far outweighs the importance of any other form of communication—for example, movies or television. Even on those rare occasions when violent motion pictures seem to provoke mass criminal episodes, these outbreaks can be more readily explained as a reaction to peer group pressure than as a reaction to the films themselves.

- **Criminal techniques are learned.** Learning criminal behavior involves learning the techniques of committing the crime, which are sometimes very complicated and sometimes very simple. This requires learning the specific direction of motives, drives, rationalizations, and attitudes. Young delinquents learn from their associates the proper way to pick a lock, shoplift, and obtain and use narcotics. In addition, novice criminals learn to use the proper terminology for their acts and then acquire "proper" reactions to law violations. For example, getting high on marijuana and learning the proper way to "smoke a joint" are behavior patterns usually acquired from more experienced companions. Moreover, criminals must learn how to react properly to their illegal acts, such as when to defend them, rationalize them, or show remorse for them.

- **Perceptions of legal code influence motives and drives.** The specific direction of motives and drives is learned from perceptions of various aspects of the legal code as being favorable or unfavorable. The reaction to social rules and laws is not uniform across society, and people constantly come into contact with others who maintain different views on the utility of obeying the legal code. Some people they admire may openly disdain or flout the law or ignore its substance. People experience what Sutherland calls culture conflict when they are exposed to different and opposing attitudes toward what is right and wrong, moral and immoral. The conflict of social attitudes and cultural norms is the basis for the concept of differential association.

A person becomes a criminal when he or she perceives more favorable than unfavorable consequences to violating the law (see Figure 8.2). According to Sutherland's theory, individuals become law violators when they are in contact with persons, groups, or events that produce an excess of definitions favorable toward criminality and are isolated from counteracting forces. A definition favorable toward criminality occurs, for example, when a person is exposed to friends sneaking into a theater to avoid paying for a ticket or talking about the virtues of getting high on drugs. A definition unfavorable toward crime occurs when friends or parents demonstrate their disapproval of crime. Neutral behavior, such as reading a book, is neither positive nor negative with respect to law violation. Cressey argues that neutral behavior is important: for example, when a child is occupied doing something neutral, it prevents him or her

from being in contact with those involved in criminal behaviors.[64]

Differential associations may vary in frequency, duration, priority, and intensity. Whether a person learns to obey the law or to disregard it is influenced by the quality of social interactions. Those of lasting *duration* have greater influence than those that are brief. Similarly, *frequent* contacts have greater effect than rare and haphazard contacts. Sutherland did not specify what he meant by *priority*, but Cressey and others have interpreted the term to mean the age of children when they first encounter definitions of criminality. Contacts made early in life probably have a greater and more far-reaching influence than those developed later on. Finally, *intensity* is generally interpreted to mean the importance and prestige attributed to the individual or groups from whom the definitions are learned. For example, the influence of a father, mother, or trusted friend far outweighs the effect of more socially distant figures.

The process of learning criminal behavior by association with criminal and anticriminal patterns involves all of the mechanisms involved in any other learning process. This suggests that learning criminal behavior patterns is similar to learning nearly all other patterns and is not a matter of mere imitation.

Figure 8.2 Differential Associations

Differential association theory assumes that criminal behavior will occur when the definitions toward crime outweigh the definitions against crime.

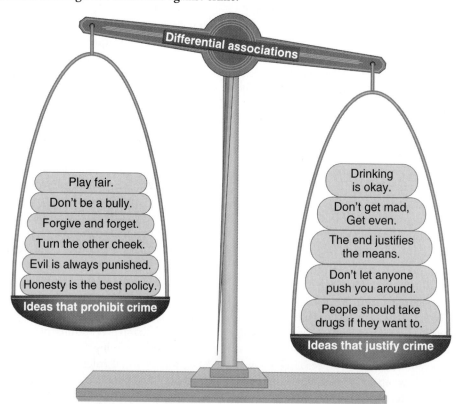

Differential associations

Ideas that prohibit crime
- Play fair.
- Don't be a bully.
- Forgive and forget.
- Turn the other cheek.
- Evil is always punished.
- Honesty is the best policy.

Ideas that justify crime
- Drinking is okay.
- Don't get mad, Get even.
- The end justifies the means.
- Don't let anyone push you around.
- People should take drugs if they want to.

Criminal behavior is an expression of general needs and values, but it is not excused by those general needs and values because noncriminal behavior is also an expression of those same needs and values. This principle suggests that the motives for criminal behavior cannot logically be the same as those for conventional behavior. Sutherland rules out such motives as desire to accumulate money or social status, personal frustration, or low self-concept as causes of crime because they are just as likely to produce noncriminal behavior, such as getting a better education or working harder on a job. It is only the learning of deviant norms through contact with an excess of definitions favorable toward criminality that produces illegal behavior.

In sum, differential association theory holds that people learn criminal attitudes and behavior while in their adolescence from close and trusted friends and/or relatives. A criminal career develops if learned antisocial values and behaviors are not at least matched or exceeded by conventional attitudes and behaviors. Criminal behavior, then, is learned in a process that is similar to learning any other human behavior.

To read a brief biography of Sutherland and learn how he formulated his ideas, go to:
   http://www.fitzroydearborn.com/chicago/ criminology/sample-sutherland-edwin.php3
For an up-to-date list of Web links, go to
   http://info.wadsworth.com/siegel ▪

Testing differential association theory   Despite the importance of differential association theory, research devoted to testing its assumptions has been relatively sparse. It has proven difficult to conceptualize the principles of the theory so that they can be empirically tested. For example, social scientists find it difficult to evaluate such vague concepts as "definition toward criminality." It is also difficult to follow people over time, establish precisely when definitions toward criminality begin to outweigh prosocial definitions, and determine if this imbalance produces criminal behavior.

Despite these limitations, several notable research efforts have supported the core principles of this theory. These generally show a correlation between (a) having deviant friends, (b) holding deviant attitudes, and (c) committing deviant acts.[65] In a classic work, criminologist James Short surveyed institutionalized youth and found that they had, in fact, maintained close associations with delinquent youths prior to their law-violating acts.[66] Mark Warr found that antisocial children who maintain delinquent friends over a long duration are much more likely to persist in their delinquent behavior than those without such peer support.[67]

Differential association also seems especially relevant in trying to explain the onset of substance abuse and a career in the drug trade. This requires learning proper techniques and attitudes from an experienced user or dealer.[68] In his interview study of low-level drug dealers, Kenneth Tunnell found that many novices were tutored by a more experienced criminal dealer who helped them make connections with buyers and sellers. One told him:

> I had a friend of mine who was an older guy, and he introduced me to selling marijuana to make a few dollars. I started selling a little and made a few dollars. For a young guy to be making a hundred dollars or so, it was a lot of money. So I got kind of tied up in that aspect of selling drugs.[69]

Tunnell found that making connections is an important part of the dealer's world. Adolescent drug users are likely to have intimate relationships with a peer friendship network that supports their substance abuse and teaches them how to deal within the drug world.[70]

Differential association may also be used to explain the gender difference in the crime rate. Males are more likely to socialize with deviant peers than females and, when they do, are more deeply influenced by peer relations.[71] Females are shielded by their unique moral sense, which makes caring about people and avoiding social harm a top priority. Males, in contrast, have a more cavalier toward others and are more interested in their own self-interests. They are therefore more susceptible to the influence of deviant peers.

Analysis of differential association theory   There have been a number of important critiques of the theory. According to the *cultural deviance critique,* differential association is invalid because it suggests that criminals are people "properly" socialized into a deviant subculture; that is, they are taught criminal norms by significant others. Supporters counter that differential association also recognizes that individuals can embrace criminality because they have been improperly socialized into the normative culture.[72]

Differential association theory also fails to explain why one youth who is exposed to delinquent definitions eventually succumbs to them, while another, living under the same conditions, is able to avoid criminal entanglements. It fails to account for the origin of delinquent definitions. How did the first "teacher" learn delinquent attitudes and definitions in order to pass them on? Another apparently valid criticism of differential association is that it assumes criminal and delinquent acts to be rational and systematic. This ignores spontaneous and wanton acts of violence and damage that appear to have little utility or purpose, such as the isolated psychopathic killing or serial rapist.

Another critique concerns the relationship between deviant peers and criminality. It is possible that youths learn about crime and then commit criminal acts, but it is also possible that experienced delinquents and criminals seek out like-minded peers after they engage in antisocial acts and that the internalization of deviant attitudes follows, rather than precedes, criminality ("birds of a feather flock together").[73]

Despite these criticisms, differential association theory maintains an important place in the study of criminal behavior. For one thing, it provides a consistent explanation of all types of delinquent and criminal behavior. Unlike social structure theories, it is not limited to the explanation of a single facet of antisocial activity, such as lower-class gang activity. The theory can also account for the extensive delinquent behavior found even in middle- and upper-class areas, where youths may be exposed to a variety of prodelinquent definitions from such sources as overly opportunistic parents and friends.

Differential Reinforcement Theory

Differential reinforcement theory is another attempt to explain crime as a type of learned behavior. First proposed by Ronald Akers in collaboration with Robert Burgess in 1966, it is a version of the social learning view that employs both differential association concepts along with elements of psychological learning theory

| CONNECTIONS |

Psychological learning theories were first discussed in Chapter 6. These trait theories maintain that human actions are developed through learning experiences. Behavior is supported by rewards and extinguished by negative reactions or punishments. Behavior is constantly being shaped by life experiences. ■

According to Akers, the same process is involved in learning both deviant and conventional behavior. People learn to be neither "all deviant" nor "all conforming" but rather strike a balance between the two opposing poles of behavior. This balance is usually stable, but it can undergo revision over time.[74]

A number of learning processes shape behavior. **Direct conditioning,** also called **differential reinforcement,** occurs when behavior is reinforced by being either rewarded or punished while interacting with others. When behavior is punished, this is referred to as **negative reinforcement.** This type of reinforcement can be distributed by using either negative stimuli (punishment) or loss of reward (negative punishment). Whether deviant or criminal behavior has been initiated or persists depends on the degree to which it has been rewarded or punished and the rewards or punishments attached to its alternatives.

According to Akers, people learn to evaluate their own behavior through their interactions with significant others and groups in their lives. These groups control sources and patterns of reinforcement, define behavior as right or wrong, and provide behaviors that can be modeled through observational learning. The more individuals learn to define their behavior as good or at least as justified, rather than

as undesirable, the more likely they are to engage in it. For example, adolescents who hook up with a drug abusing peer group whose members value drugs and alcohol, encourage their use, and provide opportunities to observe people abusing substances will be encouraged, through this social learning experience, to use drugs themselves.

Akers's theory posits that the principal influence on behavior comes from "those groups which control individuals' major sources of reinforcement and punishment and expose them to behavioral models and normative definitions."[75] The important groups are the ones with which a person is in differential association—peer and friendship groups, schools, churches, and similar institutions. Within the context of these critical groups, according to Akers, "deviant behavior can be expected to the extent that it has been differentially reinforced over alternative behavior . . . and is defined as desirable or justified."[76] Once people are indoctrinated into crime, their behavior can be reinforced by being exposed to deviant behavior models, associating with deviant peers, and lacking negative sanctions from parents or peers. The deviant behavior, originally executed by imitating someone else's behavior, is sustained by social support. It is possible that differential reinforcements help establish criminal careers and are a key factor in explaining persistent criminality.

Testing differential reinforcement   The principles of differential reinforcement have been subject to empirical review by Akers and other criminologists.[77] In an important test of his theory, Akers and his associates surveyed 3,065 male and female adolescents on drug- and alcohol-related activities and their perception of variables related to social learning and differential reinforcement. Items in the scale included the respondents' perceptions of esteemed peers' attitudes toward drug and alcohol abuse, the number of people they admired who actually used controlled substances, and whether people they admired would reward or punish them for substance abuse. Akers found a strong association between drug and alcohol abuse and social learning variables: those who believed they would be rewarded for deviance by those they respect were the ones most likely to engage in deviant behavior.[78]

Akers also found that the learning–deviant behavior link is not static. The learning experience continues within a deviant group as behavior is both influenced by, and exerts influence over, group processes. For example, adolescents may learn to smoke because their friends are smoking and, therefore, approve of this behavior. Over time, smoking influences friendships and peer group memberships as smokers seek each other out for companionship and support.[79]

Differential reinforcement theory is an important perspective that endeavors to determine the cause of criminal activity. It considers how the content of socialization conditions crime. Because not all socialization is positive, it accounts for the fact that negative social reinforcements and experiences can produce criminal results. This concurs with research that demonstrates that parental deviance is related to adolescent antisocial behavior.[80] Parents may reinforce their children's deviant behavior by supplying negative social reinforcements. Akers's work also fits well with rational choice theory because they both suggest that people learn the techniques and attitudes necessary to commit crime. Criminal knowledge is gained through experience. After considering the outcome of their past experiences, potential offenders decide which criminal acts will be profitable and which are dangerous and should be avoided.[81] Integrating these perspectives, people make rational choices about crime because they have learned to balance risks against the potential for criminal gain.

Neutralization Theory

Neutralization theory is identified with the writings of David Matza and his associate Gresham Sykes.[82] They view the process of becoming a criminal as a learning experience in which potential delinquents and criminals master techniques that enable them to counterbalance or neutralize conventional values and drift back and forth between illegitimate and conventional behavior. One reason this is possible is the subterranean value structure of American society. **Subterranean values** are morally tinged influences that have become entrenched in the culture but are publicly condemned. They exist side by side with conventional values and while condemned in public may be admired or practiced in private. Examples include viewing pornographic films, drinking alcohol to excess, and gambling on sporting events. In American culture, it is common to hold both subterranean and conventional values; few people are "all good" or "all bad."

To read more about the work and life of David Matza, go to:

http://www.criminology.fsu.edu/crimtheory/ matza.htm

For an up-to-date list of Web links, go to **http://info.wadsworth.com/siegel** ■

Matza argues that even the most committed criminals and delinquents are not involved in criminality all the time; they also attend schools, family functions, and religious services. Their behavior can be conceived as falling along a continuum between total freedom and total restraint. This process, which he calls **drift**, refers to the movement from one extreme of behavior to another, resulting in behavior that is sometimes unconventional, free, or deviant and at other times constrained and sober.[83] Learning techniques of neutralization enables a person to temporarily "drift away" from conventional behavior and get involved in more subterranean values and behaviors including crime and drug abuse.[84]

Sykes and Matza base their theoretical model on these observations:[85]

Criminals sometimes voice a sense of guilt over their illegal acts. If a stable criminal value system existed in opposition to generally held values and rules, it would be unlikely that criminals would exhibit any remorse for their acts, other than regret at being apprehended.

Offenders frequently respect and admire honest, law-abiding persons. Really honest persons are often revered; and if for some reason such persons are accused of misbehavior, the criminal is quick to defend their integrity. Those admired may include sports figures, priests and other clergy, parents, teachers, and neighbors.

Criminals draw a line between those whom they can victimize and those whom they cannot. Members of similar ethnic groups, churches, or neighborhoods are often off limits. This practice implies that criminals are aware of the wrongfulness of their acts.

Criminals are not immune to the demands of conformity. Most criminals frequently participate in many of the same social functions as law-abiding people—for example, in school, church, and family activities.

Because of these factors, Sykes and Matza conclude that criminality is the result of the neutralization of accepted social values through the learning of a standard set of techniques that allow people to counteract the moral dilemmas posed by illegal behavior.[86]

Techniques of neutralization Sykes and Matza suggest that people develop a distinct set of justifications for their law-violating behavior. These neutralization techniques enable them to temporarily drift away from the rules of the normative society and participate in subterranean behaviors. These techniques of neutralization include the following patterns:

- **Denial of responsibility.** Young offenders sometimes claim their unlawful acts were simply not their fault. Criminals' acts resulted from forces beyond their control or were accidents.

- **Denial of injury.** By denying the wrongfulness of an act, criminals are able to neutralize illegal behavior. For example, stealing is viewed as borrowing; vandalism is considered mischief that has gotten out of hand. Delinquents may find that their parents and friends support their denial of injury. In fact, they may claim that the behavior was merely a "prank," helping affirm the offender's perception that crime can be socially acceptable.

- **Denial of victim.** Criminals sometimes neutralize wrongdoing by maintaining that the victim of crime "had it coming." Vandalism may be directed against a disliked teacher or neighbor; or homosexuals may be beaten up by a gang because their behavior is considered offensive. Denying the victim may also take the form of ignoring the rights of an absent or unknown victim: for example, stealing from the unseen owner of a department store. It becomes morally acceptable for the criminal to commit such crimes as vandalism when the victims, because of their absence, cannot be sympathized with or respected.

CONNECTIONS

Denial of the victim may help explain the hate crime phenomenon in which people are victimized simply because they belong to the wrong race, religion, ethnic group, or because of their sexual orientation. Hate crimes are discussed in Chapter 11. ■

- **Condemnation of the condemners.** An offender views the world as a corrupt place with a dog-eat-dog code. Since police and judges are on the take, teachers show favoritism, and parents take out their frustrations on their kids, it is ironic and unfair for these authorities to condemn his or her misconduct. By shifting the blame to others, criminals are able to repress the feeling that their own acts are wrong.

- **Appeal to higher loyalties.** Novice criminals often argue that they are caught in the dilemma of being loyal to their own peer group while at the same time attempting to abide by the rules of the larger society. The needs of the group take precedence over the rules of society because the demands of the former are immediate and localized (see Figure 8.3).

In sum, the theory of neutralization presupposes a condition that allows people to neutralize unconventional norms and values by using such slogans as "I didn't mean to do it," "I didn't really hurt anybody," "They had it coming to them," "Everybody's picking on me," and "I didn't do it for myself." These excuses allow people to drift into criminal modes of behavior.

Testing neutralization theory Attempts have been made to verify the assumptions of neutralization theory empirically, but the results have been inconclusive.[87] One area of research has been directed at determining whether there really is a need for law violators to neutralize moral constraints. The thinking behind this research is this: If criminals hold values *in opposition* to accepted social norms, then there is really no need to neutralize. So far, the evidence is mixed. Some studies show that law violators approve of criminal behavior, such as theft and violence, and still others find evidence that even though they may be active participants themselves criminals voice disapproval of illegal behavior.[88] Some studies indicate that law violators approve of social values such as honesty and fairness; others come to the opposite conclusion.[89]

Although the existing research findings may be ambiguous, the weight of the evidence is that (a) most adolescents generally *disapprove* of deviant behaviors such as violence and that (b) neutralizations do in fact enable youths to engage in socially disproved of behavior.[90] Equally important is some recent evidence showing that, as Matza predicted, people drift in and out of antisocial behavior. Jeffery Fagan's interviews with 150 young men who had experiences with violent crimes while living in some of New York City's toughest neighborhoods found that many alternated their demeanor between "decent" and "street" codes of behavior, language, and dress. Both orientations lived side by side within the same individuals. The street code's rules for getting and maintaining respect through aggressive behavior forced many "decent" youths to situationally adopt a tough demeanor and perhaps behave violently in order to survive an otherwise hostile and possibly dangerous environment.[91]

CONNECTIONS

The concept of "decent" and "street" codes of behavior is discussed in the focal concerns section of Chapter 7. ■

The theory of neutralization, then, is a major contribution to the literature of crime and delinquency. It can account for the aging-out process: youths can forgo criminal behavior as adults because they never really rejected the morality of normative society. It helps explain the behavior of the occasional or nonchronic delinquent, who is able to successfully age out of crime. Since teens are not committed to criminality, as they mature, they simply drift back into conventional behavior patterns. While they are young, justifications and excuses neutralize guilt and enable individuals to continue to feel good about themselves.[92] In contrast, people who remain criminals as adults may be using newly learned techniques to neutralize the wrongfulness of their actions and avoid guilt. For example, psychotherapists accused of sexually exploiting their clients blame the victim for "seducing them"; some claim there was little injury caused by the sexual encounter; others seek scapegoats to blame for their actions.[93]

Are Learning Theories Valid?

Learning theories make a significant contribution to our understanding of the onset of criminal behavior. Nonetheless, the general learning model has been subject to some criticism. One complaint is that learning theorists fail to account for the origin of criminal definitions. How did the first "teacher" learn criminal techniques and definitions? Who came up with the original neutralization technique?

Learning theories also imply that people systematically learn techniques that enable them to be active and successful criminals, but they fail to adequately explain spontaneous and wanton acts of violence and damage and other

Figure 8.3 Techniques of Neutralization

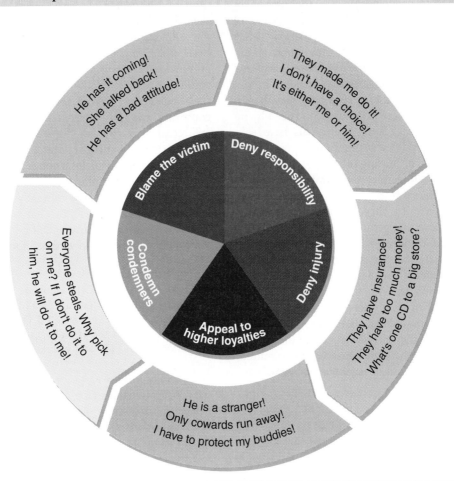

expressive crimes that appear to have little utility or purpose. Principles of differential association can easily explain shoplifting, but is it possible that a random shooting is caused by excessive deviant definitions? It is estimated that about 70 percent of all arrestees were under the influence of drugs and alcohol when they committed their crime: Do "crack heads" pause to neutralize their moral inhibitions before mugging a victim? Do drug-involved kids stop to consider what they have "learned" about moral values?[94]

Little evidence exists substantiating that people learn the techniques that enable them to become criminals before they actually commit criminal acts. It is equally plausible that people who are already deviant seek out others with similar lifestyles. Early onset of deviant behavior is now considered a key determinant of criminal careers. It is difficult to see how extremely young adolescents had the opportunity to learn criminal behavior and attitudes within a peer group setting.

Despite these criticisms, learning theories maintain an important place in the study of delinquent and criminal behavior. Unlike social structure theories, these theories are not limited to the explanation of a single facet of antisocial activity—for example, lower-class gang activity; they may be used to explain criminality across all class structures. Even corporate executives may be exposed to a variety of procriminal definitions and learn to neutralize moral constraints.

Not only can learning theories be applied to a wide assortment of criminal activity, they are also used to explain noncriminal activities. To find out more, go to InfoTrac College Edition and use "learning theory" as a key word. ■

Social Control Theory

Social control theories maintain that all people have the potential to violate the law and that modern society presents many opportunities for illegal activity. Criminal activities, such as drug abuse and car theft, are often exciting pastimes that hold the promise of immediate reward and gratification.

Considering the attractions of crime, the question control theorists pose is, "Why do people obey the rules of society?" A choice theorist would respond that it is the fear of punishment; structural theorists would say that obedience is a function of having access to legitimate opportunities; learning theorists would explain that obedience is acquired through contact with law-abiding parents and peers. In contrast, social control theorists argue that people obey the law because behavior and passions are being controlled by internal and external forces. Some individuals have **self-control,** manifested through a strong moral sense, which renders them incapable of hurting others and violating social norms. Other people develop a **commitment to conformity,** which is adhered to because there is a real, present, and logical reason to obey the rules of society.[95] Individuals may believe that getting caught at criminal activity will hurt a dearly loved parent or jeopardize their chance at a college scholarship, or perhaps they feel that their job will be forfeited if they get in trouble with the law. In other words, people's behavior, including criminal activity, is controlled by their attachment and commitment to conventional institutions, individuals, and processes. If that commitment is absent, they are free to violate the law and engage in deviant behavior. Those who are "uncommitted" are not deterred by the threat of legal punishments.[96]

Self-Concept and Crime

Early versions of control theory speculated that low self-control was a product of weak self-concept and poor self-esteem. Youths who felt good about themselves and maintained a positive attitude were able to resist the temptations of the streets. As early as 1951, sociologist Albert Reiss described how delinquents had weak egos and lacked the self-control to produce conforming behavior.[97] Scott Briar and Irving Piliavin noted that youths who believe criminal activity will damage their self-image and their relationships with others will be most likely to conform to social rules; they have a commitment to conformity. In contrast, those less concerned about their social standing are free to violate the law.[98] In his **containment theory,** pioneering control theorist Walter Reckless argued that a strong self-image insulates a youth from the pressures and pulls of crimogenic influences in the environment.[99] In a series of studies conducted within the school setting, Reckless and his colleagues found that nondelinquent youths are able to maintain a positive self-image in the face of environmental pressures toward delinquency.[100]

How does self-concept influence delinquent and criminal behavior? To find out, read this article on InfoTrac College Edition: Kenneth St.C. Levy. The contribution of self-concept in the etiology of adolescent delinquents. *Adolescence* Fall 1997 v32 n127 p671(16) ■

Sociologist Howard Kaplan believes youths with poor self-concepts are the ones most likely to engage in delinquent behavior; successful participation in criminality actually helps raise their self-esteem.[101] Kaplan's self-enhancement theory suggests that adolescents structure their behavior to enhance their self-image and to minimize negative self-attitudes.

■ Some social control theories maintain that delinquent youths suffer from low self-concept because it is difficult for them to form personal relationships. Even if kids join together to form criminal gangs, within-group relationships are actually strained and remote. Here girl gang members engage in a violent initiation ceremony. Can such violent youths have warm personal relationships?

Deborah Copaken/Liaison-Getty Images

Youth conform to social rules of society, seek membership in **normative groups** (for example, the high school "in-crowd"), and perform conventional tasks as long as their efforts pay off in positive, esteem-enhancing feedback. If they feel threatened, rebuked, or belittled, they may experience "self-rejection" (for example, "I feel I do not have much to be proud of"; "I feel useless at times"). Because of this rejection, they may then turn to deviant groups made up of youths who have been similarly rejected to meet their need for self-esteem. While conventional society may reject them, their new criminal friends give them positive feedback and support. To further enhance their new identity, they may engage in deviant behaviors.[102] Youths who maintain both the lowest self-image and the greatest need for approval are the ones most likely to seek self-enhancement by engaging in criminal activities. There is also evidence that perceptions of relative deprivation may produce the negative self-feelings imagined by Kaplan: kids who perceive economic deprivation relative to their friends, neighbors, and the general population also develop negative self-feelings, which motivate antisocial behaviors.[103]

CONNECTIONS

Kaplan's views help explain the deviance-producing effect of relative deprivation discussed in Chapter 7. Tying relative deprivation to self-concept helps to explain why some but not all people in disadvantaged areas are crime prone. It also suggests means to reduce crime rates: for example, by providing self-concept enhancing opportunities for relatively disadvantaged youth. ■

Hirschi's Social Bond Theory

Social bond theory (also called *social control theory*), articulated by Travis Hirschi in his 1969 book, *Causes of Delinquency,* is now the dominant version of control theory.[104] Hirschi links the onset of criminality to the weakening of the ties that bind people to society. Hirschi assumes that all individuals are potential law violators, but they are kept under control because they fear that illegal behavior will damage their relationships with friends, parents, neighbors, teachers, and employers. Without these social ties or bonds, and in the absence of sensitivity to and interest in others, a person is free to commit criminal acts. Hirschi does not view society as containing competing subcultures with unique value systems. Most people are aware of the

prevailing moral and legal code. He suggests, however, that in all elements of society people vary in how they respond to conventional social rules and values. Among all ethnic, religious, racial, and social groups, people whose bond to society is weak may fall prey to crimogenic behavior patterns.

Elements of the Social Bond

Hirschi argues that the **social bond** a person maintains with society is divided into four main elements: attachment, commitment, involvement, and belief (see Figure 8.4).

Attachment Attachment refers to a person's sensitivity to and interest in others.[105] Without a sense of attachment, psychologists believe a person becomes a psychopath and loses the ability to relate coherently to the world. The acceptance of social norms and the development of a social conscience depend on attachment to and caring for other human beings.

Hirschi views parents, peers, and schools as the important social institutions with which a person should maintain ties. Attachment to parents is the most important. Even if a family is shattered by divorce or separation, a child must retain a strong attachment to one or both parents. Without this attachment, it is unlikely that feelings of respect for others in authority will develop.

Commitment Commitment involves the time, energy, and effort expended in conventional lines of action, such as getting an education and saving money for the future. If people build a strong commitment to conventional society, they will be less likely to engage in acts that will jeopardize their hard-won position. Conversely, the lack of commitment to conventional values may foreshadow a condition in which risk-taking behavior, such as crime, becomes a reasonable behavior alternative.

Involvement Heavy involvement in conventional activities leaves little time for illegal behavior. When people become involved in school, recreation, and family, Hirschi believes it insulates them from the potential lure of criminal behavior, whereas idleness enhances it.

Belief People who live in the same social setting often share common moral beliefs; they may adhere to such values as sharing, sensitivity to the rights of others, and admiration for the legal code. If these beliefs are absent or weakened, individuals are more likely to participate in antisocial or illegal acts. Hirschi further suggests that the interrelationship of social bond elements controls subsequent behavior. For example, people who feel kinship and sensitivity to parents and friends should be more likely to adopt and work toward legitimate goals. A person who rejects such social relationships is more likely to lack commitment to conventional goals. Similarly, people who are

Figure 8.4 Elements of the Social Bond

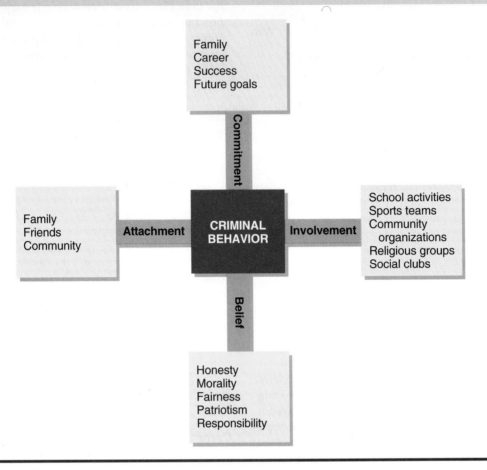

highly committed to conventional acts and beliefs are more likely to be involved in conventional activities.

Testing Social Bond Theory

One of Hirschi's most significant contributions was his attempt to test the principal hypotheses of social bond theory. He administered a detailed self-report survey to a sample of more than 4,000 junior and senior high school students in Contra Costa County, California.[106] In a detailed analysis of the data, Hirschi found considerable evidence to support the control theory model. Among Hirschi's more important findings are the following:

- Youths who were strongly attached to their parents were less likely to commit criminal acts.

- Commitment to conventional values, such as striving to get a good education and refusing to drink alcohol and "cruise around," was indicative of conventional behavior.

- Youths involved in conventional activity, such as homework, were less likely to engage in criminal behavior.

- Youths involved in unconventional behavior, such as smoking and drinking, were more delinquency prone.

- Youths who maintained weak and distant relationships with people tended toward delinquency.

- Those who shunned unconventional acts were attached to their peers.

- Delinquents and nondelinquents shared similar beliefs about society.

Hirschi's data lent important support to the validity of control theory. Even when the statistical significance of his findings was less than he expected, the direction of his research data was notably consistent. Only in very rare instances did his findings contradict the theory's most critical assumptions.

Supporting research   Hirschi's version of social control theory has been corroborated by numerous research studies showing that delinquent youth often feel detached from society.[107] Their relationships within the family, peer group, and school often appear strained, indicative of a weakened social bond.[108] Associations between indicators of attachment, belief, commitment, and involvement with measures of delinquency have tended to be positive and significant.[109] In contrast, positive attachments help control delinquency.[110] For example, youths who fail at school and are detached from the educational experience are at risk of criminality; those who do well and are committed to school are less likely to engage in delinquent acts.[111]

Teens who are attached to their parents are also able to develop the social skills that equip them both to maintain harmonious social ties and also to escape life stresses such as school failure.[112] In contrast, family detachment, including intrafamily conflict, abuse of children, and lack of affection, supervision, and family pride, are predictive of delinquent conduct.[113] Youths who are detached from the educational experience are at risk to criminality; those who are committed to school are less likely to engage in delinquent acts.[114]

Other research efforts have shown that holding positive beliefs are inversely related to criminality. Children who are involved in religious activities and hold conventional religious beliefs are less likely to become involved in substance abuse.[115] Similarly, youths who are involved in conventional leisure activities, such as supervised social activities and noncompetitive sports, are less likely to engage in delinquency than those who are involved in unconventional leisure activities and unsupervised, peer-oriented social pursuits.[116]

Cross-national surveys have also supported the general finding of Hirschi's control theory.[117] For example, one study of Canadian youth found that perceptions of parental attachment were the strongest predictor of delinquent or law-abiding behavior. Teens who are attached to their parents may develop the social skills that equip them both to maintain harmonious social ties and to escape life stresses such as school failure.[118]

Opposing views More than 70 published attempts have been made to corroborate social control theory by replicating Hirschi's original survey techniques.[119] There has been significant empirical support for Hirschi's work, but there are also those who question some or all of its elements. Here are some elements that have come under criticism and need further study.

Friendship: One significant criticism concerns Hirschi's contention that delinquents are detached loners whose bond to their family and friends has been broken. Some critics have questioned whether delinquents (1) do in fact have strained relations with family and peers and (2) whether they may, in fact, be influenced by close relationships with deviant peers and family members. A number of research efforts do show that delinquents maintain relationships with deviant peers and are influenced by members of their deviant peer group.[120] Delinquents, however, may not be "lone wolves" whose only personal relationships

are exploitive; their friendship patterns seem quite close to those of conventional youth.[121] In fact, some types of offenders, such as drug abusers, may maintain even more intimate relations with their peers than nonabusers.[122]

Not all elements of the bond are equal: Hirschi makes little distinction between the importance of each element of the social bond, yet research evidence suggests that there may be differences. Some adolescents who report high levels of "involvement," which Hirschi suggests should reduce delinquency, are involved in criminal behavior. As kids get involved in behaviors outside the home, it is possible that parental control weakens and youths have greater opportunity to commit crime.[123] When asked, children report that concepts such as "involvement" and "belief" have relatively little influence over behavior patterns.[124]

Deviant peers and parents: Hirschi's conclusion that any form of social attachment is beneficial, even to deviant peers and parents, has also been disputed. Rather than deter delinquency attachment to deviant peers, it may support and nurture antisocial behavior. Though his classic study supported the basic principles of control theory, criminologist Michael Hindelang found that attachment to delinquent peers escalated rather than restricted criminality.[125] In a similar fashion, a number of research efforts have found that youths attached to drug-abusing parents are more likely to become drug users themselves.[126] Attachment to deviant family members, peers, and associates may help motivate youths to commit crime and helped facilitate their antisocial acts.[127]

CONNECTIONS

Kaplan's self-enhancement view, discussed earlier in the chapter, posits that delinquent youth seek out similarly antisocial peers to enhance their feelings of self-esteem. This view contradicts Hirschi's control theory version of attachments in that it assumes deviant attachments have a negative effect whereas Hirschi argues that all attachments are beneficial. ■

Restricted in scope: There is some question as to whether the theory can explain all modes of criminality (as Hirschi maintains) or is restricted to particular groups or forms of criminality. For example, control variables seem better able to explain minor delinquency (such as alcohol and marijuana abuse) than more serious criminal acts.[128] Research efforts have found control variables are more predictive of female than male behavior.[129] Perhaps girls, more so than boys, are more deeply influenced by the quality of their bond to society.

Changing bonds: Social bonds seem to change over time, a phenomenon ignored by Hirschi.[130] It is possible then that at one age level weak bonds (to parents) lead to delinquency, while at another strong bonds (to peers) lead to delinquency.

Crime and social bonds: The most severe criticism of control theory has been leveled by sociologist Robert Agnew, who claims that Hirschi miscalculated the direction of the relationship between criminality and a weakened social bond.[131] Hirschi's theory projects that a weakened bond leads to delinquency, but Agnew suggests that the chain of events may flow in the opposite direction. In other words, perhaps kids who break the law find that their bond to parents, schools, and society eventually becomes weak and attenuated. Other studies have also found that criminal behavior weakens social bonds and not vice versa.[132]

Although these criticisms need to be addressed with further research, the weight of existing empirical evidence supports control theory, and it has emerged as one of the preeminent theories in criminology.[133] For many criminologists, it is perhaps the most important way of understanding the onset of youthful misbehavior.

CONNECTIONS

Though his work has achieved a prominent place in criminological literature, Hirschi, along with Michael Gottfredson, has restructured his concept of control by integrating biosocial, psychological, and rational choice theory ideas into a "general theory of crime." This theory is essentially developmental and integrated, and it will be discussed more fully in Chapter 10. ■

■ Social Reaction Theory

Social reaction theory, commonly called labeling theory (the two terms are used interchangeably here), explains how criminal careers form based on destructive social interactions and encounters. Its roots are found in the **symbolic interaction theory** of sociologists Charles Horton Cooley and George Herbert Mead, and later, Herbert Blumer.[134] Symbolic interaction theory holds that people communicate via symbols—gestures, signs, words, or images—that stand for or represent something else.

To read a selection from George Herbert Mead, *Mind, Self, and Society* (Chicago: University of Chicago Press, 1934), go to:
http://wizard.ucr.edu/~bkaplan/soc/lib/ meadself.html
For an up-to-date list of Web links, go to
http://info.wadsworth.com/siegel ■

People interpret symbolic gestures from others and incorporate them in their self-image. Symbols are used by others to let people know how well they are doing and whether they are liked or appreciated. How people view reality then depends on the content of the messages and situations they encounter, the subjective interpretation of these interactions, and how they shape future behavior. There is no objective reality. People interpret the reactions of others and this interpretation assigns meaning. Because interpretation changes over time, so do the meanings of concepts and symbols.

Social reaction theory picks up on these concepts of *interaction* and *interpretation*.[135] Throughout their lives, people are given a variety of symbolic labels and ways to interact with others. These labels represent a variety of behavior and attitude characteristics; labels help define not just one trait but the whole person. For example, people labeled "insane" are also assumed to be dangerous, dishonest, unstable, violent, strange, and otherwise unsound. Valued labels, including "smart," "honest," and "hard working," suggest overall competence. These labels can improve self-image and social standing. Research shows that people who are labeled with one positive trait, such as being physically attractive, are assumed to maintain others traits, such as being intelligent and competent.[136] In contrast, negative labels, including "troublemaker," "mentally ill," and "stupid," help stigmatize the recipients of these labels and reduce their self-image.

Both positive and negative labels involve subjective interpretation of behavior: a "troublemaker" is merely someone who people label as "troublesome." There need not be any objective proof or measure indicating that the person is actually a troublemaker. Though a label may be a function of rumor, innuendo, or unfounded suspicion, its adverse impact can be immense.

If a devalued status is conferred by a significant other—teacher, police officer, elder, parent, or valued peer—the negative label may cause permanent harm. The degree to which a person is perceived as a social deviant may affect his or her treatment at home, at work, at school, and in other social situations. Children may find that their parents consider them a "bad influence" on younger brothers and sisters. School officials may limit them to classes reserved for people with behavioral problems. Likewise, when adults are labeled as "criminal," "ex-con," or "drug addict," they may find their eligibility for employment severely restricted. Furthermore, if the label is bestowed as the result of conviction for a criminal offense, the labeled person may be subjected to official sanctions ranging from a mild reprimand to incarceration.

Beyond these immediate results, labeling advocates maintain that, depending on the visibility of the label and the manner and severity with which it is applied, a person will have an increasing commitment to a deviant career. As one national commission put it: "Thereafter he may be watched; he may be suspect . . . he may be excluded more and more from legitimate opportunities."[137] Labeled persons may find themselves turning to others similarly stigmatized for support and companionship. Isolated from conventional society, they may identify themselves as members of an outcast group and become locked into a deviant career. Figure 8.5 illustrates this process.

Because the process of acquiring stigma is essentially interactive, labeling theorists blame criminal career formation on the social agencies originally designed for its control. Often mistrustful of institutions, such as police, courts, and correctional agencies, labeling advocates find it logical that these institutions produce the stigma that is so harmful to the very people they are trying to help, treat, or correct. Rather than reduce deviant behavior, for which they were designed, such label-bestowing institutions actually help to maintain and amplify criminal behavior.

Figure 8.5   The Labeling Process

Initial criminal act
People commit crimes for a number of reasons.

Detection by the justice system
Arrest is influenced by racial, economic, and power relations.

Decision to label
Some are labeled "official" criminals by police and court authorities.

Creation of a new identity
Those labeled are known as troublemakers, criminals, etc., and shunned by conventional society.

Acceptance of labels
Labeled people begin to see themselves as outsiders (secondary deviance, self-labeling).

Deviance amplification
Stigmatized offenders are now locked into criminal careers.

CONNECTIONS

Fear of stigma has prompted efforts to reduce the impact of criminal labels through such programs as pretrial diversion and community treatment programs. These efforts are reviewed in some detail in Chapter 15. In addition, some criminologists have called for noncoercive "peacemaking" solutions to interpersonal conflict. This peacemaking, or restorative justice movement, is reviewed in Chapter 9. ■

Crime and Labeling Theory

Labeling theorists use an interactionist definition of crime. In a defining statement, sociologist Kai Erickson argues, "Deviance is not a property inherent in certain forms of behavior, it is a property conferred upon those forms by the audience which directly or indirectly witnesses them."[138] Crime and deviance, therefore, are defined by the social audience's reaction to people and their behavior and the subsequent effects of that reaction; they are not defined by the moral content of the illegal act itself.[139]

In a famous statement, Becker sums up the importance of the audience's reaction:

> Social groups create deviance by making rules whose infractions constitute deviance, and by applying those rules to particular people and labeling them as outsiders. From this point of view, deviance is not a quality of the act a person commits, but rather a consequence of the application by others of rules and sanctions to an "offender." The deviant is one to whom the label has successfully been applied; deviant behavior is behavior that people so label.[140]

In its purest form, social reaction theory argues that such crimes as murder, rape, and assault are only bad or evil because people label them as such. After all, the difference between an excusable act and a criminal one is often a matter of legal definition, which changes from place to place and from year to year. For example, acts such as abortion, marijuana use, possession of a handgun, and gambling have been legal at some points and places in history and illegal at others.

Howard Becker refers to people who create rules as **moral entrepreneurs.** An example of a moral entrepreneur today might be members of an ultra orthodox religious group who target the gay lifestyle and mount a campaign to prevent gays from adopting children or conducting same-sex marriages.[141] He says:

> Social groups create deviance by making rules whose infractions constitute deviance, and by applying those rules to particular people and labeling them as outsiders. From this point of view, deviance is not a quality of the act a person commits, but rather a consequence of the application by others of rules and sanctions to an "offender." The deviant is one to whom the label has successfully been applied; deviant behavior is behavior that people so label.[142]

A social reaction theorist views crime as a subjective concept whose definition is totally dependent on the viewing audience. An act that is considered illegal and/or criminal to one person may be perfectly acceptable behavior to another. Because crime is defined by those in power, the shape of the criminal law is defined by the values of those who rule and not by an objective standard of moral conduct.

Differential Enforcement

An important principle of social reaction theory is that the law is differentially applied, benefiting those who hold economic and social power and penalizing the powerless. The probability of being brought under the control of legal authority is a function of a person's race, wealth, gender, and social standing. A core concept of social reaction theory is that police officers are more likely to formally arrest males, minority group members, and those in the lower class and to use their discretionary powers to give beneficial treatment to more favored groups.[143] Minorities and the poor are more likely to be prosecuted for criminal offenses and to receive harsher punishments when convicted.[144] Judges may sympathize with white defendants and help them avoid criminal labels, especially if they seem to come from "good families," whereas minority youth are not afforded that luxury.[145]

This evidence is used to support the labeling concept that personal characteristics and social interactions are more important variables in developing criminal careers than merely violating the law. Social reaction theorists also argue that the content of the law reflects power relationships in society. They point to the evidence that white-collar crimes—economic crimes usually committed by members of the upper class—are most often punished by a relatively small fine and rarely result in a prison sentence. This treatment contrasts with long prison sentences given to those convicted of "street crimes," such as burglary or car theft, which are the province of the lower, powerless, classes.[146]

In sum, a major premise of social reaction theory is that the law is differentially constructed and applied, depending on the offenders. It favors the powerful members of society who direct its content and penalizes people whose actions represent a threat to those in control, such as minority group members and the poor who demand equal rights.[147]

Becoming Labeled

Social reaction theory is not especially concerned with why people originally engage in acts that result in their being labeled.[148] Crime may be a result of greed, personality, social structure, learning, or control. Regardless of why they commit crime, the less personal power and fewer resources a person has, the greater the chance he or she will become labeled. Race, class, and ethnic differences between those in power and those who are not influence the

AP/Wide World Photos

■ The Scary Guy (now his legal name) is covered from head to toe in tattoos. What do you think he is like? What are his personality traits? Would you want him to meet your family? Are you labeling him?

likelihood of labeling. For example, the poor or minority group teenager may run a greater chance of being officially processed for criminal acts by police, courts, and correctional agencies than the wealthy white youth. This helps to explain why there are significant racial and economic differences in the crime rate.

Not all labeled people have chosen to engage in label-producing activities, such as crime. Some negative labels are bestowed on people for behaviors over which they have little control. Negative labels of this sort include "mentally ill" and "mentally deficient." In these categories, the probability of being labeled may depend on how visible that person is in the community, the tolerance of the community for unusual behavior, and the person's own power to combat labels.

Consequences of Labeling

Social reaction theorists are most concerned with two effects of labeling: the creation of **stigma** and the effect on self-image. Labels are believed to produce stigma. The labeled deviant becomes a social outcast who may be prevented from enjoying a higher education, well-paying jobs, and other social benefits. Such alienation leads to a low self-image.

Labeling theorists consider public condemnation an important part of the label-producing process. It may be accomplished in such "ceremonies" as a hearing, in which a person is found to be mentally ill, or a trial, in which an individual is convicted of a crime. A public record of the deviant acts, such as an arrest or conviction record, causes the denounced person to be ritually separated from a place in the legitimate order and placed outside the world occupied by citizens of good standing. Harold Garfinkle has called transactions that produce irreversible, permanent labels "successful degradation ceremonies."[149]

Differential social control   According to the concept of **differential social control,** the process of labeling may produce a reevaluation of the self, which reflects actual or perceived appraisals made by others. Kids who view themselves as delinquents after being labeled as such are giving an inner voice to their perceptions of how parents, teachers, peers, and neighbors view them. When they believe that others view them as antisocial or troublemakers, they take on attitudes and roles that reflect this assumption; they expect to become suspects and then to be rejected.[150] This process has been linked to delinquent behavior and other social problems including depression.[151]

Tempering or enhancing the effect of this **reflective role-taking** are informal and institutional social control processes. Families, schools, peers, and the social system can either help control children and dissuade them from crime or encourage and sustain deviance. When these groups are dysfunctional, such as when parents use drugs, they encourage, rather than control, antisocial behavior.[152]

Joining deviant cliques   When children are labeled as deviant, they may join up with similarly outcast delinquent peers who facilitate their behavior. Eventually, antisocial behavior becomes habitual and automatic.[153] The desire to join deviant cliques and groups may stem from a self-rejecting attitude ("At times, I think I am no good at all"), which eventually results in a weakened commitment to conventional values and behaviors. In turn, these children may acquire motives to deviate from social norms. Facilitating this attitude and value transformation is the bond social outcasts form with similarly labeled peers in the form of a deviant subculture.[154] Membership in a deviant subculture often involves conforming to group norms that conflict with those of conventional society.

Deviant behaviors that defy conventional values can serve a number of different purposes. Some acts are defiant, designed to show contempt for the source of the negative labels. Others acts are planned to distance the transgressor from further contact with the source of criticism (for example, an adolescent runs away from critical parents).[155]

Retrospective reading   Beyond any immediate results, labels tend to redefine the whole person. For example, the label "ex-con" may create in people's imaginations a whole series of behavior descriptions—tough, mean, dangerous, aggressive, dishonest, sneaky—that a person who has been

in prison may or may not possess. People begin to react to the label description and what it signifies instead of reacting to the actual behavior of the person who bears it. This is referred to as **retrospective reading,** a process in which the past of the labeled person is reviewed and reevaluated to fit his or her current status. For example, boyhood friends of an assassin are interviewed by the media and report that the suspect was withdrawn, suspicious, and negativistic as a youth. By a retrospective reading, we can now understand what prompted his current behavior; therefore, the label must be accurate.[156]

Dramatization of evil   Labels become the basis of personal identity. As the negative feedback of law enforcement agencies, parents, friends, teachers, and other figures amplifies the force of the original label, stigmatized offenders may begin to reevaluate their own identities. If they are not really evil or bad, they may ask themselves, why is everyone making such a fuss? Frank Tannenbaum, a social reaction theory pioneer, referred to this process as the **dramatization of evil.** With respect to the consequences of labeling delinquent behavior, Tannenbaum stated:

> The process of making the criminal, therefore, is a process of tagging, defining, identifying, making conscious and self-conscious; it becomes a way of stimulating, suggesting and evoking the very traits that are complained of. If the theory of relation of response to stimulus has any meaning, the entire process of dealing with the young delinquent is mischievous insofar as it identifies him to himself or to the environment as a delinquent person. The person becomes the thing he is described as being.[157]

Primary and Secondary Deviance

One of the best-known views of the labeling process is Edwin Lemert's concept of primary deviance and secondary deviance.[158] According to Lemert, **primary deviance** involves norm violations or crimes that have very little influence on the actor and can be quickly forgotten. For example, a college student takes a "five-finger discount" at the campus bookstore. He successfully steals a textbook, uses it to get an A in a course, goes on to graduate, is admitted into law school, and later becomes a famous judge. Because his shoplifting goes unnoticed, it is a relatively unimportant event that has little bearing on his future life.

In contrast, **secondary deviance** occurs when a deviant event comes to the attention of significant others or social control agents who apply a negative label. The newly labeled offender then reorganizes his or her behavior and personality around the consequences of the deviant act. The shoplifting student is caught by a security guard and expelled from college. With his law school dreams dashed and his future cloudy, his options are limited; people who know him say he "lacks character," and he begins to share their opinion. He eventually becomes a drug dealer and winds up in prison (see Figure 8.6).

Figure 8.6 Primary and Secondary Deviance

Secondary deviance involves resocialization into a deviant role. The labeled person is transformed into one who, according to Lemert, "employs his behavior or a role based upon it as a means of defense, attack, or adjustment to the overt and covert problems created by the consequent social reaction to him."[159] Secondary deviance produces a deviance amplification effect. Offenders feel isolated from the mainstream of society and become firmly locked within their deviant role. They may seek out others similarly labeled to form deviant subcultures or groups. Ever more firmly enmeshed in their deviant role, they are locked into an escalating cycle of deviance, apprehension, more powerful labels, and identity transformation. Lemert's concept of secondary deviance expresses the core of social reaction theory: deviance is a process in which one's identity is transformed. Efforts to control the offenders, whether by treatment or punishment, simply help lock them in their deviant role.

Research on Social Reaction Theory

Research on social reaction theory can be classified into two distinct categories. The first focuses on the characteristics of offenders who are chosen for labels. The theory maintains that these offenders should be relatively powerless people who are unable to defend themselves against the negative labeling. The second type of research attempts to discover the effects of being labeled. Labeling theorists predict that people who are negatively labeled should view themselves as deviant and commit increasing amounts of criminal behavior.

Who gets labeled?   The poor and powerless people are victimized by the law and justice system; labels are not equally distributed across class and racial lines. Critics charge that although substantive and procedural laws govern almost every aspect of the American criminal justice system, discretionary decision making controls its operation at every level. From the police officer's decision on whom to arrest, to the prosecutor's decisions on whom to charge and for how many and what kind of charges, to the court's decision on whom to release or on whom to permit bail, to the grand jury's decision on indictment, to the judge's decision on the length of the sentence, discretion works to the detriment of minorities, including African Americans, Hispanics, Asian Americans, and Native Americans.[160] Reviews indicate that race bias adversely influences decision making in many critical areas of the justice system.[161] There is also evidence that those in power try to streamline the labeling process by discounting or ignoring the "protestations of innocence" made by suspects accused of socially undesirable acts such as rape, sex crimes, and child abuse.[162]

Although these arguments are persuasive, little definitive evidence exists that the justice system is inherently unfair and biased. Procedures such as arrest, prosecution, and sentencing seem to be more often based on legal factors, such as prior record and severity of the crime, than on personal characteristics, such as class and race.[163] However, it is possible that discriminatory practices in the labeling process are subtle and hidden. For example, in a thorough review of sentencing disparity, Samuel Walker, Cassia Spohn, and Miriam Delone identify what they call **contextual discrimination.** This term refers to judges' practices in some jurisdictions of imposing harsher sentences on African Americans only in some instances, such as when they victimize whites and not other African Americans.[164] They may also be more likely to impose prison sentences on racial minorities in "borderline" cases for which whites get probation. According to their view, racism is very subtle and hard to detect, but it still exerts an influence in the distribution of criminal sanctions.

The effects of labeling   There is empirical evidence that negative labels actually have a dramatic influence on the self-image of offenders. Considerable empirical evidence indicates that social sanctions lead to self-labeling and deviance amplification.[165]

Family interaction can influence the labeling process. Children negatively labeled by their parents routinely suffer a variety of problems, including antisocial behavior and school failure.[166] This process is important because once they are labeled troublemakers, adolescents begin to reassess their self-image. Parents who label their kids as troublemakers promote deviance amplification: labeling causes parents to become alienated from their child; negative labels reduce a child's self-image and increase delinquency.[167]

As they mature, children are in danger of receiving repeat and intensive official labeling, which has been shown to produce self-labeling and damaged identities.[168] Kids labeled troublemakers in school are the ones most likely to drop out; dropping out has been linked to delinquent behavior.[169] Even as adults, the labeling process can take its toll. Male drug users labeled as addicts by social control agencies eventually become self-labeled and increase their drug use.[170] People arrested in domestic violence cases, especially those with a low "stake in conformity" (for example, jobless and unmarried), increase offending after being given official labels.[171]

Labeling and criminal careers

Until recently, scant attention had been paid to the fact that stigma and negative labels may be critical factors in a criminal career.[172] In fact, the very definition of a chronic offender is a person who has been arrested and therefore labeled multiple times over the course of his or her offending career.

Empirical evidence supports the fact that labeling plays an important role in persistent offending.[173] Maintaining a damaged identity after official labeling may, along with other negative social reactions from society, produce a "cumulative disadvantage," which provokes some adolescents into repeating their antisocial behaviors.[174] Although labels may not cause adolescents to initiate criminal behaviors, experienced delinquents are significantly more likely to continue offending if they believe their parents and peers view them in a negative light.[175] Labeling may help sustain criminality over time.

In sum, there is considerable evidence that people who are negatively labeled by parents, schools, and the criminal justice system are likely to partake in criminal behaviors. However, it is still unclear whether this outcome is actually a labeling effect or the product of some other personal and social factors that also caused the labeling to occur.

Is Labeling Theory Valid?

Labeling theory has been the subject of academic debate in criminological circles. Those who criticize it point to its inability to specify the conditions that must exist before an act or individual is labeled deviant; that is, why some people are labeled and others remain "secret deviants."[176] Critics also charge that social reaction theory fails to explain differences in crime rates; if crime is a function of stigma and labels, why are crime rates higher in some parts of the country at particular times of the year?[177] Labeling also ignores the onset of deviant behavior (that is, it fails to ask why people commit the initial deviant act) and does not deal with the reasons delinquents and criminals decide to forgo a deviant career.[178]

In an in-depth analysis of research on the crime-producing effects of labels, criminologist Charles Tittle found little evidence that stigma produces crime.[179] Tittle claims that many criminal careers occur without labeling; that labeling often comes after, rather than before, chronic offending; and that criminal careers may not follow even when labeling takes place. There is growing evidence that the onset of criminal careers occurs early in life and that those who go on to a "life of crime" are burdened with so many social, physical, and psychological problems that negative labeling may be a relatively insignificant event.[180]

Labeling reexamined

Criticisms of social reaction theory have reduced the importance of labeling in the criminological literature, but its use to explain crime and deviance should not be dismissed. Criminologists Raymond Paternoster and Leeann Lovanni have identified some other features of the labeling perspective that are important contributions to the study of criminality:[181]

- The labeling perspective identifies the role played by social control agents in the process of crime causation. Criminal behavior cannot be fully understood if the agencies and individuals empowered to control and treat it are neglected.
- Labeling theory recognizes that criminality is not a disease or pathological behavior. It focuses attention on the social interactions and reactions that shape individuals and their behavior.
- Labeling theory distinguishes between criminal acts (primary deviance) and criminal careers (secondary deviance) and shows that these concepts must be interpreted and treated differently.

Labeling theory is also important because of its focus on interaction as well as the situations surrounding the crime. Rather than view the criminal as a robotlike creature whose actions are predetermined, it recognizes that crime is often the result of complex interactions and processes. The decision to commit crime involves actions of a variety of people including peers, the victim, the police, and other key characters. Labels may expedite crime because they guide the actions of all parties involved in these criminal interactions. Actions deemed innocent when performed by one person are considered provocative when someone who has been labeled as deviant engages in them. Similarly, labeled people may be quick to judge, take offense, or misinterpret behavior of others because of past experience.

■ Evaluating Social Process Theories

The branches of social process theory—social learning, social control, and social reaction—are compatible because they suggest that criminal behavior is part of the socialization process. Criminals are people whose interactions with critically important social institutions and processes—the family, schools, justice system, peer groups, employers, and

■ Social process theories suggest that people can be helped by social programs that help them become committed and attached to society. Here, Head Start children in Illinois rally with their parents and care providers for improved day care legislation. Participation in programs such as Head Start helps youngsters develop a commitment to society.

AP/Wide World Photos

neighbors—are troubled and disturbed. Though there is some disagreement about the relative importance of those influences and the form they take, there seems to be little question that social interactions shape the behavior, beliefs, values, and self-image of the offender. People who have learned deviant social values, find themselves detached from conventional social relationships, or are the subject of stigma and labels from significant others will be the most likely to fall prey to criminal behavior. These negative influences can affect people in all walks of life, beginning in their youth and continuing through their majority. The major strength of the social process view is the vast body of empirical data showing that delinquents and criminals are people who grew up in dysfunctional families, who had troubled childhoods, and who failed at school, at work, and in marriage. Prison data show that these characteristics are typical of inmates.

Although persuasive, these theories do not always account for the patterns and fluctuations in the crime rate. If social process theories are valid, for example, people in the West and South must be socialized differently from those in the midwest and New England because these latter regions have much lower crime rates. How can the fact that crime rates are lower in October than in July be explained if crime is a function of learning or control? How can social processes explain why criminals escalate their activity or why they desist from crime as they age? Once a social

bond is broken, how can it be "reattached"? Once crime is "learned," how can it be "unlearned"?

■ Social Process Theories and Public Policy

Social process theories have had a major influence on policy making since the 1950s. Learning theories have greatly influenced the way criminal offenders are dealt with and treated. The effect of these theories has mainly been felt by young offenders, who are viewed as being more salvageable than "hardened" criminals. If people become criminal by learning definitions and attitudes toward criminality, advocates of the social learning approach argue that they can "unlearn" them by being exposed to definitions toward conventional behavior. It is common today for residential and nonresidential programs to offer treatment programs that teach offenders about the harmfulness of drugs, to forgo delinquent behavior, and to stay in school. If learning did not affect behavior, such exercises would be futile.

Control theories have also influenced criminal justice and other public policy. Programs have been developed to increase people's commitment to conventional lines of action. Some work at creating and strengthening bonds early in life before the onset of criminality. The educational system has been the scene of numerous programs designed

Head Start

The Head Start program is probably the best-known effort to help lower-class youths achieve proper socialization and, in so doing, reduce their potential for future criminality. Head Start programs were instituted in the 1960s as part of President Johnson's War on Poverty. In the beginning, Head Start was a two-month summer program for children who were about to enter school and was aimed at embracing the "whole child." In embracing the whole child, the school offered comprehensive programming that helped improve physical health, enhance mental processes, and improve social and emotional development, self-image, and interpersonal relationships. Preschoolers were provided with an enriched educational environment to develop their learning and cognitive skills. They were given the opportunity to use pegs and pegboards, puzzles, toy animals, dolls, letters and numbers, and other materials that middle-class children take for granted. These opportunities provided the children with a leg up in the educational process.

Today, with annual funding approaching $5 billion, the Head Start program is administered by the Head Start Bureau, the Administration on Children, Youth, and Families (ACFY), the Administration for Children and Families (ACF), and the Department of Health and Human Services (DHHS). Head Start teachers strive to provide a variety of learning experiences appropriate to the child's age and development. These experiences encourage the child to read books, to understand cultural diversity, to express feelings, and to play with and relate to peers in an appropriate fash-

ion. Students are guided in developing gross and fine motor skills and self-confidence. Health care is also an issue, and most children enrolled in the program receive comprehensive health screening, physical and dental examinations, and appropriate follow-up. Many programs provide meals, and in so doing help children receive proper nourishment.

Head Start programs now serve parents in addition to their preschoolers. Some programs allow parents to enroll in classes that cover parenting, literacy, nutrition/weight loss, domestic violence prevention, and other social issues; social services, health, nutrition, and educational services are also available.

Considerable controversy has surrounded the success of the Head Start program. In 1970, the Westinghouse Learning Corporation issued a definitive evaluation of the Head Start effort and concluded that there was no evidence of lasting cognitive gains on the part of the participating children. Initial gains seemed to evaporate during the elementary school years, and by the third grade, the performance of the Head Start children was no different from their peers.

While disappointing, this evaluation focused on IQ levels and gave short shrift to improvement in social competence and other survival skills. More recent research has produced dramatically different results. One report found that, by age 5, children who experienced the enriched day care offered by Head Start averaged more than 10 points higher on their IQ scores than their peers who did not participate in the program. Other research that carefully compared Head Start children to similar youngsters who did not attend the program found that the former made signifi-

cant intellectual gains. Head Start children were less likely to have been retained in a grade or placed in classes for slow learners; they outperformed peers on achievement tests; and they were more likely to graduate from high school.

Head Start kids also made strides in nonacademic areas: they appear to have better health, immunization rates, nutrition, and enhanced emotional characteristics after leaving the program. Research also shows that the Head Start program can have important psychological benefits for the mothers of participants, such as decreasing depression and anxiety and increasing feelings of life satisfaction. While findings in some areas may be tentative, they are all in the same direction: Head Start enhances school readiness and has enduring effects on social competence.

If, as many experts believe, there is a close link between school performance, family life, and crime, programs such as Head Start can help some potentially criminal youths avoid problems with the law. By implication, their success indicates that programs that help socialize youngsters can be used to combat urban criminality. While some problems have been identified in individual centers, the government has shown its faith in Head Start as a socialization agent.

SOURCES: Current information, personal contact, Head Start Program, 2001; Edward Zigler and Sally Styfco, "Head Start, Criticisms in a Constructive Context," *American Psychologist* 49 (1994): 127–32; Nancy Kassebaum, "Head Start, Only the Best for America's Children," *American Psychologist* 49 (1994): 123–26; Faith Lamb Parker, Chaya Piorkowski, and Lenore Peay, "Head Start as Social Support for Mothers: The Psychological Benefits of Involvement," *American Journal of Orthopsychiatry* 57 (1987): 220–33.

to improve basic skills and create an atmosphere in which youths will develop a bond to their schools. The most famous of these efforts, the Head Start Program, is profiled in the Policy and Practice in Criminology feature.

Control theories have focused on the family and have played a key role in putting into operation programs de-

signed to strengthen the bond between parent and child. Others attempt to "repair" bonds that have been broken and frayed. Examples of this approach are the career, work furlough, and educational opportunity programs being developed in the nation's prisons. These programs are designed to help inmates maintain a stake in society so they will be less willing to resort to criminal activity on their release.

Labeling theorists caution against too much intervention. Rather than ask social agencies to attempt to rehabilitate people having problems with the law, they argue, "less is better." Put another way, the more institutions try to "help" people, the more these people will be stigmatized and labeled. For example, a special education program designed to help problem readers may cause them to label themselves and others as slow or stupid. Similarly, a mental health rehabilitation program created with the best intentions may cause clients to be labeled as crazy or dangerous.

CONNECTIONS

The social reaction perspective has had a significant influence on the criminal justice system. In Chapter 15, you will learn more about policies that the criminal justice system has put in place to help and/or treat offenders without further enmeshing them in the system and/or branding them with negative labels. ■

The influence of labeling theory can be viewed in the development of diversion and restitution programs. **Diversion programs** are designed to remove both juvenile and adult offenders from the normal channels of the criminal justice process by placing them in programs designed for rehabilitation. For example, a college student whose drunken driving causes injury to a pedestrian may, before a trial occurs, be placed for six months in an alcohol treatment program. If he successfully completes the program, charges against him will be dismissed. Thus, he avoids the stigma of a criminal label. Such programs are common throughout the nation. Often, they offer counseling; vocational, educational, and family services; and medical advice.

Another label-avoiding innovation that has gained popularity is **restitution.** Rather than face the stigma of a formal trial, an offender is asked to either pay back the victim of the crime for any loss incurred or do some useful work in the community in lieu of receiving a court-ordered sentence.

Despite their good intentions, stigma-reducing programs have not met with great success. Critics charge that they substitute one kind of stigma for another—for instance, attending a mental health program in lieu of a criminal trial. In addition, diversion and restitution programs usually screen out violent offenders and repeat offenders. Finally, there is little hard evidence that the recidivism rate of people placed in alternative programs is less than that of people sent to traditional programs.

Summary

Social process theories view criminality as a function of people's interaction with various organizations, institutions, and processes in society. People in all walks of life have the potential to become criminals if they maintain destructive social relationships. Social process theory has three main branches: social learning theory stresses that people learn how to commit crimes; social control theory analyzes the failure of society to control criminal tendencies; and labeling theory maintains that negative labels produce criminal careers. These theories are summarized in Table 8.1.

The social learning branch of social process theory suggests that people learn criminal behaviors much as they learn conventional behavior. Differential association theory, formulated by Edwin Sutherland, holds that criminality is a result of a person's perceiving an excess of definitions in favor of crime over definitions that uphold conventional values. Ronald Akers has reformulated Sutherland's work using psychological learning theory. He calls his approach differential reinforcement theory. Sykes and Matza's theory of neutralization stresses youths' learning of behavior rationalizations that enable them to overcome societal values and norms and engage in illegal behavior.

Control theory is the second branch of the social process approach. Control theories maintain that all people have the potential to become criminals but that their bonds to conventional society prevent them from violating the law. Walter Reckless's containment theory suggests that a person's self-concept aids his or her commitment to conventional action. Travis Hirschi describes the social bond as containing elements of belief, commitment, attachment, and involvement. Weakened bonds allow youths to become active in antisocial behavior.

Social reaction or labeling theory holds that criminality is promoted by becoming negatively labeled by significant others. Such labels as "criminal," "ex-con," and "junkie" serve to isolate people from society and lock them into lives of crime. Labels create expectations that the labeled person will act in a certain way; labeled people are always watched and suspected. Eventually, these people begin to accept their labels as personal identities, locking them further into lives of crime and deviance. Edwin Lemert has said that people who accept labels are involved in secondary deviance. Unfortunately, research on labeling has not supported its major premises. Consequently, critics have charged that it lacks credibility as a description of crime causation. Social process theories have had a great influence on public policy. They have controlled treatment orientations as well as community action policies.

Table 8.1 Social Process Theories

Theory	Major Premise	Strengths
Social Learning Theories		
Differential association theory	People learn to commit crime from exposure to antisocial definitions.	Explains onset of criminality. Explains the presence of crime in all elements of social structure. Explains why some people in high-crime areas refrain from criminality. Can apply to adults and juveniles.
Differential reinforcement theory	Criminal behavior depends on the person's experiences with rewards for conventional behaviors and punishment for deviant ones. Being rewarded for deviance leads to crime.	Adds psychological learning theory principles to differential association. Links sociological and psychological principles.
Neutralization theory	Youths learn ways of neutralizing moral restraints and periodically drift in and out of criminal behavior patterns.	Explains why many delinquents do not become adult criminals. Explains why youthful law violators can participate in conventional behavior.
Social Control Theories		
Containment theory	Society produces pushes and pulls toward crime. In some people, they are counteracted by internal and external containments, such as a good self-concept and group cohesiveness.	Brings together psychological and sociological principles. Can explain why some people are able to resist the strongest social pressure to commit crime.
Hirschi's social bond theory	A person's bond to society prevents him or her from violating social rules. If the bond weakens, the person is free to commit crime.	Explains the onset of crime; can apply to both middle- and lower-class crime. Explains its theoretical constructs adequately so they can be measured. Has been empirically tested.
Social Reaction Theory		
Labeling theory	People enter into law-violating careers when they are labeled for their acts and organize their personalities around the labels.	Explains the role of society in creating deviance. Explains why some juvenile offenders do not become adult criminals. Develops concepts of criminal careers.

■ Thinking Like a Criminologist

As a criminologist, you have been asked by the governor to help her deal with the state's emerging gang problem. The head of the state police views the gang problem as part of a criminal conspiracy designed to provide profits for highly motivated young criminals. Kids turn to gangs, he argues, as a method of obtaining desired goods and services, either directly through theft and extortion or indirectly through the profits generated by drug dealing and weapons sales. He argues that the best method to control this rational choice is to increase police gang control units and pass legislation heavily penalizing gang activity.

As a social process theorist, you believe the gang is a refuge for young men and women who have learned criminal attitudes and behaviors at home. Many have weak ties to their parents and families. Many do poorly in school. You are aware of research that shows that significant numbers of gang members have been sexually abused at home and that their homes are very likely to include drug users and persons arrested for crimes. Considering these data, you be-lieve joining a gang can be an assertion of independence not only from the family but also from cultural and class constraints; the gang is a substitute institution that can provide meaning and identity.

If gang control is the objective, what programs would you suggest the governor implement? Do you believe a "get tough" program could actually work, or may it backfire? How would you convince the governor that your ideas are valid and worthwhile?

Key Terms

- **social process theories** (214)
- **social process approach** (219)
- **social learning theory** (219)
- **social control theory** (219)
- **social reaction (labeling) theory** (219)
- **differential association theory (DA)** (220)
- **differential reinforcement theory** (224)
- **direct conditioning** (224)
- **differential reinforcement** (224)
- **negative reinforcement** (224)
- **neutralization theory** (225)
- **subterranean values** (225)
- **drift** (225)
- **self-control** (228)
- **commitment to conformity** (228)
- **containment theory** (228)
- **normative groups** (229)
- **social bond** (229)
- **symbolic interaction theory** (232)
- **moral entrepreneurs** (233)
- **stigma** (234)
- **differential social control** (235)
- **reflective role-taking** (235)
- **retrospective reading** (235)
- **dramatization of evil** (235)
- **primary deviance** (235)
- **secondary deviance** (235)
- **contextual discrimination** (236)
- **diversion programs** (240)
- **restitution** (240)

Critical Thinking Questions

1. Do negative labels cause crime? Or do people who commit crime become negatively labeled? That is, are labels a cause of crime or a result?

2. Once weakened, can a person's bonds to society become reattached? What social processes might help reattachment?

3. Can you devise a test of Sutherland's differential association theory? How would you go about measuring an excess of definitions toward criminality?

4. Can you think of ways you may have supported your peers' or siblings' antisocial behavior by helping them learn criminal techniques or attitudes?

5. Do you recall neutralizing any guilt you might have felt for committing a criminal or illegal act? Did your neutralizations come before or after you committed the act in question?

Notes

1. Callie Marie Rennison, *Criminal Victimization 2000 Bureau of Justice Statistics Changes 1999–2000 with Trends 1993–2000* (Washington, D.C.: Bureau of Justice Statistics, 2001).

2. Alan Lizotte, Terence Thornberry, Marvin Krohn, Deborah Chard-Wierschem, and David McDowall, "Neighborhood Context and Delinquency: A Longitudinal Analysis," in *Cross-National Longitudinal Research on Human Development and Criminal Behavior*, eds. E. M. Weitekamp and H. J. Kerner (Netherlands: Kluwer, 1994), pp. 217–27.

3. Charles Tittle and Robert Meier, "Specifying the SES/Delinquency Relationship," *Criminology* 28 (1990): 271–99, at 274.

4. Sheldon Glueck and Eleanor Glueck, *Unraveling Juvenile Delinquency* (Cambridge: Harvard University Press, 1950); Ashley Weeks, "Predicting Juvenile Delinquency," *American Sociological Review* 8 (1943): 40–46.

5. Denise Kandel, "The Parental and Peer Contexts of Adolescent Deviance: An Algebra of Interpersonal Influences," *Journal of Drug Issues* 26 (1996): 289–315; Ann Goetting, "The Parenting Crime Connection," *Journal of Primary Prevention* 14 (1994): 167–84.

6. For general reviews of the relationship between families and delinquency, see Alan Jay Lincoln and Murray Straus, *Crime and the Family* (Springfield, Ill.: Charles C. Thomas, 1985); Rolf Loeber and Magda Stouthamer-Loeber, "Family Factors as Correlates and Predictors of Juvenile Conduct Problems and Delinquency," in *Crime and Justice, An Annual Review of Research*, vol. 7, eds. Michael Tonry and Norval Morris (Chicago: University of Chicago Press, 1986), pp. 29–151; Goetting, "The Parenting Crime Connection."

7. Joseph Weis, Katherine Worsley, and Carol Zeiss, "The Family and Delinquency: Organizing the Conceptual Chaos." Monograph. (Seattle, Wash.: Center for Law and Justice, University of Washington, 1982).

8. Susan Stern and Carolyn Smith, "Family Processes and Delinquency in an Ecological Context," *Social Service Review* 37 (1995): 707–31.

9. *Families with Children Under 18 by Type: 1995 to 2010*, Series 1, 2, and 3 (Washington, D.C.: U.S. Bureau of the Census, 1996).

10. Jukka Savolainen, "Relative Cohort Size and Age-Specific Arrest Rates: A Conditional Interpretation of the Easterlin Effect," *Criminology* 38 (2000): 117–36.

11. Lawrence Rosen and Kathleen Neilson, "Broken Homes," in *Contemporary Criminology*, eds. Leonard Savitz and Norman Johnston (New York: Wiley, 1982), pp. 126–32.

12. Cesar Rebellon, "Reconsidering the Broken Homes/Delinquency Relationship and Exploring Its Mediating Factors," *Criminology* 40 (2002): 103–36.

13. L. Edward Wells and Joseph Rankin, "Families and Delinquency: A Meta-Analysis of the Impact of Broken Homes," *Social Problems* 38 (1991): 71–90.

14. Nan Marie Astone and Sara McLanahan, "Family Structure, Parental Practices and High School Completion," *American Sociological Review* 56 (1991): 309–20.

15. Mary Pat Traxler, "The Influence of the Father and Alternative Male Role Models on African-American Boys' Involvement in Antisocial Behavior." Paper presented at the annual meeting

of the American Society of Criminology, New Orleans, November 1992.

16. Paul Amato and Bruce Keith, "Parental Divorce and the Well-Being of Children: A Meta-Analysis," *Psychological Bulletin* 110 (1991): 26–46.

17. Joseph Rankin and L. Edward Wells, "The Effect of Parental Attachments and Direct Controls on Delinquency," *Journal of Research in Crime and Delinquency* 27 (1990): 140–65.

18. John Paul Wright and Francis Cullen, "Parental Efficacy and Delinquent Behavior: Do Control and Support Matter?" *Criminology* 39 (2001): 677–706.

19. Carter Hay, "Parenting, Self-Control, and Delinquency: A Test of Self-Control Theory," *Criminology* 39 (2001): 707–36.

20. Robert Roberts and Vern Bengston, "Affective Ties to Parents in Early Adulthood and Self-Esteem across 20 Years," *Social Psychology Quarterly* 59 (1996): 96–106.

21. Robert Johnson, S. Susan Su, Dean Gerstein, Hee-Choon Shin, and John Hoffman, "Parental Influences on Deviant Behavior in Early Adolescence: A Logistic Response Analysis of Age- and Gender-Differentiated Effects," *Journal of Quantitative Criminology* 11 (1995): 167–92.

22. Judith Brook and Li-Jng Tseng, "Influences of Parental Drug Use, Personality, and Child Rearing on the Toddler's Anger and Negativity," *Genetic, Social and General Psychology Monographs* 122 (1996): 107–28.

23. Thomas Ashby Wills, Donato Vaccaro, Grace McNamara, and A. Elizabeth Hirky, "Escalated Substance Use: A Longitudinal Grouping Analysis from Early to Middle Adolescence," *Journal of Abnormal Psychology* 105 (1996); 166–80.

24. John Laub and Robert Sampson, "Unraveling Families and Delinquency: A Reanalysis of the Gluecks' Data," *Criminology* 26 (1988): 355–80.

25. Richard Famularo, Karen Stone, Richard Barnum, and Robert Wharton, "Alcoholism and Severe Child Maltreatment," *American Journal of Orthopsychiatry* 56 (1987): 481–85; Richard Gelles, "Child Abuse and Violence in Single-Parent Families: Parent Absence and Economic Deprivation," *American Journal of Orthopsychiatry* 59 (1989): 492–501; Cecil Willis and Richard Wells, "The Police and Child Abuse: An Analysis of Police Decisions to Report Illegal Behavior," *Criminology* 26 (1988): 695–716; Carolyn Webster-Stratton, "Comparison of Abusive and Nonabusive Families with Conduct-Disordered Children," *American Journal of Orthopsychiatry* 55 (1985): 59–69.

26. Carolyn Smith and Terence Thornberry, "The Relationship between Childhood Maltreatment and Adolescent Involvement in Delinquency," *Criminology* 33 (1995): 451–79.

27. Murray Straus, "Discipline and Deviance: Physical Punishment of Children and Violence and Other Crime in Adulthood," *Social Problems* 38 (1991): 101–23.

28. Murray A. Straus, "Spanking and the Making of a Violent Society: The Short- and Long-Term Consequences of Corporal Punishment," *Pediatrics* 98 (1996): 837–43.

29. Ibid.

30. Lening Zhang and Steven Messner, "Family Deviance and Delinquency in China," *Criminology* 33 (1995): 359–87.

31. *The Forgotten Half: Pathways to Success for America's Youth and Young Families* (Washington, D.C.: William T. Grant Foundation, 1988); Lee Jussim, "Teacher Expectations: Self-Fulfilling Prophecies, Perceptual Biases, and Accuracy," *Journal of Personality and Social Psychology* 57 (1989): 469–80.

32. Eugene Maguin and Rolf Loeber, "Academic Performance and Delinquency," in *Crime and Justice: A Review of Research,* vol. 20, ed. Michael Tonry (Chicago: University of Chicago Press, 1996), pp. 145–264.

33. Jeannie Oakes, *Keeping Track, How Schools Structure Inequality* (New Haven: Yale University Press, 1985); Marc LeBlanc, Evelyne Valliere, and Pierre McDuff, "Adolescent's School Experience and Self-Reported Offending: A Longitudinal Test of Social Control Theory." Paper presented at the annual meeting of the American Society of Criminology, Baltimore, November 1990.

34. G. Roger Jarjoura, "Does Dropping Out of School Enhance Delinquent Involvement? Results from a Large-Scale National Probability Sample," *Criminology* 31 (1993): 149–72; Terence Thornberry, Melaine Moore, and R. L. Christenson, "The Effect of Dropping Out of High School on Subsequent Criminal Behavior," *Criminology* 23 (1985): 3–18.

35. Carolyn Smith, Alan Lizotte, Terence Thornberry, and Marvin Krohn, *Resilient Youth: Identifying Factors That Prevent High-Risk Youth from Engaging in Delinquency and Drug Use* (Albany, N.Y.: Rochester Youth Development Study, 1994), pp. 19–21.

36. Kathryn A. Chandler, Chris Chapman, Michael R. Rand, and Bruce M. Taylor, *Students' Reports of School Crime: 1989 and 1995* (Washington, D.C.: Bureau of Justice Statistics, 1998).

37. Sheila Heaviside and Shelley Burns, *Violence and Discipline Problems in U.S. Public Schools: 1996–1997* (Washington, D.C.: Department of Education, 1998). Herein cited as National Violence Survey.

38. Irving Janis, *Groupthink: Psychological Studies of Policy Decisions and Fiascoes* (Boston: Houghton Mifflin, 1982).

39. Lening Zhang and Steven Messner, "Family Deviance and Delinquency in China," *Criminology* 33 (1995): 359–87.

40. Thomas Berndt, "The Features and Effects of Friendships in Early Adolescence," *Child Development* 53 (1982): 1447–69; Thomas Berndt and T. B. Perry, "Children's Perceptions of Friendships as Supportive Relationships," *Developmental Psychology* 22 (1986): 640–48; Spencer Rathus, *Understanding Child Development* (New York: Holt, Rinehart and Winston, 1988), p. 462.

41. Peggy Giordano, "The Wider Circle of Friends in Adolescence," *American Journal of Sociology* 101 (1995): 661–97.

42. Delbert Elliott, David Huizinga, and Suzanne Ageton, *Explaining Delinquency and Drug Use* (Beverly Hills: Sage, 1985); Helene Raskin White, Robert Padina, and Randy LaGrange, "Longitudinal Predictors of Serious Substance Use and Delinquency," *Criminology* 6 (1987): 715–40.

43. See, generally, John Hagedorn, *People and Folks: Gangs, Crime and the Underclass in a Rustbelt City* (Chicago: Lakeview Press, 1988).

44. Robert Agnew and Timothy Brezina, "Relational Problems with Peers, Gender and Delinquency," *Youth and Society* 29 (1997): 84–111.

45. Scott Menard, "Demographic and Theoretical Variables in the Age-Period Cohort Analysis of Illegal Behavior," *Journal of Research in Crime and Delinquency* 29 (1992): 178–99.

46. Patrick Jackson, "Theories and Findings about Youth Gangs," *Criminal Justice Abstracts,* June 1989, pp. 313–27.

47. Marvin Krohn and Terence Thornberry, "Network Theory: A Model for Understanding Drug Abuse among African-American and Hispanic Youth," in *Drug Abuse among Minority Youth: Advances in Research and Methodology,* eds. Mario De La Rosa and Juan-Luis Recio Adrados (Washington, D.C.: U.S. Department of Health and Human Services, 1993).

48. D. Wayne Osgood, Janet Wilson, Patrick O'Malley, Jerald Bachman, and Lloyd Johnston, "Routine Activities and Individual Deviant Behavior," *American Sociological Review* 61 (1996): 635–55.

49. Mark Warr, "Age, Peers, and Delinquency," *Criminology* 31 (1993): 17–40.

50. Mark Warr, "Organization and Instigation in Delinquent Groups," *Criminology* 34 (1996): 11–35.

51. Sara Battin, Karl Hill, Robert Abbott, Richard Catalano, and J. David Hawkins, "The Contribution of Gang Membership to Delinquency Beyond Delinquent Friends," *Criminology* 36 (1998): 93–116.

52. Terence Thornberry, Alan Lizotte, Marvin Krohn, Margaret Farnworth, and Sung Joon Jang, "Delinquent Peers, Beliefs, and Delinquent Behavior: A Longitudinal Test of Interactional Theory." Working paper no. 6, rev. (Albany, N.Y.: Rochester Youth Development Study, Hindelang Criminal Justice Research Center, 1992), pp. 8–30.

53. Warr, "Age, Peers and Delinquency."

54. Travis Hirschi and Rodney Stark, "Hellfire and Delinquency," *Social Problems* 17 (1969): 202–13.

55. Colin Baier and Bradley Wright, "If You Love Me, Keep My Commandments: A Meta-Analysis of the Effect of Religion on Crime," *Journal of Research in Crime and Delinquency* 38 (2001): 3–21; Byron Johnson, Sung Joon Jang, David Larson, and Spencer De Li, "Does Adolescent Religious Commitment Matter? A Reexamination of the Effects of Religiosity on Delinquency," *Journal of Research in Crime and Delinquency* 38 (2001): 22–44.

56. Sung Joon Jang and Byron Johnson, "Neighborhood Disorder, Individual Religiosity, and Adolescent Use of Illicit Drugs: A Test of Multilevel Hypothesis," *Criminology* 39 (2001): 109–44.

57. T. David Evans, Francis Cullen, R. Gregory Dunaway, and Velmer Burton Jr., "Religion and Crime Reexamined: The Impact of Religion, Secular Controls, and Social Ecology on Adult Criminality," *Criminology* 33 (1995): 195–224.

58. Lee Ellis and James Patterson, "Crime and Religion: An International Comparison among Thirteen Industrial Nations," *Personal Individual Differences* 20 (1996): 761–68.

59. Walter Miller, *Violence by Youth Gangs and Youth Groups as a Crime Problem in Major American Cities* (Washington, D.C.: U.S. Government Printing Office, 1975).

60. Edwin H. Sutherland, *Principles of Criminology* (Philadelphia: Lippincott, 1939).

61. See, for example, Edwin Sutherland, "White-Collar Criminality," *American Sociological Review* 5 (1940): 2–10.

62. See Edwin Sutherland and Donald Cressey, *Criminology,* 8th ed. (Philadelphia: Lippincott, 1970), pp. 77–79.

63. Sandra Brown, Vicki Creamer, and Barbara Stetson, "Adolescent Alcohol Expectancies in Relation to Personal and Parental Drinking Patterns," *Journal of Abnormal Psychology* 96 (1987): 117–21.

64. Ibid.

65. Matthew Ploeger, "Youth Employment and Delinquency: Reconsidering A Problematic Relationship," *Criminology* 35 (1997): 659–75; Elton Jackson, Charles Tittle, and Mary Jean Burke, "Offense-Specific Models of the Differential Association Process," *Social Problems* 33 (1986): 335–56; Gerben J. N. Bruinsma, "Differential Association Theory Reconsidered: An Extension and Its Empirical Test," *Journal of Quantitative Criminology* 8 (1992): 29–46.

66. James Short, "Differential Association as a Hypothesis: Problems of Empirical Testing," *Social Problems* 8 (1960): 14–25.

67. Warr, "Age, Peers, and Delinquency."

68. Denise Kandel and Mark Davies, "Friendship Networks, Intimacy, and Illicit Drug Use in Young Adulthood: A Comparison of Two Competing Theories," *Criminology* 29 (1991): 441–67.

69. Kenneth Tunnell, "Inside the Drug Trade: Trafficking from the Dealer's Perspective," *Qualitative Sociology* 16 (1993): 361–81, at 367.

70. Krohn and Thornberry, "Network Theory," pp. 123–24.

71. Daniel Mears, Matthew Ploeger, and Mark Warr, "Explaining the Gender Gap in Delinquency: Peer Influence and Moral Evaluations of Behavior," *Journal of Research in Crime and Delinquency* 35 (1998): 251–66.

72. Ronald Akers, "Is Differential Association/Social Learning Cultural Deviance Theory," *Criminology* 34 (1996): 229–47; for an opposing view, see Travis Hirschi, "Theory without Ideas: Reply to Akers," *Criminology* 34 (1996): 249–56.

73. Robert Burgess and Ronald Akers, "A Differential Association–Reinforcement Theory of Criminal Behavior," *Social Problems* 14 (1966): 128–47.

74. Ronald Akers, *Deviant Behavior: A Social Learning Approach,* 2d ed. (Belmont, Calif.: Wadsworth, 1977).

75. Ronald Akers, Marvin Krohn, Lonn Lonza-Kaduce, and Marcia Radosevich, "Social Learning and Deviant Behavior: A Specific Test of a General Theory," *American Sociological Review* 44 (1979): 638.

76. Ibid.

77. Marvin Krohn, William Skinner, James Massey, and Ronald Akers, "Social Learning Theory and Adolescent Cigarette Smoking: A Longitudinal Study," *Social Problems* 32 (1985): 455–71.

78. L. Thomas Winfree, Christine Sellers, and Dennis L. Clason, "Social Learning and Adolescent Deviance Abstention: Toward Understanding the Reasons for Initiating, Quitting, and Avoiding Drugs," *Journal of Quantitative Criminology* 9 (1993): 101–25.

79. Ronald Akers and Gang Lee, "A Longitudinal Test of Social Learning Theory: Adolescent Smoking," *Journal of Drug Issues* 26 1996): 317–43.

80. Gary Jensen and David Brownfield, "Parents and Drugs," *Criminology* 21 (1983): 543–54.

81. Ronald Akers, "Rational Choice, Deterrence and Social Learning Theory in Criminology: The Path Not Taken," *Journal of Criminal Law and Criminology* 81 (1990): 653–76.

82. Gresham Sykes and David Matza, "Techniques of Neutralization: A Theory of Delinquency," *American Sociological Review* 22 (1957): 664–70; David Matza, *Delinquency and Drift* (New York: John Wiley, 1964).

83. Matza, *Delinquency and Drift,* p. 51.

84. Sykes and Matza, "Techniques of Neutralization," pp. 664–70; see also David Matza, "Subterranean Traditions of Youths," *Annals of the American Academy of Political and Social Science* 378 (1961): 116.

85. Sykes and Matza, "Techniques of Neutralization," pp. 664–70.

86. Ibid.

87. Ian Shields and George Whitehall, "Neutralization and Delinquency among Teenagers," *Criminal Justice and Behavior* 21 (1994): 223–35; Robert A. Ball, "An Empirical Exploration of Neutralization Theory," *Criminologica* 4 (1966): 22–32. See also M. William Minor, "The Neutralization of Criminal Offense," *Criminology* 18 (1980): 103–20; Robert Gordon, James Short, Desmond Cartwright, and Fred

Strodtbeck, "Values and Gang Delinquency: A Study of Street Corner Groups," *American Journal of Sociology* 69 (1963): 109–28.

88. Michael Hindelang, "The Commitment of Delinquents to Their Misdeeds: Do Delinquents Drift?" *Social Problems* 17 (1970): 500–9; Robert Regoli and Eric Poole, "The Commitment of Delinquents to Their Misdeeds: A Reexamination," *Journal of Criminal Justice* 6 (1978): 261–69.

89. Larry Siegel, Spencer Rathus, and Carol Ruppert, "Values and Delinquent Youth: An Empirical Reexamination of Theories of Delinquency," *British Journal of Criminology* 13 (1973): 237–44.

90. Robert Agnew, "The Techniques of Neutralization and Violence," *Criminology* 32 (1994): 555–80.

91. Jeffrey Fagan, "Adolescent Violence: A View from the Street," *NIJ Research Preview* (Washington, D.C.: National Institute of Justice, 1998).

92. John Hamlin, "Misplaced Role of Rational Choice in Neutralization Theory," *Criminology* 26 (1988): 425–38.

93. Mark Pogrebin, Eric Poole, and Amos Martinez, "Accounts of Professional Misdeeds: The Sexual Exploitation of Clients by Psychotherapists," *Deviant Behavior* 13 (1992): 229–52.

94. Eric Wish, *Drug Use Forecasting 1990* (Washington, D.C.: National Institute of Justice, 1991).

95. Scott Briar and Irvin Piliavin, "Delinquency: Situational Inducements and Commitment to Conformity," *Social Problems* 13 (1965–1966): 35–45.

96. Lawrence Sherman and Douglas Smith, with Janell Schmidt and Dennis Rogan, "Crime, Punishment, and Stake in Conformity: Legal and Informal Control of Domestic Violence," *American Sociological Review* 57 (1992): 680–90.

97. Albert Reiss, "Delinquency as the Failure of Personal and Social Controls," *American Sociological Review* 16 (1951): 196–207.

98. Briar and Piliavin, "Delinquency: Situational Inducements and Commitment to Conformity."

99. Walter Reckless, *The Crime Problem* (New York: Appleton-Century Crofts, 1967), pp. 469–83.

100. Among the many research reports by Reckless and his colleagues are Frank Scarpitti, Ellen Murray, Simon Dinitz, and Walter Reckless, "The Good Boy in a High Delinquency Area: Four Years Later," *American Sociological Review* 23 (1960): 555–58; Walter Reckless, Simon Dinitz, and Ellen Murray, "The Good Boy in a High Delinquency Area," *Journal of Criminal Law, Criminology, and Police Science* 48 (1957): 12–26; idem, "Self-Concept as an Insulator against Delinquency," *American Sociological Review* 21 (1956): 744–46; Walter Reckless and Simon Dinitz, "Pioneering with Self-Concept as a Vulnerability Factor in Delinquency," *Journal of Criminal Law, Criminology, and Police Science* 58 (1967): 515–23; Walter Reckless, Simon Dinitz, and Barbara Kay, "The Self-Component in Potential Delinquency and Potential Non-Delinquency," *American Sociological Review* 22 (1957): 566–70.

101. Howard Kaplan, *Deviant Behavior in Defense of Self* (New York: Academic Press, 1980); idem, "Self-Attitudes and Deviant Response," *Social Forces* 54 (1978): 788–801.

102. Howard Kaplan, *Deviant Behavior in Defense of Self* (New York: Academic Press, 1980), pp. 30–50.

103. Beverly Stiles, Xiaoru Liu, and Howard Kaplan, "Relative Deprivation and Deviant Adaptations: The Mediating Effects of Negative Self-Feelings," *Journal of Research in Crime and Delinquency* 37 (2000): 64-90.

104. Travis Hirschi, *Causes of Delinquency* (Berkeley: University of California Press, 1969).

105. Ibid., p. 231.

106. Ibid., pp. 66–74.

107. Michael Wiatrowski, David Griswold, and Mary K. Roberts, "Social Control Theory and Delinquency," *American Sociological Review* 46 (1981): 525–41.

108. Patricia Van Voorhis, Francis Cullen, Richard Mathers, and Connie Chenoweth Garner, "The Impact of Family Structure and Quality on Delinquency: A Comparative Assessment of Structural and Functional Factors," *Criminology* 26 (1988): 235–61.

109. Marc LeBlanc, "Family Dynamics, Adolescent Delinquency, and Adult Criminality." Paper presented at the Society for Life History Research Conference, Keystone, Colorado, October 1990, p. 6.

110. Bobbi Jo Anderson, Malcolm Holmes, and Erik Ostresh, "Male and Female Delinquent's Attachments and Effects of Attachments on Severity of Self-Reported Delinquency," *Criminal Justice and Behavior* 26 (1999): 435–52.

111. Patricia Jenkins, "School Delinquency and the School Social Bond," *Journal of Research in Crime and Delinquency* 34 (1997): 337–67.

112. Teresa Lagrange and Robert Silverman, "Perceived Strain and Delinquency Motivation: An Empirical Evaluation of General Strain Theory." Paper presented at the American Society of Criminology meeting, Boston, Mass., November 1995.

113. Patricia Van Voorhis, Francis Cullen, Richard Mathers, and Connie Chenoweth Garner, "The Impact of Family Structure and Quality on Delinquency: A Comparative Assessment of Structural and Functional Factors," *Criminology* 26 (1988): 235–61.

114. Thomas Vander Ven, Francis Cullen, Mark Carrozza, and John Paul Wright, "Home Alone: The Impact of Maternal Employment on Delinquency," *Social Problems* 48 (2001): 236–57; Patricia Jenkins, "School Delinquency and the School Social Bond," *Journal of Research in Crime and Delinquency* 34 (1997): 337–67.

115. John Cochran and Ronald Akers, "An Exploration of the Variable Effects of Religiosity on Adolescent Marijuana and Alcohol Use," *Journal of Research in Crime and Delinquency* 26 (1989): 198–225.

116. Robert Agnew and David Peterson, "Leisure and Delinquency," *Social Problems* 36 (1989): 332–48.

117. Marianne Junger and Ineke Haen Marshall, "The Interethnic Generalizability of Social Control Theory: An Empirical Test," *Journal of Research in Crime and Delinquency* 34 (1997): 79–112; Josine Junger-Tas, "An Empirical Test of Social Control Theory," *Journal of Quantitative Criminology* 8 (1992): 18–29.

118. Teresa Lagrange and Robert Silverman, "Perceived Strain and Delinquency Motivation: An Empirical Evaluation of General Strain Theory." Paper presented at the American Society of Criminology meeting, Boston, Mass., November 1995.

119. Kimberly Kempf, "The Empirical Status of Hirschi's Control Theory," in *Advances in Criminological Theory*, eds. Bill Laufer and Freda Adler (New Brunswick, N.J.: Transaction Publishers, 1992).

120. Vander Ven, Cullen, Carrozza, and Wright, "Home Alone: The Impact of Maternal Employment on Delinquency," p. 253.

121. Peggy Giordano, Stephen Cernkovich, and M.D. Pugh, "Friendships and Delinquency," *American Journal of Sociology* 91 (1986): 1170–1202.

122. Denise Kandel and Mark Davies, "Friendship Networks, Intimacy, and

Illicit Drug Use in Young Adulthood: A Comparison of Two Competing Theories," *Criminology* 29 (1991): 441–67.

123. Velmer Burton, Francis Cullen, T. David Evans, R. Gregory Dunaway, Sesha Kethineni, and Gary Payne, "The Impact of Parental Controls on Delinquency," *Journal of Criminal Justice* 23 (1995): 111–26.

124. Kimberly Kempf Leonard and Scott Decker, "The Theory of Social Control: Does It Apply to the Very Young," *Journal of Criminal Justice* 22 (1994): 89–105.

125. Michael Hindelang, "Causes of Delinquency: A Partial Replication and Extension," *Social Problems* 21 (1973): 471–87.

126. Gary Jensen and David Brownfield, "Parents and Drugs," *Criminology* 21 (1983): 543–54. See also M. Wiatrowski, D. Griswold, and M. Roberts, "Social Control Theory and Delinquency," *American Sociological Review* 46 (1981): 525–41.

127. Leslie Samuelson, Timothy Hartnagel, and Harvey Krahn, "Crime and Social Control among High School Dropouts," *Journal of Crime and Justice* 18 (1990): 129–61.

128. Marvin Krohn and James Massey, "Social Control and Delinquent Behavior: An Examination of the Elements of the Social Bond," *Sociological Quarterly* 21 (1980): 529–43.

129. Jill Leslie Rosenbaum and James Lasley, "School, Community Context, and Delinquency: Rethinking the Gender Gap," *Justice Quarterly* 7 (1990): 493–513.

130. Randy LaGrange and Helene Raskin White, "Age Differences in Delinquency: A Test of Theory," *Criminology* 23 (1985): 19–45.

131. Robert Agnew, "Social Control Theory and Delinquency: A Longitudinal Test," *Criminology* 23 (1985): 47–61.

132. Alan E. Liska and M. D. Reed, "Ties to Conventional Institutions and Delinquency: Estimating Reciprocal Effects," *American Sociological Review* 50 (1985): 547–60.

133. Michael Wiatrowski, David Griswold, and Mary K. Roberts, "Social Control Theory and Delinquency," *American Sociological Review* 46 (1981): 525–41.

134. George Herbert Mead, *Mind, Self and Society* (Chicago: University of Chicago Press, 1934); idem, *The Philosophy of the Act* (Chicago: University of Chicago Press, 1938); Charles Horton Cooley, *Human Nature and the Social*

Order (Schocken: New York, 1964), originally published in 1902; Herbert Blumer, *Symbolic Interactionism: Perspective and Method* (Englewood Cliffs, N.J.: Prentice-Hall, 1969).

135. Bruce Link, Elmer Streuning, Francis Cullen, Patrick Shrout, and Bruce Dohrenwend, "A Modified Labeling Theory Approach to Mental Disorders: An Empirical Assessment," *American Sociological Review* 54 (1989): 400–23.

136. Linda Jackson, John Hunter, and Carole Hodge, "Physical Attractiveness and Intellectual Competence: A Meta-Analytic Review," *Social Psychology Quarterly* 58 (1995): 108–22.

137. *President's Commission on Law Enforcement and the Administration of Youth Crime, Task Force Report: Juvenile Delinquency and Youth* (Washington, D.C.: U.S. Government Printing Office, 1967), p. 43.

138. Kai Erickson, "Notes on the Sociology of Deviance," *Social Problems* 9 (1962): 397–414.

139. Edwin Schur, *Labeling Deviant Behavior* (New York: Harper and Row, 1972), p. 21.

140. Howard Becker, *Outsiders, Studies in the Sociology of Deviance* (New York: Macmillan, 1963), p. 9.

141. Laurie Goodstein, "The Architect of the 'Gay Conversion' Campaign," *New York Times*, 13 August 1998, p. A10.

142. Howard Becker, *Outsiders, Studies in the Sociology of Deviance* (New York: Macmillan, 1963), p. 9.

143. Christy Visher, "Gender, Police Arrest Decision, and Notions of Chivalry," *Criminology* 21 (1983): 5–28.

144. Marjorie Zatz, "Race, Ethnicity and Determinate Sentencing," *Criminology* 22 (1984): 147–71.

145. Christina DeJong and Kenneth Jackson, "Putting Race into Context: Race, Juvenile Justice Processing, and Urbanization," *Justice Quarterly* 15 (1998): 487–504.

146. Roland Chilton and Jim Galvin, "Race, Crime and Criminal Justice," *Crime and Delinquency* 31 (1985): 3–14.

147. Joan Petersilia, "Racial Disparities in the Criminal Justice System: A Summary," *Crime and Delinquency* 31 (1985): 15–34.

148. Walter Gove, *The Labeling of Deviance: Evaluating a Perspective* (New York: John Wiley, 1975), p. 5.

149. Harold Garfinkle, "Conditions of Successful Degradation Ceremonies," *American Journal of Sociology* 61 (1956): 420–24.

150. Karen Heimer and Ross Matsueda, "Role-Taking, Role-Commitment and Delinquency: A Theory of Differential Social Control," *American Sociological Review* 59 (1994): 400–37.

151. Stacy DeCoster and Karen Heimer, "The Relationship between Law Violation and Depression: An Interactionist Analysis," *Criminology* 39 (2001): 799–837.

152. Karen Heimer, "Gender, Race, and the Pathways to Delinquency: An Interactionist Explanation," in *Crime and Inequality*, eds. John Hagan and Ruth Peterson (Stanford, Calif.: Stanford University Press, 1995), pp. 32–57.

153. Heimer and Matsueda, "Role-Taking, Role-Commitment and Delinquency: A Theory of Differential Social Control."

154. See, for example, Howard Kaplan and Hiroshi Fukurai, "Negative Social Sanctions, Self-Rejection, and Drug Use," *Youth and Society* 23 (1992): 275–98; Howard Kaplan and Robert Johnson, "Negative Social Sanctions and Juvenile Delinquency: Effects of Labeling in a Model of Deviant Behavior," *Social Science Quarterly* 72 91991): 98–122; Howard Kaplan, Robert Johnson, and Carol Bailey, "Deviant Peers and Deviant Behavior: Further Elaboration of a Model," *Social Psychology Quarterly* 30 (1987): 277–84.

155. Howard Kaplan, *Toward a General Theory of Deviance: Contributions from Perspectives on Deviance and Criminality* (College Station, Texas: Texas A&M University, n.d.).

156. John Lofland, *Deviance and Identity* (Englewood Cliffs, N.J.: Prentice-Hall, 1969).

157. Frank Tannenbaum, *Crime and the Community* (New York: Columbia University Press, 1938), pp. 19–20.

158. Edwin Lemert, *Social Pathology* (New York: McGraw-Hill, 1951).

159. Ibid., p. 75.

160. National Minority Advisory Council on Criminal Justice, *The Inequality of Justice* (Washington, D.C.: author, 1981), p. 200.

161. Carl Pope and William Feyerherm, "Minority Status and Juvenile Justice Processing," *Criminal Justice Abstracts* 22 (1990): 327–36; see also Carl Pope, "Race and Crime Revisited," *Crime and Delinquency* 25 (1979): 347–57.

162. Leslie Margolin, "Deviance on Record: Techniques for Labeling Child Abusers in Official Documents," *Social Problems* 39 (1992): 58–68.

163. Charles Corley, Stephen Cernkovich, and Peggy Giordano, "Sex and the Likelihood of Sanction," *Journal of Criminal Law and Criminology* 80 (1989): 540–53.

164. Samuel Walker, Cassia Spohn, and Miriam DeLone, *The Color of Justice, Race, Ethnicity and Crime in America* (Belmont, Calif.: Wadsworth, 1996), pp. 145–46.

165. Howard Kaplan and Robert Johnson, "Negative Social Sanctions and Juvenile Delinquency: Effects of Labeling in a Model of Deviant Behavior," *Social Science Quarterly* 72 (1991): 98–122.

166. Ruth Triplett, "The Conflict Perspective, Symbolic Interactionism, and the Status Characteristics Hypothesis," *Justice Quarterly* 10 (1993): 540–58.

167. Ross Matsueda, "Reflected Appraisals: Parental Labeling, and Delinquency: Specifying a Symbolic Interactionist Theory," *American Journal of Sociology* 97 (1992): 1577–1611.

168. Suzanne Ageton and Delbert Elliott, *The Effect of Legal Processing on Self-Concept* (Boulder, Colo.: Institute of Behavioral Science, 1973).

169. Christine Bowditch, "Getting Rid of Troublemakers: High School Disciplinary Procedures and the Production of Dropouts," *Social Problems* 40 (1993): 493–507.

170. Melvin Ray and William Downs, "An Empirical Test of Labeling Theory Using Longitudinal Data," *Journal of Research in Crime and Delinquency* 23 (1986): 169–94.

171. Sherman and Smith, with Schmidt and Rogan, "Crime, Punishment, and Stake in Conformity."

172. Charles Tittle, "Two Empirical Regularities (Maybe) in Search of an Explanation: Commentary on the Age/Crime Debate," *Criminology* 26 (1988): 75–85.

173. Ibid.

174. Robert Sampson and John Laub, "A Life-Course Theory of Cumulative Disadvantage and the Stability of Delinquency," in *Developmental Theories of Crime and Delinquency* ed. Terence Thornberry (New Brunswick, N.J.: Transaction Books, 1997), pp. 133–61.

175. Douglas Smith and Robert Brame, "On the Initiation and Continuation of Delinquency," *Criminology* 4 (1994): 607–30.

176. Jack Gibbs, "Conceptions of Deviant Behavior: The Old and the New," *Pacific Sociological Review* 9 (1966): 11–13.

177. Schur, *Labeling Deviant Behavior,* p. 14.

178. Ronald Akers, "Problems in the Sociology of Deviance," *Social Problems* 46 (1968): 463.

179. Charles Tittle, "Labeling and Crime: An Empirical Evaluation," in *The Labeling of Deviance: Evaluating a Perspective,* ed. Walter Gove (New York: John Wiley, 1975), pp. 157–79.

180. David Farrington, "Early Predictors of Adolescent Aggression and Adult Violence," *Violence and Victims* 4 (1989): 79–100.

181. Raymond Paternoster and Leeann Iovanni, "The Labeling Perspective and Delinquency: An Elaboration of the Theory and an Assessment of the Evidence," *Justice Quarterly* 6 (1989): 358–94.

CHAPTER 9 Conflict Theory

AP/Wide World Photos

Introduction

In July of 2001 as the Group of Eight (an association of major industrialized trading nations including the United States) were set to meet in Genoa, Italy, representatives of many international antiglobalization groups set out to disrupt the meetings.[1] Their aim was to demand that international trade agreements be linked to human rights and protection of the environment. Some wanted wealthy nations to forgive the foreign debt of the poor nations with which they trade. Protesters decried how international corporations and governments now control every aspect of life—water, genes, atmosphere, health care, culture, public spaces, land. Groups from different nations had unique agendas. For example, the Landless Movement of Brazil (MST) campaigned for land reform in Brazil in opposition to the World Bank's program of market-led land reform and corporate control of agriculture through patents on seed.

■ Carlo Giuliani, shown here, was killed during clashes between police and protesters in Genoa, Italy, on July 20, 2001. The protests centered around the demand that international trade agreements be linked to human rights and protection of the environment. Protesters wanted to bring attention to the fact that international corporations now control every aspect of life—water, genes, atmosphere, health care, culture, public spaces, and land. The resulting conflict between the mostly left-wing protesters and government authorities destroyed property and left scores injured.

The demonstrations soon got out of hand, and gangs of protesters began burning cars and gutting buildings in Genoa. The Italian police responded to the violence by a minority of protesters with violence of their own. By the time the violence subsided, one protester was dead—Carlo Giuliani, a member of MST—more than 400 people were injured, and roughly $45 million in property was damaged. The Genoa protests were a continuation of angry confrontations between government officials and antiglobalization demonstrators that began in Seattle, Washington, in 1999 and continued at meetings of the World Bank and International Monetary Fund in Washington, D.C., the Republican convention in Philadelphia, the Democratic convention in Los Angeles, the Americas summit in Quebec, and half a dozen events in Europe.

The conflict between multinational corporations, big governments, and left-wing protesters is not unique. It would be unusual to pick up the morning paper and not see headlines proclaiming renewed strife between the United States and its overseas adversaries, between terrorists and authorized governments, between union negotiators and management attorneys, between citizens and police authorities, or between feminists and reactionary males protecting their turf. The world is filled with conflict. Conflict is destructive when it leads to war, violence, and death, but it can be functional when it results in positive social change. Criminologists who view crime as a function of social conflict and economic rivalry are aligned with a number of schools of thought (see Figure 9.1). These are referred to as *conflict, critical, Marxist,* or *radical* schools of criminology, or one of their affiliated branches, including but not limited to *peacemaking, left realism, radical feminism,* and *postmodernism* (also called *deconstructionism*).

The goal of social conflict theorists is to explain crime within economic and social contexts and to express the connection between the nature of social class, crime, and social control.[2] Conflict theorists are concerned with issues such as these:

• The role government plays in creating a crimogenic environment.

• The relationship between personal or group power and the shaping of criminal law.

• The prevalence of bias in justice system operations.

• The relationship between a capitalist free-enterprise economy and crime rates.

Conflict theorists view crime as the outcome of class struggle. Conflict works to promote crime by creating a social atmosphere in which the law is a mechanism for controlling dissatisfied, have-not members of society while the wealthy maintain their position of power. That is why crimes that are the province of the wealthy, such as illegal corporate activities, are sanctioned much more leniently

Figure 9.1   **The Branches of Social Conflict Theory**

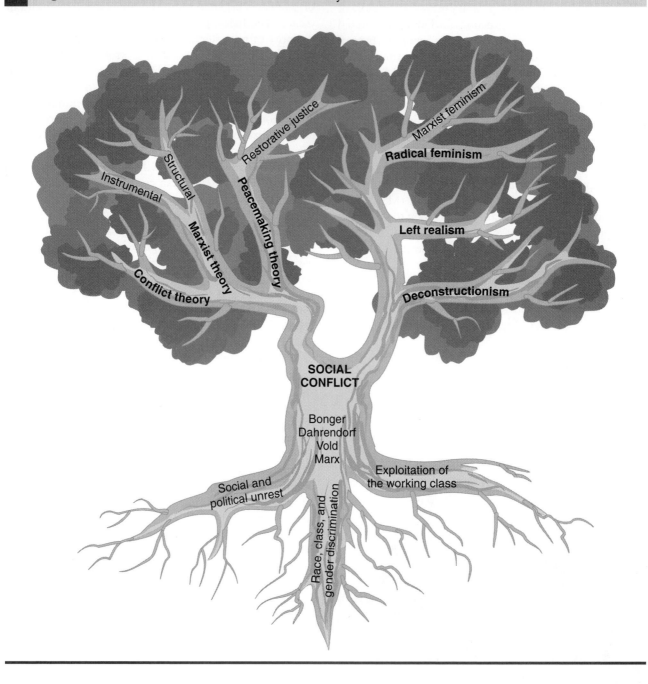

than those, such as burglary, that are considered lower-class activities.

Conflict theorists consider acts of racism, sexism, imperialism, unsafe working conditions, inadequate child care, substandard housing, pollution of the environment, and war-making as a tool of foreign policy as "true crimes." The crimes of the helpless—burglary, robbery, and assault—are more expressions of rage over unjust conditions than actual crimes.[3] By focusing on how the state uses the law to control the lower classes, conflict theory

seeks to show that crime is the inevitable result of inter-class hostility.

This chapter will review criminological theories that allege that criminal behavior is a function of conflict, a reaction to the unfair distribution of wealth and power in society. The social conflict perspective has several independent branches. One, generally referred to as **conflict theory,** assumes that the intergroup conflict and rivalry that exists in every society causes crime. A second branch focuses more directly on the crime-producing traits of capitalist society. The various schools of thought in this area of scholarship are known interchangeably as critical, radical, and Marxist criminology.[4] Other sections are devoted to feminist, new realist, peacemaking, and postmodern thought.

Marxist Thought

Karl Marx lived in an era of unrestrained capitalist expansion.[5] The tools of the Industrial Revolution had become regular features of society by 1850. Mechanized factories, the use of coal to drive steam engines, and modern transportation all inspired economic development. Production had shifted from cottage industries to large factories.

CONNECTIONS

As you may recall from Chapter 1, the philosophical and economic analysis of Karl Marx forms the historical roots of the conflict perspective of criminology. ■

Industrialists could hire workers on their own terms; as a result, conditions in factories were atrocious. Owners and government agents, who were the agents of capitalists, ruthlessly suppressed trade unions that promised workers salvation from these atrocities.

Marx's early career as a journalist was interrupted by government suppression of the newspaper where he worked because of the paper's liberal editorial policy. He then moved to Paris, where he met Friedrich Engels (1820–1895), who would become his friend and economic patron. By 1847, Marx and Engels had joined with a group of primarily German socialist revolutionaries known as the Communist League.

Productive Forces and Productive Relations

In 1848, Marx issued his famous **communist manifesto.** In this document, Marx focused his attention on the economic conditions perpetuated by the capitalist system. He stated that its development had turned workers into a dehumanized mass who lived an existence that was at the mercy of their capitalist employers. He wrote of the injustice of young children being sent to work in mines and factories from dawn to dusk. He railed against the people who were being beaten down by a system that demanded obedience and cooperation and offered little in return. These oppressive conditions led Marx to conclude that the character of every civilization is determined by its mode of production—the way its people develop and produce material goods (materialism).

Karl Marx identified the economic structures in society that control all human relations. Production has two components: (1) **productive forces,** which include such things as technology, energy sources, and material re-

sources; and (2) **productive relations,** which are the relationships that exist among the people producing goods and services. The most important relationship in industrial culture is between the owners of the means of production, the **capitalist bourgeoisie,** and the people who do the actual labor, the **proletariat.** Throughout history, society has been organized this way—master–slave, lord–serf, and now capitalist–proletarian. According to Marx and Engels, capitalist society is subject to the development of a rigid class structure with the capitalist bourgeoisie at the top. Next come the working proletariat, who actually produce goods and services. At the bottom of society are the fringe members who produce nothing and live, parasitically, off the work of others—the **lumpen proletariat** (Figure 9.2).

In Marxist theory, the term "class" does not refer to an attribute or characteristic of a person or a group; rather, it denotes position in relation to others. Thus, it is not necessary to have a particular amount of wealth or prestige to

Figure 9.2 The Marxist View of Class

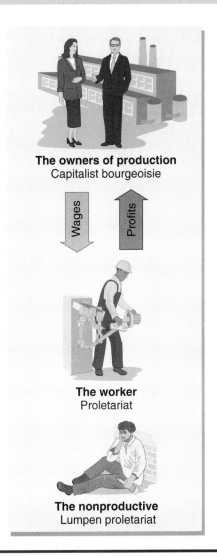

The owners of production
Capitalist bourgeoisie

Wages

Profits

The worker
Proletariat

The nonproductive
Lumpen proletariat

be a member of the capitalist class; it is more important to have the power to exploit others economically, legally, and socially. The political and economic philosophy of the dominant class influences all aspects of life. Consciously or unconsciously, artists, writers, and teachers bend their work to the whims of the capitalist system. Thus, the economic system controls all facets of human life. Consequently, people's lives revolve around the means of production. As Marx said:

> In all forms of society, there is one specific kind of production which predominates over the rest, whose relations thus assign rank and influence to the others. It is a general illumination which bathes all the other colours and modifies their particularity. It is a particular ether which determines the specific gravity of every being which has materialized within it.[6]

Marx believed societies and their structures were not stable and, therefore, could change through slow evolution or sudden violence. Historically, such change occurs because of contradictions present in a society. These contradictions are antagonism or conflicts between elements in the existing social arrangement, which in the long run are incompatible with one another. If these social conflicts are not resolved, they tend to destabilize society, leading to social change.

Surplus Value

How could social change occur in capitalist society? Marx held that the laboring class produces goods that exceed wages in value (the theory of **surplus value**). The excess value goes into the hands of the capitalists as profit; they then use most of it to acquire an ever-expanding capitalist base that relies on advanced technology for efficiency. Capitalists are in constant competition with each other, so they must find ways of producing goods more efficiently and cheaply. One way is to pay workers the lowest possible wages or to replace them with labor-saving machinery (Figure 9.3). Soon the supply of efficiently made goods outstrips the ability of the laboring classes to purchase them, a condition that precipitates an economic crisis. During this period of crisis, weaker enterprises go under and are consequently incorporated into ever-expanding, monopolistic mega-corporations strong enough to further exploit the workers. For example, between the 1980s and today, many giant corporations have merged to form even larger enterprises: Disney and ABC; AOL and Time Warner; Exxon and Mobil, and Mercedes Benz and Chrysler. This allowed management to control costs, cut excess labor, and reduce the power of workers to demand benefits or wage increases. Also, in an era of globalization, mergers enable companies to have a worldwide reach and to exploit labor in developing nations.

Marx believed the ebb and flow of the capitalist business cycle contained the seeds of its own destruction. He predicted that from its ashes would grow a socialist state in which the workers themselves would own the means of production. In his analysis, Marx used the **dialectic method,** based on the analysis developed by the philosopher Georg Hegel (1770–1831). Hegel argued that for every idea, or thesis, there exists an opposing argument, or **antithesis.** Since neither position can ever be truly accepted, the result is a merger of the two ideas, a **synthesis.** Marx adapted this analytic method for his study of

Figure 9.3 Surplus Value

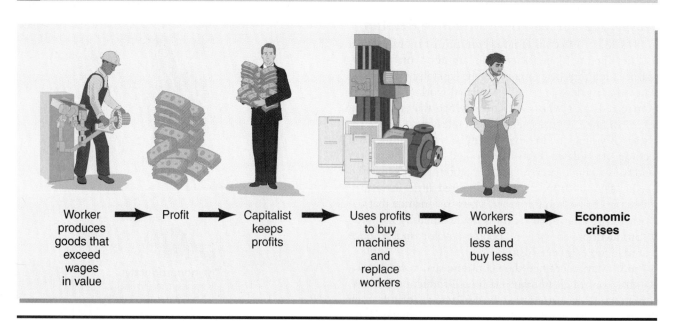

Worker produces goods that exceed wages in value ➡ Profit ➡ Capitalist keeps profits ➡ Uses profits to buy machines and replace workers ➡ Workers make less and buy less ➡ **Economic crises**

class struggle. History, argued Marx, is replete with examples of two opposing forces whose conflict promotes social change. When conditions are bad enough, the oppressed will rise up to fight the owners and eventually replace them. Thus, in the end, the capitalist system will destroy itself.

Marx on Crime

Marx did not write a great deal on the subject of crime, but he mentioned it in a variety of passages scattered throughout his writing. He viewed crime as the product of law enforcement policies akin to a labeling process theory.[7] He also saw a connection between criminality and the inequities found in the capitalist system. He reasoned: "There must be something rotten in the very core of a social system which increases in wealth without diminishing its misery, and increases in crime even more rapidly than in numbers."[8]

To read an excerpt in Marx's own words on the nature of crime, go to InfoTrac College Edition, and look up this article: Karl Marx. Criminals on the development of productive power. *Journal of Contemporary Asia* August 2001 v31 i3 p288 ■

His collaborator, Friedrich Engels, however, did spend some time on the subject in his work, *The Condition of the Working Class in England in 1844*.[9] Engels portrayed crime as a function of social demoralization—a collapse of people's humanity reflecting a decline in society. Workers, demoralized by capitalist society, are caught up in a process that leads to crime and violence. According to Engels, workers were social outcasts, ignored by the structure of capitalist society and treated as brutes.[10] Left to their own devices, working people committed crime because their choice was a slow death of starvation or a speedy one at the hands of the law. The brutality of the capitalist system, he believed, turns workers into animal-like creatures without a will of their own.

■ Developing a Conflict Theory of Crime

The writings of Karl Marx and Friedrich Engels greatly influenced the development of social conflict thinking. Even though Marx himself did not write much on the topic of crime, his views on the relationship between the economic structure and social behavior deeply influenced other thinkers.

Conflict theory was first applied to criminology by three distinguished scholars: Willem Bonger, Ralf Dahrendorf, and George Vold. In some instances, their works share the Marxist view that industrial society is wracked by conflict between the proletariat and the bourgeoisie; in other instances, their writings diverge from Marxist dogma. The writing of each of these pioneers is briefly discussed next.

The Contribution of Willem Bonger

Willem Bonger was born in 1876 in Holland and committed suicide in 1940 rather than submit to Nazi rule. He is famous for his Marxist socialist concepts of crime causation, which were first published in 1916.[11]

Bonger believed crime is of social and not biological origin, and that with the exception of a few special cases, crime lies within the boundaries of normal human behavior. According to Bonger, no act is naturally immoral or criminal. He viewed crimes as antisocial acts that reflect current morality. Since the social structure changes continually, ideas of what is moral and what is not also are in constant flux. The tension between rapidly changing morality, which is common in modern society, and a comparatively static, predominantly bourgeois criminal, can become very great. According to Bonger, the response to crime is to apply penalties considered more severe than spontaneous moral condemnation. These penalties are administered by those in political control—that is, by the state. Bonger believed society is divided into have and have-not groups, not on the basis of people's innate ability, but because of the system of production that is in force. In every society that is divided into a ruling class and an inferior class, penal law serves the will of the ruling class. Even though criminal laws may appear to protect members of both classes, hardly any act is punished that does not injure the interests of the dominant ruling class. Crimes, then, are considered to be antisocial acts because they are harmful to those who have the power at their command to control society.

Bonger argued that attempts to control law violations through force are a sign of a weak society. He viewed the capitalist system, characterized by extreme competition, as being held together by force rather than consensus, thus making it a weak system. As a consequence of this force, he claimed that the social order is maintained for the benefit of the capitalists at the expense of the population as a whole. Everyone may desire wealth, but it is only the most privileged people, with the most capital, who can enjoy luxuries and advantages. Within this society, people care only for their own lives and pleasures and ignore the plight of the disadvantaged. Because of this dramatic inequity between the haves and have-nots, Bonger claimed, people have become very egotistical and more capable of crime than if the system had developed under a socialist philosophy.

Though the capitalist system makes both the proletariat and the bourgeoisie crime prone, only the former are likely to become officially recognized criminals. The reason for this is twofold. First of all, the legal system discriminates against the poor by defending the actions of the wealthy, and second of all, it is the proletariat who are deprived of the materials that are monopolized by the bourgeoisie.

Upper-class individuals will commit crime if (a) they sense a good opportunity to make a financial gain and if (b) their lack of moral sense enables them to violate social rules. It is the drive toward success at any price that pushes wealthier individuals toward criminality.

Recognized, official crimes are a function of poverty. The relationship can be direct, as when a person steals to survive, or indirect, as when poverty kills the social sentiments in each person and between people.

It is not the absolute amount of wealth that affects crime, but its distribution, posits Bonger. If wealth is distributed unequally throughout the social structure and people are taught to equate economic advantage with superiority, then those who are poor and therefore inferior will be crime prone. The economic system will intensify any personal disadvantage people have—for example, psychological problems—and increase their propensity to commit crime.

Bonger concluded that almost all crime will disappear if society progresses from competitive capitalism, to monopoly capitalism (in which a relatively few enterprises control the means of production), to having the means of production held in common, to the ultimate socialist form of society. In other words, Bonger believed that redistribution of property according to the maxim "each according to his needs" would be the demise of crime. If this stage of society cannot be reached, a residue of crime will always remain. If socialism can be achieved, however, then remaining crimes will be of the irrational psychopathic type caused by individual mental problems. Bonger's writing continues to be one of the most often-cited sources of Marxist thought.

The Contribution of Ralf Dahrendorf

In formulating their views, today's conflict theorists also rely heavily on the writings of pioneering social thinker Ralf Dahrendorf.[12]

To read the transcript of an informative interview, go to:
http://globetrotter.berkeley.edu/Elberg/
Dahrendorf/dahrendorf0.html
For an up-to-date list of Web links, go to
http://info.wadsworth.com/siegel ∎

Dahrendorf argues that modern society is organized into what he called **imperatively coordinated associations.** These associations comprise two groups: those who possess authority and use it for social domination and those who lack authority and are dominated. Since the domination of one segment of society (for example, industry) does not mean dominating another (such as government), society is a plurality of competing interest groups.

In his classic work, *Class and Class Conflict in Industrial Society,* Dahrendorf attempted to show how society has changed since Marx formulated his concepts of class, state, and conflict. Dahrendorf argued that Marx did not foresee the changes that have occurred in the laboring classes. "The working class of today," Dahrendorf stated, "far from being a homogeneous group of equally unskilled and impoverished people, is in fact a stratum differentiated by numerous subtle and not so subtle distinctions."[13] Workers are divided into the unskilled, semiskilled, and skilled; the interests of one group may not match the needs of the others. Accordingly, Marx's concept of a cohesive proletarian class has proved inaccurate. As a result of his differing perspectives, Dahrendorf embraced a non-Marxist conflict orientation. Dahrendorf proposed a unified conflict theory of human behavior, which can be summarized as follows:

- Every society is at every point subject to processes of change; social change is everywhere.
- Every society displays at every point dissent and conflict; social conflict is everywhere.
- Every element in a society renders a contribution to its disintegration and change.
- Every society is based on the coercion of some of its members by others.

Dahrendorf did not speak directly to the issue of crime, but his model of conflict serves as a pillar of modern conflict criminology.

The Contribution of George Vold

Though Dahrendorf contributed its theoretical underpinnings, conflict theory was actually adapted to criminology by George Vold.[14] Vold argued that crime can also be explained by social conflict. Laws are created by politically oriented groups, who seek the government's assistance to help them defend their rights and protect their interests. If a group can marshal enough support, a law will be created to hamper and curb the interests of some opposition group. Every stage of the process—from passing the law, to prosecuting the case, to developing relationships between inmate and guard, parole agent and parolee—is marked by conflict. Vold found that criminal acts are a consequence of direct contact between forces struggling to control society. Though their criminal content may mask their political meaning, closer examination of even the most basic violent acts often reveals political undertones.

Vold's model cannot be used to explain all types of crime. It is limited to situations in which rival group loyalties collide. It cannot explain impulsive, irrational acts unrelated to any group's interest. Despite this limitation, Vold found that a great deal of criminal activity results from intergroup clashes.

■ Conflict Theory

Conflict theory came into criminological prominence during the 1960s. Vold and Dahrendorf had published their influential works in the late 1950s. At the same time, self-report studies began to yield data suggesting that the class–crime correlation found in official crime data was spurious. The self-reports indicated that crime and delinquency were much more evenly distributed through the social structure than was shown by the official statistics; official data indicate that crime was more often found in lower-class environments.[15] If this was true, then middle-class participation in crime was going unrecorded, while the lower class was the subject of discriminatory law enforcement practices by the criminal justice system.

To learn more about the effect of conflict on everyday life, search InfoTrac College Edition using "social conflict" as a key word. ■

Criminologists began to view the justice system as a mechanism to control the lower class and maintain the status quo rather than as the means of dispensing fair and even-handed justice.[16] The publication of important labeling perspective works, such as Lemert's *Social Pathology* and Becker's *Outsiders*, also contributed to the development of the conflict model.[17] Labeling theorists rejected the notion that crime is morally wrong; they called for an analysis of the interaction among crime, criminal, victim, and social control agencies. By focusing on social reactions to crime, labeling theory researchers found that the social context within which crimes occur plays an important role in the criminal process and that agents of social control actually may play an active role in the process that ultimately produces crime. The criminal was a person whose behavior was shaped by the social, political, and legal worlds in which he or she lived. Some criminologists charged that labeling theory did not go far enough in analyzing the important relationships in society because it was essentially apolitical and satisfied with examining the behavior of social deviants such as drug users and mental patients.[18] As a result, a group of criminologists began to produce scholarship and research directed at these issues:

- Identifying "real" crimes in U.S. society, such as profiteering, sexism, and racism
- Evaluating how the criminal law is used as a mechanism of social control
- Turning the attention of citizens to the inequities in U.S. society[19]

The theme that dominated much of the work in this area was the contention that criminal legislation was determined by the relative power of groups who wanted to use the criminal law to advance their own special interests or to impose their moral preferences on others.[20]

This movement was aided by the general and widespread social and political upheaval of the late 1960s and early 1970s. These forces included anti-Vietnam War demonstrations, counterculture movements, and various forms of political protest. Conflict theory flourished within this framework because it provided a systematic basis for challenging the legitimacy of the government's creation and application of law. The federal government agents' crackdown on political dissidents, the prosecution of draft resisters, and the like all seemed designed to maintain control in the hands of political power brokers.

Developing a Conflict Criminology

As conflict theory began to have a significant influence on criminological study, several respected scholars, inspired by the writings of Dahrendorf and Vold, abandoned the criminological mainstream. William Chambliss and Robert Seidman wrote the treatise, *Law, Order and Power*, which documented how the justice system operates to protect the rich and powerful. After closely observing its operations, Chambliss and Seidman concluded:

> In America, it is frequently argued that to have "freedom" is to have a system, which allows one group to make a profit over another. To maintain the existing legal system requires a choice. That choice is between maintaining a legal system that serves to support the existing economic system with its power structure and developing an equitable legal system accompanied by the loss of "personal freedom." But the old question comes back to plague us: Freedom for whom? Is the black man who provides such a ready source of cases for the welfare workers, the mental hospitals, and the prisons "free"? Are the slum dwellers who are arrested night after night for "loitering," "drunkenness," or being "suspicious" free? The freedom protected by the system of law is the freedom of those who can afford it. The law serves their interests, but they are not "society"; they are one element of society. They may in some complex societies even be a majority (though this is very rare), but the myth that the law serves the interests of "society" misrepresents the facts.[21]

These common objectives of conflict criminology appear in Chambliss and Seidman's writing:

- Describing how the control of the political and economic system affects how criminal justice is administered
- Showing how the definitions of crime favor those who control the justice system
- Analyzing the role of conflict in contemporary society

Their scholarship also reflects another major objective of conflict theory: to show how justice in U.S. society is skewed. It shows that those who deserve to be punished the most (wealthy white-collar criminals whose crimes cost society millions of dollars) are actually punished the least, whereas those whose crimes are relatively minor and committed out of economic necessity (petty, underclass thieves) receive the stricter sanctions.[22]

Power relations   According to the conflict view, crime is defined by those in power. Power refers to the ability of persons and groups to determine and control the behavior of others and to shape public opinion to meet their personal interests. The unequal distribution of power produces conflict, and conflict is rooted in the competition for power. The ability of the powerful majority to control people is exemplified by the relationship between the U.S. justice system and African Americans. The subtle and not-so-subtle ways the justice system victimizes African Americans has been well documented.[23] According to this view, poor inner-city youths are driven to commit crimes out of economic desperation. Racial discrimination then results in discretionary decisions by law enforcement officers, who brand them felons and not misdemeanants; they are shunted into the criminal courts and not into diversion programs.

Does race discrimination still exist in modern society, and what forms does it take? To find out, use the term "race discrimination" as a subject guide on InfoTrac College Edition. ■

Busy public defenders too often short shrift their clients into plea bargains that assure early criminal records. Health care workers and teachers are quick to report suspected violent acts to the police; this results in frequent and early arrests of minority adults and youth. Police departments routinely employ policies of searching, questioning, and detaining all African American males in an area if a violent criminal has been described as "looking or sounding black." By creating the image of pervasive African American criminality and coupling it with unfair treatment, those in power further alienated this population from the mainstream, perpetuating a class- and race-divided society. It is not surprising then that surveys show that African Americans are much more likely to perceive "criminal injustice" than are white Americans.[24]

The social reality of crime   Sociologist Richard Quinney formulated one of the best-known conflict models, known today as the **social reality of crime.** The theory's six propositions are contained in Exhibit 9.1.[25] According to Quinney, criminal definitions (law) represent the interests of those who hold power in society. Where there is conflict between social groups—for example, the wealthy and the poor—those who hold power will be the ones to create the laws that benefit themselves and hold rivals in check. This may explain the rather harsh punishments for

■ According to the conflict view, crime is defined by those in power, who use the law to control the behavior of others and to shape public opinion to meet their personal interests. The unequal distribution of power produces conflict, and conflict is rooted in the competition for power. Racial profiling and other human rights violations are a result of the unequal distribution of power. Here, protesters in Denver speak out against police racial profiling on August 29, 2000. The rally was held two doors away from a house where a Hispanic man was killed in a drug raid on the wrong house.

property crime in the United States; they are designed to help those who are already wealthy keep their possessions. In contrast, the lenient sanctions attached to corporate crimes are designed to give the already powerful a free hand at economic exploitation.

To read about Richard Quinney and his life's work, go to:

http://www.criminology.fsu.edu/crimtheory/quinney.htm

For an up-to-date list of Web links, go to

http://info.wadsworth.com/siegel ■

Quinney wrote that criminal definitions are based on such factors as (1) changing social conditions; (2) emerging interests; (3) increasing demands that political, economic, and religious interests be protected; and (4) changing conceptions of public interest. In the sixth statement on the social reality of crime, Quinney pulls together the ideas he developed in the preceding five: concepts of crime are controlled by the powerful, and the criminal justice system works to secure the needs of the powerful. When people develop behavior patterns that conflict with these needs, the agents of the rich—the justice system—define them as criminals. Because of their reliance on power relations, criminal definitions are a constantly changing set of concepts that mirror the political organization of society. Law is not an abstract body of rules that represents an absolute moral code; law is an integral part of society, a force that represents a way of life and a method of doing things.

Crime is a function of power relations and an inevitable result of social conflict. Criminals are not simply social misfits but people who have come up short in the struggle for success and are seeking alternative means of achieving wealth, status, or even survival.[26] Consequently, law violations can be viewed as political or even quasi-revolutionary acts.[27]

CONNECTIONS

Quinney has changed his outlook over his long and distinguished career. He now is a leader of the Zen-inspired peacemaking movement, which seeks to remove violence and coercion from the criminal justice system and promotes healing or "restorative justice." See the section on peacemaking later in this chapter. ■

Norm resistance Other criminological writers have made influential contributions to the general conflict criminology. Austin Turk wrote about how authority relationships are inevitable and that they produce social conflict. Those in society who dominate (that is, the authorities) are in conflict with those who are controlled by but have little ability to control the law (that is, the subjects). There is inherent conflict in this superior–subordinate relationship because both groups have their own sets of cultural norms (ideals and values) and social norms (actual group behaviors). Interaction between authorities and subjects eventually produces **norm resistance,** open conflict between the two groups that can take on a number of different forms. The probability of norm resistance is highest under the following conditions:

- Authorities and subjects are both strongly committed to their own cultural norms, which are in opposition to one another.
- Subjects receive social support from their peers; people with group support will be resistant to authority and/or change.
- Subjects lack sophistication; people who are sophisticated and can accurately assess the strengths and weaknesses of their opponents will be better able to avoid conflict with authorities.[28]

Research does show that there is more conflict between authorities and subjects when group sophistication, a key component of Turk's theory, is lacking.[29]

■ Exhibit 9.1 Propositions of the Social Reality of Crime

1. *Definition of crime:* Crime is a definition of human conduct that is created by authorized agents in a politically organized society.
2. *Formulation of criminal definition:* Criminal definitions describe behaviors that conflict with the interests of the segments of society that have the power to shape public policy.
3. *Application of criminal definitions:* Criminal definitions are applied by the segments of society that have the power to shape the enforcement and administration of criminal law.
4. *Development of behavior patterns in relation to criminal definitions:* Behavior patterns are structured in segmentally organized society in relation to criminal definitions, and within this context, persons engage in actions that have relative probabilities of being defined as criminal.
5. *Construction of criminal conceptions:* Conceptions of crime are constructed and diffused in the segments of society by various means of communication.
6. *The social reality of crime:* The social reality of crime is constructed by the formulation and application of criminal definitions, the development of behavior patterns to criminal definitions, and the construction of criminal conceptions.

SOURCE: Richard Quinney, *The Social Reality of Crime* (Boston: Little, Brown, 1970), pp. 15–23.

Research on Conflict Theory

Research efforts designed to test conflict theory attempt to show that conflict principles hold up under empirical scrutiny. One method of research is to compare the crime rates of members of powerless groups with those of members of the elite classes. Conflict researchers also examine the justice system operations to uncover bias and discrimination. To identify laws created with the intent of preserving the power of the elite classes at the expense of the poor, they attempt to chart the historical development of criminal law. Conflict theorists maintain that social inequality creates the need for people to commit some crimes, such as burglary and larceny, as a means of social and economic survival, whereas other crimes, such as assault, homicide, and drug use, are a means of expressing rage, frustration, and anger. Data show that crime rates vary according to indicators of poverty and need. For example, infant mortality rates have been associated with homicide rates, a finding that indicates that a society that cannot care for its young is also prone to social unrest and violence.[30] Crime rates seem strongly related to measures of social inequality, such as income level, deteriorated living conditions, and relative economic deprivation.[31]

Another area of conflict-oriented research involves examining criminal justice system operations. This research strives to answer the question of whether the criminal justice system operates as an instrument of class oppression or as a fair and even-handed social control agency. Some conflict researchers have found evidence of class bias. For example, some state jurisdictions with significant levels of economic disparity are also the most likely to have the largest number of people killed by police officers. Police may act more forcefully in areas where class conflict creates the perception that extreme forms of social control are needed to maintain order.[32] Criminal courts were also found to be more likely to dole out more severe punishments to members of powerless, disenfranchised groups and more lenient with affluent majority group members.[33] When criminals were convicted, both white and black offenders were found to receive stricter sentences if their personal characteristics (single, young, urban, male) showed them to be members of the "dangerous classes."[34] The unemployed, especially racial minorities, may be perceived as "social dynamite" who present a real threat to society and must be controlled and incapacitated.[35]

Conflict theorists also point to studies that show that the criminal justice system is quick to take action when the victim of crime is wealthy, white, and male; but it is disinterested when the victim is poor, black, and female. These studies illustrate how power positions affect justice.[36] It is not surprising then that analysis of national population trends and imprisonment rates shows that as the percentage of minority group members increases in a population, the imprisonment rate does likewise.[37] As minority populations increase, the majority may become less tolerant and/or feel more threatened.

One reason for such displays of discrimination may be the attitudes of decision makers. For example, justice professionals who express racist values (that is, who state that race-based differences exist) are also more punitive, believe courts should be stricter and that the death penalty is an effective deterrent, and are most likely to let race affect their judgments.[38] Critical thinkers would argue that there must be a thorough rethinking of the role and purpose of the criminal justice system, giving the powerless a greater voice to express their needs and concerns, if these inequities are to be addressed.[39]

Analysis of Conflict Theory

Conflict theorists attempt to identify the power relations in society and draw attention to their role in promoting criminal behavior. The aim is to describe how class differentials produce an ecology of human behavior that favors the wealthy and powerful over the poor and weak. To believe their view, we must reject the consensus view of crime (Chapter 1), which states that law represents the values of the majority, that legal codes are designed to create a just society, and that by breaking the law criminals are predators who violate the rights of others. To a conflict theorist, the criminal law is a weapon employed by the affluent to maintain their dominance in the class struggle. This view is not without its critics. Some criminologists consider the conflict view "naive," suggesting instead that crime is a matter of rational choice made by offenders motivated more by greed and selfishness than by poverty and hopelessness.[40]

There is little conclusive evidence that the criminal justice process, including police discretion, criminal court sentencing, and correctional policy, is racially or socially biased.[41] For example, socioeconomic status seems unrelated to the length of prison terms assigned by the courts.[42] Similarly, evidence of race bias in sentencing is inconclusive.[43] Evidence that the justice system is not class and race biased refutes conflict theory and supports consensus, traditional criminology.

CONNECTIONS

Race bias in the criminal justice system is both a highly controversial and important issue. Racial bias in police discretion is covered in Chapter 16, and inequality in sentencing is covered more fully in Chapter 17. Although the direct effect of race is often debated, there is clear evidence that factors associated with race affect criminal justice decision making. ■

Despite its critics, conflict theory has had an important niche in the criminological literature. However, more radical versions of the general conflict model have become predominant, and attention has now turned to these versions of social conflict theory.

■ Marxist Criminology

Marxist criminologists view crime as a function of the capitalist mode of production.[44] Because economic competitiveness is the essence of capitalism, it has a destabilizing effect on social institutions and social life.[45] In a capitalist society, those in political power control the legal definition of crime and the manner in which the criminal justice system enforces the law.[46] Shut out from the economic hierarchy, the poor are severely sanctioned when, out of desperation, they engage in "street crimes" such as rape, murder, theft, and mugging. In contrast, members of the middle class cheat on their taxes and engage in petty corporate crime (employee theft). These acts are rarely punished; when they are punished it typically results in a fine and community sentence.

The wealthy are immune from prosecution. They are typically involved in acts that should be described as crimes but are not, such as racism, sexism, and profiteering. When they violate the law, they typically commit business crimes, which are subject to regulatory laws that are rarely enforced and are lightly punished. Even when the wealthy are sent to prison for these white-collar offenses, they are punished much more leniently than working-class people who commit crimes of lesser magnitude. Laws regulating corporate crime are really window dressing designed to impress the working class with how fair the justice system is. In reality, the justice system is the equivalent of an army that defends the owners of property in their ongoing struggle against the workers.[47]

CONNECTIONS

The enforcement of laws against illegal business activities, such as price fixing, restraint of trade, environmental crimes, and false advertising, is discussed in Chapter 13. ■

The rich use the fear of crime as a tool to maintain their control over society: the poor are controlled through incarceration; the middle class are diverted from caring about the crimes of the powerful because they fear the crimes of the powerless.[48] Ironically, they may have more to lose from the economic crimes committed by the rich than by the street crimes of the poor. Stock market swindles and savings and loan scams cost the public billions of dollars but do not create the fear and outrage associated with a mugging or rape.

Development of a Radical Criminology

In 1968, a group of British sociologists formed the National Deviancy Conference (NDC). With about 300 members, this organization sponsored several national symposiums and dialogues. Members came from all walks of life, but at its core was a group of academics critical of the positivist criminology being taught in English and U.S. universities.

More specifically, they rejected the conservative stance of criminologists and their close financial relationship with government funding agencies. The NDC was not conceived as a Marxist-oriented group; rather, it investigated the concept of deviance from a labeling perspective. It called attention to ways in which social control might actually be a cause of deviance rather than a response to antisocial behavior. Many conference members became concerned about the political nature of social control. In time, a schism developed within the NDC, with one group clinging to the now-conservative interactionist/labeling perspective, while the second embraced Marxist thought.

In 1973, **radical theory** was given a powerful academic boost when British scholars Ian Taylor, Paul Walton, and Jock Young published *The New Criminology*.[49] This brilliant work was a thorough and well-constructed critique of existing concepts in criminology; it called for the development of new criminological methods of analysis and critique. *The New Criminology* became the standard resource for scholars critical of both the field of criminology and the existing legal process.

While these events were transpiring in Britain, a small group of scholars in the United States began to follow a new radical approach to criminology. The locus of the radical school was the criminology program at the University of California at Berkeley. The most noted Marxist scholars at that institution were Anthony Platt, Paul Takagi, Herman Schwendinger, and Julia Schwendinger. Marxist scholars at other U.S. academic institutions included Richard Quinney (originally a conflict theorist, later a peacemaker), William Chambliss, Steven Spitzer, and Barry Krisberg. The U.S. radicals were influenced by the widespread social ferment during the late 1960s and early 1970s. The war in Vietnam, prison struggles, and the civil rights and feminist movements produced a climate in which criticism of the ruling class seemed a natural by-product. Mainstream, positivist criminology was criticized as being overtly conservative, progovernment, and antihuman. Critical criminologists scoffed when their fellow scholars used statistical analysis of computerized data to describe criminal and delinquent behavior.

Barry Krisberg lamented the social inadequacies of earlier criminologists more than 20 years ago when he wrote this: "Many of our scientific heroes of the past, upon rereading, turned out to be racists or, more generally, apologists for social injustice." In response to the widespread protests on campuses and throughout society, many of the contemporary giants of social science emerged as defenders of the status quo and vocally dismissed the claims of the oppressed for social justice.[50]

To read a radical take on the criminal law and American society, go to:
   http://www.guerrillalaw.com/left.html
For an up-to-date list of Web links, go to
   http://info.wadsworth.com/siegel ■

Many of the new Marxist criminologists had enjoyed distinguished careers as positivist criminologists. Some well-known criminologists, such as William Chambliss and Richard Quinney, shifted their research interests from positivism to social conflict theory to a radical-Marxist approach to crime.

Marxists did not meet with widespread approval at major universities. Rumors that professors were being fired for their political beliefs were common during the 1970s, and the criminology school at Berkeley was eventually closed for what many believe were political reasons. Even today, conflict exists between critical thinkers and mainstream academics. Prestigious Harvard Law School and other law centers have been the scenes of conflict and charges of purges and tenure denials because some professors held critical views of law and society. Some isolated radicals are tolerated, but the majority have been heavily victimized by what has been referred to as "academic McCarthyism."[51]

In the following years, new branches of a radical criminology were developing in the United States and abroad. In the early 1980s, the **left realism** school was started by scholars affiliated with Middlesex Polytechnic and the University of Edinburgh in Great Britain. In the United States, scholars influenced in part by the pioneering work of Dennis Sullivan and Larry Tifft created the **peacemaking movement.**[52] At the same time, feminist scholars began to apply critical analysis to the relationship between gender, power, and criminality. These movements have coalesced into a rich and complex criminological tradition.

Fundamentals of Marxist Criminology

As a general rule, Marxist criminologists ignore formal theory construction with its heavy emphasis on empirical testing. They scoff at the objective, "value-free" stance of mainstream criminologists and instead argue that there should be a political, ideological basis for criminological scholarship.[53] Crime and criminal justice must be viewed in a historical, social, and economic context.

Radicals use the conflict definition of crime. Crime is a political concept designed to protect the power and position of the upper classes at the expense of the poor. Some, but not all, radicals would include in a list of "real" crimes such acts as violations of human rights due to racism, sexism, and imperialism and other violations of human dignity and physical needs and necessities. Part of the radical agenda, then, is to make the public aware that these behaviors "are crimes just as much as burglary and robbery."[54]

The nature of a society controls the direction of its criminality; criminals are not social misfits but rather a product of the society and its economic system.[55] This analysis tells us that criminals are not a group of outsiders who can be controlled by an increased law enforcement presence. Criminality, instead, is a function of society's so-cial and economic organization. To control crime and reduce criminality, we must end the social conditions that promote crime.

Economic structure and surplus value No single view or theory defines Marxist criminology today, but its general theme is the relationship between crime and the ownership and control of private property in a capitalist society.[56] That ownership and control is the principal basis of power in U.S. society.[57] Social conflict is fundamentally related to the historical and social distribution of productive private property. Destructive social conflicts inherent within the capitalist system cannot be resolved unless that system is destroyed or ended.

One important aspect of the capitalist economic system is the effect of "surplus value." As you may recall, Marx used this term to refer to the value resulting from production when the cost of labor is less than the cost of the goods it produces. The excess value, or profit, can either be reinvested or used to enrich the owners. To increase the rate of surplus value, workers can be made to work harder for less pay, be made more efficient, or be replaced by "labor-saving" machines or technology. Therefore, economic growth does not have the same benefits for all elements of the population, and in the long run, it may produce the same effect as a depression or recession.

Marginalization As the rate of surplus value increases, more people are displaced from productive relationships and the size of the "marginal" population swells. As corporations "downsize" to increase profits, high-paying labor and managerial jobs are lost to computer-driven machinery. Displaced workers are forced into service jobs at minimum wage. Many become temporary employees without benefits or a secure position.

For a discussion of surplus value, go to:
http://twincitysinc.org/~nup/ch16.htm
For an up-to-date list of Web links, go to
http://info.wadsworth.com/siegel ■

As more people are thrust outside the economic mainstream, a condition referred to as **marginalization,** a larger portion of the population is forced to live in areas conducive to crime, known as **structural locations.** Once people are marginalized, commitment to the system declines, producing another crimogenic force: a weakened bond to society.[58]

The government may be quick to respond during periods of economic decline because those in power assume that poor economic conditions breed crime and social disorder. When unemployment is increasing, public officials assume the worse and devote greater attention to the criminal justice system, perhaps funding the building of new prisons to prepare for the coming "crime wave."[59] Empir-

■ Social conflict is fundamentally related to the distribution of private property, a process that historically has been unfair, biased, and discriminatory. Here, protestors demonstrate against a meeting of the Fortune 500 in Austin, Texas. Protesters held signs denouncing corporate domination of the U.S. political system, the growing gap between rich and poor, and the militarization of the police.

ical research confirms that economic downturns are indeed linked to both crime rate increases and governmental activities such as passage of anticrime legislation.[60] For example, as the level of surplus value increases, so too does the level of police expenditures, most likely because of the perceived or real need for the state to control those on the economic margin.[61]

The effect of surplus value is not unique to the United States. Crime and violence have escalated in former socialist republics that have converted to free-market economies. Both China and the former Soviet Union have experienced an upsurge in gang activity as they embrace market economies.

Although some form of these themes can be found throughout all Marxist writing, there are actually two independent visions within the radical literature, referred to as instrumental Marxism and structural Marxism.

Instrumental Marxism

One group of Marxists is referred to as **instrumentalists.** They view the criminal law and criminal justice system solely as an instrument for controlling the poor, have-not members of society; the state is the "tool" of the capitalists.

According to the instrumental view, capitalist justice serves the powerful and rich and enables them to impose their morality and standards of behavior on the entire society. Under capitalism, those who wield economic power are able to extend their self-serving definition of illegal or criminal behavior to encompass those who might threaten the status quo or interfere with their quest for

ever-increasing profits.[62] For example, the concentration of monetary assets in the nation's largest industrial firms is translated into the political power needed to control the tax laws and limit firms' tax liabilities.[63] Some, such as Microsoft, have the economic clout to hire the top attorneys needed to defend themselves from governmental antitrust actions, making them almost immune to regulation.

The poor, according to this branch of Marxist theory, may or may not commit more crimes than the rich, but they certainly are arrested and punished more often. Under the capitalist system, the poor are driven to crime because a natural frustration exists in a society in which affluence is well publicized but unattainable. When class conflict becomes unbearable, frustration can spill out in riots, such as one that occurred in Los Angeles on April 29, 1992, which was described as a "class rebellion of the under-privileged against the privileged."[64]

Because of class conflict, a deep-rooted hostility is generated among members of the lower class toward a social order in which they are not allowed to shape or participate.[65] Instrumental Marxists consider it essential to *demystify* law and justice—that is, to unmask its true purpose. They charge that conventional criminology is devoted to identifying the social conditions that cause crime. Those criminological theories that focus on family structure, intelligence, peer relations, and school performance serve to keep the lower classes servile by showing why they are more criminal, less intelligent, and more prone to school failure and family problems than the middle class. Demystification involves identifying the destructive intent of capitalist inspired and funded criminology. Instrumental

Marxists' goal for criminology is to explicate the rule of law in capitalist society and show how it works to preserve ruling-class power. The essence of instrumental Marxist theory can be summarized in the following statements:

- U.S. society is based on an advanced capitalist economy.
- The state is organized to serve the interests of the dominant economic class—the capitalist ruling class.
- Criminal law is an instrument of the state and the ruling class to maintain and perpetuate the existing social and economic order.
- Crime control in capitalist society is accomplished through a variety of institutions and agencies established and administered by a governmental elite, representing ruling-class interests for the purpose of establishing domestic order.
- The contradictions of advanced capitalism require that the subordinate classes remain oppressed by whatever means necessary, especially through the coercion and violence of the legal system.
- Only with the collapse of capitalist society and the creation of a new society, based on socialist principles, will there be a solution to the crime problem.[66]

Concepts of instrumental Marxism The writings of a number of influential instrumental Marxist theorists have helped shape this field of inquiry. Two of the most influential are Herman Schwendinger and Julia Siegel Schwendinger. According to the Schwendingers, legal relations in the United States secure an economic infrastructure that centers around a capitalist mode of production. The legal system is designed to guard the position of the owners (bourgeoisie) at the expense of the workers (proletariat). Even common-law crimes, such as murder and rape, are implemented to protect capitalism.[67]

According to the Schwendingers, the basic laws of the land (such as constitutional laws) are based on the conditions that reproduce the class system as a whole. Laws are aimed at securing the domination of the capitalist system. Though the system may at times secure the interests of the working class—for example, when laws are created that protect collective bargaining—due to the inherent antagonisms built into the capitalist system, all laws generally contradict their stated purpose of producing justice. Legal relations maintain patterns of individualism and selfishness and, in so doing, perpetuate a class system characterized by anarchy, oppression, and crime.[68]

In another classic work, Stephen Spitzer examined how capitalist societies criminalize any behavior that threatens the power of the ownership classes or conflicts with its basic principles of consumption, exploitation, and socialization:

- Capitalist modes of appropriating the product of human labor (for example, when the poor turn to crime rather than remain wage slaves)

- The social conditions under which capitalist production takes place (for example, when some people refuse or are unable to perform wage labor)
- Patterns of distribution and consumption in capitalist society (for example, when people use drugs for escape and transcendence, rather than sociability and adjustment)
- The process of socialization for productive and nonproductive roles (for example, when youths drop out of school or deny the validity of family life)
- The ideology that supports the functioning of capitalist society (for example, when people become proponents of alternative forms of social organization)[69]

Integrative-constitutive theory Gregg Barak and Stuart Henry's **integrative-constitutive theory** is a recent effort to show how crime and its control cannot be separated from the structural and cultural contexts in which it is produced.[70] Using an instrumental Marxist approach, they define crime as the application of harm to others. In our postmodern society, unequal power relations, built on human differences, provide the conditions that define harm and therefore crime. These power relations often involve pain, conflict, and injury to others. People who are defined as committing criminal acts are at the same time being made unequal or "disrespected"; they are rendered powerless to maintain or express their humanity. In a sense then, the act of making people "criminals" is a crime. A more realistic or constitutive view of crime would (or should) include current business practices, governmental policies, and unequal social relations.

Many of the destructive relationships in family life, such as sexual harassment, emotional torment, physical beating, and child abuse, are criminal. The emotional torment inflicted on workers by managers who threaten their jobs is extremely harmful and therefore criminal. Government neglect of safety and health regulations is criminal. So is unaffordable housing, which renders so many people homeless. According to integrative-constitutive theory, crime must be defined and evaluated in its broadest sense: the amount of harm it inflicts on people.

According to Barak and Henry, there are actually two aspects of crime: crimes of repression and crimes of reduction. **Crimes of repression** occur when members of a group are prevented from achieving their fullest potential because of racism, sexism, or some other status bias. **Crimes of reduction** occur when the offended party experiences a loss of some quality relative to his or her present standing. Their loss can come about if they are victims of robbery or theft, but they also may be victimized if their dignity is stripped from them when they are taunted by racists.

To understand and prevent crime, criminologists must first develop a complete understanding of what crime truly is and the power relations that support its occurrence. This is not easy, for each element of harm may have a separate and unique history. Criminologists must focus on the social experiences of different groups (for example, African American females or lower-class white males) and how they interact with one another. Yet charting this interaction is hopelessly complex because each group is itself in a constant state of flux. For example, race-gender-class identities may reinforce criminality in some contexts while helping to neutralize it in others. It is also critical that criminologists understand that they cannot study one group at the expense of another. For example, gender bias influences females, but it also has an effect on males; racism affects majority group members as well as minorities. Crime and crime control cannot be understood independent of their cultural and definitional context.

The essence of instrumental Marxism   At its core, instrumental Marxism defines the state, the law, and the ruling class as a single entity. The law is shaped by the economic, social, and political interests of the ruling class and used by the ruling class to its own advantage.[71]

Some observers suggest that instrumental Marxist theory may be limited because it claims that the law and justice always operate in the interests of the ruling class; that members of the ruling class "conspire" to control society; and what benefits one member of the ruling class benefits them all. In reality, some laws benefit the lower classes, for example, and capitalists compete with one another rather than conspire.[72] Because of these deficiencies, some radicals have turned from instrumental theory and embraced structural Marxism.

Structural Marxism

Structural Marxists disagree with the view that the relationship between law and capitalism is unidimensional, always working for the rich and against the poor.[73] Law is not the exclusive domain of the rich, but it is used to maintain the long-term interests of the capitalist system and to control members of any class who pose a threat to its existence. If law and justice were purely instruments of the capitalist class, why would laws controlling corporate crimes, such as price-fixing, false advertising, and illegal restraint of trade, have been created and enforced? To a structuralist, the law is designed to keep the capitalist system operating efficiently, and anyone, capitalist or proletarian, who "rocks the boat" is targeted to be sanctioned. For example, antitrust legislation is designed to prevent any single capitalist from dominating the system and preventing others from "playing the game." If the capitalist system is to function, no single person can get too powerful at the expense of the economic system as a whole.

Another reason the law must moderate the behavior of capitalists is the need for legitimacy.[74] Capitalist states must gain the support of the majority to maintain a legal and financial system that provides control over labor markets, which is needed by businesspeople. This may take the form of sound monetary policies and protection of capitalist enterprise at home and abroad. To gain the support of the working classes in these endeavors, the ruling regime must create what appears to be a modicum of fairness in the justice system. Consequently, laws may be created and rules instituted that contradict the short-term needs of the capitalist class in order to ensure its long-term survival.

For more on Marxist criminology, read this article on InfoTrac College Edition: Ronnie Lippens. Critical criminologies and the reconstruction of Utopia. *Social Justice* Spring 1995 v22 n1 p32   ■

Research on Marxist Criminology

Marxist criminologists rarely use standard social science methodologies to test their views because many believe the traditional approach of measuring research subjects is antihuman and insensitive.[75] Marxists believe the research conducted by mainstream liberal/positivist criminologists is designed to unmask the weak and powerless members of society so they can be better dealt with by the legal system—a process called **correctionalism.** They are particularly offended by purely empirical studies, such as those that are designed to show that minority group members have lower IQs than the white majority or that the inner city is the site of the most serious crime whereas middle-class areas are relatively crime free.

Empirical research, however, is not considered totally incompatible with Marxist criminology, and there have been some important efforts to quantitatively test its fundamental assumptions.[76] For example, research has shown that the property crime rate reflects a change in the level of surplus value; the capitalist system's emphasis on excessive profits accounts for the need of the working class to commit property crime.[77] Nonetheless, Marxist research tends to be historical and analytical and not quantitative and empirical. Social trends are interpreted with regard to how capitalism has affected human interaction. Marxists investigate both macro-level issues, such as how the accumulation of wealth affects crime rates, and micro-level issues, such as the effect of criminal interactions on the lives of individuals living in a capitalist society. Of particular importance to Marxist critical thinkers is the analysis of the historical development of capitalist social control institutions, such as criminal law, police agencies, courts, and prison systems.

Crime, the individual, and the state   Marxists devote considerable attention to the study of the relationships between crime, victims, the criminal, and the state. Two common themes emerge: (1) crime and its control are a function of capitalism, and (2) the justice system is biased against the working class and favors upper-class interests. Marxian analysis of the criminal justice system is designed to identify the often-hidden processes that exert control over people's lives. It takes into account how conditions, processes, and structures evolved into what they are today. One issue that is considered is the process by which deviant behavior is defined as criminal or delinquent in U.S. society.[78] Another issue taken into account is the degree to which class affects the justice system's decision-making process.[79] It is not surprising to conflict theorists that police brutality complaints are highest in minority neighborhoods.[80] Also subject to analysis is how power relationships help undermine any benefit the lower class gets from sentencing reforms.[81] In general, Marxist research efforts have yielded evidence linking operations of the justice system to racial and class bias.[82]

In addition to conducting studies showing the relationship between crime and the state, some critical researchers have attempted to show how capitalism influences the distribution of punishment. For example, David Greenberg and Valerie West show that during the 20-year period from 1971 to 1991 the rate of imprisonment grew substantially in those states with (a) the highest revenues, (b) the highest unemployment rates, and (c) the largest African American populations.[83] They conclude that in wealthier states, where income is concentrated in the hands of a relatively few affluent people, those in power will be willing to spend enormous sums to keep the poor and minority group members under state control. This finding supports the suggestion that a rise in the prison population may be a function of the utility an expanding correctional system has for the capitalist system.

Robert Weis found that the expansion of the prison population is linked to the need for capitalists to acquire a captive and low paid labor force in order to compete with overseas laborers and domestic immigrant labor. Employing immigrants has its political downside because it displaces "American" workers and antagonizes their legal representatives. In contrast, using prison labor can be viewed as a humanitarian gesture. Weiss also observes that an ever-increasing prison population is politically attractive because it masks unemployment rates. Many inmates were chronically unemployed before their imprisonment; incarcerating the chronically unemployed allows politicians to claim they have lowered unemployment. When the millions of people who are on probation and parole and who must maintain jobs are added to the mix, the correctional system is now playing an ever-more important role in suppressing wages and maintaining the profitability of capitalism.[84]

This type of research does not set out to prove statistically that capitalism causes crime but rather to show that it creates an environment in which crime is inevitable. Marxist research is humanistic, situational, descriptive, and analytical rather than statistical, rigid, and methodological.

Historical analysis A second type of Marxist research focuses on the historical background of commonly held institutional beliefs and practices. One goal is to show how changes in the criminal law correspond to the development of a capitalist economy. The second goal is to investigate the development of modern police agencies.

To examine the changes in criminal law, historian Michael Rustigan analyzed historical records to show that law reform in nineteenth-century England was largely a response to pressure from the business community to increase punishments for property law violations to protect their rapidly increasing wealth.[85] Other research has focused on topics such as how the relationship between convict work and capitalism evolved during the nineteenth century. During this period, prisons became a profitable method of centralized state control over lower-class criminals whose labor was exploited by commercial concerns. These criminals were used as forced laborers in order to pay off wardens and correctional administrators.[86]

Marxists have also found that modern police agencies developed as an antilabor force that provided muscle for industrialists at the turn of the century.[87] Since police often play an active role in putting down labor disputes and controlling political dissidents' activities, their interrelationships with capitalist economics are of particular importance to Marxists.[88]

Critique of Marxist Criminology

Marxist criminology has met with a great deal of criticism from some members of the criminological mainstream who charge that its contribution has "been hot air, heat, but no real light."[89] In turn, radicals have accused mainstream criminologists of being culprits in developing state control over individual lives and "selling out" their ideals for the chance to receive government funding.

Mainstream criminologists have also attacked the substance of Marxist thought. For example, sociologist Jackson Toby argues that Marxist theory is a simple rehash of the old tradition of helping the underdog. He likens the ideas behind Marxist criminology to the ideas in such traditional literary works as *Robin Hood* and Victor Hugo's *Les Miserables*, in which the poor steal from the rich to survive.[90] In reality, Toby claims, most theft is for luxury, not survival. Moreover, he disputes the idea that the crimes committed by the rich are more reprehensible and less understandable than crimes committed by those who live in poverty. Toby acknowledges that criminality and immoral behavior occur at every social level, but he believes the relatively disadvantaged contribute disproportionately to crime and delinquency rates.[91]

Other critics, such as criminologist Carl Klockars, charge that Marxists unfairly neglect the efforts of the capitalist system to regulate itself, for example, by instituting antitrust regulations and creating social reforms aimed at helping the poor.[92] They question the logic behind giving poor people more rights as an inducement to control their behavior. They do not feel this is a workable solution to crime of the lower class. Klockars also feels that Marxists refuse to address the problems and conflicts that exist in socialist countries, such as the gulags and purges of the Soviet Union under Stalin. Similarly, they fail to explain why some highly capitalist countries, such as Japan, have extremely low crime rates. He feels that Marxists are too quick to assign blame for every human vice without adequate explanation or regard for other social and environmental factors.[93] In so doing, they ignore objective reality and refuse to acknowledge that members of the lower classes tend to victimize one another. They ignore the plight of the lower classes who must live in crime-ridden neighborhoods, while they condemn the capitalist system from the security of the "ivory tower."

Marxist scholars respond to their critics by charging that they rely on "traditional" variables, such as "class" and "poverty," in their analysis of radical thought. Although important, these variables do not reflect the key issues in the structural and economic process. In fact, like crime, they too may be the outcome of the capitalist system.[94] They also respond that other capitalist nations may have lower crime rates but this does not mean that they are crime free. As an illustration, they point out that even Japan has significant problems with teen prostitution and organized crime.

| CONNECTIONS |

In Chapter 1, the Race, Culture, Gender, and Criminology feature on international crime trends notes the rapid increase in crime in other industrialized nations. ■

■ Emerging Forms of Conflict Theory

Though radical criminologists dispute criticisms, they have also responded by creating new theoretical models that incorporate Marxist ideas in an innovative manner. In the following sections, some recent forms of radical theory are discussed in some detail.

Left Realism

Some radical scholars are now addressing the need for left-wing liberals to respond to the increasing power of right-wing conservatives. They are troubled by the emergence of a strict "law and order" philosophy, which has as its centerpiece a policy of waiving juveniles to adult court where they may be punished severely. At the same time, they find the focus of most left-wing scholarship—the abuse of power by the ruling elite—too narrow. It is wrong, they argue, to ignore the problem of inner-city gang crime and violence, which all too often targets indigent people.[95] Those who share these concerns are referred to as left realists.[96]

Left realism is most often connected to the writings of British scholars John Lea and Jock Young. In their well-respected 1984 work, *What Is to Be Done about Law and Order?*, they reject the utopian views of "idealistic" Marxists who portray street criminals as revolutionaries.[97] They take a more "realistic" approach, saying that street criminals prey on the poor and disenfranchised, thus making them doubly abused, first by the capitalist system and then by members of their own class.

Lea and Young's view of crime causation borrows from conventional sociological theory and closely resembles the relative deprivation approach, which posits that experiencing poverty in the midst of plenty creates discontent; discontent without legitimate opportunity breeds crime. As they put it, "The equation is simple: relative deprivation equals discontent; discontent plus lack of political solution equals crime."[98]

Left realists argue that crime victims in all classes need and deserve protection; crime control reflects community needs. They do not view police and the courts as inherently evil tools of capitalism whose tough tactics alienate the lower classes. In fact, they recognize that these institutions would offer life-saving public services if needed. The left realists wish for police, however, is that their use of force be reduced and their sensitivity to the public be increased.[99]

Preemptive deterrence is an approach in which community organization efforts eliminate or reduce crime before it becomes necessary to employ police forces. They reason that if the number of marginalized youth (who feel they are not part of society and have nothing to lose by committing crime) could be reduced, then delinquency rates would decline.[100]

To left-realists Martin Schwartz and Walter DeKeseredy, street crime is "real"; the fear of violence among the lower classes has allowed the right wing to seize "law and order" as a political issue.[101] According to Schwartz and DeKeseredy, gangs are not made up of "Robin Hoods," or revolutionaries who steal from the rich. Most gang kids prey on members of their own race and class and are happy to keep the proceeds for themselves. According to Schwartz and DeKeseredy, gang kids may be the "ultimate capitalists," hustling their way to obtain the coveted symbols of success.[102]

While implementing a socialist economy might help eliminate the crime problem, left realists recognize that something must be done in the meantime to control crime under the existing capitalist system. To create crime control policy, left realists welcome not only radical ideas but build on the work of strain theorists, social ecologists, and other "mainstream" views. Community-based efforts seem to hold the most promise as crime-control techniques.

Left realism has been critiqued by radical thinkers as legitimizing the existing power structure: by supporting the existing definitions of law and justice, it suggests that the "deviant" and not the capitalist system is the root cause of society's problems. They question whether the left realists are advocating the very institutions that "currently imprison us and our patterns of thought and action."[103] In rebuttal, a left realist would charge that it is unrealistic to speak of a socialist state lacking a police force or system of laws and justice. They believe that the criminal code does, in fact, represent public opinion.

Radical Feminist Theory

Like so many theories in criminology, most of the efforts of radical theorists have been devoted to explaining male criminality.[104] To remedy this theoretical lapse, a number of feminist writers have attempted to explain the cause of crime, gender differences in the crime rate, and the exploitation of female victims from a radical feminist perspective. Scholars in this area usually can be described as holding one of two related philosophical orientations: Marxist feminism or radical feminism.

Marxist feminism   The first group of writers can be described as Marxist feminists, who view gender inequality as stemming from the unequal power of men and women in a capitalist society. They view gender inequality as a function of female exploitation by fathers and husbands. They suggest that women are considered a "commodity" worth possessing, like land or money.[105] The origin of gender differences can be traced to the development of private property and male domination over the laws of inheritance, which led to their control over property and power.[106]

A patriarchal system developed in which men's work was valued and women's work was devalued. As capitalism emerged as a prevailing concept, the division of labor by gender made women responsible for the unwaged maintenance and reproduction of the current and future labor force, which was called derisively "domestic work." Though this nonwaged work done by women is crucial and profitable for capitalists, who reap these free benefits, such labor is exploitative and oppressive for women.[107] Even when women gained the right to work, they were exploited as low wage, cheap labor. The dual exploitation of women within the household and in the labor market meant that women would produce far greater surplus value for capitalists than did men.

Patriarchy, or male supremacy, has been and continues to be supported by capitalists. This serves to sustain female oppression at home and in the workplace.[108] Though the number of traditional patriarchal families is in steep decline, in those that still exist a wife's economic dependence ties men more securely to wage-earning jobs, further serving the interests of capitalists by undermining potential rebellion against the system.

Patriarchy and crime   Marxist feminists link criminal behavior patterns to the gender conflict created by the economic and social struggles common in postindustrial societies. James Messerschmidt has made important contributions to understanding the root cause of gender conflict. In *Capitalism, Patriarchy, and Crime*, Messerschmidt argues that capitalist society is marked by both patriarchy and class conflict. Capitalists control the labor of workers, and

■ Marxist feminists view gender inequality as a function of female exploitation by men. Women have become a "commodity" worth possessing, like land or money. The origin of gender differences can be traced to the development of private property and male domination over the laws of inheritance, which led to their control over property and power. Are these teen prostitutes—shown here waiting to be booked at the Maricopa, Arizona, jail—a by-product of this view of women as commodities, which was engendered by the capitalist system?

© A. Ramey/Photo Edit

men control women both economically and biologically.[109] This "double marginality" explains why females in a capitalist society commit fewer crimes than males: they are isolated in the family and have fewer opportunities to engage in **elite deviance** (white-collar and economic crimes). They are also denied access to male-dominated street crimes. For example, powerful males will commit white-collar crimes, as will powerful females. However, the female crime rate is restricted because of the patriarchal nature of the capitalist system.[110] Since capitalism renders women powerless, they are forced to commit less serious, nonviolent, self-destructive crimes, such as abusing drugs.

Powerlessness also increases the likelihood that women will become the target of violent acts.[111] When lower-class males are shut out of the economic opportunity structure, they try to build their self-image through acts of machismo; such acts may involve violence or abuse of women. This type of reaction accounts for a significant percentage of female victims who are attacked by a spouse or intimate partner.

In *Masculinities and Crime,* Messerschmidt expands on these themes.[112] He suggests that in every culture males try to emulate what are considered "ideal" masculine behaviors. In Western culture, this means being authoritative, in-charge, combative, and controlling. Failure to adopt these roles leaves men feeling effeminate and unmanly. Their struggle to dominate women to prove their manliness is called **doing gender.**

Crime is a vehicle for men to "do gender" because it separates them from the weak and allows them to demonstrate physical bravery. Violence directed toward women is an especially economical way to demonstrate manhood. Would a weak and effeminate male ever attack a woman?

Radical feminism   Radical feminists view the cause of female crime as originating with the onset of male supremacy (patriarchy), the subsequent subordination of women, male aggression, and the efforts of men to control females sexually.[113] The Race, Culture, Gender, and Criminology feature traces the history of patriarchy.

Radical feminists focus on the social forces that shape women's lives and experiences to explain female criminality.[114] For example, they attempt to show how the sexual victimization of girls is a function of male socialization because so many young males learn to be aggressive and to exploit women. Males seek out same-sex peer groups for social support; these groups serve to encourage members to exploit and sexually abuse women. On college campuses, peers encourage sexual violence against women who are considered "teasers," "bar pickups," or "loose women." These derogatory labels allow the males to justify their actions; a code of secrecy then protects the aggressors from retribution.[115] This sexual and physical exploitation triggers a reaction among young girls. They may run away or abuse substances, which is labeled deviant or delinquent behavior.[116] In a sense, the female criminal is a victim herself.

Analyses of national surveys support the radical perspective by showing that about 90 percent of adolescent girls are sexually harassed in school, including 33 percent who report having been pressured to "do something sexual" and 10 percent who report experiencing sexual violence.[117] Despite the fact that so many young girls are sexual victims, their cries for help are often ignored or demeaned by school officials. When school girls complain about harassment, teachers and school officials sometimes respond by asking the young victim, "Did you like it?" or by saying, "They [the boys] must be doing it for a reason." Because agents of social control often choose to ignore reports of abuse and harassment, young girls may feel trapped and desperate.

Research shows that a significant number of girls sent to hospital emergency rooms to be treated for sexual abuse later reported engaging in physical fighting as a teen or as an adult. Many of these abused girls later formed a romantic attachment with an abusive partner. Clearly, many girls involved in delinquency, crime, and violence have themselves been the victims of violence in their youth and later as adults.[118]

Even within the radical feminist movement, there are important differences. For example, some feminist scholars charge that the movement focuses on the problems and viewpoints of white, middle-class, heterosexual women without taking into account the special interests of lesbians and women of color.[119]

How the justice system penalizes women   Radical feminists have indicted the justice system and its patriarchal hierarchy as contributing to the onset of female delinquency. From its inception, the juvenile justice system has viewed the great majority of female delinquents as sexually precocious girls who have to be brought under control. Writing on the "girl problem," Ruth Alexander has described how working-class young women desiring autonomy and freedom in the 1920s were considered delinquents and placed in reformatories. Lacking the ability to protect themselves from the authorities, these young girls were considered outlaws in a male-dominated society because they flouted the very narrow rules of appropriate behavior applied to females in this Victorian society. Girls who rebelled against parental authority or who engaged in sexual behavior deemed inappropriate were incarcerated to protect them from a career in prostitution.[120]

In a similar vein, a study of the early Los Angeles Juvenile Court by Mary Odem and Steven Schlossman found that in 1920 so-called delinquency experts identified young female "sex delinquents" as a major social problem that required a forceful public response. Civic leaders concerned about immorality mounted a eugenics and social hygiene campaign that identified the "sex delinquent" as a moral and sexual threat to American society and advocated a policy of eugenics or sterilization to prevent these inferior individuals from having children. Los Angeles responded by

Capitalism and Patriarchy

Feminist scholar Nancy Jurik has described the historical association between patriarchy and capitalism and how both worked to subjugate women.

Patriarchy first emerged in precapitalist agricultural societies in which a male head presided over his family, controlling work and the marriages of its members. In these early societies, the household was the center of production. With the development of industrialization and the emergence of labor, capitalism interacted with patriarchy to change family life. With the advent of mass production, the factory and not the home became the center of production.

At the onset of industrialization, all family members, including children, went out to work. Gradually, however, social reformers and even some capitalists arranged for the removal of women and children from the harsh conditions of factory life. Male-controlled unions fought for job protection by forcing legislation, which prohibited women from competing for factory jobs. Capitalists eventually agreed to pay a "family wage" that would be large enough to support wives and children. Capitalism then rendered men the sole "breadwinners" while at the same time satisfying the owners' need for a stable and healthy workforce. Despite the ideology that all men should earn enough to keep their wives at home, men of color, nonunion whites, and immigrants rarely earned a family wage.

Women began to be exploited because they provided free reproductive labor in their homes. Their labor, though unappreciated, allowed men to work. Women produced and cared for the next generation of laborers (their children). Women's reproductive labor limited their ability to engage in paid work or to participate in the political process. They were denied control over their sexuality and reproduction.

Men's domination was both a function of their control of social institutions and their constant threat of physical violence. Lack of opportunity relegated women to seek men's protection in monogamous nuclear families. The law even denied a woman's right to control her own sexuality by limiting access to birth control and abortions.

For those women who did hold jobs outside the home, their role in the workplace defined the way they were viewed. In the event a woman was forced to seek work, she was reduced to "help" and "support" work, which was viewed as less skilled than the work men did and was therefore lower paid. Keeping women's wages low also helped capitalists dominate male workers by threatening to replace them with lower-paid women. This fear allowed them to deny raises and to limit benefits. This further alienated and enraged men, convincing them of the urgency of preventing women from joining unions and from gaining employment in traditional male occupations.

Patriarchy may have preceded capitalism, but beginning with the Industrial Age both capitalism and patriarchy have been intertwined in an effort to sustain the subordination of women.

Critical Thinking Questions

1. How would you respond to someone who claims that the social roles of men and women have converged and, if anything, women actually have more power today?
2. Can you think of institutions and practices that show gender discrimination to be a continuing and contemporary problem?

InfoTrac College Edition Research

For more on the concept of patriarchy and how it influences women, see:

Heidi Gottfried. Beyond patriarchy? Theorising gender and class. *Sociology* August 1998 v32 n3 p451

Stanley Rothman and Amy E. Black. Who rules now? American elites in the 1990s. *Society* Sept–Oct 1998 v35 n6 p17

SOURCE: Nancy Jurik, "Socialist Feminism, Criminology and Criminal Justice," in *Social Justice/Criminal Justice*, ed. Bruce Arrigo (Belmont, Calif.: West/Wadsworth, 1999), pp. 31–51.

---

hiring the first female police officers in the nation to deal with girls under arrest, and the first female judges to hear girls' cases in juvenile court; it also established a female detention center and a girls' reformatory.[121]

The judicial victimization of female delinquents has continued. A well-known feminist writer, Meda Chesney-Lind, has written extensively on the victimization of female delinquents by agents of the juvenile justice system in Hawaii and other locales.[122] She found:

• Police in Honolulu, Hawaii, were likely to arrest female adolescents for sexual activity and to ignore the same behavior among male delinquents.

• Some 74 percent of the females in her sample were charged with sexual activity or incorrigibility, but only 27 percent of the boys faced the same charges.

• The court ordered physical examinations in more than 70 percent of the female cases, but only about 15 percent of the males were forced to undergo this embarrassing procedure.

• Girls were more likely to be sent to a detention facility before trial, and the length of their detention averaged three times that of the boys.

• A higher percentage of females than males were institutionalized for similar delinquent acts.

Because female adolescents have a much narrower range of acceptable behavior than male adolescents, Chesney-Lind suggests that any sign of misbehavior in girls is seen as a substantial challenge to authority and to the viability of the double standard of sexual inequality. Female delinquency is viewed as relatively more serious than male delinquency and, therefore, is more likely to be severely sanctioned.

Power-Control Theory

John Hagan and his associates have created a radical feminist model that uses gender differences to explain the onset of criminality. The most significant statements of these views are contained in a series of scholarly articles and expanded in Hagan's 1989 book, *Structural Criminology*.[123] Hagan's view is that crime and delinquency rates are a function of two factors: (1) class position (power) and (2) family functions (control).[124] The link between these two variables is that within the family parents reproduce the power relationships they hold in the workplace. Parents' work experiences and class position influence the criminality of children.

A position of dominance at work is equated with control in the household. In families that are paternalistic, fathers assume the traditional role of breadwinner, and mothers tend to have menial jobs or remain at home to supervise domestic matters. Within the paternalistic home, mothers are expected to control the behavior of their daughters while granting greater freedom to sons. In such a home, the parent–daughter relationship can be viewed as a preparation for the "cult of domesticity," which makes girls' involvement in delinquency unlikely, whereas boys are freer to deviate because they are not subject to maternal control. Consequently, male siblings exhibit a higher degree of delinquent behavior than their sisters.

In egalitarian families—those in which husband and wife share similar positions of power at home and in the workplace—daughters gain a kind of freedom that reflects reduced parental control. These families produce daughters whose law-violating behavior mirrors their brothers' behavior. Ironically, these kinds of relationships also occur in female-headed households with absent fathers. Similarly, Hagan and his associates found that when both fathers and mothers hold equally valued managerial positions, the similarity between the rates of their daughters' and sons' delinquency is greatest. By implication, middle-class girls are the most likely to violate the law because they are less closely controlled than their lower-class counterparts. In homes in which both parents hold positions of power, girls are more likely to have the same expectations of career success as their brothers. Consequently, siblings of both sexes will be socialized to take risks and engage in other behavior related to delinquency. Power-control theory implies that girls in higher income families (where both mom and dad work) will have higher overall crime rates than girls in families where the father is the sole provider. The fact that girls are controlled more strictly in paternalistic families explains why female crime rates are lower in the general population.

Testing power-control theory Power-control theory has received a great deal of attention in the criminological community because it encourages a new approach to the study of criminality, one that includes gender differences, class position, and the structure of the family. Although its basic premises have not yet been thoroughly tested, there is evidence that parental power and control in the workplace increases male antisocial behavior and that in more egalitarian families female crime rates are higher. For example, Brenda Sims Blackwell's research found support for a key element of power-control theory: females in paternalistic households have been socialized to fear legal sanctions more so than their brothers.[125]

Not all research is as supportive.[126] Some critics have questioned its core assumption that power and control variables can explain crime.[127] More specifically, critics fail to replicate the finding that upper-class kids are more likely to deviate than their lower-class peers or that class and power interact to produce delinquency.[128] Some researchers have found few gender-based supervision and behavior differences in worker-, manager-, or owner-dominated households.[129] It is possible that the concept of class employed by Hagan may have to be reconsidered. Moreover, power-control theory must now consider the multitude of power and control relationships that are emerging in postmodern society: for example, blended families, and families where mothers hold managerial positions and fathers are blue-collar workers, and so forth.[130]

Power-control theory also raises an interesting dilemma when it maintains that the daughters of successful and powerful mothers are more at risk for delinquency than the daughters of stay-at-home moms, a conclusion that may be viewed as an implicit critique of feminist goals. However, as sociologist Christopher Uggen points out, there may be a bright side to this aspect of the theory: girls of powerful mothers may be encouraged to take prosocial risks such as athletic competition and break into traditional male-dominated occupations such as policing and the military.

Postmodern Theory

A number of radical thinkers, referred to as **postmodernists,** have embraced **semiotics** and/or **deconstructionist analysis** as a method of understanding all human relations, including criminal behavior. These perspectives focus on the critical analysis of communication and language in legal codes.[131] Rules and regulations are analyzed to determine whether they contain language and content that forces racism or sexism to become institutionalized.

To read more about deconstructionist theory and its founders, go to:

http://prelectur.stanford.edu/lecturers/derrida/deconstruction.html

For an up-to-date list of Web links, go to

http://info.wadsworth.com/siegel ■

Postmodernists rely on semiotics to conduct their research efforts. This means using language as signs or symbols beyond their literal meaning. For example, the term "special needs children" is designed to describe their learning needs, but it may also characterize these children as either mentally challenged, dangerous, or uncontrollable. There are many signs or language groupings in operation today. For example, sports relies very heavily on the use of signs, and to become a sports "expert" means becoming familiar with terminology such as "blitzing the quarterback" and a "hat trick." These terms convey meanings far greater than the words themselves and provide images to sports fans familiar with the signs that would be lost on others.

Postmodernists believe language is value laden and can promote the same sort of inequities that are present in the rest of the social structure. The concepts of "truth," "identity," "justice," and "power" all derive their meaning from the language dictated by those in power.[132] The law, legal skill, and justice are "commodities" that can be bought and sold like any other service or product.[133] The O. J. Simpson case is vivid proof that the affluent can purchase a different brand of justice than the indigent.[134]

Postmodernists assert that there are different languages and ways of knowing. Those in power are able to use their own language to define crime and law while excluding or dismissing those who are in opposition to their control (prisoners or the poor). By dismissing these "oppositional" languages, certain versions of how to think, feel, or act are devalued and excluded. This exclusion is the source of conflict in society.[135]

Peacemaking Criminology

One of the newer movements in radical theory is peacemaking criminology. To members of the peacemaking movement, the main purpose of criminology is to promote a peaceful and just society. Rather than standing on empirical analysis of data sets, peacemaking draws its inspiration from religious and philosophical teachings, ranging from Quakerism to Zen.

Peacemakers view the efforts of the state to punish and control as crime encouraging rather than crime discouraging. These views were first articulated in a series of books with an anarchist theme written by criminologists Larry Tifft and Dennis Sullivan in 1980.[136] In the foreword to Sullivan's book, *The Mask of Love,* Larry Tifft writes, "The violent punishing acts of the state and its controlling professions are of the same genre as the violent acts of individuals. In each instance these acts reflect an attempt to monopolize human interaction."[137]

Sullivan recognizes the futility of correcting and punishing criminals in the context of our conflict-ridden society. He comments, "The reality we must grasp is that we live in a culture of severed relationships, where every available institution provides a form of banishment but no

■ Peacemakers believe in restoration and not revenge, even for the most heinous crimes. They are firmly against the death penalty. Here, Scott Langley, Chris Banner, and Virginia Hodges sing together for death row inmates at the U.S. Federal Penitentiary in Terre Haute, Indiana, November 14, 2000. The three participated in an 80-mile march from Indianapolis to Terre Haute in protest of the death penalty.

AP/Wide World Photos

place or means for people to become connected, to be responsible to and for each other."[138] Sullivan suggests that mutual aid rather than coercive punishment is the key to a harmonious society. In their newest volume, *Restorative Justice* (2001), Sullivan and Tifft reaffirm their belief that society must seek humanitarian forms of justice without resorting to brutal punishments:

> By allowing feelings of vengeance or retribution to narrow our focus on the harmful event and the person responsible for it—as others might focus solely on a sin committed and the "sinner"—we tell ourselves we are taking steps to free ourselves from the effects of the harm or the sin in question. But, in fact, we are putting ourselves in a servile position with respect to life, human growth, and the further enjoyment of relationships with others.[139]

Today, advocates of the peacemaking movement, such as Harold Pepinsky and Richard Quinney (who has shifted his theoretical orientation from conflict theory, to Marxist theory, and now to peacemaking), try to find humanist solutions to crime and other social problems.[140] Rather than punishment and prison, they advocate such policies as mediation and conflict resolution.

■ Social Conflict Theory and Public Policy

At the core of all the varying branches of social conflict theory is the fact that conflict causes crime. If conflict and competition in society could somehow be reduced, it is possible that crime rates would fall. Some critical theorists believe this goal can only be accomplished by thoroughly reordering society so that capitalism is destroyed and a socialist state is created. Others call for a more "practical" application of conflict principles. Nowhere has this been more successful than in applying peacemaking principles in the criminal justice system.

There has been an ongoing effort to reduce the conflict created by the criminal justice system when it hands out harsh punishments to offenders, many of whom are powerless social outcasts. Rather than cast them aside, peacemakers have found a way to bring them back to the community. This peacemaking movement has adopted nonviolent methods and applied them to what is known as **restorative justice.** Springing both from academia and justice system personnel, the restorative approach relies on nonpunitive strategies for crime prevention and control.[141] The next sections discuss the foundation and principles of restorative justice.

Reintegrative Shaming

One of the key foundations of the restoration movement is contained in John Braithwaite's influential book *Crime, Shame and Reintegration.*[142] Braithwaite notes that countries such as Japan, in which conviction for crimes brings an inordinate amount of shame, have extremely low crime rates. In Japan, criminal prosecution proceeds only when the normal process of public apology, compensation, and the victim's forgiveness breaks down.

Shame is a powerful tool of informal social control. Citizens in cultures in which crime is not shameful, such as the United States, do not internalize an abhorrence for crime. When they are punished, they view themselves as mere victims of the justice system. Their punishment comes at the hands of neutral strangers (police and judges) who are being paid to act. In contrast, shaming relies on the victim's participation.[143]

Braithwaite divides the concept of shame into two distinct types. The most common form of shaming typically involves stigmatization. This form of shaming involves an ongoing process of degradation in which the offender is branded as an evil person and cast out of society. Shaming can occur at a school disciplinary hearing or a criminal court trial. Bestowing stigma and degradation may have a general deterrent effect: it makes people afraid of social rejection and public humiliation. As a specific deterrent, stigma is doomed to failure: people who suffer humiliation at the hands of the justice system "reject their rejectors" by joining a deviant subculture of like-minded people who collectively resist social control. Despite these dangers, there has been an ongoing effort to brand offenders and make their "shame" both public and permanent. For example, most states have passed sex offender registry and notification laws, which make public the names of those convicted of sex offenses and warn neighbors of their presence in the community.[144]

Braithwaite argues that crime control can be better achieved through a policy of **reintegrative shaming.** Here disapproval is extended to the offenders' evil deeds, while at the same time they are cast as respected people who can be reaccepted by society. A critical element of reintegrative shaming occurs when offenders begin to understand and recognize their wrongdoing and shame themselves. To be reintegrative, shaming must be brief and controlled and then followed by ceremonies of forgiveness, apology, and repentance.

To prevent crime, Braithwaite charges, society must encourage reintegrative shaming. For example, the women's movement can reduce domestic violence by mounting a crusade to shame spouse abusers.[145] Similarly, parents who use reintegrative shaming techniques in their child-rearing practices may improve parent–child relationships and ultimately reduce the delinquent involvement of their children.[146]

Because informal social controls may have a greater impact than legal or formal ones, it may not be surprising that the fear of personal shame can have a general deterrent effect greater than the fear of legal sanctions. It may also be applied to produce specific deterrence. One Australian program brings offenders together with victims so that the offenders can experience shame. Their close family members and peers are also present to help the offender reintegrate.[147] Efforts like these can humanize a system of justice that today relies on repression, rather than forgiveness, as the basis of specific deterrence.

CONNECTIONS

Reintegrative shaming has been advocated by criminologists who consider harsh punishment counterproductive. If shame can convince people to refrain from crime, then it follows that people are using a logical process in choosing criminal over conventional solutions to their problems. This idea is similar to that of choice theory discussed in Chapter 5. ■

Concepts of Restoration

Restoration involves turning the justice system into a "healing" process rather than being a distributor of retribution and revenge. Most people involved in offender–victim relationships actually know one another or were related in some way before the criminal incident took place. According to restorative justice advocates, instead of treating one of the involved parties as a victim deserving of sympathy and the other as a criminal deserving of punishment, it is more productive to address the issues that produced conflict between these people. Rather than take sides and choose whom to isolate and punish, society should try to reconcile the parties involved in conflict.[148] The effectiveness of justice ultimately depends on the stake a person has in the community (or a particular social group). If a person does not value membership in the group, that person will be unlikely to accept responsibility, show remorse, or repair the injuries caused by his or her actions.

The Center for Restorative Justice and Peacemaking provides links and information on the ideals of restoration and programs based on its principles. Go to their Web site, at:

http://ssw.che.umn.edu/rjp/default.html

For an up-to-date list of Web links, go to

http://info.wadsworth.com/siegel ■

Restorative versus Traditional Justice

Restorative justice can be contrasted with a legalistic view of criminal punishments.[149] According to the legalistic view of justice, society is defined as an aggregation of people who share common values over which the state has jurisdiction. This can be contrasted with the restorative justice view that society is made up of many competing interests and values, making it difficult to derive a universal code that applies to all people. It is only in smaller, less formal and more cohesive social groups, such as families, congregations, and residential communities, that such agreements can be found. Therefore, the potential for restoring social relations damaged by crime is to be found not in the state but in social groups. Without the capacity to restore damaged social relations, society's response to crime has been and can only be almost exclusively punitive, requiring the traditional justice system to be harsh and adversarial. As a result of its preoccupation with punishment, the adversarial system encourages the accused to deny, justify, or excuse their actions, thereby precluding the acceptance of responsibility. Restorative justice is guided by three essential principles:

- Community ownership of conflict (including crime)
- Material and symbolic reparation for victims and the community
- Social reintegration of the offender

The process begins by redefining crime in terms of a conflict among the offender, the victim, and affected constituencies (families, schools, workplaces, and so forth). Therefore, it is vitally important that the resolution take place within the context in which the conflict originally occurred rather than be transferred to a specialized institution that has no social connection to the community or group from which the conflict originated. By maintaining "ownership" or jurisdiction over the conflict, the community is able to express its shared outrage about the offense. Shared community outrage is directly communicated to the offender. The victim is also given a chance to voice his or her story, and the offender can directly communicate his or her need for social reintegration and treatment. In a sense, then, many different parties have a stake in the justice process; these are the primary and secondary "stakeholders" in crime and justice (Exhibit 9.2).

The restoration process is dependent on a communicative conception of law in which law is conceived of as a discussion that is cohesive rather than punitive and disruptive. Communicative law encourages people to discuss the main problems in their social life (which are typically manifested in terms of interpersonal conflict). By regularly engaging in such discourse, members of a group keep alive the sense that law unites them rather than separates them. The restoration process involves an informal communicative exchange among the victim, offender, and community. Although processes differ in structure and style, their discourse generally includes recognition of the injury to personal and social relations, a determination and acceptance of responsibility (ideally accompanied by a statement of remorse), a commitment to both material and symbolic reparation (for example, an apology), and a determination of community support and assistance for both victim and offender. The intended result of the process is to repair injuries suffered by the victim and the community while assuring reintegration of the offender.

Although there is widespread agreement among proponents of restorative justice as to what constitutes restoration, a clear division exists among those who believe justice can be achieved within the context of the existing social structure and those who contend that significant social structural change must occur for the true potential of

Exhibit 9.2 **Who Are the Stakeholders in Crime and Justice?**

Offenders

Primary offenders	Offenders who accept primary responsibility for the offense.
Secondary offenders	Offenders who accept some responsibility for contributing to the offense.

Victims

Direct victims	Those against whom the crime was committed and who suffered physical injury, monetary loss, and/or emotional suffering as a consequence of the offense.
Indirect victims	Those who suffered indirect financial loss because of their relationship to the victim or offender.

Microcommunities

Secondary victims	Those who suffer because they have a personal relationship of responsibility with a victim or offender, including family members of offenders and victims, especially their parents and/or spouses.
Communities of support	Those who have an ongoing relationship of concern for a victim or offender and are only indirectly emotionally connected to the specific offense.

Macrocommunities

Locality/neighborhood/ township	Local residents who are not personally connected to victims or offenders, and the local government that represents them. They may experience a sense of vicarious victimization, but their injury is abstract or unrelated to the specific offense in question.
Society/government	The totality of society and the agents of government responsible for justice policy, including state and federal authorities.

SOURCE: Paul McCold, *Toward a Mid-Range Theory of Restorative Criminal Justice: A Reply to the Maximalist Model* (Bethlehem, Penn.: International Institute for Restorative Practices, 2001).

justice to be realized. The former argue that the social qualities of the group can be re-created within such processes as family group conferencing, victim/offender reconciliation, and sentencing circles. The latter group suggests that such social qualities cannot be effectively re-created; rather, they must exist prior to the process.

Restoration Programs

Restorative programs typically involve diverting the formal court process. These programs encourage meeting and reconciling the conflicts between offenders and victims via victim advocacy, mediation programs, and sentencing circles. Crime victims and their families are brought together with offenders and their families in an effort to formulate a sanction that addresses the needs of each party.

Negotiation, mediation, consensus-building, and peacemaking have been part of the dispute resolution process in European and Asian communities for centuries.[150] Native American and Native Canadian people have long used this type of community participation in the adjudication process (for example, sentencing circles, sentencing panels, elders panels) that restorative justice advocates are now embracing.[151] In some Native American communities, people accused of breaking the law meet with community members, victims, if any, village elders, and agents of the justice system in a sentencing circle. Each member of the circle expresses his or her feelings about the act that was committed and raises questions or concerns. The accused can

express regret about his or her actions and a desire to change the harmful behavior. People may suggest ways the offender can make things up to the community and those he or she harmed. A treatment program, such as Alcoholics Anonymous can be suggested, if appropriate. The purpose of this process is to reduce the conflict and harm and restore rather then punish.[152] The principles of restorative justice are outlined in Exhibit 9.3.

The Challenge of Restorative Justice

Restorative justice holds great promise, but critics warn of pitfalls that may undermine it. For example, restorative justice programs must be wary of the cultural and social differences that can be found throughout our heterogeneous society. What may be considered "restorative" in one subculture may be considered insulting and damaging in another.[153]

Possibly the greatest challenge to restorative justice is the difficult task of balancing the needs of offenders with those of their victims. If programs focus solely on reconciliation of victims' needs, they may risk ignoring the offender's needs and increase the likelihood of reoffending. Sharon Levrant and her colleagues suggest that restorative justice programs that feature short-term interactions with victims fail to help offenders learn prosocial ways of behaving. Restorative justice advocates may falsely assume that relatively brief interludes of public shaming will change deeply rooted criminal predispositions.[154]

Exhibit 9.3   Principles of Restorative Justice

I. Crime is fundamentally a violation of people and interpersonal relationships.
  A. Victims and the community have been harmed and are in need of restoration. Victims include the target of the offense, but also family members, witnesses, and the community at large.
  B. Victims, offenders, and the affected communities are the key stakeholders in justice. The state must investigate crime and ensure safety, but it is not the center of the justice process. Victims are the key, and they must help in the search for restoration, healing, responsibility, and prevention.

II. Violations create obligations and liabilities.
  A. Offenders have the obligation to make things right as much as possible. They must understand the harm they have caused. Their participation should be as voluntary as possible; coercion is to be minimized.
  B. The community's obligations are to victims and to offenders and for the general welfare of its members. This includes the obligation to reintegrate the offender in the community and to ensure that the offender has the opportunity to make amends.

III. Restorative justice seeks to heal and put right the wrongs.
  A. Victims' needs are the focal concern of the justice process. Safety is a top priority, and victims should be empowered to participate in determining their needs and case outcomes.
  B. The exchange of information between victim and offender should be encouraged; when possible, face-to-face meetings might be undertaken. There should be mutual agreement over imposed outcomes.
  C. Offenders needs and competencies need to be addressed. Healing and reintegration are emphasized; isolation and removal from the community are restricted.
  D. The justice process belongs to the community; members are encouraged to "do justice." The justice process should be sensitive to community needs and geared to prevent similar harm in the future. Early interventions are encouraged.
  E. Justice is mindful of the outcomes, intended and unintended, of its responses to crime and victimization. It should monitor case outcome and provide necessary support and opportunity to all involved. The least restrictive intervention should be used, and overt social control should be avoided.

SOURCE: Howard Zehr and Harry Mika, "Fundamental Concepts of Restorative Justice," *Contemporary Justice Review* 1 (1998): 47–55.

Exhibit 9.4   Victim Concerns about Restorative Justice

1. Restorative justice processes can cast victims as little more than props in a psychodrama focused on the offender, to restore him and thereby render him less likely to offend again.
2. A victim, supported by family and intimates while engaged in restorative conferencing, and feeling genuinely free to speak directly to the offender, may press a blaming rather than restorative shaming agenda.
3. The victims' movement has focused for years on a perceived imbalance of "rights." Criminal defendants enjoy the presumption of innocence, the right to proof beyond a reasonable doubt, the right not to have to testify, and lenient treatment when found guilty of crime. Victims were extended no rights at all in the legal process. Is restorative justice another legal giveaway to criminals?
4. Victims' rights are threatened by some features of the restorative justice process, such as respectful listening to the offender's story and consensual dispositions. These features seem affronts to a victim's claim of the right to be seen as a victim, to insist on the offender being branded a criminal, to blame the offender, and not to be "victimized all over again by the process."
5. Many victims do want an apology, if it is heartfelt and easy to get, but some want even more: to put the traumatic incident behind them; to retrieve stolen property being held for use at trial; to be assured that the offender will receive treatment he is thought to need if he is not to victimize someone else. For victims such as these, restorative justice processes can seem unnecessary at best.
6. Restorative processes depend, case by case, on victims' active participation in a role more emotionally demanding than that of complaining witness in a conventional criminal prosecution—which is itself a role avoided by many, perhaps most, victims.

SOURCE: Michael E. Smith, *What Future for "Public Safety" and "Restorative Justice" in Community Corrections?* (Washington, D.C.: National Institute of Justice, 2001).

In contrast, programs that focus on the offender may turn off victims and their advocates. Some victim advocacy groups have voiced concerns about the focus of restorative justice programs (see Exhibit 9.4).

The concerns described in Exhibit 9.4 are among the obstacles restorative justice programs must overcome to be successful and productive. Yet because the method holds so much promise, criminologists are now conducting numerous demonstration projects to find the most effective means of returning the ownership of justice to the people and the community.

Summary

Social conflict theorists view crime as a function of the conflict that exists in society. Social conflict has its theoretical basis in the works of Karl Marx, as interpreted by Willem Bonger, Ralf Dahrendorf, and George Vold. Conflict theorists suggest that crime in any society is caused by class conflict. Laws are created by those in power to protect their rights and interests.

All criminal acts have political undertones. Richard Quinney has called this concept "the social reality of crime." Unfortunately, research efforts to validate the conflict approach have not produced significant findings. One of conflict theory's most important premises is that the justice system is biased and designed to protect the wealthy. Research has not been unanimous in supporting this point.

Marxist criminology views the competitive nature of the capitalist system as a major cause of crime. The poor commit crimes because of their frustration, anger, and need. The wealthy engage in illegal acts because they are used to competition and because they must do so to keep their positions in society. Marxist scholars have attempted to show that the law is designed to protect the wealthy and powerful and to control the poor, have-not members of society. There are a number of branches of radical theory referred to as instrumental Marxism and structural Marxism (see Table 9.1 for a summary of these theories).

Research on Marxist theory focuses on how the system of justice was designed and how it operates to further class interests. Quite often, this research uses historical analysis to show how the capitalist classes have exerted their control over the police, courts, and correctional agencies. Both Marxist and conflict criminology have been heavily criticized by consensus criminologists, who suggest that Marxists make fundamental errors in their concepts of ownership and class interest.

During the 1990s, new forms of conflict theory emerged. Feminist writers drew attention to the influence of patriarchal society on crime; left realism takes a centrist position on crime by showing its rational and destructive nature; peacemaking criminology brings a call for humanism to criminology; deconstructionism looks at the symbolic meaning of law and culture.

Table 9.1 Social Conflict Theories

Theory	Major Premise	Strengths
Conflict theory	Crime is a function of class conflict. Law is defined by people who hold social and political power.	Accounts for class differentials in the crime rate. Shows how class conflict influences behavior.
Marxist theory	The capitalist means of production creates class conflict. Crime is a rebellion of the lower class. The criminal justice system is an agent of class warfare.	Accounts for the associations between economic structure and crime rates.
Instrumental Marxist theory	Criminals are revolutionaries. The real crimes are sexism, racism, and profiteering.	Broadens the definition of crime and demystifies or explains the historical development of law.
Structural Marxist theory	The law is designed to sustain the capitalist economic system.	Explains the existence of white-collar crime and business control laws.
Radical feminist theory	The capital system creates patriarchy, which oppresses women.	Explains gender bias, violence against women, and repression.
Left realism	Crime is a function of relative deprivation; criminals prey on the poor.	Represents a compromise between conflict and traditional criminology.
Deconstructionism	Language controls the meaning and use of the law.	Provides a critical analysis of meaning.
Peacemaking	Peace and humanism can reduce crime; conflict resolution strategies can work.	Offers a new approach to crime control through mediation.

Thinking Like a Criminologist

An interim evaluation of Restoration House's New Hope for Families program, a community-based residential treatment program for women with dependent children, shows that 70 percent of women who completed follow-up interviews six months after treatment had maintained abstinence or reduced their drug use. The other 30 percent, however, lapse back into their old habits.

The program relies on restorative justice techniques in which community people meet with the women to discuss the harm drug use can cause and how it can damage them and their children. The communicators show their support and help the women find a niche in the community.

Women who completed the Restoration House program showed improvement in their employment, reduced parenting stress, retained custody of children, and restored their physical, mental, and emotional health. The program focuses not only on reducing drug and alcohol use but also on increasing health, safety, self-sufficiency, and positive attitudes.

As a criminologist, would you consider this program a success?

What questions would have to be answered before it gets your approval? How do you think those who do not succeed in the program should be handled? Are there any other approaches you would try with them? If so, explain.

Key Terms

- **conflict theory** (*250*)
- **communist manifesto** (*251*)
- **productive forces** (*251*)
- **productive relations** (*251*)
- **capitalist bourgeoisie** (*251*)
- **proletariat** (*251*)
- **lumpen proletariat** (*251*)
- **surplus value** (*252*)
- **dialectic method** (*252*)
- **antithesis** (*252*)
- **synthesis** (*252*)

- **imperatively coordinated associations** (*254*)
- **social reality of crime** (*256*)
- **norm resistance** (*257*)
- **radical theory** (*259*)
- **left realism** (*260*)
- **peacemaking movement** (*260*)
- **marginalization** (*260*)
- **structural locations** (*260*)
- **instrumentalists** (*261*)
- **integrative-constitutive theory** (*262*)
- **crimes of repression** (*262*)

- **crimes of reduction** (*262*)
- **structural Marxists** (*263*)
- **correctionalism** (*263*)
- **preemptive deterrence** (*265*)
- **elite deviance** (*267*)
- **doing gender** (*267*)
- **postmodernist** (*269*)
- **semiotics** (*269*)
- **deconstructionist analysis** (*269*)
- **restorative justice** (*271*)
- **reintegrative shaming** (*271*)

Critical Thinking Questions

1. How would a conservative reply to a call for more restorative justice? How would a restorative justice advocate respond to a conservative call for more prisons?

2. Considering recent changes in U.S. culture, how would a power-control theorist explain recent drops in the crime rate?

3. Is conflict inevitable in all cultures? If not, what can be done to reduce the level of conflict in our own society?

4. If Marx were alive today, what would he think about the prosperity enjoyed by the working class in industrial societies? Might he alter his vision of the capitalist system?

Notes

1. Melinda Henneberger, "Outcry Grows over Police Use of Force in Genoa," *New York Times*, 8 August 2001, p. B1; Sam Howe Verhovek and Joseph Kahn, "Talks and Turmoil: Street Rage; Dark Parallels with Anarchist Outbreaks in Oregon," *New York Times*, 3 December 1999, p. A3.

2. Michael Lynch, "Rediscovering Criminology: Lessons from the Marxist Tradition," in *Marxist Sociology: Surveys of Contemporary Theory and Research*, eds. Donald McQuarie and Patrick McGuire (New York: General Hall Press, 1994).

3. Michael Lynch and W. Byron Groves, *A Primer in Radical Criminology*, 2d ed. (Albany, N.Y.: Harrow and Heston, 1989), pp. 32–33.

4. Ibid., p. 4.

5. See, generally, Karl Marx and Friedrich Engels, *Capital: A Critique of Political Economy*, trans. E. Aveling (Chicago: Charles Kern, 1906); Karl Marx, *Selected Writings in Sociology and Social Philosophy*, trans. P. B. Bottomore (New York: McGraw-Hill, 1956). For a general discussion of Marxist thought, see Lynch and Groves, *A Primer in Radical Criminology*, pp. 6–26.

6. Karl Marx, *Grundrisse: Introduction to the Critique of Political Economy*, trans. Martin Nicolaus (New York: Vintage, 1973), pp. 106–107.

7. Lynch, "Rediscovering Criminology."

8. Karl Marx, "Population, Crime and Pauperism," in *Karl Marx and Friedrich Engels, Ireland and the Irish Question* (Moscow: Progress, 1859, reprinted 1971), p. 92.

9. Friedrich Engels, *The Condition of the Working Class in England in 1844* (London: Allen and Unwin, 1950).

10. Lynch, "Rediscovering Criminology," p. 5.

11. Willem Bonger, *Criminality and Economic Conditions*, abridged ed. (Bloomington: Indiana University Press, 1969). [Originally published 1916]

12. Ralf Dahrendorf, *Class and Class Conflict in Industrial Society* (Palo Alto, Calif.: Stanford University Press, 1959).

13. Ibid., p. 48.

14. George Vold, *Theoretical Criminology* (New York: Oxford University Press, 1958).

15. James Short and F. Ivan Nye, "Extent of Undetected Delinquency: Tentative Conclusions," *Journal of Criminal Law, Criminology, and Police Science* 49 (1958): 296–302.

16. For a general view, see David Friedrichs, "Crime, Deviance and Criminal Justice: In Search of a Radical Humanistic Perspective," *Humanity and Society* 6 (1982): 200–26.

17. Edwin Lemert, *Social Pathology* (New York: McGraw-Hill, 1951); Howard Becker, *Outsiders: Studies in the Sociology of Deviance* (New York: MacMillan, 1963).

18. Alexander Liazos, "The Poverty of the Sociology of Deviance: Nuts, Sluts and Perverts," *Social Problems* 20 (1972): 103–20.

19. See, generally, Robert Meier, "The New Criminology: Continuity in Criminological Theory," *Journal of Criminal Law and Criminology* 67 (1977): 461–69.

20. David Greenberg, ed., *Crime and Capitalism* (Palo Alto, Calif.: Mayfield, 1981), p. 3.

21. William Chambliss and Robert Seidman, *Law, Order and Power* (Reading, Mass.: Addison-Wesley, 1971), p. 503.

22. John Braithwaite, "Retributivism, Punishment and Privilege," in *Punishment and Privilege*, eds. W. Byron Groves and Graeme Newman (Albany, N.Y.: Harrow and Heston, 1986), pp. 55–66.

23. Daniel Georges-Abeyie, "Race, Ethnicity, and the Spatial Dynamic: Toward a Realistic Study of Black Crime, Crime Victimization, and Criminal Justice Processing of Blacks," *Social Justice* 16 (1989): 35–54.

24. John Hagan and Celesta Albonetti, "Race, Class and the Perception of Criminal Injustice in America," *American Journal of Sociology* 88 (1982): 329–55.

25. Richard Quinney, *The Social Reality of Crime* (Boston: Little, Brown, 1970), pp. 15–23.

26. Austin Turk, *Criminality and Legal Order* (Chicago: Rand McNally, 1969), p. 58.

27. Lynch and Groves, *A Primer in Radical Criminology*, p. 38.

28. Turk, *Criminality and Legal Order*.

29. Richard Greenleaf and Lonn Lanza-Kaduce, "Sophistication, Organization and Authority-Subject Conflict: Rediscovering and Unraveling Turk's Theory of Norm Resistance," *Criminology* 33 (1995): 565–85.

30. David McDowall, "Poverty and Homicide in Detroit, 1926–1978," *Victims and Violence* 1 (1986): 23–34; David McDowall and Sandra Norris, "Poverty and Homicide in Baltimore, Cleveland, and Memphis, 1937–1980." Paper presented at the annual meeting of the American Society of Criminology, Montreal, November 1987.

31. Judith Blau and Peter Blau, "The Cost of Inequality: Metropolitan Structure and Violent Crime," *American Sociological Review* 147 (1982): 114–29; Richard Block, "Community Environment and Violent Crime," *Criminology* 17 (1979): 46–57; Robert Sampson, "Structural Sources of Variation in Race-Age-Specific Rates of Offending across Major U.S. Cities," *Criminology* 23 (1985): 647–73.

32. David Jacobs and David Britt, "Inequality and Police Use of Deadly Force: An Empirical Assessment of a Conflict Hypothesis," *Social Problems* 26 (1979): 403–12.

33. Alan Lizotte, "Extra-Legal Factors in Chicago's Criminal Courts: Testing the Conflict Model of Criminal Justice," *Social Problems* 25 (1978): 564–80.

34. Terance Miethe and Charles Moore, "Racial Differences in Criminal Processing: The Consequences of Model Selection on Conclusions about Differential Treatment," *Sociological Quarterly* 27 (1987): 217–37.

35. Tracy Nobiling, Cassia Spohn, and Miriam DeLone, "A Tale of Two Counties: Unemployment and Sentence Severity," *Justice Quarterly* 15 (1998): 459–85.

36. Nancy Wonders, "Determinate Sentencing: A Feminist and Postmodern Story," *Justice Quarterly* 13 (1996): 610–48; Douglas Smith, Christy Visher, and Laura Davidson, "Equity and Discretionary Justice: The Influence of Race on Police Arrest Decisions," *Journal of Criminal Law and Criminology* 75 (1984): 234–49.

37. Thomas Arvanites, "Increasing Imprisonment: A Function of Crime or Socio-economic Factors?" *American Journal of Criminal Justice* 17 (1992): 19–38.

38. Michael Leiber, Anne Woodrick, and E. Michele Roudebush, "Religion, Discriminatory Attitudes and the Orientations of Juvenile Justice Personnel: A Research Note," *Criminology* 33 (1995): 431–47; Michael Leiber and Katherine Jamieson, "Race and Decision Making within Juvenile Justice: The Importance of Context," *Journal of Quantitative Criminology* 11 (1995): 363–88.

39. Dragan Milovanovic, "Postmodern Criminology: Mapping the Terrain," *Justice Quarterly* 13 (1996): 567–610.

40. Jackson Toby, "The New Criminology Is the Old Sentimentality," *Criminology* 16 (1979): 513–26.

41. See generally, William Wilbanks, *The Myth of a Racist Criminal Justice System* (Pacific Grove, Calif.: Brooks/Cole, 1987).

42. Theodore Chiricos and Gordon Waldo, "Socioeconomic Status and Criminal Sentencing: An Empirical Assessment of a Conflict Proposition," *American Sociological Review* 40 (1975): 753–72.

43. Stephen Klein, Joan Petersilia, and Susan Turner, "Race and Imprisonment Decisions in California," *Science* 247 (1990): 812–16.

44. This section borrows heavily from Richard Sparks, "A Critique of Marxist Criminology," in *Crime and Justice*, vol. 2, eds. Norval Morris and Michael Tonry (Chicago: University of Chicago Press, 1980), pp. 159–208.

45. Barbara Sims, "Crime, Punishment and the American Dream: Toward a Marxist Integration," *Journal of Research in Crime and Delinquency* 34 (1997): 5–24.

46. Jeffery Reiman, *The Rich Get Richer and the Poor Get Prison* (New York: Wiley, 1984), pp. 43–44.

47. For a general review of Marxist criminology, see Lynch and Groves, *A Primer in Radical Criminology*.

48. Sims, "Crime, Punishment and the American Dream."

49. Ian Taylor, Paul Walton, and Jock Young, *The New Criminology: For a Social Theory of Deviance* (London: Routledge and Kegan Paul, 1973).

50. Barry Krisberg, *Crime and Privilege: Toward a New Criminology* (Englewood Cliffs, N.J.: Prentice-Hall, 1975), p. 167.

51. David Friedrichs, "Critical Criminology and Critical Legal Studies," *Critical Criminologist* 1 (1989): 7.

52. See, for example, Larry Tifft and Dennis Sullivan, *The Struggle to Be Human: Crime, Criminology and Anarchism* (Orkney Islands, Over-the Water-Sanday: Cienfuegos Press, 1979); Dennis Sullivan, *The Mask of Love* (Port

Washington, N.Y.: Kennikat Press, 1980).

53. R. M. Bohm, "Radical Criminology: An Explication," *Criminology* 19 (1982): 565–89.

54. Robert Bohm, "Radical Criminology: Back to the Basics." Paper presented at the annual meeting of the American Society of Criminology, Phoenix, Arizona, November 1993, p. 2.

55. Ibid., p. 4.

56. W. Byron Groves and Robert Sampson, "Critical Theory and Criminology," *Social Problems* 33 (1986): 58–80.

57. Gregg Barak, "'Crimes of the Homeless' or the 'Crime of Homelessness': A Self-Reflexive, New-Marxist Analysis of Crime and Social Control." Paper presented at the annual meeting of the American Society of Criminology, Montreal, November 1987.

58. Michael Lynch, "Assessing the State of Radical Criminology: Toward the Year 2000." Paper presented at the annual meeting of the American Society of Criminology, Phoenix, Arizona, November 1993.

59. Steven Box, *Recession, Crime and Unemployment* (London: Macmillan, 1987).

60. David Barlow, Melissa Hickman-Barlow, and W. Wesley Johnson, "The Political Economy of Criminal Justice Policy: A Time-Series Analysis of Economic Conditions, Crime and Federal Criminal Justice Legislation, 1948–1987," *Justice Quarterly* 13 (1996): 223–41.

61. Mahesh Nalla, Michael Lynch, and Michael Leiber, "Determinants of Police Growth in Phoenix, 1950–1988," *Justice Quarterly* 14 (1997): 115–43.

62. Gresham Sykes, "The Rise of Critical Criminology," *Journal of Criminal Law and Criminology* 65 (1974): 211.

63. David Jacobs, "Corporate Economic Power and the State: A Longitudinal Assessment of Two Explanations," *American Journal of Sociology* 93 (1988): 852–81.

64. Deanna Alexander, "Victims of the L.A. Riots: A Theoretical Consideration." Paper presented at the annual meeting of the American Society of Criminology, Phoenix, Arizona, November 1993.

65. Ibid., p. 2.

66. Richard Quinney, "Crime Control in Capitalist Society," in *Critical Criminology*, eds. Ian Taylor, Paul Walton, and Jock Young (London: Routledge and Kegan Paul, 1975), p. 199.

67. Herman Schwendinger and Julia Schwendinger, "Defenders of Order or Guardians of Human Rights," *Issues in Criminology* 7 (1970): 71–81.

68. Herman Schwendinger and Julia Schwendinger, "Delinquency and Social Reform: A Radical Perspective," in *Juvenile Justice,* ed. Lamar Empey (Charlottesville: University of Virginia Press, 1979), pp. 246–90.

69. Steven Spitzer, "Toward a Marxian Theory of Deviance," *Social Problems* 22 (1975): 638–51.

70. Gregg Barak and Stuart Henry, "An Integrative-Constitutive Theory of Crime, Law and Social Justice," in *Social Justice/Criminal Justice,* ed. Bruce Arrigo (Belmont, Calif.: West/Wadsworth, 1999), pp. 152–88. For similar views, see Mark Colvin and John Pauly, "A Critique of Criminology: Toward an Integrated Structural-Marxist Theory of Delinquency Production," *American Journal of Sociology* 89 (1983): 513–51.

71. Michael Lynch, Raymond Michalowski, and W. Byron Groves, *The New Primer in Radical Criminology: Critical Perspectives on Crime, Power, and Identity,* 3d ed. (Monsey, N.Y.: Criminal Justice Press, 2000), p. 45. Herein cited as *The New Primer.*

72. Lynch, "Rediscovering Criminology," p. 14.

73. John Hagan, *Structural Criminology* (New Brunswick, N.J.: Rutgers University Press, 1989), pp. 110–19.

74. *The New Primer,* p. 50.

75. Roy Bhaskar, "Empiricism," in *A Dictionary of Marxist Thought,* ed. T. Bottomore (Cambridge: Harvard University Press, 1983), pp. 149–50.

76. Byron Groves, "Marxism and Positivism," *Crime and Social Justice* 23 (1985): 129–50; Michael Lynch, "Quantitative Analysis and Marxist Criminology: Some Old Answers to a Dilemma in Marxist Criminology," *Crime and Social Justice* 29 (1987): 110–17.

77. Alan Lizotte, James Mercy, and Eric Monkkonen, "Crime and Police Strength in an Urban Setting: Chicago, 1947–1970," in *Quantitative Criminology,* ed. John Hagan (Beverly Hills: Sage, 1982), pp. 129–48.

78. William Chambliss, "The State, the Law and the Definition of Behavior as Criminal or Delinquent," in *Handbook of Criminology,* ed. D. Glazer (Chicago: Rand McNally, 1974), pp. 7–44.

79. Timothy Carter and Donald Clelland, "A Neo-Marxian Critique, Formulation and Test of Juvenile Dispositions as a Function of Social Class," *Social Problems* 27 (1979): 96–108.

80. Malcolm Homes, "Minority Threat and Police Brutality: Determinants of Civil Rights Criminal Complaints in U.S. Municipalities," *Criminology* 38 (2000): 343–68.

81. David Greenberg, "Socio-Economic Status and Criminal Sentences: Is There an Association?" *American Sociological Review* 42 (1977): 174–75; David Greenberg and Drew Humphries, "The Co-optation of Fixed Sentencing Reform," *Crime and Delinquency* 26 (1980): 206–25.

82. Steven Box, *Power, Crime and Mystification* (London: Tavistock, 1984); Gregg Barak, *In Defense of Whom? A Critique of Criminal Justice Reform* (Cincinnati: Anderson Publishing, 1980); for an opposing view, see Franklin Williams, "Conflict Theory and Differential Processing: An Analysis of the Research Literature," in *Radical Criminology: The Coming Crisis,* ed. J. Inciardi (Beverly Hills: Sage, 1980), pp. 213–31.

83. David Greenberg and Valerie West, "State Prison Populations and Their Growth, 1971–1991," *Criminology* 39 (2001): 615–54.

84. Robert Weiss, "Repatriating Low-Wage Work: The Political Economy of Prison Labor Reprivatization in the Postindustrial United States," *Criminology* 39 (2001): 253–92.

85. Michael Rustigan, "A Reinterpretation of Criminal Law Reform in Nineteenth-Century England," in *Crime and Capitalism,* ed. D. Greenberg (Palo Alto, Calif.: Mayfield, 1981), pp. 255–78.

86. Rosalind Petchesky, "At Hard Labor: Penal Confinement and Production in Nineteenth-Century America," in *Crime and Capitalism,* ed. D. Greenberg (Palo Alto, Calif.: Mayfield, 1981), pp. 341–57; Paul Takagi, "The Walnut Street Jail: A Penal Reform to Centralize the Powers of the State," *Federal Probation* 49 (1975): 18–26.

87. Sidney Harring, "Policing a Class Society: The Expansion of the Urban Police in the Late Nineteenth and Early Twentieth Centuries," in *Crime and Capitalism,* ed. D. Greenberg (Palo Alto, Calif.: Mayfield, 1981), pp. 292–313.

88. Steven Spitzer and Andrew Scull, "Privatization and Capitalist Development: The Case of the Private Police," *Social Problems* 25 (1977): 18–29; Dennis Hoffman, "Cops and Wobblies" (Ph.D. diss., Portland State University, 1977).

89. Jack Gibbs, "An Incorrigible Positivist," *Criminologist* 12 (1987): 2–3.

90. Toby, "The New Criminology Is the Old Sentimentality."

91. Sparks, "A Critique of Marxist Criminology," pp. 198–99.

92. Carl Klockars, "The Contemporary Crises of Marxist Criminology," in *Radical Criminology: The Coming Crisis,* ed. J. Inciardi (Beverly Hills: Sage, 1980), pp. 92–123.

93. Ibid.

94. Michael Lynch, W. Byron Groves, and Alan Lizotte, "The Rate of Surplus Value and Crime: A Theoretical and Empirical Examination of Marxian Economic Theory and Criminology," *Crime, Law and Social Change* 21 (1994): 15–48.

95. Anthony Platt, "Criminology in the 1980s: Progressive Alternatives to 'Law and Order,'" *Crime and Social Justice* 21–22 (1985): 191–99.

96. See, generally, Roger Matthews and Jock Young, eds., *Confronting Crime* (London: Sage, 1986). For a thorough review of left realism, see Martin Schwartz and Walter DeKeseredy, "Left Realist Criminology: Strengths, Weaknesses and the Feminist Critique," *Crime, Law and Social Change* 15 (1991): 51–72.

97. John Lea and Jock Young, *What Is to Be Done about Law and Order?* (Harmondsworth, England: Penguin, 1984).

98. Ibid., p. 88.

99. Richard Kinsey, John Lea, and Jock Young, *Losing the Fight against Crime* (London: Blackwell, 1986).

100. Martin Schwartz and Walter DeKeseredy, *Contemporary Criminology* (Belmont, Calif.: Wadsworth, 1993), p. 249.

101. Schwartz and DeKeseredy, "Left Realist Criminology."

102. Ibid., p. 54.

103. Schwartz and DeKeseredy, "Left Realist Criminology."

104. For a general review of this issue, see Kathleen Daly and Meda Chesney-Lind, "Feminism and Criminology," *Justice Quarterly* 5 (1988): 497–538; Douglas Smith and Raymond Paternoster, "The Gender Gap in Theories of Deviance: Issues and Evidence," *Journal of Research in Crime and Delinquency* 24 (1987): 140–72; Pat Carlen, "Women, Crime, Feminism, and Realism," *Social Justice* 17 (1990): 106–23.

105. Julia Schwendinger and Herman Schwendinger, *Rape and Inequality* (Beverly Hills: Sage, 1983).

106. Daly and Chesney-Lind, "Feminism and Criminology."

107. Janet Saltzman Chafetz, "Feminist Theory and Sociology: Underutilized Contributions for Mainstream Theory," *Annual Review of Sociology* 23 (1997): 97–121.

108. Ibid.

109. James Messerschmidt, *Capitalism, Patriarchy and Crime* (Totowa, N.J.: Rowman and Littlefield, 1986). For a critique of this work, see Herman Schwendinger and Julia Schwendinger, "The World according to James Messerschmidt," *Social Justice* 15 (1988): 123–45.

110. Kathleen Daly, "Gender and Varieties of White Collar Crime," *Criminology* 27 (1989): 769–93.

111. Jane Roberts Chapman, "Violence against Women as a Violation of Human Rights," *Social Justice* 17 (1990): 54–71.

112. James Messerschmidt, *Masculinities and Crime: Critique and Reconceptualization of Theory* (Lanham, Md.: Rowman and Littlefield, 1993).

113. For a review of feminist theory, see Sally Simpson, "Feminist Theory, Crime and Justice," *Criminology* 27 (1989): 605–32.

114. Suzie Dod Thomas and Nancy Stein, "Criminality, Imprisonment, and Women's Rights in the 1990's," *Social Justice* 17 (1990): 1–5.

115. Walter DeKeseredy and Martin Schwartz, "Male Peer Support and Woman Abuse: An Expansion of DeKeseredy's Model," *Sociological Spectrum* 13 (1993): 393–413.

116. Daly and Chesney-Lind, "Feminism and Criminology." See also, Drew Humphries and Susan Caringella-MacDonald, "Murdered Mothers, Missing Wives: Reconsidering Female Victimization," *Social Justice* 17 (1990): 71–78.

117. Center for Research on Women, *Secrets in Public: Sexual Harassment in Our Schools* (Wellesley, Mass.: Wellesley College, 1993).

118. Jane Siegel and Linda Meyer Williams, "Aggressive Behavior among Women Sexually Abused as Children." Paper presented at the American Society of Criminology meeting, Phoenix, Arizona, 1993. Revised version.

119. Susan Ehrlich Martin and Nancy Jurik, *Doing Justice, Doing Gender* (Thousand Oaks, Calif.: Sage, 1996), pp. 27.

120. Ruth Alexander, *The "Girl Problem," Female Sexual Delinquency in New York, 1900–1930* (Ithaca, N.Y.: Cornell University Press, 1995).

121. Mary Odem and Steven Schlossman, "Guardians of Virtue: The Juvenile Court and Female Delinquency in Early 20th-Century Los Angeles," *Crime and Delinquency* 37 (1991): 186–203.

122. Meda Chesney-Lind, "Judicial Enforcement of the Female Sex Role: The Family Court and the Female Delinquent," *Issues in Criminology* 8 (1973): 51–69; see also idem, "Women and Crime: The Female Offender," *Signs: Journal of Women in Culture and Society* 12 (1986): 78–96; idem, "Female Offenders: Paternalism Reexamined," in *Women, the Courts, and Equality,* eds. Laura L. Crites and Winifred L. Hepperle (Newbury Park, Calif.: Sage, 1987): 114–39; idem, "Girls' Crime and a Woman's Place: Toward a Feminist Model of Female Delinquency." Paper presented at a meeting of the American Society of Criminology, Montreal, 1987.

123. Hagan, *Structural Criminology.*

124. John Hagan, A. R. Gillis, and John Simpson, "The Class Structure and Delinquency: Toward a Power-Control Theory of Common Delinquent Behavior," *American Journal of Sociology* 90 (1985): 1151–78; John Hagan, John Simpson, and A. R. Gillis, "Class in the Household: A Power-Control Theory of Gender and Delinquency," *American Journal of Sociology* 92 (1987): 788–816.

125. Brenda Sims Blackwell, "Perceived Sanction Threats, Gender, and Crime: A Test and Elaboration of Power-Control Theory," *Criminology* 38 (2000): 439–88.

126. Christopher Uggen, "Class, Gender, and Arrest: An Intergenerational Analysis of Workplace Power and Control," *Criminology* 38 (2001): 835–62.

127. Gary Jensen, "Power-Control versus Social-Control Theory: Identifying Crucial Differences for Future Research." Paper presented at the annual meeting of the American Society of Criminology, Baltimore, November 1990.

128. Gary Jensen and Kevin Thompson, "What's Class Got to Do with It? A Further Examination of Power-Control Theory," *American Journal of Sociology* 95 (1990): 1009–23. For some critical research, see Simon Singer and Murray Levine, "Power Control Theory, Gender and Delinquency: A Partial Replication with Additional Evidence on the Effects of Peers," *Criminology* 26 (1988): 627–48.

129. Kevin Thompson, "Gender and Adolescent Drinking Problems: The Effects of Occupational Structure," *Social Problems* 36 (1989): 30–38.

130. See, generally, Uggen, "Class, Gender, and Arrest: An Intergenerational

Analysis of Workplace Power and Control."

131. See, generally, Lynch, "Rediscovering Criminology," pp. 27–28.

132. See, generally, Stuart Henry and Dragan Milovanovic, *Constitutive Criminology: Beyond Postmodernism* (London: Sage, 1996).

133. Dragan Milovanovic, *A Primer in the Sociology of Law* (New York: Harrow and Heston, 1988) pp. 127–28.

134. See, generally, Henry and Milovanovic, *Constitutive Criminology: Beyond Postmodernism.*

135. Bruce Arrigo and Thomas Bernard, "Postmodern Criminology in Relation to Radical and Conflict Criminology," *Critical Criminology* 8 (1997): 39–60.

136. See, for example, Tifft and Sullivan, *The Struggle to Be Human;* and Sullivan, *The Mask of Love.*

137. Larry Tifft, "Foreword," to Sullivan, *The Mask of Love,* p. 6.

138. Ibid., p. 141.

139. Dennis Sullivan and Larry Tifft, *Restorative Justice* (Monsey, N.Y.: Willow Tree Press, 2001).

140. Richard Quinney, "The Way of Peace: On Crime, Suffering and Service," in *Criminology as Peacemaking,* eds. Harold Pepinsky and Richard Quinney (Bloomington: Indiana Univerity Press, 1991), pp. 8–9.

141. Kathleen Daly and Russ Immarigeon, "The Past, Present and Future of Restorative Justice: Some Critical Reflections," *Contemporary Justice Review* 1 (1998): 21–45.

142. John Braithwaite, *Crime, Shame, and Reintegration* (Melbourne, Australia: Cambridge University Press, 1989).

143. Ibid., p. 81.

144. Anthony Petrosino and Carolyn Petrosino, "The Public Safety Potential of Megan's Law in Massachusetts: An Assessment from a Sample of Criminal Sexual Psychopaths," *Crime and Delinquency* 45 (1999): 140–58.

145. For more on this approach, see Jane Mugford and Stephen Mugford, "Shame and Reintegration in the Punishment and Deterrence of Spouse Assault." Paper presented at the annual meeting of the American Society of Criminology, San Francisco, 1991.

146. Carter Hay, " An Exploratory Test of Braithwaite's Reintegrative Shaming Theory," *Journal of Research in Crime and Delinquency* 38 (2001): 132–53.

147. Mugford and Mugford, "Shame and Reintegration in the Punishment and Deterrence of Spouse Assault."

148. Gene Stephens, "The Future of Policing: From a War Model to a Peace Model," in *The Past, Present and Future of American Criminal Justice,* eds. Brendan Maguire and Polly Radosh (Dix Hills, N.Y.: General Hall, 1996), pp. 77–93.

149. This section developed with the help of Dr. Peter Cordella, St. Anselm College, Manchester, N.H.

150. Kay Pranis, "Peacemaking Circles: Restorative Justice in Practice Allows Victims and Offenders to Begin Repairing the Harm," *Corrections Today* 59 (1997): 72–76, at 74.

151. Carol LaPrairie, "The 'New' Justice: Some Implications for Aboriginal Communities," *Canadian Journal of Criminology* 40 (1998): 61–79.

152. Adapted from Pranis, "Peacemaking Circles."

153. David Altschuler, "Community Justice Initiatives: Issues and Challenges in the U.S. Context," *Federal Probation* 65 (2001): 28–33.

154. Sharon Levrant, Francis Cullen, Betsy Fulton, and John Wozniak, "Reconsidering Restorative Justice: The Corruption of Benevolence Revisited?" *Crime and Delinquency* 45 (1999): 3–28.

© Will Waldron/The Image Works

CHAPTER 10 Developmental Theories

■ Introduction

Gary L. Sampson, 41, addicted to alcohol and cocaine, was a deadbeat dad, a two-bit thief, and a bank robber with a long history of violence. On August 1, 2001, he turned himself in to the Vermont State Police after fleeing from a string of three murders he committed in Massachusetts and New Hampshire.

Those who knew Sampson speculated that his murders were a desperate finale to a troubled life. During his early life in New England, he once bound, gagged, and beat three elderly women in a candy store, hijacked cars at knifepoint, and had been medically diagnosed as schizophrenic. In 1977, he married a 17-year-old girl he had impregnated; two months later he was arrested and charged with rape for having "unnatural intercourse with a child under 16." Although he was acquitted of that charge, his wife noticed that Sampson had started developing a hair-trigger temper and had become increasingly violent; their marriage soon ended. As the years passed, Sampson had at least four failed marriages, was an absentee father to two children, and became an alcoholic and a drug user; he spent nearly half of his adult life behind bars. Jumping bail after being arrested for theft from an antique store, he headed south to North Carolina and took on a new identity: Gary Johnson, a construction worker. He took up with Ricki Carter, a transvestite, but their relationship was anything but stable. Sampson once put a gun to Carter's head, broke his ribs, and threatened to kill his family. After his breakup with Carter, Sampson moved in with a new girlfriend, Karen Anderson, and began pulling bank jobs.

When the police closed in, Sampson fled north. Needing transportation, he pulled three carjackings and killed the drivers, one a 19-year-old college freshman who had stopped to give Sampson a hand.

Career criminals like Gary Sampson have become a focus of contemporary criminological theory. He seems to fit the profile of the chronic offender who is responsible for a significant number of all recorded crimes. Why is it that only a relatively few offenders engage in persistent, serious criminality? If structural theories are correct and environmental factors such as poverty explain the onset of criminal activity, why is it that most kids growing up in disorganized areas, even those who engage in delinquent behaviors in their adolescence, fail to become chronic or persistent offenders? Sampson's family lived in a middle-class suburb, not an inner-city neighborhood. What factors can account for his life of crime?

Career criminals like Gary Sampson also seem to defy the aging-out process. We know that most young offenders do not become adult criminals. Why is it that some kids become delinquents and then abandon the delinquent way of life as they mature, whereas others persist in criminality into their adulthood? Some experts believe antisocial behavior is a function of some personal trait, such as a low IQ or impulsive personality, which is present at birth or soon afterward. Yet, if the onset of crime is explained by abnormally low intelligence or a defective personality, than why is it that most people desist from crime as they mature? It seems unlikely that intelligence increases as young offenders mature or that personality flaws disappear. Even

■ Gary Sampson at his arraignment in White River Junction, Vermont. Career criminals such as Sampson seem to defy the aging-out process and persist in criminality into their adulthood.

if the onset of criminality can be explained by a single biological or personal trait, some other factor must explain its termination.

CONNECTIONS

Chapter 3 addressed the issues of both chronic offending and aging out. These two issues are the cornerstones of contemporary criminological theories. ■

Concern over these two critical issues has prompted the development of some contemporary visions of criminality referred to here as **developmental theories.** They seek to chart the natural history or development of a criminal career. Why do some offenders escalate their criminal activities while others decrease or limit their law violations? Why do some offenders specialize in a particular crime while others become generalists? Why do some criminals reduce criminal activity and then resume it once again? Research now shows that some offenders begin their criminal careers at a very early age, whereas others begin later. How can early- and late-onset criminality be explained?[1]

Concern about the natural history of criminal careers is not confined to the United States. You may access the results of a study conducted in the United Kingdom at:
http://www.homeoffice.gov.uk/rds/pdfs/
hosb401.pdf
For an up-to-date list of Web links, go to
http://info.wadsworth.com/siegel ■

Developmental theories seem to fall into two distinct groups: latent trait and life course theories. **Latent trait theories** hold that criminal behavior is controlled by a "master trait," present at birth or soon after, that remains stable and unchanging throughout a person's lifetime. In contrast, **life course theorists** view criminality as a dynamic process, influenced by individual characteristics as well as social experiences. Whereas latent trait theorists believe that "people don't change, opportunities do," life course theorists expect personal change and growth (see Figure 10.1). Each of these positions is discussed in detail in the following sections.

■ The Latent Trait View

In a critical 1990 article, David Rowe, D. Wayne Osgood, and W. Alan Nicewander proposed the concept of **latent traits** to explain the flow of crime over the life cycle. Their model assumes that a number of people in the population have a personal attribute or characteristic that controls their inclination or propensity to commit crimes.[2] This disposition, or latent trait, may be either present at birth or established early in life, and it remains stable over time.

Figure 10.1   Latent Trait versus Life Course Theories

Latent trait theory
- Master trait
  - Personality
  - Intelligence
  - Genetic makeup
- People do not change, criminal opportunities change; maturity brings fewer opportunities
- Early social control and proper parenting can reduce criminal propensity

- Criminal careers are a passage
- Personal and structural factors influence crime
- Change affects crime
- Personal vs. situational

Life course theory
- Multiple traits: social, psychological, economic
- People change over the life course
- Family, job, peers influence behavior

Suspected latent traits include defective intelligence, impulsive personality, genetic abnormalities, the physical-chemical functioning of the brain, and environmental influences on brain function such as drugs, chemicals, and injuries.[3] Those who carry one of these latent traits are in danger of becoming career criminals; those who lack the traits have a much lower risk. Latent traits should affect the behavioral choices of all people equally, regardless of their gender or personal characteristics.[4]

CONNECTIONS

Individual factors seem ideally suited for a role in developmental-type theories because, as noted in Chapter 6, even ardent biosocial theorists recognize that they cannot by themselves explain crime rate patterns and changes. Some environmental force must interact with them to control criminality. ■

Because latent traits are stable, people who are antisocial during adolescence are the most likely to persist in crime. The positive association between past and future criminality detected in the cohort studies of career criminals reflects the presence of this underlying crimogenic trait. That is, if low IQ contributes to delinquency in childhood, it should also cause the same people to offend as adults because intelligence is usually stable over the life span.

Whereas the propensity to commit crime is stable, the opportunity to commit crime fluctuates over time. People age out of crime: as they mature and develop, there are simply fewer opportunities to commit crimes and greater inducements to remain "straight." They may marry, have children, and obtain jobs. The former delinquents' newfound adult responsibilities leave them little time to hang with their friends, abuse substances, and get into scrapes with the law. For example, assume that a stable latent trait such as low IQ causes some people to commit crime. Teenagers have more opportunity to commit crime than adults, so at every level of intelligence, adolescent crime rates will be higher. As they mature, however, teens with both high and low IQs will commit less crime because their adult responsibilities provide them with fewer criminal opportunities. Latent trait theories also assume a biological effect of the aging process. As people mature, they lose the strength and vigor to commit crimes. Even if the occasion arises, they may lack the energy to take advantage of criminal opportunity, hence crime slows down with age.

Crime and Human Nature

Latent trait theorists were encouraged when two prominent social scientists, James Q. Wilson and Richard Herrnstein, published *Crime and Human Nature* in 1985.[5] This book and its **human nature theory** argue that personal traits, such as genetic makeup, intelligence, and body build, may outweigh the importance of social variables as predictors of criminal activity.

To read an interview with James Q. Wilson and learn more about his ideas on the causes of crime, go to:
http://www.pbs.org/fmc/interviews/jwilson.htm
For an up-to-date list of Web links, go to
http://info.wadsworth.com/siegel ■

According to Wilson and Herrnstein, all human behavior, including criminality, is determined by its perceived consequences. A criminal incident occurs when an individual chooses criminal over conventional behavior (referred to as noncrime) after weighing the potential gains and losses of each: "the larger the ratio of net rewards of crime to the net rewards of non-crime, the greater the tendency to commit the crime."[6]

Wilson and Herrnstein's model assumes that both biological and psychological traits influence the crime–noncrime choice. They see a close link between a person's decision to choose crime and such biosocial factors as low intelligence, mesomorphic body type, genetic influences

(parental criminality), and possessing an autonomic nervous system that responds too quickly to stimuli. Psychological traits, such as an impulsive or extroverted personality or generalized hostility, also determine the potential to commit crime.

In their focus on the association between these constitutional and psychological factors and crime, Wilson and Herrnstein seem to be suggesting the existence of an elusive latent trait that predisposes people to commit crime.[7] Their vision helped inspire other criminologists to identify the elusive latent trait that causes criminal behavior.

General Theory of Crime

In their important work, *A General Theory of Crime,* Michael Gottfredson and Travis Hirschi modified and redefined some of the principles articulated in Hirschi's social control theory by integrating the concepts of control with those of biosocial, psychological, routine activities, and rational choice theories.[8]

CONNECTIONS

In his original version of control theory, discussed in Chapter 8, Hirschi focused on the social controls that attach people to conventional society and insulate them from criminality. In this newer work, he concentrates on self-control as a stabilizing force. The two views are connected, however, because both social control (or social bonds) and self-control are acquired through early experiences with effective parenting. ■

The act and the offender In their **general theory of crime (GTC),** Gottfredson and Hirschi consider the criminal offender and the criminal act as separate concepts (see Figure 10.2). On one hand, criminal acts, such as robberies or burglaries, are illegal events or deeds that people engage in when they perceive them to be advantageous. For example, burglaries are typically committed by young males looking for cash, liquor, and entertainment; the crime provides "easy, short-term gratification."[9] This aspect of the theory relies on concepts developed first as classical theory and later as rational choice and routine activities theories: crime is rational and predictable; people commit crime when it promises rewards with minimal threat of pain; the threat of punishment can deter crime. If targets are well guarded, crime rates diminish. Only the truly irrational offender would dare to strike under those circumstances.

On the other hand, criminal offenders are predisposed to commit crimes. They are not robots who commit crime without restraint; their days are also filled with conventional behaviors, such as going to school, parties, concerts, and church. But given the same set of criminal opportunities, such as having a lot of free time for mischief and living in a neighborhood with unguarded homes containing valuable merchandise, crime-prone people have a much higher prob-

Figure 10.2   The General Theory of Crime

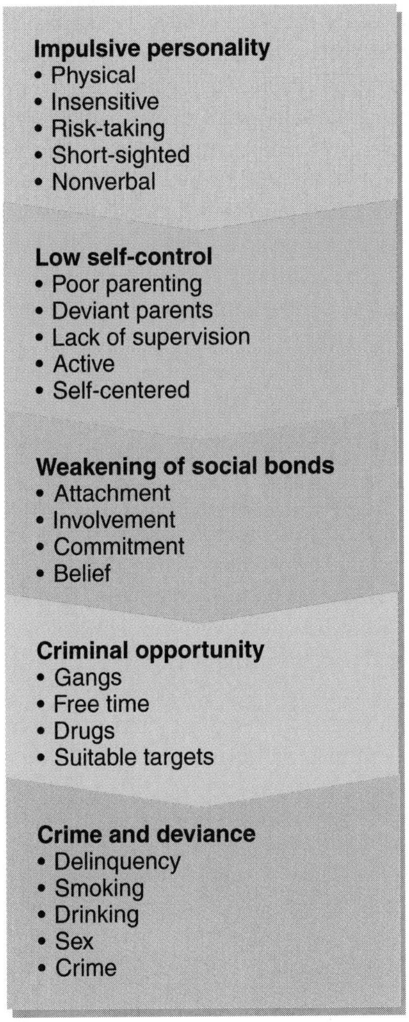

Impulsive personality
- Physical
- Insensitive
- Risk-taking
- Short-sighted
- Nonverbal

Low self-control
- Poor parenting
- Deviant parents
- Lack of supervision
- Active
- Self-centered

Weakening of social bonds
- Attachment
- Involvement
- Commitment
- Belief

Criminal opportunity
- Gangs
- Free time
- Drugs
- Suitable targets

Crime and deviance
- Delinquency
- Smoking
- Drinking
- Sex
- Crime

What makes people crime prone? What, then, causes people to become excessively crime prone? Gottfredson and Hirschi attribute the tendency to commit crimes to a person's level of self-control. People with limited self-control tend to be impulsive; they are insensitive to other people's feelings, physical (rather than mental), risk takers, shortsighted, and nonverbal.[11] They have a "here-and-now" orientation and refuse to work for distant goals; they lack diligence, tenacity, and persistence. People lacking self-control tend to be adventuresome, active, physical, and self-centered. As they mature, they often have unstable marriages, jobs, and friendships.[12] They are less likely to feel shame if they engage in deviant acts and are more likely to find them pleasurable.[13] They are also more likely to engage in dangerous behaviors such as drinking, smoking, and reckless driving; all of these behaviors are associated with criminality.[14]

Because those with low self-control enjoy risky, exciting, or thrilling behaviors with immediate gratification, they are more likely to enjoy criminal acts, which require stealth, agility, speed, and power, than conventional acts, which demand long-term study and cognitive and verbal skills. As Gottfredson and Hirschi put it, they derive satisfaction from "money without work, sex without courtship, revenge without court delays."[15] Many of these individuals who have a propensity for committing crime also engage in other behaviors such as smoking, drinking, gambling, and illicit sexuality.[16] Although these acts are not illegal, they too provide immediate, short-term gratification. Exhibit 10.1 lists the elements of low self-control.

Is there an association between low-self control and ADHD? To find out, go to this Web site:
  http://www.sciam.com/1998/0998issue/ 0998barkley.html
For an up-to-date list of Web links, go to
  http://info.wadsworth.com/siegel

ability of violating the law than do noncriminals. The propensity to commit crimes remains stable throughout a person's life. Change in the frequency of criminal activity is purely a function of change in criminal opportunity.

By recognizing that there are stable differences in people's propensity to commit crime, the GTC adds a biosocial element to the concept of social control. Individual differences are stable over the life course, and so is the propensity to commit crime; only opportunity changes. The biological and psychological factors that make people impulsive and crime prone may be inherited or may develop through incompetent or absent parenting. Biosocial theorists recognize that improper parenting can have a long-term impact on human behavior. If a child is not properly socialized, his or her neural pathways are physically affected. Once experiences are ingrained, the brain establishes a pattern of electrochemical activation that remains for life.[10]

Exhibit 10.1   The Elements of Impulsivity: Signs That a Person Has Low Self-Control

Physical	Lacks tenacity
Shortsighted	Adventuresome
Nonverbal	Self-centered
Here-and-now orientation	Shameless
Unstable social relations	Imprudent
Enjoys deviant behaviors	Lacks cognitive and
Risk taker	verbal skills
Refuses to work for distant goals	Enjoys danger and excitement
Lacks diligence	

Gottfredson and Hirschi trace the root cause of poor self-control to inadequate child-rearing practices. Parents who refuse or are unable to monitor a child's behavior, to recognize deviant behavior when it occurs, and to punish that behavior will produce children who lack self-control. Children who are not attached to their parents, who are poorly supervised, and whose parents are criminal or deviant themselves are the most likely to develop poor self-control. In a sense, lack of self-control occurs naturally when steps are not taken to stop its development.[17]

Low self-control develops early in life and remains stable into and through adulthood.[18] Considering the continuity of criminal motivation, Hirschi and Gottfredson have questioned the utility of the juvenile justice system and of giving more lenient treatment to young delinquent offenders. Why separate youthful and adult offenders legally when the source of their criminality (for example, impulsivity) is essentially the same?[19]

Self-control and crime Gottfredson and Hirschi claim that the principles of **self-control theory** can explain all varieties of criminal behavior and all the social and behavioral correlates of crime. That is, such widely disparate crimes as burglary, robbery, embezzlement, drug dealing, murder, rape, and insider trading all stem from a deficiency of self-control. Likewise, gender, racial, and ecological differences in crime rates can be explained by discrepancies in self-control. Put another way, the male crime rate is higher than the female crime rate because males have lower levels of self-control.

Unlike other theoretical models that explain only narrow segments of criminal behavior (such as theories of lower-class crime), Gottfredson and Hirschi argue that self-control applies equally to all crimes, ranging from murder to corporate theft. For example, Gottfredson and Hirschi maintain that white-collar crime rates remain low because people who lack self-control rarely attain the positions necessary to commit those crimes. However, the relatively few white-collar criminals lack self-control to the same degree and in the same manner as criminals such as rapists and burglars. Although the criminal activity of individuals with low self-control also declines as those individuals mature, they maintain an offense rate that remains consistently higher than those with strong self-control.

Supporting evidence for the GTC Following publication of *A General Theory of Crime*, researchers have attempted to test the validity of Gottfredson and Hirschi's theoretical views. One approach involved identifying indicators of impulsiveness and self-control to determine whether scales measuring these factors correlate with measures of criminal activity. A number of studies conducted both in the United States and abroad have successfully showed this type of association.[20] Some of the most

■ According to the general theory of crime, people who have low self-control are crime prone even if they are born into affluent families. Here, Malissa "Lisa" Warzeka (right) and Katie Marie Dunn, both 17, enter the courtroom during their trial in Houston. Warzeka and Dunn, both affluent suburban girls, were sentenced to seven-year prison terms for committing a string of convenience store robberies over the summer vacation. Is it possible that their crime spree was a function of their impulsive personalities and low self-control?

Exhibit 10.2   Empirical Evidence Supporting the General Theory of Crime

1. Novice offenders, lacking in self-control, commit a garden variety of criminal acts.
2. More mature and experienced criminals become more specialized in their choice of crime: for example, robbers, burglars, and drug dealers.
3. Male and female drunk drivers are impulsive individuals who manifest low self-control.
4. Repeat violent offenders are more impulsive than their less violent peers.
5. Incarcerated youth enjoy risk-taking behavior and hold values and attitudes that suggest impulsivity.
6. Kids who take drugs and commit crime are impulsive and enjoy engaging in risky behaviors.
7. Measures of self-control can predict deviant and antisocial behavior across age groups ranging from teens to adults age 50.
8. People who commit white-collar and workplace crime have lower levels of self-control than nonoffenders.
9. Gang members have lower levels of self-control than the general population; gang members report lower levels of parental management, a factor associated with lower self-control.
10. Low self-control shapes perceptions of criminal opportunity and consequently conditions the decision to commit crimes.
11. People who lack self-control expect to commit crime in the future.
12. Kids whose problems develop early in life are the most resistant to change in treatment and rehabilitation programs.
13. Gender differences in self-control are responsible for crime rate differences. Females who lack self-control are as crime prone as males with similar personalities.
14. Parents who manage their children's behavior increase their self-control, which helps reduce their delinquent activities.
15. Having parents (or stepparents) available to control behavior may reduce the opportunity to commit crime.
16. Victims have lower self-control than nonvictims. Impulsivity predicts both the likelihood that a person will engage in criminal behavior and the likelihood he or she will become a victim of crime.
17. There is little difference in the background characteristics of violent and nonviolent offenders. Because there is no tendency to specialize in crime, the root cause of crime (low self-control) may be the same for all offenders and offenses.

SOURCES: (1) Xiaogang Deng and Lening Zhang, "Correlates of Self-Control: An Empirical Test of Self-Control Theory," *Journal of Crime and Justice* 21 (1998): 89–103; (2) Alex Piquero, Raymond Paternoster, Paul Mazerolle, Robert Brame, and Charles Dean, "Onset Age and Offense Specialization," *Journal of Research in Crime and Delinquency* 36 (1999): 275–99; (3) Carl Keane, Paul Maxim, and James Teevan, "Drinking and Driving, Self-Control, and Gender: Testing a General Theory of Crime," *Journal of Research in Crime and Delinquency* 30 (1993): 30–46; (4) Judith DeJong, Matti Virkkunen, and Markku Linnoila, "Factors Associated with Recidivism in a Criminal Population," *Journal of Nervous and Mental Disease* 180 (1992): 543–50; (5) David Cantor, "Drug Involvement and Offending among Incarcerated Juveniles." Paper presented at the American Society of Criminology meeting, Boston, Mass., November 1995; (6) David Brownfield and Anne Marie Sorenson, "Self-Control and Juvenile Delinquency: Theoretical Issues and an Empirical Assessment of Selected Elements of a General Theory of Crime," *Deviant Behavior* 14 (1993): 243–64; (7) Velmer Burton, T. David Evans, Francis Cullen, Kathleen Olivares, and R. Gregory Dunaway, "Age, Self-Control, and Adults' Offending Behaviors: A Research Note Assessing a General Theory of Crime," *Journal of Criminal Justice* 27 (1999): 45–54; John Gibbs and Dennis Giever, "Self-Control and Its Manifestations among University Students: An Empirical Test of Gottfredson and Hirschi's General Theory," *Justice Quarterly* 12 (1995): 231–55; (8) Carey Herbert, "The Implications of Self-Control Theory for Workplace Offending." Paper presented at the American Society of Criminology Meeting, San Diego, Calif., 1997; (9) Dennis Giever, Dana Lynskey, and Danette Monnet, "Gottfredson and Hirschi's General Theory of Crime and Youth Gangs: An Empirical Test on a Sample of Middle School Youth." Paper presented at the American Society of Criminology Meeting, San Diego, Calif., 1997; (10) Douglas Longshore, Susan Turner, and Judith Stein, "Self-Control in a Criminal Sample: An Examination of Construct Validity," *Criminology* 34 (1996): 209–28; (11) Xiaogang Deng and Lening Zhang, "Correlates of Self-Control: An Empirical Test of Self-Control Theory"; (12) Linda Pagani, Richard Tremblay, Frank Vitaro, and Sophie Parent, "Does Preschool Help Prevent Delinquency in Boys with a History of Perinatal Complications?" *Criminology* 36 (1998): 245–68; (13) Velmer Burton, Francis Cullen, T. David Evans, Leanne Fiftal Alarid, and R. Gregory Dunaway, "Gender, Self-Control, and Crime," *Journal of Research in Crime and Delinquency* 35 (1998): 123–47; (14) Carter Hay, "Parenting, Self-Control, and Delinquency: A Test of Self-Control Theory," *Criminology* 39 (2001): 707–36; John Gibbs, Dennis Giever, and Jamie Martin, "Parental Management and Self-Control: An Empirical Test of Gottfredson and Hirschi's General Theory," *Journal of Research in Crime and Delinquency* 35 (1998): 40–70; (15) Vic Bumphus and James Anderson, "Family Structure and Race in a Sample of Offenders," *Journal of Criminal Justice* 27 (1999): 309–20; (16) Christopher Schreck, "Criminal Victimization and Low Self-Control: An Extension and Test of a General Theory of Crime," *Justice Quarterly* 16 (1999): 633–54; (17) Alex Piquero, "Frequency, Specialization and Violence in Offending Careers," *Journal of Research in Crime and Delinquency* 37 (2000): 392–418.

important findings are included in Exhibit 10.2. In an important recent study, Alexander Vazsonyi and his associates analyzed self-control and deviant behavior with samples drawn from four different countries (Hungary, Switzerland, the Netherlands, and the United States).[21] Their findings indicate that, as predicted by Gottfredson and Hirschi, low self-control is significantly related to antisocial behavior and that the association can be seen regardless of culture or national settings.

CONNECTIONS

The finding that victims are high in impulsivity supports both the lifestyle and victim precipitation view of victimization risk (Chapter 4). Impulsive people may choose a high-risk lifestyle with partying and drinking in public places, which puts them at risk to crime. It is also possible that people with low-self control will be confrontative and refuse to back away from a challenge, behaviors that may provoke a violent reaction. ■

Analyzing the general theory of crime Gottfredson and Hirschi's general theory answers many of the questions left unresolved by Hirschi's original single-factor control model. By integrating the concepts of socialization and criminality, Gottfredson and Hirschi help explain why some people who lack self-control can escape criminality, and conversely, why some people who have self-control might not escape criminality. People who are at risk because they have impulsive personalities may forgo criminal careers because there are no criminal opportunities that satisfy their impulsive needs; instead, they may find other outlets for their impulsive personalities. In contrast, if the opportunity is strong enough, even people with relatively strong self-control may be tempted to violate the law; the incentives to commit crime may overwhelm self-control.

Integrating criminal propensity and criminal opportunity can explain why some children enter into chronic offending while others living in similar environments are able to resist criminal activity. It can also help us understand why the corporate executive with a spotless record gets caught up in business fraud. Even a successful executive may find self-control inadequate if the potential for illegal gain is large. The driven executive, accustomed to both academic and financial success, may find that the fear of failure can overwhelm self-control. During tough economic times, the impulsive manager who fears dismissal may be tempted to circumvent the law to improve the bottom line.[22]

Although the general theory seems persuasive, several questions and criticisms remain unanswered. Among the most important are the following:

1. **Tautological.** Some critics argue that the theory is tautological or involves circular reasoning: How do we know when people are impulsive? When they commit crimes? Are all criminals impulsive? Of course, or else they would not have broken the law![23]

    Gottfredson and Hirschi counter by saying that impulsivity is not itself a propensity to commit crime but a condition that inhibits people from appreciating the long-term consequences of their behavior. Consequently, if given the opportunity, they are more likely to indulge in criminal acts than their nonimpulsive counterparts.[24] According to Gottfredson and Hirschi, impulsivity and criminality are neither identical nor equivalent. Some impulsive people may channel their reckless energies into noncriminal activity, such as trading on the commodities markets or real estate speculation, and make a legitimate fortune for their efforts.

2. **Personality disorder.** Saying someone lacks self-control implies a personality defect that makes him or her impulsive and rash. The view that criminals have a deviant personality is not new; psychologists have long sought evidence of a "criminal personality."[25] Yet the search for the criminal personality has proven elusive, and there is still no conclusive proof that criminals can be distinguished from noncriminals on the basis of personality alone.

3. **Ecological/individual differences.** The GTC also fails to address individual and ecological patterns in the crime rate. For example, if crime rates are higher in Los Angeles than in Albany, New York, can it be assumed that residents of Los Angeles are more impulsive than residents of Albany? There is little evidence of regional differences in impulsivity or self-control. Can these differences be explained solely by variation in criminal opportunity? Few researchers have tried to account for the influence of culture, ecology, economy, and so on.

    Gottfredson and Hirschi might counter that crime rate differences may reflect criminal opportunity: one area may have more effective law enforcement, more draconian laws, and higher levels of guardianship. In their view, opportunity is controlled by economy and culture.

4. **Racial and gender differences.** Although distinct gender differences in the crime rate exist, there is little evidence that males are more impulsive than females (although females and males differ in many other personality traits).[26] Similarly, Gottfredson and Hirschi explain racial differences in the crime rate as a failure of child-rearing practices in the African American community.[27] In so doing, they overlook issues of institutional racism, poverty, and relative deprivation, which have been shown to have a significant impact on crime rate differentials.

5. **Moral beliefs.** The general theory also ignores the moral concept of right and wrong, or "belief," which Hirschi considered a cornerstone in his earlier writings on the social bond.[28] Does this mean that learning and assimilating moral values has little effect on criminality? Belief may be the weakest of the bonds associated with crime, and the general theory reflects this relationship.[29]

6. **People change.** The general theory assumes that criminal propensity does not change; opportunities change. Is it possible that human personality and behavior patterns remain unaltered over the life course? For example, a number of research efforts show that the quality of peer relations either enhances or controls criminal behavior and that these influences vary over time.[30] As children mature, peer influence continues to grow.[31] Consequently, adolescents who spend less time with delinquent friends as they mature also reduce their criminal offending.[32] Research shows that kids who lack self-control also have trouble maintaining relationships with law-abiding peers. They may either choose (or be forced) to seek out friends who are similarly limited in their ability to maintain self-control. Establishing friendships with low-self-control

individuals appears to increase the likelihood of involvement in criminal behaviors.[33]

This finding contradicts the GTC, which suggests the influence of friends should be stable and unchanging and that a relationship established later in life (for example, making friends) should not influence criminal propensity. Research shows that other changing life circumstances, such as starting and leaving school, abusing substances, "getting straight," and starting or ending personal relationships, all influence the frequency of offending. For example, people who marry reduce their criminal activity whereas getting divorced elevates offending rates.[34]

Gottfredson and Hirschi assume that low self-control varies little with age and that low self-control is almost exclusively a product of early childhood rearing; but research shows that self-control may vary with age. As people mature, they may be better able to control their impulsive behavior.[35] These findings contradict the GTC, which assumes that levels of self-control and therefore criminal propensity are constant and independent of personal relationships.

To read a critique of the GTC, use InfoTrac College Edition to access this article: Charles R. Tittle and Harold G. Grasmick. Criminal behavior and age: a test of three provocative hypotheses. *Journal of Criminal Law and Criminology* Fall 1997 v88 n1 p309–42 ■

Although these research efforts claim to record change in behavior and personality over time, it is uncertain whether life changes affect the propensity to commit crime or merely the opportunity, as Gottfredson and Hirschi would suggest. For example, perhaps single and divorced men have more free time than married fathers who must remain at home and care for children. Also, men who spend less time with their friends as they mature may be spending more time with wives and children, who have a stabilizing influence on behavior. Increased levels of offending, then, might be more reflective of criminal opportunity than a change in criminal propensity brought on by the pacifying influence of marriage.

7. **Modest relationship.** Some research results support the proposition that self-control is a causal factor in criminal and other forms of deviant behavior but that the association is at best quite modest.[36] This would indicate that other forces influence criminal behavior and that low self-control alone cannot predict the onset of a criminal or deviant career. Perhaps antisocial behavior is best explained by a condition that either develops subsequent to the development of self-control or is independent of a person's level of impulsivity.[37] This alternative quality, which may be the real stable latent trait, is still unknown.

8. **Cross-cultural differences.** Evidence shows that criminals in some other countries do not lack self-control, indicating that the GTC may be culturally limited. For example, Otwin Marenin and Michael Resig actually found equal or higher levels of self-control in Nigerian criminals than in noncriminals.[38] Behavior that may be considered imprudent in one culture may be socially acceptable in another and therefore cannot be viewed as "lack of self-control."[39]

9. **Misreads human nature.** According to Francis Cullen, John Paul Wright, and Mitchell Chamlin, the GTC makes flawed assumptions about human character.[40] It assumes that people are essentially selfish, self-serving, and hedonistic and must therefore be controlled lest they gratify themselves at the expense of others. A more plausible view is that humans are inherently generous and kind; selfish hedonists may be a rare exception.

Although questions like these remain, the strength of the general theory lies in its scope and breadth; it attempts to explain all forms of crime and deviance, from lower-class gang delinquency to sexual harassment in the business community.[41] By integrating concepts of criminal choice, criminal opportunity, socialization, and personality, Gottfredson and Hirschi make a plausible argument that all deviant behaviors may originate at the same source. Continued efforts are needed to test the GTC and establish the validity of its core concepts. It remains one of the key developments of modern criminological theory.

Differential Coercion Theory

Gottfredson and Hirschi suggest that low-self control is a function of an impulsive personality. In *Crime and Coercion*, Mark Colvin puts a different slant on low self-control when he suggests that it is produced by experiences a person has with destructive social forces he calls *coercion*.[42]

There are actually two types of coercion: "interpersonal" and "impersonal." **Interpersonal coercion** is direct, involving the use or threat of force and intimidation from parents, peers and significant others. In contrast, **impersonal coercion** involves pressures beyond individual control, such as economic and social pressure caused by unemployment, poverty, or competition among businesses or other groups.

Colvin suggests that a person's ability to maintain self-control is a function of the amount, type, and consistency of coercion experienced as he or she goes through the life course. Prosocial behavior occurs when the amount of coercion a person is subjected to is minimal; low coercion produces low anger, high self-esteem (confidence), and a strong moral and social bond.

In contrast, some people find themselves experiencing a consistent amount of high coercive inputs, which produce high levels of self-directed anger, low self-esteem, a

Figure 10.3 Colvin's Theory of Differential Coercion

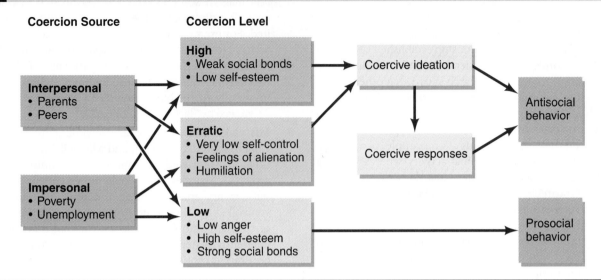

weak social bond, feelings of resignation, and declining self-control. These in turn produce a low probability of prosocial behavior and a predisposition to mental health problems, such as chronic depression. Even more debilitating, according to Colvin, is experiencing inconsistent or erratic episodes of coercive behavior, which produce high levels of anger, low self-esteem, a weak, alienated social bond, feelings of debasement and humiliation, and eventually low self-control. These social-psychological deficits create a strong predisposition for serious, chronic predatory street crime.

Coercion and criminal careers How do feelings of coercion translate into the development of a chronic criminal career? Colvin finds that chronic offenders grew up in homes where parents used erratic control and applied it in an erratic and inconsistent fashion. Moreover, coercion seems to be intergenerational, and parents who had coercive backgrounds tended to use coercive controls in their own families.

CONNECTIONS

Chapter 11 contains a discussion of the "cycle of violence" concept, which holds that abused kids grow up to become violent and abusive parents themselves, creating a consistent supply of violent youth. ∎

As the coerced child matures, his or her behavior is likely to elicit further coercive responses by family members, school officials, peers, employers, and criminal justice agencies. These new sources of coercion further increase social-psychological deficits and produce a mind-set that Colvin labels **coercive ideation,** in which the world is conceived as full of coercive forces that can only be overcome

through the application of equal or even greater coercive responses (Figure 10.3).

Colvin argues individuals who come from backgrounds of coercion, and whose self-control is therefore limited, are the ones most likely to get involved in coercive situations and to respond to them with violence and other predatory acts. They become caught up in a vicious coercive cycle, which they themselves help to create and maintain, which leads them back to crime. Breaking this coercive cycle is the key to treatment and rehabilitation.

Control Balance Theory

Another prominent latent trait theory, Charles Tittle's **control balance theory,** expands on the concept of personal control as a predisposing element for criminality.[43] Tittle also finds that the concept of control has two distinct elements: the amount of control one is subject to by others and the amount of control one can exercise over others. Conformity results when these two elements are in balance; control imbalances produce deviant and criminal behaviors.

To read a review of Tittle's book, use InfoTrac College Edition to access this article: G. David Curry. Control balance: toward a general theory of deviance. (book reviews) *Social Forces* March 1998 v76 n3 p1147(3) ∎

Tittle envisions control as a continuous variable (Figure 10.4) ranging from a control deficit, which occurs when a person's desires or impulses are limited by other people's ability to regulate or punish the person's behavior, to a control surplus, which occurs when the amount of control one can exercise over others is in excess of the ability others have to control or modify the person's behavior.

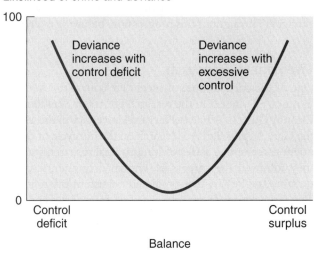

Figure 10.4 Tittle's Control Balance Theory

Likelihood of crime and deviance

Deviance increases with control deficit

Deviance increases with excessive control

Control deficit

Control surplus

Balance

Those people who sense a deficit of control turn to three types of behavior to restore balance: predation, defiance, or submission. **Predation** involves direct forms of physical violence, such as robbery, sexual assault, or other forms of physical violence. **Defiance** is designed to challenge control mechanisms but stop short of physical harm: for example, vandalism, curfew violations, and unconventional sex. **Submission** involves passive obedience to the demands of others, such as submitting to physical or sexual abuse without response.

An excess of control can also lead to deviance and crime, a contention in contradistinction to Hirschi and Gottfredson's view that only low control leads to crime. According to Tittle, those who have an excess of control engage in **exploitation,** which involves using others to commit crimes: for example, as contract killers or drug runners. They may also **plunder,** which involves using power without regard for others, such as committing a hate crime or polluting the environment. Finally, **decadence** involves spur of the moment, irrational acts such as child molesting.

Control imbalance represents a potential to commit crime and deviance. That is, possessing excessive or deficient control increases the likelihood that when presented with situational motivations a person will react in an antisocial manner. Deviant motivations emerge when a person suffering from control imbalance believes that engaging in some antisocial act will alter his or her control ratio in a favorable way. So, for example, when a person who has a surplus of control is insulted, he may tells his friends to attack the instigator; a student with a control deficit may vandalize a school after getting a bad grade on her report card.

Even when motivated to commit crime, a person may be constrained by his or her perceptions of external forces

of control. Even a highly motivated individual may be constrained if that person believes his or her deviant behavior is very serious and likely to be discovered by those who can exert corrosive control: for example, the police. Tittle also recognizes that opportunity shapes antisocial behavior: no matter how much the motivation or how little the restraint, the actual likelihood of a crime occurring depends on the opportunity.

Tittle's view, like that of Hirschi and Gottfredson, incorporates external or social concepts such as opportunity and restraint with internal or individual variables such as degree of control.

To read how control balance theory may be applied to explain the behavior of sex offenders, go to:
> **http://www.doc.state.ok.us/DOCS/OCJRC/**
> **OCJRC97-98/An%20Application%20of%20Control**
> **%20Balance%20Theory.pdf**

For an up-to-date list of Web links, go to
> **http://info.wadsworth.com/siegel** ■

■ The Life Course View

According to life course theory, even as toddlers, people begin relationships and behaviors that will determine their adult life course. At first they must learn to conform to social rules and function effectively in society. Later they are expected to begin to think about careers, leave their parental homes, find permanent relationships, and eventually marry and begin their own families.[44] These transitions are expected to take place in order, beginning with finishing school, then entering the workforce, getting married, and having children.

Some individuals, however, are incapable of maturing in a reasonable and timely fashion because of family, environmental, or personal problems. In some cases, transitions can occur too early—for example, when adolescents engage in precocious sex. In other cases, transitions may occur too late, such as when a student fails to graduate on time because of bad grades or too many incompletes. Sometimes disruption of one trajectory can harm another. A teenager who becomes pregnant may find that her educational and career development is disrupted. Because these theories focus on the associations between life events and deviant behaviors, they are sometimes referred to as life course theories.

Disruptions in life's major transitions can be destructive and ultimately can promote criminality. Those who are already at risk because of socioeconomic problems or family dysfunction are the most susceptible to these awkward transitions. The cumulative impact of these disruptions sustains criminality from childhood into adulthood.

Because a transition from one stage of life to another can be a bumpy ride, the propensity to commit crimes is neither stable nor constant: it is a developmental process. A positive life experience may help some criminals desist from crime for a while, whereas a negative one may cause them to resume their activities. Criminal careers are said to be developmental because people are influenced by the behavior of those around them and, in turn, influence others' behavior. For example, a youth's antisocial behavior may turn his more conventional friends against him; their rejection solidifies and escalates his antisocial behavior.[45]

CONNECTIONS

Life course theories mesh with labeling theory, which is discussed in Chapter 8. However, labeling theory ignores the effect of criminal behavior on those assigning the labels and instead concentrates on the effect of stigma on the development of deviant identities. Life course theories recognize that the relationship may be reciprocal. ■

Life course theories also recognize that as people mature the factors that influence their behavior change.[46] At first, family relations may be most influential; in later adolescence, school and peer relations predominate; in adulthood, vocational achievement and marital relations may be the most critical influences. For example, some antisocial children who are in trouble throughout their adolescence may manage to find stable work and maintain intact marriages as adults; these life events help them desist from crime. In contrast, less fortunate adolescents who develop arrest records and get involved with the wrong crowd may find themselves limited to menial jobs and at risk for criminal careers.

CONNECTIONS

Social process theories lay the foundation for assuming that peer, family, educational, and other interactions, which vary over the life course, influence behaviors. See the first few sections of Chapter 8 for a review of these issues. As you may recall from Chapter 3, a great deal of research has been conducted on the relationship of age and crime and the activities of chronic offenders. This scholarship has prompted interest in the life cycle of crime. ■

Life course theories are inherently multidimensional, suggesting that criminality has multiple roots, including maladaptive personality traits, educational failure, and family relations. Criminality, according to this view, cannot be attributed to a single cause, nor does it represent a single underlying tendency.[47] People are influenced by different factors as they mature. Consequently, a factor that may have an important influence at one stage of life (such as delinquent peers) may have little influence later on.[48]

Life course theorists conclude that multiple social, personal, and economic factors can influence criminality,

and as these factors change over time, so does criminal involvement.[49] As people make important life transitions—from child to adolescent, from adolescent to adult, from unwed to married—the nature of social interactions changes. Throughout this progression, behavior is altered.

The Glueck Research

One of the cornerstones of recent life course theories lies in renewed interest in the research efforts of Sheldon and Eleanor Glueck. While at Harvard University in the 1930s, the Gluecks popularized research on the life cycle of delinquent careers. In a series of longitudinal research studies, they followed the careers of known delinquents to determine the factors that predicted persistent offending.[50] The Gluecks made extensive use of interviews and records in their elaborate comparisons of delinquents and nondelinquents.[51]

The Gluecks' research focused on early onset of delinquency as a harbinger of a criminal career: "the deeper the roots of childhood maladjustment, the smaller the chance of adult adjustment."[52] They also noted the stability of offending careers: children who are antisocial early in life are the most likely to continue their offending careers into adulthood.

The Gluecks identified a number of personal and social factors related to persistent offending, the most important of which was family relations. This factor was considered in terms of quality of discipline and emotional ties with parents. The adolescent raised in a large, single-parent family of limited economic means and educational achievement was the most vulnerable to delinquency.

The Gluecks did not restrict their analysis to social variables. When they measured such biological and psychological traits as body type, intelligence, and personality, they found that physical and mental factors also played a role in determining behavior. Children with low intelligence, who had a background of mental disease, and who had a powerful (mesomorph) physique were the most likely to become persistent offenders.

The Gluecks' research was virtually ignored for nearly 30 years as the study of crime and delinquency shifted almost exclusively to social and social-psychological factors (such as poverty, neighborhood deterioration, and socialization) that formed the nucleus of structural and process theories. The Gluecks' methodology and their integration of biological, psychological, and social factors was heavily criticized by mainstream sociologists who dominated the field. For many years their work was ignored in criminology texts and overlooked in the academic curriculum.

Life Course Concepts

During the 1990s, the Glueck legacy was rediscovered in a series of papers by criminologists Robert Sampson and John Laub. These scholars argued that the Gluecks' careful empirical measurements, which had been cast aside by the criminological community, were actually an ideal platform for studying criminal careers.[53] Sampson and Laub reanalyzed the Glueck data and used them in a series of articles that have gained wide readership. Their work will be discussed in greater detail later in the chapter.

A 1990 review paper (revised in 1998) by Rolf Loeber and Marc LeBlanc was another important event in the development of life course theory.[54] In their landmark works, Loeber and LeBlanc proposed that criminologists should devote time and effort to understanding some basic questions about the evolution of criminal careers: Why do people begin committing antisocial acts? Why do some stop while others continue? Why do some escalate the severity of their criminality (that is, go from shoplifting to drug dealing to armed robbery) while others deescalate and commit less serious crimes as they mature? If some terminate their criminal activity, what, if anything, causes them to begin again? Why do some criminals specialize in certain types of crime, whereas others are generalists engaging in a variety of antisocial behaviors? According to Loeber and LeBlanc's developmental view, criminologists must pay attention to how a criminal career unfolds.

A number of key research efforts have also found that crimogenic influences change and develop. In their studies on delinquency prevention, Gerald Patterson and his colleagues at the Oregon Social Learning Center found that poor parental discipline and monitoring was a key to the onset of criminality in early childhood. Children whose socialization is ineffective because of improper, maladaptive parenting later build on this improper interactional style and engage in behavior that leads to both peer rejection and academic failure.[55] They then turn to deviant peers, from whom they learn new forms of antisocial behavior. Patterson and his colleagues have found that early childhood family conflicts and lack of a strong bond with parents open the door for social conflict in later adolescence.[56] Consequently, in middle childhood, social rejection by conventional peers and academic failure sustains antisocial behavior. In later adolescence, commitment to a deviant peer group creates a training ground for crime.[57] Although the onset of a criminal career is a function of poor parenting skills, its maintenance and support are connected to social relations that emerge later in life.[58]

From these and similar efforts, a view of crime has emerged that incorporates personal change and growth. The factors that produce crime and delinquency at one point in the life cycle may not be relevant at another; as people mature, the social, physical, and environmental influences on their behavior are transformed. Although latent traits may be important, they alone are not enough to control human behavior. People may show a propensity to offend early in their lives, but the nature and frequency of their activities are affected by outside forces beyond their control, such as the likelihood of getting arrested and punished for crime.[59]

The next sections review some of the more important concepts associated with the developmental perspective and discuss some prominent life course theories.

Problem Behavior Syndrome

Most criminological theories portray crime as resulting from, rather than causing, social problems. For example, learning theorists view a troubled home life and deviant friends as precursors of criminality; structural theorists maintain that acquiring deviant cultural values leads to criminality. In contrast, the developmental view is that criminality may best be understood as one of many social problems faced by at-risk youth. These theorists believe criminality may be part of a **problem behavior syndrome (PBS),** a group of antisocial behaviors that cluster together and typically involve family dysfunction, sexual and physical abuse, substance abuse, smoking, precocious sexuality and early pregnancy, educational underachievement, suicide attempts, sensation seeking, and unemployment.[60] People who suffer from one of these conditions typically exhibit many symptoms of the rest.[61] All varieties of criminal behavior, including violence, theft, and drug offenses, may be part of a generalized PBS, indicating that all forms of antisocial behavior have similar developmental patterns (see Exhibit 10.3).[62]

Those who suffer PBS are prone to more difficulties than the general population.[63] They find themselves with

Exhibit 10.3   Problem Behaviors

Social

- Family dysfunction
- Unemployment
- Educational underachievement
- School misconduct

Personal

- Substance abuse
- Suicide attempts
- Early sexuality and parenthood
- Sensation seeking
- Criminal behavior
- Accident-proneness
- Medical problems
- Mental disease
- Anxiety
- Eating disorders (bulimia, anorexia)

Environmental

- High-crime area
- Disorganized area
- Racism
- Exposure to poverty

■ Adolescents with multiple problems present a significant challenge for the justice system. What can be done to help them avoid more serious antisocial behavior? Some jurisdictions have developed special programs for multiproblem offenders. Here, Joey Anderson, 18, thanks his mother, Mary Sanchez, for supporting him during the juvenile DWI/Drug Court program in Albuquerque. Anderson was placed under the no-nonsense supervision of the Drug Court team led by Children's Court Judge Geraldine Rivera. Teens qualifying for this program have had several run-ins with the law.

a range of personal dilemmas ranging from drug abuse to being accident prone, to requiring more health care and hospitalization, to becoming teenage parents. PBS has been linked to personality problems (such as rebelliousness and low ego), family problems (such as intrafamily conflict and parental mental disorder), and educational failure.[64] Multisite research has shown that PBS is not unique to any single area of the country and that children who suffer PBS, including drug use, delinquency, and precocious sexuality, display symptoms at an early age.[65]

Many examples support the existence of PBS.[66] A survey of Minnesota students in grades 6, 9, and 12 shows that children who experience physical and sexual abuse at the hands of parents or other adults are also likely to have eating disorders (binge eating, purging, or anorexia), increased levels of cigarette smoking, alcohol consumption, stress, anxiety, hard drug use, and suicidal thoughts; they are raised in families with parents who are addicted to drugs and alcohol.[67] Other research efforts have linked violence to a variety of family and environmental problems that seem to cluster together: low income, single parenthood, residence in isolated urban areas, lack of family support or resources, racism, and prolonged exposure to poverty.[68] Studies of inmates show that many had mental health problems and were also undereducated, unemployed, and have histories of alcohol, marijuana, cocaine, and heroin abuse.[69]

In one important research effort that shows the nature of PBS, Helene Raskin White studied a sample of 400 youths measured repeatedly over a six-year cycle and found that behaviors that clustered together included delinquency, substance abuse, school misconduct and underachievement, precocious sexual behavior, violence, suicide, and mental health problems.[70] White found problem behaviors to be stable: subjects who experienced multiple problems at age 15 continued to experience them at age 21. In a subsequent analysis of adolescent misbehavior conducted with Erich Labouvie, White found that PBS might involve one of several clusters of behavior, including drug specialists, crime specialists, and generalists who engage in both delinquency and drug abuse. Generalists are the most likely to suffer PBS, displaying higher levels of psychological problems, lack of control, and lower emotional stability.[71]

Problem behaviors, including violence, drug abuse, and theft, may cluster in a number of different ways, affecting people as they mature from adolescence into adulthood.[72] The interconnection of problem behaviors increases the risk of teenage pregnancy, AIDS, and other sources of social distress that require a combination of behaviors (sex, drug use, violence). For example, gang members, who suffer many forms of social problems, have also been found to exhibit a garden variety of ills compatible with PBS, including living in a single-parent home, suffering poor school achievement, and having siblings who engaged in antisocial behaviors.[73] The fact that youths involved in crime have significantly higher mortality rates than the general population is perhaps the most extreme product of PBS.[74]

 What are the problems that plague troubled youth, and how are they linked? Use InfoTrac College Edition to access this article for answers to these questions: Gabriel Kuperminca and Joseph Allen. Social orientation: problem behavior and motivations toward interpersonal problem solving among high-risk adolescents. *Journal of Youth and Adolescence* Oct 2001 v30 i5 p597 ■

Pathways to Crime

Some life course theorists recognize that career criminals may travel more than a single road: some may specialize in violence and extortion; some may be involved in theft and fraud; others may engage in a variety of criminal acts. Some offenders may begin their careers early in life, whereas others are late bloomers who begin committing crime when most people desist. Are there different pathways to crime? Using data from a longitudinal cohort study conducted in Pittsburgh, Rolf Loeber and his associates have identified three distinct paths to a criminal career (see Figure 10.5):[75]

1. The **authority conflict pathway** begins at an early age with stubborn behavior. This leads to defiance (doing

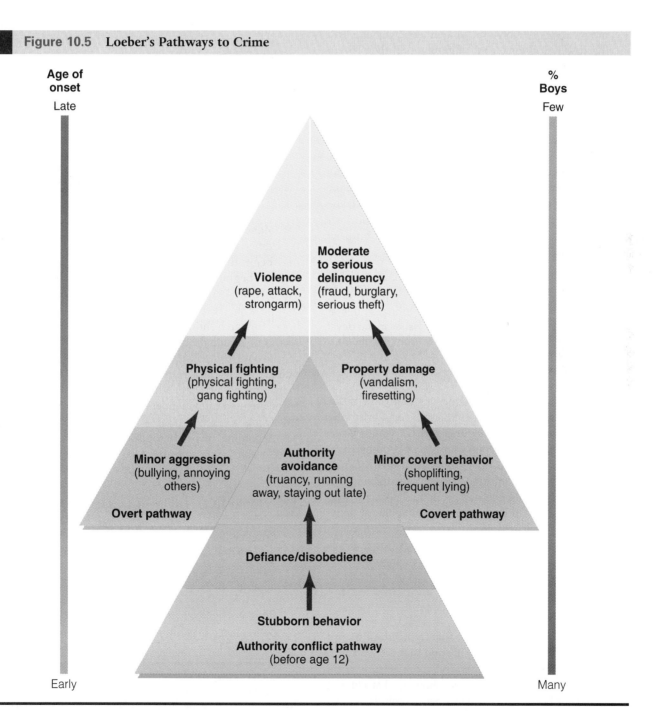

Figure 10.5 Loeber's Pathways to Crime

Age of onset — Late / Early

% Boys — Few / Many

Violence (rape, attack, strongarm)

Moderate to serious delinquency (fraud, burglary, serious theft)

Physical fighting (physical fighting, gang fighting)

Property damage (vandalism, firesetting)

Minor aggression (bullying, annoying others)

Authority avoidance (truancy, running away, staying out late)

Minor covert behavior (shoplifting, frequent lying)

Overt pathway

Covert pathway

Defiance/disobedience

Stubborn behavior

Authority conflict pathway (before age 12)

SOURCE: "Serious and Violent Juvenile Offenders," *Juvenile Justice Bulletin,* May 1998.

things one's own way, disobedience) and then to authority avoidance (staying out late, truancy, running away).

2. The **covert pathway** begins with minor, underhanded behavior (lying, shoplifting) that leads to property damage (setting nuisance fires, damaging property). This behavior eventually escalates to more serious forms of criminality, ranging from joyriding, pocket picking, larceny, and fencing to passing bad checks, using stolen credit cards, stealing cars, dealing drugs, and breaking and entering.

3. The **overt pathway** escalates to aggressive acts beginning with aggression (annoying others, bullying), leading to physical (and gang) fighting, and then to violence (attacking someone, forced theft).

The Loeber research indicates that each of these paths may lead to a sustained deviant career. Some people enter two and even three paths simultaneously: they are stubborn, lie to teachers and parents, are bullies, and commit petty thefts. These adolescents are the most likely to become persistent offenders as they mature. Although some persistent offenders may specialize in one type of behavior, others engage in varied criminal acts and antisocial behaviors as they mature. For example, they cheat on tests, bully kids in the schoolyard, take drugs, commit burglary, steal a car, and then shoplift from a store.

To read an article in which the pathways model is explained, use InfoTrac College Edition to access this article: Rolf Loeber and Dale Hay. Key issues in the development of aggression and violence from childhood to early adulthood. *Annual Review of Psychology* 1997 v48 p371(40) ■

Some recent support for Loeber's pathways model was put forward by Sheila Royo Maxwell and Christopher Maxwell in their study of the career paths of young female offenders. One distinct group consisted of women who used drugs and engaged in a variety of illegal activities, including theft and prostitution, to generate capital for further drug purchases. The second group specialized in drug-selling and avoided prostitution and other illegal activities.[76] The Maxwell research suggests the existence of a multitude of criminal career subgroupings (for example, prostitutes, drug dealers) that each have their own distinctive career paths.

Age of Onset

Most life course theories assume that the seeds of a criminal career are planted early in life and that early onset of deviance strongly predicts later and more serious criminality.[77] Research supports this by showing that children who will later become delinquents begin their deviant careers at a very early (preschool) age and that the earlier the

onset of criminality the more frequent, varied, and sustained the criminal career.[78] A thorough review of this issue by Rolf Loeber and David Farrington finds that the youngest criminals typically have a long history of disruptive behavior beginning in early childhood with truancy, cruelty to animals, lying, and theft.[79] Though most commit less serious forms of delinquency, since 1980 more than 600 murders have been committed by youngsters aged 12 or younger; 12 to 14 percent of all juveniles arrested for rape are between the ages of 7 and 12.

To learn more about the relationship between crime and age, use these terms as subject guides on InfoTrac College Edition. ■

Age of onset is associated with another key life course concept, the **continuity of crime:** children who are repeatedly in trouble during early adolescence will continue to be antisocial throughout their life course.[80] Early criminal activity is likely to be sustained because these offenders seem to lack the social survival skills necessary to find work or to develop the interpersonal relationships needed to allow them to drop out of crime.[81]

"Adolescent-limiteds" and "life course persisters"

In addition to taking different paths to criminality, people may begin their journey at different times: some are precocious, beginning their criminal careers early; others stay out of trouble until their teenage years. Some offenders may peak at an early age, whereas others persist into adulthood. Research shows that there are a number of different classes of criminal careers that seem to reflect changes in the life course (see Table 10.1). Some youth maximize their offending rates at a relatively early age and then reduce their criminal activity; others persist into their twenties. Some are high-rate offenders, whereas others offend at relatively low rates.[82]

According to psychologist Terrie Moffitt, the prevalence and frequency of antisocial behavior peak in adoles-

Table 10.1 Different Classes of Criminals

Criminal Classes	Onset	Offending Rate
Adolescent peaked	Early	High
Delinquency maximized ages 15–18	Late	Low
Chronic offender	Early	High
Delinquency maximized ages 17–21	Late	Low

SOURCE: Any D'Unger, Kenneth Land, Patricia McCall, and Daniel Nagin, "How Many Latent Classes of Delinquent/Criminal Careers? Results from Mixed Poisson Regression Analysis," *American Journal of Sociology* 103 (1998): 1593–130.

cence and then diminish for most offenders; she calls those who follow this path **adolescent-limited offenders.** These kids may be considered "typical teenagers" who get into minor scrapes and engage in what might be considered rebellious teenage behavior with their friends.[83]

CONNECTIONS

Moffitt views adolescent-limited kids as following the social learning perspective discussed in Chapter 8. Kids learn that violating the norms of society are acts of independence, and some, such as smoking and drinking, may be efforts at gaining a pseudo-maturity. These acts are neither serious nor violent. ■

Moffitt also finds that there is a small group of **life course persisters** who begin their offending career at a very early age and continue to offend well into adulthood.[84] Life course persisters combine family dysfunction with severe neurological problems that predispose them to antisocial behavior patterns. These afflictions can be the result of maternal drug abuse, poor nutrition, or exposure to toxic agents such as lead. Life course persisters may have lower verbal ability, which inhibits reasoning skills, learning ability, and school achievement. Early starters, those who begin offending before age 14, experience (1) poor parenting, which leads them into (2) deviant behaviors and then (3) involvement with delinquent groups. There may be more than one subset of life course persisters. Some begin acting out during the preschool years; these youth show signs of ADHD and do not outgrow the levels of disobedience typical of the preschool years. The second group shows few symptoms of ADHD but, from an early age, is aggressive, underhanded, and in constant opposition to authority.[85]

As they reach their midteens, adolescent-limited delinquents begin to mimic the antisocial behavior of more troubled teens, only to reduce the frequency of their offending as they mature to around age 18.[86] This group tends to focus on a specific type of misbehavior such as drug abuse.

Terrie Moffitt has written on a number of topics involving psychological issues and criminal involvement. Use her name as a subject guide on InfoTrac College Edition and read some of her research papers. ■

Supporting research Research has supported Moffitt's model, showing that early-onset delinquents are both more prevalent and more generalized in their delinquent activity and that the patterns predicted by Moffitt can be found in samples of both male and female delinquents.[87] Early-onset delinquents seem to be strongly influenced by individual-level traits such as low verbal ability, hyperactivity, and negative or impulsive personality; community-level factors such as poverty and instability seem to have

little effect on their behavior.[88] In contrast, late-onset adolescent delinquents are more strongly influenced by their delinquent peers and by conflict with parents. The path to their misbehavior may be as follows: (1) poor parenting leads to (2) identification with delinquent groups and then to (3) deviant involvement.[89]

Early-onset delinquents also appear to be more violent than their older peers, who are likely to be involved in nonviolent crimes such as theft.[90] They also experience pseudo-maturity, experimenting at an early age with substance abuse and sexuality.[91]

Research by criminologist Charles Dean and his associates found that, surprisingly, criminal punishment seems to have a greater deterrent effect on early rather than late starters.[92] It is possible that early starters learn from their punishment experiences and become more cunning criminals, increasing their offending rates while avoiding detection. Because they are more sensitive to the punishment associated with capture, they may be more motivated to find ways to avoid getting caught!

The discovery that people begin their criminal careers at different ages and follow different offense paths and trajectories provides strong support for the life course view. If all criminals possessed a singular latent trait that made them crime prone, it would be unlikely that these variations in criminal careers would be observed. It is difficult to explain such concepts as late-onset and adolescent-limited behavior from the perspective of latent trait theory. The Race, Culture, Gender, and Criminology feature titled "Violent Female Criminals" explores this issue further.

■ Theories of the Criminal Life Course

An ongoing effort has been made to track persistent offenders over their life course.[93] The early data seem to support what is already known about delinquent and criminal career patterns: early onset predicts more lasting crime; there is continuity in crime (juvenile offenders are likely to become adult criminals); and chronic offenders commit a significant portion of all crimes.[94] Based on these findings, a number of systematic theories that account for the onset, continuance, and desistance from crime have been formulated. The following sections discuss a number of life course theories in some detail.

The Social Development Model

In their **social development model (SDM),** Joseph Weis, Richard Catalano, J. David Hawkins, and their associates have attempted to integrate social control, social learning, and structural models.[95] According to the SDM, a number of community-level risk factors make some people susceptible to developing antisocial behaviors. For example, the quality of the community organization influences the

Violent Female Criminals

Although considerable research is now being devoted to gender differences in the crime rate, little has been done to chart the life course of one subset of this group: violent female street criminals. To correct this oversight, two studies—one by Deborah Baskin and Ira Sommers and the other by Henry Brownstein, Barry Spunt, Susan Crimmins, and Sandra Langley—have analyzed data based on samples of violent female felons in New York. These data provide considerable insight into the formation and maintenance of a criminal career.

Baskin and Sommers Study

Criminal justice scholars Baskin and Sommers used Census data, analyses of political and economic changes, and direct observations and interviews to examine the career patterns of violent female offenders. They also looked at the relationships these women have with their family members and their communities. They provide a detailed account of the criminal careers of 170 women who committed violent street crimes in New York City, describing their entry into criminal activities and their lives as persistent street criminals.

Baskin and Sommers found that about 60 percent of violent female offenders began their criminal careers at a very young age. About half reported regular fighting as early as 10 years old, and about 40 percent reported that they regularly left home carrying a weapon. In contrast, the others reported that they did not start fighting until much later, until they had left school. Because of the clear differential between when these females began their criminal careers, Baskin and Sommers independently analyzed the early- and late-onset offenders.

The women in both groups suffered from severe social and emotional problems. Most were raised in single-parent families and received little parental supervision. Both groups experienced physical and sexual abuse by a parent or guardian and were likely to have witnessed abuse between their guardians. Almost half were raised in households that relied on welfare. More than half had a parent who either was a substance abuser or had been incarcerated sometime during their childhood.

Women in the early-onset group could be distinguished by the severity of their childhood problems. They were most likely to reside in areas with high concentrations of poverty and to have family histories of psychiatric problems requiring hospitalization. They were more likely to be truant, leave school early, and associate with delinquent peers while in school. They also were more likely to be placed in a juvenile detention center.

The major distinction between the groups, however, could be found in the scale and direction of their offending careers. Although both groups used drugs, early-onset women began abusing substances two years ahead of the late-onset group. The women in the early-onset group were involved in a variety of crimes, including serious robberies, assaults, and burglaries, even before they became involved with drugs. In contrast, the women in the late-onset group were involved in mostly nonviolent crimes, such as shoplifting and prostitution, until they began taking drugs. The violent offending of the latter group, then, can be attributed to their drug use. In contrast, the violent behavior of the early-onset women was part of a generalized PBS.

Brownstein Study

Henry Brownstein and his associates interviewed 215 women convicted of murder. Most of these women told a familiar story: the most violent of these women had histories of juvenile violence, drug abuse, and personal victimization. Out of a sample of 215, they found that

65 percent had participated in some other violent activity,

64 percent claimed to have seriously harmed someone when they were growing up,

58 percent had been the victim of serious physical harm, and

49 percent had been sexually abused.

These women had a long-term commitment to crime beginning in early childhood, which continued through adulthood and culminated in their use of deadly violence. Brownstein also focused on the behavior of 19 women who killed in the context of dealing drugs. Some of these acts were motivated by economic interests, whereas others were motivated by a relationship to a man (either killing on behalf of a man who controlled them or killing a man who they feared would cause them injury).

The researchers found that there are, in fact, different pathways to crime that involve both environmental and serendipitous life circumstances. These conclusions support a developmental view and repudiate the latent trait approach.

Critical Thinking Questions

1. Crime data tell us that women are significantly less violent than men. Are the pathways to chronic offending different among violent females than among males?
2. Do you believe that some conditions present at birth can control future criminal behavior?

InfoTrac College Edition Research

There is a growing body of literature on the violent behavior of female offenders. To read more about this phenomenon, access these articles:

Denise Hien and Nina Hien. Women, violence with intimates, and substance abuse: relevant theory, empirical findings, and recommendations for future research. *American Journal of Drug and Alcohol Abuse* August 1998 v24 n3 p419

Karen Joe Laidler and Geoffrey Hunt. Violence and social organization in female gangs. *Social Justice* Winter 1997 v24 n4 p148

SOURCES: Deborah Baskin and Ira Sommers, *Casualties of Community Disorder: Women's Careers in Violent Crime* (Boulder, Colo.: Westview Press, 1998); Deborah Baskin and Ira Sommers, "Females' Initiation into Violent Street Crime," *Justice Quarterly* 10 (1993): 559–81; Ira Sommers, Deborah Baskin, and Jeffrey Fagan, *Workin' Hard for the Money: The Social and Economic Lives of Women Drug Sellers* (Hauppauge, N.Y.: Nova Science Publishers, 2000); Henry Brownstein, Barry Spunt, Susan Crimmins, and Sandra Langley, "Women Who Kill in Drug Market Situations," *Justice Quarterly* 12 (1995): 473–98.

AP/Wide World Photos

■ Gary Luster, an heir to the Max Factor cosmetics empire, is shown here on June 5, 2001, leaving a California courtroom where he was charged with 50 criminal counts including the use of a date rape drug; he faces a possibility of a 1,000-year prison sentence. According to the social development model, parental attachment affects a child's behavior for life, determining both school experiences and personal beliefs and values. Is it possible that a man such as Luster failed to achieve parental attachments? If not, what could have caused his serial offending?

child's risk of developing antisocial behavior. Social control is less effective when the frontline socializing institutions are weak in disorganized areas. In a low-income, disorganized community, for example, families are under great stress; educational facilities are inadequate; there are fewer material goods; and respect for the law is weak. Because crime rates are high, there are more opportunities to violate the law, which puts even greater strain on the agencies of social control.

As children mature within their environment, elements of socialization control their developmental process. Preexisting risk factors are either reinforced or neutralized by socialization. Children are socialized and develop bonds to their families through four distinct interactions and processes:

• Perceived opportunities for involvement in activities and interactions with others

• The degree of involvement and interaction with parents

• The children's ability to participate in these interactions

• The reinforcement (such as feedback) children receive for their participation

To control the risk of antisocial behavior, a child must maintain **prosocial bonds.** These are developed within the context of family life, which not only provides prosocial opportunities but reinforces them by consistent, positive feedback. Parental attachment affects a child's behavior for life, determining both school experiences and personal beliefs and values. For those with strong family relationships, school will be a meaningful experience marked by academic success and commitment to education. Youth in this category are likely to develop conventional beliefs and values, become committed to conventional activities, and form attachments to conventional others.

Children's antisocial behavior also depends on the quality of their attachments to parents and other influential relations. If they remain unattached or develop attachments to deviant others, their behavior may become deviant as well. Unlike Hirschi's control theory, which assumes that all attachments are beneficial, the SDM suggests that interaction with antisocial peers and adults promotes participation in delinquency and substance abuse.[96]

As Figure 10.6 shows, the SDM differs from Hirschi's vision of how the social bond develops. Whereas Hirschi maintains that early family attachments are the key determinant of future behavior, the SDM suggests that later involvement in prosocial or antisocial behavior determines the quality of attachments. Adolescents who perceive opportunities and rewards for antisocial behavior will form deep attachments to deviant peers and will become committed to a delinquent way of life. In contrast, those who perceive opportunities for prosocial behavior will take a different path, getting involved in conventional activities and forming attachments to others who share their conventional lifestyle.

The SDM holds that commitment and attachment to conventional institutions, activities, and beliefs insulate youths from the crimogenic influences of their environment. The prosocial path inhibits deviance by strengthening bonds to prosocial others and activities. Without the proper level of bonding, adolescents can succumb to the influence of deviant others.

Many of the core assumptions of the SDM have been tested and verified empirically.[97] The path predicted by the SDM seems an accurate picture of the onset and continuation of violent and antisocial behavior both for early-onset offenders who engage in antisocial acts in childhood and later-onset offenders who begin offending in their teens.[98]

CONNECTIONS

This finding contradicts the work of Terrie Moffitt, discussed previously, which indicates that the background and characteristics of early starters (life course persisters) is quite different from kids who begin offending later in their development (adolescent-limited). According to SDM research, the differences between early and late starters is less than anticipated by Moffitt. ■

Figure 10.6   The Social Development Model of Antisocial Behavior

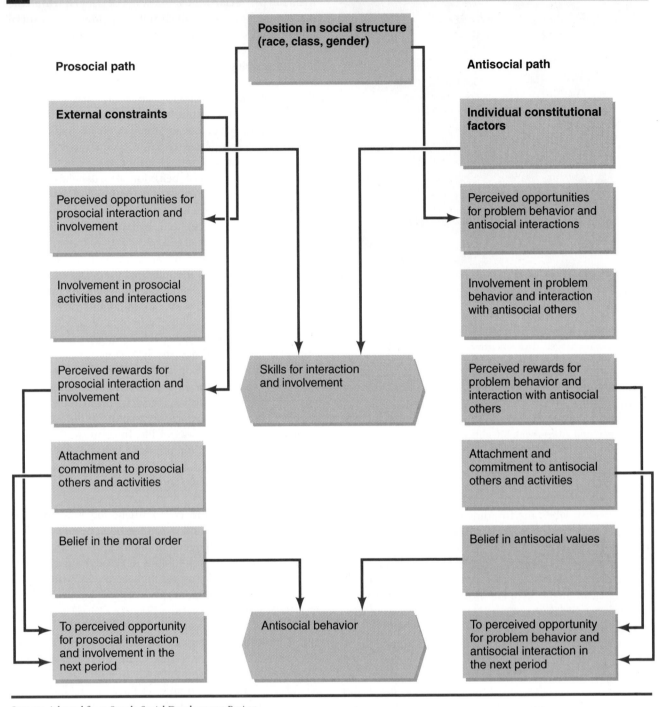

Position in social structure (race, class, gender)

Prosocial path

Antisocial path

External constraints

Individual constitutional factors

Perceived opportunities for prosocial interaction and involvement

Perceived opportunities for problem behavior and antisocial interactions

Involvement in prosocial activities and interactions

Involvement in problem behavior and interaction with antisocial others

Perceived rewards for prosocial interaction and involvement

Skills for interaction and involvement

Perceived rewards for problem behavior and interaction with antisocial others

Attachment and commitment to prosocial others and activities

Attachment and commitment to antisocial others and activities

Belief in the moral order

Belief in antisocial values

To perceived opportunity for prosocial interaction and involvement in the next period

Antisocial behavior

To perceived opportunity for problem behavior and antisocial interaction in the next period

SOURCE: Adapted from Seattle Social Development Project.

Kids who learn deviant attitudes and behaviors and who also have weak ties to conventional institutions are the most likely to engage in criminal behaviors. Kids who maintain antisocial opportunities and involvement and who also perceive that it is easy to get away with antisocial behaviors and who see them as "cool" and rewarding are also the ones most likely to engage in antisocial activities.[99]

The SDM has also guided treatment interventions, which promote the development of strong family and school bonds and help kids use these bonds to resist any opportunity or motivation to take drugs and engage in delinquent behaviors. Preliminary evaluations of one program, the Seattle Social Development Project, indicate that SDM-based interventions can help reduce delinquency and drug abuse.[100]

To read more about the Social Development Project, go to:

http://ojjdp.ncjrs.org/jjbulletin/9810_2/g1.html

For an up-to-date list of Web links, go to

http://info.wadsworth.com/siegel ■

Farrington's Theory of Delinquent Development

One of the most important longitudinal studies tracking persistent offenders is the Cambridge Study in Delinquent Development, which has followed the offending careers of 411 London boys born in 1953.[101] This cohort study, directed since 1982 by David Farrington, has made a serious attempt to isolate the factors that predict lifelong continuity of criminal behavior. The study uses self-report data as well as in-depth interviews and psychological testing. The boys have been interviewed eight times over 24 years, beginning at age 8 and continuing to age 32.[102]

The results of the Cambridge study show that many of the same patterns found in the United States are repeated in a cross-national sample: the existence of chronic offenders, the continuity of offending, and early onset of criminal activity. Each of these patterns leads to persistent criminality.

Farrington found that traits present in persistent offenders can be observed as early as age 8. The chronic criminal, typically a male, begins as a property offender; is born into a low-income, large family headed by parents who have criminal records; and has delinquent older siblings. The future criminal receives poor parental supervision, including the use of harsh or erratic punishment and child-rearing techniques; his parents are likely to divorce or separate. The chronic offender tends to associate with friends who are also future criminals. By age 8, he exhibits antisocial behavior, including dishonesty and aggressiveness; at school he tends to have low educational achievement and is restless, troublesome, hyperactive, impulsive, and often truant. After leaving school at age 18, the persistent criminal tends to take a relatively well-paid but low-status job and is likely to have an erratic work history and periods of unemployment.

Deviant behavior tends to be versatile rather than specialized. That is, the typical offender not only commits property offenses, such as theft and burglary, but also engages in violence, vandalism, drug use, excessive drinking, drunk driving, smoking, reckless driving, and sexual promiscuity—evidence of a generalized problem behavior syndrome. Chronic offenders are more likely to live away from home and have conflicts with their parents. They wear tattoos, go out most evenings, and enjoy hanging out with groups of their friends. They are much more likely than nonoffenders to get involved in fights, to carry weapons, and to use them in violent encounters. The frequency of offending reaches a peak in the teenage years (about 17 or 18) and then declines in the twenties, when the offenders marry or live with women.

By the time he reaches his thirties, the former delinquent is likely to be separated or divorced from his wife and to be an absent parent. His employment record remains spotty, and he moves often between rental units. His life is still characterized by evenings out, heavy drinking, substance abuse, and more violent behavior than his contemporaries. Because the typical offender provides the same kind of deprived and disrupted family life for his own children that he experienced, the social experiences and conditions that produce delinquency are carried on from one generation to the next.

Nonoffenders and desisters   Farrington has also identified factors that predict the discontinuity of criminal offenses. He found that people who exhibit these factors have backgrounds that put them at risk of becoming offenders; however, either they are able to remain nonoffenders, or they begin a criminal career and then later desist. The factors that protected high-risk youths from beginning criminal careers included the following:

- Having a somewhat shy personality
- Having few friends (at age 8)
- Having nondeviant families
- Being highly regarded by their mothers

Shy children with few friends avoided damaging relationships with other adolescent boys (members of a high-risk group) and were therefore able to avoid criminality.

What caused offenders to desist?   Holding a relatively good job helped reduce criminal activity. Conversely, unemployment seemed to be related to the escalation of theft offenses; violence and substance abuse were unaffected by unemployment. In a similar vein, getting married also helped diminish criminal activity. However, finding a spouse who was also involved in criminal activity and had a criminal record increased criminal involvement. Physical relocation also helped some offenders desist because they were forced to sever ties with co-offenders. For this reason, leaving the city for a more rural or suburban area was linked to reduced criminal activity.

Although employment, marriage, and relocation helped potential offenders desist, not all desisters found success. At-risk youth who managed to avoid criminal convictions were unlikely to avoid other social problems. Rather than becoming prosperous homeowners with flourishing careers, they tended to live in unkempt homes and have large debts and low-paying jobs. They were also more likely to remain single and live alone. Youth who experienced social isolation at age 8 were also found to experience it at age 32.

Farrington summarized his observations by proposing a theory of criminality based on his long-term data

Exhibit 10.4 Farrington's Theory of Criminality

1. Childhood factors predict teenage antisocial behavior and adult dysfunction. There is continuity in criminal behavior.
2. Personal and social factors are associated with criminal propensity. Kids who suffer economic deprivation, poor parenting, and antisocial families and have personalities marked by impulsivity, hyperactivity, and attention deficit disorder are the most likely to become delinquent.
3. Adolescents who have crimogenic tendencies are motivated to offend by their desire for material goods, excitement, and status with peers. Boys from less affluent families are unable to achieve these goals through legitimate means, so they tend to commit offenses.
4. Life events influence behavior. For example, family life is critical to a deviant career. Adolescents exposed to effective child rearing, including consistent discipline and close supervision, tend to build up internal inhibitions against offending in a social learning process. In contrast, this same learning process causes kids raised in antisocial families to model their beliefs and behaviors dysfunctionally.
5. The chance of offending in any particular situation depends on the perceived costs and benefits of crime and noncrime alternatives. The more impulsive boys were more likely to offend because they were less likely to consider possible future consequences (as opposed to immediate benefits).
6. Factors that encourage criminality at one period during the life course may inhibit it in another. Being nervous and withdrawn and having few friends is negatively related to adolescent and teenage offending but is positively related to adult social dysfunction.
7. Adult criminal behavior is predicted by external and internal behaviors. External behaviors include engaging in violence and getting arrested and convicted for crimes. Internal behaviors include psychiatric disorders, substance abuse, nervousness, and social isolation.

collections. Farrington's theoretical model is outlined in Exhibit 10.4. Farrington's theory suggests that life experiences shape the direction and flow of behavior choices. People are not controlled by a single, unalterable latent trait. His work is included here as a developmental theory because it is age-graded: although there may be continuity in offending, the factors that predict criminality at one point in the life course may not be the ones that predict criminality at another. Although most adult criminals begin their careers in childhood, life events may help some children forgo criminality as they mature.

Interactional Theory

Terence Thornberry has proposed a life course view of crime that he calls **interactional theory** (see Figure 10.7).[103] Thornberry agrees that the onset of crime can be traced to a deterioration of the social bond during adolescence, marked by weakened attachment to parents, commitment to school, and belief in conventional values. Thornberry's view similarly recognizes the influence of social class and other structural variables: youths growing up in socially disorganized areas also stand the greatest risk of a weakened social bond and subsequent delinquency. The onset of a criminal career is supported by residence in a social setting in which deviant values and attitudes can be learned from and reinforced by delinquent peers.

Interactional theory also holds that seriously delinquent youth form belief systems consistent with their deviant lifestyle. They seek out the company of other kids who share their interests and who are likely to reinforce their beliefs about the world and to support their delinquent behavior. According to interactional theory, delinquents find a criminal peer group for the same reason that chess buffs look for others who share their passion for the game; hanging out with other chess players helps improve their game. Similarly, deviant peers do not turn an other-

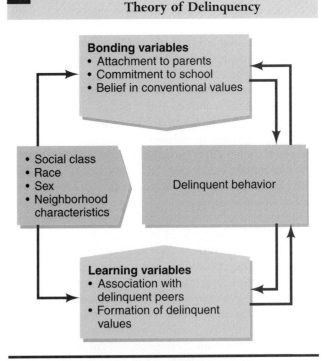

Figure 10.7 Overview of the Interactional Theory of Delinquency

SOURCE: Terrence Thornberry, Margaret Farnworth, Alan Lizotte, and Susan Stern, "A Longitudinal Examination of the Causes and Correlates of Delinquency," working paper No. 1, Rochester Youth Development Study (Albany, N.Y.: Hindelang Criminal Justice Research Center, 1987), p. 11.

■ Interactional theory posits that seriously delinquent youths form belief systems consistent with their deviant lifestyles. They seek the company of other kids who share their interests and who are likely to reinforce their beliefs about the world and support their delinquent behavior. Do interactional theory concepts explain the behavior of these four Cambodian gang members? Is their gang membership the product of seeking peers who support their preexisting behavior? Without peer support, is it likely that they would have been involved in deviant behavior?

© A. Ramey/Photo Edit

wise innocent boy into a delinquent; they support and amplify the behavior of kids who have already accepted a delinquent way of life.[104]

The key idea here is that causal influences are bidirectional. Weak bonds lead kids to develop friendships with deviant peers and get involved in delinquency. Frequent delinquency involvement further weakens bonds and makes it difficult to reestablish conventional ones. Delinquency-promoting factors tend to reinforce one another and sustain a chronic criminal career.

Interactional theory incorporates elements of the cognitive perspective in psychology. That is, as people mature, they pass through different stages of reasoning and sophistication.[105] Thornberry applies this concept when he suggests that criminality is a developmental process that takes on different meaning and form as a person matures. According to Thornberry, the causal process is a dynamic one and develops over a person's life.[106] During early adolescence, attachment to the family is the single most important determinant of whether a youth will adjust to conventional society and be shielded from delinquency. By midadolescence, the influence of the family is replaced by the "world of friends, school and youth culture."[107] By adulthood, a person's behavioral choices are shaped by his or her place in conventional society and his or her own nuclear family.

Testing interactional theory Interactional theory is now being tested by a number of criminologists, and there is ample evidence supportive of its core premise: crime and social relations are interactional.[108] For example, delin-

quent behavior has been found to influence the quality of family life, and changes in the quality of family life stimulate delinquency.[109] Kids who take drugs and use alcohol at a very young age are more likely to engage in other high-risk behaviors, such as dropping out of school and parenting children out of wedlock. These risky behaviors increase the chances that alcohol and drugs will be used into and during adulthood.[110]

Preliminary results also support interactional theory's explanation of how peer groups influence delinquency.[111] Research indicates that associating with delinquent peers does, in fact, increase delinquent involvement and that the relationship is interactional: as delinquent behavior escalates, kids are more likely to seek out deviant friends, who in turn reinforce delinquent beliefs.[112] For example, kids who join gangs typically have long histories of prior delinquent activity. Once in a gang, fellow members facilitate and support their criminal activity. The relationship between gang membership and criminal activity is therefore interactional.[113] In contrast, conventional youth seek equally conforming friends, who then reinforce their prosocial lifestyle. As this process unfolds, antisocial kids will become part of a deviant peer network that reinforces their behavior; conventional youth will be reinforced by their conventional friends.[114]

Delinquency has also been related to other weakened attachments to family and the educational process; delinquent behavior further weakens the bonds to family and school.[115] For example, Suman Kakar found that parents of gang members are subject to considerable stress and a lack of well-being.[116] Inadequate families may promote delinquency, but engaging in antisocial behaviors may have a reciprocal effect on families as well. Other researchers have supported an interactional relationship between criminal behavior and moral values (antisocial behavior weakens moral beliefs, and weakened beliefs encourage criminality).[117]

There is evidence that, as Thornberry suggests, associations with peers, parents, and school vary over time and have differential impacts on a youth's behavior choices.[118] Data also show that life events can make even high-risk youth resilient to delinquency. Kids who grow up in indigent households that experience unemployment, high mobility, and parental criminality, and who are placed in the care of social service agencies, can resist delinquent involvements if they sustain prosocial life experiences. In later adolescence, kids who are committed to school, develop attachment to teachers, and establish the goal of a college education are best able to resist delinquency. Scoring high on reading and math tests is also associated with prosocial behaviors.[119]

In sum, interactional theory suggests that criminality is part of a dynamic social process and not just an outcome of that process. Although crime is influenced by social forces, it also influences these processes and associations to create behavioral trajectories toward increasing law violations for some people.[120] Interactional theory integrates elements of social disorganization, social control, social learning, and cognitive theories into a powerful model of the development of a criminal career.

Sampson and Laub: Age-Graded Theory

If there are various pathways to crime and delinquency, are there trails back to conformity? In an important 1993 work, *Crime in the Making,* Robert Sampson and John Laub identify the **turning points** in a criminal career.[121] As devotees of the life course perspective, Sampson and Laub find that the stability of delinquent behavior can be affected by events that occur later in life, even after a chronic delinquent career has been undertaken. They agree with Hirschi and Gottfredson that formal and informal social controls restrict criminality and that crime begins early in life and continues over the life course; they disagree that once this course is set, nothing can impede its progress. Laub and Sampson reanalyzed the data originally collected by the Gluecks more than 40 years ago. Using modern statistical analysis, Laub and Sampson found evidence supporting the developmental view. They state that children who enter delinquent careers are those who have trouble at home and at school and maintain deviant friends; these findings are similar to those from earlier research on delinquent careers.

Turning points Laub and Sampson's most important contribution is identifying the life events that enable adult offenders to desist from crime (see Figure 10.8). Two critical turning points are marriage and career. For example,

adolescents who are at risk for crime can live conventional lives if they can find good jobs or achieve successful careers. Their success may hinge on a lucky break. Even those who have been in trouble with the law may turn from crime if employers are willing to give them a chance despite their records.

When they achieve adulthood, adolescents who had significant problems with the law are able to desist from crime if they become attached to a spouse who supports and sustains them even when the spouse knows they had gotten in trouble when they were young. Happy marriages are life sustaining, and marital quality improves over time (as people work less and have fewer parental responsibilities).[122] Spending time in marital and family activities also reduces exposure to deviant peers, which in turn reduces the opportunity to become involved in delinquent activities.[123] People who cannot sustain secure marital relations are less likely to desist from crime.

Sampson and Laub's age-graded theory is also supported by research that shows children who grow up in two-parent families are more likely to later have happier marriages than children who are the product of divorced or never-married parents.[124] This finding suggests the marriage–crime association may be intergenerational: if people with marital problems are more crime prone, their children will also suffer a greater long-term risk of marital failure and antisocial activity.

Social capital Social scientists recognize that people build **social capital**—positive relations with individuals and institutions that are life sustaining. In the same manner that building financial capital improves the chances for personal success, building social capital supports conventional behavior and inhibits deviant behavior. For example, a successful marriage creates social capital when it improves a person's stature, creates feelings of self-worth, and encourages people to trust the individual. A successful career inhibits crime by creating a stake in conformity; why commit crime when you are doing well at your job? The relationship is reciprocal. If people are chosen to be employees, they return the favor by doing the best job possible; if they are chosen as spouses, they blossom into devoted partners. In contrast, moving to a new city reduces social capital by closing people off from long-term relationships.[125]

Sampson and Laub's research indicates that building social capital and strong social bonds reduces the likelihood of long-term deviance. This finding suggests that, in contrast to latent trait theories, events that occur in later adolescence and adulthood do, in fact, influence the direction of delinquent and criminal careers. Life events can help either terminate or sustain deviant careers. Sampson and Laub argue that getting arrested and punished may have little direct effect on future criminality, but it can help sustain a criminal career because it reduces the chances of employment and job stability, two factors that are directly related to crime.[126]

Figure 10.8   Sampson and Laub's Age-Graded Theory

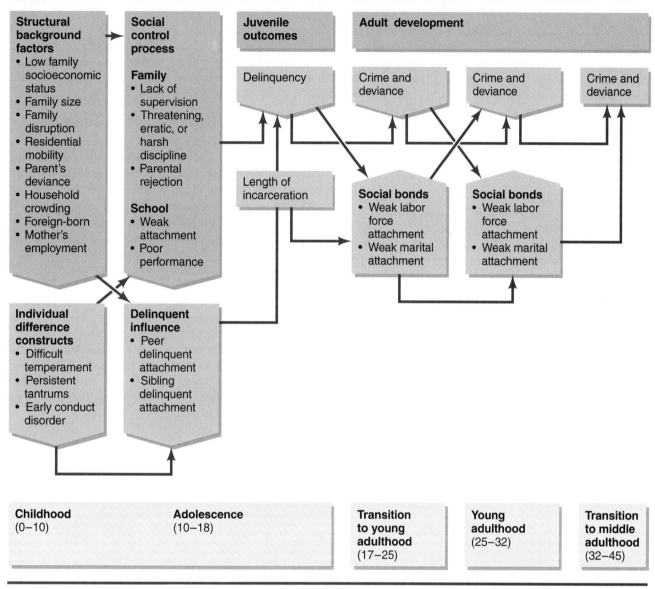

SOURCE: Robert Sampson and John Laub, *Crime in the Making: Pathways and Turning Points Through Life* (Cambridge, Mass.: Harvard University Press, 1993), pp. 244–45.

Research has been directed at identifying the sources of social capital and determining whether and how it is related to crime. Youths who accumulate social capital in childhood (for example, by doing well in school or having a tightly knit family) are also the most likely to maintain steady work as adults; employment may help insulate them from crime.[127] Also, people who maintain a successful marriage in their twenties and become parents are the most likely to mature out of crime.[128] Although it is possible that marriage stabilizes people and helps them build social capital, it is also likely, as Mark Warr suggests, that marriage may discourage crime by reducing contact with criminal peers:

For many individuals, it seems, marriage marks a transition from heavy peer involvement to a preoccupation with one's spouse. That transition is likely to reduce interaction with former friends and accomplices and thereby reduce the opportunities as well as the motivation to engage in crime.[129]

Testing age-graded theory Empirical research now shows that, as predicted by Sampson and Laub, people change over the life course and that the factors that predict delinquency in adolescence, such as a weak social bond, may have less of an impact on adult crime.[130] Criminality appears to be dynamic and is affected by behaviors occurring over the life course, such as accumulating deviant peers: the more deviant friends one accumulates over time, the more likely the person is to get involved in crime.[131] Of critical importance is early labeling by the justice system: adolescents who are convicted of crime at an early age are more likely to develop antisocial attitudes later in life. They later develop low educational achievement, declining occupational status, and unstable employment records.[132] People who get involved with the justice system as adolescents may find that their career paths are blocked well into adulthood.[133] The relationship is reciprocal: men who are unemployed or underemployed report higher criminal participation rates than employed men.[134]

CONNECTIONS

Data showing that apprehension and conviction lead to persistent offending patterns support the labeling perspective discussed in Chapter 8. Rather than deterring crime, it suggests that criminal labels help prolong its occurrence. ∎

Evidence is also available that confirms Sampson and Laub's suspicion that criminal career trajectories can be reversed once begun if life conditions improve.[135] For example, youth who have a positive high school experience, facilitated by occupationally oriented course work, small class size, and positive peer climates, are less likely to become incarcerated as adults than those who do not enjoy these social benefits.[136] Even after being involved with the justice system, people can "go straight" if they have positive life experiences. Men released from prison on parole who obtain jobs are less likely to recidivate than those who lack or lose employment.[137]

A number of research efforts have supported Sampson and Laub's position that accumulating social capital reduces crime rates. For example, delinquents who enter the military, serve overseas, and receive veterans' benefits enhance their occupational status (social capital) while reducing criminal involvement.[138] Similarly, high-risk adults who are fortunate enough to obtain high-quality jobs are likely to reduce their criminal activities even if they have a prior history of offending.[139] In contrast, research shows that people who are self-centered and present-oriented are less likely to accumulate social capital and more prone to commit criminal acts.[140]

Some important questions still need to be answered: Why do some kids change while others resist? Why do some people enter strong marriages while others fail? What is it about a military career that helps reduce future criminality? Does the connection between military service and desistance suggest universal military service as a crime prevention alternative? Why are some troubled youth able to conform to the requirements of a job or career while others cannot? Is it possible that social capital—family, friends,

education, marriage, and employment—aids in the successful recovery from crime?[141] To answer some of these questions, Laub and Sampson are currently conducting an important research study. They are contacting the surviving members of the Glueck cohort, and some of their findings are discussed in the Criminological Enterprise feature.

■ Evaluating Developmental Theories

Although the differences between the latent trait and life course views presented in this chapter may seem irreconcilable, they in fact share some common ground. They indicate that a criminal career must be understood as a passage along which people travel, that it has a beginning and an end, and that events and life circumstances influence the journey. The factors that affect a criminal career may include structural factors, such as income and status; socialization factors, such as family and peer relations; biological factors, such as size and strength; psychological factors, including intelligence and personality; and opportunity factors, such as free time, inadequate police protection, and a supply of easily stolen merchandise.

Life course theories emphasize the influence of changing interpersonal and structural factors (that is, people change along with the world they live in). Latent trait theories assume that there is a dominant trait that, once formed, is resistant to change.

In her paper, "Building the Foundation for a Side-by-Side Explanatory Model: A General Theory of Crime, the Age-Graded Life Course Theory, and Attachment Theory," Rebecca S. Katz attempts to show how these models can be linked. Read her work at:
http://wcr.sonoma.edu/v1n2/katz.html
For an up-to-date list of Web links, go to
http://info.wadsworth.com/siegel ∎

These perspectives differ in their view of human development. Do people change, as life course theories suggest, or are they stable, constant, and changeless, as the latent trait view indicates? It is actually possible that both positions may make a notable contribution to understanding the onset and continuity of a criminal career. For example, recent research by Bradley Entner Wright and his associates found evidence supporting both latent trait and life course theories.[142] Their research, conducted with subjects in New Zealand, indicates that low self-control in childhood predicts disrupted social bonds and criminal offending later in life, a finding that supports latent trait theory. They also found that maintaining positive social bonds helps reduce criminality and that maintaining prosocial bonds could even counteract the effect of low self-control. Latent traits are an important influence on crime, but their findings indicate that social relationships that form later in

THE CRIMINOLOGICAL ENTERPRISE

Tracking Down the 500 Delinquent Boys in the New Millennium

Why are some delinquents destined to become persistent criminals as adults? John Laub and Robert Sampson are now conducting a follow-up to their reanalysis of Sheldon and Eleanor Glueck's study that matched 500 delinquent boys with 500 non-delinquents. The individuals in the original sample were reinterviewed by the Glueck's at ages 25 and 32. Now Sampson and Laub have located the survivors, the oldest being 70 years old and the youngest 62, and they are reinterviewing this cohort.

Persistence and Desistance
Laub and Sampson find that delinquency and other forms of antisocial conduct in childhood are strongly related to adult crime and drug and alcohol abuse. Former delinquents also suffer consequences in other areas of social life, such as school, work, and family life. For example, delinquents are far less likely to finish high school than are nondelinquents and subsequently more likely to be unemployed, receive welfare, and experience separation or divorce as adults.

In their latest research, Laub and Sampson address one of the key questions posed by developmental theories: Is it possible for former delinquents to rehabilitate themselves as adults? They find that most antisocial children do not remain antisocial as adults. For example, of men in the study cohort who survived to age 50, 24 percent had no arrests for crimes of violence and property after age 17 (6 percent had no arrests for total crime); 48 percent had no arrests for these predatory crimes after age 25 (19 percent for total crime); 60 percent had no arrests for predatory crime after age 31 (33 percent for total crime); and 79 percent had no arrests for predatory crime after age 40 (57

percent for total crime). They conclude that desistance from crime is the norm and that most, if not all, serious delinquents desist from crime.

Why Do Delinquents Desist?
Laub and Sampson's earlier research indicated that building social capital through marriage and jobs were key components of desistance from crime. However, in this new round of research, Laub and Sampson were able to find out more about long-term desistance by interviewing 52 men as they approached age 70. Drawing on the men's own words, they find that one important element for "going straight" is the "knifing off" of individuals from their immediate environment and offering them a new script for the future. Joining the military can provide this knifing-off effect, as does marriage, or changing one's residence. One former delinquent (age 69) told them:

> I'd say the turning point was, number one, the Army. You get into an outfit, you had a sense of belonging, you made your friends. I think I became a pretty good judge of character. In the Army, you met some good ones, you met some foul balls. Then I met the wife. I'd say probably that would be the turning point. Got married, then naturally, kids come. So now you got to get a better job, you got to make more money. And that's how I got to the Navy Yard and tried to improve myself.

Former delinquents who "went straight" were able to put structure into their lives. Structure often led the men to disassociate from delinquent peers, reducing the opportunity to get into trouble. Getting married, for example, may limit the number of nights men can "hang with the guys." As one wife of a former delinquent said, "It is not how many beers you have, it's who you drink with." Even multiple offenders who did time in prison were able to desist with the help of a stabilizing marriage.

Former delinquents who can turn their life around, who have acquired a

degree of maturity by taking on family and work responsibilities, and who have forged new commitments are the ones most likely to make a fresh start and find new direction and meaning in life. It seems that men who desisted changed their identity as well, and this, in turn, affected their outlook and sense of maturity and responsibility. The ability to change did not reflect crime "specialty": violent offenders followed the same path as property offenders.

Policy Implications
Laub and Sampson find that youth problems—delinquency, substance abuse, violence, dropping out, teen pregnancy—often share common risk characteristics. Intervention strategies, therefore, should consider a broad array of antisocial, criminal, and deviant behaviors, and not limit the focus to just one subgroup or crime type. Because criminality and other social problems are linked, early prevention efforts that reduce crime will probably also reduce alcohol abuse, drunk driving, drug abuse, sexual promiscuity, and family violence. The best way to achieve these goals is through four significant life-changing events: marriage, joining the military, getting a job, and changing one's environment or neighborhood. What appears to be important about these processes is that they all involve, to varying degrees, the following items: a knifing off of the past from the present; new situations that provide both supervision and monitoring as well as new opportunities of social support and growth; and new situations that provide the opportunity for transforming identity. Prevention of crime must be a policy at all times and at all stages of life.

SOURCE: John Laub, "Crime over the Life Course," *Poverty Research News,* The Newsletter of the Northwestern University/ University of Chicago Joint Center for Poverty Research, vol. 4, no. 3, May–June 2000.

life appear to influence criminal behavior "above and be-yond" individuals' preexisting characteristics.[143] This find-ing may reflect, as Stephen Cernkovich and Peggy Gior-dano have found, that there are two classes of criminals: a less serious group who are influenced by life events, and a more chronic group whose latent traits insulate them from any positive prosocial relationships.[144]

CONNECTIONS

Earlier in this chapter Moffitt's concept of life course per-sistent and adolescent-limited offenders was discussed in some detail. The fact that there may be two classes of criminals has become a popular viewpoint in con-temporary criminology. ∎

■ Summary

Latent trait theories hold that some underlying condition present at birth or soon after controls behavior. Suspect traits include low IQ, impulsivity, and personality structure. These underlying traits explain the continuity of offending because, once present, they remain with a person through-out his or her life. The latent trait the-ories developed by Gottfredson and Hirschi and Wilson and Herrnstein both integrate choice theory con-cepts: people with latent traits choose crime over noncrime; the opportu-nity for crime mediates their choice. More recent theories have been de-veloped by Mark Colvin and Charles Tittle.

Life course theories argue that events that take place over the life course influence criminal choices. The cause of crime constantly changes as people mature. At first, the nuclear family influences behav-ior; during adolescence, the peer group dominates; in adulthood, mar-riage and career are critical. There are a variety of pathways to crime: some kids are sneaky, others hostile, and still others defiant. Crime may be part of a variety of social problems, in-cluding health, physical, and inter-personal troubles. Life course theo-ries include the social development model, which finds that living in a dis-organized area helps weaken social bonds. Other important life course theories have been formulated by Ter-ence Thornberry, David Farrington, and John Laub and Robert Sampson (see Table 10.2).

■ Table 10.2   Developmental Theories

Theory	Major Premise	Strengths
Latent Trait Theories		
General theory of crime	Crime and criminality are separate concepts. People choose to commit crime when they lack self-control. People lacking in self-control will seize criminal opportunities.	Integrates choice and social control concepts. Identifies the difference between crime and criminality.
Control balance	An excess or lack of control makes people crime prone.	Shows that control is a multidimensional concept.
Differential coercion	Low self-control is a product of impersonal and interpersonal coercion.	Provides basis for understanding the development of low self-control.
Life Course Theories		
Social development model	Weak social controls produce crime. A person's place in the structure influences his or her bond to society.	Combines elements of social structural and social process theories. Accounts for variations in the crime rate.
Farrington's theory of delinquent development	Personal and social factors control the onset and stability of criminal careers.	Makes use of data collected over a 20-year period to substantiate hypothesis.
Interactional theory	Criminals go through lifestyle changes during their offending careers.	Combines sociological and psychological theories.
Age-graded theory	As people mature, the factors that influence their propensity to commit crime change. In childhood, family factors are critical; in adulthood, marital and job factors are key.	Shows how crime is a developmental process that shifts in direction over the life course.

Thinking Like a Criminologist

Luis Francisco is the leader of the Almighty Latin Kings and Queens Nation. He was convicted of murder in 1998 and sentenced to life imprisonment plus 45 years.

Luis Francisco's life has been filled with displacement, poverty, and chronic predatory crime. The son of a prostitute in Havana, at the age of 9 he was sent to prison for robbery. He had trouble in school, and teachers described him as having attention problems; he dropped out in the seventh grade. On his nineteenth birthday in 1980, he immigrated to the United States and soon after became a gang member in Chicago, where he joined the Latin Kings. After moving to the Bronx, he shot and killed his girlfriend in 1981. He fled to Chicago and was not apprehended until 1984. Sentenced to nine years for second-degree manslaughter, Luis Francisco ended up in a New York prison, where he started a New York prison chapter of the Latin Kings. As King Blood, Inka, First Supreme Crown, Francisco ruled the 2000 Latin Kings in and out of prison. Disciplinary troubles erupted when some Kings were stealing from the organization. Infuriated, King Blood wrote to his street lieutenants and ordered their termination. Federal authorities had been monitoring Francisco's mail and arrested 35 Latin Kings. Thirty-four pled guilty; only Francisco insisted on a trial, where he was found guilty of conspiracy to commit murder.

Explain Luis's behavior patterns from a developmental view. How would a latent trait theorist explain his escalating criminal activities?

Key Terms

- developmental theories (283)
- latent trait theory (283)
- life course theory (283)
- latent trait (283)
- human nature theory (284)
- general theory of crime (GTC) (284)
- self-control theory (286)
- interpersonal coercion (289)
- impersonal coercion (289)
- coercive ideation (290)
- control balance theory (290)
- predation (291)
- defiance (291)
- submission (291)
- exploitation (291)
- plunder (291)
- decadence (291)
- problem behavior syndrome (PBS) (293)
- authority conflict pathway (295)
- covert pathway (296)
- overt pathway (296)
- continuity of crime (296)
- adolescent-limited offenders (297)
- life course persisters (297)
- social development model (SDM) (297)
- prosocial bonds (299)
- interactional theory (302)
- turning points (304)
- social capital (304)

Critical Thinking Questions

1. Do you consider yourself a holder of "social capital"? If so, what form does it take?

2. A person gets 1600 on the SAT. Without knowing him or her, what personal, family, and social characteristics do you think this person has? Another person becomes a serial killer. Without knowing him or her, what personal, family, and social characteristics do you think this person has? If "bad behavior" is explained by multiple problems, is "good behavior" explained by multiple strengths?

3. Do you believe it is a "latent trait" that makes a person crime prone, or is crime a function of environment and socialization?

4. Do you agree with Loeber's multiple pathways model? Do you know people who have traveled down those paths?

5. Do people really change, or do they stay the same but appear to be different because their life circumstances have changed?

Notes

1. Gerald Patterson and Karen Yoerger, "Developmental Models for Delinquent Behavior," in *Mental Disorder and Crime,* ed. Sheilagh Hodgins (Newbury Park, Calif.: Sage, 1993), pp. 150–59.

2. David Rowe, D. Wayne Osgood, and W. Alan Nicewander, "A Latent Trait Approach to Unifying Criminal Careers," *Criminology* 28 (1990): 237–70.

3. Lee Ellis, "Neurohormonal Bases of Varying Tendencies to Learn Delinquent and Criminal Behavior," in *Behavioral Approaches to Crime and Delinquency,* eds. E. Morris and C. Braukmann (New York: Plenum, 1988), pp. 499–518.

4. David Rowe, Alexander Vazsonyi, and Daniel Flannery, "Sex Differences in Crime: Do Means and Within-Sex Variation Have Similar Causes?" *Journal of Research in Crime and Delinquency* 32 (1995): 84–100.

5. James Q. Wilson and Richard Herrnstein, *Crime and Human Nature* (New York: Simon and Schuster, 1985).

6. Ibid., p. 44.

7. Ibid., p. 171.

8. Michael Gottfredson and Travis Hirschi, *A General Theory of Crime* (Stanford, Calif.: Stanford University Press, 1990).

9. Ibid., p. 27.

10. Anthony Walsh and Lee Ellis, "Shoring Up the Big Three: Improving Criminological Theories with Biosocial Concepts." Paper presented at the annual Society of Criminology meeting, San Diego, Calif., November 1997, p. 15.

11. Gottfredson and Hirschi, *A General Theory of Crime*, p. 90.

12. Ibid., p. 89.

13. Alex Piquero and Stephen Tibbetts, "Specifying the Direct and Indirect Effects of Low Self-Control and Situational Factors in Offenders' Decision Making: Toward a More Complete Model of Rational Offending," *Justice Quarterly* 13 (1996): 481–508.

14. David Forde and Leslie Kennedy, "Risky Lifestyles, Routine Activities, and the General Theory of Crime," *Justice Quarterly* 14 (1997): 265–94.

15. Gottfredson and Hirschi, *A General Theory of Crime*, p. 112.

16. Ibid.

17. Dennis Giever, "An Empirical Assessment of the Core Elements of Gottfredson and Hirschi's General Theory of Crime." Paper presented at the American Society of Criminology meeting, Boston, Mass., November 1995.

18. Robert Agnew, "The Contribution of Social-Psychological Strain Theory to the Explanation of Crime and Delinquency," *Anomie Theory: Advances in Criminological Theory*, vol. 6, eds. Freda Adder and William Laufer (New Brunswick, N.J.: Transaction Press, 1995), pp. 81–96.

19. Travis Hirschi and Michael Gottfredson, "Rethinking the Juvenile Justice System," *Crime and Delinquency* 39 (1993): 262–71.

20. David Brownfield and Ann Marie Sorenson, "Self-Control and Juvenile Delinquency: Theoretical Issues and an Empirical Assessment of Selected Elements of a General Theory of Crime," *Deviant Behavior* 14 (1993): 243–64; Harold Grasmick, Charles Tittle, Robert Bursik, and Bruce Arneklev, "Testing the Core Empirical Implications of Gottfredson and Hirschi's General Theory of Crime," *Journal of Research in Crime and Delinquency* 30 (1993): 5–29; John Cochran, Peter Wood, and Bruce Arneklev, "Is the Religiosity–Delinquency Relationship Spurious? A Test of Arousal and Social Control Theories," *Journal of Research in Crime and Delinquency* 31 (1994): 92–123; Marc LeBlanc, Marc Ouimet, and Richard Tremblay, "An Integrative Control Theory of Delinquent Behavior: A Validation 1976–1985," *Psychiatry* 51 (1988): 164–76.

21. Alexander Vazsonyi, Lloyd Pickering, Marianne Junger, and Dick Hessing, "An Empirical Test of a General Theory of Crime: A Four-Nation Comparative Study of Self-Control and the Prediction of Deviance," *Journal of Research in Crime and Delinquency* 38 (2001): 91–131.

22. Michael Benson and Elizabeth Moore, "Are White-Collar and Common Offenders the Same? An Empirical and Theoretical Critique of a Recently Proposed General Theory of Crime," *Journal of Research in Crime and Delinquency* 29 (1992): 251–72.

23. Ronald Akers, "Self-Control as a General Theory of Crime," *Journal of Quantitative Criminology* 7 (1991): 201–211.

24. Gottfredson and Hirschi, *A General Theory of Crime*, p. 88.

25. Samuel Yochelson and Clifford Samenow, *The Criminal Personality* (New York: Jason Aronson, 1977).

26. Alan Feingold, "Gender Differences in Personality: A Meta Analysis," *Psychological Bulletin* 116 (1994): 429–56.

27. Gottfredson and Hirschi, *A General Theory of Crime*, p. 153.

28. Ann Marie Sorenson and David Brownfield, "Normative Concepts in Social Control." Paper presented at the annual meeting of the American Society of Criminology, Phoenix, Ariz., November 1993.

29. Brent Benda, "An Examination of Reciprocal Relationship between Religiosity and Different Forms of Delinquency within a Theoretical Model," *Journal of Research in Crime and Delinquency* 34 (1997): 163–86.

30. Delbert Elliott and Scott Menard, "Delinquent Friends and Delinquent Behavior: Temporal and Developmental Patterns," in *Crime and Delinquency: Current Theories*, ed. J. David Hawkins (Cambridge: Cambridge University Press, 1996).

31. Graham Ousey and David Aday, "The Interaction Hypothesis: A Test Using Social Control Theory and Social Learning Theory." Paper presented at the American Society of Criminology Meeting, Boston, Mass., 1995.

32. Ronald Simons, Christine Johnson, Rand Conger, and Glen Elder, "A Test of Latent Trait versus Life-Course Perspectives on the Stability of Adolescent Antisocial Behavior," *Criminology* 36 (1998): 217–44.

33. Bradley Entner Wright, Avashalom Caspi, Terrie Moffitt, and Phil Silva, "The Effects of Social Ties on Crime Vary by Criminal Propensity: A Life-Course Model of Interdependence," *Criminology* 39 (2001): 321–52.

34. Julie Horney, D. Wayne Osgood, and Ineke Haen Marshall, "Criminal Careers in the Short-Term: Intra-Individual Variability in Crime and Its Relations to Local Life Circumstances," *American Sociological Review* 60 (1995): 655–73; Martin Daly and Margo Wilson, "Killing the Competition," *Human Nature* 1 (1990): 83–109.

35. Charles R. Tittle and Harold G. Grasmick, "Criminal Behavior and Age: A Test of Three Provocative Hypotheses," *Journal of Criminal Law and Criminology* 88 (1997): 309–42.

36. Carter Hay, "Parenting, Self-Control, and Delinquency: A Test of Self-Control Theory," *Criminology* 39 (2001): 707–36; Douglas Longshore, "Self-Control and Criminal Opportunity: A Prospective Test of the General Theory of Crime," *Social Problems* 45 (1998): 102–14; Finn-Aage Esbensen and Elizabeth Piper Deschenes, "A Multisite Examination of Youth Gang Membership: Does Gender Matter?" *Criminology* 36 (1998): 799–828.

37. Raymond Paternoster and Robert Brame, "The Structural Similarity of Processes Generating Criminal and Analogous Behaviors," *Criminology* 36 (1998): 633–70.

38. Otwin Marenin and Michael Resig, "A General Theory of Crime and Patterns of Crime in Nigeria: An Exploration of Methodological Assumptions," *Journal of Criminal Justice* 23 (1995): 501–18.

39. Bruce Arneklev, Harold Grasmick, Charles Tittle, and Robert Bursik, "Low Self-Control and Imprudent Behavior," *Journal of Quantitative Criminology* 9 (1993): 225–46.

40. Francis Cullen, John Paul Wright, and Mitchell Chamlin, "Social Support and Social Reform: A Progressive Crime

Control Agenda," *Crime and Delinquency* 45 (1999): 188–207.

41. Kevin Thompson, "Sexual Harassment and Low Self-Control: An Application of Gottfredson and Hirschi's General Theory of Crime." Paper presented at the annual meeting of the American Society of Criminology, Phoenix, Ariz., November 1993.

42. Mark Colvin, *Crime and Coercion: An Integrated Theory of Chronic Criminality* (New York: Palgrave Press, 2000).

43. Charles Tittle, *Control Balance: Toward a General Theory of Deviance* (Boulder, Colo.: Westview Press, 1995).

44. Marvin Krohn, Alan Lizotte, and Cynthia Perez, "The Interrelationship between Substance Use and Precocious Transitions to Adult Sexuality," *Journal of Health and Social Behavior* 38 (1997): 87–103, at 88.

45. Wright, Caspi, Moffitt, and Silva, "The Effects of Social Ties on Crime Vary by Criminal Propensity: A Life-Course Model of Interdependence," pp. 340–42.

46. G. R. Patterson, Barbara DeBaryshe, and Elizabeth Ramsey, "A Developmental Perspective on Antisocial Behavior," *American Psychologist* 44 (1989): 329–35.

47. Joan McCord, "Family Relationships, Juvenile Delinquency, and Adult Criminality," *Criminology* 29 (1991): 397–417.

48. Paul Mazerolle, "Delinquent Definitions and Participation Age: Assessing the Invariance Hypothesis," *Studies on Crime and Crime Prevention* 6 (1997): 151–68.

49. Robert Sampson and John Laub, "Crime and Deviance in the Life Course," *American Review of Sociology* 18 (1992): 63–84.

50. See, generally, Sheldon Glueck and Eleanor Glueck, *500 Criminal Careers* (New York: Knopf, 1930); Sheldon Glueck and Eleanor Glueck, *One Thousand Juvenile Delinquents* (Cambridge: Harvard University Press, 1934); Sheldon Glueck and Eleanor Glueck, *Predicting Delinquency and Crime* (Cambridge: Harvard University Press, 1967), pp. 82–83.

51. Sheldon Glueck and Eleanor Glueck, *Unraveling Juvenile Delinquency* (Cambridge: Harvard University Press, 1950).

52. Ibid., p. 48.

53. See, generally, John Laub and Robert Sampson, "The Sutherland–Glueck Debate: On the Sociology of Criminological Knowledge," *American Journal of Sociology* 96 (1991): 1402–40; John Laub and Robert Sampson, "Unravel-

ing Families and Delinquency: A Re-analysis of the Gluecks' Data," *Criminology* 26 (1988): 355–80.

54. Rolf Loeber and Marc LeBlanc, "Toward a Developmental Criminology," in *Crime and Justice,* vol. 12, eds. Norval Morris and Michael Tonry (Chicago: University of Chicago Press, 1990), pp. 375–473; Rolf Loeber and Marc Leblanc, "Developmental Criminology Updated," in *Crime and Justice,* vol. 23, ed. Michael Tonry (Chicago: University of Chicago Press, 1998), pp. 115–98.

55. Gerald Patterson, J. B. Reid, and Thomas Dishion, *A Social Interactional Approach: Antisocial Boys* (Eugene, Ore.: Castalia Press, 1992).

56. Francois Poulin, Thomas Dishion, Mike Stoolmiller, and Gerald Patterson, "Modeling Growth in Adolescent Delinquency: The Combined Effect and Developmental Specificity of Parent Bonding and Deviant Peers." Paper presented at the annual meeting of the American Society of Criminology, Chicago, Ill., November 1996.

57. G. R. Patterson, L. Crosby, and S. Vuchinich, "Predicting Risk for Early Police Arrest," *Journal of Quantitative Criminology* 8 (1992): 335–55.

58. G. R. Patterson, Barbara DeBaryshe, and Elizabeth Ramsey, "A Developmental Perspective on Antisocial Behavior," *American Psychologist* 44 (1989): 329–35, at 331–33.

59. Raymond Paternoster, Charles Dean, Alex Piquero, Paul Mazerolle, and Robert Brame, "Generality, Continuity, and Change in Offending," *Journal of Quantitative Criminology* 13 (1997): 231–66.

60. Magda Stouthamer-Loeber and Evelyn Wei, "The Precursors of Young Fatherhood and Its Effect on Delinquency of Teenage Males," *Journal of Adolescent Health* 22 (1998): 56–65; Richard Jessor, John Donovan, and Francis Costa, *Beyond Adolescence: Problem Behavior and Young Adult Development* (New York: Cambridge University Press, 1991); Xavier Coll, Fergus Law, Aurelio Tobias, Keith Hawton, and Josep Tomas, "Abuse and Deliberate Self-Poisoning in Women: A Matched Case-Control Study." *Child Abuse and Neglect* 25 (2001): 1291–93.

61. Richard Miech, Avshalom Caspi, Terrie Moffitt, Bradley Entner Wright, and Phil Silva, "Low Socioeconomic Status and Mental Disorders: A Longitudinal Study of Selection and Causation during Young Adulthood," *American Journal of Sociology* 104 (1999): 1096–1131; Marvin Krohn, Alan Li-

zotte, and Cynthia Perez, "The Interrelationship between Substance Use and Precocious Transitions to Adult Sexuality," *Journal of Health and Social Behavior* 38 (1997): 87–103, at 88; Richard Jessor, "Risk Behavior in Adolescence: A Psychosocial Framework for Understanding and Action," in *Adolescents at Risk: Medical and Social Perspectives,* eds. D. E. Rogers and E. Ginzburg (Boulder, Colo.: Westview Press, 1992).

62. Deborah Capaldi and Gerald Patterson, "Can Violent Offenders Be Distinguished from Frequent Offenders: Prediction from Childhood to Adolescence," *Journal of Research in Crime and Delinquency* 33 (1996): 206–31; D. Wayne Osgood, "The Covariation among Adolescent Problem Behaviors." Paper presented at the annual meeting of the American Society of Criminology, Baltimore, November 1990.

63. Terence Thornberry, Carolyn Smith, and Gregory Howard, "Risk Factors for Teenage Fatherhood," *Journal of Marriage and the Family* 59 (1997): 505–22; Todd Miller, Timothy Smith, Charles Turner, Margarita Guijarro, and Amanda Hallet, "A Meta-Analytic Review of Research on Hostility and Physical Health," *Psychological Bulletin* 119 (1996): 322–48; Marianne Junger, "Accidents and Crime," in *The Generality of Deviance,* eds. T. Hirschi and M. Gottfredson (New Brunswick, N.J.: Transaction Press, 1993).

64. Robert Johnson, S. Susan Su, Dean Gerstein, Hee-Choon Shin, and John Hoffman, "Parental Influences on Deviant Behavior in Early Adolescence: A Logistic Response Analysis of Age- and Gender-Differentiated Effects," *Journal of Quantitative Criminology* 11 (1995): 167–92; Judith Brooks, Martin Whiteman, and Patricia Cohen, "Stage of Drug Use, Aggression, and Theft/Vandalism," in *Drugs, Crime and Other Deviant Adaptations: Longitudinal Studies,* ed. Howard Kaplan (New York: Plenum Press, 1995), pp. 83–96; Robert Hoge, D. A. Andrews, and Alan Leschied, "Tests of Three Hypotheses Regarding the Predictors of Delinquency," *Journal of Abnormal Child Psychology* 22 (1994): 547–59.

65. David Huizinga, Rolf Loeber, and Terence Thornberry, "Longitudinal Study of Delinquency, Drug Use, Sexual Activity, and Pregnancy among Children and Youth in Three Cities," *Public Health Reports* 108 (1993): 90–96.

66. For an analysis of more than 30 studies, see Mark Lipsey and James Derzon, "Predictors of Violent or Serious

Delinquency in Adolescence and Early Adulthood: A Synthesis of Longitudinal Research," in *Serious and Violent Juvenile Offenders: Risk Factors and Successful Interventions,* eds. Rolf Loeber and David Farrington (Thousand Oaks, Calif.: Sage, 1998).

67. Jeanne Hernandez, "The Concurrence of Eating Disorders with Histories of Child Abuse among Adolescents." Paper presented at the annual meeting of the American Society of Criminology, Phoenix, Ariz., November 1993.

68. Candace Kruttschnitt, Jane McLeod, and Maude Dornfeld, "The Economic Environment of Child Abuse," *Social Problems* 41 (1994): 299–312.

69. James Marquart, Victoria Brewer, Patricia Simon, and Edward Morse, "Lifestyle Factors among Female Prisoners with Histories of Psychiatric Treatment," *Journal of Criminal Justice* 29 (2001): 319–28.

70. Helene Raskin White, "Early Problem Behavior and Later Drug Problems," *Journal of Research in Crime and Delinquency* 29 (1992): 412–29.

71. Helene Raskin White and Erich Labouvie, "Generality versus Specificity of Problem Behavior: Psychological and Functional Differences," *Journal of Drug Issues* 24 (1994): 55–74.

72. See, generally, Richard Dembo, Linda Williams, Werner Wothke, James Schmeidler, Alan Getreu, Estrellita Berry, and Eric Wish, "The Generality of Deviance: Replication of a Structural Model among High-Risk Youths," *Journal of Research in Crime and Delinquency* 29 (1992): 200–16.

73. Karl Hill, James Howell, J. David Hawkins, and Sara Battin-Pearson, "Childhood Risk Factors for Adolescent Gang Membership: Results from the Seattle Social Development Project," *Journal of Research in Crime and Delinquency* 36 (1999): 300–22.

74. Pamela Lattimore, Richard Linster, and John MacDonald, "Risk of Death among Serious Young Offenders," *Journal of Research in Crime and Delinquency* 34 (1997): 187–209.

75. Rolf Loeber, Phen Wung, Kate Keenan, Bruce Giroux, Magda Stouthamer-Loeber, Wemoet Van Kammen, and Barbara Maughan, "Developmental Pathways in Disruptive Behavior," *Development and Psychopathology* (1993): 12–48.

76. Sheila Royo Maxwell and Christopher Maxwell, "Examining the 'Criminal Careers' of Prostitutes within the Nexus of Drug Use, Drug Selling, and Other Illicit Activities," *Criminology* 38 (2000): 787–809.

77. Alex R. Piquero and He Len Chung, "On the Relationships between Gender, Early Onset, and the Seriousness of Offending," *Journal of Criminal Justice* 29 (2001): 189–206.

78. David Nurco, Timothy Kinlock, and Mitchell Balter, "The Severity of Preaddiction Criminal Behavior among Urban, Male Narcotic Addicts and Two Nonaddicted Control Groups," *Journal of Research in Crime and Delinquency* 30 (1993): 293–316.

79. Rolf Loeber and David Farrington, "Young Children Who Commit Crime: Epidemiology, Developmental Origins, Risk Factors, Early Interventions, and Policy Implications," *Development and Psychopathology* 12 (2000): 737–62.

80. Mark Lipsey and James Derzon, "Predictors of Violent or Serious Delinquency in Adolescence and Early Adulthood: A Synthesis of Longitudinal Research," in *Serious and Violent Juvenile Offenders: Risk Factors and Successful Interventions,* eds. Rolf Loeber and David Farrington (Thousand Oaks, Calif.: Sage, 1998).

81. G. R. Patterson and Karen Yoerger, "Differentiating Outcomes and Histories for Early and Late Onset Arrests." Paper presented at the annual meeting of the American Society of Criminology, Phoenix, Ariz., November 1993.

82. Amy D'Unger, Kenneth Land, Patricia McCall, and Daniel Nagin, "How Many Latent Classes of Delinquent/Criminal Careers? Results from Mixed Poisson Regression Analyses," *American Journal of Sociology* 103 (1998): 1593–1630.

83. Alex Piquero and Timothy Brezina, "Testing Moffitt's Account of Adolescent-Limited Delinquency," *Criminology* 39 (2001): 353–70.

84. Terrie Moffitt, "Natural Histories of Delinquency," in *Cross-National Longitudinal Research on Human Development and Criminal Behavior,* eds. Elmar Weitekamp and Hans-Jurgen Kerner (Dordrecht, Netherlands: Kluwer, 1994), pp. 3–65.

85. Rolf Loeber and Magda Stouthamer-Loeber, "Development of Juvenile Aggression and Violence," *American Psychologist* 53 (1998): 242–59.

86. Terrie Moffitt, "Adolescence-Limited and Life-Course Persistent Antisocial Behavior: A Developmental Taxonomy," *Psychological Review* 100 (1993): 674–701.

87. Paul Mazerolle, Robert Brame, Ray Paternoster, Alex Piquero, and Charles Dean, "Onset Age, Persistence, and Offending Versatility: Comparisons across Sex," *Criminology* 38 (2000): 1143–72.

88. Per-Olof Wikstrom and Rolf Loeber, "Do Disadvantaged Neighborhoods Cause Well-Adjusted Children to Become Adolescent Delinquents? A Study of Male Juvenile Serious Offending, Individual Risk and Protective Factors, and Neighborhood Context," *Criminology* 38 (2000): 1109–42.

89. Ronald Simons, Chyi-In Wu, Rand Conger, and Frederick Lorenz, "Two Routes to Delinquency: Differences between Early and Later Starters in the Impact of Parenting and Deviant Careers," *Criminology* 32 (1994): 247–75.

90. Dawn Jeglum Bartusch, Donald Lynam, Terrie Moffitt, and Phil Silva, "Is Age Important? Testing a General versus a Developmental Theory of Antisocial Behavior," *Criminology* 35 (1997): 13–48.

91. Michael Newcomb, "Pseudomaturity among Adolescents: Construct Validation, Sex Differences, and Associations in Adulthood," *Journal of Drug Issues* 26 (1996): 477–504.

92. Charles Dean, Robert Brame, and Alex Piquero, "Criminal Propensities, Discrete Groups of Offenders, and Persistence of Crime," *Criminology* 34 (1996): 547–73.

93. See, for example, the Rochester Youth Development Study, Hindelang Criminal Justice Research Center, 135 Western Avenue, Albany, N.Y. 12222.

94. David Farrington, "The Development of Offending and Antisocial Behavior from Childhood to Adulthood." Paper presented at the Congress on Rethinking Delinquency, University of Minho, Braga, Portugal, July 1992.

95. Joseph Weis and J. David Hawkins, *Reports of the National Juvenile Assessment Centers, Preventing Delinquency* (Washington, D.C.: U.S. Department of Justice, 1981); Joseph Weis and John Sederstrom, *Reports of the National Juvenile Justice Assessment Centers, The Prevention of Serious Delinquency: What to Do* (Washington, D.C.: U.S. Department of Justice, 1981).

96. Julie O'Donnell, J. David Hawkins, and Robert Abbott, "Predicting Serious Delinquency and Substance Use among Aggressive Boys," *Journal of Consulting and Clinical Psychology* 63 (1995): 529–37.

97. Ibid., pp. 534–36; Richard Catalano, Rick Kosterman, J. David Hawkins, Michael Newcomb, and Robert Abbott, "Modeling the Etiology of Adolescent Substance Use: A Test of the

Social Development Model," *Journal of Drug Issues* 26 (1996): 429–55.

98. Todd Herrenkohl, Bu Huang, Rick Kosterman, J. David Hawkins, Richard Catalano, and Brian Smith, "A Comparison of Social Development Processes Leading to Violent Behavior in Late Adolescence for Childhood Initiators and Adolescent Initiators of Violence," *Journal of Research in Crime and Delinquency* 38 (2001): 45–63.

99. Bu Huang, Rick Kosterman, Richard Catalano, J. David Hawkins, and Robert Abbott, "Modeling Mediation in the Etiology of Violent Behavior in Adolescence: A Test of the Social Development Model," *Criminology* 39 (2001): 75–107.

100. J. David Hawkins, Richard Catalano, Diane Morrison, Julie O'Donnell, Robert Abbott, and L. Edward Day, "The Seattle Social Development Project," in *The Prevention of Antisocial Behavior in Children,* eds. Joan McCord and Richard Tremblay (New York: Guilford Press, 1992), pp. 139–60.

101. See, generally, D. J. West and David P. Farrington, *The Delinquent Way of Life* (London: Hienemann, 1977).

102. The material in the following sections is summarized from Farrington, "The Development of Offending and Antisocial Behavior from Childhood to Adulthood"; idem, "Psychobiological Factors in the Explanation and Reduction of Delinquency," *Today's Delinquent* 7 (1988): 44–46; idem, "Childhood Origins of Teenage Antisocial Behaviour and Adult Social Dysfunction," *Journal of the Royal Society of Medicine* 86 (1993): 13–17; idem, "Psychosocial Influences on the Development of Antisocial Personality." Paper presented at the annual meeting of the American Society of Criminology, Phoenix, Ariz., November 1993.

103. Terence Thornberry, "Toward an Interactional Theory of Delinquency," *Criminology* 25 (1987): 863–91.

104. Ross Matsueda and Kathleen Anderson, "The Dynamics of Delinquent Peers and Delinquent Behavior," *Criminology* 36 (1998): 269–308.

105. See, for example, Jean Piaget, *The Grasp of Consciousness* (Cambridge: Harvard University Press, 1976).

106. Thornberry, "Toward an Interactional Theory of Delinquency."

107. Ibid., p. 863.

108. This research is known as the Rochester Youth Development Study. Thornberry's colleagues on the project include Alan Lizotte, Margaret Farnworth, Marvin Krohn, and Susan Stern.

109. Sung Joon Jang and Carolyn Smith, "A Test of Reciprocal Causal Relationships among Parental Supervision, Affective Ties, and Delinquency," *Journal of Research in Crime and Delinquency* 34 (1997): 307–36.

110. Marvin Krohn, Alan Lizotte, and Cynthia Perez, "The Interrelationship between Substance Use and Precocious Transitions to Adult Sexuality," *Journal of Health and Social Behavior* 38 (1997): 87–103, at 88; Richard Jessor, "Risk Behavior in Adolescence: A Psychosocial Framework for Understanding and Action," in *Adolescents at Risk: Medical and Social Perspectives,* eds. D. E. Rogers and E. Ginzburg (Boulder, Colo.: Westview Press, 1992).

111. Terence Thornberry, Alan Lizotte, Marvin Krohn, and Margaret Farnworth, *The Role of Delinquent Peers in the Initiation of Delinquent Behavior,* working paper No. 6, rev., Rochester Youth Development Study (Albany, N.Y.: Hindelang Criminal Justice Research Center, 1993).

112. Terence Thornberry, Alan Lizotte, Marvin Krohn, Margaret Farnworth, and Sung Joon Jang, "Delinquent Peers, Beliefs, and Delinquent Behavior: A Longitudinal Test of Interactional Theory," *Criminology* 32 (1994): 601–37.

113. Lening Zhang, John Welte, and William Wieczorek, "Youth Gangs, Drug Use and Delinquency," *Journal of Criminal Justice* 27 (1999): 101–9.

114. Terence Thornberry, Alan Lizotte, Marvin Krohn, Margaret Farnworth, and Sung Joon Jang, *Delinquent Peers, Beliefs, and Delinquent Behavior: A Longitudinal Test of Interactional Theory,* working paper No. 6, rev., Rochester Youth Development Study (Albany, N.Y.: Hindelang Criminal Justice Research Center, 1992).

115. Terence Thornberry, Alan Lizotte, Marvin Krohn, Margaret Farnworth, and Sung Joon Jang, "Testing Interactional Theory: An Examination of Reciprocal Causal Relationships among Family, School, and Delinquency," *Journal of Criminal Law and Criminology* 82 (1991): 3–35.

116. Suman Kakar, "Youth Gangs and Their Families: Effect of Gang Membership on Family's Subjective Well-Being," *Journal of Crime and Justice* 21 (1998): 157–71.

117. Scott Menard and Delbert Elliott, "Delinquent Bonding, Moral Beliefs, and Illegal Behavior: A Three Wave-Panel Model," *Justice Quarterly* 11 (1994): 173–88.

118. Sung Joon Jang, "Age-Varying Effects of Family, School and Peers on Delinquency: A Multilevel Modeling Test of Interactional Theory," *Criminology* 37 (1999): 643–86.

119. Carolyn Smith, Alan Lizotte, Terence Thornberry, and Marvin Krohn, *Resilient Youth: Identifying Factors That Prevent High-Risk Youth from Engaging in Delinquency and Drug Use* (Albany, N.Y: Rochester Youth Development Study, 1994).

120. Thornberry et al., "Delinquent Peers, Beliefs, and Delinquent Behavior," pp. 628–29.

121. Robert Sampson and John Laub, *Crime in the Making: Pathways and Turning Points Through Life* (Cambridge: Harvard University Press, 1993); John Laub and Robert Sampson, "Turning Points in the Life Course: Why Change Matters to the Study of Crime." Paper presented at the annual meeting of the American Society of Criminology, New Orleans, November 1992.

122. Terri Orbuch, James House, Richard Mero, and Pamela Webster, "Marital Quality Over the Life Course," *Social Psychology Quarterly* 59 (1996): 162–71; Lee Lillard and Linda Waite, "'Til Death Do Us Part: Marital Disruption and Mortality," *American Journal of Sociology* 100 (1995): 1131–56.

123. Mark Warr, "Life-Course Transitions and Desistance from Crime," *Criminology* 36 (1998): 183–216.

124. Pamela Webster, Terri Orbuch, and James House, "Effects of Childhood Family Background on Adult Marital Quality and Perceived Stability," *American Journal of Sociology* 101 (1995): 404–32.

125. John Hagan, Ross MacMillan, and Blair Wheaton, "New Kid in Town: Social Capital and the Life Course Effects of Family Migration on Children," *American Sociological Review* 61 (1996): 368–85.

126. Sampson and Laub, *Crime in the Making,* p. 249.

127. Avshalom Caspi, Terrie Moffitt, Bradley Entner Wright, and Phil Silva, "Early Failure in the Labor Market: Childhood and Adolescent Predictors of Unemployment in the Transition to Adulthood," *American Sociological Review* 63 (1998): 424–51.

128. Erich Labouvie, "Maturing Out of Substance Use: Selection and Self-Correction," *Journal of Drug Issues* 26 (1996): 457–74.

129. Mark Warr, "Life-Course Transitions and Desistance from Crime," *Criminology* 36 (1998): 502–35.

130. Leonore M. J. Simon, "Social Bond and Criminal Record History of Acquaintance and Stranger Violent Offenders," *Journal of Crime and Justice* 22 (1999): 131–46.

131. Raymond Paternoster and Robert Brame, "Multiple Routes to Delinquency? A Test of Developmental and General Theories of Crime," *Criminology* 35 (1997): 49–84.

132. Spencer De Li, "Legal Sanctions and Youths' Status Achievement: A Longitudinal Study," *Justice Quarterly* 16 (1999): 377–401.

133. Shawn Bushway, "The Impact of an Arrest on the Job Stability of Young White American Men," *Journal of Research on Crime and Delinquency* 35 (1999): 454–79.

134. Candace Kruttschnitt, Christopher Uggen, and Kelly Shelton, "Individual Variability in Sex Offending and Its Relationship to Informal and Formal Social Controls." Paper presented at the American Society of Criminology meeting, San Diego, Calif., 1997; Mark Collins and Don Weatherburn, "Unemployment and the Dynamics of Offender Populations," *Journal of Quantitative Criminology* 11 (1995): 231–45.

135. Robert Hoge, D. A. Andrews, and Alan Leschied, "An Investigation of Risk and Protective Factors in a Sample of Youthful Offenders," *Journal of Child Psychology and Psychiatry* 37 (1996): 419–24.

136. Richard Arum and Irenee Beattie, "High School Experience and the Risk of Adult Incarceration," *Criminology* 37 (1999): 515–40.

137. Candace Kruttschnitt, Christopher Uggen, and Kelly Shelton, "Individual Variability in Sex Offending and Its Relationship to Informal and Formal Social Controls." Paper presented at the American Society of Criminology meeting, San Diego, Calif., 1997; Mark Collins and Don Weatherburn, "Unemployment and the Dynamics of Offender Populations," *Journal of Quantitative Criminology* 11 (1995): 231–45.

138. Eloise Dunlop and Bruce Johnson, "Family and Human Resources in the Development of a Female Crack-Seller Career: Case Study of a Hidden Population," *Journal of Drug Issues* 26 (1996): 175–98.

139. Christopher Uggen, "Ex-Offenders and the Conformist Alternative: A Job Quality Model of Work and Crime," *Social Problems* 46 (1999): 127–51.

140. Daniel Nagin and Raymond Paternoster, "Personal Capital and Social Control: The Deterrence Implications of a Theory of Criminal Offending," *Criminology* 32 (1994): 581–606.

141. Eloise Dunlop and Bruce Johnson, "Family and Human Resources in the Development of a Female Crack-Seller Career: Case Study of a Hidden Population," *Journal of Drug Issues* 26 (1996): 175–98.

142. Bradley Entner Wright, Avashalom Caspi, Terrie Moffitt, and Phil Silva, "Low Self-Control, Social Bonds, and Crime: Social Causation, Social Selection, or Both?" *Criminology* 37 (1999): 479–514.

143. Ibid., p. 504.

144. Stephen Cernkovich and Peggy Giordano, "Stability and Change in Antisocial Behavior: The Transition from Adolescence to Early Adulthood," *Criminology* 39 (2001): 371–410.

Regardless of why people commit crime in the first place, their actions are defined by law as falling into particular crime categories, or typologies. Criminologists often seek to group individual criminal offenders or behaviors so they may be more easily studied and understood. These are referred to as offender typologies.

In this section, crime patterns are clustered into four typologies: violent crime (Chapter 11); economic crimes involving common theft offenses (Chapter 12); economic crimes involving white-collar criminals or criminal organizations (Chapter 13);

PART III Crime Typologies

and public order crimes, such as prostitution and drug abuse (Chapter 14). This format groups criminal behaviors by their focus and consequence: bringing physical harm to others; misappropriating other people's property; and violating laws designed to protect public morals.

Typologies can be useful in classifying large numbers of criminal offenses or offenders into easily understood categories. This text has grouped offenses and offenders on the basis of their legal definitions and their collective goals, objectives, and consequences.

the FBI's ten most wanted fugitives

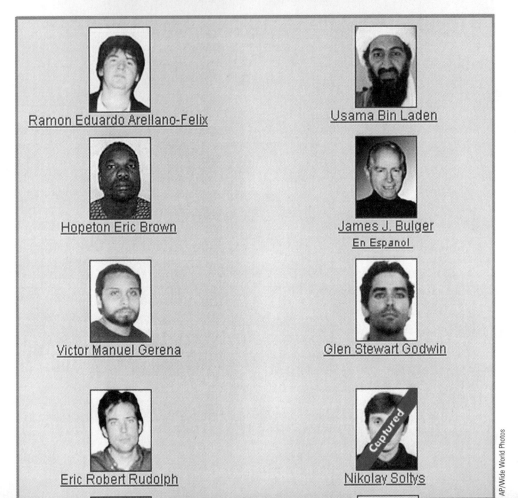

Ramon Eduardo Arellano-Felix

Hopeton Eric Brown

Victor Manuel Gerena

Eric Robert Rudolph

Usama Bin Laden

James J. Bulger
En Espanol

Glen Stewart Godwin

Captured

Nikolay Soltys

AP/Wide World Photos

CHAPTER 11 Violent Crime

Introduction

In the aftermath of the September 11, 2001, destruction of the World Trade Center in New York City, many Americans asked themselves the same simple question: Why? What could motivate someone like Osama bin Laden to order the deaths of thousands of innocent people? How could someone who had never been to the United States or suffered personally at its hands develop such lethal hatred?

Some experts believed the attacks had a political basis, claiming that Osama's anger was an outgrowth of America's Middle East policies. Others saw a religious motivation and claimed that the terrorists were radical Muslims at war with the liberal religions of the West. Another view was that Osama's rage was fueled by deep-rooted psychological problems.

On the surface, it appeared that Osama bin Laden was the favored son of a wealthy Saudi Arabian family.[1] The fortune he used to finance his terrorist activities was derived from an inheritance of more than $300 million from his family. It is also possible, however, that some deep-rooted psychological issues may have precipitated his murderous impulses. Some analysts note that bin Laden was the only son of his late father's least favorite wife, who was a Syrian and not a Saudi. Bin Laden may have been close to his mother, but he may have felt driven to achieve stature in the eyes of his father and the rest of the family. Bin Laden may have been willing to do anything to gain power and eclipse his father, who died when bin Laden was 10 years old.

The impulse for his murderous actions may have stemmed from bin Laden's unconscious efforts to gain his father's approval. He modeled his behavior after his father in many ways, including working with the Saudi royal family on construction deals. Bin Laden once told an interviewer of his desire to please his father: "My father was very keen that one of his sons should fight against the enemies of Islam. So I am the one son who is acting according to the wishes of his father." Perhaps this need for acceptance explains bin Laden's religious zeal, which was in excess of anyone else's in his large extended family.

After his father's death, bin Laden was mentored by a Jordanian named Abdullah Azzam whose motto was "Jihad and the rifle alone: no negotiations, no conferences and no dialogues." When Azzam was killed in 1989 by a car bomb in Pakistan, bin Laden vowed to carry on Azzam's "holy war" against the West. He threw himself into the Afghan conflict against the Soviet Union, and when the Russians withdrew, he was convinced that the West was vulnerable. "The myth of the superpower was destroyed not only in my mind, but also in the minds of all Muslims," bin Laden has told interviewers.

Bin Laden's motivations will probably never be fully understood, but is it possible that his violent urges stemmed from the same web of emotions that fuel the thousands of predatory criminals who prowl society looking for unwary victims? If so, his actions, although extreme, are certainly not unique. Many people have personally experienced violence or have a friend who has been victimized. Almost everyone has heard about someone being robbed, beaten, or killed. Riots and mass disturbances have ravaged urban areas; racial attacks plague schools and college campuses; assassination has claimed the lives of political, religious, and social leaders all over the world.

Violence directed toward strangers is **instrumental violence;** it is designed to improve the financial or social position of the criminal, such as through an armed robbery. In contrast, **expressive violence** refers to crimes that vent rage, anger, or frustration. This may have been the case when on April 20, 1999, Eric Harris and Dylan Klebold, two students at Columbine High School in Littleton, Colorado, went on a murderous rampage that left 12 students and one teacher dead and 24 other people wounded, before the boys committed suicide. Members of a cult group called the "Trenchcoat Mafia," Harris and Klebold had spent more than a year planning the attack and building homemade bombs. The Littleton incident is an extreme example of expressive violence.

The general public believes the government should "get tough" about violent crime. Public opinion polls indicate that about 66 percent of U.S. citizens favor the use of capital punishment for persons convicted of murder, up from 38 percent in 1965.[2] Many people believe the United States is becoming even more violent than in the past. But longing for the serenity of the pioneer days may be misplaced: American society has long been stained with violent crime, as is discussed in the Criminological Enterprise feature titled "Violent Land."

What sets off a violent person? Some experts suggest that a small number of inherently violence-prone individuals may themselves have been the victims of physical or psychological abnormalities. Another view is that violence and aggression are inherently human traits that can affect any person at any time. There may be violence-prone subcultures within society whose members value force, routinely carry weapons, and consider violence to have an acceptable place in social interaction.[3]

This chapter surveys the nature and extent of violent crime. First, it briefly reviews some hypothetical causes of violence. Then it focuses on specific types of interpersonal violence—rape, homicide, assault, robbery, and emerging forms of interpersonal violence. Finally, it briefly examines political violence, state-sponsored violence, and terrorism.

The Roots of Violence

What causes people to behave violently? There are a number of competing explanations for violent behavior. A few of the most prominent are discussed here and illustrated in Figure 11.1.

Violent Land

David Courtwright, an authority on the sociocultural roots of violence, describes a nineteenth-century American society much more violent than today. According to Courtwright, societies with the highest rates of violent crime have been populations with an overabundance of young males who are "awash with testosterone" and unrestrained by social controls such as marriage and family.

Until the mid-twentieth century, the U.S. population was disproportionately young and male. The male–female gender ratio of those who settled here involuntarily—indentured servants and slaves—was more than 2:1. Poor laborers who paid for their passage by signing labor contracts were almost all male; the gender ratio among Chinese laborers was an astounding 27:1. Aside from Ireland, which furnished slightly more female than male immigrants, Europeans who arrived voluntarily were also predominantly male. Because these young men outnumbered women, not all men were able to marry, and those who did not remained unrestrained by the calming influence of family life and parental responsibility.

Cultural factors worsened these population trends. Frontier culture was characterized by racism and a preoccupation with personal honor. Some ethnic groups drank heavily and frequented saloons and gambling halls, where petty arguments could become lethal because most patrons carried guns and knives. Violent acts often went unpunished, however, because law enforcement agencies were unable or unwilling to take action. Nowhere were these cultural and population effects felt more acutely than on the western frontier. Here the population was mostly young

bachelors who were sensitive about honor, hostile racists, heavy drinkers, morally indifferent, heavily armed, and unchecked by adequate law enforcement. It is not surprising, considering this explosive mix, that 20 percent of the 89,000 miners who arrived in California during the 1849 gold rush were dead within six months. Many died from disease, but others succumbed to drink and violence. Smoking, gambling, and heavy drinking became a cultural imperative, and those who were disinclined to indulge were considered social outcasts.

Over time, gender ratios equalized as more men brought families to the frontier and children of both sexes were born. Many men died, returned home, or drifted elsewhere. By the mid-twentieth century, America's overall male surplus was disappearing, and a balanced population helped bring down the crime rate.

According to Courtwright, rising violence rates in the 1960s and 1970s can be attributed to the fact that men were avoiding, delaying, or terminating marriage. In 1960 Americans spent an average of 62 percent of their lives with spouses and children, an all-time high; in 1980 they spent 43 percent with families, an all-time low. Both the illegitimacy and divorce rates began to spiral upward, guaranteeing that the number of poorly socialized and poorly supervised children would increase dramatically. The inner-city urban ghetto became the "frontier" community of today. Gangs such as the Crips and Bloods in Los Angeles are the modern descendants of the Old West gangs of Jesse James and Butch Cassidy and the Sundance Kid's Hole in the Wall Gang. Although the male–female ratio is more balanced today than on the western frontier, the presence of unsupervised, poorly socialized males, who have easy access to guns,

drugs, and vice, has produced a crime rate of similar proportions. Violence rates have stabilized lately, but they may rise again as the decline in the family remains unchecked.

Courtwright's analysis shows that violence is not a recent development and that demographic and cultural forces determine violent crime rates. It disputes the contention that some artifact of modern life, such as violent films and TV, is causing American violence. The factors that predispose societies to violence can be found in demographics and culture and are unique neither to our society nor to our times.

Critical Thinking Questions

1. According to Courtwright, crime rates were exceedingly high in the nineteenth century before TV, movies, and rap videos had been created. What, if anything, does this say about the effect of media on crime?

2. What were some of the other factors that provoked violence? Do you think these factors still cause violence today?

InfoTrac College Edition Research

If you are interested in reading more about the early history of violence in the West, look up:

Margaret Walsh. New horizons for the American West. *History Today* March 1994 v44 n3 p44(7)

SOURCES: David Courtwright, "Violence in America," American Heritage 47 (1996): 36–52, quote at p. 36; David Courtwright, *Violent Land: Single Men and Social Disorder from the Frontier to the Inner City* (Cambridge: Harvard University Press, 1996).

Figure 11.1 Sources of Violence

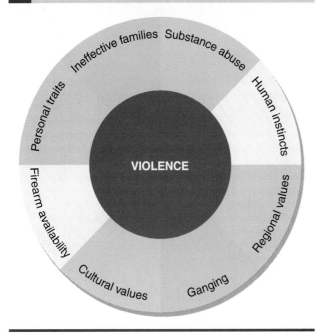

Ineffective families · Substance abuse · Personal traits · Human instincts · Firearm availability · Regional values · Cultural values · Ganging

VIOLENCE

Personal Traits

On March 13, 1995, an ex–Boy Scout leader named Thomas Hamilton took four high-powered rifles into the primary school of the peaceful Scottish town of Dunblane and slaughtered 16 children and their teacher. This horrific crime shocked the British Isles into implementing strict controls on all guns.[4] Bizarre outbursts such as Hamilton's support a link between violence and personal traits.

To read more about the Dunblane Massacre, go to:
**http://www.guardiancentury.co.uk/
1990-1999/Story/0,6051,112749,00.html**
For an up-to-date list of Web links, go to
http://info.wadsworth.com/siegel ■

Psychologist Dorothy Otnow Lewis and her associates found that murderous youths suffer signs of major neurological impairment (such as abnormal EEGs, multiple psychomotor impairments, and severe seizures), low intelligence as measured on standard IQ tests, psychotic close relatives, and psychotic symptoms such as paranoia, illogical thinking, and hallucinations.[5] In her 1998 book *Guilty by Reason of Insanity*, Lewis finds that death row inmates have a history of mental impairment and intellectual dysfunction.[6] Abnormal personality structures, including such traits as depression, impulsivity, aggression, dishonesty, pathological lying, lack of remorse, borderline personality syndrome, and psychopathology, have been associated with various forms of violence.[7] It comes as no

surprise then that many murderers kill themselves shortly after committing their crime. Even more bizarre are the cases of people who commit murder with the expectation that they will be executed for their crimes, a form of "suicide-murder."[8] Although this evidence indicates that violent offenders are more prone to psychosis than other people, no single clinical diagnosis can characterize their behavior.[9]

CONNECTIONS

As you may recall from Chapter 6, biosocial theorists link violence to a number of biological irregularities, including but not limited to genetic influences and inheritance, the action of hormones, the functioning of neurotransmitters, brain structure, and diet. Psychologists link violent behavior to observational learning from violent TV shows, traumatic childhood experiences, low intelligence, mental illness, impaired cognitive processes, and abnormal (psychopathic) personality structure. ■

To read an interview with Dorothy Otnow Lewis in which she discusses how the problems in an aggressive boy's life should be evaluated and how appropriate treatment should be provided, go to: Rena Large. New path for aggressive boys. *NEA Today* Oct 1998 v17 n2 p29(1) ■

Ineffective Families

Absent or deviant parents, inconsistent discipline, and lack of supervision have all been linked to persistent violent offending.[10] Although infants demonstrate individual temperaments, who they become may have a lot to do with how they are treated during their early years. Some children are less easy to soothe than others; in some cases, difficult infant temperament has been associated with later aggression and behavioral problems.[11] Parents who fail to set adequate limits or to use proper, consistent discipline reinforce a child's coercive behavior.[12] The effects of inadequate parenting and early rejection may affect violent behavior throughout life.[13] There is evidence that children who are maltreated and neglected in early childhood are the ones most likely to be initiated into criminality and thereafter continue or persist in a criminal career.[14]

There are also indications that children who are subject to even minimal amounts of physical punishment may be more likely one day to use violence themselves. Murray Straus reviewed the concept of discipline in a series of surveys and found a powerful relationship between exposure to physical punishment and later aggression.[15] The effect of physical punishment may be mediated or neutralized to some extent if parents also provide support, warmth, and care. When kids experience physical punishment in the absence of parental involvement, they feel angry and unjustly treated and are more willing to defy their parents and engage in antisocial behavior.[16]

■ It is difficult to imagine that a mother would kill her child; the instinct to nurture and protect young children seems to be universal. Andrea Yates, who drowned her five children in 2001, claimed she was suffering from mental disease brought about by postpartum depression. Nonetheless, a jury found her guilty of murder on March 12, 2002. The prosecution did not contest that Yates suffered from a severe mental disease but contended that she knew killing her children was wrong and that the acts were premeditated.

AP/Wide World Photos

Abused children   A number of research studies have found that children who are clinically diagnosed as abused later engage in delinquent behaviors, including violence, at a rate significantly greater than that of children who were not abused.[17] Samples of convicted murderers reveal a high percentage of seriously abused youth.[18] The abuse–violence association has been established in many cases in which parents have been killed by their children; sexual abuse is also a constant factor in father (patricide) and mother (matricide) killings.[19] Dorothy Otnow Lewis found in her study of juvenile death row inmates that all had long histories of intense child abuse.[20]

One of the most outspoken critics of physical punishment of children is Murray Straus of the Family Research Laboratory at the University of New Hampshire. Straus has used survey and record data to show that children who are physically punished by their parents are likely to physically abuse a sibling and later engage in spouse abuse and other forms of criminal violence.[21]

The brutalization process   Lonnie Athens is one well-known criminologist who links violence to early experiences with child abuse. Athens finds that people can be classified into three groups based on their aggressive tendencies: nonviolent, violent (those who attack others

physically with the intention of harming them), and incipiently violent (those who are willing and ready to attack but limit themselves to violent ultimatums and / or intimidating physical gestures). Athens also finds that there are actually four distinct types of violent acts: physically defensive (in which the perpetrator sees his violent act as one of self-defense), frustrative (in which the offender acts out of anger due to frustration when he cannot get his way), malefic (in which the victim is considered to be extremely evil or malicious), and frustrative-malefic (a combined type). Antisocial careers are often created in a series of stages that begin with brutal episodes during early adolescence.

- The first stage involves the brutalization process, during which a young victim begins the process of developing a belligerent, angry demeanor. The brutalization can come at the hands of abusive parents or caretakers. But the brutalization process is broader than parental physical or sexual abuse. It may also result from violent subjugation, personal horrification, and violent coaching by peers, neighbors, and schoolmates. Although most brutalization occurs early in life, some people can be brutalized as they mature.
- Brutalized youth may become belligerent and angry. When confronted at home, school, or on the street,

Mothers Who Kill Their Children

It is inconceivable that a mother would kill her child, because the instinct to nurture and protect young children seems to be universal. What would prompt a woman to kill her own child, who is both helpless and dependent on her for care and survival?

To answer this question, Susan Crimmins, Sandra Langley, Henry Brownstein, and Barry Spunt interviewed 42 women in New York state prisons, all of whom had been convicted of manslaughter or murder in the deaths of their children. The women described a consistent history of social and psychological trauma leading up to their fatal acts. More than two-thirds were characterized as "motherless mothers," who had either absent or abusive mothers themselves. More than one-third reported that their mothers were alcoholics.

About three-fourths of the women had been physically or sexually abused as children. Early childhood experience with abuse was carried over into abusive spousal relations: most of these women (79 percent) had been abused by a partner. Forty-one percent of these women had attempted

suicide. All 43 women interviewed experienced more than one incident that damaged their self-image prior to killing their children.

When asked why they killed their children (about three-fourths were biological parents; the others killed foster or adopted children or the children of neighbors or relatives), most reported extreme psychological stress (such as depression or schizophrenia). About one-third linked their behavior to alcohol or drug abuse. Isolation in childhood carried over to motherhood, and they felt isolated and alone; they had learned to suffer in silence.

So the link these women shared was a traumatic childhood that was filled with a variety of losses as well as insensitivity to their emotional needs. Social isolation, along with their learned ability to suffer without complaining, reinforced their already poor self-esteem. Lethal violence was connected to their years of social and economic frustration and a prior history of violence to settle disputes in their own families. Because their emotional needs were consistently unmet, their attachments to others were disrupted, and their self-esteem did not develop in a healthy way. Isolated, rejected, and feeling low self-worth, these women were unable to feel empathy with others. Such feelings gen-

erated additional rage and despair that later erupted into violent, aggressive behavior.

Critical Thinking Questions

1. What can be done to deal with the issues that produce women who kill their children?

2. Is it possible for government intervention programs to alter the lives of women who have had a long history of trauma and conflict?

 InfoTrac College Edition Research

What factors contribute to violent episodes by women? To find out more, read:

Lionel Tiger. Men, women, and aggression: from rage in marriage to violence in the streets—how gender affects the way we act. *Society* March–April 1995 v32 n3 p79A

Ofra Anson and Shifra Sagy. Marital violence: comparing women in violent and nonviolent unions. *Human Relations* March 1995 v48 n3 p285

SOURCE: Susan Crimmins, Sandra Langley, Henry Brownstein, and Barry Spunt, "Convicted Women Who Have Killed Children: A Self-Psychology Perspective," *Journal of Interpersonal Violence* 12 (1997): 49–69.

---

these belligerent youth respond with violent performances of angry, hostile behavior. The success of their violent confrontations provides them with a sense of power and achievement.

- In the virulency stage, emerging criminals develop a violent identity that makes them feared; they enjoy intimidating others. To Athens, this process takes violent youths full circle from being the victims of aggression to its initiators; they are now the same person they grew up despising, ready to begin the process with their own children.[22]

Athens recognizes that brutalization alone is not a sufficient condition to cause someone to become a dangerous violent criminal. One must complete the full cycle of the "violentization process"—belligerence, violent per-

formances, and virulency—to become socialized into violence. Many brutalized children do not go on to become violent criminals, and some later reject the fact that they were abused as youths and redefine their early years as normative.

A significant amount of evidence has shown the association between abuse and violent crime, but it is also true that many offenders have not suffered abuse and that many abused youths do not grow up to become persistent adult offenders.[23] Judith Rich Harris for one suggests that the link is spurious and that there is little reason to assume that the behavior of parents influences the behavior of their offspring.[24]

The Race, Culture, Gender, and Criminology feature titled "Mothers Who Kill Their Children" discusses one aspect of the abuse–violence link.

To learn more about the nature and extent of child abuse, use the subject guide feature of InfoTrac College Edition to search for the term "child abuse." ∎

Evolutionary Factors/Human Instinct

Perhaps violent responses and emotions are actually inherent in all humans, and the right spark can trigger them. Sigmund Freud believed that human aggression and violence are produced by instinctual drives.[25] Freud maintained that humans possess two opposing instinctual drives that interact to control behavior: **eros,** the life instinct, which drives people toward self-fulfillment and enjoyment; and **thanatos,** the death instinct, which produces self-destruction. Thanatos can be expressed externally (as violence and sadism) or internally (as suicide, alcoholism, or other self-destructive habits). Because aggression is instinctual, Freud saw little hope for its treatment.

To learn more about Freud's views, go to InfoTrac College Edition and use his name as a key word. ∎

A number of biologists and anthropologists have also speculated that instinctual violence-promoting traits may be common in the human species. One view is that aggression and violence are the results of instincts inborn in all animals, including human beings. A leading proponent of this view, Konrad Lorenz, developed this theory in his famous book, *On Aggression.*[26] Lorenz argued that aggressive energy is produced by inbred instincts that are independent of environmental forces. In the animal kingdom, aggression usually serves a productive purpose—for example, it leads members of grazing species such as zebras and antelopes to spread out over available territory to ensure an ample food supply and the survival of the fittest. Lorenz found that humans possess some of the same aggressive instincts as animals. But among lower species, aggression is rarely fatal; when a conflict occurs, the winner is determined through a test of skill or endurance. This inhibition against killing members of their own species protects animals from self-extinction. Humans, lacking this inhibition against fatal violence, are capable of killing their own kind in war or as a result of interpersonal conflicts. As technology develops and more lethal weapons are produced, the extinction of the human species becomes a significant possibility.

To read the autobiography of Lorenz, who won the Nobel Prize in Medicine in 1973, go to:
   **http://www.nobel.se/medicine/laureates/1973/
   lorenz-autobio.html**
For an up-to-date list of Web links, go to
   http://info.wadsworth.com/siegel ∎

Evolutionary theories in criminology suggest that violent behavior is committed predominantly by males. Over the course of human existence, sexually aggressive males have been the ones most likely to produce children. Their offspring carry genes that support aggression. In all species, the males' competitive success is determined by their being dangerous and aggressive enough to scare off rivals. Among humans, just the reputation for being dangerous can last a lifetime. This psychologically ingrained need to display virility and toughness comes when young men are at the peak of their physical strength. They are more willing to take risks than at any other point in the life cycle, which factors heavily into their propensity toward violence.[27]

Exposure to Violence

People who are constantly exposed to violence at home, at school, or in the environment may adopt violent methods themselves. Some are exposed at an early age to violence in the home. For example, when Ira Hutchison and J. David Hirschel studied domestic violence cases in North Carolina, they found that in more than half of the cases children had witnessed the assault and in two-thirds of the cases children were there when the police arrived.[28]

Social scientist Felton Earls is now conducting a government-funded longitudinal study of pathways to violence among 8,000 Chicago area youths in 80 different, randomly selected neighborhoods.[29] Interviews with youths ages 9 to 15 show that large numbers of these children have been victims of or witnesses to violence and that many carry weapons. Between 30 and 40 percent of the children who reported exposure to violence also displayed significant violent behavior themselves. The research also shows that girls are involved in violence as much as boys, although the nature of the violence is quite different. Girls are more likely than boys to be victims of sexual violence, and boys are more likely to see or to participate in fights, stabbings, or shootings.

Children living in these conditions become **"crusted over":** they do not let people inside, nor do they express their feelings. They exploit others and in turn are exploited by those older and stronger; as a result, they develop a sense of hopelessness. They find that parents and teachers focus on their failures and problems, not their achievements. Consequently, they are vulnerable to the lure of delinquent gangs and groups.[30]

Substance Abuse

It has become common to link violence to substance abuse. In fact, substance abuse influences violence in three ways:[31]

1. A **psychopharmacological relationship** may be the direct consequence of ingesting mood-altering substances. Experimental evidence shows that high doses of drugs such as PCP and amphetamines may produce

violent, aggressive behavior.[32] Alcohol abuse has long been associated with all forms of violence because drinking reduces cognitive ability, making miscommunication more likely while at the same time limiting the capacity for rational dialogue and compromise.[33]

2. Drug ingestion may also cause **economic compulsive behavior,** in which drug users resort to violence to support their habit.

3. Violence becomes endemic when drug gangs flex their muscle to dominate territory and drive out rivals; this is referred to as a **systemic link.** Studies of gangs that sell drugs show that their violent activities may result in a significant proportion of all urban homicides.[34]

Most drug-related deaths, in fact, are motivated by drug trafficking and interpersonal conflict that results from drug abuse rather than from any direct cause, such as drug overdoses.[35]

Firearm Availability

Although firearm availability may not cause violence, it is certainly a facilitating factor. A petty argument can escalate into a fatal encounter if one party has a handgun. It may not be coincidence that the United States, which has a huge surplus of guns and in which most firearms (80 percent) used in crimes are stolen or obtained through illegal or unregulated transactions, also has one of the world's highest violence rates.[36] Disturbing evidence indicates that more than 80 percent of inmates in juvenile correctional facilities owned a gun just before their confinement, and 55 percent said they carried one almost all the time.[37] Institutionalized youth are not the only ones to carry weapons. The nation has also been rocked by the use of firearms in schools and the resulting slew of well-publicized school shootings. Research indicates that a significant number of kids routinely carry guns to school; those who have been the victims of crime themselves and who hang with peers who carry weapons are the ones most likely to bring guns to school.[38]

The Uniform Crime Report (UCR) indicates that two-thirds of all murders and about two-fifths of all robberies involve firearms.[39] Handguns kill two-thirds of all police who die in the line of duty. The presence of firearms in the home also significantly increases the risk of suicide among adolescents, regardless of how carefully the guns are secured or stored.[40] Assaults and violence among family members and other intimates are 12 times more likely to result in death if a handgun is used than if the attacks do not involve firearms.[41]

CONNECTIONS

Although it seems logical that banning the sale and ownership of firearms might help reduce violence, those in favor of gun ownership, as discussed in a feature on gun control in Chapter 3, do not agree. Some experts believe taking guns away from citizens might endanger them against armed criminals. ■

Cultural Values

Areas that experience violence seem to cluster together.[42] To explain this phenomenon, criminologists Marvin Wolfgang and Franco Ferracuti formulated the famous concept that some areas contain an independent **subculture of violence.**[43]

CONNECTIONS

Delinquent subcultures were discussed in some detail in Chapter 7. Recall that subculture theorists portray delinquents not as rebels from the normative culture but rather as people who are in accord with the informal rules and values of their immediate culture. By adhering to cultural norms, they violate the law. ■

The subculture's norms are separate from society's central, dominant value system. In this subculture, a potent theme of violence influences lifestyles, the socialization process, and interpersonal relationships. Even though the subculture's members share some of the dominant culture's values, they expect that violence will be used to solve social conflicts and dilemmas. In some cultural subgroups, then, violence has become legitimized by custom and norms. It is considered appropriate behavior within culturally defined conflict situations in which an individual who has been offended by a negative outcome in a dispute seeks reparations through violent means (disputatiousness).[44]

Research has shown that the subculture of violence may be found in areas that experience concentrated poverty and social disorganization.[45] Though most people abhor violence, income inequality and racial disparity may help instill a sense of hopelessness that nourishes pro-violence norms and values.[46]

Social movements Membership in radical political and social movements contributes to violence. Members may be told that the group's values are highly important and must be gained at all costs, even violent ones.[47] Some may tell their followers that "the best defense is a good offense," encouraging them to take aggressive action against their enemies. For example, local militia groups who fear foreign control over the United States may encourage their members either explicitly or implicitly to defy government agents or to attack immigrants in an effort to drive them out of the country.

Because some social movements, such as the right-to-life campaign, have gone national, there is little control over membership and leadership is diffuse. Violence-prone members who take the organization's goals to the extreme have become difficult to identify and/or remove. Furthermore, individuals who are considered too extreme or dangerous to be considered for group membership can gain material on the Internet and are free to use whatever violent means they desire.

Gang values Empirical evidence shows that violence rates are highest in urban areas where subcultural values support teenage gangs, whose members typically embrace the use of violence.[48] Gang boys are more likely to own guns and other weapons than non–gang members. They are also more likely to have peers who are gun owners and are more likely to carry guns outside the home.[49]

The association between gang membership and violence has a number of roots. It can result from drug trafficking activities and turf protection but also stems from personal vendettas and a perceived need for self-protection.[50] As criminologist Scott Decker found in his interviews with St. Louis gang boys, violence is a core value of gang membership.[51] Decker found that gang violence may be initiated for a variety of reasons:

- It enables new members to show toughness during initiation ceremonies.
- It can be used to retaliate against rivals for actual or perceived grievances.
- It protects ownership, such as when violence erupts when graffiti is defaced by rivals.
- It protects turf from incursions by outsiders.[52]

Regional values Some criminologists have suggested that regional values promote violence.[53] In a classic study, sociologist Raymond Gastil found a significant relationship between murder rates and residence in the South, a relationship that predates the Civil War. He also found that outside the South regional homicide rates are related to an influx of southern migration.[54] Gastil attributes high homicide rates to a southern culture that stresses a frontier mentality, mob violence, night riders, personal vengeance, and easily available firearms. Southerners are also thought to place greater emphasis on personal honor, to own more firearms, and to use different child-rearing practices than citizens in other parts of the country.[55] It has been suggested that especially in areas dominated by white populations, southerners behave in the heritage of medieval European knights, ready to defend family and home against any perceived threat.[56]

Not all criminologists agree with the southern subculture concept.[57] Some argue that southern homicide rates are high because of economic and social factors, not any "southern culture of lethal violence."[58] Gastil has responded to his critics by stating that they missed his point—that southern culture promotes violence, not just the approval of violence.[59]

Although the southern subculture view is still debated, Uniform Crime Report data indicate that the southern states continue to have a relatively high crime rate.[60] Despite recent evidence that refutes the southern subculture of violence theory, the image of the violent southerner remains, unfortunately, an enduring myth.[61]

National values Some nations, including the United States, Sri Lanka, Angola, Uganda, and the Philippines, have relatively high violence rates; others are much more peaceful. According to research by sociologist Jerome Neapolitan, a number of national characteristics are predictive of violence. These include a high level of social disorganization, economic stress (versus support), high child abuse rates, approval of violence by the government, political corruption, and an inefficient justice system.[62] Children in high-violence nations are likely to be economically deprived and socially isolated, exposed to constant violence, and lacking in hope and respect for the law. Guns are common in these nations because, lacking an efficient justice system, people arm themselves or hire private security forces for protection.[63]

Each of these factors is believed to influence violent crime, including both traditional common-law crimes, such as rape, murder, assault, and robbery, and newly recognized problems, such as workplace violence, hate crimes, and political violence. Each of these forms of violent behavior is now discussed.

■ Forcible Rape

Rape (from the Latin *rapere,* to take by force) is defined in common law as "the carnal knowledge of a female forcibly and against her will."[64] It is one of the most loathed, misunderstood, and frightening crimes. Under traditional common-law definitions, rape involves nonconsensual sexual intercourse that a male performs against a female he is neither married to nor cohabitating with. Sexual acts that are excluded from this definition of rape are usually included in other crime categories: for example,

- A male forcing a female to participate in fellatio, cunnilingus, and, in many states, anal intercourse; these crimes are usually covered by sodomy statutes, which outlaw deviant sexual practices.
- A female or male coercing a male to participate in intercourse or other sexual activity.
- A female coercing another female to participate in sexual activity.
- A male or female coercing sexual intercourse by threatening social, economic, or vocational harm rather than physical injury.[65]

Rape was often viewed as a sexual offense in the traditional criminological literature. It was presented as a crime that involved overwhelming lust, driving a man to force his attentions on a woman. Even today, some men view rape as a sexual act, including one Tennessee judge who released an accused rapist after stating that all he needed was a girlfriend and telling the public defender's office to arrange for a dating service. Public outcry led to the release being rescinded.[66]

Criminologists now consider rape a violent, coercive act of aggression, not a forceful expression of sexuality. There has been a national campaign to alert the public to the seriousness of rape, offer help to victims, and change legal definitions to facilitate the prosecution of rape offenders. Such efforts have been only marginally effective in reducing rape rates, but there has been significant progress in overhauling rape laws and developing a vast social service network to aid victims.

Use the term "rape" as a subject guide to search for more information in InfoTrac College Edition. ■

History of Rape

Rape has been a recognized crime throughout history. It has been the subject of art, literature, film, and theater. Paintings such as the *Rape of the Sabine Women* by Nicolas Poussin, novels such as *Clarissa* by Samuel Richardson, poems such as *The Rape of Lucrece* by William Shakespeare, and films such as *The Accused* have sexual violence as their central theme.

In early civilization rape was common. Men staked a claim of ownership on women by forcibly abducting and raping them. This practice led to males' solidification of power and their historical domination of women.[67] Under Babylonian and Hebraic law, the rape of a virgin was a crime punishable by death. However, if the victim was married, then both she and her attacker were considered equally to blame, and unless her husband intervened, both were put to death.

During the Middle Ages, it was common for ambitious men to abduct and rape wealthy women in an effort to force them into marriage. The practice of "heiress stealing" illustrates how feudal law gave little thought or protection to women and equated them with property.[68] Only in the late fifteenth century, after a monetary economy developed, was forcible sex outlawed. Thereafter, the violation of a virgin caused an economic hardship on her family, who expected a significant dowry for her hand in marriage. However, the law only applied to the wealthy; peasant women and married women were not considered rape victims until well into the sixteenth century. The Christian condemnation of sex during this period was also a denunciation of women as evil, having lust in their

hearts, and redeemable only by motherhood. A woman who was raped was almost automatically suspected of contributing to her attack.

Rape and the Military

Although rape has long been associated with military conquest, the nation was still stunned when in 1996 the national media revealed the presence of a "rape ring" at the Aberdeen Proving Grounds in Maryland. Nearly 20 noncommissioned officers were accused of raping and sexually harassing 19 female trainees. The investigation prompted more than 5,000 female soldiers to call military hot lines to report similar behavior at Army bases around the country. The Army scandal was especially disturbing because it involved drill instructors, who are given almost total control over the lives of young female recruits who depend on them for support, training, and nurturing.[69]

The link between the military and rape is inescapable. Throughout recorded history, rape has been associated with armies and warfare. Soldiers of conquering armies have considered sexual possession of their enemies' women one of the spoils of war. Among the ancient Greeks, rape was socially acceptable within the rules of warfare. During the Crusades, even knights and pilgrims, ostensibly bound by vows of chivalry and Christian piety, took time to rape as they marched toward Constantinople.

The belief that women are part of the spoils of war has continued. During World War II the Japanese army forced as many as 200,000 Korean women into frontline brothels, where they were repeatedly raped. In a 1998 Japanese ruling, the surviving Korean women were awarded the equivalent of $2,300 each in compensation.[70] The systematic rape of Bosnian and Kosovar women by Serbian army officers during the civil war in the former Yugoslavia horrified the world during the 1990s. These crimes seemed particularly atrocious because they appeared to be part of an official policy of genocide: rape was deliberately used to impregnate Bosnian women with Serbian children.

CONNECTIONS

State-sponsored terrorism, often directed at minority groups who share some personal characteristic such as religion or ethnic background, will be discussed later in this chapter in the sections on political terrorism. ■

On March 9, 1998, Dragoljub Kunarac, 37, a former Bosnian Serb paramilitary commander, admitted before an international tribunal in the Netherlands that he had raped Muslim women during the Bosnian war in 1992. His confession made him the first person to plead guilty to rape as a war crime.[71] Human rights groups have estimated that more than 30,000 women and young girls were sexually abused in the Balkan fighting.

Incidence of Rape

According to the most recent UCR data, about 90,000 rapes or attempted rapes were reported to U.S. police in 2000, a rate of 32 per 100,000 inhabitants.[72] Like other violent crimes, the rape rate has been in a decade-long decline, and the 2000 totals are 6 percent below 1996 and 15 percent below 1991 levels.

Population density influences the rape rate. Metropolitan areas today have rape rates significantly higher than rural areas; nonetheless, urban areas have experienced a much greater drop in rape reports than rural areas. The police make arrests in slightly more than half of all reported rape offenses. Of the offenders arrested, about 45 percent were under 25 years of age, and 63 percent were white. The racial pattern of rape arrests has been fairly consistent for some time. Finally, rape is a warm-weather crime—most incidents occur during July and August, with the lowest rates occurring during December, January, and February.

These data must be interpreted with caution. According to the National Crime Victimization Survey (NCVS), rape is frequently underreported. For example, in 2000 the NCVS estimates that 260,000 rapes and attempted rapes took place, suggesting that fewer than half of such incidents are reported to police.[73] Many people fail to report rapes because they are embarrassed, believe nothing can be done, or blame themselves.

Because other victim surveys indicate that at least 20 percent of adult women, 15 percent of college-aged women, and 12 percent of adolescent girls have experienced sexual abuse or assault at some time during their lives, it is evident that both official and victimization statistics significantly undercount rape.[74]

Types of Rape and Rapists

Some rapes are planned, others are spontaneous; some focus on a particular victim, whereas others occur almost as an afterthought during the commission of another crime, such as a burglary. Some rapists commit a single crime, whereas others are multiple offenders; some attack alone, and others engage in group or gang rapes.[75] Because there is no single type of rape or rapist, criminologists have attempted to define and categorize the vast variety of rape situations.

Criminologists now recognize that there are numerous motivations for rape and as a result various types of rapists. One of the best-known attempts to classify the personalities of rapists was made by psychologist A. Nicholas Groth, an expert on classifying and treating sex offenders. According to Groth, every rape encounter contains at least one of these three elements: anger, power, and sadism.[76] Consequently, rapists can be classified according to one of the three dimensions described in Exhibit 11.1. In treating rape offenders, Groth found that about 55 percent were of

■ Donita Welch, a rape survivor, speaks at a news conference in Santa Fe, New Mexico, on November 6, 2001, after watching the execution of her attacker Terry Clark who had been convicted of raping and killing another woman, Dena Lynn Gore, two years after he attacked Welch. Despite the seriousness of the crime, about 20 percent of convicted rapists are given a probationary sentence.

the power type; about 40 percent, the anger type; and about 5 percent, the sadistic type. Groth's major contribution has been his recognition that rape is generally a crime of violence, not a sexual act. In all of these circumstances, rape involves a violent criminal offense in which a predatory criminal chooses to attack a victim.[77]

Exhibit 11.1 Varieties of Forcible Rape

- *Anger rape* occurs when sexuality becomes a means of expressing and discharging pent-up anger and rage. The rapist uses far more brutality than would have been necessary if his real objective had been simply to have sex with his victim. His aim is to hurt his victim as much as possible; the sexual aspect of rape may be an afterthought. Often the anger rapist acts on the spur of the moment after an upsetting incident has caused him conflict, irritation, or aggravation. Surprisingly, anger rapes are less psychologically traumatic for the victim than might be expected. Because a woman is usually physically beaten during an anger rape, she is more likely to receive sympathy from her peers, relatives, and the justice system and consequently be immune from any suggestion that she complied with the attack.

- *Power rape* involves an attacker who does not want to harm his victim as much as he wants to possess her sexually. His goal is sexual conquest, and he uses only the amount of force necessary to achieve his objective. The power rapist wants to be in control, to be able to dominate women and have them at his mercy. Yet it is not sexual gratification that drives the power rapist; in fact, he often has a consenting relationship with his wife or girlfriend. Rape is instead a way of putting personal insecurities to rest, asserting heterosexuality, and preserving a sense of manhood. The power rapist's victim usually is a woman equal in age to or younger than the rapist. The lack of physical violence may reduce the support given the victim by family and friends. Therefore, the victim's personal guilt over her rape experience is increased—perhaps, she thinks, she could have done something to get away.

- *Sadistic rape* involves both sexuality and aggression. The sadistic rapist is bound up in ritual—he may torment his victim, bind her, or torture her. Victims are usually related, in the rapist's view, to a personal characteristic that he wants to harm or destroy. The rape experience is intensely exciting to the sadist; he gets satisfaction from abusing, degrading, or humiliating his captive. This type of rape is particularly traumatic for the victim. Victims of such crimes need psychiatric care long after their physical wounds have healed.

SOURCE: A. Nicholas Groth and Jean Birnbaum, *Men Who Rape* (New York: Plenum Press, 1979).

Gang versus individual rape   Estimates of the number of women raped by multiple offenders range from about 1 percent to 26 percent.[78] There is generally little difference in the demographic characteristics of single- or multiple-victim rapes. However, women who are attacked by multiple offenders are subject to more violence, such as beatings and the use of weapons, and the rapes are more likely to be completed than individual rapes. However, gang rape victims are more likely to resist and face injury than those attacked by single offenders. Gang rape victims are more likely to call police, to seek therapy, and to contemplate suicide. **Gang rapes** then, as might be expected, are more severe in violence and outcome.

Serial rape   Some rapists are one-time offenders, but others engage in multiple or **serial rapes.** Some serial rapists constantly increase their use of force; others do not. Research by Janet Warren and her associates determined that increasers (about 25 percent of serial rapists) tend to be white males who attack multiple victims who are typically older than the norm. During these attacks, the rapist uses excessive profanity and takes more time than during typical rapes. Increasers have a limited criminal history for other crimes, a fact suggesting that their behavior is focused almost solely on sexual violence.[79]

Some serial rapists commit "blitz rapes," in which they attack their victims without warning, whereas others try to "capture" their victims by striking up a conversation or offering them a ride. Others use personal or professional relationships to gain access to their targets.[80] For example, police officers and other criminal justice personnel have been accused of using their authority to force citizens into sexual encounters. Police officers have been implicated in using telescopes to spy on women in their homes, performing unnecessary strip searches, and forcing women to have sexual relations in lieu of arrest or other official action.[81] Similarly, male correctional workers in female prisons have been accused of trading privileges for sexual favors from inmates, using their power to gain sexual access.

Acquaintance rape   **Acquaintance rape** involves someone known to the victim, including family members and friends. Included within acquaintance rapes are the subcategories of **date rape,** which involves a sexual attack during a courting relationship; **statutory rape,** in which the victim is underage; and **marital rape,** which is forcible sex between people who are legally married to each other.

It is difficult to estimate the ratio between rapes involving strangers and those in which victim and assailant were in some way acquainted because women may be more reluctant to report acts involving acquaintances. By some estimates, about 50 percent of rapes involve acquaintances.[82] Stranger rapes are typically more violent than acquaintance rapes; attackers are more likely to carry a weapon, threaten the victim, and harm her physically. However, stranger rapes may be less likely to be prosecuted than acquaintance rapes because victims may be more reluctant to recount their ordeal at trial if the attack involved a stranger than if their attacker was someone they knew or had been involved with in an earlier relationship.[83]

Date rape Although official crime data indicate that most rapists and victims are strangers to one another, it is likely that acquaintance rapes constitute the bulk of sexual assaults. One disturbing trend of rape involves people who are in some form of courting relationship. There is no single form of date rape. Some occur on first dates, others after a relationship has been developing, and still others occur after the couple has been involved for some time. In long-term or close relationships, the male partner may feel he has invested so much time and money in his partner that he is owed sexual relations or that sexual intimacy is an expression that the involvement is progressing. He may make comparisons to other couples who have dated as long and are sexually active.[84]

Date rape is not unique to the United States. A survey of Canadian college women found that, although the overall crime rate in Canada is lower than in the United States, the incidence of date rape is still extremely high. About one-third of the young women surveyed experienced an episode of physical, verbal, or psychological sexual coercion; one-quarter said they had had sexual relations when they did not want to during the past year.[85]

Another disturbing phenomenon is campus gang rape, in which a group of men attacks a defenseless or inebriated victim. Well-publicized gang rapes have occurred at the University of New Hampshire, Duke University, Florida State University, Pennsylvania State University, and Bentley College in Massachusetts in the past decade.[86]

Date rape is believed to be frequent on college campuses. It has been estimated that 15 percent to 20 percent of all college women are victims of rape or attempted rape. One self-report survey conducted on a midwestern campus found that 100 percent of all rapists knew their victims beforehand.[87] The actual incidence of date rape may be even higher than surveys indicate, because many victims blame themselves and do not recognize the incident as a rape, saying, for example, "I should have fought back harder" or "I shouldn't have gotten drunk."[88]

Despite their seriousness and prevalence, fewer than 1 in 10 date rapes may be reported to police. Some victims do not report because they do not view their experience as a "real rape," which, they believe, involves a strange man "jumping out of the bushes." Other victims are embarrassed and frightened. Some men use a variety of strategies to coerce sex, including getting their dates drunk, threatening them with termination of a relationship, threatening to disclose negative information, making them feel guilty, or uttering false promises (like "we'll get engaged") to obtain sex.[89] Coercive sexual encounters have become disturbingly common in our culture. As criminologist Martin Schwartz has stated:

> The conclusion is inescapable that a very substantial minority of women on American college campuses have experienced an event which would fit most states' definitions of felony rape or sexual assault.[90]

Does watching films that degrade women influence the commission of a date rape? To find out, use InfoTrac College Edition and read: Michael Milburn, Roxanne Mather, and Sheree D. Conrad. The effects of viewing R-rated movie scenes that objectify women on perceptions of date rape. *Sex Roles: A Journal of Research* Nov 2000 p645 ∎

Marital rape In 1978 Greta Rideout filed rape charges against her husband John. This Oregon case grabbed headlines because it was the first in which a husband was prosecuted for raping his wife while sharing a residence with her. John was acquitted, and the couple briefly reconciled; later, continued violent episodes culminated in divorce and a jail term for John.[91]

Traditionally, a legally married husband could not be charged with raping his wife; this was referred to as the **marital exemption.** The origin of this legal doctrine can be traced to the sixteenth-century pronouncement of Matthew Hale, England's chief justice, who wrote

> But the husband cannot be guilty of rape committed by himself upon his lawful wife, for by their mutual matrimonial consent and contract the wife hath given up herself in this kind unto the husband which she cannot retract.[92]

However, research indicates that many women are raped each year by their husbands as part of an overall pattern of spousal abuse, and they deserve the protection of the law. Although popular myth, illustrated by Rhett Butler overcoming the objections of his reluctant bride Scarlett O'Hara in the classic film *Gone With the Wind*, says that marital rapes are the result of "healthy male sexuality," the reality is quite the opposite. Many spousal rapes are accompanied by brutal, sadistic beatings and have little to do with normal sexual interests.[93] Not surprisingly, the marital exemption has undergone significant revision. In 1980, only three states had laws against marital rape; today almost every state recognizes marital rape as a crime.[94] Piercing the marital exemption is not unique to U.S. courts; it has also been abolished in Canada, Israel, Scotland, and New Zealand.[95] However, although marital rape is now recognized, most states do not give wives the same legal protection as they would nonmarried couples, and when courts do recognize marital rape, the perpetrators are sanctioned less harshly than are those accused of nonmarital sexual assaults. For example, some will only prosecute when women suffer severe physical harm.[96]

Statutory rape The term *statutory rape* refers to sexual relations between an underage minor female and an adult male. Although the sex is not forced or coerced, the law says that young girls are incapable of giving informed consent, so the act is legally considered nonconsensual. Typically a state's law will define an age of consent above which there can be no criminal prosecution for sexual relations.

Although each state is different, most evaluate the age differences between the parties to determine whether an offense has taken place. For example, Indiana law mandates prosecution of men aged 21 or older who have consensual sex with girls younger than 14. In some states, defendants can claim they mistakenly assumed their victims were above the age of consent, whereas in others, "mistake-of-age" defenses are ignored. A recent American Bar Association (ABA) survey found that prosecution is often difficult in statutory rape cases because the young victims are reluctant to testify. Often parents have given their blessing to the relationships, and juries are reluctant to convict men involved in consensual sex even with young teenaged girls. The ABA report calls for stricter enforcement of these cases, noting that many states are already toughening their laws by raising the age of consent to protect minors from the psychological scars of precocious sexuality with an older predatory partner.[97]

To read a report on a victim-oriented approach to dealing with statutory rape, go to:

  http://www.ojp.usdoj.gov/ovc/publications/
  infores/statutoryrape/trainguide/welcome.html
For an up-to-date list of Web links, go to
  http://info.wadsworth.com/siegel ■

The Causes of Rape

What factors predispose some men to commit rape? Criminologists' responses to this question are almost as varied as the crime itself. However, most explanations can be grouped into a few consistent categories.

Evolutionary, biological factors One explanation for rape focuses on the evolutionary, biological aspects of the male sexual drive. This perspective suggests that rape may be instinctual, developed over the ages as a means of perpetuating the species. In more primitive times, forcible sexual contact may have helped spread genes and maximize offspring. Some believe that these prehistoric drives remain: males still have a natural sexual drive that encourages them to have intimate relations with as many women as possible.[98] The evolutionary view is that the sexual urge corresponds to the unconscious need to preserve the species by spreading one's genes as widely as possible. Men who are sexually aggressive will have a reproductive edge over their more passive peers. In contrast, women are more cautious and want stable partners who seem willing to make a long-term commitment to child rearing. This difference produces sexual tension that causes men to employ forceful copulatory tactics, especially when the chance of punishment is quite low.[99] Rape is bound up with sexuality as well as violence because, according to biosocial theorist Lee Ellis, the act involves the "drive to

possess and control others to whom one is sexually attracted."[100]

Male socialization In contrast to the evolutionary biological view, some researchers argue that rape is a function of modern male socialization. Diana Russell suggests that rape is actually not a deviant act but one that conforms to the qualities regarded as masculine in U.S. society.[101] Russell maintains that from an early age boys are taught to be aggressive, forceful, tough, and dominating. Men are taught to dominate at the same time that they are led to believe that women want to be dominated. Russell describes the **virility mystique**—the belief that males must separate their sexual feelings from needs for love, respect, and affection. She believes men are socialized to be the aggressors and expect to be sexually active with many women; consequently, male virginity and sexual inexperience are shameful. Similarly, sexually aggressive women frighten some men and cause them to doubt their own masculinity. Sexual insecurity may lead some men to commit rape to bolster their self-image and masculine identity. It is not surprising then that rape is so common in the male-dominated U.S. culture.[102]

Feminists suggest that as the nation moves toward gender equality there may be an immediate increase in rape rates because of increased threats to male virility and dominance. However, in the long term, gender equality will reduce rape rates because there will be an improved social climate toward women.[103]

Hypermasculinity If rape is an expression of male anger and devaluation of women and not an act motivated by sexual desire, it follows that men who hold so-called macho attitudes will be more likely to engage in sexual violence. **Hypermasculine** men typically have a callous sexual attitude and believe violence is manly. They perceive danger as exciting and are overly sensitive to insult and ridicule. They are also impulsive, more apt to brag about sexual conquests, and more likely to lose control, especially when using alcohol.[104] These men are quicker to anger and more likely to be sexually aggressive. In fact, the sexually aggressive male may view the female as a legitimate victim of sexual violence.

CONNECTIONS

Recall that Chapter 9 described how the need to prove masculinity helps men justify their abuse of women. Sexually violent men, the argument goes, are viewed as virile and masculine by their peers. ■

Psychological abnormality Another view is that rapists suffer from some type of personality disorder or mental illness. Research shows that a significant percentage of incarcerated rapists exhibit psychotic tendencies, and many others have hostile, sadistic feelings toward women.[105] A high proportion of serial rapists and repeat sexual offenders exhibit psychopathic personality structures.[106]

Social learning This perspective submits that men learn to commit rapes much as they learn any other behavior. For example, sexual aggression may be learned through interaction with peers who articulate attitudes supportive of sexual violence.[107]

Nicholas Groth found that 40 percent of the rapists he studied were sexually victimized as adolescents.[108] A growing body of literature links personal sexual trauma with the desire to inflict sexual trauma on others.[109] Watching violent or pornographic films featuring women who are beaten, raped, or tortured has been linked to sexually aggressive behavior in men.[110] In one startling case, a 12-year-old Providence, Rhode Island, boy sexually assaulted a 10-year-old girl on a pool table after watching television trial coverage of a case in which a woman was similarly raped (the incident was made into a film, *The Accused*, starring actress Jodie Foster).[111]

CONNECTIONS

This view will be explored further in Chapter 14 when the issue of pornography and violence is analyzed in greater detail. Most research does not show that watching pornography is directly linked to sexual violence, but there may be a link between sexual aggression and viewing movies with sexual violence as their theme. ∎

Sexual motivation Most criminologists believe rape is a violent act that is not sexually motivated. Yet it might be premature to dismiss the sexual motive from all rapes.[112] NCVS data reveal that rape victims tend to be young and that rapists prefer younger, presumably more attractive, victims. Data show an association between the ages of rapists and their victims, indicating that men choose rape targets of approximately the same age as consensual sex partners. And, despite the fact that younger criminals are usually the most violent, older rapists tend to harm their victims more than younger rapists. This pattern indicates that older criminals may rape for motives of power and control, whereas younger offenders may be seeking sexual gratification and may therefore be less likely to harm their victims.

Rape and the Law

Of all violent crimes, none has created such conflict in the legal system as rape. Even if women choose to report sexual assaults to police, they are often initially reluctant because of the sexist fashion in which rape victims are treated by police, prosecutors, and court personnel and the legal technicalities that authorize invasion of women's privacy when a rape case is tried in court. Police officers may be hesitant to make arrests and testify in court when the alleged assaults do not yield obvious signs of violence or struggle (presumably showing the victim strenuously resisted the attack). Police are also loath to testify on the victim's behalf if she had previously known or dated her attacker. Some state laws have made rape so difficult to prove that women believe the slim chance that their attacker will be convicted is not sufficient to warrant their participation in the legal process. However, police and courts are now becoming more sensitive to the plight of rape victims and are just as likely to investigate acquaintance rapes as they are **aggravated rapes** involving multiple offenders, weapons, and victim injuries. In some jurisdictions, the justice system takes all rape cases seriously and does not ignore those in which victim and attacker have had a prior relationship or those that did not involve serious injury.[113]

Proving rape Proving guilt in a rape case is extremely challenging for prosecutors. First, some male psychiatrists and therapists still maintain that women fantasize that a rape has occurred and therefore may falsely accuse their alleged attackers. Some judges also fear that women may charge men with rape because of jealousy, false marriage proposals, or pregnancy. Although those concerned with protecting the rights of rape victims have campaigned for legal reforms, some well-publicized false rape accusations have hindered change. In one famous 1985 incident, Gary Dotson, convicted of raping a woman in Illinois, served more than six years in prison before his alleged victim recanted her story on national television.[114] Such incidents make it more difficult for prosecutors to gain convictions in rape cases.

Suspiciousness U.S. sexism causes a cultural suspiciousness of women, who are often seen as provocateurs in any sexual encounters with men. Consequently, the burden is shifted to the woman to prove she has not provoked or condoned the rape. Although the law does not recognize it, jurors are sometimes swayed by the insinuation that the rape was victim-precipitated; thus the blame is shifted from rapist to victim. To get a conviction, prosecutors must establish that the act was forced and violent and that no question of voluntary compliance exists. They may be reluctant to prosecute cases where they have questions about the victim's moral character or if they believe that the victim's demeanor and attitude will turn off the jury and undermine the chance of conviction.[115]

Consent Rape represents a major legal challenge to the criminal justice system for a number of reasons.[116] One issue involves the concept of **consent.** It is essential to prove that the attack was forced and that the victim did not give voluntary consent to her attacker. In a sense, the burden of proof is on the victim to show that her character is beyond question and that she in no way encouraged, enticed, or misled the accused rapist. Proving victim dissent is not a requirement in any other violent crime. For example, robbery victims do not have to prove they did not entice their attackers by flaunting expensive jewelry; yet the defense counsel in a rape case can create reasonable doubt about the woman's credibility. A common defense tactic is to introduce suspicion in the minds of the jury that the woman may have consented to the sexual act and later regretted her decision. Conversely, it is difficult for a prosecuting attorney to establish that a woman's character is so impeccable that the absence of consent is a certainty. Such distinctions are important in rape cases because male jurors may be sympathetic to the accused if the victim is portrayed as unchaste. Simply referring to the woman as "sexually liberated" or promiscuous may be enough to result in exoneration of the accused, even if violence and brutality were used in the attack.[117] Research shows that even when a defendant is found guilty in a sexual assault case his punishment is significantly reduced if the victim is believed to have negative personal characteristics such as being a transient, hitchhiker, alone in a bar, or a drug and alcohol abuser.[118]

Reform   Because of the difficulty rape victims have in obtaining justice, rape laws have been changing around the country. Efforts for reform include changing the language of statutes, dropping the condition of victim resistance, and changing the requirement of use of force to include the threat of force or injury.[119] A number of states and the federal government have replaced rape laws with the more gender-neutral term "crimes of sexual assault."[120] Sexual assault laws outlaw any type of forcible sex, including homosexual rape.[121]

Most states and the federal government have developed **shield laws,** which protect women from being questioned about their sexual history unless it directly bears on the case. In some instances these laws are quite restrictive, whereas in others they grant the trial judge considerable discretion to admit prior sexual conduct in evidence if it is deemed relevant for the defense. In an important 1991 case, *Michigan v. Lucas,* the U.S. Supreme Court upheld the validity of shield laws and ruled that excluding evidence of a prior sexual relationship between the parties did not violate the defendant's right to a fair trial.[122]

In addition to requiring evidence that consent was not given, the common law of rape required corroboration that the crime of rape actually took place. This involved the need for independent evidence from police officers, physicians, and witnesses that the accused was actually the person who committed the crime, that sexual penetration took place, and that force was present and consent absent. This requirement shielded rapists from prosecution in cases where the victim delayed reporting the crime or in which physical evidence had been compromised or lost. Corroboration is no longer required except under extraordinary circumstances, such as when the victim is too young to understand the crime, has had a previous sexual relationship with the defendant, or gives a version of events that is improbable and self-contradictory.[123]

The federal government may have given rape victims another source of redress when it passed the Violence Against Women Act in 1994. This statute allows rape victims to sue in federal court on the grounds that sexual violence violates their civil rights; the provisions of the act have so far been upheld by appellate courts.[124]

The limits of reform   Despite these reform efforts, prosecutors may be influenced in their decision to bring charges by the circumstances of a crime.[125] The victim must still establish her intimate, detailed knowledge of the act for her testimony to be believed in court. This may include searching questions about her assailant's appearance, the location in which the crime took place, and the nature of the physical assault. When Cassia Spohn and David Holleran studied prosecutors' decisions in rape cases, they found that perception of the victim's character was still a critical factor in their decision to file charges. In cases involving acquaintance rape, prosecutors were reluctant to file charges when the victim's character was questioned— for example, when police reports described the victim as sexually active or engaged in sexually oriented occupations such as "stripper." In stranger cases, prosecutors were more likely to take action if a gun or knife was used. Spohn and Holleran conclude that prosecutors are still influenced by perceptions of what constitutes "real rape" and who are "real victims."[126]

■ Murder and Homicide

Murder is defined in common law as "the unlawful killing of a human being with malice aforethought."[127] It is the most serious of all common-law crimes and the only one that can still be punished by death. Western society's abhorrence of murderers is illustrated by the fact that there is no statute of limitations in murder cases. Whereas state laws limit prosecution of other crimes to a fixed period, usually 7 to 10 years, accused killers can be brought to justice at any time after their crimes were committed. An example of the law's reach in these cases is the murder conviction of George Franklin on January 29, 1990. Franklin's daughter, Eileen Franklin-Lipsker, told legal authorities that in recent psychotherapy sessions she had remembered how her father sexually assaulted and killed her 8-year-old friend. The murder had taken place in 1969, more than 20 years earlier.[128]

To legally prove that a murder has taken place, most state jurisdictions require prosecutors to show that the accused maliciously intended to kill the victim. "Express or actual malice" is the state of mind assumed to exist when someone kills another person in the absence of any apparent provocation. "Implied or constructive malice" is considered to exist when a death results from negligent or unthinking behavior. In these cases, even though the perpetrator did not wish to kill the victim, the killing resulted from an inherently dangerous act and therefore is considered murder. An unusual example of this concept is the attempted murder conviction of Ignacio Perea, an AIDS-infected Miami man who kidnapped and raped an 11-year-old boy. Perea was sentenced to up to 25 years in prison when the jury agreed with the prosecutor's contention that the AIDS virus is a deadly weapon.[129]

Degrees of Murder

There are different levels or degrees of homicide.[130] **First-degree murder** occurs when a person kills another after premeditation and deliberation. **Premeditation** means that the killing was considered beforehand and suggests that it was motivated by more than a simple desire to engage in an act of violence. **Deliberation** means the killing was planned after careful thought rather than carried out on impulse: "To constitute a deliberate and premeditated killing, the slayer must weigh and consider the question of killing and the reasons for and against such a choice; having in mind the consequences, he decides to and does kill."[131] The planning implied by this definition need not be a long process; it may be an almost instantaneous decision to take another's life. Also, a killing accompanying a felony, such as robbery or rape, usually constitutes first-degree murder (**felony murder**).

Second-degree murder requires the killer to have malice aforethought but not premeditation or deliberation. A second-degree murder occurs when a person's wanton disregard for the victim's life and his or her desire to inflict serious bodily harm on the victim result in the victim's death.

Homicide without malice is called **manslaughter** and is usually punished by anywhere from 1 to 15 years in prison. **Voluntary or nonnegligent manslaughter** refers to a killing committed in the heat of passion or during a sudden quarrel that provoked violence. Although intent may be present, malice is not. **Involuntary or negligent manslaughter** refers to a killing that occurs when a person's acts are negligent and without regard for the harm they may cause others. Most involuntary manslaughter cases involve motor vehicle deaths—for example, when a drunk driver kills a pedestrian. However, one can be held criminally liable for the death of another when disregard of safety causes a death. For example, on February 16, 1990, Michael Patrick Berry, whose pit bull killed a child who had wandered into his yard, was sentenced to 3 years and 8 months in prison; it was the first U.S. case in which a person was convicted for manslaughter for the actions of a pet.[132]

"Born and alive" One issue that has received national attention is whether a murder victim can be a fetus that has not yet been delivered; this is referred to as **feticide.** In some instances, fetal harm involves a mother whose behavior endangers an unborn child; in other cases, feticide results from the harmful action of a third party.

Some states have prosecuted women for endangering or killing their unborn fetuses by their drug or alcohol abuse. Some of these convictions have been overturned because the law applies only to a "human being who has been born and is alive."[133] At least 200 women in 30 states have been arrested and charged in connection with harming (though not necessarily killing) a fetus; appellate courts have almost universally overturned such convictions on the basis that they were without legal merit or were unconstitutional.[134] However, in *Whitner v. State,* the Supreme Court of South Carolina ruled that a woman could be held liable for actions during pregnancy that could affect her viable fetus.[135] In holding that a fetus is a "viable person," the court opened the door for a potential homicide prosecution if a mother's action resulted in fetal death.

State laws more commonly allow prosecutions for murder when a third party's actions kill a fetus. Four states (Illinois, Missouri, South Dakota, and West Virginia) extend wrongful death action to the death of any fetus, whereas the remaining states require that the fetus be viable. A viable fetus is able to live outside the mother's body; therefore, the law extends the definition of murder to a fetus that is born alive but dies afterward due to injuries sustained in utero.[136] In a recent Texas case, a man was convicted of manslaughter in the death of a baby who was delivered prematurely after he caused an auto accident while intoxicated. It was one of the first cases to hold that a person can be held criminally liable for harming an unborn child.[137]

The Nature and Extent of Murder

It is possible to track U.S. murder rate trends from 1900 to the present with the aid of coroners' reports and UCR data. The murder rate peaked in 1933, a time of high unemployment and lawlessness, and then fell until 1958. The homicide rate doubled from the mid-1960s to the late 1970s and then peaked at 10.2 per 100,000 population in 1980. After a brief decline, the murder rate rose again in the late 1980s and early 1990s to a peak of 9.8 per 100,000 in 1991. Since then, the rate has declined, to 5.5 per 100,000 in 2000: a decline of more than 25 percent between 1996 and 2000. Although this is a welcome development, about 15,000 citizens were killed in 2000.

What else do official crime statistics tell us about murder today? Murder tends to be an urban crime. More than half of the homicides occur in cities with a population of 100,000 or more.[138] Almost one-quarter of homicides occur in cities with a population of more than one million. Not surprisingly, murder in urban areas is more commonly crime- and gang-related than in less populated areas. Large cities are much more commonly the site of drug-related killings, gang-related murders, and relatively less likely the location of family-related homicides, including murders of intimates.

Murder victims and offenders tend to be males. Males represent 75 percent of homicide victims and nearly 90 percent of offenders. In terms of rates per 100,000, males are 3 times more likely to be killed, and 8 times more likely to commit homicide, than are females. Approximately one-

AP/Wide World Photos

■ Males represent 75 percent of homicide victims and nearly 90 percent of offenders. Males are 3 times more likely to be killed and 8 times more likely to commit homicide than are females. Here, murder suspect Billy Lyon is escorted into U.S. District Court in Owensboro, Kentucky. According to the FBI, Lyons and two accomplices sat down, said grace, and had dinner after the 1999 murder of an Alabama man.

third of murder victims and almost half the offenders are under the age of 25. For both victims and offenders, the rate per 100,000 peaks in the 18- to 24-year-old age group.

About half of all victims are African Americans and the other half white. African Americans are disproportionately represented as both homicide victims and offenders. They are 6 times more likely to be victimized and 8 times more likely to commit homicide than are whites. Murder, like rape, tends to be an intraracial crime; about 90 percent of victims are slain by members of their own race. Similarly, people arrested for murder are generally young (under 35) and male (about 90 percent), a pattern that has proved consistent over time.

Some murders involve very young children, a crime referred to as **infanticide,** and others involve senior citizens, referred to as **eldercide.**[139] The UCR indicates that about 500 children under 4 years old were murdered in 2000. The younger the child, the greater the risk for infanticide. Recently, the number of infanticides of children age 1 and younger has declined. At the opposite end of the age spectrum, about 5 percent of all homicides involve people age 65 or older. Males age 65 or older were more likely than females of the same age to be homicide victims.

Although most of the offenders who committed eldercide were age 50 or younger, elderly females were more likely than elderly males to be killed by an elderly offender.[140]

Today few would deny that some relationship exists between social and ecological factors and murder. The following section explores some of the more important issues related to these factors.

Murderous Relations

One factor that has received a great deal of attention from criminologists is the relationship between the murderer and the victim.[141] Most criminologists generally agree that murders can be separated into those involving strangers, typically stemming from a felony attempt such as a robbery or drug deal, and acquaintance homicides involving disputes between family, friends, and acquaintances.[142] The quality of relationships and interpersonal interactions, then, may influence murder.

CONNECTIONS

Recall from Chapter 4 the discussion of victim precipitation. The argument made by some criminologists is that murder victims help create the "transactions" that lead to their death. ■

Spousal relations   The rate of homicide among cohabitating couples has declined significantly during the past two decades, a finding that can be attributed to the shift away from marriage in modern society. There are, however, significant gender differences in homicide trends among unmarried people. The number of unmarried men killed by their partners has declined (mirroring the overall trend in the murder rate), but the number of women killed by the men they live with has increased dramatically.

It is possible that men kill their spouses or partners because they fear losing control and power. Because unmarried people who live together have a legally and socially more open relationship, males in such relationships may be more likely to feel loss of control and exert their power with violence.[143]

In contrast, most females who kill their mates do so after suffering repeated violent attacks.[144] Perhaps the number of males killed by their partners has declined because alternatives to abusive relationships, such as battered women's shelters, are becoming more prevalent around the United States. Regions that provide greater social support for battered women and that have passed legislation to protect abuse victims also have lower rates of female-perpetrated homicide.[145]

Some people kill their mates because they find themselves involved in a *love triangle.*[146] Interestingly, women who kill out of jealousy aim their aggression at their partners; in contrast, men are more likely to kill their mates' suitors. Love triangles tend to become lethal when the offenders believe they have been lied to or betrayed. Lethal violence is more common when (1) the rival initiated the affair, (2) the killer knew the spouse was already in a steady relationship outside the marriage, and (3) the killer was repeatedly lied to or betrayed.[147]

CONNECTIONS

It is possible that men who perceive loss of face aim their aggression at rivals who are competing with them for a suitable partner. Biosocial theory (Chapter 6) suggests that this behavior is motivated by the male's instinctual need to replenish the species and protect his place in the gene pool. Killing a rival would help a spouse maintain control over a potential mother for his children. ■

Personal relations   Most murders occur among people who are acquainted. Although on the surface the killing might have seemed senseless, it often is the result of a long-simmering dispute motivated by revenge, dispute resolution, jealousy, drug deals, racial bias, or threats to identity or status.[148] For example, a prior act of violence, motivated by profit or greed, may generate revenge killing, such as when a buyer robs his dealer during a drug transaction.

Over the past decade, the number of stranger homicides has seemed to increase. Today less than half of mur-der victims knew their assailants, a significant decline from years past. Under what circumstances do stranger homicides occur? Stranger homicides are most often felony murders occurring during rapes, robberies, and burglaries. Others are random acts of urban violence that fuel public fear. For example, a homeowner tells a motorist to move his car because it is blocking the driveway, an argument ensues, and the owner gets a pistol and kills the motorist; or consider a young boy who kills a store manager because, he says, "something came into my head to hurt the lady."[149]

How do these murderous relations develop between two people who have never before met? In a well-known study, David Luckenbill studied murder transactions to determine whether particular patterns of behavior are common between the killer and the victim.[150] He found that many homicides follow a sequential pattern. First, the victim makes what the offender considers an offensive move. The offender typically retaliates verbally or physically. An agreement to end things violently is forged with the victim's provocative response. The battle ensues, leaving the victim dead or dying. The offender's escape is shaped by his or her relationship to the victim or the reaction of the audience, if any (Figure 11.2).

Student relations   Though relatively rare events, because they are so shocking, school shootings have captured

Figure 11.2   Murder Transactions

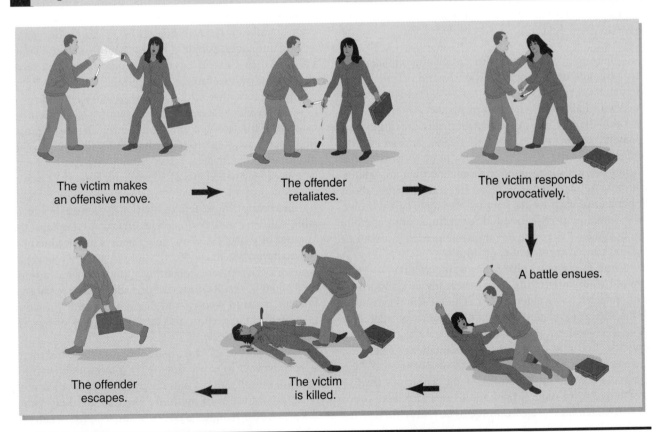

The victim makes an offensive move.

The offender retaliates.

The victim responds provocatively.

A battle ensues.

The offender escapes.

The victim is killed.

■ According to Colombian police, Luis Alfredo Garavito is one of the world's worst serial killers. In 1999 Garavito confessed to the slayings of at least 140 boys between the ages of 8 and 16 during a five-year killing spree. This monument in Pereira, Colombia, was constructed to commemorate his victims.

significant media attention. One recent study examined all school-related shootings occurring between July 1, 1994, and June 30, 1999. A total of 220 incidents on or near school grounds had resulted in 253 deaths. Of these, 202 involved a single victim and 18 had multiple victims. Although highly publicized in the media, the average annual incidence is very small, 0.068 per 100,000 students. Between 1992 and 1999, the rate of single-victim student homicides decreased significantly while multiple-victim incidents increased significantly.

The research found that most shooting incidents occur around the start of the school day, the lunch period, or the end of the school day. In most of the shootings (55 percent), a note, threat, or other action indicating risk for violence occurred prior to the event. Shooters were also likely to have expressed some form of suicidal behavior and to have been bullied by their peers.[151] Kids who have been the victims of crime themselves are the ones most likely to bring guns to school.[152]

Serial Murder

According to Colombian police, Luis Alfredo Garavito is a glib predator and a "solitary sadist" who stands accused as one of the world's worst serial killers.[153] In 1999, Garavito, a 42-year-old drifter, confessed to the slayings of at least 140 boys between the ages of 8 and 16 during a five-year killing spree. Garavito would befriend the children and take them on long walks until they were tired. Then he would tie them up with nylon rope, slit their throats or behead them, and then bury their bodies. Most of Garavito's victims were street children, children from poor families, or children sep-

arated from their parents by poverty or political violence. Authorities said it was because there was no one to notice that the children were missing or to inquire about their whereabouts that Garavito was able to go on killing for so long without being detected. Garavito is not the only Colombian **serial murderer.** Pedro Armando Lopez, known here as the "Monster of the Andes," may be the largest-scale serial killer of modern times. He is believed to have killed more than 300 girls and young women in Colombia, Ecuador, and Peru before being captured in Ecuador and convicted of 57 counts of murder there in 1980. Lopez served 16 years in an Ecuadorean prison, but because that country does not have a law that permits consecutive sentences, he was released and deported back to Colombia. His present whereabouts are unknown.

Some serial murderers, such as the American Theodore Bundy, roam the country killing at random.[154] Other serial killers terrorize a city, such as the Los Angeles–based Night Stalker; the Green River Killer, who is believed to have slain more than four dozen young women in Seattle; and the Hillside Stranglers, Kenneth Bianchi and Angelo Buono, who tortured and killed 10 women in the Los Angeles area.[155] A third type of serial murderer, such as Garavito and Milwaukee cannibal Jeffrey Dahmer, kills so cunningly that many victims are dispatched before the authorities even realize the deaths can be attributed to a single perpetrator.[156] Serial killers operate over a long period and can be distinguished from **mass murderers,** who kill many victims in a single, violent outburst.

The Criminological Enterprise feature titled "Mass Murder and Serial Killing" further discusses types of serial killers and multiple killers.

Mass Murder and Serial Killing

Criminologists Jack Levin and James Alan Fox have written extensively on two of the most frightening aspects of modern violence—mass murder and serial killing. According to Levin and Fox, it is difficult to estimate the number and extent of serial killings, but a reasoned estimate is that up to 20 serial killers are active in a given year, accounting for up to 240 killings or about 1 percent of the total number of homicides.

There are different types of serial killers. Some wander the countryside killing at random; others stay in their hometowns and lure victims to their death. Theodore Bundy, convicted killer of three young women and suspected killer of many others, roamed the country in the 1970s, killing as he went. Wayne Gacy, during the same period, killed more than 30 boys and young men without leaving Chicago. Although these men share many characteristics with the general population, one special trait stands out: serial killers are exceptionally skillful in how they present themselves. Based on appearances, they seem beyond suspicion.

Why do serial murderers kill? They kill for fun. They enjoy the thrill, the sexual gratification, and the dominance they achieve over the lives of their victims. The serial killer rarely uses a gun because this method is too quick and would deprive him of his greatest pleasure, exulting in his victim's suffering. Serial killers are not insane; they are "more cruel than crazy."

Fox and Levin have their own typology of serial killers, which they describe as follows:

1. *Thrill killers* strive for either sexual sadism or dominance. This is the most common form of serial murderer.

2. *Mission killers* want to reform the world or have a vision that drives them to kill.

3. *Expedience killers* are out for profit or want to protect themselves from a perceived threat.

In contrast to serial killers, mass murderers engage in a single, uncontrollable outburst called simultaneous killing. Examples include Charles Whitman, who killed 14 people and wounded 30 others from atop the 307-foot tower on the University of Texas campus on August 1, 1966; James Huberty, who killed 21 people in a McDonald's restaurant in San Ysidro, California, on July 18, 1984; and George Hennard, a deranged Texas man who, on October 16, 1991, smashed his truck through a plate glass window in a cafeteria in Killeen, Texas, got out, and systematically killed 22 people before committing suicide as police closed in.

Fox and Levin define four types of mass murderers:

1. *Revenge killers* seek to get even with individuals or society at large. Their typical target is an estranged wife and "her" children or an employer and "his" employees.

2. *Love killers* are motivated by a warped sense of devotion. They are often despondent people who commit suicide and take others, such as a wife and children, with them.

3. *Profit killers* are usually trying to cover up a crime, eliminate witnesses, and carry out a criminal conspiracy.

4. *Terrorist killers* are trying to send a message. Gang killings tell rivals to watch out; cult killers may actually leave a message behind to warn society about impending doom.

Levin and Fox dispute the notion that all mass murderers and serial killers have some form of biological or psychological problems, such as genetic anomalies or schizophrenia. Even the most sadistic serial murderers are not mentally ill or driven by delusions or hallucinations. Instead, they typically exhibit a sociopathic personality that deprives them of pangs of conscience or guilt to guide their behavior. Mass murderers are typically ordinary citizens driven to extreme acts. They experience long-term frustration, blame others for their problems, and then are set off by some catastrophic loss they are unable to cope with or get help for.

So far, police have been successful in capturing simultaneous killers whose outbursts are directed at family members or friends. Serial killers have proven more elusive. The U.S. Department of Justice is now coordinating efforts to gather information on unsolved murders in different jurisdictions to find patterns linking the crimes. Unfortunately, when a serial murderer is caught, it is often the result of luck—or an informant—not investigative skill.

Critical Thinking Questions

1. How should (mass) school shootings be classified?

2. Can a mass murderer be legally sane? If not, what should be done with irrational killers?

3. Is it fair to put serial killers and mass murderers to death? Explain your response.

InfoTrac College Edition Research

Serial killers are not new to this century. To read about the history of such gruesome acts, read:

Bernard Capp. Serial killers in 17th-century England. *History Today* March 1996 v46 n3 p21

For more on modern serial killers, see:

Jan Scott. Serial homicide: we need to explore behind the stereotypes and ask why. *British Medical Journal* Jan 6, 1996 v312 n7022 p2

Eugene H. Methvin. The face of evil. National Review Jan 23, 1995 v47 n1 p34(7)

SOURCE: James Alan Fox and Jack Levin, "Multiple Homicide: Patterns of Serial and Mass Murder," in *Crime and Justice, An Annual Edition*, Volume 23, ed. Michael Tonry (Chicago, Ill.: University of Chicago Press, 1998): 407–55; James Alan Fox and Jack Levin, *Overkill: Mass Murder and Serial Killing Exposed* (New York: Plenum, 1994); James Allan Fox and Jack Levin, "A Psycho-Social Analysis of Mass Murder," in *Serial and Mass Murder: Theory, Policy, and Research*, eds. Thomas O'Reilly-Fleming and Steven Egger (Toronto: University of Toronto Press, 1993); James Alan Fox and Jack Levin, "Serial Murder: A Survey," in *Serial and Mass Murder: Theory, Policy, and Research*, eds. Thomas O'Reilly-Fleming and Steven Egger (Toronto: University of Toronto Press, 1993); Jack Levin and James Alan Fox, *Mass Murder* (New York: Plenum Press, 1985).

Serial murderers and their motivations In July of 2001, Iranian authorities admitted that a serial killer had murdered at least 17 prostitutes in the holy city of Mashhad. Local officials dubbed the killings the "spider murders" because the victims were strangled with their headscarves in the same way a spider uses its web to trap victims. Authorities speculated that the killer (or killers) may have been infected with AIDS and sought revenge against women who may have been the source of the infection.[157]

What motivates serial killers? The killings in Iran may be a function of revenge, but research shows that serial killers have long histories of violence, beginning in childhood when they start by targeting other children, siblings, and small animals.[158] They maintain superficial relationships with others, have trouble relating to the opposite sex, and feel guilty about their interest in sex. Despite these common characteristics, there is no single distinct type of serial killer. Some seem to be monsters—like Edmund Kemper, who, in addition to killing six young female hitchhikers in 1972, killed his mother, cut off her head, and used it as a dart board. Others, such as Theodore Bundy, were suave ladies' men whose murders surprised even close friends.

Consequently, the cause of serial murder eludes criminologists. Such disparate factors as mental illness, sexual frustration, neurological damage, child abuse and neglect, smothering relationships with mothers (David Berkowitz, the notorious Son of Sam, slept in his parents' bed until he was 10), and childhood anxiety have been suggested as possible causes. However, most experts view serial killers as sociopaths who from early childhood demonstrate bizarre behavior, such as torturing animals. This behavior extends to the pleasure that they reap from killing, their ability to ignore or enjoy their victims' suffering, and their propensity for basking in the media limelight when apprehended for their crimes. Wayne Henley Jr., who along with Dean Corill killed 27 boys in Houston, offered to help prosecutors find the bodies of additional victims so he could break Chicago killer Wayne Gacy's record of 33 murders.[159]

Other types of serial killers include the sexual sadist and the *mysoped*, or sadistic child killer, who gain sexual satisfaction from torturing and killing.[160] These sadists wish to gain complete control over their victims through humiliation, shame, enslavement, and terror. Another type, the psychopathic killer, is motivated by a character disorder that causes an inability to experience shame, guilt, sorrow, or other normal human emotions; these murderers are concerned solely with their own needs and passions. Professional hit killers who assassinate complete strangers for economic, political, or ideological reasons; terrorists; and organized crime figures fall within this category.[161]

Female serial killers An estimated 10 to 15 percent of serial killers are women. A recent study by criminologists Belea Keeney and Kathleen Heide investigated the characteristics of a sample of 14 female serial killers and found some striking differences between the way male and female killers carried out their crimes.[162] Males were much more likely than females to use extreme violence and torture. Whereas males used a "hands-on" approach, including beating, bludgeoning, and strangling their victims, females were more likely to poison or smother their victims. Men tracked or stalked their victims, but women were more likely to lure victims to their death.

There were also gender-based personality and behavior characteristics. Female killers, somewhat older than their male counterparts, abused both alcohol and drugs; males were not likely to be substance abusers. Women were diagnosed as having histrionic, manic-depressive, borderline, dissociative, and antisocial personality disorders; men were more often diagnosed as having antisocial personalities.

The profile of the female serial killer that emerges is a person who smothers or poisons someone she knows. During childhood she suffered from an abusive relationship in a disrupted family. Female killers' education levels are below average, and if they hold jobs, they are in low-status positions.

Controlling serial killers Serial killers come from diverse backgrounds. To date, law enforcement officials have been at a loss to control random killers who leave few clues, constantly move, and have little connection to their victims. Catching serial killers is often a matter of luck. To help local law enforcement officials, the FBI has developed a profiling system to identify potential suspects. In addition, the Justice Department's Violent Criminal Apprehension Program (VICAP), a computerized information service, gathers information and matches offense characteristics on violent crimes around the country.[163] This program links crimes to determine if they are the product of a single culprit.

■ Assault and Battery

Although many people mistakenly believe the term *assault and battery* refers to a single act, they are actually two separate crimes. **Battery** requires offensive touching, such as slapping, hitting, or punching a victim. **Assault** requires no actual touching but involves either attempted battery or intentionally frightening the victim by word or deed. Although common law originally intended these twin crimes to be misdemeanors, most jurisdictions now upgrade them to felonies either when a weapon is used or when they occur during the commission of a felony (for example, when a person is assaulted during a robbery). In the UCR, the FBI defines serious assault, or aggravated assault, as "an unlawful attack by one person upon another for the purpose of inflicting severe or aggravated bodily injury"; this definition is similar to the one used in most state jurisdictions.[164]

Under common law, battery required bodily injury, such as broken limbs or wounds. However, under modern law, an assault and battery occurs if the victim suffers a temporarily painful blow, even if no injury results. Battery can also involve offensive touching, such as if a man kisses a woman against her will or puts his hands on her body.

Nature and Extent of Assault

The pattern of criminal assault is quite similar to that of homicide; one could say that the only difference between the two is that the victim survives.[165] Assaults may be common in our society simply because of common life stresses. Motorists who assault each other have become such a familiar occurrence that the term **road rage** has been coined. There have even been frequent incidents of violent assault among frustrated passengers who lose control while traveling. In 1998 British Airways began issuing printed warnings to abusive passengers, giving notice that continued misbehavior could result in hefty fines and even jail sentences.[166] These warnings were developed after an alarming increase in angry passengers, who punched, kicked, scratched, bit, and head-butted airline workers or one another.

Every citizen is bound by the law of assault, even police officers. Excessive use of force can result in criminal charges being filed even if it occurs while police officers are arresting a dangerous felony suspect. Only the minimum amount of force needed to subdue the suspect is allowed by law, and if police use more aggressive tactics than required, they may find themselves the target of criminal charges and civil lawsuits. In the 1998–99 fiscal year, New York City paid out a record $40 million to settle lawsuits stemming from brutality charges including $2.75 million paid to an African American electrician who, while walking to work in Greenwich Village on his birthday in 1996, was beaten by police officers because he fit the profile of a black suspect they were seeking.[167]

In 2000 the FBI recorded slightly less than 910,000 assaults, a rate of 324 per 100,000 inhabitants. Like other violent crimes, the number of assaults has been in decline, down 17 percent from 1996 and 25 percent from 1991.

People arrested for assault and those identified by victims are usually young, male, and white, although the number of African Americans arrested for assault (34 percent) is disproportionate to their representation in the population. Assault victims tend to be male, but as Figure 11.3 shows, women also face a significant danger. Assault rates are highest in urban areas, during summer, and in southern and western regions. The most common weapons used in assaults are blunt instruments (36 percent) and hands and feet (28 percent).

Another way of determining the nature of assault is to review the attributes and extent of injuries people suffer during violent encounters that require them to be treated in local hospital emergency rooms. At last count about 1.4 million people were treated for violence-related injuries, ranging from a nose broken in a fight to a shooting or stabbing during a robbery.[168] About 40 percent of these injuries were quite serious, resulting from rapes and

---

■ **Figure 11.3   Violence Against Women**

What did women tell NCVS interviewers about their experience with violence?

- Women age 12 or older annually sustain almost 5 million violent victimizations each year. About 75 percent of all lone-offender violence against women and 45 percent of violence involving multiple offenders was perpetrated by offenders whom the victim knew. In 29 percent of all violence against women by a lone offender, the perpetrator was an intimate (husband, ex-husband, boyfriend, or ex-boyfriend).
- Women were about 6 times more likely than men to experience violence committed by an intimate.
- Women annually reported about 500,000 rapes and sexual assaults to interviewers. Friends or acquaintances of the victims committed over half these rapes or sexual assaults. Strangers were responsible for about 1 in 5.
- Women of all races and Hispanic and non-Hispanic women were about equally vulnerable to violence by an intimate.
- Women ages 19 to 29 and women in families with incomes below $10,000 were more likely than other women to be victims of violence by an intimate.
- Among victims of violence committed by an intimate, the victimization rate of women separated from their husbands was about 3 times higher than that of divorced women and about 25 times higher than that of married women. Because the NCVS reflects a respondent's marital status at the time of the interview, which is up to 6 months after the incident, it is possible that separation or divorce followed the violence.
- Female victims of violence by an intimate were more often injured by the violence than females victimized by a stranger.

SOURCE: Ronet Bachman and Linda Saltzman, *Violence Against Women: Estimates from the Redesigned Survey* (Washington, D.C.: Bureau of Justice Statistics, 1995), p. 1.

sexual assaults, shootings, and stabbings; about 33 percent of the victims suffered only bruising. About 60 percent of the attacks did not involve a weapon, but guns or knives were used in about 12 percent of the assaults.

Although these data give the impression that assault is widespread, they most likely undercount the problem. The NCVS indicates that only about 57 percent of all serious assaults are reported to the police. Victims reported more than 1.2 million aggravated assaults in 2000 and 4 million simple or weaponless assaults.

Assault in the Home

Violent attacks in the home are one of the most frightening types of assault. Criminologists recognize that intrafamily violence is an enduring social problem in the

United States. One area of intrafamily violence that has received a great deal of media attention is **child abuse.**[169] This term describes any physical or emotional trauma to a child for which no reasonable explanation, such as an accident or ordinary disciplinary practices, can be found.[170]

Child abuse can result from actual physical beatings administered to a child by hands, feet, weapons, belts, sticks, burning, and so on. Another form of abuse results from **neglect**—not providing a child with the care and shelter to which he or she is entitled. It is difficult to estimate the actual number of child abuse cases because many incidents are never reported to the police. Nonetheless, child abuse and neglect appear to be serious social problems. The U.S. Department of Heath and Human Services conducts annual surveys to assess the nature and trends in reported abuse.[171] The most recent survey indicates that approximately 3 million referrals are received each year

■ Substance abuse has been linked to child abuse. Here, comedian Paula Poundstone and her attorney arrive in Los Angeles County Superior Court for sentencing after her conviction on abuse charges. She was ordered to serve five years of probation and placed in an alcohol rehabilitation facility for six months.

and about 60 percent are transferred for investigation. Of these, slightly less than one-third of investigations (29 percent) resulted in a disposition of either substantiated or indicated child maltreatment. Consequently, there were an estimated 826,000 substantiated victims of maltreatment nationwide in 1999, a rate of victimization of 11.8 per 1,000 children, a decline from the rate of 12.6 recorded in 1998.

Sexual abuse   Another aspect of the abuse syndrome is **sexual abuse**—the exploitation of children through rape, incest, and molestation by parents or other adults. It is difficult to estimate the incidence of sexual abuse, but a number of attempts have been made to gauge the extent of the problem. In a classic study, Diana Russell's survey of women in the San Francisco area found that 38 percent had experienced intra- or extrafamilial sexual abuse by the time they reached age 18.[172] Others have estimated that at least 20 percent of females suffer some form of sexual violence; that is, at least 1 in 5 girls suffers sexual abuse.[173]

Although sexual abuse is still quite prevalent, the number of reported cases has been in a significant decline. Research by Lisa Jones and David Finkelhor of the University of New Hampshire's Crimes Against Children Research Center shows that after a 15-year increase substantiated child sexual-abuse cases in the United States dropped 31 percent between 1992 and 1998. Most states (36 out of the 47 they reviewed) showed declines of at least 30 percent.[174] These data could mean that the actual number of cases is truly in decline because of the effectiveness of prevention programs, increased prosecution, and public awareness campaigns. It could also mean that more cases are overlooked because of (1) increased evidentiary requirements to substantiate cases, (2) increased caseworker caution due to new legal rights for caregivers, and (3) increasing limitations on the types of cases that agencies accept for investigation.[175]

Sexual abuse is of particular concern because children who have been abused experience a long list of symptoms, including fear, posttraumatic stress disorder, behavior problems, sexualized behavior, and poor self-esteem. The amount of force used during the abuse, its duration, and its frequency are all related to the extent of the long-term effects and the length of time needed for recovery.

Causes of child abuse   Why do parents physically assault their children? Such maltreatment is a highly complex problem with neither a single cause nor a readily available solution. It cuts across ethnic, religious, and socioeconomic lines. Abusive parents cannot be categorized by sex, age, or educational level; they come from all walks of life.[176]

A number of factors have been commonly linked to abuse and neglect:

• Family violence seems to be perpetuated from one generation to another within families.

• The behavior of abusive parents can often be traced to negative experiences in their own childhood—physical abuse, lack of love, emotional neglect, incest, and so on.

- Blended families, which include children living with an unrelated adult such as a stepparent or another unrelated co-resident, have also been linked to abuse. For example, children who live with a mother's boyfriend are at much greater risk for abuse than children living with two genetic parents. Some stepparents do not have strong emotional ties to their nongenetic children, nor do they reap emotional benefits from the parent–child relationship.[177]
- Parents may also become abusive if they are isolated from friends, neighbors, or relatives who can help in times of crisis. Potentially abusive parents are often alienated from society; they have carried the concept of the shrinking nuclear family to its most extreme form and are cut off from ties of kinship and contact with other people in the neighborhood.[178]

Spousal abuse   Spousal abuse has occurred throughout recorded history. Roman men had the legal right to beat their wives for minor acts such as attending public games without permission, drinking wine, or walking outdoors with their faces uncovered.[179] More serious transgressions, such as adultery, were punishable by death. During the later stages of the Roman Empire, the practice of wife beating abated; and by the fourth century A.D., excessive violence on the part of husband or wife was grounds for divorce.[180] During the early Middle Ages, there was a separation of love and marriage.[181] The ideal woman was protected, cherished, and loved from afar. In contrast, the wife, with whom marriage had been arranged by family ties, was guarded jealously and could be punished severely for violating her duties. A husband was expected to beat his wife for "misbehaviors" and might himself be punished by neighbors if he failed to do so.[182] Through the later Middle Ages and into modern times (from 1400 to 1900) there was little community objection to a man using force against his wife as long as the assault did not exceed certain limits, usually construed as death or disfigurement. By the mid-nineteenth century, severe wife beating fell into disfavor, and accused wife beaters were subject to public ridicule. Nonetheless, limited chastisement was still the rule. By the close of the nineteenth century, England and the United States outlawed wife beating. Yet the long history of husbands' domination of their wives made physical coercion hard to control. Until recent times, the subordinate position of women in the family was believed to give husbands the legal and moral obligation to manage their wives' behavior. Even after World War II, English courts found domestic assault a reasonable punishment for a wife who had disobeyed her husband.[183] These ideas form the foundation of men's traditional physical control of women and have led to severe cases of spousal assault.

The nature and extent of spousal abuse   It is difficult to estimate how widespread spousal abuse is today;

however, some statistics indicate the extent of the problem. In their classic study of family violence, Richard Gelles and Murray Straus found that 16 percent of surveyed families had experienced husband–wife assaults.[184] In police departments around the country, 60 to 70 percent of evening calls involve domestic disputes.

Nor is violence restricted to marriage: national surveys indicate that between 20 and 40 percent of females experience violence while dating.[185] According to a recently released survey conducted by researchers from the Harvard School of Public Health, 1 in 5 high school girls suffered sexual or physical abuse from a boyfriend. The study found that teen girls who had been abused by their boyfriends also were much more likely to use drugs or alcohol, to have unsafe sex, and to acquire eating disorders among other social problems.[186]

To read this study, go to the Harvard School of Public Health Web site at:

    **http://www.hsph.harvard.edu/press/releases/
press7312001.html**

For an up-to-date list of Web links, go to

    http://info.wadsworth.com/siegel ∎

There is a great variety in spouse abuse. One view is that batterers are damaged individuals who suffer a variety of neuropsychological disorders and cognitive deficits and who may have suffered brain injuries in youth.[187] Psychologists Neil Jacobson and John Mordechai Gottman studied 200 couples and found that batterers tend to fall into one of two categories, which they call "Pit bulls" and "Cobras."[188] Pit bulls, whose emotions are quick to erupt, are driven by deep insecurity and a dependence on the wives and partners they abuse. They tend to become stalkers, unable to let go of relationships once they have ended. In contrast, Cobras coolly and methodically inflict pain and humiliation on their spouses. Many Cobras have been physically or sexually abused in childhood and, as a consequence, see violence as an unavoidable part of life. The personal attributes and characteristics of spouse abusers are listed in Exhibit 11.2.

Some people view spousal abuse from an evolutionary standpoint: males are aggressive toward their mates because they have evolved with a high degree of sexual proprietariness. Men fear both losing a valued reproductive resource to a rival and making a paternal investment in a child that is not their own. Violence serves as a coercive social tool to dissuade interest in other males and to lash out in jealousy if threats are not taken seriously (that is, if the woman leaves). This explains why men often kill or injure their ex-wives; threats lose their effectiveness if they are merely a bluff.[189]

Growing support is being given to battered women. Shelters for assaulted wives are springing up around the country, and laws are being passed to protect a wife's in-

Exhibit 11.2 Factors that Predict Spousal Abuse

Presence of alcohol. Excessive alcohol use may turn otherwise docile husbands into wife abusers.

Hostility toward dependency. Some husbands who appear docile and passive may resent their dependence on their wives and react with rage and violence; this reaction has been linked to sexual inadequacy.

Excessive brooding. Obsession with a wife's behavior, however trivial, can result in violent assaults.

Social approval. Some husbands believe society approves of wife abuse and use these beliefs to justify their violent behavior.

Socioeconomic factors. Men who fail as providers and are under economic stress may take their frustrations out on their wives.

Flashes of anger. Research shows that a significant amount of family violence results from a sudden burst of anger after a verbal dispute.

Military service. Spouse abuse among men who have served in the military service is extremely high. Similarly, those serving in the military are more likely to assault their wives than civilian husbands. The reasons for this phenomenon may be the violence promoted by military training and the close proximity in which military families live to one another.

Having been battered children. Husbands who assault their wives were generally battered as children.

Unpredictableness. Batterers are unpredictable, unable to be influenced by their wives, and impossible to prevent from battering once an argument has begun.

Batterers can be classified into two distinct types: men whose temper slowly simmers until it suddenly erupts into violence, and those who strike out immediately.

SOURCE: Neil Jacobson and John Mordechai Gottman, *When Men Batter Women: New Insights into Ending Abusive Relationships* (New York: Simon and Schuster, 1998); Kenneth Leonard and Brian Quigley, "Drinking and Marital Aggression in Newlyweds: An Event-Based Analysis of Drinking and the Occurrence of Husband Marital Aggression," *Journal of Studies on Alcohol* 60 (1999):537–41; Graeme Newman, *Understanding Violence* (New York: Lippincott, 1979).

terests. Police departments have made enforcement of domestic abuse laws a top priority. It is essential that this problem be brought to public light and controlled.

Robbery

The common-law definition of **robbery** (and the one used by the FBI) is "the taking or attempting to take anything of value from the care, custody or control of a person or persons by force or threat of force or violence and/or by putting the victim in fear."[190] A robbery is considered a violent crime because it involves the use of force to obtain money or goods. Robbery is punished severely because the victim's life is put in jeopardy. In fact, the severity of punishment is based on the amount of force used during the crime, not the value of the items taken.

In 2000 the FBI recorded more than 407,000 robberies, a rate of 145 per 100,000 population. As with other violent crimes, there has been a significant reduction in the robbery rate during the 1990s. Between 1991 and 2000 the rate of robbery declined more than 40 percent.

The ecological pattern for robbery is similar to that of other violent crimes, with one significant exception: northeastern states by far have the highest robbery rate. NCVS data show that robbery is more of a problem than the FBI data indicate. According to the NCVS, about 730,000 robberies were committed or attempted in 2000.[191] The two data sources agree, however, on the age, race, and sexual makeup of the offenders: they are disproportionately young, male minority group members.

Attempts have been made to classify and explain the nature and dynamics of robbery. One approach is to characterize robberies by type (Exhibit 11.3), and another is to characterize types of robbers based on their specialties (Exhibit 11.4).

As these typologies indicate, the typical armed robber is unlikely to be a professional who carefully studies targets while planning a crime. People walking along the street, convenience stores, and gas stations are much more likely robbery targets than banks or other highly secure environments. Robbers, therefore, seem to be diverted by modest defensive measures, such as having more than one clerk in a store or locating stores in strip malls; they are more likely to try an isolated store.[192]

Acquaintance Robbery

As Exhibit 11.4 suggests, one type of robber may focus on people they know, a phenomenon referred to as **acquaintance robbery.** This seems puzzling because victims can easily identify their attackers and report them to the police. However, despite this threat, acquaintance robbery may be attractive for a number of rational reasons:[193]

- Victims may be reluctant to report these crimes because they do not want to get involved with the police: they may be involved in crime themselves (drug dealers, for example), or they may fear retaliation if they report the crime. Some victims may be reluctant to gain the label of "rat" or "fink" if they go to the police.

- Some robberies are motivated by street justice. The robber has a grievance against the victim and settles the dispute by stealing the victim's property. In this instance, robbery may be considered a substitute for an assault: the robber wants retribution and revenge rather than remuneration.[194]

- Because the robber knows the victim personally, the robber has inside information that there will be a

Exhibit 11.3   Types of Robberies

Robbery of persons who, as part of their employment, are in charge of money or goods This category includes robberies in jewelry stores, banks, offices, and other places in which money changes hands.

Robbery in an open area These robberies include street muggings, purse snatchings, and other attacks. Street robberies are the most common type, especially in urban areas where this type of robbery constitutes about 60 percent of reported totals. Street robbery is most closely associated with mugging or yoking, which refers to grabbing victims from behind and threatening them with a weapon. Street muggers often target unsavory characters such as drug dealers or pimps who carry large amounts of cash because these victims would find it awkward to report the crime to the police. Most commit their robberies within a short distance from their homes.

Commercial robbery This type of robbery occurs in businesses ranging from banks to liquor stores. Banks are among the most difficult targets to rob, usually because they have more personnel and a higher level of security.

Robbery on private premises This type of robbery involves breaking into people's homes. FBI records indicate that this type of robbery accounts for about 10 percent of all offenses.

Robbery after a short, preliminary association This type of robbery comes after a chance meeting—in a bar, at a party, or after a sexual encounter.

Robbery after a longer association between victim and offender An example of this type of robbery would be an intimate acquaintance robbing his paramour and then fleeing the jurisdiction.

Carjacking This is a completed or attempted theft of a motor vehicle by force or threat of force.

SOURCE: Patsy Klaus, *Carjackings in the United States, 1992–96* (Washington, D.C.: Bureau of Justice Statistics, 1999); Peter J. van Koppen and Robert Jansen, "The Road to the Robbery: Travel Patterns in Commercial Robberies," *British Journal of Criminology* 38 (1998): 230–47; F. H. McClintock and Evelyn Gibson, *Robbery in London* (London: Macmillan, 1961), p. 15.

Exhibit 11.4   Types of Robbers

Professional robbers have a long-term commitment to crime as a source of livelihood. This type of robber plans and organizes crimes prior to committing them and seeks money to support a hedonistic lifestyle. Some professionals are exclusively robbers, whereas others engage in additional types of crimes. Professionals are committed to robbing because it is direct, fast, and profitable. They hold no other steady job and plan three or four "big scores" a year to support themselves. Planning and skill are the trademarks of the professional robber, who usually operates in groups with assigned roles. Professionals usually steal large amounts from commercial establishments. After a score, they may stop for a few weeks until "things cool off."

Opportunist robbers steal to obtain small amounts of money when an accessible target presents itself. They are not committed to robbery but will steal from cab drivers, drunks, the elderly, and other vulnerable persons if they need some extra spending money. Opportunists are usually young minority group members who do not plan their crimes. Although they operate within the milieu of the juvenile gang, they are seldom organized and spend little time discussing weapon use, getaway plans, or other strategies.

Addict robbers steal to support their drug habits. They have a low commitment to robbery because of its danger but a high commitment to theft because it supplies needed funds. The addict is less likely to plan crime or use weapons than the professional robber but is more cautious than the opportunist. Addicts choose targets that present minimal risk; however, when desperate for funds, they are sometimes careless in selecting the victim and executing the crime. They rarely think in terms of the big score; they just want enough money to get their next fix.

Alcoholic robbers steal for reasons related to their excessive consumption of alcohol. Alcoholic robbers steal (1) when, in a disoriented state, they attempt to get some money to buy liquor or (2) when their condition makes them unemployable and they need funds. Alcoholic robbers have no real commitment to robbery as a way of life. They plan their crimes randomly and give little thought to their victim, circumstance, or escape. For that reason, they are the most likely to be caught.

SOURCE: John Conklin, *Robbery and the Criminal Justice System* (New York: Lippincott, 1972), pp. 1–80.

"good take." Offenders may target people they know to be carrying a large amount of cash or who just purchased expensive jewelry.

- When a person in desperate need for immediate cash runs out of money, the individual may target people in close proximity simply because they are convenient targets.

When Richard Felson and his associates studied acquaintance robbery, they found that victims were more likely to be injured in acquaintance robberies than in stranger robberies, indicating that revenge rather than reward was the primary motive.[195] Similarly, robberies of family members were more likely to have a bigger pay-off than stranger robberies, an indication that the offender was aware that the target had a large amount of cash on hand.

Rational Robbers

Most robbers may be opportunistic rather than professional, but the patterns of robbery suggest that it is not merely a random act committed by an alcoholic or drug abuser. Though most crime rates are higher in the sum-

A surveillance camera picks up a man as he robs the Santa Fe Federal Credit Union in Albuquerque, New Mexico, on December 19, 2001. Robberies like this one are still common, but the rate of robbery declined more than 40 percent from 1991 to 2001.

mer, robberies seem to peak during the winter months. One reason may be that the cold weather allows for greater disguise; another reason is that robbers may be attracted to the high amounts of cash people and merchants carry during the Christmas shopping season.[196] Robbers may also be attracted to the winter because days are shorter, affording them greater concealment in the dark.

Robbers also choose vulnerable victims. According to research by criminologist Jody Miller, female armed robbers are likely to choose female targets, reasoning that they will be more vulnerable and offer less resistance.[197] When robbing males, women "set them up" in order to catch them off guard; some feign sexual interest or prostitution to gain the upper hand.[198] In an important book, Scott Decker and Richard Wright interviewed active robbers in St. Louis, Missouri.[199] Their findings, presented in the Criminological Enterprise feature titled "Armed Robbers in Action," also suggest that robbers are rational decision makers.

CONNECTIONS

Chapter 5 discussed the rationality of street robbery. Even when robbers are stealing to support a drug habit, their acts do not seem haphazard or irrational. Only the most inebriated might fail to take precautions. The fact that robbery is gender-specific is also evidence that robbers are rational decision makers. ■

■ Emerging Forms of Interpersonal Violence

Assault, rape, robbery, and murder are traditional forms of interpersonal violence. As more data become available, criminologists have recognized relatively new subcategories within these crime types, such as serial murder and date rape. Additional new categories of interpersonal violence are now receiving attention in criminological literature; the next sections describe three of these forms of violent crime.

Hate Crimes

In the fall of 1998 Matthew Shepard, a gay college student, was kidnapped and severely beaten. He died five days after he was found unconscious on a Wyoming ranch, where he had been left tied to a fence for 18 hours in near freezing temperatures.[200] His two killers, Aaron J. McKinney and Russell A. Henderson, both 22, were sentenced to life in prison after the Shepard family granted them mercy. At McKinney's sentencing, Matthew's father, Dennis Shepard, addressed the young man:

> I would like nothing better than to see you die, McKinney. However, this is the time to begin the healing process, to show mercy to someone who refused to show any mercy. Mr. McKinney, I am going to grant you life, as hard as it is for me to do so, because of Matthew. Every time you

Armed Robbers in Action

Criminologists Richard Wright and Scott Decker have identified and interviewed a sample of 86 active armed robbers in St. Louis, Missouri. Their sample, primarily young African American men, helped provide an in-depth view of armed robbery that had been missing from the criminological literature.

Wright and Decker found that most armed robberies are motivated by a pressing need for cash. Many robbers careen from one financial crisis to the next, prompted by their endless quest for stimulation and thrills. Interviewees told of how they partied, gambled, drank, and abused substances until they were broke. Their partying not only provided excitement, but it helped generate a street reputation as a "hip" guy who can "make things happen." Robbers had a "here and now" mentality, which required a constant supply of cash to fuel their appetites. Those interviewed showed little long-range planning or commitment to the future. Because of their street hustler mentality, few if any of the robbers were able to obtain or keep legitimate employment, even if it was available.

Armed robbery also provided a psychic thrill. It was a chance to hurt or humiliate victims, or to get even with someone who may have wronged them in the past. As one robber explained, "This might sound stupid, but I [also] like to see a person get scared, be scared of the pistol.... You got power. I come in here with a big old pistol and I ain't playing."

Robbers show evidence of being highly rational offenders. Many choose victims who themselves are involved in illegal behavior, most often drug dealers. Ripping off a dealer kills three birds with one stone, providing both money and drugs while at the same time targeting victims who are quite unlikely to call the police. Another ideal target is a married man who is looking for illicit sexual adventures. He also is disinclined to call the police and bring attention to himself. One told them why he chose to be a robber:

I feel more safer doing a robbery because doing a burglary, I got a fear of breaking into somebody's house not knowing who might be up in there.... On robbery I can select my victims, I can select my place of business. I can watch and see who all work in there or I can rob a person and pull them around in the alley or push them up in a doorway and rob them. (p. 52)

Others target noncriminal victims. They like to stay in their own neighborhood, relying on their intimate knowledge of streets and alleys to avoid detection. Although some range far afield seeking affluent victims, others believe that residents in the city's poorest areas are more likely to carry cash (wealthy people carry checks and credit cards). Because they realize that the risk of detection and punishment is the same whether the victim is carrying a load of cash or is penniless, experienced robbers use discretion in selecting targets. People whose clothing, jewelry, and demeanor mark them as carrying substantial amounts of cash make suitable targets; people who look like they can fight back are avoided. Some station themselves at cash machines to spot targets who are flashing rolls of money.

Robbers have racial, gender, and age preferences in their selection of targets. Some African American robbers prefer white targets because they believe they are too afraid to fight back. Others concentrate on African American victims, who are more likely to carry cash than credit cards. As one interviewee revealed, "White guys can be so paranoid [that] they just want to get away.... They're not...gonna argue with you." Likewise, intoxicated victims in no condition to fight back were favored targets. Some robbers tend to target women because they feel they are easy subjects; however, others avoid them because they believe they will get emotionally upset and bring unwanted attention. Most agree that the elderly are less likely to put up a fuss than younger, stronger targets.

Some robbers choose commercial targets, such as convenience stores or markets that are cash businesses open late at night. Gas stations are a favorite victim. Security is of little consequence to experienced robbers, who may bring an accomplice to subdue guards.

Once they choose their targets, robbers carefully orchestrate the criminal incidents. They immediately impose their will on their chosen victims, leaving little room for the victims to maneuver and making sure the victims feel threatened enough to offer no resistance. Some approach from behind so they cannot be identified, and others approach victims head-on, showing that they are tough and bold. By convincing the victims of their impending death, the robber takes control.

Critical Thinking Questions

1. It is unlikely that the threat of punishment can deter robbery (most robbers refuse to think about apprehension and punishment), but Wright and Decker suggest that eliminating cash and relying on debit and credit cards may be the most productive method to reduce the incidence of robbery. Although this seems far-fetched, our society is becoming progressively more cashless; it is now possible to buy both gas and groceries with credit cards. Would a cashless society end the threat of robbery, or would innovative robbers find new targets?

2. Based on what you know about how robbers target victims, how can you better protect yourself from robbery?

InfoTrac College Edition Research

To learn more about robbery, see:

Peter J. van Koppen and Robert W. J. Jansen. The road to the robbery: travel patterns in commercial robberies. *British Journal of Criminology* Spring 1998 v38 n2 p230

D. J. Pyle and D. F. Deadman. Crime and the business cycle in post-war Britain. *British Journal of Criminology* Summer 1994 34 n3 p339–357

SOURCE: Richard Wright and Scott Decker, *Armed Robbers in Action, Stickups and Street Culture* (Boston, Mass.: Northeastern University Press, 1997).

celebrate Christmas, a birthday or the Fourth of July, remember that Matthew isn't. Every time you wake up in that prison cell, remember that you had the opportunity and the ability to stop your actions that night. You robbed me of something very precious, and I will never forgive you for that. May you live a long life and may you thank Matthew every day for it.[201]

Hate crimes or **bias crimes** are violent acts directed toward a particular person or members of a group merely because the targets share a discernible racial, ethnic, religious, or gender characteristic.[202] Hate crimes can include the desecration of a house of worship or cemetery, harassment of a minority group family that has moved into a previously all-white neighborhood, or a racially motivated murder. For example, on August 23, 1989, Yusuf Hawkins, a black youth, was killed in the Bensonhurst section of Brooklyn, New York, because he had wandered into a racially charged white neighborhood.[203]

Hate crimes usually involve convenient, vulnerable targets who are incapable of fighting back. For example, there have been numerous reported incidents of teenagers attacking vagrants and the homeless in an effort to rid their town or neighborhood of people they consider undesirable.[204] Another group targeted for hate crimes is gay men and women: *gay bashing* has become common in U.S. cities.

Racial and ethnic minorities have also been the targets of attack. In California, Mexican laborers have been attacked and killed; in New Jersey, Indian immigrants have been the targets of racial hatred.[205] Although hate crimes are often mindless attacks directed toward "traditional" minority victims, political and economic trends may cause this form of violence to be redirected. For example, Asians have been attacked by groups who resent the growing economic power of Japan and Korea as well as the commercial success of Asian Americans.[206] The factors that precipitate hate crimes are listed in Exhibit 11.5.

■ **Exhibit 11.5** **Factors that Produce Hate Crimes**

- Poor or uncertain economic conditions
- Racial stereotypes in films and on television
- Hate-filled discourse on talk shows or in political advertisements
- The use of racial code language such as "welfare mothers" and "inner-city thugs"
- An individual's personal experiences with members of particular minority groups
- Scapegoating—blaming a minority group for the misfortunes of society as a whole

SOURCE: "A Policymaker's Guide to Hate Crimes," *Bureau of Justice Assistance Monograph* (Washington, D.C.: Bureau of Justice Assistance, 1997).

The roots of hate Why do people commit bias crimes? Research by sociologist Jack McDevitt shows that hate crimes are generally spontaneous incidents motivated by victims' walking, driving, shopping, or socializing in an area in which their attackers believe they "do not belong."[207] Other factors that motivate bias attacks include a victim moving into an ethnically distinct neighborhood or dating a member of a different race or ethnic group. Although hate crimes are often unplanned, McDevitt finds that most of these crimes are serious incidents that involve assaults and robberies.[208] In their book *Hate Crimes*, McDevitt and Jack Levin say that hate crimes are typically one of three types that reflect different motives:

- **Thrill-seeking hate crimes.** In the same way some kids like to get together to shoot hoops, hate-mongers join forces to have fun by bashing minorities or destroying property. Inflicting pain on others gives them a sadistic thrill.

- **Reactive hate crimes.** Perpetrators of these crimes rationalize their behavior as a defensive stand taken against outsiders whom they believe threaten their community or way of life. A gang of teens that attacks a new family in the neighborhood because they are the "wrong" race is committing a reactive hate crime.

- **Mission hate crimes.** Some disturbed individuals see it as their duty to rid the world of evil. Those on a "mission," like Skinheads, the Ku Klux Klan (KKK), and white supremacist groups, may seek to eliminate people who threaten their religious beliefs because they are members of a different faith or threaten "racial purity" because they are of a different race.[209]

In one study of Boston police records, Levin and McDevitt found that thrill crimes were the most common (58 percent), and most of these (70 percent) involved assault. Reactive crimes (42 percent) also involved assaulting strangers who happened to be in the wrong place at the wrong time. Although there was only one mission-type crime, it was the most violent incident and involved beating two supposedly gay males with baseball bats.[210]

Nature and extent of hate crime During 2000, law enforcement reported 8,063 bias-motivated criminal acts involving 9,430 offenses, 9,924 victims, and 7,530 known offenders. These crimes resulted in 19 murders: 10 due to racial bias; 6 attributed to a bias against an ethnicity or national origin; 2 more driven by bias against a sexual orientation; and 1 resulting from a religious bias.

To examine the FBI's hate crime data, go to:
http://www.fbi.gov/ucr/cius_00/hate00.pdf
For an up-to-date list of Web links, go to
http://info.wadsworth.com/siegel ■

What form do hate crimes take, and whom do they target? A recent analysis of 3,000 hate crime cases reported to the police found that about 60 percent of hate crimes involved a violent act, most commonly intimidation or simple assault, and 40 percent of the incidents involved property crimes, most commonly damage, destruction, or vandalism of property.[211]

About 60 percent of these crimes were motivated by race, 14 percent by religion (most often anti-Semitism), 13 percent by sexual orientation, 11 percent by ethnicity, and 1 percent by victim disability. Vandalism and property crimes were the products of hate crimes motivated by religion. However, criminals were more likely to turn to violent acts when race, ethnicity, and sexual orientation were the motivation. Most targets of hate crimes, especially the violent variety, were young white men. More than half of victims of violence were age 24 or under, and nearly a third were under 18. Similarly, the majority of known hate crime offenders were young: 31 percent of violent offenders and 46 percent of property offenders were under age 18.

NIBRS data allow researchers to determine the relationship between the victim and offender for violent offenses and nonviolent sex offenses. In crimes where victims could actually identify the culprits, most victims reported that they were acquainted with their attackers (38 percent) or that their attackers were actually friends or relatives (7 percent). Younger victims were more likely to be victimized by persons known to them (of violent victims age 12 or younger, 63 percent were victimized by an acquaintance, relative, or friend).

Because of the extent and seriousness of the problem, a number of legal jurisdictions have made a special effort to control the spread of hate crimes. Boston maintains the Community Disorders Unit, and the New York City police department formed the Bias Incident Investigating Unit in 1980. When a crime anywhere in the city is suspected of being motivated by bias, the unit initiates an investigation. The unit also assists victims and works with concerned organizations such as the Commission on Human Rights and the Gay and Lesbian Task Force. These agencies deal with noncriminal bias incidents through mediation, education, and other forms of prevention.[212]

Punishing hate crimes   Almost every state jurisdiction has enacted some form of legislation designed to combat hate crimes: 39 states have enacted laws against bias-motivated violence and intimidation; 19 states have statutes that specifically mandate the collection of hate crime data.

Some critics argue that it is unfair to punish criminals motivated by hate any more severely than those who commit similar crimes whose motivation is revenge, greed, or anger. However, in his important book *Punishing Hate: Bias Crimes Under American Law*, Frederick Lawrence argues that criminals motivated by bias deserve to be pun-

■ An image of a murdered Indian immigrant, Balbir Singh Sodhi, is shown at a memorial service in Phoenix, Arizona. Sodhi was killed in a hate crime after the September 11 attack in the mistaken belief that he was of Middle Eastern descent. Should hate crimes be punished more severely than crimes motivated by revenge or greed?

ished more severely than those who commit identical crimes for other motives.[213] He suggests that a society dedicated to the equality of all its peoples must treat bias crimes differently from other crimes, and in so doing enhance the punishment of these crimes.[214] Some criminals choose their victims randomly; others select specific victims, for example, as in crimes of revenge. Bias crimes are different. They are crimes in which (a) distinct identifying characteristics of the victim are critical to the perpetrator's choice of victim, and (b) the individual identity of the victim is irrelevant.[215] He views a bias crime as one that would not have been committed but for the victim's membership in a particular group.[216] He argues that bias crimes should be punished more severely because the harm caused will exceed that caused by crimes with other motivations:[217]

1. Bias crimes are more likely to be violent and involve serious physical injury to the victim.

2. Bias crimes will have significant emotional and psychological impact on the victim; they result in a

"heightened sense of vulnerability," which causes depression, anxiety, and feelings of helplessness.

3. Bias crimes harm not only the victim but also the "target community."

4. Bias crimes violate the shared value of equality among citizens and racial and religious harmony in a heterogeneous society.

Workplace Violence

Paul Calden, a former insurance company employee, walked into a Tampa cafeteria and opened fire on a table at which his former supervisors were dining. Calden shouted, "This is what you all get for firing me!" and began shooting. When he finished, three were dead and two others were wounded.[218] It has become commonplace to read of irate employees or former employees attacking coworkers or sabotaging machinery and production lines. **Workplace violence** is now considered the third leading cause of occupational injury or death.[219]

Who engages in workplace violence? The typical offender is a middle-aged white male who faces termination in a worsening economy. The fear of economic ruin is especially strong in agencies such as the U.S. Postal Service, where long-term employees fear job loss because of automation and reorganization. In contrast, younger workers usually kill while committing a robbery or another felony.

A number of factors precipitate workplace violence. One may simply be the conflict caused by economic restructuring. As corporations cut their staffs due to recent trends such as office automation and company buyouts, long-term employees who had never thought of themselves losing a job are suddenly unemployed. There is often a correlation between sudden, unexpected layoffs and violent reactions.[220] Another trigger may be leadership styles. Some companies, including the U.S. Postal Service, have authoritarian management styles that demand performance, above all else, from employees. Unsympathetic, unsupportive managers may help trigger workplace violence.

Not all workplace violence is triggered by management-induced injustice. In some incidents coworkers have been killed because they refused romantic relationships with the assailants or reported them for sexual harassment. Others have been killed because they got a job the assailant coveted. Irate clients and customers have also killed because of poor service or perceived slights. For example, in one Los Angeles incident, a former patient shot and critically wounded three doctors because his demands for painkillers had gone unheeded.[221]

There are a variety of responses to workplace provocations. Some people take out their anger and aggression by attacking their supervisors in an effort to punish the company that dismissed them; this is a form of murder by proxy.[222] Disgruntled employees may also attack family members or friends, misdirecting the rage and frustration caused by their work situation. Others are content with sabotaging company equipment; computer databases are particularly vulnerable to tampering. The aggrieved party may do nothing to rectify the situation; this inaction is referred to as **sufferance.** Over time, the unresolved conflict may be compounded by other events that cause an eventual eruption.

The extent of workplace violence   The latest available data show that each year more than 2 million U.S. residents become victims of violent crime while they work. The most common type of victimization is assault, with an estimated 1.5 million simple assaults and 396,000 aggravated assaults reported annually. Each year sees 84,000 robberies, about 51,000 rapes or sexual assaults, and more than 1,000 workplace homicides.[223] As Figure 11.4 shows, retail sales workers have the highest risk of on-the-job injuries, followed by law enforcement officers.

CONNECTIONS

Does the fact that sales clerks and police officers have the highest injury risk support routine activities theory? People in high-risk jobs who are out late at night and, in the case of sales clerks, do business in cash seem to have the greatest risk of injury on the job. See Chapter 4 for more on routine activities and crime. ■

Can workplace violence be controlled?   One approach is to use third parties to mediate disputes. The restorative justice movement (discussed in Chapter 9) advocates the use of mediation to resolve interpersonal disputes. Restorative justice techniques may work particularly well in the workplace, where disputants know each other and tensions may be simmering over a long period. This may help control the rising tide of workplace violence. Another idea is a human resources approach, with aggressive job retraining and continued medical coverage after layoffs; it is also important to use objective, fair hearings to thwart unfair or biased terminations. Perhaps rigorous screening tests can help identify violence-prone workers so that they can be given anger management training.

Stalking

In Wes Craven's popular movies *Scream 1–3*, the heroine, Sydney (played by Neve Campbell), is stalked by a mysterious adversary who scares her half to death while killing off most of her peer group. Although obviously extreme even by Hollywood standards, the *Scream* movies focus on

Figure 11.4 Trends in Workplace Violence

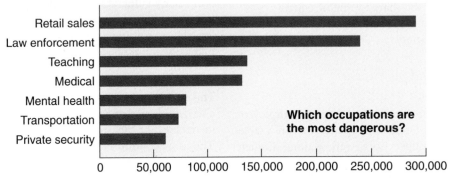

Selected occupations with a larger
number of violent victimizations

**Which occupations are
the most dangerous?**

Average annual number of violent victimizations
in the workplace, 1992–1996

• Each year between 1992 and 1996,
more than 2 million U.S. residents
were victims of a violent crime while
they were at work or on duty.

• More than 1,000 workplace homicides
occurred annually.

• The most common type of
victimization was simple assault, with
an estimated 1.5 million occurring
each year. U.S. residents also suffered
51,000 rapes and sexual assaults and
about 84,000 robberies while they
were at work.

• Annually, more than 230,000 police
officers became victims of a nonfatal
violent crime while they were working
or on duty.

• About 40 percent of victims of nonfatal
violence in the workplace reported
that they knew their offenders.

• Women were more likely than men to
be victimized by someone they knew.

• Approximately 12 percent of the
nonfatal violent workplace crimes
injured the victim. Of those injured,
about half received medical treatment.

• Intimates (current and former spouses,
boyfriends, and girlfriends) were
identified by the victims as the
perpetrators of about 1 percent of all
workplace violent crime.

SOURCE: Greg Warchol, *Workplace Violence, 1992–1996* (Washington, D.C.: Bureau of Justice Statistics, 1998).

a newly recognized form of long-term and repeat victimization: stalking.[224]

Stalking can be defined as a course of conduct directed at a specific person that involves repeated physical or visual proximity, nonconsensual communication, or verbal, written, or implied threats sufficient to cause fear in a reasonable person. Stalking is a problem that affects about 1.4 million victims annually. It is strongly linked to the controlling behavior and physical, emotional, and sexual abuse perpetrated against women by intimate partners. About half of all female stalking victims report their victimization to the police, and about one-quarter of them obtain a restraining order against their assailants. In most cases, stalking episodes last one year or less, but in a few cases, stalking continues for five or more years.

Most victims know their stalker. Women are most likely to be stalked by an intimate partner—a current spouse, a former spouse, someone they lived with, or even a date. In contrast, men typically are stalked by a stranger or an acquaintance. The typical female victim is stalked because her assailant wants to control her, scare her, or keep her in a relationship. Victims of both genders find that there is a clear relationship between stalking and other emotionally controlling and physically abusive behavior.

Stalkers behave in ways that induce fear, but they do not always make overt threats against their victims. Many followed or spied upon their victims, some threatened to kill pets, and others vandalized property. However, as criminologist Mary Brewster found, stalkers who make verbal threats are the ones most likely to later attack their victims.[225]

Although stalking usually stops within one to two years, victims experience its social and psychological consequences long afterward. About one-third seek psycho-

■ Although we often assume that the targets of stalking are women, men are not immune. Here, convicted stalker Gary Randolf appears at a court hearing in Clark County, Nevada. Randolf had been sent to a mental facility after being convicted of the aggravated stalking of comedian Jerry Lewis.

logical treatment, and about one-fifth lose time from work; some never return to work.

Why does stalking stop? Most often because the victim moved away or the police got involved or, in some cases, when the stalker met another love interest.

■ Terrorism

As we all watched on September 11, 2001, two hijacked airliners crashed into the World Trade Center Towers in New York City. Thousands were killed when the towers collapsed more than an hour after the impacts. A third hijacked airliner crashed into the Pentagon. A fourth jet, possibly bound for another target in Washington, D.C., crashed in Somerset County, Pennsylvania, after passengers were able to overpower the hijackers. The events of September 11 were quickly traced to followers of Osama bin Laden and his al-Qaeda terrorist organization based in Afghanistan.

Acting swiftly, the United States began military operations in Afghanistan to root out bin Laden and topple the Taliban government that had sheltered his activities.

The crimes of 9/11 are so monumental that they still remain difficult to comprehend, but terrorism has been with us throughout history.[226] It is often difficult to separate terrorism from interpersonal crimes of violence. For example, if a group robs a bank to obtain funds for its revolutionary struggles, should the act be treated as terrorism or as a common bank robbery? In this instance, defining a crime as terrorism depends on the kind of legal response the act evokes from those in power. To be considered **terrorism,** which is a political crime, an act must carry with it the intent to disrupt and change the government and must not be merely a common-law crime committed for greed or egotism. Criminologist Stephen Schafer referred to those who violate the law because they believe their actions will ultimately benefit society as **convictional criminals.** They know their actions may be wrong and harmful but believe these actions are necessary to create the changes they fervently desire. "A member of the Second World War Resistance," Schafer argued, "may have condemned violence, yet his own conviction overshadowed any sense of repugnance and induced him to engage in violent crimes in an effort to expel the invader from his Fatherland."[227] In these cases, political violence is not violence for violence's sake; it is violence with a higher, political purpose.

What Is Terrorism?

Because of its complexity, an all-encompassing definition of terrorism is difficult to formulate, although most experts agree that it generally involves the illegal use of force against innocent people to achieve a political objective. According to the U.S. State Department, the term *terrorism* means premeditated, politically motivated violence perpetrated against noncombatant targets by subnational groups or clandestine agents, usually intended to influence an audience. The term **international terrorism** means terrorism involving citizens or the territory of more than one country. A **terrorist group** is any group practicing, or that has significant subgroups that practice, international terrorism.[228]

Terrorism usually involves a type of political crime that emphasizes violence as a mechanism to promote change. Whereas some political criminals may demonstrate, counterfeit, sell secrets, spy, and the like, terrorists systematically murder and destroy or threaten such violence to terrorize individuals, groups, communities, or governments into conceding to the terrorists' political demands.[229] However, it may be erroneous to equate terrorism with political goals, because not all terrorist actions are aimed at political change. Some terrorists may try to bring about what they consider to be economic or social reform—for example, by attacking women wearing fur coats or sabotaging property during a labor dispute. Terrorism must also be distinguished from conventional warfare, because it requires secrecy and clandestine operations to exert social control over large populations.[230]

The term *terrorist* is often used interchangeably with the term **guerilla,** meaning "little war," which developed out of the Spanish rebellion against French troops after Napoleon's 1808 invasion of the Iberian peninsula.[231] Terrorists have an urban focus. Operating in small bands, or cadres, of three to five members, they target the property or persons of their enemy, such as members of the ruling class.[232] Guerillas, on the other hand, are located in rural areas and attack the military, the police, and government officials. Their organizations can grow quite large and eventually take the form of a conventional military force. However, guerilas can infiltrate urban areas in small bands, and terrorists can make forays into the countryside; consequently, the terms are used interchangeably.[233]

A Brief History of Terrorism

Acts of terrorism have been known throughout history. The assassination of Julius Caesar on March 15, 44 B.C., is considered an act of terrorism. Terrorism became widespread at the end of the Middle Ages, when political leaders were subject to assassination by their enemies. The word *assassin* was derived from an Arabic term meaning "hashish eater"; it originally referred to members of a drug-using Muslim terrorist organization that carried out plots against prominent Christians and other religious enemies.[234] The literal translation of assassin refers to the acts of ritual intoxication undertaken by the warriors before their missions. From A.D. 66 to 73, a Jewish sect known as the Zealots took up arms against the Roman occupation, using daggers to slit the throats of Romans and of Jews who collaborated.

When rulers had absolute power, terrorist acts were viewed as one of the only means of gaining political rights. At times European states encouraged terrorist acts against their enemies. For example, Queen Elizabeth I empowered her naval leaders, including famed captains John Hawkins and Francis Drake, to attack the Spanish fleet. These privateers would have been considered pirates had they not operated with government approval. American privateers attacked the British during the Revolutionary War and the War of 1812 and were considered heroes for their actions against the English Navy.

The term *terrorist* first became popular during the French Revolution. From the fall of the Bastille on July 14, 1789 until July 1794, thousands suspected of counterrevolutionary activity were killed on the guillotine. Here again, the relative nature of political crime is documented: whereas most victims of the French Reign of Terror were revolutionaries who had been denounced by rival factions, thousands of the hated nobility lived in relative tranquility. The end of the terror was signaled by the death of its prime mover, Maximilien Robespierre, on July 28, 1794, as the result of a successful plot to end his rule. He was executed on the same guillotine to which he had sent almost 20,000 people.

In the hundred years after the French Revolution, terrorism continued around the world. The Hur Brotherhood in India was made up of religious fanatics who carried out terrorist acts against the ruling class. In Eastern Europe the Internal Macedonian Revolutionary Organization campaigned against the Turkish government, which controlled its homeland (Macedonia became part of the former Yugoslavia). Similarly, the protest of the Union of Death Society, or Black Hand, against the Austro-Hungarian Empire's control of Serbia led to the group's assassination of Archduke Franz Ferdinand, which started World War I. The Irish Republican Army, established around 1916, steadily battled British forces from 1919 to 1923, culminating in the Republic of Ireland gaining independence. Between the world wars, right-wing terrorism existed in Germany, Spain, and Italy. Conversely, Russia was the scene of left-wing revolutionary activity, which killed the czar in 1917 and gave birth to the Marxist state.

During World War II, resistance to the occupying German troops was common throughout Europe. The Germans considered the resistance to be terrorists, but the rest of the world considers them heroes. Meanwhile, in Palestine, Jewish terrorist groups—the Haganah, Irgun, and Stern Gang, whose leaders included Menachem Begin, who later became Israel's prime minister—waged war against the British to force them to allow Jewish survivors of the Holocaust to settle in their traditional homeland. Today, of course, many of these alleged terrorists are considered freedom fighters who laid down their lives for a just cause.

Contemporary Forms of Terrorism

Today the term *terrorism* encompasses many different behaviors and goals. Some of the more common forms are briefly described here.

Revolutionary terrorists Revolutionary terrorists use violence to frighten those in power and their supporters. The ultimate goal of these acts is to replace the existing government with a regime that holds acceptable political or religious views. Terrorist actions such as kidnapping, assassination, and bombing are designed to draw repressive responses from governments trying to defend themselves. These responses help revolutionaries to expose, through the skilled use of media coverage, the government's inhumane nature. The original reason for the government's harsh response may be lost as the effect of counterterrorist activities is felt by uninvolved people. For example, since 1994 fundamentalist Muslims have attacked foreign tourists in Egypt in an effort to sabotage the tourist industry, topple the secular government, and turn Egypt into an Islamic state. On November 17, 1997, more than 60 foreign tourists were killed in an attack by Muslim terrorists near the ruins of Luxor in Southern Egypt.

Political terrorists Political terrorism is directed at people or groups who oppose the terrorists' political ideology or whom the terrorists define as "outsiders" who must be destroyed. U.S. political terrorists tend to be heavily armed groups organized around such themes as white supremacy, militant tax resistance, and religious revisionism. Identified groups have included the Aryan Republican Army, the Aryan Nation, the Posse Comitatus, and the Ku Klux Klan. Although unlikely to topple the government, these individualistic acts of terror are difficult to predict or control. On April 19, 1995, 168 people were killed during the Oklahoma City bombing. This is the most severe example of political terrorism in the United States.

Nationalist terrorism Nationalist terrorism promotes the interests of a minority ethnic or religious group that believes it has been persecuted under majority rule and wishes to carve out its own independent homeland. In the Middle East, terrorist activities have been linked to the Palestinians' desire to wrest their former homeland from Israel. The leading group, the Palestinian Liberation Organization (PLO), had directed terrorist activities against

■ A fireball explodes from the World Trade Center on September 11, 2001. The unprovoked attacks on symbols of American prosperity killed thousands of innocent civilians and were the catalyst for a worldwide crusade against transnational terrorism.

Israel. Although the PLO now has political control over the West Bank and the Gaza Strip, splinter groups have broken from the PLO. These groups, Hamas and the Iranian-backed Hizballah, are perpetuating the conflict that Israel and the PLO sought to resolve and are behind a spate of suicide bombings and terrorist attacks designed to elicit a sharp response from Israel and set back any chance for peace in the region. In the first half of 2002, hundreds on both sides of the conflict were killed during terrorist attacks and reprisals.

In India, Sikh radicals use violence to recover what they believe to be lost homelands. They assassinated Indian Prime Minister Indira Gandhi on November 6, 1984, in retaliation for the government's storming of their Golden Temple religious shrine (and revolutionary base) in June 1984.

Cause-based terrorism Some terrorists, such as bin Laden's al-Qaeda organization, direct their terrorist activities against individuals and/or governments to whom they object. They espouse a particular social or religious cause and use violence to attract followers to their standard.

Bin Laden's intention's were revealed four years before the destruction of the World Trade Center, when in a 1997 interview with CNN he claimed that his "jihad" or holy war against the United States was started because American forces were still operating in Saudi Arabia. He demanded that the United States end its "aggressive intervention against Muslims in the whole world." He claimed that his cause was based on Islamic tradition; he believed that it was not permissible for non-Muslims to remain as protectors in Saudi Arabia. He stated that the current Egyptian and Saudi governments were insufficiently devout and therefore suitable targets of his group.

Though bin Laden's brand of terrorist activity proved to be more violent than anything previously experienced, it is not unique. For example, antiabortion groups have demonstrated at abortion clinics, and some members have attacked clients, bombed offices, and killed doctors who perform abortions. On October 23, 1998, Dr. Barnett Slepian was shot by a sniper and killed in his Buffalo, New York, home; he was one of a growing number of abortion providers believed to be the victims of terrorists who ironically claim to be "pro-life."

The Race, Culture, Gender, and Criminology feature further explores this relatively new form of terrorist activity.

Environmental terrorism On October 19, 1998, several suspicious fires were set atop Vail Mountain, a luxurious ski resort in Colorado. Soon after, a militant environmental group, the Earth Liberation Front, claimed that it set the fires to stop a ski operator from expanding into animal habitats (especially that of the mountain lynx). The fires, which cost an estimated $12 million in damages, are the most costly of the more than 1,500 terrorist acts committed by environmental terrorists during the past two

Transnational Terrorism in the New Millennium

"Today, international terrorists likely to target the United States are individuals" (p. 87) and "The greatest threat to the security of the United States in the next millennium will come from the hands of the freelancer" (p. 92): these prophetic words were written by terrorism expert Harvey Kushner in 1998. As he correctly recognized, the traditional image of the armed professional terrorist group with a clear-cut goal such as nationalism or independence is giving way to a new breed of terrorists with diverse motives and sponsors. Rather than a unified central command, they are organized in far-flung nets. Not located in any particular nation or area, they have no identifiable address. They are capable of attacking anyone at any time with great destructive force. They may employ an arsenal of weapons of mass destruction—chemical, biological, nuclear—without fear of contaminating their own homelands because in reality they may not actually have one.

The new "postmodern terrorist" is becoming more lethal, and as a result, terrorism fatalities have steadily increased throughout the decade. Terrorism expert Bruce Hoffman believes this may be attributed to the rise of religiously motivated terrorist groups such as al-Qaeda, which grew sixfold from 1980 to 1992 and has continued to increase steadily ever since. He suggests that religiously inspired terrorist attacks are more likely to result in higher casualties because they are motivated not by efforts to obtain political freedom or a national homeland but because of culture conflict. Maintaining a differing value system allows the perpetrators to justify in their minds the deaths of large numbers of people: "for the religious terrorist, violence is a divine duty . . . executed in direct response to some theological demand . . . and justified by scripture" (p. 20).

Osama bin Laden and the al-Qaeda network is the paradigm of the new value-oriented terrorist organization. His masterminding of the 9/11 bombing was not designed to restore his homeland or bring about a new political state but to have his personal value structure adopted by Muslim nations. His attack may have been designed to create a military invasion of Afghanistan, which he hoped to exploit for his particular brand of revolution. According to Michael Scott Doran, bin Laden believed his acts would reach the audience that concerned him the most: the umma, or universal Islamic community. The media would show Americans killing innocent civilians in Afghanistan, and the umma would find it shocking how Americans nonchalantly caused Muslims to suffer and die. The ensuing outrage would open a chasm between the Muslim population of the Middle East and the ruling governments in states such as Saudi Arabia, which were allied with the West. On October 7, 2001, bin Laden made a broadcast in which he said that the Americans and the British "have divided the entire world into two regions—one of faith, where there is no hypocrisy, and another of infidelity, from which we hope God will protect us."

According to Doran, bin Laden's true aim was to cause an Islamic revolution within the Muslim world itself, in Saudi Arabia especially, and not to win a war with the United States. Bin Laden viewed the leaders of the Arab and Islamic worlds as hypocrites and idol worshippers propped up by American military might. His attack was designed to force those governments to choose: You are either with the idol-worshiping enemies of God, or you are with the true believers. The attack on the United States was merely an instrument designed to help his brand of extremist Islam survive and flourish among the believers who could bring down these corrupt governments. Americans, in short, were drawn into somebody else's civil war.

This new generation of terrorists is especially frightening because they have no need to live to enjoy the fruits of victory. They do not hope to regain a homeland or a political voice; hence, they are willing to engage in suicide missions to achieve their goals. The devoted members of al-Qaeda were willing to martyr themselves because they believe they are locked in a life-or-death struggle with the forces of nonbelievers. They consider themselves true believers surrounded by blasphemers and concluded that the future of religion itself, and therefore the world, depends on them and their battle against idol worship. They believe that victory and salvation can be achieved in a martyr's death.

Critical Thinking Questions

1. Are there parallels between an inner-city youth joining a gang in Los Angeles and a disaffected youth who joins an international terrorist group? Do they have the same goals? The same psychological needs?

2. Would you be willing to give up some of your civil rights, such as personal privacy, if it meant that the government could mount a more effective campaign against terrorist groups? For example, should government agents be allowed to search the homes of suspected terrorists without a warrant?

InfoTrac College Edition Research

What can be done to prevent terrorism in the new millennium? Can technology hold the key? Find out by reading:

Richard K. Betts. Fixing intelligence. *Foreign Affairs* Jan–Feb 2002 v81 i1 p43

SOURCE: Michael Scott Doran, "Somebody Else's Civil War," *Foreign Affairs* 81 (Jan–Feb 2002): 22–25; Bruce Hoffman, "Change and Continuity in Terrorism," *Studies in Conflict and Terrorism* 24 (2001); Harvey Kushner, *Terrorism in America, A Structured Approach to Understanding the Terrorist Threat* (Springfield: Charles C. Thomas, 1998); Ian Lesser, Bruce Hoffman, John Arquilla, David Ronfeldt, and Michele Zanini, *Countering the New Terrorism* (Washington, D.C.: Rand, 1999); Jessica Stern, *The Ultimate Terrorists* (Cambridge, Mass.: Harvard University Press, 1999).

responses to terrorism. Law enforcement agencies have infiltrated terrorist groups and turned members over to police. Rewards are often offered for information leading to the arrest of terrorists. "Democratic" elections have been held to discredit terrorists' complaints that the state is oppressive. Counterterrorism laws have increased penalties and decreased political rights afforded known terrorists.

The United States has followed a fourfold policy in dealing with terrorists:

First, make no concessions to terrorists and strike no deals;

Second, bring terrorists to justice for their crimes;

Third, isolate and apply pressure on states that sponsor terrorism to force them to change their behavior; and

Fourth, bolster the counterterrorism capabilities of those countries that work with the United States and require assistance.[243]

Antiterrorist legislation provides jurisdiction over terrorist acts committed abroad against U.S. citizens and gives the United States the right to punish people for killing foreign officials and politically protected persons. The 1994 Violent Crime Control Act authorized the death penalty for international terrorists who kill U.S. citizens abroad.[244]

Post 9/11 efforts   The World Trade Center attack forever changed U.S. policy on terrorism. On September 20, 2001, in response to the attack, President Bush announced the establishment of a cabinet-level Office of Homeland Security and appointed Governor Tom Ridge of Pennsylvania as director. He was given the mission of developing and coordinating a comprehensive national strategy to secure the United States from terrorist threats or attacks. Rather than field its own force, the Office of Homeland Security works with executive departments and agencies, state and local governments, and private entities to detect, prepare for, prevent, and respond to terrorist threats or attacks within the United States. On October 29, 2001, the Foreign Terrorist Tracking Task Force was created to aid in closing the borders to any illegal alien who is a representative, member, or supporter of terrorist organizations; aliens who are suspected of engaging in terrorist activity; or aliens who provide material support to terrorist activ-

ity. In addition, the FBI announced that it will expedite its Joint Terrorism Task Force program, which began in New York City in 1980. These interagency programs draw members from several agencies, including the Bureau of Alcohol Tobacco and Firearms, the Immigration and Naturalization Service, and the State Police. Nationwide there are 36 Joint Terrorism Task Forces staffed by more than 1,200 investigators from federal and other law enforcement agencies.[245]

Also in the wake of the 9/11 attacks, the United States has moved to freeze the financial assets of groups they consider to engage in, or support, terrorist activities. For example, on December 4, 2001, under authority of Executive Order 13224, Blocking Terrorist Property, the assets of the Holy Land Foundation for Relief and Development, Beit Al-Mal Holdings, and Al-Aqsa Islamic Bank were frozen because they were suspected of funding Hamas, a Middle Eastern terror group. As of December 2001, the United States had blocked more than $27 million in assets of the Taliban and al-Qaeda, and other nations have blocked at least $33 million. To help monitor terrorist assets, the Treasury Department established an interagency Foreign Terrorist Asset Tracking Center. The United States also began working with foreign allies to ensure coordinated action; 139 nations have begun seizing terrorist assets.

Ian Lesser, a terrorism expert, has created a four-pronged plan that he believes should form the core of a future national counterterrorism strategy:

- Reducing the systemic causes of terrorism by working to ameliorate social, economic, and political tensions.

- Deterring terrorists and their sponsors by pressuring states that support or harbor them and by moving against individual terrorist leaders.

- Reducing the risk of "super terrorism" involving weapons of mass destruction through preemptive military action, specialized intelligence activities, and global control and surveillance of Weapons of Mass Destruction (WMD) related materials.

- Retaliating where deterrence fails.

In light of the events of 9/11, it seems likely that Lesser's model may become the norm.[246]

■ Summary

Violence has become an all too common aspect of modern life. Among the various explanations for violent crimes are the availability of firearms, human traits, a subculture of violence that stresses violent solutions to interpersonal problems, and family conflict.

There are many types of interpersonal violent crime. Rape, the carnal knowledge of a female forcibly and against her will, has been known throughout history, but the view of rape has evolved. At present, close to 100,000 rapes are reported to U.S. police each year; the actual number of rapes is probably much higher. Rape is an extremely difficult charge to prove in court. The victim's lack of consent must be proven; therefore, it almost seems that the victim is on trial. Consequently, changes are being made in rape law and procedure.

Murder is defined as killing a human being with malice aforethought. There are different degrees of murder, and punishments vary accordingly. One important characteristic of murder is that the victim and criminal often know each other. This has led some criminologists to believe that murder is partly victim-precipitated.

Assault, another serious interpersonal violent crime, often occurs in the home, including child abuse and spouse abuse. There also appears to be a trend toward violence between dating couples.

Robbery involves theft by force, usually in a public place. Types of offenders include professional, opportunist, addict, and alcoholic robbers. Robbery is considered a violent crime because it can and often does involve violence.

Terrorism is a significant form of violence. Many terrorist groups exist at both the national and international levels. Hundreds of terrorist acts are reported each year in the United States alone. There are a variety of terrorist goals including political change, nationalism, personal causes, criminality, and environmental protection. Terrorists may be motivated by criminal gain, psychosis, grievance against the state, or ideology. The World Trade Center bombing on September 11, 2001, turned world attention to terrorism. Renewed efforts to combat this threat have included the creation of a cabinet-level Office of Homeland Security.

■ Thinking Like a Criminologist

The state legislature has asked you to prepare a report on statutory rape because of the growing number of underage girls who have been impregnated by adult men. Studies reveal that many teenage pregnancies result from affairs that underage girls have with older men, with age gaps ranging from 7 to 10 years. For example, the typical relationship that is prosecuted in California involves a 13-year-old girl and a 22-year-old male partner. Some outraged parents adamantly support a law that provides state grants to counties to prosecute statutory rape. These grants would allow more vigorous enforcement of the law and could result in the conviction of more than 1,500 offenders annually.

However, some critics suggest that implementing statutory rape laws to punish males who have relationships with minor girls does not solve the problems of teenage pregnancies and out-of-wedlock births. Liberals dislike the idea of using criminal law to solve social problems because it does not provide for the girls and their young children and focuses only on punishing offenders. In contrast, conservatives fear that such laws give the state power to prosecute people for victimless crimes, thereby adding to the government's ability to control people's private lives. Not all cases involve much older men, and critics ask whether we should criminalize the behavior of 17-year-old boys and their 15-year-old girlfriends. As a criminologist with expertise on rape and its effects, what would you recommend regarding implementation of the law?

■ Key Terms

- instrumental violence (317)
- expressive violence (317)
- eros (322)
- thanatos (322)
- crusted over (322)
- psychopharmacological relationship (322)
- economic compulsive behavior (323)
- systemic link (323)
- subculture of violence (323)
- rape (324)
- gang rape (327)
- serial rape (327)
- acquaintance rape (327)
- date rape (327)
- statutory rape (327)
- marital rape (327)

- marital exemption (328)
- virility mystique (329)
- hypermasculine (329)
- aggravated rape (330)
- consent (330)
- shield laws (331)
- murder (331)
- first-degree murder (332)
- premeditation (332)
- deliberation (332)
- felony murder (332)
- second-degree murder (332)
- manslaughter (332)
- voluntary or nonnegligent manslaughter (332)
- involuntary or negligent manslaughter (332)

- feticide (332)
- infanticide (333)
- eldercide (333)
- serial murderer (335)
- mass murderer (335)
- battery (337)
- assault (337)
- road rage (338)
- child abuse (339)
- neglect (339)
- sexual abuse (339)
- robbery (341)
- acquaintance robbery (341)
- hate crimes (345)
- bias crimes (345)
- thrill-seeking hate crimes (345)
- reactive hate crimes (345)

- **mission hate crimes** *(345)*
- **workplace violence** *(347)*
- **sufferance** *(347)*
- **stalking** *(348)*

- **terrorism** *(349)*
- **convictional criminals** *(349)*
- **international terrorism** *(349)*
- **terrorist group** *(349)*

- **guerilla** *(350)*
- **death squads** *(353)*

■ Critical Thinking Questions

1. Should different types of rape receive different legal sanctions? For example, should someone who rapes a stranger be punished more severely than someone who is convicted of marital rape or date rape? If your answer is yes, do you also think that someone who kills a stranger should be punished more severely than someone who kills his wife or girlfriend?

2. Is there a "subculture of violence" in your home city or town? If so,

how would you describe its environment and values?

3. There have been significant changes in rape laws regarding issues such as corroboration and shield laws. What other measures would you take to protect the victims of rape when they are forced to testify in court?

4. Should hate crimes be punished more severely than crimes motivated by greed, anger, or revenge? Why should crimes be distin-

guished by the motivations of the perpetrator? Is hate a more heinous motivation than revenge?

5. In light of the 9/11 attack, should acts of terrorism be treated differently from other common-law violent crimes? For example, should terrorists be executed for their acts even if no one is killed during their attack?

■ Notes

1. Peter L. Bergen, *Holy War, Inc.: Inside The Secret World of Osama bin Laden* (New York, Free Press, 2001), pp. 41–50; Yonah Alexander and Michael S. Swetnam, *Usama bin Laden's al-Qaida: Profile of a Terrorist Network* (New York: Transnational Publishers, 2001); Michael Kranish and Anthony Shadid, "Bin Laden Zeal for Stature Used Psychology, Religion," *Boston Globe,* 19 November 2001, p. 3.

2. Kathleen Maguire and Ann Pastore, eds., *Sourcebook of Criminal Justice Statistics* [Online], p. 142. Available: http://www.albany.edu/sourcebook/ [Accessed September 22, 2001].

3. Robert Nash Parker and Catherine Colony, "Relationships, Homicides, and Weapons: A Detailed Analysis." Paper presented at the annual meeting of the American Society of Criminology, Montreal, November 1987.

4. Stryker McGuire, "The Dunblane Effect," *Newsweek,* 28 October 1996, p. 46.

5. Dorothy Otnow Lewis, Ernest Moy, Lori Jackson, Robert Aaronson, Nicholas Restifo, Susan Serra, and Alexander Simos, "Biopsychosocial Characteristics of Children Who Later Murder," *American Journal of Psychiatry* 142 (1985): 1161–67.

6. Dorothy Otnow Lewis, *Guilty by Reason of Insanity* (New York: Fawcett Columbine, 1998).

7. Richard Rogers, Randall Salekin, Kenneth Sewell, and Keith Cruise, "Prototypical Analysis of Antisocial Personality Disorder," *Criminal Justice and Behavior* 27 (2000): 234–55; Amy Holtzworth-Munroe and Gregory Stuart, "Typologies of Male Batterers: Three Subtypes and the Differences among Them," *Psychological Bulletin* 116 (1994): 476–97.

8. Katherine Van Wormer and Chuk Odiah, "The Psychology of Suicide-Murder and the Death Penalty," *Journal of Criminal Justice* 27 (1999): 361–70.

9. Albert Reiss and Jeffrey Roth, *Understanding and Preventing Violence* (Washington, D.C.: National Academy Press, 1993) pp. 112–13.

10. Pamela Lattimore, Christy Visher, and Richard Linster, "Predicting Rearrest for Violence among Serious Youthful Offenders," *Journal of Research in Crime and Delinquency* 32 (1995): 54–83.

11. Rolf Loeber and Dale Hay, "Key Issues in the Development of Aggression and Violence from Childhood to Early Adulthood," *Annual Review of Psychology* 48 (1997): 371–410.

12. Deborah Capaldi and Gerald Patterson, "Can Violent Offenders Be Distinguished from Frequent Offenders: Prediction from Childhood to Adolescence," *Journal of Research in Crime and Delinquency* 33 (1996): 206–31.

13. Adrian Raine, Patricia Brennan, and Sarnoff Mednick, "Interaction between Birth Complications and Early Maternal Rejection in Predisposing Individuals to Adult Violence: Specificity to Serious, Early-Onset Violence," *American Journal of Psychiatry* 154 (1997): 1265–71.

14. John Lemmon, "How Child Maltreatment Affects Dimensions of Juvenile Delinquency in a Cohort of Low-Income Urban Youths," *Justice Quarterly* 16 (1999): 357–76.

15. Murray Straus, "Discipline and Deviance: Physical Punishment of Children and Violence and Other Crime in Adulthood," *Social Problems* 38 (1991): 101–23.

16. Ronald Simons, Chyi-In Wu, Kuei-Hsiu Lin, Leslie Gordon, and Rand Conger, "A Cross-Cultural Examination of the Link between Corporal Punishment and Adolescent Antisocial Behavior," *Criminology* 38 (2000): 47–79.

17. Robert Scudder, William Blount, Kathleen Heide, and Ira Silverman, "Important Links between Child Abuse, Neglect, and Delinquency," *International Journal of Offender Therapy* 37 (1993): 315–23.

18. Dorothy Lewis et al., "Neuropsychiatric, Psychoeducational, and Family Characteristics of 14 Juveniles Condemned to Death in the United

States," *American Journal of Psychiatry* 145 (1988): 584–88.

19. Charles Patrick Ewing, *When Children Kill* (Lexington, Mass.: Lexington Books, 1990), p. 22.

20. Lewis, *Guilty by Reason of Insanity,* pp. 11–35.

21. Murray Straus, "Discipline and Deviance: Physical Punishment of Children and Violence and Other Crime in Adulthood," *Social Problems* 38 (1991): 133–54.

22. Lonnie Athens, *The Creation of Dangerous Violent Criminals* (Urbana, Ill.: University of Illinois Press, 1992), pp. 27–80.

23. Cathy Spatz Widom, "Child Abuse, Neglect, and Violent Criminal Behavior," *Criminology* 27 (1989): 251–71; Beverly Rivera and Cathy Spatz Widom, "Childhood Victimization and Violent Offending," *Violence and Victims* 5 (1990): 19–34.

24. Judith Rich Harris, "The Outcome of Parenting: What Do We Really Know?" *Journal of Personality* 68 (2000): 625–37.

25. Sigmund Freud, *Beyond the Pleasure Principle* (London: Inter-Psychoanalytic Press, 1922).

26. Konrad Lorenz, *On Aggression* (New York: Harcourt Brace Jovanovich, 1966).

27. Martin Daly and Margo Wilson, "Evolutionary Psychology of Male Violence," in *Male Violence,* ed. J. Archer (London: Routledge, 1994), pp. 253–88.

28. Ira Hutchison and J. David Hirschel, "The Effects of Children's Presence on Women Abuse," *Violence and Victims* 16 (2001): 3–17.

29. Felton Earls, *Linking Community Factors and Individual Development* (Washington, D.C.: National Institute of Justice, 1998).

30. Michael Greene, "Chronic Exposure to Violence and Poverty: Interventions That Work for Youth," *Crime and Delinquency* 39 (1993): 106–24.

31. Paul Goldstein, Henry Brownstein, and Patrick Ryan, "Drug-Related Homicide in New York: 1984–1988," *Crime and Delinquency* 38 (1992): 459–76.

32. Reiss and Roth, *Understanding and Preventing Violence,* pp. 193–94.

33. James Collins and Pamela Messerschmidt, "Epidemiology of Alcohol-Related Violence," *Alcohol Health and Research World* 17 (1993): 93–100.

34. Paul Goldstein, Patricia Bellucci, Barry Spunt, and Thomas Miller, "Volume of Cocaine Use and Violence: A Comparison between Men and Women," *Journal of Drug Issues* 21 (1991): 345–67.

35. Goldstein, Brownstein, and Ryan, "Drug-Related Homicide in New York: 1984–1988," p. 473.

36. Reiss and Roth, *Understanding and Preventing Violence,* p. 19.

37. Joseph Sheley and James Wright, *Gun Acquisition and Possession in Selected Juvenile Samples* (Washington, D.C.: National Institute of Justice, 1993).

38. Pamela Wilcox and Richard Clayton, "A Multilevel Analysis of School-Based Weapon Possession," *Justice Quarterly* 18 (2001): 509–42

39. Federal Bureau of Investigation, *Crime in the United States, 2000* (Washington, D.C.: U.S. Government Printing Office, 2001).

40. David Brent, Joshua Perper, Christopher Allman, Grace Moritz, Mary Wartella, and Janice Zelenak, "The Presence and Accessibility of Firearms in the Home and Adolescent Suicides," *Journal of the American Medical Association* 266 (1991): 2989–95.

41. Linda Saltzman, James Mercy, Patrick O'Carroll, Mark Rosenberg, and Philip Rhodes, "Weapon Involvement and Injury Outcomes in Family and Intimate Assaults," *Journal of the American Medical Association* 267 (1992): 3043–47.

42. Robert Baller, Luc Anselin, Steven Messner, Glenn Deane and Darnell Hawkins, "Structural Covariates of U.S. County Homicide Rates Incorporating Spatial Effects," *Criminology* 39 (2001): 561–90.

43. Marvin Wolfgang and Franco Ferracuti, *The Subculture of Violence* (London: Tavistock, 1967).

44. David Luckenbill and Daniel Doyle, "Structural Position and Violence: Developing a Cultural Explanation," *Criminology* 27 (1989): 419–36.

45. Robert Sampson and William Julius Wilson, "Toward a Theory of Race, Crime and Urban Inequality," in *Crime and Inequality,* eds. John Hagan and Ruth Peterson (Stanford, Calif.: Stanford University Press, 1995), p. 51.

46. Liqun Cao, Anthony Adams, and Vickie Jensen, "A Test of the Black Subculture of Violence Thesis," *Criminology* 35 (1997): 367–79.

47. Joshua Freilich, Nelson Pichardo Almanzar, and Craig Rivera, "How Social Movement Organizations Explicitly and Implicitly Promote Deviant Behavior: The Case of the Militia Movement," *Justice Quarterly* 16 (1999): 655–83.

48. Steven Messner, "Regional and Racial Effects on the Urban Homicide Rate: The Subculture of Violence Revisited," *American Journal of Sociology* 88 (1983): 997–1007; Steven Messner and Kenneth Tardiff, "Economic Inequality and Levels of Homicide: An Analysis of Urban Neighborhoods," *Criminology* 24 (1986): 297–317.

49. Beth Bjerregaard and Alan Lizotte, "Gun Ownership and Gang Membership," *Journal of Criminal Law and Criminology* 86 (1995): 37–58.

50. James Howell, "Youth Gang Homicides: A Literature Review," *Crime and Delinquency* 45 (1999): 208–41.

51. Scott Decker, "Gangs and Violence: The Expressive Character of Collective Involvement" (unpublished manuscript, University of Missouri–St. Louis: 1994), p. 11.

52. Ibid.

53. See, generally, Kirk Williams and Robert Flewelling, "The Social Production of Criminal Homicide: A Comparative Study of Disaggregated Rates in American Cities," *American Sociological Review* 53 (1988): 421–31.

54. Raymond Gastil, "Homicide and the Regional Culture of Violence," *American Sociological Review* 36 (1971): 12–27.

55. Keith Harries, *Serious Violence: Patterns of Homicide and Assault in America* (Springfield, Ill.: Charles C. Thomas, 1990).

56. Edem Avakame, "How Different Is Violence in the Home: An Examination of Some Correlates of Stranger and Intimate Homicide," *Criminology* 36 (1998): 601–32.

57. Howard Erlanger, "Is There a Subculture of Violence in the South?" *Journal of Criminal Law and Criminology* 66 (1976): 483–90.

58. Colin Loftin and Robert Hill, "Regional Subculture of Violence: An Examination of the Gastil-Hackney Thesis," *American Sociological Review* 39 (1974): 714–24.

59. Raymond Gastil, "Comments," *Criminology* 16 (1975): 60–64.

60. FBI, *Uniform Crime Report, 2000* (Washington, D.C.: Federal Bureau of Investigation, 2001) p. 9; see also Keith Harries, "Crime and Region: Is the South Still Different?" Paper presented at the annual meeting of the American Society of Criminology, Chicago, November 1996; Gregory Kowalski and Thomas Petee, "Sunbelt Effects on Homicide Rates," *Sociology and Social Research* 76 (1991): 73–79.

61. F. Frederick Hawley and Steven Messner, "The Southern Violence Construct: A Review of Arguments, Evidence, and the Normative Context," *Justice Quarterly* 6 (1989): 481–511.

62. Jerome Neapolitan, "A Comparative Analysis of Nations with Low and High Levels of Violent Crime," *Journal of Criminal Justice* 27 (1999): 259–74.

63. Ibid., p. 271.

64. William Green, *Rape* (Lexington, Mass.: Lexington Books, 1988), p. 5.

65. Susan Randall and Vicki McNickle Rose, "Forcible Rape," in *Major Forms of Crime*, ed. Robert Meyer (Beverly Hills, Calif.: Sage, 1984), p. 47.

66. Associated Press, "Judge Who Told Rape Suspect to Get a Girlfriend Orders Him into Custody," *Manchester Union Leader*, 19 February 1994, p. 2.

67. Susan Brownmiller, *Against Our Will: Men, Women and Rape* (New York: Simon & Schuster, 1975).

68. Green, *Rape*, p. 6.

69. Gregory Vistica, "Rape in the Ranks," *Newsweek*, 25 November 1996, pp. 29–31.

70. Yuri Kageyama, "Court Orders Japan to Pay Sex Slaves," *Boston Globe*, 28 April 1998, p. A2.

71. Marlise Simons, "Bosnian Serb Pleads Guilty to Rape Charge Before War Crimes Tribunal," *New York Times*, 10 March 1998, p. 8.

72. FBI, *Uniform Crime Report, 2000*, pp. 25–28.

73. Callie Marie Rennison, *Criminal Victimization 2000: Changes 1999–2000 with Trends 1993–2000* (Washington, D.C.: Bureau of Justice Statistics, 2001).

74. Angela Browne, "Violence against Women: Relevance for Medical Practitioners," *Journal of the American Medical Association* 267 (1992): 3184–89.

75. Mark Warr, "Rape, Burglary and Opportunity," *Journal of Quantitative Criminology* 4 (1988): 275–88.

76. A. Nicholas Groth and Jean Birnbaum, *Men Who Rape* (New York: Plenum Press, 1979).

77. For another typology, see Raymond Knight, "Validation of a Typology of Rapists," in *Sex Offender Research and Treatment: State-of-the-Art in North America and Europe*, eds. W. L. Marshall and J. Frenken (Beverly Hills, Calif.: Sage, 1997), pp. 58–75.

78. Sarah Ullman, "A Comparison of Gang and Individual Rape Incidents," *Violence and Victimization* 14 (1999): 123–34.

79. Janet Warren, Roland Reboussin, Robert Hazlewood, Natalie Gibbs, Susan Trumbetta, and Andrea Cummings, "Crime Scene Analysis and the Escalation of Violence in Serial Rape," *Forensic Science International* (1998): 56–62.

80. James LeBeau, "Patterns of Stranger and Serial Rape Offending Factors Distinguishing Apprehended and At-Large Offenders," *Journal of Criminal Law and Delinquency* 78 (1987): 309–26.

81. Michael Vaughn, "Police Sexual Violence: Civil Liability Under State Tort Law," *Crime and Delinquency* 45 (1999): 334–57.

82. Julie Allison and Lawrence Wrightsman, *Rape: The Misunderstood Crime* (Newbury Park, Calif.: Sage, 1993), p. 51.

83. Cassia Spohn, Dawn Beichner, and Erika Davis-Frenzel, "Prosecutorial Justifications for Sexual Assault Case Rejection: Guarding the 'Gateway to Justice'," *Social Problems* 48 (2001): 206–35.

84. R. Lance Shotland, "A Model of the Causes of Date Rape in Developing and Close Relationships," in *Close Relationships*, ed. C. Hendrick (Newbury Park, Calif.: Sage, 1989), pp. 247–70.

85. Walter DeKeseredy, Martin Schwartz, and Karen Tait, "Sexual Assault and Stranger Aggression on a Canadian Campus," *Sex Roles* 28 (1993): 263–77.

86. Ibid.

87. Thomas Meyer, "Date Rape: A Serious Campus Problem That Few Talk About," *Chronicle of Higher Education* 29 (5 December 1984): 15.

88. Allison and Wrightsman, *Rape: The Misunderstood Crime*, p. 64.

89. Kimberly Tyler, Danny Hoyt, and Les Whitbeck, "Coercive Sexual Strategies," *Violence and Victims* 13 (1998): 47–63.

90. Martin Schwartz, "Humanist Sociology and Date Rape on the College Campus," *Humanity and Society* 15 (1991): 304–16.

91. Allison and Wrightsman, *Rape: The Misunderstood Crime*, pp. 85–87.

92. Cited in Diana Russell, "Wife Rape," in *Acquaintance Rape: The Hidden Crime*, eds. A. Parrot and L. Bechhofer (New York: John Wiley, 1991), pp. 129–39, at 129.

93. David Finkelhor and K. Yllo, *License to Rape: Sexual Abuse of Wives* (New York: Holt, Rinehart and Winston, 1985).

94. Allison and Wrightsman. *Rape: The Misunderstood Crime*, p. 89.

95. Associated Press, "British Court Rejects Precedent, Finds a Man Guilty of Raping Wife," *Boston Globe*, 15 March 1991, p. 68.

96. Jill Elaine Hasday, "Contest and Consent: A Legal History of Marital Rape," *California Law Review* 88(2000): 1373–433.

97. Sharon Elstein and Roy Davis, *Sexual Relationships between Adult Males and Young Teen Girls: Exploring the Legal and Social Responses* (Chicago, Ill.: American Bar Association, 1997).

98. Donald Symons, *The Evolution of Human Sexuality* (Oxford: Oxford University Press, 1979).

99. Lee Ellis and Anthony Walsh, "Gene-Based Evolutionary Theories in Criminology," *Criminology* 35 (1997): 229–76.

100. Lee Ellis, "A Synthesized (Biosocial) Theory of Rape," *Journal of Consulting and Clinical Psychology* 39 (1991): 631–42.

101. Diana Russell, *The Politics of Rape* (New York: Stein and Day, 1975).

102. Diana Russell and Rebecca M. Bolen, *The Epidemic of Rape and Child Sexual Abuse in the United States* (Thousand Oaks, Calif.: Sage, 2000).

103. Rachel Bridges Whaley, "The Paradoxical Relationship between Gender Inequality and Rape: Toward a Refined Theory," *Gender & Society* 15 (2001): 531–55.

104. Kala Downs and Steven Gold, "The Role of Blame, Distress, and Anger in the Hypermasculine Man," *Violence and Victims* 12 (1997): 19–36.

105. Paul Gebhard, John Gagnon, Wardell Pomeroy, and Cornelia Christenson, *Sex Offenders: An Analysis of Types* (New York: Harper & Row, 1965), pp. 198–205; Richard Rada, ed., *Clinical Aspects of the Rapist* (New York: Grune & Stratton, 1978), pp. 122–30.

106. Stephen Porter, David Fairweather, Jeff Drugge, Huues Herve, Angela Birt, and Douglas Boer, "Profiles of Psychopathy in Incarcerated Sexual Offenders," *Criminal Justice and Behavior* 27 (2000): 216–33.

107. Martin Schwartz, Walter DeKeseredy, David Tait, and Shahid Alvi, "Male Peer Support and a Feminist Routine Activities Theory: Understanding Sexual Assault on the College Campus," *Justice Quarterly* 18 (2001): 623–50.

108. Groth and Birnbaum, *Men Who Rape*, p. 101.

109. See, generally, Edward Donnerstein, Daniel Linz, and Steven Penrod, *The Question of Pornography* (New York: Free Press, 1987); Diana Russell, *Sexual Exploitation* (Beverly Hills, Calif.: Sage, 1985), pp. 115–16.

110. Neil Malamuth and John Briere, "Sexual Violence in the Media: Indirect Ef-

fects on Aggression against Women," *Journal of Social Issues* 42 (1986): 75–92.

111. Associated Press, "Trial on TV May Have Influenced Boy Facing Sexual-Assault Count," *Omaha World Herald*, 18 April 1984, p. 50.

112. Richard Felson and Marvin Krohn, "Motives for Rape," *Journal of Research in Crime and Delinquency* 27 (1990): 222–42.

113. Julie Horney and Cassia Spohn, "The Influence of Blame and Believability Factors on the Processing of Simple versus Aggravated Rape Cases," *Criminology* 34 (1996): 135–63.

114. "Woman Urges Dotson's Release," *Omaha World Herald*, 25 April 1985, p. 3.

115. Spohn, Beichner, and Davis-Frenzel, "Prosecutorial Justificiations for Sexual Assault Case Rejection."

116. Gerald Robin, "Forcible Rape: Institutionalized Sexism in the Criminal Justice System," *Crime and Delinquency* 23 (1977): 136–53.

117. Associated Press, "Jury Stirs Furor by Citing Dress in Rape Acquittal," *Boston Globe*, 6 October 1989, p. 12.

118. Rodney Kingsworth, Randall MacIntosh, and Jennifer Wentworth, "Sexual Assault: The Role of Prior Relationship and Victim Characteristics in Case Processing," *Justice Quarterly* 16 (1999): 276–302.

119. Susan Estrich, *Real Rape* (Cambridge: Harvard University Press, 1987), pp. 58–59.

120. See, for example, Mich. Comp. Laws Ann. 750.5200-(1); Florida Statutes Annotated, Sec. 794.011; see, generally, Gary LaFree, "Official Reactions to Rape," *American Sociological Review* 45 (1980): 842–54.

121. Martin Schwartz and Todd Clear, "Toward a New Law on Rape," *Crime and Delinquency* 26 (1980): 129–51.

122. *Michigan v. Lucas* 90-149 (1991); Comment, "The Rape Shield Paradox: Complainant Protection Amidst Oscillating Trends of State Judicial Interpretation," *Journal of Criminal Law and Criminology* 78 (1987): 644–98.

123. Andrew Karmen, *Crime Victims* (Pacific Grove, Calif.: Brooks/Cole, 1990), p. 252.

124. "Court Upholds Civil Rights Portion of Violence Against Women Act," *Criminal Justice Newsletter* 28 (Dec. 1, 1997), p. 3.

125. Colleen Fitzpatrick and Philip Reichel, "Conceptions of Rape and Perceptions of Prosecution." Paper presented at the American Society of Criminology meeting, San Diego, Calif., 1997.

126. Cassia Spohn and David Holleran, "Prosecuting Sexual Assault: A Comparison of Charging Decisions in Sexual Assault Cases Involving Strangers, Acquaintances, and Intimate Partners," *Justice Quarterly* 18 (2001): 651–88.

127. Donald Lunde, *Murder and Madness* (San Francisco: San Francisco Book, 1977), p. 3.

128. Amy Dockser Marcus, "Mists of Memory Cloud Some Legal Proceedings," *Wall Street Journal*, 3 December 1990, p. B1.

129. Lisa Baertlein, "HIV Ruled Deadly Weapon in Rape Case," *Boston Globe*, 2 March 1994, p. 3.

130. The legal principles here come from Wayne LaFave and Austin Scott, *Criminal Law* (St. Paul: West Publishing, 1986; updated, 1993). The definitions and discussion of legal principles used in this chapter lean heavily on this work.

131. LaFave and Scott, *Criminal Law*.

132. Reuters, "California Man Gets 3 Years for Pit Bull's Attack on Toddler," *Boston Globe*, 17 February 1990, p. 3.

133. Pauline Arrillaga, "Jurors Give Drunk Driver 16 Years in Fetus's Death," *Manchester Union Leader*, 22 October 1996, p. B20.

134. Center for Reproductive Law and Policy, *Punishing Women for Their Behavior During Pregnancy* (New York: author, 1996), pp. 1–2.

135. *Whitner v. State of South Carolina*, Supreme Court of South Carolina, Opinion Number 24468, July 15, 1996.

136. Janet Kreps, *Feticide and Wrongful Death Laws* (New York: Center for Reproductive Law and Policy, 1996), pp. 1–2.

137. Arrillaga, "Jurors Give Drunk Driver 16 Years in Fetus's Death."

138. James Alan Fox and Marianne Zawitz, *Homicide Trends in the United States* (Washington, D.C.: Bureau of Justice Statistics, 2001).

139. Ibid.

140. Ibid.

141. See, generally, Marc Reidel and Margaret Zahn, *The Nature and Pattern of American Homicide* (Washington, D.C.: U.S. Government Printing Office, 1985).

142. James L. Williams, "A Discriminant Analysis of Urban Homicide Patterns." Paper presented at the annual meeting of the American Society of Criminology, Baltimore, November 1990.

143. Angela Browne and Kirk Williams, "Gender, Intimacy, and Lethal Violence: Trends from 1976 through 1987," *Gender and Society* 7 (1993): 78–98.

144. Linda Saltzman and James Mercy, "Assaults between Intimates: The Range of Relationships Involved," in *Homicide: The Victim/Offender Connection*, ed. Anna Victoria Wilson (Cincinnati: Anderson Publishing, 1993), pp. 65–74.

145. Angela Browne and Kirk Williams, "Exploring the Effect of Resource Availability and the Likelihood of Female-Perpetrated Homicides," *Law and Society Review* 23 (1989): 75–94.

146. Richard Felson, "Anger, Aggression, and Violence in Love Triangles," *Violence and Victimization* 12 (1997): 345–63.

147. Ibid., p. 361.

148. Scott Decker, "Deviant Homicide: A New Look at the Role of Motives and Victim–Offender Relationships," *Journal of Research in Crime and Delinquency* 33 (1996): 427–49.

149. Margaret Zahn and Philip Sagi, "Stranger Homicides in Nine American Cities," *Journal of Criminal Law and Criminology* 78 (1987): 377–97.

150. David Luckenbill, "Criminal Homicide as a Situational Transaction," *Social Problems* 25 (1977): 176–86.

151. Mark Anderson, Joanne Kaufman, Thomas Simon, Lisa Barrios, Len Paulozzi, George Ryan, Rodney Hammond, William Modzeleski, Thomas Feucht, Lloyd Potter, and the School-Associated Violent Deaths Study Group, "School-Associated Violent Deaths in the United States, 1994–1999," *Journal of the American Medical Association* 286 (2001): 2695–702.

152. Pamela Wilcox and Richard Clayton, "A Multilevel Analysis of School-Based Weapon Possession," *Justice Quarterly* 18 (2001): 509–42.

153. Larry Rohter, "In the Chaos of Colombia, the Makings of a Mass Killer," *New York Times*, 1 November 1999, p. 3.

154. "Police Suspect 'Something Snapped' to Ignite Wilder's Crime Spree," *Omaha World Herald*, 15 April 1984, p. 21A.

155. Mark Starr, "The Random Killers," *Newsweek*, 26 November 1984, pp. 100–106.

156. Thomas Palmer, "Ex-Hospital Aide Admits Killing 24 in Cincinnati," *Boston Globe*, 19 August 1987, p. 3.

157. Reuters, "Pressure Growing in Iran to Solve Prostitute Killings," *New York Times*, 25 July 2001, p. B2.

158. Ronald Holmes and Stephen Homes, *Murder in America* (Thousand Oaks, Calif.: Sage, 1994), p. 6.

159. Ibid., p. 106.

160. Ibid., pp. 13–14.

161. Ibid., p. 17.

162. Belea Keeney and Kathleen Heide, "Gender Differences in Serial Murderers: A Preliminary Analysis," *Journal of Interpersonal Violence* 9 (1994): 37–56.

163. Jennifer Browdy, "VI-CAP System to Be Operational This Summer," *Law Enforcement News*, 21 May 1984, p. 1.

164. Federal Bureau of Investigation, *Crime in the United States, 2000* (Washington, D.C.: U.S. Government Printing Office, 2001), p. 34.

165. Keith Harries, "Homicide and Assault: A Comparative Analysis of Attributes in Dallas Neighborhoods, 1981–1985," *Professional Geographer* 41 (1989): 29–38.

166. Laurence Zuckerman, "The Air-Rage Rage: Taking a Cold Look at a Hot Topic," *New York Times*, 4 October 1998, p. A3.

167. Kevin Flynn, "Record Payouts in Settlements of Lawsuits against the New York City Police Are Set for Year," *New York Times*, 1 October 1999, p. 12.

168. Michael Rand, *Violence-Related Injuries Treated in Hospital Emergency Departments* (Washington, D.C.: Bureau of Justice Statistics, 1997).

169. See, generally, Joel Milner, ed., "Special Issue: Physical Child Abuse," *Criminal Justice and Behavior* 18 (1991).

170. See, generally, Ruth S. Kempe and C. Henry Kempe, *Child Abuse* (Cambridge: Harvard University Press, 1978).

171. U.S. Department of Health and Human Services, "Administration on Children, Youth and Families," *Child Maltreatment 1999* (Washington, D.C.: U.S. Government Printing Office, 2001).

172. Diana Russell, "The Incidence and Prevalence of Intrafamilial and Extrafamilial Sexual Abuse of Female Children," *Child Abuse and Neglect* 7 (1983): 133–46; see also David Finkelhor, *Sexually Victimized Children* (New York: Free Press, 1979), p. 88.

173. Jeanne Hernandez, "Eating Disorders and Sexual Abuse in Adolescents." Paper presented at the annual meeting of the American Psychosomatic Society, Charleston, S.C., March 1993; Glenn Wolfner and Richard Gelles, "A Profile of Violence toward Children: A National Study," *Child Abuse and Neglect* 17 (1993): 197–212.

174. Lisa Jones and David Finkelhor, *The Decline in Child Sexual Abuse Cases* (Washington, D.C.: Office of Juvenile Justice and Delinquency Prevention, 2001).

175. Lisa Jones, David Finkelhor, and Kathy Kopie, "Why Is Sexual Abuse Declining? A Survey of State Child Protection Administrators," *Child Abuse and Neglect* 25 (2001): 1139–41.

176. Wolfner and Gelles, "A Profile of Violence toward Children."

177. Martin Daly and Margo Wilson, "Violence against Step Children," *Current Directions in Psychological Science* 5 (1996): 77–81.

178. Ruth Inglis, *Sins of the Fathers: A Study of the Physical and Emotional Abuse of Children* (New York: St. Martins Press, 1978), p. 53.

179. R. Emerson Dobash and Russell Dobash, *Violence against Wives* (New York: Free Press, 1979).

180. Julia O'Faolain and Laura Martines, eds., *Not in God's Image: Women in History* (Glasgow: Fontana/Collins, 1974).

181. Laurence Stone, "The Rise of the Nuclear Family in Modern England: The Patriarchal Stage," in *The Family in History*, ed. Charles Rosenberg (Philadelphia: University of Pennsylvania Press, 1975), p. 53.

182. Dobash and Dobash, *Violence against Wives*, p. 46.

183. John Braithwaite, "Inequality and Republican Criminology." Paper presented at the annual meeting of the American Society of Criminology, San Francisco, November 1991, p. 20.

184. Richard Gelles and Murray Straus, "Violence in the American Family," *Journal of Social Issues* 35 (1979): 15–39.

185. Miguel Schwartz, Susan O'Leary, and Kimberly Kendziora, "Dating Aggression among High School Students," *Violence and Victimization* 12 (1997): 295–307; James Makepeace, "Social Factor and Victim–Offender Differences in Courtship Violence," *Family Relations* 33 (1987): 87–91.

186. Jay Silverman, Anita Raj, Lorelei Mucci, and Jeanne Hathaway, "Dating Violence against Adolescent Girls and Associated Substance Abuse, Unhealthy Weight Control, Sexual Risk Behavior, Pregnancy and Suicidality," *Journal of the American Medical Association* 286 (2001): 572–79.

187. Ronald Cohen, Alan Rosenbaum, Robert Kane, William Warneken, and Sheldon Benjamin, "Neuropsychological Correlates of Domestic Violence," *Violence and Victims* 15 (2000): 397–410.

188. Neil Jacobson and John Mordechai Gottman, *When Men Batter Women: New Insights into Ending Abusive Relationships* (New York: Simon and Schuster, 1998).

189. Margo Wilson and Martin Daly, "Male Sexual Proprietariness and Violence Against Wives," *Current Directions in Psychological Science* 5 (1996): 2–7.

190. FBI, *Crime in the United States, 2000*, p. 29.

191. Callie Marie Rennison, *Criminal Victimization 2000* (Washington, D.C.: Bureau of Justice Statistics, 2001) p. 3.

192. James Calder and John Bauer, "Convenience Store Robberies: Security Measures and Store Robbery Incidents," *Journal of Criminal Justice* 20 (1992): 553–66.

193. Richard Felson, Eric Baumer, and Steven Messner, "Acquaintance Robbery," *Journal of Research in Crime and Delinquency* 37 (2000): 284–305.

194. Ibid., p. 287.

195. Ibid.

196. Peter Van Koppen and Robert Jansen, "The Time to Rob: Variations in Time of Number of Commercial Robberies," *Journal of Research in Crime and Delinquency* 36 (1999): 7–29.

197. Jody Miller, "Up It Up: Gender and the Accomplishment of Street Robbery," *Criminology* 36 (1998): 37–67.

198. Ibid., pp. 54–55.

199. Richard Wright and Scott Decker, *Armed Robbers in Action, Stickups and Street Culture* (Boston, Mass.: Northeastern University Press, 1997).

200. James Brooke, "Gay Student Who Was Kidnapped and Beaten Dies," *New York Times*, 13 October 1998, A1.

201. Michael Janofsky, "Wyoming Man Gets Life Term in Gay's Death," *New York Times*, 5 November 1999, p. 1.

202. James Garofalo, "Bias and Non-Bias Crimes in New York City: Preliminary Findings." Paper presented at the annual meeting of the American Society of Criminology, Baltimore, November 1990.

203. Ronald Powers, "Bensonhurst Man Guilty," *Boston Globe*, 18 May 1990, p. 3.

204. "Boy Gets 18 Years in Fatal Park Beating of Transient," *Los Angeles Times*, 24 December 1987, p. 9B.

205. Ewing, *When Children Kill*, pp. 65–66.

206. Mike McPhee, "In Denver, Attacks Stir Fears of Racism," *Boston Globe*, 10 December 1990, p. 3.

207. Jack McDevitt, "The Study of the Character of Civil Rights Crimes in Massachusetts (1983–1987)." Paper

presented at the annual meeting of the American Society of Criminology, Reno, Nevada, November 1989.

208. Ibid., p. 8.

209. Jack Levin and Jack McDevitt, *Hate Crimes: The Rising Tide of Bigotry and Bloodshed* (New York: Plenum, 1993).

210. Jack Levin and Jack McDevitt, *Hate Crimes: A Study of Offenders' Motivations* (Boston, Mass.: Northeastern University, 1993).

211. Kevin J. Strom, *Hate Crimes Reported in NIBRS, 1997–99* (Washington, D.C.: Bureau of Justice Statistics, 2001).

212. Garofalo, "Bias and Non-Bias Crimes in New York City," p. 3.

213. Frederick M. Lawrence, *Punishing Hate: Bias Crimes Under American Law* (Cambridge, Mass., Harvard University Press, 1999).

214. Ibid., p. 3.

215. Ibid., p. 9.

216. Ibid., p. 11.

217. Ibid., pp. 39–42.

218. Carl Weiser, "This Is What You Get for Firing Me," *USA Today*, 28 January 1993, p. 3A.

219. James Alan Fox and Jack Levin, "Firing Back: The Growing Threat of Workplace Homicide," *Annals* 536 (1994): 16–30.

220. John King, "Workplace Violence: A Conceptual Framework." Paper presented at the annual meeting of the American Society of Criminology, Phoenix, Arizona, November 1993.

221. Associated Press, "Gunman Wounds 3 Doctors in L.A. Hospital," *Cleveland Plain Dealer*, 9 February 1993, p. 1B.

222. Fox and Levin, "Firing Back," p. 5.

223. Greg Warchol, *Workplace Violence, 1992–96* (Washington, D.C.: Bureau of Justice Statistics, 1998).

224. The following sections rely heavily on Patricia Tjaden, *The Crime of Stalking: How Big Is the Problem?* (Washington, D.C.: National Institute of Justice, 1997); see also, Robert M. Emerson, Kerry O. Ferris, and Carol Brooks Gardner, "On Being Stalked," *Social Problems* 45 (1998): 289–98.

225. Mary Brewster, "Stalking by Former Intimates: Verbal Threats and Other Predictors of Physical Violence," *Violence and Victims* 15 (2000): 41–51.

226. Stephen Schafer, *The Political Criminal* (New York: Free Press, 1974), p. 1.

227. Ibid., p. 150.

228. Title 22 of the United States Code section 2656f(d) (1999).

229. Paul Wilkinson, *Terrorism and the Liberal State* (New York: John Wiley, 1977), p. 49.

230. Jack Gibbs, "Conceptualization of Terrorism," *American Sociological Review* 54 (1989): 329–40, at 330.

231. Robert Friedlander, *Terrorism* (Dobbs Ferry, N.Y.: Oceana Publishers, 1979), p. 14.

232. Daniel Georges-Abeyie, "Political Crime and Terrorism," in *Crime and Deviance: A Comparative Perspective*, ed. Graeme Newman (Beverly Hills, Calif.: Sage, 1980), pp. 313–33.

233. Georges-Abeyie, "Political Crime and Terrorism," p. 319.

234. This section relies heavily on Friedlander, *Terrorism*, pp. 8–20.

235. "Brutal Elves in the Woods," *The Economist* 359 (April 14, 2001): 28–30.

236. Jeffrey Kluger, "The Nuke Pipeline: The Trade in Nuclear Contraband Is Approaching Critical Mass. Can We Turn Off the Spigot?" *Time*, 17 December 2001, p. 40.

237. Chris Dishman, "Terrorism, Crime, and Transformation," *Studies in Conflict & Terrorism* 24 (2001): 43–56.

238. Mark Jurgensmeyer, *Terror in the Mind of God* (Berkeley and Los Angeles: University of California Press, 2000).

239. Jerrold M. Post, "Terrorist Psycho-Logic: Terrorist Behavior as a Product of Psychological Forces," in *Origins of Terrorism: Psychologies, Ideologies Theologies, States of Mind*, ed. Walter Reich (Cambridge: Cambridge University Press, 1990), p. 12.

240. Haruki Murakami, *Underground* (New York: Vintage Books, 2001).

241. Reuel Marc Gerecht, "The Counterterrorist Myth," *Atlantic Monthly* 288 (Jul/Aug 2001): 288–93.

242. Stephen Flynn, "America the Vulnerable," *Foreign Affairs* 81 (Jan–Feb 2002): 60.

243. Sean Hill, "Internal Terrorism and Extradition," *Crime and Justice International* (April 2001): 5–25.

244. 18 U.S.C.A 2332 (a)(1)(West Supp., 1997).

245. FBI, *New York: The Beginning of Joint Terrorism Task Forces* [Online]. Available: http://www.fbi.gov/page2/newyork.htm [Accessed December 2001]

246. Ian O. Lesser, "Countering the New Terrorism: Implications for Strategy," in *Countering the New Terrorism*, eds. Ian Lesser, Bruce Hoffman, John Arquilla, David Ronfeldt, and Michele Zanini (Washington, D.C.: Rand, 1999).

© L. Clarke/CORBIS

CHAPTER 12 Property Crimes

◼ Introduction

The *Thomas Crown Affair* is a film so appealing that it has already been made twice, once in 1968, with Steve McQueen in the title role, and again in 1999, with Pierce Brosnan reprising the story of the self-made billionaire who can buy anything he wants except fulfillment. Crown is so bored that he hatches an elaborate theft scam just for the thrill of it. Why he needs this rush is a mystery. In both films he is incredibly handsome and fit, irresistible to almost all women including Catherine Banning, the otherwise brilliant female investigator hired to bring him to justice (Faye Dunaway in the original, Renee Russo in the remake). Despite her independence and good judgment, Banning just can't help succumbing to his manly charms. Crown already has all the toys, a gigantic house in Manhattan (McQueen's *Crown* lived in Boston) full of art treasures, a Bentley to drive from his house to his penthouse office suite, and a private plane that takes him on excursions to his mountaintop compound on a Caribbean island.

To read more about the *Thomas Crown Affair,* go to its official Web site at:
**http://www.mgm.com/thethomascrownaffair/
index_adv_frame.html**
For an up-to-date list of Web links, go to
http://info.wadsworth.com/siegel ◼

In both films, the audience admires Thomas Crown and secretly hopes he can outwit his pursuers. When we see Crown sitting in front of the stolen treasure feeling self-satisfied, few in the audience care that he has taken a priceless painting from a museum and appropriated it for his private use, even though he already owns and hoards plenty of rare art. Nor do most of us dwell on the fact that Crown's actions have deprived the public of viewing a beloved work of art so that he may enjoy it for his own private amusement.

Though average citizens may be puzzled and enraged by violent crimes, believing them to be both senseless and cruel, they often view economic crimes with a great deal more ambivalence. Society generally disapproves of crimes involving theft and corruption, but the public seems quite tolerant of the "gentleman bandit," even to the point of admiring such figures. They pop up as characters in popular myths and legends—the famed English outlaw Robin Hood, Western bank robber Jesse James, 1930s outlaws Bonnie Parker and Clyde Barrow (the subject of the 1967 award-winning film *Bonnie and Clyde* starring Warren Beatty and Faye Dunaway). In addition to Thomas Crown, there are the semiheroic subjects of books and films such as *48 Hours* (1982), in which Eddie Murphy plays a thief who helps a police officer (Nick Nolte) catch even more dangerous criminals; *Heat* (1995),

in which Robert DeNiro plays a master thief and Al Pacino the detective who tracks him down; and *Heist* (2001), in which Gene Hackman plays a clever thief who steals gold bullion by the ton.

How can such ambivalence toward criminality be explained? For one thing, if self-report surveys are accurate, national tolerance toward economic criminals may be prompted by the fact that almost every U.S. citizen has at some time been involved in economic crime. Even those among us who would never consider ourselves lawbreakers may have at one time engaged in petty theft, cheated on our income tax, stolen a textbook from a college bookstore, or pilfered from our place of employment. Consequently, it may be difficult for society to condemn economic criminals without feeling hypocritical.

People may also be somewhat more tolerant of economic crimes because they never seem to seriously hurt anyone—banks are insured, large businesses pass along losses to consumers, stolen cars can be easily replaced and, in most cases, are insured. Thomas Crown uses his considerable wit to steal a painting without causing any serious harm. The true pain of economic crime often goes unappreciated. Convicted offenders, especially businesspeople who commit white-collar crimes involving millions of dollars, often are punished rather lightly.

This chapter is the first of two that review the nature and extent of economic crime in the United States. It is divided into two principal sections. The first deals with the concept of professional crime and focuses on different types of professional criminals, including the **fence,** a buyer and seller of stolen merchandise. The chapter then turns to a discussion of common theft-related offenses, which criminologists often refer to as **street crimes.** These crimes include the major forms of common theft: larceny, embezzlement, and theft by false pretenses. Included within these general offense categories are such common crimes as auto theft, shoplifting, and credit card fraud. Next, the chapter discusses a more serious form of theft, **burglary,** which involves forcible entry into a person's home or place of work for the purpose of theft. Finally, the crime of **arson** is discussed briefly. In the following chapter, attention will be given to white-collar crimes and economic crimes that involve organizations devoted to criminal enterprise.

◼ A Brief History of Theft

As a group, **economic crimes** can be defined as acts in violation of the criminal law designed to bring financial reward to an offender. In U.S. society, the range and scope of criminal activity motivated by financial gain is tremendous: self-report studies show that property crime among the young in every social class is widespread. National surveys of criminal behavior indicate that millions of personal

■ Property crimes are not new to this century. This painting illustrates fourteenth-century thieves plundering a home in Paris.

and household thefts occur annually, including auto thefts, shoplifting incidents, embezzlements, burglaries, and larcenies. National surveys indicate that between 10 and 15 percent of the U.S. population are victims of theft offenses each year.

Theft, however, is not a phenomenon unique to modern times; the theft of personal property has been known throughout recorded history. The Crusades of the eleventh century inspired peasants and downtrodden noblemen to leave the shelter of their estates to prey on passing pilgrims.[1] Crusaders felt it within their rights to appropriate the possessions of any infidels—Greeks, Jews, or Muslims—they happened to encounter during their travels.

The Crusades actually lasted for centuries. Read about them and why they ended in this article on InfoTrac College Edition: Nigel Saul. The vanishing vision: late medieval crusading. *History Today* June 1997 v47 n6 p23(6) ■

By the thirteenth century, returning pilgrims, not content to live as serfs on feudal estates, gathered in the forests of England and the Continent to poach on game that was the rightful property of their lord or king and, when possible, to steal from passing strangers. By the fourteenth century, many such highwaymen and poachers were full-time livestock thieves, stealing great numbers of cattle and sheep.[2] The fifteenth and sixteenth centuries brought hostilities between England and France in what has come to be known as the Hundred Years' War. Foreign mercenary troops fighting for both sides roamed the countryside; loot and pillage were viewed as a rightful part of their pay. As cities developed and a permanent class of propertyless

urban poor was established,[3] theft became more professional. By the eighteenth century, three separate groups of property criminals were active: skilled thieves, smugglers, and poachers.

- **Skilled thieves** typically worked in the larger cities, such as London and Paris. This group included pickpockets, forgers, and counterfeiters, who operated freely. They congregated in **flash houses**— public meeting places, often taverns, that served as headquarters for gangs. Here, deals were made, crimes were plotted, and the sale of stolen goods was negotiated.[4]

- **Smugglers** were the second group of thieves. They moved freely in sparsely populated areas and transported goods, such as spirits, gems, gold, and spices, without bothering to pay tax or duty.

- **Poachers,** the third type of thief, typically lived in the country and supplemented their diet and income with game that belonged to a landlord.

Is poaching still a crime? To find out, use "poaching" as a subject guide on InfoTrac College Edition. ■

By the eighteenth century, professional thieves in the larger cities had banded together into gangs to protect themselves, increase the scope of their activities, and help dispose of stolen goods. Jack Wild, perhaps London's most famous thief, perfected the process of buying and selling stolen goods and gave himself the title of "Thief-Taker General of Great Britain and Ireland." Before he was hanged, Wild controlled numerous gangs and dealt harshly with any thief who violated his strict code of conduct.[5]

During this period, individual theft-related crimes began to be defined by the common law. The most important of these categories are still used today.

■ Modern Thieves

Of the millions of property and theft-related crimes that occur each year, most are committed by **occasional criminals** who do not define themselves by a criminal role or view themselves as committed career criminals; other theft-offenders are in fact skilled **professional criminals.** The following sections review these two orientations toward property crime.

Occasional Criminals

Though criminologists are not certain, they suspect that the great majority of economic crimes are the work of amateur criminals whose decision to steal is spontaneous and whose acts are unskilled, impulsive, and haphazard. Millions of theft-related crimes occur each year, and most are not reported to police agencies. Many of these theft offenses are committed by school-age youths who are unlikely to enter into a criminal career and whose behavior has been described as drifting between conventional and criminal behavior. Added to the pool of amateur thieves are the millions of adults whose behavior may occasionally violate the criminal law—shoplifters, pilferers, tax cheats—but whose main source of income comes from conventional means and whose self-identity is noncriminal. Added together, their behaviors form the bulk of theft crimes.

Occasional property crime occurs when there is an opportunity or **situational inducement** to commit crime.[6] Opportunities are available to members of all classes, but members of the upper class have the opportunity to engage in the more lucrative business-related crimes of price-fixing, bribery, embezzlement, and so on, which are closed to the lower classes. Hence, lower-class individuals are overrepresented in street crime.

Situational inducements are short-term influences on a person's behavior that increase risk-taking. These include psychological factors, such as financial problems, and social factors, such as peer pressure. Opportunity and situational inducements are not the cause of crime; rather, they are the occasion for crime, hence, the term *occasional criminal.*

The opportunity to commit crime and the short-run inducements to do so are not randomly situated; some people, typically poor young males, have an ample supply of both. Consequently, the frequency of occasional property crime varies according to age, class, sex, and so on. Occasional offenders are not professional criminals, nor do they make crime their occupation. They do not rely on skills or knowledge to commit their crimes, they do not organize their daily activities around crime, and they are not committed to crime as a way of life.

Occasional criminals have little group support for their acts. Unlike professionals, they do not receive informal peer group support for their crimes. In fact, they will deny any connection to a criminal lifestyle and instead view their transgressions as being "out of character." They may see their crimes as being motivated by necessity. For example, they were only "borrowing" the car the police caught them with; they were going to pay for the merchandise that they stole from the store—eventually. Because of their lack of commitment to a criminal lifestyle, occasional offenders may be the most likely to respond to the general deterrent effect of the law.

Professional Criminals

In contrast to occasional criminals, professional criminals make a significant portion of their income from crime. Professionals do not delude themselves with the belief that their acts are impulsive, one-time efforts, nor do they employ elaborate rationalizations to excuse the harmfulness of their action ("shoplifting doesn't really hurt anyone"). Consequently, professionals pursue their craft with vigor, attempting to learn from older, experienced criminals the techniques that will earn them the most money with the least risk. Though their numbers are relatively few, professionals engage in crimes that produce the greater losses to society and perhaps cause the more significant social harm.

Professional theft traditionally refers to nonviolent forms of criminal behavior that are undertaken with a high degree of skill for monetary gain and that exploit interests tending to maximize financial opportunities and minimize the possibilities of apprehension. The most typical forms include pocket-picking, burglary, shoplifting, forgery and counterfeiting, extortion, sneak theft, and confidence swindling.[7]

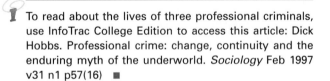

To read about the lives of three professional criminals, use InfoTrac College Edition to access this article: Dick Hobbs. Professional crime: change, continuity and the enduring myth of the underworld. *Sociology* Feb 1997 v31 n1 p57(16) ■

Relatively little is known about the career patterns of professional thieves and criminals. From the literature on crime and delinquency, three patterns emerge:

- Youth come under the influence of older, experienced criminals who teach them the trade.

- Juvenile gang members continue their illegal activities at a time when most of their peers have "dropped out" to marry, raise families, and take conventional jobs.

- Youth sent to prison for minor offenses learn the techniques of crime from more experienced thieves.

Harry King, a professional thief, relates this story about his entry into crime after being placed in a shelter-care home by his recently divorced mother:

> It was while I was at this parental school that I learned that some of the kids had been committed there by the court for stealing bikes. They taught me how to steal and where to steal them and where to sell them. Incidentally, some of the "nicer people" were the ones who bought bikes from the kids. They would dismantle the bike and use the parts: the wheels, chains, handlebars, and so forth.[8]

Here we can see how would-be criminals may be encouraged in their illegal activities by so-called "honest" people who are willing to buy stolen merchandise and gain from criminal enterprise.

There is some debate in the criminological literature over who may be defined as a professional criminal. In his classic works, Edwin Sutherland used the term to refer only to thieves who do not use force or physical violence in their crimes and who live solely by their wits and skill.[9] However, some criminologists use the term to refer to any criminal who identifies with a criminal subculture, who makes the bulk of his or her living from crime, and who possesses a degree of skill in his or her chosen trade.[10] Thus, one can become a professional safecracker, burglar, car thief, or fence. Some criminologists would not consider drug addicts who steal to support their habit as professionals; they lack skill and therefore are amateur opportunists rather than professional technicians. However, professional criminals who take drugs might still be considered under the general pattern of professional crime. If the sole criterion for being judged a professional criminal was using crime as one's primary source of income, then many drug users would have to be placed in the professional category.

Sutherland's Professional Criminal

What we know about the lives of professional criminals has come to us through their journals, diaries, autobiographies, and the first-person accounts they have given to criminologists. The best-known account of professional theft is Edwin Sutherland's recording of the life of a professional thief or con man, Chic Conwell, in Sutherland's classic book, *The Professional Thief*.[11] Conwell and Sutherland's concept of professional theft has two critical dimensions.

First, professional thieves engage in limited types of crime, which are described in Figure 12.1.[12] Professionals depend solely on their wit and skill. Thieves who use force or commit crimes that require little expertise are not considered worthy of the title "professional." Their areas of activity include "heavy rackets," such as bank robbery, car theft, burglary, and safecracking. You can see that Conwell and Sutherland's criteria for professionalism are weighted heavily toward con games and trickery and give little attention to common street crimes.

Figure 12.1 Sutherland's Typology of Professional Thieves

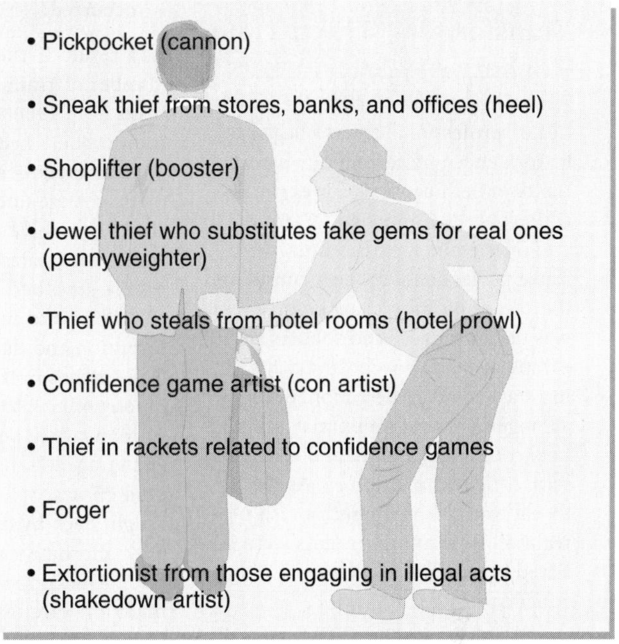

- Pickpocket (cannon)
- Sneak thief from stores, banks, and offices (heel)
- Shoplifter (booster)
- Jewel thief who substitutes fake gems for real ones (pennyweighter)
- Thief who steals from hotel rooms (hotel prowl)
- Confidence game artist (con artist)
- Thief in rackets related to confidence games
- Forger
- Extortionist from those engaging in illegal acts (shakedown artist)

SOURCE: Edwin Sutherland and Chic Conwell, *The Professional Thief* (Chicago: University of Chicago Press, 1937).

The second requirement of professional theft is the exclusive use of wits, front (a believable demeanor), and talking ability. Manual dexterity and physical force are of little importance. Professional thieves must acquire status in their profession. Status is based on their technical skill, financial standing, connections, power, dress, manners, and wide knowledge base. In their world, "thief" is a title worn with pride. Conwell and Sutherland also argue that professional thieves share feelings, sentiments, and behaviors. Of these, none is more important than the code of honor of the underworld; even under the threat of the most severe punishment, a professional thief must never inform (squeal) on his or her fellows. Sutherland and Conwell view professional theft as an occupation with much the same internal organization as that characterizing such legitimate professions as advertising, teaching, or police work. They conclude:

> A person can be a professional thief only if he is recognized and received as such by other professional thieves. Professional theft is a group way of life. One can get into the group and remain in it only by the consent of those previously in the group. Recognition as a professional thief by other professional thieves is the absolutely necessary, universal and definitive characteristic of the professional thief.[13]

Professional thieves have changed their behavior over time in response to crime control technology. As the

THE CRIMINOLOGICAL ENTERPRISE

Transforming Theft: Train Robbers and Safecrackers

According to Neal Shover, the activities of professional thieves began to be influenced by technology before the twentieth century. For example, train robbery flourished toward the end of the nineteenth century because professional robbers considered them easy pickings. Law enforcement was decentralized, and robbers could escape over the border to a neighboring state to avoid detection. Security arrangements were minimal, and robbers could stop, board, and loot trains with little fear of capture. As the threat to trains increased, a rash of technological improvements were initiated in an effort to deter would-be robbers:

- Plainclothes officers were placed on trains and rode unobtrusively among the passengers.
- Baggage cars were equipped with ramps and stalls containing fleet horses that could be used to immediately pursue bandits.
- Cars were made with finer precision and strength to make them impregnable.
- Forensic science made it easier to identify robbers, and improved communication made it easier to capture them.
- Federal involvement in train protection extended the ability of law enforcement beyond the county or

state in which the robbery occurred.

As a result of these innovations, the number of train robberies decreased from 29 in 1900 to 7 in 1905; by 1920, train robbers had all but disappeared.

Safecracking also underwent a dramatic change due to technological changes in the design of safes. In the early 1900s, safes were made of manganese steel because it was resistant to drilling and was fireproof. With the invention and distribution of acetylene torches in the latter part of the nineteenth century, safes constructed of manganese became vulnerable and encouraged "safecrackers" to commit bold crimes. Safe manufacturers fought back by constructing safes with alternative sheets of copper and steel. The copper diffused heat and made the safe resistant to being torched. In response, safecrackers shifted their approach to attacking safes' locks and locking mechanisms. They developed mechanical devices that either dismantled or destroyed locks. Some burglars developed methods of peeling the laminated layers of the safe apart. After World War II, safecrackers began using carbide and then diamond drill bits, which tore through metal. Safe manufacturers responded by lining safes with new metals designed to chip or break drill bits. They also developed sophisticated security systems featuring light beams, which would trip an alarm if the beam was interrupted by an intruder. When thieves learned how to

neutralize these alarms, they were supplanted by motion detectors and ultrasonic systems, which fill space with sound waves and set off alarms when they are disturbed. Though these systems can be defeated, it requires expensive electronic gear, which most criminals can neither afford nor operate. As a result, the number of safecrackers has declined and the crime of "safecracking" is relatively rare.

Critical Thinking Questions

1. Technology changes the nature and extent of theft crimes. Although train robbing and safecracking may be rare today, using bogus credit cards and stealing from ATM machines has increased in both number of crimes and value. What are some other crime patterns that have been created by technological innovation?
2. What types of crime involving technological innovations have been prevented or deterred?

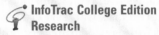

InfoTrac College Edition Research

To read about the life of an actual train robber, check out this article:

Stephen Fox. Chris Evans could always be relied on to pull a fast one. *Smithsonian* May 1995 v26 n2 p84(8)

SOURCE: Neal Shover, *Great Pretenders, Pursuits and Careers of Persistent Thieves,* (Boulder, Colo.: Westview Press, 1996), pp. 50–51.

Criminological Enterprise feature shows, these technology-inspired shifts in criminality began as early as the nineteenth century.

The Professional Fence

Some experts have argued that Sutherland's view of the professional thief may be outdated because modern thieves often work alone, are not part of a criminal subculture, and were not tutored early in their careers by other criminals.[14] However, some important research efforts show that the principles set down by Sutherland still have

value for understanding the behavior of one contemporary criminal type—the **professional fence,** who earns his or her living solely by buying and reselling stolen merchandise. The fence's critical role in criminal transactions has been recognized since the eighteenth century.[15] They act as middlemen who purchase stolen merchandise—ranging from diamonds to auto hubcaps—and resell them to merchants who market them to legitimate customers.[16]

Carl Klockars examined the life and times of one successful fence who used the alias "Vincent Swaggi." Through 400 hours of listening to and observing Vincent, Klockars found that this highly professional criminal had developed techniques that made him almost immune to prosecution. During the course of a long and profitable career in crime, Vincent spent only four months in prison. He stayed in business, in part, because of his sophisticated knowledge of the law of stolen property. To convict someone of receiving stolen goods, the prosecution must prove that the accused was in possession of the goods and knew that they had been stolen. Vincent had the skills to make sure that these elements could never be proved. Also helping Vincent stay out of the law's grasp were the close working associations he maintained with society's upper classes, including influential members of the justice system. Vincent helped them purchase stolen items at below-cost, bargain prices. He also helped authorities recover stolen goods and therefore remained in their good graces. Klockars's work strongly suggests that fences customarily cheat their thief-clients and at the same time cooperate with the law.

Sam Goodman, a fence interviewed by sociologist Darrell Steffensmeier, lived in a world similar to Vincent Swaggi's. He also purchased stolen goods from a wide variety of thieves and suppliers, including burglars, drug addicts, shoplifters, dockworkers, and truck drivers. According to Sam, to be successful, a fence must meet the following conditions:

Upfront cash—all deals are cash transactions, so an adequate supply of ready cash must always be on hand.

Knowledge of dealing: learning the ropes—the fence must be schooled in the knowledge of the trade, including developing a "larceny sense"; learning to "buy right" at acceptable prices; being able to "cover one's back" and not get caught; finding out how to make the right contacts; and knowing how to "wheel and deal" and how to create opportunities for profit.

Connections with suppliers of stolen goods—the successful fence must be able to engage in long-term relationships with suppliers of high-value stolen goods who are relatively free of police interference. The warehouse worker who pilfers is a better supplier than the narcotics addict, who is more likely to be apprehended and talk to the police.

Connections with buyers—the successful fence must have continuing access to buyers of stolen merchandise who are inaccessible to the common thief.

Complicity with law enforcers—the fence must work out a relationship with law enforcement officials who invariably find out about the fence's operations. Steffensmeier found that to stay in business the fence must either bribe officials with good deals on merchandise and cash payments or act as an informer who helps police recover particularly important merchandise and arrest thieves.

Fences handle a tremendous number of products—televisions, cigarettes, stereo equipment, watches, autos, and cameras.[17] In dealing their merchandise, they operate through many legitimate fronts, including art dealers, antique stores, furniture and appliance retailers, remodeling companies, salvage companies, trucking companies, and jewelry stores. When deciding what to pay the thief for goods, the fence uses a complex pricing policy: professional thieves who steal high-priced items are usually given the highest amounts—about 30 to 50 percent of the wholesale price. For example, furs valued at $5,000 may be bought for $1,200. However, the amateur thief or drug addict who is not in a good bargaining position may receive only ten cents on the dollar.

Fencing seems to contain many of the elements of professional theft as described by Sutherland: fences live by their wits, never engage in violence, depend on their skill in negotiating, maintain community standing based on connections and power, and share the sentiments and behaviors of their fellows. The only divergence between Sutherland's thief and the fence is the code of honor; it seems likely that the fence is much more willing to cooperate with authorities than most other professional criminals. The Criminological Enterprise feature describes the activities of a professional fencing operation in Atlanta.

The Nonprofessional Fence

Professional fences have attracted the attention of criminologists, but like other forms of theft, fencing is not dominated solely by professional criminals. A significant portion of all fencing is performed by amateur or occasional criminals. For example, novice burglars, such as juveniles and drug addicts, often find it so difficult to establish relationships with professional fences that they turn instead to nonprofessionals to unload the stolen goods.[18]

One type of occasional fence is the part-timer who, unlike professional fences, has other sources of income. Part-timers are often "legitimate" businesspeople who integrate the stolen merchandise into their regular stock. For example, the manager of a local video store who buys stolen VCRs and tapes and rents them along with his legitimate merchandise is a part-time fence. An added benefit of the illegitimate part of his work is the profit he makes on these stolen items, which are not reported for tax purposes.

Some merchants become actively involved in theft either by specifying the merchandise they want the burglars to steal or by "fingering" victims. Some businesspeople sell merchandise and then describe the customers' homes and vacation plans to known burglars so that they can steal it back!

Associational fences are amateur fences who barter stolen goods for services. These amateurs typically have legitimate professional dealings with known criminals including bail bonds agents, police officers, and attorneys. One lawyer bragged of getting a $12,000 Rolex watch from one client in exchange for legal services. Bartering for

Operation American Dream: The Anatomy of a Professional Criminal Fencing Enterprise

In the mid-1990s, a Pakistani criminal enterprise ran a large-scale fencing/repackaging business in the Atlanta metropolitan area. The groups targeted retail stores located in and on the outskirts of Atlanta from which the thieves stole over-the-counter medicines, pharmaceuticals, razors, and all types of health and beauty aids. Computers, DVDs, stereos, TVs, clothing, shoes, even jet skis and household goods disappeared from the shelves of nationally recognized retail stores.

The criminal enterprise operating out of the Atlanta area was comprised of 30 predominantly illegal Pakistani nationals who had also committed crimes in at least three other states. The leaders of the enterprise, who operated convenience stores that were receiving the stolen merchandise, recruited a group of more than 200 professional shoplifters. The shoplifters would steal from retail stores in small towns where store security, in most cases, was minimal. They would usually operate in groups of four or five, often using distraction techniques to steal merchandise. The group leaders supported the efforts of the boosters by providing them with vehicles and by posting bond for them if they

were arrested. On a good day, they could steal $50 to $1,000 worth of merchandise.

The stolen merchandise would later be taken to a warehouse where it was repackaged and shipped to co-conspirators in New York, Baltimore, and Pakistan. Subjects in New York and Baltimore would sell the stolen merchandise to wholesale companies who could often resell the merchandise to retail stores. Some of the stolen merchandise was also sold in the Atlanta area to businesses that would, in turn, put the merchandise in their stores and sell it to their customers.

Competition to buy the stolen merchandise from the shoplifters was intense. In one instance, a group member was so enraged by another member who had bought more merchandise and made more money that he hired a couple of thugs to rough up a clerk who helped operate his rival's store. The clerk was severely beaten and shot.

Then there was merchandise skimming. Some group members would keep the better, more costly shoplifted items for themselves instead of turning the merchandise in to the leader of the group.

This enterprising crime group was not afraid of the police, and for good reason—at least two Atlanta police officers were being paid to assist the group. The officers would provide security during illegal operations and transactions and warn the group of impending police action.

On October 14, 1999, after an ongoing criminal investigation by local and federal agents, a 214-count indictment was issued in Atlanta charging 29 subjects in this matter with multiple counts of conspiracy, money laundering, and interstate transportation of stolen property. One Atlanta police officer was arrested and convicted, and another chose to resign and may be indicted at a later date.

Critical Thinking Questions

1. Does this criminal enterprise fit the description of Sutherland's professional criminal?
2. How would a rational choice theorist explain the activities of this group? How would a trait theorist explain it?

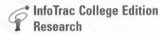
InfoTrac College Edition Research

Who commits shoplifting? Are they professionals or amateurs? To find out, read:

> Read Hayes. When shoplifters attack. *Security Management* June 1998 v42 n6 p14(1)

Can something be done to prevent shoplifting? To find out, read:

> Katherine Hobson. Hey, security tag makers: you're it. *U.S. News & World Report* 14 May 2001 v130 i19 p34

SOURCE: Federal Bureau of Investigation, *Operation American Dream, Joint Law Enforcement Efforts Shut Down Fencing Operation* (Washington, D.C.: Federal Bureau of Investigation, 2001).

---

stolen merchandise avoids taxes and becomes a transaction in the "underground economy."

Neighborhood hustlers buy and sell stolen property as one of the many ways they make a living. They keep some of the booty for themselves and sell the rest in the neighborhood. These dealmakers are familiar figures to neighborhood burglars looking to get some quick cash by selling them stolen merchandise.

Amateur receivers can be complete strangers approached in a public place by someone offering a great deal on valuable commodities. It is unlikely that anyone buying a $500 stereo for $200 cash would not suspect that it may have been stolen. Some amateur receivers make a habit of

buying suspect merchandise at reasonable prices from a "trusted friend," establishing an ongoing relationship. This practice encourages crime because the criminals know that there will always be someone to buy their merchandise. In addition to the professional fence, the nonprofessional fence may account for a great deal of criminal receiving. Both professional and amateur thieves have a niche in the crime universe.

Criminologists and legal scholars recognize that common theft offenses fall into several categories linked together because they involve the intentional misappropriation of property for personal gain. In fencing, goods are bought from another who is in illegal possession of those goods. In the case of embezzlement, burglary, and larceny, the property is taken through stealth. In other kinds of theft, such as bad checks, fraud, and false pretenses, goods are obtained through deception. Some of the major categories of common theft offenses are discussed in the next sections in some detail.

■ Larceny/Theft

Larceny/theft was one of the earliest common-law crimes created by English judges to define acts in which one person took for his or her own use the property of another.[19] According to common law, larceny was defined as "the trespassory taking and carrying away of the personal property of another with intent to steal."[20] Most state jurisdictions have incorporated the common-law crime of larceny in their legal codes. Today, definitions of larceny often include such familiar acts as shoplifting, passing bad checks, and other theft offenses that do not involve using force or

■ Receiving or buying goods that a person knows have been stolen is a form of larceny/theft. Here, Louis "Baby Shanks" Manocchio listens during his trial, April 12, 1999, in Providence Superior Court in Providence, Rhode Island. Manocchio, the reputed leader of the New England mob, was charged with a felony count of receiving stolen goods, a refrigerator and a dishwasher. Manocchio, who allegedly gave the appliances to his elderly mother, faced a maximum of 10 years in prison if convicted.

threats on the victim (robbery) or forcibly breaking into a person's home or place of work (burglary).

To learn about the law of larceny, use "larceny" as a subject guide on InfoTrac College Edition. ■

When it was originally construed, **larceny** involved taking property that was in the possession of the rightful owners. For example, it would have been considered larceny for someone to go secretly into a farmer's field and steal a cow. Thus, the original common-law definition required a "trespass in the taking"; this meant that for an act to be considered larceny, goods must have been taken from the physical possession of the rightful owner. In creating this definition of larceny, English judges were more concerned with people disturbing the peace than they were with thefts. If someone tried to steal property from another's possession, they reasoned that the act could eventually lead to a physical confrontation and possibly the death of one party or the other, thereby disturbing the peace! Consequently, the original definition of larceny did not include crimes in which the thief had come into the possession of the stolen property by trickery or deceit. For example, if someone entrusted with another person's property decided to keep it, it was not considered larceny.

The growth of manufacturing and the development of the free enterprise system required greater protection for private property. The pursuit of commercial enterprise often required that one person's legal property be entrusted to a second party; therefore, larceny evolved to include the theft of goods that had come into the thief's possession through legitimate means.

To get around the element of "trespass in the taking," English judges created the concept of **constructive possession.** This legal fiction applied to situations in which persons voluntarily and temporarily gave up custody of their property but still believed the property was legally theirs. For example, if a person gave a jeweler her watch for repair, she would still believe she owned the watch even though she had handed it over to the jeweler. Similarly, when a person misplaces his wallet and someone else finds it and keeps it—although identification of the owner can be plainly seen—the concept of constructive possession makes the person who has kept the wallet guilty of larceny.

Larceny Today

Most state jurisdictions have, as mentioned, incorporated larceny in their criminal codes. Larceny is usually separated by state statute into **petit (or petty) larceny** and **grand larceny.** The former involves small amounts of money or property; it is punished as a misdemeanor. Grand larceny, involving merchandise of greater value, is considered a felony and is punished by a sentence in the state prison. Each state sets its own boundary between grand larceny and petty larceny, but $50 to $100 is not unusual. This distinction often presents a serious problem for the justice system. Car thefts and other larcenies involving high-priced merchandise are easily classified, but it is often difficult to decide whether a particular theft should be considered petty or grand larceny. For example, if a 10-year-old watch that originally cost $500 is stolen, should its value be based on its original cost, on its current worth (say, $50), or on its replacement cost (say, $1,000)? As most statutes are worded, the current market value of the property governs its worth. Thus, the theft of the watch would be considered petty larceny because its worth today is only $50. However, if a painting originally bought for $25 has a current market value of $500, its theft would be considered grand larceny.

Larceny/theft is probably the most common criminal offense. Self-report studies indicate that a significant number of youths have engaged in theft-related activities. The FBI reports that about 7 million larcenies occur each year. Larceny rates remained stable between 1999 and 2000, but like other crimes rates they have declined during the past decade, down 12 percent since 1996 and 14 percent since 1991.[21]

There are many different varieties of larceny. Some involve small items of little value. Many of these go unreported, however, especially if the victims were business owners who do not want to take the time to get involved with police. They simply write off the losses as part of doing business. For example, hotel owners estimate that guests filch $100-million-worth a year in towels, bathrobes, ashtrays, bedspreads, shower heads, flatware, and even television sets and wall paintings.[22]

Other larcenies involve complex criminal conspiracies, and no one, not even the U.S. government, is immune. Thieves steal millions of dollars worth of government equipment and supplies each year. For example, the Department of Energy reported more than $20 million in property missing from its site in Rocky Flats, Colorado. Missing items included semi-trailers, forklifts, cameras, desks, radios, and more than 1,800 pieces of computer equipment.[23]

Shoplifting

Shoplifting is a common form of theft involving the taking of goods from retail stores. Usually shoplifters try to snatch goods—jewelry, clothes, records, or appliances—when store personnel are otherwise occupied, and they then hide the goods on their person. The "five-finger discount" is an extremely common form of crime, and retailers lose an estimated $30 billion to inventory shrinkage; on average, stores small and large lose at least 2 percent of total sales to thieves.[24] Nor is shoplifting unique to the United States. In England, about 5 percent of the population is convicted of shoplifting by age 40. Surveys of retailers in the United Kingdom suggest that there are more than 4 million known shoplifting incidents, 1.3 million apprehended shoplifters, and 800,000 shoplifters reported to the police each year. One reason for the popularity of shoplifting may

be lax treatment. Although about 1 in 7 apprehended offenders is eventually convicted in court, less than 1 in 20 shoplifting attempts result in apprehension.[25]

Retail security measures add to the already high cost of this crime, all of which is passed on to the consumer. Some studies estimate that about one in every nine shoppers steals from department stores. Moreover, the increasingly popular discount stores, such as Costco, Wal-Mart, and Target, have a minimum of sales help and depend on highly visible merchandise displays to attract purchasers, all of which makes them particularly vulnerable to shoplifters.

The profile of a shoplifter In the early 1960s, Mary Owen Cameron conducted a classic study of shoplifting.[26] In her pioneering effort, Cameron found that about 10 percent of all shoplifters were professionals who derived the majority of their income from shoplifting. Sometimes called **boosters** or **heels,** she found that professional shoplifters steal with the intention of reselling stolen merchandise to pawnshops or fences, usually at half the original price.[27]

Cameron found that the majority of shoplifters are amateur pilferers, called **snitches** in thieves' argot. Snitches are usually respectable persons who do not conceive of themselves as thieves but are systematic shoplifters who steal merchandise for their own use. They are not simply taken by an uncontrollable urge to take something that attracts them; they come equipped to steal. Snitches who are arrested usually have never been apprehended before. For the most part, they are people who lack the kinds of criminal experience that suggest extensive association with a criminal subculture.

Criminologists view shoplifters as people who are likely to reform if apprehended. Because snitches are not part of a criminal subculture and do not think of themselves as criminals, Mary Owen Cameron reasoned that they are deterred by an initial contact with the law. Getting arrested has a traumatic effect on them, and they will not risk a second offense.[28] This argument seems plausible, but some criminologists argue that apprehension may have a labeling effect that inhibits deterrence and results in repeated offending.[29]

The National Crime Prevention Council has information on shoplifting on its Web site. You may visit it at:
http://www.ncpc.org/publications/shoplifting.pdf
For an up-to-date list of Web links, go to
http://info.wadsworth.com/siegel ■

Controlling shoplifting One major problem associated with combating shoplifting is that many customers who observe pilferage are reluctant to report it to security agents. Store employees themselves are often reluctant to get involved in apprehending a shoplifter. In fact, less than 10 percent of shoplifting incidents are detected by store employees; customers who notice boosters are unwilling to report even serious cases to managers.[30] It is also likely that a store owner's decision to prosecute shoplifters will be based on the value of the goods stolen, the nature of the goods stolen, and the manner in which the theft was realized. For example, shoplifters who planned their crime by using a concealed apparatus, such as a bag pinned to the inside of their clothing, were more apt to be prosecuted than those who had impulsively put merchandise into their pockets.[31] The concealment indicated that the crime was premeditated and not a spur of the moment loss of control.

To encourage the arrest of shoplifters, a number of states have passed merchant privilege laws designed to protect retailers and their employers from litigation stemming from improper or false arrests of suspected shoplifters.[32] These laws protect but do not immunize merchants from lawsuits. They require that arrests be made on reasonable grounds or probable cause, detention be of short duration, and store employees or security guards conduct themselves in a reasonable fashion.

Prevention strategies   Retail stores are now initiating a number of strategies designed to reduce or eliminate shoplifting. **Target removal** strategies involve putting dummy or disabled goods on display while the "real" merchandise is kept under lock and key. For example, audio equipment with missing parts is displayed, and only after items are purchased are the necessary components installed. Some stores sell from a catalogue while keeping merchandise in stockrooms.

Target hardening strategies involve locking goods in place or having them monitored by electronic systems. Clothing stores may use racks designed to prevent large quantities of garments from being slipped off easily. Store owners may rely on electronic article surveillance (EAS) systems, featuring tags with small electronic sensors that trip sound and light alarms if not removed by employees before the item leaves the store. Security systems now feature source tagging, a process by which manufacturers embed the tag in the packaging or in the product itself. Thieves are hard pressed to remove or defeat such tags, and retailers save on the time and labor needed to attach the tags at their stores.[33]

Situational measures place the most valuable goods in the least vulnerable places, use warning signs to deter potential thieves, and use closed-circuit cameras. Goods may be tagged with devices that activate an alarm if they are taken out of the shop. Figure 12.2 illustrates some additional measures that stores can take to deter shoplifters.

To learn more about shoplifting control, use InfoTrac College Edition, and read: Ann Longmore-Etheridge. Bagging profits instead of thieves. *Security Management* Oct 2001 v45 i10 p70 ■

Figure 12.2   How to Stop Shoplifting: Recommendations of Retail Insurers

- Train employees to watch for suspicious behavior, such as a shopper loitering over a trivial item. Have them keep an eye out for shoppers wearing baggy clothes, carrying their own bag, or using some other method to conceal products taken from the shelf.

- Develop a call code. When employees suspect that a customer is shoplifting, they can use the call to bring store management of security to the area.

- Because products on lower floors face the greatest risk, relocate the most tempting targets to upper floors.

- Use smaller exits and avoid placing the most expensive merchandise near these exits.

- Design routes within stores to make theft less tempting and funnel customers toward cashiers.

- Place service departments (credit and packaging) near areas where shoplifters are likely to stash goods. Extra supervision reduces the problem.

- Avoid creating corners with no supervision sight lines in areas of stores favored by young males. Restrict and supervise areas where electronic tags can be removed.

SOURCES: Marcus Felson, "Preventing Retail Theft: An Application of Environmental Criminology," *Security Journal* 7 (1996): 71–75; Marc Brandeberry, $15 Billion Lost to Shoplifting, *Today's Coverage,* A Newsletter of the Grocers Insurance Group (Portland, Ore.: Grocers Insurance Group, 1997).

Bad Checks

Another form of larceny is cashing bad bank checks, knowingly and intentionally drawn on a nonexistent or underfunded bank account, to obtain money or property. In general, for a person to be guilty of passing a bad check, the bank the check is drawn on must refuse payment, and the check casher must fail to make the check good within 10 days after finding out the check was not honored.

Edwin Lemert conducted the best-known study of check forgers more than 40 years ago.[34] Lemert found that the majority of check forgers—he calls them **naive check forgers**—are amateurs who do not believe their actions will hurt anyone. Most naive check forgers come from middle-class backgrounds and have little identification with a criminal subculture. They cash bad checks because of a financial crisis that demands an immediate resolution—perhaps they have lost money at the horse track and have some pressing bills to pay. Lemert refers to this condition as **closure.** Naive check forgers are often socially isolated people who have been unsuccessful in their personal relationships. They are risk prone when faced with a situation that is unusually stressful for them. The willingness of stores and other commercial establishments to cash checks with a minimum of fuss to promote business encourages the check forger to risk committing a criminal act.

Not all check forgers are amateurs. Lemert found that a few professionals—whom he calls **systematic forgers**— make a substantial living by passing bad checks. However, professionals constitute a relatively small segment of the total population of check forgers. It is difficult to estimate the number of such forgeries committed each year or the amounts involved. Stores and banks may choose not to press charges because the effort to collect the money due them is often not worth their while. It is also difficult to separate the true check forger from the neglectful shopper.

Credit Card Theft

The use of stolen credit cards has become a major problem in U.S. society. It has been estimated that fraud has been responsible for a billion-dollar loss in the credit card industry. Most credit card abuse is the work of amateurs who acquire stolen cards through theft or mugging and then use them for two or three days. However, professional credit card rings may be getting into the act. For example, in Los Angeles, members of a credit card gang got jobs as clerks in several stores, where they collected the names and credit card numbers of customers. Gang members bought plain plastic cards and had the names and numbers of the customers embossed on them. The gang created a fictitious wholesale jewelry company and applied for and received authorization to accept credit cards from the customers. The thieves then used the phony cards to charge nonexistent jewelry purchases on the accounts of the people whose names and card numbers they had collected. The banks that issued the original cards honored more than $200,000 in payments before the thieves withdrew the money from their business account and left town.[35] To combat losses from credit card theft, Congress passed a law in 1971 limiting a person's liability to $50 per stolen card. Similarly, some states, such as California, have passed specific statutes making it a misdemeanor to obtain property or services by means of cards that have been stolen, forged, canceled, or revoked, or whose use is for any reason unauthorized.[36]

The problem of credit card misuse is being compounded by thieves who set up bogus Internet sites strictly to trick people into giving them their credit card numbers, which they then use for their own gain. The problem is growing so rapidly that a number of new technologies are being prepared, aimed at combating credit card number theft over the Internet. One method is to incorporate digital signatures into computer operating systems, which can be accessed with a digital key that comes with each computer. Owners of new systems can present three forms of identification to a notary public and trade a notarized copy of their key for a program that will sign files. The basis of the digital signature is a digital certificate, a small block of data that contains a person's "public key." This certificate is signed, in turn, by a certificate authority. This digital certificate will act like a credit card with a hologram and a photograph and identify the user to the distant Web site and vice versa.[37]

Want to avoid credit card theft? The Federal Trade Commission has some important tips:
http://www.ftc.gov/bcp/conline/pubs/credit/cards.htm
For an up-to-date list of Web links, go to
http://info.wadsworth.com/siegel

Auto Theft

Motor vehicle theft is another common larceny offense. Yet because of its frequency and seriousness, it is treated as a separate category in the UCR. The FBI recorded almost 1.2 million auto thefts in 2000, accounting for a total loss of more than $8 billion. Like other crimes, motor vehicle theft has declined during the past decade, down 16 percent from 1996 and about 30 percent from 1991. However, between 1999 and 2000, the number of cars stolen actually increased slightly (about 1 percent). It is possible that with the slowing economy car thefts are becoming more attractive.

UCR projections on auto theft are actually quite similar to the projections of the National Crime Victim Survey (almost 1 million thefts in 2000). The similarity of data between these sources occurs because almost every state jurisdiction requires owners to insure their vehicles. Auto theft is the most highly reported of all major crimes (80 percent of all auto thefts are reported to police).

A number of attempts have been made to categorize the various forms of auto theft. Distinctions typically are made between theft for temporary personal use, for resale, and for chopping or stripping cars for parts. One of the most detailed typologies was developed by Charles McCaghy and his associates after examining data from police and court files in several state jurisdictions.[38] The researchers uncovered five categories of auto theft transactions:

Joyriding—Many car thefts are motivated by teenagers' desire to acquire the power, prestige, sexual potency, and recognition associated with an automobile. Joyriders do not steal cars for profit or gain but to experience, even briefly, the benefits associated with owning an automobile.

Short-term transportation—Auto theft for short-term transportation is most similar to joyriding. It involves the theft of a car simply to go from one place to another. In more serious cases, the thief may drive to another city or state and then steal another car to continue the journey.

Long-term transportation—Thieves who steal cars for long-term transportation intend to keep the cars for their personal use. Usually older than joyriders and from a lower-class background, these auto thieves may repaint and otherwise disguise cars to avoid detection.

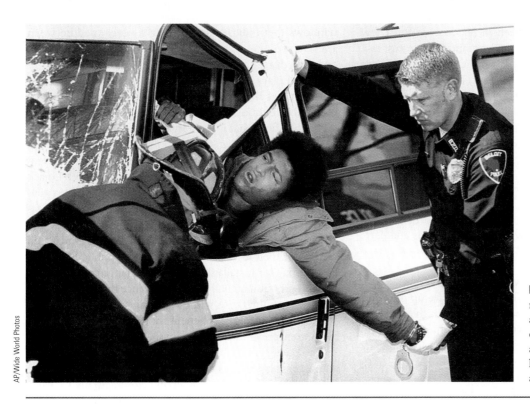

■ Suspect Jose Valadez remains inside a stolen van as Beloit, Wisconsin, police officer Mike Crall (right) and firefighters work to free him from the wreckage after a high-speed chase.

Profit—Auto theft for profit is motivated by hope for monetary gain. At one extreme are highly organized professionals who resell expensive cars after altering their identification numbers and falsifying their registration papers. At the other end of the scale are amateur auto strippers who steal batteries, tires, and wheel covers to sell them or reequip their own cars.

Commission of another crime—A small portion of auto thieves steal cars to use in other crimes, such as robberies and thefts. This type of auto thief desires both mobility and anonymity.

At one time, joyriding was the predominant motive for auto theft, and most cars were taken by relatively affluent, white, middle-class teenagers looking for excitement.[39] There appears to be a change in this pattern: fewer cars are being taking today while, concomitantly, fewer stolen cars are being recovered. Part of the reason is that there has been an increase in professional car thieves who are linked to "chop shops," export rings, or both. Export of stolen vehicles has become a global problem, and the emergence of capitalism in Eastern Europe has increased the demand for U.S.-made cars.[40]

Which cars are taken most? Car thieves show signs of rational choice when they make their target selections. Today, luxury cars and utility vehicles are in greatest demand. The Toyota Land Cruiser is 23 times more likely to be taken than the average vehicle. According to the Na-

tional Insurance Crime Bureau (NICB), the Toyota Camry and Honda Accord are the cars most often stolen (2000), followed in popularity by Oldsmobile Cutlass, Honda Civic, Jeep Cherokee/Grand Cherokee, Chevrolet full size C/K pickup, Toyota Corolla, Chevrolet Caprice, Ford Taurus, and Ford F150 pickup. The NICB also found that American cars were more attractive to thieves in some cities, such as Chicago, whereas pickups were more frequently stolen in Dallas. In the Los Angeles area, thieves preferred Japanese models.[41]

According to the NICB, thieves typically choose these vehicles because of the high profit potential when the cars are stripped of their component parts, which are then sold on the black market. These vehicles are popular overseas, and once taken, organized theft rings will illegally export them to foreign destinations. Many of the highly desired cars are never recovered because they are immediately transshipped abroad where they command prices three times higher than their U.S. sticker price.[42]

The National Insurance Crime Bureau (NICB) is dedicated to fighting insurance fraud and theft through information analysis, forecasting, criminal investigation support, training, and public awareness. The NICB is supported by approximately 1,000 property/casualty insurance companies. Their Web site can be reached at:
   http://www.nicb.org/
For an up-to-date list of Web links, go to
   http://info.wadsworth.com/siegel ■

Car models that have been in production for a few years without many design changes stand the greatest risk of theft. These vehicles are popular because their parts are most valued in the secondary market. Luxury cars, on the other hand, typically experience a sharp decline in their theft rate soon after a design change. Enduring models are also in demand because older cars are more likely to be uninsured, and demand for stolen used parts is higher for these vehicles.

CONNECTIONS

Chapter 5 discusses the rational choice view of car theft. As you may recall, cars with expensive radios and parts are more often the target of rational thieves. ■

Carjacking You may have read about gunmen approaching a car and forcing the owner to give up the keys; in some cases, people have been killed when they reacted too slowly. This type of auto theft has become so common that it has its own name, **carjacking**.[43] Carjacking is legally considered a type of robbery because it involves force to steal. About 50,000 carjackings occur each year.[44]

Both victims and offenders in carjackings tend to be young black men. Urban residents were more likely to experience carjacking than suburban or rural residents. Persons over age 50 had lower rates than younger persons, but there were no clear patterns by household income. About half of all carjackings are typically committed by gangs or groups. These crimes are most likely to occur in the evening, in the central city, in an open area or parking garage.

Although the public perceives carjackings as particularly violent crimes, most carjacking victims are not injured. Serious injuries, such as gunshot or knife wounds, broken bones, internal injuries, and loss of consciousness, occur in only about 4 percent of all carjackings. More minor injuries, such as bruises, chipped teeth, and other similar injuries, are more common and occur in about 13 percent of all carjackings.

To read more about carjacking, the Bureau of Justice Statistics Web site contains the findings of a national study:
http://www.ojp.usdoj.gov/bjs/pub/ascii/c.txt
For an up-to-date list of Web links, go to
http://info.wadsworth.com/siegel ■

Combating auto theft Auto theft is a significant target of situational crime prevention efforts. One approach to theft deterrence has been to increase the risks of apprehension. Information hot lines offer rewards for information leading to the arrest of car thieves. A Michigan-based program, Operation HEAT (Help Eliminate Auto Theft), is credited with recovering more than 900 vehicles, worth $11 million, and resulting in the arrest of 647 people. Another approach has been to place fluorescent decals on windows that indicate that the car is never used between 1 A.M. and 5 A.M.; if police spot a car with the decal being operated during this period, they know it is stolen.[45]

The Lojack system involves a hidden tracking device installed in cars that gives off a signal, enabling the police to pinpoint its location. Research evaluating the effectiveness of this device finds that it has a significant crime reduction capability.[46] Because car thieves cannot tell that Lojack has been installed, it does not reduce the likelihood that a protected car will be stolen. However, cars installed with Lojack have a much higher recovery rate. There may also be a general deterrent effect: areas with high rates of Lojack use experience significant reductions in their auto theft rates. Lojack owners actually accrue a smaller than anticipated reward for their foresight than the general public since they have to pay for installation and maintenance of the device. Those without it actually gain more since they benefit from a lower auto theft rate without paying any additional cost! It is ironic that nonusers benefit more than users.

Other prevention efforts involve making it more difficult to steal cars. Publicity campaigns have been directed at encouraging people to lock their cars. Parking lots have been equipped with theft-deterring closed-circuit TV cameras and barriers. Manufacturers have installed more sophisticated steering column locking devices and other security systems that make theft harder.

A study by the Highway Loss Data Institute (HLDI) found that most car theft prevention methods, especially alarms, have little effect on theft rates. The most effective methods appear to be devices that immobilize a vehicle by cutting off the electrical power needed to start the engine when a theft is detected.[47]

False Pretenses or Fraud

The crime of **false pretenses,** or **fraud,** involves misrepresenting a fact in a way that causes a victim to willingly give his or her property to the wrongdoer, who then keeps it.[48] In 1757, the English Parliament defined false pretenses to cover an area of law left untouched by larceny statutes. The first false pretenses law punished people who "knowingly and designedly by false pretense or pretenses, [obtained] from any person or persons, money, goods, wares or merchandise with intent to cheat or defraud any person or persons of the same."[49]

False pretense differs from traditional larceny because the victims willingly give their possessions to the offender, and the crime does not, as does larceny, involve a "trespass in the taking." An example of false pretenses would be an unscrupulous merchant selling someone a chair by claiming it was an antique, but knowing all the while that it was a cheap copy. Another example would be a phony healer selling a victim a bottle of colored sugar water as an "elixir" that would cure a disease.

Fraud may also occur when people conspire to cheat a third party or institution; for example, by selling fake IDs,

and obstruction of justice and received a four-year prison term for his efforts. In this case, there were many victims, including the testing service, universities, and the students who lost places in school because those who inflated their scores through the scheme were admitted instead.[50]

Confidence Games

Confidence games are run by swindlers, who aspire to separate a victim (or "sucker") from his or her hard-earned money. These "con games" usually involve getting a **mark,** the target of a con man or woman, interested in some get-rich-quick scheme, which may have illegal overtones. The criminal's hope is that when victims lose their money they will either be too embarrassed or too afraid to call the police. There are hundreds of varieties of con games. The most common is called the **pigeon drop.**[51] Here, a package or wallet containing money is "found" by a con man or woman. A passing victim is stopped and asked for advice about what to do, since no identification can be found. Another "stranger," who is part of the con, approaches and enters the discussion. The three decide to split the money; but first, to make sure everything is legal, one of the swindlers goes off to consult a lawyer. Upon returning, he or she says that the lawyer claims the money can be split up; first, however, each party must prove he or she has the means to reimburse the original owner, should one show up. The victim then is asked to give some good-faith money for the lawyer to hold. When the victim goes to the lawyer's office to pick up a share of the loot, he or she finds the address bogus and the money gone.

In the new millennium, the "pigeon drop" has been appropriated by corrupt telemarketers, who contact people over the phone, typically elderly victims, to bilk them out of their savings. The FBI estimates that illicit telephone pitches cost Americans some $40 billion a year.[52] In one scam, a salesman tried to get $500 out of a 78-year-old woman by telling her the money was needed as a deposit to make sure she would get $50,000 in cash she had supposedly won in a contest. With the growth of direct-mail marketing and "900" telephone numbers that charge callers more than $3.50 per minute for conversations with what are promised to be beautiful and willing sex partners, a flood of new confidence games may be about to descend on the U.S. public. In all, about 414,000 people were arrested for fraud in 2000, most likely a very small percentage of all swindlers, scam artists, and frauds.

Embezzlement

Embezzlement was mentioned in early Greek culture when, in his writings, Aristotle alluded to theft by road commissioners and other government officials.[53] It was first codified in law by the English Parliament during the sixteenth century to fill a gap in the larceny law.[54] Until then, to be guilty of theft, a person had to take goods from

■ The crime of false pretenses, or fraud, involves misrepresenting a fact in a way that causes a victim to willingly give his or her property to the wrongdoer, who then keeps it for his or her own use. Here, Kristen Clougherty leaves Suffolk Superior Court October 31, 2000, after being sentenced to two years probation for faking cancer to raise nearly $50,000 from well-meaning donors in Boston. The South Boston woman, who according to prosecutors used the money for cosmetic surgery, a new car, and weekends in luxury hotels, was also ordered to repay victims and to perform 300 hours of community service.

tickets, vouchers, tokens, or licenses, which can be used to fraudulently gain services or illegal access. One example of an innovative cheating scheme was instituted by a man named Po Chieng Ma, who conspired to sell answers to the Graduate Management Administration Test (GMAT), the Graduate Record Examinations (GRE), and the Test of English as a Foreign Language (TOEFL) to an estimated 788 customers, each of whom had paid him $2,000 to $9,000. In the scheme, people were paid to take the multiple-choice tests in Manhattan and then call California, where the same tests were to be given, with the answers. The answers were passed on to Mr. Ma, who, taking advantage of the three-hour time difference, carved the answers in code on the sides of pencils, which were then given to his customers. Ma pleaded guilty to conspiracy

the physical possession of another (trespass in the taking). However, as explained earlier, this definition did not cover instances in which one person trusted another and willfully gave that person temporary custody of his or her property. For example, in everyday commerce, store clerks, bank tellers, brokers, and merchants gain lawful possession but not legal ownership of other people's money. Embezzlement occurs when someone who is so trusted with property fraudulently converts it—that is, keeps it for his or her own use or the use of others. It can be distinguished from fraud on the basis of when the criminal intent was formed. Most U.S. courts require that a serious breach of trust must have occurred before a person can be convicted of embezzlement. The mere act of moving property without the owner's consent, or damaging it or using it, is not considered embezzlement. However, using it up, selling it, pledging it, giving it away, or holding it against the owner's will is considered to be embezzlement.[55]

Although it is impossible to know how many embezzlement incidents occur annually, the FBI found that only 19,000 people were arrested for embezzlement in 2000—probably an extremely small percentage of all embezzlers. However, the number of people arrested for embezzlement has increased more than 40 percent since 1991, indicating that either (1) more employees are willing to steal from their employers, (2) more employers are willing to report instances of embezzlement, or (3) law enforcement officials are more willing to prosecute embezzlers.

■ Burglary

In common law, the crime of burglary is defined as "the breaking and entering of a dwelling house of another in the nighttime with the intent to commit a felony within."[56] Burglary is considered a much more serious crime than larceny/theft because it often involves entering another's home, a situation in which the threat of harm to occupants is great. Even though the home may be unoccupied at the time of the burglary, the potential for harm to the occupants is so significant that most state jurisdictions punish burglary as a felony. The legal definition of burglary has undergone considerable change since its common-law origins. When first created by English judges during the late Middle Ages, laws against burglary were designed to protect people whose homes might be set upon by wandering criminals. Including the phrase "breaking and entering" in the definition protected people from unwarranted intrusions; if an invited guest stole something, it would not be considered a burglary. Similarly, the requirement that the crime be committed at nighttime was added because evening was considered the time when honest people might fall prey to criminals.[57]

In more recent times, state jurisdictions have changed the legal requirements of burglary, and most have discarded the necessity of forced entry. Many now protect all structures, not just dwelling houses. A majority of states have removed the nighttime element from burglary definitions as well. It is quite common for states to enact laws creating different degrees of burglary. In this instance, the more serious and heavily punished crimes involve a nighttime forced entry into the home; the least serious involve a daytime entry into a nonresidential structure by an unarmed offender. Several gradations of the offense may be found between these extremes.

The Nature and Extent of Burglary

The FBI's definition of burglary is not restricted to burglary from a person's home; it includes any unlawful entry of a structure to commit theft or felony. Burglary is further categorized into three subclasses: forcible entry, unlawful entry where no force is used, and attempted forcible entry.

According to the UCR, about 2 million burglaries occurred in 2000. The burglary rate has dropped by more than 23 percent since 1996 and is 41 percent below the 1991 rate. As Figure 12.3 shows, both residential and commercial burglaries have undergone steep declines; crimes committed at night have undergone a steeper decline than daytime events. Overall, the average loss for a burglary was about $1,400 per victim, for a total of about $3 billion.[58]

The NCVS reports that about 3.4 million residential burglaries occurred in 2000. The difference between the UCR and NCVS statistics is explained by the fact that little more than half of all burglary victims report the incident to police. However, similar to the UCR, the NCVS indicates that the number of burglaries has been in decline, dropping from 5.8 million in 1992. According to the NCVS, those most likely to be burglarized are relatively poor Hispanic and African American families (annual income under $7,500). Owner-occupied and single-family residences had lower burglary rates than renter-occupied and multiple dwellings.

Residential Burglary

Some burglars are crude thieves who will smash a window and enter a vacant home or structure with minimal preparation; others plan out a strategy. For example, experienced burglars learn to avoid areas of the city in which most residents are renters and not home owners, reasoning that renters are less likely to be suitable targets than are more affluent home owners.[59] Because it involves planning, risk, and skill, burglary has been a crime long associated with professional thieves who carefully learn their "craft." For example, Francis Hoheimer, an experienced professional burglar, has described how he learned the "craft of burglary" from a fellow inmate, Oklahoma Smith, when the two were serving time in the Illinois State Penitentiary. Among Smith's recommendations are these:

Figure 12.3   Burglary Types: Change in
Frequency 1996 to 2000

Residential Burglary

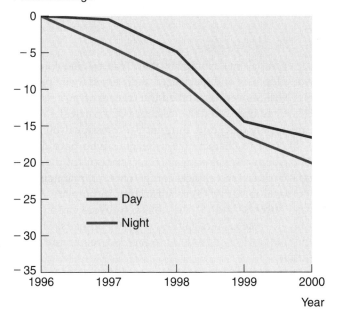

Nonresidential Burglary

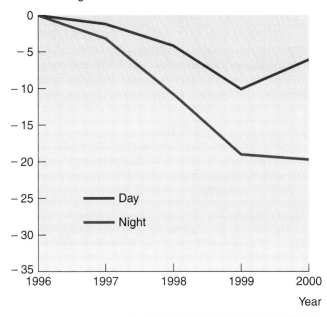

SOURCE: FBI, Uniform Crime Report, 2000, p. 44.

Never wear deodorant or shaving lotion; the strange scent might wake someone up. The more people there are in a house, the safer you are. If someone hears you moving around, they will think it's someone else.... If they call, answer in a muffled sleepy voice.... Never be afraid of dogs, they can sense fear. Most dogs are friendly, snap your finger, they come right to you.[60]

Despite his elaborate preparations, Hoheimer spent many years in confinement.

Burglars must "master" the skills of their "trade," learning to spot environmental cues "nonprofessionals" fail to notice.[61] For example, they must learn which targets contain valuables worth stealing and which are most likely to prove to be a dry hole. Research shows that burglary rates for student-occupied apartments is actually much lower than the rate for other residences in the same neighborhoods; burglars appear to have learned which apartments to avoid.[62]

In an important book titled *Burglars on the Job,* Richard Wright and Scott Decker describe the working conditions of active burglars.[63] Most are motivated by the need for cash in order to get high; they want to enjoy the good life, "keeping the party going" without having to work. As Figure 12.4 shows, they approach their "job" in a rational workmanlike fashion, but their lives are controlled by their culture and environment. Unskilled and uneducated, urban burglars make the choices they do because there are few conventional opportunities for success.

CONNECTIONS

According to the rational choice approach discussed in Chapter 5, burglars make rational and calculating decisions before committing crimes. If circumstances and culture dictate their activities, their decisions must be considered a matter of choice. ■

Commercial Burglary

Some burglars prefer to victimize commercial property rather than private homes. Of all business establishments, retail stores are their favorite targets. They display merchandise so that burglars know exactly what to look for, where it can be found, and because the prices are displayed, how much they can hope to gain in resale to a fence. Burglars can legitimately enter a retail store during business hours and gain knowledge about what the store contains and where it is stored; they can also check for security alarms and devices. Commercial burglars perceive retail establishments as quick sources of merchandise that can be easily sold.

Other commercial establishments such as service centers, warehouses, and factories are less attractive targets because it is more difficult to gain legitimate access to plan the theft. The burglar must use a great deal of guile to

Figure 12.4 Burglars on the Job

According to active burglars:

- Targets are often acquaintances.

- Drug dealers are favored targets because they tend to have a lot of cash and drugs, and victims aren't going to call police!

- Tipsters help them select attractive targets.

- Some stake out residences to learn occupants' routine.

- Many approach a target masquerading as workmen such as carpenters or house painters.

- Most avoid occupied residences, considering them high-risk targets.

- Most are not deterred by alarms and elaborate locks; in fact, these devices tell them there is something inside worth stealing.

- Some call occupants from a pay phone, and if the phone is still ringing when they arrive, they know no one is home.

- Once entering a residence, anxiety turns to calm as they first turn to the master bedroom for money and drugs. They also search kitchens believing that some people keep money in the mayonnaise jar!

- Most work in groups, one serving as a lookout while the other(s) ransacks the place.

- Some dispose of goods through a professional fence; others try to pawn the goods. Some exchange goods for drugs; some sell them to friends and relatives; and a few keep the stolen items for themselves, especially guns and jewelry.

SOURCE: Richard Wright and Scott Decker, *Burglars on the Job: Streetlife and Residential Break-Ins* (Boston, Mass: Northeastern University Press, 1994).

scope out these places, perhaps posing as a delivery person. In addition, the merchandise is more likely to be used, and it may be more difficult to fence at a premium price.

If burglars choose to attack factories, warehouses, or service centers, the most vulnerable properties are those located far from major thoroughfares and away from pedestrian traffic. Establishments located within three blocks of heavily traveled thoroughfares have been found to be less vulnerable to burglary than those located farther away; commercial establishments in wealthier communities have a higher probability of burglary.[64]

Though alarms have been found to be an effective deterrent to burglary, they are less effective in isolated areas because it takes police longer to respond than on more heavily patrolled thoroughfares and an alarm is less likely

to be heard by a pedestrian who would be able to call for help. Even in the most remote areas, however, burglars are wary of alarms and try to choose targets without elaborate or effective security systems. One study found that the probability of burglary of nonalarmed properties is 4.57 times higher than that of similar property with alarms.[65]

Careers in Burglary

Some criminals make burglary their "career" and continually develop new and specialized skills to aid their "profession." Neal Shover has studied the careers of professional burglars and uncovered the existence of a particularly successful type—the **good burglar**.[66] Professional burglars use this title to characterize colleagues who have distinguished themselves as burglars. Characteristics of the good burglar include (1) technical competence, (2) maintenance of personal integrity, (3) specialization in burglary, (4) financial success, and (5) the ability to avoid prison sentences. To receive recognition as good burglars, Shover found that novices must develop four key requirements of the trade.

First, they must learn the many skills needed to commit lucrative burglaries. This process may include learning techniques such as how to gain entry into homes and apartment houses; how to select targets with high potential payoffs; how to choose items with a high resale value; how to open safes properly, without damaging their contents; and how to use the proper equipment, including cutting torches, electric saws, explosives, and metal bars.

Second, the good burglar must be able to team up to form a criminal gang. Choosing trustworthy companions is essential if the obstacles to completing a successful job—police, alarms, and secure safes—are to be overcome.

Third, the good burglar must have inside information. Without knowledge of what awaits them inside, burglars can spend a tremendous amount of time and effort on empty safes and jewelry boxes.

Finally, the good burglar must cultivate fences or buyers for stolen wares. Once the burglar gains access to people who buy and sell stolen goods, he or she must also learn how to successfully sell these goods for a reasonable profit.

Evidence of these skills was discovered in a recent study of more than 200 career burglars in Australia. Burglars reported that they had developed a number of relatively safe methods for disposing of their loot. Some traded stolen goods directly for drugs; others used fences, legitimate businesses, pawnbrokers, and secondhand dealers as trading partners. Surprisingly, many sold their illegal gains to family or friends. Burglars report that disposing of stolen goods was actually low risk and more efficient than expected. One reason was that in many cases fences and shady businesspeople put in a request for particular items and the readymade market allowed the stolen merchandise to be disposed of quickly, often in less than one hour. Though

AP/Wide World Photos

■ Armed burglars present a very real threat to police officers trying to make an arrest. Here, police officers follow a police dog up stairs at a house in Augusta, Michigan, as they investigate the scene where an officer was wounded and a suspect killed during a burglary investigation. The suspect, James Gregory Douglas, 20, died at the scene, and Detective Larry Napp, 49, a 28-year police veteran, was shot three times.

the typical markdown was 67 to 75 percent of the price of the goods, most reported that they could still earn a good living, averaging AUS$2,000 per week (about $1,000 in U.S. dollars). Those who benefited most from these transactions were the receivers of stolen property, who make considerable profits and are unlikely to be caught.[67]

CONNECTIONS

Shover finds that the process of becoming a professional burglar is similar to the process described in Sutherland's theory of differential association. You can read more about this theory in Chapter 8. ■

According to Shover, a person becomes a good burglar by learning the techniques of the trade from older, more experienced burglars. During this process, the older burglar teaches the novice how to handle such requirements of the trade as dealing with defense attorneys, bail bond agents, and other agents of the justice system. Apprentices must be known to have the appropriate character before they are taken under the wing of the "old pro." Usually, the opportunity to learn burglary comes as a reward for being a highly respected juvenile gang member; from knowing someone in the neighborhood who has made a living at burglary; or, more often, from having built a reputation for being solid while serving time in prison. Consequently, the opportunity to become a good burglar is not open to everyone.

The burglary "career ladder" Paul Cromwell, James Olson, and D'Aunn Wester Avary interviewed 30 active bur-

glars in Texas and found that burglars go through stages of career development. They begin as young *novices* who learn the trade from older more experienced burglars, frequently siblings or relatives. Novices will continue to get this tutoring as long as they can develop their own markets (fences) for stolen goods. After their education is over, novices enter the *journeyman* stage, characterized by forays in search of lucrative targets and careful planning. At this point, they develop reputations as experienced reliable criminals. Finally, they become *professional* burglars when they have developed advanced skills and organizational abilities that give them the highest esteem among their peers.

The Texas burglars also displayed evidence of rational decision making. Most seemed to carefully evaluate potential costs and benefits before deciding to commit crime. There is evidence that burglars follow this pattern in their choice of burglary sites. Burglars show a preference for corner houses because they are easily observed and offer the maximum number of escape routes.[68] They look for houses that show evidence of long-term care and wealth. Though people may erect fences and other barriers to deter burglars, these devices may actually attract crime because they are viewed as protecting something worth stealing: If there is nothing valuable inside, why go through so much trouble to secure the premises?[69]

Cromwell, Olson, and Avary also found that many burglars had serious drug habits and that their criminal activity was, in part, aimed at supporting their substance abuse.

Repeat burglary To what extent do burglars strike the same victim more than once? Research suggests that burglars may in fact return to the "scene of the crime" to repeat their offenses. One reason is that many burgled items are indispensable (for example, televisions and VCRs); therefore, it is safe to assume that they will quickly be replaced.[70] Research shows that some burglars repeat their acts to steal these replacement goods.[71] Graham Farrell, Coretta Phillips, and Ken Pease have articulated why burglars would most likely try to hit the same target more than once:

- It takes less effort to burgle a home or apartment known to be a suitable target than an unknown or unsuitable one.

- The burglar is already aware of the target's layout.

- The ease of entry of the target has probably not changed, and escape routes are known.

- The lack of protective measures and the absence of nosy and intrusive neighbors that made the first burglary a success has probably not changed.

- Goods have been observed that could not be taken out the first time.[72]

CONNECTIONS

In Chapter 4, repeat victimization was discussed. As you may recall, it is common for particular people and places to be the targets of numerous predatory crimes. ■

■ Arson

Arson is the willful and malicious burning of a home, public building, vehicle, or commercial building. Arson is a young man's crime. FBI statistics for 2000 show that juveniles accounted for 46 percent of arson arrests; juveniles are arrested for a greater share of this crime than any other.

There are several motives for arson. Adult arsonists may be motivated by severe emotional turmoil. Some psychologists view fire starting as a function of a disturbed personality. Arson, therefore, should be viewed as a mental health problem and not a criminal act.[73] It is alleged that arsonists often experience sexual pleasure from starting fires and then observing their destructive effects. Although some arsonists may be aroused sexually by their activities, there is little evidence that most arsonists are psychosexually motivated.[74] It is equally likely that fires are started by angry people looking for revenge against property owners or by teenagers out to vandalize property.

The Bureau of Alcohol, Tobacco, and Firearms is the federal agency that has jurisdiction over violations of the federal law involving arson. You may go to their home page at:
http://www.atf.treas.gov/
For an up-to-date list of Web links, go to
http://info.wadsworth.com/siegel ■

Juveniles, the most prolific fire starters, may get involved in arson for a variety of reasons as they mature. Juvenile fire setting has long been associated with conduct problems, such as disobedience and aggressiveness, anger, hostility, and resentment over parental rejection. Juvenile fire starting is the topic of the Criminological Enterprise feature.

Other arsons are set by "professional" arsonists who engage in **arson for profit.** People looking to collect insurance money, but who are afraid or unable to set the fire themselves, hire professional arsonists. These professionals have acquired the skills to set fires yet make the cause seem accidental (for example, like an electrical short). Another form is **arson fraud,** which involves a business owner burning his or her property, or hiring someone to do it, to escape financial problems.[75] Over the years, investigators have found that businesspeople are willing to become involved in arson to collect fire insurance or for various other reasons, including but not limited to these:

- Obtaining money during a period of financial crisis

- Getting rid of outdated or slow-moving inventory

- Destroying outmoded machines and technology

- Paying off legal and illegal debt

- Relocating or remodeling a business; for example, when a theme restaurant has not been accepted by customers

- Taking advantage of government funds available for redevelopment

- Applying for government building money, pocketing it without making repairs, and then claiming that fire destroyed the "rehabilitated" building

- Planning bankruptcies to eliminate debts, after the merchandise supposedly destroyed was secretly sold before the fire

- Eliminating business competition by burning out rivals

- Employing extortion schemes that demand that victims pay up or the rest of their holdings will be burned

- Solving labor–management problems; arson may be committed by a disgruntled employee

- Concealing another crime, such as embezzlement

Some recent technological advances may help prove that many alleged arsons were actually accidental fires. There is now evidence of a fire effect called **flashover.** During the course of an ordinary fire, heat and gas at the ceiling of a room can reach 2,000 degrees. This causes clothes and furniture to burst into flame, duplicating the effects of arsonists' gasoline or explosives. It is possible that many suspected arsons are actually the result of flashover.[76]

During the past decade, hundreds of jurisdictions across the nation have established programs to address the growing concern about juvenile fire setting. Housed primarily within the fire service, these programs are designed to identify, evaluate, and treat juvenile fire setters to prevent the recurrence of fire setting behaviors.

What Motivates Juvenile Fire Setters?

What motivates young people to commit arson? According to research by sociologist Wayne Wooden, juvenile arsonists can be classified in one of four categories:

The "Playing with Matches" Fire Setter—This is the youngest fire starter, usually between the ages of 4 and 9, who sets fires because parents are careless with matches and lighters. Proper instruction on fire safety can help prevent fires set by these young children.

The "Crying for Help" Fire Setter—This type of fire setter is a 7 to 13 year old who turns to fire to reduce stress. The source of the stress is family conflict, divorce, death, or abuse. These youngsters have difficulty expressing their feelings of sorrow, rage, or anger and turn to fire as a means of relieving stress or getting back at their antagonists.

The "Delinquent" Fire Setter—Some youth set fires to school property or surrounding areas to retaliate for some slight experienced at school. These kids may break into the school to vandalize property with friends and later set a fire to cover up their activities.

The "Severely Disturbed" Fire Setter—This youngster is obsessed with fires and often dreams about them in "vibrant colors." This is

the most disturbed type of juvenile fire setter and the one most likely to set numerous fires with the potential for death and damage.

Another research effort, by Eileen M. Garry, concluded that juvenile fire setters fall into three general groups. The first is made up of children under 7 years of age. Generally, fires started by these children are the result of accidents or curiosity. In the second group of fire setters are children ranging in age from 8 to 12. Although the fire setting of some of these children is motivated by curiosity or experimentation, a greater proportion of their fire setting represents underlying psychosocial conflicts. The third group comprises adolescents between the ages of 13 and 18. These youth tend to have a long history of undetected fire play and fire starting behavior. Their current fire setting episodes are usually either the result of psychosocial conflict and turmoil or intentional criminal behavior. This behavior is summarized in Table A.

Table A   Fire Setting Groups

	Group 1 Under 7 years	Group 2 8–12 years	Group 3 13–18 years
Reason(s) for fire setting behavior	Accident or curiosity	Curiosity or psychosocial conflict	History of fire starting behavior, or psychosocial conflict, or intentional criminal behavior

Critical Thinking Questions

1. Have you ever been fascinated with fire? Did this ever result in experimenting with matches? If not, what stopped you from acting on your impulses?
2. If you knew of someone who frequently tampered with matches to the point of concern, how would you handle this situation?

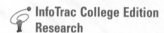

InfoTrac College Edition Research

To read more on the subject of arson, check out this article:

Herschel Prins. Arson: a review of the psychiatric literature. (book reviews) *British Journal of Criminology*, Winter 1996 36 n1 p162–63

SOURCES: Wayne Wooden, "Juvenile Firesetters in Cross-Cultural Perspective: How Should Society Respond?" in *Official Responses to Problem Juveniles: Some International Reflections,* ed. James Hackler (Onati, Spain: Onati Publications, 1991), pp. 339–48; Eileen M. Garry, *Juvenile Firesetting and Arson* (Washington, D.C.: Office of Juvenile Justice and Delinquency Prevention, 1997).

Summary

Economic crimes are designed to financially reward the offender. Opportunistic amateurs commit the majority of economic crimes. However, economic crime has also attracted professional criminals. Professionals earn the bulk of their income from crime, view themselves as criminals, and possess skills that aid them in their law-breaking behaviors. Edwin

Sutherland's classic book, *The Professional Thief,* is perhaps the most famous portrayal of professional crime. According to Sutherland and his informant, Chic Conwell, professionals live by their wits and never resort to violence. A good example of the professional criminal is the fence, who buys and sells stolen merchandise. There are also occasional thieves

whose skill level and commitment fall below the professional level.

Common theft offenses include larceny, embezzlement, fraud, and burglary. These are common-law crime definitions, created by English judges to meet social needs. Larceny involves taking the legal possessions of another. Petty larceny is theft of amounts typically under $100; grand larceny refers to amounts usually over $100. The crime of false pretenses, or fraud, is similar to larceny because it involves the theft of goods or money, but it differs because the criminal tricks victims into voluntarily giving up their possessions. Embezzlement is another larceny crime. It involves people taking something temporarily entrusted to them, such as bank tellers taking money out of the cash drawer and keeping it for themselves. Most states have codified these common-law crimes in their legal codes. New larceny crimes have also been defined to keep abreast of changing social conditions: passing bad checks, stealing or illegally using credit cards, shoplifting, and stealing automobiles.

Burglary, a more serious theft offense, was defined in the common law as the "breaking and entering of a dwelling house of another in the nighttime with the intent to commit a felony within." This definition has also evolved over time. Today, most states have modified their definitions of burglary to include theft from any structure at any time of day. Because burglary involves planning and risk, it attracts professional thieves. The most competent are known as good burglars. Good burglars have technical competence and personal integrity, specialize in burglary, are financially successful, and avoid prison sentences.

Arson is another serious property crime. Though most arsonists are teenage vandals, there are professional arsonists who specialize in burning commercial buildings for profit.

■ Thinking Like a Criminologist

You are approached by the local police chief, who is quite concerned about high burglary rates in some areas of the city. She is a former student of yours and well aware of recent developments in criminological theory. The chief is a strong advocate of rational choice theory and has already instituted a number of programs based on a deterrence/situational crime prevention model of control. The existing police initiatives include these programs:

* The police offer target hardening measures to repeat victims. They install high-tech security equipment in their homes so that the homes can be monitored on a 24-hour basis. The police plan an advertising campaign to alert would-be offenders that they are on watch at prior target residences.

* A new police initiative identifies repeat burglars in the area and provides intervention designed to supply them with legitimate economic opportunities to reduce their criminal motivation.

* A new school-based program designed to reduce criminal motivation seeks to raise young people's awareness of the dangers of burglary and how it can result in a long prison sentence.

* The police have developed a series of environmental improvements in the target area with a view to minimizing burglary opportunities. These include improved visibility, better access control, and lighting in areas that have relatively high burglary rates. They have also instituted high-visibility police patrols in these areas to deter criminals from committing crimes here.

* A "Burglary Control Model House," fitted with low-cost methods of security, such as strengthened door/window frames, bolts, locks, and so on, has been built and will be advertised to encourage residents to help themselves.

The chief has asked you to look over these initiatives and comment on their anticipated effectiveness. She wants to know whether there are any pitfalls and whether you can suggest other policy initiatives that might prove effective in reducing the opportunity to commit burglary and deter potential burglars.

■ Key Terms

- **false pretenses** *(376)*
- **fraud** *(376)*
- **confidence games** *(377)*
- **mark** *(377)*
- **pigeon drop** *(377)*
- **embezzlement** *(377)*
- **good burglar** *(380)*
- **arson for profit** *(382)*
- **arson fraud** *(382)*
- **flashover** *(382)*

▋ Critical Thinking Questions

1. Differentiate between an occasional and a professional criminal. Which one would be more likely to resort to violence? Which one would be more easily deterred?

2. What crime occurs when a person who owns an antique store sells a client an "original" Tiffany lamp that the person knows is a fake? Would it still be a crime if the person selling the lamp was not aware that it was a fake? As an antique dealer, should the seller have a duty to determine the authenticity of the products he or she sells?

3. What are the characteristics of the "good burglar"? Can you compare their career path to any other professionals, such as doctors or lawyers? Which theory of criminal behavior best predicts the development of the good burglar?

4. You have been the victim of repeat burglaries. What could you do to reduce the chances of future victimization? (Hint: buying a gun is not an option!)

▋ Notes

1. Andrew McCall, *The Medieval Underworld* (London: Hamish Hamilton, 1979), p. 86.
2. Ibid., p. 104.
3. J. J. Tobias, *Crime and Police in England, 1700–1900* (London: Gill and Macmillan, 1979).
4. Ibid., p. 9.
5. Marilyn Walsh, *The Fence* (Westport, Conn.: Greenwood Press, 1977), pp. 18–25.
6. John Hepburn, "Occasional Criminals," in *Major Forms of Crime*, ed. Robert Meier (Beverly Hills, Calif.: Sage, 1984), pp. 73–94.
7. James Inciardi, "Professional Crime," in *Major Forms of Crime*, ed. Robert Meier (Beverly Hills, Calif.: Sage, 1984), p. 223.
8. Harry King and William Chambliss, *Box Man: A Professional Thief's Journal* (New York: Harper and Row, 1972), p. 24.
9. Edwin Sutherland, "White-Collar Criminality," *American Sociological Review* 5 (1940): 2–10.
10. Gilbert Geis, "Avocational Crime," in *Handbook of Criminology*, ed. D. Glazer (Chicago: Rand McNally, 1974), p. 284.
11. Edwin Sutherland and Chic Conwell, *The Professional Thief* (Chicago: University of Chicago Press, 1937).
12. Ibid., pp. 197–98.
13. Ibid., p. 212.
14. See, for example, Edwin Lemert, "The Behavior of the Systematic Check Forger," *Social Problems* 6 (1958): 141–48.
15. Cited in Walsh, *The Fence*, p. 1.
16. Carl Klockars, *The Professional Fence* (New York: Free Press, 1976); Darrell Steffensmeier, *The Fence: In the Shadow of Two Worlds* (Totowa, N.J.: Rowman and Littlefield, 1986); Walsh, *The Fence*, pp. 25–28.
17. Walsh, *The Fence*, p. 34.
18. Paul Cromwell, James Olson, and D'Aunn Avary, "Who Buys Stolen Property? A New Look at Criminal Receiving," *Journal of Crime and Justice* 16 (1993): 75–95.
19. This section depends heavily on a classic book, Wayne La Fave and Austin Scott, *Handbook on Criminal Law* (St. Paul: West Publishing, 1972).
20. Ibid., p. 622.
21. FBI, *Crime in the United States, 2000* (Washington, D.C.: U.S. Government Printing Office, 2001), p. 46.
22. Margaret Loftus, "Gone: One TV," *U.S. News & World Report*, 14 July 1997, p. 61.
23. Timothy W. Maier, "Uncle Sam Gets Rolled," *Insight on the News*, 10 March 1997, p. 13.
24. Jill Jordan Siedfer, "To Catch a Thief, Try This: Peddling High-Tech Solutions to Shoplifting," *U.S. News & World Report*, 23 September 1996, p. 71.
25. David Farrington, "Measuring, Explaining and Preventing Shoplifting: A Review of British Research," *Security Journal* 12 (1999): 9–27.
26. Mary Owen Cameron, *The Booster and the Snitch* (New York: Free Press, 1964).
27. Ibid., p. 57.
28. Lawrence Cohen and Rodney Stark, "Discriminatory Labeling and the Five–Finger Discount: An Empirical Analysis of Differential Shoplifting Dispositions," *Journal of Research on Crime and Delinquency* 11 (1974): 25–35.
29. Lloyd Klemke, "Does Apprehension for Shoplifting Amplify or Terminate Shoplifting Activity?" *Law and Society Review* 12 (1978): 390–403.
30. Erhard Blankenburg, "The Selectivity of Legal Sanctions: An Empirical Investigation of Shoplifting," *Law and Society Review* 11 (1976): 109–29.
31. Michael Hindelang, "Decisions of Shoplifting Victims to Invoke the Criminal Justice Process," *Social Problems* 21 (1974): 580–95.
32. George Keckeisen, *Retail Security versus the Shoplifter* (Springfield, Ill.: Charles Thomas, 1993), pp. 31–32.
33. Siedfer, "To Catch a Thief, Try This: Peddling High-Tech Solutions to Shoplifting," p. 71.
34. Edwin Lemert, "An Isolation and Closure Theory of Naive Check Forgery," *Journal of Criminal Law, Criminology and Police Science* 44 (1953): 297–98.
35. Ibid.
36. La Fave and Scott, *Handbook on Criminal Law*, p. 672.
37. Peter Wayner, "Bogus Web Sites Troll for Credit Card Numbers," *New York Times*, 12 February 1997, p. A18.
38. Charles McCaghy, Peggy Giordano, and Trudy Knicely Henson, "Auto Theft," *Criminology* 15 (1977): 367–81.
39. Donald Gibbons, *Society, Crime and Criminal Careers* (Englewood Cliffs, N.J.: Prentice-Hall, 1977), p. 310.
40. Kim Hazelbaker, "Insurance Industry Analyses and the Prevention of Motor

Vehicle Theft," in *Business and Crime Prevention,* eds. Marcus Felson and Ronald Clarke (Monsey, N.Y.: Criminal Justice Press, 1997), pp. 283–93.

41. National Insurance Crime Bureau, "Auto Theft Rises for First Time in 10 Years: NICB Releases Nation's Most Commonly Stolen Vehicles." Press release. (Arlington, Va.: author, December 11, 2001).

42. Hazelbaker, "Insurance Industry Analyses and the Prevention of Motor Vehicle Theft," p. 287.

43. Michael Rand, *Carjacking* (Washington, D.C.: Bureau of Justice Statistics, 1994), p. 1.

44. Patsy Klaus, *Carjackings in the United States, 1992–96* (Washington, D.C.: Bureau of Justice Statistics, 1999).

45. Ronald Clarke and Patricia Harris, "Auto Theft and Its Prevention," in *Crime and Justice, An Annual Review,* eds. N. Morris and M. Tonry (Chicago: Chicago University Press, 1992).

46. Ian Ayres and Steven D. Levitt, "Measuring Positive Externalities from Unobservable Victim Precaution: An Empirical Analysis of Lojack," *Quarterly Journal of Economics* 113 (1998): 43–78.

47. Kim Hazelbaker, "Insurance Industry Analyses and the Prevention of Motor Vehicle Theft," p. 289.

48. La Fave and Scott, *Handbook on Criminal Law,* p. 655.

49. 30 Geo. III, C.24 (1975).

50. Benjamin Weiser, "4-Year Sentence for Mastermind of Scheme to Cheat on Graduate School Tests," *New York Times,* 3 October 1998, p. 8.

51. As described in Charles McCaghy, *Deviant Behavior* (New York: Macmillan, 1976), pp. 230–31.

52. Susan Gembrowski and Tim Dahlberg "Over 100 Here Indicted after Telemarketing Fraud Probe Around the U.S.," *San Diego Daily Transcript* [Online], 8 December 1995. Available at: http://www.sddt.com/files/library/95headlines/DN95_12_08/DN95_12_08_02.html

53. Jerome Hall, *Theft, Law and Society* (Indianapolis: Bobbs-Merrill, 1952), p. 36.

54. La Fave and Scott, *Handbook on Criminal Law,* p. 644.

55. Ibid., p. 649.

56. Ibid., p. 708.

57. E. Blackstone, *Commentaries on the Laws of England* (London: 1769), p. 224.

58. FBI, Uniform Crime Report, 2000, p. 42.

59. Elizabeth Groff and Nancy La Vigne, "Mapping an Opportunity Surface of Residential Burglary," *Journal of Research in Crime and Delinquency* 38 (2001): 257–78.

60. Frank Hoheimer, *The Home Invaders: Confessions of a Cat Burglar* (Chicago: Chicago Review, 1975).

61. Richard Wright, Robert Logie, and Scott Decker, "Criminal Expertise and Offender Decision Making: An Experimental Study of the Target Selection Process in Residential Burglary," *Journal of Research in Crime and Delinquency* 32 (1995): 39–53.

62. Matthew Robinson, "Accessible Targets, But Not Advisable Ones: The Role of 'Accessibility' in Student Apartment Burglary," *Journal of Security Administration* 21 (1998): 28–44.

63. Richard Wright and Scott Decker, *Burglars on the Job: Streetlife and Residential Break-Ins* (Boston, Mass.: Northeastern University Press, 1994).

64. Simon Hakim and Yochanan Shachmurove, "Spatial and Temporal Patterns of Commercial Burglaries," *American Journal of Economics and Sociology* 55 (1996): 443–57.

65. Ibid., pp. 443–56.

66. See, generally, Neal Shover, "Structures and Careers in Burglary," *Journal of Criminal Law, Criminology and Police Science* 63 (1972): 540–49.

67. Richard Stevenson, Lubica Forsythe, and Don Weatherburn, "The Stolen Goods Market in New South Wales, Australia: An Analysis of Disposal Avenues and Tactics," *British Journal of Criminology* 41 (Winter 2001): 101–18.

68. Paul Cromwell, James Olson, and D'Aunn Wester Avary, *Breaking and Entering: An Ethnographic Analysis of Burglary* (Newbury Park, Calif.: Sage, 1991), pp. 48–51.

69. See, M. Taylor and C. Nee, "The Role of Cues in Simulated Residential Burglary: A Preliminary Investigation," *British Journal of Criminology* 28 (1988): 398–401; Julia MacDonald and Robert Gifford, "Territorial Cues and Defensible Space Theory: The Burglar's Point of View," *Journal of Environmental Psychology* 9 (1989): 193–205.

70. Roger Litton, "Crime Prevention and the Insurance Industry," in *Business and Crime Prevention,* eds. Marcus Felson and Ronald Clarke (Monsey, N.Y.: Criminal Justice Press, 1997), pp. 162.

71. "Explaining Repeat Residential Burglaries: An Analysis of Property Stolen," Ronald Clarke, Elizabeth Perkins, and Donald Smith, in *Repeat Victimization,* Crime Prevention Studies, vol. 12, eds. Graham Farrell and Ken Pease (Monsey, N.Y.: Criminal Justice Press, 2001): 119–32.

72. Graham Farrell, Coretta Phillips, and Ken Pease, "Like Taking Candy, Why Does Repeat Victimization Occur?" *British Journal of Criminology* 35 (1995): 384–99, at 391.

73. Nancy Webb, George Sakheim, Luz Towns-Miranda, and Charles Wagner, "Collaborative Treatment of Juvenile Firestarters: Assessment and Outreach," *American Journal of Orthopsychiatry* 60 (1990): 305–10.

74. Vernon Quinsey, Terry Chaplin, and Douglas Unfold, "Arsonists and Sexual Arousal to Fire Setting: Correlations Unsupported," *Journal of Behavior Therapy and Experimental Psychiatry* 20 (1989): 203–9.

75. Leigh Edward Somers, *Economic Crimes* (New York: Clark Boardman, 1984), pp. 158–68.

76. Michael Rogers, "The Fire Next Time," *Newsweek,* 26 November 1990, p. 63.

BANK FRAUD

RICO

Casimir Jackson Flureima Charles

GRAND THEFT

Brown Chevy Fluerinord Grant Clare Dixon

Hernandez Ponce Potter Reid Rivera Smith

CO-CONSPIRATORS

Augustine Brisson Carter Kenol Napoleon Rocourt Wilson

CHAPTER 13 White-Collar and Organized Crime

AP/Wide World Photos

Introduction

For more than a decade the Gold Club in Atlanta was the hottest spot in town, the destination for conventioneers and businessmen looking for a rowdy night on the town filled with good cigars, strong drinks, and nude dancers.[1] It became the home away from home for well-known professional athletes who stopped by to receive sexual favors from the girls who worked at the club. In 2001, the shuttle buses that had regularly traveled from the club to the city's best hotels were halted when the federal government filed charges claiming that the Gold Club manager, Steven Kaplan, was in cahoots with the Gambino organized-crime family of New York. The Gambinos provided protection in exchange for money skimmed from overcharged and/or double-billed credit cards of unsuspecting customers. The club owners were also charged with ordering women in their employ to provide sexual services to professional athletes and celebrities to encourage their presence at the club. The government claimed that several dancers were sent to Charleston, South Carolina, in the spring of 1997 to perform a "lesbian sex show" and have sex with members of a professional basketball team. The government won its case when Mr. Kaplan pleaded guilty and received a three- to five-year prison sentence and a $5 million fine. Ironically, as part of the deal, the federal government took over the Gold Club, making it the manager of one of the largest strip clubs in the nation!

An ongoing scheme such as the one Kaplan and his associates were charged with takes an enormous amount of planning. Such crimes involve efforts to bend the rules of enterprise and commerce to make a profit or gain an illegal advantage over competitors. Although running a "gentlemen's club" in itself is not a crime, fraudulently billing customers and sending the profits to an organized crime family violates the rules of doing business. However, as long as there are profits to be made, people seem willing to risk violating the law to gain a competitive edge and reap undeserved gains. At the time of his conviction, Steven Kaplan had an estimated net worth of $50 million!

In this chapter we divide these crimes of illicit entrepreneurship into two distinct categories: white-collar crime and organized crime. **White-collar crime** involves illegal activities of people and institutions whose acknowledged purpose is profit through legitimate business transactions. The second category, **organized crime,** involves illegal activities of people and organizations whose acknowledged purpose is profit through illegitimate business enterprise.

Organized crime and white-collar crime are linked together here because commercial enterprise, not crime, is the governing characteristic of both phenomena. As the Gold Club case shows, the distinction between white-collar and organized crime is often blurred: white-collar criminals may partner up with organized crime figures; organized crime figures may use their criminal connections to commit white-collar crimes.[2] Both of these organizational crimes taint and corrupt the free market system;

■ Gold Club owner Steve Kaplan leaves federal court in Atlanta, August 2, 2001. Kaplan was accused of cheating customers and paying dancers to have sex with celebrities. He pleaded guilty to one count of racketeering and agreed to a three- to five-year prison sentence and a $5 million fine.

they involve all phases of illegal entrepreneurial activity. Organized crime involves individuals or groups whose marketing techniques (threat, extortion, and smuggling) and product lines (drugs, sex, gambling, and loan-sharking) have been outlawed. White-collar crimes include the use of illegal business practices (embezzlement, price-fixing, bribery, and so on) to merchandise what are ordinarily legitimate commercial products.[3]

Surprisingly to some, both forms of crime can involve violence. Although the use of force and coercion by organized crime members has been popularized in the media and therefore comes as no shock, that white-collar crimes may inflict pain and suffering seems more astonishing. Yet experts claim that more than 200,000 occupational deaths occur each year and that "corporate violence" annually kills and injures more people than all street crimes combined.[4]

It is also possible to link organized and white-collar crime because some criminal enterprises involve both forms of activity. Organized criminals may seek legitimate enterprises to launder money, diversify their source of income, increase their power and influence, and gain and enhance respectability.[5] Otherwise legitimate businesspeople may turn to organized criminals to help them with economic problems (such as breaking up a strike or dumping

AP/Wide World Photos

hazardous waste products), stifle or threaten competition, and increase their influence. The distinction between organized crime and white-collar criminals is often blurred.[6]

Some forms of white-collar crime may be more like organized crime than others.[7] Whereas some corporate executives cheat to improve their company's position in the business world, others are motivated purely for personal gain. It is this latter group, people who engage in ongoing criminal conspiracies for their own profit, that most resembles organized crime.[8]

■ White-Collar Crime

In the late 1930s, the distinguished criminologist Edwin Sutherland first used the phrase "white-collar crime" to describe the criminal activities of the rich and powerful. He defined white-collar crime as "a crime committed by a person of respectability and high social status in the course of his occupation."[9] As Sutherland saw it, white-collar crime involved conspiracies by members of the wealthy classes to use their position in commerce and industry for personal gain without regard to the law. Often these actions were handled by civil courts because injured parties were more concerned with recovering their losses than with seeing the offenders punished criminally. Consequently, Sutherland believed that the great majority of white-collar criminals did not become the subject of criminological study. Yet the cost of white-collar crime is probably several times greater than all the crimes customarily regarded as the "crime problem." And, in contrast to street crimes, white-collar offenses breed distrust in economic and social institutions, lower public morale, and undermine faith in business and government.[10]

Redefining White-Collar Crime

Although Sutherland's work is considered a milestone in criminological history, his focus was on corporate criminality, including the crimes of the rich and powerful. Contemporary definitions of white-collar crime are typically much broader and include both middle-income Americans and corporate titans who use the marketplace for their criminal activity.[11] Included within recent views of white-collar crime are such acts as income tax evasion, credit card fraud, and bankruptcy fraud. Other white-collar criminals use their positions of trust in business or government to commit crimes. Their activities might include pilfering, soliciting bribes or kickbacks, and embezzlement. Some white-collar criminals set up business for the sole purpose of victimizing the general public. They engage in land swindles (for example, representing swamps as choice building sites), securities theft, medical fraud, and so on.

In addition to acting as individuals, some white-collar criminals become involved in criminal conspiracies designed to improve the market share or profitability of their corporations. This type of white-collar crime, which includes antitrust violations, price-fixing, and false advertising, is known as **corporate crime.**[12]

The White-Collar Crime Problem

It is difficult to estimate the extent and influence of white-collar crime on victims because all too often those who suffer the consequences of white-collar crime are ignored by victimologists.[13] Some experts place its total monetary value in the hundreds of billions of dollars, far outstripping the expense of any other type of crime. For example, the loss due to employee theft from businesses alone amounts to $90 billion per year.[14] Beyond their monetary cost, white-collar crimes often damage property and kill people. Violations of safety standards, pollution of the environment, and industrial accidents due to negligence can be classified as corporate violence. It is possible that corporate crime annually results in 20 million serious injuries, including 110,000 people who become permanently disabled and 30,000 deaths.[15] White-collar crime also destroys confidence, saps the integrity of commercial life, and has the potential for devastating destruction. Think of the possible results if nuclear regulatory rules are flouted or if toxic wastes are dumped into a community's drinking water supply.[16]

■ Components of White-Collar Crime

White-collar crimes today represent a range of behaviors involving individuals acting alone and within the context of a business structure. The victims of white-collar crime can be the general public, the organization that employs the offender, or a competing organization. Numerous attempts have been made to create subcategories or typologies of white-collar criminality.[17] This text adapts a typology created by criminologist Mark Moore to organize the analysis of white-collar crime.[18] Moore's typology contains seven elements, ranging from an individual using a business enterprise to commit theft-related crimes, to an individual using his or her place within a business enterprise for illegal gain, to business enterprises collectively engaging in illegitimate activity. Because no single typology may sufficiently encompass the complex array of acts that the term usually denotes, Moore's typology has been expanded to include newly emerging high-tech crimes such as Internet fraud.[19]

Stings and Swindles

The first category of white-collar crime involves stealing through deception by individuals who use their institutional or business position to bilk people out of their money. Offenses in this category range from fraud involving the door-to-door sale of faulty merchandise to passing millions of dollars in counterfeit stock certificates to an established brokerage firm. If caught, white-collar swindlers are usually charged with common-law crimes such as embezzlement or fraud.

The collapse of the Bank of Credit and Commerce International (BCCI) was one swindle that cost depositors billions of dollars. BCCI was the world's seventh largest private bank, with assets of about $23 billion. Investigators believe bank officials made billions of dollars in loans to confederates who had no intention of repaying them; BCCI officers also used false accounting methods to defraud depositors. Its officers helped clients, such as Colombian drug cartel leaders and dictators Saddam Hussein and Ferdinand Marcos, launder money, finance terrorist organizations, and smuggle illegal arms. BCCI officers aided drug dealers and helped launder drug money so that it could be shifted to legitimate banks.[20] After the bank was closed, hundreds of millions of dollars were spent to pay auditors to liquidate the bank's holdings.[21] Despite the notoriety of the BCCI case, investors continue to bite at bogus investment schemes promising quick riches.

To read more about the infamous case of the Bank of Credit and Commerce International, go to:
http://www.apfn.org/apfn/BCCI.htm
For an up-to-date list of Web links, go to
http://info.wadsworth.com/siegel ■

Religious swindles   In 1998, 2,100 devout Christians gave Jonathan Strawder and his Sovereign Ministries International between $11 million and $14 million after he promised them not only that they would get huge returns on their investments but also that with the profits churches would be built in Kenya and Poland, poor students would have their education paid for, and other Christian ministries would get donations. When Strawder was arrested in Florida, legal authorities found that his fund-raising was a swindle and that he used the money for fancy cars, a yacht, and two apartment buildings in Chicago; most of the money has not yet been recovered.[22]

It is estimated that fake religious organizations bilk thousands of people out of $100 million per year.[23] Swindlers take in worshippers of all persuasions: Jews, Baptists, Lutherans, Catholics, Mormons, and Greek Orthodox have all fallen prey to religious swindles. How do religious swindlers operate? Many join close-knit churches and establish a position of trust that enables them to operate without the normal investor skepticism. Some use religious television and radio shows to sell their products. Others place verses from the scriptures on their promotional literature to comfort hesitant investors.

Chiseling

Chiseling, the second category of white-collar crime, involves regularly cheating an organization, its consumers, or both. Chiselers may be individuals looking to make quick profits in their own businesses or employees of large organizations who decide to cheat on obligations to their own company or its clients by doing something contrary to either the law or company policy. Chiseling can involve charging for bogus auto repairs, cheating customers on home repairs, or short-weighting (intentionally tampering with the accuracy of scales used to weigh products) in supermarkets or dairies. In one scheme, some New York City cab drivers routinely tapped the dashboards of their cabs with pens loaded with powerful magnets to "zap" their meters and jack up the fares.[24] Chiseling may even involve illegal use of information about company policies that have not been disclosed to the public. The secret information can be sold to speculators or used to make money in the stock market. Use of the information violates the obligation to keep company policy secret.

Professional chiseling   It is not uncommon for professionals to use their positions to chisel clients. Pharmacists have been known to alter prescriptions or substitute low-cost generic drugs for more expensive name brands.[25] In one case that made national headlines in 2001, Kansas City pharmacist Robert R. Courtney was charged with fraud when it was discovered that he had been selling diluted mixtures of the cancer medications Taxol, Gemzar, Paraplatin, and Platinol, which are used to treat a variety of illnesses including pancreatic and lung cancer, advanced ovarian and breast cancer, and AIDS-related Kaposi's sarcoma. In one alleged instance, Mr. Courtney provided a doctor with only 450 milligrams of Gemzar for a prescription that called for 1,900 mg, a transaction that netted him a profit of $779.[26] His actions put many patients at risk because they had been taking improper doses of medication. In another 2001 case, 172 people in New Jersey—including a medical doctor, a lawyer, and two chiropractors—were charged with staging 19 automobile accidents and filing false medical claims totaling more than $5 million. They recruited participants who were paid up to $2,500 to claim they were injured in an accident. The ringleaders coached them about the types of injuries to fake. The medical professionals would then file claims with the drivers' insurance companies for services never rendered.[27]

Securities fraud   A great deal of chiseling takes place on the commodity and stock markets, where individuals engage in deceptive practices that are prohibited by federal law. Some brokers will use their positions to cheat individual clients: for example, by **churning** the client's account by repeated, excessive, and unnecessary buying and selling of stock.[28] Other broker fraud includes **front running,** in which brokers place personal orders ahead of a large customer's order to profit from the market effects of the trade; and **bucketing,** which is skimming customer trading profits by falsifying trade information.[29] Some stock frauds involve conspiracies by financial organizations to cheat their clients. In one 1998 case, employees of Mon-

AP/Wide World Photos

■ Kansas City pharmacist Robert R. Courtney was charged with fraud after it was discovered that he had been selling diluted mixtures of the cancer medications Taxol, Gemzar, Paraplatin, and Platinol. These drugs are used to treat a variety of illnesses including pancreatic and lung cancer, advanced ovarian and breast cancer, and AIDS-related Kaposi's sarcoma. A plea bargain helped Courtney avoid a life sentence, but he will spend about 30 years in prison.

roe Parker Securities Inc., a Westchester County, New York, securities firm, were accused of using high-pressure telephone sales tactics to defraud 8,000 investors nationwide of $100 million. In the scheme, brokers at Monroe Parker would persuade a client to open an account by offering blue-chip stocks like IBM as the bait. Once a person agreed to open an account, the broker would push stocks in companies in which Monroe Parker owned a majority of shares. The traders pressured clients into buying the "house stocks" at artificially inflated prices. If an investor insisted on selling the house stock, the broker would turn the account over to a colleague, who would start the hard sell all over again.[30]

The Monroe Parker case is highly reminiscent of the plot of the 2000 film *Boiler Room,* which tells the story of aggressive young brokers who skirt the law to make millions. Visit their Web site at:

http://www.boilermovie.com/
For an up-to-date list of Web links, go to
http://info.wadsworth.com/siegel ■

Securities chiseling can also involve using one's position of trust to profit from inside business information, referred to as **insider trading.** The information can then be used to buy and sell securities, giving the trader an unfair advantage over the general public, which lacks this inside information.

Insider trading violations can occur in a variety of situations. As originally conceived, it was illegal for corporate employees with direct knowledge of market-sensitive information to use that information for their own benefit—for example, by buying stock in a company that they learn will be taken over by the larger concern for which they work. In recent years, the definition of insider trading has been expanded by federal courts to include employees of financial institutions, such as law or banking firms, who misappropriate confidential information on pending corporate actions to purchase stock or give the information to a third party so that party may buy shares in the company. Courts have ruled that such actions are deceptive and violate security trading codes.[31]

To read the most up-to-date review of securities fraud law and practice, use InfoTrac College Edition to find this article: Julia K. Cronin, Amanda R. Evansburg, and Sylvia Rae Garfinkle-Huff. Securities fraud (16th annual survey of white collar crime). *American Criminal Law Review* Summer 2001 v38 i3 p1277 ■

Individual Exploitation of Institutional Position

Another type of white-collar crime involves individuals' exploiting their power or position in organizations to take advantage of other individuals who have an interest in how that power is used. For example, a fire inspector who demands that the owner of a restaurant pay him to be granted an operating license is abusing his institutional position. In most cases, this type of offense occurs when the victim has a clear right to expect a service and the offender threatens to withhold the service unless an additional payment or bribe is forthcoming.

On the local and state levels, scandals commonly emerge in which liquor license board members, food inspectors, and fire inspectors are named as exploiters. A striking example of exploitation made national headlines on October 6, 1998, when San Francisco 49ers co-owner Eddie DeBartolo Jr. pleaded guilty to concealing an extortion plot by the former governor of Louisiana, Edwin Edwards. According to the authorities, Edwards demanded payments of $400,000 or he would use his influence to prevent DeBartolo from obtaining a license for a riverboat gambling casino.[32] Here a former politician is alleged to have used his still-considerable political clout to demand payment from a businessman desiring to engage in a legitimate business enterprise.

Exploitation can also occur in private industry. Purchasing agents in large companies often demand a piece of the action for awarding contracts to suppliers and distributors. Managing agents in some of New York City's most luxurious buildings have been convicted on charges that they routinely extorted millions of dollars from maintenance contractors and building suppliers. Building managers have been charged with steering repair and maintenance work to particular contractors in exchange for kickbacks totaling millions of dollars.[33]

In some foreign countries, soliciting bribes to do business is a common, even an expected, practice. Not surprisingly, U.S. businesses have complained that stiff penalties for bribery give foreign competitors an edge over them. In European countries, such as Italy and France, giving bribes to secure contracts was until recently legal; and in the former West Germany, corporate bribes were actually tax-deductible.[34] Some government officials solicited bribes to allow American firms to do business in their countries.[35]

Influence Peddling and Bribery

Sometimes individuals holding important institutional positions sell power, influence, and information to outsiders who have an interest in influencing or predicting the activities of the institution. Offenses within this category include government employees' taking kickbacks from contractors in return for awarding them contracts they could not have won on merit, or outsiders' bribing government officials, such as those in the Securities and Exchange Commission, who might sell information about future government activities. Political leaders have been convicted of accepting bribes to rig elections that enable their party to control state politics.[36]

One major difference distinguishes **influence peddling** from the previously discussed exploitation of an institutional position. **Exploitation** involves forcing victims to pay for services to which they have a clear right. In contrast, influence peddlers and bribe takers use their institutional positions to grant favors and sell information to which their coconspirators are not entitled. In sum, in crimes of institutional exploitation, the victim is the person forced to pay, whereas the victim of influence peddling is the organization compromised by its employees for their own interests.

Influence peddling in government   In the mid-1980s officials at the Department of Housing and Urban Development (HUD) were involved in a scheme to defraud the government of somewhere between $4 billion and $8 billion. Officials used their power to dispense huge grants to well-connected political figures. Several officials who left the department received huge consulting fees from former associates who still worked for the department. A number of officials were later convicted of taking bribes and defrauding the government, including one woman who siphoned off $5 million from the sale of repossessed homes, the largest individual theft of U.S. government funds in history. Her feat earned her the name "Robin HUD" because she claimed that she gave much of the money to charity; the judge gave her four years in prison.[37]

Federal officials are not the only ones to be accused of influence peddling. It has become all too common for legislators and other state officials to be forced to resign or even to be jailed for accepting bribes to use their influence. Two West Virginia governors have been jailed on bribery charges since 1960. The Louisiana state insurance commissioner was convicted in 1991 of money laundering, conspiracy, and fraud connected to the collapse of the Champion Insurance Company, which cost policyholders $185 million; the commissioner took $2 million in bribes in return for regulatory favors.[38] And foreign businessmen and officials have also been implicated in corruption. For example, in Italy, the former chairperson of the Montedison agricultural chemical firm admitted making illegal payments to political leaders to secure contracts.[39]

Agents of the criminal justice system have also gotten caught up in official corruption, a circumstance that is particularly disturbing because society expects a higher standard of moral integrity from people empowered to uphold the law and judge their fellow citizens. Police officers have been particularly vulnerable to charges of corruption. Thirty years ago, the Knapp Commission found that police corruption in New York City was pervasive and widespread, ranging from patrol officers' accepting small gratuities from local businesspeople to senior officers receiving payoffs in the thousands of dollars from gamblers and narcotics violators.[40] Despite years of effort to eradicate police corruption, instances still abound. For example, in 1998 more than 20 officers were alleged to have been patrons of prostitutes working at 335 West 39th Street and a nearby massage parlor; some officers were filmed demanding sex.[41]

Influence peddling in business Politicians and government officials are not the only ones accused of bribery; business has had its share of scandals. The 1970s witnessed revelations that multinational corporations regularly made payoffs to foreign officials and businesspeople to secure business contracts. Gulf Oil executives admitted paying $4 million to the South Korean ruling party; Burroughs Corporation admitted paying $1.5 million to foreign officials; and Lockheed Aircraft admitted paying $202 million. McDonnell-Douglas Aircraft Corporation was indicted for paying $1 million in bribes to officials of Pakistani International Airlines to secure orders.[42]

In response to these revelations, in 1977 Congress passed the Foreign Corrupt Practices Act (FCPA), which makes it a criminal offense to bribe foreign officials or to make other questionable overseas payments. Violations of the FCPA draw strict penalties for both the defendant company and its officers.[43] Moreover, all fines imposed on corporate officers are paid by them, not absorbed by the company. For example, for violating the antibribery provisions of the FCPA, a domestic corporation can be fined up to $1 million. Company officers, employees, or stockholders who are convicted of bribery may have to serve a prison sentence of up to five years and pay a $10,000 fine. Congressional dissatisfaction with the harshness and ambiguity of the bill has caused numerous revisions to be proposed. Despite the penalties imposed by the FCPA, corporations that deal in foreign trade have continued to give bribes to secure favorable trade agreements.[44] In 1995, for example, several former executives of the Lockheed Aircraft Corporation pleaded guilty to bribery in the sale of transport aircraft to the Egyptian government.[45]

To find out more about the FCPA and read its provisions, go to its Web site at:
    http://www.usdoj.gov/criminal/fraud/fcpa.html
For an up-to-date list of Web links, go to
    http://info.wadsworth.com/siegel ■

Embezzlement and Employee Fraud

The fifth type of white-collar crime involves individuals' use of their positions to embezzle company funds or appropriate company property for themselves. Here the company or organization that employs the criminal, rather than an outsider, is the victim of white-collar crime.

Blue-collar fraud Employee theft can reach all levels of the organizational structure. Blue-collar employees have

been involved in systematic theft of company property, commonly called **pilferage.**[46]

About 35 percent of employees report involvement in pilferage.[47] Employee theft is most accurately explained by factors relevant to the work setting, such as job dissatisfaction and the workers' belief that they are being exploited by employers or supervisors; economic problems play a relatively small role in the decision to pilfer. So, although employers attribute employee fraud to economic conditions and declining personal values, workers themselves say they steal because of strain and conflict. It is difficult to determine the value of goods taken by employees, but it has been estimated that pilferage accounts for 30 percent to 75 percent of all shrinkage and amounts to losses of up to $10 billion annually.[48]

In some cases, workers use their position in an organization to conduct illegal schemes or help others benefit illegally. For example, in July of 2001, four racetrack tellers at Belmont, Aqueduct, and Saratoga in New York were arrested when it was discovered that they used the flow of cash through betting windows to launder money for drug dealers. The tellers exchanged more than $300,000 in small bills for large ones.[49]

Where do you go to report cases of employee fraud? The National Whistleblower Center is a nonprofit educational advocacy organization that works for the enforcement of environmental laws, nuclear safety, civil rights, and government and industry accountability through the support and representation of employee whistleblowers. Go to their Web site at:
    http://www.whistleblowers.org/
For an up-to-date list of Web links, go to
    http://info.wadsworth.com/siegel ■

Management fraud Blue-collar workers are not the only employees who commit corporate theft. Management-level fraud is also quite common. Such acts include (1) converting company assets for personal benefit; (2) fraudulently receiving increases in compensation (such as raises or bonuses); (3) fraudulently increasing personal holdings of company stock; (4) retaining one's present position within the company by manipulating accounts; and (5) concealing unacceptable performance from stockholders.[50] In one strange case of management fraud that almost defies classification, the FBI uncovered a scheme by eight McDonald's employees to steal $13 million worth of McDonald's game prizes from its Monopoly game promotion, which offered a top prize of $1 million. Those involved in the scam were in a position to obtain winning game pieces, which they distributed to friends and associates who acted as recruiters. These recruiters then solicited individuals who falsely and fraudulently represented that they were the legitimate winners of the McDonald's games.[51] The McDonald's case seems quirky, but the most

■ There is an ongoing investigation into the practices of the Enron Corporation to determine if its downfall may have been caused by criminal conduct. Here, former Enron Chief Executive Officer Jeffrey Skilling (center), Enron Vice President of Corporate Development Sherron Watkins (left), and Enron President and Chief Operating Officer Jeffrey McMahon are sworn in on Capitol Hill February 26, 2002, prior to testifying before the Senate Commerce Committee's hearings on Enron.

AP/Wide World Photos

serious case of management fraud to date involves the demise of the oil and natural gas trading company Enron and the criminal involvement of its auditors, the Arthur Andersen company, one of the world's largest accounting firms.

Enron was an aggressive energy company that sought to transform itself into the world's biggest energy trader.[52] At one time it was, by stock market value, the seventh largest U.S. company. But its share price collapsed when word got out that the company had been setting up shell companies and limited partnerships to conceal debts. Enron executives lied about profits and conducted a range of shady dealings, including concealing debts so they didn't show up in the company's accounts. Some involved a series of limited partnerships controlled by its chief financial officer. In one incident, which helped sink the company, six Enron executives negotiated complex deals in which they made at least $42 million on personal investments totaling $161,000, all the while knowing that the partnerships they sold to retirement plans and private foundations were collapsing in value. It is also suspected that Enron engaged in sham transactions in late 2000 that drove up electricity prices in California and helped worsen the energy crisis that plagued the West for more than a year.

It is suspected that company officials touted the stock to perspective buyers while they themselves were selling shares. At the time of this writing, a criminal investigation by federal authorities is trying to pin down blame for the Enron debacle, which cost shareholders billions of dollars and in some instances wiped out their life savings.

The focus has been on its auditors from Arthur Andersen. How could accountants from this prestigious firm not realize that Enron was engaging in shady business practices? It was revealed that Enron's auditors actually shredded key documents to keep them out of the hands of the government. One man involved in the incident, David Duncan, a former Andersen partner who was head of the team that audited Enron, agreed to serve as a government witness after pleading guilty to obstruction of justice. Duncan admitted in court that he "knowingly, intentionally and corruptly persuaded and attempted to persuade" Andersen employees to withhold records, documents, and other objects from an investigation by the Securities and Exchange Commission.

Client Fraud

A sixth component of white-collar crime is theft by an economic client from an organization that advances credit to its clients or reimburses them for services rendered. These offenses are linked together because they involve cheating an organization (such as a government agency or insurance company) with many individual clients that the organization supports financially (such as welfare clients), reimburses for services provided (such as health care providers), covers losses of (such as insurance policyholders), or extends credit to (such as bank clients or taxpayers). Included in this category are insurance fraud, credit card fraud, fraud related to welfare and Medicare programs, and tax evasion. For example, some critics suggest that welfare recipients cheat the federal government out of billions each year. As eligibility for public assistance becomes more limited, recipients are resorting to a number of schemes to maintain their status. Some women collect government checks while working on the side or living illegally with boyfriends or husbands. Some young mothers tell children to answer exam questions incorrectly to be classified as disabled and receive government assistance.[53]

Health care fraud Under Medicaid, recipients under age 21 are entitled to dental checkups and cleanings twice a year and a limited number of other treatments. In 2001, prosecutors in Miami filed charges against two former dentists, Joel Berger and Charles Kravitz, for allegedly setting up a Medicaid fraud scheme that cost the state millions in bogus fees. Berger was charged with hiring recruiters to pick up children, some as young as 2, from street corners, school buses, and even day care centers and take them to dental facilities for unneeded procedures that included cleanings, X-rays, and even extractions. Recruiters received $25 for every child they placed in a dental chair; the kids got $5 for participating. The procedures were frequently administered by untrained dental employees. The scheme involved a dozen dentists and nearly 90 recruiters and dental workers and may have cost taxpayers up $20 million in illegal Medicaid payments. Similar, albeit smaller scale frauds have been uncovered in Texas, Kansas, and in other states.[54]

The Miami case is one of the growing number of health care frauds being perpetrated in the United States.[55] Abusive practices include such techniques as "ping-ponging" (referring patients to other physicians in the same office), "gang visits" (billing for multiple services), and "steering" (directing patients to particular pharmacies). Doctors who abuse their Medicaid or Medicare patients in this way are liable to civil suits and even criminal penalties. For example, in 1997 the Baptist Medical Center in Kansas City, Missouri, agreed to pay the government $17.5 million to settle claims that it bribed doctors to send it Medicare patients for treatment; the doctors had received over a million dollars in kickbacks.[56]

In addition to individual physicians, some large health care providers have been accused of routinely violating the law to obtain millions in illegal payments. In 1998 the federal government filed suit against two of the nation's largest hospital chains, Columbia/HCA Healthcare Corporation (320 hospitals) and Quorum Health Group (250 hospitals), alleging that they routinely overstated expenses to bilk Medicare.[57] It has been estimated that $100 billion spent annually on federal health care is lost to fraudulent practices.[58] Despite the magnitude of this abuse, state and federal governments have been reluctant to prosecute Medicaid fraud.[59]

In light of these and other health care scandals, the government has attempted to tighten control over the industry. New regulations restrict the opportunity for physicians to commit fraud. For example, in 1993 Congress passed what are known as the Stark Amendments,[60] which prohibit physicians from making a referral to a health care provider that accepts Medicare patients if that physician or a family member holds a financial interest.

Bank fraud Bank fraud can encompass such diverse schemes as check kiting (Figure 13.1), check forgery, false statements on loan applications, sale of stolen checks, bank credit card fraud, unauthorized use of automatic teller ma-

---

Figure 13.1   Check Kiting

Check kiting is a scheme whereby a client with accounts in two or more banks takes advantage of the time required for checks to clear in order to obtain unauthorized use of bank funds.

Example:

- A person has $5,000 on account in a bank and cashes a check for $3,000 from an account in another bank in which he has no funds.

- The bank cashes the check because he is already a customer.

- He then closes his account before the check clears, or...

- He may write checks on his account totalling $5,000, which are cleared because he has funds in his account.

- In some instances the kiter expects a bank to cover a withdrawal before a check is presented to another bank for collection (she simply wants a short-term, interest-free loan).

- Others have no intention of ever covering the transaction, but instead want to take cash out of the system after building accounts to artificially high amounts.

- Kiting can be a multimillion-dollar offense involving checks written and deposited in banks in two or more states or even in separate countries.

---

chines (ATMs), auto title fraud, and illegal transactions with offshore banks.[61] To be found guilty of bank fraud, one must knowingly execute or attempt to execute a scheme to fraudulently obtain money or property from a financial institution. For example, a car dealer would commit bank fraud by securing loans on titles to cars it no longer owned. A real estate owner would be guilty of bank fraud if he or she obtained a false appraisal on a piece of property with the intention of obtaining a bank loan in excess of the property's real worth. Penalties for bank fraud include a maximum fine of $1 million and up to 30 years in prison.

Tax evasion Another important aspect of client fraud is tax evasion. Here the victim is the government that is cheated by one of its clients, the errant taxpayer to whom it extended credit by allowing the taxpayer to delay paying taxes on money he or she had already earned. Tax fraud is a particularly challenging area for criminological study because (1) so many U.S. citizens regularly underreport their income, and (2) it is often difficult to separate honest error from deliberate tax evasion. The basic law on tax evasion is contained in the U.S. Internal Revenue Code, section 7201, which states:

> Any person who willfully attempts in any manner to evade or defeat any tax imposed by this title or the payment thereof shall, in addition to other penalties provided by

law, be guilty of a felony and, upon conviction thereof, shall be fined not more than $100,000 or imprisoned not more than five years, or both, together with the costs of prosecution.

To prove tax fraud, the government must find that the taxpayer either underreported his or her income or did not report taxable income. No minimum dollar amount is stated before fraud exists, but the government can take legal action when there is a "substantial underpayment of tax." A second element of tax fraud is "willfulness" on the part of the tax evader. In the major case on this issue, willfulness was defined as a "voluntary, intentional violation of a known legal duty and not the careless disregard for the truth."[62] Finally, to prove tax fraud, the government must show that the taxpayer has purposely attempted to evade or defeat a tax payment. If the offender is guilty of passive neglect, the offense is a misdemeanor. Passive neglect means simply not paying taxes, not reporting income, or not paying taxes when due. On the other hand, affirmative tax evasion, such as keeping double books, making false entries, destroying books or records, concealing assets, or covering up sources of income, constitutes a felony.

For more on tax evasion, use InfoTrac College Edition to find this article: C. Michael Chitwood, Paul J. Haase, and Kerry Halpern. Tax violations (16th annual survey of white collar crime). *American Criminal Law Review* Summer 2001 v38 i3 p1345 ■

Corporate Crime

Yet another component of white-collar crime involves situations in which powerful institutions or their representatives willfully violate the laws that restrain these institutions from doing social harm or require them to do social good. This is also known as corporate or **organizational crime.**

Interest in corporate crime first emerged in the early 1900s, when a group of writers, known as the muckrakers, targeted the unscrupulous business practices of John D. Rockefeller, Andrew Carnegie, J. P. Morgan, and other corporate business leaders.[63] In a 1907 article, sociologist E. A. Ross described the "criminaloid": a business leader who while enjoying immunity from the law victimized an unsuspecting public.[64] Edwin Sutherland focused theoretical attention on corporate crime when he began his research on the subject in the 1940s; corporate crime was probably what he had in mind when he coined the phrase *white-collar crime.*[65]

Corporate crimes are socially injurious acts committed by people who control companies to further their business interests. The target of their crimes can be the general public, the environment, or even their companies' workers. What makes these crimes unique is that the perpetrator is a legal fiction—a corporation—and not an individual. In reality, it is company employees or owners who commit corporate crimes and who ultimately benefit through career advancement or greater profits. For a corporation to be held criminally liable, the employee committing the crime must be acting within the scope of his employment and must have actual or apparent authority to engage in the particular act in question. **Actual authority** occurs when a corporation knowingly gives authority to an employee; **apparent authority** is satisfied if a third party, like a customer, reasonably believes the agent has the authority to perform the act in question. Courts have ruled that actual authority may occur even when the illegal behavior is not condoned by the corporation but is nonetheless within the scope of the employee's authority.[66]

Some of the acts included within corporate crime are price-fixing and illegal restraint of trade, false advertising, and the use of company practices that violate environmental protection statutes. The variety of crimes contained within this category is great, and they cause vast damage. The following subsections examine some of the most important offenses.

Illegal restraint of trade and price-fixing A restraint of trade involves a contract or conspiracy designed to stifle competition, create a monopoly, artificially maintain prices, or otherwise interfere with free market competition. The control of restraint of trade violations has its legal basis in the **Sherman Antitrust Act,** which subjects to criminal or civil sanctions any person "who shall make any contract or engage in any combination or conspiracy" in restraint of interstate commerce.[67] For violations of its provisions, this federal law created criminal penalties of up to three years' imprisonment and $100,000 in fines for individuals and $10 million in fines for corporations.[68] The act outlaws conspiracies between corporations designed to control the marketplace.

In most instances, the act lets the presiding court judge whether corporations have conspired to "unreasonably restrain competition." However, four types of market conditions are considered so inherently anticompetitive that federal courts, through the Sherman Antitrust Act, have defined them as illegal per se, without regard to the facts or circumstances of the case:

> **Division of markets:** firms divide a region into territories, and each firm agrees not to compete in the others' territories.
>
> **Tying arrangement:** a corporation requires customers of one of its services to use other services it offers. For example, it would be an illegal restraint of trade if a railroad required that companies doing business with it or supplying it with materials ship all goods they produce on trains owned by the rail line.[69]
>
> **Group boycotts:** an organization or company boycotts retail stores that do not comply with its rules or desires.

Price-fixing: a conspiracy to set and control the price of a necessary commodity is considered an absolute violation of the act.

Deceptive pricing   Even the largest U.S. corporations commonly use deceptive pricing schemes when they respond to contract solicitations. Deceptive pricing occurs when contractors provide the government or other corporations with incomplete or misleading information on how much it will actually cost to fulfill the contracts they are bidding on or use mischarges once the contracts are signed.[70] For example, defense contractors have been prosecuted for charging the government for costs incurred on work they are doing for private firms or shifting the costs on fixed-price contracts to ones in which the government reimburses the contractor for all expenses ("cost-plus" contracts). One well-known example of deceptive pricing occurred when the Lockheed Corporation withheld information that its labor costs would be lower than expected on the C-5 cargo plane. The resulting overcharges were an estimated $150 million. Although the government was able to negotiate a cheaper price for future C-5 orders, it did not demand repayment on the earlier contract. The government prosecutes approximately 100 cases of deceptive pricing in defense work each year, involving 59 percent of the nation's largest contractors.[71]

False claims and advertising   Executives in even the largest corporations sometimes face stockholders' expectations of ever-increasing company profits that seem to demand that sales be increased at any cost. At times executives respond to this challenge by making claims about their products that cannot be justified by actual performance. However, the line between clever, aggressive sales techniques and fraudulent claims is fine. It is traditional to show a product in its best light, even if that involves resorting to fantasy. It is not fraudulent to show a delivery service vehicle taking off into outer space or to imply that taking one sip of iced tea will make people feel they have just jumped into a swimming pool. However, it is illegal to knowingly and purposely advertise a product as possessing qualities that the manufacturer realizes it does not have.

Charges stemming from false and misleading claims have been common in several U.S. industries. For example, the Federal Trade Commission reviewed and disallowed advertising by the three major U.S. car companies that alleged that new cars got higher gas mileage than buyers actually could expect. The Warner-Lambert drug company was prohibited from claiming that Listerine mouthwash could prevent or cure colds. Sterling Drug was prohibited from claiming that Lysol disinfectant killed germs associated with colds and flu. An administrative judge ruled that the American Home Products Company (now called Wyeth Pharmaceuticals) falsely advertised Anacin as a tension reliever. The list seems endless.[72]

Environmental crimes   Much attention has been paid to intentional or negligent environmental pollution caused by many large corporations. The numerous allegations in this area involve almost every aspect of U.S. business. There are many different types of environmental crimes. Some corporations have endangered the lives of their own workers by maintaining unsafe conditions in their plants and mines. It has been estimated that 21 million workers have been exposed to hazardous materials while on the job. The National Institute of Occupational Safety and Health has estimated that it would cost about $40 million just to alert these workers to the danger of their exposure to hazardous waste and $54 billion to track whether they develop occupationally related disease.[73] Some industries have been hit particularly hard by complaints and allegations. The asbestos industry was inundated with lawsuits after environmental scientists found a close association between exposure to asbestos and the development of cancer. More than 250,000 people have filed 12,000 lawsuits against 260 asbestos manufacturers. In all, some insurance company officials estimate that asbestos-related lawsuits could amount to as much as $150 billion. Similarly, some 100,000 cotton mill workers suffer from some form of respiratory disease linked to prolonged exposure to cotton dust. About one-third of the workers are seriously disabled by brown lung disease, an illness similar to emphysema.[74] The control of workers' safety has been the province of the Occupational Safety and Health Administration (OSHA). OSHA sets industry standards for the proper use of such substances as benzene, arsenic, lead, and coke. Intentional violation of OSHA standards can result in criminal penalties.

High-Tech Crime

High-tech crimes are a new breed of white-collar offenses that can be singular or ongoing and typically involve the theft of information, resources, or funds. High-tech crimes cost consumers billions of dollars each year and will most likely increase dramatically in the years to come. What are some of these emerging forms of white-collar crime?

Internet crimes   Until it was raided by federal authorities on August 8, 2001, Landslide Productions Inc. of Fort Worth was a highly profitable Internet-based pornography ring, taking in as much as $1.4 million in one month.[75] It was the largest known commercial child pornography enterprise, having at least 250,000 subscribers worldwide. The crackdown led to convictions of Landslide's owners Thomas and Janice Reedy, who had offered subscribers access to Web sites that advertised themselves with such phrases as "Child Rape" or "Cyber Lolita." The sites, off limits to control by U.S. authorities because they were located in Russia and Indonesia, had a fee-sharing arrangement with the Reedys, who pocketed millions, drove a Mercedes, and lived in a luxury home.

Millions of people use the Internet daily in the United States and Canada alone, and the number entering cyberspace is growing rapidly. Criminal entrepreneurs view this vast pool as a target for high-tech crimes. In a number of highly publicized cases, adults have solicited teenagers in Internet "chat rooms." Others have used the Internet to sell and distribute obscene material, prompting some service providers to censor or control sexually explicit material.

CONNECTIONS

The use of the Internet in the sex industry will be discussed more fully in Chapter 14. Needless to say, being able to access pornographic material over the Internet has helped expand the sale of sexually related material. However, the federal government has recently cracked down on this type of offense, resulting in hundreds of arrests. ■

Selling pornographic material on the Internet is just one method of its illegal use. Bogus get-rich-quick schemes, weight-loss scams, and investment swindles have been pitched on the Internet. With the continuing growth of e-commerce, a January 2001 study by Meridien Research reports that payment-card fraud on the Internet will increase worldwide from $1.6 billion in 2000 to $15.5 billion by 2005.[76] Nor is Internet fraud unique to the United States. The European Commission reported that in 2000 payment-card fraud in the European Union rose by 50 percent to $553 million in fraudulent transactions; the International Chamber of Commerce reported that nearly two-thirds of all cases it handled in 2000 involved online fraud.[77] What are some of the forms Internet fraud takes?[78]

Internet securities fraud Some criminals make use of Internet chat rooms in their fraudulent schemes. In one famous case, 15-year-old Jonathan Lebed was charged with securities fraud by the SEC after he repeatedly bought low-cost, thinly traded stocks and then spread hundreds of false and misleading messages concerning them—generally baseless price predictions. After their values were artificially inflated, Lebed sold the securities at an inflated price. Lebed agreed to findings of fraud but later questioned whether he had done anything wrong.[79]

Though he might not agree, young Lebed's actions are considered Internet fraud because they involve using the Internet to intentionally manipulate the securities marketplace for profit. There are actually three major types of Internet securities fraud today:

Market manipulation: Stock market manipulation occurs when an individual tries to control the price of stock by interfering with the natural forces of supply and demand. There are two principal forms of this crime: the "pump and dump" and the "cybersmear." In a pump and dump scheme, erroneous and deceptive information is posted online to get unsuspecting investors to become interested in a stock while those spreading the information sell previously

■ Fear of identity theft has prompted changes in the way the government conducts business. Here, Department of Motor Vehicles Director Steve Gourley (right) and California's Business, Transportation, and Housing Agency Secretary Maria Contreras-Sweet display a facsimile of the state's new driver's license at a news conference in Culver City, California. The license uses new printing and ink technology in an effort to deter identity theft or fraudulent duplication.

AP/Wide World Photos

purchased stock at an inflated price. The "cyber-smear" is a reverse pump and dump: negative information is spread online about a stock, driving down its price and enabling people to buy it at an artificially low price before rebuttals by the company's officers reinflate the price.[80]

Fraudulent offerings of securities: Some cyber criminals create Web sites specifically designed to fraudulently sell securities. To make the offerings look more attractive than they are, assets may be inflated, expected returns overstated, and/or risks understated.

Illegal touting: This crime occurs when individuals make securities recommendations and fail to disclose that they are being paid to disseminate their favorable opinions. Section 17(b) of the Securities Act of 1933 requires that paid touters disclose the nature, source, and amount of their compensation. If those who tout stocks fail to disclose their relationship with the company, information misleads investors into believing that the speaker is objective and credible rather than bought and paid for.

Identity theft   Identity theft occurs when a person uses the Internet to steal someone's identity and/or impersonate them to open a new credit card account or conduct some other financial transaction. Identity information can be gathered easily from confederates because people rou-tinely share their name, address, phone numbers, personal information, credit card account numbers, and Social Security number (SSN) when making routine purchases over the Internet or in stores. An identity thief appropriates personal information to commit fraud or theft. For example, they can fill out change of address cards at the post office and obtain people's credit card bills and bank statements. They may then call the credit card issuer and, pretending to be the victim, ask for a change in address on the account. They can then charge numerous items over the Internet and have the merchandise sent to the new address. It may take months for the victim to realize the fraud because they are not getting bills from the credit card company. Some common Internet crimes are listed in Exhibit 13.1.

 Internet information theft and access violations threaten companies worldwide. To read how business leaders are fighting back, go to InfoTrac College edition and read this article: Luis Ramiro Hernandez. Integrated risk management in the Internet age. *Risk Management* June 2000 v47 i6 p29 ■

Computer crimes   Computer-related thefts are a new trend in employee theft and embezzlement. The widespread use of computers to record business transactions has encouraged some people to use them for illegal purposes. Computer crimes generally fall into one of five categories:[81]

Exhibit 13.1   Common Internet Fraud Schemes

Online Auction/Retail	The fraud attributable to the misrepresentation of a product advertised for sale through an Internet auction site or the nondelivery of merchandise or goods purchased through an Internet auction site.
Investment Fraud	An offering that uses false or fraudulent claims to solicit investments or loans, or that provides for the purchase, use, or trade of forged or counterfeit securities.
Business Opportunity/ "Work at Home"	The offering of a phony job opportunity, often with associated charges such as "processing" or "application" fees. Perpetrators frequently forge the name of a computer service or Internet service provider.
Financial Institution Fraud	Misrepresentation of the truth or concealment of a material fact by a person to induce a business, organization, or other entity that manages money, credit, or capital to perform a fraudulent activity.
Credit Card Theft/Fraud	The unauthorized use of a credit/debit card or credit/debit card number to fraudulently obtain money or property. Credit/debit card numbers can be stolen from unsecured Web sites.
Ponzi/Pyramid Schemes	An investment scheme in which investors are promised abnormally high profits on their investments. No investment is actually made. Early investors are paid returns with the investment money received from the later investors. The system usually collapses, and the later investors do not receive dividends and lose their initial investment.
Nondelivery of Goods/Services	The nondelivery of goods or services that were purchased or contracted remotely through the Internet, independent of an Internet auction.

SOURCE: FBI, *Common Internet Fraud Schemes* (Washington, D.C.: author, 2001).

1. Theft of services, in which the criminal uses the computer for unauthorized purposes or an unauthorized user penetrates the computer system. Included within this category is the theft of processing time and services not entitled to an employee.

2. Use of data in a computer system for personal gain.

3. Unauthorized use of computers employed for various types of financial processing to obtain assets.

4. Theft of property by computer for personal use or conversion to profit. For example, using a computer to illegally copy and sell software.

5. Making the computer itself the subject of a crime—for example, when a virus is placed in it to destroy data.

Although most of these types of crimes involve using computers for personal gain, the last category typically involves activities that are motivated more by malice than by profit. When computers themselves are the target, criminals are typically motivated by revenge for some perceived wrong; a need to exhibit their technical prowess and superiority; a wish to highlight the vulnerability of computer security systems; a desire to spy on other people's private financial and personal information ("computer voyeurism"); or a philosophy of open access to all systems and programs.[82]

Several common techniques are used by computer criminals. In fact, computer theft has become so common that experts have created their own jargon to describe theft styles and methods:

The Trojan horse: One computer is used to reprogram another for illicit purposes. In one incident, two high school–age computer users reprogrammed the computer at DePaul University, preventing that institution from using its own processing facilities. The youths were convicted of a misdemeanor.

The salami slice: An employee sets up a dummy account in the company's computerized records. A small amount—even a few pennies—is subtracted from customers' accounts and added to the account of the thief. Even if they detect the loss, customers don't complain because a few cents is an insignificant amount to them. The pennies picked up here and there eventually amount to thousands of dollars in losses.

Super-zapping: Most computer programs used in business have built-in antitheft safeguards. However, employees can use a repair or maintenance program to supersede the antitheft program. Some tinkering with the program is required, but the "super-zapper" is soon able to order the system to issue checks to his or her private account.

The logic bomb: A program is secretly attached to the company's computer system. The new program monitors the company's work and waits for a sign of error to appear, some illogic that was designed for

AP/Wide World Photos

■ There has been an ongoing effort by law enforcement authorities to crack down on computer crimes. Here, Richard LaMagna, head of worldwide piracy enforcement for Microsoft, holds a counterfeit instruction booklet for Windows XP, Microsoft's newest operating system. During this news conference on November 16, 2001, in Whittier, California, as Sheriff Lee Baca looks on, LaMagna announced that investigators with the Southern California High-Tech Crimes Task Force, which includes officers from the Los Angeles Sheriff's Department, U.S. Customs, and the Los Angeles Police Department, made the largest seizure of counterfeit computer software in U.S. history, material worth an estimated $100 million if sold at retail prices.

the computer to follow. Illogic causes the logic bomb to kick into action and exploit the weakness. The way the thief exploits the situation depends on his or her original intent—theft of money or defense secrets, sabotage, or the like.

Impersonation: An unauthorized person uses the identity of an authorized computer user to access the computer system.

Data leakage: A person illegally obtains data from a computer system by leaking it out in small amounts.

A different type of computer crime involves installing a virus in a computer system. A virus is a program that disrupts or destroys existing programs and networks.[83] All too often this high-tech vandalism is the work of hackers, who consider their efforts to be pranks. In one well-publicized case, a 25-year-old computer whiz named Robert Morris unleashed a program that wrecked a nationwide electronic mail network. His efforts netted him three years' probation, a $10,000 fine, and 400 hours of community service; some critics felt this punishment was too lenient to deter future virus creators.[84]

An accurate accounting of computer crime will probably never be made because so many offenses go unreported. Sometimes company managers refuse to report the crime to police lest they display their incompetence and vulnerability to stockholders and competitors.[85] In other instances, computer crimes go unreported because they involve low-visibility acts such as copying computer software in violation of copyright laws.[86]

■ Causes of White-Collar Crime

When Ivan Boesky pleaded guilty to one count of securities fraud, he agreed to pay a civil fine of $100 million, the largest at that time in SEC history. Boesky's fine was later surpassed by financier Michael Milken's fine of more than $1 billion. How, people asked, can people with so much disposable wealth get involved in a risky scheme to produce even more? There probably are as many explanations for white-collar crime as there are white-collar crimes. Many offenders feel free to engage in business crime because they can easily rationalize its effects. Some convince themselves that their actions are not really crimes because the acts involved do not resemble street crimes. For example, a banker who uses his position of trust to lend his institution's assets to a company he secretly controls may see himself as a shrewd businessman, not as a criminal. Or a pharmacist who chisels customers on prescription drugs may rationalize her behavior by telling herself that it does not really hurt anyone. Further, some businesspeople feel justified in committing white-collar crimes because they believe government regulators do not really understand the business world or the problems of competing in the free enterprise system. Even when caught, many white-collar criminals cannot see the error of their ways. For example, one offender who was convicted in an electrical industry price-fixing conspiracy categorically denied the illegality of his actions. "We did not fix prices," he said; "I am telling you that all we did was recover costs."[87] Some white-collar criminals believe that everyone violates business laws, so it is not so bad if they do so themselves. Rationalizing greed is a common trait of white-collar criminals.

Greedy or Needy?

When Kansas City pharmacist Robert Courtney was asked after his arrest why he substituted improper doses of drugs instead of what doctors had prescribed, he told investigators he cut the drugs' strength "out of greed."[88]

Greed is not the only motivation for white-collar crime; need also plays an important role. Executives may tamper with company books because they feel the need to keep or improve their jobs, satisfy their egos, or support their children. Blue-collar workers may pilfer because they need to keep pace with inflation or buy a new car. Kathleen Daly's analysis of convictions in seven federal district courts indicate that many white-collar crimes involve relatively trivial amounts. Women convicted of white-collar crime typically work in lower-echelon positions, and their acts seem motivated more by economic survival than by greed and power.[89]

Even people in the upper echelons of the financial world, such as Ivan Boesky, may carry scars from an earlier needy period in their lives that can be healed only by accumulating ever-greater amounts of money. As one of Boesky's associates put it:

> I don't know what his devils were. Maybe he's greedy beyond the wildest imaginings of mere mortals like you and me. And maybe part of what drives the guy is an inherent insecurity that was operative here even after he had arrived. Maybe he never arrived.[90]

A well-known study of embezzlers by Donald Cressey illustrates the important role need plays in white-collar crime. According to Cressey, embezzlement is caused by what he calls a "nonshareable financial problem." This condition may be the result of offenders' living beyond their means, perhaps piling up gambling debts; offenders feel they cannot let anyone know about such financial problems without ruining their reputations. Cressey claims that the door to solving personal financial problems through criminal means is opened by the rationalizations society has developed for white-collar crime: "Some of our most respectable citizens got their start in life by using other people's money temporarily"; "in the real estate business, there is nothing wrong about using deposits before the deal is closed"; "all people steal when they get in a tight spot."[91] Offenders use these and other rationalizations to resolve the conflict they experience over engaging in illegal behavior. Rationalizations allow offenders' financial needs to be met without compromising their values. The Criminological Enterprise feature discusses this view in greater detail.

There are a number of more formal theories of white-collar crime. The next sections describe two of the more prominent theories.

Corporate Culture Theory

The corporate culture view is that some business organizations promote white-collar criminality in the same way that lower-class culture encourages the development of juvenile gangs and street crime. According to the corporate

THE CRIMINOLOGICAL ENTERPRISE

Snakes and Ladders: How Otherwise Respectable People Confront Their White-Collar Crimes

How do otherwise law-abiding people cope with the emotional turmoil created when they are cast as white-collar criminals? This issue was explored by Sara Willott, Christine Griffin, and Mark Torrance through a series of interviews they conducted with groups of working-class and professional men in Great Britain who had been convicted of white-collar offenses.

Willott and her colleagues found that members of both groups used linguistic devices to justify their behavior. The working-class men argued that they were the breadwinners of their families and were forced by dire economic circumstances to commit crime. Their crimes were not for personal gain but simply to feed their families. They also viewed themselves as modern day "Robin Hoods" who were taking from the rich to help the poor, which in this case were their own families. Rather than accept blame, they positioned themselves as decent men who were forced to commit crimes: it was not their fault but the government's for failing to provide them with a safety net during a time of financial crisis. And, having been forced into crime by an unfair system, the men claimed they were revictimized and humiliated when sent to prison. They viewed themselves as the bottom of life's barrel, as pawns similar to the ones used in the children's game "snakes and ladders" (called "Chutes and Ladders" in the United States). They were being kept in place by powerful forces beyond their control.

The professional men used some similar linguistic tools to justify their behavior. They also saw themselves as breadwinners who used other people's money to help their families. But, unlike the blue-collar workers, they saw their professional responsibilities as adding to their burden. As businesspeople, they saw themselves as protectors of a wider circle of dependents, including their employees and their families. They did not steal but were "digging into funds" when the need arose. They were careful to point out that they did not use the funds to support an extravagant lifestyle but to shoulder the responsibility they had been socialized to carry.

The professionals were also aware of the high social standing demanded by their profession and lifestyle. Along with power come the obligations and trappings of power, and they were forced to violate the law to meet these obligations.

Some of the professional men viewed themselves as victims of bureaucrats who relentlessly pursued them to enhance their careers in government. They viewed law enforcers, many of whom had lower-class backgrounds, as ruthlessly ambitious people who used the prosecutions as stepping stones to success. Class envy, then, was responsible in part for their current dilemma.

The businesspeople believed the conditions that produced their descent were not of their doing and were beyond their control. Economic decline and recession had pushed them down the slippery slope. And, once in the "system," their entire world was rocked to its very foundations. They were aliens in a strange land of courts and correctional facilities: although working-class criminals might feel at home in their current surroundings, they complained that as professionals "we have fallen out of the structures of our lives" (p. 457). And, even though they viewed themselves as competent professionals in the business world, their amateurism as criminals helped get them into their current predicament. They sought to distinguish themselves as being morally superior to both working-class criminals and the justice officials who led them to their disgrace.

Critical Thinking Questions

1. Willott and her colleagues found that both working-class and professional-class white-collar offenders created elaborate justifications for their behavior. They were pawns in an economic and social system beyond their control. Do their findings seem similar to Cressey's earlier research, which indicates that white-collar criminals are more likely to view themselves as victims than predators?

2. Would you put violators in prison? Or should white-collar criminals be given economic sanctions alone?

InfoTrac College Edition Research

Use "white-collar crime" as a key word on InfoTrac College Edition and access the articles in the *American Criminal Law Review,* annual edition, which reviews all the recent case law on business-related crimes.

SOURCE: Sara Willott, Christine Griffin, and Mark Torrance, "Snakes and Ladders: Upper-Middle-Class Male Offenders Talk about Economic Crime," *Criminology* 39 (2001): 441–66.

---

culture view, some business enterprises cause crime by placing excessive demands on employees while at the same time maintaining a business climate tolerant of employee deviance. New employees learn the attitudes and techniques needed to commit white-collar crime from their business peers.

The corporate culture theory can be used to explain the collapse of Enron. A new CEO had been brought in to revitalize the company, and he wanted to become part of the "new economy" based on the Internet. Layers of management were wiped out, and hundreds of outsiders were recruited. Huge cash bonuses and stock options were granted to top performers. Young managers were given authority to make $5 million decisions without higher approval. It became common for executives to change jobs two or three times in an effort to maximize bonuses and pay. Seminars were conducted showing executives how to hide profits and avoid taxes.[92]

CONNECTIONS

The view that white-collar crime is a learning process seems reminiscent of Edwin Sutherland's description of how gang boys learn the techniques of drug dealing and burglary from older youths through differential association. See Chapter 8 for a description of this process. ■

Those holding the corporate culture view would point to the Enron scandal as a prime example of what happens when people work in organizations whose cultural values stress profit over fair play, in which government scrutiny is limited and regulators are viewed as the enemy, and in which senior members encourage newcomers to believe that "greed is good."

Self-Control View

Not all criminologists agree with corporate culture theory. Travis Hirschi and Michael Gottfredson take exception to the hypothesis that white-collar crime is a product of corporate culture.[93] If that were true, there would be much more white-collar crime than actually exists, and white-collar criminals would not be embarrassed by their misdeeds, as most seem to be. Instead, Hirschi and Gottfredson maintain that the motives that produce white-collar crimes—quick benefits with minimal effort—are the same as those that produce any other criminal behaviors.

CONNECTIONS

As you may recall from Chapter 10, Gottfredson and Hirschi's general theory of crime holds that criminals lack self-control. Since Gottfredson and Hirschi believe all crime has a similar basis, the motivation and pressure to commit white-collar crime is the same as for any other form of crime. ■

White-collar criminals have low self-control and are inclined to follow momentary impulses without considering the long-term costs of such behavior.[94] White-collar crime is relatively rare because, as a matter of course, business executives tend to hire people with self-control, thereby limiting the number of potential white-collar criminals. Hirschi and Gottfredson have collected data showing that the demographic distribution of white-collar crime is similar to other crimes. For example, gender, race, and age ratios are the same for crimes such as embezzlement and fraud as they are for street crimes such as burglary and robbery.

White-Collar Law Enforcement Systems

On the federal level, detection of white-collar crime is primarily in the hands of administrative departments and agencies.[95] The decision to pursue criminal rather than civil violations usually is based on the seriousness of the case and the perpetrator's intent, actions to conceal the violation, and prior record. Any evidence of criminal activity is then sent to the Department of Justice or the FBI for investigation. Some other federal agencies, such as the Securities and Exchange Commission and the U.S. Postal Service, have their own investigative arms. Enforcement generally is reactive (generated by complaints) rather than proactive (involving ongoing investigations or the monitoring of activities). Investigations are carried out by the various federal agencies and the FBI. The FBI has made enforcement of white-collar criminal law a top priority (along with combating terrorism, foreign counterintelligence, and organized crime). If criminal prosecution is called for, the case will be handled by attorneys from the criminal, tax, antitrust, and civil rights divisions of the Justice Department. If insufficient evidence is available to warrant a criminal prosecution, the case will be handled civilly or administratively by some other federal agency. For example, the Federal Trade Commission can issue a cease and desist order in antitrust or merchandising fraud cases.

On the state and local levels, law enforcement officials have made progress in a number of areas, such as controlling consumer fraud. For example, the Environmental Crimes Strike Force in Los Angeles County, California, is considered a model for the control of illegal dumping and pollution.[96] The number of state-funded technical assistance offices to help local prosecutors has increased significantly; more than 40 states offer such services.

Local prosecutors pursue white-collar criminals more vigorously if they are part of a team effort involving a network of law enforcement agencies.[97] National surveys of local prosecutors find that many do not consider white-collar crimes particularly serious problems. They are more willing to prosecute cases if the offense causes substantial harm and if other agencies fail to act. Relatively few prosecutors participate in interagency task forces designed to investigate white-collar criminal activity.[98]

Controlling White-Collar Crime

The prevailing wisdom is that, unlike lower-class street criminals, white-collar criminals are rarely prosecuted and, when convicted, receive relatively light sentences. In years past, it was rare for a corporate or white-collar criminal to receive a serious criminal penalty.[99] White-collar criminals are often considered nondangerous offenders because they usually are respectable, older citizens who have families to support. These "pillars of the community" are not seen in the same light as a teenager who breaks into a drugstore to steal a few dollars. Their public humiliation at being caught is usually deemed punishment enough; a prison sentence seems unnecessarily cruel.

The prevailing wisdom, then, is that many white-collar criminals avoid prosecution, and those that are prosecuted receive lenient punishment. What efforts have been made to bring violators of the public trust to justice? White-collar criminal enforcement typically involves two strategies designed to control organizational deviance: compliance and deterrence.[100]

Compliance strategies Compliance strategies aim for law conformity without the necessity of detecting, processing, or penalizing individual violators. At a minimum, they ask for cooperation and self-policing among the business community. Compliance systems attempt to create conformity by giving companies economic incentives to obey the law. They rely on administrative efforts to prevent unwanted conditions before they occur. Compliance systems depend on the threat of economic sanctions or civil penalties to control corporate violators.

One method of compliance is to set up administrative agencies to oversee business activity. For example, the Securities and Exchange Commission regulates Wall Street activities, and the Food and Drug Administration regulates drugs, cosmetics, medical devices, meats, and other foods. The legislation creating these agencies usually spells out the penalties for violating regulatory standards. This approach has been used to control environmental crimes, for example, by levying heavy fines based on the quantity and quality of pollution released into the environment.[101] It is easier and less costly to be in compliance, the theory goes, than to pay costly fines and risk criminal prosecution for repeat violations. Moreover, the federal government bars people and businesses from receiving government contracts if they have engaged in repeated business law violations.

In sum, compliance strategies attempt to create a marketplace incentive to obey the law; for example, the more a company pollutes, the more costly and unprofitable that pollution becomes. Compliance strategies also avoid stigmatizing and shaming businesspeople by focusing on the act, rather than the actor, in white-collar crime.[102]

Deterrence strategies Some criminologists say that the punishment of white-collar crimes should include a retributive component similar to that used in common-law crimes. White-collar crimes, after all, are immoral activities that have harmed social values and deserve commensurate punishment.[103] Even the largest fines and penalties are no more than a slap on the wrist to multibillion dollar companies. Corporations can get around economic sanctions by moving their rule-violating activities overseas, where legal controls over injurious corporate activities are lax or nonexistent.[104] They argue that the only way to limit white-collar crime is to deter potential offenders through fear of punishment.

Deterrence strategies involve detecting criminal violations, determining who is responsible, and penalizing the offenders to deter future violations.[105] Deterrence systems are oriented toward apprehending violators and punishing them rather than creating conditions that induce conformity to the law.

Deterrence strategies should work—and they have—because white-collar crime by its nature is a rational act whose perpetrators are extremely sensitive to the threat of criminal sanctions. Perceptions of detection and punishment for white-collar crimes appear to be a powerful deterrent to future law violations.[106] There are numerous instances in which prison sentences for corporate crimes have produced a significant decline in white-collar criminal activity.[107] Although deterrence strategies may prove effective, federal agencies have been reluctant to throw corporate executives in jail. For example, the courts have not hesitated to enforce the Sherman Antitrust Act in civil actions, but they have limited application of the criminal sanctions. Similarly, the government seeks criminal indictments in corporate violations only in "instances of outrageous conduct of undoubted illegality," such as price-fixing.[108] The government has also been lenient with companies and individuals that cooperate voluntarily after an investigation has begun; leniency is not given as part of a confession or plea arrangement. Those who comply with the leniency policy are charged criminally for the activity reported.[109]

 Some federal courts are quite likely to send convicted white-collar criminals to prison, whereas others seem reluctant to use incarceration. For a news report on this phenomenon, go to InfoTrac College Edition and read this article: Wide disparity in white-collar sentences. *USA Today* (Magazine), April 2000 v128 i2659 p11 ∎

Is the Tide Turning?

Despite years of neglect, there is growing evidence that white-collar crime deterrence strategies have become normative. Deterrence policies are now being aided because the federal government has created sentencing guidelines that control punishment for convicted criminals. Prosecutors can now control the length and type of sentence through their handling of the charging process. The guidelines also create mandatory minimum prison sentences that must be served for some crimes; judicial clemency can no longer be counted on.[110]

This new get-tough deterrence approach appears to be affecting all classes of white-collar criminals. Although many people believe affluent corporate executives usually avoid serious punishment, public displeasure with such highly publicized white-collar crimes may be producing a backlash that is resulting in more frequent use of prison sentences.[111] Some commentators now argue that the government may actually be going overboard in its efforts to punish white-collar criminals, especially for crimes that are the result of negligent business practices rather than intentional criminal conspiracy.[112] For example, in April of 2001, the United States Sentencing Commission voted to increase penalties for high-dollar fraud and theft offenses. Under the new guidelines, the perpetrator of a $590,000 investment fraud, for example, could receive more than 60 months in prison.[113]

The control of white-collar crime seems to be entering a new phase, but there are already new challenges being presented by emerging high-tech crimes. The Policy and Practice in Criminology feature on page 406 discusses some efforts being undertaken to deal with these newly emerging crimes.

■ Organized Crime

The second branch of organizational criminality involves organized crime—ongoing criminal enterprise groups whose ultimate purpose is personal economic gain through illegitimate means. Here a structured enterprise system is set up to continually supply consumers with merchandise and services banned by criminal law but for which a ready market exists: prostitution, pornography, gambling, and narcotics. The system may resemble a legitimate business run by an ambitious chief executive officer, his or her assistants, staff attorneys, and accountants, with thorough, efficient accounts receivable and complaint departments.[114]

Because of its secrecy, power, and fabulous wealth, a great mystique has grown up about organized crime. Its legendary leaders—Al Capone, Meyer Lansky, Lucky Luciano—have been the subjects of books and films. The famous *Godfather* films popularized and humanized organized crime figures; the media often glamorize organized crime figures.[115] Most citizens believe organized criminals are capable of taking over legitimate business enterprises if given the opportunity. Almost everyone is familiar with such terms as mob, underworld, Mafia, wise guys, syndicate, or La Cosa Nostra, which refer to organized crime. Although most of us have neither met nor seen members of organized crime families, we feel sure that they exist, and we fear them. This section briefly defines organized crime, reviews its history, and discusses its economic effect and control.

Characteristics of Organized Crime

A precise description of the characteristics of organized crime is difficult to formulate, but here are some of its general traits:[116]

- Organized crime is a conspiratorial activity, involving the coordination of numerous persons in the planning and execution of illegal acts or in the pursuit of a legitimate objective by unlawful means (for example, threatening a legitimate business to get a stake in it).

- Organized crime involves continuous commitment by primary members, although individuals with specialized skills may be brought in as needed.

- Organized crime is usually structured along hierarchical lines—a chieftain supported by close advisers, lower subordinates, and so on.

- Organized crime has economic gain as its primary goal, although power and status may also be motivating factors. Economic gain is achieved through maintenance of a near-monopoly on illegal goods and services, including drugs, gambling, pornography, and prostitution.

- Organized crime activities are not limited to providing illicit services. They include such sophisticated activities as laundering illegal money through legitimate businesses, land fraud, and computer crimes.

- Organized crime employs predatory tactics, such as intimidation, violence, and corruption. It appeals to greed to accomplish its objectives and preserve its gains.

- By experience, custom, and practice, organized crime's conspiratorial groups are usually very quick and effective in controlling and disciplining their members, associates, and victims. The individuals involved know that any deviation from the rules of the organization will evoke a prompt response from the other participants. This response may range from a reduction in rank and responsibility to a death sentence.

- Organized crime is not synonymous with the Mafia, the most experienced, most diversified, and possibly best-disciplined of these groups. The Mafia is actually a common stereotype of organized crime. Although several families in the organization called the Mafia are important components of organized crime activities, they do not hold a monopoly on underworld activities.

- Organized crime does not include terrorists dedicated to political change. Although violent acts are a major tactic of organized crime, the use of violence does not mean that a group is part of a confederacy of organized criminals.

Activities of Organized Crime

What are the main activities of organized crime? The traditional sources of income are derived from providing illicit materials and using force to enter into and maximize profits in legitimate businesses.[117] Most organized crime income comes from narcotics distribution, loan-sharking (lending money at illegal rates), and prostitution. However, additional billions come from gambling, theft rings, pornography, and other illegal enterprises. Organized criminals have infiltrated labor unions and taken control of their pension funds and dues.[118] Hijacking of shipments and cargo theft are other sources of income. Underworld

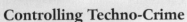

Controlling Techno-Crime

What is now being done to control the newest forms of white-collar crime, which use technology and the Internet for criminal pursuits?

Controlling Internet Crime

1. Because cyber crime is so new, existing laws sometimes are inadequate to address the problem. Therefore new legislation must be drafted to protect the public from this new breed of cyber criminals. For example, before October 30, 1998, when the Identity Theft and Assumption Act of 1998 became law, there was no federal statute that made identity theft a crime. Today, federal prosecutors are making substantial use of the statute and have prosecuted more than 90 cases of identity theft.

2. The federal government is now operating a number of organizations that are coordinating efforts to control cyber fraud. One approach is to create working groups that coordinate the activities of numerous agencies involved in investigating cyber crime. For example, the Interagency Telemarketing and Internet Fraud Working Group brings together representatives of numerous United States Attorneys' offices, the FBI, the Secret Service, the Postal Inspection Service, the Federal Trade Commission, the Securities and Exchange Commission, and other law enforcement and regulatory agencies to share information about trends and patterns in Internet fraud schemes.

3. Specialized enforcement agencies are being created. The Internet Fraud Complaint Center, based in Fairmont, West Virginia, is run by the FBI and the National White-Collar Crime Center. It brings together about 1,000 state and local law enforcement officials and regulators. It then analyzes the fraud-related complaints for patterns, develops additional information on particular cases, and sends investigative packages to law enforcement authorities in the jurisdiction that appears likely to have the greatest investigative interest in the matter In the first year of its operation, the center has received 36,000 complaints, the majority involving auction fraud. Law enforcement has made remarkable strides in dealing with identity theft as a crime problem over the last two years.

4. Some private security companies now offer services to counter Internet criminals. For example, the Equifax Corporation has launched a credit-monitoring service that alerts clients by email whenever an inquiry is made of their credit file or a new account is opened under their name. Other firms already sell credit-monitoring services and several of them offer daily alerts.

Controlling Computer Crime

As computer applications become more varied, so will the use of computers for illegal purposes. The growth of computer-related crimes prompted Congress to enact the Counterfeit Active Device and Computer Fraud and Abuse Act (amended in 1986). This statute makes it a felony for a person to illegally enter a computer to gain $5,000, to cause another to lose $5,000, or to access data affecting the national interest. Violating this act can bring up to 10 years in prison and a $10,000 fine. Repeat offenders can receive 20-year prison sentences and $100,000 fines. In 1994 the Computer Abuse Amendments Act was passed to update federal enforcement efforts. This statute addresses six areas of computer-related abuses, including obtaining information related to national defense or financial records, or using a "federal interest computer" to defraud, obtain something of value, or destroy data. The 1994 act criminalizes "reckless conduct," which means that hackers who plant viruses will now violate federal law.

In addition to the Computer Abuse Act, people who illegally copy software violate the Criminal Copyright Infringement Act, which punishes copying and distribution of software for financial gain or advantage. Computer crime may also be controlled by other federal statutes, including the Electronic Communications Privacy Act of 1986, which prohibits unauthorized interception of computer communications and prohibits obtaining, altering, or preventing authorized access to data through intentional unauthorized access to the stored data. The act is designed to prevent hackers from intercepting computer communications and invading the privacy of computer users.

Critical Thinking Questions

1. How far should the government go in protecting consumers from Internet crime? Might aggressive efforts inhibit the development of this new technology?

2. Considering the complexity of this task, should a new law enforcement agency be developed devoted solely to investigating high-tech crimes? This agency would recruit people who are computer/Internet literate but may not be able to fire guns.

InfoTrac College Edition Research

Use "Internet crime" as key words on InfoTrac College Edition to learn more about this contemporary crime problem.

SOURCES: Identity Theft and Assumption Act of 1998 (18 U.S.C. S 1028(a)(7)); Bruce Swartz, Deputy Assistant General, Criminal Division, Justice Department Internet Fraud Testimony Before the House Energy and Commerce Committee, May 23, 2001; Comprehensive Crime Control Act of 1984, PL 98-473, 2101-03, 98 Stat. 1837, 2190 (1984), adding 18 USC 1030 (1984); Counterfeit Active Device and Computer Fraud and Abuse Act Amended by PL 99-474, 100 Stat. 1213 (1986) codified at 18 U.S.C. 1030 (Supp. V 1987); Computer Abuse Amendments Act 18 U.S.C. section 1030 (1994); Copyright Infringement Act 17 U.S.C. section 506(a) 1994; Electronic Communications Privacy Act of 198618 U.S.C. 2510-2520 (1988 and Supp. II 1990).

figures fence high-value items and maintain international sales territories. In recent years they have branched into computer crime and other white-collar activities. Organized crime figures have also kept up with the information age by using computers and the Internet to sell illegal material such as pornography.

The Concept of Organized Crime

The term *organized crime* conjures up images of strong men in dark suits, machine gun–toting bodyguards, rituals of allegiance to secret organizations, professional "gangland" killings, and meetings of "family" leaders who chart the course of crime much as the board members at General Motors decide on the country's transportation needs. These images have become part of what criminologists refer to as the **alien conspiracy theory** concept of organized crime. This is the belief, adhered to by the federal government and many respected criminologists, that organized crime is a direct offshoot of a criminal society—the **Mafia**—that first originated in Italy and Sicily and now controls racketeering in major U.S. cities. A major premise of the alien conspiracy theory is that the Mafia is centrally coordinated by a national committee that settles disputes, dictates policy, and assigns territory.[119] Not all criminologists believe in this narrow concept of organized crime, and many view the alien conspiracy theory as a figment of the media's imagination.[120] Their view depicts organized crime as a group of ethnically diverse gangs or groups who compete for profit in the sale of illegal goods and services or who use force and violence to extort money from legitimate enterprises. These groups are not bound by a central national organization but act independently on their own turf. We will now examine these perspectives in some detail.

Alien Conspiracy Theory

According to the alien conspiracy theory, organized crime is made up of a national syndicate of 25 or so Italian-dominated crime families that call themselves **La Cosa Nostra.** The major families have a total membership of about 1,700 "made men," who have been inducted into organized crime families, and another 17,000 "associates," who are criminally involved with syndicate members. The families control crime in distinct geographic areas. New York City, the most important organized crime area, alone contains five families—the Gambino, Columbo (formerly Profaci), Lucchese, Bonnano, and Genovese families—named after their founding "godfathers"; in contrast, Chicago contains a single mob organization called the "outfit," which also influences racketeering in such cities as Milwaukee, Kansas City, and Phoenix.[121] The families are believed to be ruled by a "commission" made up of the heads of the five New York families and bosses from Detroit, Buffalo, Chicago, and Philadelphia, which settles personal problems and jurisdictional conflicts and enforces rules that allow members to

gain huge profits through the manufacture and sale of illegal goods and services (see Figure 13.2).

In sum, the alien conspiracy theory sees organized crime as being run by an ordered group of ethnocentric (primarily of Italian origin) criminal syndicates, maintaining unified leadership and shared values. These syndicates communicate closely with other groups and obey the decisions of a national commission charged with settling disputes and creating crime policy.

Emerging Organized Crime Groups

Even such devoted alien conspiracy advocates as the U.S. Justice Department now view organized crime as a loose confederation of ethnic and regional crime groups, bound together by a commonality of economic and political objectives.[122] Some of these groups are located in fixed geographical areas. Chicano crime families are found in areas with significant Hispanic populations, such as California and Arizona. White-ethnic crime organizations are found across the nation. Some Italian and Cuban groups operate internationally. Some have preserved their past identity, whereas others are constantly changing organizations.

One important recent change in organized crime is the interweaving of ethnic groups into the traditional structure. African American, Hispanic, and Asian racketeers now compete with the more traditional groups, overseeing the distribution of drugs, prostitution, and gambling in a symbiotic relationship with old-line racketeers.

Eastern European crime groups   Since 1970, Russian and other Eastern European groups have been operating on U.S. soil. Some groups are formed by immigrants from former satellites of the Soviet Union. For example, in 1998 the FBI established the Yugoslavian/Albanian/Croatian/Serbian (YACS) Crime Group initiative as a response to the increasing threat of criminal activity by people originating from these areas. YACS gangs focus on highly organized and specialized thefts from ATM machines in the New York City area.[123]

Some experts believe Russian crime families, thanks to their control of gasoline terminals and distributorships in the New York metropolitan area, evade as much as $5 billion a year in state and federal taxes. Some of that money then goes to pay off their allies, the Italian Mafia. To find out more, use "Russian organized crime" as a subject guide on InfoTrac College Edition. Also, read this article: Sherry Ricchiardi. The best investigative reporter you've never heard of. *American Journalism Review* Jan 2000 v22 i1 p44 ■

In addition, as many as 2,500 Russian immigrants are believed to be involved in criminal activity, primarily in Russian enclaves in New York City. Beyond extortion from immigrants, Russian organized crime groups have cooperated

Figure 13.2 Traditional Organization of the Mafia "Family"

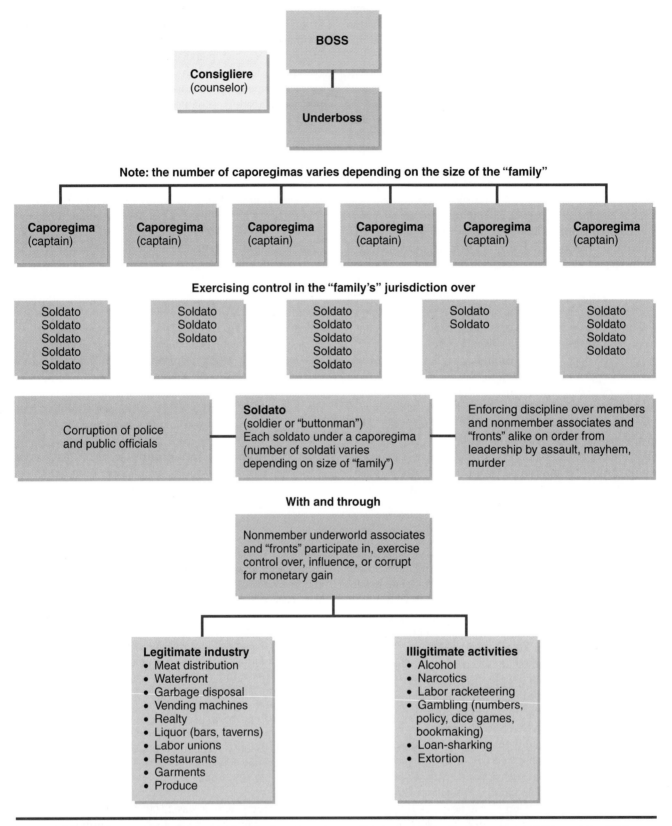

SOURCE: U.S. Senate, Permanent Subcommittee on Investigations, Committee on Government Affairs, *Hearings on Organized Crime and Use of Violence*, 96th Cong., 2d Sess., April 1980, p. 117.

with Mafia families in narcotics trafficking, fencing stolen property, money laundering, and other traditional organized crime schemes.[124] Some of these gangs have engaged in wide-ranging multinational conspiracies. In 1999, after a two-year criminal investigation in Italy, investigators turned up evidence that alleged Russian organized crime operators had funneled millions of dollars through the Bank of New York in a massive money-laundering scheme.[125] Italian prosecutors found that the Russian criminal gangs were raising money in Italy through a mixture of legitimate business activities as well as extortion and tax fraud. Their targets were the Russian businessmen and immigrants who had flooded into Italy with the collapse of communism. The illegal funds were then routed to Moscow and New York, where they were transferred to accounts belonging to suspected organized crime operators. Between 1996 and 1999, the Russian mob is believed to have moved at least $7.5 billion from Russia into the Bank of New York. For more on the Russian mob, see the Race, Culture, Gender, and Criminology feature on page 410.

The Evolution of Organized Crime

Have these newly emerging groups achieved the same level of control as traditional crime families? Some experts argue that minority gangs will have a tough time develop-

© Reuters NewMedia-CORBIS

■ The "traditional" mob is being replaced by newcomers from Latin America and Europe. Some of the major figures from the crime families are in prison or federal witness protection programs. Sometimes these one-time mobsters revert to their criminal ways. Here, former Mafia turncoat and hitman Salvatore "Sammy the Bull" Gravano sits at his hearing in Judge Ronald Reinstein's courtroom in Phoenix, Arizona. Gravano was formally charged on February 28, 2000, with helping to run a crime syndicate that peddled 30,000 pills per week of the drug Ecstasy to Arizona youths while in a Federal witness program.

ing the network of organized corruption, which involves working with government officials and unions, that traditional crime families enjoyed.[126]

As law enforcement pressure has been put on traditional organized crime figures, other groups have filled the vacuum. For example, the Hell's Angels motorcycle club is now believed to be one of the leading distributors of narcotics in the United States. Similarly, Chinese criminal gangs have taken over the dominant role in New York City's heroin market from the traditional Italian-run syndicates.[127]

In sum, most experts now agree that it is simplistic to view organized crime in the United States as a national syndicate that controls all illegitimate rackets in an orderly fashion. This view seems to ignore the variety of gangs and groups, their membership, and their relationship to the outside world.[128] Mafia-type groups may play a major role in organized crime, but they are by no means the only ones that can be considered organized criminals.[129]

For a Web page devoted to organized crime and links to other similar sites, go to:
http://organizedcrime.about.com/
For an up-to-date list of Web links, go to
http://info.wadsworth.com/siegel ■

Controlling Organized Crime

George Vold once argued that the development of organized crime parallels early capitalist enterprises. Organized crime employs ruthless monopolistic tactics to maximize profits; it is also secretive, protective of its operations, and defensive against any outside intrusion.[130] Consequently, controlling its activities is extremely difficult.

Federal and state governments actually did little to combat organized crime until fairly recently. One of the first measures aimed directly at organized crime was the Interstate and Foreign Travel or Transportation in Aid of Racketeering Enterprises Act (Travel Act).[131] The Travel Act prohibits travel in interstate commerce or use of interstate facilities with the intent to promote, manage, establish, carry on, or facilitate an unlawful activity; it also prohibits the actual or attempted engagement in these activities. In 1970 Congress passed the Organized Crime Control Act. Title IX of the act, probably its most effective measure, has been called the **Racketeer Influenced and Corrupt Organization Act (RICO)**.[132]

RICO did not create new categories of crimes but rather new categories of offenses in racketeering activity, which it defined as involvement in two or more acts prohibited by 24 existing federal and 8 state statutes. The offenses listed in RICO include state-defined crimes, such as murder, kidnapping, gambling, arson, robbery, bribery, extortion, and narcotic violations; and federally defined crimes, such as bribery, counterfeiting, transmission of

Russian Organized Crime

In the decade since the collapse of the Soviet Union, criminal organizations in Russia and other former Soviet republics such as Ukraine have engaged in a variety of crimes. Illegal drugs, arms trafficking, stolen automobiles, trafficking in women and children, and money laundering are among the most prevalent. No area of the world seems immune to this menace, especially not the United States. America is the land of opportunity for unloading criminal goods and laundering dirty money.

Unlike Colombian, Italian, Mexican, or other well-known forms of organized crime, Soviet organized crime is not primarily based on ethnic or family structures. Instead, Russian organized crime is developed out of economic necessity, which was nurtured by the oppressive Soviet regime. A professional criminal class developed in Soviet prisons during the Stalinist period, which began in 1924, the era of the gulag. These criminals adopted behaviors, rules, values, and sanctions that bound them together in what was called the thieves' world, led by the elite *"vory v zakone,"* criminals who lived according to the "thieves' law." This thieves' world, and particularly the *vory,* created and maintained the bonds and climate of trust necessary for carrying out organized crime.

Here are some specific characteristics of Russian organized crime in the post-Soviet era:

Russian criminals make extensive use of the state governmental apparatus to protect and promote their criminal activities. For example, most businesses in Russia—legal, quasi-legal, and illegal—must operate with the protection of a *krysha* (roof). The protection is often provided by police or security officials employed for this purpose outside their "official" capacities. In other cases, officials are "silent partners" in criminal enterprises that they, in turn, protect.

The criminalization of the privatization process has resulted in the massive use of state funds for criminal gain. Valuable properties are purchased through insider deals for much less than their true value and then resold for lucrative profits.

Criminals have been able to directly influence the state's domestic and foreign policy to promote the interests of organized crime, either by attaining public office themselves or by buying public officials.

Beyond these particular features, organized crime in Russia shares other characteristics that are common to some forms of organized crime elsewhere in the world:

Systematic use of violence, including both the threat and the use of force

Hierarchical structure

Limited or exclusive membership

Specialization in types of crime and a division of labor

Military-style discipline, with strict rules and regulations for the organization as a whole

High-tech equipment including military weapons, threats, blackmail, and violence used to penetrate business management and assume control of commercial enterprises, or in some instances, to found their own enterprises with money from their criminal activities

The organized crime threat to Russia's national security is now becoming a global threat. They are operating both on their own and in cooperation with foreign groups. The latter cooperation often comes in the form of joint money-laundering ven-
tures. Russian criminals have become involved in killings for hire in Central and Western Europe, Israel, Canada, and the United States. However, in the United States, with the exception of extortion and money laundering, Russians have had little or no involvement in some of the more traditional types of organized crime, such as drug trafficking, gambling, and loan sharking. Instead, these criminal groups are extensively engaged in a broad array of frauds and scams, including health care fraud, insurance scams, stock frauds, antiquities swindles, forgery, and fuel tax evasion schemes. Recently, for example, Russians have become the main purveyors of credit card fraud in the United States. Legitimate businesses such as the movie business and textile industry have become targets of criminals from the former Soviet Union, and they are often used for money laundering.

Critical Thinking Questions

The influence of new immigrant groups in organized crime seems to suggest that illegal enterprise is a common practice among "new" Americans. Do you believe some aspect of American culture causes immigrants to choose a criminal lifestyle? Or does our open culture encourage the criminal activities of people that may have been incubated in their native lands?

InfoTrac College Edition Research

To read more about Russian organized crime, go to InfoTrac College Edition and access this article:

Scott O'Neal. Russian organized crime. *FBI Law Enforcement Bulletin* May 2000 v69 i5 p1

SOURCE: James O. Finckenauer and Yuri A. Voronin, *The Threat of Russian Organized Crime* (Washington, D.C.: National Institute of Justice, 2001).

gambling information, prostitution, and mail fraud. RICO is designed to limit patterns of organized criminal activity by prohibiting involvement in acts intended to

- Derive income from racketeering or the unlawful collection of debts and to use or invest such income.
- Acquire through racketeering an interest in or control over any enterprise engaged in interstate or foreign commerce.
- Conduct business through a pattern of racketeering.
- Conspire to use racketeering as a means of making income, collecting loans, or conducting business.

An individual convicted under RICO is subject to 20 years in prison and a $25,000 fine. Additionally, the accused must forfeit to the U.S. government any interest in a business in violation of RICO. These penalties are much more potent than simple conviction and imprisonment.

RICO's success has shaped the way the FBI attacks organized crime groups. They now use the **enterprise theory of investigation (ETI)** model as their standard investigative tool. Rather than investigate crimes after they are committed, under the ETI model the focus is on criminal enterprise and investigation attacks on the structure of the criminal enterprise rather than on criminal acts viewed as isolated incidents.[133] For example, a drug trafficking organization must get involved in such processes as transportation and distribution of narcotics, finance such as money laundering, and communication with clients and dealers. The ETI identifies and then targets each of these areas simultaneously, focusing on the subsystems that are considered the most vulnerable.

The Future of Organized Crime

Indications are that the traditional organized crime syndicates are in decline. Law enforcement officials in Philadelphia, New Jersey, New England, New Orleans, Kansas City, Detroit, and Milwaukee all report that years of federal and state interventions have severely eroded the Mafia organizations in their areas.

What has caused this alleged erosion of Mafia power? First, a number of the reigning family heads are quite old, in their 70s and 80s, prompting some law enforcement of-

ficials to dub them "the Geritol gang."[134] A younger generation of mob leaders is stepping in to take control of the families, and they seem to lack the skill and leadership of the older bosses. In addition, active government enforcement policies have halved what the estimated mob membership was 20 years ago, and a number of the highest-ranking leaders have been imprisoned. Additional pressure comes from newly emerging ethnic gangs that want to muscle in on traditional syndicate activities, such as drug sales and gambling. For example, Chinese Triad gangs have been active in New York and California in the drug trade, loan sharking, and labor racketeering. Other ethnic crime groups include black and Colombian drug cartels and the Sicilian Mafia, which operates independently of U.S. groups.

Although most street gangs are too disorganized to become stable crime groups, there are some large gangs such as Chicago's Gangster Disciples whose structure, activities, and relationships are now becoming similar to traditional organized gangs. This African American gang is actively involved in politics to gain power and support. Members meet regularly, commit crime as a group, and maintain ongoing relationships with other street gangs and also with prison-based gangs. The Gangster Disciples have extensive ownership of legitimate private businesses and dealings with other businessmen. They offer "protection" against rival gangs and supply stolen merchandise to customers and employees.[135]

The Mafia has also been hurt by changing values in U.S. society. White, ethnic, inner-city neighborhoods, which were the locus of Mafia power, have been shrinking as families move to the suburbs. Organized crime groups have consequently lost their political and social base of operations. In addition, the code of silence that protected Mafia leaders is now broken regularly by younger members who turn informer rather than face prison terms. It is also possible that their success has hurt organized crime families: younger members are better educated than their forebears and are equipped to seek their fortunes through legitimate enterprise.[136] Traditonal organized gangs may be in decline, but it is unlikely, considering the demand for illegal goods and services, that organized criminal behavior will ever be eradicated.

■ Summary

White-collar and organized criminals are similar because they both use ongoing illegal business enterprises to make personal profits. There are various types of white-collar crime. Stings and swindles involve the use of deception to bilk people out of their money. Chiseling customers, businesses, or the government regularly is a second common type of white-collar crime. Surprisingly, many professionals engage in chiseling offenses. Other white-collar criminals use their positions in business and the marketplace to commit economic crimes. Their crimes include exploitation of position in a company or the government to secure illegal payments; embezzlement and employee pilferage and fraud; client fraud; and influence peddling and bribery. Further, corporate officers sometimes violate the law to improve the position and profitability of their businesses. Their crimes include price-fixing, false advertising, and environmental offenses.

So far, little has been done to combat white-collar crimes. Most offenders do not view themselves as criminals and therefore do not seem to be deterred by criminal statutes. Although thousands of white-collar criminals are prosecuted each year, their numbers are insignificant compared with the magnitude of the problem. The government has used various law enforcement strategies to combat white-collar crime. Some involve deterrence, which uses punishment to frighten potential abusers. Others involve economic or compliance strategies, which create economic incentives to obey the law.

The demand for illegal goods and services has produced a symbiotic relationship between the public and an organized criminal network. Organized crime supplies alcohol, gambling, drugs, prostitutes, and pornography to the public. It is immune from prosecution because of public apathy and because of its own strong political connections. Organized criminals used to be white ethnics—Jews, Italians, and Irish—but today African Americans, Hispanics, and other groups have become involved in organized crime activities. The old-line "families" are now more likely to use their criminal wealth and power to buy into legitimate businesses. They are being replaced by groups formed from newly arriving immigrants from Eastern Europe.

There is debate over the control of organized crime. Some experts believe a national crime cartel controls all activities. Others view organized crime as a group of disorganized, competing gangs dedicated to extortion or to providing illegal goods and services. Efforts to control organized crime have been stepped up. The federal government has used antiracketeering statutes to arrest syndicate leaders. But as long as huge profits can be made, illegal enterprises will continue to flourish.

■ Thinking Like a Criminologist

People who commit computer crime are found in every segment of society. They range in age from 10 to 60, and their skill level runs from novice to professional. They are otherwise average people, not supercriminals possessing unique abilities and talents. Any person of any age with even a little skill is a potential computer criminal.

Most studies indicate that employees represent the greatest threat to computers. Almost 90 percent of computer crimes against businesses are inside jobs. Ironically, as advances continue in remote data processing, the threat from external sources will probably increase. With the networking of systems and the adoption of more user-friendly software, the sociological profile of the computer offender may change. For example, computer criminals may soon be members of organized crime syndicates. They will use computer systems to monitor law enforcement activities. To become a made man in the twenty-first-century organized crime family, the recruit will have to develop knowledge of the equipment used for audio surveillance of law enforcement communications: computers with sound card or microphone, modems, and software programs for the remote operation of the systems.

Which theories of criminal behavior best explain the actions of computer criminals, and which ones fail to account for computer crime?

■ Key Terms

- white-collar crime (388)
- organized crime (388)
- corporate crime (389)
- churning (390)
- front running (390)
- bucketing (390)
- insider trading (391)
- influence peddling (392)
- exploitation (392)
- pilferage (393)
- organizational crime (396)
- actual authority (396)
- apparent authority (396)
- Sherman Antitrust Act (396)
- division of markets (396)
- tying arrangement (396)
- group boycott (396)
- price-fixing (397)
- alien conspiracy theory (407)
- Mafia (407)
- La Cosa Nostra (407)
- Racketeer Influenced and Corrupt Organization Act (RICO) (409)
- enterprise theory of investigation (ETI) (411)

Critical Thinking Questions

1. How would you punish a corporate executive whose product killed people if the executive had no knowledge that the product was potentially lethal? What if the executive did know?

2. Is organized crime inevitable as long as immigrant groups seek to become part of the "American Dream"?

3. Does the media glamorize organized crime? Does it paint an inaccurate picture of noble crime lords fighting to protect their families?

4. Apply traditional theories of criminal behavior to white-collar and organized crime? Which one seems to best predict why someone would engage in these behaviors?

Notes

1. David Firestone, "In Racketeering Trial, Well-Dressed Strip Club Takes the Stage," *New York Times,* 5 May 2001, p. 3.

2. Dwight Smith, "White-Collar Crime, Organized Crime and the Business Establishment: Resolving a Crisis in Criminological Theory," in *White Collar and Economic Crime: A Multidisciplinary and Crossnational Perspective,* eds. P. Wickman and T. Dailey (Lexington, Mass.: Lexington Books, 1982), p. 53.

3. Mark Haller, "Illegal Enterprise: A Theoretical and Historical Interpretation," *Criminology* 28 (1990): 207–35.

4. Nancy Frank and Michael Lynch, *Corporate Crime, Corporate Violence* (Albany, N.Y.: Harrow and Heston, 1992), p. 7.

5. Nikos Passas and David Nelken, "The Thin Line between Legitimate and Criminal Enterprises: Subsidy Frauds in the European Community," *Crime, Law and Social Change* 19 (1993): 223–43.

6. Ibid., p. 238.

7. For a thorough review, see David Friedrichs, *Trusted Criminals* (Belmont, Calif.: Wadsworth, 1996).

8. Kitty Calavita and Henry Pontell, "Savings and Loan Fraud as Organized Crime: Toward a Conceptual Typology of Corporate Illegality," *Criminology* 31 (1993): 519–48.

9. Edwin Sutherland, *White-Collar Crime: The Uncut Version* (New Haven: Yale University Press, 1983).

10. Edwin Sutherland, "White-Collar Criminality," *American Sociological Review* 5 (1940): 2–10.

11. David Weisburd and Kip Schlegel, "Returning to the Mainstream," in *White-Collar Crime Reconsidered,* eds. Kip Schlegel and David Weisburd (Boston: Northeastern University Press, 1992), pp. 352–65.

12. Ronald Kramer and Raymond Michalowski, "State-Corporate Crime." Paper presented at the annual meeting of the American Society of Criminology, Baltimore, November 1990.

13. Elizabeth Moore and Michael Mills, "The Neglected Victims and Unexamined Costs of White-Collar Crime," *Crime and Delinquency* 36 (1990): 408–18.

14. Stuart Traub, "Battling Employee Crime: A Review of Corporate Strategies and Programs," *Crime and Delinquency* 42 (1996): 244–56.

15. Laura Schrager and James Short, "Toward a Sociology of Organizational Crime," *Social Problems* 25 (1978): 415–25.

16. Gilbert Geis, "White-Collar and Corporate Crime," in *Major Forms of Crime,* ed. Robert Meier (Beverly Hills, Calif.: Sage, 1984), p. 145.

17. Marshall Clinard and Richard Quinney, *Criminal Behavior Systems: A Typology* (New York: Holt, Rinehart and Winston, 1973), p. 117.

18. Mark Moore, "Notes Toward a National Strategy to Deal with White-Collar Crime," in *A National Strategy for Containing White-Collar Crime,* eds. Herbert Edelhertz and Charles Rogovin (Lexington, Mass.: Lexington Books, 1980), pp. 32–44.

19. For a general review, see John Braithwaite, "White Collar Crime," *Annual Review* 11 (1985): 1–25.

20. Nikos Passas, "Structural Sources of International Crime: Policy Lessons from the BCCI Affair," *Crime, Law and Social Change* 19 (1994): 223–31.

21. Nikos Passas, "Accounting for Fraud: Auditors' Ethical Dilemmas in the BCCI Affair," in *The Ethics of Accounting and Finance,* eds. W. Michael Hoffman, Judith Brown Kamm, Robert Frederick, and Edward Petry (Westport, Conn.: Quorum Books, 1996), pp. 85–99.

22. Mike Schneider, "In Florida, Man Suspected of a Religious Scam," *Boston Globe,* 27 October 1998, p. B1.

23. Earl Gottschalk, "Churchgoers Are the Prey as Scams Rise," *Wall Street Journal,* 7 August 1989, p. C1.

24. Associated Press, "NYC Cab Scam Warning Given," *Boston Globe,* 19 September 1997, p. 13.

25. Richard Quinney, "Occupational Structure and Criminal Behavior: Prescription Violation of Retail Pharmacists," *Social Problems* 11 (1963): 179–85; see also John Braithwaite, *Corporate Crime in the Pharmaceutical Industry* (London: Routledge and Kegan Paul, 1984).

26. Pam Belluck, "Prosecutors Say Greed Drove Pharmacist to Dilute Drugs" *New York Times,* 18 August 2001, p. 3.

27. Metropolitan Desk, "False Claims from Fake Crashes Lead to Charges against 172," *New York Times,* 20 July 2001, p. C1

28. James Armstrong et al., "Securities Fraud," *American Criminal Law Review* 33 (1995): 973–1016.

29. Scott McMurray, "Futures Pit Trader Goes to Trial," *Wall Street Journal,* 8 May 1990, p. C1; Scott McMurray, "Chicago Pits' Dazzling Growth Permitted a Free-for-All Mecca," *Wall Street Journal,* 3 August 1989, p. A4.

30. Associated Press, "12 Westchester Stockbrokers Indicted in $100 Million Telephone-Sales Fraud," *New York Times,* 3 October 1998, p. B1.

31. *Carpenter v. United States* 484 U.S. 19 (1987); also see John Boland, "The SEC Trims the First Amendment," *Wall Street Journal,* 4 December 1986, p. 28.

32. Kevin Sack, "49ers Owner Pleads Guilty in Louisiana Casino Case," *New York Times,* 7 October 1998, p.1.

33. Charles V. Bagli, "Kickback Investigation Extends to Middle-Class Buildings in New York," *New York Times,* 14 October 1998, p. A19.

34. Marshall Clinard and Peter Yeager, *Corporate Crime* (New York: Free Press, 1980), p. 67.

35. Ibid.

36. United Press International, "Minority Leader in N.Y. Senate Is Charged," *Boston Globe,* 17 September 1987, p. 20.

37. Discussed in Friedrichs, *Trusted Criminals,* p. 147.

38. Larry Tye, "A Tide of State Corruption Sweeps from Coast to Coast," *Boston Globe,* 25 March 1991, p. 1.

39. Maureen Kline, "Italian Magistrates Query Montedison Former Chairman," *Wall Street Journal,* 19 July 1993, p. A6.

40. *The Knapp Commission Report on Police Corruption* (New York: George Braziller, 1973), pp. 1–3, 170–82.

41. David Kocieniewski and David M. Halbfinger, "New York's Most Respected Officers Led Precinct Where Sex Scandal Festered," *New York Times,* 20 July 1998, p. 1.

42. Cited in Hugh Barlow, *Introduction to Criminology,* 2d ed. (Boston: Little, Brown, 1984).

43. PL No. 95-213, 101-104, 91 Stat. 1494.

44. Thomas Burton, "The More Baxter Hides Its Israeli Boycott Role, the More Flak It Gets," *Wall Street Journal,* 25 April 1991, p. 1.

45. "Newsbreaks," *Aviation Week and Space Technology,* 10 July 1995, p. 19.

46. Charles McCaghy, *Deviant Behavior* (New York: Macmillan, 1976), p. 178.

47. John Clark and Richard Hollinger, *Theft by Employees in Work Organizations* (Washington, D.C.: U.S. Government Printing Office, 1983), pp. 2–3.

48. Associated Press, "Business Fraud Prevails, May Worsen, Study Says," *Wall Street Journal,* 17 August 1993, p. A4.

49. Richard Pérez-Peña, "Indictments Charge 4 Racetrack Tellers with Laundering Money at Betting Windows," *New York Times,* 20 July 2001, p. A4.

50. J. Sorenson, H. Grove, and T. Sorenson, "Detecting Management Fraud: The Role of the Independent Auditor," in *White-Collar Crime, Theory and Research,* eds. G. Geis and E. Stotland (Beverly Hills, Calif.: Sage, 1980), pp. 221–51.

51. The Associated Press, "F.B.I. Arrests 8 in McDonald's Prize Scheme," *New York Times,* 21 August 2001, p. B1.

52. Kurt Eichenwald, "Ex-Andersen Partner Pleads Guilty in Record-Shredding," *New York Times,* 12 April 2002, p. C1; John A. Byrne, "At Enron, the Environment Was Ripe for Abuse," *Business Week,* 25 February 2002, p.12.

53. Joe Sexton, "In Brooklyn Neighborhood, Welfare Fraud Is Nothing New," *New York Times,* 19 March 1997, p. A1.

54. Dana Canedy, "Children Are Prey in a Medicaid Dental Scheme," *New York Times,* 17 August 2001, p.1.

55. See Kristine DeBry, Bonny Harbinger, and Susan Rotkis, "Health Care Fraud," *American Criminal Law Review* 33 (1995): 818–38.

56. Associated Press, "Hospital Settles Bribe Allegation," *Boston Globe,* 19 September 1997, p. 13.

57. Kurt Eichenwald, "Hospital Chain Cheated U.S. on Expenses, Documents Show," *New York Times,* 18 December 1997, p. B1.

58. Laura Johannes and Wendy Bounds, "Corning Agrees to Pay $6.8 Million to Settle Medicare Billing Charges," *Wall Street Journal,* 22 February 1996, p. B2.

59. Ibid.

60. 42 U.S.C. section 1395nn (1993).

61. 18 U.S.C. section 1344 (1994).

62. *United States v. Bishop,* 412 U.S. 346 (1973).

63. Frank and Lynch, *Corporate Crime, Corporate Violence,* pp. 12–13.

64. Cited in Frank and Lynch, *Corporate Crime, Corporate Violence,* pp. 12–13.

65. Sutherland, "White-Collar Criminality," pp. 2–10.

66. Joseph S. Hall, "Corporate Criminal Liability," *American Criminal Law Review* 35 (1998): 549–60.

67. 15 U.S.C. section 1 (1994).

68. 15 U.S.C. 1–7 (1976).

69. *Northern Pacific Railways v. United States,* 356 U.S. 1 (1958).

70. Tim Carrington, "Federal Probes of Contractors Rise for Year," *Wall Street Journal,* 23 February 1987, p. 50.

71. Ibid.

72. Clinard and Yeager, *Corporate Crime.*

73. "Econotes," *Environmental Action* 13 (October 1981): 7.

74. "Econotes," *Environmental Action* 13 (September 1981): 5.

75. Christopher Marquis, "U.S. Says It Broke Pornography Ring Featuring Youths," *New York Times,* 9 August 2001, p. 6.

76. Jeanne Capachin and Dave Potterton, "Online Card Payments, Fraud Solu-

tions Bid to Win," *Meridien Research Report* (Newton, Mass.), 18 January 2001.

77. Bruce Swartz, Deputy Assistant General, Criminal Division, Justice Department, *Internet Fraud Testimony Before the House Energy And Commerce Committee,* 23 May 2001.

78. Ibid.

79. This section is based on Richard Walker and David M. Levine, "'You've Got Jail': Current Trends in Civil and Criminal Enforcement of Internet Securities Fraud," *American Criminal Law Review* 38 (2001): 405–30.

80. Jim Wolf, "Internet Scams Targeted in Sweep: A 10-Day Crackdown Leads to 62 Arrests and 88 Indictments," *Boston Globe,* 22 May 2001, p. A2.

81. M. Swanson and J. Terriot, "Computer Crime: Dimensions, Types, Causes and Investigations," *Journal of Political Science and Administration* 8 (1980): 305–6; see Donn Parker, "Computer-Related White-Collar Crime," in *White Collar Crime, Theory and Research,* eds. G. Geis and E. Stotland (Beverly Hills, Calif.: Sage, 1980), pp. 199–220.

82. Anne Branscomb, "Rogue Computer Programs and Computer Rogues: Tailoring Punishment to Fit the Crime," *Rutgers Computer and Technology Law Journal* 16 (1990): 24–26.

83. Carl Benson, Andrew Jablon, Paul Kaplan, and Mara Elena Rosenthal, "Computer Crimes," *American Criminal Law Review* 34 (1997): 409–43.

84. David Stipp, "Computer Virus Maker Is Given Probation, Fine," *Wall Street Journal,* 7 May 1990, p. B3.

85. Erik Larson, "Computers Turn Out to Be Valuable Aid in Employee Crime," *Wall Street Journal,* 14 January 1985, p. 1.

86. Clyde Wilson, "Software Piracy: Uncovering Mutiny on the Cyberseas," *Trial* 32 (1996): 24–31.

87. Herbert Edelhertz and Charles Rogovin, eds., *A National Strategy for Containing White-Collar Crime* (Lexington, Mass.: Lexington Books, 1980), Appendix A, pp. 122–23.

88. Belluck, "Prosecutors Say Greed Drove Pharmacist to Dilute Drugs," p. 3.

89. Kathleen Daly, "Gender and Varieties of White-Collar Crime," *Criminology* 27 (1989): 769–93.

90. Quoted in Tim Metz and Michael Miller, "Boesky's Rise and Fall Illustrate a Compulsion to Profit by Getting Inside Track on Market," *Wall Street Journal,* 17 November 1986, p. 28.

91. Donald Cressey, *Other People's Money: A Study of the Social Psychology of Embezzlement* (Glencoe, Ill.: Free Press, 1973), p. 96.

92. Byrne, "At Enron, the Environment Was Ripe for Abuse," p. 14.

93. Travis Hirschi and Michael Gottfredson, "Causes of White-Collar Crime," *Criminology* 25 (1987): 949–74.

94. Michael Gottfredson and Travis Hirschi, *A General Theory of Crime* (Stanford, Calif.: Stanford University Press, 1990), p. 191.

95. This section relies heavily on Daniel Skoler, "White-Collar Crime and the Criminal Justice System: Problems and Challenges," in *A National Strategy for Containing White-Collar Crime,* eds. Herbert Edelhertz and Charles Rogovin (Lexington, Mass.: Lexington Books, 1980), pp. 57–76.

96. Theodore Hammett and Joel Epstein, *Prosecuting Environmental Crime: Los Angeles County* (Washington, D.C.: National Institute of Justice, 1993).

97. Michael Benson, Francis Cullen, and William Maakestad, "Local Prosecutors and Corporate Crime," *Crime and Delinquency* 36 (1990): 356–72.

98. Ibid., pp. 369–70.

99. David Simon and D. Stanley Eitzen, *Elite Deviance* (Boston: Allyn and Bacon, 1982), p. 28.

100. This section relies heavily on Albert Reiss Jr., "Selecting Strategies of Social Control over Organizational Life," in *Enforcing Regulation,* eds. Keith Hawkins and John M. Thomas (Boston: Klowver Publications, 1984), pp. 25–37.

101. John Braithwaite, "The Limits of Economism in Controlling Harmful Corporate Conduct," *Law and Society Review* 16 (1981–1982): 481–504.

102. Michael Benson, "Emotions and Adjudication: Status Degradation among White-Collar Criminals," *Justice Quarterly* 7 (1990): 515–28; John Braithwaite, *Crime, Shame and Reintegration* (Sydney: Cambridge University Press, 1989).

103. Kip Schlegel, "Desert, Retribution and Corporate Criminality," *Justice Quarterly* 5 (1988): 615–34.

104. Raymond Michalowski and Ronald Kramer, "The Space between Laws: The Problem of Corporate Crime in a Transnational Context," *Social Problems* 34 (1987): 34–53.

105. Ibid.

106. Steven Klepper and Daniel Nagin, "The Deterrent Effect of Perceived Certainty and Severity of Punishment Revisited," *Criminology* 27 (1989): 721–46.

107. Geis, "White-Collar and Corporate Crime," p. 154.

108. Christopher M. Brown and Nikhil S. Singhvi, "Antitrust Violations," *American Criminal Law Review* 35 (1998): 467–501.

109. Howard Adler, "Current Trends in Criminal Antitrust Enforcement," *Business Crimes Bulletin* (April 1996): 1.

110. Robert Bennett, "Eighth Survey of White Collar Crime" (Foreword), *American Criminal Law Review* 30 (1993).

111. David Weisburd, Elin Waring, and Stanton Wheeler, "Class, Status, and the Punishment of White-Collar Criminals," *Law and Social Inquiry* 15 (1990): 223–43.

112. Mark Cohen, "Environmental Crime and Punishment: Legal/Economic Theory and Empirical Evidence on Enforcement of Federal Environmental Statutes," *Journal of Criminal Law and Criminology* 82 (1992): 1054–1109.

113. Russell Mokhiber, "White Collar Crime Penalties," *Multinational Monitor* 22 (2001): 30.

114. See, generally, President's Commission on Organized Crime, *Report to the President and the Attorney General, The Impact: Organized Crime Today* (Washington, D.C.: U.S. Government Printing Office, 1986). Herein cited as *Organized Crime Today.*

115. Frederick Martens and Michele Cunningham-Niederer, "Media Magic, Mafia Mania," *Federal Probation* 49 (1985): 60–68.

116. *Organized Crime Today,* pp. 7–8.

117. Alan Block and William Chambliss, *Organizing Crime* (New York: Elsevier, 1981).

118. Alan Block, *East Side/West Side* (New Brunswick, N.J.: Transaction Books, 1983), pp. VII, 10–11.

119. Donald Cressey, *Theft of the Nation* (New York: Harper and Row, 1969).

120. Dwight Smith, *The Mafia Mystique* (New York: Basic Books, 1975).

121. Stanley Einstein, and Menachem Amir, *Organized Crime: Uncertainties and Dilemmas* (Chicago, Ill.: University of Illinois at Chicago, Office of International Criminal Justice, 1999);

William Kleinknecht, *The New Ethnic Mobs: The Changing Face of Organized Crime in America* (New York: Free Press, 1996); Don Liddick, *An Empirical, Theoretical, and Historical Overview of Organized Crime* (Lewiston, N.Y.: Edwin Mellen Press, 1999); Maria Minniti, "Membership Has Its Privileges: Old and New Mafia Organizations," *Comparative Economic Studies* 37 (1995): 31–47.

122. *Organized Crime Today,* p. 11.

123. Richard A. Ballezza, "YACS Crime Groups: An FBI Major Crime Initiative," *FBI Law Enforcement Bulletin* 67 (1998): 7–13.

124. Omar Bartos, "Growth of Russian Organized Crime Poses Serious Threat," *CJ International* 11 (1995): 8–9.

125. John Tagliabue, "Russian Racket Linked to New York Bank," *New York Times,* 28 September 1999, p. 1.

126. Robert Kelly and Rufus Schatzberg, "Types of Minority Organized Crime: Some Considerations." Paper presented at the annual meeting of the American Society of Criminology, Montreal, November 1987.

127. Peter Kerr, "Chinese Now Dominate New York Heroin Trade," *New York Times,* 9 August 1987, p. 1.

128. Phillip Jenkins and Gary Potter, "The Politics and Mythology of Organized Crime: A Philadelphia Case Study," *Journal of Criminal Justice* 15 (1987): 473–84.

129. William Chambliss, *On the Take* (Bloomington: Indiana University Press, 1978).

130. George Vold, *Theoretical Criminology,* 2d ed., rev. Thomas Bernard (New York: Oxford University Press, 1979).

131. 18 U.S.C. 1952 (1976).

132. PL No. 91-452, Title IX, 84 Stat. 922 (1970) (codified at 18 U.S.C. 1961–68, 1976).

133. Richard McFeely, "Enterprise Theory of Investigation," *FBI Law Enforcement Bulletin* 70 (2001): 19–26.

134. Selwyn Raab, "A Battered and Ailing Mafia Is Losing Its Grip on America," *New York Times,* 22 October 1990, p. 1.

135. Scott Decker, Tim Bynum, and Deborah Weisel, "A Tale of Two Cities: Gangs and Organized Crime Groups," *Justice Quarterly* 15 (1998): 395–425.

136. Raab, "A Battered and Ailing Mafia Is Losing Its Grip on America," p. B7.

AP/Wide World Photos

CHAPTER 14 Public Order Crimes

Introduction

Stuart J. Roll built a thriving business selling mustard, ketchup, jelly and jam that did $10 million in sales each year and made him a multimillionaire. Then he decided to branch out into prostitution. Mr. Roll solicited women through ads in local newspapers seeking a "companion/ housekeeper." When women applied, he proposed that they become prostitutes. He employed at least three women and charged customers $150 for half an hour or $250 for an hour, which he split 50–50 with the women. He got customers through classified ads in New York magazines that promised "pvt. relaxation for the refined gentleman. Elegant European beauty. Private res. Upscale/Expensive."

After his arrest, Mr. Roll, 68, told the media that he set up the new business using the same kind of principles — catering to his customers' needs and paying meticulous attention to detail—that he had used to start his food business. "What we are performing here is more of a community service than breaking the law," Mr. Roll said of his new enterprise. "People need love so badly. Here a man can come in and have his sanctuary, his peace of mind and his fantasy all wrapped in a million-dollar home ready to serve him.... It is a victimless crime.... I want to take sex out of the street and put it in the home, where it belongs," he claimed.[1]

Is Mr Roll's behavior criminal, or do you agree with him that he is providing a community service that the public truly desires? Unfortunately for him, most societies have long banned or limited behaviors that are believed to run contrary to social norms, customs, and values. These behaviors are often referred to as **public order crimes** or **victimless crimes,** although this latter term can be misleading.[2] Public order crimes involve acts that interfere with the operations of society and the ability of people to function efficiently. Put another way, common-law crimes such as rape or robbery are considered inherently wrong and damaging, but other behaviors are outlawed (public order crimes) because they conflict with social policy, prevailing moral rules, and current public opinion. Statutes designed to uphold public order usually prohibit the manufacture and distribution of morally questionable goods and services such as erotic material, commercial sex, and mood-altering drugs. They may also ban acts that a few people holding political power consider morally tinged, such as homosexual contact. Statutes like these are controversial in part because millions of otherwise law-abiding citizens often engage in these outlawed activities and consequently become criminals. These statutes are also controversial because they selectively prohibit desired goods, services, and behaviors; in other words, they outlaw sin and vice.

This chapter covers these public order crimes; it first briefly discusses the relationship between law and morality. Next the chapter addresses public order crimes of a sexual nature: pornography, prostitution, deviant sex, and homosexual acts. The chapter concludes by focusing on the abuse of drugs and alcohol.

Law and Morality

Legislation of moral issues has continually frustrated lawmakers. There is little debate that the purpose of criminal law is to protect society and reduce social harm. When a store is robbed or a child assaulted, it is relatively easy to see and condemn the harm done the victim. It is, however, more difficult to sympathize with or even identify the victims of immoral acts, such as pornography or prostitution, where the parties involved may be willing participants. If there is no victim, can there be a crime? Should acts be made illegal merely because they violate prevailing moral standards? If so, who defines morality?

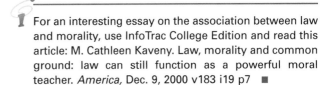

For an interesting essay on the association between law and morality, use InfoTrac College Edition and read this article: M. Cathleen Kaveny. Law, morality and common ground: law can still function as a powerful moral teacher. *America,* Dec. 9, 2000 v183 i19 p7 ■

Consider the case of Stuart J. Roll. Should he have been punished? His clients wanted to hire his sex workers and willingly purchased their services. It hardly seems possible that these clients were crime victims. What of his alleged employees? They willingly engaged in sexual activity for money, and their income was far higher than what they would have earned in legitimate jobs. Although "immoral," should Roll and his employees be considered criminals?

To answer this question, we might first consider whether there is actually a victim in so-called victimless crimes. Some participants may have been coerced into their acts; they are therefore its victims. Opponents of pornography, such as Andrea Dworkin, charge that women involved in adult films, far from being highly paid stars, are "dehumanized— turned into objects and commodities."[3] Research on prostitution shows that many young runaways and abandoned children are coerced into a life on the streets, where they are cruelly treated and held as virtual captives.[4]

For a site dedicated to the works of Andrea Dworkin, including her fiction, go to:
  http://www.igc.apc.org/Womensnet/dworkin/
For an up-to-date list of Web links, go to
  http://info.wadsworth.com/siegel ■

Even if public order crimes do not actually harm their participants, perhaps society as a whole should be considered the victim of these crimes. Is the community harmed when an adult bookstore opens or a brothel is established? Does this signal that a neighborhood is in decline? Does it teach children that deviance is to be tolerated and profited from?

Debating Morality

Some scholars argue that acts like pornography, prostitution, and drug use erode the moral fabric of society and

Alinari/Art Resource, NY

■ Michelangelo's statue of David is one of the most important and beloved pieces of Western art. Is it possible that some might consider the unclothed David obscene or prurient? If so, should children be prevented from viewing the statue? Should it be covered up? If David's nudity is not offensive or sexually suggestive, then what does it take to make a statue or photo "pornographic"?

ous."[5] In his classic statement on the function of morality in the law, legal scholar Sir Patrick Devlin states,

> Without shared ideas on politics, morals, and ethics no society can exist.... If men and women try to create a society in which there is no fundamental agreement about good and evil, they will fail; if having based it on common agreement, the agreement goes, the society will disintegrate. For society is not something that is kept together physically; it is held by the invisible bonds of common thought. If the bonds were too far relaxed, the members would drift apart. A common morality is part of the bondage. The bondage is part of the price of society; and mankind, which needs society, must pay its price.[6]

According to this view, so-called victimless crimes are prohibited because one of the functions of criminal law is to express a shared sense of public morality.[7]

Some influential legal scholars have questioned the propriety of legislating morals. H. L. A. Hart states,

> It is fatally easy to confuse the democratic principle that power should be in the hands of the majority with the utterly different claim that the majority, with power in their hands, need respect no limits. Certainly there is a special risk in a democracy that the majority may dictate how all should live.[8]

Hart may be motivated by the fact that defining morality may be an impossible task: Who defines morality? Are we not punishing differences rather than social harm? Are photographs of nude children and adults by famed photographer Robert Mapplethorpe art or obscenity?

As U.S. Supreme Court Justice William O. Douglas once so succinctly put it, "What may be trash to me may be prized by others."[9] This debate made national news in 1999 when New York City Mayor Rudolph W. Giuliani took on the Brooklyn Museum of Art over a controversial art exhibition it had scheduled.[10] The focus of Giuliani's ire was Chris Ofili's portrait of the Virgin Mary, painted on dried dung and surrounded by cutouts of female sex organs. The mayor threatened to withhold the museum's funding and evict it from the city-owned building in an effort to force the removal of the work he found offensive. On November 1, 1999, a federal judge ruled that Mayor Giuliani had violated the First Amendment when he cut city financing and began eviction proceedings against the museum. Should politicians such as Mayor Guiliani have the right to censor public art exhibitions they find offensive or immoral? After all, many of the great works of Western art depict nude males and females, some quite young. Should a politician be able to ban the paintings of Leonardo Da Vinci or the sculpture of Michelangelo because he or she considers it "porn"? Joseph Gusfield argues that the purpose of outlawing immoral acts is to show the moral superiority of those who condemn the acts over those who partake of them. The legislation of morality "enhances the social status of groups carrying the affirmed culture and degrades groups carrying that which is condemned as deviant."[11]

therefore should be prohibited and punished. They are crimes, according to the great legal scholar Morris Cohen, because "it is one of the functions of the criminal law to give expression to the collective feeling of revulsion toward certain acts, even when they are not very danger-

Should a politician use his or her power to control the content of an art exhibition? Use "Brooklyn Museum of Art" as a subject guide on InfoTrac College Edition to read articles about this art controversy. ■

Research indicates that people who define themselves as liberals are also the most tolerant of sexually explicit material. Demographic attributes such as age, educational attainment, and occupational status may also influence views of pornography: the young and better educated tend to be more tolerant than older, less-educated people.[12] Whose views should prevail?

And if the law tried to define or limit objectionable material, might it not eventually inhibit free speech and political dissent? Not so, according to social commentator Irving Kristol:

> If we start censoring pornography and obscenity, shall we not inevitably end up censoring political opinion? A lot of people seem to think this would be the case—which only shows the power of doctrinaire thinking over reality. We had censorship of pornography and obscenity for 150 years, until almost yesterday, and I am not aware that freedom of opinion in this country was in any way diminished as a consequence of this fact.[13]

Cultural clashes may ensue when behavior that is considered normative in one society is deplored by those living in another. For example, the United Nations estimates that over 130 million African women have undergone genital mutilation and that each year more than 2 million girls undergo the procedure, some of them in infancy.[14] The surgery is done to ensure virginity, remove sexual sensation, and render the women suitable for marriage. Critics of this practice, led by American author Alice Walker (*The Color Purple*), consider the procedure mutilation and torture; others argue that this ancient custom should be left to the discretion of the indigenous people who consider it part of their culture. "Torture," counters Walker, "is not culture." Can an outsider define the morality of another culture?[15] Because of outside pressure, several African nations south of the Sahara have now instituted bans that are enforced with fines and jail terms. The procedure is now barred in Senegal, Egypt, Burkina Faso, the Central African Republic, Djibouti, Ghana, Guinea, and Togo. Other countries, among them Uganda, discourage it. In North Africa, the Egyptian Supreme Court upheld a ban on the practice and also ruled it had no place in Islam.[16]

While almost universally condemned in the West, female circumcision is still quite common in Africa and the Middle East. To find out why, read this article on InfoTrac College Edition: Richard A. Shweder. What about "female genital mutilation"? and why understanding culture matters in the first place. *Daedalus*, Fall 2000 v129 i4 p209 ■

Social Harm

Many acts that most of us deem highly immoral and objectionable are not criminal. There is no law against lust, gluttony, avarice, sloth, envy, pride, or anger, although they are considered the *seven deadly sins*. Nor is it a crime in most jurisdictions to ignore the pleas of a drowning person, even though such callous behavior is quite immoral. How then do we distinguish between acts that are criminal and outlawed and those that are merely objectionable but tolerated and legal?

In our society, immoral acts can be distinguished from crimes on the basis of the **social harm** they cause. Acts that are believed to be extremely harmful to the general public are usually outlawed; those that may only harm the actor are more likely to be tolerated. Yet even this perspective does not always hold sway. Some acts that cause enormous amounts of social harm are perfectly legal. It is well documented that the consumption of tobacco and alcohol is extremely harmful, but these products remain legal to produce and sell; manufacturers continue to sell sports cars and motorcycles that can accelerate to more than 100 mph, but the legal speed limit is usually 65 mph. More people die each year from alcohol-, tobacco-, and auto-related deaths than from all illegal drugs combined. Should drugs be legalized and fast cars outlawed?

Moral Crusaders

In the early West, "Vigilance Committees" were set up in San Francisco and other boom towns to pursue cattle rustlers and stage coach robbers and to dissuade undesirables from moving in. These **vigilantes** held a strict standard of morality that, when they caught their prey, resulted in sure and swift justice.

The avenging vigilante has remained part of popular culture. Fictional "do-gooders" who take it on themselves to enforce the law, battle evil, and personally deal with those whom they consider immoral have become enmeshed in the public psyche. From the Lone Ranger to Batman, the righteous vigilante is expected to go on moral crusades without any authorization from legal authorities. The assumption that it is okay to take matters into your own hands if the cause is right and the target is immoral is not lost on the younger generation. Gang boys sometimes take on the street identity of Batman or Superman so they can battle their rivals with impunity.

Fictional characters are not the only ones who take it upon themselves to fight for moral decency; members of special interest groups are also ready to do battle. Popular targets of moral crusaders are abortion clinics, pornographers, gun dealers, and logging companies. For example, on March 21, 1993, Baylor University regents voted against allowing nude modeling in art classes after school administrators were swamped with phone calls objecting to "nudity in the classroom."[17] In 1996 Key West, Florida, prohibited nude body painting at the town's annual Fantasy

Fest, a raucous Mardi Gras–like festival. The Monroe County Christian Coalition had launched an all-out offensive against Fantasy Fest, calling it "depravity and debauchery," and the city commission responded by curbing some of the more outrageous activities.[18]

The Baylor and Key West incidents illustrate the pressure that can be placed on governing boards by **moral crusaders** (whom Howard Becker calls **moral entrepreneurs**). These rule creators, argues Becker, operate with an absolute certainty that their way is right and that any means are justified to get their way; "the crusader is fervent and righteous, often self-righteous."[19] Today moral crusaders take on such issues as prayer in school, the right to legal abortions, and the distribution of sexually explicit books and magazines.

Moral crusaders run the risk of engaging in immoral conduct in their efforts to protect society from those they consider "immoral." Abortion foes have resorted to violence and murder to rid the nation of pro-choice health care providers whom they consider "immoral" while failing to realize the depravity of their own extreme acts.

Acts that are illegal because they are viewed as a threat to morality are referred to as public order crimes. Those public order crimes discussed in this chapter are divided into two broad areas. The first relates to what conventional society considers deviant sexual practices: homosexual acts, paraphilias, prostitution, and pornography. The second area concerns the use of substances that have been outlawed or controlled because of the alleged harm they cause: drugs and alcohol.

■ Homosexuality

In October 1998 Matthew Shepard, an openly gay University of Wyoming student, was kidnapped, beaten, and left to die while tied to a fence. A passerby thought at first that his slumped, discolored body was a scarecrow. His death brought cries of outrage from national leaders. Then media stories revealed that, while Shepard lay comatose, a Colorado State University homecoming parade passed within a few blocks of his hospital bed. Propped on a fraternity float was a discolored, straw-haired scarecrow labeled in black spray paint "I'm Gay."[20]

It may be surprising that a section on homosexuality is still included in a criminology text, but today homosexual men and women not only face archaic legal restrictions that criminalize their behavior but are still targeted for so many violent hate crimes that a specific term, **gay bashing,** has been coined to describe violent acts directed at people because of their sexual orientation.

Like other crimes, assaults on homosexuals are adjudicated in the criminal courts. How have victims fared when they seek damages in civil courts? To find out, go

to InfoTrac College Edition and read this article: Lisa Gelhaus. Gay-bashing victims overcome prejudice to win civil settlements. *Trial,* Feb 1999 v35 i2 p14(1) ■

Homosexuality (the word derives from the Greek *homos,* meaning "same") refers to erotic interest in members of one's own sex. However, engaging in homosexual behavior does not necessarily mean one is a homosexual. People may engage in homosexuality because heterosexual partners are unavailable (for example, in the armed services). Some may have sex forced on them by aggressive homosexuals, a condition common in prisons. Some adolescents may experiment with partners of the same sex although their sexual affiliation is heterosexual.[21] Finally, it is possible to be a homosexual but not to engage in sexual conduct with members of the same sex. To avoid this confusion, it might be helpful to adopt the definition of a homosexual as one "who is motivated in adult life by a definite preferential erotic attraction to members of the same sex and who usually (but not necessarily) engages in overt sexual relations with them."[22]

Homosexual behavior has existed in most societies. Records of it can be found in prehistoric art and hieroglyphics.[23] Even when homosexuality was banned or sanctioned, it still persisted.[24] The U.S. Census Bureau now measures the number of unmarried, same-sex partner households in the United States; as of the year 2000, there were 601,209 gay partnerships (more than 1.2 million people), a 314 percent increase over the 145,130 same-sex, unmarried partner households tallied in the 1990 Census. More than 99 percent of all counties in the United States have same-sex households; only 22 counties in the entire country reported no same-sex households.[25]

Attitudes toward Homosexuality

Throughout much of Western history, homosexuals have been subject to discrimination, sanction, and violence. The Bible implies that God destroyed the ancient cities of Sodom and Gomorrah because of their residents' deviant behavior, presumably homosexuality; Sodom is the source of the term **sodomy** (deviant intercourse). The Bible expressly forbids homosexuality—in Leviticus in the Old Testament; Paul's Epistles, Romans, and Corinthians in the New Testament—and this prohibition has been the basis for repressing homosexual behavior.[26]

Gays were brutalized and killed by the ancient Hebrews, a practice continued by the Christians who ruled Western Europe. Laws providing the death penalty for homosexuals existed until 1791 in France, until 1861 in England, and until 1889 in Scotland. Until the Revolution, some American colonies punished homosexuality with death. In Hitler's Germany, 50,000 homosexuals were put in concentration camps; up to 400,000 more from occupied countries were killed. Negative feelings about the homosexual lifestyle are, however, not a historical oddity. In

1996 conservative Christian groups began a national campaign aimed at counteracting legislative victories won by gay rights groups in the area of discrimination and civil rights.[27] Some groups have taken out ads in local newspapers showing "former homosexuals" who "overcame" their sexual orientation through prayer and the help of Christian "ex-gay ministries."

Today many reasons are given for an extremely negative overreaction to homosexuals referred to as **homophobia**.[28] The cause of antigay feelings is uncertain. Ultraconservative religious leaders believe that the Bible condemns same-sex relations and that this behavior is therefore a sin. Some are ignorant about the lifestyle of gays and fear that homosexuality is a contagious disease or that homosexuals will seduce their children.[29] Others develop a deep-rooted hatred of gays because they are insecure about their own sexual identity. Research shows that males who express homophobic attitudes are also likely to become aroused by erotic images of homosexual behavior. Homophobia, then, may be associated with homosexual arousal that the homophobe is either unaware of or denies.[30]

CONNECTIONS

As you may recall from Chapter 11, gay men and women are still subject to thousands of incidents of violence and other hate crimes each year. ■

Homosexuality and the Law

Homosexuality, considered a legal and moral crime throughout most of Western history, is no longer a crime in the United States. In the case of *Robinson v. California,* the U.S. Supreme Court determined that people could not be criminally prosecuted because of their status (such as drug addict or homosexual).[31] Despite this protection, most states and the federal government criminalize the lifestyle and activities of homosexuals. For example, no state or locality allows same-sex marriages, and homosexuals cannot obtain a marriage license to legitimize their relationship. Twenty-six states have banned same-sex marriages, and in 1996 Congress passed the Defense of Marriage Law, which declared that states are not obligated to recognize single-sex marriages performed in other states.[32]

Despite long-standing biases, it is illegal to deprive gay men and women of due process of law. In a 1996 Colorado case, *Romer v. Evans,* the U.S. Supreme Court said that gay people cannot be stripped of legal protection and made "strangers to the law."[33] Nonetheless, the Supreme Court let stand a Cincinnati city charter amendment barring protective legislation for gay people; this amendment prevents homosexuals from obtaining special civil protections such as affirmative action.[34]

Oral and anal sex and all other forms of intercourse that are not heterosexual and genital are banned in about half the states under statutes prohibiting sodomy, deviant sexuality, or buggery. Maximum penalties range from three years to life in prison, with 10 years being the most common sentence.[35] In 1986 the Supreme Court in *Bowers v. Hardwick* upheld a Georgia statute making it a crime to engage in consensual sodomy, even within one's own home.[36] Since then, prestigious legal bodies such as the American Law Institute (ALI) have called for the abolition of statutes prohibiting homosexual sex unless force or coercion is used.[37] Nonetheless, four states—Texas, Oklahoma, Kansas, and Missouri—have sodomy laws that single out same-sex relationships (the Missouri law is currently under court review) and eleven other states have sodomy laws that outlaw some forms of both heterosexual and homosexual activity and consider it a felony. Consider the Massachusetts statute:

> GENERAL LAWS OF MASSACHUSETTS
> Chapter 272: Section 34. Crime against nature.
> Whoever commits the abominable and detestable crime against nature, either with mankind or with a beast, shall be punished by imprisonment in the state prison for not more than twenty years.

The military still bans openly gay people from serving but has compromised with a "don't ask, don't tell" policy: the military does not ask about sexual orientation; gay people can serve as long as their sexuality remains secret. In 1996 the U.S. Supreme Court tacitly approved the "don't ask" policy by declining to hear a case brought by Navy Lieutenant Paul Thomasson, who was discharged in 1994 for openly declaring himself homosexual.[38] Gays have also lost custody of their children because of their sexual orientation, although more courts are now refusing to consider a gay lifestyle alone as evidence of parental unfitness.[39]

Is the Tide Turning?

Although the unenlightened may still hold negative attitudes toward gays, there seems to be a long overdue increase in social tolerance. Surveys conducted by the National Gay and Lesbian Task Force show that strong majorities of Americans now support gays in the military and equality in employment, housing, inheritance rights, and Social Security benefits for same-sex couples. In addition, disapproval of same-sex relationships dropped a substantial 19 points from a peak of 75 percent in 1987 to about 56 percent today. The percentage of people opposed to same-sex marriage (and those opposed to adoption by gay and lesbian couples) is in decline.[40] More than half the states now include gay bashing within their definitions of hate crimes. And, significantly, in November 1998, by a vote of 6–1, the Georgia Supreme Court struck down the state's 182-year-old sodomy law that was the basis for the *Bowers v. Hardwick* decision.[41]

The NGLTF is the national progressive organization working for the civil rights of gay, lesbian, bisexual, and transgendered people, with the vision and commitment of building a powerful political movement. Visit their Web site at:

http://www.ngltf.org/

For an up-to-date list of Web links, go to

http://info.wadsworth.com/siegel ■

■ Paraphilias

In 2002, the Archdiocese of Boston was rocked by allegations that a significant number of priests had engaged in sexual relations with minor children. The Archdiocese eventually turned over the names of nearly 100 priests to prosecutors. As the scandal spread, clergy elsewhere in the United States and abroad resigned amid allegations that they had abused children or failed to stop abuse of which they had knowledge. In Ireland the Most Rev. Brendan Comiskey, the Bishop of Ferns, offered his resignation to the pope and an archbishop in Wales was forced to resign because he had ignored complaints about two priests later convicted of sexually abusing children. Responding to the crisis, Pope John Paul II called a special meeting of American Catholic leaders in April 2002 to create new policies on sex abuse. The pope issued a statement in which he said that there is "no place in the priesthood . . . for those who would harm the young." He added that sexual abuse by the clergy was not only an "appalling sin" but a crime, and he noted that "many are offended at the way in which church leaders are perceived to have acted in this matter."[42]

Paraphilias have existed and been recorded for thousands of years. From the Greek *para,* "to the side of," and *philos,* "loving," **paraphilias** are bizarre or abnormal sexual practices involving recurrent sexual urges focused on (1) nonhuman objects (such as underwear, shoes, or leather), (2) humiliation or the experience of receiving or giving pain (such as in sadomasochism or bondage), or (3) children or others who cannot grant consent. More than 2000-year-old Buddhist texts contain references to sexually deviant behaviors among monastic communities including sexual activity with animals and sexual interest in corpses. Richard von Krafft-Ebing's *Psychopathia Sexualis,* first published in 1887, was the first text to discuss such paraphilias as sadism, bestiality, and incest.[43]

Some paraphilias, such as wearing clothes normally worn by the opposite sex (transvestite fetishism), can be engaged in by adults in the privacy of their homes and do not involve a third party; these are usually out of the law's reach. Others, however, risk social harm and are subject to criminal penalties. Included in this group of outlawed sexual behaviors are these practices:

> **Asphyxiophilia (autoerotic asphyxia):** by means of a noose, ligature, plastic bag, mask, volatile chemicals, or chest compression, attempting partial asphyxia and oxygen deprivation to the brain to enhance sexual gratification. Almost all cases of hypoxyphilia involve males.

■ Demonstrators in Belgium protest the killing of young girls by pedophile Marc Dutroix. Belgian police had failed to discover two young girls held captive by Dutroix in his basement, even though they had him under arrest. The girls starved to death in a crime that shocked an entire nation.

Frotteurism: rubbing against or touching a nonconsenting person in a crowd, elevator, or other public area.

Voyeurism: obtaining sexual pleasure from spying on a stranger while he or she disrobes or engages in sexual behavior with another.

Exhibitionism: deriving sexual pleasure from exposing the genitals to surprise or shock a stranger.

Sadomasochism: deriving pleasure from receiving pain or inflicting pain on another.

Pedophilia: attaining sexual pleasure through sexual activity with prepubescent children. Research indicates that more than 20 percent of males report sexual attraction to at least one child, although the rate of sexual fantasies and the potential for sexual contacts are much lower.[44]

Paraphilias that involve unwilling or underage victims are illegal. Most state criminal codes also ban indecent exposure and voyeurism. Others prosecute paraphilias under common-law assault and battery or sodomy statutes. In their extreme, paraphilias can lead to sexual assaults in which the victims suffer severe harm.

■ Prostitution

Prostitution has been known for thousands of years. The term derives from the Latin *prostituere,* which means "to cause to stand in front of." The prostitute is viewed as publicly offering his or her body for sale. The earliest record of prostitution appears in ancient Mesopotamia, where priests engaged in sex to promote fertility in the community. All women were required to do temple duty, and passing strangers were expected to make donations to the temple after enjoying its services.[45]

Modern commercial sex appears to have its roots in ancient Greece, where Solon established licensed **brothels** in 500 B.C. The earnings of Greek prostitutes helped pay for the temple of Aphrodite. Famous men openly went to prostitutes to enjoy intellectual, aesthetic, and sexual stimulation; prostitutes, however, were prevented from marrying.[46]

Although some early Christian religious leaders, such as St. Augustine and St. Thomas Aquinas, tolerated prostitution as a necessary evil, this tolerance disappeared after the reformation. Martin Luther advocated abolishing prostitution on moral grounds, and Lutheran doctrine depicted prostitutes as emissaries of the devil who were sent to destroy the faith.[47]

During the early nineteenth century, prostitution was tied to the rise of English breweries: saloons controlled by the companies employed prostitutes to attract patrons and encourage them to drink. This relationship was repeated in major U.S. cities, such as Chicago, until breweries were forbidden to own the outlets that distributed their product.

Today there are many variations of prostitution, but in general, **prostitution** can be defined as granting non-marital sexual access, established by mutual agreement of the prostitutes, their clients, and their employers, for remuneration. This definition is sexually neutral because prostitutes can be straight or gay and male or female.

Prostitutes are referred to by sociologists as "street level sex workers" whose activities are similar to any other service industry. These conditions are usually present in a commercial sexual transaction:

Activity that has sexual significance for the customer: This includes the entire range of sexual behavior, from sexual intercourse to exhibitionism, sadomasochism, oral sex, and so on.

Economic transaction: Something of economic value, not necessarily money, is exchanged for the activity.

Emotional indifference: The sexual exchange is simply for economic consideration. Although the participants may know one another, their interaction has nothing to do with affection for one another.[48]

Sociologist Monica Prasad observed these conditions when she interviewed both men and women about their motivation to employ a prostitute. Although their choice was shaped by sexuality, she found that their decision was also influenced by pressure from friends to try something different and exciting, the wish for a sexual exchange free from obligations, and curiosity about the world of prostitution. Prasad found that most customers who became "regulars" began to view prostitution as a service occupation not different from other service occupations.[49]

Incidence of Prostitution

It is difficult to assess the number of prostitutes operating in the United States. Fifty years ago, about two-thirds of non–college-educated men and one-quarter of college-educated men had visited a prostitute.[50] It is likely that the number of men who hire prostitutes has declined sharply; the number of arrests for prostitution has remained stable for the past two decades while the population has increased.[51]

How can these changes be accounted for? The "sexual revolution" has liberalized sexuality so that men are less likely to use prostitutes because legitimate alternatives for sexuality are now available. In addition, the prevalence of sexually transmitted diseases has caused many men to avoid visiting prostitutes for fear of irreversible health hazards.

Despite such changes, the Uniform Crime Report (UCR) indicates that about 90,000 prostitution arrests are made annually, with the gender ratio being about 3:4 female.[52] More alarming is the fact that in 2000 about 1,000 arrests involved minors under the age of 18, including about 120 kids aged 15 and under. Arguments that criminal law should not interfere with sexual transactions because no one is harmed are undermined by these disturbing statistics.

Types of Prostitutes

Several different types of prostitutes operate in the United States. As you will see, each group operates in a particular venue.

Streetwalkers Prostitutes who work the streets in plain sight of police, citizens, and customers are referred to as *hustlers, hookers,* or *streetwalkers*. Although glamorized by the Julia Roberts character in the film *Pretty Woman* (who winds up with the multimillionaire character played by Richard Gere), streetwalkers are considered the least attractive, lowest paid, most vulnerable men and women in the profession. They are most likely to be impoverished members of ethnic or racial minorities. Many are young runaways who gravitate to major cities to find a new, exciting life and escape from sexual and physical abuse at home.[53] In the United States and abroad, street workers tend to be younger than other prostitutes, start working at a younger age, and have less education. More use money from sex work for drugs and use drugs at work; they are more likely than other prostitutes to be the targets of extreme forms of violence.[54]

Streetwalkers wear bright clothing, makeup, and jewelry to attract customers; they take their customers to hotels. The term "hooker," however, is not derived from the ability of streetwalkers to hook clients on their charms. It actually stems from the popular name given women who followed Union General "Fighting Joe" Hooker's army during the Civil War.[55] Because streetwalkers must openly display their occupation, they are likely to be involved with the police.

If they survive and gain experience, street workers learn to adopt sex practices that promote their chances of survival, such as refusing to trade sex for drugs and/or refusing to service clients they consider too dangerous or distasteful for sex.[56]

CONNECTIONS

Research that highlights the survival skills of streetwalkers seems to support the rational choice approach discussed in Chapter 5. Such rules of behavior would not be learned and adopted if prostitutes were compulsive or irrational. ■

Bar girls B-girls, as they are also called, spend their time in bars, drinking and waiting to be picked up by customers. Although alcoholism may be a problem, B-girls usually work out an arrangement with the bartender so they are served diluted drinks or water colored with dye or tea, for which the customer is charged an exorbitant price. In some bars, the B-girl is given a credit for each drink she gets the customer to buy. It is common to find B-girls in towns with military bases and large transient populations.[57]

Brothel prostitutes Also called bordellos, cathouses, sporting houses, and houses of ill repute, brothels flour-

ished in the nineteenth and early twentieth centuries. They were large establishments, usually run by madams, that housed several prostitutes. A **madam** is a woman who employs prostitutes, supervises their behavior, and receives a fee for her services; her cut is usually 40 to 60 percent of the prostitute's earnings. The madam's role may include recruiting women into prostitution and socializing them in the trade.[58]

Brothels declined in importance following World War II. The closing of the last brothel in Texas is chronicled in the play and movie *The Best Little Whorehouse in Texas*. Today the most well-known brothels exist in Nevada, where prostitution is legal outside large population centers (one, The Mustang Ranch, has an official Web site that sells souvenirs!). Despite their decline, some madams and their brothels have achieved national prominence. In 1984 socialite Sydney Biddle Barrows was arrested by New York police for operating a $1 million per year prostitution ring out of a bordello on West Seventy-Fourth Street.[59] Descended from a socially prominent family who traced their lineage to the Mayflower, Barrows ranked her 20 women on looks and personality from A ($125 per hour) to C ($400 per hour) and kept 60 percent of their take. Her book of clients was described by police as a mini "Who's Who" of celebrities.

Call girls The aristocrats of prostitution are **call girls.** Some charge customers thousands per night and net more than $100,000 per year. Some gain clients through employment in escort services, and others develop independent customer lists. Many call girls come from middle-class backgrounds and service upper-class customers. Attempting to dispel the notion that their service is simply sex for money, they concentrate on making their clients feel important and attractive. Working exclusively via telephone "dates," call girls get their clients by word of mouth or by making arrangements with bellhops, cab drivers, and so on. They either entertain clients in their own apartments or visit clients' hotels and apartments. Upon retiring, a call girl can sell her "date book" listing client names and sexual preferences for thousands of dollars. Despite the lucrative nature of their business, call girls suffer considerable risk by being alone and unprotected with strangers. They often request the business cards of their clients to make sure they are dealing with "upstanding citizens."

Escort services/call houses Some escort services are fronts for prostitution rings. Both male and female sex workers can be sent out after the client calls an ad in the yellow pages. In Las Vegas, 134 pages in the phone book are dedicated to such services.[60] A relatively new phenomenon, call houses, combines elements of the brothel and call girl rings: a madam receives a call from a prospective customer, and if she finds the client acceptable, she arranges a meeting between the caller and a prostitute in her service. The madam maintains a list of prostitutes who are on call rather than living together in a house. The call

■ Although call girls may be the elite in the world of prostitution, they also run the risk of exposure, apprehension, and criminal sanction. Here, Susanne Teslovich, a former Fayette County commissioner, is led into District Justice Rick Vernon's office on charges of running a prostitution ring out of her farmhouse. Among the evidence against Teslovich are statements from workers and customers and logs of phone calls from state and county offices.

house insulates the madam from arrest because she never meets the client or receives direct payment.[61]

Circuit travelers Prostitutes known as circuit travelers move around in groups of two or three to lumber, labor, and agricultural camps. They ask the foremen for permission to ply their trade, service the whole crew in an evening, and then move on. Some circuit travelers seek clients at truck stops and rest areas.

Sometimes young girls are forced to become circuit travelers by unscrupulous pimps. In 1998, 16 people were charged with enslaving at least 20 women from Mexico, some as young as 14, and forcing them to work for months as prostitutes in agricultural migrant camps in Florida and South Carolina. Their captors, known as "ticketeros," forced them to work six days a week under the threat of violence and for little pay; the women were paid $3 for each sexual act, but the ticketeros charged $20.[62]

Skeezers Surveys conducted in New York and Chicago have found that a significant portion of female prostitutes have substance abuse problems, and more than half claim that prostitution is how they support their drug habits; on the street, women who barter drugs for sex are called **skeezers.** Not all drug-addicted prostitutes barter sex for drugs, but those that do report more frequent drug abuse and sexual activity than other prostitutes.[63]

Massage parlors/photo studios Some "working girls" are based in massage parlors and/or photo studios.

Although it is unusual for a masseuse to offer all the services of prostitution, oral sex and manual stimulation are common. Most localities have attempted to limit commercial sex in massage parlors by passing ordinances specifying that the masseuse keep certain parts of her body covered and limiting the areas of the body that can be massaged. Some photo studios allow customers to put body paint on models before the photo sessions start.

Becoming a Prostitute

Why does someone turn to prostitution? In the United States, both male and female prostitutes often come from troubled homes marked by extreme conflict and hostility and from poor urban areas or rural communities. Divorce, separation, or death splits the family; most prostitutes grew up in homes with absent fathers.[64]

Lower-class girls who get into "the life" report conflict with school authorities, poor grades, and an overly regimented school experience.[65] Drug abuse, including heroin and cocaine addiction, is often a factor in the prostitute's life. A significant portion of prostitutes have long histories of drug abuse, indicating that psychological disturbance and not social-environmental factors (for example, living in poverty) are behind entry into sex work.[66] Young girls who frequently use drugs and begin using at an early age are most at risk for prostitution to support their habits.[67]

Sexual abuse and prostitution Many prostitutes were initiated into sex by family members at ages as young as 10 to 12 years; they have long histories of sexual exploitation and abuse.[68] The early experiences with sex help teach them that their bodies have value and that sexual encounters can be used to obtain affection, power, or money. In a detailed study of child sexual exploitation in North America, Richard J. Estes and Neil Alan Weiner found that the problem of child sexual abuse is much more widespread than has been previously believed or documented.[69] Their research indicated that each year in the United States 25,000 children are subjected to some form of sexual exploitation, which often begins with sexual assaults by relatives and acquaintances, such as a teacher, coach, or a neighbor. Abusers were nearly always men, and about a quarter of them were married with children.

Once they fled an abusive situation at home, kids were vulnerable to life on the streets. Some get hooked up in the sex trade, starting as strippers and lap dancers and drifting into prostitution and pornography. Some meet pimps who quickly turn them to a life of prostitution and beat them if they do not make their daily financial quotas. Others who fled to the streets exchange sex for money, food, and shelter. Some have been traded between prostitution rings, and others are shipped from city to city and even sent overseas as prostitutes. About 20 percent of sexually exploited children were involved in prostitution rings that worked across state lines.

International sex trade   Not all women enter prostitution willingly; some are kidnapped and/or lured from abroad and forced into prostitution. There is a troubling overseas trade in prostitution in which men from wealthy countries frequent semi-regulated sex areas in needy nations such as Thailand to procure young girls forced or sold into prostitution—a phenomenon known as "sex tourism." In addition, every year hundreds of thousands of women and children—primarily from Southeast Asia and Eastern Europe—are lured by the promise of good pay but end up forced into brothels or to work as circuit travelers in labor camps. It is believed that traffickers import up to 50,000 women and children every year into the United States despite legal prohibitions (in addition to prostitution, some are brought in to work in sweat shops).[70]

Controlling Prostitution

In the late nineteenth and early twentieth century, efforts were made to regulate prostitution in the United States through medical supervision and the licensing and zoning of brothels in districts outside residential neighborhoods.[71] After World War I, prostitution became associated with disease, and the desire to protect young servicemen from harm helped to end almost all experiments with legalization in the United States.[72] Some reformers attempted to paint pimps and procurers as immigrants who used their foreign ways to snare unsuspecting American girls into prostitution. Such fears prompted passage of the federal Mann Act (1925), which prohibited bringing women into the country or transporting them across state lines for the purposes of prostitution. Often called the "white slave act," it carried a $5,000 fine, five years in prison, or both.[73]

Today, prostitution is considered a misdemeanor, punishable by a fine or a short jail sentence. In practice, most law enforcement is uneven and aims at confining illegal activities to particular areas in the city.[74] Prostitution is illegal in all states except Nevada (in the counties in which Las Vegas and Reno are located), where it is a highly regulated business enterprise.

Legalize Prostitution?

Feminists have staked out conflicting views of prostitution. One position is that women must become emancipated from male oppression and reach sexual equality. The *sexual equality view* considers the prostitute a victim of male dominance. In patriarchal societies, male power is predicated on female subjugation, and prostitution is a clear example of this gender exploitation.[75] In contrast, for some feminists, the fight for equality depends on controlling all attempts by men or women to impose their will on women. The *free choice view* is that prostitution, if freely chosen, expresses women's equality and is not a symptom of subjugation.

Advocates of both positions argue that the penalties for prostitution should be reduced (decriminalized); neither side advocates outright legalization. Decriminalization would relieve already desperate women of the additional burden of severe legal punishment. In contrast, legalization might be coupled with regulation by male-dominated justice agencies. For example, required medical examinations would mean increased male control over women's bodies.

Both positions have had significant influence around the world. In Sweden, feminists have succeeded in getting legislation passed that severely restricts prostitution and criminalizes any effort to buy sexual activities.[76] In contrast, Holland legalized brothels in 2001 but ordered that they be run under a strict set of guidelines.[77] The new law was designed to protect the more than 30,000 women who work as prostitutes in the Netherlands and give them the chance to get the basic labor rights, including insurance policies and disability payments, enjoyed by other citizens. Things have not worked as planned. The rules, designed to protect both customers and sex workers, have become an administrative nightmare for brothel owners, a group not known for their careful record keeping. Reports indicate that to maintain their privacy, avoid stringent government regulations (for example, how to wash their clothes or how long their nails must be), and avoid paying tax on their earnings, they are plying their trade underground, a condition the regulations were designed to avoid. Holland's experience indicates that the regulation of prostitution is no easy task.

Should prostitution be legalized in the United States? In a recent book, *Brothel*, Alexa Albert, a Harvard trained physician who interviewed young women working at a legal brothel in Nevada, makes a compelling case for legalization. She found that the women remained HIV-free and felt safer working in a secure environment than alone on city streets. Despite long hours and rules that gave too much profit to the owners, the women actually took "pride" in their work. In addition to the added security, most earned between $300 and $1,500 per day.[78]

■ Pornography

The term **pornography** derives from the Greek *porne,* meaning "prostitute," and *graphein,* meaning "to write." In the heart of many major cities are stores that display and sell books, magazines, and films depicting every imaginable explicit sex act. Suburban video stores also rent and sell sexually explicit tapes, which make up 15 to 30 percent of the home rental market. The Internet contains at least 200,000 Web sites offering pornographic material and "adult sex films." The purpose of this material is to provide sexual titillation and excitement for paying customers. Although material depicting nudity and sex is typically legal, protected by the First Amendment's provision limiting governmental control of speech, most criminal codes prohibit the production, display, and sale of obscene material.

Obscenity, derived from the Latin *caenum,* for "filth," is defined by Webster's dictionary as "deeply offensive to morality or decency . . . designed to incite to lust or depravity."[79] The problem of controlling pornography centers on this definition of obscenity. Police and law enforcement officials can legally seize only material that is judged obscene. "But who," critics ask, "is to judge what is obscene?" At one time, such novels as *Tropic of Cancer* by Henry Miller, *Ulysses* by James Joyce, and *Lady Chatterley's Lover* by D. H. Lawrence were prohibited because they were considered obscene; today they are considered works of great literary value. Thus, what is obscene today may be considered socially acceptable at a future time. After all, *Playboy* and *Penthouse* magazines, sold openly on most college campuses, display nude models in all kinds of sexually explicit poses. Allowing individual judgments on what is obscene makes the Constitution's guarantee of free speech unworkable. Could not anti-obscenity statutes also be used to control political and social dissent? The uncertainty surrounding this issue is illustrated by Supreme Court Justice Potter Stewart's famous 1964 statement on how he defined obscenity: "I know it when I see it." Because of this legal and moral ambiguity, a global pornography industry is becoming increasingly mainstream, currently generating up to $60 billion per year in revenue. In fact, some Internet pornography companies are now listed on the NASDAQ stock exchange.[80]

Opponents of pornography argue that it degrades both the people who are photographed and members of the public who are sometimes forced to see obscene material. It has been charged that pornographers exploit their models, who often include underage children.[81]

Child Pornography

The use of children in pornography is the most controversial and reprehensible aspect of the business. Each year more than a million children are believed to be used in pornography or prostitution, many of them runaways whose plight is exploited by adults.[82] Sexual exploitation by child pornography rings can devastate victims, causing them physical problems ranging from headaches and loss of appetite to genital soreness, vomiting, and urinary tract infections and psychological problems including mood swings, withdrawal, edginess, and nervousness. In cases of extreme, prolonged victimization, children may lock onto the sex group's behavior and become prone to further victimization or even become victimizers themselves.

Child pornography has become widespread on the Internet. In his recent book, *Beyond Tolerance: Child Pornography on the Internet,* sociologist Philip Jenkins argues that activists are focused on stamping out Internet pornography but that they have not focused on its most dangerous form, *kiddie porn,* which sometimes involves pictures of 4- and 5-year-old girls in sexual encounters.

When an effort is made to target pedophilic Web sites, investigators often go in the wrong direction, failing to recognize that most sites are short-lived entities whose addresses are passed around to users. Jenkins suggests that kiddie porn is best combated by more effective law enforcement: instead of focusing on users, efforts should be directed against suppliers. He also suggests that newsgroups and bulletin boards that advertise and/or discuss kiddie porn be criminalized.[83]

Kiddie porn is a critical problem, which may be growing. The Australian Institute of Criminology Web site has an article dealing with this issue. You can read it at:
> **http://www.aic.gov.au/publications/ chpornography/**
For an up-to-date list of Web links, go to
> **http://info.wadsworth.com/siegel** ■

Does Pornography Cause Violence?

An issue critical to the debate over pornography is whether viewing it produces sexual violence or assaultive behavior. This debate was given added attention when serial killer Ted Bundy claimed his murderous rampage was fueled by reading pornography.

The evidence is mixed. Some studies indicate that viewing sexually explicit material actually has little effect on sexual violence. For example, there seems to be little difference in rape and violence rates before and after the creation of antismut laws designed to limit the sale of pornography.[84] Presidential commissions expressly created to investigate the association between pornography and violence have found no clear relationship.[85] After careful reviews of the relevant literature, some criminologists conclude that the association is modest at best.[86]

How might we account for this surprisingly modest association?[87] It is possible that viewing erotic material may act as a safety valve for those whose impulses might otherwise lead them to violence. Convicted rapists and sex offenders report less exposure to pornography than a control group of nonoffenders.[88] Viewing prurient material may have the unintended side effect of satisfying erotic impulses that otherwise might result in more sexually aggressive behavior.

While the pornography–violence link seems modest, there is more evidence that people exposed to material that portrays violence, sadism, and women enjoying being raped and degraded are also likely to be sexually aggressive toward female victims.[89] Laboratory experiments conducted by a number of leading authorities have found that men exposed to violent pornography are more likely to act aggressively and hold aggressive attitudes toward women.[90] James Fox and Jack Levin find it common for serial killers to collect and watch violent pornography. Some make their own "snuff" films starring their victims.[91] On a macro level, cross-national research indicates that nations that consume the highest levels of pornography also have extremely high rape rates.[92]

However, it is still not certain if such material drives people to sexual violence or whether people predisposed to sexual violence are drawn to pornography with a violent theme. The issue is discussed further in the Criminological Enterprise feature entitled "Pornography and Sexual Violence."

Pornography and the Law

All states and the federal government prohibit the sale and production of pornographic material. Child pornography is usually a separate legal category that involves either (1) the creation or reproduction of materials depicting minors engaged in actual or simulated sexual activity ("sexual exploitation of minors") or (2) the publication or distribution of obscene, indecent, or harmful materials to minors.[93] Under existing federal law, trafficking in obscenity (18 U.S.C. Sec. 1462, 1464, 1466), child pornography (18 U.S.C. Sec. 2252), harassment (18 U.S.C. Sec. 875(c)), illegal solicitation or luring of minors (18 U.S.C. Sec. 2423(b)), and threatening to injure someone (18 U.S.C. Sec. 875(c)) are all felonies punished by long prison sentences.

Despite the fact that state and federal laws control the production and sale of obscene materials, punishing pornography often creates moral and legal dilemmas. In one famous incident, a posthumous exhibition featuring the works of gay photographer Robert Mapplethorpe was heavily criticized by conservative politicians because it contained images of nude children and men in homoerotic poses and because it had received federal funding. When Cincinnati's Contemporary Arts Center mounted the show, obscenity charges were brought against its director; he was later found not guilty. The actions taken against the Mapplethorpe exhibit brought waves of protest from artists and performers as well as from civil libertarians, who fear governmental control over art, music, and theater. To many, these incidents represented an exercise of criminal law that was a direct attack on the First Amendment's guarantee of free speech. Should free expression be controlled if it offends some people's sense of decency?

The First Amendment of the U.S. Constitution protects free speech and prohibits police agencies from limiting the public's right of free expression. However, the Supreme Court held in the twin cases of *Roth v. United States* and *Alberts v. California* that the First Amendment protects all "ideas with even the slightest redeeming social importance—unorthodox ideas, controversial ideas, even ideas hateful to the prevailing climate of opinion...but implicit in the history of the First Amendment is the rejection of obscenity as utterly without redeeming social importance."[94] In the 1966 case of *Memoirs v. Massachusetts,* the Supreme Court again required that for a work to be considered obscene it must be shown to be "utterly without redeeming social value."[95] These decisions left unclear how obscenity is defined. If a highly erotic movie tells a "moral tale," must it be judged legal even if 95 percent of its content is objectionable? A spate of movies made after the *Roth* decision alleged that they were educational or told a moral tale, so they could not be said to lack redeeming social importance. Many state obscenity cases were appealed to federal courts so judges could decide whether the films totally lacked redeeming social importance. To rectify the situation, the Supreme Court redefined its concept of obscenity in the case of *Miller v. California:*

> The basic guidelines for the trier of fact must be (a) whether the average person applying contemporary community standards would find that the work taken as a whole appeals to the prurient interest; (b) whether the work depicts or describes, in a patently offensive way, sexual conduct specifically defined by the applicable state law, and (c) whether the work, taken as a whole, lacks serious literary, artistic, political or scientific value.[96]

To convict a person of obscenity under the *Miller* doctrine, the state or local jurisdiction must specifically define obscene conduct in its statute, and the pornographer must engage in that behavior. The Court gave some examples of what is considered obscene: "patently offensive representations or descriptions of masturbation, excretory functions and lewd exhibition of the genitals." In subsequent cases the Court overruled convictions for "offensive" or "immoral" behavior; these are not considered obscene. The *Miller* doctrine has been criticized for not spelling out

Pornography and Sexual Violence

The suspected association between violent crime and pornography is troubling considering the explosive growth in the distribution of obscene material via the Internet and other media sources. Because the true association between these two factors is still uncertain, in-depth research was conducted by sociologists Neil Malamuth, Tamara Addison, and Mary Koss to determine their true relationship. The authors first carefully reviewed the existing literature and found the following relationships:

1. Exposure to both nonviolent and violent pornography affects aggressive attitudes toward women; violent pornography has a somewhat greater effect.

2. Exposure to nudity significantly decreases aggression.

3. There is no difference between rapists and nonrapists in age of first exposure or amount of exposure to pornography. Rapists do seem to be more aroused by violent pornography than nonrapists.

4. Using and/or being exposed to pornography is related to sexual aggression in noncriminal populations and groups.

5. Overall, there appears to be an association between pornography use and sexual aggression. Most research agrees that there is an association between exposure to violent pornography and aggressive responses. For nonviolent pornography, the effects are not as strong or consistent, but they also emerge quite reliably.

Because they concluded that existing literature may have some methodological flaws, Malamuth and his colleagues conducted their own survey research with a large sample of 2,972 male college students with a mean age of 21. Eighty-six percent were white, 6 percent black, 3 percent Hispanic, 4 percent Asian, and 1 percent Native American. In addition to answering questions about their use of pornography, subjects were asked to indicate whether they had ever committed coercive sexual acts (for example, holding a woman down and causing her pain in an attempt to get her to engage in unwanted intercourse) and the frequency of such behavior since the age of 14, as well as within the last school year. Subjects were also tested on their aggressive attitudes toward women.

Malamuth, Addison, and Koss found that frequent use of pornography was not related to a high risk for sexual aggression. There were only relatively minor differences in sexual aggression between those who report different levels of exposure to pornography (never using it, seldom, somewhat frequently, or very frequently). However, men who were both at high risk for sexual aggression and who were additionally very frequent users of pornography were also much more likely to engage in sexual aggression than their counterparts who consume pornography less frequently. Put simply, if a person has relatively aggressive sexual inclinations resulting from various personal and/or cultural factors, exposure to pornography may activate and reinforce associated coercive tendencies and behaviors. But even high levels of exposure to pornography do not turn nonaggressive men into sexual predators.

The findings suggest that for the majority of American men pornography exposure (even at the highest levels) is not associated with high levels of sexual aggression. But among those already at the highest "predisposing" risk level for sexual aggression (about 7 percent of men), those who are very frequent pornography users (about 12 percent of this high risk group) have sexual aggression levels approximately four times higher than their counterparts who do not very frequently consume pornography.

Critical Thinking Questions

1. The authors conclude that if pornography consumption is not a per se cause of aggressiveness toward women it may still be a contributing factor. Is it possible that sexually aggressive men are drawn to the images in pornography because it reinforces their preexisting hostile orientation to sexuality?

2. The findings suggest the need for increased research attention on the use and impact of pornography in men at elevated risk for sexual aggression. Given the potential for problems, should Internet pornography be strictly controlled and/or banned until conclusive research is conducted?

InfoTrac College Edition Research

In a thoughtful analysis, conservative columnist William F. Buckley argues that pornography has insinuated itself everywhere in American culture:

> William F. Buckley. Porn, pervasive presence: The creepy wallpaper of our daily lives. *National Review*, Nov 19, 2001 v53 i22 pNA

SOURCE: Neil Malamuth, Tamara Addison, and Mary Koss, "Pornography and Sexual Aggression: Are There Reliable Effects and Can We Understand Them?" *Annual Review of Sex Research* 11 (2000): 26–94.

---

how community standards are to be determined. Obviously, a plebiscite cannot be held to determine the community's attitude for every trial concerning the sale of pornography. Works that are considered obscene in Omaha might be considered routine in New York, but how can we be sure? To resolve this dilemma, the Supreme Court articulated in *Pope v. Illinois* a reasonableness doctrine: a work is obscene if a reasonable person applying objective standards would find the material lacking in any social value.[97] Although *Pope* should help clarify the legal definition of obscenity, the issue is far from settled. Justice John Paul Stevens in his dissent offered one interesting alternative: The First Amendment protects material "if some reasonable persons could [find] serious literary[,] artistic, political or scientific value" in it.[98] If anyone could find merit in a work, Stevens believes it should be protected by law. Do you?

To read *Pope v. Illinois,* go to:
http://caselaw.lp.findlaw.com/scripts/
getcase.pl?court=US&vol=481&invol=497
For an up-to-date list of Web links, go to
http://info.wadsworth.com/siegel ◾

Controlling Pornography

Sex for profit predates Western civilization. Considering its longevity, there seems to be little evidence that it can be controlled or eliminated by legal means alone. In 1986, the Attorney General's Commission on Pornography advocated a strict law enforcement policy to control obscenity, directing that "the prosecution of obscene materials that portray sexual violence be treated as a matter of special urgency."[99] Since then, there has been a concerted effort by the federal government to prosecute adult movie distributors. Law enforcement has been so fervent that industry members have filed suit claiming they are the victims of a "moral crusade" by right-wing zealots.[100]

Although politically appealing, controlling sex for profit is difficult because of the public's desire to purchase sexually related material and services. It is ironic that while there has been ongoing worldwide effort to criminalize sexually related activities, such as possession of child pornography, there has also been a soaring demand for pornography, strip clubs, lap-dancing, escorts, telephone sex, and "sex tours" in developing countries.[101] Law enforcement crusades may not necessarily obtain the desired effect. A get-tough policy could make sex-related goods and services scarce, driving up prices and making their sale even more desirable and profitable. Going after national distributors may help decentralize the adult movie and photo business and encourage local rings to expand their activities, for example, by making and marketing videos as well as still photos or distributing them through computer networks.

An alternative approach has been to restrict the sale of pornography within acceptable boundaries. For example, municipal governments have tolerated or even established adult entertainment zones in which obscene material can be openly sold. In the case of *Young v. American Mini Theaters,* the Supreme Court permitted a zoning ordinance that restricted theaters showing erotic movies to one area of the city, even though it did not find that any of the movies shown were obscene.[102] The state, therefore, has the right to regulate adult films as long as the public has

the right to view them. Some jurisdictions have responded by limiting the sale of sexually explicit material in residential areas and restricting the number of adult stores that can operate in a particular area. For example, New York City has enacted zoning that seeks to break up the concentration of peep shows, topless bars, and X-rated businesses in several neighborhoods, particularly in Times Square.[103] The law forbids sex-oriented businesses within 500 feet of residential zones, schools, churches, or day care centers. Sex shops cannot be located within 500 feet of each other, so concentrated "red light" districts must be dispersed. Rather than close their doors, sex shops got around the law by adding products like luggage, cameras, T-shirts, and classic films. The courts have upheld the law, ruling that stores can stay in business if no more than 40 percent of their floor space and inventory are dedicated to adult entertainment.[104]

Technological Change

A 1993 letter to advice columnist Ann Landers gave this cry for help:

> Dear Ann Landers,
> [S]everal months ago, I caught my husband making calls to a 900-sex number. After a week of denial, he admitted that for several years he had been hooked on porn magazines, porn movies, peep shows, strippers, and phone sex. This addiction can start early in life. With my husband it began at age 12 with just one simple, "harmless" magazine. By the time he was 19, it had become completely out of control.... For years my husband hated himself, and it affected his entire life.[105]

A 1998 letter asking Ann for help updates the problem:

> Dear Ann Landers,
> My husband and I have had a fabulous marriage. We have two wonderful children, ages 22 and 25.... Here's the problem. Phil has become obsessed with porn on the Internet.... Recently, when I returned from an evening out, I noticed Phil appeared quite nervous and upset. I looked at the computer, and sure enough, he had been looking at some unbelievably raunchy stuff. He said he was sincere when he promised to give it up, but he just couldn't stay away from it. I now believe he is obsessed and self-destructive.[106]

Technological change will provide the greatest challenge to those seeking to control the sex-for-profit industry. Adult movie theaters are closing as people are able to buy or rent tapes in their local video stores and play them in the privacy of their homes.[107] Adult CD-ROMs are now a staple of the computer industry. Internet sex services include live, interactive stripping and sexual activities.[108] The government has moved to control the broadcast of obscene films via satellite and other technological innovations. On February 15, 1991, Home Dish Only Satellite Networks, Inc. was fined $150,000 for broadcasting pornographic movies to its 30,000 clients throughout the United States; it was

AP/Wide World Photos

■ The technological revolution represented by the Internet poses a major obstacle for people who want to control or limit sex-related entertainment. Here, Ashley West, one of the roommates on the VoyeurDorm.com Web site, poses in front of a new recreational vehicle owned by the site while Faith Gardner demonstrates the real-time video being shot inside. Clients pay a monthly fee to watch the girls 24 hours a day. Should such activities be criminalized? Or are they legitimate and harmless business transactions between consenting adults?

the first prosecution of the illegal use of satellites to broadcast obscene films.[109]

To control the spread of Internet pornography, Congress passed the Communications Decency Act (CDA), which made all Internet service providers, commercial online services, bulletin board systems, and electronic mail providers criminally liable whenever their services are used to transmit any material considered "obscene, lewd, lascivious, filthy, or indecent" (S 314, 1996). In *Reno v. ACLU* (1997) the Supreme Court upheld an ACLU claim that the CDA unconstitutionally restricted free speech.[110] In a landmark 7–2 decision written by Justice Stevens, the Court ruled that the CDA places an "unacceptably heavy burden on protected speech" that "threatens to torch a large segment of the Internet community."

The defeat of the CDA does not mean that efforts at regulating the content of the Internet have ended. For example, a more recent law, the Child Online Protection Act (H.R. 3783), bans Web postings of material deemed "harmful to minors."[111] On May 13, 2002 the Supreme Court partly upheld the law when it ruled that the law's use of what it calls "community standards" to define what is harmful to children does not by itself make the law unconstitutional (*Ashcroft v. ACLU*, 00-1293). However, there may be future challenges to COPA on the grounds that it controls free speech.

In 1996, Congress passed the Child Pornography Prevention Act (CPPA), criminalizing virtual child pornogra-

phy—sexually explicit images that appear to involve children but are actually computer-simulated images of virtual children engaged in virtual sex. The act sets mandatory prison sentences of at least 15 years for production and distribution of child pornography, 5 years for possession of child pornography, and life imprisonment for repeat offenders convicted of sexual abuse of a minor. In *Ashcroft v. Free Speech Coalition* (2002), the U.S. Supreme Court struck down provisions of the CPPA that ban the creation, distribution, or possession of "virtual" child pornography, which uses computer images or young adults rather than actual children. The Court reasoned that pictures of what appear to be 17-year-olds engaging in sexually explicit activity do not in every case violate existing community standards. It also held that as enacted the CPPA prohibited speech having serious redeeming value because it banned the visual depiction of teenagers engaging in sexual activity, something that the Court found to be a fact not only of modern society but a theme in art and literature for centuries. The justices cited a number of acclaimed movies, such as *American Beauty* and *Traffic,* which explore child sexual themes covered by the CPPA even though they did not use underage actors. If the legislation was upheld, those who created those movies would be subject to severe punishment without regard to the literary and artistic value of the work. The Court's decision forces Congress to reassess the CPPA and remove the provisions on "virtual pornography."[112]

■ Substance Abuse

The problem of substance abuse stretches across the United States. Large urban areas are beset by drug-dealing gangs, drug users who engage in crime to support their habits, and alcohol-related violence. Rural areas are important staging centers for the shipment of drugs across the country and are often the production sites for synthetic drugs and marijuana farming.[113] Nor is the United States alone in experiencing a problem with substance abuse. In Australia 19 percent of youths in detention centers and 40 percent of adult prisoners report having used heroin at least once; in Canada, cocaine and crack are considered serious urban problems; South Africa reports increased cocaine and heroin abuse; Thailand has a serious heroin and methamphetamine problem; and British police have found a major increase in heroin abuse.[114]

Another indication of the concern about drugs has been the increasing number of drug-related arrests: from less than half a million in 1977 to more than 1.5 million in 2000.[115] Similarly, the proportion of prison inmates incarcerated for drug offenses has increased by 300 percent since 1986.[116] Clearly the justice system views drug abuse as a major problem and is taking what decision makers regard as decisive measures to control it.

Despite the scope of the drug problem, some still view it as another type of victimless public order crime. There is great debate over the legalization of drugs and the control of alcohol. Some consider drug use a private matter and drug control another example of government intrusion into people's private lives. Furthermore, legalization could reduce the profit of selling illegal substances and drive suppliers out of the market.[117] Others see these substances as dangerous, believing that the criminal activity of users makes the term "victimless" nonsensical. Still another position is that the possession and use of all drugs and alcohol should be legalized but that the sale and distribution of drugs should be heavily penalized. This would punish those profiting from drugs and would enable users to be helped without fear of criminal punishment.

The National Center on Addiction and Substance Abuse is devoted to informing Americans about the economic and social costs of substance abuse and its impact on their lives. Their Web site can be found at:
   http://www.casacolumbia.org/index.htm
For an up-to-date list of Web links, go to
   http://info.wadsworth.com/siegel ■

When Did Drug Use Begin?

The use of chemical substances to change reality and to provide stimulation, relief, or relaxation has gone on for thousands of years. Mesopotamian writings indicate that opium was used 4,000 years ago—it was known as the "plant of joy."[118] The ancient Greeks knew and understood the problem of drug use. At the time of the Crusades, the Arabs were using marijuana. In the Western hemisphere, natives of Mexico and South America chewed coca leaves and used "magic mushrooms" in their religious ceremonies.[119] Drug use was also accepted in Europe well into the twentieth century. Recently uncovered pharmacy records circa 1900 to 1920 showed sales of cocaine and heroin solutions to members of the British royal family; records from 1912 show that Winston Churchill, then a member of Parliament, was sold a cocaine solution while staying in Scotland.[120]

In the early years of the United States, opium and its derivatives were easily obtained. Opium-based drugs were used in various patent medicine cure-alls. Morphine was used extensively to relieve the pain of wounded soldiers in the Civil War. By the turn of the century, an estimated 1 million U.S. citizens were opiate users.[121]

Several factors precipitated the current stringent U.S. drug laws. The rural religious creeds of the nineteenth century—for example, those of the Methodists, Presbyterians, and Baptists—emphasized individual human toil and self-sufficiency while designating the use of intoxicating substances as an unwholesome surrender to the evils of urban morality. Religious leaders were thoroughly opposed to the use and sale of narcotics. The medical literature of the late 1800s began to designate the use of morphine and opium as a vice, a habit, an appetite, and a disease. Nineteenth- and early twentieth-century police literature described drug users as habitual criminals. Moral crusaders in the nineteenth century defined drug use as evil and directed that local and national entities should outlaw the sale and possession of drugs. Some well-publicized research efforts categorized drug use as highly dangerous.[122] Drug use was also associated with the foreign immigrants recruited to work in factories and mines; they brought with them their national drug habits. Early antidrug legislation appears to be tied to prejudice against immigrating ethnic minorities.[123]

After the Spanish-American War of 1898, the United States inherited Spain's opium monopoly in the Philippines. Concern over this international situation, along with the domestic issues just outlined, led the U.S. government to participate in the First International Drug Conference, held in Shanghai in 1908, and a second one at The Hague in 1912. Participants in these two conferences were asked to strongly oppose free trade in drugs. The international pressure, coupled with a growing national concern, led to the passage of the antidrug laws discussed here.

Alcohol and Its Prohibition

The history of alcohol and the law in the United States has also been controversial and dramatic. At the turn of the century, a drive was mustered to prohibit the sale of alcohol. This **temperance movement** was fueled by the belief that the purity of the U.S. agrarian culture was being destroyed by the growth of the city. Urbanism was viewed as a threat to the lifestyle of the majority of the nation's population, then living on farms and in villages. The forces behind the temperance movement were such lobbying groups as the Anti-Saloon League led by Carrie Nation, the Women's Temperance Union, and the Protestant clergy of the Baptist, Methodist, and Congregationalist faiths.[124] They viewed the growing city, filled with newly arriving Irish, Italian, and Eastern European immigrants, as centers of degradation and wickedness. The propensity of these ethnic people to drink heavily was viewed as the main force behind their degenerate lifestyle. The eventual prohibition of the sale of alcoholic beverages brought about by ratification of the Eighteenth Amendment in 1919 was viewed as a triumph of the morality of middle- and upper-class Americans over the threat posed to their culture by the "new Americans."[125]

Prohibition failed. It was enforced by the Volstead Act, which defined intoxicating beverages as those containing one-half of one percent, or more, alcohol.[126] What doomed prohibition? One factor was the use of organized crime to supply illicit liquor. Also, the law made it illegal only to sell alcohol, not to purchase it; this cut into the law's deterrent capability. Finally, despite the work of Elliot Ness and his "Untouchables," law enforcement agencies were inadequate, and officials were likely to be corrupted by wealthy bootleggers.[127] Eventually, in 1933, the Twenty-First Amendment to the Constitution repealed prohibition, signaling the end of the "noble experiment."

The Extent of Substance Abuse

Despite continuing efforts at control, the use of mood-altering substances persists in the United States. Some of the most commonly abused drugs are described in Exhibit 14.1. What is the extent of the substance abuse problem today? A number of national surveys attempt to chart trends in drug abuse in the general population. Results from two of the most important sources are described in the next sections.

Monitoring the Future (MTF)
One important source of information on drug use is the annual self-report survey of drug abuse among high school students conducted by the Institute of Social Research (ISR) at the University of Michigan.[128] This survey is based on the self-report responses of about 44,000 high school students in the eighth, tenth, and twelfth grades in 424 schools across the United States (eighth and tenth graders were added to the survey in 1991).

As Figure 14.1 shows, drug use declined from a high point around 1980 until 1990, when it began once again to increase until 1996; since then teenage drug use has either stabilized or declined. Marijuana, the most widely used of the illicit drugs, accounted for most of the increase in overall illicit drug use during the 1990s, and it now accounts for much of the observed decrease. All three grades showed a

gradual decrease in marijuana use in the prior 12 months. Even though marijuana use is decreasing, more than one-third of all seniors said they smoked pot at least once during the prior 12 months.[129] The MTF survey shows that the drug Ecstasy has been increasing in popularity among the nation's youth; about 12 percent of seniors report having ever used Ecstasy, making it now more popular than cocaine. Though alcohol use has stabilized since 1990, nearly one-quarter of eighth graders and half of all seniors reported drinking in the past month.

To get the full and most recent reports on drug use among high school students, go the MTF Web site at:
http://monitoringthefuture.org/
For an up-to-date list of Web links, go to
http://info.wadsworth.com/siegel

National Household Survey of Drug Abuse
Conducted by the Department of Health and Human Services' National Institute on Drug Abuse (NIDA), the National Household Survey of Drug Abuse interviews approximately 70,000 people at home each year.[130] The highlights of the most recent survey are contained in Exhibit 14.2 on page 436. Like the MTF survey, the Household Survey shows that drug and alcohol use, though still a significant problem, has stabilized or declined. For example, alcohol use has stabilized, but heavy drinking was reported by 5.6 percent of the population aged 12 and older, or 12.6 million people; more than 40 percent of college students engaged in "binge drinking," having five or more alcoholic beverages at the same occasion.

Are the Surveys Accurate?
The ISR survey is methodologically sophisticated, but it relies on self-report evidence that is subject to error. Drug users may boastfully overinflate the extent of their substance abuse, underreport out of fear, or simply be unaware or forgetful. About 20 percent of the ISR survey respondents say they would not provide or are not sure if they provide honest answers.

Another problem is that these national surveys overlook important segments of the drug-using population. For example, the NIDA survey misses people who are homeless, in prison, in drug rehabilitation or AIDS clinics, and those (about 20 percent of the people contacted) who refuse to participate in the interview. The ISR survey omits kids who are institutionalized, who are absent on the day the survey is administered, who refuse to answer target questions such as their racial background, and who have dropped out of school. Research indicates that dropouts may, in fact, be the most frequent users of dangerous drugs.[131] The surveys also rely on accurate self-reporting by drug users, a group whose recall and dependability may both be questionable. A number of studies indicate that serious abusers underreport drug use in surveys.[132] There is evidence that reporting may be affected by social and

Exhibit 14.1 Commonly Used Drugs

Anesthetics Anesthetics, such as PCP or "angel dust," are drugs used as nervous system depressants. They act on the brain to produce a generalized loss of sensation, stupor, or unconsciousness (called narcosis).

Volatile liquids Volatile liquids are liquids that are easily vaporized. Some substance abusers inhale vapors from lighter fluid, paint thinner, cleaning fluid, and model airplane glue to reach a drowsy, dizzy state sometimes accompanied by hallucinations. The psychological effect produced by inhaling these substances is a short-term sense of excitement and euphoria followed by a period of disorientation, slurred speech, and drowsiness.

Barbiturates These hypnotic, sedative drugs depress the central nervous system into a sleeplike condition. On the illegal market, barbiturates are called "goofballs" or "downers" or are known by the color of the capsules—"reds" (Seconal), "blue dragons" (Amytal), and "rainbows" (Tuinal).

Tranquilizers Tranquilizers relieve uncomfortable emotional feelings by reducing levels of anxiety; they ease tension and promote a state of relaxation. The major tranquilizers are used to control the behavior of the mentally ill who are suffering from psychoses, aggressiveness, and agitation. They are known by their brand names—Ampazine, Thorazine, Pacatal, Largactil, and Sparine. Improper dosages can lead to addiction, and withdrawal can be painful and hazardous.

Amphetamines Amphetamines (Dexedrine, "dex"), Dexamyl, Bephetamine ("whites"), and Methedrine ("meth," "speed," "crystal meth," "ice") are synthetic drugs that stimulate action in the central nervous system. They produce an intense physical reaction: mood elevation and increased blood pressure, breathing rate, and bodily activity. Amphetamines also produce psychological effects, such as increased confidence, euphoria, fearlessness, talkativeness, impulsive behavior, and loss of appetite. Methedrine is probably the most widely used and most dangerous amphetamine. Long-term heavy use can result in exhaustion, anxiety, prolonged depression, and hallucinations.

Cannabis (marijuana) Commonly called "pot," "grass," "ganja," "maryjane," "dope," and a variety of other names, marijuana is produced from the leaves of Cannabis sativa, a plant grown throughout the world. Hashish (hash) is a concentrated form of cannabis made from unadulterated resin from the female plant. Smoking large amounts of pot or hash can cause drastic distortion in auditory and visual perception, even producing hallucinatory effects.

Hallucinogens Hallucinogens are drugs, either natural or synthetic, that produce vivid distortions of the senses without greatly disturbing the viewer's consciousness. Some produce hallucinations, and others cause psychotic behavior in otherwise normal people. D-lysergic acid diethylamide-25, commonly called LSD, is a powerful substance that stimulates cerebral sensory centers to produce visual hallucinations in all ranges of colors, to intensify hearing, and to increase sensitivity.

Cocaine Cocaine is an alkaloid derivative of the coca leaf first isolated in 1860 by Albert Niemann of Göttingen, Germany. When originally discovered, it was considered a medicinal breakthrough that could relieve fatigue, depression, and various other symptoms. Cocaine, or coke, is the most powerful natural stimulant. Its use produces euphoria, laughter, restlessness, and excitement. Overdoses can cause delirium, increased reflexes, violent manic behavior, and possible respiratory failure.

Freebase Freebase is a chemical produced from street cocaine by treating it with a liquid to remove the hydrochloric acid with which pure cocaine is bonded during manufacture. The free cocaine, or cocaine base (hence the term "freebase") is then dissolved in a solvent, usually ether, that crystallizes the purified cocaine. The resulting crystals are crushed and smoked in a special glass pipe; the high produced is more immediate and powerful than snorting street-strength coke.

Crack Crack is processed street cocaine. Its manufacture involves using ammonia or baking soda to remove the hydrochlorides and create a crystalline form of cocaine base that can then be smoked. Crack is not a pure form of cocaine and contains both remnants of hydrochloride and additional residue from the baking soda (sodium bicarbonate); it gets its name from the fact that the sodium bicarbonate often emits a crackling sound when the substance is smoked. It is relatively cheap and provides a powerful high; users rapidly become psychologically addicted to crack.

Narcotics/ Heroin Narcotic drugs produce insensibility to pain (analgesia) and free the mind of anxiety and emotion (sedation). Users experience a rush of euphoria, relief from fear and apprehension, release of tension, and elevation of spirits. After experiencing this uplifting mood for a short period, users become apathetic and drowsy and nod off. Heroin, the most commonly used narcotic, was first produced in 1875 and used as a painkiller (the drug's name derives from the fact it was considered a "hero" because of its painkilling ability when it was first isolated). It is also possible to create synthetic narcotics in the laboratory. Synthetics include Demerol, Methadone, Nalline, and Darvon.

Steroids Anabolic steroids are used to gain muscle bulk and strength for athletics and bodybuilding. Although not physically addicting, steroid use can be an obsession among people who desire athletic success. Steroids are dangerous because of the significant health problems associated with long-term use: liver ailments, tumors, hepatitis, kidney problems, sexual dysfunction, hypertension, and mental problems such as depression.

Exhibit 14.1 **Continued**

Alcohol	Although the purchase and sale of alcohol are legal today in most U.S. jurisdictions, excessive alcohol consumption is considered a major substance abuse problem. Drinkers report that alcohol reduces tension, diverts worries, enhances pleasure, improves social skills, and transforms experiences for the better. Long-term use has been linked with depression and numerous physical ailments ranging from heart disease to cirrhosis of the liver (although some research links moderate drinking to a reduction in the probability of heart attack).
Club drugs	Club drugs are primarily synthetic substances that are commonly used at nightclubs, bars, and raves. Within this category are MDMA (Ecstasy), GHB (gamma hydroxybutyrate), Rohypnol, DMT and 2c-B or "Nexus", Ketamine, and methamphetamine. MDMA (Ecstasy) combines an amphetaminelike rush with hallucinogenic experiences. Rohypnol is a central nervous system depressant that has been connected with sexual assault, rape, and robbery. OxyContin (also known by its generic name oxycodone) is widely used as a painkiller. Though it should be released slowly into the system, abusers grind tablets into powder and snort or inject the drug to produce feelings of euphoria.

Figure 14.1 **Trends in Annual Prevalence of Teenage Illicit Drug Use**

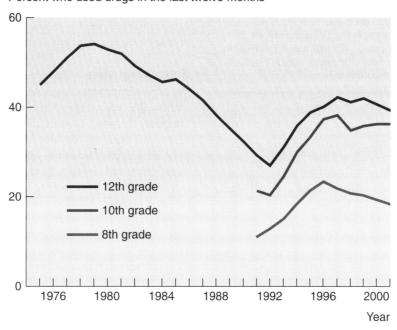

SOURCE: Monitoring the Future, 2001.

personal traits: girls are more willing than boys to admit taking drugs; kids from two-parent homes are less willing to admit taking drugs than kids growing up in single-parent homes.[133]

These surveys also use statistical estimating methods to project national use trends from relatively small samples.[134] Although these weaknesses are troubling, the surveys are administered yearly, in a consistent fashion, so that the effects of over- and underreporting and missing subjects should have a consistent effect in every survey year. The surveys have attempted to improve their methodologies to increase validity. For example, the ISR survey now includes eighth- and tenth-graders in an attempt to survey youths before they drop out of school.

Exhibit 14.2   Findings from the 2000 National Household Survey on Drug Abuse

- About 4 million Americans, or about 6.3 percent of the population 12 years old and older, were current illicit drug users.
- Drug use remained stable between 1999 and 2000.
- Men continued to have a higher rate of illicit drug use than women (7.7 percent versus 5 percent). However, the rates of pain relievers, tranquilizers, stimulants, and sedatives were similar for males (1.8 percent) and females (1.7 percent).
- Among youth aged 12 to 17, 9.7 percent had used an illicit drug within the 30 days prior to interview in 2000. This rate is almost identical to the rate for youth in 1999 (9.8 percent).
- Among youths who were heavy drinkers in 2000, 65.5 percent were also current illicit drug users. Among nondrinkers, only 4.2 percent were current illicit drug users. Similarly, among youths who smoked cigarettes, the rate of past month illicit drug use was 42.7 percent, compared with 4.6 percent for nonsmokers.
- Heavy drinking was reported by 5.6 percent of the population aged 12 and older, or 12.6 million people. About 9.7 million persons aged 12 to 20 reported drinking alcohol in the prior month, or 28 percent of this age group. An estimated 6.6 million (18.7 percent) were binge drinkers, and 2.1 million (6 percent) were heavy drinkers.

SOURCE: 2000 National Household Survey on Drug Abuse, 2001.

AIDS and Drug Use

IV drug use is closely tied to the threat of AIDS.[135] Since monitoring the spread of AIDS began in 1981, about one-fourth of all adult AIDS cases reported to the Centers for Disease Control in Atlanta have occurred among intravenous (IV) drug users. It is now estimated that as many as one-third of all IV drug users are AIDS carriers.[136]

One reason for the AIDS–drug use relationship is the widespread habit of needle sharing among IV users. For example, a recent study of Los Angeles drug "shooting galleries" conducted by researcher Douglas Longshore found that about one-quarter of users shoot drugs in these abandoned buildings, private apartments, or other sites, where for a small entry fee injection equipment can be borrowed or rented.[137] Most users (72 percent) shared needles, and although some tried to use bleach as a disinfectant, the majority ignored this safety precaution. Asking for or bringing bleach ruined the moment because it reminded the addicts of the risk of AIDS; others were too high to be bothered. As one user told Longshore,

> After I started shooting coke, all hell broke loose, no holds barred, couldn't be bothered to get bleach. That was out of the question. Literally picking needles up that I had no idea who had used.... I was just out of my mind insane.

[HIV] wasn't a consideration. It was more like, I hope this is going to be okay. You just aren't in your right mind anymore.[138]

Needle sharing has been encouraged by efforts to control drugs by outlawing the over-the-counter sale of hypodermic needles. Consequently, some jurisdictions have developed outreach programs to help these drug users; others have made an effort to teach users how to clean their needles and syringes; a few states have gone so far as to give addicts sterile needles.[139]

The threat of AIDS may be changing the behavior of recreational and middle-class users, but drug use may still be increasing among the poor, high school dropouts, and other disadvantaged groups. If that pattern is correct, then the recently observed decline in substance abuse may be restricted to one segment of the at-risk population while another is continuing to use drugs at ever-increasing rates.

What Causes Substance Abuse?

What causes people to abuse substances? Although there are many different views on the causes of drug use, most can be characterized as seeing the onset of an addictive career as being either an environmental or a personal matter.

Subcultural view   Those who view drug abuse as having an environmental basis concentrate on lower-class addiction. Because a disproportionate number of drug abusers are poor, the onset of drug use can be tied to such factors as racial prejudice, devalued identities, low self-esteem, poor socioeconomic status, and the high level of mistrust, negativism, and defiance found in impoverished areas.

Youths may join peers to learn the techniques of drug use and receive social support for their habit. Research shows that peer influence is a significant predictor of drug careers that actually grows stronger as people mature.[140] Drug use splits some communities into distinct groups of relatively affluent abstainers and desperately poor abusers.[141]

Psychodynamic view   Psychodynamic explanations of substance abuse suggest that drugs help youths control or express unconscious needs and impulses. Drinking alcohol may reflect an oral fixation that is associated with other nonfunctional behaviors, such as dependence and depression.[142] A young teen may resort to drug abuse to remain dependent on an overprotective mother, to reduce the emotional turmoil of adolescence, or to cope with troubling impulses.[143]

Research on the psychological characteristics of drug abusers does in fact reveal the presence of a significant degree of personal pathology. Studies have found that addicts suffer personality disorders characterized by a weak ego, low frustration tolerance, anxiety, and fantasies of omnipotence. Many addicts exhibit psychopathic or sociopathic behavior characteristics, forming what is called an addiction-prone personality.[144] One study of abusers conducted in five large U.S. cities found a significant association between mental illness and drug abuse: about 53 percent of drug abusers and 37 percent of alcohol abusers have at least one serious mental illness. Conversely, 29 percent of the diagnosed mentally ill people in the survey have substance abuse problems.[145]

Genetic factors   It is also possible that substance abuse may have a genetic basis. For example, a number of studies comparing alcoholism among identical twins and fraternal twins have found that the degree of concordance (both siblings behaving identically) is twice as high among the identical twin groups.[146]

AP/Wide World Photos

■ Is the use of drugs a rational choice? Did baseball star Darryl Strawberry, shown here during a closed circuit court hearing, ruin his career and forfeit his high salary because he "chose" to use crack cocaine? Or is his addiction the symptom of some uncontrollable psychological problem?

Taken as a group, studies of the genetic basis of substance abuse suggest that people whose parents were alcoholic or drug dependent have a greater chance of developing a problem than the children of nonabusers. However, not all children of abusing parents become drug dependent themselves, suggesting that even if drug abuse is heritable, environment and socialization must play some role in the onset of abuse.[147]

Social learning   Social psychologists suggest that drug abuse may also result from observing parental drug use. Parental drug abuse begins to have a damaging effect on children as young as 2 years old, especially when parents manifest drug-related personality problems such as depression or poor impulse control.[148] Children whose parents abuse drugs are more likely to have persistent abuse problems than the children of nonabusers.[149]

People who learn that drugs provide pleasurable sensations may be the most likely to experiment with illegal substances; a habit may develop if the user experiences lower anxiety, fear, and tension levels.[150] Having a history of family drug and alcohol abuse has been found to be a characteristic of violent teenage sexual abusers.[151] Heroin abusers report an unhappy childhood that included harsh physical punishment and parental neglect and rejection.[152]

Problem behavior syndrome (PBS)   For many people, substance abuse is just one of many problem behaviors. Longitudinal studies show that drug abusers are maladjusted, alienated, and emotionally distressed and that drug use is only one among many social problems.[153] Having a deviant lifestyle begins early in life and is punctuated with criminal relationships, family history of substance abuse, educational failure, and alienation. Crack cocaine use has been linked to sexual abuse as children and social isolation as adults.[154] There is robust support for the interconnection of problem drinking and drug abuse, delinquency, precocious sexual behavior, school failure, family conflict, and other similar social problems.[155]

Rational choice   Not all people who abuse drugs do so because of personal pathology. Some may use drugs and alcohol because they want to enjoy their effects: get high, relax, improve creativity, escape reality, and increase sexual responsiveness. Research indicates that adolescent alcohol abusers believe that getting high will make them powerful, increase their sexual performance, and facilitate their social behavior; they care little about negative future consequences.[156] Claire Sterk's research on middle-class drug-abusing women shows that most were introduced by friends in the context of "just having some fun."[157]

Substance abuse, then, may be a function of the rational but mistaken belief that drugs can benefit the user. The decision to use drugs involves evaluations of personal consequences (such as addiction, disease, and legal punishment) and the expected benefits of drug use (such as peer approval, positive affective states, heightened awareness, and relaxation). Adolescents may begin using drugs because they believe their peers expect them to do so.[158]

Is There a Drug Gateway?

Some experts believe that, regardless of its cause, most people fall into drug abuse slowly, beginning with alcohol and then following with marijuana and more serious drugs as the need for a more powerful high intensifies. A number of research efforts have confirmed this **gateway model.** For example, James Inciardi, Ruth Horowitz, and Anne Pottieger found a clear pattern of adult involvement in adolescent drug abuse. Kids on crack started their careers with early experimentation with alcohol at age 7, began getting drunk at age 8, had alcohol with an adult present by age 9, and became regular drinkers by the time they were 11 years old.[159] Drinking with an adult present, presumably a parent, was a significant precursor of future substance abuse and delinquency. "Adults who gave children alcohol," they argue, "were also giving them a head start in a delinquent career."[160] Other research efforts support this view when they find that the most serious drug users have a history of alcohol abuse.[161] Kids who begin using alcohol in adolescence become involved in increasing levels of deviant behavior as they mature.[162]

The "drug gateway" vision is popular, but not all research efforts find that users progress to ever-more potent drugs and some show that, surprisingly, many hard-core drug abusers never actually smoked pot or used alcohol.[163] And although many American youths have tried marijuana, few actually progress to crack or heroin abuse.[164]

In sum, there may be no single cause of substance abuse. People may try and continue to use illegal substances for a variety of reasons. As James Inciardi points out,

> There are as many reasons people use drugs as there are individuals who use drugs. For some, it may be a function of family disorganization, or cultural learning, or maladjusted personality, or an "addiction-prone" personality.... For others, heroin use may be no more than a normal response to the world in which they live.[165]

Types of Drug Users

The general public often groups all drug users together without recognizing that there are many varieties, ranging from adolescent recreational drug users to adults who run large smuggling operations.[166]

Adolescents who distribute small amounts of drugs
Many adolescents begin their involvement in the drug trade by using and distributing small amounts of drugs; they do not commit any other serious criminal acts. Kenneth Tunnell found in his interviews with low-level drug dealers that many started out as "stash dealers" who sold drugs to maintain a consistent access to drugs for their own consumption; their customers are almost always personal acquaintances, including friends and relatives.[167] They are insulated from the legal system because their activities rarely result in apprehension and sanction.

Adolescents who frequently sell drugs A small number of adolescents, most often multiple-drug users or heroin or cocaine users, are high-rate dealers who bridge the gap between adult drug distributors and the adolescent user. Frequent dealers often have adults who "front" for them—that is, loan them drugs to sell without upfront cash. The teenagers then distribute the drugs to friends and acquaintances, returning most of the proceeds to the supplier while keeping a commission for themselves. Frequent dealers are more likely to sell drugs in public and can be seen in known drug user hangouts in parks, schools, or other public places. Deals are irregular, so the chances of apprehension are slight.

Teenage drug dealers who commit other delinquent acts A more serious type of drug-involved youth comprises those who use and distribute multiple substances and also commit both property and violent crimes; many are gang members.[168] Although these youngsters make up about 2 percent of the teenage population, they commit 40 percent of the robberies and assaults and about 60 percent of all teenage felony thefts and drug sales.

These youths are frequently hired by older dealers to act as street-level drug runners. Each member of a crew of 3 to 12 boys will handle small quantities of drugs, perhaps three bags of heroin, which are received on consignment and sold on the street; the supplier receives 50 to 70 percent of the drug's street value. The crew members also act as lookouts, recruiters, and guards. Between drug sales, the young dealers commit robberies, burglaries, and other thefts.[169]

Adolescents who cycle in and out of the justice system Some drug-involved youths are failures at both dealing and crime. They do not have the savvy to join gangs or groups and instead begin committing unplanned, opportunistic crimes that increase their chances of arrest. They are heavy drug users, which both increases apprehension risk and decreases their value for organized drug distribution networks. Drug-involved "losers" can earn a living steering customers to a seller in a "copping" area, "touting" drug availability for a dealer, or acting as a lookout. However, they are not considered trustworthy or deft enough to handle drugs or money. They may bungle other criminal acts, which solidifies their reputation as undesirable.

Drug-involved youth who continue to commit crimes as adults Although about two-thirds of substance-abusing youths continue to use drugs after they reach adulthood, about half desist from other criminal activities. Those who persist in both substance abuse and crime as adults exhibit a garden variety of social and developmental problems. Some evidence also exists that these drug-using persisters have low nonverbal IQs and poor physical coordination.

Outwardly respectable adults who are top-level dealers A few outwardly respectable adult dealers sell large quantities of drugs to support themselves in high-class lifestyles. Outwardly respectable dealers often seem indistinguishable from other young professionals. Upscale dealers seem to drift into dealing from many different walks of life. Some begin as campus dealers whose lifestyle and outward appearance are indistinguishable from other students (though they are more frequently involved in illegal behavior outside of drug dealing).[170] Frequently they are drawn from professions and occupations that are unstable, have irregular working hours, and accept drug abuse. Former graduate students, musicians, performing artists, and barkeepers are among those who are likely to fit the profile of the adult who begins dealing drugs in his or her twenties. Some use their business skills and drug profits to get into legitimate enterprises or illegal scams. Others drop out of the drug trade because they are the victims of violent crime committed by competitors or disgruntled customers; a few wind up in jail or prison.

Smugglers Smugglers import drugs into the United States. They are generally men, middle-aged or older, who have strong organizational skills, established connections, capital to invest, and a willingness to take large business risks. Smugglers are a loosely organized, competitive group of individual entrepreneurs. There is a constant flow in and out of the business as some sources become the target of law enforcement activities, new drug sources become available, older smugglers become dealers, and former dealers become smugglers.

Adult predatory drug users who are frequently arrested Many users who begin abusing substances in early adolescence continue in drugs and crime in their adulthood. Getting arrested, doing time, using multiple drugs, and committing predatory crimes are a way of life for them. They have few skills, did poorly in school, and have long criminal records. The threat of conviction and punishment has little effect on their criminal activities. These "losers" have friends and relatives involved in drugs and crime. They specialize in robberies, burglaries, thefts, and drug sales. They filter in and out of the justice system and begin committing crimes as soon as they are released. In some populations, at least one-third of adult males are involved in drug trafficking and other criminal acts well into their adulthood.[171]

If they make a "big score," perhaps through a successful drug deal, they may significantly increase their drug use. Their increased narcotics consumption then destabilizes their lifestyle, destroying family and career

ties. When their finances dry up, they may become street junkies, people whose traditional lifestyle has been destroyed, who turn to petty crime to maintain an adequate supply of drugs. Cut off from a stable source of quality heroin, not knowing from where their next fixes or the money to pay for them will come, looking for any opportunity to make a buck, getting sick or "jonesing," being pathetically unkempt and unable to maintain even the most primitive routines of health or hygiene, street junkies live a very difficult existence. Because they are unreliable and likely to become police informants, street junkies pay the highest prices for the poorest quality heroin; lack of availability increases their need to commit habit-supporting crimes.[172]

Adult predatory drug users who are rarely arrested Some drug users are "winners." They commit hundreds of crimes each year but are rarely arrested. On the streets, they are known for their calculated violence. Their crimes are carefully planned and coordinated. They often work with partners and use lookouts to carry out the parts of their crimes that have the highest risk of apprehension. These "winners" are more likely to use recreational drugs, such as coke and pot, than the more addicting heroin or opiates. Some become high-frequency users and risk apprehension and punishment. But for the lucky few, their criminal careers can stretch for up to 15 years without interruption by the justice system.

These users are sometimes referred to as *stabilized junkies* who have learned the skills needed to purchase and process larger amounts of heroin. Their addiction enables them to maintain normal lifestyles, although they may turn to drug dealing to create contacts with drug suppliers. They are employable, but earning legitimate income does little to reduce their drug use or dealing activities.[173]

Less predatory drug-involved adult offenders Most adult drug users are petty criminals who avoid violent crime. These occasional users are people just beginning their addiction, who use small amounts of narcotics, and whose habit can be supported by income from conventional jobs; narcotics have relatively little influence on their lifestyles.[174] They are typically high school graduates and have regular employment that supports their drug use. They usually commit petty thefts or pass bad checks. They stay on the periphery of the drug trade by engaging in such acts as helping addicts shoot up, bagging drugs for dealers, operating shooting galleries, renting needles and syringes, and selling small amounts of drugs. These petty criminal drug users do not have the stomach for a life of hard crime and drug dealing. They violate the law in proportion to the amount and cost of the drugs they are using. Pot smokers have a significantly lower frequency of theft violations than daily heroin users, whose habit is considerably more costly.

Women who are drug-involved offenders Women who are drug-involved offenders constitute a separate type of substance abuser. Although women are far less likely than men to use addictive drugs, female offenders are just as likely to be involved in drugs as male offenders. Though infrequently violent criminals, they are often involved in prostitution and low-level drug dealing; a few become top-level dealers. Many are pregnant and/or already mothers and because they share needles, they are at high risk of contracting AIDS, and many pass the HIV virus to their newborn children. They maintain a high risk of victimization. One study of 171 crack cocaine using women found that since initiating crack use, 62 percent of the women reported suffering a physical attack and 32 percent suffered rape; more than half were forced to seek medical care for their injuries.[175]

Drugs and Crime

One of the main reasons for the criminalization of particular substances is the assumed association between drug abuse and crime. Research suggests that many criminal offenders have extensive experience with drug use and that drug users commit an enormous amount of crime; alcohol abuse has also been linked to criminality.[176] Research shows that almost 4 in 10 violent crimes and fatal motor vehicle accidents involve alcohol.[177] This pattern is not unique to the United States. Research conducted in England found that about 61 percent of arrestees tested positively for at least one drug, a finding comparable to arrestees in the United States.[178]

Although the drug–crime connection is powerful, the relationship is still uncertain because many users have had a history of criminal activity before the onset of their substance abuse.[179] It is just as likely that chronic criminal offenders begin to abuse drugs and alcohol as it is that substance abusers turn to a life of crime.

There is also evidence that the relationship may be structured by the order of initiation into addiction and/or crime. For example, research shows that those addicts who have committed serious crime before their addiction constitute a particularly dangerous subgroup of users who continue to commit significant numbers of violent and theft crimes after their drug use begins.[180] In contrast, those who begin criminal careers postaddiction are more likely to engage in a diverse variety of crimes but are less likely to commit predatory crimes and more likely to engage in victimless crimes.[181] In addition, the type of drug used may influence criminality: those dependent on cocaine and heroin are less likely to commit predatory crimes than those who are alcohol dependent.[182] Nonetheless, if drug use does not turn otherwise law-abiding citizens into criminals, it certainly amplifies the extent of their criminal activities.[183] And, as addiction levels increase, so does the frequency and seriousness of criminality.[184]

Two approaches have been used to study the relationship between drugs and crime. One has been to survey known addicts to assess the extent of their law violations; the other has been to survey known criminals to see if they were or are drug users. These are discussed separately next.

User surveys Numerous studies have examined the criminal activity of drug users. As a group, they show that people who take drugs have extensive involvement in crime.[185] Youths who abuse alcohol are also the most likely to engage in violence during their life course; violent adolescents report histories of alcohol abuse; adults with long histories of drinking are also more likely to report violent offending patterns.[186] One often-cited study of this type was conducted by sociologist James Inciardi. After interviewing 356 addicts in Miami, Inciardi found that they reported 118,134 criminal offenses during a 12-month period; of these, 27,464 were index crimes.[187] If this behavior is typical, the country's estimated 300,000 to 700,000 heroin users could be responsible for a significant amount of all criminal behavior. A recent English study using a sample of 100 known abusers found that more than half of the subjects reported involvement in crime in the month prior. The most common offenses were shoplifting, receiving stolen goods, and theft; violence was used relatively rarely (11 percent).[188]

Surveys of known criminals The second method used to link drugs and crime involves testing known criminals to determine the extent of their substance abuse. Surveys of prison inmates disclose that many (80 percent) are lifelong substance abusers. More than one-third claim to have been under the influence of drugs when they committed their last offense.[189] These data support the view that a strong association exists between substance abuse and serious crime.

Another important source of data on the drug abuse–crime connection is the federally sponsored Arrestee Drug Abuse Monitoring Program (ADAM), which interviews and tests thousands of arrestees for drug abuse each year. ADAM finds that though drug use is abating it is still quite common. In 15 sites, about two-thirds of the adult arrestees and more than half of the juvenile male arrestees tested positive for at least one drug. ADAM also finds that multiple drug use remains a persistent problem among arrestees: more than three-fourths of the individuals who test positive for opiates also tested positive for another drug.

The National Institute of Justice's Arrestee Drug Abuse Monitoring (ADAM) program tracks trends in the prevalence and types of drug use among booked arrestees in urban areas. You can visit their Web site at:
   http://www.adam-nij.net/
For an up-to-date list of Web links, go to
   http://info.wadsworth.com/siegel ∎

Exhibit 14.3 Summary of Drug–Crime Relationship

Drugs and Crime Relationship	Definition	Examples
Drug-defined offenses	Violations of laws prohibiting or regulating the possession, use, distribution, or manufacture of illegal drugs	Drug possession or use; marijuana cultivation; methamphetamine production; cocaine, heroin, or marijuana sales
Drug-related offenses	Offenses in which a drug's pharmacologic effects contribute; offenses motivated by the user's need for money to support continued use; and offenses connected to drug distribution itself	Violent behavior resulting from drug effects; stealing to get money to buy drugs; violence against rival drug dealers
Drug-using lifestyle	Drug use and crime are common aspects of a deviant lifestyle. The likelihood and frequency of involvement in illegal activity is increased because drug users may not participate in the legitimate economy and are exposed to situations that encourage crime.	A life orientation with an emphasis on short-term goals supported by illegal activities; opportunities to offend resulting from contacts with offenders and illegal markets; criminal skills learned from other offenders

SOURCE: White House Office of National Drug Control Policy, *Fact Sheet: Drug-Related Crime* (Washington, D.C., 1997).

The drug–crime connection It is of course possible that most criminals are not actually drug users but that police are more likely to apprehend muddle-headed substance abusers than clear-thinking abstainers. A second, and probably more plausible, interpretation is that most criminals are in fact substance abusers. Drug use interferes with maturation and socialization. Drug abusers are more likely to drop out of school, be underemployed, engage in premarital sex, and become unmarried parents. These factors have been linked to a weakening of the social bond that leads to antisocial behaviors.[190] As Exhibit 14.3 shows, the typical drug–crime relationship may be explained in one of three ways.

In sum, research testing both the criminality of known narcotics users and the narcotics use of known criminals produces a very strong association between drug use and crime. Even if the crime rate of drug users were actually half that reported in the research literature, users would be responsible for a significant portion of the total criminal activity in the United States. The Criminological Enterprise feature titled "Does Substance Abuse Provoke Violence?" discusses research efforts designed to find out how drug use relates to criminality.

Drugs and the Law

The federal government first initiated legal action to curtail the use of some drugs early in the twentieth century.[191] In 1906 the Pure Food and Drug Act required manufacturers to list the amounts of habit-forming drugs in products on the labels but did not restrict their use. However, the act prohibited the importation and sale of opiates except for medicinal purposes. In 1914 the Harrison Narcotics Act restricted importation, manufacture, sale, and dispensing of narcotics. It defined narcotic as any drug that produces sleep and relieves pain, such as heroin, morphine, and opium. The act was revised in 1922 to allow importation of opium and coca (cocaine) leaves for qualified medical practitioners. The Marijuana Tax Act of 1937 required registration and payment of a tax by all persons who imported, sold, or manufactured marijuana. Because marijuana was classified as a narcotic, those registering would also be subject to criminal penalty.

In later years, other federal laws were passed to clarify existing drug statutes and revise penalties. For example, the Boggs Act of 1951 provided mandatory sentences for violating federal drug laws. The Durham-Humphrey Act of 1951 made it illegal to dispense barbiturates and amphetamines without a prescription. The Narcotic Control Act of 1956 increased penalties for drug offenders. In 1965 the Drug Abuse Control Act set up stringent guidelines for the legal use and sale of mood-modifying drugs, such as barbiturates, amphetamines, LSD, and any other "dangerous drugs," except narcotics prescribed by doctors and pharmacists. Illegal possession was punished as a misdemeanor and manufacture or sale as a felony. And in 1970 the Comprehensive Drug Abuse Prevention and Control Act set up unified categories of illegal drugs and associated penalties with their sale, manufacture, or possession. The law gave the U.S. attorney general discretion to decide in which category to place any new drug.

Since then, various federal laws have attempted to increase penalties imposed on drug smugglers and limit the manufacture and sale of newly developed substances. For example, the 1984 Controlled Substances Act set new, stringent penalties for drug dealers and created five categories

Does Substance Abuse Provoke Violence?

Criminologists have looked at the drug–violence connection in a number of different ways.

Structural Factors

Henry Brownstein, Susan Crimmins, and Barry Spunt find that violence can be linked to the way drugs are bought, sold, and distributed. In some areas, drug markets are quite stable. Dealers use businesslike operations. Manufacturing, distribution, and trade are organized, and the relationships between producers and distributors, employers and employees, and merchants and consumers are tightly controlled. Drug deals are oriented toward interactions within established businesses. Dealers, workers, and customers view themselves as "business-people" who see violence as unprofitable. In these areas, drug-related violence is less common.

However, in less-stable markets freelance entrepreneurs run the drug trade. Here, operators, workers, and customers are free from the social controls of any established drug business hierarchies. Dealers competing with one another over access to customers and resources are more likely to employ violence in these unstable areas. Brownstein and his colleagues found that in New York City drug markets were quite unstable in the 1980s; this was also a period of high violence rates. They also note that drug markets in the city were observed to have been more stable in the 1990s. Not surprisingly, this is a period when violence rates declined.

Individual Factors

Jeffrey Fagan and his fellow researchers at Columbia University's Center for Violence Research and Prevention are conducting a multistage study on adolescent violence to construct a situational framework for understanding violent behavior. The research design includes three samples of young men, ages 16 to 24, with histories of involvement in violent activities and currently (or, if incarcerated, formerly) residing in two of New York City's neighborhoods with the highest rates of youth homicide—

East New York (Brooklyn) and Mott Haven (South Bronx). The criminal justice sample includes young men convicted on gun-related charges and incarcerated in the Rikers Island Correctional Facility and facilities under the auspices of the New York State Division for Youth Facilities. The second sample consists of victims of violence identified in the emergency rooms of two hospitals, one near each of the two neighborhoods. The community sample consists of young men who are involved in violence but have avoided both the criminal justice system and the emergency room.

The study has found that alcohol and drugs can influence social interactions in two ways that may lead to violence. First, alcohol can shape the dynamics, decisions, and strategies in a violent or near-violent episode. That is, interactions in which one or both individuals have been drinking will turn out differently than those in which one or both are sober. Second, the context in which drinking occurs independently affects how violent or near-violent events unfold. The young men reported that intoxication increased the likelihood that a person's language would become provocative and boastful, turning minor disputes into violent encounters. Alcohol exaggerated the sense of outrage over perceived transgressions of personal codes, resulting in violence to exert control or exact retribution. Some drinkers acted on bystanders' provocations to fight more seriously; others felt invincible and started fights that they then lost. In addition, certain bars were frequent scenes of violence, regardless of who was present or how much alcohol had been consumed; being in the wrong place at the wrong time resulted in injuries, including gunshot wounds, to a number of respondents.

Interestingly, the effects of drugs on violence were much less clear. Marijuana made some subjects less prone to violence, whereas other users sought out victims to exploit or dominate. Another type of user became paranoid and either avoided human contact or became hostile and prone to defensive violence. Yet, if a fight broke out, even the most relaxed, "mellow" individual would im-

mediately snap out of his stupor to defend himself.

Not all of the young men who were interviewed blamed their violent behavior on alcohol or drugs. A number of young men used alcohol or drugs after violent events as a form of self-medication. This finding is substantiated by research conducted by Howard Kaplan and his associates, who found that aggressive youth who later use drugs reduced the frequency of their violent behavior. They conclude that some drugs have a direct, dampening effect on violent impulses whereas others may create feelings of potency or competence, which reduces the need for the use of aggression to prove masculinity or self-worth.

Critical Thinking Questions

The Fagan research shows how substance abuse can facilitate violent episodes. Interestingly, alcohol seems to have a greater influence on violent behavior than do other drugs. Some drugs, like marijuana, may even help regulate violence if they provide a sense of euphoria that reduces conflict. Could this be used as an argument for drug legalization?

InfoTrac College Edition Research

Treating alcohol abusers is a major social goal. To research current treatment programs, read these articles:

Deborah Pappas, Chudley E. Werch, and Joan M. Carlson. Recruitment and retention in an alcohol prevention program of two inner-city middle schools. *Journal of School Health* August 1998 v68 n6 p231(6)

John P. Allen. Project MATCH: a clarification. *Behavioral Health Management* July–August 1998 v18 n4 p42(2)

SOURCES: Henry H. Brownstein, Susan M. Crimmins, and Barry J. Spunt, "A Conceptual Framework for Operationalizing the Relationship between Violence and Drug Market Stability," *Contemporary Drug Problems* 27 (2000): 867–93; Howard Kaplan, Glen Tolle Jr., and Takuji Yoshida, "Substance Use-Induced Diminution of Violence: A Countervailing Effect in Longitudinal Perspective," *Criminology* 39 (2001): 205–24; Jeffrey Fagan, "Adolescent Violence: A View from the Street," *NIJ Research Preview* (Washington, D.C.: National Institute of Justice, 1998).

■ Although drug use per se may not be a cause of crime, it does involve people in highly risky behaviors and increases the frequency of offending. Here, investigators inspect a charred vehicle containing the remains of Jeremy Lindsey and Joseph Clayton. According to police, the men had driven from Erie to Pittsburgh so that one of them could buy $7,000 worth of marijuana, but the drug dealers robbed and killed them before lighting their car and bodies on fire.

of narcotic and nonnarcotic substances subject to federal laws.[192] The Anti–Drug Abuse Act of 1986 again set new standards for minimum and maximum sentences for drug offenders, increased penalties for most offenses, and created a new drug penalty classification for large-scale offenses (such as trafficking in more than one kilogram of heroin), for which the penalty for a first offense was 10 years to life in prison.[193] With then-President George Bush's endorsement, Congress passed the Anti–Drug Abuse Act of 1988, which created a coordinated national drug policy under a "drug czar," set treatment and prevention priorities, and, symbolizing the government's hard-line stance against drug dealing, imposed the death penalty for drug-related killings.[194]

For the most part, state laws mirror federal statutes. Some states now apply extremely heavy penalties for selling or distributing dangerous drugs, involving long prison sentences of up to 25 years.

Drug Control Strategies

Substance abuse remains a major social problem in the United States. Politicians looking for a safe campaign issue can take advantage of the public's fear of drug addiction by calling for a war on drugs. These wars have been declared even when drug usage is stable or in decline.[195] Can these efforts pay off? Can illegal drug use be eliminated or controlled?

A number of different drug control strategies have been tried with varying degrees of success. Some aim to deter drug use by stopping the flow of drugs into the coun-

try, apprehending and punishing dealers, and cracking down on street-level drug deals. Others focus on preventing drug use by educating potential users to the dangers of substance abuse (convincing them to "say no to drugs") and by organizing community groups to work with the at-risk population in their area. Still another approach is to treat known users so they can control their addictions. Some of these efforts are discussed here.

Source control One approach to drug control is to deter the sale and importation of drugs through the systematic apprehension of large-volume drug dealers, coupled with the enforcement of strict drug laws that carry heavy penalties. This approach is designed to capture and punish known international drug dealers and deter those who are considering entering the drug trade. A major effort has been made to cut off supplies of drugs by destroying overseas crops and arresting members of drug cartels in Central and South America, Asia, and the Middle East, where many drugs are grown and manufactured. The federal government has been in the vanguard of encouraging exporting nations to step up efforts to destroy drug crops and prosecute dealers. However, translating words into deeds is a formidable task. Drug lords are willing and able to fight back through intimidation, violence, and corruption when necessary. The Colombian drug cartels do not hesitate to use violence and assassination to protect their interests.

The amount of narcotics grown each year is so vast that even if three-quarters of the opium crop were destroyed, the U.S. market would still require only 10 percent of the remainder to sustain the drug trade. Radically reducing the amount of illegal drugs produced each year might have little effect on U.S. consumption. Drug users in the United States are able and willing to pay more for drugs than anyone else in the world. Even if the supply were reduced, whatever drugs there were would find their way to the United States.

Adding to control problems is the fact that the drug trade is an important source of foreign revenue, and destroying the drug trade undermines the economies of Third World nations. Even if the government of one nation were willing to cooperate in vigorous drug suppression efforts, suppliers in other nations, eager to cash in on the sellers' market, would be encouraged to turn more acreage over to coca or poppy production. For example, between 1994 and 1999, enforcement efforts in Peru and Bolivia were so successful that they altered cocaine cultivation patterns. Colombia became the premier coca cultivating country, displacing Peru and Bolivia, due to a long-term strategy on the part of the Colombian drug syndicate, which refines 80 percent of the world's cocaine supply. Rather than rely on shaky foreign sources, the drug cartels are encouraging local growers to cultivate coca plants. When the Colombian government mounted an effective eradication campaign in the traditional growing areas, the cartel linked up with rebel groups in remote parts of the country for their drug supply.[196] There are also indications that the drug syndicates may be planting a higher yield variety of coca and improving refining techniques to replace crops lost to government crackdowns.

Adding to the problem of source control is the fact that the United States has little influence in some key drug-producing areas such as Vietnam, Cambodia, and Myanmar (formerly Burma).[197]

Interdiction strategies Law enforcement efforts have also been directed at intercepting drug supplies as they enter the country. Border patrols and military personnel using sophisticated hardware have been involved in massive interdiction efforts; many impressive multimillion-dollar seizures have been made. Yet the U.S. borders are so vast and unprotected that meaningful interdiction is impossible. And even if all importation were shut down, homegrown marijuana and laboratory-made drugs, such as "ice," LSD, and PCP, could become the drugs of choice. Even now, their easy availability and relatively low cost are increasing their popularity among the at-risk population.

Law enforcement strategies Local, state, and federal law enforcement agencies have been actively fighting against drugs. One approach is to direct efforts at large-scale drug rings. The long-term consequence has been to decentralize drug dealing and encourage young independent dealers to become major suppliers. Ironically, it has proven easier for federal agents to infiltrate and prosecute traditional organized crime groups than to take on drug-

dealing gangs. Consequently, some nontraditional groups have broken into the drug trade. For example, the Hell's Angels motorcycle club has become one of the primary distributors of cocaine and amphetamines in the United States.

Police can also target, intimidate, and arrest street-level dealers and users in an effort to make drug use so much of a hassle that consumption is cut back and the crime rate reduced. Approaches that have been tried are reverse stings, in which undercover agents pose as dealers to arrest users who approach them for a buy. One approach is to direct efforts at large-scale drug rings. However, this effort has merely served to decentralize drug dealing. Asian, Latin American, and Jamaican groups, motorcycle clubs, and local gangs, such as Los Angeles's Crips and Bloods are all involved in large-scale dealing. Colombian syndicates have established cocaine distribution centers on every continent, and Mexican organizations are responsible for large methamphetamine shipments to U.S., Russian, Turkish, Italian, Nigerian, Chinese, Lebanese, and Pakistani heroin trafficking syndicates, which are now competing for dominance. In terms of weight and availability, there is still no commodity more lucrative than illegal drugs. They cost relatively little to produce and provide large profit margins to dealers and traffickers. At an average street price of $100 per gram in the United States, a metric ton of pure cocaine is worth $100 million; cutting it and reducing purity can double or triple the value. It is difficult for law enforcement agencies to counteract the inducement of drug profits. When large-scale drug busts are made, supplies become scarce and market values increase, encouraging more people to enter the drug trade. There are also suspicions that a displacement effect occurs: stepped-up efforts to curb drug dealing in one area or city simply encourage dealers to seek out friendlier territory.[198]

Despite questions about their effectiveness, drug sweeps have clogged courts and correctional facilities. For example, between 1984 and 1999, the number of defendants charged with a drug offense in the federal courts increased from 11,854 to 29,306; more than 30 percent of these cases involved marijuana. Clearly the "war on drugs" is having a great impact on court processing.[199]

Punishment strategies Even if law enforcement efforts cannot produce a general deterrent effect, the courts may achieve the required result by severely punishing known drug dealers and traffickers. A number of initiatives have made the prosecution and punishment of drug offenders a top priority. State prosecutors have expanded their investigations into drug importation and distribution and created special prosecutors to focus on drug dealers. The fact that drugs such as crack are considered a serious problem may have convinced judges and prosecutors to expedite substance abuse cases. One study of court processing in New York found that cases involving crack had a higher probability of pretrial detention, felony indictment,

■ By handing down harsh sentences for drug trafficking, the government hopes to deter would-be dealers and convince them that the potential cost of their illegal activities is far greater than the gains. Here, Laura Hiett pauses to think during an interview at the women's federal prison at Carswell Joint Air Station in Fort Worth, Texas. Hiett, 37, is serving five years for her part in a cocaine and heroin smuggling scheme that ultimately wrecked the military career of her husband, an Army colonel once in charge of the U.S. military's antidrug program in Colombia.

and incarceration sentences than other criminal cases.[200] Some states, such as New Jersey and Pennsylvania, report that these efforts have resulted in sharp increases in the number of convictions for drug-related offenses.[201] Once convicted, drug dealers can get very long sentences. Research by the federal government shows that the average sentence for drug offenders sent to federal prison is about six years.[202]

However, these efforts often have their downside. Defense attorneys consider delay tactics to be sound legal maneuvering in drug-related cases. Courts are so backlogged that prosecutors are anxious to plea-bargain. The consequence of this legal maneuvering is that about 25 percent of people convicted on federal drug charges are granted probation or some other form of community release.[203] Even so, prisons have become jammed with inmates, many of whom were involved in drug-related cases. Many drug offenders sent to prison do not serve their entire sentences because they are released in an effort to relieve prison overcrowding. The average prison stay is about two years, or about one-third of the original sentence.[204] It is unlikely that the public would approve of a drug control strategy that locks up large numbers of traffickers; research indicates that the public already believes drug trafficking penalties are too harsh (while supporting the level of punishment for other crimes).[205] And some critics are disturbed

because punishment strategies seem to have a disproportionate effect on minority group members and the impoverished. Some have gone as far as suggesting that government agencies are either ignoring or covering up the toll harsh drug penalties have on society's disadvantaged because it is politically expedient to be a tough defender of the nation's moral climate.[206]

Community strategies   Another type of drug-control effort relies on the involvement of local community groups to lead the fight against drugs. Representatives of various local government agencies, churches, civic organizations, and similar institutions are being brought together to create drug prevention and awareness programs.

Citizen-sponsored programs attempt to restore a sense of community in drug-infested areas, reduce fear, and promote conventional norms and values.[207] These efforts can be classified into one of four distinct categories.[208] The first involves law enforcement–type efforts, which may include block watches, cooperative police–community efforts, and citizen patrols. Some of these citizen groups are nonconfrontational: they simply observe or photograph dealers, write down their license plate numbers, and then notify police. On occasion, telephone hot lines have been set up to take anonymous tips on drug activity. Other groups engage in confrontational tactics that may even include citizens' arrests. Area residents have gone as far as contracting with private security firms to conduct neighborhood patrols.

Another tactic is to use the civil justice system to harass offenders. Landlords have been sued for owning properties that house drug dealers; neighborhood groups have scrutinized drug houses for building code violations. Information acquired from these various sources is turned over to local authorities, such as police and housing agencies, for more formal action.

There are also community-based treatment efforts in which citizen volunteers participate in self-help support programs, such as Narcotics Anonymous or Cocaine Anonymous, which have more than 1,000 chapters nationally. Other programs provide youths with martial arts training, dancing, and social events as an alternative to the drug life.

Cocaine Anonymous is a fellowship of men and women who share their experience, strength, and hope with each other so that they may solve their common problem and help others to recover from their addiction. Their Web site is at:
   http://www.ca.org/
Narcotics Anonymous can be reached at:
   http://www.na.org/
For an up-to-date list of Web links, go to
   http://info.wadsworth.com/siegel   ■

The fourth drug prevention effort is designed to enhance the quality of life, improve interpersonal relationships, and upgrade the neighborhood's physical environment. Activities might include the creation of drug-free school zones (which encourage police to keep drug dealers away from the vicinity of schools). Consciousness-raising efforts include demonstrations and marches to publicize the drug problem and build solidarity among participants. Politicians have been lobbied to get better police protection or tougher laws passed; New York City residents even sent bags filled with crack collected from street corners to the mayor and police commissioner to protest drug dealing. Residents have cleaned up streets, fixed broken streetlights, and planted gardens in empty lots to broadcast the message that they have local pride and do not want drug dealers in their neighborhoods.

Community crime prevention efforts seem appealing, but there is little conclusive evidence that they are an effective drug-control strategy. Some surveys indicate that most residents do not participate in programs. There is also evidence that community programs work better in stable, middle-income areas than in those that are crime ridden and disorganized.[209] Although these findings are discouraging, some studies do find that on occasion deteriorated areas can sustain successful antidrug programs.[210] Future evaluations of community control efforts should determine whether they can work in the most economically depressed areas. The most common community based program is Drug Abuse Resistance Education (DARE), which is discussed more fully in the Policy and Practice in Criminology feature.

Drug-testing programs   Drug testing of private employees, government workers, and criminal offenders is believed to deter substance abuse. In the workplace, employees are tested to enhance on-the-job safety and productivity. In some industries, such as mining and transportation, drug testing is considered essential because abuse can pose a threat to the public.[211] Business leaders have been enlisted in the fight against drugs. Mandatory drug-testing programs in government and industry are common: more than 40 percent of the country's largest companies, including IBM and AT&T, have drug-testing programs. The federal government requires employee testing in regulated industries such as nuclear energy and defense contracting. About 4 million transportation workers are subject to testing.

Drug testing is also common in government and criminal justice agencies. About 30 percent of local police departments test applicants, and 16 percent routinely test field officers. However, larger jurisdictions serving populations over 250,000 are much more likely to test applicants (84 percent) and field officers (75 percent). Drug testing is also part of the federal government's Drug-Free Workplace Program, which has the goal of improving productivity and safety. Employees most likely to be tested include presidential appointees, law enforcement officers, and people in positions of national security.

Criminal defendants are now routinely tested at all stages of the justice system, from arrest to parole. The goal is to reduce criminal behavior by detecting current users and curbing their abuse. Can such programs reduce criminal activity? Two evaluations of pretrial drug-testing programs found little evidence that monitoring defendants' drug use influenced their behavior.[212]

Treatment strategies   A number of approaches are taken to treat known users, getting them clean of drugs and alcohol and thereby reducing the at-risk population. One approach rests on the assumption that users have low self-esteem and treatment efforts must focus on building a sense of self. For example, users have been placed in worthwhile programs of outdoor activities and wilderness training to create self-reliance and a sense of accomplishment.[213] More intensive efforts use group therapy approaches relying on group leaders who have been substance abusers; through such sessions users get the skills and support to help them reject social pressure to use drugs. These programs are based on the Alcoholics Anonymous approach, which holds that users must find within themselves the strength to stay clean and that peer support from those who understand their experiences can help them achieve a drug-free life.

There are also residential programs for the more heavily involved, and a large network of drug treatment centers has been developed. Some detoxification units use medical procedures to wean patients from the more addicting drugs to others, such as methadone, that can be more easily regulated. Methadone is a drug similar to heroin, and addicts can be treated at clinics where they receive methadone under controlled conditions. However, methadone programs have been undermined because some users sell their methadone in the black market, and others supplement their dosages with illegally obtained heroin.

Did you know that the state of New York is implementing sweeping new drug court reforms that will increase the number of nonviolent drug-addicted offenders who go into court-mandated substance abuse treatment? To learn more, go to InfoTrac College Edition and read this article: New York drug reforms call for drug treatment, not incarceration. *Alcoholism & Drug Abuse Weekly*, July 3, 2000 v12 i27 p1   ■

Other therapeutic programs attempt to deal with the psychological causes of drug use. Hypnosis, aversion therapy (getting users to associate drugs with unpleasant sensations, such as nausea), counseling, biofeedback, and other techniques are often used.

The long-term effects of treatment on drug abuse are still uncertain. Critics charge that a stay in a residential program can help stigmatize people as addicts even if they

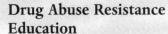

Drug Abuse Resistance Education

The most widely known drug education program, Drug Abuse Resistance Education (DARE), is an elementary school course designed to give students the skills for resisting peer pressure to experiment with tobacco, drugs, and alcohol. It is unique because it employs uniformed police officers to carry the antidrug message to the students before they enter junior high school. The program focuses on five major areas:

1. Providing accurate information about tobacco, alcohol, and drugs
2. Teaching students techniques to resist peer pressure
3. Teaching students respect for the law and law enforcers
4. Giving students ideas for alternatives to drug use
5. Building the self-esteem of students

DARE is based on the concept that the young students need specific analytical and social skills to resist peer pressure and say no to drugs. Instructors work with children to raise their self-esteem, provide them with decision-making tools, and help them identify positive alternatives to substance abuse. Millions of students have already taken the DARE program. More than 40 percent of all school districts incorporate assistance from local law enforcement agencies in their drug-prevention programming. New community policing strategies commonly incorporate the DARE program in their efforts to provide services to local neighborhoods at the grassroots level.

Does DARE Work?

DARE is quite popular with both schools and police agencies, but a highly sophisticated evaluation of the program by Dennis Rosenbaum and his associates found that it had only a marginal impact on student drug use and attitudes. A longitudinal study by psychologist Donald Lynam and his colleagues found that DARE had no effect on students' drug use at any time through tenth grade, and a 10-year follow-up failed to find any hidden or delayed "sleeper" effects. At age 20, there were no differences in drug use between those who received DARE and those who did not; the only difference was that those who received DARE reported slightly lower levels of self-esteem at age 20, an effect that proponents were not aiming for.

Changing the DARE Curriculum

Although national evaluations have questioned the validity of DARE and a few communities have discontinued its use, it is still widely employed in school districts around the United States. To meet criticism head on, DARE began testing a new curriculum in 2001. The new program is aimed at older students and relies more on having them question their assumptions about drug use than on listening to lectures on the subject. Among other changes, the new program will work largely on changing social norms, teaching students to question whether they really have to use drugs to fit in with their peers. Police officers will now serve more as coaches than as lecturers, encouraging students to challenge the social norm of drug use in discussion groups. Students also do more role playing in an effort to learn decision-making skills. There will also be an emphasis on the role of media and advertising in shaping behavior.

Critical Thinking Questions

1. If DARE does not work as expected, what policy might be the best strategy to reduce teenage drug use? Source control? Reliance on treatment? Community-level enforcement?
2. Should all teens who are receiving a free education from the state be tested for drugs and alcohol in order to remain in school?
3. Do you think that the DARE program would be more successful if taught by people other than police officers? What about ex-addicts?

InfoTrac College Edition Research

Use "Drug Abuse Resistance Education" as a subject guide in InfoTrac College Edition. To learn more about the Lynam research, read this article:

DARE: doubtful after 10 years. *Harvard Mental Health Letter,* August 2000 v17 i2 pITEM00224005

SOURCES: Kate Zernike, "Antidrug Program Says It Will Adopt a New Strategy," *New York Times,* 15 February 2001, p.1; Donald R. Lynam, Rich Milich, Rick Zimmerman, Scott Novak, T. K. Logan, Catherine Martin, Carl Leukefeld, and Richard Clayton, "Project D.A.R.E.: No Effects at 10-Year Follow-Up," *Journal of Consulting and Clinical Psychology* 67 (1999): 590–93; Dennis Rosenbaum, Robert Flewelling, Susan Bailey, Chris Ringwalt, and Deanna Wilkinson, "Cops in the Classroom: A Longitudinal Evaluation of Drug Abuse Resistance Education (D.A.R.E.)," *Journal of Research in Crime and Delinquency* 31 (1994): 3–31; David Carter, *Community Policing and D.A.R.E.: A Practitioner's Perspective* (Washington, D.C.: Bureau of Justice Assistance, 1995).

never used hard drugs; and in treatment they may be introduced to hard-core users with whom they will associate after release. Users do not often enter these programs voluntarily and have little motivation to change.[214] And even those who could be helped soon learn that there are simply more users who need treatment than there are beds in treatment facilities. Many facilities are restricted to users whose health insurance will pay for short-term residential care; when their insurance coverage ends, patients are often released, even though their treatment is incomplete.

Supporters of treatment argue that any addicts are helped by intensive in- and outpatient treatment. As one District of Columbia program shows, clients who complete treatment programs are less likely to use drugs than those who drop out.[215] Although such data support treatment strategies, it is also possible that completers are motivated individuals who would have stopped using drugs even if they had not been treated.

Although these and similar results are encouraging, treatment strategies have been thwarted because relatively few drug-dependent people actually receive the rehabilitation efforts they so desperately need. Unfortunately, those requiring treatment may not often receive the proper care. More than 4.1 million people may now be drug dependent, but less than 1 million are receiving treatment. The treatment gap is most pronounced for adolescents: the number of persons ages 12 to 25 dependent on illicit drugs is nearly six times greater than the number receiving treatment.

Employment programs   Research indicates that drug abusers who obtain and keep employment will end or reduce the incidence of their substance abuse.[216] Not surprisingly, then, there have been a number of efforts to provide vocational rehabilitation for drug abusers. One approach is the supported work program, which typically involves job-site training, ongoing assessment, and job-site intervention. Rather than teach work skills in a classroom, support programs rely on helping drug abusers deal with real work settings. Other programs provide training to overcome the barriers to employment, including help with motivation, education, experience, the job market, job-seeking skills, and personal issues.

Drug Legalization

Despite the massive effort to control drugs through prevention, deterrence, education, and treatment strategies, the fight against substance abuse has not proved successful. It is difficult to get people out of the drug culture because of the enormous profits involved in the drug trade. It has also proved difficult to control drugs by convincing known users to quit; few treatment efforts have been successful. The so-called war on drugs is expensive, costing more than $500 billion over the past 20 years—money that could have been spent on education and economic development. Drug enforcement now costs federal, state, and local governments more than $30 billion per year.[217]

Considering these problems, some commentators have called for the legalization or decriminalization of restricted drugs. Legalization is warranted, according to Ethan Nadelmann, because the use of mood-altering substances is customary in almost all human societies; people have always wanted, and will find ways of obtaining, psychoactive drugs.[218] Banning drugs creates networks of manufacturers and distributors, many of whom use violence as part of their standard operating procedures. Although some believe drug use is immoral, Nadelmann questions whether it is any worse than the unrestricted use of alcohol and cigarettes, both of which are addicting and

unhealthful. Far more people die each year because they abuse these legal substances than are killed in drug wars or from abusing illegal substances.[219]

Nadelmann also states that just as prohibition failed to stop the flow of alcohol in the 1920s, while it increased the power of organized crime, the policy of prohibiting drugs is similarly doomed to failure. When drugs were legal and freely available earlier in this century, the proportion of Americans using drugs was not much greater than today; most users led normal lives, most likely because of the legal status of their drug use.[220]

If drugs were legalized, the argument goes, price and distribution could be controlled by the government. This would reduce addicts' cash requirements, so crime rates would drop because users would no longer need the same cash flow to support their habits. Drug-related deaths would decline because government control would reduce needle sharing and the spread of AIDS. Legalization would also destroy the drug-importing cartels and gangs. Because drugs would be bought and sold openly, the government would reap a tax windfall both from taxes on the sale of drugs and from income taxes paid by drug dealers on profits that have been part of the hidden economy. Of course, drug distribution would be regulated, like alcohol, keeping drugs away from adolescents, public servants such as police and airline pilots, and known felons. Those who favor legalization point to the Netherlands as a country that has legalized drugs and remains relatively crime-free.[221]

The consequences of legalization   Critics claim the legalization approach might have the short-term effect of reducing the association between drug use and crime, but it might also have grave social consequences. Legalization might increase the nation's rate of drug usage, creating an even larger group of nonproductive, drug-dependent people who must be cared for by the rest of society.[222] For example, the state of Florida reports that in a single year (1997) nearly 40,000 hospitalizations were linked to drug abuse, increasing the state's hospital costs by $304 million. This included more than $250 million for treating diseases and other health disorders caused by substance abuse; $46 million for detoxifying substance-addicted patients; and about $8 million for the delivery and care of newborns affected by maternal substance abuse and addiction.[223]

If drugs were legalized and freely available, drug users might significantly increase their daily intake. In countries like Iran and Thailand, where drugs are cheap and readily available, the rate of narcotics use is quite high. Historically, the availability of cheap narcotics has preceded drug-use epidemics, as was the case when British and American merchants sold opium in nineteenth-century China.

If the government tried to raise money by taxing legal drugs, as it now does with liquor and cigarettes, that might encourage drug smuggling to avoid tax payments; these "illegal" drugs might then fall into the hands of adolescents.

The lesson of alcohol The problems of alcoholism should serve as a warning of what can happen when controlled substances are made readily available. For example, because women may more easily become dependent on crack than men, the number of drug-dependent babies could begin to match or exceed the number delivered with fetal alcohol syndrome.[224] Drunk-driving fatalities, which today number about 25,000 per year, might be matched by deaths due to driving under the influence of pot or crack. And although distribution would be regulated, it is likely that adolescents would have the same opportunity to obtain potent drugs as they now have to obtain alcoholic beverages.

Decriminalization or legalization of controlled substances is unlikely in the near term, but further study is warranted. What effect would a policy of partial decriminalization (for example, legalizing small amounts of marijuana) have on drug use rates? Would a get-tough policy help to "widen the net" of the justice system and actually deepen some youths' involvement in substance abuse? Can society provide alternatives to drugs that will reduce teenage drug dependency?[225] The answers to these questions have proven elusive.

■ Summary

Public order crimes are acts considered illegal because they conflict with social policy, accepted moral rules, and public opinion. There is usually great debate over public order crimes. Some charge that they are not really crimes at all and that it is foolish to legislate morality. Others view such morally tinged acts as prostitution, gambling, and drug abuse as harmful and therefore subject to public control. Many public order crimes are sex-related. Although homosexuality is not a crime, homosexual acts are subject to legal control. Some states still follow the archaic custom of legislating long prison terms for consensual homosexual sex.

Prostitution is another sex-related public order crime. Although prostitution has been practiced for thousands of years and is legal in some areas, most states outlaw commercial sex. There are a variety of prostitutes, including streetwalkers, B-girls, and call girls. Studies indicate that prostitutes come from poor, troubled families and have abusive parents. However, there is little evidence that prostitutes are emotionally disturbed, addicted to drugs, or sexually abnormal. Although prostitution is illegal, some cities have set up adult entertainment areas where commercial sex is tolerated by law enforcement agents.

Pornography involves the sale of sexually explicit material intended to sexually excite paying customers. The depiction of sex and nudity is not illegal, but it does violate the law when it is judged obscene. Obscene material is a legal term that today is defined as material offensive to community standards. Thus each local jurisdiction must decide what pornographic material is obscene. A growing problem is the exploitation of children in obscene materials (kiddie porn). There is no hard evidence that pornography is related to crime or aggression, but data suggest that sexual material with a violent theme is related to sexual violence by those who view it.

Substance abuse is another type of public order crime. Most states and the federal government outlaw a wide variety of drugs they consider harmful, including narcotics, amphetamines, barbiturates, cocaine, hallucinogens, and marijuana. One of the main reasons for the continued ban on drugs is their relationship to crime. Numerous studies have found that drug addicts commit enormous amounts of property crime.

There are many different strategies to control substance abuse, ranging from source control to treatment. So far, no single method seems effective. Although legalization is debated, the fact that so many people already take drugs and the association of drug abuse with crime make legalization unlikely in the near term.

■ Thinking Like a Criminologist

The President's "Drug Czar" has asked you to suggest a response to groups asking the government to legalize "recreational" drugs such as marijuana and "Ecstasy." Before you make your recommendations, he asks that you review the most recent National Household Survey on Drug Abuse (NHSDA). This survey asks youths aged 12 to 17 to report on their participation in violent behavior during the year before the survey, including serious fighting at school or work, group-against-group fighting, and attacking others with the intent to seriously hurt them. Youths were also asked about their use of alcohol and illicit drugs during the month before the survey.

The most recent NHSDA data indicate that violence among young people has increased during the past 15 years. Of the estimated 23 million youths in the United States aged 12 to 17, the NHSDA showed that more than 5 million reported participating in serious fighting at school or work, almost 4 million took part in a group-against-group fight, and almost 2 million attacked others with the intent of seriously hurting them during the past year. Youths aged 14 or 15 were more likely than 16 or 17 year olds to report being involved in serious fighting at school or work during the past year, and youths aged 14 to 17 were more likely than 12 or 13 year olds to report attacking others with the intent to seriously hurt them in the past year. There were no significant differences between age groups in reporting group-against-group fighting. Males were more likely than females to participate in these violent behaviors. Asian youths (13 percent) were less likely than youths from other racial/ethnic groups (white, 21 percent; American Indian/Alaska Native, 21 percent; Hispanic, 25 percent; and black, 26 percent) to participate in serious fighting at school or work during the past year or to attack others with the intent to seriously hurt them (Asian, 4 percent; white, 7 percent; Hispanic, 9 percent; American Indian/Alaska Native, 9 percent; and black, 13 percent). There were no clear differences between racial/ethnic groups in reporting past year group-against-group fighting. Also, no clear differences in violent behaviors emerged between youths who lived in metropolitan versus non-metropolitan counties.

Considering these findings, would you recommend drug legalization? If so, why? If not, why not?

Key Terms

- **public order crimes** *(417)*
- **victimless crimes** *(417)*
- **social harm** *(419)*
- **vigilantes** *(419)*
- **moral crusaders** *(420)*
- **moral entrepreneurs** *(420)*
- **gay bashing** *(420)*

- **homosexuality** *(420)*
- **sodomy** *(420)*
- **homophobia** *(421)*
- **paraphilias** *(422)*
- **brothels** *(423)*
- **prostitution** *(423)*
- **madam** *(424)*

- **call girls** *(424)*
- **skeezers** *(425)*
- **pornography** *(427)*
- **obscenity** *(427)*
- **temperance movement** *(432)*
- **gateway model** *(438)*

Critical Thinking Questions

1. Under what circumstances, if any, might the legalization or decriminalization of drugs be beneficial to society?

2. Do you consider alcohol a drug? Should greater control be placed on the sale of alcohol?

3. Do TV shows and films glorify drug usage and encourage youths to enter the drug trade? Should all images on TV of drugs and alcohol be banned?

4. Is prostitution really a crime? Should a man or woman have the right to sell sexual favors if they so choose?

5. Do you believe there should be greater controls placed on the distribution of sexually explicit material on the Internet? Would you approve of the online sale of sexually explicit photos of children if they were artificial images created by computer animation? In other words, do you agree or disagree with the Supreme Court decision allowing the sales of such items?

6. Are there objective standards of morality? Does the existing criminal code reflect contemporary national moral standards? Or are laws banning sexual behaviors and substance abuse the product of a relatively few "moral entrepreneurs" who seek to control other people's behaviors?

Notes

1. Al Baker, "L. I. Millionaire's Newest Venture Was Oldest Profession, Police Say," *New York Times*, 21 July 2001.

2. Edwin Schur, *Crimes without Victims* (Englewood Cliffs, N.J.: Prentice-Hall, 1965).

3. Andrea Dworkin, quoted in "Where Do We Stand on Pornography," *Ms* (January–February 1994), p. 34.

4. Jennifer Williard, *Juvenile Prostitution* (Washington, D.C.: National Victim Resource Center, 1991).

5. Morris Cohen, "Moral Aspects of the Criminal Law," *Yale Law Journal* 49 (1940): 1017.

6. Sir Patrick Devlin, *The Enforcement of Morals* (New York: Oxford University Press, 1959), p. 20.

7. See Joel Feinberg, *Social Philosophy* (Englewood Cliffs, N.J.: Prentice-Hall, 1973), chap. 2, 3.

8. H. L. A. Hart, "Immorality and Treason," *Listener* 62 (1959): 163.

9. *United States v. 12 200-ft Reels of Super 8mm Film*, 413 U.S. 123 (1973) at 137.

10. Dan Barry and Carol Cogel, "Giuliani Vows to Cut Subsidy over Art He

Calls Offensive," *New York Times,* 23 September 1999, p. 1; David Barstow, "Brooklyn Museum Official Discussed Removing an Offending Work, *New York Times,* 28 September 1999, p.1; David Barstow, "Exhibit Was Heavily Financed by Those with Much to Gain," *New York Times,* 31October 1999, p.1; David Barstow, "Giuliani Is Ordered to Halt Attacks against Museum," *New York Times,* 2 November 1999, p.1.

11. Joseph Gusfield, "On Legislating Morals: The Symbolic Process of Designating Deviancy," *California Law Review* 56 (1968): 58–59.

12. John Franks, "The Evaluation of Community Standards," *The Journal of Social Psychology,* 139 (1999): 253–55.

13. Irving Kristol, "Liberal Censorship and the Common Culture," *Society* 36 (September 1999): 5.

14. Barbara Crossette, "Senegal Bans Cutting of Genitals of Girls," *New York Times,* 18 January 1999, p. A11.

15. David Kaplan, "Is It Torture or Tradition?" *Newsweek,* 20 December 1993, p. 124.

16. Crossette, "Senegal Bans Cutting of Genitals of Girls."

17. "Baylor U. Cancels Art Class on Nudes," *Boston Globe,* 22 March 1993, p. 21.

18. Reuters, "In Key West, Body Paint No Longer Counts as Clothes," *Boston Globe,* 22 October 1996, p. A14.

19. Howard Becker, *Outsiders* (New York: Macmillan, 1963), pp. 13–14.

20. James Brooke, "Gay Leaders Say Student's Death Just Tip of the Iceberg," *New York Times,* 14 October 1998, p. A1.

21. Albert Reiss, "The Social Integration of Queers and Peers," *Social Problems* 9 (1961): 102–20.

22. Judd Marmor, "The Multiple Roots of Homosexual Behavior," in *Homosexual Behavior,* ed. J. Marmor (New York: Basic Books, 1980), p. 5.

23. J. Money, "Sin, Sickness, or Status? Homosexual Gender Identity and Psychoneuroendocrinology," *American Psychologist* 42 (1987): 384–99.

24. C. S. Ford and F. A. Beach, *Patterns of Sexual Behavior* (New York: Harper, 1951).

25. U.S. Census Department, *Current Population Survey,* March 2000.

26. J. McNeil, *The Church and the Homosexual* (Kansas City, Mo.: Sheed, Andrews, and McNeel, 1976).

27. Laurie Goodstein, "The Architect of the 'Gay Conversion' Campaign," *New York Times,* 13 August 1998, p. A10.

28. Marmor, "The Multiple Roots of Homosexual Behavior," pp. 18–19.

29. Ibid., p. 19.

30. Henry Adams, Lester Wright, and Bethany Lohr, "Is Homophobia Associated with Homosexual Arousal?" *Journal of Abnormal Psychology* 105 (1996): 440–45.

31. 376 U.S. 660; 82 S.Ct. 1417; 8 L.Ed.2d 758 (1962).

32. Elsa Arnett, "Efforts Grow to Cap Gay-Rights Gains," *Boston Globe,* 12 April 1998, p. A10.

33. *Romer v. Evans,* 517 U.S. 620 (1996).

34. *Equality Foundation of Greater Cincinnati v. City of Cincinnati,* No. 97–1795, 1998.

35. F. Inbau, J. Thompson, and J. Zagel, *Criminal Law and Its Administration* (Mineola, N.Y.: Foundation Press, 1974), p. 287.

36. *Bowers v. Hardwick,* 106 S.Ct. 2841 (1986); reh. den. 107 S.Ct. 29 (1986).

37. American Law Institute, *Model Penal Code,* Section 207.5.

38. John Biskupic, "Justice Let Stand 'Don't Ask, Don't Tell' Policy," *Boston Globe,* 22 October 1996, p. A6.

39. Associated Press, "Court Gives Sons Back to Gay Father," *Boston Globe,* 16 October 1996, p. A5.

40. National Gay and Lesbian Task Force, "Eye on Equality: Pride and Public Opinion." Press Release, 5 July 1998.

41. American Civil Liberties Union, Press Release, 23 November 1998.

42. Charles M. Sennott, "Pope Calls Sex Abuse Crime, Pontiff Says Cases Mishandled, Voices Solidarity with Victims," *Boston Globe,* 24 April 2002, p. A1; Kevin Cullen, "Irish Bishop Quits over Priest Case, Prelate Admits He Failed to Stop Abuse of Children," *Boston Globe,* 2 April 2002, p. A6.

43. W. P. de Silva, "Sexual Variations," *British Medical Journal* 318 (1999): 654–55.

44. Kathy Smiljanich and John Briere, "Self-Reported Sexual Interest in Children: Sex Differences and Psychosocial Correlates in a University Sample," *Violence and Victims* 11 (1996): 39–50.

45. See, generally, V. Bullogh, *Sexual Variance in Society and History* (Chicago: University of Chicago Press, 1958), pp. 143–44.

46. Spencer Rathus, *Human Sexuality* (New York: Holt, Rinehart and Winston, 1983), p. 463.

47. Annette Jolin, "On the Backs of Working Prostitutes: Feminist Theory and Prostitution Policy," *Crime and Delinquency* 40 (1994): 60–83.

48. Charles McCaghy, *Deviant Behavior* (New York: Macmillan, 1976), pp. 348–49.

49. Monica Prasad, "The Morality of Market Exchange: Love, Money, and Contractual Justice," *Sociological Perspectives* 42 (1999): 181–87.

50. Cited in McCaghy, *Deviant Behavior.*

51. FBI, *Crime in the United States, 1999* (Washington, D.C.: U.S. Government Printing Office, 2000), p. 217; updated with data from FBI, *Crime in the United States, 2000* (Washington, D.C.: U.S. Government Printing Office, 2001), p. 217.

52. FBI, *Crime in the United States, 2000,* p. 216.

53. Mark-David Janus, Barbara Scanlon, and Virginia Price, "Youth Prostitution," in *Child Pornography and Sex Rings,* ed. Ann Wolbert Burgess (Lexington, Mass.: Lexington Books, 1989), pp. 127–46.

54. Libby Plumridge and Gillian Abel, "A 'Segmented' Sex Industry in New Zealand: Sexual and Personal Safety of Female Sex Workers," *Australian and New Zealand Journal of Public Health* 25 (2000): 78–83.

55. Charles Winick and Paul Kinsie, *The Lively Commerce* (Chicago: Quadrangle Books, 1971), p. 58.

56. Lisa Maher, "Hidden in the Light: Occupational Norms among Crack-Using Street-Level Sex Workers," *Journal of Drug Issues* 26 (1996): 143–73.

57. Winick and Kinsie, *The Lively Commerce,* pp. 172–73.

58. Paul Goldstein, "Occupational Mobility in the World of Prostitution: Becoming a Madam," *Deviant Behavior* 4 (1983): 267–79.

59. Alessandra Stanley, "Case of the Classy Madam," *Time,* 29 October 1984, p. 39.

60. The Associated Press, "Mob Seen in Las Vegas Sex Trade," *New York Times,* 17 October 1998, p. A7.

61. Goldstein, "Occupational Mobility in the World of Prostitution," pp. 267–70.

62. Mireya Navarro, "Group Forced Illegal Aliens into Prostitution, U.S. Says," *New York Times,* 24 April 1998, p. A10.

63. Paul Goldstein, Lawrence Ouellet, and Michael Fendrich, "From Bag Brides to Skeezers: A Historical Perspective on Sex-for-Drugs Behavior," *Journal of Psychoactive Drugs* 24 (1992): 349–61.

64. D. Kelly Weisberg, *Children of the Night: A Study of Adolescent Prostitution* (Lexington, Mass.: Lexington Books, 1985), pp. 44–55.

65. N. Jackman, Richard O'Toole, and Gilbert Geis, "The Self-Image of the Prostitute," in *Sexual Deviance,* eds. J. Gagnon and W. Simon (New York: Harper and Row, 1967), pp. 152–53.

66. John Potterat, Richard Rothenberg, Stephen Muth, William Darrow, and Lynanne Phillips-Plummer, "Pathways to Prostitution: The Chronology of Sexual and Drug Abuse Milestones," *Journal of Sex Research* 35 (1998): 333–42.

67. Sheila Royo Maxwell and Christopher Maxwell, "Examining the 'Criminal Careers' of Prostitutes within the Nexus of Drug Use, Drug Selling, and Other Illicit Activities," *Criminology* 38 (2000): 787–809.

68. Gerald Hotaling and David Finkelhor, *The Sexual Exploitation of Missing Children* (Washington, D.C.: U.S. Department of Justice, 1988).

69. Richard Estes and Neil Alan Weiner, *The Commercial Sexual Exploitation of Children in the U.S., Canada and Mexico* (Philadelphia, Pa.: University of Pennsylvania, 2001).

70. David Enrich, "Trafficking in People," *U.S. News & World Report* 131 (July 23, 2001): 34.

71. Barbara G. Brents and Kathryn Hausbeck, "State-Sanctioned Sex: Negotiating Formal and Informal Regulatory Practices in Nevada Brothels," *Sociological Perspectives* 44 (2001): 307–35.

72. Ibid.

73. Mara Keire, "The Vice Trust: A Reinterpretation of the White Slavery Scare in the United States, 1907–1917," *Journal of Social History* 35 (2001): 5–42.

74. Ronald Weitzer, "The Politics of Prostitution in America," in *Sex for Sale,* ed. Ronald Weitzer (New York: Routledge, 2000): 159–80.

75. Andrea Dworkin, *Pornography* (New York: Dutton, 1989).

76. Arthur Gould, "The Criminalisation of Buying Sex: The Politics of Prostitution in Sweden," *Journal of Social Policy* 30 (2001): 437–38.

77. Suzanne Daley, "New Rights for Dutch Prostitutes, But No Gain," *New York Times,* 12 August 2001, A4.

78. Alexa Albert, *Brothel: Mustang Ranch and Its Women* (New York: Random House, 2001).

79. *Merriam-Webster Dictionary* (New York: Pocket Books, 1974), p. 484.

80. Neil Malamuth, Tamara Addison, and Mary Koss, "Pornography and Sexual Aggression: Are There Reliable Effects and Can We Understand Them?" *Annual Review of Sex Research* 11 (2000): 26–94.

81. Attorney General's Commission, *Report on Pornography, Final Report* (Washington, D.C.: U.S. Government Printing Office, 1986), pp. 837–901. Hereinafter cited as *Pornography Commission.*

82. Albert Belanger et al., "Typology of Sex Rings Exploiting Children," in *Child Pornography and Sex Rings,* ed. Ann Wolbert Burgess (Lexington, Mass.: Lexington Books, 1984), pp. 51–81.

83. Philip Jenkins, *Beyond Tolerance: Child Pornography Online* (New York: New York University Press, 2001).

84. Charles Winick and John Evans, "The Relationship between Nonenforcement of State Pornography Laws and Rates of Sex Crime Arrests," *Archives of Sexual Behavior* 25 (1996): 439–44.

85. *The Report of the Commission on Obscenity and Pornography* (Washington, D.C.: U.S. Government Printing Office, 1970).

86. W. Fisher and G. Grenier, "Violent Pornography, Antiwoman Thoughts, and Antiwoman Acts: In Search of Reliable Effects," *Journal of Sex Research* 31 (1994): 23–38.

87. Berl Kutchinsky, "The Effect of Easy Availability of Pornography on the Incidence of Sex Crimes," *Journal of Social Issues* 29 (1973): 95–112.

88. Michael Goldstein, "Exposure to Erotic Stimuli and Sexual Deviance," *Journal of Social Issues* 29 (1973): 197–219.

89. See Edward Donnerstein, Daniel Linz, and Steven Penrod, *The Question of Pornography* (New York: Free Press, 1987).

90. Edward Donnerstein, "Pornography and Violence against Women," *Annals of the New York Academy of Science* 347 (1980): 277–88; E. Donnerstein and J. Hallam, "Facilitating Effects of Erotica on Aggression against Women," *Journal of Personality and Social Psychology* 36 (1977): 1270–77.

91. James Alan Fox and Jack Levin, "Multiple Homicide: Patterns of Serial and Mass Murder," in *Crime and Justice, An Annual Edition, Vol. 23,* ed. Michael Tonry (Chicago, Ill.: University of Chicago Press, 1998): 418–19.

92. John Court, "Sex and Violence: A Ripple Effect," *Pornography and Aggression,* eds. Neil Malamuth and Edward Donnerstein (Orlando, Fla.: Academic Press, 1984).

93. State Laws on Obscenity, Child Pornography, and Harassment [Online]. Available at: http://www.itaa.org/porn1.htm

94. *Roth v. United States,* 354 U.S. 476 (1957).

95. *A Book Named "John Cleland's Memoirs of a Woman of Pleasure" v. Attorney General of Massachusetts* 383 U.S. 413 (1966).

96. *Miller v. California,* 413 U.S. 15 (1973).

97. R. George Wright, "Defining Obscenity: The Criterion of Value," *New England Law Review* 22 (1987): 315–41.

98. *Pope v. Illinois,* at 1927 (J. Stevens dissenting).

99. *Pornography Commission,* pp. 376–77.

100. Bob Cohn, "The Trials of Adam and Eve," *Newsweek,* 7 January 1991, p. 48.

101. Elizabeth Bernstein, "The Meaning of the Purchase: Desire, Demand and the Commerce of Sex," *Ethnography* 2 (2001): 389–420.

102. 427 U.S. 50 (1976).

103. Thomas J. Lueck, "At Sex Shops, Fear That Ruling Means the End Is Near," *New York Times,* 25 February 1998, p.1.

104. David Rohde, "In Giuliani's Crackdown on Porn Shops, Court Ruling Is a Setback," *New York Times,* 29 August 1998, p. A11.

105. Ann Landers, "Pornography Can Be an Addiction," *Boston Globe,* 19 July 1993, p. 36.

106. Ann Landers, "Husband Is Obsessed with Internet Porn," *Boston Globe,* 22 May 1998, p. D12.

107. Joseph Scott, "Violence and Erotic Material—The Relationship between Adult Entertainment and Rape." Paper presented at the annual meeting of the American Association for the Advancement of Science, Los Angeles, 1985.

108. Anthony Flint, "Skin Trade Spreading across U.S.," *Boston Globe,* 1 December 1996, pp. 1, 36–37.

109. Associated Press, "N.Y. Firm Fined for Broadcasting Pornographic Films by Satellite," *Boston Globe,* 16 February 1991, p. 12.

110. ACLU, *Reno v. ACLU,* No. 96–511.

111. ACLU, "*ACLU v. Reno,* Round 2: Broad Coalition Files Challenge to New Federal Net Censorship Law." News Release, 22 October 1998.

112. 18 U.S.C. 2256(8); *Ashcroft, Attorney General, et al. v. Free Speech Coalition et al.* No. 00795. Decided April 16, 2002.

113. Ralph Weisheit, "Studying Drugs in Rural Areas: Notes from the Field," *Journal of Research in Crime and Delinquency* 30 (1993): 213–32.

114. "British Officials Report Skyrocketing Heroin Use," *Alcoholism & Drug Abuse Weekly* 10 (August 17, 1998): 7; Na-

tional Institute on Drug Abuse, Community Epidemiology Work Group, *Epidemiological Trends in Drug Abuse, Advance Report* (Washington, D.C.: National Institute on Drug Abuse, 1997).

115. FBI, *Uniform Crime Report,* 2000, p. 116.

116. Allen Beck and Paige Harrison, *Prisoners in 2000* (Washington, D.C.: Bureau of Justice Statistics, 2002), p. 2.

117. Arnold Trebach, *The Heroin Solution* (New Haven, Conn.: Yale University Press, 1982).

118. James Inciardi, *The War on Drugs* (Palo Alto, Calif.: Mayfield, 1986), p. 2.

119. See, generally, David Pittman, "Drug Addiction and Crime," in *Handbook of Criminology,* ed. D. Glazer (Chicago: Rand McNally, 1974), pp. 209–32; Board of Directors, National Council on Crime and Delinquency, "Drug Addiction: A Medical, Not a Law Enforcement, Problem," *Crime and Delinquency* 20 (1974): 4–9.

120. Associated Press, "Records Detail Royals' Turn-of-Century Drug Use," *Boston Globe,* 29 August 1993, p. 13.

121. See Edward Brecher, *Licit and Illicit Drugs* (Boston: Little, Brown, 1972).

122. James Inciardi, *Reflections on Crime* (New York: Holt, Rinehart and Winston, 1978), p. 15.

123. William Bates and Betty Crowther, "Drug Abuse," in *Deviants: Voluntary Actors in a Hostile World,* eds. E. Sagarin and F. Montanino (New York: Foresman and Co., 1977), p. 269.

124. Inciardi, *Reflections on Crime,* pp. 8–10. See also, A. Greeley, William McCready, and Gary Theisen, *Ethnic Drinking Subcultures* (New York: Praeger, 1980).

125. Joseph Gusfield, *Symbolic Crusade* (Urbana: University of Illinois Press, 1963), chap. 3.

126. McCaghy, *Deviant Behavior,* p. 280.

127. Ibid.

128. The annual survey is conducted by Lloyd Johnston, Jerald Bachman, and Patrick O'Malley of the Institute of Social Research, University of Michigan, Ann Arbor, Michigan.

129. Monitoring the Future Study. The most recent data from the study is contained in a Press Release, "Rise in Ecstasy Use among American Teens Begins to Slow," 19 December 2001.

130. Data in this section come from Department of Health and Human Services, *The Household Survey on Drug Abuse, 2000* (Washington, D.C.: author, 2000).

131. Eric Wish, *Drug Use Forecasting Program, Annual Report 1990* (Washington, D.C.: National Institute of Justice, 1990).

132. Thomas Gray and Eric Wish, *Maryland Youth at Risk: A Study of Drug Use in Juvenile Detainees* (College Park, Md.: Center for Substance Abuse Research, 1993); Eric Wish and Christina Polsenberg, "Arrestee Urine Tests and Self-Reports of Drug Use: Which Is More Related to Rearrest?" Paper presented at the annual meeting of the American Society of Criminology, Phoenix, Arizona, November 1993.

133. Julia Yun Soo Kim, Michael Fendrich, and Joseph Wislar, "The Validity of Juvenile Arrestees' Drug Use Reporting: A Gender Comparison," *Journal of Research in Crime and Delinquency* 37 (2000): 419–32.

134. Thomas Mieczkowski, "The Prevalence of Drug Use in the United States," in *Crime and Justice, A Review of Research,* vol. 20, ed. Michael Tonry (Chicago: University of Chicago Press, 1996), 349–414, at 376.

135. See, generally, Mark Blumberg, ed., *AIDS: The Impact on the Criminal Justice System* (Columbus, Ohio: Merrill Publishing, 1990).

136. Scott Decker and Richard Rosenfeld, "Intravenous Drug Use and the AIDS Epidemic: Findings for a Twenty-City Sample of Arrestees." Paper presented at the annual meeting of the American Society of Criminology, Baltimore, November 1990.

137. Douglas Longshore, "Prevalence and Circumstances of Drug Injection at Los Angeles Shooting Galleries," *Crime and Delinquency* 42 (1996): 21–35.

138. Ibid., p. 30.

139. Mark Blumberg, "AIDS and the Criminal Justice System: An Overview," in *AIDS: The Impact on the Criminal Justice System,* ed. Mark Blumberg (Columbus, Ohio: Merrill Publishing, 1990), p. 11.

140. Marvin Krohn, Alan Lizotte, Terence Thornberry, Carolyn Smith, and David McDowall, "Reciprocal Causal Relationships among Drug Use, Peers, and Beliefs: A Five-Wave Panel Model," *Journal of Drug Issues* 26 (1996): 205–428.

141. Kellie Barr, Michael Farrell, Grace Barnes, and John Welte, "Race, Class, and Gender Differences in Substance Abuse: Evidence of Middle-Class/Underclass Polarization among Black Males," *Social Problems* 40 (1993): 314–26.

142. Rathus and Nevid, *Abnormal Psychology,* p. 361.

143. Spencer Rathus, *Psychology,* 4th ed. (New York: Holt, Rinehart, and Winston, 1990), p. 158.

144. Jerome J. Platt, *Heroin Addiction and Theory, Research and Treatment: The Addict, the Treatment Process and Social Control* (Melbourne, Fl.: Krieser Publishing, 1995), p. 127.

145. Alison Bass, "Mental Ills, Drug Abuse Linked," *Boston Globe,* 21 November 1990, p. 3.

146. D. W. Goodwin, "Alcoholism and Genetics," *Archives of General Psychiatry* 42 (1985): 171–74.

147. For a thorough review of this issue, see John Petraitis, Brian Flay, and Todd Miller, "Reviewing Theories of Adolescent Substance Use: Organizing Pieces in the Puzzle," *Psychological Bulletin* 117 (1995): 67–86.

148. Judith Brooks and Li-Jung Tseng, "Influences of Parental Drug Use, Personality, and Child Rearing on the Toddler's Anger and Negativity," *Genetic, Social and General Psychology Monographs* 122 (1996): 107–28.

149. Thomas Ashby Wills, Donato Vaccaro, Grace McNamara, and A. Elizabeth Hirky, "Escalated Substance Use: A Longitudinal Grouping Analysis from Early to Middle Adolescence," *Journal of Abnormal Psychology* 105 (1996): 166–80.

150. Denise Kandel and Mark Davies, "Friendship Networks, Intimacy, and Illicit Drug Use in Young Adulthood: A Comparison of Two Competing Theories," *Criminology* 29 (1991): 441–71.

151. J. S. Mio, G. Nanjundappa, D. E. Verlur, and M. D. DeRios, "Drug Abuse and the Adolescent Sex Offender: A Preliminary Analysis," *Journal of Psychoactive Drugs* 18 (1986): 65–72.

152. D. Baer and J. Corrado, "Heroin Addict Relationships with Parents During Childhood and Early Adolescent Years," *Journal of Genetic Psychology* 124 (1974): 99–103.

153. John Wallace and Jerald Bachman, "Explaining Racial/Ethnic Differences in Adolescent Drug Use: The Impact of Background and Lifestyle," *Social Problems* 38 (1991): 333–57.

154. Amy Young, Carol Boyd, and Amy Hubbell, "Social Isolation and Sexual Abuse among Women Who Smoke Crack," *Journal of Psychosocial Nursing* 39 (2001): 16–19.

155. John Donovan, "Problem-Behavior Theory and the Explanation of Adolescent Marijuana Use," *Journal of Drug Issues* 26 (1996): 379–404.

156. A. Christiansen, G. T. Smith, P. V. Roehling, and M. S. Goldman, "Using Alcohol Expectancies to Predict Adolescent Drinking Behavior After One Year," *Journal of Counseling and Clinical Psychology* 57 (1989): 93–99.

157. Claire Sterk-Elifson, "Just for Fun?: Cocaine Use Among Middle-Class Women," *Journal of Drug Issues* 26 (1996): 63–76, at 69.

158. Icek Ajzen, *Attitudes, Personality and Behavior* (Homewood, Ill.: Dorsey Press, 1988).

159. James Inciardi, Ruth Horowitz, and Anne Pottieger, *Street Kids, Street Drugs, Street Crime: An Examination of Drug Use and Serious Delinquency in Miami* (Belmont, Calif.: Wadsworth, 1993), p. 43.

160. Ibid.

161. Mary Ellen Mackesy-Amiti, Michael Fendrich, and Paul Goldstein, "Sequence of Drug Use among Serious Drug Users: Typical vs. Atypical Progression," *Drug and Alcohol Dependence* 45 (1997): 185–96.

162. Bu Huang, Helene White, Rick Kosterman, Richard Catalano, and J. David Hawkins, "Developmental Associations between Alcohol and Interpersonal Aggression during Adolescence," *Journal of Research in Crime and Delinquency* 38 (2001): 64–83.

163. Andrew Golub and Bruce Johnson, "The Multiple Paths Through Alcohol, Tobacco and Marijuana to Hard Drug Use among Arrestees." Paper presented at the annual Society of Criminology meeting, San Diego, Calif., November 1997.

164. Andrew Golub and Bruce D. Johnson, *The Rise of Marijuana as the Drug of Choice among Youthful Adult Arrestees* (Washington, D.C.: National Institute of Justice, 2001).

165. Inciardi, *The War on Drugs*, p. 60.

166. These lifestyles are described in Marcia Chaiken and Bruce Johnson, *Characteristics of Different Types of Drug-Involved Offenders* (Washington, D.C.: National Institute of Justice, 1988).

167. Kenneth Tunnell, "Inside the Drug Trade: Trafficking from the Dealer's Perspective," *Qualitative Sociology* 16 (1993): 361–81.

168. Lening Zhang, John Welte, and William Wieczorek, "Youth Gangs, Drug Use and Delinquency," *Journal of Criminal Justice* 27 (1999): 101–9.

169. Carolyn Rebecca Block, Antigone Christakos, Ayad Jacob, and Roger Przybylski, *Street Gangs and Crime* (Chicago: Illinois Criminal Justice Information Authority, 1996).

170. Richard Tewksbury and Elizabeth Ehrhardt Mustaine, "Lifestyle of the Wheelers and Dealers: Drug Dealing among American College Students," *Journal of Crime and Justice* 21 (1998): 37.

171. Hilary Saner, Robert MacCoun, and Peter Reuter, "On the Ubiquity of Drug Selling among Youthful Offenders in Washington, D.C., 1985–1991: Age, Period, or Cohort Effect?" *Journal of Quantitative Criminology* 11 (1995): 362–73.

172. Charles Faupel and Carl Klockars, "Drugs–Crime Connections: Elaborations from the Life Histories of Hard-Core Heroin Addicts," *Social Problems* 34 (1987): 54–68.

173. Charles Faupel, "Heroin Use, Crime and Unemployment Status," *Journal of Drug Issues* 18 (1988): 467–79.

174. Faupel and Klockars, "Drugs–Crime Connections."

175. Russel Falck, Jichuan Wang, and Robert Carlson, "The Epidemiology of Physical Attack and Rape among Crack-Using Women," *Violence and Victims* 16 (2001): 79–89.

176. Marvin Dawkins, "Drug Use and Violent Crime among Adolescents," *Adolescence* 32 (1997): 395–406.

177. U.S. Department of Justice, "Four in Ten Criminal Offenders Report Alcohol as a Factor in Violence." Press Release, 5 April 1998.

178. Arrestee Drug Abuse Monitoring Program, *1997 Drug Use Forecasting, Annual Report on Adult and Juvenile Arrestees* (Washington, D.C.: National Institute of Justice, 1998); *Center for Substance Abuse Research Report*, 7 September 1998.

179. George Speckart and M. Douglas Anglin, "Narcotics Use and Crime: An Overview of Recent Research Advances," *Contemporary Drug Problems* 13 (1986): 741–69; Faupel and Klockars, "Drugs–Crime Connections."

180. David Nurco, Thomas Hanlon, Mitchell Balter, et al., "A Classification of Narcotic Addicts Based on Type, Amount and Severity of Crime," *Journal of Drug Issues* 21 (1991): 429–48.

181. David Farabee, Vandana Joshi, and M. Douglas Anglin, "Addiction Careers and Criminal Specialization," *Crime and Delinquency* 47 (2001): 196–220.

182. Ibid.

183. M. Douglas Anglin, Elizabeth Piper Deschenes, and George Speckart, "The Effect of Legal Supervision on Narcotic Addiction and Criminal Behavior." Paper presented at the annual meeting of the American Society of Criminology, Montreal, November 1987, p. 2.

184. Speckart and Anglin, "Narcotics Use and Crime: An Overview of Recent Research Advances," p. 752.

185. Ibid.

186. Bu Huang, Helene White, Rick Kosterman, Richard Catalano, and J. David Hawkins, "Developmental Associations between Alcohol and Interpersonal Aggression during Adolescence," *Journal of Research in Crime and Delinquency* 38 (2001): 64–83; Helene Raskin White and Stephen Hansell, "The Moderating Effects of Gender and Hostility on the Alcohol–Aggression Relationship," *Journal of Research in Crime and Delinquency* 33 (1996): 450–70.

187. James Inciardi, "Heroin Use and Street Crime," *Crime and Delinquency* 25 (1979): 335–46; see also, W. McGlothlin, M. Anglin, and B. Wilson, "Narcotic Addiction and Crime," *Criminology* 16 (1978): 293–311.

188. David Best, Clare Sidwell, Michael Gossop, et al., "Crime and Expenditure amongst Polydrug Misusers Seeking Treatment: The Connection between Prescribed Methadone and Crack Use, and Criminal Involvement," *British Journal of Criminology* 41 (2001): 119–26.

189. Allen Beck, Darrell Gilliard, Lawrence Greenfeld, Caroline Harlow, Thomas Hester, Lewis Jankowski, Tracy Snell, James Stephen, and Danielle Morton, *Survey of State Prison Inmates, 1991* (Washington, D.C.: Bureau of Justice Statistics, 1993). The survey of prison inmates is conducted by the Bureau of Justice Statistics every five to seven years.

190. Paul Goldstein, "The Drugs–Violence Nexus: A Tripartite Conceptual Framework," *Journal of Drug Issues* 15 (1985): 493–506; Marvin Krohn, Alan Lizotte, and Cynthia Perez, "The Interrelationship between Substance Use and Precocious Transitions to Adult Sexuality," *Journal of Health and Social Behavior* 38 (1997): 87–103, at 88; Richard Jessor, "Risk Behavior in Adolescence: A Psychosocial Framework for Understanding and Action," in *Adolescents at Risk: Medical and Social Perspectives*, eds. D. E. Rogers and E. Ginzburg (Boulder, Colo.: Westview, 1992).

191. See Kenneth Jones, Louis Shainberg, and Carter Byer, *Drugs and Alcohol* (New York: Harper & Row, 1979), pp. 137–46.

192. Controlled Substance Act, 21 U.S.C. 848 (1984).

193. Anti–Drug Abuse Act of 1986, PL No. 99-570, U.S.C. 841 (1986).

194. Anti–Drug Abuse Act of 1988, PL No. 100-690; 21 U.S.C. 1501; Subtitle A—Death Penalty, Sec. 7001, Amending the Controlled Substances Abuse Act, 21 U.S.C. 848.

195. Eric Jensen, Jurg Gerber, and Ginna Babcock, "The New War on Drugs: Grass Roots Movement or Political Construction?" *Journal of Drug Issues* 21 (1991): 651–67.

196. U.S. Department of State, *1998 International Narcotics Control Strategy Report*, February 1999.

197. George Rengert, *The Geography of Illegal Drugs* (Boulder, Colo.: Westview Press, 1996), p. 2.

198. Mark Moore, *Drug Trafficking* (Washington, D.C.: National Institute of Justice, 1988).

199. John Scalia, *Federal Drug Offenders, 1999 with Trends 1984–99* (Washington, D.C.: Bureau of Justice Statistics, 2001).

200. Steven Belenko, Jeffrey Fagan, and Ko-Lin Chin, "Criminal Justice Responses to Crack," *Journal of Research in Crime and Delinquency* 28 (1991): 55–74.

201. *FY 1988 Report on Drug Control* (Washington, D.C.: National Institute of Justice, 1989), p. 103.

202. Carol Kaplan, *Sentencing and Time Served* (Washington, D.C.: Bureau of Justice Statistics, 1987).

203. Ibid., p. 2.

204. Patrick Langan and Jodi Brown, *Felony Sentences in the United States, 1994* (Washington, D.C.: Bureau of Justice Statistics, 1997).

205. Peter Rossi, Richard Berk, and Alec Campbell, "Just Punishments: Guideline Sentences and Normative Consensus," *Journal of Quantitative Criminology* 13 (1997): 267–83.

206. Michael Welch, Russell Wolff, and Nicole Bryan, "Recontextualizing the War on Drugs: A Content Analysis of NIJ Publications and Their Neglect of Race and Class," *Justice Quarterly* 15 (1998): 719–42.

207. Robert Davis, Arthur Lurigio, and Dennis Rosenbaum, eds., *Drugs and the Community* (Springfield, Ill.: Charles Thomas, 1993), pp. xii–xv.

208. Saul Weingart, "A Typology of Community Responses to Drugs," in *Drugs and the Community*, eds. Robert Davis, Arthur Lurigio, and Dennis Rosenbaum (Springfield, Ill.: Charles Thomas, 1993), pp. 85–105.

209. Davis, Lurigio, and Rosenbaum, *Drugs and the Community*, pp. xii–xiii.

210. Marianne Zawitz, *Drugs, Crime and the Justice System* (Washington, D.C.: Bureau of Justice Statistics, 1992), pp. 109–112.

211. Ibid., pp. 115–22.

212. John Goldkamp and Peter Jones, "Pretrial Drug-Testing Experiments in Milwaukee and Prince George's County: The Context of Implementation," *Journal of Research in Crime and Delinquency* 29 (1992): 430–65; Chester Britt, Michael Gottfredson, and John Goldkamp, "Drug Testing and Pretrial Misconduct: An Experiment on the Specific Deterrent Effects of Drug Monitoring Defendants on Pretrial Release," *Journal of Research in Crime and Delinquency* 29 (1992): 62–78.

213. See, generally, Peter Greenwood and Franklin Zimring, *One More Chance* (Santa Monica, Calif.: Rand Corporation, 1985).

214. Eli Ginzberg, Howard Berliner, and Miriam Ostrow, *Young People at Risk: Is Prevention Possible?* (Boulder, Colo.: Westview Press, 1988), p. 99.

215. National Evaluation Data and Technical Assistance Center, *The District of Columbia's Drug Treatment Initiative (DCI)*, (Washington, D.C.: author, February 1998).

216. The following section is based on material found in Jerome Platt, "Vocational Rehabilitation of Drug Abusers," *Psychological Bulletin* 117 (1995): 416–33.

217. Ernest Drucker, "Drug Prohibition and Public Health: 25 Years of Evidence," *Public Health Reports* 114 (1999): 14–15.

218. Ethan Nadelmann, "America's Drug Problem," *Bulletin of the American Academy of Arts and Sciences* 65 (1991): 24–40.

219. Ibid., p. 24.

220. Ethan Nadelmann, "Should We Legalize Drugs? History Answers Yes," *American Heritage* (February/March 1993): 41–56.

221. See, generally, Ralph Weisheit, *Drugs, Crime and the Criminal Justice System* (Cincinnati: Anderson, 1990).

222. David Courtwright, "Should We Legalize Drugs? History Answers No," *American Heritage* (February/March 1993): 43–56.

223. State of Florida Agency for Health Care Administration (AHCA), *Drug Abuse Hospitalization Costs Study, May 1999* (College Park, Md.: Center for Substance Abuse Research [CESAR], 23 June 1999).

224. James Inciardi and Duane McBride, "Legalizing Drugs: A Gormless, Naive Idea," *Criminologist* 15 (1990): 1–4.

225. Kathryn Ann Farr, "Revitalizing the Drug Decriminalization Debate," *Crime and Delinquency* 36 (1990): 223–37.

This final section reviews the agencies and the process of justice designed to exert social control over criminal offenders. Chapter 15 provides an overview of the justice system and describes its major institutions and processes. Chapter 16 looks at the police; Chapters 17 and 18 analyze the courts and correctional systems. This vast array of people and institutions is beset by conflicting goals and values. Some view the justice system as a mammoth agency of social control; others see it as a great social agency dispensing therapy to those who cannot fit within the boundaries of society.

PART IV The Criminal Justice System

Consequently, a major goal of justice system policymakers is to formulate and disseminate effective models of crime prevention and control. Efforts are now being undertaken at all levels of the justice system to improve information flow, experiment with new program concepts, and evaluate current operating procedures.

AP/Wide World Photos

CHAPTER 15 Overview of the Criminal Justice System

■ Introduction

In 2001, Michael and Sarah Dalton were shocked when they read the explicit sexual fantasies they found in their son Brian's journal.[1] The diary told a story about the abduction, rape, and torture of three young children. The story was entirely fictional, and Brian never intended for anybody else to see or read his work; it was his private property. His parents, however, were frightened that this writing might portend future sex crimes because Brian was already on probation for possessing child pornography. They decided to tell his probation officer about the diary hoping that his probation would be revoked for a year or two and he would be able to receive intensive sex-offender treatment in a community institution. They didn't expect he would be charged with a new crime of pandering obscenity. Afraid that a trial would be extremely embarrassing to family and friends, Brian pleaded guilty and received a seven-year prison sentence rather than the treatment in a community facility his parents had desired. After the trial, when the Daltons suggested that Brian withdraw his plea, they claimed that the prosecutor's office threatened to file more charges and to bring in other writings describing Brian's fantasies about molesting young children.

The Dalton case illustrates a number of the complex issues facing the criminal justice system:

- Brian Dalton's diary was private and fictional; there was no evidence that the children he described actually existed. Is it fair to punish someone for writing offensive fictional material, or is it a violation of his or her constitutional right to free speech?

- It is possible that Brian Dalton was prosecuted because legal authorities feared he would one day act out his fantasies. Should a person be punished for future behaviors and crimes—even though there is no real evidence that he will actually commit them—or is that a violation of due process?

- The prosecutor threatened further legal action when Dalton's family advised him to renege on his plea arrangement. Is it fair to coerce a criminal defendant with the threat of increased punishment if he demands his constitutional right to trial? After all, if the district attorney believed Brian had committed other serious crimes, why had he not been charged with them in the first place?

- Brian Dalton was described as a troubled young man with attention deficit disorder. He was a high school dropout and had trouble holding a job. Should he be sent to prison for his sexual problems or placed in a treatment facility where he might be successfully rehabilitated?

The Dalton case shows the dilemmas faced by the component agencies of the criminal justice system—police, courts, and corrections—which have been established

to apprehend, adjudicate, sanction, and treat criminal offenders. These government institutions are charged by law with dispensing fair, equal justice to all who come before them; maintaining the rule of law in a society beset by racial and social injustice and conflict; deterring crime; and treating both offenders and victims in a just, evenhanded manner.

Was Brian Dalton's journal a private matter, or should it have been made available to law enforcement authorities? To read some views on this issue, go to these Web sites:

    http://www.commondreams.org/views01/ 0808-04.htm
    http://www.nationalreview.com/coulter/ coulter080201.shtml
For an up-to-date list of Web links, go to
    http://info.wadsworth.com/siegel ■

Questions are still being asked about the general direction the justice system should take, how the problem of crime control should be approached, and what is the most effective method of dealing with known criminal offenders. This chapter reviews the various components and processes of criminal justice and then discusses the legal constraints on criminal justice agencies. Some of the philosophical concepts that dominate the system will be mentioned and explained.

■ Early Origins of American Justice

Until fairly recently, there was little recognition that the agencies of criminal justice worked in concert or formed a system.[2] The formalized police agencies, now so familiar, simply did not exist. After the Civil War, frontier towns set up "vigilance committees" and asked their **vigilantes** to keep order and go after badmen.

Are vigilantes still active today? Use "vigilante" as a key word on InfoTrac College Edition to find out how modern-day vigilantes take the law into their own hands. ■

Although firmly entrenched in our culture, common criminal justice agencies have existed for only 150 years or so. At first these institutions operated independently, with little notion that their functions could be coordinated or have common ground. In fact, it was not until 1919 that a unified criminal justice system received recognition. In that year the **Chicago Crime Commission,** a professional association funded by private contributions, was created. This organization acts as a citizens' advocacy group and keeps track of the ongoing activities of local justice agencies.

In 1931, President Herbert Hoover appointed the National Commission of Law Observance and Enforcement, commonly known today as the **Wickersham Commission.** This national study group analyzed the U.S. justice system in detail and helped usher in the era of treatment and rehabilitation. It showed the complex rules and regulations that govern the system and exposed how difficult it was for justice personnel to keep track of its legal and administrative complexity.

The Modern Era of Justice

The modern era of criminal justice study began with a series of explorations of the criminal justice process conducted under the auspices of the American Bar Foundation.[3] As a group, the foundation studies brought to light some of the hidden or low-visibility processes that were at the heart of justice system operations. They showed how informal decision making and the use of personal discretion were essential ingredients of the justice process.

The American Bar Foundation is a nonprofit, independent national research institute committed to basic empirical research on law and legal institutions. For more than 40 years, the foundation's research products have served to expand knowledge of the theory and functioning of law, legal institutions, and the legal profession. Visit their Web site at:
   http://www.abf-sociolegal.org/
For an up-to-date list of Web links, go to
   http://info.wadsworth.com/siegel ■

Another milestone occurred in 1967, when the President's Commission on Law Enforcement and the Administration of Justice (the Crime Commission), which had been appointed by President Lyndon Johnson, published its final report, titled *The Challenge of Crime in a Free Society*.[4] This group of practitioners, educators, and attorneys had been charged with creating a comprehensive view of the criminal justice process and offering recommendations for its reform. Its efforts resulted in Congress passing the Safe Streets and Crime Control Act of 1968, which provided federal funds for state and local crime control efforts. This act helped launch a massive campaign to restructure the justice system by funding the Law Enforcement Assistance Administration (LEAA), an agency that provided hundreds of millions of dollars in aid to local and state justice agencies. Federal intervention through the LEAA ushered in a new era in research and development in criminal justice and established the concept that its component agencies actually make up a system.[5] Rather than viewing police, court, and correctional agencies as thousands of independent institutions, it has become common to view them as components in a large, integrated, people-

processing system that manages law violators from the time of their arrest through trial, punishment, and release.

What Is the Criminal Justice System?

Criminal justice refers to the agencies of government charged with enforcing law, adjudicating crime, and correcting criminal conduct. The criminal justice system is essentially an instrument of social control: society considers some behaviors so dangerous and destructive that it either strictly controls their occurrence or outlaws them outright. It is the job of the agencies of justice to prevent these behaviors by apprehending and punishing transgressors or deterring their future occurrence. Although society maintains other forms of **social control,** such as the family, school, and church, these entities are designed to deal with moral, not legal, misbehavior. Only the criminal justice system has the power to control crime and punish criminals.

The contemporary criminal justice system is monumental in size. It consists of more than 55,000 public agencies, and now costs federal, state, and local governments nearly $150 billion for civil and criminal justice; this amounts to more than $500 for every resident in the United States. As Figure 15.1 shows, the federal government alone spends more than $25 billion on criminal and civil justice, compared with more than $50 billion spent by state governments, and $75 billion by counties and municipalities. At every level of government, the cost of operating the justice system has increased significantly since 1982.[6]

Within the confines of these agencies, the justice system today employs more than 2 million people, including about 900,000 individuals in law enforcement. They are employed in 17,000 police agencies, nearly 17,000 courts, more than 8,000 prosecutorial agencies, about 6,000 correctional institutions, and more than 3,500 probation and parole departments.

There are also capital costs. State jurisdictions are now conducting a massive correctional building campaign, adding tens of thousands of prison cells. It costs about $70,000 to build a prison cell, and about $22,000 per year is needed to keep an inmate in prison. Juvenile institutions cost about $30,000 per year per resident. And beyond the direct costs of funding police, court, and corrections, there are many additional crime-related expenses incurred by federal, state, and local governments. For example, federal drug-control efforts now cost an additional $19 billion per year.[7]

The rising costs of the justice system are discussed in this article on InfoTrac College Edition: Kathryn Casa. Prisons: the new growth industry. *National Catholic Reporter,* 2 July 1999 v35 i33 p1 ■

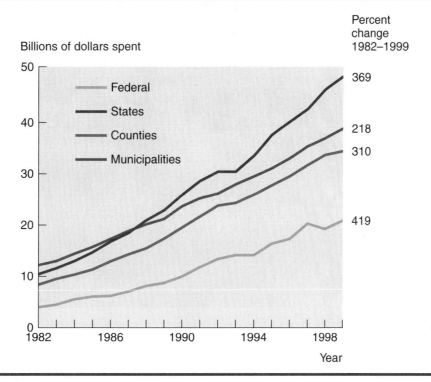

SOURCE: Sidra Lee Gifford, *Justice Expenditure and Employment Extracts* (Washington, D.C.: Bureau of Justice Statistics, 2002), p. 1.

The system is so big because it must process, treat, and care for millions of people. Although the crime rate has declined substantially during the past decade, about 15 million people are still being arrested each year, including more than 2 million for serious felony offenses;[8] about 1.5 million juveniles are handled by the juvenile courts. Today state and federal courts convict a combined total of more than 1 million adults on felony charges each year.

In addition, we are now punishing criminals more harshly and forcing them to spend more of their sentence behind bars than ever before. Consequently, the correctional system population is at an all-time high. As of 2001, there were 3,839,532 men and women on probation, 725,527 on parole, 1,312,354 in prison, and 621,149 in local jails, for a total of more than 6.5 million.[9] In 2001, almost 3 percent of the adult U.S. population, or about 1 in every 30 adults, was incarcerated or on probation or on parole.

The National Insititute of Justice, or NIJ, is the research and development agency of the U.S. Department of Justice and is the only federal agency solely dedicated to researching crime control and justice issues. You can visit their Web site and access online publications at:
   http://www.ojp.usdoj.gov/nij/welcome.html
For an up-to-date list of Web links, go to
   http://info.wadsworth.com/siegel ▪

The major components of this immense system—the police, courts, and correctional agencies—are described in the next sections.

Police and Law Enforcement

Since their origin in early nineteenth-century Britain, law enforcement agencies have been charged with peacekeeping, deterring potential criminals, and apprehending law violators.[10] The traditional police role involved maintaining order through patrolling public streets and highways, responding to calls for assistance, investigating crimes, and identifying criminal suspects. The police role has gradually expanded to include a variety of human service functions, such as preventing youth crime and diverting juvenile offenders from the criminal justice system, resolving family conflicts, facilitating the movement of people and vehicles, preserving civil order during emergencies, providing emergency medical care, and improving police–community relations.[11]

Police are the most visible agents of the justice process. Their reactions to victims and offenders are carefully scrutinized in the news media. On numerous occasions police have been criticized for being too harsh or too lenient, too violent or too passive. Police control of such groups as minority citizens, youths, political dissidents, protesters,

■ The police role is not limited to crime prevention and control and now includes a variety of human service functions, such as preventing youth crime and diverting juvenile offenders from the criminal justice system, resolving family conflicts, facilitating the movement of people and vehicles, preserving civil order during emergencies, providing emergency medical care, and improving police–community relations. Here, police in New York control a crowd of demonstrators on February 4, 2002, as they protest against the World Economic Forum.

AP/Wide World Photos

and union workers has been publicly debated. An ongoing problem has been charges that police use **racial profiling**—selecting suspects on the basis of their ethnic or racial background.

CONNECTIONS

On Christmas day 2001, a 33-year-old armed Secret Service agent of Arab descent, on his way to protect President Bush on his Texas ranch, was barred from a flight at Baltimore/Washington International Airport when the Captain questioned the agent's credentials. Was this racial profiling or a realistic security measure? See more on this case and racial profiling in Chapter 16. ■

Compounding the problem is the tremendous discretion afforded police officers, who determine when a domestic dispute becomes disorderly conduct or criminal assault, whether it is appropriate to arrest juveniles or refer them to a social agency, and when to assume that probable cause exists to arrest a suspect for a crime.[12] At the same time, police agencies have been criticized for such problems as internal corruption, inefficiency, lack of effectiveness, brutality, and discriminatory hiring.[13] Widely publicized cases of police brutality, such as the beatings of Rodney King in Los Angeles and Abner Louima in New York City, have prompted calls for the investigation and prosecution of police officers.

The Criminal Courts

The **criminal courts** are the core element in the administration of criminal justice. In the purest sense of justice, they are expected to try, convict, and sentence those who commit crimes while ensuring that the falsely accused are freed without any consequence or burden. The courts are formally required to seek the truth, obtain justice, and maintain the integrity of the government's rule of law.

During the entire criminal court process, the rights of the individual are protected at all times by federal and state constitutional mandates, statutes, and case law. They include such basic concepts as the right to an attorney, the right to a jury trial, and the right to a speedy trial. Under the Fifth and Fourteenth Amendments of the U.S. Constitution, defendants also have the right to **due process** and the right to be treated with **fundamental fairness.** Under the protective umbrella of due process are included the rights to be present at trial, to be notified of the charges, to have an opportunity to confront hostile witnesses, and to have favorable witnesses appear. Such practices are an integral part of a system and process that seek to balance the interests of the individual and the state.

The National Center for State Courts is an independent, nonprofit organization dedicated to the improvement of justice. NCSC activities include developing policies to enhance state courts, advancing state courts' interests within the federal government, fostering state court adaptation to future changes, securing sufficient resources for state courts, strengthening state court leadership, facilitating state court collaboration, and providing a model for organizational administration. To access their Web site, go to:

http://www.ncsc.dni.us
For an up-to-date list of Web links, go to
http://info.wadsworth.com/siegel ∎

Unfortunately, the ideal conditions of objectivity, fairness, and equal rights under which the nation's courts should operate are rarely achieved. Court dockets are too crowded and funds too scarce to grant each defendant the full share of justice. Consequently, a system known as **plea bargaining** has developed: defendants are asked to plead guilty as charged in return for consideration of leniency or mercy.[14] Such "bargain justice" is estimated to occur in more than 90 percent of all criminal trials. Although the criminal court system is founded on the concept of equality before the law, poor and wealthy citizens unquestionably receive different treatment when they are accused of crimes.

Corrections

After conviction and sentencing, the offender enters the correctional system. Correctional agencies administer the postjudicatory care given to offenders, which, depending on the seriousness of the crimes and the individual needs of offenders, can range from casual monitoring in the community to solitary confinement in a maximum-security prison.

The most common correctional treatment, **probation,** is a legal disposition that allows the convicted offender to remain in the community, subject to conditions imposed by court order, under the supervision of a probation officer. A probationary sentence allows an offender to continue working and to avoid the crippling effects of incarceration.

A person given a sentence involving incarceration ordinarily is confined to a correctional institution for a specified period. Different types of institutions are used to hold offenders. **Jails** or **houses of correction** hold offenders convicted of misdemeanors and those awaiting trial or those involved in other proceedings, such as grand jury deliberations, arraignments, or preliminary hearings. Many of these institutions for short-term detention are administered by county governments, and consequently, little is done to treat inmates because the personnel and institutions lack the qualifications, services, and resources.

State and federally operated correctional facilities that receive felony offenders sentenced by the criminal courts are called **prisons** or **penitentiaries.** They may be minimum-, medium-, or maximum-security institutions. Prison facilities vary throughout the country. Some have high walls, cells, and large, heterogeneous inmate populations; others offer much freedom, good correctional programs, and small, homogeneous populations.

The last segment of the corrections system, **parole,** is a process whereby an inmate is selected for early release and serves the remainder of the sentence in the community under the supervision of a parole officer. The main purpose of parole is to help the ex-inmate bridge the gap between institutional confinement and a positive adjustment within the community. All parolees must adhere to a set of rules of behavior while they are "on the outside." If these rules are violated, the parole privilege can be terminated (revoked), and the parolee will be sent back to the institution to serve the remainder of the sentence.

Other ways an offender may be released from an institution include **mandatory release** upon completion of the sentence and the **pardon,** a form of executive clemency.

Along with the criminal justice system, there is an independent juvenile justice system, which manages and treats minors who violate the law. This system is described in the Policy and Practice in Criminology feature titled "The Juvenile Justice System in the New Millennium."

∎ The Process of Justice

In addition to viewing the criminal justice system as a collection of agencies, it is possible to see it as a series of decision points through which offenders flow. This process, illustrated in Figure 15.2 on page 466, begins with initial contact with police and ends with the offender's reentry into society. At any point in the process, a decision may be made to drop further proceedings and allow the accused back into society without further penalty.

Although each jurisdiction is somewhat different, a comprehensive view of the processing of a felony offender would probably contain the following decision points:

1. **Initial contact.** The initial contact an offender has with the justice system is usually with police. Police officers may observe a criminal act during their patrol of city streets, parks, or highways. They may also find out about a crime through a citizen or victim complaint. Similarly, an informer can alert them about criminal activity in return for financial or other consideration. Sometimes political officials, such as the mayor or city council, ask police to look into ongoing criminal activity, such as gambling, and during their subsequent investigations police officers encounter an illegal act.

2. **Investigation.** Once a crime is recognized, police officers conduct an investigation to gather sufficient facts, or evidence, to identify the perpetrator, justify an

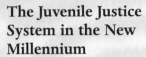

The Juvenile Justice System in the New Millennium

Independent of but interrelated with the adult criminal justice system, the juvenile justice system is primarily responsible for dealing with juveniles who commit crimes (delinquents) and those who are incorrigible, truants, runaways, or unmanageable (status offenders).

The policy of treating juveniles who commit criminal acts separately from adults is a relatively new one. Until the late nineteenth century, youthful criminals were tried in adult courts and punished in adult institutions. However, nineteenth-century reformers, today known as "child savers," lobbied to separate young offenders from serious adult criminals. Their efforts were rewarded when the first separate juvenile court was set up in Chicago in 1899. Over the next 20 years, most other states created separate juvenile court and correctional systems.

At first, the juvenile system was based on the philosophy of *parens patriae*. This meant that the state was acting in the best interests of children in trouble who could not care for themselves. Under the *parens patriae* doctrine, delinquents and status offenders (sometimes called "wayward minors" or "children in need of supervision," these youths are truants, runaways, or simply beyond control of parental authority) were tried in an informal juvenile court hearing without the benefit of counsel or other procedural rights. The juvenile correctional system, designed for treatment rather than punishment, was usually located in small institutions referred to as schools or camps. (The first juvenile reform school was opened in 1847 in Massachusetts.) After the separate juvenile justice system was developed, almost all incarcerated youths were maintained in separate juvenile institutions that stressed individualized treatment, education, and counseling.

Critics charged that the juvenile justice system's reliance on informal procedure often violated a child's constitutional rights to due process of law. It seemed unfair to place a minor child, tried without benefit of an attorney or other legal safeguards granted to adult defendants, in a remote incarceration facility. In the 1960s, the Supreme Court revolutionized the juvenile justice system when, in a series of cases—the most important being *In re Gault*—it granted procedural and due process rights, such as the right to legal counsel, to juveniles at trial. The Court recognized that many youths were receiving long sentences without the benefit of counsel and other Fifth and Sixth Amendment rights and that many institutions did not carry out their treatment role. Consequently, the juvenile justice process became similar to the adult process.

In the 1970s, recognizing the "stigma" placed on a youth by the "delinquency label," every effort was made to remove or divert youths from the official justice process and place them in alternative, community-based treatment programs. Massachusetts went so far as to close its secure correctional facilities and place all youths, no matter how serious their crimes, in community programs.

The juvenile court is a vast enterprise, handling nearly 1.8 million delinquency cases each year and conducting more than 1 million formal hearings. In 1998 (the most recent data available), juveniles were adjudicated delinquent in 63 percent of the 1,000,300 cases brought before a judge. Once adjudicated, juveniles in 58 percent (365,100) of the cases were placed on formal probation; in 26 percent (163,800) of the cases juveniles were placed in a residential facility.

Today, concern over juvenile violence has caused some critics to question the juvenile justice system's treatment philosophy. Some states have created mandatory waiver laws, making it easier to try serious juvenile offenders in the adult system. The general trend has been to remove as many nonviolent and status offenders as possible from secure placements in juvenile institutions and at the same time to lengthen the sentences of serious offenders or to move such offenders to the adult system. Each year about 8,000 kids are "waived" to the adult system and face long prison sentences and even the death penalty.

Some of the similarities and differences between the adult and juvenile justice systems are listed in Table A. Though there are many similarities between rights and privileges in both systems, there are some important differences. Juveniles can be taken into custody and placed in an institution for acts (status offenses) made illegal because of their age, such as being truant from school or running away from home. They do not have the right to a jury trial, and juvenile hearings are still closed to the public. However, juveniles who are *waived* to the adult court can be incarcerated in prisons and even subject to the death penalty.

Abolish Juvenile Justice?

In an important work, *Bad Kids: Race and the Transformation of the Juvenile Court*, legal expert Barry Feld makes the rather controversial suggestion that the juvenile court system should be discontinued and/or replaced by an alternative method of justice. He suggests that the current structure of the court makes it almost impossible for the court to fulfill or achieve the purpose for which it was originally intended.

The rehabilitative vision of the juvenile court was undercut by the fear and consequent racism created by postwar migration and economic trends, which led to the development of large enclaves of poor and underemployed African Americans living in northern cities. Then, in the 1980s, the sudden rise in gang membership, gun violence, and homicide committed by juveniles further undermined the juvenile court mission and resulted in legislation that created mandatory sentences for juvenile offenders and mandatory waiver to the adult court. As a result, the focus of the court has been on dealing with the offense rather than treating the offender. In Feld's words, the juvenile court has become a "deficient second-rate criminal court." The welfare and rehabilitative purposes of the juvenile court have been subordinated to its role of law enforcement agent.

Table A   Similarities and Differences between Juvenile and Adult Justice Systems

Similarities

Police officers, judges, and correctional personnel use discretion in decision making in both the adult and the juvenile systems.

The right to receive *Miranda* warnings applies to juveniles as well as to adults.

Juveniles and adults are protected from prejudicial lineups or other identification procedures.

Similar procedural safeguards protect juveniles and adults when they admit guilt.

Prosecutors and defense attorneys play equally critical roles in juvenile and adult advocacy.

Juveniles and adults have the right to counsel at most key stages of the court process.

Pretrial motions are available in juvenile and criminal court proceedings.

Negotiations and plea bargaining exist for juvenile and adult offenders.

Children and adults have the right to a hearing and an appeal.

The standard of evidence in juvenile delinquency adjudications, as in adult criminal trials, is proof beyond a reasonable doubt.

Juveniles and adults can be placed on probation by the court.

Both juveniles and adults can be placed in pretrial detention facilities.

Juveniles and adults can be kept in detention without bail if they are considered dangerous.

After trial, juveniles and adults can be placed in community treatment programs.

Differences

The primary purpose of juvenile procedures is protection and treatment. With adults, the aim is to punish the guilty.

Age determines the jurisdiction of the juvenile court. The nature of the offense determines jurisdiction in the adult system.

Juveniles can be apprehended for acts that would not be criminal if they were committed by an adult (status offenses).

Juvenile proceedings are not considered criminal; adult proceedings are.

Juvenile court procedures are generally informal and private. Those of adult courts are more formal and are open to the public.

Courts cannot release identifying information about a juvenile to the media, but they must release information about an adult.

Parents are highly involved in the juvenile process but not in the adult process.

The standard of arrest is more stringent for adults than for juveniles.

Juveniles are released into parental custody. Adults are generally given the opportunity for bail.

Juveniles have no constitutional right to a jury trial. Adults have this right.

Juveniles can be searched in school without probable cause or a warrant.

A juvenile's record is sealed when the age of majority is reached. The record of an adult is permanent.

A juvenile court cannot sentence juveniles to county jails or state prisons; these are reserved for adults.

There is no death penalty in the juvenile justice system. However, the U.S. Supreme Court has declared that the Eighth Amendment does not prohibit the death penalty for crimes committed by juveniles ages 16 and 17.

Critical Thinking Questions

1. Some experts disagree with Feld, but there is little question that the concept of juvenile justice is being reconsidered. Do you believe children should be tried in adult courts and sent to adult prisons if they commit serious crimes? If so, why do we need a juvenile justice system?

2. Is it fair to place kids who repeatedly run away from home in the same facilities as kids who steal cars? Is it possible that both groups of offenders are motivated by the same types of personal problems and therefore deserve similar treatments?

 InfoTrac College Edition Research

For additional information that may help you answer the first critical thinking question, read this article:

Katti Gray. Juvenile injustice. *Essence*, Sept 2001 v32 i5 p147

SOURCES: Anne L. Stahl, *Delinquency Cases in Juvenile Courts, 1998* (Washington, D.C.: Office of Juvenile Justice and Delinquency Prevention, 2001); Charles M. Puzzanchera, *Delinquency Cases Waived to Criminal Court, 1989–1998* (Washington, D.C.: Office of Juvenile Justice and Delinquency Prevention, 2001); Barry C. Feld, *Bad Kids: Race and the Transformation of the Juvenile Court* (New York: Oxford University Press, 1999); John Johnson Kerbs, "(Un)equal Justice: Juvenile Court Abolition and African Americans," *Annals, AAPSS*, 564 (1999): 109–25; Larry Siegel, *Juvenile Delinquency: The Core* (Belmont, Calif.: Wadsworth/West, 2001).

Figure 15.2   Critical Stages in the Justice Process

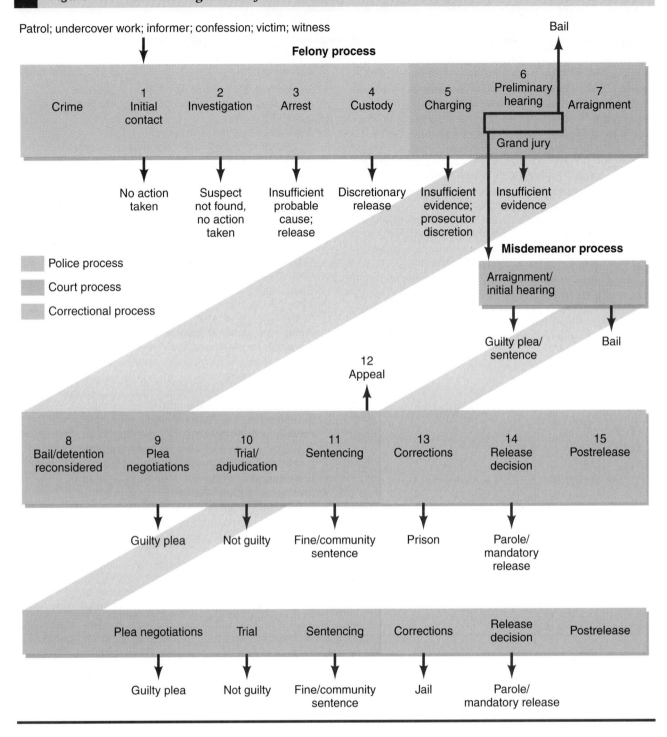

Patrol; undercover work; informer; confession; victim; witness

Felony process

Bail

| Crime | 1 Initial contact | 2 Investigation | 3 Arrest | 4 Custody | 5 Charging | 6 Preliminary hearing | 7 Arraignment |

Grand jury

No action taken | Suspect not found, no action taken | Insufficient probable cause; release | Discretionary release | Insufficient evidence; prosecutor discretion | Insufficient evidence

Police process
Court process
Correctional process

Misdemeanor process

Arraignment/ initial hearing

Guilty plea/ sentence | Bail

12 Appeal

| 8 Bail/detention reconsidered | 9 Plea negotiations | 10 Trial/ adjudication | 11 Sentencing | 13 Corrections | 14 Release decision | 15 Postrelease |

Guilty plea | Not guilty | Fine/community sentence | Prison | Parole/ mandatory release

| Plea negotiations | Trial | Sentencing | Corrections | Release decision | Postrelease |

Guilty plea | Not guilty | Fine/community sentence | Jail | Parole/ mandatory release

arrest, and bring the offender to trial. An investigation can take but a few minutes, for example, when a patrol officer sees a burglary in progress and apprehends the burglar at the scene of the crime. An investigation may also take years to complete and involve numerous investigators, such as the case of Theodore Kaczinski (aka *The Unabomber*), whom federal agents tracked and captured in 1996 after a 10-year investigation.

3. **Arrest.** An **arrest** occurs when the police take a person into custody for allegedly committing a criminal act. An arrest is legal when all of the following conditions exist: (a) the officer believes there is sufficient ev-

■ After a crime is committed, police officers conduct an investigation to gather sufficient facts, or evidence, to identify the perpetrator, justify an arrest, and bring the offender to trial. Sometimes things do not work out as planned. Here, members of the Tampa Police Department Tactical Response Team check an apartment building in Tampa, Florida, where a bank robbery suspect had barricaded himself after fatally shooting a police officer July 6, 2001. For more than two hours police tried to talk the gunman, Nester Luis DeJesus, into surrendering. Despite on and off talks with a negotiator and with his mother, DeJesus, 25, shot himself.

idence (**probable cause**) that a crime is being or has been committed and that the suspect committed the crime; (b) the officer deprives the individual of freedom; and (c) the suspect believes that he or she is in the custody of a police officer and cannot voluntarily leave. The police officer is not required to use the word "arrest" or any similar word to initiate an arrest; nor does the officer first have to bring the suspect to the police station. For all practical purposes, a person who has been deprived of liberty is under arrest. Arrests can be made at the scene of a crime or after a warrant is issued by a magistrate.

4. **Custody.** After arrest, the suspect remains in police custody. The person may be taken to the police station to be fingerprinted and photographed and to have personal information recorded—a procedure popularly referred to as "booking." Witnesses may be brought in to view the suspect (in a **lineup**), and further evidence may be gathered on the case. Suspects may be interrogated by police officers to get their side of the story, they may be asked to sign a confession of guilt, or they may be asked to identify others involved in the crime. The law allows suspects to have their lawyers present when police conduct in-custody interrogations.

5. **Complaint/charging.** If sufficient evidence is gathered, the police will turn the case over to the prosecutor's office. A decision will then be made whether to file a **complaint,** with the court having jurisdiction over the case. The prosecutor must determine the extent of the charge. For example, in a homicide case, is there enough evidence to convict a person of first degree murder, or should a lesser charge such as manslaughter be filed?

6. **Preliminary hearing; grand jury.** Because it is a tremendous personal and financial burden, the U.S. Constitution mandates that before a person is forced to stand trial for a serious crime the state must first prove there is at least probable cause that the accused committed the criminal act. In about half the states and in the federal system, this decision is made by a **grand jury,** a group of citizens brought together to form a grand jury. The grand jury considers the case in a closed hearing, in which only the prosecutor presents evidence. If the evidence is sufficient, the grand jury will issue a "true bill of indictment," which means that the accused must stand trial; insufficient evidence will result in a "no bill" and freedom for the accused.

In the remaining states, the prosecutor will file a charging document called an **information** before a lower court. A **preliminary hearing** or **probable cause hearing** is then held to determine if there is sufficient evidence to warrant a trial. The defendant may appear at a preliminary hearing and dispute the prosecutor's charges.

7. **Arraignment.** At an **arraignment,** the accused defendant is brought for the first time before the court that

■ In some jurisdictions, arraignments have gone high-tech and defendants do not have to be in court to be arraigned. Here, Tina Page (seated right) is arraigned by videoconference for a misdemeanor in front of Kanawha County Magistrate Jeanie Moore (left screen) without having to leave the South Central Regional Jail in Charleston, West Virginia, November 2, 2001. Assisting Page is Corrections Officer C. D. Fleming (left position on right screen) and First Sgt. R. E. Rogers (center of right screen).

will actually try the case. Here the accused is told of the formal charges being brought against him or her, informed of his or her constitutional rights (such as the right to legal counsel), has bail considered, and has the trial date set.

8. **Bail or detention.** If the bail decision has not been considered previously, it is evaluated at arraignment. **Bail** is a money bond, the amount of which is set by judicial authority; it is intended to ensure the presence of suspects at trial while allowing them their freedom until that time. Suspects who do not show up for trial forfeit their bail. Those suspects who cannot afford bail or are refused bail because they are a danger to society or a flight risk must remain in detention until trial.

9. **Plea bargaining.** After arraignment, it is common for the prosecutor to meet with the defendant and his or her attorney to discuss a possible guilty plea arrangement. If a bargain can be struck, the accused pleads guilty as charged, thus ending the criminal trial process. In return for the plea, the prosecutor may reduce the charges, request a lenient sentence, or grant the defendant some other consideration.

10. **Trial/adjudication.** If a plea bargain cannot be arranged, a **criminal trial** takes place. This involves a full-scale inquiry into the facts of the case before a judge, a jury, or both. The defendant can be found guilty or not guilty, or the jury can fail to reach a decision (**hung jury**), thereby leaving the case unresolved and open for a possible retrial.

Use the term "trial" on InfoTrac College Edition to read a slew of articles on this important stage in the justice process. ■

11. **Disposition.** After a criminal trial, a defendant who is found guilty as charged is sentenced by the presiding judge. **Disposition** usually involves a fine, a term of community supervision (probation), a period of incarceration in a penal institution, or some combination of these penalties. In the most serious capital cases, it is possible to sentence the offender to death. Dispositions are usually made after a presentencing investigation is conducted by the court's probation staff. After disposition, the defendant may appeal the conviction to a higher court.

12. **Postconviction remedies.** After conviction, if the defendant believes he or she was not treated fairly by the justice system, the individual may appeal the conviction. An appellate court reviews trial procedures to determine whether an error was made. It considers such questions as whether evidence was used properly, whether the judge conducted the trial in an approved fashion, whether the jury was representative, and whether the attorneys in the case acted appropriately. If the court rules that the appeal has merit, it can hold

that the defendant be given a new trial or, in some instances, order his or her outright release.

13. **Correctional treatment.** Offenders who are found guilty and are formally sentenced come under the jurisdiction of correctional authorities. They may serve a term of community supervision under control of the county probation department; they may have a term in a community correctional center; or they may be incarcerated in a large penal institution.

14. **Release.** At the end of the correctional sentence, the offender is released into the community. Most incarcerated offenders are granted parole before the expiration of the maximum term and therefore finish their prison sentences in the community under supervision of the parole department. Offenders sentenced to community supervision, if successful, simply finish their terms and resume their lives unsupervised by court authorities.

15. **Postrelease/aftercare.** After termination of correctional treatment, the offender must successfully return to the community. The offender may be asked to spend some time in a community correctional center, which acts as a bridge between a secure treatment facility and absolute freedom. Offenders may find that their conviction has cost them some personal privileges, such as the right to hold certain kinds of jobs. These privileges may be returned by court order once offenders have proven their trustworthiness and willingness to adjust to society's rules. Successful completion of the postrelease period marks the end of the criminal justice process.

Going through the Process

At every stage of the process, a decision is made by an agency of criminal justice whether to send the case further down the line or "kick it" from the system (see Exhibit 15.1). For example, an investigation is pursued for a few days, and if a suspect is not identified, the case is dropped. A prosecutor decides not to charge a person in police custody because he or she believes there is insufficient evidence to sustain a finding of guilt. A grand jury fails to hand down indictments because it finds that the prosecutor presented insufficient evidence. A jury fails to convict the accused because it doubts his or her guilt. A parole board decides to release one inmate but denies another's request for early release.

These decisions transform the identity of the individual passing through the system from an accused to a defendant, convicted criminal, inmate, and ex-con. Conversely, if decision makers take no action, people accused of crime can return to their daily lives with minimal interference in their lives or identities. Their friends and neighbors may not even know that they were once the subject of a criminal investigation. Decision making and dis-

| Exhibit 15.1 | The Interrelationship of the Criminal Justice System and the Criminal Justice Process |

The System: Agencies of Crime Control

The System: Agencies of Crime Control	The Process
1. Police	1. Contact
	2. Investigation
	3. Arrest
	4. Custody
2. Prosecution and defense	5. Complaint/charging
	6. Grand jury/preliminary hearing
	7. Arraignment
	8. Bail/detention
	9. Plea negotiations
3. Court	10. Adjudication
	11. Disposition
	12. Appeal/postconviction remedies
4. Corrections	13. Correction
	14. Release
	15. Postrelease

cretion mark each stage of the system. As Figure 15.3 shows, few people who commit crime are actually caught, and even fewer make it all the way throught the justice process.

The "Wedding Cake" Model

The traditional model of the criminal justice process depicts it as a uniform series of decision points through which cases flow, each characterized by uniform procedures and rights. Yet many experts view this model as fanciful; they argue that the justice system is a political entity that actually works much more subjectively. Some cases receive the full attention of the law, but most are settled with a minimum of legal and procedural due process.

Samuel Walker, a justice historian, suggests that the criminal justice process is best conceived of as a four-layer cake, depicted in Figure 15.4.[15] The relatively small first layer of Walker's model is made up of the celebrated cases involving the famous, wealthy, or powerful, such as O. J. Simpson, Robert Blake, and John Gotti, or the not-so-powerful whose crimes make them media sensations, such as Charles Manson and Oklahoma City bomber Timothy McVeigh. Also included within this category are unknown criminals whose cases become celebrated either because they are brought before the Supreme Court for some procedural irregularity, such as those of Ernesto Miranda and Clarence Gideon, or because they involve media events, such as the case of British nanny Louise Woodward, accused of killing the baby she was hired to care for.

Figure 15.3 The Criminal Justice Funnel

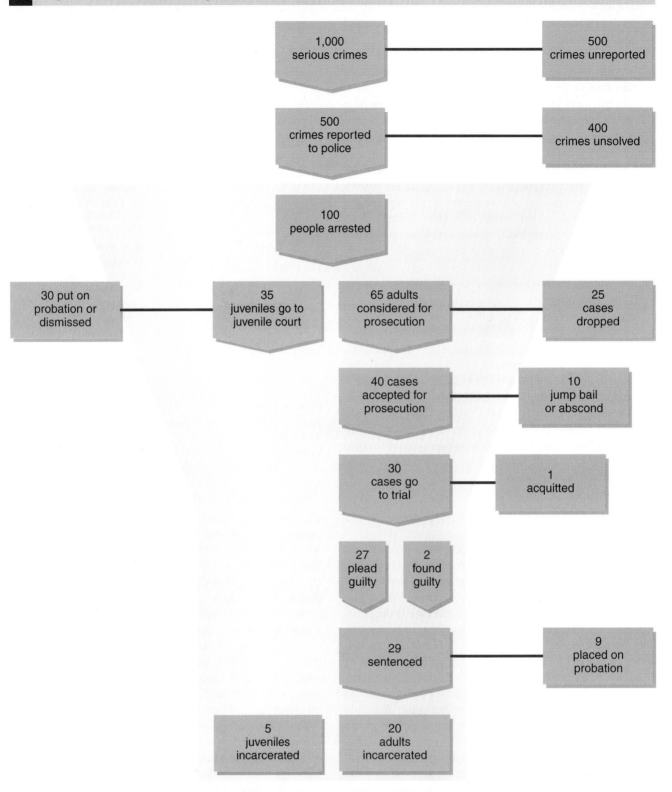

SOURCE: Brian Reaves, *Felony Defendants in Large Urban Counties, 1998* (Washington, D.C.: Bureau of Justice Statistics, 2001).

■ The courtroom work group seeks to hammer out deals and plea bargains in even the most serious and heinous crimes. The courtroom scene shown here is a "tier II" crime in Walker's "Wedding Cake" model. Lawrence Michael Hensley, with his family behind him, awaits sentencing in a Sidney, Ohio, courtroom. To avoid a possible death sentence, Hensley pleaded guilty to aggravated murder, attempted aggravated murder, and kidnapping. He received a life sentence for killing three teenage girls and a Bible studies teacher.

Figure 15.4   The Criminal Justice "Wedding Cake"

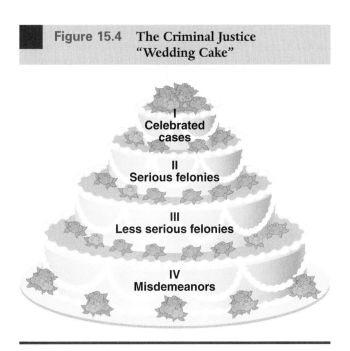

I
Celebrated cases

II
Serious felonies

III
Less serious felonies

IV
Misdemeanors

SOURCE: Based on Samuel Walker, *Sense and Nonsense about Crime* (Pacific Grove, Calif.: Brooks/Cole, 1985).

People in the first layer of the criminal justice wedding cake receive a great deal of public attention, and their cases usually involve the full panoply of criminal justice procedures, including famous defense attorneys, jury trials, and elaborate appeals. Because the public hears so much about these cases, they believe them to be the norm; but they do not represent how the system really operates.

The second and third layers of the cake are made up of those serious felonies encountered daily in urban jurisdictions, such as robberies, burglaries, rapes, and homicides. Those cases that fall in the second layer do so by virtue of their seriousness, the prior record of the defendant, and the defendant's relationship to the victim. For example, police treat a burglary in which thousands of dollars are stolen differently from a simple break-in that netted the criminal a stereo.[16] Similarly, an assault on an affluent merchant is perceived by criminal justice decision makers as more serious than punching a friend during a fraternity beer party. The more serious second-layer crimes are likely to be prosecuted to the fullest extent of the law, and if convicted, these offenders receive lengthy prison sentences. In contrast, felonies relegated to the third layer because the amount of money taken is relatively small or the damage done trivial usually receive an outright dismissal, a plea bargain, a reduction in charges, or a probationary sentence.

The fourth layer of the cake is made up of the millions of misdemeanors, such as disorderly conduct, shoplifting, public drunkenness, passing bad checks, and minor assault. These are handled by the lower criminal courts in assembly-line fashion. Few defendants insist on exercising their constitutional rights because the delay would cost them valuable time and money. Because the typical penalty is a small fine, the experience and expense of going to court may be the real punishment in a misdemeanor case; few (4.9 percent) of the cases involve any jail time.[17]

Is There a Criminal Justice Wedding Cake?

The wedding cake model is an intriguing alternative to the traditional criminal justice flow chart. According to Walker's view, the outcome of cases in the criminal justice system is a function of how they are evaluated by decision makers. Within each layer, there is a high degree of consistency; regardless of the size of the jurisdiction, high-profile cases get serious treatment that differs markedly from the attention and time given to run-of-the-mill felonies.

The Walker model helps us realize that public opinion about criminal justice is often formed on the basis of what happens in a few celebrated cases. In fact, criminal justice experts commonly view the process as being dominated by judges, prosecutors, and defense attorneys who work in concert to get cases processed; this spirit of cooperation is referred to as the **courtroom work group.** The tired assistant district attorney, irritable judge, and overworked public defender who get together to settle cases involving lower-class victims and offenders are now common characters in TV shows, films, and books. In contrast are the celebrated cases that inspire movies and TV miniseries and attract top criminal lawyers.

Can the criminal justice system be reformed and be made more fair to all defendants? Read this article on InfoTrac College Edition for one answer to this question: Stephen Pomper. Reasonable doubts. *Washington Monthly,* June 2000 v32 i6 p21 ■

■ Criminal Justice and the Rule of Law

For many years U.S. courts exercised little control over the operations of criminal justice agencies, believing that their actions were not an area of judicial concern. This policy is referred to as the hands-off doctrine. However, in the 1960s, under the guidance of Chief Justice Earl Warren, the U.S. Supreme Court became more active in the affairs of the justice system. Today each component of the justice system is closely supervised by state and federal courts through the **law of criminal procedure,** which sets out and guarantees citizens certain rights and privileges when they are accused of crime.

Procedural laws control the actions of the agencies of justice and define the rights of criminal defendants. They first come into play when people are suspected of committing crimes and the police wish to investigate them, search their property, interrogate them, and so on. Here the law dictates, for example, whether police can search the homes of or interrogate unwilling suspects. If a formal charge is filed, procedural laws guide pretrial and trial activities; for example, they determine when and if people can obtain state-financed attorneys and when they can be released on bail. If a person is found guilty of committing a criminal offense, procedural laws guide the posttrial and correctional processes; for example, they determine when a conviction can be appealed.

Procedural laws have several different sources. Most important are the first 10 amendments of the U.S. Constitution, ratified in 1791 and generally called the **Bill of Rights.** Included within these amendments to the Constitution are the right of the people to be secure in their homes from unwarranted intrusion by government agents, to be free from self-incrimination, and to be protected against cruel punishments, such as torture.

The guarantees of freedom contained in the Bill of Rights initially applied only to the federal government and did not affect the individual states. In 1868 the Fourteenth Amendment made the first 10 amendments to the U.S. Constitution binding on state governments. However, it has remained the duty of state and federal court systems to interpret constitutional law and develop a body of case law that spells out the exact procedural rights to which a person is entitled. For example, the Sixth Amendment states that a person has the right to be represented by legal counsel at a criminal trial. This right once had little meaning because many criminal defendants were indigent and could not afford to pay for their legal defense. Then, in 1963, the U.S. Supreme Court interpreted the Sixth Amendment to mean that all people accused of felonies had the right to counsel; if they could not afford an attorney, the state had to provide the funds to hire one for them. Thus it is the U.S. Supreme Court that interprets the Constitution and sets out the procedural laws that must be followed by the lower federal and state courts. If the Supreme Court has not ruled on a procedural issue, then the lower courts are free to interpret the Constitution as they see fit.

Some of the most important cases granting criminal suspects civil and procedural rights and their holding are listed in Exhibit 15.2.

■ Concepts of Justice

Many justice system operations are controlled by the rule of law, but they are also influenced by the various philosophies or viewpoints held by its practitioners and policymakers. These, in turn, have been influenced by criminological theory and research. Knowledge about crime, its causes, and its control has significantly affected perceptions of how criminal justice should be managed.

Not surprisingly, many competing views of justice exist simultaneously in our culture. Those in favor of one position or another try to win public opinion to their side, hoping to influence legislative, judicial, or administrative decision making. Over the years, different philosophical viewpoints tend to predominate, only to fall into disfavor as programs based on their principles fail to prove effective. The following sections briefly discuss the most important concepts of criminal justice.

Exhibit 15.2   Critical Cases in Criminal Procedure

Case	Stage and Ruling
Escobedo v. Illinois 378 U.S. 478 (1964)	The defendant has the right to counsel during the course of any police interrogation.
Miranda v. Arizona 384 U.S. 436 (1966)	Procedural safeguards, including the right to counsel, must be followed at custodial interrogation to secure the privilege against self-incrimination.
Massiah v. United States 377 U.S. 201 (1964)	The defendant has the right to counsel during postindictment interrogation.
Powell v. Alabama 287 U.S. 45 (1932)	Defendants have the right to counsel at their trial in a state capital case.
Gideon v. Wainwright 372 U.S. 335 (1963)	An indigent defendant charged in a state court with a noncapital felony has the right to the assistance of free counsel at trial under the due process clause of the Fourteenth Amendment.
Argersinger v. Hamlin 407 U.S. 25 (1972)	A defendant has the right to counsel at trial whenever he or she may be imprisoned, even for one day, for any offense, whether classified as a misdemeanor or a felony.
Faretta v. California 422 U.S. 806 (1975)	The defendant has a constitutional right to defend her- or himself if her or his waiver of the right to counsel is knowing and intelligent.
In re Gault 387 U.S. 1 (1967)	Procedural due process, including the right to counsel, applies to juvenile delinquency adjudication that may lead to a child's commitment to a state institution.
Mempa v. Rhay 389 U.S. 128 (1967)	A convicted offender has the right to assistance of counsel at probation revocation hearings where the sentence has been deferred.
Gagnon v. Scarpelli 411 U.S. 778 (1973) *Morrissey v. Brewer* 408 U.S. 471 (1972)	The defendant has a right to counsel at the court's discretion at probation revocation and parole board revocation hearings.

Crime Control Model

Those espousing the **crime control model** believe crime rates trend upward when criminals do not sufficiently fear apprehension and punishment. If the efficiency of the justice system could be increased and the criminal law could be toughened, crime rates would eventually decline. Crime control advocates attribute recent reductions in the crime rate to a "get tough" attitude toward crime, which has resulted in mandatory punishments and expanding prison populations. Though crime control may be expensive, reducing the pains of criminal activity is well worth the price.

According to this view, the overriding purpose of the justice system is to protect the public, deter criminal behavior, and incapacitate known criminals. Those who embrace its principles view the justice system as a barrier between destructive criminal elements and conventional society. Speedy, efficient justice—unencumbered by legal red tape and followed by punishment designed to fit the crime—is the goal of advocates of the crime control model. Its disciples promote such policies as increasing the size of police forces, maximizing the use of discretion, building more prisons, using the death penalty, and reducing legal controls on the justice system. They lobby for the abolition of procedural rights for criminal defendants and applaud when the Supreme Court hands down rulings that increase police power.[18]

The crime control philosophy emphasizes protecting society and compensating victims. The criminal is responsible for his or her actions, has broken faith with society, and has chosen to violate the law for reasons of anger, greed, revenge, and so forth. Therefore, money spent should be directed not at making criminals more comfortable but on increasing the efficiency of police to apprehend them and the courts to effectively try them. As David Garland suggests, criminal punishment enforces conventional cultural values and expresses the conviction that crime will not be tolerated. Punishment symbolizes the legitimate social order and the power societies have to regulate behavior and punish those who break social rules.[19]

The crime control philosophy has become a dominant force in American justice. Fear of crime in the 1960s and 1970s was coupled with a growing skepticism about the effectiveness of rehabilitation efforts. A number of important reviews claimed that treatment and rehabilitation efforts directed at known criminals just did not work.[20] The lack of clear evidence that criminals can be successfully treated has produced a climate in which conservative, hardline solutions to the crime problem are being sought. The results of this swing can be seen in such phenomena as the increasing use of the death penalty, erosion of the exclusionary rule, prison overcrowding, and attacks on the insanity defense. In the past few years, a number of states have changed their juvenile codes, making it easier to try juveniles as adults. Other states have expanded their control over ex-offenders, such as by requiring registration of sex offenders. New York has passed a death penalty statute, and other states, including Delaware and South Dakota, have expanded the circumstances under which a person could be eligible for the death penalty.[21]

Can such measures deter crime? There is some evidence that strict crime control measures can in fact have a deterrent effect.[22] Crime control advocates point out that the introduction of get tough measures has coincided with a decade-long decline in the crime rate. Surely, they claim, this is not a mere coincidence! For example, research indicates that people arrested for domestic violence violations who receive more severe sentences (such as jail) are less likely to repeat their offenses than those who receive more lenient treatment (such as probation).[23] A 1997 study by the National Center for Policy Analysis uncovered a direct correlation between the probability of imprisonment for a particular crime and a subsequent decline in the rate of that crime.[24] The probability of going to prison for murder increased 17 percent between 1993 and 1997, and the murder rate dropped 23 percent during that period; robbery declined 21 percent as the probability of prison increased 14 percent. These data support the crime control model.

CONNECTIONS

Crime control supporters embrace the rational choice theory discussed in Chapter 5. Harsh punishments are endorsed as a way of making crime less attractive and gratifying; the pains must outweigh the pleasures. Tough state crime control measures can be used to restrain human choice. ∎

Justice Model

People who believe in the **justice model** are most concerned about the presence of unequal treatment in the justice system. It is unfair if two people commit the same crime but receive different sentences because only one is receptive to treatment. The consequence is a sense of injustice in the criminal justice system. Justice model advocates also are concerned with unfairness in the system, such as racism and discrimination, that causes sentencing disparity and unequal treatment before the law.[25] Why is it that some offenders receive probation or a lenient sentence while others who commit essentially the same criminal offense are handed a strict prison sentence? As an alternative to sentencing disparity, the justice model calls for adoption of sentencing policies that require that all offenders who commit the same types of crime receive the same sentence.

Advocates of the justice perspective have had considerable influence in molding the nation's sentencing policy. There have been a number of initiatives designed to

achieve "justice," including adoption of sentencing guidelines that control judicial discretion, mandatory sentences that require all people convicted of the same crime to receive the same prison sentence, and "truth in sentencing laws" that require offenders to serve a substantial portion of their prison sentence behind bars, limiting their eligibility for early release on parole.[26]

Due Process Model

Those who adhere to due process principles believe the civil rights of the accused should be protected at all costs. This requires practices such as strict scrutiny of police search and interrogation procedures, the presence of legal counsel at all stages of the process, review of sentencing policies, and development of prisoners' rights.

Advocates of the **due process model** have demanded that competent defense counsel, jury trials, and other procedural safeguards be offered to every criminal defendant. They have also called for making public the operations of the justice system and placing controls over its discretionary power.

Due process advocates serve as watchdogs over government practices they believe are unconstitutional or threaten a suspect's civil liberties. Their concern seems justified by charges of racial profiling by police and the overrepresentation of the poor and minority group members in the criminal justice system. In some jurisdictions, such as Washington, D.C., almost half of the African American young men are under control of the justice system.[27]

Due process advocates believe everyone deserves fairness before the law no matter how heinous the crime. For example, when President Bush ordered military tribunals to be set up to try suspected al-Qaeda terrorists, the American Civil Liberties Union condemned the use of military justice. On January 16, 2002, they issued a statement that if military courts must be used to try terrorists they should offer the accused certain fundamental due process rights. These include the right of the accused to confront the evidence against him or her, the right to a speedy trial, a prohibition against evidence obtained through torture or coercive interrogation, insurance that the tribunals be impartial and independent of any improper command or political influence, strong limitations on the use of secret evidence, and the opportunity for court review of the tribunal's verdicts.[28]

For a brief review of the due process issues raised by military tribunals, go to InfoTrac College Edition and read this article: Will our sense of justice be a second casualty of war? *U.S. News & World Report,* Nov 26, 2001 p22 ∎

Advocates of the due process orientation are quick to point out that the justice system remains an adversary process that pits the forces of an all-powerful state against those of a solitary individual accused of crime. If an overwhelming concern for justice and fairness did not exist, the defendant who lacked resources could easily be overwhelmed. They point to miscarriages of justice like the case of Jeffrey Blake, who went to prison for a double murder in 1991 and spent seven years behind bars before his conviction was overturned in 1998. The prosecution's star witness conceded that he lied on the stand, forcing Blake to spend a quarter of his life in prison for a crime he did not commit.[29]

AP/Wide World Photos

■ Advocates of the rehabilitation model believe the justice system can develop programs that will help former law violators embrace a more conventional lifestyle and become productive members of the community. Some of these programs operate within prisons and jails. Here, Richard Gallegos, who hasn't had a visitor for more than a year, poses in his jail cell at Utah State Prison in Draper, July 5, 2001. Like 46 percent of Draper's 3,600 inmates, Gallegos sits alone when others fill the visiting room to chat with loved ones. A new program scheduled to begin in August 2001 will match lonely inmates with a "mentor" to chat about life in prison, goals, sports, or anything else on their minds.

Numerous cases of rape and murder have been overturned because DNA evidence later proved that the convicted men could not have committed the crimes; some inmates spent years in prison before their release.[30] There is even evidence that innocent people may have been executed for crimes they did not commit. Between 1976 and 1999, 566 people were executed; during that same period of time, 82 people awaiting execution were exonerated—a ratio of one freed for every seven put to death.[31] Since such mistakes can happen, even the most apparently guilty offender deserves all the protection the justice system can offer.

To read about such critical due process issues as defending judicial independence, controversial judicial opinions, federal judicial selection, state judicial elections, judicial appointments in the states, impeachment and disciplining of judges, judicial reform, and other similar issues, go to the home page of the Brennan Judicial Center at New York University:
   http://brennancenter.org/
For an up-to-date list of Web links, go to
   http://info.wadsworth.com/siegel ■

Rehabilitation Model

The **rehabilitation model** embraces the notion that, given proper care and treatment, criminals can be changed into productive, law-abiding citizens. People commit crimes because they themselves are the victims of social injustice, poverty, and racism. And because of their disturbed and impoverished upbringing, they may be suffering psychological problems and personality disturbances that further enhance their crime-committing capabilities.

Although the general public wants protection from crime, the argument goes, it also favors programs designed to help unfortunate people who commit crime because of emotional or social problems.[32] Even those people who say they want to "get tough" on crime are willing to make exceptions to help younger offenders turn their lives around.[33]

According to the rehabilitation view, to deal effectively with crime, its root causes must be attacked. This requires supporting such programs as public assistance, educational opportunity, and job training. Increasing economic opportunities through job training, family counseling, educational services, and crisis intervention are more effective crime reducers than prisons and jails. As legitimate opportunities increase, violence rates decline.[34]

If individuals run afoul of the law, efforts should be made to treat them, not punish them, by emphasizing counseling and psychological care in community-based treatment programs. This view of the justice system portrays it as a method for dispensing "treatment" to needy "patients." Also known as the "medical model," it portrays offenders as people who, because they have failed to exercise self-control, need the help of the state. The medical model rejects the crime control philosophy on the ground that it ignores the needs of offenders, who are people society has failed to help. Consequently, whenever possible, offenders should be placed on probation, in halfway houses, or in other rehabilitation-oriented programs.

Rehabilitation advocates believe effective treatment can make a significant difference in reducing offender recidivism. Programs that teach interpersonal skills and use individual counseling and behavioral modification techniques have produced positive results both in the community and within correctional institutions.[35] Offender rehabilitation programs that help people develop interpersonal skills, induce a prosocial change in attitudes, and improve cognitive thinking patterns have been shown to significantly reduce recidivism rates.[36]

Nonintervention Model

Noninterventionists believe that, whenever possible, justice agencies should limit their involvement with criminal defendants. Regardless of whether intervention is designed to punish or treat people, the ultimate effect of any involvement is harmful. Once involved with an agency of criminal justice, a person is stigmatized as being dangerous and untrustworthy. They are given labels such as "rapist" or "child abuser" that will stick with them forever. Once labeled, people may find it difficult to ever be accepted back into society, even after they have completed their sentence.

Noninterventionists are fearful of the harmful effects of stigma and negative labels. They want to **decriminalize** (reduction of penalties) and/or legalize nonserious, victimless crimes, such as the possession of small amounts of marijuana, public drunkenness, and vagrancy. They also want nonviolent offenders to be removed from the nation's correctional system, a policy referred to as **deinstitutionalization.** Instead, they ask that first offenders who commit minor crimes be placed in informal, community-based treatment programs, a process referred to as **pretrial diversion.**

Noninterventionists then call for limiting government intrusion into the lives of people who run afoul of the law. They believe the justice system should interact as little as possible with offenders. Police, courts, and correctional agencies should concentrate their efforts on diverting law violators out of the formal justice system, thereby helping them avoid the stigma of formal labels like "delinquent" or "ex-con." Programs instituted under this model include mediation (instead of trial), diversion (instead of formal processing), and community-based corrections (instead of secure corrections).

Nonintervention advocates are also skeptical about the creation of laws that criminalize acts that previously were legal, thus expanding the reach of justice and creating new classes of offenders. For example, it has become popular to expand control over youthful offenders by creating local curfew laws that make it a crime for young people to be out at night after a certain hour, such as 11 P.M. An adolescent who formerly was a night owl is now a criminal![37]

There are many examples of nonintervention ideas in practice. For example, the juvenile justice system has made a major effort to remove youths from adult jails and reduce the use of pretrial detention. Mediation programs have proven to be successful alternatives to the formal trial process.[38] In the adult system, pretrial release programs (alternatives to bail) are now the norm. Probation and community treatment have become the most common forms of criminal sanction.

In the future, the nonintervention philosophy will be aided by the rising cost of justice. Although low-impact, nonintrusive programs may work no better than prison, they are certainly cheaper; program costs may receive greater consideration than program effectiveness.

CONNECTIONS

One key nonintervention initiative is the legalization of drugs. If controlled substances were legalized, the argument goes, crime rates would drop because addicts would not be forced into crime to pay the prohibitive costs of narcotics, nor would gangs use violence to control the drug trade. For more on this view, see Chapter 14. ■

Restorative Justice Perspective

A number of liberal and left-oriented scholars have devised the concept of **restorative justice.** They believe the true purpose of the criminal justice system is to promote a peaceful, just society; they advocate peacemaking, not punishment.[39]

Advocates of restorative justice say that state efforts to punish and control actually encourage crime. The violent punishing acts of the state, they claim, are not dissimilar from the violent acts of individuals.[40] Whereas crime control advocates associate lower crime rates with increased punishment, restorative justice advocates counter that studies show that punitive methods of correction (such as jail) are no more effective than more humanitarian efforts (such as probation with treatment).[41] Therefore, mutual aid rather than coercive punishment is the key to a harmonious society. Without the capacity to restore damaged social relations, society's response to crime has been almost exclusively punitive.

Numerous restorative justice–based programs are now in operation. Police officer–citizen dispute mediation programs are an essential element of community policing.[42] Mediation and conflict resolution programs are now common. Financial and community service restitution programs as an alternative to imprisonment have been in operation for more than two decades.

Although restorative justice programs are becoming increasingly popular, some critics charge that, rather than providing a blueprint for crime control, restorative justice programs rely on untested principles and beliefs that sound humane but may not work effectively in actual practice.[43] So far there is little empirical evidence that restorative programs can reduce crime, prevent victimization, or rebuild communities.[44] However, more thorough evaluation research may eventually verify the effectiveness of the restorative approach to reduce recidivism and reintegrate offenders into the community.[45]

Concepts of Justice Today

The various philosophies of justice compete today for dominance in the criminal justice system (see Figure 15.5). Each has supporters who lobby diligently for their positions. At the time of this writing, it seems that the crime control and justice models have captured the support of legislators and the general public. There is a growing emphasis on protecting the public by increasing criminal sentences and swelling prison populations. Yet advocates of the rehabilitation model claim that the recent imprisonment binge may be a false panacea. For example, in his book *Crime and Punishment in America,* liberal scholar Elliott Currie concedes that the crime rate has declined as the incarceration rate has increased.[46] Nonetheless, he claims that the association may be misleading because the crime rate is undergoing a natural revision from the abnormally high, unprecedented increases brought about by the crack cocaine epidemic in the 1980s. He claims that punitive, incarceration-based models of justice are doomed to fail in the long run. Most offenders eventually return to society, and if the justice system neglects to successfully help inmates achieve a productive lifestyle, a steadily increasing cohort of ex-offenders with limited life chances will be on the street. Their chances of success in the legitimate world have, if anything, been severely diminished by their prison experiences. Punishment may produce short-term reductions in the crime rate, but only rehabilitation and treatment can produce long-term gains.

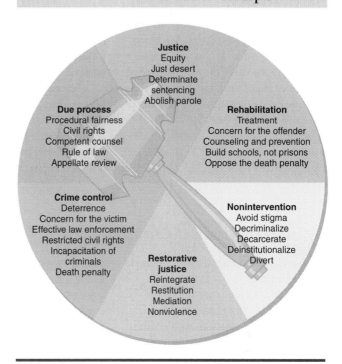

Figure 15.5   Perspectives on Justice: Key Concerns and Concepts

Justice
Equity
Just desert
Determinate sentencing
Abolish parole

Due process
Procedural fairness
Civil rights
Competent counsel
Rule of law
Appellate review

Rehabilitation
Treatment
Concern for the offender
Counseling and prevention
Build schools, not prisons
Oppose the death penalty

Crime control
Deterrence
Concern for the victim
Effective law enforcement
Restricted civil rights
Incapacitation of criminals
Death penalty

Nonintervention
Avoid stigma
Decriminalize
Decarcerate
Deinstitutionalize
Divert

Restorative justice
Reintegrate
Restitution
Mediation
Nonviolence

So despite the demand for punishing serious, chronic offenders, the door to treatment for nonviolent, nonchronic offenders has not been closed. The number of noninterventionist and restorative justice programs featuring restitution and nonpunitive sanctions is growing. As the cost of justice skyrockets and the correctional system becomes increasingly overcrowded, alternatives such as house arrest, electronic monitoring, intensive probation supervision, and other cost-effective programs have come to the forefront.

In sum, there are a number of competing views on the core values of criminal justice. These have influenced everyday policy in the justice system.

Summary

Criminal justice refers to the formal processes and institutions that have been established to apprehend, try, punish, and treat law violators. The major components of the criminal justice system are the police, courts, and correctional agencies. Police maintain public order, deter crime, and apprehend law violators. The courts determine the criminal liability of accused offenders brought before them and dispense sanctions to those found guilty of crime. Corrections agencies provide postjudicatory care to offenders who are sentenced by the courts to confinement or community supervision. Dissatisfaction with traditional forms of corrections has spurred the development of community-based facilities and work-release and work-furlough programs. There are about 55,000 justice-related agencies in the United States. About 20,000 of them are police-related, 25,000 are court-related, and 9,000 are correctional agencies. They employ over 1 million people and cost taxpayers about $75 billion per year.

Justice can also be conceived of as a process through which offenders flow. The justice process begins with initial contact by a police agency and proceeds through investigation and custody, trial stages, and correctional system processing. At any stage of the process, the offender can be excused because a lack of evidence exists, the case is trivial, or a decision maker simply decides to discontinue interest in the case.

Procedures, policies, and practices employed within the criminal justice system are scrutinized by the courts to make sure they do not violate the guidelines in the first 10 amendments to the U.S. Constitution. If a violation occurs, the defendant can appeal the case and seek to overturn the conviction. Among the rights that must be honored are freedom from illegal searches and seizures and treatment with overall fairness and due process.

Several different philosophies or perspectives dominate the justice process. One is the crime control model, which asserts that the goals of justice are protection of the public and incapacitation of known offenders. In contrast, the due process model emphasizes liberal principles, such as legal rights and procedural fairness for the offender. The rehabilitation model views the justice system as a wise and caring parent; the noninterventionist perspective calls for minimal interference in offenders' lives; the justice model calls for fair, equal treatment for all offenders. The restorative justice model attempts nonpunitive, humane solutions to the conflict inherent in crime and victimization.

■ Thinking Like a Criminologist

You have been appointed as the assistant to the president's "Drug Czar," who is in charge of coordinating the nation's drug control policy. She has asked you to develop a plan to reduce drug abuse by 25 percent within three years. You realize that multiple perspectives of justice exist and that the agencies of the criminal justice system can use a number of strategies to reduce drug trafficking and the use of drugs. It might be possible to control the drug trade through a strict crime control effort, for example, by using law enforcement officers to cut off supplies of drugs by destroying crops and arresting members of drug cartels in drug-producing countries. Border patrols and military personnel using sophisticated hardware could also prevent drugs from entering the country. According to the justice model, if drug violations were punished with criminal sentences commensurate with their harm, then the rational drug trafficker might look for a new line of employment. The adoption of mandatory sentences for drug crimes to ensure that all offenders receive similar punishment for their acts might reduce crime. The rehabilitation model suggests that strategies should be aimed at reducing the desire to use drugs and increasing incentives for users to eliminate substance abuse. A noninterventionist strategy calls for the legalization of drugs so distribution could be controlled by the government. Crime rates would be cut because drug users would no longer need the same cash flow to support their habit.

Considering these different approaches, how would you shape drug control strategies?

■ Key Terms

- vigilantes (459)
- Chicago Crime Commission (459)
- Wickersham Commission (460)
- criminal justice (460)
- social control (460)
- racial profiling (462)
- criminal courts (462)
- due process (462)
- fundamental fairness (462)
- plea bargaining (463)
- probation (463)
- jail (463)
- house of correction (463)
- prison (463)
- penitentiary (463)
- parole (463)
- mandatory release (463)
- pardon (463)
- arrest (466)
- probable cause (467)
- lineup (467)
- complaint (467)
- grand jury (467)
- information (467)
- preliminary hearing (467)
- probable cause hearing (467)
- arraignment (467)
- bail (468)
- criminal trial (468)
- hung jury (468)
- disposition (468)
- courtroom work group (472)
- law of criminal procedure (472)
- Bill of Rights (472)
- crime control model (473)
- justice model (474)
- due process model (474)
- rehabilitation model (475)
- decriminalize (476)
- deinstitutionalization (476)
- pretrial diverson (476)
- restorative justice (476)

Critical Thinking Questions

1. What are the layers of the criminal justice "wedding cake"? Give an example of a crime that would fall into each level.

2. What are the basic elements of each model or perspective on justice? Which best represents your own point of view?

3. How would an advocate of each perspective on criminal justice consider the use of the death penalty as a sanction for first-degree murder? Would someone who believes in the "justice model" be for or against capital punishment?

4. Should all forms of discretion be removed from the justice system? Would you want to live in a country where all law violations were punished, or should decision makers be allowed to treat some people more leniently than others?

5. Is the justice system really a "system" or merely a collection of agencies linked together because they deal with the same types of people? Should police agencies coordinate their actions with correctional agencies?

Notes

1. Kevin Mayhood, "Sex-Diary Prosecution: Parents Turned in Son to Get Him Care," *Columbus Dispatch*, 2 August 2001, p.1.

2. This section leans heavily on Samuel Walker, *Popular Justice* (New York: Oxford University Press, 1980).

3. For a detailed analysis of this work, see Samuel Walker, "Origins of the Contemporary Criminal Justice Paradigm: The American Bar Foundation Survey, 1953–1969," *Justice Quarterly* 9 (1992): 47–76.

4. President's Commission on Law Enforcement and the Administration of Justice, *The Challenge of Crime in a Free Society* (Washington, D.C.: U.S. Government Printing Office, 1967).

5. See Public Law 90-351, Title I—Omnibus Crime Control Safe Streets Act of 1968, 90th Congress, June 19, 1968.

6. Sidra Lee Gifford, *Justice Expenditures and Employment, 1999 Data* (Washington, D.C.: Bureau of Justice Statistics, 2002).

7. Office of National Drug Control Policy, "National Drug Control Strategy." Executive Summary, Fiscal Year 2002.

8. Federal Bureau of Investigation, *Crime in the United States, 2000* (Washington, D.C.: U.S. Government Printing Office, 2001), p. 208.

9. Bureau of Justice Statistics, "National Correctional Population Reaches New High—Grows by 126,400 during 2000 to Total 6.5 Million Adults." Press Release, 28 August 2001.

10. See Albert Reiss, *Police and the Public* (New Haven: Yale University Press, 1972).

11. American Bar Association, *Standards Relating to the Urban Police Function* (New York: Institute of Judicial Administration, 1973), Standard 2.2, p. 9.

12. Kenneth L. Davis, *Police Discretion* (St. Paul: West, 1975).

13. See Peter Manning and John Van Maanen, eds., *Policing: A View from the Streets* (Santa Monica, Calif.: Goodyear Publishing, 1978).

14. See Donald Newman, *Conviction: The Determination of Guilt or Innocence without Trial* (Boston: Little, Brown, 1966).

15. Samuel Walker, *Sense and Nonsense about Crime and Drugs*, 3d ed. (Belmont, Calif.: Wadsworth, 1994).

16. Steven Brandl, "The Impact of Case Characteristics on Detectives' Decision Making," *Justice Quarterly* 10 (1993): 395–415.

17. Malcolm Feeley, *The Process Is the Punishment* (New York: Russell Sage Foundation, 1979).

18. *Ohio v. Robinette*, 95-891 (1996).

19. David Garland, *Punishment and Modern Society* (Chicago: University of Chicago Press, 1990).

20. The most often cited of these is Douglas Lipton, Robert Martinson, and Judith Wilks, *The Effectiveness of Correctional Treatment: A Survey of Treatment Evaluation Studies* (New York: Praeger, 1975).

21. "Many State Legislatures Focused on Crime in 1995, Study Finds," *Criminal Justice Newsletter* 27 (January 1996), pp. 1–2.

22. Daniel Nagin, "Criminal Deterrence Research: A Review of the Evidence and a Research Agenda for the Outset of the 21st Century," in *Crime and Justice: An Annual Review*, ed. Michael Tonry (Chicago: University of Chicago Press, 1997), pp. 126–58.

23. Amy Thistlewaite, John Wooldredge, and David Gibbs, "Severity of Dispositions and Domestic Violence Recidivism," *Crime and Delinquency* 44 (1998): 388–98.

24. National Center for Policy Analysis, "Crime and Punishment in America: 1997 Update," author: Dallas, Texas, 1997.

25. Travis Pratt, "Race and Sentencing: A Meta-Analysis of Conflicting Empirical Research Results," *Journal of Criminal Justice* 26 (1998): 513–25.

26. Paula M. Ditton and Doris James Wilson, *Truth in Sentencing in State Prisons* (Washington, D.C.: Bureau of Justice Statistics, 1999).

27. Eric Lotke, "Hobbling a Generation: Young African-American Men in Washington, D.C.'s Criminal Justice System—Five Years Later," *Crime and Delinquency* 44 (1998): 355–66.

28. American Civil Liberties Union, "ACLU Submits Recommendations for Military Tribunals; Urges Adherence to Bush Demand for 'Full and Fair' Trials." Press Release, 16 January 2002.

29. Jim Yardley, "Convicted in Murder Case, Man Cleared 7 Years Later," *New York Times*, 29 October 1998.

30. "DNA Testing Has Exonerated 28 Prison Inmates, Study Finds," *Criminal Justice Newsletter*, 17 June 1996, p. 2.

31. Caitlin Lovinger "Death Row's Living Alumni," *New York Times*, 22 August 1999, p.1.

32. Francis Cullen, John Paul Wright, Shayna Brown, Melissa Moon, Michael Blankenship, and Brandon Applegate, "Public Support for Early Intervention Programs: Implications for a Progressive Policy Agenda," *Crime and Delinquency* 44 (1998): 187–204.

33. Jane Sprott, "Are Members of the Public Tough on Crime? The Dimensions of Public Punitiveness," *Journal of Criminal Justice* 27 (1999): 467–74.

34. Karen Parker and Patricia McCall, "Structural Conditions and Racial

Homicide Patterns: A Look at the Multiple Disadvantages in Urban Areas," *Criminology* 37 (1999): 447–48.

35. Mark Lipsey and David Wilson, "Effective Intervention for Serious Juvenile Offenders: A Synthesis of Research," in *Serious and Violent Juvenile Offenders: Risk Factors and Successful Interventions*, eds. Rolf Loeber and David Farrington (Thousand Oaks, Calif.: Sage, 1998), pp. 39–53.

36. Francis Cullen, John Paul Wright, and Mitchell Chamlin, "Social Support and Social Reform: A Progressive Crime Control Agenda," *Crime and Delinquency* 45 (1999): 188–207.

37. Craig Hemmens and Katherine Bennett, "Juvenile Curfews and the Courts: Judicial Response to a Not-So-New Crime Control Strategy," *Crime and Delinquency* 45 (1999): 99–121.

38. Mark Umbreit and Robert Coates, "Cross-Site Analysis of Victim–Offender Mediation in Four States," *Crime and Delinquency* 39 (1993): 565–85.

39. Herbert Bianchi, *Justice as Sanctuary* (Bloomington: Indiana University Press, 1994); Nils Christie, "Conflicts as Property," *British Journal of Criminology* 17 (1977) 1–15; L. Hulsman, "Critical Criminology and the Concept of Crime," *Contemporary Crises* 10 (1986): 63–80.

40. Larry Tifft, Foreword, to Dennis Sullivan, *The Mask of Love* (Port Washington, N.Y.: Kennikat Press, 1980), p. 6.

41. Robert Davis, Barbara Smith, and Laura Nickles, "The Deterrent Effect of Prosecuting Domestic Violence Misdemeanors," *Crime and Delinquency* 44 (1998): 434–42.

42. Christopher Cooper, "Patrol Police Officer Conflict Resolution Processes," *Journal of Criminal Justice* 25 (1997): 87–101.

43. Sharon Levrant, Francis Cullen, Betsy Fulton, and John Wozniak, "Reconsidering Restorative Justice: The Corruption of Benevolence Revisited," *Crime and Delinquency* 45 (1999): 3–27.

44. Leena Kurki, "Restorative and Community Justice in the United States," in *Crime and Justice: An Annual Review*, vol. 27, eds. Michael Tonry and Norval Morris (Chicago: University of Chicago Press, 2000): 235–304.

45. Ibid.

46. Elliott Currie, *Crime and Punishment in America* (New York: Henry Holt, 1998). See also Elliott Currie, *Confronting Crime: An American Challenge* (New York: Pantheon, 1985); Elliott Currie, *Reckoning, Drugs, the Cities, and the American Future* (New York: Hill and Wang, 1993).

AP/Wide World Photos

CHAPTER 16 Police and Law Enforcement

Introduction

On Christmas Day 2001, a Secret Service agent of Middle Eastern ancestry was en route to protect President Bush who was vacationing in Texas.[1] A mechanical failure caused the cancellation of the officer's original flight, forcing him to board a later one. The officer had already filled out forms required for carrying firearms on board commercial flights, but after the cancellation of his flight, airline employees were unable to find blank forms, so they simply crossed out the flight and seat numbers on the original form. When he was presented with the forms, the pilot on his new flight found that they were unreadable and missing information. Also, while the agent was boarding, the crew saw that he had a Middle Eastern history book tucked into his carry-on luggage, a discovery that made them uncomfortable. Based on this information, the pilot refused to allow him to depart on the aircraft. When the incident was reported to the airline's operation manager, he suggested that the Secret Service office should be called and asked to verify that the passenger was in fact an agent. However, the captain insisted that this was risky because if the passenger was indeed a terrorist he could have a friend answering the phone.

Was the captain being properly cautious about possible terrorism in light of the 9/11 attacks, or was he engaging in a form of racial profiling? Would he have been suspicious if the agent had had blonde hair, blue eyes, and had been named Johanson? Is this incident different from the racial profiling that goes on in big city police departments?

Racial profiling is but one of many critical issues facing big city police departments. These incidents highlight the critical and controversial role police play in the justice system and the need for developing a professional, competent police force.

What are the legal issues surrounding the use of racial profiling in identifying suspects? To find out, use Info-Trac College Edition to access this article: Richard G. Schott. The role of race in law enforcement: racial profiling or legitimate use? *FBI Law Enforcement Bulletin*, Nov 2001 v70 i11 p24(9) ∎

Police are the **gatekeepers** of the criminal justice process. They initiate contact with law violators and decide whether to formally arrest them and start their journey through the criminal justice system, settle the issue informally (such as by issuing a warning), or simply take no action at all. The strategic position of law enforcement officers, their visibility and contact with the public, and their use of weapons and arrest power have kept them in the forefront of public thought for most of the twentieth century.

In the late 1960s and early 1970s, great issue was taken with the political and social roles of the police. Critics viewed police agencies as biased organizations that ha-

rassed minority citizens, controlled political dissidents, and generally seemed out of touch with the changing times. The major issues appeared to be controlling the abuse of police power and making police agencies more responsive to public control. During this period, major efforts were undertaken in the nation's largest cities to curb police power.

Since the mid-1970s, the relationship between police and the public has changed. Police departments have become more sensitive to their public image. Programs have been created to improve relations between police and the community and to help police officers on the beat to be more sensitive to the needs of the public and to cope more effectively with the stress of their jobs.[2] Nonetheless, there are many areas of interaction, such as racial profiling, that have proven to be troubling to the public in general, especially in the minority community. Even when community members believe police officers are competent and dependable, many question their priorities and often consider them disrespectful.[3]

There is continuing concern over police use of force and treatment of citizens. Municipal police agencies have been rocked with charges that some of their officers are corrupt and/or apply the law in an improper fashion. Minority citizens are suspicious of police, and their mistrust may be justified: research shows that minorities are more adversely affected than whites by police misconduct.[4] Compounding the problem is the fact that police behavior is now more visible than ever before because it is commonly captured on video; when police make the local news, these real accounts of the use of force can have an extremely negative impact on public perceptions of police behavior.[5]

This chapter reviews the function and role of police in U.S. society. First the history of police is briefly discussed. Then the role and structure of police agencies is reviewed. Finally, some of the critical issues facing the police in society are analyzed.

History of Police

The origin of U.S. police agencies can be traced back to early English society.[6] Before the Norman conquest, there was no regular English police force. Every man living in the villages scattered throughout the countryside was responsible for aiding his neighbors and protecting the settlement from thieves and marauders. This was known as the **pledge system.** People were grouped into a collective of 10 families, called a tithing, and entrusted with policing their own minor problems. Ten tithings were grouped into a hundred, whose affairs were supervised by a constable appointed by the local nobleman. The **constable,** who might be considered the first real police officer, dealt with more serious breaches of the law.[7] They supervised the **watch system** created to protect cities and towns. Watchmen patrolled at night and helped protect against robberies, fires, and disturbances.

Two other offices were created to provide early law enforcement. The **shire reeve,** forerunner of today's sheriff, was appointed by the crown to supervise a certain territory and assure the local nobleman that order would be kept. In 1326 the office of **justice of the peace** was created to assist the shire reeve in controlling the county. Eventually the justices took on judicial functions in addition to their primary duty as peacekeepers. A system developed in which the local constable became the operational assistant to the justice of the peace, supervising the night watchmen, investigating offenses, serving summonses, executing warrants, and securing prisoners. This working format helped delineate the relationship between police and the judiciary that endured intact for 500 years.

The London Police

At the end of the eighteenth century, the Industrial Revolution lured thousands from the English countryside to work in the larger factory towns. The swelling population of urban poor, whose minuscule wages could hardly sustain them, increased crime rates and heightened the need for police protection.

In 1829 Sir Robert Peel, England's home secretary, guided through Parliament an "Act for Improving the Police In and Near the Metropolis." The act established the first organized police force in London. Composed of more than a thousand men, the London police force was structured along military lines. Its members wore a distinctive uniform and were led by two magistrates, who were later given the title of commissioner. However, the ultimate responsibility for the police fell to the home secretary and consequently to the Parliament.

To learn more about the history of the London Metropolitan Police, go to their Web page at:
http://www.met.police.uk/history/ index.htm
For an up-to-date list of Web links, go to
http://info.wadsworth.com/siegel

The London experiment proved so successful that the metropolitan police soon began helping outlying areas that requested law enforcement assistance. Another act of Parliament allowed justices of the peace to establish local police forces; by 1856 every borough and county in England was required to form its own police force.

Policing the American Colonies

Law enforcement in colonial America paralleled the British model. In the colonies, the county sheriff became the most important law enforcement agent.[8] In addition to peace-keeping and crime fighting, these sheriffs collected taxes, supervised elections, and handled a great deal of other legal business. The colonial sheriff did not patrol or seek out crime; instead, he reacted to citizens' complaints and investigated crimes that had already occurred. His salary was related to his effectiveness. Sheriffs were paid by the fee system: they were given a fixed amount for every arrest made, subpoena served, or court appearance made. Unfortunately, their tax-collecting chores were more lucrative than crime fighting, so law enforcement was not one of their primary concerns.

In the cities, law enforcement was the province of the town marshal, who was aided, often unwillingly, by a variety of constables, night watchmen, police justices, and city council members. However, local governments had little administrative power, and criminal law enforcement was largely an individual or community responsibility. Individual initiative was encouraged by the practice of offering rewards for the capture of felons.[9] If trouble arose, citizens might be called on to form a posse to chase offenders or break up an angry mob.

After the American Revolution, larger cities relied on a variety of elected or appointed officials, such as marshals, sheriffs, or constables, to serve warrants and recover stolen property, sometimes in cooperation with the thieves themselves. Night watchmen, referred to as "leatherheads" because of the leather helmets they wore, patrolled the streets calling the hour; they were equipped with a rattle to summon help and a nightstick to ward off lawbreakers. Watchmen were not widely respected: rowdy young men enjoyed tipping over the watch houses with the leatherhead inside, and a favorite saying in New York was "while the city sleeps, the watchmen do too."[10]

As the size of cities grew, it became exceedingly difficult for local leaders to organize citizens' groups. Moreover, the early nineteenth century was an era of widespread urban unrest and mob violence. Local leaders began to realize that a more structured police function was needed to control demonstrators and to keep the peace.

Early American Police Agencies

The modern police department was born out of urban mob violence, which wracked the nation's cities in the nineteenth century. Boston created the nation's first formal police department in 1838. New York formed its police department in 1844; Philadelphia, in 1854. The new police departments replaced the night watch system and relegated constables and sheriffs to serving court orders and running the jail.

At first the urban police departments inherited the functions of the older institutions they replaced. For example, Boston police were charged with maintaining public health until 1853; New York police were responsible for street sweeping until 1881.

Politics dominated the departments and determined the recruitment of new officers and promotion of supervisors.

An individual with the right connections could be hired despite a lack of qualifications. In New York City during the 1880s, potential police recruits had to be connected to a local politician and pay $300 to be hired as officers; promotion to captain required a payment of $15,000.[11] "In addition to the pervasive brutality and corruption," writes one justice historian, Samuel Walker, "the police did little to effectively prevent crime or provide public services. Officers were primarily tools of local politicians; they were not impartial and professional public servants."[12]

At mid-nineteenth century, the detective bureau was set up as part of the Boston police. Until then, thief taking had been the province of amateur bounty hunters who hired themselves out to victims. When professional police departments replaced bounty hunters, the close working relationships that developed between police detectives and their underworld informants produced many scandals and, consequently, high personnel turnover.

Police during the nineteenth century were generally incompetent, corrupt, and disliked by the people they served. The police role was only minimally directed at law enforcement. Its primary function was serving as the enforcement arm of the reigning political power, protecting private property, and keeping control of the ever-rising numbers of foreign immigrants.

Reform Movements

Police agencies evolved slowly through the latter half of the nineteenth century. Uniforms were introduced in 1853 in New York. Technological innovations, such as linking precincts to central headquarters by telegraph, appeared in the late 1850s; somewhat later, call boxes enabled patrol officers on the beat to communicate with their commanders. Nonpolice functions, such as care of the streets, began to be abandoned after the Civil War.

Despite any steps they may have made toward improvement, big city police were not respected by the public, successful in their role as crime stoppers, or involved in progressive activities. The control of police departments by local politicians impeded effective law enforcement and fostered graft and corruption.

In an effort to prevent police corruption, civic leaders in some jurisdictions created police administrative boards to reduce the control over police exercised by local officials. These tribunals were given the responsibility for appointing police administrators and controlling police affairs. In many instances these measures failed because the private citizens appointed to the review boards lacked expertise in the intricacies of police work.

The Boston police strike of 1914 heightened interest in police reform. The strike was brought about by dissatisfaction with the status of police officers in society. While other professions were unionizing and increasing their standard of living, police salaries lagged behind. The Boston police officers' organization, the Boston Social Club, voted

■ African Americans have served on police forces since the mid-nineteenth century. Thirty years after the Civil War, the streets of Lawrence, Kansas, were patrolled by African American policeman Sam Jeans, shown here. A Republican mayor appointed the first black police officer in Chicago in 1872; by 1884 there were 23 African American officers serving in that city.

to become a union affiliated with the American Federation of Labor. The officers struck on September 9, 1914. Rioting and looting broke out, resulting in Governor Calvin Coolidge's mobilization of the state militia to take over the city. Public support turned against the police, and the strike was broken. Eventually, all the striking officers were fired and replaced by new recruits. The Boston police strike ended police unionism for decades and solidified power in the hands of a reactionary, autocratic police administration.

The Advent of Professionalism

The onset of police professionalism might be traced to the 1920s and the influence of August Vollmer.[13] While serving as police chief of Berkeley, California, Vollmer instituted university training as an important part of his development of young officers. He also helped develop the School of Criminology at the University of California at

1. The intellectual caliber of the police has risen dramatically. American police today at all ranks are smarter, better informed, and more sophisticated than police in the 1960s.
2. Senior police managers are more ambitious for their organizations than they used to be. Chiefs and their deputies want to leave their own distinctive stamp on their organizations. Many recognize that management is an important specialized skill that must be developed.
3. An explicit scientific mindset has taken hold in American policing that involves an appreciation of the importance of evaluation and the timely availability of information.
4. The standards of police conduct have risen. Despite recent well-publicized incidents of brutality and corruption, American police today treat the public more fairly, more equitably, and less venally than police did 30 years ago.

5. Police are remarkably more diverse in terms of race and gender than a generation ago. This amounts to a revolution in American policing, changing both its appearance and, more slowly, its behavior.
6. Police work has become intellectually more demanding, requiring an array of new specialized knowledge about technology, forensic analysis, and crime. This has had profound effects on recruitment, notably civilianization, organizational structure, career patterns, and operational coordination.
7. Civilian review of police discipline has gradually become accepted by police. Although the struggle is not yet over, expansion is inevitable as more senior police executives see that civilian review reassures the public and validates their own favorable opinion of the overall quality of police performance.

SOURCE: David H. Bayley, "Policing in America," *Society* 36 (December 1998): 16–20.

Berkeley, which became the model for justice-related programs around the country.

One important aspect of professionalism was the technological breakthroughs that significantly increased and expanded the scope of police operations. The first innovation came in the area of communications, when telegraph police boxes were installed in 1867; an officer could turn a key in a box and his location and number would automatically register at headquarters. The Detroit police department outfitted some of its patrol officers with bicycles in 1897. By 1913 the motorcycle was employed by departments in the eastern part of the country. The first police car was used in Akron, Ohio, in 1910; the police wagon became popular in Cincinnati in 1912.

In the early 1960s police professionalism was interpreted as being a tough, highly trained, rule-oriented law enforcement department organized along militaristic lines. The urban unrest of the late 1960s changed the course of police department development. Efforts were made to promote understanding between police and the community, reduce police brutality, and recognize the stresses of police work. Efforts have also been made to add members of minority groups and women to police departments. With increasing professionalism, the ideal police officer came to be viewed as a product of the computer age, skilled in using the most advanced techniques to fight crime.[14]

Despite technological and professional achievements, the effectiveness of police is still questioned, and their ability to control crime is still considered problematic. Critics argue that plans to increase police professionalism place too much emphasis on hardware and not enough on police–citizen cooperation. As a result, there has been an ongoing effort to make police "user friendly" by decentralizing police departments and making them responsive to community needs. Some police experts, such as David Bayley, believe the police have made many notable strides over the past three decades, some of the most important of which are listed in Exhibit 16.1.

Law Enforcement Agencies Today

Today, law enforcement duties are distributed across local, county, state, and federal jurisdictions. This section discusses the role of federal, state, county, and local law enforcement/police agencies.

Federal Law Enforcement

The federal government maintains about 50 organizations involved in law enforcement. Some of the most important of these are discussed here.

Federal Bureau of Investigation In 1870 the U.S. Department of Justice became involved in actual policing when the attorney general hired investigators to enforce the Mann Act (which prohibited prostitution across state lines). In 1908 this group of investigators was formally made a distinct branch of the government, the Bureau of Investigation; in the 1930s the agency was reorganized into the Federal Bureau of Investigation under the direction of J. Edgar Hoover.

Today's FBI is not a police agency but an investigative agency, with jurisdiction over all matters in which the United States is, or may be, an interested party. It limits its jurisdiction to federal laws, including all federal statutes not specifically assigned to other agencies. These include statutes dealing with espionage, sabotage, treason, civil rights violations, the murder and assault of federal officers, mail fraud, robbery and burglary of federally insured banks, kidnapping, and interstate transportation of stolen vehicles and property. In the aftermath of the September 11 attacks, the FBI is being reorganized with a new emphasis on counterterrorism. Among the changes being proposed as of June 2002 are the development of a highly trained and specialized counterintelligence workforce with an ongoing system of accountability that integrates counterintelligence with communications, policy, plans, priorities, and management concerns throughout the counterintelligence program. There are plans for the establishment of a counterespionage section within the counterintelligence division which will have responsibility for managing all major espionage investigations. There are also plans to build a national terrorism response capability that is more mobile, agile, and flexible—for example, use of "flying squads" to get to the scene of suspected terrorism as quickly as possible. The agency also plans to recruit agents, analysts, translators, and others with specialized skills and backgrounds in terrorism and to enhance counterterrorism training for FBI agents. The programs and divisions of the FBI are described further in Exhibit 16.2.

Other Federal Agencies

Agents of the **Drug Enforcement Administration (DEA)** investigate illegal drug use and carry out independent surveillance and enforcement activities to control the importation of narcotics.

The **U.S. marshals** are court officers who help implement federal court rulings, transport prisoners, and enforce court orders.

The **Immigration and Naturalization Service** administers immigration laws, deports illegal aliens, and naturalizes aliens lawfully present in the United States. Under a new restructuring plan, Immigration Services and Immigration Enforcement (border patrol) will be separated into two independent bureaus within the INS.

Alcohol, Tobacco, and Firearms (ATF) Bureau has jurisdiction over the sale and distribution of firearms, explosives, alcohol, and tobacco products. The ATF made national headlines with its 1993 tragic confrontation and shootout with the Branch Davidian cult in Waco, Texas.

The **Internal Revenue Service,** established in 1862, enforces violations of income, excise, stamp, and other tax laws. Its intelligence division actively pursues gamblers, narcotics dealers, and other violators who do not report their illegal financial gains as taxable income.

The **Customs Bureau** guards points of entry into the United States and prevents smuggling of contraband into or out of the country.

▮ **Exhibit 16.2** Special Programs and Divisions of the Federal Bureau of Investigation

The Criminal Justice Information Services (CJIS) Division Located in Clarksburg, West Virginia, the CJIS centralizes criminal justice information. It serves as the national repository for fingerprint information and criminal record data and also manages Law Enforcement On-Line (LEO), a law enforcement "intranet" that provides secure communications, distance learning, and information services to the law enforcement community. It operates the National Instant Check System (NICS), mandated by the Brady law to check on the background of people desiring to purchase firearms. It is currently developing the Integrated Automated Fingerprint Identification System (IAFIS).

Crime Laboratory The FBI Crime Laboratory, one of the largest and most comprehensive forensic laboratories in the world, examines evidence free of charge for federal, state, and local law enforcement agencies. Among its activities are these:

- Scientific analysis of physical evidence submitted for examination followed by expert testimony in court
- Operational and technical support to investigations
- Research and development of forensic techniques and procedures
- Development and deployment of new forensic technologies

- Training programs and symposia for U.S. and international crime laboratory practitioners and law enforcement personnel

Child Abduction and Serial Killer Unit (CASKU) Created in 1994, CASKU responds upon request from local law enforcement agencies to kidnappings and serial killer cases.

Combined DNA Index System (CODIS) This is a national database of DNA profiles from convicted offenders, unsolved crime scenes, and missing persons. CODIS enables state and local law enforcement crime labs to exchange and compare DNA profiles electronically.

Critical Incident Response Group (CIRG) This group is ready to assist law enforcement agencies in hostage-taking and barricade situations, terrorist activities, and other critical incidents.

Uniform Crime Report (UCR) This is another service of the FBI. The UCR is an annual compilation of crimes reported to local police agencies, arrests, police killed or wounded in action, and other information.

National Crime Information Center (NCIC) The NCIC is a computerized network linked to local police departments, which provides ready information on stolen vehicles, wanted persons, stolen guns, and other crime related materials.

SOURCE: Federal Bureau of Investigation, *FBI Facts and Figures* (Washington, D.C.; author, 2001).

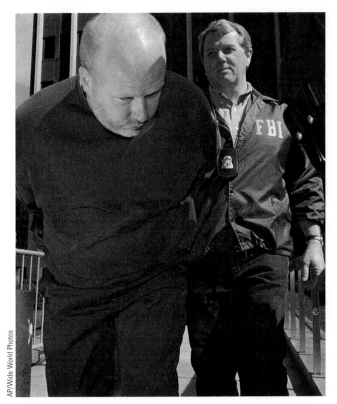

■ The FBI now plays an active role in combating Internet crime. Here, Brian Matthews, a former New York City police officer, holds his head down as he is led in handcuffs to a waiting bus outside the building that houses the FBI's New York headquarters, March 21, 2002. Matthews was among 21 suspects charged in the FBI's ongoing nationwide "Operation Candyman" crackdown on Internet-based child pornography. According to the police department, Matthews was dismissed from the force in 1998 for ordering child pornography through the mail.

The **Secret Service,** an arm of the Treasury Department, was originally charged with enforcing laws against counterfeiting. Today it also protects the president and vice president and their families, presidential candidates, and former presidents.

County Law Enforcement

The county police department is an independent agency whose senior officer, the **sheriff,** is usually elected. The county sheriff's role has evolved from that of the early English shire reeve, whose main duty was to assist royal judges in trying prisoners and enforcing the law outside cities. From the time of U.S. westward expansion until municipal departments were developed, the sheriff often was the sole legal authority in vast territories.

Today, there are nearly 3,100 sheriffs' offices operating nationwide, employing more than 290,000 full-time employees, including about 186,000 sworn personnel.[15] Nearly

all sheriffs' offices provided basic law enforcement services such as routine patrol (97 percent), responding to citizen calls for service (95 percent), and investigating crimes (92 percent). It is also common for the sheriff's department to be keepers of the county jail, court attendants, and executors of criminal and civil processes. Typically, the sheriff's law enforcement functions today are carried out only in unincorporated areas within a county or in response to city departments' requests for aid in such matters as patrol or investigation.

State Police

The Texas Rangers, organized in 1835, are considered the first **state police** force. However, the Rangers were more a quasi-military force that supported the Texas state militia than a law enforcement body. The first true state police forces emerged at the turn of the twentieth century, with Pennsylvania's leading the way.

The impetus for creating state police agencies can be traced both to the low regard of the public for the crime-fighting ability of local police agencies and to the increasingly greater mobility of law violators. Using automobiles, thieves could strike at will and be out of the jurisdiction of local police before an investigation could be mounted. Therefore, a law enforcement agency with statewide jurisdiction was needed. Also, state police gave governors a powerful enforcement arm that was under their personal control and not that of city politicians.

Today there are about 56,000 full-time state police officers and 29,000 other full-time employees in 49 departments (Hawaii has no state police).[16] The major role of state police is controlling traffic on the highway system, tracing stolen automobiles, and aiding in disturbances and crowd control.

In states with large, powerful county sheriff's departments, the state police function is usually restricted to highway patrol. In others, where the county sheriff's law enforcement role is limited, state police usually maintain a more active investigative and enforcement role and aid cities and town police departments in criminal investigation.

Metropolitan Police

Metropolitan police agencies make up the vast majority of the law enforcement community's members. Today, there are an estimated 556,631 full-time law enforcement employees, including about 436,000 sworn personnel.[17] Forty-six departments now employ 1,000 or more officers, and these agencies accounted for about a third of all local police officers; in contrast, nearly 800 departments employ just one officer.

Most larger urban departments are independent agencies operating without specific administrative control from any higher governmental authority. They are organized at

Figure 16.1 Organization of a Metropolitan Police Department

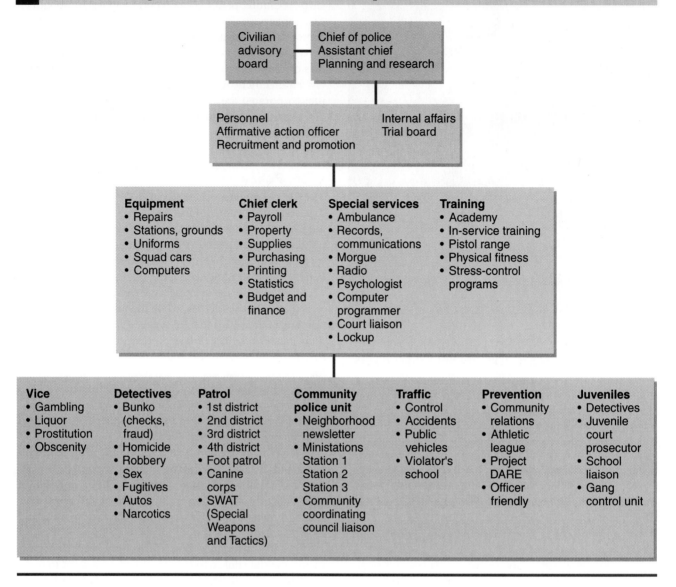

the executive level of government. It is therefore common for the city mayor (or the equivalent) to control the hiring and firing of the police chief and, consequently, determine departmental policies.

The organization of a typical metropolitan police department is illustrated in Figure 16.1. This complex structure is a function of the multiplicity of roles police are entrusted with. Among the daily activities of police agencies are these:

- Identifying criminal suspects
- Investigating crimes
- Apprehending offenders and participating in their trials

- Deterring crime through patrol
- Aiding individuals in danger or in need of assistance; providing emergency services
- Resolving conflict and keeping the peace
- Maintaining a sense of community security
- Keeping vehicular and pedestrian movement efficient
- Promoting civil order
- Operating and administering the police department

The remaining sections focus more fully on the major roles and activities of local police agencies.

■ Police Functions

What do local police actually do? What are their major functions, and how well do they perform them? This section discusses these issues.

Patrol Function

Patrol entails police officers' visible presence on the streets and public places of their jurisdiction. The purpose of patrol is to deter crime, maintain order, enforce laws, and aid in service functions, such as emergency medical care. There are a large variety of patrol techniques. In early police forces, **foot patrol** was almost exclusively used. Each officer had a particular area, or beat, to walk; the police officer was the symbol of state authority in that area. The beat officer dispensed "street justice," and some became infamous for their use of clubs or nightsticks.

When the old-style beat officer needed assistance, he would pound the pavement with his stick to summon his colleagues from nearby areas. Later, call boxes were introduced so the officer could communicate more easily with headquarters. Today, patrol cars, motorcycles, helicopters, and other types of mechanized transportation have all but ended walking the beat. Although the patrol car enables police to supervise more territory with fewer officers, it has removed and isolated patrol officers from the communities they serve. In some communities, **aggressive preventive patrol,** designed to deter crime, has heightened tensions between the police and minorities.

Considerable tension is involved in patrolling, especially in high-crime areas where police feel they are open targets. The patrol officer must learn to work the street, taking whatever action is necessary to control the situation and no more. When patrol officers take inappropriate action or when their behavior results in violence or death, they are subject to intense scrutiny by public agencies and may be subject to disciplinary measures from the police department's internal affairs division. Patrol officers are expected to make mature, reasoned decisions while facing a constant flow of people in emotional crisis.

How effective is patrol? In the aftermath of the Kansas City patrol study (see Chapter 5), experts began to question whether the mere presence of police officers was an effective deterrent to crime.[18] Some criminolgists, citing research showing the effectiveness of aggressively arresting and detaining suspicious persons as a crime deterrent, have called for more proactive police policies.[19]

Why does proactive, aggressive policing seem to work? Aggressive policing may have a direct deterrent effect: it increases community perception that police arrest a lot of criminals and that most violators get caught. Aggressive police arrest more suspects, and their subsequent conviction gets them off the street; fewer criminals pro-

duce lower crime rates. The recent downturn in New York City violent crime has been attributed by some to aggressive police work aimed at lifestyle crimes such as vandalism, panhandling, and graffiti. Is it possible that aggressive policing efforts for one type of crime may help reduce the incidence of other serious crimes?[20]

Traditionally, criminologists believed that the number of law enforcement officers in a jurisdiction had little effect on area crimes.[21] However, more contemporary research shows that jurisdictions that have increased the size of their police forces are now experiencing a drop in crime rates. Cities that have more officers per capita than the norm also experience lower levels of violent crimes.[22] It is possible that larger, more focused and aggressive police forces may now be a more effective deterrent to crime.[23]

CONNECTIONS

Chapter 5 reviewed the deterrent effect of police and noted that more recent research efforts have found that patrol may be a more effective deterrent than previously believed. ■

Before a general policy of vigorous police work can be adopted, more research is needed on proactive policing. Not all evaluations have found that aggressive patrol efforts actually bring the crime rate down.[24] Aggressive patrol seems to work best when it targets particular offenders (such as gang members) or offenses (such as gun possession).[25] Proactive police strategies also breed resentment in minority areas where citizens believe they are the target of police suspicion and reaction.[26] Evidence exists that aggressive police tactics such as random stop-and-frisks and rousting teenagers who congregate on street corners are the seeds from which racial conflict grows.[27] The Policy and Practice in Criminology feature titled "Does Aggressive Policing Work?" further explores this issue.

 To find out more about the effectiveness of patrol, use "police patrol" as a subject guide on InfoTrac College Edition. ■

Investigation Function

The second prominent police role is investigation and crime detection. The detective has been a figure of great romantic appeal since the first independent bureau was established by the London Metropolitan Police in 1841. The detective has been portrayed as the elite of the police force in films and television shows such as *Dirty Harry, NYPD Blue,* and *Lethal Weapon,* to name but a few.

Detective branches are organized on the individual precinct level or out of a central headquarters and perform various functions. Some jurisdictions maintain **morals** or

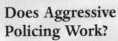

Does Aggressive Policing Work?

During the 1990s, New York City experienced a significant reduction in street crime. Much of the crime reduction has been attributed to the aggressive effort of the NYPD to rid the city of seemingly minor lifestyle offenses such as prostitution, low-level drug dealing, and panhandling. City and law enforcement officials believe dangerous criminals will be deterred if they get tough on these crimes and maintain a "zero tolerance" policy toward any offense. Was this policy truly responsible for the city's crime drop?

When Mayor Rudolph Giuliani took office in 1993, he promised to make New York City a safer place. One of Guiliani's first acts was to hire then–Boston Police Chief William Bratton to run New York City's police department. Bratton brought a fresh approach to policing. He helped to update the technology of the New York City police by creating the crime mapping Compstat program, which put crime data into the hands of precinct commanders. Bratton instituted a policy that held local commanders accountable if crime problems were not taken care of in a timely fashion. He also replaced officers whose performances he deemed inadequate. Finally, Bratton increased the freedom of police officers to stop, search, and question people who had committed even minor legal infractions, a practice that helped turn up concealed weapons and led to the gathering of information about more serious crimes.

The numbers seemed to support the new practices. Between 1993 and 1997, the city saw dramatic reductions in the number of murders, nonnegligent homicides, robberies, and burglaries.

While the numbers appear to support the effectiveness of the NYPD's "zero-tolerance" approach, the city paid a price for its aggressive crime control strategy. Filings of civil rights violations committed by the NYPD climbed 75 percent in four years once the zero-tolerance strategy was begun. By 1996 citizen complaints filed with New York's Civilian Complaint Review Board had risen by 60 percent. Complaints against the police in cases in which no arrests were made doubled within a year of the zero-tolerance approach being implemented; most incidents occurred in minority neighborhoods. Amnesty International claimed that New York had problems with police brutality and the use of unjustifiable force.

The zero-tolerance approach seemed to reduce crime in New York, but other urban areas that employed less aggressive police tactics were able to achieve similar results. For example, San Diego, California's police department took a more community-oriented approach to crime prevention, adopting what they refer to as the Neighborhood Policing Philosophy. In San Diego, law enforcement personnel work in conjunction with community organizations such as Neighborhood Watch programs to prevent and control crime. The SDPD works closely with citizens and businesses to try to create change in areas where chronic crime problems exist. Information sharing is the norm, and teams work with residents to find solutions to long-term problems.

The crime reduction results achieved by San Diego's Neighborhood Policing Philosophy are similar to those attained with New York City's heralded "zero-tolerance" program and the results were achieved at less cost and with fewer negative consequences. New York's 37.4 percent drop in crime from 1990 to 1995 was bolstered by a 39.5 percent increase in personnel; San Diego's 36.8 percent crime rate drop during the same time period was accomplished with a 6.2 percent increase in staff. Perhaps even more important to the community, San Diego's crime rate decrease was accompanied by a decrease in the number of citizen complaints filed against the police.

While New York's aggressive patrol program has been given credit for the declining crime rate, it is possible that the crime drop would have occurred even if the police had chosen a less aggressive stance. The booming economy, declining use of crack cocaine, and other social factors may have been the key reasons for the reduction in the crime rate.

Critical Thinking Questions

1. Would you want to live in a city with extremely aggressive police officers who routinely stop and frisk suspicious-looking people and use their arrest power for every violation of the law, no matter how minor or petty?

2. If police become overly aggressive, are charges of minority harassment and racial profiling inevitable?

InfoTrac College Edition Research

To read more about the dangers of zero-tolerance policing, read this article:

Dorothy E Roberts. Foreword: race, vagueness, and the social meaning of order-maintenance policing. *Journal of Criminal Law and Criminology,* Spring 1999 v89 p 775

SOURCE: Judith Greene, "Zero Tolerance: A Case Study of Police Policies and Practices in New York City," *Crime and Delinquency* 45 (1999): 171–88.

vice squads, which are usually staffed by plainclothes officers or detectives specializing in victimless crimes such as prostitution or gambling. Vice squad officers may set themselves up as customers for illicit activities to make arrests. For example, undercover detectives may frequent public men's rooms and make advances toward men; those who respond are arrested for homosexual soliciting. In other instances, female police officers may pose as prostitutes. These covert police activities have often been criticized as violating the personal rights of citizens, and their appropriateness and fairness have been questioned.

Investigators must often enter a case after it has been reported to police and attempt to accumulate enough evidence to identify the perpetrator.[28] Detectives use various investigatory techniques. Sometimes they obtain fingerprints from a crime scene and match them with those on file. Other cases demand the aid of informers to help identify perpetrators. In some instances, victims or witnesses are asked to identify offenders by viewing their pictures, or **mug shots,** or by pulling them out of lineups. It is also possible for detectives to solve a crime by being familiar with the working methods of particular offenders—their **modus operandi** or **MO.** The detective identifies the criminal by matching the facts of the crime with the criminal's peculiar habits or actions. In some cases, stolen property is located, and then the case is cleared. Either the suspect is arrested on another matter and subsequently found to possess stolen merchandise, or during routine questioning, a person confesses to criminal acts the police did not suspect of him or her.

Finally, detectives can use their own initiative in solving a case. For example, the **sting** operation has received widespread publicity.[29] Here detectives pose as fences with thieves interested in selling stolen merchandise. Transactions are videotaped to provide prosecutors with strong cases. Sting-type undercover operations are controversial because they involve a police officer's becoming involved in illegal activity and encouraging offenders to break the law. Stings may encourage crime when area residents realize that a new group is offering cash for stolen goods.[30] The ethics of these operations have been questioned, especially when the police actively recruit criminals. Nonetheless, sting operations seem to have found a permanent place in the law enforcement repertoire.

 To learn more about modern police detectives and how they go about their their business, use the term "criminal investigation" as a subject guide on InfoTrac College Edition. ■

Are investigations effective? Although detectives in the movies and on television always capture the villains, research indicates that real detectives are much less suc-

cessful. The Rand Corporation, in a classic 1975 study of 153 detective bureaus, found that a great deal of detectives' time was spent in nonproductive work and that investigative expertise did little to help them solve cases.[31] In more than half of the cases cleared, simple, routine actions solved the case; there was little need for scientific, highly trained investigators. The Rand researchers estimated that half of all detectives could be removed without reducing crime clearance rates.

Replications of the Rand study have found that when a suspect was identified it usually occurred before the case was assigned to a detective. Initial identification of suspects usually took place at the crime scene or through routine follow-up procedures.[32] Similarly, the Police Executive Research Forum found that most solved cases involved data gathered at the crime scene by patrol officers; detectives dropped 75 percent of cases after one day and spent an average of four hours on each case.[33]

Efforts have been made to revamp investigation procedures. Patrol officers have been given greater responsibilities in conducting preliminary investigations at crime scenes. In addition, the precinct detective is being replaced by specialized units, such as homicide or burglary squads, that operate over larger areas and can bring specific expertise to bear on a particular case. Another trend has been the development of regional squads of local, state, and federal officers (called regional strike forces) that concentrate on major crimes and organized crime activities and use their wider jurisdiction and expertise to provide services beyond the capabilities of a metropolitan police department. An additional common operation is to focus on the investigation and arrest of hard-core career criminals.[34] Ever more specialized units are being created. For example, Washington, D.C.'s metropolitan police department has a Cold Case Homicide Squad (CCS), which, in cooperation with FBI agents who work directly with the squad, specializes in unsolved crimes at least a year old.[35]

■ Changing the Police Role

Unlike their fictional counterparts, contemporary police officers do not spend their time in car chases and shootouts. James Q. Wilson's pioneering work, *Varieties of Police Behavior,* viewed the major police role as "handling the situation."[36] Wilson found that police encounter many troubling incidents that need some sort of "fixing up." Enforcing the law might be one tool a police officer uses; threat, coercion, sympathy, understanding, and apathy might be others. Most important is "keeping things under control" so that there are no complaints that the police officer is doing nothing or that he or she is doing too much.

The peacekeeping role of the police has been documented by several different studies, which found that the police function essentially as order-keeping, dispute-settling

AP/Wide World Photos

■ Some police departments have created cold case squads that specialize in unsolved crimes at least a year old. Here, James F. Sullivan, escorted by Pennsylvania State Trooper Beverly Ashton, is led to his arraignment for the murder of Linda May Covach. Covach's murder occurred in 1978 and Sullivan was arrested on December 15, 2000.

agents of public health and safety.[37] Figure 16.2 shows the results of a national survey of police behavior. About 44 million Americans have contacts with the police each year, and about half of these involve some form of motor vehicle or traffic-related issue.[38] About 5 million annual contacts involve citizens asking for assistance: for example, responding to a neighbor's complaint about music being too loud during a party, or warning kids not to shoot fireworks. Relatively few incidents involve force. This survey indicates that the police role is both varied and complex.[39]

The burdens of police work have helped set law enforcement officers outside the mainstream of society and have encouraged the development of a police subculture marked by insulation from the outside world and a code of secrecy.[40]

Community-Oriented Policing

In a highly regarded article, "Broken Windows: The Police and Neighborhood Safety," criminologists James Q. Wilson and George Kelling called for a return to a nineteenth-century style of **community-oriented policing (COP)** in which police maintained a presence in the community, walked beats, got to know citizens, and inspired feelings of public safety.[41] Wilson and Kelling asked police administrators to get their officers out of depersonalizing patrol cars. Instead of deploying police on the basis of crime rates or in areas where citizens make the most calls for help, police ad-

ministrators should station their officers where they can do the most to promote public confidence and elicit citizen cooperation. Community preservation, public safety, and order maintenance—not crime fighting—should become the primary focus of police. Implied in the Wilson and Kelling model was a proactive police role. Instead of merely responding to calls for help (known as **reactive policing**), police should play an active role in the community, identify neighborhood problems and needs, and set a course of action for an effective response. Wilson and Kelling conclude,

> Just as physicians now recognize the importance of fostering health rather than simply treating illness, so the police—and the rest of us—ought to recognize the importance of maintaining intact communities without broken windows.[42]

The "broken windows" article had an important impact on policing, and since its publication there has been a continuing reanalysis of the police role.

How does the broken windows concept impact the police use of discretion? What can be done to control police behaviors that violate community standards? Read "'Broken Windows' and Police Discretion" by criminologist George Kelling at this Web site:
 http://www.ncjrs.org/pdffiles1/nij/178259.pdf
For an up-to-date list of Web links, go to
 http://info.wadsworth.com/siegel ▪

Figure 16.2   Police Encounters with Citizens

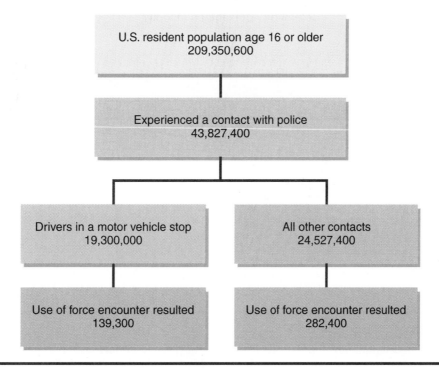

SOURCE: Patrick A. Langan, Lawrence A. Greenfeld, Steven K. Smith, Matthew R. Durose, and David J. Levin, *Contacts between Police and the Public: Findings from the 1999 National Survey* (Washington, D.C.: Bureau of Justice Statistics, 2001).

Implementing COP   The current COP movement began when the old-time foot patrol was reintroduced in a limited number of jurisdictions as an experiment in improving community relations. Foot patrol was believed to be an effective device to help police monitor community concerns and control drug dealers, vandals, and other petty criminals associated with community decline. Officers on foot are more easily approachable and offer a comforting presence to citizens. Although foot patrols had little effect on community crime rates, evaluations of these programs found that they did help to improve citizens' attitudes toward police.[43]

The success of these early experiments encouraged other cities to implement innovative patrol strategies such as Neighborhood Watch and other programs in which police involved local citizens in crime prevention efforts. Some featured decentralized command structures, in which police operate out of neighborhood ministations, and others employed newsletters and other devices that brought the police and the community closer.[44] These early efforts signaled a change in policing that culminated in a concerted effort to actively pursue citizen involvement in police activities, to orient police strategies toward the neighborhood or block level, and to identify community-level problems and seek their solutions.[45]

Is it possible that police could attack community problems in the same way doctors combat diseases? Before you answer, use InfoTrac College Edition to access this article: Joseph Harpold. Medical model for community policing. *FBI Law Enforcement Bulletin,* June 2000 v69 i6 p23 ■

Community policing in action   Today COP programs have been implemented in large cities, suburban areas, and rural communities (see Figure 16.3).[46] Some COP programs assign officers to neighborhoods, organize training programs for community leaders, and feature a bottom-up approach to dealing with community problems: decision making involves the officer on the scene, not a directive from central headquarters. Some departments have created programs for juveniles such as neighborhood cleanup efforts, whereas others contact local businesspeople and community groups to get them involved in planning.[47]

In Spokane, Washington, the community police effort created a program called COPY Kids, a summer outreach program for disadvantaged youth that promotes a positive work ethic, emphasizes the values of community involvement, and helps create a positive image of the police department. Spokane's Neighborhood Investigative Resource

Figure 16.3 **Tempe, Arizona, Police Department Planning Model**

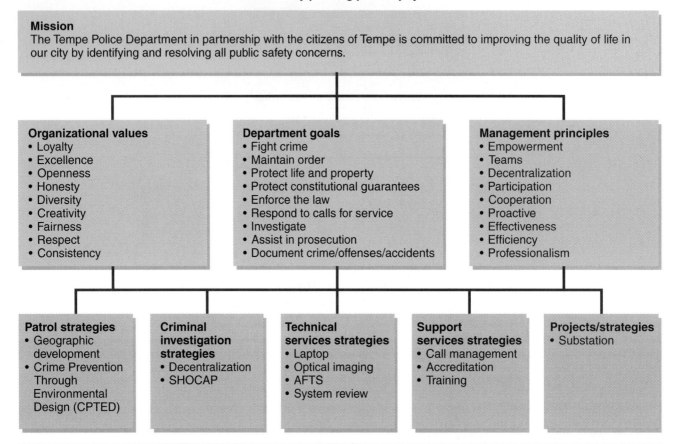

Community policing philosophy

Mission
The Tempe Police Department in partnership with the citizens of Tempe is committed to improving the quality of life in our city by identifying and resolving all public safety concerns.

Organizational values
- Loyalty
- Excellence
- Openness
- Honesty
- Diversity
- Creativity
- Fairness
- Respect
- Consistency

Department goals
- Fight crime
- Maintain order
- Protect life and property
- Protect constitutional guarantees
- Enforce the law
- Respond to calls for service
- Investigate
- Assist in prosecution
- Document crime/offenses/accidents

Management principles
- Empowerment
- Teams
- Decentralization
- Participation
- Cooperation
- Proactive
- Effectiveness
- Efficiency
- Professionalism

Patrol strategies
- Geographic development
- Crime Prevention Through Environmental Design (CPTED)

Criminal investigation strategies
- Decentralization
- SHOCAP

Technical services strategies
- Laptop
- Optical imaging
- AFTS
- System review

Support services strategies
- Call management
- Accreditation
- Training

Projects/strategies
- Substation

SOURCE: Tempe, Arizona, Police Department.

Officer (NIRO) program reassigned detectives to patrol sectors based on efforts to detect and prevent crime.[48]

One group dedicated to providing the latest information, training, advice, and discussion on community policing shares this view: "community policing is a philosophy based on the recognition that nothing can outperform dedicated people working together to make their communities better and safer places in which to live and work and raise children." To find out more, go to:
http://www.policing.com
For an up-to-date list of Web links, go to
http://info.wadsworth.com/siegel ∎

Neighborhood policing Some problems are best solved at the neighborhood level where issues originate, not at a far-off central headquarters. Because each neighborhood has its own particular needs, police decision making must be flexible and adaptive. For example, neighborhoods undergoing change in ethnic composition often experience high levels of racially motivated violence.[49] Po-

lice must be able to distinguish these neighborhoods and allocate resources to meet their needs.

Because COP also stresses sharing power with local groups and individuals, neighborhood initiatives are considered an ideal way to fight crime. Citizens actively participate by providing information in area crime investigations or helping police reach out to troubled area youths. In 1983, police in Houston adopted the Positive Interaction Program (PIP), in which captains in each of the city's nine (decentralized) substations were required to meet monthly with area business leaders and prominent residents to discuss neighborhood problems. Substation captains were then charged with using available resources to resolve the problems. PIP now has 30 groups that meet every month throughout the city to help people learn more about their police department.[50]

Does Community-Oriented Policing Work?

Many police experts and administrators have embraced the community and problem-oriented policing concepts as a revolutionary revision of the basic police role. COP efforts have been credited with helping to reduce crime rates in large cities such as New York and Boston. The most professional and highly motivated officers are the ones most likely to support COP efforts.[51]

Not all criminologists agree that a return to the older model of policing is a panacea. For example, justice historian Samuel Walker has criticized the "broken windows" concept on the grounds that it misinterprets and romanticizes police history: old-style police were neither liked nor respected.[52] Police expert Jack Greene has argued that COP strategies fail to accurately define the concept of community, which he defines as an ecological area with common norms, shared values, and interpersonal bonds.[53] Community policing often ignores community boundaries for administrative convenience.

It may also be difficult to retrain and reorient police from their traditional roles into more of a social service orientation.[54] Most police officers do not have the social service skills required of effective community agents. Some are reluctant to develop new skills—for example, considering it a waste of time when asked to take courses in cultural diversity to make them more sensitive to community needs.[55] Surveys of police officers involved report that they are generally favorable to COP but that they also suffer ridicule from their peers because of the "cushy" assignment that is not "real" police work, that they are often unsure of what to do, and that their program has little effect on the crime rate.[56] If police are in fact mistrustful and cynical, then community police efforts will be difficult to implement. Police administrators, while enjoying the public support created by COP, are reluctant to give up the autonomy and authority that power sharing with the public demands.[57] They may find that the practices demanded by COP conflict with what they consider to be effective, efficient law enforcement.

National surveys find that police administrators still consider law enforcement their top priority; providing community and social services is not considered a significant police role.[58] They find that the core functions and priorities of American policing largely remain unchanged since the advent of community policing. Rather than reflect community needs, most police agencies seek to provide crime control while pursuing professional standards. The addition of community policing officers, the provision of funds for COP training, or adoption of COP programs seem to have little effect on the core values of policing.[59]

Some police supervisors may stress acceptance of community policing activities and, not surprisingly, officers under their command will be much more likely to engage in COP activities than those who follow a more traditional policing model.[60] One national survey of police organizations found that they had actually undergone relatively little structural change since the advent of the COP movement. Police departments have become even more specialized in the new millennium, an organizational de-

velopment in opposition to the COP vision of police as informal problem solvers.[61]

These concerns are valid; but a number of research evaluations indicate that COP programs improve community relations, upgrade the image of local police, and reduce levels of community fear.[62] There is also evidence that local police departments can implement community programs without straining or sacrificing their ability to provide emergency services.[63]

Problem-Oriented Policing

Traditional policing models were reactive, responding to calls for help rather than attempting to prevent crimes before they occurred. According to a recent, aggressive strategy referred to as **problem-oriented policing (POP),** police play an active role in first identifying particular community problems—street-level drug dealers, prostitution rings, gang hangouts—and then developing strategies to counteract them.[64] Problems are typically defined narrowly; for example, reducing larceny from the mall on weekends, not a general reduction in the crime rate. Rather than stifle or control creativity, problem-oriented policing encourages new solutions to old problems, such as involving a variety of community agencies in crime control efforts.

Problem-oriented policing techniques are now being used in a number of police departments around the nation. For example, Operation Ceasefire is a problem-oriented policing intervention aimed at reducing youth homicide and youth firearms violence in Boston. The Ceasefire plan assumes that a relatively small number of gang-involved youth are responsible for most of the shooting incidents in the area and focuses police attention on these persistent offenders. Evaluations of the program have found that the Ceasefire program produced significant reductions in youth homicide victimizations, shots-fired calls for service, and gun assault incidents in Boston, which were not experienced in other communities in New England or elsewhere in the nation.[65]

The evaluation report on Operation Ceasefire can be accessed directly at the NIJ Web site:
http://www.ncjrs.org/pdffiles1/nij/188741.pdf
For an up-to-date list of Web links, go to
http://info.wadsworth.com/siegel

Crackdowns and hotspots POP strategies sometimes involve **crackdowns,** in which particular problem areas in a city are the target of increased police resources.[66] Research shows that a significant portion of all police calls emanate from relatively few locations—bars, malls, the bus depot, hotels, certain apartment buildings—referred to as the **hot spots** of crime.[67] By implication, concentrating police resources on these hot spots can appreciably

■ Some community policing programs assign police officers to outreach programs for disadvantaged youths to promote a positive work ethic, emphasize the values of community involvement, and help create a positive image of the police department. Here, two police officers assigned to a local substation in New Orleans get involved in a basketball league with neighborhood kids.

Steve Liss/TimePix. Copyright Time, Inc.

reduce crime.[68] For example, in 1999 the Richmond, Virginia, police department began a crackdown and cleanup in seven city neighborhoods. Evaluations indicate that a 92 percent reduction in reported crime occurred in the target area during the month-long crackdown period, and crime reductions persisted in some parts of the neighborhood six months after the crackdown ended. The crime reduction was achieved without displacing crime into surrounding neighborhoods.[69]

A recent review by Anthony Braga of existing programs of allocating police resources to hot spots found that such tactics can measurably reduce crime in the target areas without displacing it to nearby areas.[70] In some programs, unintended crime reductions were recorded, a phenomenon referred to as **diffusion of benefits.** The Braga research underscores the fact that proactive, problem-oriented policing may have significant benefits for crime control.

www The Police Foundation is a nonprofit organization dedicated to conducting research on law enforcement, including issues such as the effectiveness of problem-oriented policing. To check out their activities and publications, go to their Web site at:
   http://www.policefoundation.org/
For an up-to-date list of Web links, go to
   http://info.wadsworth.com/siegel ■

COPPS Little question exists that community and problem-oriented policing will continue to find support.

They fit well with efforts to reduce crime among high-risk populations.[71] It is becoming difficult to separate innovative policing models from more traditional ones, and in the future the norm may be a blend that includes elements of problem solving, community actions, and public security.[72] Some experts are already beginning to combine innovative policing strategies into a unified concept and are using the acronym COPPS to stand for a community-oriented policing and problem-solving approach to identify, assess, and address crime-related community issues.[73]

■ Police and the Rule of Law

Like other areas of criminal justice, police behavior is carefully controlled by court action. On one hand, police want a free hand to enforce the law as they see fit. On the other hand, the courts must balance the needs of efficient law enforcement with the constitutional rights of citizens. Some important legal issues have emerged from this conflict, the most critical being citizen rights during police interrogation and the right to be free from illegal searches and seizures by police officers.

Custodial Interrogation

The Fifth Amendment guarantees people the right to be free from self-incrimination. This has been interpreted as meaning that law enforcement agents cannot use physical or psychological coercion while interrogating suspects under their control to get them to confess or give information.

In 1966 the Supreme Court, in the case of *Miranda v. Arizona,* created objective standards for questioning by police after a defendant has been taken into custody.[74] The Court maintained that before the police can question a person who has been arrested or is in custody they must inform the individual of the Fifth Amendment right to be free from self-incrimination. This is accomplished by the police issuing what is known as the **Miranda warning,** which informs the suspect that

- He or she has the right to remain silent.
- If he or she makes a statement, it can be used against him or her in court.
- He or she has the right to consult an attorney and to have the attorney present at the time of the interrogation.
- If he or she cannot afford an attorney, one will be appointed by the state.

If the defendant is not given the Miranda warning before the investigation, the evidence obtained from the interrogation cannot be admitted at trial. The accused can waive his or her Miranda rights at any time. However, for the waiver to be effective, the state must first show that the defendant was aware of all the Miranda rights and must then prove that the waiver was made with the full knowledge of constitutional rights.

Miranda was a turning point in criminal procedure because it introduced attorneys into an early stage of the justice process. Police were concerned that the presence of an attorney would significantly impede the investigation process and hinder their ability to interrogate suspects and/or pressure them to confess. Without confessions, the ability to obtain evidence and convict defendants would be lost.

The Miranda rule today   The Supreme Court has used case law to define the boundaries of the Miranda warning since its inception. Important Supreme Court rulings on the Miranda warning have created a number of exceptions to the rule and guidelines for its implementation; some of the most important exceptions are listed here:

1. If individuals perjure themselves during trial, evidence obtained in violation of the Miranda warning can be used by the government to impeach a defendant's testimony.[75]

2. At trial, the testimony of a witness is permissible even though his or her identity was revealed by the defendant in violation of the Miranda rule.[76]

3. The Miranda warning applies only to the right to have an attorney present; the suspect cannot demand to speak to a priest, probation officer, or any other official.[77]

4. Information provided by a suspect that leads to the seizure of incriminating evidence is permissible if the evidence would have been obtained anyway by other means or sources; this is now referred to as the **inevitable discovery rule.**[78]

5. Admissable evidence can be obtained without a Miranda warning if the information the police seek is needed to protect public safety; for example, in an emergency, suspects can be asked where they hid their weapons.[79] Their answer can be used in a court of law even though they had not received the Miranda warning; this is referred to as the **public safety doctrine.**

6. Initial errors by police in getting statements do not make subsequent statements inadmissible; a subsequent Miranda warning that is properly given can "cure the condition" that made the initial statements inadmissible.[80]

7. Suspects need not be aware of all the possible outcomes of waiving their rights for the Miranda warning to be considered properly given.[81]

8. The admissions of mentally impaired defendants can be admitted in evidence as long as the police acted properly and there is a "preponderance of the evidence" that they understood the meaning of Miranda.[82]

9. An attorney's request to see the defendant does not affect the validity of the defendant's waiver of the right to counsel; police misinformation to an attorney does not affect waiver of Miranda rights.[83]

10. People who are mentally ill due to clinically diagnosed schizophrenia may voluntarily confess and waive their Miranda rights.[84]

11. Once a criminal suspect has invoked his or her Miranda rights, police officials cannot reinitiate interrogation in the absence of counsel even if the accused has consulted with an attorney in the meantime.[85]

12. The erroneous admission of a coerced confession at trial can be ruled a "harmless error" that would not automatically result in overturning a conviction.[86]

13. A suspect who makes an ambiguous reference to an attorney during questioning, such as "Maybe I should talk to an attorney," is not protected under Miranda; the police may continue their questioning.[87]

In the 2000 case *Dickerson v. United States,* the Supreme Court established *Miranda* as an indisputable cornerstone of the justice process.[88] While the future of the warning itself seems certain, recent rulings have narrowed the scope of *Miranda* and given police greater leeway in their actions. It is not surprising that today police administrators who in the past might have been wary of the restrictions forced by *Miranda* now actually favor its use.[89] They view the warning as irrefutable evidence that they did not pressure suspects or use unfair tactics.

Critics, however, warn that this easing of the rule's restrictions may encourage police to pressure suspects to confess. One recent analysis of 60 cases where a confession later proved false showed that police routinely induce confessions from suspects before they ask for a lawyer, a practice that imposes substantial deprivations of liberty on the defendants. At trial, these false confessions are considered important evidence in the minds of jurors and criminal justice officials even if they seem inconsistent with the facts of the case.[90]

Search and Seizure

In order to conduct investigations, the police may want to search people, their cars, and homes. To do so, they must under normal circumstances obtain a **search warrant,** a judicial order, based on probable cause, allowing police officers to search for evidence in a particular place, seize that evidence, and carry it away. If seized with a valid warrant, the evidence can be used against the suspect at trial.

To make it easier for police to conduct investigations and to protect public safety, the Court has ruled that under certain circumstances a valid search may be conducted without a search warrant. The six major exceptions are searches incident to a valid arrest, threshold inquiry (stop-and-frisk), automobile search, consent search, plain-sight search, and seizure of nonphysical evidence.

> **Search incident to an arrest:** A warrantless search is valid if it is made incident to a lawful arrest. The reason for this exception is that the arresting officer must have the power to disarm the accused, protect him- or herself, preserve the evidence of the crime, and prevent the accused's escape from custody. Because the search is lawful, the officer retains what he or she finds if it is connected with a crime. The officer is permitted to search only the defendant's person and the areas in the defendant's immediate physical surroundings that are under his or her control.[91]
>
> **Threshold inquiry (stop-and-frisk):** A threshold inquiry occurs when an officer does not have probable cause to arrest but his or her suspicions are legitimately aroused by the unusual or suspicious behavior of an individual. In such a case, the officer has a right to stop and question the individual; if the officer has reason to believe the person is carrying a concealed weapon, he or she may frisk the suspect. Frisking is limited to a pat-down of the outer clothing for the purpose of finding a concealed weapon. If an illegal weapon is found, then an arrest can be made and a search incident to the arrest performed.[92] If, while conducting a pat down for weapons, an officer discovers other contraband, the officer may seize it and hold it for trial.
>
> **Automobile search:** An automobile may be searched without a warrant if there is probable cause to believe the car was involved in a crime.[93] Because automobiles

are inherently mobile, there is a significant chance that the evidence will be lost if the search is not conducted immediately. Also, people should not expect as much privacy in their cars as in their homes.[94] Police officers who have legitimately stopped an automobile and who have probable cause to believe contraband is concealed somewhere within it may conduct a warrantless search of the vehicle that is as thorough as a magistrate could authorize by warrant. The Supreme Court has also ruled that police who have stopped a motorist for a routine traffic violation can conduct a search if they find probable cause that the vehicle was also involved in a crime; for example, after stopping a car for an illegal U-turn if they spot drug paraphernalia in the front seat.[95]

> Traffic stops can be dangerous, and the Court has ruled that if a police officer perceives danger during a routine traffic stop the officer can order drivers and passengers from the car without suspicion and conduct a limited search of their persons to ensure police officer safety.[96] Taken as a whole, these rulings are designed to ensure the safety of officers.
>
> **Consent search:** People and their property may be searched without a warrant if they willingly consent to the search. However, for the search to be legal, the consent must be given voluntarily; threat or compulsion invalidates the search.[97] Police are under no obligation to inform individuals of their right to refuse the search. For example, police do not have to tell motorists they have stopped for a traffic violation that they are actually free to go before asking permission to search the car.[98]
>
> **Plain sight search:** Contraband can be seized without a warrant if it is in plain view. For example, if a police officer looks through a fence and sees marijuana growing in a suspect's fields, no search warrant is needed for the property to be seized.[99]
>
> **Seizure of nonphysical evidence:** Police can seize nonphysical evidence, such as a conversation, if the suspects had no reason to expect privacy—for example, if police overhear and record a conversation in which two people conspire to kill a third party.[100]

In recent years the Court has given police greater latitude to search for and seize evidence and has eased restrictions on how police operate. The Court's policy has reflected the legal orientation of its more conservative members.

■ Issues in Policing

A number of important issues face police departments today. Although an all-encompassing discussion of each is beyond the scope of this text, a few of the more important aspects of policing are discussed here.

Police Personality and Subculture

It has become commonplace to argue that a majority of U.S. police officers have unique personality traits that place them apart from the average citizen. The typical police personality is thought to include authoritarianism, suspicion, racism, hostility, insecurity, conservatism, and cynicism.[101] These negative values and attitudes are believed to cause police officers to be secretive and isolated from the rest of society, producing what has been described by William Westly as the **blue curtain subculture**.[102] Isolation and conflict may also contribute to the extreme stress that is an occupational hazard of police work.[103] Studies of police officers show that their stress levels increase substantially after urban unrest, when some officers may feel estranged from the community they are forced to control.[104]

There are two opposing viewpoints on the cause of this phenomenon. One position holds that police departments attract recruits who are by nature cynical, authoritarian, secretive, and so on; other experts maintain that socialization and experience on the police force cause these character traits to develop in police officers.[105] Because research evidence supportive of both viewpoints has been produced, neither position dominates on the issue of how the police personality develops; it is not even certain that such a personality actually exists.

The police subculture   More than 40 years ago, police expert William Westly argued that most police officers develop into cynics because of their daily duties.[106] Westly maintained that police officers learn to mistrust the citizens they protect because they are constantly faced with keeping people in line and come to believe that most people are out to break the law or harm a police officer. As a consequence, most officers band together in a police subculture characterized by clannishness, secrecy, and insulation from others in society. Policing expert John Crank has described how the sources of police culture can be traced to the need to be a moral force on their beat, to the fear of the unknown and hidden dangers, and to the overwhelming need for peer support to cope with adversity. The police culture, then, has its roots in morality, solidarity, and the need for common sense or "street smarts."[107]

Both the daily routines of police work and their close peer relations support the subculture. Police officers tend to socialize with each other and believe their occupation cuts them off from relationships with civilians. Joining the police subculture means having to support fellow officers against outsiders; maintaining a tough, macho exterior personality; and mistrusting the motives and behavior of outsiders.[108] Normative behavior might include a tough, almost cold-hearted exterior that makes them immune to the emotional turmoil a civilian might feel when encountering a shooting victim or a body that has been left for a week in a sealed apartment.[109] The police subculture encourages its members to draw a sharp distinction between good and evil. Officers are more than mere enforcers of the law; they are warriors in the "age-old battle between right and wrong."[110] In contrast, criminals are referred to as "terrorists" and "predators"—terms that portray them as evil individuals ready to prey upon the poor and vulnerable. Because the "predators" represent a real danger, police culture demands that its members be both competent and concerned with the safety of their peers and partners. Competence is often translated into respect and authority, and citizens must obey lest they face "payback."[111]

The myths of police work   Because many police–citizen encounters involve more than one officer, some sort of cooperative arrangement is necessary between the officers involved. Shared group norms may take precedence over individual style in handling daily activities.[112] Because of this solidarity, strong myths develop about police work that, after becoming institutionalized, help shape the structure and activities of police departments themselves.[113] Some officers may be frustrated by a criminal justice system that seems to favor the rights of the criminal and "handcuffs" the police; others might be sensitive to a perceived lack of support from government officials and the general public. Officers who perceive strain may be less likely to embrace innovative ideas such as community policing.[114] The most serious consequences of the police subculture are police officers' resistance to change and mistrust of the public they serve. Opening the police to change will be a prime task of police officials who seek professionalism and progress in their departments.

Police Use of Discretion

In one of the most important justice-related papers, Joseph Goldstein argued in 1960 that the law enforcement function of police is not merely a matter of enforcing the rule of law but also involves an enormous amount of personal discretion as to whether to invoke the power of arrest.[115] Since then, police discretion has been recognized as a crucial force in all law enforcement decision making.[116]

Police discretion involves the selective enforcement of the law by duly authorized police agents. However, unlike members of almost every other criminal justice agency, police officers are neither regulated in their daily procedures by administrative scrutiny nor subjected to judicial review (except when their behavior clearly violates an offender's constitutional rights). As a result, the exercise of discretion by police may sometimes deteriorate into discrimination, violence, and other abusive practices.[117] The factors that are believed to influence police discretion are illustrated in Figure 16.4.

Environmental and community factors   Various factors have been associated with the exercise of police discretion.[118] Community crime levels influence police perception and activities. In areas where social problems abound and deviant behavior is the norm, police officers

Figure 16.4   Influences on Police Discretion

Departmental norms, peers, directives, supervisors

Social climate, community attitudes, treatment facilities, alternatives

Departmental

Community/environmental

Demeanor, crime scene, witness, backup

Situational

POLICE DISCRETION

Extralegal

Income, race, gender

Legal

Type of crime, seriousness of crime

Departmental factors   The policies, practices, and customs of the local police department and its administrators also influence discretion. Departments often issue written policies that limit or expand police discretion, spelling out when an arrest should be made and which behaviors can be handled informally.

Organizational behavior may also determine how police deal with different groups in society. Police departments may routinely patrol particular areas of the city while leaving others relatively unattended. Consequently, some residents have a greater chance of experiencing detection and arrest. Although racial profiling in arrest decisions violates constitutional rights, courts have upheld the use of race as a personal identifying factor that helps narrow police searches for suspects. Police manuals also suggest that officers be aware of race when watching for suspicious characters (for example, questioning those who do not "belong" on their beat). Similarly, courts have upheld the government's use of race as a condition of determining probable cause in searches for illegal aliens and in drug courier profiles.[121]

An individual supervisor, such as a sergeant or lieutenant, can influence subordinates' decisions by making known his or her personal preferences and attitudes. Peer pressure also influences decision making. Fellow police officers dictate acceptable responses to street-level problems by displaying or withholding approval in squad room discussions. The officer who takes the job seriously and desires the respect and friendship of others will take their advice, abide by their norms, and seek out the most experienced and most influential patrol officers on the force and follow their behavior models.

Situational influences   Another discretionary influence is the way that a crime or a situation is encountered. If, for example, a police officer stumbles on an altercation or a break-in, the discretionary response may be quite different than if the officer had been summoned by police radio. If official police recognition has been given to an act, action must be taken or an explanation made as to why it was not taken. If a matter is brought to an officer's attention by a citizen observer, the officer can ignore the request and risk a complaint or take discretionary action. When an officer chooses to become involved in a situation without benefit of a summons or complaint, maximum discretion can be used. Even in this circumstance, however, the presence of a crowd or witnesses may contribute to the officer's decision. Police officers may also be influenced by their physical condition, mental state, whether there are other duties to perform, and so on. For example, research by Geoffrey Alpert and his associates finds that when police arrest someone after a car chase they are more likely to use excessive force; the excitement and danger of the pursuit seem to prompt an aggressive response in the subjects they interviewed.[122]

may become cynical and view crime victims as being undeserving of their full attention; the line between criminal and victim becomes blurred.[119] Police are overburdened in these deteriorated neighborhoods and begin to put routine crimes on the back burner. Informal rules among experienced police officers hold that deviant acts in these areas deserve less vigorous reactions than the same acts would generate in a more stable, low-crime area.[120]

Community structure, attitudes, and beliefs also influence the enforcement or nonenforcement of certain laws (for example, obscenity statutes). Conservative communities may demand a higher level of police activity than jurisdictions whose population holds more moderate or tolerant attitudes. The community's ability to fund treatment and rehabilitation programs may influence an officer's judgment because these programs provide alternatives to official police intervention or processing. A police officer may exercise discretion and arrest an individual in a particular circumstance if it seems that nothing else can be done, even if the officer does not believe that an arrest is good police work. In an environment with abundant social agencies—detoxification units, drug control centers, and child care services, for example—a police officer has more alternatives from which to choose. In fact, referring cases to these agencies saves the officer both time and effort—no records need be made out, and court appearances can be avoided. Thus social agencies provide for greater latitude in police decision making.

Legal factors The likelihood of legal action may depend on how officers view the severity of the offense. An altercation between two friends or relatives may be handled quite differently than an assault on a stranger. For example, research shows that at least in some jurisdictions police are likely to treat domestic violence cases more casually than other assault cases.[123] There is evidence that police intentionally delay responding to domestic disputes, hoping that by the time they arrive the incident will be settled.[124] Research by James Fyfe and his associates found that even in cases involving serious felony incidents, police are more than twice as likely to make arrests (13 percent as compared to 28 percent) in incidents where the parties are unrelated than those in which the people were involved in a romantic relationship.[125] However, in some jurisdictions domestic violence is treated similarly to other types of interpersonal conflict, indicating that the use of police discretion may vary between jurisdictions.[126] Other legal factors that might influence police are the use of a weapon, seriousness of injury, and the presence of alcohol or drugs.

Extralegal factors The demeanor, attitude, race, age, and gender of the offender may be considered when police officers decide to invoke their arrest powers. Most early empirical studies found that police discretion works against the young, the poor, and members of minority groups and favors the wealthy, the politically well connected, and members of the majority group.[127] Studies confirm that three-quarters of all complaints filed against the police involve conflicts with nonwhite males under the age of 30. Over one-half of the complainants were divorced or single and unemployed or blue-collar workers.[128] These findings indicate that police encounters are not the same with citizens of different races and economic status.

Suspect demeanor has long been thought to influence police discretion. The prevailing wisdom held that being contrite and remorseful can result in a break; acting defiant is more likely to result in arrest.[129] More recent research has failed to show a clear association between suspect demeanor and arrest outcome. Although suspect attitude may influence police in some encounters, it has little effect in others.[130] One reason may be that experienced officers have learned to ignore verbal taunts and bad attitudes. In his study of police in Dade County, Florida, criminologist David Klinger found that suspect behavior influences discretion only in the event that suspects display "extreme hostility" toward the officer.[131]

The most important extralegal factor in the use of police discretion involves charges that police take race into account when deciding whether to treat a case informally with a warning or arrest a suspect. This issue is discussed in the Race, Culture, Gender, and Criminology feature titled "Racial Profiling: Does Race Influence the Police Use of Discretion?"

Limiting police discretion Numerous efforts have been made to limit police discretion. Police administrators have attempted to establish guidelines for police officers' operating behavior.[132] Most departments have created rules to guide police officers' daily activities. Some departments have established special units to oversee patrol activities; others have created boundaries of police behavior, suggesting that any conduct in excess of these limits, such as racial profiling, will not be tolerated.[133]

Perhaps limiting police discretion can be carried out only by outside review. One approach is to develop civilian review boards that monitor police behavior and tactics and investigate civilian complaints. No two models are alike, but a national study of the 50 largest police departments by Samuel Walker indicates that the review board model is gaining acceptance. About 30 departments have adopted some form of civilian board, most since 1986.[134]

Diversity in Policing

For the past decade, U.S. police departments have made a concerted effort to attract women and minority police officers. The latter group includes African Americans, Asians, Hispanics, Native Americans, and members of other racial minorities. The reasons for recruiting minority and female officers are varied. Viewed in its most positive light, such recruitment reflects police departments' desire to field a more balanced force that truly represents the community it serves. A culturally diverse police force can be instrumental in gaining the public's confidence by helping to dispel the view that police departments are generally bigoted or biased organizations.

Another important reason for recruiting female and minority police officers is the need to comply with various federal guidelines on hiring.[135] Legal actions brought by minority representatives have resulted in local, state, and federal courts ordering police departments to either create hiring quotas to increase minority representation or rewrite entrance exams and requirements to encourage the employment of women and minorities. In one important case, *United States v. Paradise,* the Supreme Court upheld the use of racial quotas to counter the effects of past discrimination. The decision upheld a lower court ruling that ordered the Alabama Department of Public Safety to promote one black trooper for every white candidate elevated in rank as long as qualified black candidates were available, until 25 percent of each rank was filled by minorities; this would represent the actual racial makeup of the labor market.[136] Several such lawsuits have resulted in either court-ordered hiring judgments or voluntary compliance.

While women and minorities are still underrepresented in many police departments, their numbers have been increasing and now amount to about 20 percent of all sworn officers. Minority and female representation is

Racial Profiling: Does Race Influence the Police Use of Discretion?

In the late summer of 1997 New Yorkers were shocked as an astounding police brutality case began to unfold in the daily newspapers. Abner Louima, 33, a Haitian immigrant, had been arrested outside Club Rendezvous, a Brooklyn nightclub, on August 9, 1997, after a fight had broken out. Louima later claimed that the arresting officers had become furious when he protested his arrest, twice stopping the patrol car to beat him with their fists. When they arrived at the station house, two officers, apparently angry because some of the club goers had fought with the police, led Louima to the men's room, removed his trousers and attacked him with the handle of a toilet plunger, first shoving it into his rectum and then into his mouth, breaking teeth while Louima screamed "Why are you doing this to me? Why? Why?" The officers also shouted racial slurs at Louima, who was rushed to a hospital for emergency surgery to repair a puncture in his small intestine and injuries to his bladder. Louima, who witnesses said had no bruises or injuries when officers took him into custody, arrived at the hospital three hours later bleeding profusely.

In the aftermath of the case, NYPD investigators granted departmental immunity to nearly 100 officers to gain information. By cracking the "blue curtain" of silence, a number of police officers were convicted and given long prison sentences on charges of sexual abuse and first-degree assault.

The Louima case and other incidents involving the police and the minority community has re-ignited the long debate over whether police use race as a factor when making decisions such as stopping and questioning a suspect or deciding to make an arrest. There are two opposing views on this point.

Some experts question whether profiling and racial discrimination is as widespread as currently feared. Police expert Ronald Weitzer has conducted research that finds that the frequency and scope of police discrimination may be less than anticipated. In a study of three Washington, D.C. neighborhoods, Weitzer found that African Americans value racially integrated police services and welcome the presence of both white and black police officers, a finding that would seem improbable if most white officers were racially biased. Similarly, Thomas Priest and Deborah Brown Carter have found that the African American community is generally supportive of the local police, especially when officers respond

quickly to calls for service. It is unlikely that African Americans would appreciate rapid responses from racist police. In a research project by sociologists, Matt DeLisi and Robert Regoli found that whites are nine times more likely to suffer DWI arrests than blacks, a finding that would be unlikely if racial profiling was routine.

Profiling Remains a Problem
In contrast to these views, many experts remain concerned about the police use of profiling and discrimination. After thoroughly reviewing the literature on police bias, Samuel Walker, Cassia Spohn, and Miriam DeLone conclude that police discriminate against racial minorities and that significant problems persist between the police and racial and ethnic communities in the United States. Similarly, in *No Equal Justice: Race and Class in the American Criminal Justice System*, constitutional scholar David Cole argues that, despite efforts to create racial neutrality, a race-based double standard operates in virtually every aspect of criminal justice. These disparities allow the privileged to enjoy constitutional protections from police power without extending these protections across the board to minorities and the poor.

Is the Tide Turning?
Efforts to control racial profiling and discrimination are now ongoing in most major police departments, and

highest in the nation's largest police departments, reflecting both the population of their locale and their sensitivity to affirmative action issues. As might be expected, cities with large minority populations have a higher proportion of minority officers in their municipal police departments.[137] Many cities, such as Los Angeles, have had, or now have, African American police chiefs, and a few, most notably Houston, have promoted women to command positions, including chief. However, police expert Samuel Walker notes that only about 20 percent of police departments now have a proportionate number of Hispanic officers and that ethnic and racial minorities are still seriously underrepresented in supervisory positions.

Minority Police Officers

For the past 30 years there has been an ongoing effort to recruit minority police officers in order to field a more diverse force that truly represents the communities they serve. Part of this recruitment effort is to shore up relations between the local police department and the minority community. African Americans generally have less confidence in the police than whites and are skeptical of the ability of police to protect them from harm.[138] African Americans also seem to be more adversely affected than whites when well-publicized incidents of police misconduct occur.[139] It comes as no surprise then that public opinion polls and research surveys show that African American

there is some evidence that these programs and policies are paying off. For example, a recent national study of police contact with civilians found most drivers, regardless of race, who experienced a traffic stop said that they felt the officer had a legitimate reason for making the stop. Nearly 9 out of 10 white drivers and 3 out of 4 black drivers described the officer as having had a legitimate reason for the stop. Both African American and white drivers maintained these perceptions regardless of the race of the officer making the stop. The survey found that a clear majority of members of both racial groups believe the police acted in a forthright fashion, that they were not victims of profiling, and that the race of the police officer had no influence on his or her performance.

According to legal experts Dan Kahan and Tracey Meares, racial discrimination may be on the decline because minorities now possess sufficient political status to protect them from abuses within the justice system. Community policing efforts may also be helping police officers become more sensitive to issues that concern the public, such as profiling.

Although these signs are encouraging, some experts argue that the police should not become so overly concerned about offending suspects that they fail to do their job. Harvard University law professor Randall Kennedy

forcefully argues that it would be wrong to tie the hands of police: African Americans are more likely than whites to become crime victims and, therefore, are the group most likely to benefit from aggressive law enforcement efforts.

Critical Thinking Questions

1. What, if anything, can be done to reduce racial bias on the part of police? Would adding minority officers help? Would it be a form of racism to assign minority officers to minority neighborhoods?
2. Would research showing that police are more likely to make arrests in interracial incidents than intraracial incidents constitute evidence of racism?

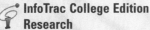
InfoTrac College Edition Research

Use "racial profiling" as a key word to review articles on the use of race as a determining factor in the police use of discretion.

SOURCES: Patrick A. Langan, Lawrence A. Greenfeld, Steven K. Smith, Matthew R. Durose, and David J. Levin, *Contacts between Police and the Public: Findings from the 1999 National Survey* (Washington, D.C.: Bureau of Justice Statistics, 2001); Richard Felson and Jeff Ackerman, "Arrest for Domestic and Other Assaults," *Criminology* 39 (2001): 655–76; Ronald Weitzer "White, Black or Blue Cops? Race and Citizen Assessments of Police Officers," *Journal of Criminal Justice* 28 (2000): 313–24; Sidney L. Harring, "The Diallo Verdict: Another 'Tragic Accident' in New York's War on Street Crime?" *Social Justice* 27

(2000): 9–14; Robert Worden and Robin Shepard, "Demeanor, Crime and Police Behavior: A Reexamination of the Police Services Study Data," *Criminology* 34 (1996): 83–105; Stephen Mastrofski, Robert Worden, and Jeffrey Snipes, "Law Enforcement in a Time of Community Policing," *Criminology* 33 (1995): 539–63; Thomas Priest and Deborah Brown Carter, "Evaluations of Police Performance in an African American Sample," *Journal of Criminal Justice* 27 (1999): 457–65; Matt De Lisi and Bob Regoli, "Race, Conventional Crime, and Criminal Justice: The Declining Importance of Skin Color," *Journal of Criminal Justice* 27 (1999): 549–57; David Cole, *No Equal Justice: Race and Class in the American Criminal Justice System* (New York: New Press, 2000); Randall Kennedy, *Race, Crime and the Law* (New York: Vintage Books, 1998); Dan M. Kahan and Tracey L. Meares, "The Coming Crisis of Criminal Procedure," *Georgetown Law Journal* 86 (1998): 1153–84; David Kocieniewski, "Man Says Officers Tortured Him after Arrest," *New York Times*, 13 August 1997, p. 1; Ronald Weitzer, "Racial Discrimination in the Criminal Justice System: Findings and Problems in the Literature," *Journal of Criminal Justice* 24 (1996): 309–22; Samuel Walker, Cassia Spohn, and Miriam DeLone, *The Color of Justice, Race, Ethnicity and Crime in America* (Belmont, Calif.: Wadsworth, 1996), p. 115; Sandra Lee Browning, Francis Cullen, Liqun Cao, Renee Kopache, and Thomas Stevenson, "Race and Getting Hassled by the Police: A Research Note," *Police Studies* 17 (1994): 1–10.

---

citizens report having little confidence in the police when compared to both Hispanics and whites.[140] African American juveniles seem particularly suspicious of police even when they deny having had a negative encounter with a police officer.[141]

African Americans have served on police forces since the mid-nineteenth century. A Republican mayor appointed the first black police officer in Chicago in 1872; by 1884 there were 23 African American officers serving in that city.[142] Black officers are still underrepresented on the nation's police forces, but legal and social pressure has been mounting to increase their numbers. Some cities have made great strides in minority recruitment.

As African Americans were appointed to police forces, it was assumed that they would face numerous challenges. In a classic work published more than 30 years ago, Nicholas Alex found that black police officers suffered "double marginality."[143] On one hand, African American officers must deal with the expectation that they will give members of their own race a break. On the other hand, they often experience overt racism from police colleagues.

Alex found that black officers' treatment of other blacks ranged from denying that African Americans should be treated differently from whites to treating black offenders more harshly than white offenders to prove lack of bias. Alex offered various reasons why some black police officers are tougher on black offenders: they desire acceptance from their white colleagues; they are particularly sensitive to any disrespect shown them by black teenagers; they view themselves as the protectors of the black community.[144] Considering Alex's findings, it is not surprising that research shows that minority citizens may actually be more likely to accuse a minority officer of misconduct than a white officer.[145]

When affirmative action was first instituted, white police officers viewed it as a threat to their job security.[146] As more minorities join U.S. police forces, their situation appears to be changing, and white officers now are more likely to appreciate the contribution of minority officers. For example, when Charles Katz examined the formation of a police gang unit in a midwestern city, he found that commanders chose minority officers so that the unit could be representative of the community it served.[147] One Hispanic officer told Katz, "when you talk to Hispanics, you have to know and be familiar with their culture . . . you always talk to the man of the house, never presenting your position to the kid or to the mother."[148]

Female Police Officers

The first female police officers were appointed in New York as early as 1845, but they were designated as "matrons," and their duties were restricted to handling females in custody.[149] In 1893 Chicago hired policewomen but again restricted their activities to making court visitations and assisting male detectives with cases involving women and children. In 1910 Alice Stebbins Wells of the Los Angeles Police Department became the first woman to hold the title of police officer and have full arrest powers. It was not until the 1972 passage of the final version of Title VII of the Civil Rights Act that police departments around the nation began to hire females and assign them to regular patrol duties.

How effective are female police officers? In general, evaluations of policewomen show them to be equal or superior to male officers in most areas of police work.[150] Women are more likely to receive support from the community and less likely to be charged with police misconduct.[151] The fewer complaints filed against female officers may be a function of their superior ability to avoid violent encounters with citizens and to deescalate potentially violent arrest situations.[152]

Despite their relative proficiency, female police officers have not received general support from their colleagues. Some male police officers believe female officers are more likely to use deadly force than males because their smaller stature prevents them from using unarmed techniques to subdue suspects. Females do not do as well as males on strength tests and are much more likely to fail the entrance physical than male recruits; critics contend that many of these tests do not reflect the actual tasks police do on the job.[153] Ironically, research shows that female officers are ac-

■ Beverly Harvard is one of the best-known minority females to hold command rank in a U.S. police force. Here, she confers with Atlanta Mayor Bill Campbell outside the Richard B. Russell Federal Building during a press conference July 8, 1999, to announce a program to send convicted felons caught in Atlanta with a firearm to federal court. The program, called FACE 5, is modeled after one in Richmond, Virginia, called Project Exile. Felons caught with firearms could face five years in federal prison with no parole. Looking on is Richard H. Deane Jr., U.S. Attorney for the Northern District of Georgia.

tually less likely to use firearms than male officers and that when male and female officers are partners, it is the male who is more likely to use a firearm.[154]

Studies of policewomen indicate that they are still struggling for acceptance, believe that they do not receive equal credit for their job performance, and report that it is common for them to be sexually harassed by their coworkers.[155] Female police officers may also be targeted for more disciplinary actions by administrators and, if cited, are more likely to receive harsher punishments than male officers (for example, a greater percentage receive punishments greater than a reprimand).[156] Considering the sometimes hostile reception they receive from male colleagues and supervisors, it may not be surprising that female officers report significantly higher levels of job-related stress than male officers.[157]

While improvement is certainly needed, it is likely that as the number of women on police forces increases so too will their job satisfaction and work experiences. Research by Joanne Belknap and Jill Kastens Shelley shows that women who work in departments with a large proportion of female officers report that they are viewed as more professionally competent and also perceive greater acceptance by fellow officers and police administrators.[158]

Is the experience of female police officers in the United States unique? Do women on police forces abroad share the same professional issues? To find out, use InfoTrac College Edition and read these articles: Jennifer M. Brown. Aspects of discriminatory treatment of women police officers serving in forces in England and Wales. *British Journal of Criminology*, Spring 1998 v38 n2 p265(18)

Simon Holdaway and Sharon K. Parker. Policing women police: uniform patrol, promotion and representation in the CID. *British Journal of Criminology*, Wntr 1998 v38 n1 p40(21) ■

Black female police officers Black women, who account for only about 2 percent of police officers, occupy a unique status because of both race and gender issues. A recent study conducted by Susan Martin of black female police serving in five large municipal departments found that they perceive significantly more racial discrimination than either other female officers or black male officers.[159] White female officers were significantly more likely to perceive sexual discrimination than black female officers.

Martin found that black female officers often incur the hostility of both white women and black men, who feel threatened that they will take their place. On patrol, black female officers were treated differently than white female officers by male officers: although neither group of females was viewed as equals, white female officers were protected and coddled, whereas black females were viewed as passive, lazy, and unequal. In the station house, male officers had very little respect for black females, who faced "widespread racial stereotypes as well as outright racial harassment."[160] Black women also report having difficult relationships with black male officers, their relationships strained by tensions and dilemmas "associated with sexuality and competition for desirable assignments and promotions."[161] Surprisingly, there was little unity among the female officers. Martin concludes,

> Despite changes in the past two decades, the idealized image of the representative of the forces of "law and order" and protector who maintains "the thin blue line" between "them" and "us" remains white and male.[162]

■ The Police and Violence

Anthony Baez was playing touch football in the street with his brothers in December 1994 when an errantly thrown ball struck New York City Police Officer Francis Livoti's patrol car. The officer tried to stop the game, and Baez, 29, of Orlando, Florida, died in the ensuing struggle. A police department investigation found that Livoti had used an illegal chokehold to subdue Baez. Although Livoti was acquitted in 1996 of negligent homicide, he was fired from the force and in June 1998 was convicted of violating Baez's civil rights in federal court. On October 1, 1998, the city agreed to pay nearly $3 million to settle lawsuits filed by the family of the man choked to death by a police officer.[163]

The Baez case illustrates the persistent problems police departments have in regulating violent contacts with citizens. Police officers are empowered to use force and violence in pursuit of their daily tasks. Some scholars argue that this is the core of the police role:

> The role of the police is best understood as a mechanism for the distribution of non-negotiable coercive force employed in accordance with the dictates of an intuitive group of situational exigencies.[164]

Police violence first became a major topic for discussion in the 1940s when rioting provoked serious police backlash. Thurgood Marshall, then of the National Association for the Advancement of Colored People, referred to the Detroit police as a "gestapo" after a 1943 race riot left 34 people dead.[165] Twenty-five years later, excessive police force was again an issue when television cameras captured police violence against protesters at the Democratic National Convention in Chicago. However, general day-to-day police brutality against individual citizens seems to be diminishing. In 1967 the President's Commission on Criminal Justice concluded,

> The Commission believes that physical abuse is not as serious a problem as it was in the past. The few statistics which do exist suggest small numbers of cases involving excessive use of force. Although the relatively small number of reported complaints cannot be considered an accurate measurement of the total problem, most persons, including civil rights leaders, believe that verbal abuse and harassment, not excessive use of force, is the major police–community relations problem today.[166]

The diminution of police force was noted in the classic study by Albert Reiss of police–citizen interactions in high-crime areas in Washington, D.C., Chicago, and Boston.[167] Verbal abuse of citizens was quite common, but the excessive use of physical force was relatively rare, occurring in 44 cases out of the 5,360 observations made. There were actually few racial differences in the use of force; when force was used, it was against more selective groups—those who showed disrespect for police authority once they were arrested. Subsequent researchers also found that violent interactions are quite rare; when force is used, it typically involves grabbing and restraining; weapons are rarely used.[168]

How Common Is the Use of Force Today?

How much force is being used by the police today?[169] A recent survey on police contacts with civilians found that in a single year (1999), of an estimated 43 million police–citizen interactions, approximately one percent or 422,000 involved the use or threatened use of force. Of these, an estimated 2 in 10 involved the threat of force only. Respondents reported that police use or threat of force primarily involved the citizen being pushed or grabbed: less than 20 percent of those experiencing force reported an injury.[170] Research does in fact show that the least intrusive types of force, such as handcuffing, are used much more often than the most intrusive, such as lethal violence. The use of weapons is quite rare: for every 1,000 police officers, there are about four incidents in which an officer shoots at a civilian.[171]

Race and force   The routine use of force may be diminishing, but there is still debate over whether police are more likely to get rough with minority suspects. The survey of police contacts found that blacks (2 percent) and Hispanics (2 percent) were more likely than whites (just under 1 percent) to experience police threat or use of force as a consequence of police contact.[172] These differences may not be conclusive evidence that police unfairly use more force against minorities, but minority citizens are much more likely to perceive that police are more likely to "hassle them," stopping them or watching them closely when they have done nothing wrong. They are also more likely to know someone who has been mistreated by police. Perceptions of "hassling" may erode an individual's future relations with police and affect police–community relations as a whole.[173]

Deadly force   A more recent area of concern has been the use of **deadly force** in apprehending fleeing or violent offenders. As commonly used, deadly force refers to the actions of a police officer who shoots and kills a suspect who is either fleeing from arrest, assaulting a victim, or attacking the officer.[174]

The justification for the use of deadly force can be traced to English common law, in which almost every criminal offense merited a felony status and subsequent death penalty. Thus execution effected during the arrest of a felon was considered expedient, saving the state from the burden of trial. It is estimated that somewhere between 250 and 1,000 citizens are now killed by police each year, although these figures are highly speculative.[175] The numbers of shooting incidents have been declining, reflecting efforts to control police use of deadly force.

Research indicates that the following factors are related to police violence:[176]

Exposure to threat and stress: Areas with an unusually high incidence of violent crime are likely to experience shootings by police.

Police workload: Levels of violence are related to the number of police officers on the street, the number of calls for service, the number and nature of police dispatches, and the number of arrests made in a given jurisdiction.

Firearm availability: Cities that have many crimes committed with firearms are also likely to have high police violence rates. For example, Houston, which ranks first in firearm availability, has many more police shootings per 1,000 arrests than San Francisco, which ranks tenth.

Population type and density: Jurisdictions swollen by large numbers and varied types of transients and nonresidents also experience a disproportionate number of police shootings. Research findings suggest that many individuals shot by police are nonresidents caught at or near the scenes of robberies or burglaries of commercial establishments.

Race and class discrimination: It is alleged that blacks and other racial minorities are killed at a significantly higher rate than whites. It is common to focus on race as the primary predictive factor in police violence. The poorest areas with high degrees of income inequality and a large percentage of minority citizens experienced the highest levels of police shootings.[177]

Controlling Force

In 1985 the Supreme Court moved to restrict police use of deadly force when, in *Tennessee v. Garner*, it banned the shooting of unarmed or nondangerous fleeing felons.[178] The Court based its decision on the premise that shooting an unarmed, nondangerous suspect was an illegal seizure of his or her body under the Fourth Amendment. According to the ruling, police could not justifiably use force unless it was necessary to prevent the escape and the officer has probable cause to believe that the suspect poses a significant threat of death or serious physical injury to the officers or others—for example, if the suspect threatens the officer or the officer has probable cause to believe that the suspect has committed a crime involving serious physical harm. Before *Garner*, the policy of shooting unarmed fleeing felons had still been used in 17 states.

There are other methods of controlling police shootings. One is through developing administrative policies that stress limiting the use of deadly force and containing armed offenders until specially trained backup teams are sent to take charge of the situation. Administrative policies have been found to be an effective control on deadly force, but their influence can be undercut or enhanced depending on the personal philosophies and policies of the chief.[179]

Deadly force situations often involve ambiguity and surprise.[180] Officers trained to take advantage of what little information is available to make quick, accurate decisions may be the most likely to avoid a potentially fatal confrontation.

Some departments have created elaborate shooting review procedures in an effort to control deadly force. The New York Police Department also created the Firearm Discharge Review Board to evaluate shooting incidents. In examining the effects of this policy, James Fyfe found that a considerable reduction in the frequency of police shootings followed the policy change.[181]

In addition to state and local policy, the Federal Crime Control Act of 1994 enables the attorney general to obtain a judicial injunction eliminating police practices that encourage excessive force and to obtain damages for injured parties.[182]

Killing police Police use of force continues to be an important issue, but there is little question that control measures seem to be working.[183] Fewer people are being killed by police, and fewer officers are being killed in the line of duty than ever before. According to the FBI, 140 law enforcement officers were feloniously killed in the line of duty in 2001, a significant increase from the prior year, and due to the 71 officers killed in the September 11 attacks. Before this increase, the number of officers slain in the line of duty had been trending downward for the past decade.[184] Excluding the September 11 deaths, about 50 to 70 police officers are killed each year.

Nonlethal weapons In the last few years, about 1,000 local police forces have started using some sort of less-than-lethal weapon designed to subdue suspects. The most widely used nonlethal weapons are wood, rubber, or polyurethane bullets shot out of modified 37-mm pistols or 12-gauge shotguns. At short distances, officers use pepper spray and tasers, which deliver electric shocks with long wire tentacles, producing intense muscle spasms. Other technologies still in development include guns that shoot giant nets, guns that squirt sticky glue, and lights that can temporarily blind a suspect. For example, Cincinnati police officers now use shotguns that fire bean bags filled with lead pellets; the weapons have a range of 100 feet and pack the wallop of a pro boxer's punch.[185]

Recent research efforts indicate that nonlethal weapons may help reduce police use of force.[186] Greater effort must be made to regulate these nonlethal weapons and create effective policies for their use.[187]

■ Summary

Police officers are the gatekeepers of the criminal justice process. They use their power of arrest to initiate the justice process. U.S. police agencies are modeled after their British counterparts. Early in British history, law enforcement was a personal matter. Later constables were appointed to keep peace among groups of one hundred families. This rudimentary beginning was the seed of today's police departments.

In 1838 the first true U.S. police department was born in Boston. The first U.S. police departments were created because of the need to control mob violence, which was common during the nineteenth century. The police were viewed as being dominated by political bosses who controlled their hiring practices and policies. Reform movements, begun during the 1920s, culminated in the concept of professionalism in the 1950s and 1960s. Police professionalism was interpreted to mean tough, rule-oriented police work featuring advanced technology and hardware. However, the view that these measures would quickly reduce crime proved incorrect.

There are several major law enforcement agencies. On the federal level, the FBI is the premier law enforcement organization. Other agencies include the Drug Enforcement Administration, the U.S. marshals, and the Secret Service. County-level law enforcement is provided by sheriff's departments, and most states maintain state police agencies. However, most law enforcement activities are carried out by local police agencies.

The police role is multilevel. Police officers fight crime, keep the peace, and provide community services. The conflicts and burdens involved in their work insulate them from the community and create great stress that has been linked to burnout.

Some criminologists question whether police patrol is actually effective. One important study conducted in Kansas City found that the extent of patrol had little effect on the crime rate or citizens' satisfaction.

The second prominent police role is investigation. Detectives collect evidence to identify perpetrators. Although detectives use various techniques, including sting operations, studies have shown that detective work is generally ineffective. Other police functions include traffic control, departmental administration and maintenance, and improvement of relations between police and community. In recent years many police operations have been constrained by court decisions. Most important, the courts have set limits on the extent of police interrogations and search and seizure of evidence.

Police departments face crucial issues today. One involves understanding the police personality and its effect on performance. Another involves police officers' use of discretion and how it can be controlled. Women and minority officers probably will become more prevalent in police departments, and their worth must be more fully appreciated by rank-and-file patrol officers. Police violence has received much attention. There is some debate over whether police officers kill members of minority groups more frequently than white citizens.

■ Thinking Like a Criminologist

You are a consultant to the local police department. The chief has recently read Malcolm Sparrow, Mark Moore, and David Kennedy's book *Beyond 911: A New Era for Policing*, in which they define the core values of the typical police officer as follows:

1. Police officers are the only real crime fighters. The public wants the police officer to fight crime; other agencies, both public and private, only play at fighting crime.

2. No one else understands the real nature of police work. Lawyers, academics, politicians, and the public in general have little concept of what it means to be a police officer.

3. Loyalty to colleagues counts above everything else. Police officers have to stick together because everyone is out to get the police and make the job more difficult.

4. It is impossible to win the war against crime without bending the rules. Courts have awarded criminal defendants too many civil rights.

5. Members of the public are basically unsupportive and unreasonably demanding. People are quick to criticize police unless they need an officer themselves.

6. Patrol work is the pits. Detective work is glamorous and exciting.

The chief is planning a major policy initiative that will emphasize community policing. He wants to know if these values will help his initiative or make it more difficult to implement. He wants your opinion on the issue. What would you do to change police values if they conflict with community policing?

■ Key Terms

- gatekeepers (482)
- pledge system (482)
- constable (482)
- watch system (482)
- shire reeve (483)
- justice of the peace (483)
- Drug Enforcement Administration (DEA) (486)
- U.S. marshal (486)
- Immigration and Naturalization Service (486)
- Alcohol, Tobacco, and Firearms (ATF) Bureau (486)
- Internal Revenue Service (486)
- Customs Bureau (486)
- Secret Service (487)
- sheriff (487)
- state police (487)
- foot patrol (489)
- aggressive preventive patrol (489)
- morals squad (489)
- vice squad (491)
- mug shots (491)
- modus operandi (MO) (491)
- sting (491)
- community-oriented policing (COP) (492)
- reactive policing (492)
- problem-oriented policing (POP) (495)
- crackdowns (495)
- hot spots (495)
- diffusion of benefits (496)
- Miranda warning (497)
- inevitable discovery rule (497)
- public safety doctrine (497)
- search warrant (498)
- blue curtain subculture (499)
- deadly force (506)

■ Critical Thinking Questions

1. List the problems faced by police departments today that were also present during the early days of policing.

2. Distinguish between the duties of the state police, sheriff's department, and local police department.

3. Discuss the trends that will influence policing during the coming decade. What social factors may affect police?

4. Do the advantages of proactive policing outweigh the disadvantages?

5. Should male and female officers have exactly the same duties in a police department?

6. A police officer orders an unarmed person running away from a burglary to stop; the suspect keeps running and is shot and killed by the officer. Has the officer committed murder?

7. Would you like to live in a society that abolished police discretion and used a full enforcement policy?

Notes

1. "The Secret Service Officer: Pilot Says Officer's Actions Led to Refusal of Passage," *New York Times*, 4 January 2002, p. 3.

2. Bernie Patterson, "Job Experience and Perceived Job Stress among Police, Correctional, and Probation/Parole Officers," *Criminal Justice and Behavior* 19 (1992): 260–85.

3. Sara Stoutland, "The Multiple Dimensions of Trust in Resident/Police Relations in Boston," *Journal of Research in Crime and Delinquency* 38 (2001): 226–56.

4. Steven Tuch and Ronald Weitzer, "The Polls—Trends, Racial Differences in Attitudes Toward the Police," *Public Opinion Quarterly* 61 (1997): 642–63.

5. Eric Jefferis, Robert Kaminski, Stephen Holmes, and Dena Hanley, "The Effect of a Videotaped Arrest on Public Perceptions of Police Use of Force," *Journal of Criminal Justice* 25 (1997): 381–95.

6. This section relies heavily on Daniel Devlin, *Police Procedure, Administration and Organization* (London: Butterworth, 1966); Robert Fogelson, *Big City Police* (Cambridge: Harvard University Press, 1977); Roger Lane, *Policing the City: Boston 1822–1885* (Cambridge: Harvard University Press, 1967); Roger Lane, "Urban Police and Crime in Nineteenth Century America," in *Crime and Justice*, vol. 2, eds. N. Morris and M. Tonry (Chicago: University of Chicago Press, 1980), pp. 1–45; J. J. Tobias, *Crime and Industrial Society in the Nineteenth Century* (New York: Schocken Books, 1967); Samuel Walker, *A Critical History of Police Reform: The Emergence of Professionalism* (Lexington, Mass.: Lexington Books, 1977); Samuel Walker, *Popular Justice* (New York: Oxford University Press, 1980); President's Commission on Law Enforcement and the Administration of Justice, *Task Force Report: The Police* (Washington, D.C.: U.S. Government Printing Office, 1967), pp. 1–9.

7. Devlin, *Police Procedure, Administration and Organization*, p. 3.

8. Walker, *Popular Justice*, p. 18.

9. Lane, "Urban Police and Crime in Nineteenth Century America," p. 5.

10. Wilbur Miller, "The Good, the Bad and the Ugly: Policing America," *History Today* 50 (2000): 29–32.

11. Michael Vaughn, "Political Patronage in Law Enforcement: Civil Liability against Police Supervisors for Violating Their Subordinates' First Amendment Rights," *Journal of Criminal Justice* 25 (1997): 347–66.

12. Walker, *Popular Justice*, p. 61.

13. See, generally, Walker, *A Critical History of Police Reform*.

14. This section was adapted from Law Enforcement Assistance Administration, *Two Hundred Years of American Criminal Justice* (Washington, D.C.: U.S. Government Printing Office, 1976).

15. Brian Reaves and Matthew Hickman, *Sheriffs' Office 1999* (Washington, D.C.: Bureau of Justice Statistics, 2001).

16. Matthew J. Hickman and Brian Reaves, *Local Police Departments 1999* (Washington, D.C.: Bureau of Justice Statistics, 2001), p. 1.

17. Ibid.

18. George Kelling, Tony Pate, Duane Dieckman, and Charles Brown, *The Kansas City Preventive Patrol Experiment: A Summary Report* (Washington, D.C.: Police Foundation, 1974).

19. James Q. Wilson and Barbara Boland, "The Effect of Police on Crime," *Law and Society Review* 12 (1978): 367–84; Robert Sampson and Jacqueline Cohen, "Deterrent Effects of the Police on Crime: A Replication and Theoretical Extension," *Law and Society Review* 22 (1988): 163–91.

20. For a thorough review of this issue, see Andrew Karmen, *Why Is New York City's Murder Rate Dropping So Sharply?* (New York: John Jay College, 1996).

21. Colin Loftin and David McDowall, "The Police, Crime, and Economic Theory: An Assessment," *American Sociological Review* 47 (1982): 393–401.

22. David Jacobs and Katherine Woods, "Interracial Conflict and Interracial Homicide: Do Political and Economic Rivalries Explain White Killings of Blacks or Black Killings of Whites?" *American Journal of Sociology* 105 (1999): 157–90.

23. Tomislav V. Kovandzic and John J. Sloan, "Police Levels and Crime Rates Revisited, A County-Level Analysis from Florida (1980–1998)," *Journal of Criminal Justice* 30 (2002): 65–76; Steven Levitt, "Using Electoral Cycles in Police Hiring to Estimate the Effect of Police on Crime," *American Economic Review* 87 (1997): 270–91.

24. Alexander Weiss and Sally Freels, "The Effects of Aggressive Policing: The Dayton Traffic Enforcement Experiment," *American Journal of Police* 15 (1996): 45–63.

25. Eric Fritsch, Tory Caeti, and Robert Taylor, "Gang Suppression Through Saturation Patrol, Aggressive Curfew, and Truancy Enforcement: A Quasi-Experimental Test of the Dallas Anti-Gang Initiative," *Crime and Delinquency* 45 (1999): 122–39.

26. Lawrence Sherman, "Policing Communities: What Works," in *Crime and Justice*, vol. 8, eds. Al Reiss and Michael Tonry (Chicago: University of Chicago Press, 1986), pp. 366–79.

27. Ibid., p. 368.

28. See, generally, Peter Greenwood and Joan Petersilia, *The Criminal Investigation Process, Vol. 1: Summary and Policy Implications* (Santa Monica, Calif.: Rand Corporation, 1975); P. Greenwood, J. Chaiken, J. Petersilia, and L. Prusoff, *The Criminal Investigation Process, Vol. 3: Observations and Analysis* (Santa Monica, Calif.: Rand Corporation, 1975).

29. C. Cotter and J. Burrows, *Property Crime Program, A Special Report: Overview of the STING Program and Project Summaries* (Washington, D.C.: Criminal Conspiracies Division, Office of Criminal Justice Programs, Law Enforcement Assistance Administration, U.S. Department of Justice, 1981).

30. Robert Langworthy, "Stings: A Crime Control Tool." Paper presented at the American Society of Criminology, Atlanta, November 1986.

31. Greenwood and Petersilia, *The Criminal Investigation Process*.

32. Mark T. Willman and John R. Snortum, "Detective Work: The Criminal Investigation Process in a Medium-Size Police Department," *Criminal Justice Review* 9 (1984): 33–39.

33. John Eck, *Solving Crimes: The Investigation of Burglary and Robbery* (Washington, D.C.: Police Executive Research Forum, 1984).

34. See, for example, Susan Martin, "Policing Career Criminals: An Examination of an Innovative Crime Control Program," *Journal of Criminal Law and Criminology* 77 (1986): 1159–82.

35. Charles L. Regini, "The Cold Case Concept," *FBI Law Enforcement Bulletin* 66 (1997): 1.

36. J. Q. Wilson, *Varieties of Police Behavior: The Management of Law and Order in Eight Communities* (Cambridge: Harvard University Press, 1968).

37. Richard Sykes and Edward Brent, *Policing: A Social Behaviorist Perspective* (New Brunswick, N.J.: Rutgers University Press, 1983).

38. Patrick A. Langan, Lawrence A. Greenfeld, Steven K. Smith, Matthew R. Durose, and David J. Levin, *Contacts between Police and the Public: Findings from the 1999 National Survey* (Washington, D.C.: Bureau of Justice Statistics, 2001).

39. Lawrence A. Greenfeld, Patrick A. Langan, and Steven K. Smith, *Police Use of Force: Collection of National Data* (Washington, D.C.: Bureau of Justice Statistics, 1997).

40. Egon Bittner, *The Functions of Police in Modern Society* (Cambridge, Mass.: Delgeschlager, Gunn, and Hain, 1980), pp. 63–72.

41. James Q. Wilson and George Kelling, "Broken Windows: The Police and Neighborhood Safety," *Atlantic Monthly,* March 1982, pp. 29–38.

42. Ibid., p. 37.

43. "Many Cities Experimenting with Foot Patrol," *Criminal Justice Newsletter* 16 (15 May 1985): 1–2.

44. Jerome Skolnick and David Bayley, "Theme and Variation in Community Policing," in *Crime and Justice, A Review of Research,* vol. 12, eds. Michael Tonry and Norval Morris (Chicago: University of Chicago Press, 1988), pp. 1–38.

45. Edward Maguire and Charles Katz, "The Validity and Reliability of Police Agencies Community Policing Claims." Paper presented at the American Society of Criminology meeting, San Diego, Calif., 1997.

46. Albert Cardarelli, Jack McDevitt, and Katrina Baum, "The Rhetoric and Reality of Community Policing in Small and Medium-Sized Cities and Towns," *Policing* 21 (1998): 397–415.

47. Police Foundation, *The Effects of Police Fear Reduction Strategies: A Summary of Findings from Houston and Newark* (Washington, D.C.: Police Foundation, 1986).

48. Quint Thurman and Phil Bogen, "Research Note: Spokane Community Policing Officers Revisited," *American Journal of Police* 15 (1996): 97–114.

49. Donald Green, Dara Strolovitch, and Janelle Wong, "Defended Neighborhoods, Integration, and Racially Motivated Crime," *American Journal of Sociology* 104 (1998): 372–403.

50. Lee Brown, "Neighborhood-Oriented Policing," *American Journal of Police* 9 (1990): 197–207. You can reach their Web site at: http://www.ci.houston.tx.us/departme/police/pip.htm

51. L. Thomas Winfree, Gregory Bartku, and George Seibel, "Support for Community Policing versus Traditional Policing among Nonmetropolitan Police Officers: A Survey of Four New Mexico Police Departments," *American Journal of Police* 15 (1996): 23–47.

52. Samuel Walker, "Broken Windows and Fractured History: The Use and Misuse of History in Recent Police Patrol Analysis," *Justice Quarterly* 1 (1984): 75–90.

53. Jack R. Greene, "The Effects of Community Policing on American Law Enforcement: A Look at the Evidence." Paper presented at the International Congress on Criminology, Hamburg, Germany, September 1988, p. 19.

54. For a review of how to recruit police officers, see Wesley Skogan and Susan Hartnett, *Community Policing, Chicago Style* (New York: Oxford University Press, 1997), chap. 4.

55. Larry Gould, "Can an Old Dog Be Taught New Tricks? Teaching Cultural Diversity to Police Officers," *Policing* 20 (1997): 339–57.

56. "Community Policing Officers See Benefits in Citizen Relations," *Criminal Justice Newsletter* 27 (15 February 1996), pp. 4–5.

57. Annette Jolin and Charles Moose, "Evaluating a Domestic Violence Program in a Community Policing Environment: Research Implementation Issues," *Crime and Delinquency* 43 (1997): 279–97.

58. Jihong Zhao and Quint Thurman, "Community Policing: Where Are We Now?" *Crime and Delinquency* 43 (1997): 345–57.

59. Jihong Zhao, Nicholas Lovrich and T. Hank Robinson, "Community Policing: Is It Changing the Basic Functions of Policing? Findings from a Longitudinal Study of 200+ Municipal Police Agencies," *Journal of Criminal Justice* 29 (2001): 365–77.

60. Robin Shepard Engel, "Patrol Officer Supervision in the Community Policing Era," *Journal of Criminal Justice* 30 (2002): 51–64.

61. Edward Maguire, "Structural Change in Large Municipal Police Organizations During the Community Policing Era," *Justice Quarterly* 14 (1997): 547–76.

62. Quint Thurman, Andrew Giacomazzi, and Phil Bogen, "Research Note: Cops, Kids, and Community Policing—An Assessment of a Community Policing Demonstration Project," *Crime and Delinquency* 39 (1993): 554–664; Bonnie Fisher, "What Works: Block Watch Meetings or Crime Prevention Seminars," *Journal of Crime and Justice* 16 (1993): 1–20.

63. David Kessler, "Integrating Calls for Services with Community- and Problem-Oriented Policing: A Case Study," *Crime and Delinquency* 39 (1993): 485–508.

64. Herman Goldstein, *Problem-Oriented Policing* (New York: McGraw-Hill, 1990).

65. Anthony Braga, David Kennedy, Elin Waring, and Anne Morrison Piehl, "Problem-Oriented Policing, Deterrence, and Youth Violence: An Evaluation of Boston's Operation Ceasefire," *Journal of Research in Crime and Delinquency* 38 (2001): 195–225.

66. Lawrence Sherman, "Police Crackdowns: Initial and Residual Deterrence," in *Crime and Justice, A Review of Research,* vol. 12, eds. Michael Tonry and Norval Morris (Chicago: University of Chicago Press, 1990), pp. 1–48.

67. Lawrence Sherman, Patrick Gartin, and Michael Buerger, "Hot Spots of Predatory Crime: Routine Activities and the Criminology of Place," *Criminology* 27 (1989): 27–55.

68. Dennis Roncek and Pamela Maier, "Bars, Blocks, and Crimes Revisited: Linking the Theory of Routine Activities to the Empiricism of 'Hot Spots,'" *Criminology* 29 (1991): 725–53.

69. Michael R. Smith, "Police-Led Crackdowns and Cleanups: An Evaluation of a Crime Control Initiative in Richmond, Virginia," *Crime and Delinquency* 47 (2001): 60–83.

70. Anthony Braga, "The Effects of Hot Spots Policing on Crime," *Annals, AAPSS* 578 (2001): 104–25.

71. Susan Guarino-Ghezzi, "Reintegrative Police Surveillance of Juvenile Offenders: Forging an Urban Model," *Crime and Delinquency* 40 (1994): 131–53.

72. Allan Jiao, "Factoring Police Models," *Policing* 20 (1997): 454–73.

73. Ronald W. Glensor and Ken Peak, "Implementing Change: Community-Oriented Policing and Problem Solving," *FBI Law Enforcement Bulletin* 65 (1996): 14–22.

74. *Miranda v. Arizona,* 384 U.S. 436 (1966).

75. *Harris v. New York,* 401 U.S. 222 (1971).

76. *Michigan v. Tucker,* 417 U.S. 433 (1974).

77. *Moran v. Burbine,* 106 S.Ct. 1135 (1986); *Michigan v. Mosley,* 423 U.S. 96 (1975); *Fare v. Michael C.,* 442 U.S. 23 (1979).

78. *Nix v. Williams,* 104 S.Ct. 2501 (1984).

79. *New York v. Quarles,* 104 S.Ct. 2626 (1984).

80. *Oregon v. Elstad,* 105 S.Ct. 1285 (1985).

81. *Colorado v. Spring,* 107 S.Ct. 851 (1987).

82. *Colorado v. Connelly,* 107 S.Ct. 515 (1986).

83. *Moran v. Burbine,* 106 S.Ct. 1135 (1986).

84. *Colorado v. Connelly,* 107 S.Ct. 515 (1986).

85. *Minnick v. Miss.,* 498 U.S. 46; 111 S.Ct. 486; 112 L.Ed. 2d. 489 (1990).

86. *Arizona v. Fulminante,* 499 U.S. 279, 111 S.Ct. 1246; 113 L.Ed. 2d. 302 (1991).

87. *Davis v. United States,* 114 S.Ct. 2350 (1994).

88. *Dickerson v. United States,* No. 99—5525. Argued April 19, 2000–Decided June 26, 2000

89. Victoria Time and Brian Payne, "Police Chiefs' Perceptions about *Miranda:* An Analysis of Survey Data," *Journal of Criminal Justice* 30 (2002): 77–86.

90. Richard A. Leo and Richard J. Ofshe, "The Consequences of False Confessions: Deprivations of Liberty and Miscarriages of Justice in the Age of Psychological Interrogation," *Journal of Criminal Law and Criminology* 88 (1998): 429–96.

91. *Chimel v. California,* 395 U.S. 752 (1969).

92. *Terry v. Ohio,* 392 U.S. 1 (1968).

93. *Carroll v. United States,* 267 U.S. 132 (1925).

94. *United States v. Ross,* 102 S.Ct. 2147 (1982).

95. *Whren et al. v. U.S.,* no. 95-5841 (1996).

96. Drivers, *Pennsylvania v. Mimms,* 434 U.S. 106, 1977; and passengers, *Maryland v. Wilson,* 117 U.S. 882, 1997.

97. *Bumper v. North Carolina,* 391 U.S. 543 (1960).

98. *Ohio v. Robinette,* 117 S. Ct. 417 (1996).

99. Limitations on the plain view doctrine have been defined in *Arizona v. Hicks,* 107 S.Ct. 1149 (1987); the recording of serial numbers from stereo components in a suspect's apartment could not be justified as being in plain view.

100. *Katz v. United States,* 389 U.S. 347 (1967).

101. Richard Lundman, *Police and Policing* (New York: Holt, Rinehart and Winston, 1980); see also Jerome Skolnick, *Justice without Trial* (New York: Wiley, 1966).

102. Cited in Arthur Neiderhoffer, *Behind the Shield: The Police in Urban Society* (Garden City, N.Y.: Doubleday, 1967), p. 65.

103. For an impressive review, see Peter Finn, "Reducing Stress: An Organization-Centered Approach," *FBI Law Enforcement Bulletin* 66 (1997): 20.

104. Terri Harvey-Lintz and Romeria Tidwell, "Effects of the 1992 Los Angeles Civil Unrest: Post Traumatic Stress Disorder Symptomatology among Law Enforcement Officers," *Social Science Journal* 34 (1997): 171–84.

105. See, for example, Richard Bennett and Theodore Greenstein, "The Police Personality: A Test of the Predispositional Model," *Journal of Police Science and Administration* 3 (1975): 439–45.

106. William Westly, *Violence and the Police: A Sociological Study of Law, Custom and Morality* (Cambridge: MIT Press, 1970); idem, "Violence and the Police," *American Journal of Sociology* 49 (1953): 34–41.

107. John Crank, *Understanding Police Culture* (Cincinnati, Ohio: Anderson, 1997).

108. See, for example, Richard Harris, *The Police Academy: An Inside View* (New York: John Wiley, 1973); John Van Maanen, "Observations on the Making of Policemen," *Human Organization* 32 (1973): 407–18; Jonathan Rubenstein, *City Police* (New York: Ballantine, 1973); John Broderick, *Police in a Time of Change* (Morristown, N.J.: General Learning Press, 1977).

109. Steve Herbert, "Police Subculture Reconsidered," *Criminology* 36 (1998): 343–69.

110. Ibid., p. 360.

111. Ibid., p. 359.

112. David Klinger, "Negotiating Order in Patrol Work: An Ecological Theory of Police Response to Deviance," *Criminology* 35 (1997): 277–306.

113. John Crank and Robert Langworthy, "An Institutional Perspective of Policing," *Journal of Criminal Law and Criminology* 83 (1992): 338–457.

114. Donald Yates and Vijayan Pillai, "Attitudes Toward Community Policing: A Causal Analysis," *Social Science Journal* 33 (1996): 193–209.

115. Joseph Goldstein, "Police Discretion Not to Invoke the Criminal Process," *Yale Law Journal* 69 (1960): 543–94.

116. Richard C. Donnelly, "Police Authority and Practices," *Annals of the American Academy of Political and Social Science* 339 (January 1962): 91–92.

117. See, generally, Kenneth C. Davis, *Discretionary Justice—A Preliminary Inquiry* (Baton Rouge: Louisiana State University Press, 1969).

118. Stephen Mastrofski, R. Richard Ritti, and Debra Hoffmaster, "Organizational Determinants of Police Discretion: The Case of Drinking and Driving," *Journal of Criminal Justice* 15 (1987): 387–402.

119. David Klinger, "Negotiating Order in Patrol Work: An Ecological Theory of Police Response to Deviance," *Criminology* 35 (1997): 277–306.

120. Ibid., p. 296.

121. Sherri Lynn Johnson, "Race and the Decision to Detain a Suspect," *Yale Law Journal* 93 (1983): 214–58.

122. Geoffrey Alpert, Dennis Kenney, and Roger Dunham, "Police Pursuits and the Use of Force: Recognizing and Managing the 'Pucker Factor'—A Research Note," *Justice Quarterly* 14 (1997): 371–86.

123. Helen Eigenberg, Kathryn Scarborough, and Victor Kappeler, "Contributory Factors Affecting Arrest in Domestic and Non-Domestic Assaults," *American Journal of Police* 15 (1996): 27–51.

124. Leonore Simon, "A Therapeutic Jurisprudence Approach to the Legal Processing of Domestic Violence Cases," *Psychology Public Policy and Law* 1 (1995): 43–79.

125. James Fyfe, David Klinger, and Jeanne Flaving, "Differential Police Treatment of Male-on-Female Spousal Violence," *Criminology* 35 (1997): 455–73.

126. David Klinger, "Policing Spousal Assault," *Journal of Research in Crime and Delinquency* 32 (1995): 308–24.

127. See, for example, Nathan Goldman, *The Differential Selection of Juvenile Offenders for Court Appearance* (New York: National Council on Crime and Delinquency, 1963); Aaron Cicourel, *The Social Organization of Juvenile Justice* (New York: John Wiley, 1968); Irving Piliavin and Scott Briar, "Police Encounters with Juveniles," *American Journal of Sociology* 70 (1964): 206.

128. Richard R. Johnson, "Citizen Complaints: What the Police Should Know," *FBI Law Enforcement Bulletin* 67 (1998): 1–6.

129. Donald Black, "The Social Organization of Arrest," *Stanford Law Review* 23 (1971): 1087–1111.

130. Richard Lundman, "Demeanor or Crime? The Midwest City Police–Citizen Encounters Study," *Criminology* 36 (1994): 631–56.

131. David Klinger, "More on Demeanor and Arrest in Dade County," *Criminology* 34 (1996): 61–82.

132. Jerome Skolnick and J. Richard Woodworth, "Bureaucracy, Information and Social Control: A Study of a Morals Detail," in *The Police, Six Sociological Essays,* ed. David Bordua (New York: John Wiley, 1960).

133. John Gardiner, *Traffic and the Police: Variations in Law Enforcement Policy* (Cambridge: Harvard University Press, 1969).

134. Samuel Walker, *Civilian Review of the Police: A National Survey of the 50 Largest Cities, 1991* (Omaha: University

of Nebraska, Department of Criminal Justice, 1991).

135. Most important is the Equal Employment Opportunity Act of 1972, amending Title VII of the Civil Rights Act of 1964.

136. *United States v. Paradise,* 55 L.W. 4211 (1987).

137. Jihong Zhao and Nicholas Lovrich, "Determinants of Minority Employment in American Municipal Police Agencies: The Representation of African American Officers," *Journal of Criminal Justice* 26 (1998): 267–78.

138. David Murphy and John Worrall, "Residency Requirements and Public Perceptions of the Police in Large Municipalities," *Policing* 22 (1999): 327–42.

139. Steven Tuch and Ronald Weitzer, "The Polls-Trends, Racial Differences in Attitudes Toward the Police," *Public Opinion Quarterly* 61 (1997): 642–63.

140. Sutham Cheurprakobkit, "Police–Citizen Contact and Police Performance, Attitudinal Differences between Hispanics and Non-Hispanics," *Journal of Criminal Justice* 28 (2000): 325–36; Maguire, Kathleen and Ann L. Pastore, eds. *Sourcebook of Criminal Justice Statistics (1999)* [Online]. Available at: http://www.albany.edu/sourcebook [Accessed January 2002]

141. Yolander G. Hurst, James Frank, and Sandra Lee Browning, "The Attitudes of Juveniles toward the Police: A Comparison of Black and White Youth," *Policing: An International Journal of Police Strategies and Management* 23 (2000): 37–53.

142. Walker, *Popular Justice,* p. 61.

143. Nicholas Alex, *Black in Blue: A Study of the Negro Policeman* (New York: Appleton Century Crofts, 1969).

144. Ibid., p. 154.

145. Kim Michelle Lersch, "Predicting Citizens' Race in Allegations of Misconduct against the Police," *Journal of Criminal Justice* 26 (1998): 87–99.

146. James Jacobs and Jay Cohen, "The Impact of Racial Integration on the Police," *Journal of Police Science and Administration* 6 (1978): 182.

147. Charles Katz, "The Establishment of a Police Gang Unit: An Examination of Organizational and Environmental Factors," *Criminology* 39 (2001): 37–73.

148. Ibid., p. 61.

149. See, generally, David J. Bell, "Policewomen: Myths and Reality," *Journal of Police Science and Administration* 10 (1982): 112–20.

150. Catherine Milton, *Women in Policing* (Washington, D.C.: Police Foundation, 1972).

151. See, generally, A. Bouza, "Women in Policing," *FBI Law Enforcement Bulletin* 44 (1975): 2–7; Joyce Sichel, Lucy Friedman, Janet Quint, and Micall Smith, *Women on Patrol: A Pilot Study of Police Performance in New York City* (Washington, D.C.: National Criminal Justice Reference Service, 1978); William Weldy, "Women in Policing: A Positive Step toward Increased Police Enthusiasm," *Police Chief* 43 (1976): 47.

152. Steven Brandl, Meghan Stroshine, and James Frank, "Who Are the Complaint-Prone Officers? An Examination of the Relationship between Police Officers' Attributes, Arrest Activity, Assignment, and Citizens' Complaints about Excessive Force," *Journal of Criminal Justice* 29 (2001): 521–29.

153. Michael Birzer and Delores Craig, "Gender Differences in Police Physical Ability Test Performance," *American Journal of Police* 15 (1996): 93–106.

154. Sean Grennan, "Findings on the Role of Officer Gender in Violent Encounters with Citizens," *Journal of Police Science and Administration* 15 (1987): 79–85.

155. James Daum and Cindy Johns, "Police Work from a Woman's Perspective," *Police Chief* 61 (1994): 46–49.

156. Matthew Hickman, Alex Piquero, and Jack Greene, "Discretion and Gender Disproportionality in Police Disciplinary Systems," *Policing: An International Journal of Police Strategies and Management* 23 (2000): 105–16.

157. Robin Harr and Merry Morash, "Gender, Race, and Strategies of Coping with Occupational Stress in Policing," *Justice Quarterly* 16 (1999): 303–36.

158. Joanne Belknap and Jill Kastens Shelley, "The New Lone Ranger: Policewomen on Patrol," *American Journal of Police* 12 (1993): 47–75.

159. Susan Martin, "'Outsider Within' the Station House: The Impact of Race and Gender on Black Women Police," *Social Problems* 41 (1994): 383–400, at 387.

160. Ibid., p. 392.

161. Ibid., p. 394.

162. Ibid., p. 397.

163. Associated Press, "NY Pays $3M to Police Victim Kin," *New York Times,* 2 October 1998, p. A1.

164. Bittner, *The Functions of Police in Modern Society,* p. 46.

165. Walker, *Popular Justice,* p. 197.

166. President's Commission on Law Enforcement and the Administration of Justice, *Task Force Report: The Police,* pp. 181–82.

167. Albert Reiss, *The Police and the Public* (New Haven: Yale University Press, 1972).

168. David Bayley and James Garofalo, "The Management of Violence by Police Patrol Officers," *Criminology* 27 (1989): 1–27; Lawrence Sherman, "Causes of Police Behavior: The Current State of Quantitative Research," *Journal of Research in Crime and Delinquency* 17 (1980): 80–81.

169. For a general review, see Tom McEwen, *National Data Collection on Police Use of Force* (Washington, D.C.: National Institute of Justice, 1996).

170. Patrick A. Langan, Lawrence A. Greenfeld, Steven K. Smith, Matthew R. Durose, and David J. Levin, *Contacts between Police and the Public: Findings from the 1999 National Survey* (Washington, D.C.: Bureau of Justice Statistics, 2001).

171. Antony Pate and Lorie Fridell, *Police Use of Force: Official Reports, Citizen Complaints, and Legal Consequences* (Washington, D.C.: Police Foundation, 1993).

172. Patrick A. Langan, Lawrence A. Greenfeld, Steven K. Smith, Matthew R. Durose, and David J. Levin, *Contacts between Police and the Public: Findings from the 1999 National Survey* (Washington, D.C.: Bureau of Justice Statistics, 2001).

173. Sandra Lee Browning, Francis Cullen, Liqun Cao, Renee Kopache, and Thomas Stevenson, "Race and Getting Hassled by the Police: A Research Note," *Police Studies* 17 (1994): 1–11.

174. For a comprehensive view of this issue, see William Geller and Michael Scott, "Deadly Force: What We Know," in *Thinking about Police,* eds. Carl Klockars and Stephen Mastrofski (New York: McGraw-Hill, 1991), pp. 446–77; James Fyfe, "Police Use of Deadly Force: Research and Reform," *Justice Quarterly* 5 (1988): 165–205.

175. Fyfe, "Police Use of Deadly Force: Research and Reform," p. 178; Kenneth Mattulla, *A Balance of Forces* (Washington, D.C.: U.S. Government Printing Office, 1982), p. 17.

176. This discussion is adapted from James Fyfe, "Toward a Typology of Police Shootings." Paper presented at the annual meeting of the Academy of Criminal Justice Sciences, Oklahoma City, March 1980.

177. Jonathan Sorensen, James Marquart, and Deon Brock, "Factors Related to Killings of Felons by Police Officers: A Test of the Community Violence and

Conflict Hypotheses," *Justice Quarterly* 10 (1993): 417–40.

178. *Tennessee v. Garner*, 105 S.Ct. 1694 (1985).

179. Michael D. White, "Controlling Police Decisions to Use Deadly Force: Reexamining the Importance of Administrative Policy." *Crime and Delinquency* 47 (2001): 131.

180. Lorie Fridell and Arnold Binder, "Police Officer Decisionmaking in Potentially Violent Confrontations," *Journal of Criminal Justice* 20 (1992): 385–99.

181. James Fyfe, "Administrative Interventions on Police Shooting Discretion: An Empirical Examination," *Journal of Criminal Justice* 7 (1979): 309–23.

182. Crime Control Act of 1994, Section 210401.

183. Estimate based on Geller and Scott, "Deadly Force: What We Know," p. 452.

184. FBI, "Law Enforcement Officers Killed and Assaulted, 2000." (Washington, D.C.: Federal Bureau of Investigation, 2002).

185. Warren Cohen, "When Lethal Force Won't Do," *U.S. News & World Report* 122 (23 June 1997): 12.

186. Richard Lumb and Paul Friday, "Impact of Pepper Spray Availability on Police Officer Use-of-Force Decisions," *Policing* 20 (1997): 136–49.

187. Tom McEwen, "Policies on Less-Than-Lethal Force in Law Enforcement Agencies," *Policing* 20 (1997): 39–60.

AP/Wide World Photos

CHAPTER 17 The Judicatory Process

■ Introduction

In April of 2000, Matthew Kaminer, then a freshman at the University of Florida, was having a few drinks when he was given an innocent-looking pill by a friend. The next morning he was found dead. It turns out that the pill was the potent painkiller OxyContin, a type of synthetic morphine. It seems that Ying Che "Dan" Lo, a 19-year-old pharmacy student, had taken a bottle from the drugstore where he worked and given the pills to Naeem Diamond Lakhani, 19, a friend of Kaminer. Prosecutors charged the boys with manslaughter, a charge that carried a sentence of up to 15 years in prison. However, on June 18, 2001, the two boys received reduced sentences under plea agreements. Dan Lo received about three months in jail, and his roommate, Naeem Lakhani, about a month. They were also ordered, as requested by the victim's mother, to keep a photograph of Matthew Kaminer on their night stands for 15 years.[1]

The Kaminer case illustrates the tremendous burden placed on the court system. It must render fair, impartial justice in deciding the outcome of a conflict between criminal and victim, law enforcement agents and violators of the law, parent and child, federal government and violators of governmental regulations, or other parties. Should college students go to prison for giving a friend a pill that later turns out to cause his death? Should people be allowed to negotiate pleas that allow them to avoid the full extent of the law?

Regardless of the issues involved, the parties' presence in a courtroom should guarantee that they will have a hearing conducted under rules of procedure in an atmosphere of fair play and objectivity and that the outcome of the hearing will be clear. If a party believes the ground rules have been violated, he or she may take the case to a higher court, where the procedures of the original trial will be examined. If this court finds that a violation of legal rights has occurred, the appellate court may deem the findings of the original trial improper and either order a new hearing or hold that some other measure must be carried out; for example, the court may dismiss the charge outright.

The court is a complex social agency with many independent but interrelated subsystems—clerk, prosecutor, defense attorney, judge, and probation department—each having a role in the court's operation. It is also the scene of many important elements of criminal justice decision making—detention, jury selection, trial, and sentencing.

Ideally, the judicatory process operates with absolute fairness and equality. The entire process—from filing the initial complaint to final sentencing of the defendant—is governed by precise rules of law designed to ensure fairness. No defendant tried before a U.S. court should suffer or benefit because of his or her personal characteristics, beliefs, or affiliations.

However, U.S. criminal justice can be selective. Discretion accompanies defendants through every step of the process, determining what will happen to them and how their cases will be resolved. Discretion means that two people committing similar crimes will receive highly dissimilar treatment. For example, most people convicted of homicide receive a prison sentence, but about 4 percent receive probation as a sole sentence; more murderers get probation than get the death penalty.[2]

This chapter reviews some of the institutions and processes involved in adjudication and trial. The chapter briefly describes the court structure and then discusses the actors in the process—prosecution, defense, judges, and juries. The pretrial stage of the justice process is the next focus of attention, as such issues as bail and plea bargaining are described. The criminal trial is then discussed in some detail; finally, sentencing formats are explained.

AP/Wide World Photos

■ Ying Che "Dan" Lo (right), a 19-year-old pharmacy student, and Naeem Diamond Lakhani, 19 (left), gave the painkiller OxyContin to a friend, Matthew Kaminer, who died suddenly after taking the potent drug. Although the prosecutors charged the young men with manslaughter, they received reduced sentences under plea agreements.

■ Court Structure

Criminal adjudication is played out within the court system. The nation's 16,000 courts are organized on the municipal, county, state, and federal levels.

State Courts

The typical state court structure is illustrated in Figure 17.1. Most states employ a multitiered court structure.

Lower courts try misdemeanors and conduct the preliminary processing of felony offenses. Superior trial courts try felony cases. Some states have a municipal court system in larger cities that handles petty or less serious cases. Appellate courts review the criminal procedures of trial courts to determine whether the offenders were treated fairly. Superior appellate courts or state supreme courts review lower appellate court decisions.

Figure 17.1   Structure of a State Judicial System

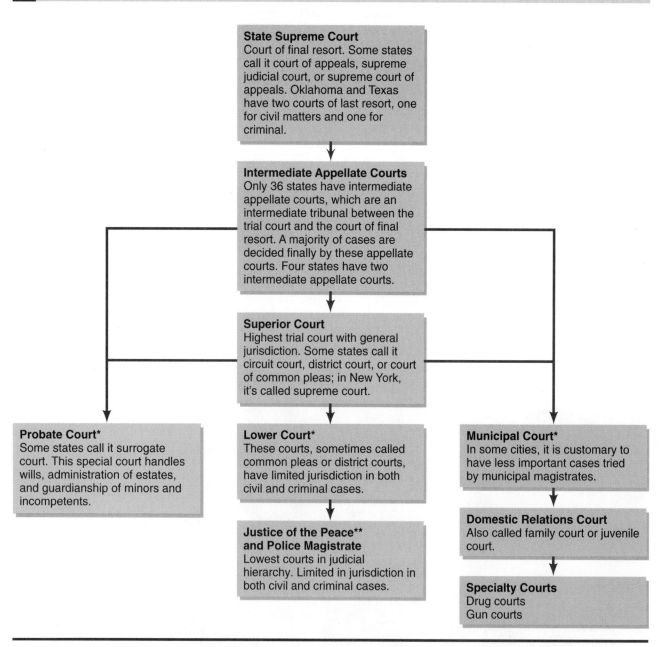

*Courts of special jurisdiction, such as probate, family, or juvenile courts, and the so-called inferior courts, such as common pleas or municipal courts, may be separate courts or part of the trial court of general jurisdiction.

**Justices of the peace do not exist in all states. Where they do exist, their jurisdictions vary greatly from state to state.

SOURCE: American Bar Association, *Law and the Courts* (Chicago: ABA, 1974), p. 20; updated information provided by West Publishing, St. Paul, Minnesota.

Use "state courts" as a subject guide on InfoTrac College Edition to find out more about recent developments in their operations. ■

A recent trend has been to develop specialized courts to handle specific justice-related problems. The Policy and Practice in Criminology feature on page 518 highlights these new courts.

Federal Courts

The federal court system has three tiers, as shown in Figure 17.2. The **U.S. district courts** are the trial courts of the system; they have jurisdiction over cases involving violations of federal law, such as interstate transportation of stolen vehicles and racketeering.

Appeals from the district court are heard in one of the intermediate **federal courts of appeal.** However, the highest federal appeals court, the **U.S. Supreme Court,** is the court of last resort for all cases tried in the various federal and state courts.

The Supreme Court maintains a Web site that has a wealth of information on its history, judges, procedures, cases filings, rules, handling guides, opinions, and other relevant court-related material. To access the site, go to:
http://www.supremecourtus.gov/
For an up-to-date list of Web links, go to
http://info.wadsworth.com/siegel ■

The Supreme Court is composed of nine members, appointed for lifetime terms by the president with the approval of Congress. In general, the Court hears only cases it deems important and appropriate. When the Court decides to hear a case, it usually grants a **writ of certiorari,** requesting a transcript of the case proceedings for review. The process by which a case gets to the Supreme Court is set out in Figure 17.3.

The Supreme Court can word a decision so that it becomes a **precedent** that must be honored by all lower courts. For example, if the Court grants a particular litigant the right to counsel at a police lineup, then all people in similar situations must be given the same right. This type of ruling is usually referred to as a **landmark decision.** The use of precedent in the legal system gives the Supreme Court power to influence and mold the everyday operating procedures of police agencies, trial courts, and corrections institutions. This influence was quite pronounced during the tenure of Chief Justice Earl Warren,

Figure 17.2   The Federal Judicial System

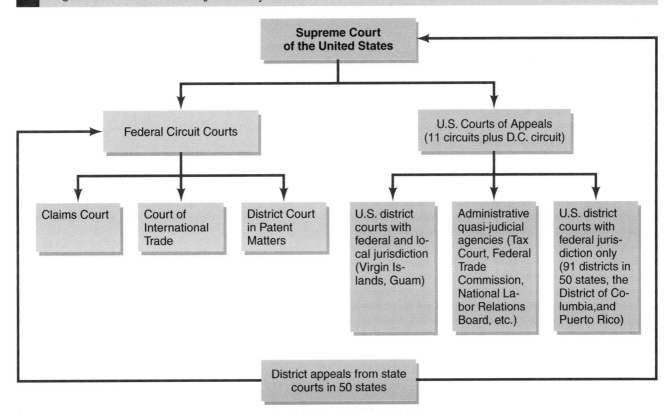

SOURCE: American Bar Association, *Law and the Courts* (Chicago: ABA, 1974), p. 21; updated information provided by the Federal Courts Improvement Act of 1982 and West Publishing, St. Paul, Minnesota.

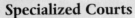

Specialized Courts

A growing phenomenon in the United States is the creation of specialty courts that focus on one type of criminal act: for example, drug courts or gun courts. All cases within the jurisdiction that involve this particular type of crime are funneled to the specialty court, where presumably they will get prompt resolution.

One well-known example is the *Gun Court* in Providence, Rhode Island. All felony cases in Bristol and Providence counties are automatically routed to Gun Court, where once a preliminary hearing has begun, the cases must be heard within 60 days. The purpose is to make sure that violent felons are not lost in the shuffle of crowded urban courts, where witnesses disappear and offenders are free to abscond.

Another specialty court is the *drug court,* which has jurisdiction over the burgeoning number of cases involving substance abuse and trafficking. The aim is to place nonviolent first offenders into intensive treatment programs rather than in jail or prison. One such court, the Drug Night Court program in Cook County, Illinois, was set up in 1975 as an emergency measure to deal with the rapidly expanding number of narcotics cases being filed. Today there are 327 drug courts across 43 states, the District of Columbia, and Puerto Rico. Drug courts address the overlap between the public health threats of drug abuse and crime: crimes are often drug related, and drug abusers are frequently involved with the criminal justice system. Drug courts provide an ideal setting to address these problems by linking the justice system with health services and drug treatment providers while easing the burden on the already overtaxed correctional system.

Some early evaluations have praised the drug court program, indicating that it is an efficient method, dramatically reducing the processing time of drug cases. However, recent research finds that drug courts may not be as effective as originally believed and that recidivism for drug court participants is significantly higher than for similar offenders who are processed in traditional courts. It is possible that drug courts stigmatize defendants as substance abusers and, consequently, impede their rehabilitation.

Other Specialized Courts

By 1998, all but 17 states had *family courts* that served some number of counties, districts, or were statewide. These courts typically had jurisdiction over domestic and marital matters such as divorce, child custody and support, and domestic violence. There are also *juvenile courts,* which specialize in cases of underage minors who violate the criminal law (juvenile delinquents), who are uncontrollable or unmanageable (status offenders, who may be truants and runaways), or who are not provided with adequate care by their parents (neglected children).

To relieve overcrowding and provide an alternative to traditional forms of juvenile courts, more than 300 jurisdictions are now experimenting with *teen courts.* These differ from other juvenile justice programs because young people rather than adults determine the disposition in the case. Cases handled in these courts typically involve young juveniles (ages 10 to 15) with no prior arrest records who are being charged with minor law violations (shoplifting, vandalism, and disorderly conduct). Typically, young offenders are asked to volunteer to have their case heard in a teen court instead of the more formal court of the traditional juvenile justice system. Though decisions are made by juveniles, adults are also involved in teen courts. They often administer the programs, and they are usually responsible for essential functions such as budgeting, planning, and personnel. In many programs, adults supervise the courtroom activities, and they often coordinate the community service placements, where youth work to fulfill the terms of their dispositions. In some programs, adults act as the judges and teens serve as attorneys and jurors.

There are currently more than 450 *tribal justice forums* among the 556 federally recognized tribes in the United States. Sixteen states have assumed mandatory or optional jurisdiction over tribal lands, pursuant to Public Law 280.

Although the specialized court movement holds the promise of bringing efficiency and specialization to the justice system, not all evaluations have proven that they are more effective than traditional court models. In addition to the problems uncovered in the drug courts, evaluations of teen courts indicate that recidivism rates range from 25 to 30 percent. Considering that these cases typically involve offenses of only moderate seriousness, the findings do not suggest that the program can play a significant role in reducing teenage crime rates. It remains to be seen whether specialized courts are simply a fad or a significant contribution to crime prevention and treatment.

Critical Thinking Questions

1. Do you believe specialized courts are needed for other crime types, such as sex offenses and/or domestic violence?
2. Should a judge preside over a specialized court, or should it be administered by treatment personnel?

InfoTrac College Edition Research

To learn more about the "drug court" movement, use it as a subject guide on InfoTrac College Edition.

SOURCES: Bureau of Justice Assistance, *Drug Night Courts: The Cook County Experience* (Washington, D.C.: National Institute of Justice, 1994); Terance Miethe, Hong Lu, and Eric Reese, "Reintegrative Shaming and Recidivism Risks in Drug Court: Explanations for Some Unexpected Findings," *Crime and Delinquency* 46 (2000): 522–41; Jeffrey A. Butts and Janeen Buck, "Teen Courts: A Focus on Research," *Juvenile Justice Bulletin October 2000* (Washington, D.C.: Office of Juvenile Justice and Delinquency Prevention, 2000); Kevin Minor, James Wells, Irina Soderstrom, Rachel Bingham, and Deborah Williamson, "Sentence Completion and Recidivism among Juveniles Referred to Teen Courts," *Crime and Delinquency* 45 (1999): 467–80; Paige Harrison, James R. Maupin, and G. Larry Mays, "Teen Court: An Examination of Processes and Outcomes," *Crime and Delinquency* 47(2001): 243–64; Suzanne Wenzel, Douglas Longshore, Susan Turner, and Susan Ridgely, "Drug Courts: A Bridge between Criminal Justice and Health Services," *Journal of Criminal Justice* 29 (2001): 241–53.

Figure 17.3   Tracing a Case to the U.S. Supreme Court

Full judicial decision by the U.S. Supreme Court
(majority and dissenting opinions)
The Court affirms or reverses lower court decisions. (Exception: The decision is not always a final judicial action. Lower courts may try the case again or, as in civil litigation, the case may be retried.) Note: There is no appeal process beyond the U.S. Supreme Court.

↓

Decision-making conferences by the justices
Four votes govern the acceptance or rejection of a case: (1) a decision and full opinion; (2) if the case is accepted, there may be a summary decision of a dismissal or affirmation of a lower-court decision (per curiam); (3) if the case is rejected, no explanation (reconsideration is possible); and (4) a rehearing after an unfavorable decision is possible.

↓

Prescreening
(discussion of the case list)
The chief justice places cases on a list, including in forma pauperis petitions.

Discretionary decisions
(special circumstances)
A writ of certiorari or a writ of habeas corpus

Mandatory decisions
Hears *direct statutory appeals* in which the state is in conflict with the federal law or Constitution, and *original jurisdiction* disputes between states.

↓

Decision making

Federal courts
(U.S. appellate courts)
The U.S. Court of Appeals, the U.S. Court of Claims, and the U.S. Customs Court

State Supreme Court
(State court of last resort)
State supreme court cases that are not an issue of federal law are ineligible for hearing by the Court.

↓

Federal or State Trial Court Cases
(processing of case through federal or state court systems)

who, during the 1960s, greatly amplified and extended the power of the Court to affect criminal justice policies.

 There are a variety of issues surrounding the operations of the federal court system. Use the term "federal courts" as a subject guide on InfoTrac College Edition to learn more about today's most pressing issues. ■

Court Case Flow

The U.S. court system is a vast enterprise. About 90 million new cases of all kinds and 280,000 appeals are brought before the courts of the 50 states and the District of Columbia.[3] As Figure 17.4 shows, the number of serious cases has trended upward over the past decade; domestic violence cases have increased 75 percent since 1984. The extent of this caseload has placed great pressure on the major actors in the pretrial, trial, and sentencing process: the prosecutor, the defense attorney, and the judge.

One reason for the increase in court caseloads is the recent attempt in some communities to lower the crime rate by aggressively prosecuting petty offenses and nuisance crimes such as panhandling or vagrancy. In New York City, for example, the number of felonies has stayed roughly the same since the early 1990s, whereas the number of misdemeanor cases has soared by 85 percent. In 1998, 77 New York City judges handled 275,379 cases—about 3,500 cases each—in the city's lower criminal courts, which handle misdemeanors involving sentences of less than a year in jail. For defendants who want to fight charges, the average waiting time for a misdemeanor trial is 284 days, up from 208 days in 1991.[4]

■ Actors in the Judicatory Process

The judge, the prosecutor, and the defense attorney are the key players in the adversary process. The prosecution and defense oppose each other in a hotly disputed contest—the criminal trial—in accordance with rules of law and procedure. In every criminal case, the prosecutor represents the state's interests and the defense attorney the criminal defendant's, with each side trying to bring evidence and arguments forward to advance its case. Theoretically, the ultimate objective of the adversary system is to seek the truth: to determine whether the evidence presented at trial is sufficient to prove the facts of the charge. So that the defendant is given a fair trial, the judge acts as an impartial arbiter of procedure, ensuring that neither side violates the rules of trial conduct.

Prosecutor

The **prosecution** represents the state in criminal matters that come before the courts. The prosecutor's major duties are listed in Exhibit 17.1.

At last count, state court prosecutors' offices employed about 71,000 attorneys, investigators, and support staff, an increase of more than 25 percent since 1992.[5] Typically, the most active prosecutors are employed in larger counties with populations of more than 500,000; Exhibit 17.2 gives a profile of these attorneys.

 How do prosecutors make decisions? What are some of the critical issues they face before, during, and after trial? Use "prosecutor" as a key term on InfoTrac College Edition to find out. ■

Prosecutors' jobs are changing with the times as they confront new crime patterns and become more sensitive to old ones. For example, a recent survey found that almost 90 percent of all offices now prosecute felony domestic violence and child abuse cases, and about half the offices prosecute cases involving new kinds of firearms offenses.[6]

Types of prosecutors In the federal system, the chief prosecuting officer is the U.S. attorney general; his or her assistant prosecutors are known as U.S. attorneys and are appointed by the president. They represent the government in federal district courts. The chief prosecutor is usually an administrator; assistants normally handle the actual preparation and trial work. Federal prosecutors are professional civil service employees with reasonable salaries and job security.

Office titles for state court prosecutors include district attorney, county attorney, prosecuting attorney, commonwealth attorney, and state's attorney. They are typically elected officials. Again, most criminal prosecution and staff work is performed by scores of full-time and part-time attorneys, police investigators, and clerical personnel. Most attorneys who work for prosecutors at state and county levels are political appointees who earn low salaries, handle many cases, and in some jurisdictions, maintain private law practices. Many young lawyers serve in this capacity to gain trial experience, then leave for better-paying positions. In some state, county, and municipal jurisdictions, however, the office of the prosecutor can be described as meeting the highest standards of professional skill, personal integrity, and working conditions.

In urban settings, the structure of the district attorney's office is often specialized, with separate divisions for felonies, misdemeanors, and trial and appeal assignments. In rural offices, chief prosecutors handle many of the criminal cases themselves. The job is stressful because of both work pressure and the danger of the job. Almost half of all prosecutors' offices indicate that a staff member experienced a work-related threat or assault. In 1992, 17 percent of offices reported that their chief prosecutor was threatened or assaulted; by 1996 that had risen to 30 percent.[7]

Prosecutorial discretion Prosecutors maintain broad discretion in the exercise of their duties. In fact, for nearly

Figure 17.4   Caseload Growth in State and Federal Courts

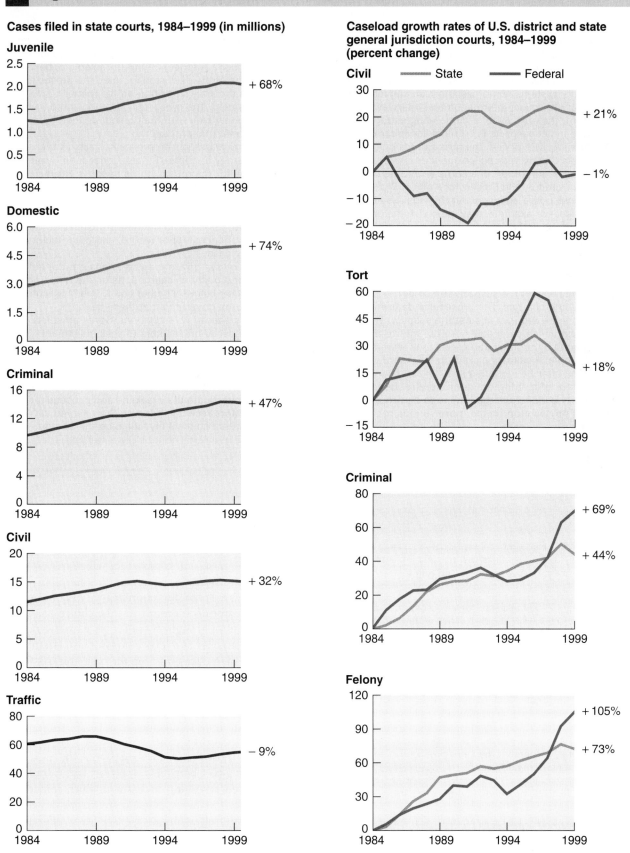

Cases filed in state courts, 1984–1999 (in millions)

Juvenile + 68%

Domestic + 74%

Criminal + 47%

Civil + 32%

Traffic − 9%

Year

Caseload growth rates of U.S. district and state general jurisdiction courts, 1984–1999 (percent change)

Civil   State   Federal   + 21%   − 1%

Tort + 18%

Criminal + 69%   + 44%

Felony + 105%   + 73%

Year

Source: National Center for State Courts, *Examining the Work of State Courts, 1999–2000* (Williamsburg, Va.: National Center for State Courts, 2001).

Exhibit 17.1   The Prosecutor's Most Significant Responsibilities

- *Investigating law violations.* Prosecutors are empowered to conduct their own investigations into alleged violations of the law. In some jurisdictions, they maintain a staff of detectives and investigators; in others they rely on local or state police. In jurisdictions with grand jury systems, the prosecutor can convene the grand jury to collect information and interview witnesses for the purpose of accumulating enough evidence to indict suspects in criminal conspiracies.
- *Cooperating with police.* The prosecutor's office usually works closely with police agencies. Police prepare the investigation report of a crime according to the format desired by the prosecutor's office. Prosecutors also advise police agents about the legal issues in a given case. For example, they supervise the drawing up of requests (affidavits) for search warrants and then make sure that the police understand the limitations presented by the warrant. Some prosecutors' offices help train police officers, making them aware of the legal issues involved in securing a warrant or a legal arrest, interrogating a suspect, and so on.
- *Determining charges.* The prosecutor determines the charges to be brought against the suspect. The charge on which defendants are brought to trial may not resemble the original reasons they were arrested. For example, a suspect picked up for disorderly conduct may later be identified at a police lineup as the perpetrator of a string of liquor store robberies. The disorderly conduct charge may then be dropped in favor of prosecution on the more serious robbery charges.
- *Representing the government in pretrial hearings and motions.* The prosecutor brings the case to trial. Prose-

cutors contact witnesses and prepare them to testify, secure physical evidence, and discuss the victim's testimony. If the defendant attempts to have evidence suppressed at a pretrial hearing (for example, because of violations of the exclusionary rule), the prosecutor represents the state's position on the matter.
- *Plea bargaining.* The prosecutor is empowered to negotiate a guilty plea with the defendant, thereby ending the formal trial process.
- *Trying criminal cases.* The prosecutor acts as the state's attorney at criminal trials. Consequently, another name for the prosecutor is people's attorney.
- *Sentencing.* The prosecutor recommends dispositions at the completion of the trial. Usually, the type of sentence recommended is influenced by plea bargaining cooperation, public opinion, the seriousness of the crime, the offender's prior record, and other factors related to the case.
- *Representing the government at appeals.* If the defendant is found guilty as charged, he or she may appeal the conviction before a higher court. The prosecutor represents the government at these hearings.
- *Conducting special investigations.* Some jurisdictions empower special prosecutors to seek indictments for serious crimes considered important to the public interest. This practice became well known during the Watergate investigation, when first Archibald Cox and then Leon Jaworski were appointed as special prosecutors to investigate the break-ins and subsequent cover-up. More recently, Kenneth Starr served as an independent counsel investigating the Clinton presidency.

Exhibit 17.2   Prosecutors in Large Courts (Population 500,000+)

- More than 14,000 assistant prosecutors and supervisory attorneys who litigated cases were employed by prosecutors' offices in large districts.
- Large district offices had combined total budgets of $2.9 billion for prosecutorial functions in 2001. The median office budget was $14 million.
- Annually, prosecutors' offices in large districts closed more than 1 million felony cases, with a median conviction rate of 85 percent.
- In large districts, 65 percent of prosecutors' offices reported a threat or assault against an assistant prosecutor, 41 percent the chief prosecutor, and 22 percent a staff investigator.
- During the previous 12 months, prosecutors' offices in large districts proceeded against in almost 11,000 juvenile cases.

SOURCE: Carol J. DeFrances, *State Court Prosecutors in Large Districts, 2001* (Washington, D.C.: Bureau of Justice Statistics, 2001).

70 years, full enforcement of the law has been so rare that it has been assumed that prosecutors will choose which cases to bring to court.[8]

Prosecutors exercise discretion in a variety of circumstances. One major decision involves the choice of acting on the information brought by police or deciding not to file for an indictment. The prosecutor can also attempt to prosecute and then decide to drop the case; this is known as a **nolle prosequi.** About half of all arrests are dismissed before they reach the trial stage. Some are diverted into treatment programs; others are rejected after being screened by the prosecutor; and another group is dealt with in a lower court by either dismissal or misdemeanor conviction. Of those carried forward to trial, the great majority end with a plea bargain.

By effectively screening out cases in which conviction could not reasonably be expected, cases inappropriate for criminal action (such as minor thefts by first offenders), and cases involving offenders with special needs (such as the emotionally disturbed or mentally retarded), the pros-

AP/Wide World Photos

■ One of the prosecutor's most important tasks is to bring cases to trial. Here, prosecutor Jim Hammer uses a cast of the gaping teeth of a dog that killed Diane Whipple during closing arguments in the highly publicized 2002 San Francisco dog mauling trial. The dogs' owners, Marjorie Knoller and her husband Robert Noel, were convicted in Whipple's death.

ecutor can concentrate on bringing to trial those who commit more serious criminal offenses. The relatively few cases that do get to trial are most often settled through plea negotiations conducted by the prosecutor's office.

Factors influencing decision making   Research indicates that widely varied factors influence prosecutorial discretion in invoking criminal sanctions, including the characteristics of the crime, the criminal, and the victim. A defendant who is a known drug user, who has a long history of criminal offending, and who causes the victim extensive physical injuries will more likely be prosecuted than one who is a first offender, does not use drugs, and does not seriously injure a victim.[9] The effect of race on prosecutorial decision making is uncertain. Although some research efforts have found that the race of the offender or victim influences prosecutorial discretion, others show that decisions are relatively unbiased.[10]

In some instances, the victim's behavior may influence charging decisions. When Myrna Dawson and Ronit Dinovitzer examined the prosecution of domestic violence cases, they found that victim cooperation is a key factor in the decision to prosecute cases; the odds of a case being prosecuted are seven times greater when victims are considered "cooperative." Significantly, Dawson and Dinovitzer found that victim cooperation was linked to prosecutorial sensitivity. Prosecutors were able to gain the cooperation

of victims and proceed to trial when they showed interest in the victim's plight by, for example, allowing victims to videotape their statements and/or provided victim-witness assistance.[11]

CONNECTIONS

The prosecution of rape cases was discussed in Chapter 11. The prosecutor's perception of the "suitability" of victims may guide their decision making. The likelihood of prosecution was reduced if women were considered unchaste or immoral. Would the victim's character enter into the decision to prosecute a case involving theft or robbery?   ■

Numerous attempts have been made to examine the charging decision. In his classic work *Prosecution: The Decision to Charge a Subject with a Crime,* Frank Miller pinpoints the factors that influence prosecutorial discretion:[12]

• The attitude of the victim
• The cost of prosecution to the criminal justice system
• The possibility of undue harm to the suspect
• The availability of alternative procedures
• The availability of civil sanctions
• The willingness of the suspect to cooperate with law enforcement authorities

In another classic work, Wayne LaFave also identified factors related to prosecutorial discretion.[13] According to LaFave, when acts have been overcriminalized—such as when laws provide stiff sentences for possessing small quantities of recreational drugs—they are not prosecuted. Limited resources force the prosecutor to select only the most serious cases. Also, alternatives to prosecution are used whenever possible to spare offenders the stigma of a criminal conviction.

In some instances, LaFave found that the prosecutor may decide to take no action; this occurs when the victim expresses the desire not to prosecute, the cost would be excessive, the harm of prosecution outweighs the benefits, or the harm done by the offender can be corrected without a criminal trial. LaFave also points out that prosecutors can invoke obscure statutes to punish unrepentant offenders or refuse leniency to defendants who will not cooperate with them. Thus, to LaFave, prosecutorial discretion is a two-edged sword. Exhibit 17.3 lists some of the other factors that have been identified as influencing prosecutorial discretion.

Case pressure is also considered an important influence on prosecutorial discretion. Although some criminologists dispute whether prosecutors' decisions are based on their work schedule, others say that the prosecutor who is deluged by serious cases is likely to not prosecute or to offer a plea bargain. Prosecutors in large counties are less likely to bring felons to trial than those in smaller, less crime-ridden counties. This is not conclusive proof of the effect of case pressure; an alternative explanation is that police work is sloppier in urban areas, forcing prosecutors to drop cases. However, it shows that jurisdictions in which prosecutors are forced to deal with more serious, violent felonies are also the ones in which the most selectivity is used.[14]

Prosecutors are political creatures. They are charged with serving the people, but they also must be wary of their reputations; losing too many high-profile cases may jeopardize their chances of reelection. They therefore may be unwilling to prosecute cases in which the odds of conviction are low; they are worried about *convictability*.[15]

Is prosecutorial discretion inherently harmful? Not necessarily, argues Judge Charles Breitel, who, in a famous statement, asserted that prosecutorial discretion is indispensable to ensure efficiency in the criminal justice system:

> If every policeman, every prosecutor, every court, and every post-sentence agency performed his or its responsibility in strict accordance with rules of law, precisely and narrowly laid down, the criminal law would be ordered but intolerable. Living would be a sterile compliance with soul-killing rules and taboos. By comparison, a primitive tribal society would seem free, indeed.[16]

Although eliminating prosecutorial discretion may not always be desirable, efforts have been made to control its content and direction. For example, national commissions have established guidelines for the exercise of appropriate prosecutorial actions.[17] Other methods of controlling prosecutorial decision making include these:

- Identification of the reasons for charging decisions
- Publication of prosecution office policies
- Review by nonprosecutorial groups
- Charging conferences
- Evaluation of charging policies and decisions and development of screening, diversion, and plea negotiation procedures[18]

Defense Attorney

While representing the accused in the criminal process, the defense counsel performs many functions (see Exhibit 17.4). Because the Supreme Court has ruled that all people facing trial have the right to legal counsel, three systems have been developed to provide legal counsel to the indigent: public defender, assigned counsel, and contract (Exhibit 17.5).[19]

These three systems can be used independently or in combination.[20] For example, in Maine the majority of its indigent criminal defense services are provided through an assigned counsel program; Oregon primarily uses a system of awarded contracts; Minnesota and New Mexico do not have assigned counsel programs but instead rely on statewide public defender programs and contract attorney programs.[21]

In general, the **assigned counsel system** is used in less populated areas, where case flow is minimal and a full-time public defender is not needed. **Public defenders** are

---

Exhibit 17.3 Factors Influencing Prosecutorial Discretion

- Evidence problems that result from a failure to find sufficient physical evidence linking the defendant to the offense
- Witness problems that arise, for example, when a witness fails to appear, gives unclear or inconsistent statements, is reluctant to testify, or is unsure of the identity of the offender
- Office policy, wherein the prosecutor decides not to prosecute certain types of offenses, particularly those that violate the letter but not the spirit of the law (for example, offenses involving insignificant amounts of property damage)
- Due process problems that involve violations of the constitutional requirements for seizing evidence and questioning the accused
- Combination with other cases, for example, when the accused is charged in several cases and the prosecutor pursues all of the charges in a single case
- Pretrial diversion, which occurs when the prosecutor and the court agree to drop charges when the accused successfully meets the conditions for diversion, such as completion of a treatment program

SOURCE: Joseph Senna and Larry Siegel, *Introduction to Criminal Justice*, 9th ed. (Belmont, Calif.: Wadsworth/West, 2001).

Exhibit 17.4   The Role of the Defense Attorney

- Investigating the incident
- Interviewing the client, police officers, and other witnesses
- Discussing the matter with the prosecutor
- Representing the defendant at the various pretrial procedures, such as arrest, interrogation, lineup, and arraignment
- Entering into plea negotiations
- Preparing the case for trial, including developing the tactics and strategy to be used
- Filing and arguing legal motions with the court
- Representing the defendant at trial
- Providing assistance at sentencing
- Determining the appropriate basis for appeal

SOURCE: Joseph Senna and Larry Siegel, *Introduction to Criminal Justice*, 9th ed. (Belmont, Calif.: Wadsworth/West, 2001).

Exhibit 17.5   The Principal Forms of Indigent Defense

Public defender	A salaried staff of full-time or part-time attorneys that render indigent criminal defense services through a public or private nonprofit organization, or as direct government paid employees. Public defenders can be part of a statewide agency, county government, the judiciary, or an independent nonprofit organization or other institution.
Assigned counsel	The appointment from a list of private bar members who accept cases on a judge-by-judge, court-by-court, or case-by-case basis. This may include an administrative component and a set of rules and guidelines governing the appointment and processing of cases handled by the private bar members.
Contract	Nonsalaried private attorneys, bar associations, law firms, consortiums or groups of attorneys, or nonprofit corporations that contract with a funding source to provide court-appointed representation in a jurisdiction.

SOURCE: Carol J. DeFrances, *State-Funded Indigent Defense Services, 1999* (Washington, D.C.: Bureau of Justice Statistics, 2001).

usually found in larger urban areas with high case flow rates. So, although a proportionately larger area of the country is served by the assigned counsel system, a significant proportion of criminal defendants receive public defenders.

A survey of the indigent defense system found that it is a vast enterprise supported by billions of dollars in tax-

payers' money. About 21 state governments funded virtually all indigent criminal defense services; 20 states had a combination of state and county funds; and 9 states relied solely on county funds.[22]

Conflicts of defense   Because of how the U.S. system of justice operates today, criminal defense attorneys face many role conflicts. As members of the legal profession, defense attorneys must be aware of their role as **officers of the court.** As an attorney, the defense counsel is obligated to uphold the integrity of the legal profession and to observe the requirements of the Code of Professional Responsibility of the American Bar Association in the defense of a client. The code makes the following statement regarding the duties of the lawyer in the **adversary system of justice:**

> Our legal system provides for the adjudication of disputes governed by the rules of substantive, evidentiary, and procedural law. An adversary presentation counters the natural human tendency to judge too swiftly in terms of the familiar that which is not yet fully known; the advocate, by his zealous preparation of facts and law, enables the tribunal to come to the hearing with an open and neutral mind and to render impartial judgements. The duty of a lawyer to his client and his duty to the legal system are the same: To present his client zealously within the boundaries of the law.[23]

In this dual capacity of being both a defensive advocate and an officer of the court, the attorney often faces conflicting obligations to client and profession. In *Nix v. Whiteside*, the Court sustained an attorney's right to refuse to represent a client whom he suspected would commit perjury. The Court also ruled that an attorney's threat to withdraw from the case and tell the court about the perjury did not violate the client's right to competent assistance of counsel.[24]

 To read more about the ethical standards of criminal defense lawyers, use InfoTrac College Edition to access this article: Joseph F. McSorley. "Criminal lawyers" or "lawyer criminals"? Ethics of criminal defense bar under attack. *Florida Bar Journal,* Feb 1998 v72 n2 p35(5) ■

Judge

The third major participant in the criminal trial is the **judge**—the senior officer in a court of criminal law. Judges' duties are quite varied and are far more extensive than the average citizen might suspect. During trials, the judge rules on the appropriateness of conduct, settles questions of evidence and procedure, and guides the questioning of witnesses. When a jury trial occurs, the judge must instruct jury members on which evidence can be examined and which should be ignored. The judge also formally charges the jury by instructing its members on what points of law and evidence they must consider before reaching a decision of guilty or innocent. When a jury trial is waived, the judge must decide for the complainant or the defendant. Finally, if a defendant is found guilty, the judge decides on the sentence (in some cases the sentence is legislatively determined). This duty includes choosing the type of sentence, its length, and in the case of probation, the conditions under which it may be revoked. Obviously this decision has a significant effect on an offender's future.[25]

The purposes of the American Judges Association are to improve the effective and impartial administration of justice, to enhance the independence and status of the judiciary, to provide for continuing education of its members, and to promote the interchange of ideas of a judicial nature among judges, court organization, and the public. Go to their Web site at:

http://aja.ncsc.dni.us/

For an up-to-date list of Web links, go to

http://info.wadsworth.com/siegel ■

Beyond these stated duties, the trial judge has extensive control and influence over the other service agencies of the court: probation agencies, court clerks, police agencies, and the district attorney's office. In some courts, the operations, philosophy, and procedures of these agencies are within the magistrate's administrative domain. In other courts—for example, where a state agency controls the probation department—the attitude of the county or district court judge still influences how a probation department is run.

Judicial selection Several methods are used to select state court judges. In some jurisdictions, the governor simply appoints judges. In others, judicial recommendations must be confirmed by the state senate, the governor's council, a special confirmation committee, an executive council elected by the state assembly, or an elected review board. Some states employ screening bodies that submit names to the governor for approval. Another form of judicial selection is through popular election, either partisan or nonpartisan. This practice is used in a majority of states.

About 16 states have adopted what is known as the **Missouri Plan** to select judges. This three-part approach consists of (1) a judicial nominating commission to nominate candidates for the bench, (2) an elected official (usually from the executive branch) to make appointments from the list submitted by the commission, and (3) subsequent nonpartisan, noncompetitive elections in which incumbent judges run on their records. Some states, such as New York and Texas, use different methods to select judges on the appellate and trial levels. New York appellate court judges are appointed by the governor; trial court judges are elected; and criminal court and family court judges in New York City are appointed by the mayor.[26]

■ Judges' duties are quite varied. During trials, they rule on the appropriateness of conduct, settle questions of evidence and procedure, and guide the questioning of witnesses. The judge also formally charges the jury. When a jury trial is waived, the judge must decide the case. Finally, if a defendant is found guilty, the judge decides on the sentence (in some cases the sentence is legislatively determined). Here, Judge Belinda Hill is shown during the trial of Andrea Yates, the Houston mother who was convicted of killing her five children in 2002.

Do research on the role of the "trial judge" by using it as a key word on InfoTrac College Edition. ■

Judicial overload There has been great concern about stress placed on judges by case pressure. In most states, people appointed to the bench have had little or no training in the role of judge. Others may have held administrative posts and may not have appeared before a court in years. Once they are appointed to the bench, judges are given an overwhelming amount of work, which has risen dramatically over the years. The number of civil and criminal filings per state court judge has increased significantly since 1985. Annually there are about 1,500 civil and criminal case filings per state court judge and 450 per federal judge.[27] State court judges deal with far more cases, but federal cases may be more complex and demand more judicial time. In any event, the number of civil and criminal cases, especially in state courts, seems to be outstripping the ability of states to create new judgeships; as Figure 17.4 on page 521 shows, caseloads have increased substantially during the past decade.

Now that the actors in the judicatory process have been introduced and the structure within which they work defined, our attention will turn to the the most important decisions and processes under their control: bail, plea negotiations, trial, and sentencing.

Bail

Bail represents money or some other security provided to the court to ensure the appearance of the defendant at trial. The amount of bail is set by a magistrate who reviews the facts of the case and the history of the defendant. Defendants who cannot afford or are denied bail are detained, usually in a county jail or lockup, until their trial date. Those who make bail are free to pursue their defense before trial.

The bail system goes back to English common law. At one time the legal relationship existing in the contract law of bailment even permitted the trying and sentencing of the bailor (the person who posted bail) if the bailee did not appear for trial.[28]

Under the U.S. system of justice, the right to reasonable bail comes from the Eighth Amendment of the Constitution. In most cases, accused persons have the right to be released on reasonable bail to prepare their defense and continue their life in the community.

Making Bail Today

The most recent national data available indicate that most defendants (64 percent) made bail; an estimated 36 percent of all defendants were detained until the courts disposed of their cases, including 7 percent who were denied bail. Murder defendants (13 percent) were the least likely to be released prior to case disposition, followed by defendants whose most serious arrest charge was robbery (38 percent), rape (47 percent), burglary (50 percent), or motor vehicle theft (50 percent).[29] About a third of released defendants were either rearrested for a new offense, failed to appear in court as scheduled, or committed some other violation that resulted in the revocation of their pretrial release.

Not all defendants make bail. Some defendants are detained because they cannot afford to make bail; others are denied bail because of the danger they present to the community, a practice called **preventive detention.**

The likelihood of making bail is directly related to the criminal charge: drug and public order offenders are the most likely to be bailed; violent offenders are more likely to be detained. A prior history of absconding before trial is also related to a lower probability of release. More than half of all defendants with an active criminal justice status (such as out on bail or on probation) were detained until case disposition, compared to about 30 percent of those without such a status. Defendants on parole were the most likely to be detained, followed by those on probation.

The Problems of Bail

Bail is quite controversial because it penalizes the indigent offender who does not have the means to pay the bond. Because people denied bail are often held in dreary, dangerous detention centers, they can be victims of the justice system even if they are innocent of all charges. The bail system is also costly, because the state must pay for the detention of offenders who are unable to raise bail and who might otherwise remain in the community.[30] Other significant problems associated with bail today include increased punishment risk and concerns regarding bonding and recovery agents.

Those who do not make bail have a much greater likelihood of conviction and receive longer prison sentences after conviction.[31] Upon conviction, 87 percent of detained defendants were sentenced to incarceration, with 50 percent receiving a prison sentence and 38 percent a jail term. In contrast, 51 percent of the released defendants who were convicted were sentenced to incarceration, with more receiving a jail sentence (32 percent) than a prison sentence (19 percent). Convicted defendants who were detained until case disposition (50 percent) were more than twice as likely as released defendants to receive a state prison sentence. Among defendants who were detained through trial and sentencing, 67 percent were convicted and sentenced to incarceration, compared to 29 percent of those who were released.[32]

Another problem of the bail system is the institution of the professional **bail bonding agent.** Normally the bail bonding agent puts up 90 percent of a bond fee and the defendant the remaining 10 percent (this is called a **surety bond**). When the defendant appears at trial, the bail is returned and the bonding agent keeps the entire amount; the defendant's 10 percent serves as the bonding agent's commission. If the defendant does not show up for trial, the bonding agent must pay the entire bail. Bonding agents usually expect defendants, their friends, or their relatives to put up further collateral (such as the deed to their house) to cover the risk; they may also purchase insurance to reduce their risk. If collateral is unavailable or the bonding agent believes the offender presents too great a risk, the bonding agent will refuse to lend bail money, relegating the defendant to a jail stay until the trial date. Bail bonding agents have often been accused of unscrupulous practices, such as bribing police and court personnel to secure referrals. Some judges have been accused of refusing to collect forfeited bail owed to bonding agents.[33]

If a bailee fails to return for trial, the bonding agent may hire **skip tracers** or **recovery agents** to track down the fugitive in order to recover the lost bond. These modern bounty hunters receive a share of the recovery. Unlike police, bounty hunters can enter a suspect's home without a warrant in most states, thanks to an 1873 Supreme Court ruling that gives agents of bail bonding agents sweeping powers. Each year bounty hunters catch about 25,000 fugitives according to the National Institute of Bail Enforcement.[34]

Bail Reform

The bail reform movement was started in 1961 to help alleviate the problems presented by the bail process. In New York the Vera Foundation, set up by philanthropist Louis Schweitzer and later supported by the Ford Foundation, pioneered the concept of **release on recognizance** (ROR).[35] This project found that if the court had sufficient background information about the defendant it could make a reasonably good judgment about whether the accused would return to court.

The project proved to be a great success. A significant majority of clients returned for trial when released on their own recognizance. The success of ROR in New York prompted its adoption in many other large cities around the country. The Federal Bail Reform Act of 1984 has made release on recognizance an assumption unless the need for greater control can be shown in court.[36]

Abuses by bail bonding agents have prompted a number of jurisdictions, including Wisconsin, Nebraska, Kentucky, Oregon, and Illinois, to set up systems that allow defendants to post a percentage of their bond (usually 10 percent) with the court; the full amount is required only if the defendant fails to show for trial. This **deposit bail system** is designed to replace the bonding agents. The major forms of bail are set out in Exhibit 17.6.

Bail reform has been considered one of the great successes in criminal justice reform, but some research efforts indicate great disparity in the way judges handle bail decisions. They also show that racial and socioeconomic disparity might be a factor in decision making.[37] If this is so, then the original purposes of reforming bail would be negated by bias in the justice system. One approach to limiting disparity is the use of **bail guidelines,** which set standard bail amounts based on such factors as criminal history and the current charge.[38]

In sum, bail reform movements have encouraged the use of pretrial release. Studies show that most defendants return for trial and most bailees do not commit more crime while in the community.

Exhibit 17.6 Bail Systems

Program	Description
Nonfinancial Release	
1. Release on recognizance	The defendant is released on a promise to appear, without any requirement of money bond. This form of release is unconditional—that is, without imposition of special conditions, supervision, or specially provided services. The defendant must simply appear in court for all scheduled hearings.
2. Conditional release	The defendant is released on a promise to fulfill some stated requirements that go beyond those associated with release on recognizance. Four types of conditions are placed on defendants, all of which share the common aims of increasing the defendant's likelihood of returning to court and maintaining community safety: (1) status quo conditions, such as requiring that the defendant maintain residence or employment status; (2) restrictive conditions, such as requiring that the defendant remain in the jurisdiction, stay away from the complainant, or maintain a curfew; (3) contact conditions, such as requiring that the defendant report by telephone or in person to the release program or a third party at various intervals; and (4) problem-oriented conditions, such as requiring that the defendant participate in drug or alcohol treatment programs.
Financial release	
3. Unsecured bail	The defendant is released with no immediate requirement of payment. However, if the defendant fails to appear, he or she is liable for the full amount.
4. Privately secured bail	A private organization or individual posts the bail amount, which is returned when the defendant appears in court. In effect, the organization provides services akin to those of a professional bonding agent, but without cost to the defendant.
5. Property bail	The defendant may post evidence of real property in lieu of money.
6. Deposit bail	The defendant deposits a percentage of the bail amount, typically 10 percent, with the court. When the defendant appears in court, the deposit is returned, sometimes minus an administrative fee. If the defendant fails to appear, he or she is liable for the full amount of the bail.
7. Surety bail	The defendant pays a percentage of the bond, usually 10 percent, to a bonding agent who posts the full bail. The fee paid to the bonding agent is not returned to the defendant if he or she appears in court. The bonding agent is liable for the full amount of the bond should the defendant fail to appear. Bonding agents often require posting of collateral to cover the full bail amount.
8. Cash bail	The defendant pays the entire amount of bail set by the judge in order to secure release. The bail is returned to the defendant when he or she appears in court.

SOURCE: Adapted from Andy Hall, *Pretrial Release Program Options* (Washington, D.C.: National Institute of Justice, 1984), pp. 32–33.

Preventive Detention

Although only about 16 percent of bailees are rearrested for committing other crimes before trial, the threat they present to the public is disturbing. After all, about 2 million people are arrested each year for felony offenses; about 65 percent, or 1.3 million of them, receive bail. About 16 percent of bailees, or about 200,000 people, are arrested for new crimes.[39] Assuming a five to one ratio of crimes to arrests, it is possible that bailees may be responsible for 1 million serious crimes each year, or about 10 percent of the total number of serious Part I crimes committed in the United States.

Because of the concern over defendant misconduct while on bail, about 30 states have limited bail for certain offenses and offenders, such as those who previously absconded, are recidivists, or have violent histories. Similarly, the federal Bail Reform Act of 1984 provides that federal offenders may be detained without bail if "no condition or combination of conditions (of bail) will reasonably assure . . the safety of any other person and the community."[40]

The issue of preventive detention is particularly vexing because a person who has not been convicted of any crime is incarcerated for an extended period without the chance to participate in his or her own defense. Those supporting preventive detention argue that it helps control witness intimidation and reduces avoidable criminal acts.

In a landmark decision, *United States v. Salerno*, the Supreme Court upheld the Bail Reform Act's preventive detention provision on the grounds that its purpose was public safety, that it was not excessive for its stated purpose, and that it contained no punitive intent but was designed to regulate the behavior of accused criminals in a legally permissible way.[41] Similarly, in the case of *Schall v. Martin*, the court upheld a New York law providing for the preventive detention of a juvenile offender if the judicial authority believes the offender threatens community safety.[42]

An analysis of the federal Bail Reform Act shows that it increased the number of people held before trial. Before the act took effect, about 24 percent of all defendants were detained or did not make bail. After the act took effect, that number rose to 29 percent; 19 percent of the detainees did not qualify for bail consideration under the new guidelines.[43] Most of those held without bail had used firearms, were drug offenders, or had violated immigration laws.

Despite years of reform efforts, bail remains a troubling aspect of the criminal justice process. It is one of the few areas in which people are seriously penalized because of their economic circumstances. Whereas some defendants are kept in jail for lack of a few hundred dollars, others are released because they can afford bail in the millions. Those who cannot make bail face a greater chance of conviction and a harsher penalty if convicted.

■ Plea Bargaining

After arraignment it is common for the prosecution and defense to arrange a **plea bargain** to settle the case without the need for a trial. Overall, more than two-thirds of defendants in felony cases enter a guilty plea at some point, with 50 percent pleading guilty to a felony, and 15 percent to a misdemeanor.[44] The ways a bargain can be struck in exchange for a guilty plea are set out in Exhibit 17.7.

There are a number of different motivations for plea bargaining. Defendants, aware of the prosecutor's strong case, plea bargain to minimize their sentences and avoid the harmful effects of a criminal conviction. Some may plead guilty to protect accomplices or confederates by "taking the rap" themselves.[45]

The defense attorney may seek a bargain to limit his or her own involvement in the case. In some instances, defense attorneys may wish to increase their operating profits by minimizing the effort they put forth for an obviously guilty client.[46] In other instances, they may simply wish to adapt to the bureaucratic structure favorable to plea bargaining that exists in most U.S. criminal courts.[47] Defense

Exhibit 17.7   Methods of Plea Bargaining

- The initial charges may be reduced to those of a lesser offense, thus automatically reducing the sentence imposed. For example, a first-degree murder charge may be reduced to second-degree murder, eliminating the threat of the death penalty.
- The charge may be reduced from a felony to a misdemeanor. For example, a felony burglary charge may be reduced to breaking and entering, a misdemeanor for which time can be served in the local jail.
- In cases where there are multiple offenses or counts (multiple charges for the same crime, such as three rape accusations), only a single charge may be filed. For example, a person is accused of raping five women. By his pleading guilty on one charge, the other four are dropped. People convicted of a single crime are less likely to be given a long sentence than those convicted of several. A defendant who commits armed robbery may plead guilty to unarmed robbery. Possessing a gun during a robbery adds an automatic three years to the sentence, which the defendant can avoid with his or her plea.
- The prosecutor may promise to recommend a lenient sentence, such as probation or a short prison term, in exchange for a plea.
- When the charge imposed has a negative label attached (such as child molester), the prosecutor may alter the charge to a less damaging one (such as assault) in exchange for a plea of guilty.
- Prosecutors may promise to get a defendant into a specific treatment program in exchange for his or her plea. For example, a substance abuser may be promised admission into the state's detoxification unit in exchange for a guilty plea.

attorneys may wish to secure noncriminal dispositions for their clients, such as placement in a treatment program, and may advise them to plead guilty in exchange for this consideration.

The prosecution also can benefit from a plea bargain. The prosecutor's case may be weaker than hoped for, convincing him or her that a trial is too risky. A prosecutor may also believe the arresting officers made a serious procedural error in securing evidence that would be brought out during pretrial motions. When a defendant pleads guilty, it voids all prior constitutional errors made in that case. And, of course, no matter how strong the state's case, there is always the chance that a jury will render an unfavorable decision. Prosecutors also bargain to gain the cooperation of informers and codefendants.

Plea Bargaining Issues

Those who favor plea bargaining argue that it actually benefits both the state and the defendant for these reasons:

- The overall financial costs of criminal prosecution are reduced.
- The administrative efficiency of the courts is greatly improved.
- The prosecution is able to devote more time to cases of greater seriousness and importance.
- The defendant avoids possible detention and extended trial and may receive a reduced sentence.[48]

Thus, those who favor plea bargaining believe it is appropriate to enter into plea discussions where the effective administration of justice will be served.

It has been argued, however, that plea bargaining encourages defendants to waive their constitutional right to a trial. In addition, some experts suggest that sentences tend to be less severe in guilty plea situations than as a result of trials and that plea bargains result in even greater sentencing disparity.

Particularly in the eyes of the general public, plea bargaining allows the defendant to beat the system and further tarnishes the criminal justice process. Plea bargaining also raises the danger that an innocent person will be convicted of a crime if the individual is convinced that the lighter treatment resulting from a guilty plea is preferable to the possible risk of a harsher sentence following a formal trial. Some suggest that plea bargaining allows dangerous offenders to get off lightly and therefore weakens the deterrent effect of the criminal law.[49] It may also undermine public confidence in the law.[50]

Control of Plea Bargaining

It is unlikely that plea negotiations will be eliminated or severely curtailed in the near future. Those who support their total abolition are in the minority. As a result of abuses, however, efforts are being made to improve plea bargaining operations. Such reforms include the development of uniform plea practices, the presence of counsel during plea negotiations, and the establishment of time limits on plea negotiations.[51]

Some recent efforts have been made to convert plea bargaining into a more visible, understandable, and fair dispositional process. Safeguards and guidelines have been developed in many jurisdictions to prevent violations of due process and to ensure that innocent defendants do not plead guilty under coercion. For example, the judge questions the defendant about the facts of the guilty plea before accepting the plea; the defense counsel is present and able to advise the defendant of his or her rights. Open discussions about the plea occur between the prosecutor and the defense attorney; and full information regarding the offender and the offense is made available at this stage of the process. Judicial supervision is also an effective mechanism to ensure that plea bargaining is undertaken fairly.

The most extreme method of reforming plea bargaining has been to abolish it completely. A ban on plea bargaining has been tried in numerous jurisdictions throughout the country. Alaska eliminated the practice in 1975. In Honolulu, Hawaii, efforts were made to abolish plea bargaining. Jurisdictions in other states, including Iowa, Arizona, and Delaware, along with the District of Columbia, have also sought to limit the use of plea bargaining.[52] These jurisdictions give no consideration or concessions to the defendant in exchange for a guilty plea.

Efforts to control plea bargaining have met with mixed results. Evaluation of the Alaska experiment found that the number of guilty pleas did not change significantly after plea bargaining was eliminated, nor did the ban increase the prison sentences given to the most serious offenders.[53] This and similar efforts indicate that attempts to eliminate plea bargaining most likely move prosecutorial discretion further up in the system. For example, eliminating felony plea bargaining may cause prosecutors to automatically charge offenders with a misdemeanor so they can retain the option of offering them a "deal" in exchange for their cooperation before trial.

■ The Criminal Trial

The jury trial is relatively rare, but it is still one of the cornerstones of the criminal justice process. Although most criminal prosecutions result in plea bargains and do not involve the adversary determination of guilt or innocence, the trial process remains vitally important to the criminal justice system. The opportunity to go to trial guards against abuse of informal processing and encourages faith in the criminal justice system.[54] Because of its importance, jury trial stages, critical issues, and associated legal rights are discussed here.

Jury Selection

The first stage of the trial process involves jury selection. Jurors are selected randomly in both civil and criminal cases, usually from voter registration lists within each court's jurisdiction. The initial list of persons chosen, which is called a **venire** or **jury array,** provides the state with a group of citizens potentially capable of serving on a jury. Many states, by law, review the venire to eliminate unqualified persons and to exempt those who by reason of their professions are not allowed to be jurors; this latter group may include, but is not limited to, physicians, the clergy, and government officials. The actual jury selection process begins with those remaining on the list.

The court clerk, who handles the administrative affairs of the trial—including the processing of the complaint, the evidence, and other documents—randomly selects enough names to supply the required number of jurors. In most cases, a criminal trial jury consists of 12 persons, with two alternate jurors standing by to serve should one of the regular jurors be unable to complete the trial. Once the prospective jurors have been chosen, the process of **voir dire** begins: all persons selected are questioned by both the prosecution and the defense to determine their appropriateness to sit on the jury. They are examined under oath by the government, the defense, and sometimes the judge about their background, occupation, residence, and possible knowledge about or interest in the case. A juror who acknowledges any bias for or prejudice against the defendant—a juror who is a friend or relative of the defendant, for example, or who has already formed an opinion about the case—is **removed for cause** and replaced with another. Thus any prospective juror who reveals an inability to be impartial and render a verdict solely on the basis of the evidence presented at the trial may be removed by either the prosecution or the defense. Because normally no limit is placed on the number of challenges for cause that can be offered, it often takes considerable time to select a jury for controversial criminal cases.

In addition to challenges for cause, both the prosecution and the defense are allowed **peremptory challenges,** through which they can excuse jurors for no particular reason or for an undisclosed reason. For example, a prosecutor might not want a bartender as a juror in a drunken driving case, believing that a person in that occupation might be sympathetic to the accused. Or a defense attorney might excuse a male prospective juror to try to obtain a predominantly female jury for the client. The number of peremptory challenges permitted is limited by statute and often varies by case and jurisdiction.

The peremptory challenge has long been criticized by legal experts who question its fairness and propriety.[55] Of particular concern was the challenging of African American jurors in interracial crimes that resulted in the trying of African American defendants by all-white juries. In a significant case, *Batson v. Kentucky,* the Supreme Court ruled that the use of peremptory challenges to dismiss all black jurors violated the defendant's right to equal protection of the law.[56] Since *Batson,* the Supreme Court has further limited the use of peremptory challenges, including jury selection in civil trials and jury selection on the basis of gender.

Impartial Juries

The Sixth Amendment to the Constitution provides for the right to a speedy, public trial by an impartial jury. Throughout the 1960s and 1970s, the Supreme Court sought to ensure compliance with this constitutional mandate of impartiality through decisions eliminating racial discrimination in jury selection. For instance, in *Ham v. South Carolina* in 1973, the Court held that the defense counsel of an African American civil rights leader was entitled to question each juror on the issue of racial prejudice.[57] In *Turner v. Murray,* the Court ruled that African American defendants accused of murdering whites are entitled to have jurors questioned about their racial bias.[58] In *Taylor v. Louisiana,* the Court overturned the conviction of a man by an all-male jury because a Louisiana statute allowed women but not men to exempt themselves from jury duty.[59]

These and similar decisions have provided safeguards against jury bias. However, in many instances, potential jury bias is not part of the trial process. For example, while the Supreme Court in *Ham* ruled that bias was a consideration in a trial involving a civil rights worker, it ruled in another case that in "ordinary crimes"—noncapital cases, such as a robbery—defense counsel may not examine the racial bias of jurors even if the crime is interracial.[60]

The Trial Process

The trial of a criminal case is a formal process conducted in a specific, orderly fashion in accordance with rules of criminal law, procedure, and evidence (see Figure 17.5).

Unlike trials in popular television programs, where witnesses are often asked leading and prejudicial questions and where judges go far beyond their supervisory role, the modern criminal trial is a complicated and often time-consuming technical affair. It is a structured adversary proceeding in which both the prosecution and the defense follow specific rules and argue the merits of their cases before the judge and the jury. Each side seeks to present its case in the most favorable light. Where possible, the prosecutor and the defense attorney object to evidence they consider damaging to their individual points of view. The prosecutor uses direct testimony, physical evidence, and a confession, if available, to convince the jury that the accused is guilty beyond a reasonable doubt. The defense attorney rebuts the government's case with his or her own evidence, makes certain that the constitutional rights of the defendant are considered during all phases of the trial,

Figure 17.5 The Steps of a Jury Trial

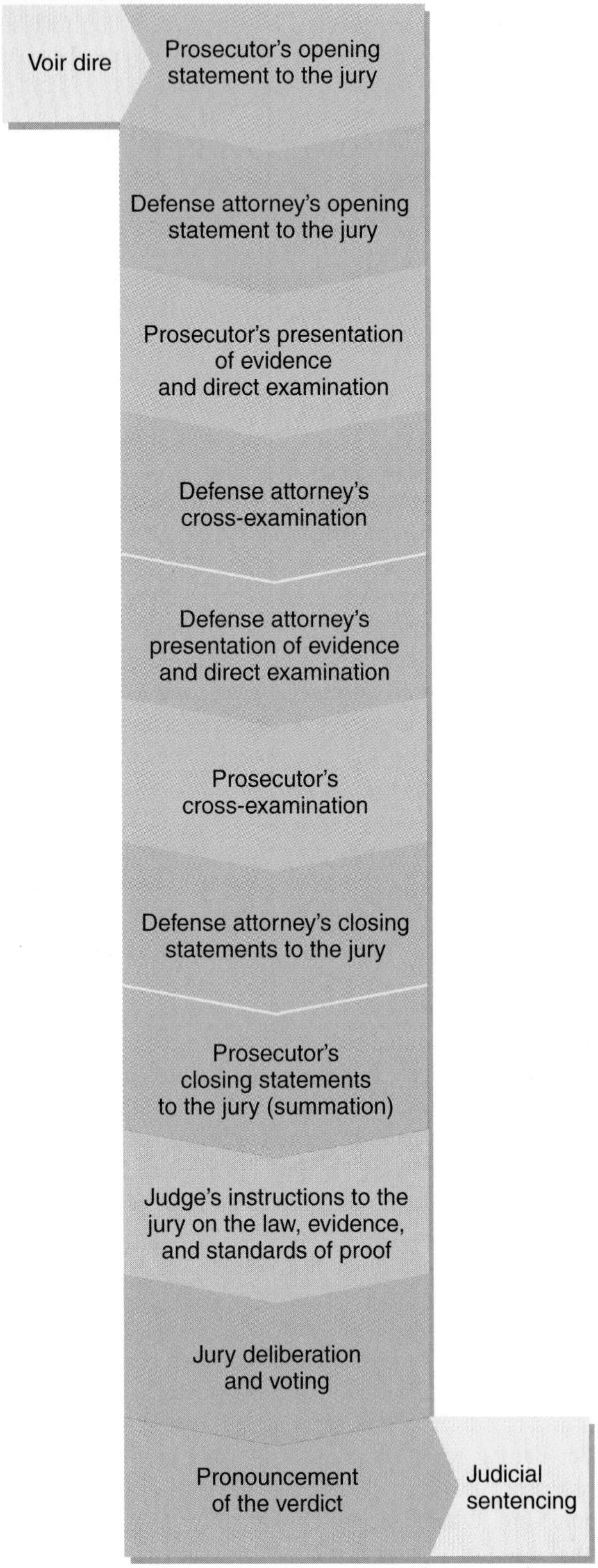

Voir dire

Prosecutor's opening statement to the jury

Defense attorney's opening statement to the jury

Prosecutor's presentation of evidence and direct examination

Defense attorney's cross-examination

Defense attorney's presentation of evidence and direct examination

Prosecutor's cross-examination

Defense attorney's closing statements to the jury

Prosecutor's closing statements to the jury (summation)

Judge's instructions to the jury on the law, evidence, and standards of proof

Jury deliberation and voting

Pronouncement of the verdict

Judicial sentencing

SOURCE: Marvin Zalman and Larry Siegel, *Criminal Procedure: Constitution and Society* (St. Paul, Minn.: West Publishing, 1991), p. 655.

and determines whether an appeal is appropriate if the client is found guilty. Throughout the process, the judge promotes an orderly, fair trial.

The basic steps of the criminal trial proceed as follows:

Opening statements: As the trial begins, both prosecution and defense address the jury and present their cases. They describe what they will attempt to prove and the major facts of the case. They introduce the witnesses, prepare the jury for their testimony, and tell them what information to listen for. The defense begins to emphasize that any doubts about the guilt of the accused must be translated into an acquittal; the prosecution dwells on civic duty and responsibility.

The prosecution's case: Following the opening statement, the government begins its case by presenting evidence to the court through its witnesses. Those called as witnesses—such as police officers, victims, or expert witnesses—provide testimony via **direct examination,** during which the prosecutor questions the witness to reveal the facts believed pertinent to the government case. Testimony involves what the witness actually saw, heard, or touched; it does not include opinions. However, a witness's opinion can be given in certain situations, such as in describing the motion of a vehicle or indicating whether a defendant appeared to act intoxicated or insane. Witnesses may also give their opinions if they are experts on a particular subject relevant to the case; for example, a psychiatrist may testify as to a defendant's mental capacity at the time of the crime.

Cross-examination: After the prosecutor finishes questioning a witness, the defense **cross-examines** the same witness by asking questions in an attempt to clarify the defendant's role in the crime. The prosecutor may seek a **redirect examination** after the defense attorney has completed cross-examination; this allows the prosecutor to ask additional questions about information brought out during cross-examination. Finally, the defense attorney may question or cross-examine the witness once again. All witnesses for the trial are sworn in and questioned in the same basic manner.

The defense's case: At the close of the prosecution's case, the defense may ask the presiding judge to rule on a motion for a **directed verdict.** If this motion is sustained, the judge directs the jury to acquit the defendant, thereby ending the trial. A directed verdict means that the prosecution did not present enough evidence to prove all the elements of the alleged crime. If the judge fails to sustain the motion, the defense presents its case. Witnesses are called to testify in the same manner used by the prosecution.

Rebuttal: After the defense concludes its case, the government may present **rebuttal evidence.** This normally involves bringing forward evidence that was not used when the prosecution initially presented its case. The defense may examine the rebuttal witnesses and introduce new witnesses in a process called surrebuttal. After all the evidence has been presented to the court, the defense attorney may again submit a motion for a directed verdict. If the motion is denied, both the prosecution and the defense prepare to make closing arguments; and the case on the evidence is ready for consideration by the jury.

Closing arguments: Closing arguments are used by the attorneys to review the facts and evidence of the case in a manner favorable to their positions. At this stage of the trial, both prosecution and defense are permitted to draw reasonable inferences and show how the facts prove or refute the defendant's guilt. Often both attorneys have a free hand in arguing about facts, issues, and evidence, including the applicable law. They cannot comment, however, on matters not in evidence, nor, where applicable, can they comment on the defendant's failure to testify. Normally, the defense attorney makes a closing statement first, followed by the prosecutor. Either party can elect to forgo the final summation to the jury.

Instructions to the jury: In a criminal trial, the judge instructs, or charges, the jury on the principles of law that ought to guide and control the decision on the defendant's innocence or guilt. Included in the charge is information about the elements of the alleged offense, the type of evidence needed to prove each element, and the burden of proof required to obtain a guilty verdict. Although the judge commonly provides the instructions, he or she may ask the prosecutor and the defense attorney to submit instructions for consideration; the judge then uses discretion in determining whether to use any of their instructions. The instructions that cover the law applicable to the case are extremely important because they may serve as the basis for a subsequent appeal.

One important aspect of instructing the jury is explaining the level of proof needed to find the person guilty of a crime. As mentioned, the U.S. system of justice requires guilt to be proved beyond a reasonable doubt. The judge must inform the jurors that if they have even the slightest suspicion that the defendant is not guilty, then they cannot find for the prosecution. Also, the judge must explain how, in criminal cases, the burden of proof is on the prosecution to prove the defendant guilty; the accused does not have to prove his or her innocence.

Verdict: Once the charge has been given to the jury, the jurors retire to deliberate on a verdict. The verdict in a criminal case is usually required to be unanimous. A review of the case by the jury may take hours or even days. The jurors are always sequestered during their deliberations; in some lengthy, highly publicized cases, they are kept overnight in a hotel until the verdict is reached. In less sensational cases, the jurors may be allowed to go home but are often cautioned not to discuss the case with anyone. If a verdict cannot be reached, the trial may result in a hung jury; in this case the prosecutor has to bring the defendant to trial again to get a conviction.

Sentence: If found not guilty, the defendant is released. If the defendant is convicted, the judge normally orders a presentence investigation by the probation department preparatory to imposing a sentence. Before sentencing, the defense attorney often submits a motion for a new trial, alleging that legal errors occurred in the trial proceedings. The judge may deny the motion and impose a sentence immediately, a practice quite common in most misdemeanor offenses. In felony cases, however, the judge sets a date for sentencing, and the defendant is either placed on bail or held in custody until that time. Sentencing usually occurs a short time after trial. At the sentencing hearing, the judge may consider evidence that is relevant to the case, including victim impact statements.[61] In most jurisdictions, typical criminal penalties include fines, community supervision, incarceration, and the death penalty.

Appeal: After sentencing, defendants have the right to appeal the case, charging either that the law under which they were tried was unconstitutional (for example, discriminatory or vague) or that the procedures used by agents of the justice system violated their constitutional rights (for example, police did not give them a proper Miranda warning, or improperly obtained evidence was used at trial). If the appeal is granted, a new trial may be ordered. If the appeal is not sustained, the convicted offender begins serving the sentence imposed, thus marking the end of the judicatory process.

■ Trials and the Rule of Law

Every trial has its constitutional issues, complex legal procedures, rules of court, and interpretations of statutes, all designed to ensure that the accused gets a fair trial. This section discusses the most important constitutional rights of the accused at trial and reviews the legal nature of the trial process.

Right to a Speedy and Public Trial

The Sixth Amendment guarantees a defendant the right to a speedy trial. This means that an accused is entitled to be tried within a reasonable period. If a person's right to a speedy trial is violated, then a complete dismissal of the charges against him or her is required according to *Strunk v. United States*.[62] The right to a speedy trial was made applicable to state courts through the due process clause of the Fourteenth Amendment in the case of *Klopfer v. North Carolina*.[63] It should be noted, however, that a defendant can waive the right to a speedy trial. A waiver of the right is implied when defendants cause the delay or when they do not assert their right when the trial takes too long to get under way.

There is no set standard of what constitutes a speedy trial, but the Federal Speedy Trial Act of 1974 mandates 30 days from arrest to indictment and 70 days from indictment to trial.

Right to a Jury Trial

Because a jury trial is considered a fundamental right, the Supreme Court, in the case of *Duncan v. Louisiana,* made the guarantee applicable to the states through the Fourteenth Amendment.[64] However, the question arises as to whether this right extends to all defendants—those charged with misdemeanors as well as felonies. The Supreme Court addressed this issue in the case of *Baldwin v. New York,* in which it decided that defendants are entitled to a jury trial only if they face the possibility of a prison sentence of more than six months.[65] Later, in *Blanton v. City of North Las Vegas,* the Court upheld the six month–plus jail sentence requirement for a jury trial but did not rule out that a lesser term accompanied by the possibility of other punishment, such as a large fine or loss of a driver's license for a year, might warrant a jury trial.[66]

Although most people think of a jury as having 12 members and, historically, most have had 12, the Sixth Amendment does not specify a jury size. In fact, in the case of *Williams v. Florida,* the Supreme Court held that a six-person jury fulfilled a defendant's right to a trial by jury.[67] However, a unanimous verdict is required when a six-person jury is used. When a 12-person jury is used, the Supreme Court has maintained that the Sixth Amendment does not require a unanimous verdict, except in first-degree murder cases. In *Apodica v. Oregon,* the Court found constitutional an Oregon statute that required a finding of guilt by 10 out of 12 jurors in cases of assault with a deadly weapon, burglary, and larceny.[68] However, it should be noted that the majority of states and the federal courts still require a unanimous verdict.

Right to Be Free from Double Jeopardy

The Fifth Amendment provides that no person shall "be subject for the same offense to be twice put in jeopardy of life or limb." This means that a defendant cannot be prosecuted by a jurisdiction more than once for a single offense. For example, if a defendant is tried and acquitted of murder in Texas, he cannot be tried again for the same murder in Texas. The right to be protected from **double**

jeopardy was made applicable to the states through the Fourteenth Amendment in the case of *Benton v. Maryland*.[69] However, a person tried in federal court can be tried in state court, and vice versa.[70] And in 1985 the Court ruled in *Heath v. Alabama* that if a single act violates the laws of two states the offender may be punished for each offense under the **dual sovereignty doctrine:** legal jurisdictions have the right to enforce their own laws, and a single act can violate the laws of two separate jurisdictions.[71]

Right to Legal Counsel

Regardless of the legal rights citizens command at trial, without legal counsel to aid them, they would be rendered defenseless before the law. Consequently, the Sixth Amendment provides the right to be represented by an attorney in criminal trials. However, the vast majority of criminal defendants are indigents who cannot afford private legal services. In a series of cases beginning in the 1930s, the U.S. Supreme Court established the defendant's right to be represented by an attorney and, in the event he or she cannot pay for representation, to have the state provide free legal services. First, in *Powell v. Alabama,* the Court held that an attorney was essential in capital cases where the defendant's life was at stake.[72] Then, in the critically important case of *Gideon v. Wainwright,* the Court granted the absolute right to counsel in all felony cases.[73] Finally, in *Argersinger v. Hamlin,* the defendant's right to counsel in misdemeanor cases was established.[74]

Right to Confront Witnesses

The accused has the right to confront witnesses to challenge their assertions and perceptions: Did they really hear what they thought they did? Or see what they think they saw? Are they biased? Honest? Trustworthy?

An important confrontation issue is the ability to shield child witnesses from the trauma of a court appearance. In *Maryland v. Craig,* the Supreme Court ruled that child witnesses could testify via closed-circuit television as long as safeguards were set up to protect the defendant's rights.[75] Protections included the defendant being able to view the witness and being in communication with the witness's attorney at all times.

■ Sentencing

After a defendant has been found guilty of a criminal offense or has pleaded guilty, he or she is brought before the court for imposition of a criminal penalty—sentencing. Historically, a full range of punishment has been meted out to criminal offenders: corporal punishment, such as whipping or mutilation; fines; banishment; incarceration; and death.

In U.S. society, incarceration in a federal, state, or local institution is generally the most serious penalty given out

Exhibit 17.8 The Goals of Sentencing

Deterrence	By punishing known offenders for their misdeeds, society hopes to convince would-be offenders that the pains of punishment outweigh the potential benefits of criminal behavior. The validity of deterrence rests on the premise that punishing one offender will convince other potential criminals to abstain from crime. According to deterrence theory, people are not punished for what they have done but for the effect their punishment will have on the future behavior of others.
Incapacitation	By incapacitating convicted offenders in a secure facility, such as a prison or jail, the state seeks to reduce or eliminate their opportunity to commit future crimes. In some instances, incapacitation involves supervising offenders while they remain in the community. It is hoped that close monitoring will restrict opportunities to commit future crime without the necessity of secure lockup. Incapacitation involves anticipating behavior patterns: offenders are confined not for what they have done but for what it is feared they might do in the future.
Rehabilitation	Correctional rehabilitation is aimed at reducing future criminality by treating and eliminating the underlying causes of crime. Offenders are believed to have one or more emotional and/or behavioral deficits, which cause them to violate the law. Criminal behavior would cease if this problem can be successfully treated. Rehabilitation efforts focus on emotional stress, vocational training, education, or substance abuse. Rehabilitation also involves predicting future behavior: unless the offenders receive treatment, they will commit future crimes; treatment reduces the likelihood of their reoffending.
Desert/retribution	Because of their heinous acts, criminals deserve to be punished. Furthermore, if the state did not punish people for their misconduct (retribution), victims would be encouraged to seek personal vengeance for their loss (revenge), creating a chaotic society. In a just society, criminals are punished in a manner proportionate to the severity of their crimes. According to this view, it is only fair that criminals who have committed the most serious crime, murder, receive the most severe penalty, death.
Equity/restitution	Because criminals gain from their misdeeds, it seems both fair and just to demand that they reimburse society for the loss caused by their crimes. In the early common law, wergild and fines represented the concept of creating an equitable solution to crime by requiring the convicted offender to make restitution to both the victim and the state. The equity goal of punishment means that convicted criminals must pay back their victims for their loss, the justice system for the costs of processing their case, and society for any disruption they may have caused.

to offenders. In addition, the death penalty remains on the statute books of most jurisdictions and has been used at an increasing rate in recent years.

Purposes of Sentencing

On January 18, 2002, Sara Jane Olson was sentenced to 20 years to life in prison for her role in a failed bomb plot to kill Los Angeles police officers in 1975.[76] Then known as Kathy Soliah, a member of the radical Symbonese Liberation Army, Olson escaped capture and fled to Minnesota, where she led a quiet life. She married a doctor, raised a family, and became an upstanding member of the community, engaging in many charitable works. Why should this now middle-aged woman be sent to prison for a failed crime committed more than 25 years ago?

In general, five major goals—deterrence, incapacitation, rehabilitation, equity, and desert/retribution—are associated with imposition of a sentence.[77] These are examined in Exhibit 17.8.

Each of these sentencing goals is considered when a person is sentenced. A judge may consider someone like

Sarah Jane Olson as being a changed person who poses no threat to the community and sentence her to community service. Or a judge may feel that she remains a danger to others and needs to be confined in a secure setting such as a state prison. A judge may also believe that too lenient a sentence might encourage other radicals to engage in terrorism and that strict punishment may deter others from committing similar crimes. It is also possible that the judge may conclude that the defendant deserves to be punished for the harm inflicted on society and/or that the individual somehow benefited from the crime and must now be made to pay back those who have been harmed.

Sentencing Dispositions

Generally, five kinds of sentences or dispositions are available to the court: fines, probation, alternative or intermediate sanctions, incarceration, and capital punishment.

A **fine** is usually exacted for a minor crime and may also be combined with other sentencing alternatives, such as probation or confinement.[78] **Probation** allows the offender to live in the community subject to compliance

CHAPTER 17 ■ The Judiciary Process   **535**

with legally imposed conditions. **Alternative sanctions** involve probation plus some other sanction, such as house arrest, electronic monitoring, or forfeiture of property. Confinement, or **incarceration,** is imposed when it has been decided that the general public needs to be protected from further criminal activity by the defendant. **Capital punishment** or the death penalty is reserved for people who commit first-degree murder under aggravated circumstances, such as with extreme cruelty, violence, or torture.

Imposing the Sentence

Sentencing is one of the most crucial functions of judges. Sentencing authority may also be exercised by the jury, an administrative body, or a group of judges, or it may be mandated by statute.

In most felony cases, except where the law dictates **mandatory prison terms,** sentencing is usually based on a variety of information available to the judge. Some jurisdictions allow victims to make **impact statements** that are considered at sentencing hearings, although these often have little impact on sentencing outcomes.[79] Most judges consider a **presentence investigation report** by the probation department. This report, which is a social and personal history as well as an evaluation of the defendant, is used by the judge in making a sentencing decision.[80] Some judges heavily weigh the presentence investigation report; others may dismiss it completely or rely on only certain portions.

When an accused is convicted of two or more charges, he or she must be sentenced on each charge. A **concurrent sentence** means that both sentences are served at the same time, and the term of imprisonment is completed after the longest term has been served. For example, a defendant is sentenced to 3 years' imprisonment on a charge of assault and 10 years for burglary, the sentences to be served concurrently. After the offender serves 10 years in prison, the sentences would be completed. Conversely, a **consecutive sentence** means that upon completion of one sentence, the other term of incarceration begins. For example, a defendant sentenced to 10 years' imprisonment on a charge of rape, 3 years for possession of a handgun, and 4 years for drug possession, the sentences to be served consecutively, would serve a total of 17 years. In most instances sentences are given concurrently.

■ Sentencing Structures

When a convicted offender is sentenced to prison, the statutes of the jurisdiction in which the crime was committed determine the penalties that may be imposed by the court. Over the years, a variety of sentencing structures have been used, including indeterminate sentences, determinate sentences, and mandatory sentences.

■ Former Symbionese Liberation Army fugitive Sara Jane Olson (left) weeps as her mother, Elsie Soliah, comes over to embrace her after speaking on Olson's behalf during a sentencing hearing January 18, 2002, in Los Angeles. With friends and family sobbing in the courtroom, Olson was sentenced to 20 years to life in prison for conspiring to blow up police cars in 1975. Immediately afterward, Olson pleaded innocent to robbery and murder charges in another decades-old crime, the 1975 SLA bank holdup in which a bystander, Myrna Opsahl, was killed. Should a person be punished for her or his misdeeds even if the crime that was committed occurred many years ago and the defendant has turned over a new leaf? Is it fair to give someone lenient treatment simply because the person has successfully evaded capture?

Indeterminate Sentences

The first U.S. prison sentences were for a fixed period that the offender was forced to serve before release. Harsh prison conditions and rules enforced by physical punishment left inmates with little incentive for rehabilitation or self-improvement. During the latter half of the nineteenth century, reformers attempted to apply progressive views of human behavior and change to the penal system and called for modernization in sentencing laws. What developed over the next 50 years was a type of **indeterminate sentence** with very brief minimums and very long maximums, allowing inmates to be released as soon as a parole board concluded they were rehabilitated.

The indeterminate sentence is still used in a majority of states. Under most sentencing models, convicted offenders who are not eligible for community supervision are given a short minimum sentence that must be served and a lengthy maximum sentence that is the outer boundary of the time that can possibly be served. For example, the legislature might set a sentence of a minimum of 1 year and a maximum of 20 years for burglary.

Under this scheme, the actual length of time served is controlled by the corrections agency. The inmate can be paroled after serving the minimum sentence whenever the institution and parole personnel believe he or she is ready

536   PART IV ■ *The Criminal Justice System*

to live in the community. The minimum (or maximum) might also be reduced by inmates earning "time off for good behavior" or for participating in counseling and vocational training programs. In many instances, sentencing reduction programs enable inmates to serve only a fraction of their minimum sentences. Inmates today serve about one-third of their original sentence.

Most jurisdictions that use indeterminate sentences specify minimum and maximum terms but allow judges discretion to fix the actual sentence within those limits. For example, if burglary is punishable by a sentence of 2 to 20 years, the judge can give one offender 5 to 10 and another 2 to 5 years. The sentence must be no less than the minimum nor more than the maximum range of years set by the legislature.

The underlying purpose of indeterminate sentencing is to individualize each sentence in the interests of rehabilitating the offender. This type of sentencing allows for flexibility not only in the type of sentence imposed but also in the length of time served.

Determinate Sentences

Determinate sentences were actually the first kind used in the United States. As originally constructed, the judge could impose a sentence, based on personal and professional judgment, that fell within limits set by statute. For example, a state criminal code could set the sentence for burglary at up to 20 years in prison. After evaluating the case, the judge could impose a sentence of 5 years on a

■ Marjorie Knoller, shown here, was charged with manslaughter and second-degree murder in the San Francisco dog mauling trial. California, a determinate sentencing state, allows sentences to be reduced by "time off for good behavior." Sentencing reduction programs allow inmates to serve only a fraction of their sentences. Such programs enable convicted killers to reduce their sentences and reenter the community.

first-time defendant, 10 on a more experienced criminal, and the full 20 on a third who may have been a repeater and carried a weapon to the crime scene. Unlike the indeterminate models in which release dates are controlled by correctional authorities, in a determinate sentence the duration of the offender's prison stay is determined by the judiciary when the sentence is imposed.

When the original determinate sentencing statutes were replaced by indeterminate sentences early in the twentieth century, judicial discretion remained quite broad. Both determinate and indeterminate sentences allowed judges to place one defendant on probation while sentencing another to a lengthy prison term for essentially the same crime. Such unbridled discretion allowed disparity and unfairness in the sentencing process. In addition, indeterminate sentences gave correctional authorities quasi-judicial power, allowing them to decide when an inmate was to be returned to society.[81] Correctional discretion could then be used to control the inmate population.[82]

In response to these concerns, a number of jurisdictions replaced indeterminate sentences and discretionary parole with a system of determinate sentencing that featured a single term of years without discretionary parole. Earned good time can reduce sentences, in some cases, by up to one-half. These modern versions of determinate sentencing reflect an orientation toward desert, deterrence, and equality at the expense of treatment and rehabilitation. Most jurisdictions have attempted to structure judicial decision making by suggesting appropriate prison terms for particular crimes.[83]

Structured Sentencing

To ensure that the new determinate sentences would be applied in a fair manner, those jurisdictions that embraced determinate sentencing have also sought to develop guidelines to control and structure the sentencing process and make it more "rational." **Sentencing guidelines** are usually based on the seriousness of a crime and the background of an offender: the more serious the crime and the more extensive the offender's criminal background, the longer the prison term recommended by the guidelines. For example, guidelines might require that all people convicted of robbery who had no prior offense record and who did not use excessive force or violence be given an average of a five-year sentence; those who used force and had a prior record will have three years added on their sentence. Guidelines eliminate discretionary parole but also allow inmates to reduce their sentence by acquiring time off for good behavior. By eliminating judicial discretion, these guidelines are designed to reduce racial and gender disparity.[84]

How are guidelines used? Today 17 states and the federal government use some form of structured sentencing. In the 7 "voluntary / advisory sentencing guidelines states," the guidelines (sometimes called "descriptive guidelines") are used merely to suggest rather than mandate sentencing. In the 10 "presumptive sentencing guidelines states," judges are required to use the guidelines (sometimes called "prescriptive guidelines") to shape their sentencing decisions, and these sentencing decisions may be open to appellate review if judges stray from the mandated sentences. Michigan, Washington, Oregon, Pennsylvania, Minnesota, North Carolina, and the federal government mandate that judges follow a set of comprehensive guidelines.[85]

The United States Sentencing Commission, an independent federal agency in the judicial branch of government, has a number of duties including developing guidelines for sentencing in federal courts; collecting data about crime and sentencing; and serving as a resource to Congress, the Executive Branch, and the Judiciary on crime and sentencing policy. Visit their Web site at:
>   **http://www.ussc.gov/**
>   For an up-to-date list of Web links, go to
>   **http://info.wadsworth.com/siegel** ∎

Prescriptive guidelines are created by appointed sentencing commissions. The commission members determine what an "ideal" sentence would be for a particular crime and offender. There is, however, a great deal of variation within prescriptive sentencing. Some guidelines coexist with parole release, and some do not. Some deal with all crimes, and others only with felonies. Some set narrow sentencing ranges, and some set broad ones. Some address sentences of all types, and some address only state prison sentences.[86] North Carolina, Pennsylvania, and Ohio employ what is known as a "comprehensive structured sentencing system," which sets sentencing standards for felonies and misdemeanors and for prison, jail, intermediate, and community punishments. They also include mechanisms for tying sentencing policy to correctional capacity and for distributing state funds to stimulate and support local corrections programs.[87]

Configuring guidelines   There are a number of ways to formulate guidelines. One method is to create a grid with prior record and current offense as the two coordinates and setting out specific punishments. Table 17.1 shows Minnesota's guidelines. Note that as prior record and offense severity increase, so does recommended sentence length. After a certain point, probation is no longer an option, and the defendant must do prison time. A burglar with no prior convictions can expect to receive probation or an 18-month sentence for a house break-in; an experienced burglar with six or more prior convictions can get 54 months for the same crime, and probation is not an option.

Future of structured sentencing   Despite the widespread acceptance of guidelines, some nagging problems remain. Research indicates that judges sometimes diverge from the guidelines.[88] Legislators have also backtracked on guidelines, creating loopholes that undercut their determinacy, such as allowing for early release from prison by administrative order.[89]

The federal guidelines have also been criticized because they punish possession of crack cocaine much more heavily than powdered cocaine; the former is a crime associated with African American offenders and the latter with white offenders.[90] The federal guidelines also require incarceration sentences for minor crimes that, in preguideline days, would have been eligible for a probationary sentence.[91]

The Coalition for Federal Sentencing Reform is a private group of individuals and organizations united by a concern that the Federal Sentencing Guidelines are not fulfilling their promise, and by a desire for reform. To find out their reasons, go to:
>   **http://www.sentencing.org/**
>   For an up-to-date list of Web links, go to
>   **http://info.wadsworth.com/siegel** ∎

Some defense attorneys oppose the use of guidelines because they result in longer prison terms, prevent judges from considering mitigating circumstances, and reduce the use of probation. However, there is little evidence that states using determinate sentences have experienced an above-normal increase in their prison populations, and in at least two states that use guidelines, Minnesota and Washington, prison populations have been reduced.[92]

The ultimate test of guidelines or other determinate sentencing models is whether they can ease crime rates. So far there is little evidence that these laws alone reduce the incidence of crime.[93]

Mandatory Sentences

Another effort to limit judicial discretion has been the development of mandatory (minimum) sentences that require the incarceration of all offenders convicted of specific crimes. Some states, for example, exclude offenders convicted of certain offenses, such as drug trafficking or handgun crimes, from even the possibility of being placed on probation; some exclude recidivists; and others bar certain offenders from being considered for parole. Mandatory sentencing generally limits the judge's discretionary power to impose any disposition but that authorized by the legislature.

Mandatory sentencing legislation may supplement an indeterminate sentencing structure or be a feature of structured sentencing. For example, in Massachusetts, which uses indeterminate sentencing, conviction for possessing an unregistered handgun brings with it a mandatory prison term of at least one year.[94]

Severity Level of Conviction Offense		Criminal History Score						
		0	1	2	3	4	5	6 or more
Murder, 2nd degree (intentional murder; drive-by-shootings)	X	306 *299–313*	326 *319–333*	346 *339–353*	366 *359–373*	386 *379–393*	406 *399–413*	426 *419–433*
Murder, 3rd degree Murder, 2nd degree (unintentional murder)	IX	150 *144–156*	165 *159–171*	180 *174–186*	195 *189–201*	210 *204–216*	225 *219–231*	240 *234–246*
Criminal sexual conduct, 1st degree† Assault, 1st degree	VIII	86 *81–91*	98 *93–103*	110 *105–115*	122 *117–127*	134 *129–139*	146 *141–151*	158 *153–163*
Aggravated robbery, 1st degree	VII	48 *44–52*	58 *54–62*	68 *64–72*	78 *74–82*	88 *84–92*	98 *94–102*	108 *104–112*
Criminal sexual conduct, 2nd degree (a) & (b)	VI	21	27	33	39 *37–41*	45 *43–47*	51 *49–53*	57 *55–59*
Residential burglary Simple robbery	V	18	23	28	33 *31–35*	38 *36–40*	43 *41–45*	48 *46–50*
Nonresidential burglary	IV	12*	15	18	21	24 *23–25*	27 *26–28*	30 *29–31*
Theft crimes (over $2,500)	III	12*	13	15	17	19 *18–20*	22 *20–22*	23 *22–24*
Theft crimes ($2,500 or less) Check forgery ($200–$2,500)	II	12*	12*	13	15	17	19	21 *20–22*
Sale of simulated controlled substance	I	12*	12*	12*	13	15	17	19 *18–20*

Italicized numbers within the grid denote the range within which a judge may sentence without the sentence being deemed a departure. Offenders with nonimprisonment felony sentences are subject to jail time according to law.

*One year and one day.

†Pursuant to M.S.• 609.342, subd. 2, the presumptive sentence for Criminal Sexual Conduct in the First Degree is a minimum of 144 months (see II.C. Presumptive Sentence and II.G. Convictions for Attempts, Conspiracies, and Other Sentence Modifiers).

☐ Presumptive commitment to state imprisonment. First-degree murder is excluded from the guidelines by law and continues to have a mandatory life sentence. See section II.E. Mandatory Sentences for policy regarding those sentences controlled by law, including minimum periods of supervision for sex offenders released from prison.

☐ Presumptive stayed sentence; at the discretion of the judge, up to a year in jail and/or other nonjail sanctions can be imposed as conditions of probation. However, certain offenses in this section of the grid always carry a presumptive commitment to a state prison. These offenses include 3rd-degree controlled substance crimes when the offender has a prior felony drug conviction, burglary of an occupied dwelling when the offender has a prior felony burglary conviction, second and subsequent criminal sexual conduct offenses, and offenses carrying a mandatory minimum prison term due to the use of a dangerous weapon (e.g., 2nd-degree assault). See sections II.C. Presumptive Sentence and II.E. Mandatory Sentences.

SOURCE: Minnesota Sentencing Guideline Commission, 2001.

Some critics charge that mandatory sentences are overly restrictive and that prosecutors and judges are reluctant to use them because the penalties are too severe. For example, research shows that armed drug traffickers are rarely charged with possession of handguns because judges and prosecutors believe that, given the already severe sentences for drugs, the additional mandatory prison sentence for carrying a firearm would be a matter of overkill.[95]

Truth in sentencing   First enacted in 1984, **truth-in-sentencing laws** require offenders to serve a substantial portion of their prison sentence behind bars.[96] Parole eligibility and good-time credits are restricted or eliminated. The truth-in-sentencing movement has been a response to prison crowding that in some instances has forced the early release of inmates from overcrowded institutions. The Violent Offender Incarceration and Truth-in-Sentencing Incentive Grants Program in the 1994 Crime Act offered the states funds to support the costs of longer sentences.[97] To qualify for federal funds, states must require persons convicted of violent felony crimes to serve not less than 85 percent of their prison sentences. More than 27 states and the District of Columbia met the federal Truth-in-Sentencing Incentive Grant Program eligibility criteria.[98] It is ironic that the United States is embracing these extremely punitive sentencing policies at the same time many other Western nations are moving in the opposite direction by employing more humane, moderate criminal punishments such as fines and community sentencing orders.[99]

Three strikes laws   During his lifetime, Michael Riggs had been convicted eight times in California for such offenses as car theft and robbery. In 1996 he was once again in trouble, this time for shoplifting a $20 bottle of vitamins. Riggs was sentenced to a term of 25 years to life under California's "three strikes" law and must serve a minimum of 20.8 years before parole eligibility. Without the three strikes law, he would ordinarily have earned a maximum sentence of six months; if he had been convicted of murder he would have had to serve only 17 years. Riggs appealed his conviction to the Supreme Court in 1999, but the justices refused to rule on the case, letting his sentence stand.[100]

Public concern over crime has convinced lawmakers to toughen sentences for repeat offenders. One new group of laws mandates lengthy periods of incarceration for repeat offenders, which in some cases can mean a life sentence for a minor felony.[101] The new "three strikes and you're out" laws provide these lengthy terms for any person convicted of three felony offenses, even if the third crime is relatively trivial. California's three strikes statute is aimed at getting habitual criminals off the street. Anyone convicted of a third felony must do a minimum term of 25 years to life; the third felony does not have to be serious or violent.[102] The Federal Crime Bill of 1994 also

adopted a three strikes and you're out provision, requiring a mandatory life sentence for any offender convicted of three felony offenses; 22 states have followed suit.

Although welcomed by conservatives looking for a remedy for violent crime, the three strikes policy is quite controversial because it can give a life sentence to a person convicted of an extremely minor felony. There are reports that some judges are defying three strikes provisions because they consider them unduly harsh. A study by the Rand Corporation concluded that the state's three strikes law may actually reduce serious felonies by between 22 and 34 percent. However, the price of this reduction is an extra $4.5 billion to $6.5 billion per year in correctional costs in California alone.[103] Three strikes laws are now being challenged legally, and their future is uncertain.

The Sentencing Project Web site is designed to provide resources and information for the news media and a public concerned with criminal justice and sentencing issues. Go to their site at:
 http://www.sentencingproject.org/
For an up-to-date list of Web links, go to
 http://info.wadsworth.com/siegel ■

How People Are Sentenced

Some of the most important information about how people are sentenced comes from national studies sponsored by the Bureau of Justice Statistics.[104] In 1998 (the most recent data available), state courts convicted a combined total of nearly 930,000 adults of felonies (federal courts convicted another 50,000 felons). As Table 17.2 shows, 68 percent of all felons convicted in state courts were sentenced to a period of confinement (44 percent to state prisons and 24 percent to local jails); 32 percent of convicted felons went straight to probation with no jail or prison time to serve. Those convicted felons sentenced to a state prison had an average sentence of five years but were likely to serve less than half (47 percent) of that sentence, or just over two years, before release; the average sentence to local jail was six months.

Though the crime rate has dropped, the correctional population continues to rise. One reason may be because the amount of time spent behind bars before release has been increasing. In 1988 the typical felon received a six-year sentence and served about two years, or a third of that sentence, before being released. By contrast, in 1998 the typical felon received a five-year sentence and served about half of that before being released, or 2.5 years. In 1988 the average murderer spent 79 months in prison, whereas by 1998 they were averaging 136 months. The increased time spent behind bars may in part be due to the passage of tough sentencing laws, which require offenders to spend a considerable portion of their sentence behind bars.

Table 17.2 Type of Felony Sentence Imposed by State Courts, Mean Prison Sentence, and Estimated Time to Be Served

Most Serious Conviction Offense	Total Incarcerated (%)	Sentenced to Prison (%)	Of Those Sentenced to Prison			Sentenced to Jail (%)	Sentenced to Probation (%)
			Mean Prison Sentence (months)	Sentence Served in Prison (%)	Time Incarcerated (months)		
All offenses	68	44	57	47	27	24	32
Violent offenses	78	59	100	54	54	19	22
Murder	96	94	263	52	136	2	4
Sexual assault	82	67	111	56	62	15	18
Rape	84	70	147	58	81	14	16
Other sexual assault	80	64	88	55	45	16	20
Robbery	88	76	106	51	54	12	12
Aggravated assault	72	46	66	57	38	26	28
Other violent	67	41	56	55	31	26	33
Property offenses	65	43	44	45	20	22	35
Burglary	75	54	52	45	24	21	25
Larceny	64	40	37	45	17	24	36
Motor vehicle theft	76	43	35	43	15	33	24
Fraud	55	35	40	42	17	20	45
Drug offenses	68	42	47	41	19	26	32
Possession	65	36	35	40	14	29	35
Trafficking	71	45	54	41	22	26	29
Weapon offenses	66	42	42	60	25	24	34
Other offenses	63	35	40	51	20	28	37

SOURCE: *State Court Sentencing of Convicted Felons, 1998* (Washington, D.C.: Bureau of Justice Statistics, 2001).

Sentencing Disparity

Sentencing disparity has long been a problem in the justice system. Simply put, it is common for people convicted of similar criminal acts to receive widely different sentences. For example, one person convicted of burglary receives a three-year prison sentence, whereas another is granted probation. Few defendants actually serve their entire sentences, causing even greater disparity. Such differences seem to violate the constitutional rights of due process and equal protection. State sentencing codes usually include various factors that can legitimately influence the length of prison sentences, including these:

- How severe the offense is
- The offender's prior criminal record
- Whether the offender used violence
- Whether the offender used weapons
- Whether the crime was committed for money

Research in fact shows a strong correlation between these legal variables and the type and length of sentence received. For example, judges seem less willing to use discretion in cases involving the most serious criminal charges, such as terrorism, while employing greater control in minor cases.[105]

The suspicion remains, however, that such extralegal factors as age, race, gender, and economic status influence sentencing outcomes. These extralegal factors appear to influence sentencing because the inmate population is disproportionately male, African American, young, and lower class. Although this phenomenon may be a result of discrimination, it could also be simply a function of existing crime patterns—males, minorities, and members of the lower class commit the crimes that are most likely to result in prison sentences (homicide, rape, armed robbery, and so on).

Numerous studies have been conducted to determine the cause of sentencing disparity in the United States.[106]

Race and Sentencing

Although critics of American race relations may think otherwise, research on sentencing has failed to show a definitive pattern of racial discrimination. Some works do indicate that a defendant's race has a direct impact on sentencing outcomes, but other efforts show that the influence of race on sentencing is less clear-cut than anticipated. It is possible that the disproportionate number of minority group members in prison are a result of crime and arrest patterns and not racial bias by judges when they hand out criminal sentences; racial and ethnic minorities commit more crime, the argument goes, and therefore they are more likely to wind up in prison.

Despite this inconclusive evidence, racial disparity in sentencing has been suspected because a disproportionate number of minority inmates are in state prisons and on death row. Research efforts show that minority defendants suffer discrimination in a variety of court actions: they are more likely to be detained before trial than whites and, upon conviction, are more likely to receive jail sentences rather than fines. Prosecutors are less likely to divert minorities from the legal system than whites who commit the same crimes; minorities are less likely to win *appeals* than white appellants.

The relationship between race and sentencing may be difficult to establish because their association may not be linear: while minority defendants may be punished more severely for some crimes, and under some circumstances, they are treated leniently for others. The most recent sentencing data indicate that minorities do in fact receive longer and harsher sentences for some crimes (such as robberies), but whites actually receive longer sentences for other criminal offenses (such as drug trafficking).

Sociologist Darnell Hawkins explains this phenomenon as a matter of "appropriateness":

Certain crime types are considered less "appropriate" for blacks than for whites. Blacks who are charged with committing these offenses will be treated more severely than blacks who commit crimes that are considered more "appropriate." Included in the former category are various white-collar offenses and crimes against political and social structures of authority. The latter groups of offenses would include various forms of victimless crimes associated with lower social status (e.g., prostitution, minor drug use, or drunkenness). This may also include various crimes against the person, especially those involving black victims.

Race may have an impact on sentencing because some race-specific crimes are punished more harshly than others. For example, as noted under the federal sentencing guidelines, African Americans receive longer sentences for drug crimes than whites because (a) they are more likely to be arrested for crack possession and sales and (b) crack dealing is more severely punished under the guidelines than is possession or sale of powered cocaine. Also, because whites are more likely to use marijuana and methamphetamines, prosecutors are more willing to plea bargain and offer shorter jail terms for these crimes.

Racial bias has also been linked to the victim–offender status. Minority defendants are sanctioned more severely if their victim is white than if their target is a fellow minority group member; minorities who kill whites are more likely to get the death penalty than those who kill other minorities. Judges may base sentencing decisions on the race of the victim and not the race of the defendant. For example, Charles Crawford, Ted Chiricos, and Gary Kleck found that African American defendants are more likely to be prosecuted under habitual offender statutes if they commit crimes where there is a greater likelihood of a white victim (for example, larceny and burglary) than if they commit violent crimes which are largely intraracial. Where there is a perceived "racial threat" due to interracial crime, punishments are enhanced.

System Effects

Sentencing disparity may also reflect race-based differences in criminal justice practices and policies associated with sentencing outcome. Probation presentence reports may favor white over minority defendants, causing judges to award whites probation more often than minorities. Whites are more likely to receive probation in jurisdictions where African Americans and whites receive prison sentences of similar duration; this is referred to as the "in-out" decision.

Defendants who can afford bail receive more lenient sentences than those who remain in pretrial detention; minority defendants are less likely to make bail because they suffer a higher degree of income inequality. That is, minorities earn less on average and therefore are less likely to be able to make bail. Sentencing out-

---

Some have found a pattern of racial discrimination in sentencing, whereas others indicate that class bias exists.[107] There is also considerable evidence being assembled that the race and class of the victim, not the offender, may be the most important factor in sentencing decisions. Crimes involving a white victim seem to be more heavily punished than those in which a minority group member is the target.[108] Sentencing disparity is the topic of the Race, Culture, Gender, and Criminology feature titled "Race and Sentencing."

■ The Death Penalty

Although the execution of convicted criminals has been common throughout human history, it is a topic that has

come is also affected by the defendant's ability to afford a private attorney and to put on a vigorous legal defense that makes use of high-paid expert witnesses. These factors place the poor and minority group members at a disadvantage in the sentencing process and result in sentencing disparity. And while considerations of prior record may be legitimate in forming sentencing decisions, there is evidence that minorities are more likely to have prior records because of organizational and individual bias on the part of police.

Are Sentencing Practices Changing? If in fact racial discrepancies exist, new sentencing laws featuring determinate and mandatory sentences may be helping to reduce disparity. For example, Jon'a Meyer and Tara Gray found that jurisdictions in California that use mandatory sentences for crimes such as drunk driving also show little racial disparity in sentences between whites and minority group members. Similarly, a national survey of sentencing practices conducted by the Bureau of Justice Statistics found that while white defendants are somewhat more likely to receive probation and other nonincarceration sentences than black defendants (34 percent versus 31 percent) there was little racial disparity in the length of prison sentences.

These results are encouraging, but it is also possible that some studies miss a racial effect because they combine white and Hispanic cases into a single category of "white" defendants and then compare them with the sentencing of "black" defendants. Darrell Steffensmeier and Stephen Demuth's

analysis of sentencing in Pennsylvania found that Hispanics are punished considerably more severely than non-Hispanics and that combining the two groups masks the racial differences in sentencing. However, Steffensmeier and Demuth also found that federal judges in Pennsylvania were less likely to consider race and ethnic origin in their sentencing decisions than state judges. This outcome suggests that federal judges, insulated from community pressures and values and holding a lifetime appointment, are better able to render objective decisions. This finding suggests ways of reducing racial disparity in sentencing.

Critical Thinking Questions

1. Do you feel that sentences should be influenced by the fact that one ethnic or racial group is more likely to commit that crime? For example, critics have called for change in the way federal sentencing guidelines are designed, asking that the provisions that punish crack possession more heavily than powdered cocaine possession be repealed because African Americans are more likely to use crack and whites powdered cocaine. Do you approve of such a change?

2. Because of the lingering problem of racial and class bias in the sentencing process, one primary goal of the criminal justice system in the 1990s was to reduce disparity by creating new forms of criminal sentences that limit judicial discretion and are aimed at uniformity and fairness. How well do you think this objective has been achieved? Can you suggest some

other ways to address this kind of bias in sentencing?

 InfoTrac College Edition Research

Use the terms "race" and "sentencing" as key words on InfoTrac College Edition to find out more about the relationship between these two factors.

SOURCES: Marian R. Williams and Jefferson E. Holcomb, "Racial Disparity and Death Sentences in Ohio," *Journal of Criminal Justice* 29 (2001): 207–18; Rodney Engen and Randy Gainey, "Modeling the Effects of Legally Relevant and Extra-Legal Factors Under Sentencing Guidelines: The Rules Have Changed," *Criminology* 38 (2000): 1207–30; Darrell Steffensmeier and Stephen Demuth, "Ethnicity and Judges' Sentencing Decisions: Hispanic-Black-White Comparisons," *Criminology* 39 (2001): 145–78; Travis Pratt, "Race and Sentencing: A Meta-Analysis of Conflicting Empirical Research Results," *Journal of Criminal Justice* 26 (1998): 513–25; Charles Crawford, Ted Chiricos, and Gary Kleck, "Race, Racial Threat, and Sentencing of Habitual Offenders," *Criminology* 36 (1998): 481–511; Jon'a Meyer and Tara Gray, "Drunk Drivers in the Courts: Legal and Extra-Legal Factors Affecting Pleas and Sentences," *Journal of Criminal Justice* 25 (1997): 155–63; Alexander Alvarez and Ronet Bachman, "American Indians and Sentencing Disparity: An Arizona Test," *Journal of Criminal Justice* 24 (1996): 549–61; Carole Wolff Barnes and Rodney Kingsworth, "Race, Drugs, and Criminal Sentencing: Hidden Effects of the Criminal Law," *Journal of Criminal Justice* 24 (1996): 39–55; Samuel Walker, Cassia Spohn, and Miriam DeLone, *The Color of Justice: Race, Ethnicity and Crime in America* (Belmont, Calif.: Wadsworth, 1996), pp. 145–46; Jo Dixon, "The Organizational Context of Sentencing," *American Journal of Sociology* 100 (1995): 1157–98; Alfred Blumstein, "On the Racial Disproportionality of the United States Prison Population," *Journal of Criminal Law and Criminology* 73 (1982): 1259–81; Celesta Albonetti and John Hepburn, "Prosecutorial Discretion to Defer Criminalization: The Effects of Defendant's Ascribed and Achieved Status Characteristics," *Journal of Quantitative Criminology* 12 (1996): 63–81; Darnell Hawkins, "Race, Crime Type and Imprisonment," *Justice Quarterly* 3 (1986): 251–69.

long perplexed social thinkers. Today the death penalty for murder is used in 38 states and by the federal government with the approval of about 75 percent of the population. At year-end 2000, 37 states and the federal government held 3,539 men and 54 women on death row. California had the most (586), followed by Texas (450), Florida (371), and Pennsylvania (238).[109] Fourteen states executed 85 prisoners in 2000, 83 men and 2 women; in 2001 the number of executions dropped to 66. The executed prisoners had spent an average of 11 years and 5 months on death row before being put to death, which was about 6 months less than those executed in 1999. During 2000, Texas executed 40 people, conducting about half of all executions. As of 2001, lethal injection was the predominant method of death, although a number of states use the gas chamber and electric chair. In 1999 the Supreme Court refused to hear a case against Florida's use of the electric chair as the sole means of execution. Even though the chair has malfunctioned several times, sending up smoke and flames, the Court refused to consider whether this amounted to cruel and unusual punishment. Of the 38 death penalty states, only Alabama, Georgia, Nebraska, and Florida still use the electric chair as the only means of execution.[110]

The Death Penalty Debate

The death penalty has long been one of the most controversial aspects of the justice system, and it likely will continue to be a source of significant debate.[111]

There is quite a bit of information on captial punishment on InfoTrac College Edition. Use "death penalty" as a key word to look for more information on this topic. ■

Arguments for the death penalty Various arguments have been offered in support of the death penalty. Some of the best-known arguments for the use of the death penalty are discussed here.

- Executions have always been used, and capital punishment is inherent in human nature. It is fair to punish the wicked, and consequently the death penalty is favored by most Americans and used in three-quarters of the nations of the world, including Japan, which has an extremely low murder rate.[112] See the Race, Culture, Gender, and Criminology feature titled "The International Use of the Death Penalty" for a closer look at how other nations have dealt with this issue.

- The Bible describes methods of executing criminals. Many moral philosophers and religious leaders, such as Thomas Moore, John Locke, and Immanuel Kant, did not oppose the death penalty; neither did the framers of the U.S. Constitution.

- The death penalty also seems to be in keeping with the current mode of dispensing punishment. Criminal law exacts proportionately harsher penalties for crimes based on their seriousness; this practice is testimony to a retributionist philosophy. Therefore, the harshest penalty for the most severe crime represents a logical step in the process.

- The death penalty is sometimes the only real threat available to deter crime. For example, prison inmates serving life sentences can be controlled only if they know that further transgressions can lead to death. Or a person committing a crime that carries with it a long prison sentence might be more likely to kill witnesses if the threat of death did not exist.

- Death is the ultimate incapacitation. Some offenders are so dangerous that they can never be safely let out

Springfield News Leader photo © Christini Dicken

■ Convicted serial killer Tommy Lynn Sells has been indicted in the murder of 9-year-old Mary B. Perez. Sells, 36, is already on death row for the murder of 13-year-old Kaylene Harris on December 31, 1999, in Del Rio, Texas. Sells has confessed to at least 12 murders in seven states, claiming he used guns, knives, a bat, a shovel, an ice pick, and his bare hands to kill. Should someone like Sells be spared the death sentence?

in society. The death penalty is a sure way of preventing these people from ever harming others. More than 280 inmates on death row today had prior homicide convictions; if they had been executed for their first offenses, at least 280 innocent people would still be alive.

- The death penalty is cost-effective. Considering the crowded prison system and the expense of keeping an inmate locked up for many years, an execution makes financial sense.

- Despite some allegations of racism, more whites are on death row than minorities, and there appears to be little racial difference in the rate of capital sentencing over the past 30 years.

In summary, supporters view capital punishment as the ultimate deterrent to crime. They believe that so serious a

The International Use of the Death Penalty

In July of 2001 two Saudi brothers, Saud and Musaid bin Abdul-Rahman al-Aulian, were beheaded for kidnapping, raping, and robbing a woman whom they had lured to a secluded area. The Saudis behead about 125 people each year for crimes such as murder, rape, drug trafficking, and armed robbery. But not all Saudi executions concern violent crime: On February 28, 2001, Hassan bin Awad al-Zubair, a Sudanese national, was beheaded after he was convicted on charges of "sorcery"; al-Zubair claimed the power to heal the sick and to "separate married couples."

The United States is not alone in using the death penalty. According to the latest data from watchdog group Amnesty International, executions are now being carried out in 34 countries, and prisoners were under sentence of death in at least 55 countries. The countries in which the most executions take place are China, Iran, Saudi Arabia, and the Democratic Republic of Congo. Amnesty International estimates that during 2000 at least 1,457 prisoners were executed in 27 countries and 3,058 people were sentenced to death in 65 countries (though the numbers may be much higher). The 2001 data had not been gathered at the time of this writing, but the numbers should be much higher because China has instituted a "Strike Hard" campaign against crime. In its first three months, at least 2,960 people were sentenced to death and 1,781 executed. In addition to violent crimes, executions were carried out for stealing gasoline, bribery, pimping, embezzlement, tax fraud, drug offenses, and selling harmful foodstuffs.

Despite its use abroad, abolition movements have been very successful. About 75 countries and territories have abolished the death penalty for all crimes and another 14 countries have abolished the death penalty for all but exceptional crimes, such as wartime crimes. An additional 20 countries retain the death penalty in law but have not carried out any executions for the past 10 years or more. In all, about 109 countries have abolished the death penalty in law or practice. On December 29, 1999, Turkmenistan became the first of the five former Soviet central Asian republics to abolish the death penalty.

Although opposition to executions is growing in many areas, in some nations the public still demands the use of the death penalty. In addition to China, nations that operate under Islamic law routinely employ the death penalty. At least 125 executions were carried out in Saudi Arabia during 2000. The governments of Jamaica, Guyana, and Barbados have all expressed interest in speeding the use of the death penalty, and more than 250 prisoners are currently on death row across the English-speaking Caribbean.

Japan, a nation that prides itself on nonviolence, routinely uses the death penalty. Prisoners are told less than two hours before execution, and the families and lawyers are never told of the decision to carry out the death penalty. As of 2001, there were at least 110 people under sentence of death in Japan, 50 of whom have had their sentences upheld by the Supreme Court and can be executed at any time. Some of the prisoners were more than 70 years old and had been incarcerated for decades.

Executions of Juveniles

International human rights treaties prohibit anyone under 18 years old at the time of the crime being sentenced to death. The International Covenant on Civil and Political Rights, the American Convention on Human Rights, and the U.N. Convention on the Rights of the Child all have provisions to this effect. More than 100 countries either have laws specifically excluding the execution of juvenile offenders or may be presumed to exclude such executions by being parties to one or another of these treaties. A small number of countries, however, continue to execute juvenile offenders. Six countries since 1990 are known to have executed prisoners who were under 18 years old at the time of the crime: Iran, Nigeria, Pakistan, Saudi Arabia, the United States, and Yemen. Between 1997 and 2001, there were 12 executions of juvenile offenders worldwide: three in Iran, one in the Democratic Republic of Congo, and eight in the United States.

Critical Thinking Questions

1. The movement toward abolition in the United States is encouraged by the fact that so many nations have abandoned the death penalty. Should we model our own system of punishments after other nations, or is our crime problem so unique that it requires the use of capital punishment?
2. Do you believe that someone who joins a terrorist group and trains to kill Americans deserves the death penalty, even if they have never actually killed anyone?

InfoTrac College Edition Research

Are there really innocent people on death row? To find out, read this article:

Peter Vilbig. Innocent on death row. *New York Times Upfront*, 18 Sept 2000 v133 i2 p10

SOURCES: "Death Penalty News: Saudi Arabia Executes Man for Sorcery," Amnesty International, March 2000; "USA Set to Break a Global Consensus—Execution of Child Offender Due," Amnesty International, News Release, 22 October 2001; "China 'Striking Harder' Than Ever Before," Amnesty International, News Release, 7 June 2001; Associated Press, "Saudi Brothers Beheaded for Raping," *New York Times*, 20 July 2001, p. 3; Amnesty International USA, *Annual Report 2000: The Death Penalty: An Affront to Our Humanity* (Washington, D.C: Amnesty International, 2000); Amnesty International, "The Death Penalty: List of Abolitionist and Retentionist Countries," 1 January 2000; Amnesty International, "Facts and Figures on the Death Penalty," April 2000; Larry Rohter, "In Caribbean, Support Growing for Death Penalty," *New York Times*, 4 October 1998; Associated Press, "Chechen Pair Executed in Public," *Boston Globe*, 19 September 1997, p. 9; Reuters, "Saudi Beheadings over 100 for 1997," *Boston Globe*, 28 September 1997, p. A29.

sanction prevents many potential criminals from taking the lives of innocent victims. The justification for the death penalty, therefore, relies on the premise that sacrificing the lives of a few evil people is a cost-effective way to save the lives of many innocent ones.

Arguments against the death penalty The death penalty has little deterrent effect. The most thorough research efforts fail to find any relationship between the use of capital punishment and reductions in the violence rate. For example, Keith Harries and Derral Cheatwood studied differences in homicide rates in 293 contiguous counties within the United States that differed in the use of capital punishment and found that there were actually higher violent crime rates in counties that routinely employed the death penalty.[113]

Although it is still uncertain why the threat of capital punishment has failed as a deterrent, the cause may lie in the nature of homicide itself. Murder is often an expressive "crime of passion," involving people who know each other and who may be under the influence of drugs and alcohol; murder is also a by-product of the criminal activity of people who suffer from the burdens of poverty and income inequality.[114] Those who argue against the use of the death penalty make the following points.

- Executions may actually increase the likelihood of murders being committed as a consequence referred to as the **brutalization effect.** The basis of this theory is that potential criminals may begin to model their behavior after state authorities: if the government can kill its enemies, so can they.[115] The brutalization effect means that after an execution murders may increase, causing even more deaths of innocent victims.[116] There may even be a vicarious brutalization effect in which murder rates in a state that does not practice capital punishment are influenced by news reports of executions in states that do.[117]

- Capital punishment may be tarnished by gender, racial, ethnic, and other biases. There is evidence that homicides with male offenders and female victims are more likely to result in a death sentence than homicides with female offenders and male victims.[118] Homicides involving strangers are more likely to result in a death sentence than homicides involving non-strangers and acquaintances. Prosecutors are more likely to recommend the death sentence for people who kill white victims than they are any other racial combination of victim and criminal (for example, whites who kill blacks).[119]

- Even if the general public voices approval of the death penalty, abolitionists argue that "social vengeance by death is a primitive way of revenge which stands in the way of moral progress."[120] People who support the death penalty may be motivated by racial prejudice.[121]

- The inherent brutality of the death penalty places it in violation of the Eighth Amendment of the U.S. Constitution, which prohibits cruel and unusual punishment. Deborah Denno has documented the cruel nature of the existing means of execution. For example, electrocution is often accompanied by charring of the skin and severe external burns; some condemned criminals literally burst into flames during botched executions.[122] Although the current application of the death penalty seems to fall outside the Eighth Amendment's "cruel and unusual" standard, Denno finds that many legislators and judges want to keep the death penalty and therefore are reluctant to question its legality.

- Critics also question whether the general public gives blanket approval to the application of capital punishment. Research suggests that most people may accept capital punishment in principle but also believe it should be used only rarely.[123] Surveys show that the general public is usually willing to forgo use of the death penalty when given choices of other penalties, such as life in prison without parole and compensation to the victim's family.[124] In a 2002 case, *Kelly v. South Carolina,* the Supreme Court ruled that jurors must be apprised of state laws that prohibit people convicted of first-degree murder from being eligible for parole.[125] Abolitionists believe jurors who understand that dangerous criminals will never be released from prison may be less willing to recommend the death penalty.

- Opponents also object to the finality of the death penalty. It of course precludes any possibility of rehabilitation. Studies indicate that death row inmates released because of legal changes rarely recidivate and present little threat to the community.[126] It is also quite possible for an innocent person to be convicted of a crime; once the person is executed, the mistake can never be rectified.[127] Many people convicted of murder are later released because of mistaken identity or perjured testimony. For example, Rolando Cruz and Alejandro Hernandez, wrongfully convicted of murder, were released in 1995 after spending more than a decade on death row in the Illinois prison system; three former prosecutors and four deputy sheriffs who worked on the case were later charged with fabricating evidence against the pair.[128]

- "It is better that a thousand guilty go free than one innocent man be executed" is a statement abolitionists often make. This point has been convincingly made by Michael Radelet and Hugo Bedeau, who claim that there have been about 350 wrongful convictions this century, of which 23 led to executions. They estimate that about three death sentences are returned every two years in cases where the defendants have been falsely accused. More than half the errors stem from perjured testimony, false identification, coerced confessions, and suppression of evidence. In addition to the 23 who were executed, 128 of the falsely convicted served more than 6 years in prison; 39 served more than 16 years; and 8 died while serving their sentences.[129] Even though the system attempts to be especially cautious in capital cases, it is evident that unacceptable mistakes can occur.

- The death penalty is capricious; receiving death is similar to losing a lottery.[130] Of the 10,000 people who are convicted of murder each year, more receive probation as a sole sentence than get the death penalty. Is it fair to release one person who has taken a life into the community and execute another?

- Because discretion and personal beliefs influence decision making, the death penalty can be employed in a discriminatory fashion. Between 1930 and 1967, 3,859 alleged criminals were executed in the United States. Of those executed, 53.5 percent were African American and 45.4 percent were white. A moratorium was then put on executions, during which the legality of capital punishment was debated (discussed next). During the 22-year period (1977–1999) since executions resumed, more than 450 executions have taken place in 26 states.

- Abolitionists claim that capital punishment has never proven to be a deterrent, any more than has life in prison. In fact, capital punishment may encourage murder because it sets an example of violence and brutality.[131]

- Abolitionists also point out that such nations as Denmark and Sweden have long abandoned the death penalty and that 40 percent of the countries with a death penalty have active abolitionist movements.[132]

The American Civil Liberties Union maintains a Web site that lists their various anti–capital punishment activities. You can access it at:
   http://www.aclu.org/death-penalty/
For an up-to-date list of Web links, go to
   http://info.wadsworth.com/siegel ∎

Legality of the Death Penalty

For most of this country's history, capital punishment was used in a discretionary, haphazard manner without strict legal controls. As a result, its application was marked by extreme racial disparity; more than half the executions conducted in the United States involved African Americans. Then, in 1972, the U.S. Supreme Court, in *Furman v. Georgia,* ruled that the discretionary imposition of the death penalty was cruel and unusual punishment under the Eighth and Fourteenth Amendments of the Constitution.[133] The Court did not rule out the use of capital punishment as a penalty; rather, it objected to the arbitrary and capricious manner in which it was imposed. After *Furman,* many states changed statutes that had allowed juries discretion in imposing the death penalty. Some states enacted guidelines that spelled out specific conditions of aggravation that must be met for the death penalty to be considered.

Despite these changes, no further executions were carried out while the Supreme Court pondered additional cases concerning the death penalty. In July 1976, the Supreme Court ruled on the constitutionality of five states' death penalty statutes. In the first case, *Gregg v. Georgia,* the Court found valid the Georgia statute that held that a jury must find at least one "aggravating circumstance" before the death penalty can be imposed in murder cases.[134] In the Gregg case, for example, the jury imposed the death penalty after establishing beyond a reasonable doubt the presence of two aggravating circumstances:

- The murder was committed while the offender was committing two other capital felonies.

- The offender committed the murder for the purpose of receiving money and other financial gain (an automobile).

The Court also upheld the constitutionality of a Texas statute on capital punishment in *Jurek v. Texas*[135] and a Florida statute in *Proffitt v. Florida.*[136] These statutes are similar to Georgia's in that they limit sentencing discretion, not only by specifying the crimes for which capital punishment can be handed down but also by stipulating criteria concerning the circumstances surrounding the crimes. However, the Supreme Court declared that mandatory death sentences were unconstitutional.

In the late 1970s and early 1980s, a more conservative Supreme Court eased the way for executions by lifting some of the legal roadblocks to capital punishment, such as allowing the removal of jurors who are opposed to the death penalty.[137] In a 1987 case, *Tison v. Arizona,* the Court permitted executions of people who were major participants in a murder case and displayed reckless indifference to human life but did not actually kill anybody.[138]

In what may have been the last major challenge to the death penalty, *McCleskey v. Kemp,* the Supreme Court upheld the capital sentence of an African American man in Georgia despite social science evidence that a black criminal who kills a white victim has a much greater chance of receiving the death penalty than a white criminal who kills a black victim.[139] Many observers felt that this case was the last legal obstacle the death penalty had to overcome to become a standard mode of punishment in the American justice system. The Court subsequently upheld the states' right to execute youthful offenders who killed after reaching the age of 16.[140] Ironically, when McCleskey reappealed his case on other procedural grounds, the Court used that case as a vehicle to limit the access of death row inmates to the appeals process; Warren McCleskey was executed in 1993.[141] The legality of the death penalty seems secure, but the fact that states have reduced the number of actual executions (from 85 in 2000 to 66 in 2001) suggests that the continued uncertainty about the fairness and accuracy of capital punishment may limit its use in the near future.

■ Summary

The judicatory process provides a forum for deciding the outcome of a conflict between two or more parties. Unfortunately, discretion and personal decision making interfere with the equality that should be built into the law.

The judicatory process is played out in the nation's court system. State courts usually involve a multitiered system—lower trial courts, superior trial courts, appellate courts, and supreme court. The federal system is similar; it contains trial courts, appellate courts, and the Supreme Court. The U.S. Supreme Court is the final court of appeals for all state and federal cases.

There are three main actors in the judicatory process. The prosecutor brings charges against the offender and then represents the state in all criminal matters. The defense attorney represents the accused at all stages of the judicatory process. Some defendants can afford to hire private attorneys for their defense, but the majority are represented by defense counsel appointed and paid for by the state. The judge controls the trial, rules on issues of evidence, charges the jury, and in some cases can choose the type and length of sentence.

The pretrial stage of the justice process involves such issues as bail and plea bargaining. Bail is a money bond the defendant puts up to secure freedom before trial. It is controversial because those who cannot make bail must spend their time in detention. Critics charge that bail discriminates against the poor, who can neither afford bond nor borrow it from bonding agents. Consequently, reform programs, such as release on recognizance, have been started.

Plea bargaining involves the prosecutor's allowing defendants to plead guilty as charged in return for some consideration—for example, a reduced sentence or dropped charges. Plea bargaining has been criticized because it represents the unchecked use of discretion by prosecutors. Often, serious criminals can receive light sentences by bargaining, and some people may be coerced into pleading guilty because they fear a harsh sentence if they go to trial. An effort has been made to control plea bargains, but they are still frequently used.

The second stage of the judicatory process is the criminal trial. The trial has a number of distinct stages, including jury selection, opening statements, presentation of evidence by prosecution and defense, closing arguments, instructions to the jury, verdict, sentence, and appeal. The rule of law also affects criminal trials. The Supreme Court has required that trials be speedy, public, and fair and has ruled that people have a right to be free from double jeopardy and to be represented by competent counsel.

After a conviction, sentencing occurs. Each state, as well as the federal government, has its own types of sentences and punishments. Fines, suspended sentences, community supervision, and prison are the most common forms of punishment. Prison sentences are divided into determinate and indeterminate types. There are also mandatory sentences that must be served upon conviction and that carry no hope of probation. Efforts to control sentencing disparity include the use of sentencing guidelines as well as determinate and mandatory sentences.

■ Thinking Like a Criminologist

The director of the American Civil Liberties Union has contacted you, asking for your professional opinion. She has read a paper by criminologists William Bowers and Glenn Pierce, who argue that, far from being a deterrent, capital punishment actually produces more violence than it prevents; they label this the "brutalization effect." Executions, they say, actually increase murder rates because they raise the general violence level in society and because violence-prone people identify with the executioner, not with the target of the death penalty. Consequently, when someone gets in a conflict with them or challenges their authority, they execute them in the same manner that the state executes people who violate its rules.

Assuming that Bowers and Pierce are correct, the ACLU director asks, does this mean that the death penalty violates the general public's civil rights? She wonders whether it might be possible to turn public opinion against the death penalty on the basis that it actually does more harm than good, thereby endangering their lives. How would you respond?

Key Terms

- U.S. district courts (517)
- federal courts of appeal (517)
- U.S. Supreme Court (517)
- writ of certiorari (517)
- precedent (517)
- landmark decision (517)
- prosecution (520)
- nolle prosequi (522)
- assigned counsel system (524)
- public defenders (524)
- officers of the court (525)
- adversary system of justice (525)
- judge (525)
- Missouri Plan (526)
- bail (527)
- preventive detention (527)
- bail bonding agent (527)
- surety bond (527)

- skip tracer (527)
- recovery agent (527)
- release on recognizance (ROR) (528)
- deposit bail system (528)
- bail guidelines (528)
- plea bargaining (529)
- venire (531)
- jury array (531)
- voir dire (531)
- removed for cause (531)
- peremptory challenge (531)
- direct examination (532)
- cross-examination (532)
- redirect examination (532)
- directed verdict (532)
- rebuttal evidence (532)
- double jeopardy (534)

- dual sovereignty doctrine (534)
- fine (535)
- probation (535)
- alternative sanctions (536)
- incarceration (536)
- capital punishment (536)
- mandatory prison term (536)
- impact statement (536)
- presentence investigation report (536)
- concurrent sentence (536)
- consecutive sentence (536)
- indeterminate sentence (536)
- determinate sentence (537)
- sentencing guidelines (537)
- truth-in-sentencing laws (540)
- sentencing disparity (541)
- brutalization effect (546)

Critical Thinking Questions

1. Compare the various types of incarceration sentences. What are the similarities and differences? Why are many jurisdictions considering the passage of mandatory sentencing laws?

2. Why does the problem of sentencing disparity exist? Do programs exist that can reduce disparate sentences? If so, what are they? Should all people who commit the same crime receive the same sentence? Explain.

3. Should convicted criminals be released from prison when correctional authorities are convinced they are rehabilitated? Why or why not?

4. The U.S. Supreme Court has ruled that prosecutors have the right to discharge those jurors who would not consider the death penalty under any circumstances, thereby creating "death qualified" juries. Does this create inherently unfair juries by removing people who are opposed to capital punishment? Doesn't this procedure create a jury that is not representative of the community because all members favor the death penalty?

5. According to the concept of specific deterrence, experiencing harsh criminal punishments should convince convicted offenders that crime does not pay and recidivism is not in their best inter-

est. Does the fact that so many people convicted of felonies receive a probationary sentence undermine the concept of specific deterrence?

6. Should plea bargaining be abolished? Does it give dangerous offenders the opportunity to avoid the full extent of the law? Is it fair to punish people more harshly simply because they asked for their constitutional right to a jury trial?

7. Should people considered to be dangerous be denied the right to bail? How can we tell for sure that someone will be dangerous in the future? Is this a violation of due process?

Notes

1. Associated Press, "Two on Trial for Painkiller Death," *New York Times,* 3 June 2001, p. 3; Associated Press, "Two Sentenced in OxyContin Death of Student," *USA Today,* 20 June 2001, p. 4.

2. Matthew Durose and Patrick A. Langan, *State Court Sentencing of Convicted Felons, 1998* (Washington, D.C.: Bureau of Justice Statistics, February 2001).

3. The data in these sections are taken from Brian Ostrom, Neal Kauder, and Robert LaFountain, *Examining the Work of State Courts, 1999–2000: A National Perspective from the Court Statistics Project* (Williamsburg, Va.: National Center for State Courts, 2001). Herein cited as *Examining the Work of State Courts, 2000.*

4. David Rohde, "Arrests Soar in Giuliani Crackdown," *New York Times,* 2 February 1999.

5. Carol J. DeFrances and Greg W. Steadman, *Prosecutors in State Courts, 1996* (Washington, D.C.: Bureau of Justice Statistics, 1998).

6. Ibid.

7. Ibid.

8. Newman Baker, "The Prosecutor Initiation of Prosecution," *Journal of Criminal Law, Criminology and Police Science* 23 (1933): 770–71.

9. Janell Schmidt and Ellen Hochstedler Steury, "Prosecutorial Discretion in Filing Charges in Domestic Violence Cases," *Criminology* 27 (1989): 487–510.

10. Rodney Kingsworth, John Lopez, Jennifer Wentworth, and Debra Cummings, "Adult Sexual Assault: The Role of Racial/Ethnic Composition in Prosecution and Sentencing," *Journal of Criminal Justice* 26 (1998): 359–72.

11. Myrna Dawson and Ronit Dinovitzer, "Victim Cooperation and the Prosecution of Domestic Violence in a Specialized Court," *Justice Quarterly* 18 (2001): 593–622.

12. Frank W. Miller, *Prosecution: The Decision to Charge a Suspect with a Crime* (Boston: Little, Brown, 1970).

13. Wayne LaFave, "The Prosecutor's Discretion in the United States," *American Journal of Comparative Law* 18 (1970): 532–48.

14. Carol J. DeFrances, Steven K. Smith, and Louise van der Does, *Prosecutors in State Courts, 1994* (Washington, D.C.: Bureau of Justice Statistics, 1996).

15. Cassia Spohn, Dawn Beichner, and Erika Davis-Frenzel," "Prosecutorial Justifications for Sexual Assault Case Rejection: Guarding the 'Gateway to Justice,'" *Social Problems* 48 (2001): 206–35.

16. Charles Breitel, "Controls in Criminal Law Enforcement," *University of Chicago Law Review* 27 (1960): 427–35.

17. See, generally, "A Symposium on Prosecutorial Discretion," *American Criminal Law Review* (1976): 379–99.

18. George Cole, "The Decision to Prosecute," *Law and Society Review* 4 (1970): 331–43.

19. *Gideon v. Wainwright*, 372 U.S. 335 (1963); *Argersinger v. Hamlin*, 407 U.S. 25 (1972).

20. Steven K. Smith and Carol J. DeFrances, *Indigent Defense* (Washington, D.C.: Bureau of Justice Statistics, 1996).

21. Carol J. DeFrances, *State-Funded Indigent Defense Services, 1999* (Washington, D.C.: Bureau of Justice Statistics, 2001).

22. Ibid.

23. See American Bar Association, *Special Committee on Evaluation of Ethical Standards, Code of Professional Responsibility* (Chicago: American Bar Association 1968), p. 81.

24. *Nix v. Whiteside*, 106 S.Ct. 988 (1986).

25. William Lineberry, ed., *Justice in America: Law, Order and the Courts* (New York: H. W. Wilson, 1972).

26. National Center for State Courts, *Examining the Work of State Courts, 1996: A National Perspective from the Court Statistics Project* (Williamsburg, Va.: National Center for State Courts, 1998). Herein cited as *Examining the Work of State Courts, 1996.*

27. *Examining the Work of State Courts, 2000.*

28. M. Ozanne, R. Wilson, and D. Gedney Jr., "Toward a Theory of Bail Risk," *Criminology* 18 (1980): 149.

29. Brian Reaves, *Felony Defendants in Large Urban Counties, 1998* (Washington, D.C.: Bureau of Justice Statistics, 2001).

30. Caleb Foote, "A Study of the Administration of Bail in New York," *University of Pennsylvania Law Review* 106 (1960): 693–730; William Rhodes, *Pretrial Release and Misconduct* (Washington, D.C.: Bureau of Justice Statistics, 1985).

31. John Goldkamp, *Two Classes of Accused* (Cambridge, Mass.: Ballinger, 1979).

32. Brian A. Reaves and Jacob Perez, *Pretrial Release of Felony Defendants, 1992: National Pretrial Reporting Program* (Washington, D.C.: Bureau of Justice Statistics, 1994).

33. Goldkamp, *Two Classes of Accused.*

34. Timothy M. Ito, "Wild West Saga: Have Gun, Will Shoot," *U.S. News & World Report* 123 (15 September 1997), p. 7.

35. Vera Institute of Justice, *Programs in Criminal Justice* (New York: Vera Institute, 1972).

36. Reaves and Perez, *Pretrial Release of Felony Defendants, 1992,* p. 5.

37. Malcolm Feeley, *Court Reform on Trial* (New York: Basic Books, 1983); John Goldkamp, "Judicial Reform of Bail Practices: The Philadelphia Experiment," *Court Management Journal* (1983): 16–20.

38. John Goldkamp and Michael Gottfredson, *Judicial Decision Guidelines for Bail: The Philadelphia Experiment* (Washington, D.C.: National Institute of Justice, 1983).

39. Reaves, *Felony Defendants in Large Urban Counties, 1998.*

40. 18 U.S.C. Sec. 3142 (e) (1985).

41. *United States v. Salerno*, 107 S.Ct. 2095 (1987).

42. *Schall v. Martin*, 104 S.Ct. 2403 (1984).

43. Stephen Kennedy and Kenneth Carlson, *Pretrial Release and Detention: The Bail Reform Act of 1984* (Washington, D.C.: Bureau of Justice Statistics, 1988).

44. Reaves, *Felony Defendants in Large Urban Counties, 1998.*

45. Donald Newman, "Making a Deal," in *Legal Process and Corrections,* eds. N. Johnston and L. Savitz (New York: John Wiley, 1982), pp. 96–97.

46. These sentiments are similar to those expressed by Abraham Blumberg in "The Practice of Law as a Confidence Game: Organizational Co-optation of a Profession," *Law and Society Review* 1 (1967): 15–39.

47. Again, these thoughts are similar to Blumberg's views as expressed in "The Practice of Law as a Confidence Game."

48. National Advisory Commission on Criminal Justice Standards and Goals, *Courts* (Washington, D.C.: U.S. Government Printing Office, 1976).

49. Richard Kuh, "Plea Copping," *Bar Bulletin* 24 (1966–1967): 160.

50. Alan Alschuler, "The Defense Counsel's Role in Plea Bargaining," *Yale Law Journal* 84 (1975): 1179.

51. See, generally, Milton Heumann, "A Note on Plea Bargaining and Case Pressure," *Law and Society Review* 9 (1975): 515.

52. National Institute of Law Enforcement and Criminal Justice, *Plea Bargaining in the United States* (Washington, D.C.: Georgetown University, 1978), p. 8.

53. Michael Rubenstein, Stevens Clarke, and Teresa White, *Alaska Bans Plea Bargaining* (Washington, D.C.: U.S. Department of Justice, 1980).

54. National Advisory Commission on Criminal Justice Standards and Goals, *Courts,* p. 66.

55. See, for example, "Limiting the Peremptory Challenge: Representation of Groups on Petit Juries," *Yale Law Journal* 86 (1977): 1715.

56. *Batson v. Kentucky*, 476 U.S. 79 (1986).

57. *Ham v. South Carolina*, 409 U.S. 524, 93 S.Ct. 848, 35 L.Ed.2d 46 (1973).

58. *Turner v. Murray*, 106 S.Ct. 1683 (1986).

59. *Taylor v. Louisiana*, 419 U.S. 522, 42 L.Ed.2d 690, 95 S.Ct. 692 (1975).

60. In *Ristaino v. Ross* [424 U.S. 589 (1976)], the Court said questioning the jury on racial issues was not automatic in all interracial crimes.

61. Edna Erez, "Victim Participation in Sentencing: Rhetoric and Reality," *Journal of Criminal Justice* 18 (1990): 19–31.

62. *Strunk v. United States*, 412 U.S. 434 (1973).

63. *Klopfer v. North Carolina,* 38 U.S. 213 (1967).

64. *Duncan v. Louisiana,* 391 U.S. 145 (1968).

65. *Baldwin v. New York,* 399 U.S. 66 (1970).

66. *Blanton v. City of North Las Vegas,* 489 U.S. 538, 109 S.Ct. 1289, 103 L.Ed.2d 550 (1989).

67. *Williams v. Florida,* 399 U.S. 78 (1970).

68. *Apodica v. Oregon,* 406 U.S. 404 (1972).

69. *Benton v. Maryland,* 395 U.S. 784 (1969).

70. *United States v. Lanza,* 260 U.S. 377 (1922); *Bartkus v. Illinois,* 359 U.S. 121 (1959); *Abbate v. U.S.,* 359 U.S. 187 (1959).

71. *Heath v. Alabama,* 106 S.Ct. 433 (1985).

72. *Powell v. Alabama,* 287 U.S. 45 (1932).

73. *Gideon v. Wainwright,* 372 U.S. 335 (1963).

74. *Argersinger v. Hamlin,* 407 U.S. 25 (1972).

75. *Maryland v. Craig,* 110 S.Ct. 3157, 111 L.Ed.2d 666 (1990).

76. Anna Gorman And Nancy Vogel, "Bomb Plot Gets Olson 20 to Life," *Los Angeles Times,* 19 January 2002, p. 1.

77. See V. O'Leary, M. Gottfredson, and A. Gelman, "Contemporary Sentencing Proposals," *Criminal Law Bulletin* 11 (1975): 558–60.

78. Sally Hillsman, Barry Mahoney, George Cole, and Bernard Auchter, *Fines as Criminal Sanctions* (Washington, D.C.: National Institute of Justice, 1987).

79. Edna Erez and Pamela Tontodonato, "The Effect of Victim Participation in Sentencing on Sentencing Outcome," *Criminology* 28 (1990): 451–74.

80. Kriss Drass and J. William Spencer, "Accounting for Presentencing Recommendations: Typologies and Probation Officers' Theory of Office," *Social Problems* 34 (1987): 277–93.

81. Kenneth Culp Davis, *Discretionary Justice: A Preliminary Inquiry* (Baton Rouge: Louisiana State University Press, 1969).

82. See Marvin Frankel, *Criminal Sentences—Law without Order* (New York: Hill and Wang, 1972), p. 5.

83. Thomas Marvell and Carlisle Moody, "Determinate Sentencing and Abolishing Parole: The Long-Term Impacts on Prisons and Crime," *Criminology* 34 (1996): 105–28.

84. Jo Dixon, "The Organizational Context of Criminal Sentencing," *American Journal of Sociology* 100 (1995): 1157–98.

85. Michael Tonry, *Reconsidering Indeterminate and Structured Sentencing Series: Sentencing & Corrections: Issues for the 21st Century* (Washington, D.C.: National Institute of Justice, 1999).

86. Michael Tonry, *The Fragmentation of Sentencing and Corrections in America* (Washington, D.C.: National Institute of Justice, 1999).

87. Ibid., p. 11.

88. David Griswold, "Deviation from Sentencing Guidelines: The Issue of Unwarranted Disparity," *Journal of Criminal Justice* 16 (1988): 317–29; Minnesota Sentencing Guidelines Commission, *The Impact of the Minnesota Sentencing Guidelines: Three-Year Evaluation* (St. Paul: Minnesota Sentencing Guidelines Commission, 1984), p. 162.

89. Pamala Griset, "Determinate Sentencing and Administrative over Time Served in Prison: A Case Study of Florida," *Crime and Delinquency* 42 (1996): 127–43.

90. Samuel Walker, Cassia Spohn, and Miriam DeLone, *The Color of Justice: Race, Ethnicity and Crime in America* (Belmont, Calif.: Wadsworth, 1996), p. 159.

91. Elaine Wolf and Marsha Weissman, "Revising Federal Sentencing Policy: Some Consequences of Expanding Eligibility for Alternative Sanctions," *Crime and Delinquency* 42 (1996): 192–205.

92. Marvell and Moody, "Determinate Sentencing and Abolishing Parole," p. 123.

93. Ibid., p. 122.

94. Michael Tonry, *Sentencing Reform Impacts* (Washington, D.C.: U.S. Government Printing Office, 1987), pp. 26–27.

95. Paul J. Hofer, "Federal Sentencing for Violent and Drug Trafficking Crimes Involving Firearms: Recent Changes and Prospects for Improvement," *American Criminal Law Review* 37 (2000): 41–74.

96. This section is based on Paula M. Ditton and Doris James Wilson, *Truth in Sentencing in State Prisons* (Washington, D.C.: Bureau of Justice Statistics, 1999).

97. PL No. 103-322, 108 Stat. 1796 (1994).

98. Ditton and Wilson, *Truth in Sentencing in State Prisons.*

99. Michael Tonry, "Parochialism in U.S. Sentencing Policy," *Crime and Delinquency* 45 (1999): 48–65.

100. *Riggs v. California,* No. 98–5021 (1999).

101. Michael Vitiello, "Three Strikes: Can We Return to Rationality?" *Journal of Criminal Law and Criminology* 87 (1997): 395–481.

102. "California Passes a Tough Three-Strikes-You're-Out Law," *Criminal Justice Newsletter* 24 (4 April 1993), p. 4.

103. Rand Research Brief, *California's New Three-Strikes Law: Benefits, Costs, and Alternatives* (Santa Monica, Calif.: Rand Corp., 1994).

104. Matthew Durose and Patrick A. Langan, *State Court Sentencing of Convicted Felons, 1998* (Washington, D.C.: Bureau of Justice Statistics, February 2001).

105. Brent Smith and Kelly Damphouse, "Terrorism, Politics, and Punishment: A Test of Structural-Contextual Theory and the 'Liberation Hypothesis,'" *Criminology* 36 (1998): 67–92.

106. For a general review of this issue, see Florence Ferguson, "Sentencing Guidelines: Are (Black) Offenders Given Just Treatment?" Paper presented at the American Society of Criminology meeting, Montreal, November 1987.

107. Alfred Blumstein, "On the Racial Disproportionality of the United States Prison Population," *Journal of Criminal Law and Criminology* 73 (1982): 1259–81; Darnell Hawkins, "Race, Crime Type, and Imprisonment," *Justice Quarterly* 3 (1986): 251–69; Martha Myers, "Offended Parties and Official Reactions: Victims and the Sentencing of Criminal Defendants," *Sociological Quarterly* 20 (1979): 529–40.

108. Raymond Paternoster, "Race of the Victim and Location of the Crime: The Decision to Seek the Death Penalty in South Carolina," *Journal of Criminal Law and Criminology* 74 (1983): 754–85.

109. Bureau of Justice Statistics, "Eighty-Five Offenders Executed during 2000, 13 Percent Drop from Previous Year, Thirty-Seven States and Federal Government Held Almost 3,600 Inmates on Death Row." Press Release, 11 December 2001.

110. *Lopez v. Singletary,* No. 98-6065.

111. For two impressive views on the death penalty, see Robert Bohm, "Humanism and the Death Penalty with Special Emphasis on the Post-*Furman* Experience," *Justice Quarterly* 6 (1989): 173–96; and David Friedrichs, "Comment—Humanism and the Death Penalty: An Alternative Perspective," *Justice Quarterly* 6 (1989): 197–211.

112. Dennis Wiechman, Jerry Kendall, and Ronald Bae, "International Use of the Death Penalty," *International Journal of Comparative and Applied Criminal Justice* 14 (1990): 239–59.

113. Keith Harries and Derral Cheatwood, *The Geography of Executions: The Capital Punishment Quagmire in America*

(Lanham, Md.: Rowman and Little-field, 1997).

114. Steven Messner and Kenneth Tardiff, "Economic Inequality and Level of Homicide: An Analysis of Urban Neighborhoods," *Criminology* 24 (1986): 297–317.

115. William Bowers and Glenn Pierce, "Deterrence or Brutalization: What Is the Effect of Executions?" *Crime and Delinquency* 26 (1980): 453–84.

116. John Cochran, Mitchell Chamlin, and Mark Seth, "Deterrence or Brutalization? An Impact Assessment of Oklahoma's Return to Capital Punishment," *Criminology* 32 (1994): 107–34.

117. William Bailey, "Deterrence, Brutalization, and the Death Penalty: Another Examination of Oklahoma's Return to Capital Punishment," *Justice Quarterly* 36 (1998): 711–34.

118. Marian Williams and Jefferson Holcomb, "Racial Disparity and Death Sentences in Ohio," *Journal of Criminal Justice* 29 (2001): 207–18.

119. Jon Sorenson and Danold Wallace, "Prosecutorial Discretion in Seeking Death: An Analysis of Racial Disparity in the Pretrial Stages of Case Processing in a Midwestern County," *Justice Quarterly* 16 (1999): 559–78.

120. See, for example, Ernest Van Den Haag, *Punishing Criminals: Concerning a Very Old and Painful Question* (New York: Basic Books, 1975), pp. 209–11; Walter Berns, "Defending the Death Penalty," *Crime and Delinquency* 26 (1980): 503–11.

121. Marian Borg, "The Southern Subculture of Punitiveness? Regional Variation in Support for Capital Punishment," *Journal of Research in Crime and Delinquency* 34 (1997): 24–45.

122. Deborah Denno, "Getting to Death: Are Executions Constitutional?" *Iowa Law Review* 82 (1997): 319–464.

123. Norman Finkel and Stefanie Smith, "Principals and Accessories in Capital Felony Murder: The Proportionality Principle Reigns Supreme," *Law and Society Review* 27 (1993): 129–46.

124. Marla Sandys and Edmund McGarrell, "Attitudes toward Capital Punishment: Preference for the Penalty or Mere Acceptance?" *Journal of Research in Crime and Delinquency* 32 (1995): 191–213.

125. *Kelly v. South Carolina,* No. 00-9280 (2002).

126. James Marquart and Jonathan Sorensen, "Institutional and Postrelease Behavior of *Furman*-Commuted Inmates in Texas," *Justice Quarterly* 26 (1988): 677–93.

127. Kilman Shin, *Death Penalty and Crime* (Fairfax, Va.: George Mason University, 1978), p. 1.

128. "Illinois Ex-Prosecutors Charged with Framing Murder Defendants," *Criminal Justice Newsletter* 28 (2 January 1997), p. 3.

129. Michael Radelet and Hugo Bedeau, "Miscarriages of Justice in Potentially Capital Cases," *Stanford Law Review* 40 (1987): 21–181. For an opposing view, see Stephen Markman and Paul Cassell, "Protecting the Innocent: A Response to the Bedeau-Radelet Study,"

Stanford Law Review 41 (1988): 121–70; for their response, see Hugo Adam Bedeau and Michael Radelet, "The Myth of Infallibility: A Reply to Markman and Cassell," *Stanford Law Review* 42 (1988): 161–70.

130. Richard Berk, Robert Weiss, and Jack Boger, "Chance and the Death Penalty," *Law and Society Review* 27 (1993): 89–108. For an opposing view, see Raymond Paternoster, "Assessing Capriciousness in Capital Cases," *Law and Society Review* 27 (1993): 111–22.

131. William Bowers and Glenn Pierce, "Deterrence or Brutalization: What Is the Effect of Executions?" *Crime and Delinquency* 26 (1980): 453–84.

132. Joseph Schumacher, "An International Look at the Death Penalty," *International Journal of Comparative and Applied Criminal Justice* 14 (1990): 307–15.

133. *Furman v. Georgia,* 408 U.S. 238, 92 S.Ct. 2726, 33 L.Ed.2d 346 (1972).

134. *Gregg v. Georgia,* 428 U.S. 153, 96 S.Ct. 2909, 49 L.Ed.2d 859 (1976).

135. *Jurek v. Texas,* 428 U.S. 262, 96 S.Ct. 2950, 49 L.Ed.2d 929 (1976).

136. *Proffitt v. Florida,* 428 U.S. 325, 96 S.Ct. 3001, 49 L.Ed.2d 944 (1976).

137. *Witherspoon v. Illinois,* 391 U.S. 510 (1968); *Wainwright v. Witt,* 469 U.S. 412 (1985).

138. *Tison v. Arizona,* 481 U.S. 137 (1987).

139. *McCleskey v. Kemp,* 106 S.Ct. 1331 (1986).

140. *Stanford v. Kentucky* and *Wilkins v. Missouri,* 109 S.Ct. 2969 (1989).

141. *McCleskey v. Zant,* 49 Cr.L. 2031 (1991).

© CORBIS

CHAPTER 18 Corrections

Introduction

On December 2001, a New Hampshire judge ordered the early release of Carl Graf, a 36-year-old man convicted of molesting a 10-year-old New Hampshire boy in 1993.[1] Graf was up for parole but would most likely have been denied early release because he had refused to complete a sex offender treatment program while in prison. The program requires inmates to admit their crimes and give a complete sexual history. Graf's attorney, however, argued before a New Hampshire Superior Court judge that, because his client had denied his guilt at trial, being forced to admit in a treatment program that he molested the boy would amount to a violation of his constitutional right against self-incrimination. Consequently, Graf's lawyer claimed, keeping him behind bars amounts to punishing him for exercising his constitutional rights. His argument was positively received by the hearing judge whom, to the chagrin of prosecutors and correctional officials, ordered Graf's release with the proviso that he not be allowed to have any unsupervised contact with minors and must get weekly counseling with a qualified sexual offender treatment provider. After the ruling was made, the prosecuting attorney retorted, "Allowing a defendant to determine his own sentence or to decide when he has satisfied the penal requirements makes the system laughable. Our justice system is designed for the protection of our citizens and the victims of crime are due no less consideration."[2]

The Graf case illustrates some of the complex issues faced by the contemporary correctional system. Are offenders better served by being treated in the community or in a secure institution? Do prison inmates retain their constitutional rights after conviction? Is the deterrent effect of prison weakened when inmates are granted early release? Over the centuries, there has been significant debate as to why people should be punished and what type of punishment is most appropriate to correct, treat, or deter criminal offenders. The style and purpose of criminal corrections have gone through many stages and have featured a variety of penal sanctions.

This chapter considers some of the basic elements of U.S. correctional treatment. First, the history of corrections is reviewed to show how our current system evolved. Then modern correctional institutions are explored, including such issues as penal institutions, the prisoner's social world, correctional treatment, and prisoners' rights.

History of Punishment and Corrections

Throughout history, the punishment of criminal offenders has undergone many noteworthy changes, reflecting custom, economic conditions, and religious and political ideals.[3]

In ancient times, the most common state-administered punishment was banishment or exile. Only slaves were commonly subject to harsh physical punishment for their misdeeds. In Rome, for example, the only crime for which capital punishment could be administered was *furtum manifestum*—a thief caught in the act was executed on the spot. More common were economic sanctions and fines, levied for such crimes as assault on a slave, arson, or housebreaking.

In both ancient Greece and Rome, interpersonal violence, even murder, was viewed as a private matter. Neither Greek nor Roman (until quite late in history) state laws punished violent crime. Execution of an offender was a prerogative of the deceased's family.

To read more about Roman law and punishment, use "Roman Law" as a subject guide on InfoTrac College Edition. ∎

The Middle Ages

Little law or governmental control existed during the early Middle Ages (fifth century to eleventh century A.D.). Offenses were settled by blood feuds between the families of the injured parties. When possible, the Roman custom of settling disputes by fine or an exchange of property was adopted as a means of resolving interpersonal conflicts with a minimum of bloodshed.

After the eleventh century, during the feudal period, forfeiture of land and property was common punishment for people who violated law and customs or who failed in the feudal obligations to their lord. The word "felony" comes from the twelfth century, when the term *felonia* referred to a breach of faith with one's feudal lord.

During this period, the main emphasis of criminal law and punishment lay in maintaining public order.[4] If, in the heat of passion or in a state of intoxication, a person severely injured or killed a neighbor, free men in the area would gather to pronounce judgment and make the culprit do penance or make a payment to the injured party, called *wergild*. The purpose of the wergild was to pacify the injured party and ensure that the conflict would not develop into a blood feud and anarchy. The inability of lower-class offenders to pay a fine led to the development of **corporal punishment,** such as whipping or branding, as a substitute penalty.

By the fifteenth century, changing social conditions influenced the relationship between crime and punishment. First, the population of England and Europe began to increase after a century of decimation by constant warfare and plague. At the same time, the developing commercial system caused large tracts of agricultural fields to be converted to grazing lands. Soon unemployed peasants and landless noblemen began flocking to newly developing urban centers, such as London and Paris, or taking to the roads as highwaymen, beggars, or vagabonds.

The later Middle Ages also saw the rise of strong monarchs, such as Henry VIII and Elizabeth I of England, who were determined to keep a powerful grip on their realm. The administration of the "King's Peace" under the shire reeve and constable became stronger.

These developments led to the increased use of capital and corporal punishment to control the criminal poor. Whereas the wealthy could buy their way out of punishment and into exile, the poor were executed and mutilated at ever-increasing rates. It is estimated that 72,000 thieves were hanged during the reign of Henry VIII alone.[5] Execution, banishment, mutilation, branding, and flogging were used on a wide range of offenders, from murderers and robbers to vagrants and gypsies. Punishments became unmatched in their cruelty, featuring a gruesome variety of physical tortures. Also during this period, punishment became a public spectacle, presumably so the sadistic sanctions would act as a deterrent. But the variety and imagination of the tortures inflicted on even minor criminals before their death suggest that sadism and spectacle were more important than any presumed deterrent effect.

What was torture like in the Middle Ages? To find out, use InfoTrac College Edition to access this article: Gavin Yamey. Torture: European instruments of torture and capital punishment from the middle ages to the present. *British Medical Journal,* 11 Aug 2001 v323 i7308 p346 ∎

Although criminologists generally view the rise of the prison as an eighteenth-century phenomenon, Marvin Wolfgang has written about Le Stinche, a prison in Florence, Italy, which was used to punish offenders as early as 1301. Prisoners were enclosed in separate cells and classified on the basis of gender, age, mental state, and crime seriousness. Furloughs and conditional release were permitted, and perhaps for the first time, a period of incarceration replaced corporal punishment for some offenses. Le Stinche existed for 500 years, but relatively little is known about its administration or whether this early example of incarceration is unique to Florence.[6]

Punishment in the Seventeenth and Eighteenth Centuries

By the end of the sixteenth century, the rise of the city and overseas colonization provided tremendous markets for manufactured goods. In England and France, population growth was checked by constant warfare and internal disturbances. Labor was scarce in many manufacturing areas of England, Germany, and Holland. The Thirty Years' War in Germany and the constant warfare among England, France, and Spain helped drain the population.

The punishment of criminals changed to meet the demands created by these social conditions. Instead of the wholesale use of capital and corporal punishment, many offenders were forced to labor for their crimes. Poor laws, developed in the early seventeenth century, required that

the poor, vagrants, and vagabonds be put to work in public or private enterprise. Houses of correction were developed to make it convenient for petty law violators to be assigned to work details. Many convicted offenders were pressed into sea duty as galley slaves, a fate considered so loathsome that convicts often mutilated themselves rather than submit to it.

The constant labor shortage in the colonies also prompted the authorities to transport convicts overseas. In England, the Vagrancy Act of 1597 legalized deportation for the first time. An Order in Council of 1617 granted a reprieve and stay of execution to people convicted of robbery and other felonies who were strong enough to be employed overseas. Similar measures were used in France and Italy to recruit galley slaves and workers.

Transportation to the colonies became popular; it supplied labor, cost little, and was actually profitable for the government because manufacturers and plantation owners paid for convicts' services. The Old Bailey Court in London supplied at least 10,000 convicts between 1717 and 1775.[7] Convicts would serve a period as workers and then become free again.

Transportation to the colonies waned as a method of punishment with the increase in colonial population, the further development of the land, and the increasing importation of African slaves in the eighteenth century. The American Revolution ended transportation of felons to North America; the remaining areas used were Australia, New Zealand, and African colonies.

Corrections in the Late Eighteenth and Nineteenth Centuries

Between the American Revolution in 1776 and the first decades of the nineteenth century, the population of Europe and America increased rapidly. The gulf between poor workers and wealthy landowners and merchants widened. The crime rate rose significantly, prompting a return to physical punishment and the increased use of the death penalty. During the last part of the eighteenth century, 350 types of crime in England were punishable by death.[8] Although many people sentenced to death for trivial offenses were spared the gallows, there is little question that the use of capital punishment rose significantly between 1750 and 1800.[9]

Correctional reform in the United States was first instituted in Pennsylvania under the leadership of William Penn.[10] At the end of the seventeenth century, Penn revised Pennsylvania's criminal code to forbid torture and the capricious use of mutilation and physical punishment. These devices were replaced by the penalties of imprisonment at hard labor, moderate flogging, fines, and forfeiture of property. All lands and goods belonging to felons were used to make restitution to the victims of crimes, with restitution limited to twice the value of the damages. Felons who owned no property were required by law to labor in the prison workhouse until the victim was compensated.

Penn ordered that a new type of institution be built to replace the widely used public forms of punishment—stocks, pillories, the gallows, and the branding iron. Each county was instructed to build a house of corrections similar to today's jails. These measures remained in effect until Penn's death in 1718, when the penal code reverted to its earlier emphasis on open public punishment and harsh brutality.

In 1776, postrevolutionary Pennsylvania again adopted William Penn's code, and in 1787 a group of Quakers led by Dr. Benjamin Rush formed the Philadelphia Society for Alleviating the Miseries of Public Prisons. The aim of the society was to bring humane and orderly treatment to the growing penal system. The Quakers' influence on the legislature resulted in limiting the use of the death penalty to cases involving treason, murder, rape, and arson.

Under pressure from the Quakers, the Pennsylvania Legislature in 1790 called for the renovation of the prison system. The ultimate result was the creation of Philadelphia's **Walnut Street Prison.** At this institution, most prisoners were placed in solitary cells, where they remained in isolation and did not have the right to work.[11] Quarters that contained the solitary or separate cells were called the penitentiary house, as was already the custom in England.

The new Pennsylvania prison system took credit for a rapid decrease in the crime rate—from 131 convictions in 1789 to 45 in 1793.[12] The prison became known as a school for reform. The Walnut Street Prison's equitable conditions were credited with reducing escapes to none in the first four years of its existence (except for 14 on opening day).

However, the Walnut Street Prison was not a total success. Overcrowding undermined the goal of solitary confinement of serious offenders, and soon more than one inmate was placed in each cell. Despite these difficulties, similar institutions were erected in New York (Newgate in 1791), New Jersey (Trenton in 1798), Virginia (1800), Massachusetts (Castle Island in 1785), and Kentucky (1800). Alexis Durham III has described the Newgate prison of Connecticut, which was constructed in an old copper mine in 1773, as the first "prison" in America.[13]

The Auburn system

In the early 1800s both the Pennsylvania and New York prison systems were experiencing difficulties maintaining the ever-increasing numbers of convicted criminals. Initially administrators dealt with the problem by increasing the use of pardons, relaxing prison discipline, and limiting supervision.

In 1816 New York built a new prison at Auburn, hoping to alleviate some of the overcrowding at Newgate. The Auburn prison design became known as the tier system because cells were built vertically on five floors of the structure. It was sometimes also referred to as the congregate system because most prisoners ate and worked in groups. In 1819 construction was started on a wing of solitary cells to house unruly prisoners. Three classes of prisoners were then created: one group remained continually in solitary confinement as a result of breaches of prison discipline; the second group was allowed labor as an occasional form of recreation; and the third and largest class worked and ate together during the days and went into seclusion only at night.

The philosophy of the **Auburn system** was crime prevention through fear of punishment and silent confinement. The worst felons were cut off from all contact with other prisoners; and although they were treated and fed relatively well, they had no hope of pardon to relieve their isolation. For a time, some of the worst convicts were forced to remain totally alone and silent during the entire day. This caused many prisoners to have mental breakdowns, resulting in many suicides and self-mutilations, and the practice was abolished in 1823.[14]

The combination of silence and solitude as a method of punishment was not abandoned easily. Prison officials sought to overcome the side effects of total isolation while maintaining the penitentiary system. The solution Auburn adopted was to keep convicts in separate cells at night but allow them to work together during the day under enforced silence. Hard work and silence became the foundation of the Auburn system wherever it was adopted. Silence was the key to prison discipline; it prevented the formulation of escape plans, averted plots and riots, and allowed prisoners to contemplate their infractions.

When discipline was breached in the Auburn system, punishment was applied in the form of a rawhide whip on the inmate's back. Immediate and effective, Auburn discipline was so successful that when 100 inmates were chosen to build the famous Sing-Sing prison in 1825 not one dared escape even though they were housed in an open field with only minimal supervision.[15]

The new Pennsylvania system

In 1818 Pennsylvania took the radical step of establishing a prison that placed each inmate in a single cell with no work to do. Classifications were abolished because each cell was intended as a miniature prison that would prevent inmates from contaminating one another.

The new Pennsylvania prison, called the Western Penitentiary, had an unusual architectural design. It was built in a semicircle, with the cells positioned along its circumference. Built back-to-back, some cells faced the boundary wall and others faced the internal area of the circle. Its inmates were kept in solitary confinement almost constantly, being allowed about an hour a day for exercise. In 1820 a second, similar penitentiary using the isolate system was built in Philadelphia and called the Eastern Penitentiary.

The Eastern State Pennitentiary became the most expensive and most copied building of its time. It is estimated that more than 300 prisons worldwide are based on the Penitentiary's wagon-wheel, or "radial" floor plan. Some of America's most notorious criminals were held in the Penitentiary's vaulted, sky-lit cells, including Al Capone. After 142 years of consecutive use, Eastern State Penitentiary was completely abandoned in 1971. However, you can still see pictures of the structure and read about its history at this Web site:

http://www.EasternState.com/

For an up-to-date list of Web links, go to

http://info.wadsworth.com/siegel ■

The supporters of the Pennsylvania system believed the penitentiary was truly a place to do penance. By advocating totally removing the sinner from society and allowing the prisoner a period of isolation in which to reflect alone upon the evils of crime, the supporters of the Pennsylvania system reflected the influence of religious philosophy on corrections. In fact, its advocates believed that solitary confinement (with in-cell labor as a recreation) would eventually make working so attractive that upon release the inmate would be well suited to resume a productive existence in society. The Pennsylvania system eliminated the need for large numbers of guards or disciplinary measures. Isolated from each other, inmates could not plan escapes or collectively break rules. When discipline was a problem, whips and iron gags were used (iron gags were jammed in inmates' mouths so they could not speak, causing great discomfort).

The **congregate system** eventually prevailed, however, and spread throughout the United States; many of its features are still used today. Its innovations included congregate working conditions, the use of solitary confinement to punish unruly inmates, military regimentation, and discipline. In Auburn-like institutions, prisoners were marched from place to place; their time was regulated by bells telling them to sleep, wake up, and work. The system was so like the military that many of its early administrators were recruited from the armed services.

Although the prison was viewed as an improvement over capital and corporal punishment, it quickly became the scene of depressed conditions; inmates were treated harshly and routinely whipped and tortured. As historian Samuel Walker notes,

> Prison brutality flourished. It was ironic that the prison had been devised as a more humane alternative to corporal and capital punishment. Instead, it simply moved corporal punishment indoors where, hidden from public view, it became even more savage.[16]

Yet in the midst of such savagery some inmates were able to adjust to institutional living and even improve their lives through prison-administered literacy programs.[17]

Post–Civil War developments The prison of the late nineteenth century was remarkably similar to that of today. The congregate system was adopted in all states except Pennsylvania. Prisons experienced overcrowding, and

the single-cell principle was often ignored. The prison, like the police department, became the scene of political intrigue and efforts by political administrators to control the hiring of personnel and dispensing of patronage.

Prison industry developed and became the predominant theme around which institutions were organized. Some prisons used the **contract system,** in which officials sold the labor of inmates to private businesses. Sometimes the contractor supervised the inmates inside the prison itself. Under the **convict-lease system** the state leased its prisoners to a business for a fixed annual fee and gave up supervision and control. Finally, the **state account system** had prisoners produce goods in prison for state use.[18]

The development of prison industry quickly led to abuse of inmates, who were forced to work for almost no wages, and to profiteering by dishonest administrators and businessmen. During the Civil War era, prisons were major manufacturers of clothes, shoes, boots, furniture, and the like. During the 1880s, opposition by trade unions sparked restrictions on interstate commerce in prison goods and ended their profitability.

There were also reforms in prison operations. **Z. R. Brockway,** warden at the Elmira Reformatory in New York, advocated individualized treatment, indeterminate sentences, and parole. The reformatory program initiated by Brockway included elementary education for illiterates, designated library hours, lectures by local college faculty members, and a group of vocational training shops. The cost to the state of the institution's operations was to be held to a minimum. Although Brockway proclaimed Elmira an ideal reformatory, his actual achievements were limited. The greatest significance of his contribution was the injection of a degree of humanitarianism into the industrial prisons of that day. Although many institutions were constructed across the country and labeled reformatories as a result of the Elmira model, most of them continued to be industrially oriented.[19]

Corrections in the Twentieth Century

The early twentieth century was a time of contrasts in the U.S. prison system.[20] At one extreme were those who advocated reform, such as the Mutual Welfare League, led by Thomas Mott Osborne. Prison reform groups proposed better treatment for inmates, an end to harsh corporal punishment, and the creation of meaningful prison industries and educational programs. Reformers argued that prisoners should not be isolated from society; rather, the best elements of society—education, religion, meaningful work, self-governance—should be brought to the prison. Osborne even spent one week in New York's notorious Sing-Sing Prison to learn about its conditions firsthand.

Opposed to the reformers were conservative prison administrators and state officials, who believed stern discipline was needed to control dangerous prison inmates.

They continued the time-honored system of regimentation. Although the whip was eventually abolished, solitary confinement in dark, bare cells became a common penal practice.

In time, some of the more rigid prison rules gave way to liberal reform. By the mid-1930s few prisons required inmates to wear the red-and-white-striped convict suit and substituted nondescript gray uniforms. The code of silence ended, as did the lockstep shuffle. Prisoners were allowed to mingle and exercise an hour or two each day.[21] Movies and radio appeared in the prisons in the 1930s. Visiting policies and mail privileges were liberalized.

A more important trend was the development of specialized prisons designed to treat particular types of offenders. For example, in New York, the prisons at Clinton and Auburn were viewed as industrial facilities for hard-core inmates, Great Meadow as an agricultural center to house nondangerous offenders, and Dannemora as a facility for the criminally insane. In California, San Quentin housed inmates considered salvageable by correctional authorities, whereas Folsom was reserved for hard-core offenders.[22]

Prison industry also evolved. Opposition by organized labor helped end the convict-lease system and forced inmate labor. Although some vestiges of private prison industry existed into the 1920s, most convict labor was devoted to state-use items, such as license plates and laundry.

Despite these changes and reforms, the prison in the mid-twentieth century remained a destructive total institution. Although some aspects of inmate life improved, severe discipline, harsh rules, and solitary confinement were the way of life in prison.

The Modern Era

The modern era has witnessed change and turmoil in the nation's correctional system. Three trends stand out. First, between 1960 and 1980, a great deal of litigation was brought by inmates seeking greater rights and privileges. State and federal court rulings gave inmates rights to freedom of religion and speech, medical care, due process, and proper living conditions. Since 1980, the "prisoners' rights" movement has slowed as judicial activism waned during the Reagan–Bush era.

Second, violence within the correctional system became a national scandal. Well-publicized riots at New York's Attica Prison and the New Mexico State Penitentiary have drawn attention to the potential for death and destruction that lurks in every prison. One reaction has been to improve conditions and provide innovative programs that give inmates a voice in running the institution. Another has been to tighten discipline and build maximum-security prisons to control dangerous offenders.

Third, the alleged failure of correctional rehabilitation has prompted many penologists to reconsider the purpose of incapacitating criminals. Today it is more common to view the correctional system as a mechanism for control and punishment than as a device for rehabilitation and reform.

The inability of the prison to reduce recidivism has prompted the development of alternatives to incarceration, including diversion, restitution, and community-based corrections. The nation's correctional policy seems to keep as many nonthreatening offenders out of the correctional system as possible by means of community-based programs and, conversely, to incarcerate dangerous, violent offenders for long periods.[23] Unfortunately, despite the development of alternatives to incarceration, the number of people under lock and key has skyrocketed.

Today correctional treatment can be divided into community-based programs and secure confinement. Community-based corrections include **probation,** which involves supervision under the control of the sentencing court, and an array of intermediate sanctions, which provide greater supervision and treatment than traditional probation but are less intrusive than incarceration.

Treatment in the community is viewed as a viable alternative to traditional correctional practices.[24] First, it is significantly less expensive to supervise inmates in the community than to house them in secure institutional facilities. Second, community-based corrections are necessary if the prison system is not to be overwhelmed by an influx of offenders. Third, community-based treatment is designed so that first-time or nonserious offenders can avoid the stigma and pain of imprisonment and be rehabilitated in the community.

In secure confinement, the jail houses misdemeanants (and some felons) serving their sentences, as well as felons and misdemeanants awaiting trial who have not been released on bail. State and federal prisons incarcerate felons for extended periods. Parole and aftercare agencies supervise prisoners who have been given early release from their sentences. Although parolees are actually in the community, **parole** is usually considered both organizationally and philosophically part of the secure correctional system. These institutions are discussed in the next sections.

■ Probation

Probation typically involves the suspension of the offender's sentence in return for the promise of good behavior in the community under the supervision of the probation department. It usually replaces a term in an institution, although minors can be placed on probation without the threat of detention. In some cases, the offender is first sentenced to a prison term, and then the sentence is suspended and the defendant placed on probation. In others, the imposition of a prison sentence is delayed or suspended while the offender is put on probation. Probation is not limited to minor or petty criminals; a significant proportion of people convicted of felony offenses receive probation, including about 4 percent of murderers and 16 percent of rapists.[25]

As practiced in all 50 states and by the federal government, probation implies a contract between the court and the offender in which the former promises to hold a prison term in abeyance and the latter promises to adhere to a set of rules or conditions required by the court. If the rules are violated, and especially if the probationer commits another criminal offense, probation may be **revoked;** this means that the contract is terminated and the original sentence enforced. If an offender on probation commits a second offense that is more severe than the first, he or she may be indicted, tried, and sentenced on that second offense. Probation may also be revoked simply because its rules and conditions have not been met, even if the offender has not committed another crime. In a series of cases, most importantly *Gagnon v. Scarpelli,*[26] the Supreme Court ruled that before probation can be revoked the offender must (1) be given a hearing before the sentencing court and (2) be provided with counsel if there is a substantial reason for him or her to require legal assistance.

Each probationary sentence is for a fixed period, depending on the seriousness of the offense and the statutory law of the jurisdiction. Probation is considered served when the offender fulfills the conditions set by the court for that period; after that, he or she can live without interference from the state.

Probationary Sentences

Probationary sentences may be granted by state and federal district courts and state superior (felony) courts. Probation has become an accepted, widely used sentence for adult felons and misdemeanants and juvenile delinquents.

In most jurisdictions, juries can recommend probation, but the judge has the final say in the matter. In nonjury trials, probation is granted solely by judicial mandate. Except where state law expressly prohibits a community supervision option, almost all offenders are eligible for probation, even those convicted of violent felonies, such as rape and homicide. Only mandatory sentencing laws that require incarceration preclude the probation option.

The term of the probationary sentence may extend to the limit of the suspended prison term. Misdemeanor probation usually extends for the entire period of the jail sentence. Felony probationary periods are likely to be shorter than the prison sentences would have been.

Probation Organizations

About 2,000 agencies nationwide list adult probation as their major function; as of 2001, approximately 3,840,000 adults were under federal, state, or local probation.[27]

Among offenders on probation, slightly more than half (52 percent) had been convicted for committing a felony, 46 percent for a misdemeanor, and 2 percent for other infractions.

Most probation agencies function at the state level; the remainder are organized at the county or municipal level. About 30 states combine probation and parole supervision into a single state agency.[28]

There are arguments for both placing probation services under the supervision of individual courts and creating statewide agencies. Local supervision makes probation more responsive to court discretion and helps judges get better information on the effectiveness of their decisions. Because the bulk of the probation department's work is in the local courts, it seems appropriate that the agencies should be organized at the county level.

Those who advocate large state probation agencies argue that probation is a correctional service and therefore should be part of the executive level of government.[29] Larger agencies can coordinate programs and staff, establish training programs, and distribute funds.

Probation Services

After a person is convicted of a crime, the probation department investigates the case to determine the factors related to the criminality of the offender. Based on this presentence investigation, the department recommends to the sentencing judge whether the offender is eligible for community release. In the event the offender is placed on probation, the investigation findings will be used as the basis for treatment and supervision. If the offender is placed on probation, the department diagnoses his or her personality and treatment needs; this is referred to as **offender classification.** Based on this evaluation, offenders classified as minimal risks will be given little supervision, perhaps a monthly phone call or visit, whereas those classified as high risk will receive close supervision and intensive care and treatment. Developing accurate risk classification methods is a major goal of probation.[30] Some studies show these methods to be effective predictors of probationer success in the community.[31]

Probation officers once commonly supervised treatment. Today clients are more often placed in community mental health, substance abuse, and family counseling clinics. There has also been an explosion of privately run community-based treatment programs that provide comprehensive for-profit correctional treatment. Probation officers can mandate that offenders attend biweekly treatment sessions, attend support groups, report for polygraph testing and urinalysis, and complete homework assignments.[32]

The treatment function is a product of both the investigative and the diagnostic aspects of probation. A probation officer who discovers that a client has a drinking

■ A probation officer confers with a police officer in San Fernando, California. If an offender violates the rules of probation, local police may be called upon to make an arrest and take the offender into custody. Probation is generally successful, but a significant number of felons granted probation eventually have it revoked for committing new crimes.

problem may help find a detoxification center willing to accept the case; a chronically underemployed offender may be placed with a job counseling center. Or, in the case of juvenile delinquency, a probation officer may work with teachers and other school officials to help a young offender stay in school. Although outside treatment placements are the norm, it is not unknown for probation officers to provide direct treatment to offenders who have substance abuse problems in communities that lack adequate, effective community-based programs.[33] Probation officers also conduct special programs for clients, such as teaching child-rearing skills to parents of juvenile offenders in their caseloads.[34] Of course, most cases do not (or cannot) receive such individualized treatment; some treatment mechanisms merely involve a yearly phone call to determine whether the offender is maintaining a job or attending school.[35] Regardless of how it is handled, probationers who complete their treatment plans are less likely to recidivate than offenders who fail at treatment.[36]

Probation Rules and Revocation

Each offender granted probation is given a set of rules to guide his or her behavior. Most jurisdictions have a standard set of rules that include these requirements:

*   Maintain steady employment
*   Make restitution for loss or damage
*   Cooperate with the probation officer
*   Obey all laws
*   Meet family responsibilities

Sometimes an individual probationer is given specific rules that relate to his or her particular circumstances, such as the requirement to enroll in a drug treatment program.

To read how corrections departments are trying to treat drug dependent inmates in the prison setting, go to:
http://www.ojp.usdoj.gov/docs/psrsa.txt
For an up-to-date list of Web links, go to
http://info.wadsworth.com/siegel ■

If rules are violated, a person's probation may be revoked by the court, and the person either begins serving the sentence or, if he or she has not yet been sentenced, receives a prison sentence from the court. Revocation for violation of probation rules is called a **technical violation;** probation also can be revoked if the offender commits another offense.

Success of Probation

How successful is probation? How often do probationers commit new crimes while they are under supervision? Some research studies have found that probation is not as successful as hoped. In an often-cited 1985 study, Joan Petersilia and her colleagues at the Rand Corporation followed the careers of 1,672 California men granted probation for felony offenses.[37] They found that 1,087 (65 percent) were rearrested, 853 (51 percent) were convicted, and 568 (34 percent) were incarcerated. The researchers uncovered the disturbing fact that 75 percent of the new arrests were for serious crimes, including larceny, burglary, and robbery; 18 percent of the probationers were convicted of serious violent crimes. They also found that about 25 percent of felons granted probation had personal and legal characteristics indistinguishable from people put in prison for the same original charges. The Petersilia research was an early indication that felons often qualified for and later failed on probation.

National data indicate that about 60 percent of probationers successfully complete their probationary sentence, and about 40 percent are either rearrested, violate probation rules, or abscond. Findings indicate that most probation violations were for technical reasons, a significant proportion of which are committed during the first three months of probation.[38] In 2000, 15 percent of probationers who were discharged from supervision were incarcerated because of a rule violation or a new offense.[39]

Although the recidivism rate of probationers seems high, it is lower than the recidivism rate of prison inmates.[40] And some studies have found a lower recidivism rate among particular classes of probationers (such as young, non–drug-using property offenders), indicating that probation may be a relatively effective correctional alternative for some groups of offenders.[41]

Probation remains the sentence of choice for about one-third of all felony cases.[42] Because it costs far less to maintain an offender in the community than in prison, and because prison overcrowding continues, there is constant economic pressure to grant probation to serious felony offenders. Even if probation is no more successful than prison, it costs less and is therefore extremely attractive to policymakers. However, some believe the risk of probation failure is too high and that judges should think carefully before sentencing felons to probation.

■ Intermediate Sanctions

At a time when overcrowding has produced a crisis in the nation's prison system, alternative sanctions are viewed as a new form of corrections that fall somewhere between probation and incarceration.[43] Alternative sanctions include fines, forfeiture, home confinement, electronic monitoring, intensive probation supervision, restitution, community corrections, and boot camps.

The development of these **intermediate sanctions** can be tied to a number of different sources. Primary is the need to develop alternatives to prisons, which have proved both ineffective and injurious. Research indicates that about half of all prison inmates are likely to be rearrested and returned to prison, many soon after their release from an institution.[44] High revocation rates indicate that probation alone may not be an effective solution to the prison crowding problem. Therefore, a sanction that falls somewhere between prison and probation might be a more effective alternative to traditional forms of correction.

Intermediate sanctions also meet the need to develop punishments that are fair, equitable, and proportional. It seems unfair to treat both a rapist and a shoplifter with the same type of sentence, considering the differences in their criminal acts. Intermediate sanctions can provide the successive steps for a meaningful "ladder" of scaled punishments outside prison (see Figure 18.1), thereby restoring fairness and equity to nonincarceration sentences.[45] For example, a forger may be ordered to make restitution to the victim, and an abusive husband can be ordered to reside in a community correctional center, whereas a rapist would be sent to state prison. This feature of intermediate sanctions allows judges to fit the punishment to the crime without resorting to a prison sentence.

Intermediate sanctions can be designed to be punitive by increasing punishments for people whose serious or repeat crimes make straight probation sentences inappropriate yet for whom prison sentences would be unduly harsh and dysfunctional.[46] In fact, the punitive nature of intermediate sanctions is not lost on offenders, some of whom prefer prison to the new, tougher forms of probation.[47] The most likely candidates are convicted criminals who would normally be sent to prison but either have a low risk of recidivating or pose little threat to society (such as nonviolent property offenders). Used in this sense, intermediate sanctions are a viable solution to the critical problem of prison overcrowding.

The following sections more thoroughly discuss the forms of intermediate sanctions in use.

Fines

An off-shoot of the medieval custom of wergild, criminal fines are monetary payments imposed on an offender as an intermediate punishment for criminal acts. Although fines are most commonly used in misdemeanors, they are also frequently employed in felonies where the offender benefited financially. Investor Ivan Boesky paid more than $100 million in fines for violating insider stock trading rules; the firm of Drexel, Burnham Lambert paid $650 million in 1988 for securities violations.[48] Fines may be used as a sole sanction or combined with other punishment, such as probation or confinement. Quite commonly judges levy other monetary sanctions along with fines, such as court costs, public defender fees, probation and treatment fees, and victim restitution, to increase the force of the financial punishment.[49]

Some jurisdictions are experimenting with **day fines,** a concept originated in Europe that gears fines to an offender's net daily income in an effort to make them more equitable. In contrast to the traditional fixed-sum fining system, in which the fine amount is governed principally by the nature of the crime, the day-fine approach tailors the fine amount to the defendant's ability to pay. Thus, for a given crime, the day fine is larger for a high-income offender than for an irregularly employed or low-paid

Figure 18.1 The Punishment Ladder

Death penalty

Prison

Boot camps

Split sentences

Residential community center

Electronic monitoring

House arrest

Intensive probation

Restitution

Probation

Forfeiture

Fines

offender. The impact of the fine on each should be approximately equal. Under the traditional approach, a given fine amount could be relatively severe for a low-income offender but trivial for a person of substantial means.

Although it is far from certain that fines are an effective sanction, either alone or in combination with other penalties, they remain one of the most commonly used criminal penalties. Research sponsored by the federal government found that lower-court judges impose fines alone or in tandem with other penalties in 86 percent of their cases, whereas superior court judges impose fines in 42 percent of their cases.[50]

Forfeiture

Another financially based alternative sanction is criminal (*in personam*) and civil (*in rem*) **forfeiture.** Both involve the seizure of goods and instrumentalities related to the commission or outcome of a criminal act. The difference is that criminal forfeiture proceedings target criminal defendants and can only follow a criminal conviction. In contrast, civil forfeiture proceedings target *property* used in a crime and do not require that formal criminal proceedings be initiated against a person or that they be proven guilty of a crime.[51] For example, federal law provides that after arresting drug traffickers the government may seize the boat they used to import the narcotics, the car they used to carry them overland, the warehouse in which drugs were stored, and the home paid for with drug money; upon conviction, the drug dealers permanently lose ownership of these instrumentalities of crime.

Forfeiture is not a new sanction. During the Middle Ages forfeiture of estate was a mandatory result of most felony convictions. The Crown could seize all of a felon's real and personal property. Forfeiture derived from the common-law concept of "corruption of blood" or "attaint," which prohibited a felon's family from receiving his or her estate. Common law mandated that descendants could not inherit property from a relative who may have attained the property illegally: "(T)he Corruption of Blood stops the Course of Regular Descent, as to Estates, over which the Criminal could have no Power, because he never enjoyed them."[52]

The use of forfeiture was reintroduced in U.S. law with the passage of the Racketeer Influenced and Corrupt Organizations (RICO) and the Continuing Criminal Enterprises acts, both of which allow the seizure of any property derived from illegal enterprises or conspiracies.

While extremely effective because of the threat it imposes on the illegal fruits of criminality, some critics warn that forfeiture can cause a conflict of interest with the goal of effective crime control. Because law enforcement agencies can use forfeited assets to supplement their budgets, they may direct their efforts to cases that promise the greatest "payoff" rather than ones that have the highest law enforcement priority.[53]

Restitution

Another popular intermediate sanction is restitution, which can take the form of requiring convicted defendants to either repay the victims of crime (**monetary restitution**) or serve the community to compensate for their criminal acts (**community service restitution**).[54]

Restitution programs offer convicted offenders a chance to avoid jail or prison sentences or lengthy probation. Restitution may also be used as a diversionary device that allows some offenders to avoid a criminal record altogether. In this instance, a judge continues the case "without a finding" while the defendant completes the restitution order; after the probation department determines that restitution has been made, the case is dismissed.[55]

Because restitution appears to benefit the crime victim, the offender, the criminal justice system, and society as a whole, national interest in the concept has been tremendous. Restitution is inexpensive, avoids stigma, and helps compensate crime victims. Offenders doing community service have worked in schools, hospitals, and nursing homes. Helping them avoid jail can save the public thousands of dollars that would have maintained them in secure institutions, free needed resources, and give the community the feeling that equity has been returned to the justice system.

Does restitution work? Most reviews give it a qualified success rating. It is estimated that almost 90 percent of eligible offenders successfully complete their restitution orders and that restitutioners have equal or lower recidivism rates when compared to control groups of various kinds.[56]

Shock Probation and Split Sentencing

Split sentences and shock probation are alternative sanctions that allow judges to grant offenders community release only after they have sampled prison life. These sanctions are based on the premise that if offenders are given a taste of incarceration sufficient to "shock" them into law-abiding behavior they will be reluctant to violate the rules of probation or commit other criminal acts.

In a number of states and in the federal criminal code, a jail term can actually be a condition of probation; this is known as **split sentencing.** Under current federal practices, about 25 percent of all convicted federal offenders receive some form of split sentence, including both prison and jail as a condition of probation.[57]

Another approach, known as **shock probation,** involves resentencing an offender after a short prison stay. The shock comes because the offender originally receives a long maximum sentence but is then eligible for release to community supervision at the discretion of the judge (usually within 90 days of incarceration). Shock probation has been praised as a program that limits prison time and allows offenders to be quickly integrated into the community, a mechanism that can maintain family ties, and a way of reducing prison populations and the costs of corrections.

Intensive Probation Supervision

Intensive probation supervision (IPS) programs are another important form of intermediate sanction. IPS programs, which have been implemented in some form in about 45 states, involve small caseloads of 15 to 40 clients who are kept under close watch by probation officers. The primary goal of IPS is diversion: without intensive supervision, clients would normally have been sent to already overcrowded prisons or jails. The second goal is control: high-risk offenders can stay in the community under much closer security than traditional probation efforts can provide. A third goal is reintegration: offenders can maintain community ties and be reoriented toward a more productive life while avoiding the pain of imprisonment.

Who is eligible for IPS? Most programs have admissions criteria based on the nature of the offense and the offender's criminal background. Some programs exclude violent offenders; others will not consider substance abusers. In contrast, some jurisdictions, such as Massachusetts, do not exclude offenders based on their prior criminal history. About 60 percent of IPS programs exclude offenders who have already violated probation orders or otherwise failed on probation.

Despite its promise, the failure rate in IPS caseloads is quite high, approaching 50 percent.[58] Younger offenders who commit petty crimes are the most likely to fail on IPS; ironically, people with these characteristics are the most likely to be included in IPS programs.[59] It is possible that closer supervision "produces" failures because supervisors are better able to detect technical and legal violations. Continuous drug testing alone should produce a higher failure rate among IPS clients than traditional probationers.

These failure rates seem high, but IPS is designed for clients who have more serious prior records and histories of drug abuse than regular probationers. However, in an important analysis of IPS in three California counties, Joan Petersilia found that IPS clients were actually less dangerous than those sent to prison and just as likely to recidivate as clients in traditional probation caseloads.[60] IPS is a waste of taxpayers' money if it works no better than traditional probation while serving a similar clientele.

Home Confinement/Electronic Monitoring

A number of states, including Florida, Oklahoma, Oregon, Kentucky, and California, have developed **home confinement (HC)** programs (also called house arrest or home detention) as an intermediate sanction. The HC concept requires convicted offenders to spend extended periods in their own homes as an alternative to incarceration. For example, an individual convicted of drunk driving might be sentenced to spend the period between 6 P.M. Friday and 8 A.M. Monday and every weekday after 5:30 P.M. in his or her home for the next six months. Some estimates indicate that as many as 10,000 people are placed under HC yearly.[61]

Like IPS programs, there is a great deal of variation in HC initiatives: some are administered by probation departments, whereas others are simply judicial sentences monitored by surveillance officers; some check clients 10 or more times a month, whereas others make only a few curfew checks; some use 24-hour confinement, whereas others allow offenders to attend work or school. Regardless of the model used, house arrest programs are designed to be more punitive than IPS and are considered a "last chance" before prison: if you are caught violating a house arrest order, the next logical stop is a secure correctional facility.[62]

As yet, no definitive data indicate that HC effectively deters crime, nor is there sufficient evidence to conclude that it lowers recidivism rates. Nonetheless, considering its cost advantages and the overcrowded status of prisons and jails, it is evident that house arrest will continue to grow in the new millennium.

For house arrest to work, sentencing authorities must be assured that arrestees are actually at home during their assigned times. Random calls and visits are one way to check on compliance with house arrest orders. However, a more advanced method of control has been the introduction of **electronic monitoring** (EM) devices to manage offender obedience to home confinement orders.

To read all about EM, go to Keeping Track of Electronic Monitoring, published by the National Law Enforcement Corrections Technology Center, at:
> **http://www.nlectc.org/txtfiles/ElecMonasc.html**
For an up-to-date list of Web links, go to
> **http://info.wadsworth.com/siegel** ∎

Electronically monitored offenders wear devices attached to their ankles, wrists, or neck that send signals back to a control office. Two basic types of systems are used: active and passive. Active systems constantly monitor the offender by continuously sending a signal back to the central office. If the offender leaves his or her home at an unauthorized time, the signal is broken and the "failure" recorded. In some cases the control officer is automatically notified electronically through a beeper. In contrast, passive systems usually involve random phone calls generated by computers to which the offender has to respond within a particular time (such as 30 seconds). Some passive systems require the offender to place the monitoring device into a verifier box, which then sends a signal back to the control computer; another approach is to have the arrestee repeat words that are analyzed by a voice verifier. Most electronic surveillance systems use telephone lines, but some employ radio transmitters that receive a signal from a device worn by the offender and relay it back to a computer monitoring system.

Growth in the number of electronically monitored offenders has been explosive. Up to 1 million people may eventually be monitored electronically in the United States.[63] EM is being hailed as one of the most important developments in correctional policy.[64] It has the benefits of relatively low cost and high security while at the same time helping offenders avoid imprisonment in overcrowded, dangerous state facilities. Electronic monitoring is capital rather than labor intensive. Because offenders are monitored by computers, an initial investment in hardware rules out the need for hiring many more supervisory officers to handle large numbers of clients. It can also be used at many stages of the justice process, including at the front end as a condition of pretrial release and at the back end as part of parole.

A general review of EM programs indicates that recidivism rates are lower than recorded for comparable groups of probationers or parolees.[65] There are variations in the success rates of programs, and EM may be more effective with some offenders than others and at certain stages of the justice process than at others. EM seems to work much more efficiently with convicted offenders than as a pretrial detention; juveniles respond better than adults.[66] Among those convicted, serious felony offenders, substance abusers, and repeat offenders are the most likely to fail on EM.[67] EM may effectively reduce recidivism among targeted groups of nonviolent offenders, especially drunk drivers, whose incarceration helps clog the correctional system.[68]

Residential Community Corrections

A more secure intermediate sanction is a sentence to a **residential community corrections** (RCC) program. These programs have been defined by the National Institute of Corrections as "a freestanding nonsecure building that is not part of a prison or jail and houses pre-trial and adjudicated adults. The residents regularly depart to work, to attend school, and/or participate in community corrections activities and programs."[69]

The traditional role of community corrections was to provide a nonsecure "halfway house" environment designed to reintegrate soon-to-be-paroled prison inmates into the community. Inmates spend the last few months of their sentences in halfway houses acquiring suitable employment, building up cash reserves, obtaining apartments, and developing job-related wardrobes. These facilities often look like residential homes because many were originally private residences. In urban centers, small apartment buildings have been used to house clients. Usually these facilities have a central treatment theme—such as group therapy or reality therapy—for rehabilitating and reintegrating clients. Another popular approach in community-based corrections is the use of ex-offenders as staff members. These individuals have experienced making the transition between the closed institution and society and can be invaluable in helping residents overcome the many hurdles to proper readjustment. Clients learn how to reestablish family and friendship ties, and the shock of sudden reentry into society is considerably reduced.

The traditional concept of community corrections has expanded recently. Today the community correctional facility provides intermediate sanctions as well as a prerelease center for those about to be paroled from prison. For example, RCC has been used as a direct sentencing option for judges who believe particular offenders need a correctional alternative halfway between traditional probation and a stay in prison. Placement in an RCC center can be used as a condition of probation for offenders who need a nonsecure community facility that provides a more structured treatment environment than traditional probation.

In addition to being a sole sentence and a halfway house, RCC programs have also been used as a residential pretrial release center for offenders who need immediate social services before their trial and as a halfway-back alternative for both parole and probation violators who might otherwise have to be imprisoned. In this capacity, RCC programs serve as a base from which offenders can be placed in outpatient psychiatric facilities, drug and alcohol treatment programs, job training, and so on.

Boot Camps/Shock Incarceration

Another intermediate sanction gaining popularity around the United States is **shock incarceration (SI)** or **boot camps.** These programs typically include youthful, first-time offenders and feature military discipline and physical training. The concept is that short periods (90 to 180 days) of high-intensity exercise and work will shock young criminals into going straight. (Figure 18.2 describes the day in a typical boot camp.) Tough physical training is designed to promote responsibility and improve decision-making skills, build self-confidence, and teach socialization skills. Inmates are treated with rough intensity by drill masters, who may call them names and punish the entire group for the failure of one of its members.

There is wide variety in the programs now operating around the United States.[70] Some programs include educational and training components, counseling sessions, and treatment for special-needs populations; others devote little or no time to therapeutic activities. Some receive program participants directly from court sentencing, whereas others choose potential candidates from the general inmate population. Some allow voluntary participation, and others voluntary termination.[71] One unique program, the Specialized Treatment and Rehabilitation (STAR) for juvenile offenders actually operates in a public school setting and is administered by the school, the juvenile court, and the juvenile probation department. Though the program has had a relatively small impact on recidivism, participants generally approved of the experience.[72]

Is shock incarceration a correctional panacea or another fad doomed to failure? The results so far are mixed. The costs of boot camps are no lower than those of tradi-

Figure 18.2 Shock Incarceration: Typical Daily Routines and Schedule in a Boot Camp Program

Rita finishes 50 sit-ups and springs to her feet. At 6 A.M. her platoon begins a 5-mile run, the last portion of this morning's physical training. After five months in New York's Lakeview Shock Incarceration Correctional Facility, the morning workout is easy. Rita even enjoys it, taking pride in her physical conditioning.

When Rita graduates and returns to New York City, she will face six months of intensive supervision before moving to regular parole. More than two-fifths of Rita's platoon did not make it this far; some withdrew voluntarily, and the rest were removed for misconduct or failure to participate satisfactorily. By completing shock incarceration, she will enter parole 11 months before her minimum release date.

The requirements for completing shock incarceration are the same for male and female inmates. The women live in a separate housing area of Lakeview. Otherwise, men and women participate in the same education, physical training, drill and ceremony, drug education, and counseling programs. Men and women are assigned to separate work details and attend network group meetings held in inmates' living units.

Daily schedule

A.M.
5:30	Wake up and standing count
5:45–6:30	Calisthenics and drill
6:30–7:00	Run
7:00–8:00	Mandatory breakfast/cleanup
8:15	Standing count and company formation
8:30–11:55	Work/school schedules

P.M.
12:00–12:30	Mandatory lunch and standing count
12:30–3:30	Afternoon work/school schedule
3:30–4:00	Shower
4:00–4:45	Network community meeting
4:45–5:45	Mandatory dinner, prepare for evening
6:00–9:00	School, group counseling, drug counseling, prerelease counseling, decision-making classes
8:00	Count while in programs
9:15–9:30	Squad bay, prepare for bed
9:30	Standing count, lights out

SOURCE: Cherie Clark, David Aziz, and Doris Mackenzie, *Shock Incarceration in New York: Focus on Treatment* (Washington, D.C.: National Institute of Justice, 1994), p. 5.

tional prisons, but because sentences are shorter, boot camps provide long-term savings. Some programs suffer high failure-to-complete rates, which makes program evaluations difficult (even if "graduates" are successful, it is possible that success is achieved because troublesome cases drop out and are placed in the general inmate population). What evaluations exist indicate that the recidivism rates of inmates who attend shock programs are in some cases no lower than those released from traditional prisons. Many of these evaluations have been conducted by Doris Layton Mackenzie and her associates. Although boot camp inmates may have lower recidivism rates than probationers and parolees, she has found that they have higher rates of technical violations and revocations.[73] These results are disappointing, but Mackenzie reports that both staff and inmates seem excited by the programs, and even those who fail on parole report they felt SI was a valuable experience.[74] She also finds that carefully managed boot camp programs can make a major dent in prison overcrowding.[75] Nonetheless, Mackenzie's extensive evaluations of the boot camp experience generate little evidence that they can significantly lower recidivism rates. Programs that seem to work, such as those in New York, stress treatment and therapeutic activities, are voluntary, and are longer in duration.[76] Perhaps the therapeutic aspect of the programs, not the military part, provides any achieved benefits.

Can Alternatives Work?

There is little evidence that alternative sanctions can prevent crime, reduce recidivism, or work much better than traditional probation or prison. Those who favor this approach argue that even without conclusive evidence that alternative sanctions are better than prison, they are certainly cheaper. Yet this rationale is valid only if the client population served would have been placed in more restrictive, costly secure confinement absent the opportunity for alternative sentencing. If, as some critics contend, placement is restricted to people who would have ordinarily been granted straight probation, then alternative sanctions are actually a more expensive method to achieve about the same result.

While evaluations of alternative sanctions have not produced clear evidence of their utility, it is probably too early to dismiss them as a significant correctional alternative. Recent research by Patricia Harris and her associates found that they are in fact being used to provide proportionality in sentencing; people who present the greatest risk are given the most restrictive sanctions.[77] If Harris is correct, then alternative sanctions have met their goal of providing correctional alternatives that fall between probation and prison.

■ Jails

The **jail** is a secure institution used (1) to detain offenders before trial if they cannot afford or are not eligible for bail and (2) to house misdemeanants sentenced to terms of one year or less, as well as some nonserious felons. The jail is

■ A Florida boot camp inmate marches while holding his bedroll. Boot camps seem to hold promise as an effective correctional treatment mode, but evaluation research indicates that they are no more successful than traditional institutions.

a multipurpose correctional institution whose other main functions are set out in Exhibit 18.1.

The jail originated in Europe in the sixteenth century and was used to house those awaiting trial and punishment. Jails were not used to house sentenced criminals because at that time punishment was achieved by fine, exile, corporal punishment, or death. Throughout their history, jails have been considered hellholes of pestilence and cruelty. In early English history, they housed offenders awaiting trial, as well as vagabonds, debtors, the mentally ill, and assorted others.[78] The early colonists adopted the European custom of detaining prisoners in jail. As noted previously, William Penn instituted the first jails to house convicted offenders while they worked off their sentences. The Walnut Street Prison, built in 1790, is considered the first modern jail.

Jail Populations

There has been a national effort to remove as many people from local jails as possible through bail reform measures and pretrial diversion. Nonetheless, jail populations have been steadily increasing, due in part to the increased use of mandatory jail sentences for such common crimes as drunk driving and the use of local jails to house inmates for whom there is no room in state prisons.

How many people are in jail today?[79] The nation's confined jail population increased by more than 33 percent in the seven years between 1993 and 2000 (from 459,804 inmates at midyear 1993 to 621,149 at midyear 2000). Further evidence of the increasing reliance on jails is the per capita increase in incarceration rates: between 1990 and 2000, the number of jail inmates per 100,000 U.S. residents rose from 163 to 226.

There is a trend toward fewer but larger jails. Whereas the number of jails has declined from a high of 4,037 in

Exhibit 18.1   Jail Functions and Services

- Receive individuals pending arraignment and hold them awaiting trial, conviction, or sentencing
- Readmit probation, parole, and bail-bond violators and absconders
- Temporarily detain juveniles pending transfer to juvenile authorities
- Hold mentally ill persons pending their movement to appropriate health facilities
- Hold individuals for the military, for protective custody, for contempt, and for the courts as witnesses
- Release convicted inmates to the community upon completion of sentence
- Transfer inmates to federal, state, or other authorities
- House inmates for federal, state, or other authorities because of crowding of their facilities
- Relinquish custody of temporary detainees to juvenile and medical authorities
- Sometimes operate community-based programs as alternatives to incarceration
- Hold inmates sentenced to short terms (generally under one year)

SOURCE: Darrell K. Gilliard and Allen J. Beck, *Prison and Jail Inmates at Midyear 1996* (Washington, D.C.: Bureau of Justice Statistics, 1997), p. 3.

1970 to about 3,500 today, the number of inmates has increased more than 400 percent (from 160,683).

Who Are Jail Inmates?

Male inmates make up about 90 percent of the local jail inmate population. There were 110 female inmates per 100,000 women in the United States, compared to 1,297 male inmates per 100,000 men. The female inmate population, like the crime rate, has been growing at a faster pace, however, and more women are entering jails than ever before. On average the adult female jail population has grown 6.6 percent annually since 1990, while the adult male inmate population has grown 4 percent.

As of 2001, a majority of local jail inmates are either black or Hispanic. White non-Hispanics made up 42 percent of the jail population; black non-Hispanics, 41 percent; Hispanics, 15 percent; members of other races made up about 1.6 percent of the jail population. In 2001, relative to their number in the U.S. population, black non-Hispanics were more than five and a half times more likely than white non-Hispanics, more than two and a half times more likely than Hispanics, and more than nine times more likely than persons of other races to have been held in a local jail.

Although removing juveniles from adult jails has long been a national priority, it is likely that more than 50,000 youths are admitted to adult jails each year. More than 8,000 persons under age 18 are housed in adult jails on any given day, and more than two-thirds of these young inmates have been convicted or are being held for trial as adults in criminal court.

New Generation Jails

To relieve overcrowding and improve effectiveness, a jail-building boom has been under way. Many of the new jails are using modern designs to improve effectiveness; these are referred to as **new generation jails.**[80] Traditional jails are constructed and use what is referred to as the linear/intermittent surveillance model. Jails using this design are rectangular, with corridors leading to either single- or multiple-occupancy cells arranged at right angles to the corridor. Correctional officers must patrol to see into cells or housing areas, and when they are in position to observe one cell, they cannot observe others; unobserved inmates are essentially unsupervised.

The new generation jails allow for continuous observation of residents. There are two types, direct and indirect supervision. Direct supervision jails contain a cluster of cells surrounding a living area or "pod," which contains tables, chairs, TVs, and other material. A correctional officer is stationed within the pod. The officer has visual observation of inmates and maintains the ability to relate to them on a personal level. By placing the officer in the pod, there is an increased awareness of the behaviors and needs of the inmates. This results in creating a safer environment for both staff and inmates. Interaction between inmates is constantly and closely monitored, and dissension can be quickly detected before it escalates. During the day, inmates stay in the open area (dayroom) and typically are not permitted to go into their rooms except with permission of the officer in charge. The officer controls door locks to cells from the control panel. In case of trouble or if the officer leaves the station for an extended period of time, command of this panel can be switched to a panel at a remote location, known as "central control." The officer usually wears a device that permits immediate communication with central control in case of trouble, and the area is also covered by a video camera monitored by an officer in the central control room.

Indirect supervision jails use similar construction, but the correctional officer's station is located inside a secure room. Microphones and speakers inside the living unit permit the officer to hear and communicate with inmates. Although these institutions have not yet undergone extensive evaluation, research shows that they may help reduce postrelease offending in some situations.[81]

To read more about new generation jails, go to:
http://www.justiceconcepts.com/design.pdf
For an up-to-date list of Web links, go to
http://info.wadsworth.com/siegel ◾

The Prison System

The Federal Bureau of Prisons and every state government maintain closed correctional facilities, also called **prisons, penitentiaries,** or **reformatories.**[82] It is a vast and costly system. According to the Bureau of Justice Statistics, the various states and the District of Columbia spend about $22 billion to build, staff, and maintain their prison facilities and to house the prisoners. The Federal Bureau of Prisons spends an additional $2.5 billion or about $20,000 per year per inmate. There has been a rapid escalation of prison costs. State prison expenditures have increased 83 percent since 1990, an average of about 11 percent per year. Federal prison expenditures rose 160 percent during the same period, or an average of about 17 percent per year.[83]

State and federal governments maintain closed correctional facilities to house convicted felons; these institutions have become familiar to most people as harsh, frightening places filled with dangerous men and women. San Quentin (California), Attica (New York), Joliet (Illinois), and Florence (Colorado) are but a few of the large state or federal prisons made well known by films, books, or other media.

This section discusses types of correctional institutions, life and treatment in prison, and the prisoners' rights movement.

Types of Institutions

As of 2002, there were more than 1,550 public and private adult correctional facilities housing state prisoners. In addition, there are 84 federal facilities and 26 private facilities that housed federal inmates. These prisons are usually categorized according to their level of security and inmate populations as maximum-, medium-, and minimum-security institutions.

Large maximum-security prisons are surrounded by high walls, have elaborate security measures and armed guards, and house inmates classified as potentially dangerous. High security and stone walls give the inmates the sense that the facility is impregnable and reassures citizens that convicts will be completely incapacitated. During the day, the inmates engage in closely controlled activities: meals, workshops, education, and so on. Rule violators may be confined to their cells; working and other shared recreational activities are viewed as privileges. Some inmates are considered so dangerous that they are housed in a new kind of prison, which is described in the Policy and Practice in Criminology feature titled "Ultra-Maximum-Security Prisons."

Medium-security prisons have similar protective measures but usually contain less violent inmates. Consequently, they are more likely to offer a variety of treatment and educational programs to their residents. They may be similar in appearance to the maximum-security prison; however, security and atmosphere are neither so tense nor so vigilant. Medium-security prisons are also surrounded by walls, but there may be fewer guard towers or other security precautions. For example, visitor privileges may be more extensive, and personal contact may be allowed; in a maximum-security prison, visitors may be separated from inmates by Plexiglas or other barriers (to prohibit the passing of contraband). Although most prisoners are housed in cells, individual honor rooms in medium-security prisons are used to reward those who make exemplary rehabilitation efforts. Finally, medium-security prisons promote greater treatment efforts, and the relaxed atmosphere allows freedom of movement for rehabilitation workers and other therapeutic personnel.

Minimum-security prisons operate without armed guards or walls; usually they are constructed in compounds surrounded by chain-link fences. Minimum-security prisons house the most trustworthy and least violent offenders; white-collar criminals may be their most common occupants. Inmates may be transferred to these nonrestrictive institutions as a reward for good behavior prior to their release. A great deal of personal freedom is allowed inmates. Instead of being marched to activities by guards, they are summoned by bells or loudspeaker announcements and assemble on their own. Work furloughs and educational releases are encouraged, and vocational training is of the highest level. Minimum-security prisons have been scoffed at for being too much like country clubs; some federal facilities catering to white-collar criminals even have tennis courts and pools. Yet they remain prisons, and the isolation and loneliness of prison life deeply affects the inmates at these facilities. And, of course, if an inmate cannot adjust to the relaxed security or if the inmate attempts to escape, he or she will be transferred to a higher-security institution.

Farms and camps In addition to closed institutions, prison farms and camps are used to detain offenders. This type of facility is found primarily in the South and the West. Prisoners on farms produce dairy products, grain, and vegetable crops that are used in the state correctional system and other government facilities, such as hospitals and schools. Forestry camp inmates maintain state parks, fight forest fires, and do reforestation work. Ranches, primarily a western phenomenon, employ inmates in cattle raising and horse breeding, among other activities. Road gangs repair roads and state highways.

Private prisons On January 6, 1986, the U.S. Corrections Corporation opened the first privately run state prison, in Marion, Kentucky: a 300-bed minimum-security facility for inmates who are within three years' of parole. Today more than 20 companies run private prisons.[84] For-profit incarceration has grown from a sole 350-bed lockup in 1983 to housing about 90,000 inmates today (5.8 pecent of state and 10.7 percent of federal inmates); local jails housed 63,140 state and federal inmates (4.6 percent of all prisoners).[85]

Though privately run institutions are now common, their increased use may present a number of problems. For example, will private providers be able to effectively evaluate programs knowing that a negative evaluation might cause them to lose their contracts? Will they skimp on services and programs to reduce costs? Might they not skim off the easy cases and leave the hard-core inmates for state care? And will the need to keep business booming require "widening the net" to fill empty cells? The notion of running prisons for profit may be unpalatable to large segments of the population. However, is this much different from a private hospital or college, both of which offer services also provided by the state? A recent review of private prisons by Richard Harding finds that they now play an important correctional role in the United States, Australia, and the United Kingdom. Harding finds clear evidence that the development of private prisons has stimulated improvement in the correctional system but also that private prisons can experience the same failures and problems as public institutions.[86]

The issues that may determine the future of private corrections are their ability to be both efficient and cost-effective: Can privately run correctional institutions provide better services at lower cost than public facilities? A 1999 evaluation of recidivism among inmates released from private and public facilities found that recidivism rates were actually lower among the private prison group than among state prison inmates.[87] Inmates released from private prisons who did reoffend committed less serious offenses than those released from public institutions. These findings help support the concept of the private correctional institution.

The American Correctional Association is a multidisciplinary organization of professionals representing all facets of corrections and criminal justice, including federal, state, and military correctional facilities and prisons, county jails, and detention centers, probation/parole agencies, and community corrections/halfway houses. Their Web site provides information on all types of correctional institutions:

http://www.corrections.com/aca/
For an up-to-date list of Web links, go to
http://info.wadsworth.com/siegel ■

Prisoners in the United States

One of the most significant problems in the criminal justice system has been the meteoric rise in the prison population. As of 2001, there were about 1.4 million prisoners under federal or state jurisdiction. As Figure 18.3 shows, the prison population has increased substantially since 1980.

Although the number of prison inmates is at an all-time high, the rise in this population may be leveling off. The total number of inmates increased 1.3 percent be-

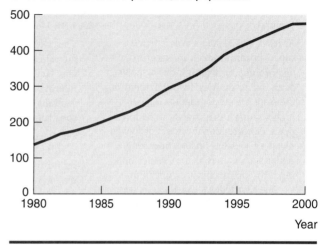

Figure 18.3 Incarceration Rate Has More Than Tripled Since 1980

Offenders incarcerated per 100,000 population

SOURCE: *Correctional Populations in the United States, 1997, and Prisoners in 2000* (Washington, D.C.: Bureau of Justice Statistics, 2001).

tween year-end 1999 and year-end 2000, far less than the average annual growth of 6 percent since 1990. During the last six months of 2000, the nation's state prison population declined by more than 6,200 inmates, the first measured decline since 1972.

Prison populations remain stubbornly high despite a declining crime rate between 1990 and 2000 mainly because (a) the conviction rate increased and (b) recently adopted determinate, mandatory and truth-in-sentencing laws increase eligibility for incarceration and limit the availability of parole.[88] For example, the amount of time served by offenders convicted of violent crimes is about double in states that apply truth-in-sentencing (88 months) as opposed to those states that have chosen not to implement this form of sentencing (45 months).[89] The long-term effect of declining crime rates may now be sufficient to stablize the prison population.

Profile of Prison Inmates

What are the personal characteristics of U.S. prison inmates?[90] As expected, prisoners reflect the same qualities that are found in samples of arrestees. Inmates of state prisons are predominantly poor, young adult males with less than a high school education. However, although inmates tend to be young, longer sentences have dictated an aging inmate population. The state prison population grew increasingly middle-aged after 1991. In 1991 inmates ages 35 to 44 comprised 23 percent of the population; the same group accounts for about 30 percent of the population today. Overall, the median inmate age increased from 30 years in 1991 to about 32 years today. Prison inmates

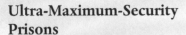
Ultra-Maximum-Security Prisons

At least 34 U.S. states now operate super- or ultra-maximum-security prisons or units, providing nearly 20,000 beds and accounting for 1.8 percent of the state prison population. These high-security institutions can be independent correctional centers or locked wings of existing prisons operating under such names as the "secure housing unit" or "maximum control unit."

The first federal maxi-prison was located in Marion, Illinois, which was infamous for its tight security and isolated conditions. Marion has been supplanted by a new 484-bed facility in Florence, Colorado. This new prison has the most sophisticated security measures in the United States, including 168 video cameras and 1,400 electronically controlled gates. Inside the cells all furniture is unmovable; the desk, bed, and TV stand are made of cement. All potential weapons, including soap dishes, toilet seats, and toilet handles, have been removed. The cement walls are 5,000-pound quality, and steel bars are placed so they crisscross every 8 inches inside the walls. Cells are angled so that inmates cannot see each other or the outside scenery (see Figure A). This cuts down on communications and denies inmates a sense of location, which prevents escapes.

Escape from the prison seems impossible. There are six guard towers at different heights to prevent air attacks. To get out, the inmates would have to pass through seven 3-inch-thick steel doors, each of which can be opened only after the previous one has closed. If a guard tower is ever seized, all controls are switched to the next station. If the whole prison is seized, it can be controlled from the outside. It appears that the only way out is via good works and behavior, through which an inmate can earn transfer to another prison within three years.

A national survey of super-max prisons conducted by the American Correctional Association found that, though the costs of running these institutions is generally higher than in less secure facilities, they tend to be popular with correctional administrators who believe that isolating troublemakers helps them maintain order. Here are the major findings of this survey:

- Thirty-four prison systems are either operating or building super-max facilities. Four others are considering the need for super-max facilities or are actively pursuing construction funds.

- Thirty-six prison systems cited the need to better manage violent and seriously disruptive inmates as a major factor in their jurisdiction's development of super-max housing; 17 of these systems include gang members as appropriate candidates for super-max housing.

- Jurisdictions vary greatly in the length of time inmates are confined in super-max facilities and the criteria for admission and release. Approval authority for admission and release of inmates varies from the warden or superintendent to the director/commissioner of the prison system.

- Programs in super-max facilities range from "none available" to "cell-front only" television/video programming or limited group programming.

- Jurisdictions differ in whether mentally ill and/or developmentally disabled inmates are placed in super-max housing.

- Transitional programming is available only in some jurisdictions.

Critiquing the Super-Max Prison
Threat of transfer to a super-max institution is used to deter inmate misbehavior in less restrictive institutions. Civil rights watchdog groups charge that these super-max prisons violate the United Nations' standards for the treatment of inmates. They are typically located in rural areas, which makes staffing difficult in the professional areas of dentistry, medicine, and counseling. Senior officers would rather not work in these institutions, leaving the most difficult inmates in the hands of the least experienced correctional officers.

A recent survey by Leena Kurki and Norval Morris found that although conditions vary from state to state many super-maxes subject inmates to nearly complete isolation and deprivation of sensory stimuli. The long-term effects of such conditions on inmates is still uncertain, but they believe it is likely to have an extremely harmful effect, especially on inmates who suffer from a preexisting mental illness or those with subnormal intelligence.

The development of the ultra-max prison represents a shift from previous correctional policy, which favored dispersing the most troublesome inmates to different prisons to prevent them from joining forces or planning escapes. Housing the most dangerous inmates in an ultra-secure facility eases their control while reducing violence levels in the general prison population. The super-max prison is considered the ultimate control mechanism for disruptive inmates, but Kurki and Morris argue that individual inmates are actually less to blame for prison violence and disruption than the dysfunctional prison regimes and misguided prison administrators that make prisons the violent institutions that they are.

Critical Thinking Questions

Ultra-max prisons are reminiscent of the old Pennsylvania system, which made use of solitary confinement and high security. Is this inhumane in our more enlightened age? Why or why not?

InfoTrac College Edition Research

For a look into the Florence Penitentiary, go to InfoTrac College Edition and read this article:

The bomber next door: What are the most dangerous men in America talking about at the Supermax prison in Colorado? *Time*, 22 March 1999 v153 i11 p55(1)

SOURCES: Leena Kurki and Norval Morris, "The Purpose, Practices, and Problems of Supermax Prisons," in *Crime and Justice, an Annual Edition*, ed. Michael Tonry (Chicago: University of Chicago Press, 2001), pp. 385–422; Richard H. Franklin, "Assessing Supermax Operations," *Corrections Today* 60 (1998): 126–28; Chase Riveland, *Supermax Prison: Overview and General Considerations* (Longmont, Colo.: National Institute of Corrections, 1998); Federal Bureau of Prisons, *State of the Bureau, 1995* (Washington, D.C.: U.S. Government Printing Office, 1996); Dennis Cauchon, "The Alcatraz of the Rockies," *USA Today*, 16 November 1994, p. 6A.

Figure A   A Typical Cell in an Ultra-Maximum-Security Prison

Few parts are movable or can be used as weapons. For example, buttons replace switches or levers; furniture and appliances are secured to the floor or walls.

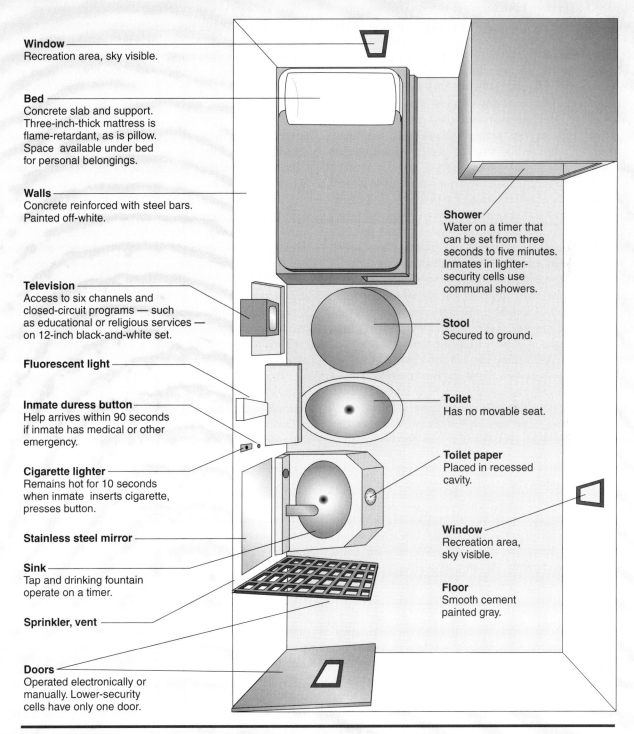

Window
Recreation area, sky visible.

Bed
Concrete slab and support. Three-inch-thick mattress is flame-retardant, as is pillow. Space available under bed for personal belongings.

Walls
Concrete reinforced with steel bars. Painted off-white.

Television
Access to six channels and closed-circuit programs — such as educational or religious services — on 12-inch black-and-white set.

Fluorescent light

Inmate duress button
Help arrives within 90 seconds if inmate has medical or other emergency.

Cigarette lighter
Remains hot for 10 seconds when inmate inserts cigarette, presses button.

Stainless steel mirror

Sink
Tap and drinking fountain operate on a timer.

Sprinkler, vent

Doors
Operated electronically or manually. Lower-security cells have only one door.

Shower
Water on a timer that can be set from three seconds to five minutes. Inmates in lighter-security cells use communal showers.

Stool
Secured to ground.

Toilet
Has no movable seat.

Toilet paper
Placed in recessed cavity.

Window
Recreation area, sky visible.

Floor
Smooth cement painted gray.

SOURCE: Louis Winn, United States Penitentiary, Administrative Maximum—Florence, Colorado.

who are aged 51 and beyond will make up 33 percent of the total prison population by the year 2010, placing pressure on prison administrators to devise ways of keeping aging inmates in the prison workforce, helping them maintain family ties, and assuring them access to medical and mental health specialists.[91]

Prison is not a new experience for many inmates: more than 60 percent have been incarcerated before; more than 15 percent have six or more prior incarcerations. About half of all inmates were either on probation or parole at the time of their incarceration.

The profile of inmates reinforces the presumed association between criminal behavior and social problems. Many inmates grew up in single-parent households. More than a quarter say their parents abused drugs or alcohol; the great majority (80 percent) have been substance abusers themselves; more than 60 percent were regular drug users.

Males and minorities are overrepresented in the prison population. At the end of 2000, 9.7 percent of all black males between 25 and 29 years of age were in prison, compared to 2.9 percent of all Hispanic males, and 1.1 percent of all white males in the same age group. There were 91,612 women in state and federal prisons at the end of 2001, making up 6.6 percent of all prison inmates. Though they make up less than 10 percent of the inmate population, the number of female inmates is growing at a faster pace than male inmates. Since 1990 the number of male prisoners has grown 77 percent, while the number of female prisoners has increased by 108 percent.

Inmates are educational and vocational underachievers. Only one-third graduated from high school or had some college; more than 40 percent never finished high school. Less than 20 percent were married, far below the standard rate for adult Americans.

CONNECTIONS

The profile of the prison inmate supports the reality of problem behavior syndrome. From birth, the path that led the inmate to prison was littered with insurmountable family, economic, and social problems. Read more about PBS in Chapter 10. ■

Prison Life: Males

Inmates in large, inaccessible prisons find themselves physically cut off from families, friends, and former associates. Those who are fathers may become depressed because they are anxious about their kids.[92] Their families and friends may find it difficult to travel great distances to visit them; mail is censored and sometimes destroyed. The prison is a "total institution," regulating dress, work, sleep, and eating habits.[93]

Inmates soon find themselves in a totally new world with its own logic, behavior, rules, and language. They must learn to live with the stress of prison life; the major losses are goods and services, liberty, heterosexual relationships, autonomy, and security.[94] Prisoners find they have no privacy; even when locked in their own cells, they are surrounded and observed by others.

Inmates must adjust to the incentives prison administrators have created to promote security and control behavior.[95] One type of incentive involves the level of comfort provided the inmate. Those obeying rules are given choice work assignments, privileges, and educational opportunities. Those who flout prison rules may be segregated, locked in their cells, or put in solitary confinement (**the hole**).

Administrators can also control the amount of time spent in prison. Furloughs can be dispensed to allow prisoners the opportunity to work or visit outside prison walls. Good-time credit can be extended to lessen sentences. Parole decisions can be influenced by reports on inmates' behavior.

The inmate must learn to deal with sexual exploitation and violence in the prison. One position says that this phenomenon is a function of racial conflict; another holds that inmates who become victims are physically weaker and less likely to form cohesive defensive groups.[96] Inmate aggressors come from a street culture that stresses violence, and they continue to behave violently while in prison.[97] Young males may be raped and kept as sexual slaves by older, more aggressive inmates. When these "slave holders" are released, they often sell their "prison wives" to other inmates.[98]

To avoid victimization, inmates must learn to adopt a lifestyle that shields them from victimization.[99] They must discover areas of safety and danger, whom to trust and whom to avoid. Some learn how to fight back to prove they are not people who can be taken advantage of. Whereas some kill their attackers and get even longer sentences, others join cliques and gangs that provide protection and the ability to acquire power within the institution. Gangs are powerful in the larger prison systems, especially in California. Some inmates seek transfers to a different cell block or prison, ask for protective custody, or simply remain in their cells all the time.

Part of inmates' early adjustment involves becoming familiar with and perhaps participating in the hidden, black-market economy of the prison—the *hustle*. Hustling provides inmates with a source of steady income and the satisfaction of believing they are beating the system.[100] Hustling involves the sale of such illegal commodities as drugs (uppers, downers, pot), alcohol, weapons, and illegally obtained food and supplies. When prison officials crack down on hustled goods, it merely drives the price up—giving hustlers a greater incentive to promote their black-market activities.[101]

Inmates must also learn to deal with daily racial conflict. Prisoners tend to segregate themselves and, if peace is to reign in the institution, stay out of each other's way.

Often racial groupings are quite exact; for example, Hispanics may separate themselves according to their national origin (Mexicans, Puerto Ricans, Colombians, and so on). In large California prisons, segregation and power struggles create even narrower divisions. For example, Hispanic gangs are now organized by area of origin: northern California (Nortenos), southern California (Surenos), and Mexican-born (Border Brothers).[102] Prisons represent one area in which minorities often hold power; as sociologist James B. Jacobs observed, "Prison may be the one institution in American society that blacks control."[103]

Prisoners must learn to deal with their frustrations over getting a "rotten deal." They may find that some other inmates received far lower sentences for similar crimes. They may be turned down for parole and then observe that others with similar records are granted early release. There is some evidence that perceived discrimination in the distribution of rewards and treatment may contribute to dissatisfaction, maladjustment, and prison violence.[104]

Finally, as the inmates' sentences wind down and their parole dates near, they must learn to cope with the anxiety of being released into the outside world. During this period, inmates may question their ability to make it in an environment in which they have failed before. Have their families stood by them? Are they outcasts? Facing release, these inmates often experience low self-esteem, become depressed, and suffer anxiety.[105]

Inmate society   A significant element of the inmate's adjustment to prison is the encounter with what is commonly known as the **inmate subculture.**[106] One major aspect of the inmate subculture is a unique **social code**—unwritten guidelines that express the values, attitudes, and types of behavior older inmates demand of younger inmates. Passed on from one generation of inmates to another, the inmate social code represents the values of interpersonal relations within the prison.

National attention was first drawn to the inmate social code and subculture by Donald Clemmer. In *The Prison Community*, Clemmer presented a detailed sociological study of life in a maximum-security prison.[107] Clemmer was able to identify a unique language (argot) of prisoners. In addition, Clemmer found that prisoners tend to group themselves into cliques on the basis of such personal criteria as sexual preference, political beliefs, and offense history. He found that there were complex sexual relationships in prison and concluded that many heterosexual men will turn to homosexual relationships when faced with long sentences and the loneliness of prison life.

Clemmer's most important contribution may have been his identification of the **prisonization process.** This he defined as the inmate's assimilation into the prison culture through acceptance of its language, sexual code, and norms of behavior. Those who become the most prisonized will be the least likely to reform on the outside.

Not all prison experts believe the prison culture is a function of the harsh conditions in a total institution. In 1962 John Irwin and Donald Cressey published a paper in which they conceded that a prison culture exists but claimed that its principles are actually imported from the outside world.[108] In their **importation model,** Irwin and Cressey conclude that inmate culture is affected by the values of newcomers: many inmates come to prison with a record of many terms in correctional institutions. These men, some of whom have institutional records dating back to early childhood, bring with them a ready-made set of patterns they apply to the new situation, taking control of the prison culture's content.

The new inmate culture   Although the "old" inmate subculture may have been harmful because its norms and values insulated the inmate from change efforts, it also helped create order within the institution and prevented violence among the inmates. People who violated the code and victimized others were sanctioned by their peers. An understanding developed between guards and inmate leaders: the guards would let the inmates have things their own way, and the inmates would not let things get out of hand and draw the attention of the administration.

The old system may be dying or already dead in most institutions. The change seems to have been precipitated by the black power movement in the 1960s and 1970s. Black inmates were no longer content to fill a subservient role and challenged the power of established white inmates. As the black power movement gained prominence, racial tension in prisons created divisions that severely altered the inmate subculture. Older, respected inmates could no longer cross racial lines to mediate disputes. Predatory inmates could victimize others without fear of retaliation.[109] Consequently, more inmates than ever are assigned for their safety to protective custody.

Sociologist James B. Jacobs is perhaps the most influential expert on the changing inmate subculture. His research has helped him to conclude that the development of "black (and Latino) power" in the 1960s, spurred by the Black Muslim movement, significantly influenced the nature of prison life.[110]

According to Jacobs, black and Latin inmates are much more cohesively organized than whites. Their groups are sometimes rooted in religious and political affiliations, such as the Black Muslims; are created specifically to combat discrimination in prison, such as the Latin group La Familia; or are reformations of street gangs, such as the Vice Lords, Disciples, or Blackstone Rangers in the Illinois prison system and the Crips in California. Only in California have white inmates successfully organized, and there it is in the form of neo-Nazi groups, such as the Aryan Brotherhood. Racially homogeneous gangs are so cohesive and powerful that they are able to supplant the original inmate code with their own. Consider the oath taken by new members of Nuestra Familia (Our Family), a Latin gang operating in California prisons: "If I go forward, follow me. If I hesitate, push me. If they kill me, avenge me. If I am a traitor, kill me."

Racial conflict prompted Jacobs to suggest that it may be humane and appropriate to segregate inmates along racial lines to maintain order and protect individual rights. In some prisons, Jacobs believes administrators use integration as a threat to keep inmates in line: to be transferred to a racially mixed setting may mean beatings or death.

Although Jacobs paints the new prison culture as one of danger and chaos, in some areas, prison life has become even more disorganized, with new gangs forming and engaging in ever-increasing violent confrontations. The new breed of inmate is younger, more dangerous, and disdainful of older gang members.[111] As the prison population expands, the violence and danger of the streets will be imported into the prison culture.

Prison Life: Females

Women are typically housed in minimum-security institutions more likely to resemble college dormitories than high-security male prisons.

Daily life in the women's prison community is somewhat different from that in male institutions. For one thing, women usually do not present the immediate physical danger to staff and fellow inmates that many male prisoners do. For another, the rigid, antiauthority inmate social code found in many male institutions does not exist in female prisons.[112] Recent research conducted in the California prison system finds that few female inmates experience the violent atmosphere common in male institutions, nor do they suffer the racial and ethnic conflicts and divisiveness.[113]

Are women inmates victimized because of their gender? How do sex-role stereotypes influence correctional programming and practices for female inmates? To find out, access this article on InfoTrac College Edition: Pamela J. Schram. Stereotypes about vocational programming for female inmates. *Prison Journal* v78 (Sept 1998) p244 ■

Female inmates may experience less discomfort than males, but that does not mean their experiences are a bed of roses. When Mark Pogrebin and Mary Dodge interviewed former female inmates who had done time in a

■ Corrections officials are now experimenting with new methods of helping female inmates maintain close ties with their families. While demonstrating the Family Virtual Visitation Program at the Pennsylvania Prison Society in Philadelphia, June 28, 2001, Komoya Goodjoines, 4, waves to her mother Sonya Goodjoines (extreme right of video screen). Sonya Goodjoines is imprisoned at Cambridge Springs in Crawford County. About 100 inmates and their families have been making "virtual visits" in a pilot program operated by the Pennsylvania Department of Corrections and the Pennsylvania Prison Society and paid for by a $134,000 federal grant allocated by the Pennsylvania Commission on Crime and Delinquency.

western state, they discovered that an important element of prison life for many women was dealing with fear and violence. Some reported that violence in women's prisons is common and that many female inmates undergo a process of socialization fraught with danger and volatile situations.[114]

Women in confinement often experience severe anxiety and anger because they are separated from families and loved ones and unable to function in normal female roles. Low self-esteem is a major problem among female inmates.[115] Unlike men, who direct their anger outward, female prisoners may revert to more self-destructive acts to cope with their problems. Female inmates are perhaps more likely than males to mutilate their own bodies and to attempt suicide. For example, one common practice among female inmates is self-mutilation or "carving." This ranges from simple scratches to carving the name of their boyfriend on their body or even complex statements or sentences ("To mother, with hate").[116] It is not surprising, considering these circumstances, that female inmates are more likely to be treated with mood-altering drugs and placed in psychiatric care, whereas male inmates' adjustment difficulties are viewed as disciplinary problems.[117]

One common form of adaptation to prison employed by women is the **surrogate family.** This group contains masculine and feminine figures acting as fathers and mothers; some even act as children and take on the role of either brother or sister. Formalized marriages and divorces may be conducted. Sometimes multiple roles are held by one inmate, so that a "sister" in one family may "marry" and become the "wife" in another.[118]

The special needs of female inmates must be addressed by correctional authorities. Health care is an issue. Many institutions have inadequate facilities to care for women who are pregnant when they enter prison or become pregnant during their prison stay.[119] There is a growing problem of HIV-related illnesses as the ongoing war on drugs increases the number of substance-abusing female inmates who are at risk for AIDS.[120]

Helping women to adjust after they leave the institution is another goal. Surveys indicate that the prison experience does little to prepare women to reenter the workforce after their sentences have been completed. Gender stereotypes still shape vocational opportunities.[121] Female inmates are still being trained for "women's roles," such as child rearing, and are not given the programming to make successful adjustments in the community.[122]

Sexual exploitation   There have been numerous reports of female prisoners being sexually abused and exploited by male correctional workers who either use brute force or psychological coercion to gain sexual control over inmates.[123] Staff-on-inmate sexual misconduct covers a wide range of behaviors, from lewd remarks to voyeurism to assault and rape. A recent (1999) survey by the federal government General Accounting Office (GAO) found that

sexual misconduct persists in the three correctional systems with the largest number of female inmates (the Federal Bureau of Prisons, the California Department of Corrections, the Texas Department of Criminal Justice) despite efforts to correct problems and train staff. Between 1995 and 1998, female inmates made 506 allegations of staff sexual misconduct; 92 of them were sustained, generally resulting in staff firings or resignations. Each of these jurisdictions was involved in at least two civil lawsuits arising from staff sexual misconduct during this period.[124]

Under antidiscrimination employment laws, U.S. prisons and jails cannot refuse to employ men to supervise female inmates (or women to supervise male inmates) and in many states there are few restrictions on their duties. It is estimated that about 40 percent of the correctional officers working with female inmates are men.[125] The presence of male correctional workers means that the prison experience often includes routine activities that greatly distress female inmates, such as routine searches for contraband that require male staff to touch women's bodies and surveillance when they are dressing.[126]

I   What can be done to control the sexual abuse of female inmates? To learn more about this topic, use InfoTrac College Edition to access this article: Nina Siegal. Stopping abuse in prison. *The Progressive,* April 1999 v63 i4 p31(1)   ■

Correctional Treatment

Correctional treatment has been an integral part of prison life since Z. R. Brockway introduced it as part of the daily regimen at the Elmira Reformatory. Today more than 90 percent of all prison inmates participate in some form of program or activity after admission.[127] There are many approaches to treatment. Some, based on a medical model, rely heavily on counseling and clinical therapy. Others attempt to prepare inmates for reintegration into the community; they rely on work release, vocational training, and educational opportunities. Others stress self-help through 12-step or Alcoholics Anonymous programs. The most popular programs have a religious theme and involve Bible clubs and other pious activities. Although it is beyond the scope of this book to describe the vast number of correctional treatment programs, a few important types will be discussed.

Therapy and counseling   The most traditional type of treatment in prison involves psychological counseling and therapy. Counseling programs exist in almost every major institution. Some stress individual treatment with psychotherapy or other techniques. However, because of lack of resources, it is more common for group methods to be used. Some groups are led by trained social workers, counselors, or therapists; others rely on lay personnel as leaders.

■ Most prisons operate numerous vocational training programs designed to help inmates develop skills for securing employment upon their release. Programs stress such marketable skills as dental laboratory work, computer programming, auto repair, and radio and television work. Some encourage employers to recruit inmates who will soon be released. Here, Duane Fleming (left), an inmate at Northern State Prison in Newark, New Jersey, talks with Jim Durkin (right foreground), of Jersey Tractor Trailer Training, during a job fair for inmates at Northern State Prison, May 16, 2001. About 20 businesses and organizations attended the job fair where 188 inmates as much as a year and a half away from release were drawing serious interest.

Group counseling in prison usually tries to stimulate inmates' self-awareness and their ability to deal with everyday problems.[128] Various innovative psychological treatment approaches have been used in the prison system:

- *Behavior therapy* uses tokens to reward conformity and help develop positive behavior traits.

- *Reality therapy* is meant to help satisfy individuals' needs to feel worthwhile to themselves and others.[129]

- *Transactional analysis* encourages inmates to identify the different aspects of their personalities and to be their own therapists.

- *Milieu therapy* uses the social structure and processes of the institution to influence the behavior patterns of offenders.

Educational programs The first prison treatment programs were educational. A prison school was opened at the Walnut Street Prison in 1784. Elementary courses were offered in New York's prison system in 1801 and in Pennsylvania's in 1844. An actual school system was established in Detroit's House of Corrections in 1870, and Elmira Reformatory opened a vocational trade school in 1876.

Today most institutions provide some type of education. Some prisons allow inmates to obtain a high school diploma through equivalency exams or general educational development (GED) certificates. Some prisons provide college courses, usually staffed by teachers who work at nearby institutions. Nearly one-half of all inmates have received some form of academic education, and about one-third have had vocational training since entering prison.[130]

Vocational rehabilitation Most prisons operate numerous vocational training programs designed to help inmates develop skills for securing employment on their release. In the past, the traditional prison industries of laundry and license plate manufacture failed to provide these skills. Today programs stress such marketable skills as dental laboratory work, computer programming, auto repair, and radio and television work.

Unfortunately, prisons often have difficulty obtaining the necessary equipment to run meaningful programs. Therefore, many have adopted work furlough programs that allow inmates to work in the community during the day and return to the institution at night.

Several state correctional departments also have instituted prerelease and postrelease employment services. Employment program staff members assess inmates' backgrounds to determine their abilities, interests, goals, and capabilities. They also help them create job plans (which are essential to their receiving early parole) and help them obtain placements in sheltered environments so that inmates can bridge the gap between the institution and the outside world; services include job placement, skill development, family counseling, and legal and medical attention.

Private industry in prisons A new version of vocational rehabilitation is the development of private industry in prison. This can take many different forms, including private citizens sitting on prison industry boards, private vendors marketing goods from prison industry, inmates manufacturing and marketing their own goods, private management of state-owned prison industry, franchising within the prison system in which manufactured goods are marketed under license from a private firm, and privately owned industries on prison grounds employing inmate labor.[131]

On paper, private industry in prison is quite attractive. It teaches inmates skills in usually desirable commercial areas, such as data processing. It increases employment opportunities on the outside in areas where the ex-offender can earn enough to forgo a life of crime. Various evaluations of the programs have given them high marks. However, private industry programs have so far used relatively few inmates. It is questionable whether they could be applied to the general prison population, which contains many people with educational deficiencies and a history of substance abuse. Yet a policy of full employment in prison may be one way of reducing future recidivism.[132]

Inmate self-help Recognizing that the probability of failure on the outside is acute, inmates have attempted to organize self-help groups to provide the psychological tools needed to prevent recidivism.[133] Some are chapters of common national organizations such as Alcoholics Anonymous. Membership in these programs is designed to improve inmates' self-esteem and help them cope with common problems such as alcoholism, narcotics abuse, or depression. Special-needs inmates at the Kentucky State Reformatory outside Louisville have taken the unusual step of forming a Boy Scout Troop within prison walls to serve as a vehicle for self-help and group solidarity.[134]

Other groups are organized along racial and ethnic lines. For example, there are chapters of the Chicanos Organizados Pintos Aztlan (COPA), the Afro-American Coalition, and the Native American Brotherhood in prisons stretching from California to Massachusetts. These groups try to establish a sense of brotherhood in order to work together for individual betterment. Members hold literacy, language, and religious classes as well as offering counseling, legal advice, and prerelease support. Ethnic groups seek ties with outside minority organizations such as the NAACP, Urban League, La Raza, and American Indian Movement as well as the religious and university communities.

A third type of self-help group includes those developed specifically to help inmates find the strength to make it on the outside. The most well known are the Fortune society, which claims 30,000 members, and the Seventh Step organization, which was developed by ex-offender Bill Sands. The Prison Fellowship is a religiously oriented group that sponsors seminars and Bible studies. Inmates who frequently attend services and seminars appear to have lower recidivism rates than other inmates.[135]

Does rehabilitation work? Despite the variety and number of treatment programs in operation, some question their effectiveness. More than 25 years ago, Robert Martinson and his associates found, in an oft-cited study, that with few exceptions rehabilitative efforts seemed to have no appreciable effect on recidivism.[136]

Martinson's work was followed by efforts that found, embarrassingly, that some high-risk offenders were more likely to commit crimes after they had been placed in treatment programs than before the onset of rehabilitation efforts.[137] Even California's highly touted community treatment program, which matched youthful offenders and counselors on the basis of their psychological profiles, was found by Paul Lerman to exert negligible influence on its clients.[138]

These less than enthusiastic reviews of correctional rehabilitation helped develop a more conservative view of corrections, which means that prisons are viewed as places of incapacitation and confinement; their purpose is punishment, not treatment.[139] Current public policy stresses eliminating the nonserious offender from the correctional system while increasing the sentences of serious, violent offenders. The development of lengthy mandatory and determinate sentences to punish serious offenders and the simultaneous evolution of alternative sanctions to limit the nonserious offender's interface with the system are manifestations of this view.

Some criminologists continue to challenge the "nothing works" philosophy.[140] Recent analysis of education, vocation, and work programs indicates that they may be able to lower recidivism rates and increase postrelease employment.[141] Inmates who have completed higher levels of education find it easier to gain employment upon release and consequently are less likely to recidivate over long periods.[142]

In general, treatment seems to be most effective if it is matched with the needs of inmates.[143] Among the characteristics associated with the most successful programs are these:

- Services are intensive, lasting only a few months.
- Programs are cognitive, aimed at helping inmates learn new skills to better cope with personality problems such as impulsivity.
- Program goals are reinforced firmly and fairly, using positive rewards rather than negative punishment.

- Therapists relate to clients sensitively and positively. Therapists are trained and supervised appropriately.
- Clients are insulated from disruptive interpersonal networks and placed in environments where prosocial activities predominate.[144]

Although the concept of correctional treatment is often questioned, many criminologists still believe it is possible to help some inmates within prison walls.

Programs that help inmates develop better cognitive skills have proven to be effective. Read about one program used in Vermont on InfoTrac College Edition: Thomas Powell, Jack Bush, and Brian Bilodeau. Vermont's cognitive self-change program: a 15-year review. *Corrections Today,* July 2001 v63 i4 p116 ■

Prison Violence

One of the more significant problems facing prison administrators is the constant fear of interpersonal and collective violence. Hans Toch, an expert on violence, has said,

Jails and prisons . . . have a climate of violence which has no free-world counterpart. Inmates are terrorized by other inmates and spend years in fear of harm. Some inmates request segregation, others lock themselves in and some are hermits by choice. Many inmates injure themselves.[145]

What are the causes of prison violence? There is no single explanation for either collective or individual violence, but theories abound. One position holds that inmates are often violence-prone individuals, many of whom suffer from personality disorders. Recent research shows that among institutionalized offenders psychopathy is the strongest predictor of violent recidivism and indifferent response to treatment.[146] In the crowded, dehumanizing world of the prison, it is not surprising that people with extreme psychological distress may resort to violence to dominate others.[147]

A second view is that prisons convert people to violence by their inhumane conditions, including overcrowding, depersonalization, and threats of rape. One social scientist, Charles Silberman, suggests that even in the most humane prisons, life is a constant put-down, and prison conditions threaten the inmates' sense of self-worth; violence is a consequence of these conditions.[148]

To read more about the effects of prison rape and efforts to control sexual violence in prison, use InfoTrac College Edition to access this article: Eli Lehrer. Hell behind bars: the crime that dare not speak its name. *National Review,* 5 Feb 2001 v53 i2 pNA ■

Still another view is that prison violence stems from mismanagement, lack of strong security, and inadequate control by prison officials.[149] This view has contributed to the escalated use of solitary confinement in recent years as a means of control. Also contributing to prison violence is the changing prison population. Younger, more violent in-

■ A guard keeps visual watch over the main courtyard in the Pontiac Correctional Center in Illinois. One of the more significant problems facing prison administrators is the constant fear of interpersonal and collective violence. Some experts say prisons convert people to violence by their inhumane conditions whereas others view violence as the by-product of the inmates' pre-incarceration lifestyle. Offenders are often violence-prone individuals who have always used force to get their own way.

AP/Wide World Photos

mates, who often have been members of teenage gangs, now dominate prison life. The old code of "do your own time" and "be a right guy" may be giving way to a prison culture dominated by gangs, whose very nature breeds violence.

Prison violence may also be associated with the overcrowding caused by rapid increases in the prison population. Data from Texas indicate that a large increase in the inmate population, unmatched by creation of new space, was associated with increases in suicide, violent death, and disciplinary action rates. The largest prisons in Texas (with populations of more than 1,600 inmates) demonstrated violence rates higher than the smaller prisons (800 inmates or less).[150]

Corrections and the Rule of Law

For many years, the nation's courts did not interfere in prison operations, maintaining what is called the **hands-off doctrine.** The judiciary's reluctance to interfere in prison matters was based on the belief that it lacked technical competence in prison administration, society's general apathy toward prisons, and the belief that prisoners' complaints involved privileges rather than rights. Consequently, prisoners had no legal rights and were "slaves of the state."[151]

The hands-off doctrine was lifted in the 1960s. General concern with civil and human rights, increasing militancy in the prison population, and the reformist nature of the Warren Court created a climate conducive to reform. The first area of change came in the First Amendment right of freedom of religion. The Black Muslims, a politically active religious organization led by Elijah Muhammed of Chicago, recruited many members in the prison system (including Malcolm X). Using their legal and financial clout, the Muslims litigated claims that their followers were being denied the right to worship according to their faith. A series of Supreme Court cases upheld the Muslims' freedom of religion and opened the door to other issues of inmates' rights.[152]

Today most litigation is brought under the federal Civil Rights Act (28 U.S.C. 1982), which states,

> Every person who, under color of any statute, ordinance, regulation, custom, or usage of any State or Territory subjects, or causes to be subjected, any citizen of the United States or other person within the jurisdiction thereof to the deprivation of any rights, privileges, or immunities secured by the Constitution and laws shall be liable to the party injured in an action at law, suit in equity or other proper proceeding for redress.

For many years the Supreme Court upheld inmates' rights, granting them access to the courts to seek legal redress for improper or damaging prison conditions. Recently claims that prisoner-inspired lawsuits are clogging the courts swayed a more conservative Court to limit the methods by which inmates can seek release or redress: for example, by discouraging inmates from filing "frivolous" lawsuits.[153] Nonetheless, some of the gains won by inmates continue in force, including the freedom of press and speech, medical rights, and safeguards against cruel and unusual punishment.

Freedom of press and speech   The courts have ruled that inmates retain freedom of speech and press unless correctional authorities can show that it interferes with or threatens institutional freedom and that restrictions are permissable if they are "reasonably related to legitimate penological interests."[154] For example, in *Procunier v. Martinez,* a court ruled that an inmate's mail could be censored only if there existed substantial belief that its contents would threaten security.

In a 2001 case, *Shaw v. Murphy,* the Court ruled that inmates do not have a right to correspond with other inmates even if it concerns legal advice. If prison administrators believe such correspondence undermines prison security, the First Amendment rights of inmates can be curtailed.[155]

Medical rights   After many years of indifference, inmates have only recently been given the right to secure proper medical attention. To gain their medical rights, prisoners have generally resorted to class action suits to ask courts to require adequate medical care.[156] In 1976, after reviewing the legal principles established over the preceding 20 years, the Supreme Court in *Estelle v. Gamble* clearly stated the inmate's right to medical care:[157]

> Deliberate indifference to serious medical needs of prisoners constitutes the "unnecessary and wanton infliction of pain," . . . proscribed by the Eighth Amendment. This is true whether the indifference is manifested by prison doctors in their response to the prisoner's needs or by prison guards in intentionally denying or delaying access to medical care or intentionally interfering with the treatment once prescribed.[158]

Lower courts will now decide, case by case, whether "deliberate indifference" has actually occurred.

Cruel and unusual punishment and overall conditions   Prisoners have long suffered severe physical punishment in prison, ranging from whipping to extended periods of solitary confinement. The courts have held that such treatment is unconstitutional when it does the following:

- Degrades the dignity of human beings[159]
- Is more severe than the offense for which it has been given[160]
- Shocks the general conscience and is fundamentally unfair[161]

The courts have also ruled on the necessity for maintaining the general prison system in a humane manner. For example, in 1970 the entire prison system in Arkansas was declared unconstitutional because its practices of overt physical punishment were ruled to violate the Eighth Amendment.[162]

In *Rhodes v. Chapman*[163] the Supreme Court upheld the practice of double-bunking two or more inmates in a small cell (50 square feet). "Conditions of confinement," the court argued, "must not involve the wanton and unnecessary infliction of pain nor may they be grossly disproportionate to the severity of the crime warranting imprisonment," but "conditions that cannot be said to be cruel and unusual under contemporary standards are not unconstitutional. To the extent that such conditions are restrictive and even harsh, they are part of the penalty that criminal offenders pay for their offenses against society."[164]

Although *Rhodes* limited inmates' rights to better living conditions, a number of state cases, especially *Estelle v. Ruiz*, have put corrections departments on notice that overcrowding will not be tolerated, and no new inmates can be admitted to prison unless the number of inmates is reduced.[165]

■ Parole

Parole is the planned release and community supervision of incarcerated offenders before the expiration of their prison sentences. It is usually considered a way of completing a prison sentence in the community and is not the same as a pardon; the paroled offender can be legally recalled to serve the remainder of his or her sentence in an institution if parole authorities deem the offender's adjustment inadequate or if the offender commits another crime while on parole. The decision to parole is determined by statutory requirement and usually involves the completion of a minimum sentence. For example, an inmate given an indeterminate sentence of two to five years for burglary will be eligible for parole consideration after serving a minimum sentence (two years) less good time.

In 2001, there were more than 650,000 people on parole, up 30 percent since 1990. About 312 adults per 100,000 adult U.S. residents were on state-supervised parole in 2000, compared to 271 in 1990.[166]

CONNECTIONS

In some states that have adopted "truth-in-sentencing laws," inmates must serve 85 percent of their sentence before being eligible for parole. Some states interpret this to mean 85 percent of the minimum sentence. See Chapter 17 for a review of "truth in sentencing." ■

Discretionary Parole

In some jurisdictions, parole is granted by the decision of a **state parole board,** a body of men and women who review cases and determine whether an offender has been rehabilitated sufficiently to deal with the outside world.

The board also dictates the specific parole rules a parolee must obey. In states where discretionary parole is used, the release decision is made at a **parole grant hearing.** There the full board or a subcommittee reviews information, may meet with the offender, and then decides whether the parole applicant has a reasonable chance of succeeding outside prison. Good time credits reduce the minimum sentence and hasten eligibility for parole. In making its decision, the board considers the inmate's offense, time served, evidence of adjustment, and opportunities on the outside.

Mandatory Parole

States with determinate sentencing statutes, such as Indiana and California, do not use parole boards but release inmates at the conclusion of their predetermined sentence less accumulated good time. About 15 states have abolished parole board authority for releasing all offenders, and another 5 states have abolished parole board authority for releasing certain violent offenders.

The popularity of determinate sentencing has radically changed the way people are being released from prison. The number of state inmates released from prison as a result of a parole board decision has dropped from 39 percent of all releases in 1990 to about 24 percent today; during the same period, mandatory releases increased from 29 percent to 41 percent of all parole releases.[167]

The Parolee in the Community

Once community release has begun, the offender is supervised by a trained staff of parole officers who help the offender adjust to the community and search for employment as they monitor behavior and activities to ensure that the offender conforms to the conditions of parole.

Parolees are subject to strict standardized or personalized rules that guide their behavior and limit their activities. If at any time these rules are violated (a technical parole violation), the offender can be returned to the institution to serve the remainder of the sentence. Inmates released in determinate sentencing states can have part or all of their good time revoked if they violate the conditions of their release.

Parole can also be revoked if the offender commits a second offense; the offender may be tried and sentenced for this crime. The Supreme Court has granted parolees due process rights similar to those of probationers at revocation hearings.

Parole is viewed as an act of grace on the part of the criminal justice system. It is a manifestation of the policy of returning the offender to the community. There are two conflicting sides to parole, however: the paroled offender is given a break and allowed to serve part of the sentence in the community; on the other hand, the sentiment exists that parole is a privilege, not a right, and that the parolee is in reality a dangerous criminal who must be carefully watched and supervised. The conflict between the treatment and enforcement aspects of parole has not been reconciled by the criminal justice system, and the parole process still contains elements of both orientations.

How Effective Is Parole?

Persons released from prison face a multitude of difficulties. They remain largely uneducated, unskilled, and usually without solid family support systems—to which are added the burdens of a prison record. Not surprisingly, most parolees fail, and rather quickly—rearrests are most common in the first six months after release.[168]

Most surveys of parole inmates indicate that more than half eventually return to prison. For example, a federal survey found that only 4 in every 10 persons discharged from parole in 1999 had successfully completed their term of supervision in the community; success rates have remained relatively stable since 1990. Parolees age 55 or older (54 percent) and females (48 percent) had higher success rates than those younger than 25 (36 percent) and males (39 percent).[169]

What factors predict parole failure? Most research efforts indicate that a long history of criminal behavior, an antisocial personality, a record of substance abuse, and childhood experiences with family dysfunction are all correlated with postrelease recidivism.[170] Parolees who have had a good employment record in the past and who maintain jobs after their release are the most likely to avoid recidivating.[171]

The specter of recidivism is especially frustrating to the American public: it is so difficult to apprehend and successfully prosecute criminal offenders that it seems foolish to grant them early release so they can prey on more victims. This problem is exacerbated when the parolee is a chronic, frequent offender. Research indicates that many of these returning prisoners are less prepared for reintegration and less connected to community-based social structures than in the past.[172]

CONNECTIONS

In Chapter 7 we noted that the large number of inmates now returning to their old neighborhoods can help destabilize communities and increase crime rates. This unforeseen consequence of the "prison boom" may have a long-term impact on the crime rate. ■

In sum, many parolees are returned to prison for technical violations. It is therefore likely that one of the reasons for prison overcrowding is the large number of technical parole violators who are returned within three years of their release. If overcrowding is to be successfully dealt with, a more realistic parole violation policy may have to be developed in areas where the correctional system is under stress.

■ Summary

Corrections involve the punishment, treatment, and incapacitation of convicted criminal offenders. Methods of punishing offenders have undergone many changes throughout history. At first, fines were levied to compensate the victims and their families for losses. Then cruel corporal and capital punishments were developed. The mercantile system and the development of overseas colonies created the need for labor, so slavery and forced labor began to replace physical punishment. In the late eighteenth century, the death penalty began to be used once again.

Reformers pushed for alternatives to harsh, physical punishment. The prison developed as an alternative that promised to reform and rehabilitate offenders. However, early institutions were brutal places featuring silence, corporal punishment,

work details, and warehousing of prisoners. Around the turn of the century, reformers began to introduce such measures as educational training and counseling for inmates. Today corrections can be divided into four components: community-based corrections, jails, prisons, and parole programs.

Many convicted offenders are treated in the community. Some are put on probation under the supervision of local probation departments. If they obey the rules of probation, they are allowed to serve their sentences in the community. A new development is intermediate sanctions, including fines, forfeiture, intensive probation supervision, house arrest, electronic monitoring, and community-based correction facilities. These programs fall somewhere between placement in a closed correctional institution

and the freedom of probation. Despite their promise, the effectiveness of alternative corrections methods has not been adequately tested.

The jail is the second element of corrections. It houses misdemeanant offenders serving their sentences and both felons and misdemeanants awaiting trial. The jail is a sore spot in the criminal justice system because jails are usually old and dilapidated and lack rehabilitation programs.

Prisons house convicted felony offenders. Recent shifts in criminal justice philosophy and the passage of laws requiring mandatory sentences have caused a large increase in the U.S. prison population and consequent overcrowding. Prisons are total institutions. Inmates must adjust to a new regimen that controls every aspect of their lives. Prison is a violent, stressful place with its own unique subculture and language. Various rehabilitation devices are used in the prison system, including counseling, educational programs, and vocational training. However, critics charge that these methods do not work. Consequently, the most recent philosophy to dominate the justice system holds that prisons are places of punishment and incapacitation, not treatment.

In the past 20 years, prisoners have been awarded some legal rights by the nation's courts, including rights to medical treatment, freedom of religion, procedural due process, and correspondence with the media.

The fourth component of corrections is aftercare or parole. Parole officers supervise inmates in the community while they complete their sentences. There is little evidence that corrections and parole actually work, and a significant number of released inmates recidivate.

■ Thinking Like a Criminologist

You are a corrections expert, and the governor has asked for your opinion on a proposed program that will allow prisoners to have completely private regular meetings with their families. The explicit purpose of this visitation program is to grant inmates access to normal family and sexual outlets and thereby counteract the pain of imprisonment.

Those who favor family visitation argue that, if properly administered, it could provide a number of important benefits: inmate frustration levels would diminish, family ties would be strengthened, and normal sexual patterns would continue. Those opposed argue that such visits can serve only the minority of inmates who are married; appropriate facilities are almost universally lacking; family visits can create jealousy among the unmarried inmates; spouses may feel embarrassment at openly sexual visits; and children may be born to parents who cannot support them.

Given the controversy surrounding the issue of family visits, would you recommend the program to the governor?

■ Key Terms

- corporal punishment (554)
- Walnut Street Prison (556)
- Auburn system (556)
- congregate system (557)
- contract system (557)
- convict-lease system (557)
- state account system (557)
- Z. R. Brockway (557)
- probation (558)
- parole (558)
- revoke (559)
- offender classification (559)
- technical violation (560)
- intermediate sanctions (561)

- day fines (561)
- forfeiture (562)
- monetary restitution (563)
- community service restitution (563)
- split sentencing (563)
- shock probation (563)
- intensive probation supervision (IPS) (563)
- home confinement (HC) (563)
- electronic monitoring (EM) (564)
- residential community corrections (RCC) (564)
- shock incarceration (SI) (565)
- boot camps (565)

- jail (566)
- new generation jails (567)
- prison (568)
- penitentiary (568)
- reformatory (568)
- the hole (572)
- inmate subculture (573)
- social code (573)
- prisonization process (573)
- importation model (573)
- surrogate family (575)
- hands-off doctrine (579)
- state parole board (580)
- parole grant hearing (580)

■ Critical Thinking Questions

1. Should a convicted criminal make restitution to the victim? When is restitution inappropriate? Is it fair to make poor, desperate people repay the wealthy for their misdeeds or is this merely compounding the problems that may have caused them to commit crime in the first place?

2. Should offenders be fined based on the severity of what they did or according to their ability to pay? Is it fair to gear day fines to wages? Should offenders be punished more severely because they are financially successful?

3. Does house arrest involve a violation of personal freedom? Does

wearing an ankle bracelet smack of "Big Brother"? Would you want the government monitoring your daily activities? Could this be expanded, for example, to monitoring the whereabouts of AIDS patients?

4. Should private companies be allowed to run correctional institu-

tions? After all, we have private colleges and hospitals? Or is there something inherently wrong with making a profit off of other people's suffering?

5. Should prison inmates be allowed a free college education while noncriminals are forced to pay tuition? Should people be allowed to benefit from their misdeeds?

6. Should a former prisoner have all the civil rights afforded the average citizen? Should people be further penalized after they have paid their debt to society by losing rights and privileges, such as the right to vote?

■ Notes

1. Carol Carter, "Appeal Sought on Decision to Release Molester," *Manchester Union Leader*, 30 December 2001, p. A1; Doug Hanchett, "Loophole May Free Molester—Prosecutors Blast Ruling," *Boston Herald*, 30 December 2001, p. 18.

2. Hanchett, "Loophole May Free Molester," p. 18.

3. Among the most helpful sources for this section are Graeme Newman, *The Punishment Response* (Philadelphia: J. B. Lippincott, 1978); Benedict Alper, *Prisons Inside-Out* (Cambridge, Mass.: Ballinger, 1974); Gustave de Beaumont and Alexis de Tocqueville, *On the Penitentiary System in the United States and Its Application in France* (Carbondale: Southern Illinois University Press, 1964); Orlando Lewis, *The Development of American Prisons and Prison Customs 1776–1845* (Montclair, N.J.: Patterson-Smith, 1967); Leonard Orland, ed., *Justice, Punishment and Treatment* (New York: Free Press, 1973); J. Goebel, *Felony and Misdemeanor* (Philadelphia: University of Pennsylvania Press, 1976); Georg Rusche and Otto Kircheimer, *Punishment and Social Structure* (New York: Russell and Russell, 1939); Samuel Walker, *Popular Justice* (New York: Oxford University Press, 1980).

4. Rusche and Kircheimer, *Punishment and Social Structure*, p. 9.

5. Ibid., p. 19.

6. Marvin Wolfgang, "Crime and Punishment in Renaissance Florence," *Journal of Criminal Law and Criminology* 81 (1990): 567–84.

7. G. Ives, *A History of Penal Methods* (Montclair, N.J.: Patterson-Smith, 1970).

8. Leon Radzinowicz, *A History of English Criminal Law*, vol. 1 (London: Stevens, 1943), p. 5.

9. Newman, *The Punishment Response*, p. 139.

10. Walker, *Popular Justice*, p. 34.

11. Lewis, *The Development of American Prisons and Prison Customs*, p. 17.

12. Ibid., p. 29.

13. Alexis Durham III, "Social Control and Imprisonment during the American Revolution: Newgate of Connecticut," *Justice Quarterly* 7 (1990): 293–324.

14. De Beaumont and de Tocqueville, *On the Penitentiary System in the United States*, p. 49.

15. Orland, *Justice, Punishment and Treatment*, p. 143.

16. Walker, *Popular Justice*, p. 70.

17. Larry Goldsmith, "History from the Inside Out: Prison Life in Nineteenth-Century Massachusetts," *Journal of Social History* 31 (1997): 109–36.

18. Walker, *Popular Justice*, p. 71.

19. See Z. R. Brockway, "The Ideal of a True Prison System for a State," in *Transactions of the National Congress on Penitentiary and Reformatory Discipline*, reprint ed. (Washington, D.C.: American Correctional Association, 1970), pp. 38–65.

20. This section relies heavily on David Rothman, *Conscience and Convenience* (Boston: Little, Brown, 1980). See also David Rothman, *The Discovery of the Asylum* (Boston: Little, Brown, 1970).

21. Rothman, *Conscience and Convenience*, p. 23.

22. Ibid., p. 133.

23. See, generally, Jameson Doig, *Criminal Corrections: Ideals and Realities* (Lexington, Mass.: Lexington Books, 1983).

24. See, generally, Chris Eskridge, Richard Seiter, and Eric Carlson, "Community Based Corrections: From the Community to the Community," in *Critical Issues in Corrections*, eds. V. Webb and R. Roberg (St. Paul: West Publishing, 1981), pp. 171–203.

25. Matthew Durose and Patrick A. Langan, *State Court Sentencing of Convicted Felons, 1998* (Washington, D.C.: Bureau of Justice Statistics, February 2001).

26. *Gagnon v. Scarpelli*, 411 U.S. 778, 93 S.Ct. 1756, 36 L.Ed.2d 655 (1973).

27. Bureau of Justice Statistics, "National Correctional Population Reaches New High—Grows By 126,400 during 2000 to Total 6.5 Million Adults." Press Release, 28 August 2001.

28. H. Allen, E. Carlson, and E. Parks, *Critical Issues in Adult Probation* (Washington, D.C.: U.S. Government Printing Office, 1979), p. 47.

29. Ibid.

30. Patricia Harris, "Client Management Classification and Prediction of Probation Outcomes," *Crime and Delinquency* 40 (1994): 154–74.

31. Barbara Sims and Mark Jones, "Predicting Success or Failure on Probation: Factors Associated with Felony Probation Outcomes," *Crime and Delinquency* 43 (1997): 314–27.

32. Karol Lucken, "Privatizing Discretion: 'Rehabilitating' Treatment in Community Corrections," *Crime and Delinquency* 43 (1997): 243–59.

33. David Duffee and Bonnie Carlson, "Competing Value Premises for the Provision of Drug Treatment to Probationers," *Crime and Delinquency* 42 (1996): 574–92.

34. Laurie Schaffner, "Families on Probation: Court-Ordered Parenting Skills Classes for Parents of Juvenile Offenders," *Crime and Delinquency* 43 (1997): 412–37.

35. See, generally, Patrick McAnany, Doug Thomson, and David Fogel, *Probation and Justice: Reconsideration of Mission* (Cambridge, Mass.: Oelgeschlager, Gunn and Hain, 1984).

36. Kit Van Stelle, Elizabeth Mauser, and D. Paul Moberg, "Recidivism to the Criminal Justice System of Substance-Abusing Offenders Diverted into Treatment," *Crime and Delinquency* 40 (1994): 175–96.

37. Joan Petersilia, Susan Turner, James Kahan, and Joyce Peterson, *Granting Felons Probation: Public Risks and Alternatives* (Santa Monica, Calif.: Rand Corporation, 1985).

38. M. Kevin Gray, Monique Fields, and Sheila Royo Maxwell, "Examining Probation Violations: Who, What, and When," *Crime and Delinquency* 47 (2001): 537–57.

39. Bureau of Justice Statistics, "National Correctional Population Reaches New High."

40. Robyn L. Cohen, *Probation and Parole Violators in State Prison, 1991* (Washington, D.C.: Bureau of Justice Statistics, 1995).

41. W. Reed Benedict and Lin Huff-Corzine, "Return to the Scene of the Punishment: Recidivism of Adult Male Property Offenders on Felony Probation, 1986–1989," *Journal of Research in Crime and Delinquency* 34 (1997): 237–52.

42. Durose and Langan, *State Court Sentencing of Convicted Felons, 1998.*

43. For a thorough review, see James Byrne, Arthur Lurigio, and Joan Petersilia, eds., *Smart Sentencing: The Emergence of Intermediate Sanctions* (Newbury Park, Calif.: Sage, 1992).

44. Allen Beck, *Recidivism of Prisoners Released in 1983* (Washington, D.C.: Bureau of Justice Statistics, 1989).

45. Michael Tonry "Intermediate Sanctions in Sentencing Guidelines," in *Crime and Justice: A Review of Research,* vol. 23, ed. Michael Tonry (University of Chicago Press, Chicago, 1998): 199–252; Michael Tonry and Richard Will, *Intermediate Sanctions, Preliminary Report to the National Institute of Justice* (Washington, D.C.: National Institute of Justice, 1988), p. 6.

46. Tonry and Will, *Intermediate Sanctions,* p. 8.

47. Ben Crouch, "Is Incarceration Really Worse? Analysis of Offenders' Preferences for Prison over Probation," *Justice Quarterly* 10 (1993): 67–88.

48. David Pauly and Carolyn Friday, "Drexel's Crumbling Defense," *Newsweek,* 19 December 1988, p. 44.

49. George Cole, Barry Mahoney, Marlene Thorton, and Roger Hanson, *The Practices and Attitudes of Trial Court Judges Regarding Fines as a Criminal Sanction* (Washington, D.C.: U.S. Government Printing Office, 1987).

50. Ibid.

51. John L. Worrall, "Addicted to the Drug War: The Role of Civil Asset Forfeiture as a Budgetary Necessity in Contemporary Law Enforcement," *Journal of Criminal Justice* 29 (2001): 171–87.

52. C. Yorke, Some Consideration on the Law of Forfeiture for High Treason 26 (2d ed. 1746), cited in David Freid, "Rationalizing Criminal Forfeiture," *Journal of Criminal Law and Criminology* 79 (1988): 328–436, at 329.

53. Worrall, "Addicted to the Drug War."

54. For a general review, see Robert Carter, Jay Cocks, and Daniel Glazer, "Community Service: A Review of the Basic Issues," *Federal Probation* 51 (1987): 4–11.

55. For a further analysis of restitution, see Larry Siegel, "Court Ordered Victim-Restitution: An Overview of Theory and Action," *New England Journal of Prison Law* 5 (1979): 135–50.

56. Peter Schneider, Anne Schneider, and William Griffith, *Two-Year Report on the National Evaluation of the Juvenile Restitution Initiative: An Overview of Program Performance* (Eugene, Ore.: Institute of Policy Analysis, 1982); Anne Schneider, "Restitution and Recidivism Rates of Juvenile Offenders: Four Experimental Studies," *Criminology* 24 (1936): 533–52.

57. Michael Block and William Rhodes, *The Impact of Federal Sentencing Guidelines* (Washington, D.C.: National Institute of Justice, 1987).

58. Michael Agopian, "The Impact of Intensive Supervision Probation on Gang-Drug Offenders," *Criminal Justice Policy Review* 4 (1990): 214–22; Peter Jones, "Expanding the Use of Non-Custodial Sentencing Options: An Evaluation of the Kansas Community Corrections Act," *Howard Journal* 29 (1990): 114–29; Patrick Langan and Mark Cuniff, *Recidivism of Felons on Probation, 1986–1989* (Washington, D.C.: Bureau of Justice Statistics, 1992), pp. 1–4.

59. James Ryan, "Who Gets Revoked? A Comparison of Intensive Supervision Successes and Failures in Vermont," *Crime and Delinquency* 43 (1997): 104–18.

60. Joan Petersilia, "An Evaluation of Intensive Probation in California," *Journal of Criminal Law and Criminology* 82 (1992): 610–58; Joan Petersilia, "Comparing Intensive and Regular Supervision for High-Risk Probationers: Early Results from an Experiment in California," *Crime and Delinquency* 36 (1990): 87–111; see also Joan Petersilia, "Conditions That Permit Intensive Supervision Programs to Survive," *Crime and Delinquency* 36 (1990): 126–45.

61. Joan Petersilia, *Expanding Options for Criminal Sentencing* (Santa Monica, Calif.: Rand Corporation, 1987), p. 32.

62. Ibid., p. 28.

63. Ibid., p. 13.

64. Kenneth Moran and Charles Lindner, "Probation and the Hi-Technology Revolution: Is Reconceptualization of the Traditional Probation Officer Role Model Inevitable?" *Criminal Justice Review* 3 (1987): 25–32.

65. For an extensive review, see Frank Cullen, "Control in the Community: The Limits of Reform." Paper presented at the annual meeting of the International Association of Residential and Community Alternatives, Philadelphia, 1993.

66. Terry Baumer, Michael Maxfield, and Robert Mendelsohn, "A Comparative Analysis of Three Electronically Monitored Home Detention Programs," *Justice Quarterly* 10 (1993): 121–42.

67. Sudipto Roy, "Five Years of Electronic Monitoring of Adults and Juveniles in Lake County, Indiana: A Comparative Study on Factors Related to Failure," *Journal of Crime and Justice* 20 (1997): 141–57.

68. J. Robert Lilly, Richard Ball, G. David Curry, and John McMullen, "Electronic Monitoring of the Drunk Driver: A Seven-Year Study of the Home Confinement Alternative," *Crime and Delinquency* 39 (1993): 462–84.

69. James Byrne and Linda Kelly, "Restructuring Probation as an Intermediate Sanction: An Evaluation of the Massachusetts Intensive Probation Supervision Program." Final Report to the National Institute of Justice, Research Program on the Punishment and Control of Offenders, 1989, p. 33.

70. Doris Layton Mackenzie, Robert Brame, David McDowall, and Claire Souryal, "Boot Camp Prisons and Recidivism in Eight States," *Criminology* 33 (1995): 327–57.

71. Ibid., pp. 328–29.

72. Chad Trulson, Ruth Triplett, and Clete Snell, "Social Control in a School Setting: Evaluating a School-Based Boot Camp," *Crime and Delinquency* 47 (2001): 573–609.

73. Doris Layton Mackenzie and James Shaw, "The Impact of Shock Incarceration on Technical Violations and New Criminal Activities," *Justice Quarterly* 10 (1993): 463–87.

74. Doris Layton Mackenzie, "Boot Camp Prisons: Components, Evaluations, and Empirical Issues," *Federal Probation* 54 (1990): 44–52.

75. Doris Layton Mackenzie and Alex Piquero, "The Impact of Shock Incarceration Programs on Prison Crowding," *Crime and Delinquency* 40 (1994): 222–49.

76. Mackenzie, Brame, McDowall, and Souryal, "Boot Camp Prisons and Recidivism in Eight States," pp. 352–53.

77. Patricia Harris, Rebecca Petersen, and Samantha Rapoza, "Between Probation and Revocation: A Study of Intermediate Sanctions Decision-Making," *Journal of Criminal Justice* 29 (2001): 307–18.

78. Margaret Wilson, *The Crime of Punishment,* Life and Letter Series, no. 64

(London: Jonathan Cape Ltd., 1934), p. 186.

79. Data in this and the following sections come from Allen J. Beck and Jennifer Karberg, *Prison and Jail Inmates at Midyear 2000* (Washington, D.C.: Bureau of Justice Statistics, 2001).

80. Brandon Applegate, Ray Surette, and Bernard McCarthy, "Detention and Desistance from Crime: Evaluating the Influence of a New Generation of Jail on Recidivism," *Journal of Criminal Justice* 27 (1999): 539–48.

81. Ibid.

82. Data in this section come from Allen J. Beck and Paige M. Harrison, *Prisoners in 2000* (Washington, D.C.: Bureau of Justice Statistics, 2001).

83. James J. Stephan, *State Prison Expenditures, 1996* (Washington, D.C.: Bureau of Justice Statistics, 1999).

84. "Many State Legislatures Focused on Crime in 1995, Study Finds," *Criminal Justice Newsletter* 27 (2 January 1996), p. 2.

85. Beck and Harrison, *Prisoners in 2000.*

86. Richard Harding, "Private Prisons," in *Crime and Justice, an Annual Edition,* ed. Michael Tonry (Chicago: University of Chicago Press, 2001), 265–347.

87. Lonn Lanza-Kaduce, Karen Parker, and Charles Thomas, "A Comparative Recidivism Analysis of Releases from Private and Public Prisons," *Crime and Delinquency* 45 (1999): 28–47, at 42–43.

88. Paula Ditton and Doris James Wilson, *Truth in Sentencing in State Prisons* (Washington, D.C.: Bureau of Justice Statistics, 1999); Todd Clear, *Harm in American Penology: Offenders, Victims and Their Communities* (Albany: State University of New York Press, 1994).

89. Ditton and Wilson, *Truth in Sentencing in State Prisons,* p. 1.

90. Data here are taken from a variety of sources, including Beck and Harrison, *Prisoners in 2000*; Caroline Wolf Harlow, Tracy Snell, and Christopher Murnola, *Survey of State Prison Inmates, 1997* (Washington, D.C.: Bureau of Justice Statistics, 2000).

91. Connie L. Neeley, Laura Addison, and Delores Craig-Moreland, "Addressing the Needs of Elderly Offenders," *Corrections Today* 59 (1997): 120–24.

92. C. S. Lanier, "Affective States of Fathers in Prison," *Justice Quarterly* 10 (1993): 48–65.

93. See E. Goffman, "Characteristics of Total Institutions," in *Justice, Punishment and Treatment,* ed. Leonard Orland (New York: Free Press, 1973), pp. 153–58.

94. Gresham Sykes, *The Society of Captives* (Princeton, N.J.: Princeton University Press, 1958), pp. 79–82.

95. Nicolette Parisi, "The Prisoner's Pressures and Responses," in *Coping with Imprisonment,* ed. N. Parisi (Beverly Hills, Calif.: Sage, 1982), pp. 9–16.

96. Daniel Lockwood, "The Contribution of Sexual Harassment to Stress and Coping in Confinement," in *Coping with Imprisonment,* ed. N. Parisi (Beverly Hills, Calif.: Sage, 1982), p. 47.

97. Lockwood, "The Contribution of Sexual Harassment to Stress and Coping in Confinement."

98. Wilbert Rideau and Ron Wikberg, *Life Sentences: Rage and Survival Behind Bars* (New York: Times Books, 1992), pp. 78–80.

99. John Wooldredge, "Inmate Lifestyles and Opportunities for Victimization," *Journal of Research in Crime and Delinquency* 35 (1998): 480–502.

100. Sandra Gleason, "Hustling: The 'Inside' Economy of a Prison," *Federal Probation* 42 (1978): 32–39.

101. Ibid., p. 39.

102. Geoffrey Hunt, Stephanie Riegel, Tomas Morales, and Dan Waldorf, "Changes in Prison Culture: Prison Gangs and the Case of the 'Pepsi Generation,'" *Social Problems* 40 (1993): 398–407.

103. James B. Jacobs, "The Killing Ground," *Newsweek,* 18 February 1980, p. 75.

104. Parisi, "The Prisoner's Pressures and Responses."

105. Thomas Castellano and Irina Soderstrom, "Self-Esteem, Depression, and Anxiety Evidenced by a Prison Inmate Sample: Interrelationships and Consequences for Prison Programming," *Prison Journal* 77 (1997): 259–71.

106. John Irwin, "Adaptation to Being Corrected: Corrections from the Convict's Perspective," in *Handbook of Criminology,* ed. Daniel Glazer (Chicago: Rand McNally, 1974), pp. 971–93.

107. Donald Clemmer, *The Prison Community* (New York: Holt, Rinehart & Winston, 1958).

108. John Irwin and Donald Cressey, "Thieves, Convicts, and the Inmate Culture," *Social Problems* 10 (1962): 142–55.

109. Paul Gendreau, Marie-Claude Tellier, and J. Stephen Wormith, "Protective Custody: The Emerging Crisis within Our Prisons," *Federal Probation* 69 (1985): 55–64.

110. James B. Jacobs, *New Perspectives on Prisons and Imprisonment* (Ithaca, N.Y.: Cornell University Press, 1983); James

B. Jacobs, "Street Gangs Behind Bars," *Social Problems* 21 (1974): 395–409; James B. Jacobs, "Race Relations and the Prison Subculture," in *Crime and Justice,* eds. N. Morris and M. Tonry (Chicago: University of Chicago Press, 1979), pp. 1–28.

111. Hunt, Riegel, Morales, and Waldorf, "Changes in Prison Culture," pp. 405–8.

112. Candace Kruttschnitt, Rosemary Gartner, and Amy Miller, "Doing Her Own Time? Women's Responses to Prison in the Context of the Old and New Penology," *Criminology* 38 (2000): 681–718.

113. Mark Pogrebin and Mary Dodge, "Women's Accounts of Their Prison Experiences: A Retrospective View of Their Subjective Realities," *Journal of Criminal Justice* 29 (2001): 531–41.

114. Beverly Fletcher, Lynda Dixon Shaver, and Dreama Moon, *Women Prisoners: A Forgotten Population* (Westport, Conn.: Greenwood Press, 1993), chap. 3.

115. Edna Erez, "The Myth of the New Female Offender: Some Evidence from Attitudes Toward Law and Justice," *Journal of Criminal Justice* 16 (1988): 499–509.

116. Robert Ross and Hugh McKay, *Self-Mutilation* (Lexington, Mass.: Lexington Books, 1979).

117. Ira Sommers and Deborah Baskin, "The Prescription of Psychiatric Medications in Prison: Psychiatric versus Labeling Perspectives," *Justice Quarterly* 7 (1990): 739–55.

118. Rose Giallombardo, *Society of Women: A Study of a Women's Prison* (New York: John Wiley, 1966), pp. 165–89.

119. John Wooldredge and Kimberly Masters, "Confronting Problems Faced by Pregnant Inmates in State Prisons," *Crime and Delinquency* 39 (1993): 195–203.

120. James Marquart, Victoria Brewer, Janet Mullings, and Ben Crouch, "The Implications of Crime Control Policy on HIV/AIDS-Related Risk among Women Prisoners," *Crime and Delinquency* 45 (1999): 82–98.

121. Pamela Schram, "Stereotypes about Vocational Programming for Female Inmates," *Prison Journal* 78 (1998): 244–71.

122. Merry Morash, Robin Harr, and Lila Rucker, "A Comparison of Programming for Women and Men in U.S. Prisons in the 1980's," *Crime and Delinquency* 40 (1994): 197–221, at 214–17.

123. "Sex Abuse of Female Inmates Is Common, Rights Group Says,"

Criminal Justice Newsletter 16 December 1996, p. 2.

124. General Accounting Office, *Women in Prison: Sexual Misconduct by Correctional Staff* (Washington, D.C.: U.S Government Printing Office, 1999).

125. "Female Offenders: As Their Numbers Grow, So Does the Need for Gender-Specific Programming," *Corrections Compendium* (March 1998): 1.

126. Amnesty International, *United States of America Rights for All "Not Part of My Sentence," Violations of the Human Rights of Women in Custody* (Washington, D.C.: author, 1999).

127. Allen Beck, *Survey of State Prison Inmates, 1991* (Washington, D.C.: Bureau of Justice Statistics, 1993), p. 27.

128. See, generally, G. Kassebaum, D. Ward, and D. Wilner, "Group Counseling," in *Legal Process and Corrections*, eds. N. Johnston and L. Savitz (New York: John Wiley, 1982), pp. 255–70.

129. See William Glasser, *Reality Therapy* (New York: Harper and Row, 1965).

130. Beck, *Survey of State Prison Inmates, 1991*, p. 27.

131. See, generally, Michael Fedo, "Free Enterprise Goes to Prison," *Corrections* 7 (1981): 11–18.

132. Timothy Flanagan and Kathleen Maguire, "A Full Employment Policy for Prisons in the United States: Some Arguments, Estimates and Implications," *Journal of Criminal Justice* 21 (1993): 117–30.

133. This section leans heavily on Mark Hamm, "Current Perspectives on the Prisoner Self-Help Movement," *Federal Probation* 52 (1988): 49–56.

134. Al Parke, "Bringing the Boy Scouts of America into Prison," *Corrections Today* 53 (1991): 154–57.

135. Byron Johnson, David Larson, and Timothy Pitts, "Religious Programs, Institutional Adjustment, and Recidivism among Former Inmates in Prison Fellowship Programs," *Justice Quarterly* 14 (1997): 145–66.

136. D. Lipton, R. Martinson, and J. Wilks, *The Effectiveness of Correctional Treatment: A Survey of Treatment Evaluation Studies* (New York: Praeger, 1975).

137. Charles Murray and Louis Cox, *Beyond Probation: Juvenile Corrections and the Chronic Delinquent* (Beverly Hills, Calif.: Sage, 1979).

138. Paul Lerman, *Community Treatment and Social Control* (Chicago: University of Chicago Press, 1975).

139. John Whitehead and Steven Lab, "A Meta-Analysis of Juvenile Correctional Treatment," *Journal of Research in Crime and Delinquency* 26 (1989): 276–95.

140. Francis Cullen and Karen Gilbert, *Reaffirming Rehabilitation* (Cincinnati: Anderson Publications, 1982).

141. David Wilson, Catherine Gallagher, and Doris Mackenzie, "A Meta-Analysis of Corrections-Based Education, Vocation, and Work Programs for Adult Offenders," *Journal of Research in Crime and Delinquency* 37 (2000): 347–68.

142. Mary Ellen Batiuk, Paul Moke, and Pamela Wilcox Rountree, "Crime and Rehabilitation: Correctional Education as an Agent of Change—A Research Note," *Justice Quarterly* 14 (1997): 167–80.

143. D. A. Andrews, Ivan Zinger, Robert Hoge, James Bonta, Paul Gendreau, and Francis Cullen, "Does Correctional Treatment Work? A Clinically Relevant and Psychologically Informed Meta-Analysis," *Criminology* 28 (1990): 369–405; for an alternative view, see Steven Lab and John Whitehead, "From Nothing Works to the Appropriate Works: The Latest Stop on the Search for the Secular Grail," *Criminology* 28 (1990): 405–19.

144. Paul Gendreau and Claire Goffin, "Principles of Effective Correctional Programming," *Forum on Correctional Research* 2 (1996): 38–41.

145. Hans Toch, *Police, Prisons and the Problems of Violence* (Washington, D.C.: U.S. Government Printing Office, 1977), p. 53.

146. Grant Harris, Tracey Skilling, and Marnie Rice, "The Construct of Psychopathy," in *Crime and Justice, an Annual Edition*, ed. Michael Tonry (Chicago: University of Chicago Press, 2001), 197–265.

147. For a series of papers on the issue, see A. Cohen, G. Cole, and R. Baily, eds., *Prison Violence* (Lexington, Mass.: Lexington Books, 1976).

148. Charles Silberman, *Criminal Violence, Criminal Justice* (New York: Vintage Books, 1978).

149. See Hans Toch, "Social Climate and Prison Violence," *Federal Probation* 42 (1978): 21–23.

150. Cited in G. McCain, V. Cox, and P. Paulus, *The Effect of Prison Crowding on Inmate Behavior* (Washington, D.C.: U.S. Government Printing Office, 1981), p. vi.

151. National Advisory Commission on Criminal Justice Standards and Goals, *Volume on Corrections* (Washington, D.C.: U.S. Government Printing Office, 1973), p. 18.

152. See, for example, *Cooper v. Pate,* 378 U.S. 546 (1964).

153. *Lewis v. Casey,* 94.1511 (1996).

154. *Turner v. Safley,* 482 U.S. 78 (1987) at 89.

155. *Shaw v. Murphy* (99-1613) 2001.

156. *Newman v. Alabama,* 349 F.Supp. 278 (M.D.Ala., 1974).

157. *Estelle v. Gamble,* 429 U.S. 97 (1976).

158. 97 S.Ct. 291 (1976).

159. See, for example, *Trop v. Dulles,* 356 U.S. 86, 78 S.Ct. 590 (1958); see also *Furman v. Georgia,* 408 U.S. 238, 92 S.Ct. 2726, 33 L.Ed.2d 346 (1972).

160. See, for example, *Weems v. United States,* 217 U.S. 349, 30 S.Ct. 544, 54 L.Ed. 793 (1910).

161. See, for example, *Lee v. Tahash,* 352 F.2d 970 (8th Cir., 1965).

162. 309 F. Supp. 362 (E.D. Ark. 1970); aff'd 442 F.2d 304 (Ninth Cir., 1971).

163. *Rhodes v. Chapman,* 452 U.S. 337 (1981).

164. Ibid.

165. *Estelle v. Ruiz,* 74-329 (E.D. Texas, 1980).

166. Bureau of Justice Statistics, "Forty-Two Percent of State Parole Discharges Were Successful." News Release, 3 October 2001.

167. Timothy A. Hughes, Doris James Wilson, and Allen J. Beck, *Trends in State Parole, 1990–2000* (Washington, D.C.: Bureau of Justice Statistics, 2001).

168. Joan Petersilia, "When Prisoners Return to Communities: Political, Economic, and Social Consequences," *Federal Probation* 65 (2001): 3–9.

169. Hughes, Wilson, and Beck, *Trends in State Parole, 1990–2000.*

170. James Bonta, Moira Law, and Karl Hanson, "The Prediction of Criminal and Violent Recidivism among Mentally Disordered Offenders: A Meta-Analysis," *Psychological Bulletin* 123 (1998): 123–42.

171. Thomas Hanlon, David Nurco, Richard Bateman, and Kevin O'Grady, "The Response of Drug Abuser Parolees to a Combination of Treatment and Intensive Supervision," *Prison Journal* 78 (1998): 31–45.

172. Jeremy Travis and Joan Petersilia, "Reentry Reconsidered: A New Look at an Old Question," *Crime and Delinquency* 47 (2001): 291–313.

acquaintance rape Forcible sex in which offender and victim are acquainted with one another.

acquaintance robbery Robbers who focus their thefts on people they know.

active precipitation The view that the source of many criminal incidents is the aggressive or provocative behavior of victims.

actual authority The authority a corporation knowingly gives to an employee.

actus reus An illegal act. The *actus reus* can be an affirmative act, such as taking money or shooting someone, or a failure to act, such as failing to take proper precautions while driving a car.

adolescent-limited offender Offender who follows the most common criminal trajectory, in which antisocial behavior peaks in adolescence and then diminishes.

adversary system of justice The procedure used to determine truth in the adjudication of guilt or innocence in which the defense (advocate for the accused) is pitted against the prosecution (advocate for the state), with the judge acting as arbiter of the legal rules. Under the adversary system, the burden is on the state to prove the charges beyond a reasonable doubt. This system of having the two parties publicly debate has proved to be the most effective method of achieving the truth regarding a set of circumstances. (Under the accusatory, or inquisitorial, system, which is used in continental Europe, the charge is evidence of guilt that the accused must disprove, and the judge takes an active part in the proceedings.)

aggravated rape Rape involving multiple offenders, weapons, and victim injuries.

aggressive preventive patrol A patrol technique designed to suppress crime before it occurs.

aging out The process by which individuals reduce the frequency of their offending behavior as they age. It is also known as spontaneous remission, because people are believed to spontaneously reduce the rate of their criminal behavior as they mature. Aging out is thought to occur among all groups of offenders.

Alcohol, Tobacco and Firearms Bureau (ATF) Government agency that has jurisdiction over the sale and distribution of firearms, explosives, alcohol, and tobacco products.

alien conspiracy theory The view that organized crime was imported to the United States by Europeans and that crime cartels have a policy of restricting their membership to people of their own ethnic background.

alternative sanctions The group of punishments falling between probation and prison; "probation plus." Community-based sanctions, including house arrest and intensive supervision, serve as alternatives to incarceration.

altruistic fear Fear for others.

American Dream The goal of accumulating material goods and wealth through individual competition; the process of being socialized to pursue material success and to believe it is achievable.

anal stage In Freud's schema, the second and third years of life, when the focus of sexual attention is on the elimination of bodily wastes.

androgens Male sex hormones.

anomie A condition produced by normlessness. Because of rapidly shifting moral values, the individual has few guides to what is socially acceptable. According to Merton, anomie is a condition that occurs when personal goals cannot be achieved by available means. In Agnew's revision anomie can occur when positive or valued stimuli are removed or negative or painful ones applied.

antithesis An opposing argument.

apparent authority Authority that a third party, like a customer, reasonably believes the agent has to perform the act in question.

appellate courts Courts that reconsider a case that has already been tried to determine whether the measures used complied with accepted rules of criminal procedure and were in line with constitutional doctrines.

arousal theory A view of crime suggesting that people who have a high arousal level seek powerful stimuli in their environment to maintain an optimal level of arousal. These stimuli are often associated with violence and aggression. Sociopaths may need greater than average stimulation to bring them up to comfortable levels of living; this need explains their criminal tendencies.

arraignment The step in the criminal justice process at which the accused are read the charges against them, asked how they plead, and advised of their rights. Possible pleas are guilty, not guilty, *nolo contendere,* and not guilty by reason of insanity.

arrest The taking of a person into the custody of the law, the legal purpose of which is to restrain the accused until he or she can be held accountable for the offense at court proceedings. The legal requirement for an arrest is probable cause. Arrests for investigation, suspicion, or harassment are improper and of doubtful legality. The police have the responsibility to use only the reasonable physical force necessary to make an arrest. The summons has been used as a substitute for arrest.

arson The intentional or negligent burning of a home, structure, or vehicle for criminal purposes such as profit, revenge, fraud, or crime concealment.

arson for profit People looking to collect insurance money, but who are afraid or unable to set the fire themselves, hire professional arsonists. These professionals have acquired the skills to set fires yet make the cause seem accidental.

arson fraud A business owner burns his or her property, or hires someone to do it, to escape financial problems.

assault An attack that may not involve physical contact; includes attempted battery or intentionally frightening the victim by word or deed.

assigned counsel system A list of private bar members who accept cases of indigent criminals on a judge-by-judge, court-by-court, or case-by-case basis; this system is used in less populated areas, where case flow is minimal and a full-time public defender is not needed.

atavistic anomalies According to Lombroso, the physical characteristics that distinguish born criminals from the general population and are throwbacks to animals or primitive people.

at-risk Children and adults who lack the education and skills needed to be effectively in demand in modern society.

attention deficit hyperactive disorder (ADHD) A psychological disorder in which a child shows developmentally inappropriate impulsivity, hyperactivity, and lack of attention.

attitude survey Surveys that measure the attitudes, beliefs, and values of different groups.

Auburn system The prison system developed in New York during the nineteenth century that stressed congregate working conditions.

authority conflict pathway The path to a criminal career that begins with early stubborn behavior and defiance of parents.

bail The monetary amount for or condition of pretrial release, normally set by a judge at the initial appearance. The purpose of bail is to ensure the return of the accused at subsequent proceedings. If the accused is unable to make bail, he or she is detained in jail. The Eighth Amendment provides that excessive bail shall not be required.

bail bonding agent A person whose business is providing bail to needy offenders, usually at an exorbitant rate of interest.

bail guidelines Standard bail amounts set based on such factors as criminal history and the current charge.

battery A physical attack that includes hitting, punching, slapping, or other offensive touching of a victim.

behavior modeling Process of learning behavior (notably aggression) by observing others. Aggressive models may be parents, criminals in the neighborhood, or characters on television or in movies.

behaviorism The branch of psychology concerned with the study of observable behavior rather than unconscious motives. It focuses on the relationship between particular stimuli and people's responses to them.

beyond a reasonable doubt Degree of proof required for conviction of a defendant in criminal and juvenile delinquency proceedings. It is less than absolute certainty but more than high probability. If there is doubt based on reason, the accused is entitled to the benefit of that doubt by acquittal.

bias crimes Violent acts directed toward a particular person or members of a group merely because the targets share a discernible racial, ethnic, religious, or gender characteristic; also called hate crimes.

Bill of Rights The first 10 amendments to the U.S. Constitution.

biological determinism A belief that crimogenic traits can be acquired through indirect heredity from a degenerate family whose members suffered from such ills as insanity, syphilis, and alcoholism, or through direct heredity—being related to a family of criminals.

biophobia Sociologists who held the view that no serious consideration should be given to biological factors when attempting to understand human nature.

biosocial theory An approach to criminology that focuses on the interaction between biological and social factors as they relate to crime.

bipolar disorder An emotional disturbance in which moods alternate between periods of wild elation and deep depression.

blue curtain subculture According to William Westly, the secretive, insulated police culture that isolates the officer from the rest of society.

booster Professional shoplifter who steals with the intention of reselling stolen merchandise.

boot camp A short-term militaristic correctional facility in which inmates undergo intensive physical conditioning and discipline.

bot Under Anglo-Saxon law, the restitution paid for killing someone in an open fight.

bourgeoisie In Marxist theory, the owners of the means of production; the capitalist ruling class.

Z. R. Brockway The warden at the Elmira Reformatory in New York, he advocated individualized treatment, indeterminate sentences, and parole. The reformatory program initiated by Brockway included elementary education for illiterates, designated library hours, lectures by local college faculty members, and a group of vocational training shops.

brothel A house of prostitution, typically run by a madam who sets prices and handles "business" arrangements.

brutalization effect The belief that capital punishment creates an atmosphere of brutality that enhances rather than deters the level of violence in society. The death penalty reinforces the view that violence is an appropriate response to provocation.

bucketing A form of stockbroker chiseling in which brokers skim customer trading profits by falsifying trade information.

burglary Breaking into and entering a home or structure for the purposes of committing a felony.

California Personality Inventory (CPI) A frequently administered personality test used to distinguish deviants from nondeviant groups.

call girls Prostitutes who make dates via the phone and then service customers in hotel rooms or apartments. Call girls typically have a steady clientele who are repeat customers.

capable guardians Effective deterrents to crime, such as police or watchful neighbors.

capital punishment The use of the death penalty to punish transgressors.

capitalist bourgeoisie The owners of the means of production.

career criminal A person who repeatedly violates the law and organizes his or her lifestyle around criminality.

carjacking Theft of a car by force or threat of force.

cartographic school of criminology This approach made use of social statistics that were being developed in Europe in the early nineteenth century that provided important demographic information on the population, including density, gender, religious affiliations, and wealth. Many of the relationships between crime and social phenomena identified then still serve as a basis for criminology today.

case law When judicial decisions began to be written and published, judicial precedents were established, and more concrete examples of common-law decisions began to emerge. Together these cases and decisions filtered through the national court system and eventually produced a fixed body of legal rule and principles, or case law.

cerebral allergies A physical condition that causes brain malfunction due to exposure to some environmental or biochemical irritant.

chemical restraints Antipsychotic drugs such as Haldol, Stelazine, Prolixin, and Risperdal, which help control levels of neurotransmitters (such as serotonin/dopamine), that are used to treat violence-prone people; also called chemical straightjackets.

chemical straightjackets Another term for chemical restraints; antipsychotic drugs used to treat violence-prone people.

Chicago Crime Commission A citizens' action group set up in Chicago to investigate problems in the criminal justice system and explore avenues for positive change; the forerunner of many such groups around the country.

Chicago School Group of urban sociologists who studied the relationship between environmental conditions and crime.

child abuse Any physical, emotional, or sexual trauma to a child for which no reasonable explanation, such as an accident, can be found. Child abuse can also be a function of neglecting to give proper care and attention to a young child.

chivalry hypothesis The idea that low female crime and delinquency rates are a reflection of the leniency with which police treat female offenders.

chronic offender According to Wolfgang, a delinquent offender who is arrested five or more times before he or she is 18 and who stands a good chance of becoming an adult criminal; such offenders are responsible for more than half of all serious crimes.

chronic victimization Those who have been crime victims maintain a significantly higher chance of future victimization than people who have remained nonvictims. Most repeat victimizations occur soon after a previous crime has occurred, suggesting that repeat victims share some personal characteristic that makes them a magnet for predators.

churning A white-collar crime in which a stockbroker makes repeated trades to fraudulently increase his or her commissions.

circuit A specific route traveled by King Henry's circuit judges who heard cases that previously had been under the jurisdiction of local courts.

circuit judges Traveling judges appointed by King Henry of England.

civil law All law that is not criminal, including torts (personal wrongs), contract, property, maritime, and commercial law.

classical criminology The theoretical perspective suggesting that (1) people have free will to choose criminal or conventional behaviors; (2) people choose to commit crime for reasons of greed or personal need; and (3) crime can be controlled only by the fear of criminal sanctions.

cleared crimes Crimes are cleared in two ways: (1) when at least one person is arrested, charged, and turned over to the court for prosecution; or (2) by exceptional means, when some element beyond police control precludes the physical arrest of an offender (for example, the offender leaves the country).

closure A term used by Lemert to describe people from a middle-class background who have little identification with a criminal subculture but cash bad checks because of a financial crisis that demands an immediate resolution.

Code of Hammurabi The first written criminal code developed in Babylonia about 2000 B.C.

coercive ideation The world is conceived as full of coercive forces that can only be overcome through the application of equal or even greater coercive responses.

cognitive theory The study of the perception of reality and of the mental processes required to understand the world we live in.

cohort A sample of subjects whose behavior is followed over a period of time.

collective efficacy Social control exerted by cohesive communities, based on mutual trust, including intervention in the supervision of children and maintenance of public order.

college boy A disadvantaged youth who embraces the cultural and social values of the middle class and actively strives to be successful by those standards. This type of youth is embarking on an almost hopeless path, since he is ill-equipped academically, socially, and linguistically to achieve the rewards of middle-class life.

commercial theft Business theft that is part of the criminal law; without such laws the free enterprise system could not exist.

commitment to conformity A strong personal investment in conventional institutions, individuals, and processes that prevents people from engaging in behavior that might jeopardize their reputation and achievements.

common law Early English law, developed by judges, that incorporated Anglo-Saxon tribal custom, feudal rules and practices, and the everyday rules of behavior of local villages. Common law became the standardized law of the land in England and eventually formed the basis of the criminal law in the United States.

communist manifesto In this document, Marx focused his attention on the economic conditions perpetuated by the capitalist system. He stated that its development had turned workers into a dehumanized mass who lived an existence that was at the mercy of their capitalist employers.

community notification laws Recent legislative efforts that require convicted sex offenders to register with local police when they move into an area or neighborhood.

community-oriented policing A police strategy that emphasizes fear reduction, community organization, and order maintenance rather than crime fighting.

community service restitution An alternative sanction that requires an offender to work in the community at such tasks as cleaning public parks or helping handicapped children in lieu of an incarceration sentence.

complaint A sworn allegation made in writing to a court or judge that an individual is guilty of some designated (complained of) offense. This is often the first legal document filed regarding a criminal offense. The complaint can be "taken out" by the victim, the police officer, the district attorney, or another interested party. Although the complaint charges an offense, an indictment or information may be the formal charging document.

compurgation In early English law, a process whereby an accused person swore an oath of innocence while being backed up by a group of 12 to 25 "oath-helpers," who would attest to his character and claims of innocence.

concentration effect As working- and middle-class families flee inner-city poverty areas, the most disadvantaged population is consolidated in urban ghettos.

concurrent sentences Literally, running sentences together. Someone who is convicted of two or more charges must be sentenced on each charge. If the sentences are concurrent, they begin the same day and are completed after the longest term has been served.

conduct disorder (CD) A psychological condition marked by repeated and severe episodes of antisocial behaviors.

conduct norms Behaviors expected of social group members. If group norms conflict with those of the general culture, members of the group may find themselves described as outcasts or criminals.

confidence game A swindle, usually involving a get-rich-quick scheme, often with illegal overtones, so that the victim will be afraid or embarrassed to call the police.

conflict view The view that human behavior is shaped by interpersonal conflict and that those who maintain social power will use it to further their own needs.

congregate system This prison system included congregate working conditions, the use of solitary confinement to punish unruly inmates, military regimentation, and discipline.

conscience One of two parts of the superego; it distinguishes between what is right and wrong.

consecutive sentences Prison sentences for two or more criminal acts that are served one after the other.

consensus view of crime The belief that the majority of citizens in a society share common ideals and work toward a common good and that crimes are acts that are outlawed because they conflict with the rules of the majority and are harmful to society.

consent In prosecuting rape cases, it is essential to prove that the attack was forced and that the victim did not give voluntary consent to her attacker. In a sense, the burden of proof is on the victim to show that her character is beyond question and that she in no way encouraged, enticed, or misled the accused rapist. Proving victim dissent is not a requirement in any other violent crime.

constable The peacekeeper in early English towns. The constable organized citizens to protect his territory and supervised the night watch.

constructive possession In the crime of larceny, willingly giving up temporary physical possession of property but retaining legal ownership.

contagion effect Genetic predispositions and early experiences make some people, including twins, susceptible to deviant behavior, which is transmitted by the presence of antisocial siblings in the household.

containment theory The idea that a strong self-image insulates a youth from the pressures and pulls of crimogenic influences in the environment.

contextual discrimination A practice in which African Americans receive harsher punishments in some instances (as when they victimize whites) but not in others (as when they victimize other blacks).

continuity of crime The view that crime begins early in life and continues throughout the life course. Thus, the best predictor of future criminality is past criminality.

contract law The law of personal agreements.

contract system (attorney) Providing counsel to indigent offenders by having attorneys under contract to the county to handle all (or some) such cases.

control balance theory A developmental theory that attributes deviant and criminal behaviors to imbalances between the amount of control that the individual has over others and that others have over him or her.

convictional criminals Those who violate the law because they believe their actions will ultimately benefit society.

convict-lease system The system used earlier in the century in which inmates were leased out to private industry to work.

corner boy According to Cohen, a role in the lower-class culture in which young men remain in their birth neighborhood, acquire families and menial jobs, and adjust to the demands of their environment.

corporal punishment The use of physical chastisement, such as whipping or electroshock, to punish criminals.

corporate crime White-collar crime involving a legal violation by a corporate entity, such as price fixing, restraint of trade, or hazardous waste dumping.

correctionalism Research conducted by mainstream liberal/positivist criminologists designed to unmask the weak and powerless members of society so they can be better dealt with by the legal system.

courtroom work group All the parties in the adversary process who work together to settle cases with the least amount of effort and conflict.

covert pathway A path to a criminal career that begins with minor underhanded behavior and progresses to fire starting and theft.

crackdown The concentration of police resources on a particular problem area, such as street-level drug dealing, to eradicate or displace criminal activity.

crime A violation of societal rules of behavior as interpreted and expressed by a criminal legal code created by people holding social and political power. Individuals who violate these rules are subject to sanctions by state authority, social stigma, and loss of status.

crime control model A model of criminal justice that emphasizes the control of dangerous offenders and the protection of society. Its advocates call for harsh punishments, such as the death penalty, as a deterrent to crime.

crime discouragers Discouragers can be grouped into three categories: guardians, who monitor targets (such as store security guards); handlers, who monitor potential offenders (such as parole officers and parents); and managers, who monitor places (such as homeowners and doorway attendants).

crime displacement An effect of crime prevention efforts in which efforts to control crime in one area shift illegal activities to another.

crime typology The study of criminal behavior involving research on the links between different types of crime and criminals. Because people often disagree about types of crimes and criminal motivation, no standard exists within the field. Some typologies focus on the criminal, suggesting the existence of offender groups, such as professional criminals, psychotic criminals, occasional criminals, and so on. Others focus on the crimes, clustering them into categories such as property crimes, sex crimes, and so on.

crimes of reduction Crimes that are committed when the offended party experiences a loss of some quality relative to his or her present standing. Their loss can come about if they are victims of robbery or theft, but they also may be victimized if their dignity is stripped from them when they are taunted by racists.

crimes of repression Crimes that are committed when members of a group are prevented from achieving their fullest potential because of racism, sexism, or some other status bias.

criminal anthropology Early efforts to discover a biological basis of crime through measurement of physical and mental processes.

criminal attempt law The intent may make an act, innocent in itself, criminal; also called inchoate crimes.

criminal court The core element in the administration of criminal justice; criminal courts are expected to try, convict, and sentence those who commit crimes while

ensuring that the falsely accused are freed without any consequence or burden.

criminal justice process The decision-making points from the initial investigation or arrest by police to the eventual release of the offender and his or her reentry into society; the various sequential criminal justice stages through which the offender passes.

criminal trial A full-scale inquiry into the facts of the case before a judge, a jury, or both.

criminality A personal trait of the individual as distinct from a "crime," which is an event.

criminological enterprise The areas of study and research that taken together make up the field of criminology. Criminologists typically specialize in one of the subareas of criminology, such as victimology or the sociology of law.

criminologists Researchers who use scientific methods to study the nature, extent, cause, and control of criminal behavior.

criminology The scientific study of the nature, extent, cause, and control of criminal behavior.

crisis intervention Emergency counseling for crime victims.

cross-examination The process in which the defense and the prosecution interrogate witnesses during a trial.

cross-sectional research Uses survey data derived from all age, race, gender, and income segments of the population measured simultaneously. Since people from every age group are represented, age-specific crime rates can be determined. Proponents believe this is a sufficient substitute for the more expensive longitudinal approach that follows a group of subjects over time to measure crime rate changes.

crusted over Children who have been victims of or witnesses to violence and do not let people inside, nor do they express their feelings. They exploit others and in turn are exploited by those older and stronger; as a result, they develop a sense of hopelessness.

cultural deviance theory Branch of social structure theory that sees strain and social disorganization together resulting in a unique lower-class culture that conflicts with conventional social norms.

cultural transmission The concept that conduct norms are passed down from

one generation to the next so that they become stable within the boundaries of a culture. Cultural transmission guarantees that group lifestyle and behavior are stable and predictable.

culture conflict According to Sellin, a condition brought about when the rules and norms of an individual's subcultural affiliation conflict with the role demands of conventional society.

culture of poverty The view that people in the lower class of society form a separate culture with its own values and norms that are in conflict with conventional society; the culture is self-maintaining and ongoing.

Customs Bureau Government agency that guards points of entry into the United States and prevents smuggling of contraband into or out of the country.

cycle of violence The idea that victims of crime, especially childhood abuse, are more likely to commit crimes themselves.

date rape Forcible sex during a courting relationship.

day fines Fines geared to the average daily income of the convicted offender in an effort to bring equity to the sentencing process.

deadly force The ability of the police to kill suspects if they resist arrest or present a danger to an officer or the community. The police cannot use deadly force against an unarmed fleeing felon.

death squads Government troops used to destroy political opposition parties.

decadence Spur of the moment, irrational acts such as child molesting.

deconstructionist analysis An approach that focuses on the use of language by those in power to define crime based on their own values and biases; also called postmodernist.

decriminalization Reducing the penalty for a criminal act but not actually legalizing it.

defective intelligence Traits such as feeblemindedness, epilepsy, insanity, and defective social instinct, which Goring believed had a significant relationship to criminal behavior.

defensible space The principle that crime prevention can be achieved through modifying the physical environment to reduce the opportunity individuals have to commit crime.

defiance Challenging control mechanisms but stopping short of physical harm: for example, vandalism, curfew violations, and unconventional sex.

deinstitutionalization The movement to remove as many offenders as possible from secure confinement and treat them in the community.

deliberation Planning a homicide after careful thought, however brief, rather than acting on sudden impulse.

delinquent boy A youth who adopts a set of norms and principles in direct opposition to middle-class values, engaging in short-run hedonism and living for today and letting "tomorrow take care of itself."

deposit bail system A system that allow defendants to post a percentage of their bond (usually 10 percent) with the court; the full amount is required only if the defendant fails to show for trial.

determinate sentence A fixed term of incarceration, such as three years' imprisonment. Determinate sentences are felt by many to be too restrictive for rehabilitative purposes; the advantage is that offenders know how much time they have to serve—that is, when they will be released.

deterrence theory The view that if the probability of arrest, conviction, and sanctioning increases, crime rates should decline.

developmental theory A branch of criminology that examines change in a criminal career over the life course. Developmental factors include biological, social, and psychological change. Among the topics of developmental criminology are desistance, resistance, escalation, and specialization.

deviant behavior Behavior that departs from the social norm.

dialectic method For every idea, or thesis, there exists an opposing argument, or antithesis. Since neither position can ever be truly accepted, the result is a merger of the two ideas, a synthesis. Marx adapted this analytic method for his study of class struggle.

differential association theory According to Sutherland, the principle that criminal acts are related to a person's exposure to an excess amount of antisocial attitudes and values.

differential opportunity The view that lower-class youths, whose legitimate opportunities are limited, join gangs and pursue criminal careers as alternative means to achieve universal success goals.

differential reinforcement Behavior is reinforced by being either rewarded or punished while interacting with others; also called direct conditioning.

differential reinforcement theory An attempt to explain crime as a type of learned behavior. First proposed by Ronald Akers in collaboration with Robert Burgess in 1966, it is a version of the social learning view that employs both differential association concepts along with elements of psychological learning theory.

differential social control A process of labeling that may produce a reevaluation of the self, which reflects actual or perceived appraisals made by others.

diffusion of benefits An effect that occurs when an effort to control one type of crime has the unexpected benefit of reducing the incidence of another.

direct conditioning Behavior is reinforced by being either rewarded or punished while interacting with others; also called differential reinforcement.

direct examination The questioning of one's own (prosecution or defense) witness during a trial.

directed verdict The right of a judge to direct a jury to acquit a defendant because the state has not proven the elements of the crime or otherwise has not established guilt according to law.

discouragement An effect that occurs when an effort made to eliminate one type of crime also controls others, because it reduces the value of criminal activity by limiting access to desirable targets.

disorder Any type of psychological problem (formerly labeled neurotic or psychotic), such as anxiety disorders, mood disorders, and conduct disorders.

disposition For juvenile offenders, the equivalent of sentencing for adult offenders. The theory is that disposition is more rehabilitative than retributive. Possible dispositions may be to dismiss the case, release the youth to the custody of his or her parents, place the offender on probation, or send him or her to a correctional institution.

diversion programs Programs of rehabilitation that remove offenders from the normal channels of the criminal justice process, thus avoiding the stigma of a criminal label.

division of markets Firms divide a region into territories, and each firm agrees not to compete in the others' territories.

doing gender Men's struggle to dominate women to prove their manliness. Crime is a vehicle for men to "do gender" because it separates them from the weak and allows them to demonstrate physical bravery. Violence directed toward women is an especially economical way to demonstrate manhood.

double jeopardy A defendant cannot be prosecuted by a jurisdiction more than once for a single offense.

dramatization of evil As the negative feedback of law enforcement agencies, parents, friends, teachers, and other figures amplifies the force of the original label, stigmatized offenders may begin to reevaluate their own identities. The person becomes the thing he is described as being.

drift According to Matza, the view that youths move in and out of delinquency and that their lifestyles can embrace both conventional and deviant values.

Drug Enforcement Administration (DEA) The federal agency that enforces federal drug control laws.

dual sovereignty doctrine If a single act violates the laws of two states, the offender may be punished for each offense.

due process model View that focuses on protecting the civil rights of those accused of crime.

due process The constitutional principle based on the concept of the primacy of the individual and the complementary concept of limitation on governmental power; a safeguard against arbitrary and unfair state procedures in judicial or administrative proceedings. Embodied in the due process concept are the basic rights of a defendant in criminal proceedings and the requisites for a fair trial. These rights and requirements have been expanded by appellate court decisions and include (1) timely notice of a hearing or trial that informs the accused of the charges against him or her; (2) the opportunity to confront accusers and to present evidence on the accused's own behalf before an impartial jury or judge; (3) the presumption of innocence under which guilt must be proven by legally obtained evidence and the verdict must be supported by the evidence presented; (4) the right of an accused to be warned of constitutional rights at the earliest stage of the criminal process; (5) protection against self-incrimination; (6) assistance of counsel at every critical stage of the criminal process; and (7) the guarantee that an individual will not be tried more than once for the same offense (double jeopardy).

early onset A term that refers to the assumption that a criminal career begins early in life and that people who are deviant at a very young age are the ones most likely to persist in crime.

ecclesiastics See holy-motes; church courts in England in the eleventh century.

ecological view A belief that social forces operating in urban areas create criminal interactions; some neighborhoods become "natural areas" for crime.

economic compulsive behavior Behavior that occurs when drug users resort to violence to gain funds to support their habit.

economic crime An act in violation of the criminal law that is designed to bring financial gain to the offender.

edgework The excitement or exhilaration of successfully executing illegal activities in dangerous situations.

ego The part of the personality, developed in early childhood, that helps control the id and keep people's actions within the boundaries of social convention.

ego ideal Part of superego; directs the individual into morally acceptable and responsible behaviors, which may not be pleasurable.

elder abuse A disturbing form of domestic violence by children and other relatives with whom elderly people live.

eldercide The murder of a senior citizen.

Electra complex A stage of development when girls begin to have sexual feelings for their fathers.

electroencephalograph (EEG) A device that can record the electronic impulses given off by the brain, commonly called brain waves.

electronic monitoring (EM) Offenders wear devices attached to their ankles, wrists, or neck that send signals back to a control office; used to monitor home confinements.

elite deviance White-collar and economic crimes.

embezzlement A type of larceny that involves taking the possessions of another (fraudulent conversion) that have been placed in the thief's lawful possession for safekeeping, such as a bank teller misappropriating deposits or a stockbroker making off with a customer's account.

enterprise theory of investigation (ETI) A standard investigation tool of the FBI that focuses on criminal enterprise and investigation attacks on the structure of the criminal enterprise rather than on criminal acts viewed as isolated incidents.

equipotentiality View that all individuals are equal at birth and are thereafter influenced by their environment.

eros The instinct to preserve and create life; eros is expressed sexually.

exclusionary rule The principle that prohibits using evidence illegally obtained in a trial. Based on the Fourth Amendment "right of the people to be secure in their persons, houses, papers, and effects, against unreasonable searches and seizures," the rule is not a bar to prosecution, as legally obtained evidence may be available that may be used in a trial.

exploitation (of criminals) Using others to commit crimes: for example, as contract killers or drug runners.

exploitation (of victims) Forcing victims to pay for services to which they have a clear right.

expressive crime A crime that has no purpose except to accomplish the behavior at hand, such as shooting someone.

expressive violence Violence that is designed not for profit or gain but to vent rage, anger, or frustration.

extinction The phenomenon in which a crime prevention effort has an immediate impact that then dissipates as criminals adjust to new conditions.

false pretenses Illegally obtaining money, goods, or merchandise from another by fraud or misrepresentation.

Federal Bureau of Investigation (FBI) The arm of the U.S. Justice Department that investigates violations of federal law, gathers crime statistics, runs a comprehensive crime laboratory, and helps train local law enforcement officers.

federal courts of appeal Court that hears appeals from the U.S. district courts.

felony A serious offense that carries a penalty of incarceration in a state prison, usually for one year or more. Persons convicted of felony offenses lose the right to vote, hold elective office, or maintain certain licenses.

felony murder A homicide in the context of another felony, such as robbery or rape; legally defined as first-degree murder.

fence A buyer and seller of stolen merchandise.

feticide Endangering or killing an unborn fetus.

fine A dollar amount usually exacted as punishment for a minor crime; fines may also be combined with other sentencing alternatives, such as probation or confinement.

first-degree murder The killing of another person after premeditation and deliberation.

fixated An adult that exhibits behavior traits characteristic of those encountered during infantile sexual development.

flash houses Public meeting places in England, often taverns, that served as headquarters for gangs.

flashover An effect in a fire when heat and gas at the ceiling of a room reach 2,000 degrees and clothes and furniture burst into flame, duplicating the effects of arsonists' gasoline or explosives. It is possible that many suspected arsons are actually the result of flashover.

focal concerns According to Miller, the value orientations of lower-class cultures; features include the needs for excitement, trouble, smartness, fate, and personal autonomy.

folkways Generally followed customs that do not have moral values attached to them, such as not interrupting people when they are speaking.

foot patrols Police patrols that take officers out of cars and put them on a walking beat to strengthen ties with the community.

forfeiture The seizure of personal property by the state as a civil or criminal penalty.

fraud Taking the possessions of another through deception or cheating, such as selling a person a desk that is represented as an antique but is known to be a copy.

free-venture program Privately run industries in a prison setting in which the inmates work for wages and the goods are sold for profit.

front running A form of stockbroker chiseling in which brokers place personal orders ahead of a large order from a customer to profit from the market effects of the trade.

fundamental fairness The legal principle that all people should be equal before the law and treated so.

gang rape Forcible sex involving multiple attackers.

gatekeepers The police, who initiate contact with law violators and decide whether to formally arrest them and start their journey through the criminal justice system, settle the issue informally (such as by issuing a warning), or simply take no action at all.

gateway model An explanation of drug abuse that posits that users begin with a more benign drug (alcohol or marijuana) and progress to ever-more potent drugs.

gay bashing Violent hate crimes directed toward people because of their sexual orientation.

general deterrence A crime control policy that depends on the fear of criminal penalties. General deterrence measures, such as long prison sentences for violent crimes, are aimed at convincing the potential law violator that the pains associated with crime outweigh its benefits.

general strain theory (GST) The view that multiple sources of strain interact with an individual's emotional traits and responses to produce criminality.

general theory of crime (GTC) A developmental theory that modifies social control theory by integrating concepts from biosocial, psychological, routine activities, and rational choice theories.

gentrification A residential renewal stage in which obsolete housing is replaced and upgraded; areas undergoing such change seem to experience an increase in their crime rates.

good burglar Professional burglars use this title to characterize colleagues who have distinguished themselves as burglars. Characteristics of the good burglar

include (1) technical competence, (2) maintenance of personal integrity, (3) specialization in burglary, (4) financial success, and (5) the ability to avoid prison sentences.

grand jury A group (usually consisting of 23 citizens) chosen to hear testimony in secret and to issue formal criminal accusations (indictments). It also serves an investigatory function.

grand larceny Theft of money or property of substantial value, punished as a felony.

group boycott A company's refusal to do business with retail stores that do not comply with its rules or desires.

guerilla The term means "little war" and developed out of the Spanish rebellion against French troops after Napoleon's 1808 invasion of the Iberian peninsula. Today the term is used interchangeably with the term terrorist.

hali-gemot The manorial court of the local nobleman in England in the eleventh century.

hands-off doctrine The judicial policy of not interfering in the administrative affairs of a prison.

hate crimes Acts of violence or intimidation designed to terrorize or frighten people considered undesirable because of their race, religion, ethnic origin, or sexual orientation.

heels Professional shoplifters who steal with the intention of reselling stolen merchandise to pawnshops or fences, usually at half the original price.

(the) hole Solitary confinement used as punishment for prisons who flout prison rules.

holy-motes Acts of a spiritual nature were judged by clergymen and church officials in these courts in England in the eleventh century; also called ecclesiastics.

home confinement (HC) Convicted offenders must spend extended periods in their own homes as an alternative to incarceration; also called house arrest or home detention.

homophobia Extremely negative overreaction to homosexuals.

homosexuality Erotic interest in members of one's own sex.

hot spots of crime The locations of a significant portion of all police calls. These hot spots include taverns and housing projects.

house of correction A county correctional institution generally used for the incarceration of more serious misdemeanants, whose sentences are usually less than one year.

human nature theory A belief that personal traits, such as genetic makeup, intelligence, and body build, may outweigh the importance of social variables as predictors of criminal activity.

humanistic psychology A branch of psychology that stresses self-awareness and "getting in touch with feelings."

hundred In medieval England, a group of 100 families who were responsible for maintaining the order and trying minor offenses.

hundred-gemot Literally, the hundred group, whose courts tried petty cases of criminal conduct.

hung jury A jury that cannot reach a decision in a criminal case. If a jury is hung, the prosecution can retry the case.

hypermasculine Men who typically have a callous sexual attitude and believe violence is manly. They perceive danger as exciting and are overly sensitive to insult and ridicule. They are also impulsive, more apt to brag about sexual conquests, and more likely to lose control, especially when using alcohol.

hypoglycemia A condition that occurs when glucose (sugar) in the blood falls below levels necessary for normal and efficient brain functioning.

id The primitive part of people's mental makeup, present at birth, that represents unconscious biological drives for food, sex, and other life-sustaining necessities. The id seeks instant gratification without concern for the rights of others.

identity crisis A psychological state, identified by Erikson, in which youth face inner turmoil and uncertainty about life roles.

Immigration and Naturalization Service Government agency that administers immigration laws, deports illegal aliens, and naturalizes aliens lawfully present in the United States.

impact statement A victim's statement considered at a sentencing hearing.

imperatively coordinated associations These associations are composed of two groups: those who possess authority and use it for social domination and those who lack authority and are dominated.

impersonal coercion Pressures beyond individual control, such as economic and social pressure caused by unemployment, poverty, or business competition.

importation model The view that the violent prison culture reflects the criminal culture of the outside world and is neither developed in nor unique to prisons.

incapacitation effect The idea that keeping offenders in confinement will eliminate the risk of their committing further offenses.

incarceration Confinement in jail or prison.

inchoate crimes Incomplete or contemplated crimes such as criminal solicitation or criminal attempts.

indeterminate sentence A term of incarceration with a stated minimum and maximum length, such as a sentence to prison for a period of from 3 to 10 years. The prisoner would be eligible for parole after the minimum sentence had been served. Based on the belief that sentences should fit the criminal, indeterminate sentences allow individualized sentences and provide for sentencing flexibility. Judges can set a high minimum to override the purpose of the indeterminate sentence.

index crimes The eight crimes that, because of their seriousness and frequency, the FBI reports the incidence of in the annual Uniform Crime Reports. Index crimes include murder, rape, assault, robbery, burglary, arson, larceny, and motor vehicle theft.

inevitable discovery rule A rule of law stating that evidence that almost assuredly would be independently discovered can be used in a court of law, even though it was obtained in violation of legal rules and practices.

infanticide The murder of a very young child.

inferiority complex People who have feelings of inferiority and compensate for them with a drive for superiority.

influence peddling Using an institutional position to grant favors and sell information to which their coconspirators are not entitled.

informal sanctions Disapproval, stigma, or anger directed toward an offender by significant others (parents, peers, neighbors, teachers), resulting in shame, embarrassment, and loss of respect.

information Like an indictment, a formal charging document. The prosecuting attorney makes out the information and files it in court. Probable cause is determined at the preliminary hearing, which, unlike grand jury proceedings, is public and attended by the accused and his or her attorney.

information processing A branch of cognitive psychology that focuses on the way people process, store, encode, retrieve, and manipulate information to make decisions and solve problems.

inheritance school Advocates of this view trace the activities of several generations of families believed to have an especially large number of criminal members.

inmate subculture The loosely defined culture that pervades prisons and has its own norms, rules, and language.

insider trading Illegal buying of stock in a company based on information provided by someone who has a fiduciary interest in the company, such as an employee or an attorney or accountant retained by the firm. Federal laws and the rules of the Securities and Exchange Commission require that all profits from such trading be returned and provide for both fines and a prison sentence.

institutional anomie theory The view that anomie pervades U.S. culture because the drive for material wealth dominates and undermines social and community values.

instrumental crimes Offenses designed to improve the financial or social position of the criminal.

instrumental violence Violence used in an attempt to improve the financial or social position of the criminal.

instrumentalists The view that the criminal law and criminal justice system are solely an instrument for controlling the poor, have-not members of society; the state is the "tool" of the capitalists.

integrative-constitutive theory This theory attempts to show how crime and its control cannot be separated from the structural and cultural contexts in which it is produced. In our postmodern society, unequal power relations, built on human differences, provide the conditions that define harm and therefore crime.

intensive probation supervision (IPS) A type of intermediate sanction involving small probation caseloads and strict daily or weekly monitoring.

interactional theory The idea that interaction with institutions and events during the life course determines criminal behavior patterns; crimogenic influences evolve over time.

interactionist view The view that one's perception of reality is significantly influenced by one's interpretations of the reactions of others to similar events and stimuli.

interdisciplinary science Involving two or more academic fields.

intermediate sanctions An alternative to prison; these sanctions include fines, forfeiture, home confinement, electronic monitoring, intensive probation supervision, restitution, community corrections, and boot camps.

Internal Revenue Service Government agency that enforces violations of income, excise, stamp, and other tax laws.

international terrorism Terrorism involving citizens or the territory of more than one country.

interpersonal coercion The use of force, threat of force, or intimidation by parents, peers, or significant others.

involuntary manslaughter A homicide that occurs as a result of acts that are negligent and without regard for the harm they may cause others, such as driving under the influence of alcohol or drugs.

jail A place to detain people awaiting trial, hold drunks and disorderly individuals, and confine convicted misdemeanants serving sentences of less than one year.

judge The senior officer in a court of criminal law.

juries In England, groups of local landholders whom the circuit judges called not only to decide the facts of cases but also to investigate the crimes, accuse suspected offenders, and even give testimony at trials.

jury array The initial list of persons chosen, which provides the state with a group of citizens potentially capable of serving on a jury; also called a venire.

just desert The philosophy of justice that asserts that those who violate the rights of others deserve to be punished. The severity of punishment should be commensurate with the seriousness of the crime.

justice model A philosophy of corrections that stresses determinate sentences, abolition of parole, and the view that prisons are places of punishment and not rehabilitation.

justice of the peace Established in 1326 in England to assist the shire reeve in controlling the county, these justices eventually took on judicial functions in addition to being peacekeepers.

justification A defense to a criminal charge in which the accused maintains that his or her actions were justified by the circumstances and therefore he or she should not be held criminally liable.

La Cosa Nostra A national syndicate of 25 or so Italian-dominated crime families who control crime in distinct geographic areas.

labeling theory Theory that views society as creating deviance through a system of social control agencies that designate certain individuals as deviants. The stigmatized individual is made to feel unwanted in the normal social order. Eventually, the individual begins to believe that the label is accurate, assumes it as a personal identity, and enters into a deviant or criminal career.

landmark decision A decision handed down by the Supreme Court that becomes the law of the land and serves as a precedent for similar legal issues.

larceny Taking for one's own use the property of another, by means other than force or threats on the victim or forcibly breaking into a person's home or workplace; theft.

latency A developmental stage that begins at age 6. During this period, feelings of sexuality are repressed until the genital stage begins at puberty; this marks the beginning of adult sexuality.

latent delinquency A psychological predisposition to commit antisocial acts because of an id-dominated personality that renders an individual incapable of controlling impulsive, pleasure-seeking drives.

latent trait A stable feature, characteristic, property, or condition, present at birth or soon after, that makes some people crime prone over the life course.

latent trait theory The view that criminal behavior is controlled by a "master trait," present at birth or soon after, that

remains stable and unchanging throughout a person's lifetime.

law of criminal procedure Judicial precedents that define and guarantee the rights of criminal defendants and control the various components of the criminal justice sytem.

left realism A branch of conflict theory that holds that crime is a "real" social problem experienced by the lower classes and that lower-class concerns about crime must be addressed by radical scholars.

legal code The specific laws that fall within the scope of criminal law.

lex talionis Physical retaliation; "an eye for an eye."

libel False and injurious writings.

liberal feminist theory This theory suggested that the traditionally lower crime rate for women could be explained by their "second-class" economic and social position. As women's social roles changed and their lifestyles became more like those of males, it was believed that their crime rates would converge.

life course persister One of the small group of offenders whose criminal career continues well into adulthood.

life course theory The study of changes in criminal offending patterns over a person's entire life. Are there conditions or events that occur later in life that influence the way people behave, or is behavior predetermined by social or personal conditions at birth?

lineup Witnesses may be brought in to view the suspect in a group of people with similar characteristics and asked to pick out the suspect.

lumpen proletariat The fringe members at the bottom of society who produce nothing and live, parasitically, off the work of others.

madam A woman who employs prostitutes, supervises their behavior, and receives a fee for her services.

Mafia A criminal society that originated in Sicily, Italy, and is believed to control racketeering in the United States.

mala in se **crimes** Acts that are outlawed because they violate basic moral values, such as rape, murder, assault, and robbery.

mala prohibitum **crimes** Acts that are outlawed because they clash with current

norms and public opinion, such as tax, traffic, and drug laws.

mandatory prison term A statutory requirement that a certain penalty shall be set and carried out in all cases on conviction for a specified offense or series of offenses.

mandatory release Prisoners must be released upon completion of their sentence.

manorial courts The local hundred who dealt with most secular violations in eleventh-century England.

manslaughter A homicide without malice.

marginalization Displacement of workers, pushing them outside the economic and social mainstream.

marital exemption The practice in some states of prohibiting the prosecution of husbands for the rape of their wives.

marital rape Forcible sex between people who are legally married to each other.

mark The target of a con man or woman.

masculinity hypothesis The view that women who commit crimes have biological and psychological traits similar to those of men.

mass murder The killing of a large number of people in a single incident by an offender who typically does not seek concealment or escape.

mechanical solidarity A characteristic of a pre-industrial society, which is held together by traditions, shared values, and unquestioned beliefs.

mens rea "Guilty mind." The mental element of a crime or the intent to commit a criminal act.

middle-class measuring rods According to Cohen, the standards by which teachers and other representatives of state authority evaluate lower-class youths. Because they cannot live up to middle-class standards, lower-class youths are bound for failure, which gives rise to frustration and anger at conventional society.

Minnesota Multiphasic Personality Inventory (MMPI) A widely used psychology test that has subscales designed to measure many different personality traits, including psychopathic deviation (Pd scale), schizophrenia (Sc), and hypomania (Ma).

Miranda warning The result of two U.S. Supreme Court decisions (*Escobedo v. Illinois* [378 U.S. 478] and *Miranda v. Arizona* [384 U.S. 436]) that require police officers to inform individuals under arrest of their constitutional right to remain silent and to know that their statements can later be used against them in court, that they can have an attorney present to help them, and that the state will pay for an attorney if they cannot afford to hire one. Although aimed at protecting an individual during in-custody interrogation, the warning must also be given when the investigation shifts from the investigatory to the accusatory stage—that is, when suspicion begins to focus on an individual.

mission hate crime Violent crimes committed by disturbed individuals who see it as their duty to rid the world of evil.

Missouri Plan A way of picking judges through nonpartisan elections as a means of ensuring judicial performance standards.

modus operandi (MO) The working methods of particular offenders.

monetary restitution A sanction requiring that convicted offenders compensate crime victims by reimbursing them for out-of-pocket losses caused by the crime. Losses can include property damage, lost wages, and medical costs.

moral crusades Efforts by interest-group members to stamp out behavior they find objectionable. Typically, moral crusades are directed at public order crimes, such as drug abuse or pornography.

moral development The way people morally represent and reason about the world.

moral entrepreneurs Interest groups that attempt to control social life and the legal order in such as way as to promote their own personal set of moral values. People who use their influence to shape the legal process in ways they see fit.

morals Generally followed behavior based on societal codes of conduct; society norms.

morals squad Plainclothes police officers or detectives specializing in victimless crimes such as prostitution or gambling.

mores In preliterate societies, common customs and traditions that were the equivalents of law.

Mosaic Code The laws of the ancient Israelites, found in the Old Testament of the Judeo-Christian Bible.

motivated offenders The potential offenders in a population. According to rational choice theory, crime rates will vary according to the number of motivated offenders.

mug shots Pictures of offenders that can be viewed by victims in an attempt to identify the perpetrator.

Multidimensional Personality Questionnaire (MPQ) A test that allows researchers to assess such personality traits as control, aggression, alienation, and well-being. Evaluations using this scale indicate that adolescent offenders who are "crime prone" maintain "negative emotionality," a tendency to experience aversive affective states such as anger, anxiety, and irritability.

murder The unlawful killing of a human being (homicide) with malicious intent.

naive check forgers Amateurs who cash bad checks because of some financial crisis but have little identification with a criminal subculture.

National Crime Victimization Survey (NCVS) The ongoing victimization study conducted jointly by the Justice Department and the U.S. Census Bureau that surveys victims about their experiences with law violation.

National Incident-Based Reporting System (NIBRS) A new program that will require local police agencies to provide a brief account of each incident and arrest within 22 crime patterns, including incident, victim, and offender information.

natural law Laws rooted in the core values inherent in Western civilization; actions contrary to natural law are also called *mala in se* crimes.

nature theory The view that intelligence is largely determined genetically and that low intelligence is linked to criminal behavior.

negative affective states According to Agnew, the anger, depression, disappointment, fear, and other adverse emotions that derive from strain.

negative reinforcement Using either negative stimuli (punishment) or loss of reward (negative punishment) to curtail unwanted behaviors.

neglect Not providing a child with the care and shelter to which he or she is entitled.

negligent manslaughter A homicide that occurs as a result of acts that are negligent and without regard for the harm they may cause others, such as driving under the influence of alcohol or drugs; also called involuntary manslaughter.

neocortex A part of the human brain; the left side of the neocortex controls sympathetic feelings toward others.

neuroallergies Allergies that affect the nervous system and cause the allergic person to produce enzymes that attack wholesome foods as if they were dangerous to the body. They may also cause swelling of the brain and produce sensitivity in the central nervous system, conditions linked to mental, emotional, and behavioral problems.

neurophysiology The study of brain activity.

neurotics People who fear that their primitive id impulses will dominate their personality.

neutralization theory Neutralization theory holds that offenders adhere to conventional values while "drifting" into periods of illegal behavior. In order to drift, people must first overcome (neutralize) legal and moral values.

new generation jails Jails that allow for continuous observation of residents. There are two types, direct and indirect supervision.

nolle prosequi The term used when a prosecutor decides to drop a case after a complaint has been formally made. Reasons for a *nolle prosequi* include insufficient evidence, reluctance of witnesses to testify, police error, and office policy.

nonnegligent manslaughter A homicide committed in the heat of passion or during a sudden quarrel; although intent may be present, malice is not; also called voluntary manslaughter.

normative groups Groups, such as the high school in-crowd, that conform to the social rules of society.

norm resistance Interaction between authorities and subjects that eventually produces open conflict between the two groups that can take on a number of different forms.

norms Unwritten rules of conduct and universally followed behavior.

nuture theory The view that intelligence is not inherited but is largely a product of environment. Low IQ scores do not cause crime but may result from the same environmental factors.

obitiatry According to Jack Kevorkian, the practice of helping people take their own lives.

obscenity According to current legal theory, sexually explicit material that lacks a serious purpose and appeals solely to the prurient interest of the viewer. While nudity per se is not usually considered obscene, open sexual behavior, masturbation, and exhibition of the genitals is banned in most communities.

obsessive-compulsive disorder An extreme preoccupation with certain thoughts and compulsive performance of certain behaviors.

occasional criminals Offenders who do not define themselves by a criminal role or view themselves as committed career criminals.

Oedipus complex A stage of development when males begin to have sexual feelings for their mothers.

offender classification If the offender is placed on probation, the department diagnoses his or her personality and treatment needs; offenders classified as minimal risks will be given little supervision, perhaps a monthly phone call or visit, whereas those classified as high risk will receive close supervision and intensive care and treatment.

offender-specific The idea that offenders evaluate their skills, motives, needs, and fears before deciding to commit crime.

offense-specific The idea that offenders react selectively to the characteristics of particular crimes.

officers of the court The courtroom work group, including the judge, prosecutor, and defense counsel.

oral stage In Freud's schema, the first year of life, when a child attains pleasure by sucking and biting.

ordeal Based on the principle of divine intervention and the then-prevalent belief that divine forces would not allow an innocent person to be harmed, this was a way of determining guilt involving such measures as having the accused place his or her hand in boiling water or hold a hot iron to see if God would intervene and heal the wounds. If the wound healed, the person wasn't found guilty; conversely, if the wound didn't heal, the accused was deemed guilty of the crime for which he or she was being punished.

organic solidarity Postindustrial social systems, which are highly developed and dependent upon the division of labor; people are connected by their interdependent needs for each other's services and production.

organizational crime Crime that involves large corporations and their efforts to control the marketplace and earn huge profits through unlawful bidding, unfair advertising, monopolistic practices, or other illegal means.

organized crime Illegal activities of people and organizations whose acknowledged purpose is profit through illegitimate business enterprise.

overt pathway Pathway to a criminal career that begins with minor aggression, leads to physical fighting, and eventually escalates to violent crime.

paranoid schizophrenics Individuals who suffer complex behavior delusions involving wrongdoing or persecution—they think everyone is out to get them.

paraphilias Bizarre or abnormal sexual practices that may involve recurrent sexual urges focused on objects, humiliation, or children.

pardon A form of executive clemency.

parole The early release of a prisoner subject to conditions set by a parole board. Depending on the jurisdiction, inmates must serve a certain proportion of their sentences before becoming eligible for parole. If an inmate is granted parole, the conditions may require him or her to report regularly to a parole officer, refrain from criminal conduct, maintain and support his or her family, avoid contact with other convicted criminals, abstain from using alcohol and drugs, remain within the jurisdiction, and so on. Violations of the conditions of parole may result in revocation of parole, in which case the individual will be returned to prison. The concept behind parole is to allow the release of the offender to community supervision, where rehabilitation and readjustment will be facilitated.

parole grant hearing A meeting of the full parole board or a subcommittee that reviews information, may meet with the offender, and then decides whether the parole applicant has a reasonable chance of succeeding outside prison. Good time credits reduce the minimum sentence and hasten eligibility for parole. In making its decision, the board considers the

inmate's offense, time served, evidence of adjustment, and opportunities on the outside.

Part I crimes Another term for index crimes; eight categories of serious, frequent crimes.

Part II crimes All crimes other than index and minor traffic offenses. The FBI records annual arrest information for Part II offenses.

passive precipitation The view that some people become victims because of personal and social characteristics that make them "attractive" targets for predatory criminals.

patricians In ancient Rome, the wealthy classes who served as magistrates.

peacemaking movement A branch of conflict theory that stresses humanism, mediation, and conflict resolution as a means to end crime.

pedophiles Sexual offenders who target children.

penitentiary State or federally operated facility for the incarceration of felony offenders sentenced by the criminal courts; prison.

peremptory challenge The dismissal of a potential juror by either the prosecution or the defense for unexplained, discretionary reasons.

permeable neighborhood Areas with a greater than usual number of access streets from traffic arteries into the neighborhood.

persistence The idea that those who started their delinquent careers early and who committed serious violent crimes throughout adolescence were the most likely to persist as adults.

personality The reasonably stable patterns of behavior, including thoughts and emotions, that distinguish one person from another.

petit (petty) larceny Theft of a small amount of money or property, punished as a misdemeanor.

phallic stage In Freud's schema, the third year, when children focus their attention on their genitals.

phrenologist Scientists who studied the shape of the skull and bumps on the head to determine whether these physical attributes were linked to criminal behavior; they believed that external cranial characteristics dictated which areas of the brain control physical activity.

physiognomist Scientists who studied the facial features of criminals to determine whether the shape of ears, nose, and eyes and the distance between them were associated with antisocial behavior.

pigeon drop A con game in which a package or wallet containing money is "found" by a con man or woman. A passing victim is stopped and asked for advice about what to do, and soon another "stranger," who is part of the con, approaches and enters the discussion. The three decide to split the money; but first, one of the swindlers goes off to consult a lawyer. The lawyer claims the money can be split up, but each party must prove he or she has the means to reimburse the original owner, should one show up. The victim then is asked to give some good-faith money for the lawyer to hold. When the victim goes to the lawyer's office to pick up a share of the loot, he or she finds the address bogus and the money gone. In the new millennium, the "pigeon drop" has been appropriated by corrupt telemarketers, who contact people over the phone, typically elderly victims, to bilk them out of their savings.

pilferage Theft by employees through stealth or deception.

plea bargaining The discussion between the defense counsel and the prosecution by which the accused agrees to plead guilty for certain considerations. The advantage to the defendant may be a reduction of the charges, a lenient sentence, or (in the case of multiple charges) dropped charges. The advantage to the prosecution is that a conviction is obtained without the time and expense of lengthy trial proceedings.

pleasure principle According to Freud, a theory in which id-dominated people are driven to increase their personal pleasure without regard to consequences.

plebeians In ancient Rome, the name for the lower classes.

pledge system An early method of law enforcement that relied on self-help and mutual aid.

plunder Using power without regard for others, such as committing a hate crime or polluting the environment.

poachers Early English thieves who typically lived in the country and supplemented their diet and income with game that belonged to a landlord.

population All people who share a particular personal characteristic, such as all high school students or all police officers.

pornography Sexually explicit books, magazines, films, or tapes intended to provide sexual titillation and excitement for paying customers.

positivism The branch of social science that uses the scientific method of the natural sciences and suggests that human behavior is a product of social, biological, psychological, or economic forces.

postmodernist Approach that focuses on the use of language by those in power to define crime based on their own values and biases; also called deconstructionist.

posttraumatic stress disorder Psychological reaction to a highly stressful event; symptoms may include depression, anxiety, flashbacks, and recurring nightmares.

precedent A rule derived from previous judicial decisions and applied to future cases; the basis of common law.

predation Direct forms of physical violence, such as robbery, sexual assault, or other forms of physical violence.

preemptive deterrence Efforts to prevent crime through community organization and youth involvement.

preliminary hearings The step at which criminal charges initiated by an information are tested for probable cause; the prosecution presents enough evidence to establish probable cause—that is, a *prima facie* case. The hearing is public and may be attended by the accused and his or her attorney.

premeditation Consideration of a homicide before it occurs.

premenstrual syndrome (PMS) The stereotype that several days prior to and during menstruation females are beset by irritability and poor judgment as a result of hormonal changes.

preponderance of the evidence The level of proof in civil cases; more than half the evidence supports the allegations of one side.

presentence investigation report An investigation performed by a probation officer attached to a trial court after the conviction of a defendant. The report contains information about the defendant's background, education, previous employment, and family; his or her own statement concerning the offense; the person's prior criminal record; interviews with neighbors or acquaintances; and his or her mental and physical condition (that is, information that would not be made part of the record in the case of a guilty plea or that would be inadmissible as evidence at a trial but could be influential and important at the sentencing stage). After conviction, a judge sets a date for sentencing (usually 10 days to two weeks from the date of conviction), during which time the presentence report is made. The report is required in felony cases in federal courts and in many states, is optional with the judge in some states, and in others is mandatory before convicted offenders can be placed on probation. In the case of juvenile offenders, the presentence report is also known as a social history report.

pretrial diverson Placing first offenders who commit minor crimes in informal, community-based treatment programs.

preventive detention The practice of holding dangerous suspects before trial without bail.

price-fixing A conspiracy to set and control the price of a necessary commodity.

primary deviance According to Lemert, deviant acts that do not help redefine the self- and public image of the offender.

prison A state or federal correctional institution for incarceration of felony offenders for terms of one year or more.

prisonization process The inmate's assimilation into the prison culture through acceptance of its language, sexual code, and norms of behavior. Those who become the most prisonized will be the least likely to reform on the outside.

probable cause The evidentiary criterion necessary to sustain an arrest or the issuance of an arrest or search warrant; less than absolute certainty or "beyond a reasonable doubt" but greater than mere suspicion or "hunch." A set of facts, information, circumstances, or conditions that would lead a reasonable person to believe that an offense was committed and that the accused committed that offense. An arrest made without probable cause may be susceptible to prosecution as an illegal arrest under "false imprisonment" statutes.

probable cause hearing A hearing to determine if there is sufficient evidence to warrant a trial; also called a preliminary hearing.

probation A sentence entailing the conditional release of a convicted offender into the community under the supervision of the court (in the form of a probation officer), subject to certain conditions for a specified time. The conditions are usually similar to those of parole. (Probation is a sentence, an alternative to incarceration; parole is administrative release from incarceration.) Violation of the conditions of probation may result in revocation of probation.

problem behavior syndrome (PBS) A cluster of antisocial behaviors that may include family dysfunction, substance abuse, smoking, precocious sexuality and early pregnancy, educational underachievement, suicide attempts, sensation seeking, and unemployment, as well as crime.

problem-oriented policing A style of police management that stresses proactive problem solving rather than reactive crime fighting.

productive forces Technology, energy sources, and material resources.

productive relations The relationships that exist among the people producing goods and services.

professional criminals Offenders who make a signficant portion of their income from crime.

professional fence An individual who earns his or her living solely by buying and reselling stolen merchandise.

proletariat A term used by Marx to refer to the working class members of society who produce goods and services but who do not own the means of production.

property law The law governing transfer and ownership of property.

prosecutor Representative of the state (executive branch) in criminal proceedings; advocate for the state's case—the charge—in the adversary trial; for example, the attorney general of the United States, U.S. attorneys, attorneys general of the states, district attorneys, and police prosecutors. The prosecutor participates in investigations both before and after arrest, prepares legal documents, participates in obtaining arrest or search warrants, decides whether to charge a suspect and, if so, with which offense. The prosecutor argues the state's case at trial, advises the police, partici-

pates in plea negotiations, and makes sentencing recommendations.

prosocial bonds Socialized attachment to conventional institutions, activities, and beliefs.

prostitution The granting of nonmarital sexual access for remuneration.

psychoanalytic (psychodynamic) perspective Branch of psychology holding that the human personality is controlled by unconscious mental processes developed early in childhood.

psychopathic personality A personality characterized by a lack of warmth and feeling, inappropriate behavior responses, and an inability to learn from experience. Some psychologists view psychopathy as a result of childhood trauma; others see it as a result of biological abnormality.

psychopharmacological relationship Violent, aggressive behavior that is the direct consequence of ingesting mood-altering substances.

psychotics In Freudian theory, people whose id has broken free and now dominates their personality. Psychotics suffer from delusions and experience hallucinations and sudden mood shifts.

public defender An attorney employed by the state whose job is to provide free legal counsel to indigent defendants.

public order crimes Acts that are considered illegal because they threaten the general well-being of society and challenge its accepted moral principles. Prostitution, drug use, and the sale of pornography are considered public order crimes.

public safety doctrine Evidence can be obtained without a Miranda warning if the information the police seek is needed to protect public safety.

racial profiling Selecting suspects on the basis of their ethnic or racial background.

Racketeer Influenced and Corrupt Organizations Act (RICO) Federal legislation that enables prosecutors to bring additional criminal or civil charges against people whose multiple criminal acts constitute a conspiracy. RICO features monetary penalties that allow the government to confiscate all profits derived from criminal activities. Originally intended to be used against organized criminals, RICO has also been used against white-collar criminals.

radical theory The view that crime is a product of the capitalist system; Marxist criminology.

rape The carnal knowledge of a female forcibly and against her will.

rational choice The view that crime is a function of a decision-making process in which the potential offender weighs the potential costs and benefits of an illegal act.

reaction formation According to Cohen, rejecting goals and standards that seem impossible to achieve. Because a boy cannot hope to get into college, for example, he considers higher education a waste of time.

reactive hate crime Perpetrators believe they are taking a defensive stand against outsiders who they believe threaten their community or way of life.

reactive policing Police officers responding only to calls for help.

reality principle According to Freud, the ability to learn about the consequences of one's actions through experience.

reasoning criminal According to the rational choice approach, law-violating behavior occurs when an offender decides to risk breaking the law after considering both personal factors (such as the need for money, revenge, thrills, and entertainment) and situational factors (how well a target is protected and the efficiency of the local police force).

rebuttal evidence Evidence that was not used when the prosecution initially presented its case.

reciprocal altruism According to sociobiology, acts that are outwardly designed to help others but that have at their core benefits to the self.

recovery agent An individual hired by the bonding agent to track down a fugitive in order to recover the lost bond. These modern bounty hunters receive a share of the recovery, and unlike police, bounty hunters can enter a suspect's home without a warrant in most states; also called a skip tracer.

redirect examination Questions asked by the prosecutor about information brought out during cross-examination.

reeve In early England, the senior law enforcement figure in a county, the forerunner of today's sheriff.

reflective role-taking According to Matsueda and Heimer, the phenomenon that occurs when youths who view themselves as delinquents give an inner voice to their perceptions of how significant others feel about them.

reformatories State and federal government closed correctional facilities that house convicted felons.

rehabilitation model View that sees criminals as victims of social injustice, poverty, and racism and suggests that appropriate treatment can change them into productive, law-abiding citizens.

reintegrative shaming A method of correction that encourages offenders to confront their misdeeds, experience shame because of the harm they caused, and then be reincluded in society.

relative deprivation The condition that exists when people of wealth and poverty live in close proximity to one another. Some criminologists attribute crime rate differentials to relative deprivation.

release on recognizance (ROR) A nonmonetary condition for the pretrial release of an accused individual; an alternative to monetary bail that is granted after the court determines that the accused has ties in the community, has no prior record of default, and is likely to appear at subsequent proceedings.

removal for cause Removing a juror because he or she is biased, has prior knowledge about a case, or otherwise is unable to render a fair and impartial judgment in a case.

residential community corrections (RCC) A freestanding nonsecure building that is not part of a prison or jail and houses pretrial and adjudicated adults. The residents regularly depart to work, to attend school, and/or to participate in community corrections activities and programs.

restitution agreement A condition of probation in which the offender repays society or the victim of crime for the trouble the offender caused. Monetary restitution involves a direct payment to the victim as a form of compensation. Community service restitution may be used in victimless crimes and involves work in the community in lieu of more severe criminal penalties.

restorative justice Using humanistic, nonpunitive strategies to right wrongs and restore social harmony.

retrospective cohort study A study that uses an intact cohort of known offenders and looks back into their early life experiences by checking their educational, family, police, and hospital records.

retrospective reading The reassessment of a person's past to fit a current generalized label.

revocation An administrative act performed by a parole authority that removes a person from parole or a judicial order by a court removing a person from parole or probation, in response to a violation on the part of the parolee or probationer.

road rage A term used to describe motorists who assault each other.

robbery Taking or attempting to take something of value by force or threat of force and/or by putting the victim in fear.

royal prosecutors Representatives of the Crown who submitted evidence and brought witnesses to testify before the jury in the reign of King Henry II.

sampling Selecting a limited number of people for study as representative of a larger group.

schizophrenia A type of psychosis often marked by bizarre behavior, hallucinations, loss of thought control, and inappropriate emotional responses. Schizophrenic types include catatonic, which characteristically involves impairment of motor activity; paranoid, which is characterized by delusions of persecution; and hebephrenic, which is characterized by immature behavior and giddiness.

search warrant A judicial order, based on probable cause, allowing police officers to search for evidence in a particular place, seize that evidence, and carry it away.

secondary deviance According to Lemert, accepting deviant labels as a personal identity. Acts become secondary when they form a basis for self-concept, as when a drug experimenter becomes an "addict."

second-degree murder A homicide with malice but not premeditation or deliberation, as when a desire to inflict serious bodily harm and a wanton disregard for life result in the victim's death.

Secret Service An arm of the Treasury Department, it was originally charged with enforcing laws against counterfeiting. Today it also protects the president and vice president and their families, presidential candidates, and former presidents.

selective incapacitation The policy of creating enhanced prison sentences for the relatively small group of dangerous chronic offenders.

self-control A strong moral sense that renders a person incapable of hurting others or violating social norms.

self-control theory According to Gottfredson and Hirschi, the view that the cause of delinquent behavior is an impulsive personality. Kids who are impulsive may find that their bond to society is weak.

self-report survey A research approach that requires subjects to reveal their own participation in delinquent or criminal acts.

semiotics The use of language elements as signs or symbols beyond their literal meaning.

sentencing disparity People convicted of similar criminal acts may receive widely different sentences.

sentencing guidelines Guidelines to control and structure the sentencing process and make it more "rational"; the more serious the crime and the more extensive the offender's criminal background, the longer the prison term recommended by the guidelines.

serial murder The killing of a large number of people over time by an offender who seeks to escape detection.

serial rape Multiple rapes committed by one person over time.

sexual abuse Exploitation of a child through rape, incest, or molestation by a parent or other adult.

sexual predator law Law that allows authorities to keep some criminals convicted of sexually violent crimes in custody even after their sentences are served.

sheriff The chief law enforcement officer in a county.

Sherman Antitrust Act Law that subjects to criminal or civil sanctions any person "who shall make any contract or engage in any combination or conspiracy" in restraint of interstate commerce.

shield laws Laws designed to protect rape victims by prohibiting the defense attorney from inquiring about their previous sexual relationships.

shire Counties in England and much of Europe in the eleventh century.

shire-gemot During the Middle Ages, an assemblage of local landholders who heard more serious and important criminal cases.

shock incarceration A short prison sentence served in boot camp–type facilities.

shock probation A sentence in which offenders serve a short prison term to impress them with the pains of imprisonment before they begin probation.

shoplifting The taking of goods from retail stores.

siblicide Sibling homicide. The median age of sibling homicide offenders is 23 years old, and the median age of their victims is 25 years old. The vast majority of sibling homicide offenders are males (87 percent), and they are most likely to kill their brothers. When lethal violence by brothers against their sisters occurs, it is more likely in juvenile sibling relationships rather than adult sibling relationships (31 percent versus 14 percent). Sisters killing their brothers or sisters are relatively rare events.

siege mentality Residents who become so suspicious of authority that they consider the outside world to be the enemy out to destroy the neighborhood.

situational crime prevention A method of crime prevention that stresses tactics and strategies to eliminate or reduce particular crimes in narrow settings, such as reducing burglaries in a housing project by increasing lighting and installing security alarms.

situational inducement Short-term influence on a person's behavior, such as financial problems or peer pressure, that increases risk-taking.

skeezers Prostitutes who trade sex for drugs, usually crack.

skilled thieves Thieves who typically work in the larger cities, such as London and Paris. This group includes pickpockets, forgers, and counterfeiters, who operated freely.

skip tracer An individual hired by the bonding agent to track down a fugitive in order to recover the lost bond. These modern bounty hunters receive a share of the recovery, and unlike police, bounty hunters can enter a suspect's home without a warrant in most states; also called a recovery agent.

slander False and injurious statements.

smugglers Thieves who move freely in sparsely populated areas and transport goods, such as spirits, gems, gold, and spices, without bothering to pay tax or duty.

snitch Amateur shoplifter who does not self-identify as a thief but who systematically steals merchandise for personal use.

social altruism Voluntary mutual support systems, such as neighborhood associations and self-help groups, that reinforce moral and social obligations.

social bond Ties a person has to the institutions and processes of society. According to Hirschi, elements of the social bond include commitment, attachment, involvement, and belief.

social capital Positive relations with individuals and institutions that are life sustaining.

social code The unwritten guidelines that express the values, attitudes, and types of behavior older inmates demand of younger inmates. Passed on from one generation of inmates to another, the inmate social code represents the values of interpersonal relations within the prison.

social control function The ability of society and its institutions to control, manage, restrain, or direct human behavior.

social control theory The view that people commit crime when the forces that bind them to society are weakened or broken.

social development model (SDM) A developmental theory that attributes criminal behavior patterns to childhood socialization and pro- or antisocial attachments over the life course.

social disorganization theory Branch of social structure theory that focuses on the breakdown of institutions such as the family, school, and employment in inner-city neighborhoods.

social ecology Environmental forces that have a direct influence on human behavior.

social harm A view that behaviors harmful to other people and society in general must be controlled. These acts are usually outlawed, but some acts that cause enormous amounts of social harm are perfectly legal, such as the consumption of tobacco and alcohol.

social learning theory The view that human behavior is modeled through observation of human social interactions, either directly from observing those who are close and from intimate contact, or indirectly through the media. Interactions that are rewarded are copied, while those that are punished are avoided.

social process theory The view that criminality is a function of people's interactions with various organizations, institutions, and processes in society.

social reaction theory (labeling theory) The view that people become criminals when significant members of society label them as such and they accept those labels as a personal identity.

social reality of crime The view that the main purpose of criminology is to promote a peaceful, just society.

social structure theory The view that disadvantaged economic class position is a primary cause of crime.

socialization Process of human development and enculturation. Socialization is influenced by key social processes and institutions.

socialization view One view is that people learn criminal attitudes from older, more experienced law violators. Another view is that crime occurs when children develop an inadequate self-image, which renders them incapable of controlling their own misbehavior. Both of these views link criminality to the failure of socialization, the interactions people have with the various individuals, organizations, institutions, and processes of society that help them mature and develop.

sodomy Illegal sexual intercourse. Sodomy has no single definition, and acts included within its scope are usually defined by state statute.

somatotype A system developed for categorizing people on the basis of their body build.

specific deterrence A crime control policy suggesting that punishment be severe enough to convince convicted offenders never to repeat their criminal activity.

split sentencing A jail term is part of the sentence and is a condition of probation.

stalking A pattern of behavior directed at a specific person that includes repeated physical or visual proximity, unwanted communications, and/or threats sufficient to cause fear in a reasonable person.

stare decisis To stand by decided cases; the legal principle by which the decision or holding in an earlier case becomes the standard by which subsequent similar cases are judged.

state account system Prisoners produce goods in prison for state use.

state parole board A body of men and women who review cases and determine whether an offender has been rehabilitated sufficiently to deal with the outside world.

state police A law enforcement agency with statewide jurisdiction; the major role of state police is controlling traffic on the highway system, tracing stolen automobiles, and aiding in disturbances and crowd control.

state prison An institution where felony offenders are held.

status frustration A form of culture conflict experienced by lower-class youths because social conditions prevent them from achieving success as defined by the larger society.

statute of limitations Specifies the amount of time by which action must be taken by the state in a criminal matter.

statutory crimes Crimes defined by legislative bodies in response to changing social conditions, public opinion, and custom.

statutory rape Sexual relations between an underage minor female and an adult male; though not coerced, an underage partner is considered incapable of giving informed consent.

stigma An enduring label that taints a person's identity and changes him or her in the eyes of others.

sting An undercover police operation in which police pose as criminals to trap law violators.

strain The emotional turmoil and conflict caused when people believe they cannot achieve their desires and goals through legitimate means. Members of the lower class might feel strain because they are denied access to adequate educational opportunities and social support.

strain theorists Criminologists who view crime as a direct result of lower-class frustration and anger.

strain theory Branch of social structure theory that sees crime as a function of the conflict between people's goals and the means available to obtain them.

stratified society Grouping according to social strata or levels. American society is considered stratified on the basis of economic class and wealth.

street crime Illegal acts designed to prey on the public through theft, damage, and violence.

strict-liability crimes Illegal acts whose elements do not contain the need for intent, or *mens rea;* they are usually acts that endanger the public welfare, such as illegal dumping of toxic wastes.

structural locations Areas conducive to crime.

structural Marxist theory The view that the law and the justice system are designed to maintain the capitalist system and that members of both the owner and worker classes whose behavior threatens the stability of the system will be sanctioned.

subculture A group that is loosely part of the dominant culture but maintains a unique set of values, beliefs, and traditions.

subculture of violence Norms and customs that, in contrast to society's dominant value system, legitimize and expect the use of violence to resolve social conflicts.

submission Passive obedience to the demands of others, such as submitting to physical or sexual abuse without response.

substantive criminal law A body of specific rules that declare what conduct is criminal and prescribe the punishment to be imposed for such conduct.

subterranean values Morally tinged influences that have become entrenched in the culture but are publicly condemned. They exist side by side with conventional values and while condemned in public may be admired or practiced in private.

sufferance The aggrieved party does nothing to rectify a conflict situation; over time, the unresolved conflict may be compounded by other events that cause an eventual eruption.

suitable target According to routine activities theory, a target for crime that is relatively valuable, easily transportable, and not capably guarded.

superego Incorporation within the personality of the moral standards and values of parents, community, and significant others.

surety bond The 10 percent the defendant pays to the bonding agent, which serves as the bonding agent's commission.

surplus value The Marxist view that the laboring classes produce wealth that far exceeds their wages and goes to the capitalist class as profits.

surrogate family A common form of adaptation to prison employed by women, this group contains masculine and feminine figures acting as fathers and mothers; some even act as children and take on the role of either brother or sister. Formalized marriages and divorces may be conducted. Sometimes multiple roles are held by one inmate, so that a "sister" in one family may "marry" and become the "wife" in another.

symbolic interaction theory The sociological view that people communicate through symbols. People interpret symbolic communication and incorporate it within their personality. A person's view of reality, then, depends on his or her interpretation of symbolic gestures.

synthesis A merger of two opposing ideas.

systematic forgers Professionals who make a living by passing bad checks.

systemic link Violent behavior that results from the conflict inherent in the drug trade.

target hardening Making one's home or business crime proof through the use of locks, bars, alarms, and other devices.

target removal strategy Displaying dummy or disabled goods as a means of preventing shoplifting.

technical violation Revocation of parole because conditions set by correctional authorities have been violated.

temperance movement An effort to prohibit the sale of liquor in the United States that resulted in the passage of the Eighteenth Amendment to the Constitution in 1919, which prohibited the sale of alcoholic beverages.

terrorism The illegal use of force against innocent people to achieve a political objective.

terrorist group Any group practicing, or that has significant subgroups that practice, international terrorism.

testosterone The principal male steroid hormone. Testosterone levels decline during the life cycle and may explain why violence rates diminish over time.

thanatos According to Freud, the instinctual drive toward aggression and violence.

theory of anomie A modified version of the concept of anomie developed by Merton to fit social, economic, and cultural conditions found in modern U.S. society. He found that two elements of culture interact to produce potentially anomic conditions: culturally defined goals and socially approved means for obtaining them.

three stikes and you're out Policy whereby people convicted of three felony offenses receive a mandatory life sentence.

thrill-seeking hate crime Hate-mongers who join forces to have fun by bashing minorities or destroying property; inflicting pain on others gives them a sadistic thrill.

time-series design Choosing an event in time (such as passage of a DWI law) and examining specific data prior to and subsequent to this event to determine whether the law can be linked to a change in behavior.

tithings During the Middle Ages, groups of about 10 families who were responsible for maintaining order among themselves and dealing with disturbances, fires, wild animals, and so on.

tort The law of personal wrongs and damage. Tort actions include negligence, libel, slander, assault, and trespass.

tort law The law of personal wrongs and damage; most similar in intent and form to the criminal law.

trait theory The view that criminality is a product of abnormal biological and/or psychological traits.

transitional neighborhood An area undergoing a shift in population and structure, usually from middle-class residential to lower-class mixed use.

treasonous acts Siding with an enemy in a dispute over territory or succession.

truly disadvantaged The lowest level of the underclass; urban, inner-city, socially isolated people who occupy the bottom rung of the social ladder and are the victims of discrimination.

truth-in-sentencing laws Laws that require offenders to serve a substantial portion of their prison sentence behind bars.

turning points According to Laub and Sampson, the life events that alter the development of a criminal career.

Twelve Tables A special commission of 10 noble Roman men formulated the Twelve Tables in 451 B.C. in response to pressure from the lower classes, who believed an unwritten code gave arbitrary and unlimited power to the wealthy classes. The original code was written on bronze plaques, which have been lost, but records of sections, which were memorized by every Roman male, survive. The remaining laws deal with debt, family relations, property, and other daily matters.

tying arrangement A corporation requires customers of one of its services to use other services it offers.

U.S. district courts Trial courts that have jurisdiction over cases involving violations of federal law, such as interstate transportation of stolen vehicles and racketeering.

U.S. marshal Court officers who help implement federal court rulings, transport prisoners, and enforce court orders.

U.S. Supreme Court The court of last resort for all cases tried in the various federal and state courts.

underclass The lowest social stratum in any country, whose members lack the education and skills needed to function successfully in modern society.

Uniform Crime Report (UCR) Large database, compiled by the Federal Bureau of Investigation, of crimes reported and arrests made each year throughout the United States.

utilitarianism The view that people's behavior is motivated by the pursuit of pleasure and the avoidance of pain.

vagrancy The crime of being a vagrant or homeless person. The first vagrancy laws were aimed at preventing workers from leaving their estates to secure higher wages elsewhere. They punished migration and permissionless travel.

vagrant A person who goes from place to place without visible means of support and who, though able to work for his or her maintenance, refuses to do so.

venire The group called for jury duty from which jury panels are selected.

vice squad Police officers assigned to enforce morally tinged laws, such as those governing prostitution, gambling, and pornography.

victim compensation The victim ordinarily receives compensation from the state to pay for damages associated with the crime. Rarely are two compensation schemes alike, however, and many state programs suffer from lack of both adequate funding and proper organization within the criminal justice system. Compensation may be made for medical bills, loss of wages, loss of future earnings, and counseling. In the case of death, the victim's survivors can receive burial expenses and aid for loss of support.

victim precipitation view The idea that the victim's behavior was the spark that ignited the subsequent offense, as when the victim abused the offender verbally or physically.

victimization (by the justice system) While the crime is still fresh in their minds, victims may find that the police interrogation following the crime is handled callously, with innuendos or insinuations that they were somehow at fault. Victims have difficulty learning what is going on in the case; property is often kept for a long time as evidence and may never be returned. Some rape victims report that the treatment they receive from legal, medical, and mental health services is so destructive that they can't help but feel "re-raped."

victimless crimes Crimes that violate the moral order but in which there is no actual victim or target. In these crimes, which include drug abuse and sex offenses, it is society as a whole and not an individual who is considered the victim.

victimologist A person who studies the victim's role in criminal transactions.

victim-witness assistance programs Government programs that help crime victims and witnesses; may include compensation, court services, and/or crisis intervention.

vigilantes Individuals who go on moral crusades without any authorization from legal authorities. The assumption is that it is okay to take matters into your own hands if the cause is right and the target is immoral.

virility mystique The belief that males must separate their sexual feelings from needs for love, respect, and affection.

voir dire The process in which a potential jury panel is questioned by the prosecution and the defense to select jurors who are unbiased and objective.

voluntary manslaughter A homicide committed in the heat of passion or during a sudden quarrel; although intent may be present, malice is not.

Walnut Street Prison At this institution, most prisoners were placed in solitary cells, where they remained in isolation and did not have the right to work.

watch system In medieval England, men organized in church parishes to guard against disturbances and breaches of the peace at night; they were under the direction of the local constable.

Wechsler Adult Intelligence Scale One of the standard IQ tests.

wergild Under medieval law, the money paid by the offender to compensate the victim and the state for a criminal offense.

Wernicke-Korsakoff disease A deadly neurological disorder.

white-collar crime Illegal acts that capitalize on a person's status in the marketplace. White-collar crimes can involve theft, embezzlement, fraud, market manipulation, restraint of trade, and false advertising.

Wickersham Commission Created in 1931 by President Herbert Hoover to investigate the state of the nation's police forces, a commission that found police training to be inadequate and the average officer incapable of effectively carrying out his duties.

wite The portion of the wergild that went to the victim's family.

workplace violence Irate employees or former employees attack coworkers or sabotage machinery and production lines; now considered the third leading cause of occupational injury or death.

writ of certiorari An order of a superior court requesting that the record of an inferior court (or administrative body) be brought forward for review or inspection.

Barak, Gregg, 262, 278 nn.57, 70, 82
Barlow, David, 278 n.60
Barlow, Hugh, 414 n.42
Barnes, Carole Wolff, 543
Barnes, Grace, 453 n.141
Barnett, Arnold, 78 n.84
Barnum, Richard, 243 n.25
Baron, R. A., 77 n.44
Barr, Kellie, 453 n.141
Barr, Robert, 133 n.90
Barrios, Lisa, 360 n.151
Barrow, Clyde, 364
Barrows, Sydney Biddle, 424
Barry, Dan, 450 n.10
Barstow, David, 451 n.10
Bartko, J., 172 n.99
Bartku, Gregory, 510 n.51
Bartos, Omar, 415 n.124
Bartusch, Dawn Jeglum, 312 n.90
Baskin, Deborah, 298, 585 n.117
Bass, Alison, 453 n.145
Bass, Patricia, 136 n.164
Bateman, Richard, 586 n.171
Bates, Marsha, 165
Bates, William, 453 n.123
Batiuk, Mary Ellen, 586 n.142
Battin, Sara, 244 n.51
Battin-Pearson, Sara, 312 n.73
Bauer, John, 361 n.192
Baum, Katrina, 510 n.46
Baumer, Eric, 112, 132 n.38, 361 nn.193,
    194, 195
Baumer, Terry, 584 n.66
Baumhover, Lorin, 133 n.94
Bayer, Ronald, 131 n.9
Bayley, David, 134 n.98, 510 n.44, 512 n.168
Bayley, David H., 485
Beach, F. A., 451 n.24
Beattie, Irenee, 314 n.136
Beatty, Warren, 364
Beaumont, James, 65
Beccaria, Cesare, 5, 22, 107, 108, 124, 129
Bechhofer, L., 359 n.92
Beck, Allen, 135 n.147, 453 n.116, 454 n.189,
    584 n.44, 586 nn.127, 130
Beck, Allen J., 567, 585 nn.79, 82, 85, 90;
    586 nn.167, 169
Becker, Howard, 17, 24 nn.8, 9, 31, 32; 233,
    246 nn.140, 142; 255, 277 n.17, 420,
    451 n.19
Becker, Jill, 170 n.39
Bedeau, Hugo, 546, 552 n.129
Begin, Menachem, 350
Beichner, Dawn, 359 n.83, 360 n.115, 550
    n.15
Beittel, Marc, 134 nn.113, 114
Belanger, Albert, 452 n.82
Belenko, Steven, 455 n.200
Belkin, Douglas, 208 n.1
Belknap, Joanne, 127, 505, 512 n.158
Bell, Daniel, 76 n.5

Bell, David J., 512 n.149
Bellair, Paul, 103 n.56, 113, 133 n.59, 210
    nn.61, 73, 76
Bellamy, Richard, 108
Bellucci, Patricia, 358 n.34
Belluck, Pam, 169 n.1, 413 n.26, 414 n.88
Benda, Brent, 310 n.29
Benedict, W. Reed, 584 n.41
Bengston, Vern, 243 n.20
Benjamin, Sheldon, 361 n.187
Bennett, Katherine, 480 n.37
Bennett, Neil, 169 n.2
Bennett, Richard, 511 n.105
Bennett, Robert, 415 n.110
Benson, Carl, 414 n.83
Benson, Michael, 310 n.22, 415 n.102, 415
    nn.97, 98
Bentham, Jeremy, 108, 129, 131 nn.5, 6
Bergen, Peter L., 357 n.1
Berger, Joel, 395
Berk, Richard, 126, 127, 455 n.205, 552
    n.130
Berkowitz, David, 155, 337
Berliner, Howard, 455 n.214
Bernard, Thomas, 76 n.33, 212 n.133, 280
    n.135
Bernburg, Jon Gunnar, 103 n.64
Berndt, Thomas, 243 n.40
Berns, Walter, 552 n.120
Bernstein, Elizabeth, 452 n.101
Bernstein, Mark I., 31
Berry, Estrellita, 312 n.72
Berry, Michael Patrick, 332
Best, Connie, 103 n.73
Best, David, 454 n.188
Betts, Richard K., 352
Bhaskar, Roy, 278 n.75
Bianchi, Herbert, 480 n.39
Bianchi, Kenneth, 335
Bibel, Daniel, 79 n.101, 173 n.147
Bier, I., 169 n.21
Biesecker, Gretchen, 171 n.65
Bilodeau, Brian, 578
bin Abdul-Rahman al-Aulian, Musaid, 545
bin Abdul-Rahman al-Aulian, Saud, 545
bin Awad al-Zubair, Hassan, 545
Binder, Arnold, 513 n.180
Bingham, Rachel, 518
bin Laden, Osama, 316, 317, 349, 351, 352,
    354
Binns, Helen J., 165
Binsfield, Peter, 4
Birkbeck, Christopher, 116, 133 n.70
Birnbaum, Jean, 327, 359 nn.76, 108
Birt, Angela, 359 n.106
Birzer, Michael, 512 n.153
Biskupic, John, 451 n.38
Bittner, Egon, 510 n.40, 512 n.164
Bjarnason, Thoroddur, 96
Bjerregaard, Beth, 76 n.24, 358 n.49
Black, Amy E., 268

Black, Donald, 210 n.72, 511 n.129
Blackmore, John, 76 n.19
Blackstone, E., 386 n.57
Blackwell, Brenda Sims, 135 n.130, 269,
    279 n.125
Blake, Jeffrey, 475
Blake, Robert, 469
Blankenburg, Erhard, 385 n.30
Blankenship, Michael, 479 n.32
Blau, Judith, 77 n.64, 211 n.107, 277 n.31
Blau, Peter, 77 n.64, 211 n.107, 277 n.31
Block, Alan, 415 nn.117, 118
Block, Carolyn Rebecca, 454 n.169
Block, Michael, 584 n.57
Block, Richard, 77 n.64, 211 n.108, 277 n.31
Blount, William, 357 n.17
Blumberg, Abraham, 550 nn.46, 47
Blumberg, Mark, 453 nn.135, 139
Blumer, Herbert, 24 n.30, 232, 246 n.134
Blumstein, Alfred, 57, 76 n.29, 78 n.84, 136
    nn.163, 167; 543, 551 n.107
Boehnke, Klaus, 210 n.97, 211 n.100
Boer, Douglas, 359 n.106
Boesky, Ivan, 112, 401, 561
Bogen, Phil, 510 nn.48, 62
Boger, Jack, 552 n.130
Bohm, R. M., 278 n.53
Bohm, Robert, 278 nn.54, 55, 551 n.111
Bohman, Michael, 173 n.138
Boland, Barbara, 509 n.19
Boland, John, 413 n.31
Bolen, Rebecca M., 359 n.102
Bonett, Douglas, 171 n.68
Bonger, Willem, 9, 253, 254, 275, 277 n.11
Bonnie, Richard J., 41
Bonta, James, 173 n.160, 174 n.188, 586
    nn.144, 171
Boomsma, Dorret, 172 n.126
Booth, Alan, 78 n.88, 170 nn.37, 41
Bordua, David, 185, 209 n.31
Borg, Marian, 552 n.121
Borgatta, E., 78 n.73
Boruch, Victor, 24 n.43
Borum, Randy, 174 n.192
Bosket, Willie, 70
Bouchard, Thomas, 172 n.128
Boulerice, Bernard, 171 n.70
Bounds, Wendy, 414 nn.58, 59
Bouza, A., 512 n.151
Bowditch, Christine, 247 n.169
Bowers, William, 548, 552 n.115, 552 n.131
Bowker, Lee, 135 n.155
Box, Steven, 79 n.99, 278 nn.59, 82
Boyd, Carol, 453 n.154
Brady, James, 64
Braga, Anthony, 65, 134 n.105, 496, 510
    nn.65, 70
Bragg, Rick, 174 n.180
Braithwaite, John, 77 n.59, 211 n.105, 271,
    277 n.22, 280 nn.142, 143; 361 n.183,
    413 nn.19, 25; 415 nn.101, 102

Brame, Robert, 247 n.175, 287, 310 n.37, 311 n.59, 312 nn.87, 92; 314 n.131, 584 nn.70, 71, 76
Brandenberry, Marc, 373
Brandl, Steven, 479 n.16, 512 n.152
Branscomb, Anne, 414 n.82
Bratton, William, 490
Braukmann, C., 309 n.3
Brecher, Edward, 24 nn.26, 27, 453 n.121
Breitel, Charles, 524, 550 n.16
Brelis, Mathew, 45 n.13
Brennan, Patricia, 171 n.71, 173 n.151, 357 n.13
Brent, David, 358 n.40
Brent, Edward, 509 n.37
Brents, Barbara G., 452 nn.71, 72
Brewer, Victoria, 77 n.52, 102 n.24, 134 n.115, 136 n.162, 312 n.69, 585 n.118
Brewster, Mary, 348, 362 n.225
Brezina, Timothy, 116, 170 n.40, 211 nn.115, 119, 120, 127, 129; 243 n.44, 312 n.83
Briar, Scott, 228, 245 nn.95, 98
Brienza, Julie, 95
Briere, John, 359 n.110, 451 n.44
Britain, R. P., 171 n.77
Britt, Chester, 455 n.212
Britt, David, 277 n.32
Brock, Deon, 512 n.177
Brockway, Z. R., 557, 575, 583 n.19
Broderick, John, 511 n.108
Broidy, Lisa, 211 nn.128, 131, 212 n.132
Bronner, Augusta, 163, 174 n.207
Brook, Judith, 159, 243 n.22
Brooke, James, 169 n.1, 361 n.200, 451 n.20
Brooks, Judith, 311 n.64, 453 n.148
Brooks, Michael, 119
Brooks-Gunn, Jeanne, 208 nn.10, 11; 209 n.13
Brosnan, Pierce, 364
Browdy, Jennifer, 361 n.163
Brown, Charles, 134 n.101, 509 n.18
Brown, Christopher M., 415 n.108
Brown, Hopeton Eric, 316
Brown, Jennifer M., 505
Brown, Jodi, 455 n.204
Brown, Lee, 510 n.50
Brown, Sandra, 244 nn.63, 64
Brown, Shayna, 479 n.32
Browne, Angela, 359 n.74, 360 nn.143, 145
Brownfield, David, 77 n.60, 102 n.46, 209 n.20, 244 n.80, 246 n.126, 287, 310 nn.20, 28
Browning, Sandra Lee, 503, 512 nn.141, 173
Brownmiller, Susan, 359 n.67
Brownstein, Henry, 298, 321, 358 nn.31, 35, 442
Bruinsma, Gerben J. N., 244 n.65
Bryan, Nicole, 455 n.206
Bryant, Susan Leslie, 101 n.11

Buchanan, Christy Miller, 170 n.39
Buchsbaum, Monte, 171 nn.79, 84
Buck, Andrew, 104 n.92, 132 n.45
Buck, Janeen, 518
Buckley, R. E., 170 n.61
Buckley, William F., 429
Buerger, Michael, 510 n.67
Buffet, Warren, 194
Bulger, James J., 316
Bullogh, V., 451 n.45
Bumphus, Vic, 287
Bundy, Theodore, 36, 335, 336, 337, 427
Buono, Angelo, 335
Bureau of Justice Statistics, 479 n.9, 551 n.109, 583 nn.27, 39; 586 n.166
Burge, Kathleen, 45 n.23
Burgess, Ann Wolbert, 451 n.53, 452 n.82
Burgess, Ernest, 208 n.4
Burgess, Ernest W., 8, 24 n.18, 177, 183
Burgess, Robert, 224, 244 n.73
Burke, Mary Jean, 244 n.65
Burkett, Steven, 134 nn.124, 125
Burns, Andrew, 165
Burns, Barbara, 174 n.192
Burns, Shelley, 243 n.37
Burrows, J., 509 n.29
Bursik, Robert, 133 n.95, 134 n.122, 135 nn.128, 129, 130; 209 nn.27, 33, 42; 210 nn.63, 67, 68, 77, 82; 310 nn.20, 39
Burton, Thomas, 414 n.44
Burton, Velmer, 77 nn.57, 62; 133 n.62, 211 n.117, 246 n.123, 287
Burton, Velmer, Jr., 244 n.57
Bush, George H., 443
Bush, George W., 355, 474, 482
Bush, Jack, 578
Bushman, Brad, 159
Bushway, Shawn, 314 n.133
Buswell, Brenda, 78 n.93
Butterfield, Fox, 45 n.22, 70, 79 n.114
Butts, Jeffrey A., 518
Byer, Carter, 454 n.191
Bynum, Tim, 415 n.135
Byrne, Donn, 173 n.157
Byrne, James, 209 nn.32, 48; 210 n.67, 211 n.108, 584 nn.43, 69
Byrne, John A., 414 n.52, 415 n.92

Cachere, J. Gregory, 159
Cadoret, R. J., 173 n.135
Caesar, Julius, 350
Caeti, Tory, 134 n.106, 509 n.25
Cain, C., 173 n.135
Calavita, Kitty, 413 n.8
Calden, Paul, 347
Calder, James, 361 n.192
Cameron, Mary Owen, 372, 385 nn.26, 27
Campbell, Alec, 455 n.205
Campbell, Anne, 78 n.94, 79 n.101, 173 n.147
Campbell, Bill, 504

Campbell, Neve, 347
Campbell, Rebecca, 101 n.9
Canedy, Dana, 414 n.54
Canela-Cacho, Jose, 136 nn.163, 167
Cantor, David, 104 n.92, 287
Cao, Liqun, 358 n.46, 503, 512 n.173
Capachin, Jeanne, 414 n.76
Capaldi, Deborah, 311 n.62, 357 n.12
Capone, Al, 405, 557
Caporael, Linda R., 150
Capowich, George E., 211 n.118
Capp, Bernard, 336
Carbonell, Joyce, 174 n.197
Cardarelli, Albert, 510 n.46
Carey, Gregory, 172 nn.110, 130
Carlen, Pat, 279 n.104
Carlson, Bonnie, 583 n.33
Carlson, E., 583 nn.28, 29
Carlson, Eric, 583 n.24
Carlson, Joan M., 442
Carlson, Kenneth, 550 n.43
Carlson, Robert, 454 n.175
Carnegie, Andrew, 396
Carr, Jackson, 90
Carr, Jason, 87
Carrington, Frank, 98, 103 n.84
Carrington, Tim, 414 nn.70, 71
Carroll, Douglas, 175 n.224
Carrozza, Mark, 245 nn.114, 120
Carter, Carol, 583 n.1
Carter, David, 447
Carter, Deborah Brown, 502, 503
Carter, Ricki, 282
Carter, Robert, 584 n.54
Carter, Timothy, 278 n.79
Cartwright, Desmond, 244 n.87
Caryl, Christian, 12
Casa, Kathryn, 460
Caspi, Avshalom, 77 n.66, 151, 173 nn.152, 162; 174 n.205, 310 n.33, 311 nn.45, 61; 313 n.127, 314 nn.142, 143
Cassell, Paul, 136 n.168, 552 n.129
Cassidy, Butch, 318
Castellano, Thomas, 585 n.105
Catalano, Richard, 244 n.51, 297, 312 n.97, 313 nn.98, 99, 100; 454 nn.162, 186
Cauce, Mari, 102 n.44
Cauchon, Dennis, 570
Cauffman, Elizabeth, 165
Cecchi, Matthew, 114, 115
Cecil, Joe, 24 n.43
Census Bureau, U.S., 178, 451 n.25
Center for Reproductive Law and Policy, 360 n.134
Center for Research on Women, 279 n.117
Cernkovich, Stephen, 76 n.23, 195, 211 n.102, 245 n.121, 247 n.163, 308, 314 n.144
Chafetz, Janet Saltzman, 279 nn.107, 108
Chaiken, J., 509 n.28
Chaiken, Marcia, 454 n.166

Chambliss, William, 35–36, 45 *n*.16, 255, 259, 260, 277 *n*.21, 278 *n*.78, 385 *n*.8, 415 *nn*.117, 129

Chamlin, Mitchell, 133 *n*.95, 195, 210 *n*.86, 211 *n*.101, 289, 310 *n*.40, 480 *n*.36, 552 *n*.116

Chandler, Kathryn A., 243 *n*.36

Chaplin, Terry, 386 *n*.74

Chapman, Chris, 243 *n*.36

Chapman, Jane Roberts, 279 *n*.111

Chappell, Duncan, 76 *n*.6

Chard-Wierschem, Deborah, 78 *n*.70, 242 *n*.2

Charlebois, P., 80 *n*.140

Chayet, Ellen, 135 *n*.149

Cheatwood, Derral, 77 *n*.46, 546, 551 *n*.113

Chermak, Steven, 79 *n*.117

Chesney-Lind, Meda, 79 *n*.100, 268, 269, 279 *nn*.104, 105, 116, 122

Cheurprakobkit, Suthan, 512 *n*.140

Children's Defense Fund, 209 *n*.12

Chilton, Roland, 185, 209 *n*.31, 246 *n*.146

Chin, Ko-Lin, 455 *n*.200

Chiricos, Ted, 24 *n*.2, 187, 209 *nn*.53, 54; 210 *n*.55, 542, 543

Chiricos, Theodore, 133–134 *n*.95, 134–135 *nn*.127, 136; 277 *n*.42

Chitwood, C. Michael, 396

Christakos, Antigone, 454 *n*.169

Christenson, Cornelia, 359 *n*.105

Christenson, R. L., 243 *n*.34

Christiansen, A., 454 *n*.156

Christiansen, Karl O., 148, 172 *n*.124, 173 *n*.136

Christie, Nils, 480 *n*.39

Christoffel, Katherine Kaufer, 165

Chung, He Len, 312 *n*.77

Churchill, Winston, 432

Cicourel, Aaron, 511 *n*.127

Cirillo, Kathleen, 174 *n*.178

Cirincione, Carmen, 174 *n*.187

Clark, Cherie, 565

Clark, John, 76 *nn*.17, 18; 414 *n*.47

Clark, Ronald, 78 *n*.89

Clark, Terry, 326

Clark-Daniels, Carolyn, 133 *n*.94

Clarke, Ronald, 94, 103 *n*.67, 104 *n*.90, 117, 118, 132 *nn*.15, 17; 133 *nn*.77, 79, 82, 86, 91, 92; 386 *nn*.45, 70, 71

Clarke, Stevens, 550 *n*.53

Clason, Dennis L., 244 *n*.78

Classen, Gabriele, 211 *n*.100

Clayton, Richard, 358 *n*.38, 360 *n*.152, 447

Clear, Todd, 45 *n*.18, 190, 191, 360 *n*.121, 585 *n*.88

Cleckley, Hervey, 164, 165

Clelland, Donald, 278 *n*.79

Clemmer, Donald, 573, 585 *n*.107

Cleveland, H. Harrington, 174 *n*.108

Clinard, Marshall, 413 *n*.17, 414 *nn*.34, 35, 72

Clinton, William J., 522

Clougherty, Kristen, 377

Cloward, Richard, 202, 203, 204, 205, 206, 212 *nn*.152, 153, 154, 155, 156, 157, 158

Coates, Robert, 480 *n*.38

Coatsworth, J. Douglas, 102 *n*.23

Cochran, John, 116, 133 *n*.71, 195, 210 *n*.86, 211 *n*.101, 245 *n*.115, 310 *n*.20, 552 *n*.116

Cocks, Jay, 584 *n*.54

Cohen, A., 586 *n*.147

Cohen, Albert, 201, 202, 203, 205, 206, 210 *n*.93, 212 *nn*.143, 144, 145, 146, 148, 149, 150

Cohen, Jacqueline, 76 *n*.29, 102 *n*.47, 132 *n*.49, 136 *nn*.163, 167; 509 *n*.19

Cohen, Jay, 512 *n*.146

Cohen, Lawrence, 92, 95, 103 *nn*.57, 69; 165, 173 *n*.139, 385 *n*.28

Cohen, Mark, 83, 101 *n*.6, 415 *n*.112

Cohen, Morris, 418, 450 *n*.5

Cohen, Patricia, 159, 311 *n*.64

Cohen, Robyn L., 584 *n*.40

Cohen, Ronald, 361 *n*.187

Cohen, Sheldon, 169 *n*.13

Cohen, Warren, 513 *n*.185

Cohn, Bob, 452 *n*.100

Cohn, Ellen, 61, 77 *nn*.43, 45, 47, 127

Cole, David, 502

Cole, G., 586 *n*.147

Cole, George, 550 *n*.18, 551 *n*.78, 584 *nn*.49, 50

Coll, Xavier, 311 *n*.60

Collins, Dean, 127

Collins, James, 358 *n*.33

Collins, Mark, 314 *nn*.134, 137

Collins, Melissa Lassiter, 219

Colony, Catherine, 357 *n*.3

Colvin, Mark, 278 *n*.70, 289, 290, 308, 311 *n*.42

Colwell, Brian, 174 *n*.178

Comer, James, 79 *n*.113

Comiskey, Brendan, 422

Comte, Auguste, 6

Conger, Rand, 310 *n*.32, 312 *n*.89, 357 *n*.16

Conklin, John, 170 *n*.54, 342

Conley, Dalton, 169 *n*.2

Conrad, John, 78 *n*.80

Conrad, Sheree D., 328

Contreras-Sweet, Maria, 398

Conwell, Chic, 367, 383, 385 *nn*.11, 12, 13

Cook, James, 7

Cook, Kimberly, 132 *n*.14

Cook, Philip, 64, 65, 132 *n*.15

Cooley, Charles Horton, 17, 232, 246 *n*.134

Coolidge, Calvin, 484

Coontz, Phyllis, 170 *nn*.46, 47

Cooper, Christopher, 480 *n*.42

Cordella, Peter, 172 *n*.105, 280 *n*.149

Coren, S., 172 *n*.101

Corill, Dean, 337

Corley, Charles, 247 *n*.163

Corneau, Rebecca, 38

Cornish, Derek, 132 *nn*.15, 17

Corrado, J., 453 *n*.152

Costa, Francis, 311 *n*.60

Costanzo, Michael, 132 *n*.47

Costin, Michael, 39

Cotter, C., 509 *n*.29

Cottey, Talbert, 65

Court, John, 452 *n*.92

Courtney, Robert R., 390, 391, 401

Courtwright, David, 318, 455 *n*.222

Couzens, Michael, 76 *n*.9

Covach, Linda May, 492

Covington, Jeanette, 209 *n*.52, 210 *n*.64, 211 *n*.108

Cox, Archibald, 522

Cox, Louis, 108, 131 *n*.8, 135 *n*.151, 586 *n*.137

Cox, V., 586 *n*.151

Craig, Delores, 512 *n*.153

Craig-Moreland, Delores, 585 *n*.91

Crall, Mike, 375

Crane, Jonathan, 209 *n*.14

Crank, John, 499, 511 *nn*.107, 113

Craven, Wes, 347

Crawford, Charles, 542, 543

Creamer, Vicki, 244 *nn*.63, 64

Cressey, Donald, 4, 15, 24 *n*.3, 24; 220, 222, 244 *n*.62, 401, 402, 415 *nn*.91, 119; 573, 585 *n*.108

Crimmins, Susan, 298, 321, 442

Crites, Laura, 79 *n*.100, 279 *n*.122

Cromwell, Paul, 132 *nn*.35, 40, 41, 44; 381, 385 *n*.18, 386 *n*.68

Cronin, Julia K., 391

Crosby, L., 311 *n*.57

Crossette, Barbara, 451 *nn*.14, 16

Crouch, Ben, 136 *n*.162, 584 *n*.47, 585 *n*.120

Crowe, R. R., 173 *n*.135

Crowther, Betty, 453 *n*.123

Cruise, Keith, 357 *n*.7

Cruz, Rolando, 546

Cullen, Francis, 77 *nn*.57, 62; 102 *n*.48, 133 *n*.62, 174 *n*.185, 211 *nn*.117, 120; 242 *n*.18, 244 *n*.57, 245 *nn*.108, 113, 114, 120; 246 *nn*.123, 135; 280 *n*.154, 287, 289, 310 *n*.40, 415 *nn*.97, 98; 479 *n*.32, 480 *nn*.36, 43; 503, 512 *n*.173, 586 *nn*.140, 143

Cullen, Frank, 584 *n*.65

Cullen, Kevin, 451 *n*.42

Cummings, Andrea, 133 *n*.69, 359 *n*.79

Cummings, Debra, 550 *n*.10

Cuniff, Mark, 584 *n*.58

Cunningham-Niederer, Michele, 415 *n*.115

Currie, Elliott, 477, 480 *n*.46

Curry, G. David, 210 *n*.56, 290, 584 *n*.68

Curry, Timothy, 64, 65

Curtis, Lynn, 79 *n*.113

Cuvelier, Steven, 133 *n*.62

Dahlberg, Tim, 386 n.52
Dahmer, Jeffrey, 36, 335
Dahrendorf, Ralf, 9, 253, 254, 255, 275, 277
  nn.12, 13
Dailey, T., 413 n.2
Daley, Suzanne, 452 n.77
Dalton, Brian, 459
Dalton, Katharina, 143, 170 n.52
Dalton, Michael, 459
Dalton, Sarah, 459
Daly, Kathleen, 279 nn.104, 105, 110, 116;
  280 n.141, 401, 414 n.89
Daly, Martin, 78 n.75, 102 n.41, 150, 173
  nn.140, 144, 145, 146; 209 n.49, 211
  n.106, 310 n.34, 358 n.27, 361 nn.177,
  189
Damphouse, Kelly, 551 n.105
Daniels, R. Steven, 133 n.94
Dann, Robert, 122, 134 n.111
Dannefer, Dale, 79 n.105
Darrow, William, 452 n.66
Darwin, Charles, 6
Daum, James, 512 n.155
Davidson, Laura, 77 n.61, 277 n.36
Davies, Mark, 244 n.68, 245 n.122, 453
  n.150
Davies, Priscilla, 175 n.218
Davies, Scott, 217
Davies-Netley, Sally, 101 n.11
Da Vinci, Leonardo, 418
Davis, Kenneth C., 511 n.117
Davis, Kenneth Culp, 551 n.80
Davis, Kenneth L., 479 n.12
Davis, Richard Allen, 36
Davis, Robert, 76 n.10, 102 n.18, 103 n.77,
  127, 455 nn.207, 208, 209; 480 n.41
Davis, Robert C., 88, 104 n.91
Davis, Roy, 359 n.97
Davis-Frenzel, Erika, 359 n.83, 360 n.115,
  550 n.15
Davison, Elizabeth, 133 n.58
Dawkins, Marvin, 454 n.176
Dawson, Myrna, 523, 550 n.11
Day, H. D., 175 n.220
Day, L. Edward, 313 n.100
Deadman, D. F., 344
Dean, Charles, 127, 287, 297, 311 n.59, 312
  nn.87, 92
Deane, Glenn, 358 n.42
Deane, Richard H., Jr., 504
DeBartolo, Eddie, Jr., 392
DeBaryshe, Barbara, 311 nn.46, 58
De Beaumont, Gusto, 583 nn.3, 14
DeBry, Kristine, 414 n.55
Decker, Scott, 133 n.66, 246 n.124, 324,
  343, 344, 358 nn.51, 52, 360 n.148, 361
  n.199, 379, 380, 386 nn.61, 63, 415
  n.135, 453 n.136
DeCoster, Stacy, 174 n.191, 246 n.151
DeFrances, Carol J., 522, 525, 549 nn.5, 6;
  550 n.7, 550 nn.14, 20, 21, 22

DeFrancesco, Susan, 65
Defronzo, James, 78 n.69, 210 n.87, 212
  n.167
DeJesus, Nester Luis, 467
Dejong, Christina, 135 nn.144, 148, 150;
  246 n.145
DeJong, Judith, 287
DeJong, M. J., 172 n.99
DeJoria, John Paul, 202
DeKeseredy, Walter, 103 n.65, 265, 279
  nn.96, 100, 101, 102, 103, 115; 359
  nn.85, 86, 107
DeLamatre, Mary, 102 n.47
De La Rosa, Mario, 243 n.47
De Li, Spencer, 244 n.55, 314 n.132
DeLisi, Matt, 502, 503
DeLone, Miriam, 79 n.116, 236, 247 n.164,
  277 n.35, 502, 503, 543, 551 n.90
Dembo, Richard, 312 n.72
Demuth, Stephen, 543
Deng, Xiaogang, 287
DeNiro, Robert, 364
Denno, Deborah, 144, 171 nn.64, 70, 72;
  173 nn.149, 150; 175 nn.212, 220; 546,
  552 n.122
Denno, Deborah W., 46 n.30
Dentler, Robert, 77 n.54
DeRios, M. D., 453 n.151
Derzon, James, 311 n.66, 312 n.80
Deschenes, Elizabeth Piper, 79 n.102, 310
  n.36, 454 n.183
de Silva, W. P., 451 n.43
Deutsch, Joseph, 132 n.48
Devine, Francis Edward, 131 nn.2, 3
Devlin, Daniel, 509 nn.6, 7
Devlin, Sir Patrick, 418, 450 n.6
Diallo, Amadou, 84
Dieckman, Duane, 134 n.101, 509 n.18
DiLalla, David, 172 n.110
Dilulio, John J., 114
Dinitz, Simon, 78 n.80, 245 n.100
Dinovitzer, Ronit, 523, 550 n.11
Dishion, Thomas, 311 nn.55, 56
Dishman, Chris, 353, 362 n.237
Ditton, Paula, 585 nn.88, 89
Ditton, Paula M., 479 n.26, 551 nn.96, 98
Dixon, Jo, 543, 551 n.84
Dobash, R. Emerson, 361 nn.179, 182
Dobash, Russell, 361 nn.179, 182
Dobrin, Adam, 103 n.49
Dodder, Richard, 76 n.25
Dodge, K. A., 173 n.171
Dodge, Mary, 574, 585 n.113
Dohrenwend, Bruce, 246 n.135
Doig, Jameson, 583 n.23
Dole, Robert, 158
Donnelly, Patrick, 103 n.70
Donnelly, Richard C., 511 n.116
Donnerstein, Edward, 359 n.109, 452 n.92,
  452 nn.89, 90
Donohue, John J., III, 56, 57

Donovan, John, 311 n.60, 453 n.155
Doran, Michael Scott, 352
Doraz, Walter, 170 n.25
Dornfeld, Maude, 312 n.68
Dotson, Gary, 330
Douglas, James Gregory, 381
Douglas, William O., 418
Downey, Douglas, 209 n.17
Downey, Robert, Jr., 113
Downs, Kala, 359 n.104
Downs, William, 101 n.11, 247 n.170
Doyle, Daniel, 358 n.44
Drake, Christina, 65
Drake, Francis, 350
Drake, J. J. P., 170 n.56
Drass, Kriss, 79 n.124, 211 n.108, 551 n.80
Driver, Edwin, 173 n.155
Drucker, Ernest, 455 n.217
Drugge, Jeff, 359 n.106
Duffee, David, 583 n.33
Dugdale, Richard, 169 n.5
Dunaway, Faye, 364
Dunaway, R. Gregory, 77 nn.57, 62; 244
  n.57, 246 n.123, 287
Duncan, David, 394
Duncan, Greg J., 208 nn.10, 11, 209 n.13
Dunford, Franklyn, 127
D'Unger, Amy, 80 n.143, 296, 312 n.82
Dungi (king of Sumer), 27
Dunham, Roger, 511 n.122
Dunlop, Eloise, 314 nn.138, 141
Dunn, Katie Marie, 286
Durham, Alexis, III, 556, 583 n.13
Durkheim, Émile, 7, 8, 10, 11, 22, 24 nn.15,
  17; 184, 185, 192, 193
Durkin, Jim, 576
Durose, Matthew, 549 n.2, 551 n.104, 583
  n.25, 584 n.42
Durose, Matthew R., 493, 503, 510 n.38,
  512 n.172
Dutroix, Marc, 422
Dworkin, Andrea, 417, 450 n.3, 452 n.75
Dyson, Laronistine, 102 n.15

Earls, Felton, 80 n.141, 210 nn.69, 71, 88;
  322, 358 n.29
Eaves, Lindon, 172 n.127
Eccles, Jacquelynne, 170 n.39
Eck, John, 120, 133 n.83, 84, 509 n.33
Edelhertz, Herbert, 413 n.18, 414 n.87, 415
  n.95
Edward Confessor (king of England), 29
Edwards, Edwin, 392
Egger, Steven, 336
Ehrlich, Isaac, 135 n.155
Eichenwald, Kurt, 414 nn.52, 57
Eigenberg, Helen, 511 n.123
Einstein, Stanley, 415 n.121
Eisenberg, Marlene, 41
Eitzen, D. Stanley, 415 n.99
Elder, Glen, 310 n.32

Elis, Lori, 66, 77 *n.63*

Elizabeth I (queen of England and Ireland), 350, 554

Ellingworth, Dan, 102 *n.30*

Elliott, Amanda, 210 *nn.83, 84*

Elliott, Delbert, 77 *nn.58, 59;* 79 *n.105,* 127, 133 *n.80,* 209 *n.44,* 210 *nn.83, 84;* 243 *n.42,* 247 *n.168,* 310 *n.30,* 313 *n.117*

Elliott, F. A., 171 *n.91*

Ellis, Desmond, 57, 102 *n.28*

Ellis, Lee, 140, 152, 169 *nn.8, 11, 12, 13, 15;* 170 *nn.45, 46, 47;* 172 *nn.101, 102, 105;* 173 *nn.141, 148;* 244 *n.58,* 309 *n.3,* 310 *n.10,* 329, 359 *nn.99, 100*

Ellison, Christopher G., 102 *n.19*

Elstein, Sharon, 359 *n.97*

Emerson, Robert M., 362 *n.224*

Empey, LaMar, 76 *n.19,* 278 *n.69*

Engel, Robin Shepard, 174 *n.186,* 510 *n.60*

Engels, Friedrich, 24 *n.19,* 251, 253, 276 *nn.5, 9*

Engen, Rodney, 543

Ennett, Susan, 79 *n.125*

Enos, V. Pualani, 99

Enrich, David, 452 *n.70*

Ensley, Margaret, 63

Ensley, Michael, 63

Epstein, Gil, 132 *n.48*

Epstein, Joel, 415 *n.96*

Erez, Edna, 550 *n.61,* 551 *n.79,* 585 *n.115*

Erickson, Kai, 233, 246 *n.138*

Erickson, Maynard, 76 *n.19,* 135 *n.127*

Erikson, Erik, 155

Erlanger, Howard, 358 *n.57*

Eron, L., 174 *n.173*

Erwin, Brigette, 102 *n.21*

Esbensen, Finn-Aage, 79 *n.102,* 210 *n.60,* 212 *n.160,* 310 *n.36*

Eskridge, Chris, 583 *n.24*

Estes, Richard, 101 *n.2,* 452 *n.69*

Estes, Richard J., 426

Estrich, Susan, 102 *n.39,* 360 *n.119*

Evans, Chris, 368

Evans, John, 452 *n.84*

Evans, T. David, 77 *nn.57, 62;* 211 *n.117,* 244 *n.57,* 246 *n.123,* 287

Evansburg, Amanda R., 391

Eve, Raymond, 78 *n.98*

Ewing, Charles Patrick, 358 *n.19,* 361 *n.205*

Eysenck, Hans, 162, 174 *nn.196, 198*

Eysenck, M. W., 174 *n.198*

Ezell, Michael, 80 *n.143*

Fader, James, 80 *n.136*

Fagan, Jeffrey, 57, 209 *n.29,* 212 *n.141,* 245 *n.91,* 298, 442, 455 *n.200*

Fagan, Jeffrey A., 127, 226

Fairweather, David, 359 *n.106*

Falck, Russel, 454 *n.175*

Famularo, Richard, 174 *n.183,* 243 *n.25*

Farabee, David, 454 *nn.181, 182*

Faraone, Stephen, 171 *nn.85 86*

Farley, Chris, 113

Farley, Reynolds, 79 *n.129*

Farnworth, Margaret, 77 *n.54,* 244 *n.52,* 302, 313 *nn.108, 111, 112, 114, 115*

Farr, Kathryn Ann, 455 *n.225*

Farrell, Graham, 102 *nn.31, 32, 34;* 382, 386 *nn.71, 72*

Farrell, Michael, 453 *n.141*

Farrington, David, 24 *n.34,* 76 *n.20,* 78 *n.84,* 94, 102 *n.47,* 103 *n.67,* 172 *nn.116, 120;* 247 *n.180,* 296, 301, 302, 308, 312 *nn.66, 79, 80, 94;* 313 *n.102,* 385 *n.25,* 480 *n.35*

Farrington, David P., 13, 78 *n.80,* 80 *n.134,* 148, 313 *n.101*

Farrington, D. P., 172 *nn.114, 121, 122, 123*

Faupel, Charles, 454 *nn.172, 173, 174*

Fay, Michael, 13

Federal Bureau of Investigation, 10 *n.5,* 49, 50, 55, 58, 62, 67, 76 *n.2,* 13; 358 *nn.39, 60;* 359 *n.72,* 361 *nn.164, 190;* 362 *n.245,* 385 *n.21,* 386 *n.58,* 451 *nn.51, 52;* 453 *n.115,* 479 *n.8,* 486, 513 *n.184*

Fedo, Michael, 586 *n.131*

Fedora, Orestes, 171 *nn.92, 93*

Feeley, Malcolm, 479 *n.17,* 550 *n.37*

Feinberg, Joel, 450 *n.7*

Feingold, Alan, 310 *n.26*

Feld, Barry, 464, 465

Feldman, Shirley, 165

Felson, Marcus, 92, 95, 96, 103 *nn.57, 69;* 117, 119, 120, 133 *nn.78, 83;* 373

Felson, Richard, 103 *n.63,* 132 *n.54,* 133 *n.67,* 212 *n.140,* 342, 360 *nn.112, 146, 147,* 361 *nn.192, 194, 195;* 386 *n.70,* 503

Fendrich, Michael, 451 *n.63,* 453 *n.133,* 454 *n.161*

Fenton, Terence, 174 *n.183*

Fenton, Tom, 13

Ferdinand, Franz, 350

Ferguson, Florence, 551 *n.106*

Ferguson, H. Bruce, 170 *n.27*

Ferracuti, Franco, 11, 24 *n.20,* 323, 358 *n.44*

Ferrell, Jeff, 116, 133 *n.72*

Ferri, Enrico, 139, 169 *n.4*

Ferris, Kerry O., 362 *n.224*

Feucht, Thomas, 360 *n.151*

Feyerherm, William, 246 *n.161*

Fields, Monique, 583 *n.38*

Figert, Anne, 170 *n.51*

Figlio, Robert, 72, 78 *n.80,* 79 *nn.106, 130, 132;* 80 *n.137,* 132 *n.47*

Figuerdo, Aurelio Jose, 173 *nn.142, 143*

Finckenauer, James, 13, 24 *n.44,* 410

Finkel, Norman, 552 *n.123*

Finkelstein, Claire, 6

Finklehor, David, 89, 102 *n.33,* 339, 359 *n.93,* 361 *nn.172, 174, 175;* 452 *n.68*

Finn, Peter, 101 *n.10,* 103 *n.78,* 104 *n.101,* 102, 511 *n.103*

Firestone, David, 413 *n.1*

Fishbein, Diana, 143, 170 *nn.30, 54;* 171 *n.73*

Fisher, Bonnie, 102 *n.48,* 510 *n.62*

Fisher, W., 452 *n.86*

Fitzpatrick, Colleen, 360 *n.125*

Flaherty, Austin, 103 *n.87*

Flaherty, Sara, 103 *n.87*

Flanagan, Timothy, 77 *n.36,* 586 *n.132*

Flannery, Daniel, 78 *n.98,* 310 *n.4*

Flaving, Jeanne, 511 *n.125*

Flay, Brian, 133 *n.61,* 453 *n.147*

Fleming, C. D., 468

Fleming, Duane, 576

Fletcher, Beverly, 585 *n.114*

Fletcher, George P., 13

Flewelling, Robert, 76 *n.21,* 79 *n.125,* 358 *n.53,* 447

Flint, Anthony, 452 *n.108*

Flynn, Kevin, 24 *n.1,* 361 *n.167*

Flynn, Stephen, 362 *n.242*

Flynn, Stephen E., 354

Foch, Terryl, 172 *n.107*

Fogel, C. A., 171 *n.68*

Fogel, David, 583 *n.35*

Fogelson, Robert, 509 *n.6*

Foglia, Wanda, 134 *n.121,* 135 *nn.136, 137*

Foote, Caleb, 550 *n.30*

Ford, C. S., 451 *n.24*

Forde, David, 310 *n.14*

Formby, William, 133 *n.94*

Forsythe, Lubica, 386 *n.67*

Foster, Hilliard, 174 *n.186*

Foster, Jodie, 158, 330

Fox, Ben, 133 *n.63*

Fox, James A., 60, 77 *n.37*

Fox, James Alan, 336, 360 *nn.138, 139, 140;* 362 *nn.218, 222;* 428, 452 *n.91*

Fox, Stephen, 368

Francisco, Luis, 309

Frank, James, 512 *nn.141, 152*

Frank, Nancy, 413 *n.4,* 414 *nn.63, 64*

Frankel, Marvin, 551 *n.82*

Franklin, George, 331

Franklin, J. M., 175 *n.220*

Franklin, Richard H., 570

Franklin-Lipsker, Eileen, 331

Franks, John, 451 *n.12*

Frazee, Sharon Glave, 133 *n.58*

Frederick, Robert, 413 *n.21*

Freedman, Jonathan, 159

Freels, Sally, 509 *n.24*

Freid, David, 584 *n.52*

Freilich, Joshua, 358 *n.47*

Frenken, J., 359 n.77
Freud, Sigmund, 154, 155, 167, 322, 358 n.25
Frey, William, 79 n.129
Friday, Carolyn, 584 n.48
Friday, Paul, 513 n.186
Fridell, Lorie, 512 n.171, 513 n.180
Fridman, Daniel, 103 n.71
Friedlander, Robert, 362 nn.231, 234
Friedman, Lucy, 512 n.151
Friedrichs, David, 277 nn.16, 51; 413 n.7, 414 n.37, 551 n.111
Fritsch, Eric, 134 n.106, 509 n.25
Fromm, Delee, 171 n.92, 93
Fromm-Auch, Delee, 175 n.218
Frost, Laurie, 165
Fukurai, Hiroshi, 246 n.154
Fulton, Betsy, 280 n.154, 480 n.43
Furr, Allen, 65
Fyfe, James, 501, 507, 511 n.125, 512 nn.174, 175, 176; 513 n.181

Gabrielli, William, 173 n.137, 175 nn.217, 225
Gacy, Wayne, 336, 337
Gagnon, C., 80 n.140
Gagnon, John, 359 n.105
Gainey, Randy, 543
Gajewski, Francis, 134 n.105
Galaway, Burt, 98, 103 n.84
Gale, Nathan, 132 n.47
Gall, Franz Joseph, 6
Gallagher, Catherine, 586 n.142
Gallegos, Richard, 475
Galvin, Jim, 246 n.146
Gandhi, Indira, 351
Gans, Dian, 170 n.29
Garavito, Luis Alfredo, 335
Garcia, Agustin, 26
Gardiner, John, 511 n.133
Gardner, Carol Brooks, 362 n.224
Gardner, Faith, 431
Garfinkle, Harold, 235, 246 n.149
Garfinkle-Huff, Sylvia Rae, 391
Garland, David, 473, 479 n.19
Garner, Connie Chenoweth, 245 nn.108, 113
Garner, Joel H., 127
Garofalo, James, 103 n.51, 104 n.100, 361 n.202, 362 n.212, 512 n.168
Garofalo, Raffaele, 139, 169 n.3
Garry, Eileen M., 383
Gartin, Patrick, 127, 135 n.151, 510 n.67
Gartner, Rosemary, 57, 102 n.42, 134 nn.113, 114; 585 n.112
Gastil, Raymond, 324, 358 nn.54, 59
Gates, Bill, 194
Gebhard, Paul, 359 n.105
Gebo, Erika, 90
Gedney, D., Jr., 550 n.28

Geis, G., 414 nn.50, 81
Geis, Gilbert, 76 n.6, 385 n.10, 413 n.16, 415 n.107, 452 n.65
Gelhaus, Lisa, 127, 420
Geller, William, 512 n.174, 513 n.183
Gelles, Richard, 243 n.25, 340, 361 nn.173, 176, 184
Gelman, A., 551 n.77
Gembrowski, Susan, 386 n.52
Gendreau, Paul, 585 n.109, 586 nn.143, 144
Georges-Abeyie, Daniel, 79 nn.110, 111; 277 n.23, 362 nn.232, 233
Gerber, Jurg, 455 n.195
Gere, Richard, 424
Gerecht, Reuel Marc, 354, 362 n.241
Gerena, Victor Manuel, 316
Gerstein, Dean, 243 n.21, 311 n.64
Gertz, Marc, 24 n.2, 63, 65, 77 n.50, 132 n.56, 209 nn.53, 54; 210 n.55
Getreu, Alan, 312 n.72
Giacomazzi, Andrew, 510 n.62
Giallombardo, Rose, 585 n.118
Gibbons, Donald, 174 n.194, 385 n.39
Gibbs, David, 127, 479 n.23
Gibbs, Jack, 135 n.127, 247 n.176, 278 n.89, 362 n.230
Gibbs, John, 132 n.42, 133 n.60, 287
Gibbs, Natalie, 133 n.69, 359 n.79
Gibson, Evelyn, 342
Gibson, H. B., 76 n.19
Gideon, Clarence, 469
Giever, Dennis, 78 n.91, 287, 310 n.17
Gifford, Robert, 386 n.69
Gifford, Sidra Lee, 461, 479 n.6
Giglio, Greg, 57, 187
Giglliard, Darrell K., 567
Gilbert, Karen, 586 n.140
Gilliard, Darrell, 454 n.189
Gillis, A. R., 279 n.124
Ginzberg, Eli, 455 n.214
Ginzburg, E., 77 n.66, 311 n.61, 313 n.110, 454 n.190
Giordano, Peggy, 76 n.23, 211 n.102, 243 n.41, 245 n.121, 247 n.163, 308, 314 n.144, 385 n.38
Giordano, Philip, 82
Girling, Evi, 12, 13
Giroux, Bruce, 312 n.75
Giuliana, Carol Cogel, 450 n.10
Giuliani, Carlo, 249
Giuliani, Rudolph W., 418, 490
Glasser, William, 586 n.129
Glazer, D., 453 n.119
Glazer, Daniel, 169 n.16, 584 n.54, 585 n.106
Gleason, Sandra, 585 nn.100, 101
Gleason, Walter, 102 n.13
Glensor, Ronald W., 510 n.73
Glick, Barry, 76 n.8

Glueck, Eleanor, 162, 174 n.195, 242 n.4, 292, 293, 304, 306, 307, 311 nn.50, 51, 52
Glueck, Sheldon, 162, 174 n.195, 242 n.4, 292, 293, 304, 306, 307, 311 nn.50, 51, 52
Goddard, Henry, 163, 164, 174 n.206
Godfrey of Viterbo, 28
Godwin, Glen Stewart, 316
Godwinson, Harold, 29
Goebel, J., 583 n.3
Goetting, Ann, 242 n.5
Goetz, Bernhard, 119
Goffin, Claire, 586 n.144
Goffman, E., 585 n.93
Gold, Martin, 76 n.34, 78 n.98
Gold, Steven, 359 n.104
Goldkamp, John, 455 n.212, 550 nn.31, 33, 38
Goldman, David, 172 n.100
Goldman, M. S., 454 n.156
Goldman, Nathan, 511 n.127
Goldsmith, Larry, 583 n.17
Goldstein, Herman, 510 n.64
Goldstein, Joseph, 499, 511 n.115
Goldstein, Michael, 452 n.88
Goldstein, Paul, 358 nn.31, 34, 35; 451 nn.58, 61, 63; 454 nn.161, 190
Golub, Andrew, 57, 454 nn.163, 164
Gondolf, Edward, 127
Goodjoines, Komoya, 574
Goodjoines, Sonya, 574
Goodman, Sam, 369
Goodstein, Laurie, 246 n.142, 451 n.27
Goodwin, D. W., 453 n.146
Gordon, Leslie, 357 n.16
Gordon, Robert, 175 n.212, 244 n.87
Gore, Dena Lynn, 326
Goring, Charles, 153, 173 n.154
Gorman, Anna, 551 n.76
Gossop, Michael, 454 n.188
Gottfredson, Denise, 102 n.45, 210 n.75
Gottfredson, Gary, 102 n.45, 210 n.75
Gottfredson, M., 551 n.77
Gottfredson, Michael, 24 n.33, 67, 68, 78 nn.71, 74; 103 n.51, 132 n.20, 162, 232, 284, 285, 286, 287, 288, 289, 291, 304, 308, 310 nn.8, 9, 11, 12, 15, 16, 19, 24, 27; 311 n.63, 403, 415 nn.93, 94; 455 n.212, 550 n.38
Gottfredson, Stephen, 132 n.46
Gottfried, Heidi, 268
Gotti, John, 469
Gottman, John Mordechai, 340, 341, 361 n.188
Gottschalk, Earl, 413 n.23
Gould, Arthur, 452 n.76
Gould, Larry, 510 n.55
Gould, Leroy, 70, 79 n.103
Gourley, Steve, 398

Gove, Walter, 116, 133 n.71, 170 n.36, 172 n.103, 246 n.148, 247 n.179
Goyer, P. F., 171 n.78
Graf, Carl, 554
Grandison, Terry, 102 n.15
Grasmick, Harold, 133 n.95, 134 n.122, 135 nn.128, 129, 130; 210 nn.63, 77, 82; 310 nn.20, 35, 39
Grasmick, Harold G., 289
Gravano, Salvatore "Sammy the Bull," 409
Gray, Gregory, 170 n.27
Gray, Katti, 465
Gray, M. Kevin, 583 n.38
Gray, Tara, 543
Gray, Thomas, 76 n.26, 453 n.132
Greeley, A., 453 n.124
Green, Donald, 57, 134 n.127, 510 n.49
Green, Lorraine, 120, 133 n.87, 88
Green, William, 359 nn.64, 68
Greenberg, D., 278 nn.85, 86
Greenberg, David, 135 nn.156, 157, 160; 179, 209 n.18, 264, 277 n.20, 278 nn.81, 83
Greenberg, Stephanie, 209 n.48
Greene, Jack, 495, 512 n.156
Greene, Jack R., 510 n.53
Greene, Judith, 490
Greene, Michael, 358 n.30
Greenfeld, Lawrence, 102 n.35, 135 n.145, 454 n.189
Greenfeld, Lawrence A., 493, 503, 510 nn.38, 39; 512 n.172
Greenleaf, Richard, 277 n.29
Greenohouse, Joel, 171 n.65
Greenstein, Theodore, 511 n.105
Greenwood, Peter, 128, 136 n.165, 455 n.213, 509 nn.28, 31
Grenier, G., 452 n.86
Grennan, Sean, 512 n.154
Griffin, Christine, 402
Griffith, William, 584 n.56
Griset, Pamala, 551 n.89
Griswold, D., 246 n.126
Griswold, David, 245 n.107, 246 n.133, 551 n.88
Groff, Elizabeth, 386 n.59
Groff, M., 175 nn.212, 217
Groth, A. Nicholas, 326, 327, 330, 359 nn.76, 108
Grove, H., 414 n.50
Groves, W. Byron, 24 nn.19, 28, 29; 210 nn.75, 276 n.3, 4, 5; 277 nn.22, 27, 47; 278 nn.56, 71, 76; 279 n.94
Grubstein, Lori, 80 n.136
Guarino-Ghezzi, Susan, 510 n.71
Guerry, Andre-Michel, 8
Guest, Avery, 181
Guijarro, Margarita, 311 n.63
Gulley, Bill, 173 n.133
Gundry, Gwen, 172 nn.121, 122, 123

Gusfield, Joseph, 418, 451 n.11, 453 n.125
Gwlasda, Victoria, 133 n.93

Haase, Paul J., 396
Hackler, James, 383
Hackman, Gene, 364
Hagan, John, 116, 210 n.97, 211 n.100, 212 n.161, 246 n.152, 269, 277 n.24, 278 n.73, 279 nn.123, 124; 313 n.125, 358 n.45
Hagedorn, John, 187, 243 n.43
Hagedorn, John M., 57
Hageman, Hans, 221
Hageman, Irvin, 221
Hakim, Simon, 104 n.92, 132 nn.45, 47; 386 nn.64, 65
Halbfinger, David M., 414 n.41
Hale, Chris, 79 n.99
Hale, Matthew, 328
Hall, Andy, 528
Hall, Jerome, 45 nn.9, 19; 386 n.53
Hall, Joseph S., 414 n.66
Hallam, J., 452 n.90
Halleck, Seymour, 173 n.163
Haller, Mark, 413 n.3
Hallet, Amanda, 311 n.63
Halperin, William, 132 n.47
Hamilton, Thomas, 319
Hamlin, John, 245 n.92
Hamm, Mark, 586 n.133
Hammer, Jim, 523
Hammett, Theodore, 415 n.96
Hammock, Georgina, 103 n.59
Hammond, Rodney, 360 n.151
Hammurabi (king of Babylon), 27
Hamparian, Donna, 78 n.80
Hanchett, Doug, 583 nn.1, 2
Hanley, Dana, 509 n.5
Hanlon, Thomas, 454 n.180, 586 n.171
Hannon, Lance, 78 n.69
Hansell, Stephen, 454 n.186
Hanson, Karl, 174 n.188, 586 n.170
Hanson, Roger, 584 nn.49, 50
Harakas, Nicki, 74
Harbinger, Bonny, 414 n.55
Harden, Philip, 171 n.70, 172 n.117
Harding, Richard, 569, 585 n.86
Harer, Miles, 57, 60, 77 nn.39, 40, 41; 78 n.82
Hargarten, Stephen W., 65
Harlow, Caroline, 454 n.189
Harlow, Caroline Wolf, 104 n.95, 585 n.90
Harpold, Joseph, 493
Harr, Robin, 512 n.157, 585 n.120
Harrelson, Woody, 158
Harries, Keith, 209 n.35, 358 nn.55, 60; 361 n.165, 546, 551 n.113
Harring, Sidney L., 278 n.87, 503
Harris, Eric, 317
Harris, Grant, 165, 586 n.147

Harris, Judith Rich, 321, 358 n.24
Harris, Kaylene, 544
Harris, Mark, 210 n.78
Harris, Patricia, 386 n.45, 566, 583 n.30, 584 n.77
Harris, Philip, 80 n.136
Harris, Richard, 511 n.108
Harrison, Paige, 453 n.116, 518
Harrison, Paige M., 585 nn.82, 85, 90
Harry, Joseph, 135 n.136, 212 n.151
Hart, Elizabeth, 171 n.89
Hart, H. L. A., 418, 450 n.8
Hartman, Jennifer, 134 n.102
Hartnagel, Timothy, 134 n.109, 246 n.127
Hartnett, Susan, 510 n.54
Hartstone, Eliot, 209 n.29
Harvard, Beverly, 504
Harvey-Lintz, Terri, 511 n.104
Hasday, Jill Elaine, 359 n.96
Hathaway, Jeanne, 361 n.186
Hathaway, R. Starke, 174 nn.202, 203
Hausbeck, Kathryn, 452 nn.71, 72
Hawke, W., 169 n.22
Hawkins, Darnell, 358 n.42, 542, 543, 551 n.107
Hawkins, Gordon, 62, 77 nn.48, 49
Hawkins, J. David, 244 n.51, 297, 310 n.30, 312 nn.73, 95, 96, 97; 313 nn.98, 99, 100; 454 nn.162, 186
Hawkins, John, 350
Hawkins, Keith, 415 n.100
Hawkins, Yusuf, 345
Hawley, C., 170 n.61
Hawley, F. Frederick, 359 n.61
Hawton, Keith, 311 n.60
Hay, Carter, 243 n.19, 280 n.146, 287, 310 n.36
Hay, Dale, 174 n.174, 296, 357 n.11
Hay, Douglas, 45 n.8
Hayes, Read, 370
Hayes, Roxanne, 125
Haynie, Dana, 209 n.43
Hazelbaker, Kim, 385 n.40, 386 nn.42, 47
Hazlewood, Robert, 133 n.69, 359 n.79
Heald, F. P., 171 n.81
Health and Human Services Department, 361 n.171, 453 n.130
Healy, William, 163, 174 n.207
Heath, James, 45 n.2
Heath, Linda, 159
Heaviside, Sheila, 243 n.37
Heckert, D. Alex, 127
Hefler, Gerd, 211 n.100
Hegel, Georg, 252
Heide, Kathleen, 337, 357 n.17, 361 n.162
Heimer, Karen, 116, 133 n.70, 174 n.191, 246 nn.150, 151, 152, 153
Heitgerd, Janet, 210 n.68
Hemmens, Craig, 480 n.37
Henderson, Russell A., 343
Henggeler, Scott, 173 n.169

Henley, Wayne, Jr., 337

Hennard, George, 336

Henneberger, Melinda, 276 n.1

Hennessy, James, 145, 171 nn.78, 80

Henry II (king of England), 30, 31

Henry VII (king of England), 554, 555

Henry, Stuart, 262, 278 n.70, 280 nn.132, 134

Henry, William, 45 n.12

Hensley, Lawrence Michael, 471

Henslin, James, 76 n.6

Henson, Trudy Knicely, 385 n.38

Hepburn, John, 385 n.6, 543

Hepperle, Winifred, 79 n.100, 279 n.122

Herbert, Carey, 287

Herbert, Steve, 511 nn.109, 110, 112

Herbert, Tracy Bennett, 169 n.13

Hernandez, Alejandro, 546

Hernandez, Jeanne, 312 n.67, 361 n.173

Hernandez, Luis Ramiro, 399

Herrenkohl, Todd, 313 n.98

Herrnstein, Richard, 22, 24 n.42, 67, 78 nn.77, 78; 135 n.143, 165, 166, 175 nn.215, 216, 222; 212 n.164, 284, 308, 310 nn.5, 6, 7

Herve, Huues, 359 n.106

Hessing, Dick, 310 n.21

Hester, Thomas, 454 n.189

Heumann, Milton, 550 n.51

Hewitt, John, 172 n.127

Hickey, Eric, 133 n.68

Hickey, J., 173 n.168

Hickman, Matthew, 509 n.15, 512 n.156

Hickman, Matthew J., 509 nn.16, 17

Hickman-Barlow, Melissa, 278 n.60

Hidaym, Virginia, 174 n.192

Hien, Denise, 298

Hien, Nina, 298

Hiett, Laura, 445

Hilbert, Richard, 210 nn.91, 92

Hill, Belinda, 526

Hill, D., 170 n.31

Hill, Karl, 244 n.51, 312 n.73

Hill, Robert, 358 n.58

Hill, Sean, 362 n.243

Hillbrand, Marc, 174 n.186

Hillsman, Sally, 551 n.78

Hinckley, John, 37, 41, 64, 158

Hindelang, Michael, 24 n.41, 54, 76 n.28, 77 nn.34, 59; 78 n.98, 164, 165, 166, 174 n.203, 175 n.211, 231, 245 n.88, 246 n.125, 385 n.31

Hippchen, Leonard, 169 nn.16, 18, 20; 170 nn.57, 62

Hirky, A. Elizabeth, 211 n.126, 243 n.23, 453 n.149

Hirschel, J. David, 127, 322, 358 n.28

Hirschi, Travis, 24 nn.33, 41; 54, 67, 68, 76 n.28, 77 n.59, 78 nn.71, 74; 103 n.51, 132 n.20, 162, 164, 165, 166, 175 n.211, 218, 228, 229, 230, 231, 232, 240, 241,

244 nn.54, 72; 245 nn.104, 105, 106; 284, 285, 286, 287, 288, 289, 291, 299, 304, 308, 310 nn.8, 9, 11, 12, 15, 16, 19, 24, 27; 311 n.63, 403, 415 nn.93, 94

Hitchcock, Alfred, 138

Hitler, Adolph, 36, 420

Hobbs, Dick, 366

Hobson, Katherine, 370

Hochstetler, Andy, 103 n.62, 116

Hodge, Carole, 246 n.136

Hodges, Virginia, 270

Hodgins, Sheilagh, 309 n.1

Hofer, Paul J., 551 n.95

Hoffar, Joe, 121

Hoffer, A., 170 n.25

Hoffman, Bruce, 352

Hoffman, Dennis, 278 n.88

Hoffman, Harry, 169 n.12

Hoffman, John, 211 n.124, 243 n.21, 311 n.64

Hoffman, W. Michael, 413 n.21

Hoffmann, John, 211 n.130

Hoffmaster, Debra, 511 n.118

Hogan, Michael, 65, 209 nn.53, 54

Hoge, Robert, 78 n.96, 314 n.135, 586 n.144

Hoge, Steven K., 41

Hoheimer, Francis, 378, 379

Hoheimer, Frank, 386 n.60

Holcomb, Jefferson E., 543, 552 n.118

Holdaway, Simon, 505

Holleran, David, 331, 360 n.126

Hollinger, Richard, 414 n.47

Holmes, Malcolm, 245 n.110, 278 n.80

Holmes, Oliver Wendell, 35, 45 n.15

Holmes, Ronald, 361 nn.158, 159, 160, 161

Holsinger, Alexander, 134 n.102

Holton, Gerald, 140

Holtzworth-Munroe, Amy, 357 n.7

Homel, Ross, 118

Homes, Stephen, 361 nn.158, 159, 160, 161; 509 n.5

Hood, Roger, 76 n.14

Hooker, "Fighting Joe," 424

Hoover, Herbert, 460

Hoover, J. Edgar, 485

Hope, Tim, 102 n.30

Horney, Julie, 170 n.53, 310 n.34, 360 n.113

Horowitz, Ruth, 438, 454 nn.159, 160

Hoskin, Anthony, 64, 65

Hotaling, Gerald, 452 n.68

Hough, Richard, 101 n.11

Hoult, David, 33

Hoult, Jennifer, 33

House, James, 313 nn.122, 124

Howard, Gregory, 57, 133 n.65, 311 n.63

Howell, James, 73, 80 n.139, 133 n.65, 312 n.73, 358 n.50

Hoyt, Dan, 102 n.44

Hoyt, Danny, 359 n.89

Hsieh, Chin-Chi, 77 n.65

Huang, Bu, 313 nn.98, 99; 454 nn.162, 186

Hubbell, Amy, 453 n.154

Hubble, L., 175 nn.212, 217

Huberty, James, 336

Hudson, Joe, 98, 103 n.84

Hudson, John, 45 n.5

Huesman, L., 174 n.173

Huesman, L. Rowell, 24 n.40

Huff-Corzine, Lin, 584 n.41

Hughes, Timothy A., 586 nn.168, 170

Hugo, Victor, 264

Huizinga, David, 77 n.59, 79 n.105, 103 n.50, 127, 210 nn.60, 83, 84; 212 n.160, 243 n.42, 311 n.65

Hulsman, L., 480 n.39

Humphries, Drew, 278 n.81

Hunt, Geoffrey, 298, 585 nn.102, 111

Hunter, Denis, 45 n.25

Hunter, John, 246 n.136

Hurlburt, Michael, 101 n.11

Hurley, Robert S., 174 n.178

Hurst, Yolander G., 512 n.141

Hussein, Saddam, 390

Hutchings, Barry, 150, 173 nn.136, 137; 175 n.225

Hutchinson, Ira, 127, 322, 358 n.28

Hyde, Janet Shibley, 78 n.93

Iheduru, Chris Ahamefule, 40

Immarigeon, Russ, 280 n.141

Immerwahr, George, 181

Inbau, F., 451 n.35

Inbau, Fred, 45 n.2

Inciardi, J., 278 n.82, 279 nn.92, 93

Inciardi, James, 385 n.7, 438, 453 nn.118, 122, 124; 454 nn.159, 160, 165, 187; 455 n.224

Ingham, Denise, 219

Inglis, Ruth, 361 n.178

Innes, Christopher, 102 n.35

Institute for Social Research, 79 n.104

Iovanni, Leeann, 127, 247 n.181

Ireland, Timothy, 102 n.20

Irwin, John, 132 n.13, 573, 585 nn.106, 108

Isaac, Nancy E., 99

Isaacson, Lynne, 57

Ito, Timothy M., 550 n.34

Ivanko, Katarina, 191

Ives, G., 583 n.7

Jablon, Andrew, 414 n.83

Jackman, N., 452 n.65

Jackson, Elton, 244 n.65

Jackson, Kenneth, 246 n.145

Jackson, Linda, 246 n.136

Jackson, Lori, 357 n.5

Jackson, Patrick, 76 n.7, 243 n.45

Jacob, Ayad, 454 n.169

Jacobs, Bruce, 110, 111, 132 nn.27, 28, 29, 31, 32, 33, 34
Jacobs, David, 79 n.122, 277 n.32, 278 n.63, 509 n.22
Jacobs, James, 512 n.146
Jacobs, James B., 573, 574, 585 nn.103, 110
Jacobs, K. J., 170 n.59
Jacobson, Neil, 340, 341, 361 n.188
Jaffe, Pater, 103 n.82
James, Jesse, 318, 364
James, William, 157
Jamieson, Katherine, 277 n.38
Jang, Kerry, 172 n.108
Jang, Sung Joon, 244 nn.52, 55, 56; 313 nn.109, 112, 114, 115, 118
Janis, Irving, 243 n.38
Jankowski, Lewis, 454 n.189
Janofsky, Michael, 361 n.201
Jansen, Robert, 132 n.57, 342, 344, 361 n.196
Janus, Mark-David, 451 n.53
Jarjoura, G. Roger, 211 n.125, 243 n.34
Jaworski, Leon, 522
Jeans, Sam, 484
Jefferis, Eric, 509 n.5
Jeffery, C. Ray, 117, 133 n.75
Jenkins, Patricia, 245 nn.111, 114
Jenkins, Philip, 427, 452 n.83
Jenkins, Phillip, 415 n.128
Jensen, Eric, 455 n.195
Jensen, Gary, 78 n.98, 79 n.103, 102 n.46, 244 n.80, 246 n.126, 279 nn.127, 128
Jensen, Vickie, 358 n.46
Jessor, Richard, 77 n.66, 311 nn.60, 61; 313 n.110, 454 n.190
Jeynes, William, 215
Jiao, Allan, 510 n.72
Jiobu, Robert, 64, 65
Joe, Karen Ann, 110, 132 nn.25, 26
Johannes, Laura, 414 nn.58, 59
John Paul II (pope), 422
Johns, Cindy, 512 n.155
Johnson, Bruce, 57, 314 nn.138, 141; 454 nn.163, 164, 166
Johnson, Byron, 244 nn.55, 56; 586 n.135
Johnson, Christine, 310 n.32
Johnson, Elmer, 207
Johnson, Gary, 282
Johnson, Holly, 173 n.145
Johnson, Jeffery G., 159
Johnson, Lyndon B., 239, 460
Johnson, R., 171 n.69
Johnson, Richard R., 511 n.128
Johnson, Robert, 243 n.21, 246 n.154, 247 n.165, 311 n.64
Johnson, Sherri Lynn, 511 n.121
Johnson, Wendell, 133 n.93
Johnson, W. Wesley, 278 n.60
Johnston, Lloyd, 24 n.16, 77 nn.35, 36; 244 n.48, 453 n.128

Johnston, N., 550 n.45, 586 n.128
Johnstone, J., 212 n.151
Jolin, Annette, 451 n.47, 510 n.57
Jones, Dana, 127
Jones, David, 45 n.2
Jones, Donald, 149, 172 n.132, 173 n.134
Jones, Kenneth, 454 n.191
Jones, Lisa, 339, 361 nn.174, 175
Jones, Mark, 583 n.31
Jones, Marshall, 149, 172 n.132, 173 n.134
Jones, Peter, 80 n.136, 455 n.212, 584 n.58
Jorge, Antonio, 97
Jorge, Kristen M., 97
Jorge, Laura, 97
Joshi, Vandana, 454 nn.181, 182
Joyce, James, 427
Junger, Marianne, 245 n.117, 310 n.21, 311 n.63
Junger-Tas, Josine, 245 n.117
Junta, Thomas, 39, 40
Jurgensmeyer, Mark, 362 n.238
Jurik, Nancy, 268, 279 n.119
Jussim, Lee, 243 n.31
Justice Department, 103 nn.75, 76; 454 n.177

Kaczinski, Theodore, 466
Kadish, Sanford, 45 n.2
Kadleck, Colleen, 133 n.85
Kageyama, Yuri, 359 n.70
Kahan, Dan, 503
Kahan, James, 583 n.37
Kahn, Joseph, 276 n.1
Kaiser, Gunther, 13
Kakar, Suman, 303, 313 n.116
Kalb, Larry, 103 n.50
Kaloupek, Danny, 102 n.21
Kaminer, Matthew, 515
Kaminski, Robert, 509 n.5
Kamm, Judith Brown, 413 n.21
Kandel, Denise, 244 n.68, 245 n.122, 453 n.150
Kandel, Elizabeth, 171 n.68, 242 n.5
Kane, Robert, 127, 361 n.187
Kanka, Megan, 42
Kant, Immanuel, 544
Kaplan, Carol, 455 nn.202, 203
Kaplan, David, 451 n.15
Kaplan, Howard, 196, 228, 229, 231, 245 nn.101, 102, 103; 246 nn.154, 155; 247 n.165, 311 n.64, 442
Kaplan, Paul, 414 n.83
Kaplan, Steven, 388
Kappeler, Victor, 511 n.123
Karberg, Jennifer, 585 n.79
Karmen, Andrew, 103 nn.83, 85, 86; 135 n.154, 360 n.123, 509 n.20
Kasen, Stephanie, 159
Kassebaum, G., 586 n.128
Kassebaum, Nancy, 239
Kates, Don, 132 n.51

Katz, Charles, 504, 510 n.45, 512 nn.147, 148
Katz, Jack, 116, 147, 172 n.104
Katz, Janet, 159
Katz, Rebecca S., 306
Kauder, Neal, 549 n.3
Kauffman, K., 173 n.168
Kaufman, Jeanne, 102 n.12
Kaufman, Joanne, 360 n.151
Kaveny, M. Cathleen, 417
Kay, Barbara, 245 n.100
Keane, Carl, 287
Keckeisen, George, 385 n.32
Keeney, Belea, 337, 361 n.162
Keire, Mara, 452 n.73
Keith, Bruce, 243 n.16
Kelling, George, 134 n.101, 492, 509 n.18, 510 nn.41, 42
Kelly, Kathryn, 173 n.157
Kelly, Linda, 584 n.69
Kelly, Robert, 415 n.126
Kempe, C. Henry, 361 n.170
Kempe, Ruth S., 361 n.170
Kemper, Edmund, 337
Kempf, Kimberly, 245 n.119
Kempf-Leonard, Kimberly, 73, 80 nn.138, 139; 135 n.145, 246 n.124
Kendall, Jerry, 551 n.112
Kendziora, Kimberly, 361 n.185
Kennan, Kate, 312 n.75
Kennedy, David, 65, 508, 510 n.65
Kennedy, Leslie, 104 n.89, 310 n.14
Kennedy, Randall, 503
Kennedy, Stephen, 550 n.43
Kenney, Dennis, 511 n.122
Kenney, T. J., 171 n.81
Kerbs, John Johnson, 465
Kercher, Kyle, 78 n.73
Kerner, Hans-Jurgen, 312 n.84
Kerner, H. J., 78 n.70, 242 n.2
Kerr, Peter, 415 n.127
Kershner, J., 169 n.22
Kessler, David, 510 n.63
Kethineni, Sesha, 246 n.123
Kevorkian, Jack, 14, 42
Kifner, John, 169 n.1
Killip, Steve, 103 n.82
Kilpatrick, Dean, 103 n.73
Kimble, Charles, 103 n.70
Kim, Julia Yun Soo, 453 n.133
Kimble, Charles, 103 n.70
King, Harry, 367, 385 n.8
King, John, 13, 211 n.110, 362 n.220
King, Kate, 136 n.164
King, Rodney, 462
Kingery, Paul M., 174 n.178
Kingsworth, Rodney, 360 n.118, 543, 550 n.10
Kinlock, Timothy, 312 n.78
Kinscherff, Robert, 174 n.183
Kinsey, Karyl, 134 n.122, 135 n.129
Kinsey, Richard, 279 n.99
Kinsie, Paul, 451 nn.55, 57

Parent, Sophie, 287
Parham, Carrie, 65
Parisi, Nicolette, 585 nn.95, 96, 104
Park, Robert Ezra, 8, 24 n.18, 177, 183, 208 nn.3, 4
Parke, Al, 586 n.134
Parker, Bonnie, 364
Parker, Donn, 414 n.81
Parker, Faith Lamb, 239
Parker, Karen, 79 n.121, 209 nn.38, 39; 479 n.34, 585 n.87
Parker, Robert Nash, 77 n.51, 357 n.3
Parker, Sharon K., 505
Parks, E., 583 nn.28, 29
Parrot, A., 359 n.92
Paschall, Mallie, 76 n.21, 79 n.125
Passas, Nikos, 211 n.112, 413 nn.5, 6, 20, 21
Pastore, Ann, 212 n.166, 357 n.2
Pastore, Ann L., 512 n.140
Pataki, Gov. George B., 3
Pate, Antony, 512 n.171
Pate, Tony, 134 n.101, 509 n.18
Paternoster, Raymond, 124, 135 nn.127, 134, 136, 140, 150; 211 n.124, 237, 247 n.181, 279 n.104, 287, 310 n.37, 311 n.59, 312 n.87, 314 nn.131, 140; 551 n.108, 552 n.130
Patterson, Bernie, 509 n.2
Patterson, Gerald, 293, 309 n.1, 311 nn.55, 56, 62; 357 n.12
Patterson, G. R., 311 nn.46, 57, 58; 312 n.81
Patterson, James, 244 n.58
Pattillo, Mary E., 57
Pattinson, Jeffrey, 156
Paulozzi, Len, 360 n.151
Paulsen, Monrad, 45 n.2
Paulus, P., 586 n.151
Pauly, David, 584 n.48
Pauly, John, 278 n.70
Payne, Brian, 134 n.110, 511 n.89
Payne, Gary, 211 n.117, 246 n.123
Pazniokas, Mark, 101 n.1
Peak, Ken, 510 n.73
Pease, Ken, 102 n.34, 133 n.90, 382, 386 nn.71, 72
Pease, Susan, 175 n.223
Peay, Lenore, 239
Peel, Sir Robert, 483
Peete, Thomas, 135 n.131
Penn, William, 31, 555, 556, 566
Penrod, Steven, 359 n.109, 452 n.89
Pepinsky, Harold, 271, 280 n.140
Perea, Ignacio, 332
Perez, Cynthia, 77 n.66, 311 nn.44, 61; 313 n.110, 454 n.190
Perez, Jacob, 550 nn.32, 36
Perez, Mary B., 544
Pérez-Peña, Richard, 414 n.49
Perkins, Elizabeth, 386 n.71

Perlmutter, M., 173 n.171
Perper, Joshua, 358 n.40
Perry, T. B., 243 n.40
Petchesky, Rosalind, 278 n.86
Petee, Thomas, 358 n.60
Petersen, Rebecca, 584 n.77
Petersilia, Joan, 190, 191, 246 n.147, 277 n.43, 509 nn.28, 31; 560, 561, 563, 583 n.37, 584 nn.43, 60, 61, 62, 63; 586 nn.168, 172
Peterson, David, 245 n.116
Peterson, Joyce, 583 n.37
Peterson, Ruth, 134 n.119, 210 n.78, 212 n.161, 246 n.152, 358 n.45
Petraitis, John, 133 n.61, 453 n.147
Petrosino, Anthony, 24 n.44, 280 n.144
Petrosino, Carolyn, 280 n.144
Petry, Edward, 413 n.21
Pezzin, Liliana, 132 n.22
Philip, Michael, 79 n.111
Phillips, Coretta, 102 n.34, 382, 386 n.72
Phillips, David, 134 n.118, 156, 173 n.165
Phillips, Julie, 79 n.127
Phillips, Lloyd, 132 nn.18, 19
Phillips-Plummer, Lynanne, 452 n.66
Piaget, Jean, 157, 173 n.166, 313 n.105
Pickering, Lloyd, 310 n.21
Pickles, Andrew, 172 n.127
Piehl, Anne Morrison, 510 n.65
Pierce, Glenn, 209 n.40, 548, 552 n.115, 131
Pihl, Robert, 171 n.70, 172 n.117
Piliavin, Irving, 228, 245 nn.95, 98, 511 n.127
Pillai, Vijayan, 511 n.114
Pinel, Phillipe, 7, 153
Piorkowski, Chaya, 239
Piquero, Alex, 124, 135 nn.138, 150; 165, 170 n.40, 175 n.214, 211 nn.116, 117, 118; 287, 310 n.13, 311 n.59, 312 nn.77, 83, 87, 92; 512 n.156, 584 n.75
Pittman, David, 453 n.119
Pitts, Timothy, 586 n.135
Platt, Anthony, 209 n.24, 259, 279 n.95
Platt, Jerome J., 453 n.144, 455 n.216
Ploeger, Matthew, 78 n.95, 244 nn.65, 71
Plumridge, Libby, 451 n.54
Podolsky, E., 170 n.31
Pogarsky, Greg, 134 nn.96, 108
Pogrebin, Mark, 245 n.93, 574, 585 n.113
Police Foundation, 510 n.47
Polk, Kenneth, 212 n.165
Pollack, Otto, 78 n.86
Polsenberg, Christina, 76 n.27, 453 n.132
Pomeroy, Wardell, 359 n.105
Pomper, Stephen, 472
Pontell, Henry, 413 n.8
Ponton, Lynn E., 155
Poole, Eric, 245 nn.88, 93
Pope, Carl, 246 n.161
Popkin, Susan, 133 n.93

Porter, Stephen, 359 n.106
Post, Jerrold M., 354, 362 n.239
Potter, Gary, 415 n.128
Potter, Lloyd, 360 n.151
Potterat, John, 452 n.66
Potterton, Dave, 414 n.76
Pottieger, Anne, 438, 454 nn.159, 160
Poulin, Francois, 311 n.56
Poundstone, Paula, 339
Poussin, Nicolas, 325
Powell, Andrea, 209 n.35
Powell, Thomas, 578
Powers, Ronald, 361 n.203
Poythress, Norman G., 41
Pranis, Kay, 280 nn.150, 152
Prasad, Monica, 423, 451 n.49
Pratt, Travis, 479 n.25, 543
President's Commission on Law Enforcement and the Administration of Justice, 479 n.4, 509 n.6, 512 n.166
President's Commission on Organized Crime, 415 n.114
Pribesh, Shana, 210 n.58
Price, Virginia, 451 n.53
Priest, Thomas, 502, 503
Prins, Herschel, 383
Prinz, Ronald, 170 nn.24, 26
Pruitt, B. E., 174 n.178
Pruitt, Matthew, 209 nn.38, 39
Prusoff, L., 509 n.28
Przybylski, Roger, 454 n.169
Pugh, M. D., 77 n.65, 245 n.121
Pugh, Meredith, 76 n.23
Puzzanchera, Charles M., 465
Pyle, D. J., 344

Quetelet, L. A. J. (Adolphe), 7, 8, 10, 24 nn.13, 14
Quigley, Brian, 341
Quinet, Kenna Davis, 102 n.29
Quinney, Richard, 256, 257, 259, 260, 271, 275, 277 n.25, 278 n.66, 280 n.140, 413 nn.17, 25
Quinsey, Vernon, 386 n.74
Quint, Janet, 512 n.151

Raab, Selwyn, 415 nn.134, 136
Rada, Richard, 359 n.105
Radelet, Michael, 546, 552 n.129
Radosevich, Marcia, 79 n.103, 244 nn.75, 76
Radosh, Polly, 280 n.148
Radzinowicz, Leon, 583 n.8
Rafter, Nicole Hahn, 24 nn.10, 11
Raine, Adrian, 171 nn.71, 79, 84, 172 n.106, 173 n.151, 174 n.172, 357 n.13
Raj, Anita, 361 n.186
Raja, Sheela, 101 n.9
Raley, R. Kelly, 79 n.126

Ryan, Kimberly, 102 n.44
Ryan, Patrick, 358 nn.31, 35

Sack, Kevin, 414 n.32
Sagarin, E., 453 n.123
Sagi, Philip, 360 n.149
Sagy, Shifra, 321
Sakheim, George, 386 n.73
Salekin, Randall, 357 n.7
Salley, Sean, 3
Saltzman, Linda, 135 n.136, 338, 360 n.144
Samenow, Clifford, 310 n.25
Sample, Barry, 79 n.111
Sampson, Robert, 77 n.64, 79 n.110, 80
    n.142, 132 n.49, 172 nn.113, 118; 207,
    208, 209 nn.28, 32, 37, 48; 210 nn.67,
    75, 83, 84, 88; 211 nn.104, 108; 212
    n.161, 216, 243 n.24, 247 n.174, 277
    n.31, 278 n.56, 292, 293, 304, 305, 306,
    307, 308, 311 nn.49, 53; 313 nn.121,
    126; 358 n.45, 509 n.19
Sampson, Robert J., 210 nn.70, 71
Samuelson, Leslie, 246 n.127
Sanchez, Mary, 294
Sandhu, Harjit, 76 n.25
Sands, Bill, 577
Sandys, Marla, 552 n.124
Saner, Hilary, 78 n.83, 454 n.171
Sansone, Lori, 101 n.11
Sansone, Randy, 101 n.11
Santello, Mark, 103 n.74
Sarbin, T. R., 172 n.111
Sargent, W., 170 n.31
Saul, Nigel, 365
Saunders, Benjamin, 103 n.73
Saunders, Daniel, 102 n.13
Savitz, L., 550 n.45, 586 n.128
Savitz, Leonard, 76 n.11
Savolainen, Jukka, 211 n.103, 242 n.10
Scalia, John, 455 n.199
Scanlon, Barbara, 451 n.53
Scarborough, Kathryn, 159, 511 n.123
Scarpitti, Frank, 245 n.100
Scary Guy, 234
Schafer, Stephen, 14, 24 n.23, 76 n.6, 349,
    362 nn.226, 227
Schafer, Walter, 212 n.165
Schaffner, Laurie, 583 n.34
Scharf, P., 173 n.168
Schatzberg, Rufus, 415 n.126
Schauss, A. G., 170 n.25
Schauss, Alexander, 170 n.60
Scheurman, Leo, 210 nn.65, 66
Schlegel, Kip, 413 n.11, 415 n.103
Schlossman, Steven, 267, 279 n.121
Schmeidelr, James, 312 n.72
Schmidt, Janell, 127, 245 n.96, 247 n.171,
    550 n.9
Schmidt, Laura, 76 n.20
Schmidt, Randall, 103 nn.80, 81

Schmutte, Pamela, 174 n.205
Schneider, Anne, 584 n.56
Schneider, Mike, 413 n.22
Schneider, Peter, 584 n.56
Schoen, Cathy, 85
Schoenthaler, Stephen, 142, 169 n.21, 170
    n.25
School-Associated Violent Deaths Study
    Group, 360 n.151
Schott, Richard G., 482
Schrag, Clarence, 76 n.32, 212 n.147
Schrager, Laura, 413 n.15
Schram, Pamela J., 574, 585 n.119
Schreck, Christopher, 287
Schulsinger, Fini, 175 n.217
Schumacher, Joseph, 552 n.132
Schumacher, Michael, 73, 80 n.135
Schur, Edwin, 246 n.139, 247 n.177, 450
    n.2
Schuster, Richard, 78 n.80
Schutt, Russell, 79 n.105
Schwaner, Shawn, 65
Schwartz, Martin, 93, 103 n.65, 265, 279
    nn.96, 100, 101, 102, 103, 115; 328, 359
    nn.85, 86, 90, 107; 360 n.121
Schwartz, Miguel, 361 n.185
Schweietzer, Louis, 527
Schwendinger, Herman, 24 n.39, 259, 262,
    278 nn.67, 68; 279 nn.105, 109
Schwendinger, Julia, 24 n.39, 259, 262, 278
    nn.67, 68; 279 nn.105, 109
Scofield, 32
Scott, Austin, 45 nn.2, 6; 360 nn.130, 131;
    385 nn.19, 20, 36; 386 nn.48, 54, 55, 56
Scott, Jan, 336
Scott, Joseph, 452 n.107
Scott, Michael, 512 n.174, 513 n.183
Scott, Peter, 24 n.7
Scudder, Robert, 357 n.17
Scull, Andrew, 278 n.88
Sealock, Miriam, 79 n.108
Sederstrom, John, 312 n.95
Seger, Cynthia, 65
Seguin, Jean, 171 n.70
Seibel, George, 510 n.51
Seidman, David, 76 n.9
Seidman, Robert, 255, 277 n.21
Seiter, Richard, 583 n.24
Sellars, James, 45 n.25
Sellers, Christine, 244 n.78
Sellin, Thorsten, 72, 78 n.80, 79 nn.130,
    131; 134 n.112, 200, 205, 212 nn.134,
    135, 136, 137
Sells, Tommy Lee, 544
Semple, W. E., 171 n.78
Senna, Joseph, 524, 525
Sennott, Charles M., 451 n.42
Serra, Susan, 357 n.5
Seth, Mark, 552 n.116
Sewell, Kenneth, 357 n.7

Sexton, Joe, 414 n.53
Shachmurove, Yochanan, 386 nn.64, 65
Shah, Saleem, 169 n.16
Shainberg, Louis, 454 n.191
Shakespeare, William, 325
Shannon, Lyle, 78 n.80, 80 n.133
Shapiro, Perry, 135 n.151
Sharpe, Kimberly, 174 n.186
Shaushnessy, Rita, 171 n.94
Shaver, Lynda Dixon, 585 n.114
Shaw, Clifford R., 183, 184, 185, 186, 204,
    205, 209 nn.23, 25, 26
Shaw, James, 584 n.73
Sheldon, William, 139, 169 n.6
Sheley, Joseph, 57, 358 n.37
Shelley, Jill Kastens, 505, 512 n.158
Shelly, Peggy, 132 n.42, 133 n.60
Shelton, Kelly, 314 nn.134, 137
Shepard, Matthew, 343, 345, 420
Shepard, Robin, 503
Sherman, Lawrence, 76 n.8, 126, 127, 134
    n.103, 245 n.96, 247 n.171, 509 nn.26,
    27; 510 nn.66, 67; 512 n.168
Shields, Edgar, 48
Shields, Ian, 244 n.87
Shin, Hee-Choon, 243 n.21, 311 n.64
Shin, Kilman, 552 n.127
Shinnar, Reuel, 127, 135 n.158
Shinnar, Shlomo, 127, 135 n.158
Shipley, Bernard, 135 n.147
Short, James, 63, 76–77 nn.34, 53, 54; 223,
    244 nn.66, 87; 277 n.15, 413 n.15
Shotland, R. Lance, 359 n.84
Shover, Neal, 132 n.24, 368, 380, 381, 386
    n.66
Showers, Carolin, 78 n.93
Shrout, Patrick, 246 n.135
Shweder, Richard A., 419
Sichel, Joyce, 512 n.151
Sidwell, Clare, 454 n.188
Siedfer, Jill Jordan, 385 nn.24, 33
Siegal, Nina, 575
Siegel, Jane, 279 n.118
Siegel, Larry, 76 nn.6, 17; 172 n.105, 174
    n.203, 245 n.89, 465, 524, 525, 532,
    584 n.55
Sigel, S., 170–171 n.62
Sigurdardottir, Thordis J., 96
Silberg, Judy, 172 n.127
Silberman, Charles, 578, 586 n.148
Silberman, Matthew, 134 n.127
Silva, Phil, 77 n.66, 80 n.141, 171 nn.68, 88;
    173 nn.152, 162; 174 n.205, 310 n.33,
    311 nn.45, 61; 312 n.90, 313 n.127, 314
    nn.142, 143
Silver, Eric, 174 nn.186, 190
Silverman, Ira, 357 n.17
Silverman, Jay, 361 n.186
Silverman, Robert, 134 n.109, 245 nn.112,
    118

Styfco, Saly, 239
Su, S. Susan, 211 *n*.130, 243 *n*.21, 311 *n*.64
Sudermann, Marlies, 103 *n*.82
Sullivan, Dennis, 260, 270, 271, 277 *n*.52, 280 *nn*.136, 138; 480 *n*.40
Sullivan, James F., 492
Sundance Kid, 318
Surette, Ray, 585 *nn*.80, 81
Sutherland, Edwin, 4, 9, 14, 15, 24 *nn*.3, 24; 164, 174 *n*.206, 175 *n*.210, 220, 221, 222, 223, 240, 244 *nn*.61, 62; 367, 368, 369, 370, 381, 383, 385 *nn*.9, 11, 12, 13; 389, 396, 403, 413 *nn*.9, 10; 414 *n*.65
Sutherland, Edwin H., 244 *n*.60
Swaggi, Vincent, 368, 369
Swanson, M., 414 *n*.81
Swartz, Bruce, 406, 414 *nn*.77, 78
Swartz, Marvin, 174 *n*.192
Swetnam, Michael S., 357 *n*.1
Sykes, Gresham, 225, 240, 244 *nn*.82, 84, 85, 86; 278 *n*.62, 585 *n*.94
Sykes, Richard, 509 *n*.37
Symons, Donald, 359 *n*.98

Tagliabue, John, 415 *n*.125
Tait, David, 103 *n*.65, 359 *n*.107
Tait, Karen, 359 *nn*.85, 86
Takagi, Paul, 259, 278 *n*.86
Tannenbaum, Frank, 235, 246 *n*.157
Tanner, Julian, 217
Tappan, Paul, 76 *n*.4
Tarde, Gabriel, 153, 173 *n*.156
Tardiff, Kenneth, 134 *n*.117, 358 *n*.48, 552 *n*.114
Taylor, Bruce, 76 *n*.10, 102 *n*.18
Taylor, Bruce M., 243 *n*.36
Taylor, Dawn, 174 *n*.184
Taylor, Ian, 259, 277 *n*.49, 278 *n*.66
Taylor, M., 386 *n*.69
Taylor, Ralph, 132 *n*.46, 209 *nn*.36, 52; 210 *nn*.64, 85; 211 *n*.108
Taylor, Robert, 134 *n*.106, 509 *n*.25
Teevan, James, 287
Tellier, Marie-Claude, 585 *n*.109
Teret, Stephen P., 65
Territo, J., 414 *n*.81
Teslovich, Sisanne, 425
Tewksbury, Richard, 132 *n*.50, 454 *n*.170
Thatcher, Robert, 171 *n*.73
Theerathorn, Pochara, 133 *n*.76
Theisen, Gary, 453 *n*.124
Thistlewaite, Amy, 127, 479 *n*.23
Thomas, Charles, 585 *n*.87
Thomas, Charles C., 352
Thomas, John M., 415 *n*.100
Thomas, Melvin, 79 *n*.123
Thomas, Suzie Dod, 279 *n*.114
Thomas, W. I., 17
Thomas Aquinas, Saint, 423
Thomasson, Paul, 421

Thompson, J., 451 *n*.35
Thompson, James, 45 *n*.2
Thompson, Kevin, 279 *nn*.128, 129; 311 *n*.41
Thomson, Doug, 583 *n*.35
Thorlindsson, Thorolfur, 96, 103 *n*.64
Thornberry, Terence, 57, 76 *n*.24, 77 *n*.54, 78 *n*.70, 79 *n*.106, 80 *n*.137, 211 *n*.120, 242 *n*.2, 243 *nn*.26, 34, 35, 47; 244 *nn*.52, 70; 247 *n*.174, 302, 303, 304, 308, 311 *nn*.63, 65, 313 *nn*.103, 106, 107, 108, 111, 112, 114, 115, 119, 120, 453 *n*.140
Thorton, Marlene, 584 *nn*.49, 50
Thrasher, Frederick, 177, 208 *n*.6
Thurman, Quint, 510 *nn*.48, 58, 62
Tibbetts, Stephen, 310 *n*.13
Tidwell, Romeria, 511 *n*.104
Tifft, Larry, 76 *nn*.17, 18; 260, 270, 271, 277 *n*.52, 280 *nn*.136, 138, 139; 480 *n*.40
Tiger, Lionel, 321
Time, Victoria, 511 *n*.89
Tita, George, 102 *n*.47
Titchener, Edward, 157
Tittle, Charles, 66, 77 *nn*.55, 56; 134 *nn*.97, 123; 209 *n*.21, 212 *n*.163, 237, 242 *n*.3, 244 *n*.65, 247 *nn*.172, 173, 179; 289, 290, 291, 308, 310 *nn*.20, 35, 39; 311 *n*.43
Tjaden, Patricia, 362 *n*.224
Tobias, Aurelio, 311 *n*.60
Tobias, J. J., 385 *nn*.3, 4; 509 *n*.6
Tobin, Kimberly, 133 *n*.65
Tobin, Michael, 171 *n*.65
Toby, Jackson, 264, 277 *n*.40, 278 *n*.90
Toch, Hans, 173 *nn*.159, 164; 578, 586 *nn*.146, 150
Tocqueville, Alexis de, 583 *nn*.3, 14
Tolle, Glen, Jr., 442
Tomas, Josep, 311 *n*.60
Tonry, Michael, 45 *n*.8, 94, 103 *n*.67, 104 *n*.90, 132 *nn*.12, 15; 133 *n*.90, 169 *n*.16, 171 *n*.67, 172 *n*.116, 173 *n*.140, 209 *nn*.43, 47; 210 *nn*.65, 66; 242 *n*.6, 311 *n*.54, 336, 386 *n*.45, 452 *n*.91, 453 *n*.134, 509 *nn*.6, 26; 510 *n*.66, 551 *nn*.85, 86, 87, 94, 99, 584 *nn*.45, 46, 585 *n*.110, 586 *n*.146
Tontodonato, Pamela, 551 *n*.79
Torrance, Mark, 402
Torres, Jose, 57, 187
Towns-Miranda, Luz, 386 *n*.73
Tracy, Paul, 73, 79 *nn*.106, 132; 80 *nn*.138, 139; 135 *n*.145
Traub, Stuart, 413 *n*.14
Travis, Jeremy, 586 *n*.173
Traxler, Mary Pat, 242 *n*.15
Trebach, Arnold, 453 *n*.117
Tremblay, R., 80 *n*.140
Tremblay, Richard, 132 *n*.21, 171 *n*.70, 287, 310 *n*.20, 313 *n*.100

Trickett, Alan, 102 *n*.30
Triplett, Ruth, 247 *n*.166, 584 *n*.72
Trulson, Chad, 584 *n*.72
Trumbetta, Susan, 133 *n*.69, 359 *n*.79
Trump, Donald, 194
Tseng, Li-Jng, 243 *n*.22, 453 *n*.148
Tuch, Steven, 79 *n*.120, 509 *n*.4, 512 *n*.139
Tunnell, Kenneth, 112, 132 *n*.52, 223, 244 *n*.69, 438, 454 *n*.167
Turk, Austin, 257, 277 *nn*.26, 28
Turner, Charles, 311 *n*.63
Turner, Michael, 134 *n*.102
Turner, Susan, 277 *n*.43, 287, 518, 583 *n*.37
Turpin-Petrosino, Carolyn, 24 *n*.44
Tye, Larry, 414 *n*.38
Tyler, Kimberly, 359 *n*.89

Uggen, Christopher, 212 *n*.159, 269, 279 *nn*.126, 130; 314 *nn*.134, 137, 139
Ullman, Sarah, 359 *n*.78
Ulmer, Jeffrey, 79 *n*.115
Umbreit, Mark, 480 *n*.38
Unfold, Douglas, 386 *n*.74

Vaccaro, Donato, 211 *n*.126, 243 *n*.23, 453 *n*.149
Valdez, Joe, 374
Valliere, Evelyne, 243 *n*.33
van den Bergle, Pierre, 169 *n*.7
Van Den Haag, Ernest, 135 *n*.132, 552 *n*.120
van den Oord, Edwin, 174 *n*.108
van den Oord, Edwin J. C. G., 172 *n*.126
van der Does, Louise, 550 *n*.14
Vander ven, Thomas, 245 *nn*.114, 120
Van Dusen, Katherine Teilmann, 79–80 *n*.132, 173 *n*.137
Van Kammen, Welmoet, 76 *n*.20, 312 *n*.75
Van Koppen, Peter, 132 *n*.57, 361 *n*.196
Van Koppen, Peter J., 342, 344
Van Maanen, John, 479 *n*.13, 511 *n*.108
Van Stelle, 583 *n*.36
Van Voorhis, Patricia, 245 *nn*.108, 113
Van Wormer, Katherine, 357 *n*.8
Vasonyi, Alexander, 287
Vaughn, Michael, 359 *n*.81, 509 *n*.11
Vaughn (British Chief Judge), 31
Vazsonyi, Alexander, 78 *n*.98, 173 *nn*.142, 143; 310 *nn*.4, 21
Velez, Maria, 210 *n*.79
Venables, Peter, 172 *n*.106, 174 *n*.172
Veneziano, Carol, 173 *n*.170
Veneziano, Louis, 173 *n*.170
Vera Institute of Justice, 550 *n*.35
Verhovek, Sam Howe, 276 *n*.1
Verhulst, Frank, 172 *n*.126
Verlur, D. E., 453 *n*.151
Vernon, Philip, 172 *n*.108
Verona, Edelyn, 174 *n*.197
Veronen, Lois, 103 *n*.73
Veysey, Bonita, 78 *n*.68

Victor, Timothy, 24 *n*.43
Vieraitis, Lynne, 211 *n*.109
Vila, Bryan, 165
Vilbig, Peter, 545
Villemez, Wayne, 66, 77 *n*.55
Vincent, Mary, 125
Virkkunen, Matti, 170 *n*.34, 171 *n*.68, 172
    nn.99, 100, 287
Visher, Christy, 246 *n*.143, 277 *n*.36, 357
    n.10
Vistica, Gregory, 359 *n*.69
Vitaro, Frank, 287
Vitiello, Michael, 551 *n*.101
Vivian, Dina, 102 *n*.13
Voety, Harold, 132 *nn*.18, 19
Vogel, Nancy, 551 *n*.76
Volavka, Jan, 169 *n*.16, 170 *n*.50, 171 *n*.77,
    172 *n*.112
Vold, George, 9, 253, 254, 255, 275, 277
    n.14, 409, 415 *n*.130
Vollmer, August, 484
Von, Judith, 103 *n*.73
Von Hentig, Hans, 14, 24 *n*.23, 102 *n*.36
Von Hirsch, Andrew, 129, 136 *nn*.170, 171,
    172
von Krafft-Ebing, Richard, 422
Voronin, Yuri A., 410
Voss, Harwin, 70, 76 *n*.19, 79 *n*.103
Votey, Harold, 135 *n*.151
Vuchinich, S., 311 *n*.57

Wachtel, Julius, 65
Wagner, Charles, 386 *n*.73
Wagner, H. Ryan, 174 *n*.192
Wagner, Richard, 174 *n*.184
Waite, Linda, 313 *n*.122
Waldo, Gordon, 133–134 *n*.95, 134–135
    nn.127, 136; 277 *n*.42
Waldorf, Dan, 585 *nn*.102, 111
Walker, Alice, 419
Walker, Richard, 414 *n*.79
Walker, Samuel, 236, 247 *n*.164, 469, 471,
    472, 479 *nn*.2, 3, 15; 484, 495, 501,
    502, 503, 509 *nn*.6, 8, 12, 13; 510 *n*.52,
    511 *n*.134, 512 *nn*.142, 165; 543, 551
    n.90, 557, 583 *nn*.3, 10, 16, 18
Wallace, Danold, 552 *n*.119
Wallace, John, 453 *n*.153
Wallace, Rodrick, 209 *n*.14
Wallerstedt, John, 135 *n*.161
Walsh, Anthony, 140, 152, 169 *nn*.10, 11;
    170 *nn*.38, 44; 173 *n*.148, 211 *n*.122,
    310 *n*.10, 359 *n*.99
Walsh, Margaret, 318
Walsh, Marilyn, 385 *nn*.5, 15, 17
Walters, Glenn, 172 *n*.131, 173 *n*.153
Walton, Paul, 259, 277 *n*.49, 278 *n*.66
Wang, Jichuan, 454 *n*.175
Wanson, Jeffrey, 174 *n*.192
Warchol, Greg, 348, 362 *n*.223

Ward, D., 586 *n*.128
Ward, David, 159, 175 *n*.212
Waring, Elin, 134 *n*.105, 135 *n*.149, 415
    n.111, 510 *n*.65
Warneken, William, 361 *n*.187
Warner, Barbara, 209 *n*.40
Warr, Mark, 78 *n*.95, 102 *n*.19, 217, 223, 244
    nn.49, 50, 53, 67, 71; 305, 313 *nn*.123,
    129; 359 *n*.75
Warren, Earl, 472
Warren, James Earl, 517
Warren, Janet, 133 *n*.69, 327, 359 *n*.79
Warren, Mark R., 207
Warzeka, Malissa, 286
Wasilchick, John, 132 *nn*.16, 39
Wassef, Adel, 219
Waterman, Jaime, 165
Watkins, Sheron, 394
Wayner, Peter, 385 *n*.37
Weatherburn, Don, 103 *n*.61, 314 *n*.134,
    386 *n*.67
Webb, Barry, 133 *n*.79
Webb, Nancy, 386 *n*.73
Webb, V., 583 *n*.24
Weber, Eugene, 24 *n*.4, 45 *nn*.2, 4
Webster, Pamela, 313 *nn*.122, 124
Wei, Evelyn, 311 *n*.60
Weinberg, Daniel H., 208 *n*.8
Weinberg, Heather, 174 *n*.184
Weiner, Neil Alan, 101 *n*.2, 426, 452 *n*.69
Weingart, Saul, 455 *n*.208
Weis, Joseph, 54, 76 *n*.28, 77 *n*.59, 78–79
    n.99, 174 *n*.203, 242 *n*.7, 297, 312 *n*.95
Weis, Robert, 264
Weisberg, D. Kelly, 451 *n*.64
Weisburd, David, 120, 133 *n*.83, 86, 87, 134
    n.105, 135 *n*.149, 413 *n*.11, 415 *n*.111
Weisel, Deborah, 415 *n*.135
Weiser, Benjamin, 386 *n*.50
Weiser, Carl, 362 *n*.218
Weisheit, Ralph, 77 *n*.42, 452 *n*.113, 455
    n.221
Weiss, Alexander, 79 *n*.117, 509 *n*.24
Weiss, Robert, 278 *n*.84, 552 *n*.130
Weissman, Marsha, 551 *n*.91
Weitekamp, E., 312 *n*.84
Weitekamp, E. M., 78 *n*.70, 242 *n*.2
Weitzer, Ronald, 79 *n*.120, 452 *n*.74, 502,
    503, 509 *n*.4, 512 *n*.139
Welch, Donita, 326
Welch, Michael, 135 *n*.131, 455 *n*.206
Weldy, William, 512 *n*.151
Wells, Alice Stebbins, 504
Wells, James, 518
Wells, L. Edward, 76 *n*.16, 77 *n*.42, 242
    n.13, 243 *n*.17
Wells, Richard, 243 *n*.25
Welsh, Sandy, 102 *n*.16
Welte, John, 78 *n*.81, 313 *n*.113, 453 *n*.141,
    454 *n*.168

Welte, John W., 102 *n*.43
Wentworth, Jennifer, 360 *n*.118, 550 *n*.10
Wenzel, Suzanne, 518
Werch, Chudley E., 442
West, Ashley, 431
West, D. J., 76 *n*.19, 78 *n*.80, 80 *n*.134, 172
    nn.114, 115, 121, 122, 123; 313 *n*.101
West, Donald J., 148
West, Valerie, 179, 209 *n*.18, 264, 278
    n.83
Wester-Stratton, Carolyn, 243 *n*.25
Westly, William, 499, 511 *n*.106
Weston, Russell Eugene, Jr., 138, 155
Whaley, Rachel Bridges, 359 *n*.103
Wharton, Robert, 243 *n*.25
Wheaton, Blair, 313 *n*.125
Wheeler, Stanton, 415 *n*.111
Whipple, Dianee, 523
Whitbeck, Les, 359 *n*.89
White, Garland, 132 *n*.36, 37, 159
White, Helene, 454 *nn*.162, 186
White, Helene Raskin, 165, 211 *n*.123, 243
    n.42, 246 *n*.130, 294, 312 *nn*.70, 71,
    454 *n*.186
White, Jennifer, 80 *n*.141
White, Michael D., 513 *n*.179
White, Teresa, 550 *n*.53
White, Thomas, 173 *n*.153
Whitehall, George, 244 *n*.87
Whitehead, John, 586 *nn*.139, 144
Whiteman, Martin, 311 *n*.64
Whitman, Charles, 144, 146, 336
Whyte, William F., 20, 24 *n*.38
Wiatrowski, Michael, 245 *n*.107, 246
    nn.126, 133
Wickman, P., 413 *n*.2
Widom, Cathy Spatz, 102 *nn*.12, 20, 22;
    358 *n*.23
Wiechman, Dennis, 551 *n*.112
Wieczorek, William, 78 *n*.81, 102 *n*.43, 313
    n.113, 454 *n*.168
Wiederman, Michael, 101 *n*.11
Wiersma, Brian, 65, 83, 101 *n*.6
Wikberg, Ron, 585 *n*.98
Wikstrom, Per-Olof, 312 *n*.88
Wilbanks, William, 277 *n*.40
Wilcox, Pamela, 358 *n*.38, 360 *n*.152
Wild, Jack, 365
Wilkinson, Deanna, 447
Wilkinson, Paul, 362 *n*.229
Wilks, J., 586 *n*.136
Wilks, Judith, 479 *n*.20
Will, Richard, 584 *nn*.45, 46
Williams, Franklin, 278 *n*.82
Williams, James, 135 *n*.141
Williams, James L., 360 *n*.142
Williams, Kirk, 358 *n*.53, 360 *nn*.143, 145
Williams, Linda, 312 *n*.72
Williams, Linda Meyer, 279 *n*.118
Williams, Marian, 552 *n*.118

Allergies, 144
All God's Children (Butterfield), 70
Al-Qaeda, 349, 351, 352, 353, 354, 355, 474
Alternative sanctions, 536
Altruistic fear, 85
Amateur receivers, 370
American Bar Association, 48
American Bar Foundation, 460
American Beauty, 431
American Civil Liberties Union, 474
American Dream, 194, 195, 202
American Judges Association, 526
American Psychological Association, 158
America's Most Wanted, 3
Amnesty International, 353, 545
Amphetamines, 434
Anal stage, 154
Androgens, 68, 69, 143, 146
Anesthetics, 434
Anger rape, 326–327
Animal Liberation Front (ALF), 353
Annie E. Casey Foundation, 178
Anomie, 8, 192–193
Anomie theory, 193–194, 205
Antiabortion groups, 351
Anti-Drug Abuse Act (1986), 443
Anti-Drug Abuse Act (1988), 443
Anti-Saloon League, 433
Antisocial behavior
    biochemical conditions and, 141, 142, 143, 144
    control balance theory and, 291
    delinquent development theory and, 301
    developmental theories and, 307
    genetics and, 147
    latent trait theories and, 283
    life course theories and, 292, 293
    neurophysiological conditions and, 145, 146
    peer relations and, 217
    personality and, 162–165
    problem behavior syndrome and, 293
    punishment and, 125
    rational choice theory and, 116
    self-control and, 287, 289
    social development model and, 299, 300
    social reaction theory and, 235
    trait theories and, 139, 140
    victimization and, 85
Antithesis, 252
Anxiety disorder, 84
Anxiety disorders, 67
Apparent authority, 396
Appeal, 533
Appeal to higher loyalties, 226, 227
Appellate court, 43
Arousal theory, 115, 147, 164–165, 218
Arraignment, 467–468
Arrest-avoidance techniques, 111

Arrestee Drug Abuse Monitoring Program
    (ADAM), 440
Arrests
    child abuse and, 85
    chronic offenders and, 72, 73–74
    crimes cleared by, 50
    gender and, 69
    justice process and, 466–467
    race and, 70, 72
    self-report surveys and, 53
    social class and, 63, 66
    spousal abuse and, 126–127
    substance abuse and, 432, 439
    Uniform Crime Reports and, 51
Arson, 32, 34, 49, 364, 382, 383
Arson for profit, 382
Arson fraud, 382
Arthur Andersen company, 394
Aryan Nation, 351
Aryan Republican Army, 351
Asian Americans
    hate crimes and, 345
    organized crime and, 407
    as police, 501
    social class and, 181
    social reaction theory and, 236
Asphyxiophilia (autoerotic asphyxia), 422
Assassin, 350
Assault
    aging out and, 68
    chronic offenders and, 72
    as common-law crime, 34
    crime trends and, 58, 59
    definition of, 337
    ecological factors and, 61
    firearms and, 62, 65
    gender and, 68, 69
    history of, 29
    in home, 338–341
    National Crime Victimization Survey
        and, 52
    nature/extent of, 338
    as Part I index crime, 49
    social class and, 63, 66, 67
    victimization and, 83, 85
    victim service programs and, 98
    as violent crime, 337–341
    workplace violence and, 347
Assisted suicide, 4, 14, 42
Associational fences, 369–370
Atavistic anomalies, 7
At-risk, 179
Attachment, 229, 230, 231
Attempt, 34
Attention deficit hyperactivity disorder
    (ADHD), 145–146, 164, 297
Attica Prison, 558
Attitude surveys, 19
Attorney list/assigned counsel system, 524
Auburn system, 556

Aum Shinrikyo, 354
Authority conflict pathway, 295–296
Automobile search, 498
Awareness space, 113

Babe, 20
Bad checks, 373–374
Bad Kids (Feld), 464
Bail, 468, 527–529
Bail bonding agent, 527
Bail guidelines, 528
Bail Reform Act (1984), 529
Balashikha criminal gang, 353
Bank fraud, 395
Bank of Credit and Commerce
    International (BCCI), 390
Barbiturates, 434
Bar girls, 424
Bartley-Fox Law, 64
Battered Woman Syndrome, 43
Battery, 29, 34, 337–338
BCCI (Bank of Credit and Commerce
    International), 390
BEAM (Brain Electrical Activity Mapping),
    145
Behavioral Science Institute, 70
Behavior modeling, 156
Behavior problems, chronic offenders and,
    73
Behavior theories, 153, 154, 155–156, 168
Behavior therapy, 576
Beit Al-Mal Holdings, 355
Belief, 229–230, 231
Bell Curve, The (Herrnstein & Murray), 22,
    166
Best Little Whorehouse in Texas, The, 424
Beyond a reasonable doubt, 33
Beyond Probation (Murray & Cox), 108
*Beyond Tolerance: Child Pornography on the
    Internet* (Jenkins), 427
Bias crimes. *See* Hate crimes
Bill of Rights, 472
Biochemical conditions, biosocial trait
    theories and, 141–144, 168
Biological determinism, 7
Biological trait theories, criminological
    perspectives and, 10, 139–140
Biophobia, 140
Biosocial theory, 7
Biosocial trait theories
    arousal theory and, 147
    biochemical conditions and, 141–144, 168
    evaluation of, 151, 153
    evolutionary theory and, 141, 150–151,
        152, 168
    genetics and, 141, 147–150, 168
    murder and, 334
    neurophysiological conditions and, 141,
        144–147, 168
    psychological trait theories and, 154

Columbine High School massacre, 48, 60, 317
Combined DNA Index System (CODIS), 486
Commercial burglary, 379–380
Commercial robbery, 342
Commercial theft, 37
Commission of another crime, 375
Commitment, 229, 230, 231
Commitment to conformity, 228
Common law, 4, 29, 30–33, 34, 366, 527
Communications Decency Act (CDA), 431
Communist League, 251
Communist manifesto, 251
Communist Manifesto (Marx), 9
Communities in Schools program, 218–219
Community Action Program, 204
Community-based corrections, 558
Community change, 187–188
Community deterioration, 185
Community notification laws, 42
Community organization, 99
Community-oriented policing (COP), 206, 492–495, 496
Community sentencing, 125
Community service restitution, 563
Community sources of strain, 197–198
Community strategies, 445–446
Comparative research, 122–123
Complaint/charging, 467
Compliance strategies, 404
Comprehensive Crime Control Act, 95
Comprehensive Drug Abuse Prevention and Control Act (1970), 441
Compurgation, 28
Computer Abuse Amendments Act (1994), 406
Computer crimes, 399–401, 406
Computer viruses, 400–401
Concentration effect, 185
Concentric zones, 183–184, 205
Concurrent sentence, 536
Condemnation of condemners, 226, 227
Condition of the Working Class in England in 1844, The (Engels), 253
Conduct disorder (CD), 67, 146
Conduct norms, 200
Confidence games, 377
Configuring guidelines, 538
Conflict criminology, 9, 10, 16–17, 249, 255–257
Conflict gangs, 203
Conflict resolution, 476
Conflict theory, social conflict theory and, 250, 255–258
Conflict view of crime, 16–17, 260. *See also* Social conflict theory
Conformity, 193
Congregate system, 557
Conscience, 154

Conscientiousness, 162
Consecutive sentence, 536
Consensus-building, 273
Consensus view of crime, 15–16, 17
Consent, 330–331
Consent search, 498
Conspiracy, 34
Constables, 482, 555
Constituent Assembly (1789), 108
Constitution, U.S.
    First Amendment, 418, 427, 428, 430, 579
    Second Amendment, 64
    Fourth Amendment, 506
    Fifth Amendment, 462, 464, 497
    Sixth Amendment, 464, 472, 531, 533–534
    Eighth Amendment, 108, 546, 547, 579, 580
    Fourteenth Amendment, 462, 472, 534, 547
    Eighteenth Amendment, 433
    Twenty-First Amendment, 433
Constructive possession, 371
Contagion effect, 149
Containment theory, 228, 229, 241
Contextual discrimination, 236
Continuing Criminal Enterprises acts, 562
Continuity of crime, 73, 296
Contract law, 33
Contract system, 557
Control balance theory, 290–291, 308
Controlled Substances Act (1984), 441, 443
Controlling disinhibitors, 118
Controlling facilitators, 118
Convictional criminals, 349
Convict-lease system, 557, 558
COPA (Chicanos Organizados Pintos Aztlan), 577
COP (community-oriented policing), 206, 492–495, 496
COPPS, 496
Corner boy, 202
Corporal punishment, 554, 555
Corporate crime, 389, 396–397
Corporate culture theory, 401–403
Correctionalism, 263
Corrections. *See also* Criminal justice system; Incarceration; Intermediate sanctions; Probation; Punishment; Sentencing
    correctional treatment, 469
    criminal justice process and, 469
    criminal justice system and, 463
    felonies vs. misdemeanors and, 34
    history of, 554–558
    introduction to, 554
    parole and, 580–581
Counseling, 575–576
Counterfeit Active Device and Computer Fraud and Abuse Act (1986), 406
County law enforcement, 487

Courtroom work group, 472
Courts. *See* Judicatory process
Covert pathway, 296
CPI (California Personality Inventory), 163
CPPA (Child Pornography Prevention Act), 431
Crack, 434, 538, 542
Crackdowns, 122, 495–496
Credit card theft, 374
Crime
    benefits of, 116, 185
    common-law crimes, 34
    compensation for, 29
    conflict view of, 16–17, 18
    consensus view of, 15–16, 17, 18
    criminality distinguished from, 109
    definitions of, 17–18
    interactionist view of, 17–18
    legal definition of, 26, 37–39
    structuring of, 111–112
Crime, Shame and Reintegration (Braithwaite), 271
Crime and Coercion (Colvin), 289
Crime and Everyday Life (Felson), 96
Crime and Human Nature (Wilson & Herrnstein), 165, 284
Crime and Punishment in America (Currie), 477
Crime and the American Dream (Messner & Rosenfeld), 194
Crime Commission, 460
Crime control model, 473–474, 477
Crime data collection, 48–49
Crime discouragers, 118–119, 120, 121
Crime displacement, 120
Crime in the Making (Sampson & Laub), 304
Crime Laboratory, 486
Crime patterns
    age and, 67–68
    criminal careers and, 72–74
    criminological enterprise and, 11, 14
    ecology of crime and, 61
    firearms and, 62
    gender and, 68–70
    gun control and, 64–65
    race and, 70–72
    social class and, 63, 66–67
    victimization and, 82, 85–86
Crime prevention
    general deterrence strategies, 117, 120–124, 126
    incapacitation strategies, 117, 125–129
    self-protection and, 99
    situational crime prevention, 117–120
    social structure theories and, 206–207
    specific deterrence strategies, 117, 124–127, 130
    trait theories and, 166
Crime Prevention through Environmental Design (Jeffery), 117
Crime rates, 12–13, 14, 51, 55

Crimes of reduction, 262
Crimes of repression, 262
Crime trends, 55–60
Crime typology, 14
Crime Victims Board of New York, 97
Criminal anthropology, 7
Criminal attempt law, 32
Criminal behavior systems, 11, 14
Criminal careers
    age of onset and, 296–297
    antisocial behavior and, 164, 165
    burglary and, 380–382
    cohort research and, 19, 21
    crime patterns and, 72–74
    cultural deviance theory and, 200
    developmental theories and, 282, 283,
        306
    differential association theory and, 223
    differential opportunity theory and, 203
    differential reinforcement theory and,
        224
    educational experience and, 216
    incarceration and, 191
    juvenile crime and, 292, 307
    labeling theory and, 17
    life course theories and, 292, 293
    lifestyle theory of victimization and, 92
    pathways to crime and, 295–296
    peer group influence and, 217
    rational choice theory and, 110–111
    selective incapacitation and, 128
    social process theory and, 214
    social reaction theory and, 233, 237
    strain theory and, 192, 198–199
    theft and, 366–368
    trait theories and, 140
    violent crimes and, 3
Criminal Copyright Infringement Act, 406
Criminal courts, criminal justice system
        and, 462–463
Criminal defenses, 39–40, 43
Criminal gangs, 203
Criminality
    crime distinguished from, 109
    structuring of, 109–111
Criminal justice field, 4, 14
Criminal Justice Information Services
        (CJIS), 486
Criminal justice system. *See also*
        Discrimination in criminal justice
        system
    age-graded theory and, 306
    biosocial trait theory and, 166
    components of, 460–463
    corrections and, 463
    costs of, 460–461, 477
    crime control model, 473–474, 477
    criminal courts and, 462–463
    criminal justice funnel, 470
    due process model, 474–475, 477
    general deterrence strategies and, 124

history of, 459–460
influence peddling and, 392–393
introduction to, 459
justice concepts and, 472–477
justice model, 474, 477
justice process and, 463, 466–472
juvenile justice system compared to,
    464, 465
law enforcement and, 461–462
Marxist criminology and, 263
modern era of, 460
nonintervention model, 476, 477
police and, 461–462, 482
rape and, 330
rehabilitation model, 475–476, 477
restorative justice and, 476–477
rule of law and, 472
social conflict theory and, 249, 257
social reaction theory and, 233, 237, 240
stage in justice process, 466
victimization and, 84
victim service programs and, 97–98
victims' rights and, 98–99
wedding cake model of, 469, 471, 472
Criminal law. *See* Law
Criminal life course theories
    age-graded theory and, 304–306, 308
    as developmental theories, 297–306
    Farrington's delinquent development
        theory and, 301–302, 308
    interactional theory and, 302–304
    social development model and, 297,
        299–301, 308
Criminal procedure, 472, 473
Criminal statistics
    compatibility of sources, 54–55
    criminological enterprise and, 11–12
    murder and, 332
    self-report surveys and, 53–54
    Uniform Crime Report and, 49–52
Criminal terrorism, 353
Criminological enterprise, 11–15
Criminologists, 3–4, 11
Criminology field
    as academic discipline, 3–4
    Chicago School and, 8–9
    classical criminology and, 5–6, 10
    conflict criminology and, 9, 10
    contemporary criminology and, 10–11
    criminological enterprise and, 11–15
    definition of, 4
    definition of crime and, 17–18
    ethical issues and, 20, 21–22
    history of, 4–11
    nineteenth-century positivism and, 6–7,
        10
    perspectives of, 10
    research methods and, 4, 18–20
    sociological criminology and, 7–8, 10
    view of crime and, 15–17
Crisis intervention, 98

Critical criminology, 249
Critical Incident Response Group (CIRG),
    486
Cross-examination, 532
Cross-sectional research, 19
Crusades, 365
Crush, The, 138
Crusted over, 322
"Crying for help" fire setter, 383
Cultural deviance theory
    culture conflict and, 200, 205
    delinquent subcultures theory, 201–202,
        205
    differential association theory and, 223
    differential opportunity theory and,
        202–203, 205
    focal concerns and, 200–201, 205
    as social structure theory, 182, 199–200,
        205
Cultural transmission, 182
Cultural values, 323–324
Culture conflict, 200, 205, 222
Culture Conflict and Crime (Sellin), 200
Culture of poverty, 179
Custodial interrogation, 496–498
Custody, 467
Customs Bureau, 486
Cycle of violence, 85

DARE (Drug Abuse Resistance
    Education), 446, 447
Dark Ages, 27, 29
Data leakage, 400
Date rape, 93–94, 160, 327, 328
Day fines, 561–562
Deadly force, 506
DEA (Drug Enforcement Administration),
    486
Death penalty. *See* Capital punishment
Death squads, 353
Decadence, 291
*Decemviri Consulari Imperio Legibus
    Scribundis,* 27
Deceptive pricing, 397
Declaration of the Rights of Man, 108
Deconstructionism, 249, 269–270, 275
Deconstructionist analysis, 269
Decriminalization, 42, 476
Defective intelligence, 153
Defense attorneys, 469, 524–525
Defense of Marriage Law (1996), 421
Defense's case, 532
Defensible space, 117
Defiance, 291
Deflecting offenders, 118
Deinstitutionalization, 476
Deliberation, 332
Delinquency and Opportunity (Cloward &
    Ohlin), 202
Delinquency in a Birth Cohort (Wolfgang,
    Figlio & Sellin), 72

Delinquent boys, 202
Delinquent Boys (Cohen), 201
Delinquent development theory, 301–302, 308
"Delinquent" fire setters, 383
Delinquent subcultures theory, 201–202, 205, 323
Denial of injury, 225, 227
Denial of responsibility, 225, 227
Denial of victim, 225–226, 227
Denying benefits, 118
Departmental factors, 500
Deposit bail system, 528
Depression, 84
Desert/retribution, 535
Detection avoidance techniques, 111
Detention, 468
Determinate sentences, 537, 543, 569, 580
Deterministic biology, 151
Deterrence strategies, 404
Deterrence theory
    capital punishment and, 544, 546
    classical criminology and, 10
    general deterrence strategies, 117, 120–124, 126
    punishment and, 121, 122–124
    sentencing and, 535
    specific deterrence strategies and, 117, 124–125, 129
Developmental theories
    criminal life course theories and, 297–306
    evaluation of, 306–308
    introduction to, 282–283
    latent trait theories and, 283–291, 308
    life course theories, 283, 291–297, 308
Deviance, 4, 8, 17
Deviance amplification, 236
Deviant behavior, 16
Deviant cliques, 235
Deviant place theory, 92, 100
Dialectic method, 252
Diet, 141–142
Differential association theory, 220–224
Differential coercion theory, 289–290, 308
Differential enforcement, 234
Differential opportunity theory, 202–203, 205
Differential reinforcement, 224
Differential reinforcement theory, 224–225
Differential social control, 235
Diffusion, 119–120
Diffusion of benefits, 496
Direct conditioning, 224
Directed verdict, 532
Direct examination, 532
Dirty Harry, 489
Discouragement, 120
Discretion
    police and, 499–501, 502
    prosecutorial discretion, 520, 522–524

sentencing and, 537, 538–540
social conflict theory and, 258
social reaction theory and, 236
Discrimination in criminal justice system
    capital punishment and, 544, 546, 547
    crime patterns and, 70–71
    institutional racism and, 71
    jury selection and, 531
    juvenile justice system and, 464
    Marxist criminology and, 259, 264
    police and, 70, 482, 502–503
    prison life and, 573
    radical feminist theory and, 267–269
    rehabilitation model and, 475
    sentencing and, 542–543
    social conflict theory and, 255, 256, 258
    social reaction theory and, 236
    structured sentencing and, 538
Disinhibition, 158
Disorders, 155
Disposition, 468
Disturbing the peace, 34
Diversion programs, 240, 448
Division of Labor in Society, The (Durkheim), 8
Division of markets, 396
DNA evidence, 475
Doing gender, 267
Doing Justice (Von Hirsch), 129
Domestic violence. *See* Spousal abuse
Double jeopardy, 534
Dramatization of evil, 235
Dressed to Kill, 138
Drift, 225
Driving While Black, 70, 71
Drug Abuse Control Act (1965), 441
Drug Abuse Resistance Education (DARE), 446, 447
Drug court, 518
Drug dealing/trafficking
    anomie theory and, 193
    chronic offenders and, 74
    crime trends and, 57
    criminal terrorism and, 353
    drug control strategies and, 443–444
    drug court and, 518
    drug legalization and, 448
    fear and, 187
    gangs and, 111
    high-risk lifestyle and, 92
    incarceration and, 128
    law enforcement and, 444
    mandatory sentencing and, 538
    murder and, 13, 86
    National Incident-Based Reporting System and, 52
    organized crime and, 405
    rational choice theory and, 107, 110–111, 112, 113–114, 115
    robbery and, 344
    routine activities theory and, 96, 111

sentencing and, 541
situational crime prevention and, 120
social class and, 63
social learning theory and, 223
violence and, 324, 442
violent crimes and, 3
Drug Enforcement Administration (DEA), 486
Drug-Free Workplace Program, 446
Drug legalization/decriminalization, 3, 4, 33, 42, 43, 432, 448–449
Drug marts, 114
Drug-testing programs, 446
Dual sovereignty doctrine, 534
Due process, 462, 464, 541, 580
Due process model, 474–475, 477
Dunblane Massacre, 319
Duress, 39
Durham-Humphrey Act (1951), 441

Early onset, 68, 298, 301
Earth Liberation Front (ELF), 351, 353
EAS (electronic article surveillance), 373
Eastern European crime groups, 407, 409
Eastern Penitentiary, 556–557
Ecclesiastics, 29
Ecological factors
    crime patterns and, 61, 62
    robbery and, 341
    self-control and, 286, 288
Ecological view of crime, 9
E-commerce, 60
Economic compulsive behavior, 323
Economic crimes, 364–365. *See also* Property crimes
Economic issues. *See also* Social class; Social conflict theory; Social structure theories
    bail and, 529
    chronic offenders and, 73
    crime trends and, 56, 60
    gender and, 69
    general deterrence strategies and, 124
    hate crimes and, 345
    incarceration and, 128–129
    institutional anomie theory and, 194–195
    Marxist criminology and, 259, 260–261
    Marxist thought and, 252, 253
    race and, 71–72
    radical feminist theory and, 266–267
    rational choice theory and, 109–110
    routine activities theory and, 95
    social class and, 66, 67
    social conflict theory and, 249, 254, 256
    social reaction theory and, 234
    victimization and, 83, 84
    white-collar crime and, 110
Economics, 4
Ectomorphs, 139
Edgework, 115

Edna McConnell Clark Foundation, 21

Educational experience, socialization and, 216–217

Educational programs in prisons, 576, 577

EEG (electroencephalograph), 144–145

Ego, 154, 155

Ego ideal, 154

Eighteenth Amendment, 433

Eighth Amendment, 108, 546, 547, 579, 580

Elder abuse, 87, 88

Eldercide, 333

Electra complex, 154

Electroencephalograph (EEG), 144–145

Electronic article surveillance (EAS), 373

Electronic Communications Privacy Act of 1986, 406

Electronic monitoring (EM), 564

ELF (Earth Liberation Front), 351, 353

Elite deviance, 267

Embezzlement
  aging out and, 68
  business enterprise and, 32, 37
  computer crime and, 399
  history of, 377–378
  National Incident-Based Reporting System and, 52
  white-collar crime and, 388, 390, 393–394, 401

EM (electronic monitoring), 564

Empirical methods, 6

Employment
  age-graded theory and, 304, 305, 306
  criminal careers and, 307
  delinquent development theory and, 301
  incarceration and, 190, 191
  Marxist criminology and, 260–261, 264
  probation services and, 560
  radical feminist theory and, 266, 268
  recidivism and, 581
  social class and, 180–181
  social disorganization theory and, 186
  social reaction theory and, 232
  social structure theories and, 178
  substance abuse programs, 448
  vocational rehabilitation, 576–577
  workplace violence, 347

Endomorphs, 139

English common law, 4, 29, 30–33, 34, 366, 527

English Convict, The (Goring), 153

Enron Corporation, 394, 402–403

Enterprise theory of investigation (ETI), 411

Entrapment, 39

Entry/exit screening, 118

Environmental contaminants, 39, 144

Environmental crimes
  compliance strategies and, 404
  corporate crime and, 396, 397

crime trends and, 60
terrorism and, 351, 353
white-collar crime and, 389

Environmental factors
  Marxist criminology and, 265
  nurture theory and, 163–164
  personality and, 162
  police discretion and, 499–500
  social disorganization theory and, 181–182
  social learning theory and, 156

Environmental terrorism, 351, 353

Equipotentiality, 141

Equity/restitution, 535

Equivalent group hypothesis, 100

Eros, 154, 322

Escort services/call houses, 424–425

Estrogen, 143

Ethical issues
  capital punishment and, 123
  criminology field and, 20, 21–22

ETI (enterprise theory of investigation), 411

Evolutionary theory
  biosocial trait theories and, 141, 150–151, 152, 168
  rape and, 329
  spousal abuse and, 340
  violence and, 322

Exclusionary rule, 98

Exhibitionism, 423

Expedience killers, 336

Experimental research, 20

Exploitation, 291, 392

Expressive crimes, 63

Expressive violence, 317

Extinction, 120

Extralegal factors, 501

Extroversion-introversion, 162

Facilitation compliance, 118

False claims and advertising, 397

False pretenses/fraud, 32, 37, 68, 112, 376–377

Family courts, 418

Family environment
  antisocial behavior and, 164
  assault and, 338–341
  chronic offenders and, 73
  delinquent development theory and, 301
  female crime and, 298
  incarceration and, 190
  interactional theory and, 302, 304
  life course theories and, 292
  murder and, 333–334
  parental deviance and, 147–148
  personality and, 163
  power-control theory and, 269
  problem behavior syndrome and, 294
  social bonds and, 229, 231, 232

social class and, 67
social development model and, 299
socialization and, 214–216
social learning theory and, 156
social reaction theory and, 236
substance abuse and, 437, 438
surrogate families in prisons, 575
violence and, 319–322

Family structure
  age-graded theory and, 304, 305
  crime patterns and, 68
  criminal careers and, 307
  delinquent development theory and, 301
  homosexuality and, 421
  prostitution and, 425
  race and, 72
  socialization and, 214–216
  victimization and, 86, 88–89
  violence and, 318

Family Virtual Visitation Program, 574

Fan, The, 138

FARC (Revolutionary Armed Forces of Columbia), 353

Fatal Attraction, 138

FCPA (Foreign Corrupt Practices Act), 393

Fear, 138

Fear
  antisocial behavior and, 165
  crime control model and, 473
  gangs and, 187
  incarceration and, 191
  Marxist criminology and, 259
  media and, 3
  murder and, 334
  race and, 187
  self-control and, 288
  self-protection and, 99
  sexual abuse and, 339
  situational crime prevention and, 120
  social disorganization theory and, 186–187
  stalking and, 348
  victimization and, 84–85, 186
  workplace violence and, 347

Federal Bureau of Investigation (FBI). *See also* Uniform Crime Reports (UCR)
  aggregate data research and, 20
  law enforcement and, 485–486
  victimization and, 82–83

Federal Bureau of Prisons, 568

Federal courts, 517–520, 521

Federal courts of appeal, 517

Federal Crime Control Act (1994), 507, 540

Federal government. *See also* Governmental role; Policy issues
  influence peddling and, 392
  law enforcement and, 485–487
  social conflict theory and, 255
  social structure theory and, 204
  victimization and, 95

Federal Gun Control Act of 1968, 64

Federal Speedy Trial Act (1974), 534
Federal Welfare Reform Act of 1996, 204
Felonies
    classification of, 33–34
    criminal justice system and, 471
    gun control and, 64
    history of, 554
    incarceration and, 558
    murder and, 332
    probation and, 559, 561
    social class and, 66
Female crime. *See also* Gender; Women
    chronic offenders and, 72
    criminal careers and, 296
    evolutionary theory and, 151
    feminist views of, 69
    intelligence and, 166
    masculinity hypothesis and, 68
    murder and, 333
    observational research and, 20
    radical feminist theory and, 267
    rational choice theory and, 110, 113
    robbery and, 343
    serial murder and, 337
    social class and, 69
    socialization and, 69
    violence and, 298
    white-collar crime and, 401
Female Offender, The (Lombroso), 68
Feminist theory, 69, 151, 249, 260,
    266–269, 329, 426
Fences, 364, 368–371, 380, 381, 407
Feticide, 332
Fifth Amendment, 462, 464, 497
Fines, 535, 555
Firearms
    change in law and, 43
    children and, 85
    crime trends and, 56
    handgun possession legalization and, 4
    high-risk lifestyle and, 92
    juvenile crime and, 64, 65, 323, 495
    mandatory sentencing and, 538
    rational choice theory and, 113, 115
    self-protection and, 99
    subculture of violence and, 324
    violence and, 323
    violent crimes and, 3
First Amendment, 418, 427, 428, 430, 579
First-degree murder, 32, 34, 332
First International Drug Conference, 432
Fixated development, 154
Fixed-site neighborhoods, 114
Flash houses, 365
Flashover, 382
Focal concerns, 200–201, 205
Folkways, 27, 35, 36–37
Foot patrol, 489
Foreign Corrupt Practices Act (FCPA), 393
Foreign Terrorist Asset Tracking Center,
    355

Foreign Terrorist Tracking Task Force, 355
Forfeiture, 29, 555, 562
Formal surveillance, 118
Fortune society, 577
48 Hours, 364
Fourteenth Amendment, 462, 472, 534,
    547
Fourth Amendment and, 506
Fourth Lateran Council, 31
Fraud, 32, 37, 68, 112, 376–377, 390
Fraudulent offerings of securities, 399
Freebase, 434
Free choice view, 426
Free will, 5
French Reign of Terror, 350
French Revolution, 350
Friday the 13th, Part 1, 138
Front running, 390
Frotteurism, 423
Fugitives, 64
Fundamental fairness, 462

Gambling, 17, 32, 68, 405
Gang, The (Thrasher), 177
Gang rapes, 327, 328
Gangs
    carjacking and, 376
    credit card theft and, 374
    crime trends and, 56–57
    differential opportunity theory and,
        202–203
    drug dealing/trafficking and, 111
    fear and, 187
    gender and, 70
    high-risk lifestyle and, 92
    interactional theory and, 302
    international perspective on, 12
    juvenile justice system and, 464
    left realism and, 265
    murder and, 86, 332, 336
    in prisons, 572, 579
    rational choice theory and, 116
    social disorganization theory and, 184,
        186, 188
    social structure theories and, 177, 204
    strain theory and, 192
    violence and, 323, 324
Gangster Disciples, 411
Gatekeepers, 482
Gateway model, 438
Gay bashing, 343, 345, 420
Gender. *See also* Men; Sexism; Women
    assault and, 338
    brain chemistry and, 147
    capital punishment and, 546
    cartographic school of criminology
        and, 8
    crime patterns and, 68–70
    criminal defenses and, 43
    differential association theory and, 223
    evolutionary theory and, 150

    general theory of crime and, 288
    hormonal influences and, 143
    male/female ratio, 318
    mothers who kill children and, 321
    parole and, 581
    power-control theory and, 269
    property crimes and, 366
    radical feminist theory and, 266–267
    robbery and, 341, 344
    self-control and, 286
    self-report surveys and, 53
    sentencing and, 541
    serial murder and, 337
    social control theory and, 231
    stalking and, 348
    strain theory and, 199
    victimization and, 86
    violence and, 322
General deterrence strategies, 117,
    120–124, 126, 130
General strain theory (GST), 196–199, 205
General Theory of Crime, A (Gottfredson &
    Hirschi), 284, 286
General theory of crime (GTC), 68,
    284–289, 308
Genetics
    biosocial trait theories and, 141,
        147–150, 168
    nature theory and, 163
    sociobiology and, 140
    substance abuse and, 437
Gentrification, 188
Ghetto, The (Wirth), 177
Glucose metabolism, 142
Godfather, 405
Gold Coast and the Slum, The (Zorbaugh),
    177
Gone With the Wind, 328
Good burglar, 3880
Good Son, The, 138
Governmental role
    Marxist criminology and, 259, 260–261,
        263–264
    nonintervention model and, 476
    peacemaking movement and, 270
    social conflict theory and, 249, 250, 255
    terrorism and, 325, 349, 353
    violence and, 317
Government crime, 22
Grand jury, 467
Grand larceny, 371–372
Greed, 401
Group boycotts, 396
Group counseling, 576
Group of Eight, 249
GST (general strain theory), 196–199, 205
GTC (general theory of crime), 68,
    284–289
Guardians, 118, 119
Guerilla, 350
Guilty by Reason of Insanity (Lewis), 319

Passive precipitation, 91
Patriarchy, 266–267, 268
Patricians, 27
Patrol function, 489
Patterns in Criminal Homicide (Wolfgang), 14
PBS (problem behavior syndrome), 293–295, 437
Peacemaking movement, 233, 249, 257, 260, 270–271, 273, 275
Pedophiles, 42
Pedophilia, 423
Peer group influence
  age-graded theory and, 306
  Chicago school and, 9
  criminal careers and, 307
  date rape and, 93–94
  differential association theory and, 221, 223–224
  differential reinforcement theory and, 224
  general theory of crime and, 288–289
  interactional theory and, 302
  life course theories and, 292, 293
  neutralization theory and, 226
  occasional criminals and, 366
  social control theory and, 228, 229, 231
  socialization and, 217
  social learning theory and, 227
  social sources of strain and, 197, 199
  substance abuse and, 436, 447
Penitentiaries, 463, 568. *See also* Incarceration
Pennsylvania system, 556–557
Penology, 11, 14
Penthouse, 17
Peremptory challenges, 531
Periodic markets, 114
Permeable neighborhoods, 111
Persistence of crime, 73, 74
Personality
  general theory of crime and, 288
  mass murderers and, 3365
  police and, 499
  psychological trait theories and, 153, 162–163
  rape and, 329–330
  serial murderers and, 336, 337
Personal relations, 334
PET (Positron Emission Tomography), 145
Petty larceny, 34, 371–372
Phallic stage, 154
Philadelphia Society for Alleviating the Miseries of Public Prisons, 556
Phrenologists, 6
Physiognomists, 6
Pigeon drop, 377
Pilferage, 393, 401
Plain sight search, 498
"Playing with matches" fire setter, 383

Plea bargaining, 98, 463, 468, 522, 524, 529–530
Pleasure principle, 154, 155
Plebeians, 27
Pledge system, 482
PLO (Palestinian Liberation Organization), 351
Plunder, 291
PMS (Premenstrual syndrome), 43, 143–144
Poachers, 365
Police
  aggressive policing and, 489, 490
  assault and, 338
  citizen encounters and, 493
  clearance rate and, 50
  collective efficacy and, 189
  community-oriented policing, 492–495
  crime displacement and, 120
  criminal justice process and, 469
  criminal justice system and, 461–462, 482
  custodial interrogation and, 496–498
  differential enforcement and, 234
  discretion and, 499–501, 502
  diversity of, 501–502
  elder abuse and, 88
  fear and, 187
  firearms and, 64
  gender and, 68
  general deterrence strategies and, 121–122
  history of, 482–485
  influence peddling and, 392–393
  introduction to, 482
  investigative function, 489, 491
  issues of, 498–505
  left realism and, 265
  Marxist criminology and, 264
  metropolitan police, 487–488
  minority police officers, 502–504
  notable achievements of, 485
  patrol function, 489
  problem-oriented policing, 495–496
  prosecutor and, 522
  race and, 70, 71, 501–504
  radical feminist theory and, 268
  rape and, 326, 327, 330
  rational choice theory and, 111, 112
  role of, 491–496
  rule of law and, 496–498
  search and seizure and, 498
  social class and, 63, 66
  social conflict theory and, 256, 258
  social disorganization theory and, 185
  social structure theories and, 206
  spousal abuse and, 340, 341
  state police, 487
  subculture of, 499
  Uniform Crime Reports and, 51
  victim advocacy and, 99

  victimization and, 84
  violence and, 505–507
  women as police officers, 501, 502, 504–505
Police Foundation, 496
Policy issues
  chronic offenders and, 74
  drug abuse resistance education and, 447
  elder abuse and, 88
  gun control and, 64–65
  incarceration and, 190–191, 570
  insanity plea and, 41
  internet crime and, 406
  jury trials and, 31
  juvenile crime and, 307
  juvenile justice system and, 464
  rational choice theory and, 109, 129
  rehabilitation and, 577
  situational crime prevention and, 119
  social class and, 181
  social conflict theory and, 271–274
  social process theories and, 238–239
  social structure theories and, 204, 206–207
  specialized courts and, 518
  trait theories and, 166–167
  ultra-maximum-security prisons and, 570
Political crimes, terrorism as, 349–355
Political science, 4
Political terrorists, 351
Poor laws, 555
Population density, 61
Populations, 19
Pornography
  child pornography, 82, 427, 428, 431
  control of, 430
  interactionist view of crime and, 17
  Internet crime and, 398
  law and, 428–430
  organized crime and, 405
  as public order crime, 427–431
  technological change and, 430–431
  victimization and, 35
  violence and, 427–428, 429
Positivism, 6–7, 10, 139
Positivist criminology, 6–7, 108, 109, 259, 260
Positron Emission Tomography (PET), 145
Posse Comitatus, 351
Postconviction remedies, 468–469
Postmodernism, 249, 269–270
Postrelease/aftercare, 469
Posttraumatic stress disorder, 84, 85, 95, 339
Poverty. *See* Social class
Poverty concentration, 185–186
Power-control theory, 269
Power rape, 326–327

Power relations
  left realism and, 265
  Marxist criminology and, 259, 261,
    262–263, 264
  Marxist thought and, 252
  radical feminist theory and, 266, 267
  social conflict theory and, 249, 250, 255,
    256–257, 258
  social reaction theory and, 234, 236
Precedents, 517
Predation, 291
Preemptive deterrence, 265
Preliminary hearing, 467
Premeditation, 332
Premenstrual syndrome (PMS), 43, 143–144
Preponderance of the evidence, 33
Prescriptive sentencing, 538
Presentence investigation report, 536
Present federal law, 40
Press, freedom of, 579
Pretrial diversion, 476
Pretrial procedures, 527–530
Pretrial release, 528
Pretty Woman, 424
Preventive detention, 98, 527, 529
Price-fixing, 388, 389, 396, 397
Primary deviance, 235–236, 237
Princess Diaries, 20
Principles of Criminology (Sutherland), 220
Prison camps, 568
Prison Community, The (Clemmer), 573
Prisoners' rights movement, 558
Prison farms, 568
Prisonization process, 573
Prisons, 463, 568–569. *See also*
    Incarceration
Private industry in prison, 577
Private prisons, 568–569
Probable cause, 467
Probable cause hearing, 467
Probation
  as community-based corrections, 558
  definition of, 33, 463, 558–559
  probationary sentences, 559
  probation organizations, 559
  probation services, 559–560
  rules and revocation of, 560
  sentencing and, 535–536
  success of, 560–561
Probationary sentences, 559
Probation organizations, 559
Probation services, 559–560
Problem behavior syndrome (PBS),
    293–295, 437
Problem-oriented policing, 495–496
Productive forces, 251
Productive relations, 251
Professional chiseling, 390
Professional criminals, 366–368
Professional fence, 368–369, 370

Professional robbers, 342
Professional Thief, The (Sutherland &
    Conwell), 367
Profit, 375
Profit killers, 336
Progesterone, 143
Proletariat, 9, 251, 253–254, 262
Property crimes. *See also* Burglary
  arson, 32, 34, 49, 364, 382, 383
  chronic offenders and, 74
  crime patterns and, 62, 85, 86
  crime trends and, 58
  gender and, 69
  history of theft, 364–366
  incarceration and, 127
  introduction to, 364
  larceny, 34, 37, 49, 52, 58, 68, 96,
    364–378
  Marxist criminology and, 263, 264
  punishment and, 37
  race and, 70
  self-protection and, 99
  self-report surveys and, 59
  sentencing and, 541
  social conflict theory and, 257
Property law, 33
Prosecution (Miller), 523
Prosecution's case, 532
Prosecutorial discretion, 520, 522–524
Prosecutors, 469, 520–524, 532
Prosocial bonds, 299
Prostitution
  becoming a prostitute, 425–426
  children and, 82
  consensus view of crime and, 16
  control of, 426
  incidence of, 423–424
  interactionist view of crime and, 17
  legalization of, 426–427
  organized crime and, 405
  as public order crime, 423–427
  situational crime prevention and, 118
  types of, 424–425
  vice squads and, 491
Proximity hypothesis, 100
Psycho, 20, 138
Psychoanalytic perspective, 154
Psychodynamic theory
  psychological trait theories and, 153,
    154–155, 168
  substance abuse and, 436–437
Psychological abuse, 84
Psychological trait theories
  behavior theories and, 153, 154, 155–156,
    168
  cognitive theory and, 153, 154, 157, 160,
    168
  criminological perspectives and, 10
  history of, 153–154
  intelligence and, 153, 163–166

  mental illness and, 153, 161–162
  personality and, 153, 162–163
  psychodynamic perspective and, 153,
    154–155, 168
  social learning theory and, 153, 156–157
Psychology, 4
Psychopathia Sexualis (von Krafft-Ebing),
    422
Psychopathic personality, 7, 162–163, 164
Psychopharmacological relationship,
    322–323
Psychosexual stages of human
    development, 154
Psychosurgery, 166
Psychotics, 155
Public defenders, 524–525
Public education, 98
Public opinion, 35–36, 40
Public order crimes
  homosexuality and, 420–422
  introduction to, 417
  morality and, 417–420
  paraphilias and, 422–423
  pornography and, 427–431
  prostitution and, 423–427
  substance abuse and, 432–449
Public safety doctrine, 497
Public social control, 189
Pulp Fiction, 17
Punishing Hate (Lawrence), 346
Punishment
  chronic offenders and, 72, 73
  classical criminology and, 5–6, 107, 108
  Code of Hammurabi and, 27
  common law and, 32
  crime trends and, 57
  deterrence theory and, 121, 122–124, 129
  discrimination in criminal justice
    system and, 71
  felonies vs. misdemeanors and, 34
  feudal period and, 28–29
  general deterrence strategies and, 121
  hate crimes and, 346–347
  history of, 4–5, 27, 28–29, 32, 534,
    554–558, 566
  inmates' rights and, 579–580
  international perspective on, 13
  just desert and, 129
  law's function and, 36–37
  Marxist criminology and, 264
  Middle Ages and, 4–5
  peacemaking movement and, 270–271
  property crimes and, 37
  punishment ladder, 562
  rational choice theory and, 108, 109, 117
  restorative justice and, 476
  severity of, 122–124
  specific deterrence strategies and,
    124–125
  substance abuse and, 444–445

wergild and, 28
white-collar crime and, 364, 403–405
Pure Food and Drug Act (1906), 441

Quakers, 556

Race. *See also* Discrimination in criminal
  justice system
    biosocial trait theory and, 151
    capital punishment and, 546
    conflict view of crime and, 17
    crime patterns and, 70–72
    crime trends and, 56
    evolutionary theory and, 152
    fear and, 187
    general theory of crime and, 288
    hate crimes and, 345
    IQ tests and, 164, 166
    murder and, 333
    police and, 70, 71, 501–504
    police use of force and, 506
    in prisons, 572–573, 574
    prosecutor and, 523
    prostitution and, 424
    rape and, 326
    robbery and, 341, 344
    self-control and, 286
    self-report surveys and, 53
    sentencing and, 541
    social class and, 71, 178, 180–181
    social disorganization theory and, 185
    social reaction theory and, 234, 236
    victim/criminal relationship and, 89
    victimization and, 89
Race, Evolution and Behavior (Rushton), 152
Racial assaults, 12
Racial profiling, 70, 462, 482, 501, 502–503
Racism. *See* Discrimination in criminal
  justice system; Hate crimes; Race;
  Social structure theories
Racketeer Influenced and Corrupt
  Organization Act (RICO), 409, 411,
  562
Radical criminology, 249
Radical feminist theory, 249, 266–269, 275
Radical theory, 259
Rape
    causes of, 329–330
    changes in law and, 42, 331
    chronic offenders and, 72
    as common-law crime, 34
    consensus view of crime and, 16
    crime trends and, 58, 59
    date rape, 93
    definition of, 324
    as felony, 34
    female inmates and, 575
    firearms and, 62, 65
    history of, 325
    incarceration and, 572

incidence of, 326
instinctual drives and, 141
law and, 330–331
as *mala in se* crime, 35
military and, 325
National Crime Victimization Survey
  and, 52
as Part I index crime, 49
prosecutor and, 523
rational choice theory and, 115
social class and, 63
social reaction theory and, 236
statute of limitations and, 33
types of, 326–329
victimization and, 83, 84, 86
victim precipitation theory and, 91
as violent crime, 324–331
workplace violence and, 347
Rape of Lucrece, The (Shakespeare), 325
Rape of the Sabine Women (Poussin), 325
Rational choice, 107
Rational choice theory
    benefits of crime and, 116
    classical criminology and, 10
    concepts of, 109, 130
    crime control model and, 474
    criminological perspectives and, 10, 11
    development of, 107–112
    differential reinforcement theory and,
      225
    elimination of crime and, 115, 117–129
    general deterrence strategies, 117,
      120–124, 130
    general theory of crime and, 284
    incapacitation strategies, 117, 125–129,
      130
    introduction to, 107
    just desert and, 129
    policy issues and, 109, 129
    rationality of crime and, 112–115
    robbery and, 113, 343
    routine activities theory and, 111, 130
    situational crime prevention and,
      117–120
    specific deterrence strategies, 117,
      124–127, 130
    structuring crime and, 111–112
    structuring criminality and, 109–111
    substance abuse and, 437–438
    violence and, 114–115
RCC (residential community corrections),
  564–565
Reaction formation, 202
Reactive hate crimes, 345
Reactive policing, 492
Reality principle, 154
Reality therapy, 576
Reasoning criminal, 109
Rebellion, 193
Rebuttal, 532–533

Rebuttal evidence, 532–533
Recidivism
    alternative sanctions and, 566
    arrests and, 126
    electronic monitoring and, 564
    incarceration and, 125, 558
    inmate reentry and, 128
    parole and, 581
    private prisons and, 569
    probation and, 561
    rehabilitation and, 577
    trait theories and, 140
Reciprocal altruism, 140
Recovery agents, 527
Redirect examination, 532
Reducing temptation, 118
Reeves, 29, 555
Reflective role-taking, 235
Reformatories, 568
Region, 61, 62
Regional values, 324
Rehabilitation
    alleged failure of, 558
    biosocial trait theory and, 166–167
    effectiveness of, 577–578
    ethical issues and, 21
    juvenile justice system and, 464
    police discretion and, 500
    positivist criminology and, 108
    sentencing and, 535
    vocational rehabilitation, 576–577
Rehabilitation model, 475–476, 477
Reintegrative shaming, 271–272
Relative deprivation, 72
Relative deprivation theory, 195–196, 205,
  229, 265
Release, 469
Release on recognizance (ROR), 528
Religion, 218, 231, 346, 352, 390, 432, 579
Religious revisionism, 351
Removed for cause, 531
Repeat burglary, 381–382
Reporting practices, 51
Research. *See also* Criminal statistics;
  specific theories
    Chicago School and, 8
    criminology and, 4, 18–21
    ethical issues and, 21–22
Residential burglary, 378–379
Residential community corrections (RCC),
  564–565
Restitution, 95, 98, 240, 476, 535, 558, 563
Restitution agreements, 98
Restorative justice
    challenge of, 273–274
    concepts of, 272
    criminal justice system and, 476–477
    peacemaking movement and, 271
    principles of, 274
    programs of, 273

Sentencing Project Web site, 540
September 11 attacks, 317, 349, 351, 352, 354, 355, 482
Serial murder, 335–337, 428
Serial rapes, 327
Seventh Step organization, 577
"Severely disturbed" fire setter, 383
Sexism
    conflict view of crime and, 17
    rape and, 330
Sexual abuse. *See also* Child abuse; Sexual assault
    assault and, 339
    female crime and, 298
    female inmates and, 575
    problem behavior syndrome and, 294
    prostitution and, 425–426
    radical feminist theory and, 267
    stalking and, 348
    violence and, 320
Sexual assault
    crime trends and, 59
    incarceration and, 572
    National Crime Victimization Survey and, 52
    sexual predator law and, 42
    victimization and, 83, 86, 95
    workplace violence and, 347
Sexual equality view, 426
Sexual harassment, 84–85, 267
Sexual motivation, 330
Sexual orientation, 343, 345, 346
Sexual predator law, 42
Shame
    deterrence theory and, 123–124
    informal sanctions and, 123
    moral development and, 160
    reintegrative shaming, 271–272
    restorative justice and, 271, 273
    social learning theory and, 220
Shelters, 340–341
Sheriff, 487
Sherman Antitrust Act, 396, 404
Shield laws, 331
Shire, 29
Shire-gemot, 29
Shire reeve, 29, 483
Shock incarceration (SI), 565–566
Shock probation, 563
Shoplifting, 372–373
Shopping malls, 96
Short-term transportation, 374
Siblicide, 90
Siege mentality, 187
Sikh radicals, 351
Silence of the Lambs, 138
Simultaneous killing, 336
Single, White Female, 138
Sing-Sing prison, 556
SI (shock incarceration), 565–566
Situational crime prevention, 117–120

Situational Crime Prevention (Clarke), 117
Situational inducement, 366
Situational influences, 500
Sixth Amendment, 464, 472, 531, 533–534
Skeezers, 425
Skilled thieves, 365
Skinheads, 12
Skip tracers, 527
Slander, 33
Slavery, 70, 554, 555
Sleeping with the Enemy, 138
SMART program, 120
Smugglers, 365, 439
Snitches, 372
Social adaptations, 193
Social altruism, 190–191
Social bonds
    age-graded theory and, 305
    developmental theories and, 306
    elements of, 229–232
    general theory of crime and, 285
    interactional theory and, 302
    social development model and, 299
Social capital, 304–305, 306, 307
Social class
    cartographic school of criminology and, 8
    conflict criminology and, 9
    conflict view of crime and, 16
    crime patterns and, 63, 66–67
    cultural deviance theory and, 199–203
    deviant place theory and, 92
    differential association theory and, 224
    differential enforcement and, 234
    ethical issues and, 22
    female crime and, 69
    history of punishment, 554–555
    interactional theory and, 302
    IQ tests and, 164, 166
    Marxist criminology and, 259, 261–262, 264, 265
    Marxist thought and, 251–252
    positivism and, 6
    power-control theory and, 269
    race and, 71, 178, 180–181
    self-report surveys and, 53, 63, 66, 214, 255
    sentencing and, 541, 542
    social conflict theory and, 249–250, 253–256, 258
    social learning theory and, 157, 227
    social process theory and, 214
    social reaction theory and, 236
    social structure theories and, 177–179, 180, 204
    strain theory and, 192–199
    substance abuse and, 63, 214
    terrorism and, 350
    theft and, 366
    Twelve Tables and, 27
    victimization and, 86, 87–88

white-collar crime and, 389
Social conflict theory
    Bonger on, 253–254
    conflict theory and, 250, 255–258, 275
    Dahrendorf on, 254
    development of, 253–254
    emerging forms of, 265–271
    introduction to, 249–251
    Marxist criminology and, 259–265, 275
    Marxist thought and, 251–253
    policy issues and, 271–274
    Vold on, 254
Social control, 460
Social control function, 35, 36, 37, 192
Social control theory
    containment theory, 228–229, 241
    self-concept and, 228–229
    social bond and, 229–230
    as social process theories, 227–232, 241
    testing of, 230–232
Social development model (SDM), 297, 299–301, 308
Social disorganization theory
    concentric zones and, 183–184, 205
    Shaw and McKay on, 183–185
    social class and, 66
    social ecology school and, 185–192, 205
    transitional neighborhoods and, 183
Social ecology
    Chicago School and, 8
    social disorganization theory and, 185–192, 205
    social structure theories and, 177
    of victimization, 86
Social harm, 16, 419
Social issues
    chronic offenders and, 73, 74
    crime trends and, 56, 60
    gender and, 69
    Marxist criminology and, 265
    positivist criminology and, 108
    race and, 71–72
    social class and, 66, 67
Socialization
    cultural deviance theory and, 200
    definition of, 9
    differential reinforcement theory and, 224–225
    gender and, 69
    general theory of crime and, 288
    Marxist criminology and, 262
    race and, 70
    rape and, 329
    social development model and, 299
    social process theories and, 214–220, 237, 239
    substance abuse and, 441
Socialization view of crime, 9
Social learning theory
    differential association theory and, 220–224, 241

firearms and, 64
gateway model and, 438
high-risk lifestyles and, 92
history of, 32–33, 432
interactionist view of crime and, 17
law and, 441, 443
mental illness and, 161
nonprofessional fence and, 369
observational research and, 20
parental deviance and, 148
prohibition and, 432–433
prostitutes and, 425
as public order crime, 432–449
radical feminist theory and, 267
rational choice theory and, 113–114, 116
routine activities theory and, 95
self-report surveys and, 53, 54, 59
sentencing and, 541
social class and, 63, 214
social process theory and, 216
social reaction theory and, 237
statutory laws and, 32
strain theory and, 199
types of drug users, 438–440
victimization and, 90
violence and, 322–323, 442
violent crimes and, 3
Substantial capacity test, 40
Substantive criminal law, 15, 35
Subterranean values, 225
Suburban areas
routine activities theory and, 95, 96
victimization and, 86
Sufferance, 347
Suffering, victimization and, 83–84
Sugar, 142
Suicide, 8, 64, 143
Suitable targets, 92, 93, 112
Superconducting Interference Device (SQUID), 145
Superego, 154, 155
Super-zapping, 400
Supreme Court, U.S.
automobile searches and, 498
bail and, 527, 529
capital punishment and, 543–544, 546, 547
as court of last resort, 517
criminal justice system and, 472
gun control and, 64
inmates' rights and, 579
juries and, 531
juvenile justice system and, 464
parole and, 580
police use of deadly force and, 506
probation and, 559
racial quotas and, 501
sentencing and, 540
tracing case to, 519

Surety bond, 527
Surplus value, 252–253, 260–261, 263
Surrogate family, 575
Surveillance by employees, 118
Survey research, 19
Swindles, 389–390
Symbolic interaction theory, 232
Synthesis, 252
Systematic forgers, 374
Systemic link, 323

Taliban, 355
Target antagonism, 89
Target gratifiability, 89
Target hardening, 99, 118, 373
Target removal, 118, 373
Target vulnerability, 89, 112
Task Force on Victims of Crime, 95
Taxation, 31
Tax evasion, 395–396
Taxi Driver, 158
Technical violation of probation, 560
Technology
arraignment and, 468
arson and, 382
change in law and, 43
crime trends and, 60
general deterrence strategies and, 121
high-tech crime and, 397–401, 406
organized crime and, 407
police and, 485, 490
pornography and, 430–431
professional thieves and, 367–368
situational crime prevention and, 118
Uniform Crime Reports and, 51
violence and, 322
Teenage pregnancy, 56, 294
Teen courts, 518
Teen crime. *See* Juvenile crime
Telemarketers, 377
Television. *See* Media
Temp, The, 138
Temperance movement, 432–433
Temperature, 61
Terrorism
contemporary forms of, 350–353
definition of, 349–350
history of, 350
motivation for, 354
responses to, 354–355
Terrorist groups, 349
Terrorist killers, 336
Testosterone levels, 43, 143, 318
Thanatos, 322
Theft. *See* Property crimes
Theory construction, criminological enterprise and, 11, 14
Therapy, 575–576
Thinking about Crime (Wilson), 109
Thirty Years' War, 555

Thomas Crown Affair, 364
Three strikes and you're out, 74, 128–129, 540
Threshold inquiry (stop-and-frisk), 498
Thrill killers, 336
Thrill-seeking hate crimes, 345
Time-series design, 20
Time-series studies, 123
Tithings, 29
Tort, 33
Tort law, 33
Torture, 5, 108, 555
Traffic, 431
Train robbery, 368
Trait theories
biosocial trait theories, 141–153
foundations of, 139–140
introduction to, 138–139
policy issues and, 166–167
psychological trait theories, 153–166
Tranquilizers, 434
Transactional analysis, 576
Transitional neighborhoods, 183
Transnational terrorism, 352
Travel Act, 409
Treasonous acts, 29
Treatment. *See also* Rehabilitation
corrections and, 558
ethical issues and, 21
incarceration and, 575–578
juvenile justice system and, 464
medium-security prisons and, 568
nonintervention model and, 476
police discretion and, 500
probation services and, 559–560
rehabilitation model and, 476
restorative justice and, 476
substance abuse and, 446–448
Trial/adjudication, 468
Trial by combat, 28, 30, 31
Trial by fire, 28, 31
Trials, 30, 31, 468, 530–534
Tribal justice forums, 518
Trojan horse, 400
Tropic of Cancer (Miller), 427
Truancy, 59
Truly disadvantaged, 179, 180, 194
Truth-in-Sentencing Incentive Grants Program, 540
Truth-in-sentencing laws, 540, 569
Turbulence, 138
Turning points, 304
Twelve Tables, 27
Twenty-First Amendment, 433
Twin behavior, 148–149
Tying arrangement, 396

Ultra-maximum-security prisons, 570–571
Ulysses (Joyce), 427
Underclass, 179, 180

Walnut Street Prison, 556, 576
Waltham Black Act (1723), 32
War on Poverty, 204, 239
Watch system, 482–483
Wechsler Adult Intelligence Scale, 166
Wedding cake model, 469, 471, 472
Wer, 29, 30
Wergild, 28, 29, 30, 554, 561
Wernicke-Korsakoff disease, 141
Western Penitentiary, 556
Westinghouse Learning Corporation, 239
What Is to Be Done about Law and Order?
   (Lea & Young), 265
When Work Disappears (Wilson), 180
White Americans
   capital punishment and, 547
   differential enforcement and, 234
   ethical issues and, 22
   fear and, 187
   institutional anomie theory and, 195
   in jails, 567
   murder and, 333
   organized crime and, 407
   police use of force and, 506
   robbery and, 344
   sentencing and, 542, 543
   social class and, 66, 67
   victimization and, 86, 89
   workplace violence and, 347
White-collar crime
   biosocial trait theory and, 151
   causes of, 401–403
   chiseling and, 390–391

client fraud and, 394–396
components of, 389–401
conflict view of crime and, 16
corporate crime and, 389, 396–397
definition of, 388
differential association theory and, 220
economic issues and, 110
embezzlement and, 388, 390, 393–394
evolutionary theory and, 152
forfeiture and, 29
high-tech crime and, 397–401
individual exploitation of institutional
   position, 391–392
influence peddling and bribery, 392–393
introduction to, 388–389
law enforcement and, 403–405
Marxist criminology and, 259
minimum-security prisons and, 568
punishment and, 364
radical feminist theory and, 267
recidivism and, 125
redefining of, 389
relative deprivation theory and, 196
self-control and, 286
social reaction theory and, 234
stings/swindles and, 389–390
strict-liability crime and, 39
study of, 14, 22
White supremacy, 351
Wickersham Commission, 460
Witchcraft, Middle Ages and, 4–5
Wite, 29, 30
Witnesses, 50

Women. *See also* Female crime; Feminist
   theory; Rape; Sexual assault
   androgen and, 143
   evolutionary theory and, 152
   feticide and, 332
   in jails, 567
   mothers who kill children and, 321
   as police officers, 501, 502, 504–505
   as prison inmates, 572
   prison life and, 574–575
   routine activities theory and, 93–94, 95
   shame and, 123
   social class and, 66, 67
   stalking statutes and, 42
   substance abuse and, 440
   victimization and, 84, 86, 87, 89, 338
   violence against, 338
Women's Temperance Union, 433
Workplace violence, 347, 348
World Trade Center Towers, 317, 349, 351,
   355
Writ of certiorari, 517
Writ of Novel Disseisin, 31

Younger brother syndrome, 57
Youth crime. *See* Juvenile crime
Yugoslavian/Albanian/Croatian/Serbian
   (YACS) Crime Group, 407

Zealots, 350
Zero tolerance policies, 48, 490

PHOTO CREDITS

This page constitutes an extension of the copyright page. We have made every effort to trace the ownership of all copyrighted material and to secure permission from copyright holders. In the event of any question arising as to the use of any material, we will be pleased to make the necessary corrections in future printings. Thanks are due to the following authors, publishers, and agents for permission to use the material indicated.

Synopsis of Criminological Theories

Classical Theory

Origin About 1764

Founders Cesare Beccaria, Jeremy Bentham

Most Important Works Beccaria, *On Crimes and Punishments* (1764); Bentham, *Moral Calculus* (1789)

Core Ideas People choose to commit crime after weighing the benefits and costs of their actions. Crime can be deterred by certain, severe, and swift punishment.

Modern Outgrowths Rational Choice Theory, Routine Activities Theory, General Deterrence Theory, Specific Deterrence, Incapacitation

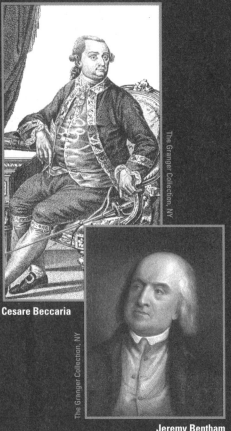

Cesare Beccaria

The Granger Collection, NY

The Granger Collection, NY

Jeremy Bentham

Marxist/Conflict Theory

Origin About 1848

Founders Karl Marx, Willem Bonger, Ralf Dahrendorf, George Vold

Most Important Works Marx and Friedrich Engels, *The Communist Manifesto* (1848); Bonger, *Criminality and Economic Conditions* (1916); George Rusche and Otto Kircheimer, *Punishment and Social Structure* (1939); Dahrendorf, *Class and Class Conflict in Industrial Society* (1959)

Core Ideas Crime is a function of class struggle. The capitalist system's emphasis on competition and wealth produces an economic and social environment in which crime is inevitable.

Modern Outgrowths Conflict Theory, Radical Theory, Radical Feminist Theory, Left Realism, Peacemaking, Power-Control Theory, Postmodern Theory, Reintegrative Shaming, Restorative Justice

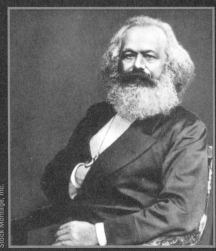

Stock Montage, Inc.

Karl Marx